TWENTIETH-CENTURY SCOTTISH DRAMA

CAIRNS CRAIG was born in Kilmarnock and educated at the University of Edinburgh where he is Head of the English Literature Department and Director of the Centre for the History of Ideas in Scotland. He has written widely on Scottish literature and culture and was General Editor of the four-volume *History of Scottish Literature* (1987-9). His books on Scottish subjects include *Out of History: Narrative Paradigms in Scottish and English Culture* (1996), and *The Modern Scottish Novel: Narrative and the National Imagination* (1999). He is a member of the editorial board for Canongate Classics.

RANDALL STEVENSON is Reader in English Literature at the University of Edinburgh. He was born in Banff, grew up in Glasgow, and went to university in Edinburgh and Oxford. He is the editor of *Scottish Theatre Since the Seventies* (1996) and the author of *Modernist Fiction* (1992, 1998); *A Reader's Guide to the Twentieth Century Novel in Britain* (1993); *The British Novel since the Thirties* (1986), as well as many articles on modernist and postmodernist fiction. He regularly reviews Scottish theatre for the *Times Literary Supplement*.

Twentieth-Century Scottish Drama

An Anthology

★

Edited and Introduced by
Cairns Craig and
Randall Stevenson

★

CANONGATE
CLASSICS
98

This edition first published as a Canongate Classic
in 2001 by Canongate Books Ltd, 14 High Street,
Edinburgh EH1 1TE. For details of copyright of the
individual plays, please see page 803. Introduction,
selection and introductory notes © Cairns Craig and
Randall Stevenson, 2001.

The publishers gratefully acknowledge general
subsidy from the Scottish Arts Council towards
the Canongate Classics series and a specific grant
towards the publication of this volume.

10 9 8 7 6 5 4 3 2 1

Canongate Classics
Series editor: Roderick Watson
Editorial Board: J. B. Pick, Cairns Craig
and Dorothy McMillan

British Library Cataloguing-in-Publication Data
A catalogue record for this book
is available from the British Library

ISBN 0 86241 979 4

Typeset by the Editors
Printed and bound by WS Bookwell, Finland
Juva

www.canongate.net

Contents

Introduction   vii

Mary Rose
   J.M. Barrie   1

In Time o' Strife
   Joe Corrie   61

Jamie the Saxt
   Robert McLellan   115

Mr Bolfry
   James Bridie   207

Men Should Weep
   Ena Lamont Stewart   269

The Bevellers
   Roddy McMillan   339

The Jesuit
   Donald Campbell   397

Mary Queen of Scots Got Her Head
  Chopped Off
   Liz Lochhead   463

Your Cheatin' Heart
   John Byrne   515

Bondagers
   Sue Glover   669

Shining Souls
   Chris Hannan   725

Copyright Permissions   803

Introduction

Scottish literature has often been seen as significantly weakened by the lack of a strong native tradition of drama. Isolated works of great power, such as David Lindsay's *Ane Satyre of the Thrie Estaitis* (1554) point towards how much was lost when the Court of James VI moved to London to preside over the glories of English Jacobean theatre, leaving the Reformed Church seeking to suppress all dramatic performances in Scotland on the grounds that they were inherently evil. Theatrical art in Scotland long continued to struggle against the censures of Calvinism: formal theatre was often a private rather than a public event, and it was not until the eighteenth century that permanent playhouses were established. Even in the mid-eighteenth century the enormous success of John Home's *Douglas* (1756) — which some believed had given Scotland an equivalent of Shakespeare's work — was met with a torrent of criticism from the Church, especially since Home himself was a clergyman.

Douglas, however, did initiate a taste for Scottish historical drama further encouraged by Macpherson's Ossian in the 1760s, and by the plays of Joanna Baillie in the 1790s. *The Family Legend*, her dark tale of Highland intrigue and violence was produced at the Theatre Royal in Edinburgh in 1811, under the guidance of Walter Scott, and it was Scott who went on to dominate nineteenth-century theatre through adaptations of his novels: plays based on his works formed the backbone of a flourishing theatrical culture in Scotland down to the 1880s. Adaptations of *Guy Mannering*, *Rob Roy*, *The Heart of Mid-Lothian*, and *The Bride of Lammermoor*, together with plays based on Ossian and on historical figures such as William Wallace and Bonnie Prince Charlie constituted a National Drama which exercised a powerful influence on nineteenth-century Scottish culture in general.

It was, however, a drama largely without dramatists. In the late nineteenth century, the music-hall and variety provided alternative forms of entertainment whose broader popularity encouraged the building of more and grander theatres, but still without much encouraging native drama. Any conventional dramatic performances mounted in the new theatres generally took the form of

touring productions sent round the country by London-based
managements: any Scottish component survived almost entirely
in the form of pantomime. As Bill Findlay's *History of Scottish Theatre* (1998) shows, traditions of Scottish *theatre*, before
the twentieth century, were never as weak as some critics have
suggested, yet it was often a theatre centred on spectacle and
performance rather than on playwrights and developing dramatic
styles. Scottish drama entered the early years of the twentieth
century with no strong place in the Scottish culture which was
beginning to reshape itself at this time. Significantly, the first
major Scottish dramatist of the new century, J. M. Barrie, had
all his plays produced in London and New York.

Until the Second World War, serious theatre in Scotland
remained almost entirely a matter of short-lived professional
organisations and long-running amateur groups. The example of
the Abbey Theatre in Dublin encouraged both the Scottish Repertory Theatre in Glasgow in the years before the First World
War — an early inspiration for James Bridie — and the establishment in the 1920s of the Scottish National Players, who organised
regular seasons in Glasgow and tours of the Scottish regions.
With work by Robert Bain, John Brandane and Joe Corrie, the
Players did much to fulfil their commitment 'to develop Scottish
national drama through . . . plays of Scottish life and character', their influence sometimes extended by the direct transfer of
some productions for radio broadcasting in the early days of BBC
Scotland. They remained, however, an amateur or at most semi-
professional organisation. It was not until the establishment of the
Citizens' Theatre in 1943, under the guidance of O. H. Mavor
('James Bridie'), and its move to a permanent site in the Gorbals
in 1945, financed by the industrialist Sir Frederick Stewart, that
a reliable stage was set up for the skills of Scottish dramatists
and actors — ones further encouraged, in the latter case, by the
foundation of the Royal Scottish Academy of Music and Drama,
also with Bridie's help, in 1950.

Between the wars, Scottish theatre was dominated by the
Scottish Community Drama Association and the various groups
which it spawned. The SCDA's annual festival of one-act plays —
attracting over 300 entries in 1926, only four years after its
foundation — was the highlight of the amateur season, and did
allow Scottish dramatists to reach a wide audience. Yet the styles
required for amateur performance could be destructive of serious
talent. Writers such as Joe Corrie — whose plays sometimes came
first, second and third in SCDA festivals — and T. M. Weston
found that they could earn a living by turning out what David

Hutchison has described as 'amusing but empty Scottish comedies', full of 'facile humour and neat solutions'. Nevertheless, the amateur movement did provide a pool of actors accustomed to the presentation of Scots character: without it, great performers such as Roddy McMillan or Duncan Macrae (who played the lead role in the first, amateur production of *Jamie the Saxt*, 1937) might not have found a way onto the stage.

The most significant development from the amateur movement, however, was the Glasgow-based Unity Theatre company. Unity combined an amateur base with a small team of professionals — including Roddy McMillan — and encouraged Scottish drama dealing directly with contemporary urban society, rather than the rural life often favoured by the Scottish National Players. Plays such as Robert McLeish's *The Gorbals Story* (1946), depicting the consequences of the post-war housing shortage, and Ena Lamont Stewart's presentation of unemployment in *Men Should Weep* (1947) illustrated the belief emphasised in the company's manifesto, drawn from the Russian writer Maxim Gorki: that 'the theatre is the school of the people — it makes them think and it makes them feel'. Unity's example both encouraged a long line of Scottish companies, such as 7:84 and Wildcat, combining theatrical innovation with a strong political message, and helped establish a style of realistic drama — including Roddy McMillan's *All in Good Faith* (1954) and *The Bevellers* (1973) — depicting the harsh realities of working life, in the west of Scotland particularly. Like many of its successors, Unity was also to run foul of the Arts Council, which had provided some of its early funding, and the company had to cease work in the early 1950s. By then, however, it had helped initiate the Edinburgh Festival Fringe by putting on plays without official support at the first Edinburgh Festival in 1947.

Begun with the intention of helping international relations in the aftermath of the war, the Edinburgh International Festival was to have a key role in the development both of theatre in Scotland and of the work of Scottish playwrights, one sustained throughout the latter half of the century. The Festival brought the new theatrical styles of post-war Europe and the United States to Scotland, allowing dramatists and actors access to an international culture from which Britain had been largely cut off since the Depression of the 1930s. It also provided a venue in which significant audiences and serious critical attention could sometimes be directed on Scottish drama — in particular, in the first festivals, through the ground-breaking production of Lindsay's *Ane Satyre of the Thrie Estaitis* by the American director

Tyrone Guthrie. Regularly revived in the following half-century.
Lindsay's play was performed, in Guthrie's staging, in the open
theatrical space of the Assembly Hall of the Church of Scotland.
Given the Kirk's centuries-old suspicion of drama, the setting
was ironic: symbolic, too, of the extent to which theatre was to
take the place of the church as an arena of public debate — or at
any rate to benefit from a more liberated climate — in the years
of declining religious faith which followed.

Practically, because it had been designed for debate rather than
as an acting chamber, the Assembly Hall posed immediate theatrical problems, solved by Guthrie's reinvention of the Elizabethan
thrust stage, jutting out among the spectators so that the actors
are surrounded by the audience. Involving the audience much
more immediately than a proscenium stage, his tactics set a
pattern regularly followed by later Scottish theatre, often drawing its spectators into close complicity with performers through
shared outlooks or simple physical proximity. Such tactics were
followed by 7:84 in their their 'ceilidh house' style of theatre. In
other ways, they were also very influentially sustained by a new
theatre spawned by the Edinburgh Festival and the 'alternative'
styles of its Fringe — the Traverse, opened in a tiny room in
a former brothel in the High Street in 1963, before moving on
to more permanent bases in the Grassmarket and Cambridge
Street. Virtually the first professional studio space in Britain,
the Traverse quickly influenced theatre and theatre architecture
throughout the world, while its commitment to staging new plays,
local ones particularly, was crucial to the development of theatre
within Scotland in the last decades of the century — of plays
included in this volume, *The Jesuit*, *Bondagers*, and *Shining Souls*
all received at the Traverse first productions which might not
have been easily or so effectively available elsewhere.

That early Festival production of *Ane Satyre of the Thrie Estaitis*
established proximities between stage and audience which were
not only physical, but above all linguistic, reminding its audiences — and a generation of writers, actors and directors — of
the continuing vitality of Scots as a dramatic medium. Guthrie's
production helped consolidate for the drama particular powers
of writing in Scots which authors of Scottish Renaissance movement had developed in other ways for poetry and the novel in the
1920s, and to establish in the theatre a kind of unique and naturally political performative space for Scots language and identity.
In the theatre, the Scottish voice could be heard, live and direct,
and not silent on the page as in poetry, or interpreted and masked
by the 'standard' speech of a narrator. While poets such as Hugh

MacDiarmid had tried to remake the possibility of poetry written in a literary Scots going back to the Middle Ages, dramatists such as Joe Corrie and Ena Lamont Stewart were providing, by the very requirements of their stage realism, a liberating sense of the contemporary Scottish voice as a theatrical experience. From the 1920s to the 1940s, in a period of profound economic and political crisis, it was in drama that the experiences of the working classes and the urban world of industrial Scotland — barely registered in fiction at the time — were most directly captured, with the liberating voice of the stage symbolically enacting a kind of freedom characters were so often denied in their lives. Characters and audiences in an often divided society were united in mutual recognition of shared accent, shared experience, shared outlook.

Such possibilities were even more significant after the Second World War. In the mid-twentieth century, after the end of Empire, Scotland was a country engaged in a fundamental redefinition of its identity, yet the media in which Scottish life and experience could be represented — film, radio, television — were all organised within a British society still rigidly hierarchical and deeply marked by the centralisation which had been required by government control of broadcasting during the Second World War. There was little space in any of the mass media for serious engagement with Scottish experience. An agenda designed in London for a British audience could only allow Scots to address themselves in stereotypical forms such as the BBC's *Doctor Finlay's Casebook*, offering Scottish actors only a limited range of parts, while Received Pronunciation — ironically, sometimes imposed by Scots such as Lord Reith at the BBC — was still used to censor class and regional expression. Audiences found live theatre, on the other hand, readily able to speak their own language, metaphorically as well as literally — able to communicate, immediately and intimately, new representations of Scottish experience and new ways of understanding it. From the 1960s to the 1980s, concurrently with the expansion of nationalism in the 1970s and the increasing momentum of political debate in the lead-up to the Devolution Referendum of 1979, theatre became a driving force for Scottish cultural change.

Paradoxically, in the later twentieth century, what had been, apparently, the weakest of Scotland's literary traditions came to have the most profound impact on Scottish cultural affairs, with a whole new generation of dramatists emerging to build on earlier successes and develop the new accents of a liberated Scottish voice, suddenly imbued again with a sense both of its history

and its contemporary significance. This encouraged further concentration on working-class experience, homes and workplaces,
where voices were most distinctively Scottish, with playwrights
such as George Munro, Bill Bryden, C. P. Taylor, Stewart Conn,
and John Byrne — in his *Slab Boys* Trilogy (1978–82) — extending along with Roddy McMillan the idiom established by Joe
Corrie and Glasgow Unity. It also encouraged further concentration — as in Robert McLellan's *Jamie the Saxt* (1937) — on
periods of history before English became the dominant language
in Scottish life and affairs. The Scottish voice became the real
protagonist in some of these plays — in Donald Campbell's *The
Jesuit* (1976), for example, in which audiences' sympathies are
shaped by contrasts between the standard English of the wilful
martyr Ogilvie and the rough tones of the Scots soldiery obliged
to look after him. For other dramatists such as Sidney Goodsir
Smith in *The Wallace* (1960) or Hector McMillan in *The Rising*
(1973), Scottish history provided contexts — rather like those
W. B. Yeats created for the Irish theatre — around which nationalist sentiments could be focused and directed. By no means all
of Scottish historical drama, of course, was nationalist in orientation. John McGrath's *The Cheviot, the Stag and the Black,
Black Oil* (1973), probably the most successful Scottish play of
the 1970s (not included in this volume as it is widely available
elsewhere) used past events to warn of the contemporary threat
of a multi-national capitalism: whether it was better resisted by
socialism or nationalism was an issue on which dramatist and
audience were often to disagree. For other historical dramatists
such as Liz Lochhead in *Mary Queen of Scots Got Her Head
Chopped Off* (1987) and Sue Glover in *Bondagers* (1991), the politics of gender rather than party became a primary interest. All
these writers nevertheless continued to demonstrate some form
of Robert McLellan's conviction that — especially given the thin-
ness of surviving Scottish dramatic tradition in early centuries —
a return to the past was necessary in order to create for Scottish
history a coherence and significance of the kind long established
for England by Shakespeare; and to show, as Lochhead does in
the last scene of her play, how heavily the Scottish past bears on
the present.

Lochhead's *Mary Queen of Scots Got Her Head Chopped Off*,
however, marks a kind of terminus in this project, and a
change of direction for Scottish theatre. A new generation of
playwrights entered the limelight in the late 1980s and 1990s,
including Chris Hannan, David Greig, Simon Donald, Rona
Munro, Duncan McLean, Ann Mari di Mambro. For these

writers — even for Lochhead herself in *Perfect Days* (1998) — Scottish history, identity and experience no longer demanded the kind of direct interrogation which shapes the opening scene of *Mary Queen of Scots Got Her Head Chopped Off*. Instead, they had become a matter of shared assumption with audiences — a familiar, immediately recognisable base for the investigation of wider issues or forces — such as the 'thrones dominions, powers, virtues, principalities, archangels, angels' that Chris Hannan shows brooding over a Glasgow otherwise entirely recognisable, in language and behaviour, in *Shining Souls* (1996). This new, relaxed mood in Scottish drama was also in evidence in *Your Cheatin' Heart* (1990), employing the once inaccessible medium of television in confident expectation that a mass audience would follow the accents of the west of Scotland, and the kind of frictions between stylishness — verbal, musical and sartorial — and the urban squalor it seeks to disguise which John Byrne had first explored in *The Slab Boys*. Scottish drama had good reason for such confidence, given how far the dynamic it had generated has passed into other genres by the end of the century. Novels such as those of James Kelman or Irvine Welsh had translated into prose narrative some of the accents and vocal effects explored by dramatists, and these passed on in due course into the wave of Scottish film-making of the 1990s, from *Trainspotting* to *The Rat Catcher* (1999).

Scottish drama also gained in confidence from the expansion in resources and performance spaces throughout the country in the latter part of the century. Strongly supported by the Scottish Arts Council, repertory companies continued to work in Edinburgh, Dundee, Glasgow and Perth. Increasing numbers of civic spaces throughout the country provided venues for touring companies, encouraging groups such as 7:84 who set out to take theatre to the people, and to create audiences in areas, especially in the Highlands, often starved of live theatre in the past. New theatres were constructed in Dundee and Pitlochry, with many refurbished elsewhere, and the new Tron and Tramway spaces, alongside the continuing unique success of the Citizens', contributing substantially to Glasgow's shifting cultural profile and its adoption as European City of Culture in 1990. New theatrical spaces and new dramatic energies also produced a generation of outstanding directors: Clive Perry and Bill Bryden in the early 1970s at the Edinburgh Lyceum, venue for *The Bevellers* as well as Bryden's own plays; Max Stafford-Clark and Chris Parr, encouraging new Scottish writing at the Traverse; Giles Havergal, bringing with his associates Robert David MacDonald and Philip Prowse a huge range of the European repertoire to the Citizens'; Gerry Mulgrew, channelling with Communicado Theatre Company some of the energies of the European avant-garde into productions of plays such as *Mary Queen of Scots Got Her Head Chopped Off*.

Even an anthology as large as this one cannot cover anything but a small sample of the achievements of the twentieth-century Scottish drama. We have chosen plays to illustrate both the historical development of Scottish drama during the century, and some of the different traditions and movements discussed above, with J. M. Barrie's *Mary Rose* (1920) and James Bridie's *Mr Bolfry* (1941) representing the mainstream, bourgeois theatre as it appeared in the earlier part of the century. Many other authors might have been included, and other plays by those who are; some of this work is in print in other editions, and some, we hope, may be included in future anthologies. Meanwhile, it should be a matter of congratulation as well as regret that twentieth-century Scottish drama so comprehensively transcends the bounds of what any single volume can contain.

Cairns Craig and Randall Stevenson

J. M. Barrie

Mary Rose

(1920)

CHARACTERS

Mrs Otery
Harry Morland Blake
Mr Morland
Mrs Morland
Mr Amy
Mary Rose
Simon Blake
Mr Cameron

Introduction

J. M. Barrie (1860–1937) is best remembered as the author of *Peter Pan*, which was first performed in London in 1904. In terms of Scottish traditions of writing he is also often cited as the founder of the 'Kailyard School'. Its sentimental representations of rural Scottish life, starting from Barrie's *Auld Licht Idylls* in 1888, were to be attacked by almost all the major writers of the early twentieth century, and were a stimulus to the dark realism of many Scottish novels that followed in the tradition established by George Douglas Brown's anti-Kailyard tragedy, *The House with the Green Shutters* (1901).

As a result, Barrie has rarely been accorded the retrospective critical status that his enormous success as short-story writer, novelist and dramatist in his own lifetime might seem to require. The reason is that Barrie's mixture of satire and whimsy, his play with the relations of childhood and adulthood, have seemed to many twentieth-century critics both to lack maturity and to imply a false view, in particular, of Scottish experience. In *Mary Rose*, for instance, the presentation of the Highlander, Cameron, combines what might seem to be a patronising presentation of his Gaelic-inflected speech — 'That iss so, ma'am. You may haf noticed that I always address you as "ma'am". It iss my way of indicating that I consider you a ferry genteel young matron' — with a stereotypic view of the Highlander as living in a world of the supernatural. Barrie's art, however, depended on the exploitation and subversion of such stereotypes in order to undermine the certainties of modern life, both its confident scientific materialism and its belief in the stability of British social structures.

In Barrie's plays, the stability and certainty of the modern world is always on the edge of disintegration, quivering on the brink of an alternative reality which is both more terrifying, but may also be more consoling, than the materialism which it displaces. Barrie's use of the modern technology of the stage to dramatise these indeterminate states is particularly pronounced in *Mary Rose*.

The scene is a room in a small Sussex manor house that has long
been for sale. It is such a silent room that whoever speaks first
here is a bold one, unless indeed he merely mutters to himself,
which they perhaps allow. All of this room's past which can be
taken away has gone. Such light as there is comes from the only
window, which is at the back and is incompletely shrouded in
sacking. For a moment this is a mellow light, and if a photograph could be taken quickly we might find a disturbing smile
on the room's face, perhaps like the Monna Lisa's, which came,
surely, of her knowing what only the dead should know. There
are two doors, one leading downstairs; the other is at the back,
very insignificant, though it is the centre of this disturbing history. The wallpaper, heavy in the adherence of other papers of a
still older date, has peeled and leans forward here and there in a
grotesque bow, as men have hung in chains; one might predict
that the next sound heard here will be in the distant future when
another piece of paper loosens. Save for two packing-cases, the
only furniture is a worn easy-chair doddering by the unlit fire, like
some foolish old man. We might play with the disquieting fancy
that this room, once warm with love, is still alive but is shrinking
from observation, and that with our departure they cunningly set
to again at the apparently never-ending search which goes on in
some empty old houses.

Some one is heard clumping up the stair, and the caretaker
enters. It is not she, however, who clumps; she has been here
for several years, and has become sufficiently a part of the house
to move noiselessly in it. The first thing we know about her
is that she does not like to be in this room. She is an elderly
woman of gaunt frame and with a singular control over herself.
There may be some one, somewhere, who can make her laugh
still, one never knows, but the effort would hurt her face. Even
the war, lately ended, meant very little to her. She has shown
a number of possible purchasers over the house, just as she
is showing one over it now, with the true caretaker's indiffer-
ence whether you buy or not. The few duties imposed on her
here she performs conscientiously, but her greatest capacity is
for sitting still in the dark. Her work over, her mind a blank,
she sits thus rather than pay for a candle. One knows a little
more about life when he knows the Mrs Oterys, but she herself is unaware that she is peculiar, and probably thinks that in
some such way do people in general pass the hour before bed-
time. Nevertheless, though saving of her candle in other empty

houses, she always lights it on the approach of evening in this one.

The man who has clumped up the stairs in her wake is a young Australian soldier, a private, such as in those days you met by the dozen in any London street, slouching along it forlornly if alone, with sudden stoppages to pass the time (in which you ran against him), or in affable converse with a young lady. In his voice is the Australian tang that became such a friendly sound to us. He is a rough fellow, sinewy, with the clear eye of the man with the axe whose chief life-struggle till the war came was to fell trees and see to it that they did not crash down on him. Mrs Otery is showing him the house, which he has evidently known in other days, but though interested he is unsentimental and looks about him with a tolerant grin.

MRS OTERY: This was the drawing-room.

HARRY: Not it, no, no, never. This wasn't the drawing-room, my cabbage;[1] at least not in my time.

MRS OTERY: (*indifferently*) I only came here about three years ago and I never saw the house furnished, but I was told to say this was the drawing-room. (*With a flicker of spirit*) And I would thank you not to call me your cabbage.

HARRY: (*whom this kind of retort helps to put at his ease*) No offence. It's a French expression, and many a happy moment have I given to the mademoiselles by calling them cabbages. But the drawing-room! I was a little shaver when I was here last, but I mind we called the drawing-room the Big Room; it wasn't a little box like this.

MRS OTERY: This is the biggest room in the house. (*She quotes drearily from some advertisement which is probably hanging in rags on the gate*) Specially charming is the drawing-room with its superb view of the Downs. This room is upstairs and is approached by —

HARRY: By a stair, containing some romantic rat-holes. Snakes, whether it's the room or not, it strikes cold; there is something shiversome about it.

　　(*For the first time she gives him a sharp glance*)

I've shivered in many a shanty in Australy, and thought of the big room at home and the warmth of it. The warmth! And now this is the best it can do for the prodigal[2] when he returns to it expecting to see that calf done to a turn. We live and learn, missis.

MRS OTERY: We live, at any rate.

HARRY: Well said, my cabbage.

MRS OTERY: Thank you, my rhododendron.

HARRY: (*cheered*) I like your spirit. You and me would get on great if I had time to devote to your amusement. But, see here, I can make sure whether this was the drawing-room. If it was, there is an apple-tree outside there, with one of its branches scraping on the window. I ought to know, for it was out at the window down that apple-tree to the ground that I slided one dark night when I was a twelve-year-old, ran away from home, the naughty blue-eyed angel that I was, and set off to make my fortune on the blasted ocean. The fortune, my — my lady friend — has still got the start of me, but the apple-tree should be there to welcome her darling boy.

> (*He pulls down the sacking, which lets a little more light into the room. We see that the window, which reaches to the floor, opens outwards. There were probably long ago steps from it down into the garden, but they are gone now, and gone too is the apple-tree*)

I've won! No tree: no drawing-room.

MRS OTERY: I have heard tell there was once a tree there; and you can see the root if you look down.

HARRY: Yes, yes, I see it in the long grass, and a bit of the seat that used to be round it. This is the drawing-room right enough, Harry, my boy. There were blue curtains to that window, and I used to hide behind them and pounce out upon Robinson Crusoe. There was a sofa at this end, and I had my first lessons in swimming on it. You are a fortunate woman, my petite, to be here drinking in these moving memories. There used to be a peacock, too. Now, what the hell could a peacock be doing in this noble apartment?

MRS OTERY: I have been told a cloth used to hang on the wall here, tapestries they're called, and that it had pictures of peacocks on it. I dare say that was your peacock.

HARRY: Gone, even my peacock! And I could have sworn I used to pull the feathers out of its tail. The clock was in this corner, and it had a wheezy little figure of a smith that used to come out and strike the hour on an anvil. My old man used to wind that clock up every night, and I mind his rage when he found out it was an eight-day clock. The padre had to reprove him for swearing. Padre? What's the English for padre? Damme, I'm forgetting my own language. Oh yes, parson. Is *he* in the land of the living still? I can see him clear, a long thin man with a hard sharp face. He was always quarrelling about pictures he collected.

MRS OTERY: The parson here is a very old man, but he is not

tall and thin, he is little and roundish with a soft face and white whiskers.

HARRY: Whiskers? I can't think he had whiskers. (*Ruminating*) *Had* he whiskers? Stop a bit, I believe it is his wife I'm thinking about. I doubt I don't give satisfaction as a sentimental character. Is there any objection, your ladyship, to smoking in the drawing-room?

MRS OTERY: (*ungraciously*) Smoke if you want.

(*He hacks into a cake of tobacco with a large clasp knife*)
That's a fearsome-looking knife.

HARRY: Useful in trench warfare. It's not a knife, it's a visiting-card. You leave it on favoured parties like this.

(*He casts it at one of the packing-cases, and it sticks quivering in the wood*)

MRS OTERY: Were you an officer?

HARRY: For a few minutes now and again.

MRS OTERY: You're playing with me.

HARRY: You're so *ir*resistible.

MRS OTERY: Do you want to see the other rooms?

HARRY: I was fondly hoping you would ask me that.

MRS OTERY: Come along, then. (*She wants to lead him downstairs, but the little door at the back has caught his eye*)

HARRY: What does that door open on?

MRS OTERY: (*avoiding looking at it*) Nothing, it's just a cupboard door.

HARRY: (*considering her*) Who is playing with me now?

MRS OTERY: I don't know what you mean. Come this way.

HARRY: (*not budging*) I'll explain what I mean. That door — it's coming back to me — it leads into a little dark passage.

MRS OTERY: That's all.

HARRY: That can't be all. Who ever heard of a passage wandering about by itself in a respectable house! It leads — yes — to a single room, and the door of the room faces this way.

(*He opens the door, and a door beyond is disclosed*)
There's a memory for you! But what the hell made you want to deceive me?

MRS OTERY: It's of no consequence.

HARRY: I think — yes — the room in there has two stone windows — and wooden rafters.

MRS OTERY: It's the oldest part of the house.

HARRY: It comes back to me that I used to sleep there.

MRS OTERY: That may be. If you'll come down with me —

HARRY: I'm curious to see that room first.

(*She bars the way*)

MRS OTERY: (*thin-lipped and determined*) You can't go in there.

HARRY: Your reasons?

MRS OTERY: It's — locked. I tell you it's just an empty room.

HARRY: There must be a key.

MRS OTERY: It's — lost.

HARRY: Queer your anxiety to stop me, when you knew I would find the door locked.

MRS OTERY: Sometimes it's locked; sometimes not.

HARRY: Is it not you that locks it?

MRS OTERY: (*reluctantly*) It's never locked, it's held.

HARRY: Who holds it?

MRS OTERY: (*in a little outburst*) Quiet, man.

HARRY: You're all shivering.

MRS OTERY: I'm not.

HARRY: (*cunningly*) I suppose you are just shivering because the room is so chilly.

MRS OTERY: (*falling into the trap*) That's it.

HARRY: So you *are* shivering!

(*She makes no answer, and he reflects with the help of his pipe*) May I put a light to these bits of sticks?

MRS OTERY: If you like. My orders are to have fires once a week.

(*He lights the twigs in the fireplace, and they burn up easily, but will be ashes in a few minutes*)

You can't have the money to buy a house like this.

HARRY: Not me. It was just my manly curiosity to see the old home that brought me. I'm for Australy again. (*Suddenly turning on her*) What is wrong with this house?

MRS OTERY: (*on her guard*) There is nothing wrong with it.

HARRY: Then how is it going so cheap?

MRS OTERY: It's — in bad repair.

HARRY: Why has it stood empty so long?

MRS OTERY: It's — far from a town.

HARRY: What made the last tenant leave in such a hurry?

MRS OTERY: (*wetting her lips*) You have heard that, have you? Gossiping in the village, I suppose?

HARRY: I have heard some other things as well. I have heard they had to get a caretaker from a distance, because no woman hereabout would live alone in this house.

MRS OTERY: A pack o' cowards.

HARRY: I have heard that that caretaker was bold and buxom when she came, and that now she is a scared woman.

MRS OTERY: I'm not.

HARRY: I have heard she's been known to run out into the fields and stay there trembling half the night.

(*She does not answer, and he resorts to cunning again*)

Of course, I see they couldn't have meant you. Just foolish stories that gather about an old house.

MRS OTERY: (*relieved*) That's all.

HARRY: (*quickly, as he looks at the little door*) What's that?

(*Mrs Otery screams*)

I got you that time! What was it you expected to see?

(*No answer*)

Is it a ghost? They say it's a ghost. What is it gives this house an ill name?

MRS OTERY: Use as brave words as you like when you have gone, but I advise you, my lad, to keep a civil tongue while you are here. (*In her everyday voice*) There is no use showing you the rest of the house. If you want to be stepping, I have my work to do.

HARRY: We have got on so nicely, I wonder if you would give me a mug of tea. Not a cup, we drink it by the mugful where I hail from.

MRS OTERY: (*ungraciously*) I have no objection.

HARRY: Since you are so pressing, I accept.

MRS OTERY: Come down, then, to the kitchen.

HARRY: No, no, I'm sure the Prodigal got his tea in the drawing-room, though what made them make such a fuss about that man beats me.

MRS OTERY: (*sullenly*) You are meaning to go into that room. I wouldn't if I was you.

HARRY: If you were me you would.

MRS OTERY: (*closing the little door*) Until I have your promise—

HARRY: (*liking the tenacity of her*) Very well, I promise — unless, of course, she comes peeping out at the handsome gentleman. Your ghost has naught to do wi' me. It's a woman, isn't it?

(*Her silence is perhaps an assent*)

See here, I'll sit in this chair till you come back, saying my prayers. (*Feeling the chair*) You're clammy cold, old dear. It's not the ghost's chair by any chance, is it?

(*No answer*)

You needn't look so scared, woman; she doesn't walk till midnight, does she?

MRS OTERY: (*looking at his knife in the wood*) I wouldn't leave that knife lying about.

HARRY: Oh, come, give the old girl a chance.

MRS OTERY: I'll not be more than ten minutes.

HARRY: She can't do much in ten minutes.

    (*at which remark Mrs Otery fixes him with her eyes and departs*)

Harry is now sitting sunk in the chair, staring at the fire. It goes
out, but he remains there motionless, and in the increasing dusk
he ceases to be an intruder. He is now part of the room, the
part long waited for, come back at last. The house is shaken
to its foundation by his presence, we may conceive a thousand
whispers. Then the crafty work begins. The little door at the
back opens slowly to the extent of a foot. Thus might a breath
of wind blow it if there were any wind. Presently Harry starts to
his feet, convinced that there is some one in the room, very near
his knife. He is so sure of the exact spot where she is that for a
moment he looks nowhere else.

  In that moment the door slowly closes. He has not seen it
close, but he opens it and calls out, 'Who is that? Is any one
there?' With some distaste he enters the passage and tries the
inner door, but whether it be locked or held it will not open. He
is about to pocket his knife, then with a shrug of bravado sends
it quivering back into the wood — for her if she can get it. He
returns to the chair, but not to close his eyes: to watch and to be
watched. The room is in a tremble of desire to get started upon
that nightly travail which can never be completed till this man
is here to provide the end.

  The figure of Harry becomes indistinct and fades from sight.
When the haze lifts we are looking at the room as it was some
thirty years earlier on the serene afternoon that began its troubled story. There are rooms that are always smiling, so that you
may see them at it if you peep through the keyhole, and Mrs
Morland's little drawing-room is one of them. Perhaps these are
smiles that she has left lying about. She leaves many things lying about; for instance, one could deduce the shape of her from
studying that corner of the sofa which is her favourite seat, and
all her garments grow so like her that her wardrobes are full of
herself hanging on nails or folded away in drawers. The pictures
on her walls in time take on a resemblance to her or hers though
they may be meant to represent a waterfall, every present given
to her assumes some characteristic of the donor, and no doubt
the necktie she is at present knitting will soon be able to pass as
the person for whom it is being knit. It is only delightful ladies
at the most agreeable age who have this personal way with their
belongings. Among Mrs Morland's friends in the room are several of whom we have already heard, such as the blue curtains
from which Harry pounced upon the castaway, the sofa on which

he had his first swimming lessons, the peacock on the wall, the clock with the smart smith ready to step out and strike his anvil, and the apple-tree is in full blossom at the open window, one of its branches has even stepped into the room.

Mr Morland and the local clergyman are chatting importantly about some matter of no importance, while Mrs Morland is on her sofa at the other side of the room, coming into the conversation occasionally with a cough or a click of her needles, which is her clandestine way of telling her husband not to be so assertive to his guest. They are all middle-aged people who have found life to be on the whole an easy and happy adventure, and have done their tranquil best to make it so for their neighbours. The squire is lean, the clergyman of full habit, but could you enter into them you would have difficulty in deciding which was clergyman and which was squire; both can be peppery, the same pepper. They are benignant creatures, but could exchange benignancies without altering. Mrs Morland knows everything about her husband except that she does nearly all his work for him. She really does not know this. His work, though he rises early to be at it, is not much larger than a lady's handkerchief, and consists of magisterial duties, with now and then an impressive scene about a tenant's cowshed. She then makes up his mind for him, and is still unaware that she is doing it. He has so often heard her say (believing it, too) that he is difficult to move when once he puts his foot down that he accepts himself modestly as a man of this character, and never tries to remember when it was that he last put down his foot. In the odd talks which the happily married sometimes hold about the future he always hopes he will be taken first, being the managing one, and she says little beyond pressing his hand, but privately she has decided that there must be another arrangement. Probably life at the vicarage is on not dissimilar lines, but we cannot tell, as we never meet Mr Amy's wife. Mr Amy is even more sociable than Mr Morland; he is reputed to know every one in the county, and has several times fallen off his horse because he will salute all passers-by. On his visits to London he usually returns depressed because there are so many people in the streets to whom he may not give a friendly bow. He likes to read a book if he knows the residence or a relative of the author, and at the play it is far more to him to learn that the actress has three children, one of them down with measles, than to follow her histrionic genius. He and his host have the pleasant habit of print-collecting, and a very common scene between them is that which now follows. They are bent over the squire's latest purchase.

MR AMY: Very interesting. A nice little lot. I must say, James, you have the collector's flair.

MR MORLAND: Oh, well, I'm keen, you know, and when I run up to London I can't resist going a bust in my small way. I picked these up quite cheap.

MR AMY: The flair. That is what you have.

MR MORLAND: Oh, I don't know.

MR AMY: Yes, you have, James. You got them at Peterkin's in Dean Street, didn't you? Yes, I know you did. I saw them there. I wanted them too, but they told me you had already got the refusal.

MR MORLAND: Sorry to have been too quick for you, George, but it is my way to nip in. You have some nice prints yourself.

MR AMY: I haven't got your flair, James.

MR MORLAND: I admit I don't miss much.

(So far it has been a competition in saintliness)

MR AMY: No. *(The saint leaves him)* You missed something yesterday at Peterkin's, though.

MR MORLAND: How do you mean?

MR AMY: You didn't examine the little lot lying beneath this lot.

MR MORLAND: I turned them over; just a few odds and ends of no account.

MR AMY: *(with horrible complacency)* All except one, James.

MR MORLAND: *(twitching)* Something good?

MR AMY: *(at his meekest)* Just a little trifle of a Gainsborough.[3]

MR MORLAND: *(faintly)* What! You've got it?

MR AMY: I've got it. I am a poor man, but I thought ten pounds wasn't too much for a Gainsborough.

(The devil now has them both)

MR MORLAND: Ten pounds! Is it signed?

MR AMY: No, it isn't signed.

MR MORLAND: *(almost his friend again)* Ah!

MR AMY: What do you precisely mean by that 'Ah,' James? If it had been signed, could I have got it for ten pounds? You are always speaking about your flair; I suppose I can have a little flair sometimes too.

MR MORLAND: I am not always speaking about my flair, and I don't believe it is a Gainsborough.

MR AMY: *(with dignity)* Please don't get hot, James. If I had thought you would grudge me my little find — which *you* missed — I wouldn't have brought it to show you.

(With shocking exultation he produces a roll of paper)

MR MORLAND: (*backing from it*) So that's it.

MR AMY: This is it. (*The squire has to examine it like a Christian*) There! I have the luck this time. I hope you will have it next. (*The exultation passes from the one face into the other*)

MR MORLAND: Interesting, George — quite. But definitely not a Gainsborough.

MR AMY: I say definitely a Gainsborough.

MR MORLAND: Definitely not a Gainsborough.

(*By this time the needles have entered into the controversy, but they are disregarded*)

I should say the work of a clever amateur.

MR AMY: Look at the drawing of the cart and the figure beside it.

MR MORLAND: Weak and laboured. Look at that horse.

MR AMY: Gainsborough did some very funny horses.

MR MORLAND: Granted, but he never placed them badly. That horse destroys the whole balance of the composition.

MR AMY: James, I had no idea you had such a small nature.

MR MORLAND: I don't like that remark; for your sake I don't like it. No one would have been more pleased than myself if you had picked up a Gainsborough. But this! Besides, look at the paper.

MR AMY: What is wrong with the paper, Mr Morland?

MR MORLAND: It is machine-made. Gainsborough was in his grave years before that paper was made.

(*After further inspection Mr Amy is convinced against his will, and the find is returned to his pocket less carefully than it had been produced*)

Don't get into a tantrum about it, George.

MR AMY: (*grandly*) I am not in a tantrum, and I should be obliged if you wouldn't George me. Smile on, Mr Morland, I congratulate you on your triumph; you have hurt an old friend to the quick. Bravo, bravo. Thank you, Mrs Morland, for a very pleasant visit. Good-day.

MRS MORLAND: (*prepared*) I shall see you into your coat, George.

MR AMY: I thank you, Mrs Morland, but I need no one to see me into my coat. Good-day.

(*He goes, and she blandly follows him. She returns with the culprit*)

MRS MORLAND: Now which of you is to say it first?

MR AMY: James, I am heartily ashamed of myself.

MR MORLAND: George, I apologise.

MR AMY: I quite see that it isn't a Gainsborough.

MR MORLAND: After all, it's certainly in the Gainsborough school.

(They clasp hands sheepishly, but the peacemaker helps the situation by showing a roguish face, and Mr Amy departs shaking a humorous fist at her)

MRS MORLAND: I coughed so often, James; and you must have heard me clicking.

MR MORLAND: I heard all right. Good old George! It's a pity he has no flair. He might as well order his prints by wireless.

MRS MORLAND: What is that?

MR MORLAND: Wireless it's to be called. There is an article about it in that paper. The fellow says that before many years have passed we shall be able to talk to ships on the ocean.

MRS MORLAND: *(who has resumed her knitting)* Nonsense, James.

MR MORLAND: Of course it's nonsense. And yet there is no denying, as he says, that there are more things in heaven and earth than are dreamt of in our philosophy.

MRS MORLAND: *(becoming grave)* You and I know that to be true, James.

(For a moment he does not know to what she is referring)

MR MORLAND: *(edging away from trouble)* Oh, that. My dear, that is all dead and done long ago.

MRS MORLAND: *(thankfully)* Yes. But sometimes when I look at Mary Rose — so happy —

MR MORLAND: She will never know anything about it.

MRS MORLAND: No, indeed. But some day she will fall in love—

MR MORLAND: *(wriggling)* That infant! Fanny, is it wise to seek trouble before it comes?

MRS MORLAND: She can't marry, James, without your first telling the man. We agreed.

MR MORLAND: Yes, I suppose I must — though I'm not certain I ought to. Sleeping dogs — Still, I'll keep my word, I'll tell him everything.

MRS MORLAND: Poor Mary Rose.

MR MORLAND: *(manfully)* Now then, none of that. Where is she now?

MRS MORLAND: Down at the boat-house with Simon, I think.

MR MORLAND: That is all right. Let her play about with Simon and the like. It may make a tomboy of her, but it will keep young men out of her head.

(She wonders at his obtuseness)

MRS MORLAND: You still think of Simon as a boy?

MR MORLAND: Bless the woman, he is only a midshipman.[4]

MRS MORLAND: A sub-lieutenant now.

MR MORLAND: Same thing. Why, Fanny, I still tip him. At least I did a year ago. And he liked it: 'Thanks no end, you are a trump,' he said, and then slipped behind the screen to see how much it was.

MRS MORLAND: He is a very delightful creature; but he isn't a boy any more.

MR MORLAND: It's not nice of you to put such ideas into my head. I'll go down to the boat-house at once. If this new invention was in working order, Fanny, I could send him packing without rising from my seat. I should simply say from this sofa, 'Is my little Mary Rose there?'

(To their surprise there is an answer from Mary Rose unseen)

MARY ROSE: *(in a voice more quaking than is its wont)* I'm here, Daddy.

MR MORLAND: *(rising)* Where are you, Mary Rose?

MARY ROSE: I am in the apple-tree.

(Mrs Morland smiles and is going to the window, but her husband checks her with a further exhibition of the marvel of the future)

MR MORLAND: What are you doing in the apple-tree, hoyden?

MARY ROSE: I'm hiding.

MR MORLAND: From Simon?

MARY ROSE: No; I'm not sure whom I'm hiding from. From myself, I think. Daddy, I'm frightened.

MR MORLAND: What has frightened you? Simon?

MARY ROSE: Yes — partly.

MR MORLAND: Who else?

MARY ROSE: I am most afraid of my daddy.

MR MORLAND: *(rather flattered)* Of me?

(If there is anything strange about this girl of eighteen who steps from the tree into the room, it is an elusiveness of which she is unaware. It has remained hidden from her girl friends, though in the after years, in the brief space before they forget her, they will probably say, because of what happened, that there was always something a little odd about Mary Rose. This oddness might be expressed thus, that the happiness and the glee of which she is almost overfull know of another attribute of her that never plays with them.

There is nothing splendid about Mary Rose, never can she become one of those secret women so much less innocent than she, yet perhaps so much sweeter in the kernel, who are the bane or glory, or the bane and glory, of greater lovers than she could ever

understand. She is just a rare and lovely flower, far less fitted
than those others for the tragic role.

She butts her head into Mrs Morland with a childish
impulsiveness that might overthrow a less accustomed bosom)

MARY ROSE: (*telling everything*) Mother!

MR MORLAND: You don't mean that anything has really
frightened you, Mary Rose?

MARY ROSE: I am not sure. Hold me tight, Mother.

MRS MORLAND: Darling, has Simon been disturbing you?

MARY ROSE: (*liking this way of putting it*) Yes, he has. It is all
Simon's fault.

MR MORLAND: But you said you were afraid even of me.

MARY ROSE: You are the only one.

MR MORLAND: Is this some game? Where is Simon?

MARY ROSE: (*in little mouthfuls*) He is at the foot of the tree.
He is not coming up by the tree. He wants to come in by the
door. That shows how important it is.

MR MORLAND: What is?

MARY ROSE: You see, his leave is up tomorrow, and he — wants
to see you, Daddy, before he goes.

MR MORLAND: I am sure he does. And I know why. I told you,
Fanny. Mary Rose, do you see my purse lying about?

MARY ROSE: Your purse, Dad?

MR MORLAND: Yes, you gosling. There is a fiver in it, and *that*
is what Master Simon wants to see me about.

(*Mary Rose again seeks her mother's breast*)

MRS MORLAND: Oh, James! Dearest, tell me what Simon has
been saying to you; whisper it, my love.

(*Mary Rose whispers*)

Yes, I thought it was that.

MARY ROSE: I am frightened to tell Daddy.

MRS MORLAND: James, you may as well be told bluntly; it isn't
your fiver that Simon wants, it is your daughter.

(*Mr Morland is aghast, and Mary Rose rushes into his arms to help*
him in this terrible hour)

MARY ROSE: (*as the injured party*) You will scold him, won't
you, Dad?

MR MORLAND: (*vainly trying to push her from him*) By — by —
by the — by all that is horrible I'll do more than scold him.
The puppy, I'll — I'll —

MARY ROSE: (*entreating*) Not more than scold him, Daddy —
not more. Mary Rose couldn't bear it if it was more.

MR MORLAND: (*blankly*) You are not in love with Simon, are
you?

MARY ROSE: Oh-h-h-h!

> (*She makes little runnings from the one parent to the other, carrying kisses for the wounds*)

Daddy, I am so awfully sorry that this has occurred. Mummy, what can we do? (*She cries*)

MRS MORLAND: (*soothing her*) My own, my pet. But he is only a boy, Mary Rose, just a very nice boy.

MARY ROSE: (*awed*) Mother, that is the wonderful, wonderful thing. He was just a boy — I quite understand that — he was a mere boy till today; and then, Daddy, he suddenly changed; all at once he became a man. It was while he was — telling me. You will scarcely know him now, Mother.

MRS MORLAND: Darling, he breakfasted with us; I think I shall know him still.

MARY ROSE: He is quite different from breakfast-time. He doesn't laugh any more, he would never think of capsizing the punt intentionally now, he has grown so grave, so manly, so — so *protective*, he thinks of everything now, of freeholds and leaseholds, and gravel soil, and hot and cold, and the hire system.[5]

> (*She cries again, but her eyes are sparkling through the rain*)

MR MORLAND: (*with spirit*) He has got as far as that, has he! Does he propose that this marriage should take place tomorrow?

MARY ROSE: (*eager to soften the blow*) Oh no, not for quite a long time. At earliest, not till his next leave.

MRS MORLAND: Mary Rose!

MARY ROSE: He is waiting down there, Mummy. May I bring him in?

MRS MORLAND: Of course, dearest.

MR MORLAND: Don't come with him, though.

MARY ROSE: Oh! (*She wonders what this means*) You know how shy Simon is.

MR MORLAND: I do not.

MRS MORLAND: Your father and I must have a talk with him alone, you see.

MARY ROSE: I — I suppose so. He so wants to do the right thing, Mother.

MRS MORLAND: I am sure he does.

MARY ROSE: Do you mind my going upstairs into the apple-room and sometimes knocking on the floor? I think it would be a help to him to know I am so near by.

MRS MORLAND: It would be a help to all of us, my sweet.

MARY ROSE: (*plaintively*) You — you won't try to put him against me, Daddy?

MR MORLAND: I would try my hardest if I thought I had any chance.

> (*When she has gone they are a somewhat forlorn pair*)

Poor old mother!

MRS MORLAND: Poor old father! There couldn't be a nicer boy, though.

MR MORLAND: No, but — (*He has a distressing thought*)

MRS MORLAND: (*quietly*) Yes, there's that.

MR MORLAND: It got me on the quick when she said, 'You won't try to put him against me, Daddy' — because that is just what I suppose I have got to do.

MRS MORLAND: He must be told.

MR MORLAND: (*weakly*) Fanny, let us keep it to ourselves.

MRS MORLAND: It would not be fair to him.

MR MORLAND: No, it wouldn't. (*Testily*) He will be an ass if it bothers him.

MRS MORLAND: (*timidly*) Yes.

> (*Simon comes in, a manly youth of twenty-three in naval uni-form. Whether he has changed much since breakfast-time we have no means of determining, but he is sufficiently attractive to make one hope that there will be no further change in the im-mediate future. He seems younger even than his years, because he is trying to look as if a decade or so had passed since the incident of the boat-house and he were now a married man of approved standing. He has come with honeyed words upon his lips, but suddenly finds that he is in the dock. His judges survey him silently, and he can only reply with an idiotic but perhaps ingratiating laugh*)

SIMON: Ha, ha, ha, ha, ha, ha, ha, ha! (*He ceases uncomfortably, like one who has made his statement*)

MR MORLAND: You will need to say more than that, you know, Simon, to justify your conduct.

MRS MORLAND: Oh, Simon, how could you!

SIMON: (*with a sinking*) It seems almost like stealing.

MR MORLAND: It is stealing.

SIMON: (*prudently*) Ha, ha, ha, ha, ha, ha!

> (*From the ceiling there comes a gentle tapping, as from a senior officer who is indicating that England expects her lieutenant this day to do his duty. Simon inflates*)

It is beastly hard on you, of course; but if you knew what Mary Rose is!

MRS MORLAND: (*pardonably*) We feel that even we know to some extent what Mary Rose is.

SIMON: (*tacking* [6]) Yes, rather; and so you can see how it has come about. (*This effort cheers him*) I would let myself be cut into little chips for her; I should almost like it. (*With a brief glance at his misspent youth*) Perhaps you have thought that I was a rather larky sort in the past?

MR MORLAND: (*sarcastically*) We see an extraordinary change in you, Simon.

SIMON: (*eagerly*) Have you noticed that? Mary Rose has noticed it too. That is my inner man coming out. (*Carefully*) To some young people marriage is a thing to be entered on lightly, but that is not my style. What I want is to give up larks, and all that, and insure my life, and read the political articles.

(*Further knocking from above reminds him of something else*)
Yes, and I promise you it won't be like losing a daughter but like gaining a son.

MRS MORLAND: Did Mary Rose tell you to say that?

SIMON: (*guiltily*) Well — (*Tap, tap*) Oh, another thing, I should consider it well worth being married to Mary Rose just to have you, Mrs Morland, for a mother-in-law.

MR MORLAND: (*pleased*) Well said, Simon; I like you the better for that.

MRS MORLAND: (*a demon*) Did she tell you to say that also?

SIMON: Well — At any rate, never shall I forget the respect and affection I owe to the parents of my beloved wife.

MR MORLAND: She is not your wife yet, you know.

SIMON: (*handsomely*) No, she isn't. But can she be? Mrs Morland, can she be?

MRS MORLAND: That is as may be, Simon. It is only a possible engagement that we are discussing at present.

SIMON: Yes, yes, of course. (*Becoming more difficult to resist as his reason goes*) I used to be careless about money, but I have thought of a trick of writing the word Economy in the inside of my watch, so that I'll see it every time I wind up. My people —

MR MORLAND: We like them, Simon.

(*The tapping is resumed*)

SIMON: I don't know whether you have noticed a sound from up above?

MR MORLAND: I did think I heard something.

SIMON: That is Mary Rose in the apple-room.

MRS MORLAND: No!

SIMON: Yes; she is doing that to help me. I promised to knock back as soon as I thought things were going well. What do you say? May I?

(*He gives them an imploring look, and mounts a chair, part of a fishing-rod in his hand*)

MR MORLAND: (*an easy road in sight*) I think, Fanny, he might?

MRS MORLAND: (*braver*) No. (*Tremulously*) There is a little thing, Simon, that Mary Rose's father and I feel we ought to tell you about her before — before you knock, my dear. It is not very important, I think, but it is something she doesn't know of herself, and it makes her a little different from other girls.

SIMON: (*alighting — sharply*) I won't believe anything against Mary Rose.

MRS MORLAND: We have nothing to tell you against her.

MR MORLAND: It is just something that happened, Simon. She couldn't help it. It hasn't troubled us in the least for years, but we always agreed that she mustn't be engaged before we told the man. We must have your promise, before we tell you, that you will keep it to yourself.

SIMON: (*frowning*) I promise.

MRS MORLAND: You must never speak of it even to her.

SIMON: Not to Mary Rose? I wish you would say quickly what it is.

(*They are now sitting round the little table*)

MR MORLAND: It can't be told quite in a word. It happened seven years ago, when Mary Rose was eleven. We were in a remote part of Scotland — in the Outer Hebrides.

SIMON: I once went on shore there from the *Gadfly*, very bleak and barren, rocks and rough grass, I never saw a tree.

MR MORLAND: It is mostly like that. There is a whaling-station. We went because I was fond of fishing. I haven't had the heart to fish since. Quite close to the inn where we put up there is — a little island.

(*He sees that little island so clearly that he forgets to go on*)

MRS MORLAND: It is quite a small island, Simon, uninhabited, no sheep even. I suppose there are only about six acres of it. There are trees there, quite a number of them, Scotch firs and a few rowan-trees, — they have red berries, you know. There seemed to us to be nothing very particular about the island, unless, perhaps, that it is curiously complete in itself. There is a tiny pool in it that might be called a lake, out of which a stream flows. It has hillocks and a glade, a sort of miniature land. That was all we noticed, though it became the most dreaded place in the world to us.

MR MORLAND: (*considerately*) I can tell him without your being here, Fanny.

MRS MORLAND: I prefer to stay, James.

MR MORLAND: I fished a great deal in the loch between that

island and the larger one. The sea-trout were wonderful. I often rowed Mary Rose across to the island and left her there to sketch. She was fond of sketching in those days, we thought them pretty things. I could see her from the boat most of the time, and we used to wave to each other. Then I would go back for her when I stopped fishing.

MRS MORLAND: I didn't often go with them. We didn't know at the time that the natives had a superstition against landing on the island, and that it was supposed to resent this. It had a Gaelic name which means 'The Island that Likes to be Visited.' Mary Rose knew nothing of this, and she was very fond of her island. She used to talk to it, call it her darling, things like that.

SIMON: (*restless*) Tell me what happened.

MR MORLAND: It was on what was to be our last day. I had landed her on this island as usual, and in the early evening I pulled across to take her off. From the boat I saw her, sitting on a stump of a tree that was her favourite seat, and she waved gaily to me and I to her. Then I rowed over, with, of course, my back to her. I had less than a hundred yards to go, but, Simon, when I got across she wasn't there.

SIMON: You seem so serious about it. She was hiding from you?

MRS MORLAND: She wasn't on the island, Simon.

SIMON: But — but — oh, but —

MR MORLAND: Don't you think I searched and searched?

MRS MORLAND: All of us. No one in the village went to bed that night. It was then we learned how they feared the island.

MR MORLAND: The little pool was dragged. There was nothing we didn't try; but she was gone.

SIMON: (*distressed*) I can't — there couldn't — but never mind that. Tell me how you found her.

MRS MORLAND: It was the twentieth day after she disappeared. Twenty days!

SIMON: Some boat —?

MR MORLAND: There was no boat but mine.

SIMON: Tell me.

MRS MORLAND: The search had long been given up, but we couldn't come away.

MR MORLAND: I was wandering one day along the shore of the loch, you can imagine in what state of mind. I stopped and stood looking across the water at the island, and, Simon, I saw her sitting on the tree-trunk sketching.

MRS MORLAND: Mary Rose!

MR MORLAND: She waved to me and went on sketching. I —

I waved back to her. I got into the boat and rowed across just in the old way, except that I sat facing her, so that I could see her all the time. When I landed, the first thing she said to me was, 'Why did you row in that funny way, Dad?' Then I saw at once that she didn't know anything had happened.

SIMON: Mr Morland! How could —? Where did she say she had been?

MRS MORLAND: She didn't know she had been anywhere, Simon.

MR MORLAND: She thought I had just come for her at the usual time.

SIMON: Twenty days. You mean she had been on the island all that time?

MR MORLAND: We don't know.

MRS MORLAND: James brought her back to me just the same merry unselfconscious girl, with no idea that she had been away from me for more than an hour or two.

SIMON: But when you told her —

MRS MORLAND: We never told her; she doesn't know now.

SIMON: Surely you —

MRS MORLAND: We had her back again, Simon; that was the great thing. At first we thought to tell her after we got her home; and then, it was all so inexplicable, we were afraid to alarm her, to take the bloom off her. In the end we decided never to tell her.

SIMON: You told no one?

MR MORLAND: Several doctors.

SIMON: How did they explain it?

MR MORLAND: They had no explanation for it except that it never took place. You can think that, too, if you like.

SIMON: I don't know what to think. It has had no effect on her, at any rate.

MR MORLAND: None whatever — and you can guess how we used to watch.

MRS MORLAND: Simon, I am very anxious to be honest with you. I have sometimes thought that our girl is curiously young for her age — as if — you know how just a touch of frost may stop the growth of a plant and yet leave it blooming — it has sometimes seemed to me as if a cold finger had once touched my Mary Rose.

SIMON: Mrs Morland!

MRS MORLAND: There is nothing in it.

SIMON: What you are worrying about is just her innocence — which seems a holy thing to me.

MRS MORLAND: And indeed it is.

SIMON: If that is all —

MR MORLAND: We have sometimes thought that she had momentary glimpses back into that time, but before we could question her in a cautious way about them the gates had closed and she remembered nothing. You never saw her talking to — to some person who wasn't there?

SIMON: No.

MRS MORLAND: Nor listening, as it were, for some sound that never came?

SIMON: A sound? Do you mean a sound from the island?

MRS MORLAND: Yes, we think so. But at any rate she has long outgrown those fancies.

    (*She fetches a sketch-book from a drawer*)

Here are the sketches she made. You can take the book away with you and look at them at your leisure.

SIMON: It is a little curious that she has never spoken to me of that holiday. She tells me everything.

MRS MORLAND: No, that isn't curious, it is just that the island has faded from her memory. I should be troubled if she began to recall it. Well, Simon, we felt we had to tell you. That is all we know, I am sure it is all we shall ever know. What are you going to do?

SIMON: What do you think!

    (*He mounts the chair again, and knocks triumphantly. A happy
    tapping replies*)

You heard? That means it's all right. You'll see how she'll come tearing down to us!

MRS MORLAND: (*kissing him*) You dear boy, you will see how I shall go tearing up to her. (*She goes off*)

SIMON: I do love Mary Rose, sir.

MR MORLAND: So do we, Simon. I suppose that made us love her a little more than other daughters are loved. Well, it is dead and done with, and it doesn't disturb me now at all. I hope you won't let it disturb you.

SIMON: (*undisturbed*) Rather not. (*Disturbed*) I say, I wonder whether I *have* noticed her listening for a sound?

MR MORLAND: Not you. We did wisely, didn't we, in not questioning her?

SIMON: Oh lord, yes. 'The Island that Likes to be Visited.' It is a queer name. (*Boyishly*) I say, let's forget all about it. (*He looks at the ceiling*) I almost wish her mother hadn't gone up to her. It will make Mary Rose longer in coming down.

MR MORLAND: (*humorous*) Fanny will think of nicer things to say to her than you could think of, Simon.

SIMON: Yes, I know. Ah, now you are chaffing me. (*Apologetically*) You see, sir, my leave is up to-morrow.

(*Mary Rose comes rushing in*)

Mary Rose!

(*She darts past him into her father's arms*)

MARY ROSE: It isn't you I am thinking of; it is father, it is poor father. Oh, Simon, how could you? Isn't it hateful of him, Daddy!

MR MORLAND: I should just say it is. Is your mother crying too?

MARY ROSE: (*squeaking*) Yes.

MR MORLAND: I see I am going to have an abominable day. If you two don't mind very much being left alone, I think I'll go and sit in the apple-room and cry with your mother. It is close and dark and musty up there, and when we feel we can't stick it any longer I'll knock on the floor, Simon, as a sign that we are coming down.

(*He departs on this light note. We see how the minds of these two children match*)

SIMON: Mary Rose!

MARY ROSE: Oh, Simon — you and me.

SIMON: You and me, that's it. We are *us*, now. Do you like it?

MARY ROSE: It is so fearfully solemn.

SIMON: You are not frightened, are you?

(*She nods*)

Not at me?

(*She shakes her head*)

What at?

MARY ROSE: At *it* — Being — married. Simon, after we are married you will sometimes let me play, won't you?

SIMON: Games?

(*She nods*)

Rather. Why, I'll go on playing rugger myself. Lots of married people play games.

MARY ROSE: (*relieved*) I'm glad; Simon, do you love me?

SIMON: Dearest — precious — my life — my sweetheart. Which name do you like best?

MARY ROSE: I'm not sure. They are all very nice. (*She is conscious of the ceiling*) Oughtn't we to knock to those beloveds to come down?

SIMON: Please don't. I know a lot about old people, darling. I assure you they don't mind very much sitting in dull places.

MARY ROSE: We mustn't be selfish.

SIMON: Honest Injun,[7] it isn't selfishness. You see, I have a ton of things to tell you. About how I put it to them, and how I remembered what you told me to say, and the way I got the soft side of them. They have heard it all already, so it would really be selfish to bring them down.

MARY ROSE: I'm not so sure.

SIMON: I'll tell you what we'll do. Let's go back to the boat-house, and then they can come down and be cosy here.

MARY ROSE: (*gleeful*) Let's! We can stay there till tea-time. (*She wants to whirl him away at once.*)

SIMON: It is fresh down there; put on a jacket, my star.

MARY ROSE: Oh, bother!

SIMON: (*firmly*) My child, you are in my care now; I am responsible for you, and I order you to put on a jacket.

MARY ROSE: Order! Simon, you do say the loveliest things. I'll put it on at once.

> (*She is going towards the little door at the back, but turns to say something important*)

Simon, I'll tell you a funny thing about me. I may be wrong, but I think I'll sometimes love you to kiss me, and sometimes it will be better not.

SIMON: All right. Tell me, what were you thinking as you sat up there in the apple-room, waiting?

MARY ROSE: Holy things.

SIMON: About love?

> (*She nods*)

MARY ROSE: We'll try to be good, won't we, Simon, please?

SIMON: Rather. Honest Injun, we'll be nailers.[8] Did you think of — our wedding-day?

MARY ROSE: A little

SIMON: Only a little?

MARY ROSE: But frightfully clearly. (*Suddenly*) Simon, I had such a delicious idea about our honeymoon. There is a place in Scotland — in the Hebrides — I should love to go there.

SIMON: (*taken aback*) The Hebrides?

MARY ROSE: We once went to it when I was little. Isn't it funny, I had almost forgotten about that island, and then suddenly I saw it quite clearly as I was sitting up there. (*Senselessly*) Of course it was the little old woman who pointed it out to me.

> (*Simon is disturbed*)

SIMON: (*gently*) Mary Rose, there are only yourselves and the three maids in the house, aren't there?

MARY ROSE: (*surprised*) You know there are. Whatever makes you ask?

SIMON: (*cautiously*) I thought — I thought I had a glimpse of a little old woman on the stair today.

MARY ROSE: (*interested*) Who on earth could that be?

SIMON: It doesn't matter, I had made a mistake. Tell me, what was there particular about that place in the Hebrides?

MARY ROSE: Oh, the fishing for father. But there was an island where I often — My little island!

SIMON: (*perhaps quite unnecessarily*) What are you listening for, Mary Rose?

MARY ROSE: Was I? I don't hear anything. Oh, my dear, my dear, I should love to show you the tree-trunk and the rowan-tree where I used to sketch while father was in the boat. I expect he used to land me on the island because it was such a safe place.

SIMON: (*troubled*) That had been the idea. I am not going to spend my honeymoon by the sea, though. And yet I should like to go to the Hebrides — some day — to see that island.

MARY ROSE: Yes, let's.

(*She darts off through the little door for her jacket*)

ACT TWO

An island in the Outer Hebrides. A hundred yards away, across the loch at the back, may be seen the greater island of which this might be but a stone cast into the sea by some giant hand: perhaps an evil stone which the big island had to spew forth but could not sink. It is fair to look upon today, all its menace hidden under mosses of various hues that are a bath to the eye; an island placid as a cow grazing or a sulky lady asleep. The sun which has left the bleak hills beyond is playing hide and seek on it; one suddenly has the curious fancy to ask, with whom? A blessed spot it might be thought, rather than sinister, were there not those two trees, a fir and a rowan, their arms outstretched for ever southward, as if they had been struck while in full flight and could no longer pray to their gods to carry them away from this island. A young Highlander, a Cameron, passes in a boat at the back. Mary Rose and Simon come into view on the island. We have already heard them swishing a way through whins and bracken that are unseen. They are dressed as English people dress in Scotland. They have been married for four years and are still the gay young creatures of their engagement day. Their talk is the happy nonsense that leaves no ripple unless the unexpected happens.

MARY ROSE: (*thrilled*) I think, I think, I don't think at all, I am quite sure. This is the place. Simon, kiss me, kiss me quick. You promised to kiss me quick when we found the place.

SIMON: (*obeying*) I am not the man to break my word. At the same time, Mary Rose, I would point out to you that this is the third spot you have picked out as being the place, and three times have I kissed you quick on that understanding. This can't go on, you know. As for your wonderful island, it turns out to be about the size of the Round Pond.[9]

MARY ROSE: I always said it was little like myself.

SIMON: It was obviously made to fit you, or you to fit it; one of you was measured for the other. At any rate, we have now been all round it, and all through it, as my bleeding limbs testify.
(*The whins have been tearing at him, and he rubs his legs*)

MARY ROSE: They didn't hurt me at all.

SIMON: Perhaps they like you better than me. Well, we have made a good search for the place where you used to sit and sketch, and you must now take your choice.

MARY ROSE: It was here. I told you of the fir and the rowan-tree.

SIMON: There were a fir and a rowan at each of the other places.

MARY ROSE: Not this fir, not this rowan.

SIMON: You have me there.

MARY ROSE: Simon, I know I'm not clever, but I'm always right. The rowan-berries! I used to put them in my hair. (*She puts them in her hair again*) Darling rowan-tree, are you glad to see me back? You don't look a bit older, how do you think *I* am wearing? I shall tell you a secret. You too, firry. Come closer, both of you. Put your arms around me, and listen: I am married!
(*The branch of which she has been making a scarf disengages itself*)
It didn't like that, Simon, it is jealous. After all, it knew me first. Dearest trees, if I had known that you felt for me in that way — but it is too late now. I have been married for nearly four years, and this is the man. His name is Lieutenant Simon Sobersides. (*She darts about making discoveries*)

SIMON: (*tranquilly smoking*) What is it now?

MARY ROSE: That moss! I feel sure there is a tree-trunk beneath it, the very root on which I used to sit and sketch.
(*He clears away some of the moss*)

SIMON: It is a tree-trunk right enough.

MARY ROSE: I believe — I believe I cut my name on it with a knife.

SIMON: This looks like it. 'M–A–R–' and there it stops. That is always where the blade of the knife breaks.

MARY ROSE: My ownest seat, how I have missed you.

SIMON: Don't you believe it, old tree-trunk. She had forgotten all about you, and you just came vaguely back to her mind because we happened to be in the neighbourhood.

MARY ROSE: Yes, I suppose that is true. You were the one who wanted to come, Simon. I wonder why?

SIMON: (*with his answer ready*) No particular reason. I wanted to see a place you had visited as a child; that was all. But what a trumpery island it proves to be.

MARY ROSE: (*who perhaps agrees with him*) How can you? Even if it is true, you needn't say it before them all, hurting their feelings. Dear seat, here is one for each year I have been away. (*She kisses the trunk a number of times*)

SIMON: (*counting*) Eleven. Go on, give it all the news. Tell it we don't have a house of our own yet.

MARY ROSE: You see, dear seat, we live with my daddy and mother, because Simon is so often away at sea. You know, the loveliest thing in the world is the navy, and the loveliest thing in the navy is HMS *Valiant*, and the loveliest thing on HMS *Valiant* is Lietenant Simon Sobersides, and the loveliest thing on Lieutenant Simon Sobersides is the little tuft of hair which will keep standing up at the back of his head.

(*Simon, who is lolling on the moss, is so used to her prattle that his eyes close*)

But, listen, you trees, I have a much more wonderful secret than that. You can have three guesses. It is this . . . I — have — got — a baby! A girl? No thank you. He is two years and nine months, and he says such beautiful things to me about loving me. Oh, rowan, do you think he means them?

SIMON: I distinctly heard it say yes.

(*He opens his eyes, to see her gazing entranced across the water*) You needn't pretend that you can see him.

MARY ROSE: I do. Can't you? He is waving his bib to us.

SIMON: That is nurse's cap.

MARY ROSE: Then he is waving it. How clever of him. (*She waves her handkerchief*) Now they are gone. Isn't it funny to think that from this very spot I used to wave to father? That was a happy time.

SIMON: I should be happier here if I wasn't so hungry. I wonder where Cameron is. I told him after he landed us to tie up the boat at any good place and make a fire. I suppose I had better try to make it myself.

MARY ROSE: Do you know, Simon, I don't think daddy and mother like this island.

SIMON: (*on his guard*) Help me with the fire, you chatterbox.
  (*He has long ceased to credit the story he heard four years ago, but he is ever watchful for Mary Rose*)

MARY ROSE: They never seem to want to speak of it.

SIMON: Forgotten it, I suppose.

MARY ROSE: I shall write to them from the inn this evening. How surprised they will be to know I am there again.

SIMON: (*casually*) I wouldn't write from there. Wait till we cross to the mainland.

MARY ROSE: Why not from there?

SIMON: Oh, no reason. But if they have a distaste for the place, perhaps they wouldn't like our coming. I say, praise me, I have got this fire alight.

MARY ROSE: (*who is occasionally pertinacious*) Simon, why did you want to come to my island without me?

SIMON: Did I? Oh, I merely suggested your remaining at the inn because I thought you seemed tired. I wonder where Cameron can have got to?

MARY ROSE: Here he comes. (*Solicitously*) Do be polite to him, dear; you know how touchy they are.

SIMON: I am learning!
  (*The boat, with Cameron, draws in. He is a gawky youth of twenty, in the poor but honourable garb of the gillie, and is not specially impressive until you question him about the universe*)

CAMERON: (*in the soft voice of the Highlander*) Iss it the wish of Mr Blake that I should land?

SIMON: Yes, yes, Cameron, with the luncheon.
  (*Cameron steps ashore with a fishing basket*)

CAMERON: Iss it the wish of Mr Blake that I open the basket?

SIMON: We shall tumble out the luncheon if you bring a trout or two. I want you to show my wife, Cameron, how one cooks fish by the water's edge.

CAMERON: I will do it with pleasure. (*He pauses*) There iss one little matter; it iss of small importance. You may haf noticed that I always address you as Mr Blake. I notice that you always address me as Cameron; I take no offence.

MARY ROSE: Oh dear, I am sure I always address you as Mr Cameron.

CAMERON: That iss so, ma'am. You may haf noticed that I always address you as 'ma'am'. It iss my way of indicating that

I consider you a ferry genteel young matron, and of all such I
am the humble servant. (*He pauses*) In saying I am your humble
servant I do not imply that I am not as good as you are. With
this brief explanation, ma'am, I will now fetch the trouts.

SIMON: (*taking advantage of his departure*) That is one in the eye
for me. But I'm hanged if I mister him.

MARY ROSE: Simon, do be careful. If you want to say anything
to me that is dangerous, say it in French.

    (*Cameron returns with two small sea-trout*)

CAMERON: The trouts, ma'am, having been cleaned in a thor-
ough and yet easy manner by pulling them up and down in the
water, the next procedure iss as follows.

    (*He wraps up the trout in a piece of newspaper and soaks them
    in the water*)

I now place the soaking little parcels on the fire, and when the
paper begins to burn it will be a sure sign that the trouts iss now
ready, like myself, ma'am, to be your humble servants. (*He is
returning to the boat*)

MARY ROSE: (*who has been preparing the feast*) Don't go away.

CAMERON: If it iss agreeable to Mistress Blake I would wish to
go back to the boat.

MARY ROSE: Why?

    (*Cameron is not comfortable*)

It would be more agreeable to me if you would stay.

CAMERON: (*shuffling*) I will stay.

SIMON: Good man — and look after the trout. It is the most
heavenly way of cooking fish, Mary Rose.

CAMERON: It iss a tasty way, Mr Blake, but I would not use
the word heavenly in this connection.

SIMON: I stand corrected. (*Tartly*) I must say —

MARY ROSE: *Prenez garde, mon brave!*

SIMON: *Mon dieu! Qu'il est un drôle!*

MARY ROSE: *Mais moi, je l'aime; il est tellement*[10] — What is the
French for an original?

SIMON: That stumps me.

CAMERON: Colloquially *coquin*[11] might be used, though the
classic writers would probably say simply *un original*.

SIMON: (*with a groan*) Phew, this is serious. What was that book
you were reading, Cameron, while I was fishing?

CAMERON: It iss a small Euripides[12] I carry in the pocket, Mr
Blake.

SIMON: Latin, Mary Rose!

CAMERON: It may be Latin, but in these parts we know no
better than to call it Greek.

SIMON: Crushed again! But I dare say it is good for me. Sit down and have pot-luck with us.

CAMERON: I thank you, Mr Blake, but it would not be good manners for a paid man to sit with his employers.

MARY ROSE: When I ask you, Mr Cameron?

CAMERON: It iss kindly meant, but I haf not been introduced to you.

MARY ROSE: Oh, but — oh, do let me. My husband Mr Blake — Mr Cameron.

CAMERON: I hope you are ferry well, sir.

SIMON: The same to you, Mr Cameron. How do you do? Lovely day, isn't it?

CAMERON: It iss a fairly fine day. (*He is not yet appeased*)

MARY ROSE: (*to the rescue*) Simon!

SIMON: Ah! Do you know my wife? Mr Cameron — Mrs Blake.

CAMERON: I am ferry pleased to make Mistress Blake's acquaintance. Iss Mistress Blake making a long stay in these parts?

MARY ROSE: No, alas, we go across tomorrow.

CAMERON: I hope the weather will be favourable.

MARY ROSE: Thank you (*passing him the sandwiches*). And now, you know, you are our guest.

CAMERON: I am much obliged. (*He examines the sandwiches with curiosity*) Butcher-meat! This iss ferry excellent.

(*He bursts into a surprising fit of laughter, and suddenly cuts it off*)

Please to excuse my behaviour. You haf been laughing at me all this time, but you did not know I haf been laughing at myself also, though keeping a remarkable control over my features. I will now haf my laugh out, and then I will explain. (*He finishes his laugh*) I will now explain. I am not the solemn prig I haf pretended to you to be, I am really a fairly attractive young man, but I am shy and I haf been guarding against your taking liberties with me, not because of myself, who am nothing, but because of the noble profession it iss my ambition to enter. (*They discover that they like him*)

MARY ROSE: Do tell us what that is.

CAMERON: It iss the ministry. I am a student of Aberdeen University, and in the vacation I am a boatman, or a gillie, or anything you please, to help to pay my fees.

SIMON: Well done!

CAMERON: I am obliged to Mr Blake. And I may say, now that we know one another socially, that there iss much in Mr Blake which I am trying to copy.

SIMON: Something in me worth copying!

CAMERON: It iss not Mr Blake's learning; he has not much learning, but I haf always understood that the English manage without it. What I admire in you iss your ferry nice manners and your general deportment, in all which I haf a great deal to learn yet, and I watch these things in Mr Blake and take memoranda of them in a little note-book.

(*Simon expands*)

MARY ROSE: Mr Cameron, do tell me that I also am in the little note-book?

CAMERON: You are not, ma'am, it would not be seemly in me. But it iss written in my heart, and also I haf said it to my father, that I will remain a bachelor unless I can marry some lady who iss ferry like Mistress Blake.

MARY ROSE: Simon, you never said anything to me as pretty as that. Is your father a crofter in the village?

CAMERON: Yes, ma'am, when he iss not at the University of Aberdeen.

SIMON: My stars, does he go there too?

CAMERON: He does so. We share a ferry small room between us.

SIMON: Father and son. Is he going into the ministry also?

CAMERON: Such iss not his purpose. When he has taken his degree he will return and be a crofter again.

SIMON: In that case I don't see what he is getting out of it.

CAMERON: He iss getting the grandest thing in the world out of it; he iss getting education.

(*Simon feels that he is being gradually rubbed out, and it is a relief to him that Cameron has now to attend to the trout. The paper they are wrapped in has begun to burn*)

MARY ROSE: (*for the first time eating of trout as it should be cooked*) Delicious! (*She offers a portion to Cameron*)

CAMERON: No, I thank you. I haf lived on trouts most of my life. This butcher-meat iss more of an excellent novelty to me.

(*He has been standing all this time*)

MARY ROSE: Do sit down, Mr Cameron.

CAMERON: I am doing ferry well here, I thank you.

MARY ROSE: But, please.

CAMERON: (*with decision*) I will not sit down on this island.

SIMON: (*curiously*) Come, come, are you superstitious, you who are going into the ministry?

CAMERON: This island has a bad name. I haf never landed on it before.

MARY ROSE: A bad name, Mr Cameron? Oh, but what a

shame! When I was here long ago, I often came to the island.

CAMERON: Iss that so? It was not a chancey thing to do.

MARY ROSE: But it is a darling island.

CAMERON: That iss the proper way to speak of it.

MARY ROSE: I am sure I never heard a word against it. Have you, Simon?.

SIMON: (*brazenly*) Not I. I have heard that its Gaelic name has an odd meaning — 'The Island that Likes to be Visited', but there is nothing terrifying in that.

MARY ROSE: The name is new to me, Mr Cameron. I think it is sweet.

CAMERON: That iss as it may be, Mistress Blake.

SIMON: What is there against the island?

CAMERON: For one thing, they are saying it has no authority to be here. It was not always here, so they are saying. Then one day it was here.

SIMON: That little incident happened before your time, I should say, Mr Cameron.

CAMERON: It happened before the time of anyone now alive, Mr Blake.

SIMON: I thought so. And does the island ever go away for a jaunt in the same way?

CAMERON: There are some who say that it does.

SIMON: But you have not seen it on the move yourself?

CAMERON: I am not always watching it, Mr Blake.

SIMON: Anything else against it?

CAMERON: There iss the birds. Too many birds come here. The birds like this island more than iss seemly.

SIMON: Birds here! What could bring them here?

CAMERON: It iss said they come to listen.

SIMON: To listen to the silence? An island that is as still as an empty church.

CAMERON: I do not know; that iss what they say.

MARY ROSE: I think it is a lovely story about the birds. I expect the kind things come because this island likes to be visited.

CAMERON: That iss another thing; for, mark you, Mistress Blake, an island that had visitors would not need to want to be visited. And why has it not visitors? Because they are afraid to visit it.

MARY ROSE: Whatever are they afraid of?

CAMERON: That iss what I say to them. Whateffer are you afraid of, I say.

MARY ROSE: But what are *you* afraid of, Mr Cameron?

CAMERON: The same thing that they are afraid of. There are stories, ma'am

MARY ROSE: Do tell us. Simon, wouldn't it be lovely if he would tell us some misty, eerie Highland stories?

SIMON: I don't know; not unless they are pretty ones.

MARY ROSE: Please, Mr Cameron! I love to have my blood curdled.

CAMERON: There iss many stories. There iss that one of the boy who was brought to this island. He was no older than your baby.

SIMON: What happened to him?

CAMERON: No one knows, Mr Blake. His father and mother and their friends, they were gathering rowans on the island, and when they looked round he was gone.

SIMON: Lost?

CAMERON: He could not be found. He was never found.

MARY ROSE: Never! He had fallen into the water?

CAMERON: That iss a good thing to say, that he had fallen into the water. That iss what I say.

SIMON: But you don't believe it?

CAMERON: I do not.

MARY ROSE: What do the people in the village say?

CAMERON: Some say he iss on the island still.

SIMON: Mr Cameron! Oh, Mr Cameron! What does your father say?

CAMERON: He will be saying that they are not here always, but that they come and go.

SIMON: They? Who are they?

CAMERON: (*uncomfortably*) I do not know.

SIMON: Perhaps he heard what the birds come to listen to!

CAMERON: That iss what they say. He had heard the island calling.

SIMON: (*hesitating*) How does the island call?

CAMERON: I do not know.

SIMON: Do you know anyone who has heard the call?

CAMERON: I do not. No one can hear it but those for whom it iss meant.

MARY ROSE: But if that child heard it, the others must have heard it also, as they were with him.

CAMERON: They heard nothing. This iss how it will be. I might be standing close to you, Mistress Blake, as it were here, and I might hear it, ferry loud, terrible, or in soft whispers — no one knows — but I would haf to go, and you will not haf heard a sound.

MARY ROSE: Simon, isn't it creepy!

SIMON: But full of holes, I have no doubt. How long ago is this supposed to have happened, credulous one?

CAMERON: It was before I was born.

SIMON: I thought so.

MARY ROSE: Simon, don't make fun of my island. Do you know any more ducky stories about it, Mr Cameron?

CAMERON: I cannot tell them if Mr Blake will be saying things the island might not like to hear.

SIMON: Not 'chancey' I suppose.

MARY ROSE: Simon, promise to be good.

SIMON: All right, Cameron.

CAMERON: This one iss about a young English miss, and they say she was about ten years of age.

MARY ROSE: Not so much younger than I was when I came here. How long ago was it?

CAMERON: I think it iss ten years ago this summer.

MARY ROSE: Simon, it must have been the year after I was here!
   (*Simon thinks she has heard enough*)

SIMON: Very likely. But, I say, we mustn't stay on gossiping. We must be getting back. Did you bail out the boat?

CAMERON: I did not, but I will do it now if such iss your wish.

MARY ROSE: The story first; I won't go without the story.

CAMERON: Well, then, the father of this miss he will be fond of the fishing, and he sometimes landed the little one on the island while he fished round it from the boat.

MARY ROSE: Just as father used to do with me!

SIMON: I dare say lots of bold tourists come over here.

CAMERON: That iss so, if ignorance be boldness, and some-times —

SIMON: Quite so. But I really think we must be starting.

MARY ROSE: No, dear. Please go on, Mr Cameron.

CAMERON: One day the father pulled over for his little one as usual. He saw her from the boat, and it iss said she kissed her hand to him. Then in a moment more he reached the island, but she was gone.

MARY ROSE: Gone?

CAMERON: She had heard the call of the island, though no sound came to him.

MARY ROSE: Doesn't it make one shiver!

CAMERON: My father was one of the searchers; for many days they searched.

MARY ROSE: But it would not take many minutes to search this darling little island.

CAMERON: They searched, ma'am, long after there was no sense in searching.

MARY ROSE: What a curdling story! Simon dear, it might have been Mary Rose. Is there any more?

CAMERON: There iss more. It was about a month afterwards. Her father was walking on the shore, over there, and he saw something moving on the island. All in a tremble, ma'am, he came across in the boat, and it was his little miss.

MARY ROSE: Alive?

CAMERON: Yes, ma'am.

MARY ROSE: I am glad: but it rather spoils the mystery.

SIMON: How, Mary Rose?

MARY ROSE: Because she could tell them what happened, stupid. Whatever was it?

CAMERON: It iss not so easy as that. She did not know that anything had happened. She thought she had been parted from her father for but an hour.

(*Mary Rose shivers and takes her husband's hand*)

SIMON: (*speaking more lightly than he is feeling*) You and your bogies and wraiths, you man of the mists.

MARY ROSE: (*smiling*) Don't be alarmed, Simon; I was only pretending.

CAMERON: It iss not good to disbelieve the stories when you are in these parts. I believe them all when I am here, though I turn the cold light of remorseless Reason on them when I am in Aberdeen.

SIMON: Is that 'chancey', my friend? An island that has such extraordinary powers could surely send its call to Aberdeen or farther.

CAMERON: (*troubled*) I had not thought of that. That may be ferry true.

SIMON: Beware, Mr Cameron, lest some day when you are preaching far from here the call plucks you out of the very pulpit and brings you back to the island like a trout on a long cast.

CAMERON: I do not like Mr Blake's way of talking. I will go and bail the boat.

(*He goes back to the boat, which soon drifts out of sight*)

MARY ROSE: (*pleasantly thrilled*) Suppose it were true, Simon!

SIMON: (*stoutly*) But it isn't

MARY ROSE: No, of course not; but if it had been, how awful for the girl when her father told her that she had been away for weeks.

SIMON: Perhaps she was never told. He may have thought it wiser not to disturb her.

MARY ROSE: Poor girl! Yes, I suppose that would have been best. And yet — it was taking a risk.

SIMON: How?

MARY ROSE: Well, not knowing what had happened before, she might come back and — and be caught again. (*She draws closer to him*) Little island, I don't think I like you today.

SIMON: If she ever comes back, let us hope it is with an able-bodied husband to protect her.

MARY ROSE: (*comfortably*) Nice people, husbands. You won't let them catch me, will you, Simon?

SIMON: Let 'em try. (*Gaily*) And now to pack up the remnants of the feast and escape from the scene of the crime. We will never come back again, Mary Rose, I'm too frightened!

(*She helps him to pack*)

MARY ROSE: It is a shame to be funny about my island. You poor, lonely isle. I never knew about your liking to be visited, and I dare say I shall never visit you any more. The last time of anything is always sad, don't you think, Simon?

SIMON: (*briskly*) There must always be a last time, dearest dear.

MARY ROSE: Yes — I suppose — for everything. There must be a last time I shall see you, Simon. (*Playing with his hair*) Some day I shall flatten this tuft for the thousandth time, and then never do it again.

SIMON: Some day I shall look for it and it won't be there. That day I shall say 'Good riddance.'

MARY ROSE: I shall cry. (*She is whimsical rather than merry and merry rather than sad*)

(*Simon touches her hair with his lips*)

Some day, Simon, you will kiss me for the last time.

SIMON: That wasn't the last time, at any rate. (*To prove it he kisses her again, sportively, little thinking that this may be the last time. She quivers*) What is it?

MARY ROSE: I don't know; something seemed to pass over me.

SIMON: You and your last times. Let me tell you, Mistress Blake, there will be a last time of seeing your baby. (*Hurriedly*) I mean only that he can't always be infantile; but the day after you have seen him for the last time as a baby you will see him for the first time as a little gentleman. Think of that.

MARY ROSE: (*clapping her hands*) The loveliest time of all will be when he is a man and takes me on his knee instead of my putting him on mine. Oh, gorgeous! (*With one of her sudden changes*) Don't you think the sad thing is that we seldom know when the last time has come? We could make so much more of it.

SIMON: Don't you believe that. To know would spoil it all.

(*The packing is nearly completed*)

I suppose I ought to stamp out the fire?

MARY ROSE: Let Cameron do that. I want you to come and sit beside me, Simon, and make love to me.

SIMON: What a life. Let me see now, how does one begin? Which arm is it? I believe I have forgotten the way.

MARY ROSE: Then I shall make love to you. (*Playing with his hair*) Have I been a nice wife to you, Simon? I don't mean always and always. There was that awful day when I threw the butter-dish at you. I am so sorry. But have I been a tolerably good wife on the whole, not a wonderful one, but a wife that would pass in a crowd?

SIMON: Look here, if you are going to butt me with your head in that way, you must take that pin out of your hair.

MARY ROSE: Have I been all right as a mother, Simon? Have I been the sort of mother a child could both love and respect?

SIMON: That is a very awkward question. You must ask that of Harry Morland Blake.

MARY ROSE: Have I —?

SIMON: Shut up, Mary Rose. I know you: you will be crying in a moment, and you don't have a handkerchief, for I wrapped it round the trout whose head came off.

MARY ROSE: At any rate, Simon Blake, say you forgive me about the butter-dish.

SIMON: I am not so sure of that.

MARY ROSE: And there were some other things — almost worse than the butter-dish.

SIMON: I should just say there were.

MARY ROSE: Simon, how can you? There was nothing so bad as that.

SIMON: (*shaking his head*) I can smile at it now, but at the time I was a miserable man. I wonder I didn't take to drink.

MARY ROSE: Poor old Simon. But how stupid you were, dear, not to understand.

SIMON: How could an ignorant young husband understand that it was a good sign when his wife threw the butter-dish at him?

MARY ROSE: You should have guessed.

SIMON: No doubt I was a ninny. But I had always understood that when a young wife — that when she took the husband aside and went red, or white, and hid her head on his bosom, and whispered the rest. I admit I was hoping for that; but all I got was the butter-dish.

MARY ROSE: I suppose different women have different ways.

SIMON: I hope so. (*Severely*) And that was a dastard trick you played me afterwards.

MARY ROSE: Which? Oh, that! I just wanted you to be out of the way till all was over.

SIMON: I don't mean your getting me out of the house, sending me to Plymouth. The dastardliness was in not letting them tell me, when I got back, that — that he had arrived.

MARY ROSE: It was very naughty of me. You remember, Simon, when you came in to my room you tried to comfort me by saying it wouldn't be long now — and I let you maunder on, you darling.

SIMON: Gazing at me with solemn, innocent eyes. You unutterable brat, Mary Rose!

MARY ROSE: You should have been able to read in my face how clever I had been. Oh, Simon, when I said at last, 'Dearest, what is that funny thing in the bassinette?' and you went and looked, never shall I forget your face.

SIMON: I thought at first it was some baby you had borrowed.

MARY ROSE: I sometimes think so still. I didn't, did I?

SIMON: You are a droll one. Always just when I think I know you at last I have to begin at the beginning again.

MARY ROSE: (*suddenly*) Simon, if one of us had to — to go — and we could choose which one —

SIMON: (*sighing*) She's off again.

MARY ROSE: Well, but if — I wonder which would be best? I mean for Harry, of course.

SIMON: Oh, I should have to hop it.

MARY ROSE: Dear!

SIMON: Oh, I haven't popped off yet. Steady, you nearly knocked over the pickles. (*He regards her curiously*) If I did go, I know your first thought would be 'The happiness of Harry must not be interfered with for a moment.' You would blot me out for ever, Mary Rose, rather than he should lose one of his hundred laughs a day.

(*She hides her face*)

It's true, isn't it?

MARY ROSE: It is true, at any rate, that if I was the one to go, that is what I should like you to do.

SIMON: Get off the table-cloth.

(*Her mouth opens*)

Don't step on the marmalade.

MARY ROSE: (*gloriously*) Simon, isn't life lovely! I am so happy, happy, happy. Aren't you?

SIMON: Rather.

MARY ROSE: But you can tie up marmalade. Why don't you scream with happiness? One of us has got to scream.

SIMON: Then I know which one it will be. Scream away, it will give Cameron the jumps.

(*Cameron draws in*)

There you are, Cameron. We are still safe, you see. You can count us — two.

CAMERON: I am ferry glad.

SIMON: Here you are (*handing him the luncheon basket*). You needn't tie the boat up. Stay there and I'll stamp out the fire myself.

CAMERON: As Mr Blake pleases.

SIMON: Ready, Mary Rose?

MARY ROSE: I must say good-bye to my island first. Good-bye, old mossy seat, nice rowan. Good-bye little island that likes too much to be visited. Perhaps I shall come back when I am an old lady with wrinkles, and you won't know your Mary Rose.

SIMON: I say, dear, do dry up. I can't help listening to you when I ought to be getting this fire out.

MARY ROSE: I won't say another word.

SIMON: Just as it seems to be out, sparks come again. Do you think if I were to get some stones —?

(*He looks up and she signs that she has promised not to talk. They laugh to each other. He is then occupied for a little time in dumping wet stones from the loch upon the fire. Cameron is in the boat with his Euripides. Mary Rose is sitting demure but gay, holding her tongue with her fingers like a child.*

Something else is happening; the call has come to Mary Rose. It is at first as soft and furtive as whisperings from holes in the ground, 'Mary Rose, Mary Rose.' Then in a fury as of storm and whistling winds that might be an unholy organ it rushes upon the island, raking every bush for her. These sounds increase rapidly in volume till the mere loudness of them is horrible. They are not without an opponent. Struggling through them, and also calling her name, is to be heard music of an unearthly sweetness that is seeking perhaps to beat them back and put a girdle of safety round her. Once Mary Rose's arms go out to her husband for help, but thereafter she is oblivious of his existence. Her face is rapt, but there is neither fear nor joy in it. Thus she passes from view. The island immediately resumes its stillness. The sun has gone down. Simon by the fire and Cameron in the boat have heard nothing)

SIMON: (*on his knees*) I think the fire is done for at last, and that we can go now. How cold and grey it has become. (*Smiling, but without looking up*) You needn't grip your tongue any longer, you know. (*He rises*) Mary Rose, where have you got to? Please don't hide. Dearest, don't. Cameron, where is my wife?

(*Cameron rises in the boat, and he is afraid to land. His face alarms Simon, who runs this way and that and is lost to sight calling her by name again and again. He returns livid*)

Cameron, I can't find her. Mary Rose! Mary Rose! Mary Rose!

ACT THREE

Twenty-five years have passed, and the scene is again that cosy room in the Morlands' house, not much changed since we last saw it. If chintzes have faded, others as smiling have taken their place. The time is a crisp autumn afternoon just before twilight comes. The apple-tree, not so easy to renew as the chintzes, has become smaller, but there are a few gallant apples on it. The fire is burning, and round it sit Mr and Mrs Morland and Mr Amy, the Morlands gone smaller like the apple-tree and Mr Amy bulky, but all three on the whole still bearing their apples. Inwardly they have changed still less; hear them at it as of yore.

MR MORLAND: What are you laughing over, Fanny?

MRS MORLAND: It is this week's *Punch*,[13] so very amusing.

MR AMY: Ah, *Punch*, it isn't what it used to be.

MR MORLAND: No, indeed.

MRS MORLAND: I disagree. You two try if you can look at this picture without laughing.

(*They are unable to stand the test*)

MR MORLAND: I think I can say that I enjoy a joke as much as ever.

MRS MORLAND: You light-hearted old man!

MR MORLAND: (*humorously*) Not so old, Fanny. Please to remember that I am two months younger than you.

MRS MORLAND: How can I forget it when you have been casting it up against me all our married life?

MR MORLAND: (*not without curiosity*) Fanny and I are seventy-three; you are a bit younger, George, I think?

MR AMY: Oh yes, oh dear yes.

MR MORLAND: You never say precisely what your age is.

MR AMY: I am in the late sixties. I am sure I have told you that before.

MR MORLAND: It seems to me you have been in the sixties longer than it is usual to be in them.

MRS MORLAND: (*with her needles*) James!

MR MORLAND: No offence, George. I was only going to say that at seventy-three I certainly don't feel my age. How do you feel, George, at — at sixty-six? (*More loudly, as if Mr Amy were a little deaf*) Do you feel your sixty-six years?

MR AMY: (*testily*) I am more than sixty-six. But I certainly don't feel my age. It was only last winter that I learned to skate.

MR MORLAND: I still go out with the hounds. You forgot to come last time, George.

MR AMY: If you are implying anything against my memory, James.

MR MORLAND: (*peering through his glasses*) What do you say?

MR AMY: I was saying that I have never used glasses in my life.

MR MORLAND: If I wear glasses occasionally it certainly isn't because there is anything defective in my eyesight. But the type used by newspapers nowadays is so vile —

MR AMY: There I agree with you. Especially Bradshaw.[14]

MR MORLAND: (*not hearing him*) I say the type used by newspapers of today is vile. Don't you think so?

MR AMY: I have just said so. (*Pleasantly*) You are getting rather dull of hearing, James.

MR MORLAND: I am? I like that, George! Why, I have constantly to shout to you nowadays.

MR AMY: What annoys me is not that you are a little deaf, you can't help that. But from the nature of your replies I often see that you are pretending to have heard what I said when you did not. That is rather vain, James.

MR MORLAND: Vain! Now you brought this on yourself, George. I have got something here I might well be vain of, and I meant not to show it to you because it will make you squirm.

　　(*Mrs Morland taps warningly*)

MR MORLAND: I didn't mean that, George. I am sure that you will be delighted. What do you think of this?

　　(*He produces a water-colour which his friend examines at arm's length*)

Let me hold it out for you, as your arms are so short.

　　(*The offer is declined*)

MR AMY: (*with a sinking*) Very nice. What do you call it?

MR MORLAND: Have you any doubt? I haven't the slightest. I am sure that it is an early Turner.[15]

MR AMY: (*paling*) Turner!

MR MORLAND: What else can it be? Holman suggested a Girtin or even a Dayes.[16] Absurd! Why, Dayes was only a glorified drawing-master. I flatter myself I can't make a mistake about a

Turner. There is something about a Turner difficult to define, but unmistakable, an absolute something. It is a charming view, too; Kirkstall Abbey obviously.

MR AMY: Rievaulx, I am convinced.

MR MORLAND: I say Kirkstall.

MRS MORLAND: (*with her needles*) James!

MR MORLAND: Well, you may be right, the place doesn't matter.

MR AMY: There is an engraving of Rievaulx in that Copperplate Magazine[17] we were looking at. (*He turns up the page*) I have got it, Rievaulx. (*He brightens*) Why, this is funny. It is an engraving of that very picture. Hello, hello, hello. (*Examining it through his private glass*) And it is signed E. Dayes.

> (*Mr Morland holds the sketch so close to him that it brushes his eyelashes*)

I wouldn't eat it, James. So it is by Dayes, the drawing-master, after all. I am sorry you have had this disappointment.

> (*Mrs Morland taps warningly, but her husband is now possessed*)

MR MORLAND: You sixty-six, Mr Amy, you sixty-six!

MR AMY: James, this is very painful. Your chagrin I can well understand, but surely your sense of manhood — I regret that I have outstayed my welcome. I bid you good afternoon. Thank you, Mrs Morland, for your unvarying hospitality.

MRS MORLAND: I shall see you into your coat, George.

MR AMY: It is very kind of you, but I need no one to see me into my coat.

MR MORLAND: You will never see your way into it by yourself.

> (*This unworthy remark is perhaps not heard, for Mrs Morland succeeds once more in bringing the guest back*)

MR AMY: James, I cannot leave this friendly house in wrath.

MR MORLAND: I am an irascible old beggar, George. What I should do without you—

MR AMY: Or I without you. Or either of us without that little old dear, to whom we are a never-failing source of mirth.

> (*The little old dear curtseys, looking very frail as she does so*)

Tell Simon when he comes that I shall be in to see him tomorrow. Good-bye, Fanny; I suppose you think of the pair of us as in our second childhood?

MRS MORLAND: Not your second, George. I have never known any men who have quite passed their first.

> (*He goes smiling*)

MR MORLAND: (*ruminating by the fire*) He is a good fellow, George, but how touchy he is about his age! And he has a way of tottering off to sleep while one is talking to him.

MRS MORLAND: He is not the only one of us who does that.
(She is standing by the window)

MR MORLAND: What are you thinking about, Fanny?

MRS MORLAND: I was thinking about the apple-tree, and that
you have given the order for its destruction.

MR MORLAND: It must come down. It is becoming a danger,
might fall on some one down there any day.

MRS MORLAND: I quite see that it has to go. *(She can speak of
Mary Rose without a tremor now)* But her tree! How often she
made it a ladder from this room to the ground!

(Mr Morland does not ask who, but he very nearly does so)

MR MORLAND: Oh yes, of course. Did she use to climb the
apple-tree? Yes, I think she did.

(He goes to his wife, as it were for protection)

MRS MORLAND: *(not failing him)* Had you forgotten that also,
James?

MR MORLAND: I am afraid I forget a lot of things.

MRS MORLAND: Just as well.

MR MORLAND: It is so long since she — how long is it, Fanny?

MRS MORLAND: Twenty-five years, a third of our lifetime. It
will soon be dark; I can see the twilight running across the
fields. Draw the curtains, dear.

(He does so and turns on the lights; they are electric lights now)
Simon's train must be nearly due, is it not?

MR MORLAND: In ten minutes or so. Did you forward his
telegram?

MRS MORLAND: No, I thought he would probably get it sooner
if I kept it here.

MR MORLAND: I dare say. *(He joins her on the sofa, and she sees
that he is troubled)*

MRS MORLAND: What is it, dear?

MR MORLAND: I am afraid I was rather thoughtless about the
apple-tree, Fanny. I hurt you.

MRS MORLAND: *(brightly)* Such nonsense! Have another pipe,
James.

MR MORLAND: *(doggedly)* I will not have another pipe. I hereby
undertake to give up smoking for a week as a punishment to
myself. *(His breast swells a little)*

MRS MORLAND: You will regret this, you know.

MR MORLAND: *(his breast ceasing to swell)* Why is my heart not
broken? If I had been a man of real feeling it would have broken
twenty-five years ago, just as yours did.

MRS MORLAND: Mine didn't, dear.

MR MORLAND: In a way it did. As for me, at the time I thought

I could never raise my head again, but there is a deal of the old Adam in me still. I ride and shoot and laugh and give pompous decisions on the bench and wrangle with old George as if nothing much had happened to me. I never think of the island now; I dare say I could go back there and fish. (*He finds that despite his outburst his hand has strayed towards his tobacco-pouch*) See what I am doing! (*He casts his pouch aside as if it were the culprit*) I am a man enamoured of myself. Why, I have actually been considering, Fanny, whether I should have another dress suit.

MRS MORLAND: (*picking up the pouch*) And why shouldn't you?

MR MORLAND: At my age! Fanny, this should be put on my tombstone: 'In spite of some adversity he remained a lively old blade to the end.'

MRS MORLAND: Perhaps that would be a rather creditable epitaph for any man, James, who has gone through as much as you have. What better encouragement to the young than to be able to tell them that happiness keeps breaking through? (*She puts the pipe, which she has been filling, in his mouth*)

MR MORLAND: If I smoke, Fanny, I shall despise myself more than ever.

MRS MORLAND: To please me.

MR MORLAND: (*as she holds the light*) I don't feel easy about it, not at all easy. (*With a happy thought*) At any rate, I won't get the dress suit.

MRS MORLAND: Your dress suit is shining like a mirror.

MR MORLAND: Isn't it! I thought of a jacket suit only. The V-shaped waistcoat seems to be what they are all wearing now.

MRS MORLAND: Would you have braid on the trousers?

MR MORLAND: I was wondering. You see — Oh, Fanny, you are just humouring me.

MRS MORLAND: Not at all. And as for the old Adam in you, dear Adam, there is still something of the old Eve in me. Our trip to Switzerland two years ago, with Simon, I enjoyed every hour of it. The little card parties here, am I not called the noisy one? Think of the girls I have chaperoned and teased and laughed with, just as if I had never had a girl myself.

MR MORLAND: Your brightness hasn't been all pretence?

MRS MORLAND: No, indeed; I have passed through the valley of the shadow, dear, but I can say thankfully that I have come out again into the sunlight. (*A little tremulously*) I suppose it is all to the good that as the years go by the dead should recede farther from us.

MR MORLAND: Some say they don't.

MRS MORLAND: You and I know better, James.

MR MORLAND: Up there in the misty Hebrides I dare say they think of her as on the island still. Fanny, how long is it since — since you half thought *that* yourself?

MRS MORLAND: Ever so many years. Perhaps not the first year. I did cling for a time —

MR MORLAND: The neighbours here didn't like it.

MRS MORLAND: She wasn't their Mary Rose, you see.

MR MORLAND: And yet her first disappearance —

MRS MORLAND: It is all unfathomable. It is as if Mary Rose was just something beautiful that you and I and Simon had dreamt together. You have forgotten much, but so have I. Even that room (*she looks towards the little door*) that was hers and her child's during all her short married life — I often go into it now without remembering that it was theirs.

MR MORLAND: It is strange. It is rather terrible. You are pretty nigh forgotten, Mary Rose.

MRS MORLAND: That isn't true, dear. Mary Rose belongs to the past, and we have to live in the present, for a very little longer. Just a little longer, and then we shall understand all. Even if we could drag her back to tell us now what these things mean, I think it would be a shame.

MR MORLAND: Yes, I suppose so. Do you think Simon is a philosopher about it also?

MRS MORLAND: Don't be bitter, James, to your old wife. Simon was very fond of her. He was a true lover.

MR MORLAND: Was, was! Is it all 'was' about Mary Rose?

MRS MORLAND: It just has to be. He had all the clever ones of the day advising, suggesting, probing. He went back to the island every year for a long time.

MR MORLAND: Yes, and then he missed a year, and that somehow ended it.

MRS MORLAND: He never married again. Most men would.

MR MORLAND: His work took her place. What a jolly, hearty fellow he is!

MRS MORLAND: If you mean he isn't heart-broken, he isn't. Mercifully the wound has healed.

MR MORLAND: I am not criticising, Fanny. I suppose anyone who came back after twenty-five years — however much they had been loved — it might — we — should we know what to say to them, Fanny?

MRS MORLAND: Don't James. (*She rises*) Simon is late, isn't he?

MR MORLAND: Very little. I heard the train a short time ago, and he might be here — just — if he had the luck to find a cab. But not if he is walking across the fields.

MRS MORLAND: Listen!

MR MORLAND: Yes, wheels. That is probably Simon. He has got a cab.

MRS MORLAND: I do hope he won't laugh at me for having lit a fire in his room.

MR MORLAND: (*with masculine humour*) I hope you put him out some bed-socks.

MRS MORLAND: (*eagerly*)Do you think he would let me? You wretch!

> (*She hurries out, and returns in Simon's arms.*
> *He is in a greatcoat and mufti. He looks his years, grizzled with grey hair and not very much of it, and the tuft is gone. He is heavier and more commanding, full of vigour, a rollicking sea-dog for the moment, but it is a face that could be stern to harshness*)

SIMON: (*saluting*) Come aboard, sir.

MRS MORLAND: Let me down, you great bear. You know how I hate to be rumpled.

MR MORLAND: Not she, loves it. Always did. Get off your greatcoat, Simon. Down with it anywhere.

MRS MORLAND: (*fussing delightedly*) How cold your hands are. Come nearer to the fire.

MR MORLAND: He is looking fit, though.

SIMON: We need to be fit — these days.

MRS MORLAND: So nice to have you again. You do like duck, don't you? The train was late, wasn't it?

SIMON: A few minutes only. I made a selfish bolt for the one cab, and got it.

MR MORLAND: We thought you might be walking across the fields.

SIMON: No, I left the fields to the two other people who got out of the train. One of them was a lady; I thought something about her walk was familiar to me, but it was darkish, and I didn't make her out.

MRS MORLAND: Bertha Colinton, I expect. She was in London today.

SIMON: If I had thought it was Mrs Colinton I would have offered her a lift. (*For a moment he gleams boyishly like the young husband of other days*) Mother, I have news; I have got the *Bellerophon*, honest Injun!

MRS MORLAND: The very ship you wanted.

SIMON: Rather.

MR MORLAND: Bravo, Simon.

SIMON: It is like realising the ambition of one's life. I'm one of the lucky folk, I admit.

(*He says this, and neither of them notices it as a strange remark*)

MR MORLAND: (*twinkling*) Beastly life, a sailor's.

SIMON: (*cordially*) Beastly. I have loathed it ever since I slept in the old *Britannia*, with my feet out at the port-hole to give them air. We all slept that way; must have been a pretty sight from the water. Oh, a beast of a life, but I wouldn't exchange it for any other in the world. (*Lowering*) And if this war does come —

MR MORLAND: (*characteristically*) It won't, I'm sure.

SIMON: I dare say not. But they say — however.

MRS MORLAND: Simon, I had forgotten. There is a telegram for you.

SIMON: Avaunt! I do trust it is not recalling me. I had hoped for at least five clear days.

MRS MORLAND: (*giving it to him*) We didn't open it.

SIMON: Two to one it is recalling me.

MRS MORLAND: It came two days ago. I don't like them, Simon, never did; they have broken so many hearts.

SIMON: They have made many a heart glad too. It may be from my Harry — at last. Mother, do you think I was sometimes a bit harsh to him?

MRS MORLAND: I think you sometimes were, my son.

MR MORLAND: Open it, Simon.

(*Simon opens the telegram and many unseen devils steal into the room*)

MRS MORLAND: (*shrinking from his face*) It can't be so bad as that. We are all here, Simon.

(*For a moment he has not been here himself, he has been on an island. He is a good son to Mrs Morland now, thinking of her only, placing her on the sofa, going on his knees beside her and stroking her kind face. Her arms go out to her husband, who has been reading the telegram*)

MR MORLAND: (*dazed*) Can't be, can't be!

SIMON: (*like some better father than he perhaps has been*) It is all right, Mother. Don't you be afraid. It is good news. You are a brave one, you have come through much, you will be brave for another minute, won't you?

(*She nods, with a frightened smile*)

Mother dear, it is Mary Rose.

MR MORLAND: It can't be true. It is too — too glorious to be true.

MRS MORLAND: Glorious? Is my Mary Rose alive?

SIMON: It is all right, all right. I wouldn't say it, surely, if it wasn't true. Mary Rose has come back. The telegram is from Cameron. You remember who he was. He is minister there now. Hold my hand, and I'll read it. 'Your wife has come back. She was found today on the island. I am bringing her to you. She is quite well, but you will all have to be very careful.'

MRS MORLAND: Simon, can it be?

SIMON: I believe it absolutely. Cameron would not deceive me.

MR MORLAND: He might be deceived himself; he was a mere acquaintance.

SIMON: I am sure it is true. He knew her by sight as well as any of us.

MR MORLAND: But after twenty-five years!

SIMON: Do you think I wouldn't know her after twenty-five years?

MRS MORLAND: My — my — she will be — very changed.

SIMON: However changed, Mother, wouldn't I know my Mary Rose at once! Her hair may be as grey as mine — her face — her little figure — her pretty ways — though they were all gone, don't you think I would know Mary Rose at once? (*He is suddenly stricken with a painful thought*) Oh, my God, I saw her, and I didn't know her!

MRS MORLAND: Simon!

SIMON: It had been Cameron with her. They must have come in my train. Mother, it was she I saw going across the fields — her little walk when she was excited, half a run, I recognised it, but I didn't remember it was hers.

(*Those unseen devils chuckle*)

MR MORLAND: It was getting dark.

SIMON: (*slowly*) Mary Rose is coming across the fields.

(*He goes out. Morland peers weakly through the window curtains. Mrs Morland goes on her knees to pray*)

MR MORLAND: It is rather dark. I — I shouldn't wonder though there was a touch of frost tonight. I wish I was more use.

(*Cameron enters, a bearded clergyman now*)

MRS MORLAND: Mr Cameron? Tell us quickly, Mr Cameron, is it true?

CAMERON: It iss true, ma'am. Mr Blake met us at the gate and he iss with her now. I hurried on to tell you the things necessary. It iss good for her you should know them at once.

MRS MORLAND: Please, quick.

CAMERON: You must be prepared to find her — different.

MRS MORLAND: We are all different. Her age —

CAMERON: I mean, Mrs Morland, different from what you expect. She iss not different as we are different. They will be
saying she iss just as she was on the day she went away.

(*Mrs Morland shrinks*)

These five-and-twenty years, she will be thinking they were
just an hour in which Mr Blake and I had left her in some
incomprehensible jest.

MRS MORLAND: James, just as it was before!

MR MORLAND: But when you told her the truth?

CAMERON: She will not have it.

MRS MORLAND: She must have seen how much older you are.

CAMERON: She does not know me, ma'am, as the boy who was
with her on that day. When she did not recognise me I thought
it best — she was so troubled already — not to tell her.

MR MORLAND: (*appealing*) But now that she has seen Simon.
His appearance, his grey hair — when she saw him she would
know.

CAMERON: (*unhappy*) I am not sure; it iss dark out there.

MR MORLAND: She must have known that he would never have
left her and come home.

CAMERON: That secretly troubles her, but she will not speak
of it. There iss some terrible dread lying on her heart.

MR MORLAND: A dread?

MRS MORLAND: Harry. James, if she should think that Harry
is still a child!

CAMERON: I never heard what became of the boy.

MRS MORLAND: He ran away to sea when he was twelve years
old. We had a few letters from Australia, very few; we don't
know where he is now.

MR MORLAND: How was she found, Mr Cameron?

CAMERON: Two men fishing from a boat saw her. She was
asleep by the shore at the very spot where Mr Blake made a
fire so long ago. There was a rowan-tree beside it. At first they
were afraid to land, but they did. They said there was such a
joy on her face as she slept that it was a shame to waken her.

MR MORLAND: Joy?

CAMERON: That iss so, sir. I have sometimes thought —

(*There is a gleeful clattering on the stairs of some one to whom
they must be familiar; and if her father and mother have doubted
they know now before they see her that Mary Rose has come
back. She enters. She is just as we saw her last except that we
cannot see her quite so clearly. She is leaping towards her mother
in the old impulsive way, and the mother responds in her way,
but something steps between them*)

MARY ROSE: (*puzzled*) What is it?

(*It is the years*)

MRS MORLAND: My love.

MR MORLAND: Mary Rose.

MARY ROSE: Father.

(*But the obstacle is still there. She turns timidly to Simon, who has come in with her*)

What is it, Simon?

(*She goes confidently to him till she sees what the years have done with him. She shakes now*)

SIMON: My beloved wife.

(*He takes her in his arms and so does her mother, and she is glad to be there, but it is not of them she is thinking, and soon she softly disengages herself*)

MR MORLAND: We are so glad you — had you a comfortable journey, Mary Rose? You would like a cup of tea, wouldn't you? Is there anything *I* can do?

(*Mary Rose's eyes go from him to the little door at the back*)

MARY ROSE: (*coaxingly to her father*) Tell me.

MR MORLAND: Tell you what, dear?

MARY ROSE: (*appealing to Cameron*) You?

(*He presses her hand and turns away. She goes to Simon and makes much of him, cajoling him*)

Simon, my Simon. Be nice to me, Simon. Be nice to me dear Simon, and tell me.

SIMON: Dearest love, since I lost you — it was a long time ago —

MARY ROSE: (*petulant*) It wasn't — please, it wasn't. (*She goes to her mother*) Tell me, my mother dear.

MR MORLAND: I don't know what she wants to be told.

MRS MORLAND: I know.

MARY ROSE: (*an unhappy child*) Where is my baby?

(*They cannot face her, and she goes to seek an answer from the room that lies beyond the little door. Her mother and husband follow her.*

Mr Morland and Cameron left alone are very conscious of what may be going on in that inner room)

MR MORLAND: Have you been in this part of the country before, Mr Cameron?

CAMERON: I haf not, sir. It iss my first visit to England. You cannot hear the sea in this house at all, which iss very strange to me.

MR MORLAND: If I might show you our Downs —

CAMERON: I thank you, Mr Morland, but — in such circumstances do not trouble about me at all.

(*They listen*)

MR MORLAND: I do not know if you are interested in prints. I have a pencil sketch by Cozens[18] — undoubtedly genuine —

CAMERON: I regret my ignorance on the subject. This matter, so strange — so inexplicable —

MR MORLAND: Please don't talk of it to me, sir. I am — an old man. I have been so occupied all my life with little things — very pleasant — I cannot cope — cannot cope —

(*A hand is placed on his shoulder so sympathetically that he dares to ask a question*)

Do you think she should have come back, Mr Cameron?

(*The stage darkens and they are blotted out. Into this darkness Mrs Otery enters with a candle, and we see that the scene has changed to the dismantled room of the first act. Harry is sunk in the chair as we last saw him*)

MRS OTERY: (*who in her other hand has a large cup and saucer*) Here is your tea, mister. Are you sitting in the dark? I haven't been more than the ten minutes I promised you. I was —

(*She stops short, struck by his appearance. She holds the candle nearer him. He is staring wide-eyed into the fire, motionless*)

What is the matter, mister? Here is the tea, mister.

(*He looks at her blankly*)

I have brought you a cup of tea, I have just been the ten minutes.

HARRY: (*rising*) Wait a mo.

(*He looks about him, like one taking his bearings*)

Gimme the tea. That's better. Thank you, missis.

MRS OTERY: Have you seen anything?

HARRY: See here, as I sat in that chair — I wasn't sleeping, mind you — it's no dream — but things of the far past connected with this old house — things I knew naught of — they came crowding out of their holes and gathered round me till I saw — I saw them all so clear that I don't know what to think, woman. (*He is a grave man now*) Never mind about that. Tell me about this — ghost.

MRS OTERY: It's no concern of yours.

HARRY: Yes, it is some concern of mine. The folk that used to live here — the Morlands —

MRS OTERY: That was the name. I suppose you heard it in the village.

HARRY: I have heard it all my days. It is one of the names I bear. I am one of the family.

MRS OTERY: I suspicioned that.

HARRY: I suppose that is what made them come to me as I sat here. Tell me about them.

MRS OTERY: It is little I know. They were dead and gone before my time, the old man and his wife.

HARRY: It's not them I am asking you about.

MRS OTERY: They had a son-in-law, a sailor. The war made a great man of him before it drowned him.

HARRY: I know that; he was my father. Hard I used to think him, but I know better now. Go on, there's the other one.

MRS OTERY: (*reluctantly*) That was all.

HARRY: There is one more.

MRS OTERY: If you must speak of her, she is dead too. I never saw her in life.

HARRY: Where is she buried?

MRS OTERY: Down by the church.

HARRY: Is there a stone?

MRS OTERY: Yes.

HARRY: Does it say her age?

MRS OTERY: No.

HARRY: Is that holy spot well taken care of?

MRS OTERY: You can see for yourself.

HARRY: I will see for myself. And so it is her ghost that haunts this house?

(*She makes no answer. He struggles with himself*)

There is no such thing as ghosts. And yet — Is it true about folk having lived in this house and left in a hurry?

MRS OTERY: It's true.

HARRY: Because of a ghost — a thing that can't be.

MRS OTERY: When I came in your eyes were staring; I thought you had seen her.

HARRY: Have you ever seen her yourself?

(*She shivers*)

Where? In this room?

(*She looks at the little door*)

In there? Has she ever been seen out of that room?

MRS OTERY: All over the house, in every room and on the stairs. I tell you I've met her on the stairs, and she drew back to let me pass and said 'Good evening' too, timidlike, and at another time she has gone by me like a rush of wind.

HARRY: What is she like? Is she dressed in white? They are allus dressed in white, aren't they?

MRS OTERY: She looks just like you or me. But for all that she's as light as air. I've seen — things.

HARRY: You look like it, too. But she is harmless, it seems?

MRS OTERY: There's some wouldn't say that; them that left in a hurry. If she thought you were keeping it from her she would do you a mischief.

HARRY: Keeping what from her?

MRS OTERY: Whatever it is she prowls about this cold house searching for, searching, searching. I don't know what it is.

HARRY: (*grimly*) Maybe I could tell you. I dare say I could even put her in the way of finding him.

MRS OTERY: Then I wish to God you would, and let her rest.

HARRY: My old dear, there are worse things than not finding what you are looking for; there is finding them so different from what you had hoped. (*He moves about*) A ghost. Oh no — and yet, and yet — See here, I am going into that room.

MRS OTERY: As you like; I care not.

HARRY: I'll burst open the door.

MRS OTERY: No need; it's not locked; I cheated you about that.

HARRY: But I tried it and it wouldn't open.

> (*Mrs Otery is very unhappy*)

You think she is in there?

MRS OTERY: She may be.

HARRY: (*taking a deep breath*) Give me air.

> (*He throws open the window and we see that it is a night of stars*)

Leave me here now. I have a call to make.

MRS OTERY: (*hesitating*) I dunno. You think you're in no danger, but —

HARRY: That is how it is to be, missis. Just ten minutes you were out of the room, did you say?

MRS OTERY: That was all.

HARRY: God!

> (*She leaves him. After a moment's irresolution he sets off upon his quest carrying the candle, which takes with it all the light of the room. He is visible on the other side of the darkness, in the little passage and opening the door beyond. He returns, and now we see the pale ghost of Mary Rose standing in the middle of the room, as if made out of the light he has brought back with him*)

MARY ROSE: (*bowing to him timidly*) Have you come to buy the house?

HARRY: (*more startled by his own voice than by hers*) Not me.

MARY ROSE: It is a very nice house. (*Doubtfully*) Isn't it?

HARRY: It was a nice house once.

MARY ROSE: (*pleased*) Wasn't it! (*Suspiciously*) Did you know this house?

HARRY: When I was a young shaver.

MARY ROSE: Young? Was it you who laughed?

HARRY: When was that?

MARY ROSE: (*puzzled*) There was once some one who laughed in this house. Don't you think laughter is a very pretty sound?

HARRY: (*out of his depths*) Is it? I dare say. I never thought about it.

MARY ROSE: You are quite old.

HARRY: I'm getting on.

MARY ROSE: (*confidentially*) Would you mind telling me why every one is so old? I don't know you, do I?

HARRY: I wonder. Take a look. You might have seen me in the old days — playing about — outside in the garden — or even inside.

MARY ROSE: You — you are not Simon, are you?

HARRY: No. (*Venturing*) My name is Harry.

MARY ROSE: (*stiffening*) *I* don't think so. I strongly object to your saying that.

HARRY: I'm a queer sort of cove, and I would like to hear you call me Harry.

MARY ROSE: (*firmly*) I decline. I regret, but I absolutely decline.

HARRY: No offence.

MARY ROSE: I think you are sorry for me.

HARRY: I am that.

MARY ROSE: I am sorry for me, too.

HARRY: (*desperately desirous to help her*) If only there was something I — I know nothing about ghosts — not a thing; can they sit down? Could you —?

(*He turns the chair toward her*)

MARY ROSE: That is your chair.

HARRY: What do you mean by that?

MARY ROSE: That is where you were sitting.

HARRY: Were you in this room when I was sitting there?

MARY ROSE: I came in to look at you.

(*A sudden thought makes him cross with the candle to where he had left his knife. It is gone*)

HARRY: Where is my knife? Were you standing looking at me with my knife in your hand?

(*She is sullenly silent*)

Give me my knife.

(*She gives it to him*)

What made you take it?

MARY ROSE: I thought you were perhaps the one.

HARRY: The one?

MARY ROSE: The one who stole him from me.

HARRY: I see. Godsake, in a sort of way I suppose I am.
(*He sits in the chair*)

MARY ROSE: Give him back to me.

HARRY: I wish I could. But I'm doubting he is gone beyond recall.

MARY ROSE: (*unexpectedly*) Who is he?

HARRY: Do you mean you have forgotten who it is you are searching for?

MARY ROSE: I knew once. It is such a long time ago. I am so tired; please can I go away and play now?

HARRY: Go away? Where? You mean back to that — that place?
(*She nods*)
What sort of a place is it? Is it good to be there?

MARY ROSE: Lovely, lovely, lovely.

HARRY: It's not just the island, is it, that's so lovely, lovely?
(*She is perplexed*)
Have you forgotten the island too?

MARY ROSE: I am sorry.

HARRY: The island, the place where you heard the call.

MARY ROSE: What is that?

HARRY: You have even forgotten the call! (*With vision*) As far as I can make out, it was as if, in a way, there were two kinds of dogs out hunting you — the good and the bad.

MARY ROSE: (*who thinks he is chiding her*) Please don't be cross with me.

HARRY: I am far from cross with you. I begin to think it was the good dogs that got you. Are they ghosts in that place?

MARY ROSE: (*with surprising certainty*) No.

HARRY: You are sure?

MARY ROSE: Honest Injun!

HARRY: What fairly does me is, if the place is so lovely, what made you leave it?

MARY ROSE: (*frightened*) I don't know.

HARRY: Do you think you could have fallen out?

MARY ROSE: I don't know. (*She thinks his power is great*) Please, I don't want to be a ghost any more.

HARRY: As far as I can see, if you wasn't a ghost there you made yourself one by coming back. But it's no use your expecting me to be able to help you. (*She droops at this and he holds out his arms*) Come to me, ghostie; I wish you would.

MARY ROSE: (*prim again*) Certainly not.

HARRY: If you come, I'll try to help you.
(*She goes at once and sits on his knee*)
See here, when I was sitting by the fire alone I seemed to hear

you as you once were saying that some day when he was a man
you would like to sit on your Harry's knee.

MARY ROSE: (*vaguely quoting she knows not whom*) The loveliest
time of all will be when he is a man and takes me on his knee
instead of me taking him on mine.

HARRY: Do you see who I am now?

MARY ROSE: Nice man.

HARRY: Is that all you know about me?

MARY ROSE: Yes.

HARRY: There is a name I would like to call you by, but my
best course is not to worry you. Poor soul, I wonder if there
was ever a man with a ghost on his knee before.

MARY ROSE: I don't know.

HARRY: Seems to me you're feared of being a ghost. I dare say,
to a timid thing, being a ghost is worse than seeing them.

MARY ROSE: Yes.

HARRY: Is it lonely being a ghost?

MARY ROSE: Yes.

HARRY: Do you know any other ghost?

MARY ROSE: No.

HARRY: Would you like to know other ghosts?

MARY ROSE: Yes.

HARRY: I can understand that. And now you would like to go
away and play?

MARY ROSE: Please.

HARRY: In this cold house, when you should be searching, do
you sometimes play by yourself instead?

MARY ROSE: (*whispering*) Don't tell.

HARRY: Not me. You're a pretty thing. What beautiful shoes
you have.

(*She holds out her feet complacently*)

MARY ROSE: Nice buckles.

HARRY: I like your hair.

MARY ROSE: Pretty hair.

HARRY: Do you mind the tuft that used to stand up at the back
of — of Simon's head?

MARY ROSE: (*merrily*) Naughty tuft.

HARRY: I have one like that.

MARY ROSE: (*smoothing it down*) Oh dear, oh dear, what a
naughty tuft!

HARRY: My name is Harry.

MARY ROSE: (*liking the pretty sound*) Harry, Harry, Harry, Harry.

HARRY: But you don't know what Harry I am.

MARY ROSE: No.

HARRY: And this brings us no nearer what's to be done with you. I would willingly stay here though I have my clearing in Australy, but you're just a ghost. They say there are ways of laying ghosts, but I am so ignorant.

MARY ROSE: (*imploringly*) Tell me.

HARRY: I wish I could; you are even more ignorant than I am.

MARY ROSE: Tell me.

HARRY: All I know about them for certain is that they are unhappy because they can't find something, and then once they've got the thing they want, they go away happy and never come back.

MARY ROSE: Oh, nice!

HARRY: The one thing clear to me is that you have got that thing at last, but you are too dog-tired to know or care. What you need now is to get back to the place you say is lovely, lovely.

MARY ROSE: Yes, yes.

HARRY: It sounds as if it might be Heaven, or near thereby.

(*She wants him to find out for her*)

Queer, you that know so much can tell nothing, and them that know nothing can tell so much. If there was any way of getting you to that glory place!

MARY ROSE: Tell me.

HARRY: (*desperate*) He would surely send for you, if He wanted you.

MARY ROSE: (*crushed*) Yes.

HARRY: It's like as if He had forgotten you.

MARY ROSE: Yes.

HARRY: It's as if nobody wanted you, either there or here.

MARY ROSE: Yes. (*She rises*) Bad man.

HARRY: It's easy to call me names, but the thing fair beats me. There is nothing I wouldn't do for you, but a mere man is so helpless. How should the likes of me know what to do with a ghost that has lost her way on earth? I wonder if what it means is that you broke some law, just to come back for the sake of — of that Harry? If it was that, it's surely time He overlooked it.

MARY ROSE: Yes.

(*He looks at the open window*)

HARRY: What a night of stars! Good old glitterers, I dare say they are in the know, but I am thinking you are too small a thing to get a helping hand from them.

MARY ROSE: Yes.

(*The call is again heard, but there is in it no unholy sound. It is a celestial music that is calling for Mary Rose, Mary Rose, first in whispers and soon so loudly that, for one who can hear, it is the only sound in the world. Mary Rose, Mary Rose. As it wraps her round, the weary little ghost knows that her long day is done. Her face is shining. The smallest star shoots down for her, and with her arms stretched forth to it trustingly she walks out through the window into the empyrean. The music passes with her. Harry hears nothing, but he knows that somehow a prayer has been answered)*

Notes

1. *my cabbage*: Harry's literal translation of the French, 'mon chou', used as a term of endearment.
2. *prodigal*: parable of the Prodigal Son, *Luke* 15: 11–32.
3. *Thomas Gainsborough* (1727–88), famous English landscape artist.
4. *midshipman*: lowest officer rank in the Royal Navy.
5. *freehold* and *leasehold* are forms of holding property under English law: *freehold* is outright ownership and *leasehold* tenure for a limited, though often extensive, period.
6. *tacking*: naval term for changing course in order to negotiate the direction of the wind.
7. *Honest Injun*: on my Honour, from accounts of Native American Indians' assurances of good faith.
8. *nailers*: 'an exceptionally good hand at something' (*OED*), suggesting that they will be naturally excellent.
9. Pond in Kensington Gardens, where Barrie walked his dogs and met the children of the Llewellyn-Davies family, for whom he first developed the idea of Peter Pan.
10. *Prennez garde . . . tellement*: 'Be careful, my dear.' 'My God! What a comic he is!' 'But as for me, I like him — he is such a character.'
11. *coquin*: a joker. Cameron's grasp of idiomatic French is used by Barrie to play up the limitations of Simon and Mary Rose's schoolroom French.
12. *Euripides*: Greek dramatist of ancient Athens, 484–406 BC.
13. *Punch*: famous satirical magazine founded in the nineteenth century.
14. *Bradshaw*: standard railway timetable guide (and therefore printed cheaply in small type).
15. *J. M. W. Turner* (1775–1851), one of the most innovative landscape and seascape painters of the nineteenth century, whose major works included views of Kirkstall and Rievaulx abbeys.
16. *Thomas Girtin* (1775–1802) and *Edward Dayes* (1763–1804): topographical painters of Turner's time.
17. *Copperplate Magazine*: magazine in which black and white engraved copies of paintings were reproduced.
18. *Cozens*: John Robert Cozens (1752–97), sometimes regarded as a forerunner of Turner.

Joe Corrie

In Time o' Strife

(1927)

CHARACTERS

Jock Smith, a Miner
Jean Smith, his Wife
Jenny Smith, their Daughter (22)
Lizzie Smith, their Daughter (13)
Bob Smith, their Son (17)
Tam Pettigrew, a Miner
Agnes Pettigrew, his Wife
Kate Pettigrew, their Daughter (22)
Tam Anderson, a Young Miner
Wull Baxter, a Young Miner

Introduction

Joe Corrie was born in 1894 in Galloway but his family moved shortly afterwards to Cardenden in Fife, where his father worked in the mine and his mother was a casual worker on local farms. Corrie followed in his father's footsteps at the age of fourteen and was as a miner in Ayrshire throughout the First World War. In its aftermath, in a period of much unemployment, he began to write poetry, some of which was collected in *The Image o' God and Other Poems* (1927, 1937) and *Scottish Pride and Other Poems* (1955).

During the General Strike of 1926, he started to write plays for unemployed miners who called themselves the Bowhill Players, *In Time o' Strife* being their first success. The play was performed in mining villages from 1926 to 1928 and another amateur group, the Fife Miner Players, toured this and other Corrie plays until the early 1930s. The play was also produced in London (March 1927) and in Leipzig (1930), though it did not receive a performance in any of the major Scottish cities.

In the 1930s, Corrie came to depend on the Scottish Community Drama Association for production of his works, and they tended to prefer his comic to his more serious works. Corrie himself felt that his serious work had been neglected because of its political content: as he wrote in 'A Scots Dramatist's Future', 'can we expect a vital Scots drama before the people of a country, especially the youth, have a vision of a fuller life and the will to strive for it and before the stage is a free institution? I don't think so'.

Corrie's most successful later works, such as *Hewers of Coal* (1937) and *A Master of Men* (1944) remained firmly based in the working-class naturalism that he had first adopted in the 1920s. 'I have always written to the other fellow, shouting at him to try to get him round to my way of thinking', he wrote in the 1950s, contrasting himself with the modern writers who 'seem to talk so much to themselves'. Joe Corrie died in Edinburgh in 1968.

ACT ONE

The kitchen of the Smiths' home in the mining village of Carhill, in Scotland.

A bed, heavily curtained, occupies almost the whole of the left side of the room (Spectators). A dresser covered with nick-nacks, stands at the back. To the right of the dresser is a four-paned window through which can be seen the colliery in the distance.

The table stands in the centre of the floor.

Between dresser and window is a stool, on which stands the water pail and a tinnie.

The door leading to the outside is at left back.

The door to room at right is at right back.

The time is night, and the lamp has been lit and window curtains drawn.

The period of the play is the mining crisis of 1926.[1]

At rise of curtain LIZZIE, pencil in her mouth, is on her knees on a chair at the table-side, poring over her home-lessons.

JENNY sits at fireside, converting an old hat into a new one with a piece of blue ribbon.

> (*The sound of marching people can be heard singing:*)
> We'll hang every blackleg[2] to the sour apple tree,
> We'll hang every blackleg to the sour apple tree,
> We'll hang every blackleg to the sour apple tree,
> As we go marching on.
> (*The tune is 'John Brown's Body'. When they have faded away in the distance,*)

LIZZIE: (*sings*)
> We'll hang every blackleg to the sour apple tree,
> We'll hang every blackleg to the sour apple tree,
> We'll hang every blackleg to the sour apple tree,
> As we go marching . . .

JENNY: Here! You get thae sums done.

LIZZIE: (*shortly*) I canna dae them, you better ha'e a shot at them, Jenny.

JENNY: What kind are they, thae kind wi' the dots?

LIZZIE: Ay.

JENNY: Weel, you'll need to try Bob.

LIZZIE: Bob! He canna dae decimals . . . I'll get the strap[3] the morn if I dinna ha'e them done.

JENNY: Let him try and gi'e you the strap, and there'll be some fun.

LIZZIE: He's done it before.

JENNY: Ay, but there's a strike on noo, and we're lookin' for blood. But does he no' let you see hoo to dae your sums?

LIZZIE: Ay, but he thinks we're a' as clever as him. I wish I was awa' frae the schule, Jenny, I dinna like it.

JENNY: We a' wish we were awa' frae the schule, but we're no' lang till we wish we were back to it.

(*Singing of crowd can be heard faintly in distance*)

LIZZIE: Is the strike aboot finished, Jenny?

JENNY: God knows. It was as like finishin' six weeks ago as it is the day.

LIZZIE: Will we ha'e ony tea the nicht before we go to bed?

JENNY: I'll be able to tell you that at bed-time. Get your lessons done.

LIZZIE: It's no' easy daein' lessons when you're hungry. (*Sings*)
   We'll hang every blackleg to the sour apple tree,
   We'll hang every blackleg to the sour apple tree,
   We'll hang every . . .

JENNY: Shut it! D'ye want to wauken him?

(JENNY *nods her head in direction of room. The door opens, and* AGNES PETTIGREW *enters. She is rather shabby, and there is the look of illness on her face. She walks wearily, and is troubled with a little, harsh cough*)

AGNES: Is your mither in, Jenny?

JENNY: No, she's awa' doon the street, auntie . . . Sit doon.

(AGNES *sits at left side of table*)

JENNY: What's a' the noise aboot the nicht?

AGNES: I dinna ken. There's been a meetin' in the hall aboot something. Oor Tam'll no' go to the meetin's to let us ken what's gaun on.

LIZZIE: Can you dae sums, auntie?

JENNY: Here! shut that book till Bob comes in.

LIZZIE: Bob canna dae them.

JENNY: Weel, awa' to the schoolmaister and get him to do them, that's what he's gettin' payed for.

(AGNES *coughs*)

JENNY: That cauld's no' leavin' you in a hurry, auntie.

AGNES: No . . . It's no' sae bad in the daytime, but it keeps me off my sleep at nicht.

JENNY: Ha'e ye seen the doctor yet?

AGNES: What guid would he dae? He'd just order me to my bed, and gi'e me a line for medicine. And what guid is that when there's no' a penny in the house?

JENNY: It's true, auntie.

LIZZIE: I wish the strike was finished till I get my new frock.

JENNY: Where is Kate the nicht, auntie?

AGNES: She's sitting mendin' wee Wullie's troosers. I think she's gaun to the soup-kitchen dance the nicht.

JENNY: She's lucky. A nicht's dancin' noo and I'd ha'e nae shoon left. Anither month o' this strike and we'll be gaun aboot as naked as savages.

AGNES: It canna last much langer noo, Jenny, it canna, or the half o' us'll gang mad.

JENNY: This is the worst week we have had, it'll be the same wi' you, I suppose?

AGNES: I dinna ken hoo to turn, Jenny; we're clean knocked oot. We'll need to hunger noo till we get the Pairish relief[4] the morn . . . I'm gettin' tired, Jenny.

JENNY: The strike canna last lang noo, auntie, and twa weeks' work'll put us on oor feet again.

AGNES: We've been sayin' that for the last twa months, but the end doesna seem to be ony nearer.

(*She takes a fit of coughing.* JENNY *goes to her, and gives her a drink of water*)

JENNY: You'll need to see the doctor, auntie, that cough's gettin' worse.

AGNES: Ay, I'll need to see him, Jenny. But I'll wait a day or twa . . . If he puts me to my bed I'll never rise again, I doot.

JENNY: That's nonsense: he'll gi'e ye a bottle that'll stop that cough in a nicht . . . You should ha'e mair claes on tae.

AGNES: Mair claes! (*She laughs hysterically*) Mair claes! . . . I wonder if I'll get a sleep the nicht? . . . When the cough does stop I canna sleep for thinkin' o' the bairns.

JENNY: You'll need to stop thinkin' o' the bairns.

AGNES: That's no' easy, Jenny, when you're a mither you'll see that . . . Puir wee things, they seem to ken, for they just sit and look like wee lambes and never say a word when I've to put them to bed to sleep the hunger of them. (*She holds her brow with her hand*) Jenny, I'm no' weel.

JENNY: I ken you're no' weel, it's your bed you should be in. Kate can look after the bairns weel enough.

AGNES: I'm feart to go to bed. I ha'e the feelin' that if I lie doon . . . (*Rises*) Ach: God kens what we have been broucht on the face o' this earth for.

JENNY: You get awa' doon hame, and ha'e a rest for a while. A guid nicht's sleep, and you'll be like anither woman in the mornin'.

AGNES: (*going off*) Peace! . . . peace! . . . I wonder when we'll ever get peace?

(*She goes out coughing.* JENNY *goes with her*)

LIZZIE: (*singing*):

We'll hang every blackleg to the sour apple tree,

We'll hang every blackleg to the sour apple tree,

We'll hang every blackleg to the sour —

JOCK: (*loudly from room*) Shut up, in there!

(LIZZIE *shuts up suddenly, and puts her finger in her mouth.* JENNY *re-enters*)

JENNY: Was that him shoutin'?

LIZZIE: No.

JENNY: It's a wonder he hasna been cryin' for water.

(*Enter* BOB, *a reckless kind of youth, light of foot as an Irish ragman*)

BOB: What aboot some chuck?

JENNY: What aboot it?

BOB: Weel, what aboot it?

JENNY: You'll need to rin and play hide and seek till my mither comes hame — and mebbe efter she comes hame tae.

LIZZIE: Can you dae decimals, Bob?

BOB: Can I dae what?

LIZZIE: Decimals?

BOB: What's decimals?

LIZZIE: Sums, fatheid.

BOB: What are you askin' that for?

LIZZIE: I have to dae them for my hame lessons, and I canna dae them.

BOB: Decimals! Och, ay, they're easy.

LIZZIE: Dae them for me, Bob.

BOB: You surely think it, I'm on strike, and I'm no gaun to blackleg noo . . . By gee! I'm hungry.

JENNY: (*to* BOB) What's a' the noise aboot the nicht?

BOB: D'ye mean to tell me you dinna ken that there's likely to be a break awa' the morn?

JENNY: Is there?

BOB: Ay, and that sweethe'rt o' yours is yin that would like to start . . . By gee! If he tries to go to the pit . . .

JENNY: Wha tellt you that?

BOB: Never you mind, but it's true. Some man, him! My uncle Tam is anither yin. (*A shout is heard in the distance*) Listen! . . . that's anither meetin' in the fitba park. (*He goes to fire and puts the poker up his sleeve*)

JENNY: Where are you gaun wi' that poker?

BOB: I'll be yin o' the pickets.

JENNY: Put that poker doon and no' be daft. (*She struggles with him and takes the poker from him*)

If the polis catch you wi' that you'd get penal servitude. You stay here and leave the picketin' to the men.

BOB: Am I no' a man?

LIZZIE: Some man.

BOB: I don't want ony o' your auld buck, see!

JENNY: And I don't want ony o' yours. Awa' doon and meet my mither.

BOB: I'm on strike.

(*Enter* KATE, *a dark, handsome lass, with a proud air*)

LIZZIE: Can you dae decimals, Kate?

JENNY: No, she canna dae decimals.

KATE: I used to could dae them, Lizzie, I'll ha'e a try before I go oot . . . I'm up to see if you're gaun to the dance, Jenny?

JENNY: Your mither was sayin' you were gaun.

KATE: Too true I am.

JENNY: Where did you get the money?

KATE: Threepence for some auld jam jars . . . I think you should come, Jenny; it'll be a good dance.

JENNY: My shoon wouldna stand it, Kate . . . are you in a hurry?

KATE: I'm finished hurryin', it's a mug's game.

JENNY: Tak' off your coat then, and sit doon.

(*She takes off her coat and hangs it over a chair. She sees BOB, who is trying to light a stump of cigarette with a lighted paper*)

KATE: You're there, Bob? . . . No' thinkin' aboot startin' to your work?

BOB: D'ye see ony green in my eye?

(*Holds down his eyelash*)

KATE: There's some thinkin' aboot startin', I hear.

BOB: Ay, and your faither's yin o' them.

KATE: Wha said that?

BOB: He said it himsel' at the street corner.

KATE: And did naebody bump him?

BOB: Tam Anderson tellt him that if he tried it he would knock his bloody heid off.

JENNY: Here! keep that kind o' language for the street corner.

KATE: I'll knock his bloody heid off mysel' if he tries it.

BOB: And the worm that rins efter Jenny here is talkin' aboot gaun to his work tae. By gee! let him try it. I don't know where I'll be if he gets there withoot gettin' his skull cracked.

KATE: Wull Baxter! . . . Surely he's no' gaun to try and break awa', Jenny?

JENNY: He'll no' blackleg, Kate.

BOB: He was ay a gaffer's man, a belly-crawler.

JENNY: Shut up!

BOB: I ken him, Kate, for I worked beside him.

KATE: (*to break conversation*) Where's your faither, Jenny?

JENNY: (*jerking her thumb towards room*) Oh, lyin' in there wi' a fat heid . . . D'ye ken what he did yesterday?

KATE: No.

JENNY: He backed a double⁵ and came hame as drunk as a lord, singin' like a canary. And no' a crust in the hoose. He met in wi' some auld pal that's here on holiday frae America — so he says — and didna come oot the pub till the double was spent.

KATE: Was your mither wild?

JENNY: Wild! she was mad. I bet ye she put the singin' oot o' his heid.

KATE: Is your mither no' in?

JENNY: No, she's awa' lookin' for grub. That auld McIntyre the grocer wouldna gi'e her ony things this mornin'. 'I'll gi'e ye plenty,' says he, 'if you send your man back to his work.'

KATE: Eh! And what did she say to that?

JENNY: She spat in his face.

KATE: That's the stuff to gi'e them. I canna understand the tradesmen aboot here, they're a' up against the miners, but bad conditions for the miners means bad conditions for them, tae. They'll mebbe learn that some day when they're puttin' up their shutters . . . Let me see your sums, Lizzie.

(LIZZIE *goes to her with book and pencil*)

BOB: Don't dae them for her, Kate.

LIZZIE: You mind your ain business.

BOB: I'll wallop your ear for ye if you set up ony auld gas to me. (*To* KATE) She's as thick in the heid as a wudden leg. I wouldna dae them for her, I would let her get the strap.

LIZZIE: You couldna dae them onywey. A' you can dae is play cairds and toss up pennies at the street corner — and swear.

BOB: Mind, I'll melt ye!

JENNY: That'll dae, noo, we a' ken hoo clever you are.

BOB: Would you like to hear a tune on my gramophone, Kate?

KATE: Ay, put it on, Bob, we're needin' something to cheer us up.

JENNY: (*nodding towards room*) You'll wauken him.

BOB: What dae I care for him!

(*Puts the gramophone on the table and takes some records from a drawer in the dresser*)

KATE: Here you are, Lizzie; I think that's richt.

LIZZIE: I wish you had been my sister, Kate, Jenny's just a dunce.

BOB: (*to* KATE) By gee! you're a right mug, I would let her get the strap.

(*Lizzie puts out her tongue at him as she packs her books in her bag*)

BOB: What d'ye want? Danny boy?

KATE: Oh, for God's sake, put on something cheery, and let Jenny and me get a dance.

(BOB *starts the gramophone.* KATE *takes a hold of* JENNY, *and they begin to dance.* BOB *watches them for a time, then he grabs hold of* LIZZIE. BOB *and* LIZZIE *are footing it at the room door when it opens, and* JOCK SMITH, *a typical miner, in his shirt and trousers and stockinged feet, enters. He brushes* BOB *and* LIZZIE *aside in an irritated manner, and goes directly to water pail. He drinks greedily two 'Tinnie' full. Then he makes for fireside*)

JOCK: Oh! stop that damned thing!

(BOB *jumps and puts the gramaphone off.* KATE *winks at* JENNY)

JOCK: What kind o' dance d'ye ca' that?

KATE: That's what you ca' the Charleston, John.

JOCK: God kens what the world's comin' tae. Nae wonder you're a' knocked-kneed and in-taed gettin'.

KATE: Wha's in-taed?

JOCK: The half o' ye are gaun aboot like a lot o' hens. (*To* JENNY, *curtly*) Did you get a paper the nicht?

JENNY: (*just as curtly*) You're sittin' on it. (JOCK *rises and gets paper under the cushion*)

JOCK: (*opening paper*) You're damned lucky that can think aboot dancin', that's what I have to say. (*Irritably*) Where's the racin' page? . . . Ay, damned lucky that can think aboot dancin' . . . (*Looking at race results*) Weel, I'm damned if that's no hard lines.

BOB: It'll be a' the same to us.

JOCK: (*making a rush at him*) I'll warm your ear for you, my lad.

(BOB *scoots out*)

LIZZIE: He's a cheeky devil that.

JOCK: (*to* JENNY) Where's your mither?

JENNY: She's awa' seein' where she can get something to fill hungry bellies till we get some money frae the pairish: awa' beggin', and lowerin' hersel' again. And there was nae need for it if you had played the game yesterday.

JOCK: If the double had went doon what difference would it have made?

JENNY: But the double came up, and you gied the winnin's to the publican to help him to buy anither motor car.

JOCK: Hoo would you like to be me, Kate?

KATE: Onything fresh in the paper aboot the strike?

JOCK: To hell wi' the strike. It should never have happened. I'm payin' nae mair Union money after this. I've got enough o' it this time. For thirty years I ha'e peyed it, but never anither penny will they get frae me.

KATE: What?

JOCK: Oor leaders. It's easy seen that this has a' been planned in Russia.[6]

KATE: (*with a smile*) What makes you think that, Jock?

JOCK: Look at the papers and you'll see pages aboot it every nicht. It's the Socialists to blame . . . I ken what they want, it's a revolution they want.

KATE: D'ye mean to tell me, Jock, that you've been locked oot for six months and doesna ken ony better than that?

JOCK: It's you that doesna ken ony better . . . I was makin' a pound a shift before they broucht us oot on strike, Jenny there'll tell you that.

KATE: You must have been well in the know. My faither wasna makin' as much as feed a canary.

JOCK: Twenty white shillin's a shift (*going to pail for another drink*) and the best o' conditions at that.

KATE: Are ye a Mason?

JOCK: No, I'm no' a Mason.

KATE: It's a mystery to me.

JOCK: God, but I'm dry . . . Make a drink o' tea, Jenny.

JENNY: The caddie's empty.

JOCK: (*drinks and returns to chair*) No, this strike! strike! strike! idea'll no' dae.

KATE: But it couldna be helped.

JOCK: Hoo could it no' be helped?

KATE: Weel, the maister wanted to reduce your wages and make you work langer 'oors, what else could you dae but strike?

JOCK: We could have knuckled doon.

KATE: But you're a Scotsman, Jock.

JOCK: I am, and prood o' it.

KATE: It doesna say much for Scotland.

JOCK: No, of coorse, no', it says mair for Russia. I ken what I would dae if I was the Gover'ment. I'd get a boat and ship the hale damned lot to Russia.

KATE: Wha, the coalmaisters?

JOCK: No, thae Socialists and Communionists.

KATE: But they didna reduce your wages?

JOCK: I ken that fine.

JENNY: And if you ken that fine, what is the argument aboot?

JOCK: What I'm sayin' is, that we'd been far better if we had knuckled doon. I kent we were gaun to be defeated.

KATE: (*jumping*) Wha said we were defeated!

JOCK: I ken we are defeated.

JENNY: D'ye ken onything aboot backin' doubles and gi'en the winnin's to the publican?

JOCK: Oh, here! we've heard enough aboot that, give it a rest . . . Bring me a drink, Lizzie.

LIZZIE: What kind o' drink, daddy?

JOCK: Ha'e some savvy.

    (LIZZIE *goes to pail.* WULL BAXTER *enters*)

WULL: Hullo, Kate. And how's the health?

KATE: Not too bad, considerin' we're slowly fadin' away.

WULL: That's a fine nicht, John.

JOCK: Is it?

(*He takes 'Tinnie' from* LIZZIE *and drinks*)

WULL: You're lookin' raither wild like, John. What's wrang?

JOCK: Oh Kate and me have been ha'ein' an argument.

WULL: Ay. What's the trouble?

JOCK: The strike.

WULL: We're a' thinkin' gey seriously aboot it noo . . . We werena expectin' it to last as lang as this.

JOCK: A piece o' damned nonsense and thrawnness. I've been tellin' her that I've payed my last penny to the Union.

WULL: I'm finished wi' the Union tae.

KATE: What's that you say, Wull?

WULL: The Union has failed us, Kate. They ken damned fine the battle's lost long ago, and they should have cried the strike off.

KATE: We've naething to lose noo, and we may as well fight to the finish.

WULL: If we saw ony signs o' the finish it wouldna be sae bad. But it's likely to go on for months yet, if it's left to oor leaders.

KATE: Weel, let it go on. The coalmaisters'll mebbe no' be sae keen to lock us oot again.

WULL: We dinna ha'e a very guid case, either. We can see noo that the pits havena been payin'.

KATE: Havena been payin'! But has that no' ay been their cry? Was that no' their cry when the women worked doon the pits?

WULL: There wasna mony women worked doon the pits.

JOCK: They were in the pits, Wull. My faither was born doon the pit.

WULL: Born doon the pit.

JOCK: Ay, born doon the pit . . . It's no' everybody can bum aboot that.

KATE: Something to bum aboot: a woman workin' doon the pit till the very minute o' confinement . . . And still the pits didna pay.

JOCK: Ay, my grannie carried coal up the auld stair pit for mony a lang day. What's mair, she helped to lift the stane off my grandfaither when he was killed.

WULL: Is that true, Jock?

JOCK: Helped to lift the stane off him; helped to cairry him hame a corpse . . . And you're grumblin', Kate, but you dinna ken you're alive. Frae daylicht to dark they had to work then; the only time they saw daylicht was on the Sunday.

KATE: And still the pits didna pay.

JOCK: I ken that fine, you didna need to tell me that.

KATE: And if the miners hadna foucht against it your women micht have been workin' in the pits yet.

JOCK: I ken that fine!

KATE: They had to fight to make things easier for you.

WULL: We're fightin' a losin' fight, Kate, you canna deny that.

KATE: We are, if a' the men are like you. But they're no', and we're gaun to win yet.

WULL: It's too late in the day to win noo. And the sooner it comes to an end the better for everybody concerned.

KATE: Mebbe you're yin o' them aboot the place that wants to bring it to an end.

WULL: I have been thinkin' aboot it, but I havena made up my mind yet.

KATE: If you've been thinkin' aboot it, Wull, you've made up your mind.

WULL: Weel, to tell you the truth, I didna see the use o' carryin' on much langer.

KATE: Then you're no the man I thoucht you were.

WULL: No?

KATE: No, you are not. I never thoucht you would stoop sae low as split on us.

WULL: I'm no' splittin'. But when word comes that the Pairish Cooncil is no' payin' ony mair relief, it's time something was done to bring it to an end.

KATE: No payin' ony mair relief! Wha tellt you that.

(*They are all attentive*)

WULL: The cooncil had a meetin' the noo, and that's their decision.

KATE: I've been expectin' it.

JOCK: That'll put us in a nice mess.

WULL: It's as weel it has come to that, Jock, for it'll bring the issue to a heid. It'll end the strike here.

KATE: Starve the women and bairns to force the men back to their work. (*Rising and facing* WULL) And you agree wi' that policy.

WULL: There's nae ither way that I see.

KATE: I have only yin answer for you, and it's THIS!
     (*She hits* WULL *a severe slap on the face.* WULL *staggers. They all rise excitedly*)

JOCK: Kate!

WULL: (*rushing at* KATE, *who stands her ground*) You flamin' tinker! ye . . .

JOCK: (*Holding* WULL *back*) Never heed her, man!
     (JENNY *goes to room crying*)

KATE: Keep your hands off me, ye blackleg . . .

JOCK: Kate!

KATE: (*to* WULL) Ye traitor.
     (BOB *enters excitedly*)

BOB: That's it noo; nae pairish money the morn, and a hunner polis in at the pit to smash up the pickets.

KATE: (*with a hysterical laugh*) And Britons, never, NEVER shall be slaves.

BOB: It's a revolution that's needed here.

JOCK: See here! If I hear tell o' you gaun to ony mair o' thae Bolshie[7] meetin's I'll scud your ear for ye.

WULL: I'll be in later, John, I want to ha'e a talk wi' ye.

KATE: Ay, awa' oot o' the sicht o' decent folk — ye scab!
     (WULL, *would return to her, but* JOCK *signs to him to go out*)

BOB: Was he sayin' he was gaun to his work in the mornin'. He has been in the office wi' the manager, and his mither has been gettin' his pit buits mended at the store. By gee! if he goes to his work in the mornin' there'll be nothing left o' him but a big bubble.

JOCK: Did you see your mither doon the street?

BOB: No, I've mair to think aboot than look for my mither . . . A flamin' worm like that . . .

JOCK: Awa' and look for your mither!

BOB: He's worse than a worm, he's a dirty rotten blackleg.

JOCK: D'ye no' hear me speakin' to ye!

BOB: If he goes to his work I'll flatten his face wi' a half brick. (JOCK *rushes at him, and he scoots out*)

JOCK: Nae pairish relief, Kate. Hoo dae they think we're gaun tae live?

KATE: It's murder, Jock. And the likes o' Wull Baxter, a workin' man, agreein' wi' it. I canna understand it. It's laughable.

JOCK: Something to laugh at; no' a crust in the hoose the nicht, and nae hopes o' gettin' ony the morn. Ach, I'm fed up wi' the hale blasted thing.

(*He goes to room*)

LIZZIE: Is that the strike finished noo, Kate?

KATE: No, it's no' finished, hen, it's just startin'.

LIZZIE: I wish it was finished till I get my new frock.

(*JENNY enters*)

KATE: What d'ye think o' that, Jenny?

JENNY: I canna understand him, Kate, I didna think he was yin o' thae kind.

KATE: Neither did I. But dinna break your he'rt ower him, he's a guid riddance. (*JENNY sobs*) Noo, noo, Jenny. Dinna greet; thank your lucky stars you ha'e got rid o' him.

JENNY: We were to get mairrit when the strike was finished.

KATE: The dirty swine!

(*The door opens and* TAM PETTIGREW *enters, standing at door*)

TAM: (*to* KATE) Are you gaun to stay here a' nicht?

KATE: What d'ye want?

TAM: Your mither's in her bed, and I want you to get my pit claes ready.

KATE: Your what?

TAM: My pit claes; I'm gaun oot to my work.

KATE: Oh, are ye! And are we to have nae say in this?

TAM: Wha?

KATE: My mither and me?

TAM: What the hell have you to do wi' it?

KATE: D'ye think I could walk through the streets o' Carhill again if you blackleg? D'ye think my mither could speak to the neebours again?

TAM: It'll soon be forgotten.

KATE: Blackleggin' is a thing that can never be forgotten.

TAM: But, Kate, we're in utter starvation, that's what has put your mither to her bed ... And there's nae pairish money the morn.

KATE: If you march a thousand strong to the parish offices they'll pay oot the money.

TAM: The polis are here to keep us frae marchin'.

KATE: It takes mair than polis to stop a hungry mob.

TAM: I'm gaun oot tae my work.

KATE: If you go to your work you'll come hame to an empty hoose. I'd rather tramp the country and beg my crust than stay in the same hoose as a blackleg.

TAM: But something has to be done, Kate.

KATE: Fight on to the finish, that's what can be done.

  (*Enter* JOCK)

JOCK: Did onybody see my pipe?

LIZZIE: It's on the fender, daddy.

  (*She goes for it*)

JOCK: Weel, Tam!

TAM: Weel!

JOCK: What are we gaun to dae aboot it noo?

TAM: God knows.

LIZZIE: You'll need to go back to the pit, daddy.

JOCK: The pit'll come to me before I go to the pit. I'll stay awa' frae it noo, just for spite. Stop the pairish relief, what the hell'll be their game?

KATE: There'll be a riot here the morn if they try to stop it.

JOCK: A lot o' guid that'll dae.

TAM: Ay, a lot o' guid that'll dae, Jock; half o' us clouted wi' a polisman's baton, and landed in the jile.

KATE: It's mair honourable to be clouted wi' a policeman's baton than clouted wi' a miner's fist, and that's what'll happen to the men wha try to blackleg.

JOCK: (*looking at pipe*) No' a smoke either, Kate. It's a wash-oot!

KATE: (*donning her coat*) Keep up your pecker, Jock, there's a guid time comin' yet.

JOCK: It's been comin' a' my time, but it's a damned sicht farther awa' noo than ever it's been.

TAM: Ay, a body would be better deid.

KATE: Did you ever hear such a crowd o' men? And they wonder why they're losin' the strike.

TAM: It's a' richt for you speakin', you havena the responsibility o' a hoose on your heid.

JOCK: Ay, they're young, Tam, and doesna ken what it means to the likes o' us.

KATE: Puir sowls, without your baccy and your beer you're no' much use. (*To* JOCK) Stick oot your chest, man! Let them see you're a Scotsman and a man. Fight like hell, and never say die till a deid horse kicks ye.

JOCK: It's no' easy for a hungry man to stick oot his chest.

TAM: It is not, Jock.

KATE: Well, stick your fingers to your nose at them. Guid nicht.

JOCK: Guid nicht

(KATE *and* JENNY *go out*)

JOCK: God kens what's to be done. For thirty years I have worked in the pit, and has come through many a hard time o't, but never the likes o' this.

TAM: I wouldna have troubled mysel' sae much, but the wife's no' keeping weel ava: that cough o' hers is gettin' worse.

JOCK: She'll need to take care o' hersel', Tam.

TAM: Tak' care o' hersel'! and hasna had a meal the day! I'll need to do something, Jock, I canna let things go on like this.

JOCK: But what can you dae?

TAM: I can go to my work. It's the only thing I can dae.

JOCK: It's a problem, Tam. I wish I could help ye, but I'm needin' help mysel'.

(*The sound of singing can be heard faintly*. We'll hang every blackleg . . .)

TAM: Ach, to hell, I dinna ken what to dae.

(*He goes out*)

JOCK: Ay, it's a problem, Tam.

LIZZIE: Will my mammie be long, daddy? . . . Does she no ken I'm hungry? . . . I wish the strike was finished, I'm needin' a new frock . . . see, I'm in rags . . . And I'm needin' shoon tae, my feet are ay wet.

(JOCK *is sitting gazing into the fire*)

LIZZIE: My mammie was greetin' when I came hame frae the schule the day . . . Gimmie a piece, daddy.

(*Enter* JEAN, *wearily; an empty bucket in her hand. She is followed by* JENNY. LIZZIE *runs to her mother, but* JEAN *takes no notice of her: She puts the basket on the table, takes off her shawl, and sits down at table side, as if she was exhausted*)

JOCK: Hoo did you get on, wife?

JEAN: I'm beat, Jock, there's no' a grocer or a baker in the toon'll gi'e me a crust.

JOCK: (*rising*) Get oot my pit claes.

JEAN: (*rising*) No, you're no dain' that.

JOCK: What else can be done?

JEAN: You came oot wi' your neebours, and you'll go back wi' them.

JOCK: And have we to dee o' hunger?

JEAN: Something'll turn up yet.

JOCK: Oh! for God's sake ha'e some sense. What can turn up?

(JEAN *sits and breaks down*)

JENNY: (*with her hand on* JEAN's *shoulder*) Ha'e ye nae he'rt! barkin' at my mither like that when you ha'e mair need to be comfortin' her. For six months she has scraped through, and you've never kent what it was to want a bite or a smoke till the nicht; lowered hersel' mony a time to keep things gaun, and noo, when she's beat, you can only bark at her.

JOCK: I dinna mean it, Jean.

JEAN: I ken that, Jock, I'm no' worth a haet gettin'.

JENNY: Mebbe my uncle, Bob, would help us?

JEAN: Supposin' we should dee you're no' gaun near him.

JOCK: Bob would help us if he kent we were in this hole.

JEAN: He's a blackleg, and we're no askin' help frae him.

JOCK: Weel, something has to be done . . . Can we no' sell that gramophone?

JEAN: No, it's the laddie's.

JOCK: But something'll need to go, Jean?

JEAN: That gramophone's no' gaun. The laddie boucht it wi' the first pocket-money ever he earned; he'd break his he'rt if he were to lose it.

JOCK: Right o! I'm gaun to the pit, for I'll starve for nae white man.

JEAN: (*rising and going to room*) You're gaun to drive me mad yet.

(LIZZIE *follows her mother*)

JENNY: For God's sake, faither, ha'e some sense.

JOCK: It's your mither that has nae sense. I'm shair that gramophone's no' needed at a time like this. And yet you'd starve rather than hurt his feelin's. I canna understand it.

JENNY: If you were a woman you would understand it, you men ha'e nae he'rts.

JOCK: It's past the time for silly sentiment. We're up against it Jenny, and some o' us have to make a sacrifice.

JENNY: Weel, you should have sacrificed your beer yesterday. This wouldna have happened if you had played the game yesterday.

JOCK: I ken that fine, you dinna need to tell me that, but it's past and canna be helped noo. Hoo are we gaun to get a crust o' breid, that's the question . . . Folk that ha'e toiled and battled a' their days, workin' frae hand to mooth, even in the best o' times, slaves, if ever there were slaves, and to think we've to go back to that pit on worse conditions! It's hellish to think o' it. It would be a God's blessin' if the roof came doon the first day and crushed the life oot o' us, they'd be responsible for oor wives and bairns, and we'd be awa' frae a' the bloody sufferin'

JENNY: That's a selfish wey oot o' it, and it's selfishness and greed that's the cause o' a' the sorrow and sufferin' the day.

(LIZZIE *enters from room*)

LIZZIE: Jenny, my ma' wants ye.

(JENNY *goes to room.* LIZZIE *follows.* JOCK *sits to put on his boots.* WULL BAXTER *enters*)

WULL: Weel that was some row the nicht, John . . . She's a right tartar, isn't she?

JOCK: Ay, she has a temper.

WULL: Ye ken, it's the women o' this place that's keepin' this strike gaun on.

JOCK: They seem to ha'e got their birz up.

WULL: Hoo are things wi' you the nicht, John?

JOCK: No' too bad, we've been worse mony a time.

WULL: The morn'll tell a tale when there's nae pairish relief.

JOCK: It'll tell a tale someway or ither.

WULL: I'm thinkin' aboot tryin' to get oot to Canada. There's naething here for a young chap.

JOCK: It's no easy gettin' out there.

WULL: I'll manage . . . The men that are startin' the morn are gettin' a guid chance.

JOCK: Are they?

WULL: Five pounds when they make a start, and a pound a day.

JOCK: That's the stuff, eh!

WULL: Isn't it. It's no' often the miner gets a chance like that.

JOCK: No, I can hardly believe it.

WULL: You can take it frae me, Jock, it's the truth . . . What about it?

JOCK: What aboot what?

WULL: Makin' a start in the mornin' wi' the rest o' us?

JOCK: Eh! D'ye mean to tell me you're canvassin' for blacklegs?

WULL: It's no' blackleggin'. You ken as weel as me that if it's left to the leaders it'll never be finished. The place is in ruination: if the pit doesna open soon it'll never open . . . A week's work would put you on your feet again.

JOCK: Would put wha on their feet?

WULL: Don't be silly, John, this chance only comes yince in a lifetime.

JOCK: Wull, I'm hungry, richt enough, and money o' ony kind is a big temptation, but before I would touch their blood money I would eat grass at the roadside.

WULL: Are you feart for the Socialists and the pickets?

JOCK: I don't want ony insults, Wull.

(JENNY *makes to enter, but when she sees* WULL *she returns*)

WULL: (*rising*) I thought you had mair pluck than that, Jock.

JOCK: (*rising and gripping him*) Ye flamin' twister! if ye insult me like that I'll choke the life oot o' ye. (JENNY *and* JEAN *come to door*)

WULL: I thought the wey you were speakin' . . .

JOCK: Oot o' my sicht, ye traitor! (*Throws him from him*) And if ever I see Jenny speakin' to ye again, I'll cut the tongue oot o' her heid. (JEAN *returns to room*) Oot o' that door, I say!

    (WULL *goes out*)

JOCK: Blackleg! No, I'm damned sure though it was a hunner pounds a shift . . . Jenny, I came oot like a man, and I'll go back like a man; it'll never be said that Jock Smith was a blackleg.

    (*Enter* BOB)

BOB: Was Wull Baxter in here?

JOCK: Ay.

BOB: Was he wantin' you oot to your work?

JOCK: Never you mind.

BOB: If you go to your work I'll leave the hoose.

JOCK: Is there a meetin' the nicht?

BOB: There's a meetin' the noo to get pickets.

JOCK: Awa' to the meetin' and let me ken what gangs on. I'll let you go this time.

    (BOB *is at the door when* JOCK *speaks*)

Bob! Come here a minute.

    (BOB *returns*)

We're up against it the nicht, Bob. Would you be vexed if we sellt your gramophone.

    (BOB *is silent*)

We'll get you anither yin when the strike's finished.

    (BOB *is on the verge of tears*)

We're at oor wits' end. Your mither has been in every shop in the toon, and canna get a crust withoot the money. And Wull Baxter was in here the noo offerin' me a pound a shift if I went to my work. I dinna want to go, Bob, but if we have to starve, weel.

BOB: You can sell it, faither.

JOCK: Your mither doesna want to pairt wi' it.

BOB: I'll tell her.

    (*He goes to room*)

JENNY: They've even to draw the blood frae the he'rt o' the bairns.

JOCK: I didna think I was sae sentimental.

    (*Re-enter* BOB)

BOB: It's a' richt, faither, I tellt her I was tired o' it. (*Going off*) I ken what's needed, it's a revolution that's needed.

JOCK: I'll need to get a breath o' fresh air, this nicht has me about suffocated.

> (*He dons muffler and jacket. A knock comes to the door.* JENNY *goes to answer*)

JENNY: It's Tam Anderson.

JOCK: Come in, Tam!

> (TAM *enters, and* JENNY *goes to room*)

TAM: Was Wull Baxter in here soundin' you aboot gaun to the pit in the mornin'?

JOCK: He was.

TAM: Are ye gaun, Jock?

JOCK: Am I hell!

TAM: Isn't he a richt traitor? Did you think he was yin o' thae kind?

JOCK: No, or he'd been coortin' some ither place . . . D'ye think there'll be mony that'll try to go oot, Tam?

TAM: I couldna say. I heard that Tam Pettigrew was thinkin' aboot it tae.

JOCK: I dinna think Tam'll be there, though Tam's up against it the nicht . . . If the pairish doesna pay ower the morn I doot there'll be a big breakawa'.

TAM: The pairish'll pay ower, Jock, or we'll tear doon the buildin'. We're formin' pickets for the morn, Jock, will you gi'e us a hand?

JOCK: I will, and if that Wull Baxter tried to pass me it'll be a face withoot a nose. Is there onything I can dae the nicht?

TAM: We're ha'in' a secret meetin' to discuss the plans for the morn, you can come if you like.

> (JOCK *claps his hand. Then singing can be heard, the tune is 'The Red Flag'*)[8]

JOCK: That's the stuff to gi'e them! Blaw their blasted pits in the air, and the blacklegs wi' them. (*As they go out*) A pound a shift! No, I may sell my muscle; but I'll never sell my soul.

> (*The singing fades away.* LIZZIE *enters*)

LIZZIE: That's my daddie awa' oot, ma!

> (JENNY *enters with her coat on. She lifts gramophone, and is near door when* JEAN *enters*)

JEAN: Jenny. We canna sell that gramophone yet. Tak' this ring instead.

> (*She takes the ring from her finger*)

JENNY: You canna sell that ring, mither. Bob wouldna let you pairt wi' that.

JEAN: I can pairt wi' it easier than the gramophone. Noo, Jenny, dinna argue aboot it. Hurry, and bring up some groceries, you're a' hungry. Hurry, Jenny.

(JENNY *goes out.* JEAN *puts the kettle on the fire, then she sits*)

LIZZIE: (*after a pause*) Maw!

JEAN: What is it, dearie.

LIZZIE: I'm sleepy.

(JEAN *takes her on her knee.* LIZZIE *lays her head against her mother's breast. There is a short pause, then* JEAN *speaks dreamily*)

JEAN: We were a prood pair that day, Jock, a prood pair. Blue skies and sunshine, and the birds singin' on every tree. But that was lang, lang syne . . . nae struggle then, and nae tears, just sang and laughter. (*Sighs*) Ay, changed days noo, Jock.

(LIZZIE *looks up in her mother's face. They kiss as the curtain falls*)

ACT TWO

The same as Act One. The following day, afternoon. The canary in the cage at the window sings merrily. JOCK sits at the fireside reading a racing paper. JENNY sits at the table side, in centre of floor, trying to knock a few tackets in her shoes.

JOCK: Canaries are like human bein's, Jenny, they canna sing when their stomachs are empty.

(JENNY *makes no answer.* JOCK *takes a stump of pencil from his pocket, wets it in his mouth and begins to write the names of horses on a slip of paper which he also takes from his pocket*)

If thae three dinna make the bookie squeal the day I'll never look at a horse in the face again. (*Puts paper in his pocket, rises and goes to the window*) I wonder wha it is that's workin' the day? I could bet you a thousand pounds it's that Wull Baxter. The dirty swine, if ever he comes aboot this hoose again I'll swing for him.

(*Enter* JEAN)

JEAN: There's nae pairish money the day yet.

JOCK: What! Are they no' payin' oot?

JEAN: No, there's a deputation awa' to Edinburgh, to see the Board o' Health, wha'ever he is. I thoucht your mairch to the Parish Council wouldna frighten them.

JOCK: Weel, I could have sworn they were gaun to pay oot, for they had the wind up properly.

JEAN: It was a' in the game, to get you awa' hame again. They ken fine that if they diddle you the first time you'll no' get the same crowd to mairch a second time.

JOCK: I believe you're richt, Jean.

JEAN: Did you ever see me wrang?

JOCK: We ha'e a lot to learn before we win a strike.

JEAN: I hear them sayin' that Tam Anderson's likely to be arrested for the speech he made. What did he say?

JOCK: He made a great speech, Jean. He had the blood boilin' in my veins. 'Fellow workers,' he says, 'are ye gaun to stand and see your wives and bairns starve to death before your e'en? Are you content to dae this and ca' yoursel's men? Fellow workers! we have been far ower meek in the past, the time has come when we've got to be prepared to let them see that we're prepared to die . . .'

JEAN: (*interrupting*) Some hope.

JOCK: D'ye think I wouldna shed my blood for you?

JEAN: You'll no' shed your hair for me, let alane your blood.

JOCK: Just wait till the time comes and I'll let you see . . . Have you heard wha it is that's workin'?

JEAN: Ay, it's Wull Baxter.

JOCK: I thoucht that. Hoo did he get through the pickets?

JEAN: He was at his work before the pickets were oot o' their beds. Some pickets!

JOCK: Weel, God pity him when he tries to get hame, he'll be torn frae limb to limb.

(JENNY *rises and goes to room*)

JEAN: Would you ha'e thoucht it o' him?

JOCK: I ay had my suspicions o' him; he was too damned nice and too damned wise, beware o' thae kind every time.

JEAN: If he had been a mairit man wi' a family there would have been some excuse, but he has naebody to keep but that auld tinker o' a mither o' his. He's made a fine fool o' Jenny onywey.

JOCK: She'll soon forget aboot him.

JEAN: It's no' sae easy forgettin', Jock. They were to be mairrit after the strike, and she has been layin' by wee bits o' things for a while.

JOCK: There's nae weddin' takin' place noo.

JEAN: It's that mither o' his that's to blame, she's been nagging at him to start to his work.

JOCK: It's no' her to blame ava', he wants to make a wheen pounds and slip off to Canada, I saw that was in his mind last nicht when he was in here.

JEAN: Jenny has been speakin' aboot Canada tae.

JOCK: Ay, a fine thing that would be, a douchter o' mine gaun to Canada on blood money. Jean, if he ever comes aboot this hoose again I'll leave him deid on that floor.

(*Enter* AGNES)

JEAN: Hullo! Agnes, I thoucht you were in your bed?

AGNES: I canna lie, Jean.

JEAN: Did you get a sleep last nicht?

AGNES: (*hopelessly*) No.

JOCK: You'll need to see the doctor, Agnes, you're lettin' it gang ower far.

JEAN: (*decisively*) The doctor's comin' the day, Jock, I'm sendin' for him mysel', we're standin' nae mair o' this nonsense.

AGNES: But, Jean, what's the use o' sendin' . . .

JEAN: (*interrupting*) He's comin', and that's a' that's aboot it. D'ye ken you're like a ghost?

AGNES: There's nae Pairish money the day.

JEAN: No. God kens what we'll dae, Agnes.

JOCK: I ken what I would dae, I would get the miners to mairch to London and blaw Parliament in the air.

JEAN: And where'll we be by the time you get to London?

AGNES: I dinna ken what to do, Jean. I'm just aboot mad.

(AGNES *begins to cry*)

JEAN: Wheesht! Agnes, I'll see if I can dae anything for ye.

AGNES: The weans are a' greetin' for something to eat, and I ha'e naething. God, but I'm weary. I just want to lie doon and dee.

(*She has a fit of coughing.* JENNY *enters*)

JEAN: (*taking her kindly by the shoulders*) Come doon wi' me Agnes, and get to your bed. I'll see that you get something to tide ower till they pay oot the Pairish money.

AGNES: (*holding her brow*) I'm tired, Jean . . . tired . . . tired . . . tired, but there's nae rest.

JEAN: I'll see that you dae get rest, supposin' I should sit at your bedside till you fa' asleep.

AGNES: It's no sleep, Jean, it's . . .

(*She had another fit of coughing, and* JEAN *leads her out, shaking her head sadly at* JOCK *as she goes*)

JOCK: You better go for a doctor, Jenny, there's something gey far wrang wi' Agnes.

JENNY: It's hunger that's wrang. I don't believe she has tasted a bite for days.

JOCK: It's hellish! And we can dae naething tae help, naething ava. And they wonder why we mairch in oor thoosan's wavin' the red flag. If they could only suffer oor lot for a week they wouldna wonder sae much. And that Wull Baxter oot workin'! cutting oor very throats.

JENNY: I didna ask him to gang, faither.

JOCK: I ken, Jenny, and I'm vexed for ye. But the first time I'll meet him I'll take it o' his hide, the traitor.

(JENNY *dons her coat*)

JOCK: Forget aboot him, Jenny.

JENNY: I canna understand him, it was the last thing in the world I was expectin'.

JOCK: Ay, ay, but things'll come a' richt for you yet, lass.

JENNY: I was lookin' forward to happy days, but everything has a' gane crash and in the yin day.

JOCK: There's naebody escapin' the strike, Jenny, we're a' gettin' a blow o' some kind. But we're learnin' and some day we'll mebbe get oor ain back.

(JEAN *enters, followed by* LIZZIE)

JEAN: (*to* JENNY) Awa' and get the doctor, Jenny. And bring up a gill o' whisky when you're doon; that woman'll need to get a sleep or she'll be deid in the mornin'. You'll get a bottle in that end drawer.

(JEAN *takes money from her purse*)

JEAN: (*to* JOCK) Thae weans are in utter starvation.

JOCK: Can you help her, Jean?

JEAN: I'll gi'e her the half o' what I ha'e, I can dae nae mair.

(*She gives* JENNY *the money for the whisky*)

JEAN: (*to* JENNY) If Dr Morrison's no' in, go for the ither yin; the sooner we ken what's what, the better.

(JENNY *goes out*. JEAN *begins to put food in the basket*)

JEAN: God be thanked we ha'e oor health and strength.

JOCK: If she could get a sleep she would be a' richt; though I dinna like that cough, Jean, it's something deeper than a cauld.

JEAN: I dinna ken, but we'll need to watch her weel, or she'll no' last long.

(TAM *enters*)

TAM: Is Jenny awa' for the doctor?

JEAN: Ay, he'll no' likely be long till he's up, Tam. I'm puttin' something in this basket for the weans. When had you onything last?

TAM: Yesterday mornin'.

JEAN: And Agnes?

TAM: I dinna ken . . . she's had naething the day.

JEAN: And what wey did she no' come and tell me?

TAM: She's no' a guid moocher, Jean, she would dee before she would ask onything.

JEAN: I'm sure she kens she needna ha'e ony fears o' comin' here.

TAM: She's ay been queer that wey.

JOCK: (*to* TAM) Was you in the mairch to the Pairish Council this mornin'?

TAM: No, I was not; you'll no' get me takin' pairt in any o' your Bolshie stunts.

JOCK: No, but you'll take the Pairish money when it comes.

TAM: Ay, WHEN it comes.

JOCK: We'll never get it sittin' at the fireside or lyin' on the grass . . . Were you no' on the pickets this mornin' either?

TAM: No, I think mair o' my bed.

JOCK: Ay, but strikes are no' won in bed.

JEAN: Not in the pub, either?

TAM: (*to* JOCK) Was you on the picket?

JOCK: Too true I was. Up at the pit at five o'clock.

JEAN: He's been singin' 'The Red Flag' since he came hame.

JOCK: This country's gaun to be a wee Russia if this strike lasts much langer.

TAM: And would you like to see it a wee Russia?

JOCK: Yes! and the sooner the better.

TAM: You had ay plenty to say against the Bolshies and Russia before.

JOCK: Ay, but my brains seem to be in my stomach.

TAM: Weel, I don't want to see this country made into a wee Russia, it would bring it to ruination.

JOCK: Ruination! That's the worst o' havin' a three-course breakfast, it makes a man a hunner per cent Britisher.

TAM: If there's nae Pairish money the morn I'm gaun to work.

JOCK: A man that's feart to mairch to the Pairish Council, doesna ha'e the pluck to face the pickets. You'd been at your work this mornin' if you hadna been feart.

TAM: I ken, and so would anither hunner men in the place. It's the damned Bolshies that's keepin' us frae startin'.

JOCK: And here's luck to them, says I.

TAM: And it's them that dinna want to work that's on the pickets.

JOCK: D'ye mean that I dinna want to work?

TAM: I never mentioned you.

JOCK: I was on the picket, and I'm damned sure I'll work beside you ony day.

TAM: Did I say you couldna?

JOCK: No, and you better no'.

JEAN: Ye look like a pair that'll dee wi' the shovel in your hand. (*To* TAM *handing him the basket*) Here! take this doon, and look slippy.

TAM: Did I say he couldna work, Jean?

JOCK: Of coorse you did.

TAM: I did naething o' the kind.

JEAN: Did I tell you to look slippy?

TAM: (*as he goes out*) Oh, aye, take his pairt.
    (*He shuts door rather loudly*)

JOCK: Isn't he an agitator? Ay talkin' aboot work, and has never worked a' his days; he has starved his wife off the face o' the earth.

JEAN: I've lost aboot ten stane mysel' since I got mairrit.

JOCK: You're a delicate lookin' cratur.
    (JEAN *pours out tea into a 'tinnie' and gives it to* LIZZIE *with a piece of bread.* LIZZIE *sits on fender*)

JEAN: If it wasna for my guid nature I'd been a walkin' skeleton.

JOCK: (*puttin' on his coat*) There's yin thing I admire aboot ye, Jean, and that's your pluck.

JEAN: I'm glad you appreciate it.

JOCK: I do, and I thank my lucky stars mony a time that I got the wife I did.

JEAN: Weel, what's the use o' continually grumblin' and grousin', it does nae guid.

JOCK: Not a bit. D'ye ken, Jean, I'm prood o' ye.

JEAN: (*looking at him in surprise*) Ay!

JOCK: I am, as prood as Punch. (*Coughs*) Can you spare eighteenpence for a three-cross double?

JEAN: I kent there was something comin'. No, I can not. I ha'e mair need o' eighteenpence than gi'ein' it to the bookie.

JOCK: They're three solid pinches, Jean, I could stake my shirt that twa o' them'll win.

JEAN: Weel, you can stake your shirt.

JOCK: Can you no spare ninepence then.

JEAN: Ninepence gets a loaf, and there's a family doon there in starvation.

JOCK: If it comes up I'll promise to gi'e ye every penny . . . If you don't speculate, Jean, you'll never accumulate . . . If I don't win money wi' this line the day, I'll list up in the Salvation Army.

JEAN: (*taking coppers from her purse*) Oh! here! there's a bob, you can get a glass o' beer wi' the extra threepence.

JOCK: (*Taking money*) You're a sport, Jean.

JEAN: Hook it! That's a' you're gettin'.

> (JOCK *is on his way out when* BOB *enters, boisterously bumping into him*)

JOCK: Here! Can you no watch where you're gaun, ye muckle nowte!

BOB: It was you that wasna watchin' where you were gaun.

JOCK: If you gi'e me ony o' your lip I'll slap your ear for ye.

JEAN: (*to* JOCK) Awa' you and attend to the bookie.

JOCK: He's daft, that's what's wrang wi' him.

> (JOCK *goes out*)

JEAN: (*to* BOB) Where ha'e you been?

BOB: Washin' tatties at the soup kitchen. Is there onything for me to eat?

JEAN: See here! you'll need to try to control your belly a bit, it would take a Carnegie[9] to keep this hoose gaun the noo.

BOB: Eat when you can get it, and when you canna get it, weel, you canna eat.

LIZZIE: I heard him swearin' the day, maw.

BOB: Wha heard me swearin'?

LIZZIE: Me.

BOB: You're a flamin' wee liar. Where did you hear me swearin'?

LIZZIE: At the street corner.

BOB: What did I say?

LIZZIE: You just want me tae swear tae, but I'm no'.

> (*She puts out her tongue at him. He makes a rush at her*)

BOB: I'll warm your ear for ye.

JEAN: Here! That'll dae!

BOB: She's a flamin' wee liar.

JEAN: That'll dae I'm sayin'!

BOB: Just wait till I get her ootside. I'll bump her.

JEAN: D'ye want ony tea?

BOB: Is there ony ham left?

JEAN: No.

BOB: Never mind tea, then, just gimmie a piece in my hand.

> (JEAN *spreads bread with treacle*)

BOB: I'm fed up wi' this treacle. I'll soon be like a darkie.

JEAN: Be damned thankfu' you're gettin' treacle. If the Pairish doesna pay oot you'll be doon on your knees on the grass.

BOB: Ha'e you heard the latest?

JEAN: No, what is it?

BOB: Tam Anderson's coortin' Kate.

JEAN: That's auld news.

BOB: Did you ken?

JEAN: Surely I kent when it was me that gi'ed him the wink that she had a notion o' him.

BOB: Can you no' gi'e somebody the wink to tak' a notion o' me?.

JEAN: Wha would tak' a notion o' you?

BOB: What's wrang wi' me?

JEAN: There's a lookin' glass there.

(Enter JENNY)

JEAN: Did you get the doctor?

JENNY: He's comin' doon after he gets his dinner.

(She hands her mother the whisky)

JEAN: You'll rin doon wi' this to your auntie's, Bob, and tell Kate that I'll come doon when the doctor comes.

BOB: *(to* JENNY) That Wull Baxter o' yours is gaun to get a maulin' when he comes up the pit; a' the women o' the place are gaun to be there; they'll skin him alive.

JEAN: *(to* BOB) Tell Kate to make the half o' that into toddy, and gi'e it to her mither.

BOB: He's just a flamin' reactionary, but just wait till he gets a taste o' the dictatorship o' the proletariat.

JEAN: Here! chuck that Bolshie stuff and rin doon wi' that whisky.

BOB: *(going off)* There's nothing like direct action for the revolutionary movement.

(He goes out)

JEAN: I wouldna worry mysel' ower Wull Baxter, he's no worth it.

JENNY: I'm no' worried, mither, just disappointed.

JEAN: Was he speakin' aboot gaun to Canada after the strike?

JENNY: We were baith gaun there.

JEAN: That's the reason he's workin' Jenny.

JENNY: I canna understaun' it, mither.

JEAN: He'll get his deserts yet, Jenny, just bide your time. Every dog gets its day.

*(*JENNY *looks out window wearily)*

LIZZIE: *(rising and handing her mug to* JEAN) Read my cup, maw.

*(*JEAN *takes mug and looks into it with a serious air.* LIZZIE *is serious too)*

JEAN: There's a new frock comin' to you, dearie . . . but I doot it'll no be till the strike's finished.

LIZZIE: Nae stockin's?

JEAN: Ay, there's stockin's and shoon tae.

LIZZIE: Nae money?

JEAN: No, there's nae money, daurlin'.

LIZZIE: And hoo will I get a new frock, and shoon, and stockin's withoot money?

JEAN: Rin awa' for a pail o' water, darlin', and I'll mebbe be able to tell you when you come back.

(LIZZIE *goes for pail*)

LIZZIE: (*going out*) This should be Bob's work, no' mine. Nae wonder I'm gettin' grey heided.

(*The canary sings*)

JEAN: I wish I'd been a bird.

(KATE *enters*)

KATE: Is Jock in, auntie?

JEAN: No. What d'ye want wi' him, Kate?

KATE: Will there be ony chance o' me gettin' some money if I go to the Pairish clerk? I'll need to get some nourishment for my mither . . . she's beginnin' to rave noo . . . Oh, Jean! I dinna ken what to dae.

JEAN: Where's your faither?

KATE: He sittin' at her bedside.

JEAN: It's him that'll need to go to the Pairish, Kate, they'll no' listen to you.

KATE: He'll no' gang.

JEAN: He'll gang if I go doon to him, and in a hurry.

(*Enter* LIZZIE *with water*)

JEAN: Is her cough ony better yet?

KATE: Ay, she's no coughin' noo, just ravin' aboot the weans.

JEAN: The doctor'll gi'e her a bottle that'll make her sleep, and she'll be like a new woman in the mornin'. She's been worryin' hersel' ower much, that's a' that's wrang wi' her. You should have had the doctor lang syne, Kate. But that's what's wrang wi' the working women, they want tae dee on their feet . . . Tam Anderson would tell you what was the best thing to do to get some money frae the Pairish.

KATE: I hear them sayin' that he's likely to be arrested if he takes pairt in the demonstration against Wull Baxter.

JEAN: If I see him, Kate, I'll ha'e a talk wi' him aboot it. He canna afford to take the risk o' gettin' the jile noo when the strike's aboot finished.

KATE: If he has his mind made up, Jean, you'll no put him off it . . . Everything seems to be gaun wrang thigither . . . I'm fed up.

(*She buries her head in her hands at table and sobs*)

JEAN: (*comforting*) It'll no' dae to lose he'rt, Kate. When things go against us we've still got to battle. Lyin' doon to things doesna help ony. Na, na, let us keep up oor he'rts . . . Wheesht!

lass things'll come a' richt for us yet. Awa' doon to the hoose and get your faither to go to the Pairish clerk; if he doesna get onything I'll go for Tam Anderson and see what he has to say about it. Go doon and attend to your mither, gi'e her the rest o' the toddie till the doctor comes, then I'll come doon and see what's trumph.

(KATE *rises*)

JEAN: That's the spirit, hen, keep up your pecker ... Go doon wi' her, Jenny, and keep her company till the doctor comes ... Your mither will be a' richt the morn', Kate, dinna worry aboot that.

(KATE *and* JENNY *go out*)

JEAN: Puir sowl, she hasna had much pleasure in life to be a young lass.

LIZZIE: What's wrang wi' my auntie, maw?

JEAN: Hunger, dear, that's what's wrang.

LIZZIE: What wey are folk hungry?

JEAN: Because some are ower fu' fed.

(TAM ANDERSON *knocks and enters*)

JEAN: Did you meet Kate and Jenny, Tam?

TAM: I dinna want to meet them, Jean.

JEAN: She's lookin' for you.

TAM: Is her mither nae better?

JEAN: She's wantin' to ken hoo she'll get some money frae the Pairish clerk; they're in utter starvation.

TAM: If she gets a line frae the doctor I'll see that she gets something. Tell her that, will ye?

JEAN: What wey dae you no' want tae see her?

TAM: I'm likely to be arrested the nicht, Jean.

JEAN: Hoo d'ye ken?

TAM: The sergeant o' the police warned me that if I took pairt in the demonstration against Wull Baxter I'd be arrested.

JEAN: And are ye?

TAM: If we let him get hame withoot a demonstration there'll be mair men oot the morn. We've got to nip it in the bud, Jean.

JEAN: Is it worth it, Tam? It means the jile for ye, and the breakawa'll take place some time or ither. You nor onybody else can stem it, and you ken that, for it has happened before in your time.

TAM: And it'll happen again, Jean, and will happen till the workers control their ain destiny. But we've got to fight till the last ditch every time, whether it means the jile or no'.

JEAN: It'll hurt Kate, Tam.

TAM: I ken it will, but there's nae escape. I'll no' likely get ony
mair than three months, and it'll be worth the sufferin' to come
back again and ken that I did my bit.

JEAN: And you'll get a' your thanks for it in the yin day. The
miners are a queer crowd, they forget about the fight when they
get their first week's pay in their hand. You ken the trouble
you had after the last strike collectin' money to pay the debts,
you had to pawn your ain watch to help.

TAM: I ken a' that, Jean, but it has a' to be suffered, there's
never onything won withoot a struggle . . . But I didna come
up to argue wi' ye, Jean, I want you to take a message to Kate.
I'm no' likely to see her for a while noo.

JEAN: What d'ye want?

TAM: Will you ask her to stick to me, Jean?

JEAN: You needna ha'e ony fear o' that, Tam. But would you
no' be better to ha'e a talk wi' her yoursel'?

TAM: I'm feart she micht put me aff takin' a pairt in the demonstration, you ken what women are, and she micht keep me
back; at least we micht quarrel aboot it, and I dinna want that
to happen . . . Tell her, Jean, that whenever I get oot we'll get
marrit . . . And, Jean, I want you to gi'e her this; it'll mebbe
tide them ower the strike.

JEAN: What is it?

TAM: (*holding out his hand*) Three pounds, a' I ha'e left o' my
savin's. It's no' much, but it'll ay help a wee thing. I'll no' need
it, I'll be gettin' free digs where I go. (*He smiles*)

JEAN: I wish you would put this affair off, Tam. No, I dinna
wish it either, laddie, for if you did you wouldna be Tam Anderson. But, Tam, you'll no' dae very weel in the jile, you're
no' the jile bird type.

TAM: If my health doesna break doon, Jean, I dinna care, but
this strike has been a tryin' time, and my nerves are a' knocked
to bits. But never mind, auld yin, we'll come through it. You'll
keep Kate's he'rt up till I come back?

JEAN: She'll be waitin' on ye comin' back, Tam, ha'e nae fear
o' that.

TAM: Weel . . . Guid bye! Jean.
    (*He holds out his hand*)

JEAN: Guid bye! Tam . . . This strike's gaun to break a' oor
he'rts. (*She sobs*)
    (TAM *wants to say more, but is not able. He goes out rather
    suddenly.* JEAN *sits at tableside.* BOB *enters*)

BOB: By gee, there's gaun to be some fun when that worm,
Baxter, comes up the pit; a' the women o' the place are gettin'

ready for him. They're no' half wild because there's nae pairish money the day. And the polis are comin' in their hunners.

JEAN: You'll keep awa' frae it.

BOB: You surely think it! I'm gaun to be in at the death.

JEAN: You're keepin' awa' frae it, I'm sayin' — and leavin' it to the men.

BOB: Leave it to the MEN! What am I!

LIZZIE: A mug.

BOB: I'm no' gaun to warn you again.

LIZZIE: You're worse than a mug, you're a' . . .

BOB: A what?

JEAN: That'll dae, the pair o' ye.

BOB: What am I?

JEAN: (*angrily*) That'll dae, I'm sayin'!

LIZZIE: (*running out*) You're a puddin'.

(BOB *chases her the length of door*)

BOB: I'm wantin' a lend o' that poker.

JEAN: What for?

BOB: A man's nae guid wi' his bare fists against a polisman wi' a baton.

JEAN: Your faither'll be gaun, and that's plenty oot o' the yin hoose. I dinna want two o' ye to get the jile.

BOB: The jile! Will we get the jile?

JEAN: Certainly you will.

BOB: I didna ken that. Will I get anither piece?

JEAN: You'll get your tea at tea time.

BOB: By gee! when this strike's finished I bet ye I'll have yin solid tightener, I'll no' be able to eat onything for a week efter it. What aboot tuppence for a packet o' Woodbines?

JEAN: I dinna ha'e tuppence; your smokin' ower much onywey.

BOB: (*going out*) I ken what's needed, it's a revolution that's needed.

(JEAN *goes to cage and gives the bird some seed. Then* JOCK *bursts in*)

JOCK: That's twa o' my horses up, Jean! thirty-five bob.

(*He catches hold of her and swings her round the room*)

JEAN: Thirty-five bob!

JOCK: Thirty-five bob! and, if the ither horse comes up, you'll ha'e twa pound ten.

JEAN: When will you ken aboot it?

JOCK: No' till the mornin', but the thirty-five bob is as safe as the bank.

JEAN: You'll see and come hame wi' it, Jock, and no' dae as you did the last time.

JOCK: I'm safe enough noo, Jean, I got a lesson last nicht I'll no' forget in a a hurry. (*Sits and lights pipe*) A bit win like that fairly lifts up a body's he'rt, doesn't it?

JEAN: It tak's something to lift up oor he'rts nooadays. I had Tam Anderson in the noo; he's to be arrested if he tak's part in the demonstration.

JOCK: So I heard doon the street. But Jean, if they arrest Tam Anderson there'll be a riot.

JEAN: Mebbe! I ken the Carhill miners; they're gey feart o' their ain skins whiles.

JOCK: That's richt enough tae. Let them sit on their hunkers at the street corner, and let the likes o' Tam Anderson risk everything for them.

JEAN: Are you gaun to the demonstration?

JOCK: There'll be plenty there withoot me. (*Then, to break the conversation*) We'll get oot your weddin' ring wi' the bookie's money.

JEAN: Let it stay where it is, we ha'e mair need o' the money than a ring on the finger.

JOCK: I wouldna care if the strike was finished, it's been a hell o' a time.

JEAN: You're no' gaun to be much better if you've to go back to the pit on the maister' terms. It's been a hard time, richt enough, and mony a nicht I have lain doon wonderin' where oor breakfast was to come frae, but, Jock, it's nae mair he'rt-rendin' than watchin' thae wheels turnin' every day, and never lookin' oot the windie but dreadin' to see some o' ye cairit hame a corpse or maimed for life. There are plenty o' women never bother their heids, they have seen that much and come through that much, that they have got hardened to it. But I havena reached that stage yet, na, thae wheels are ay between me and the sun, throwin' their lang, black shadows on the doorstep. It's mebbe been a time o' want since the strike started, but it's been a time o' peace; I was ay sure o' you and Bob comin' hame at nichts; but there's nae such faith when the wheels are turnin'. But you men dinna think o' thae things, you'll likely laugh at us when we tell ye aboot it?

JOCK: It's a fact, Jean, we put nae value on oor lives.

JEAN: You talk aboot a weddin' ring! I would gie the very he'rt oot o' my breist if I thought it would keep ye awa' frae that Hell.

JOCK: I'll need to try and get you awa' frae the pits, Jean, but it'll no' be easy noo they ha'e us gey weel chained, and I doot there's naething else for us but the same auld grind. Seven months' rent on oor heids noo, and we're a' needin' buits and claes. Ach. Christ kens what it'll be like.

JEAN: Ay but keep up your pecker, Jock, there's a silver linin' to every cloud.

JOCK: So it says in the school books.

(*Enter* JENNY)

JENNY: Mither, that's the doctor here, and he's takin' my auntie awa' to the hospital.

JEAN: The hospital! what's wrang?

JENNY: I dinna ken, she has to go through an operation.

JEAN: Good God! it's surely gey serious.

JOCK: Did the doctor no' say what was wrang?

JENNY: No, he wouldna tell us.

JEAN: (*putting on shawl*) Puir sowl, I thoucht there was something gey far wrang wi' her.

(JEAN *goes out, followed by* JENNY)

JOCK: Starvation! And they write to America to say that there's nae distress in the coalfields. Christians! I wonder what Christ would think o' them if He was here?

(BOB *enters*)

LIZZIE: I heard him swearin' the day, daddy.

BOB: I'll warm your ear for you if you say that again.

LIZZIE: (*running out*) So you were, I heard ye.

(BOB *chases her to door*)

BOB: Where's my mither?

JOCK: Awa' wi' the lodger.

BOB: I could dae wi' something to eat.

JOCK: Weel, get it yoursel'. God knows where some o' ye get the appetites. Are ye aye hungry?

BOB: I can ay eat mair than I get.

(*He goes to dresser and puts bread and margarine on the table*)

BOB: (*cutting bread*) There's gaun to be some fun at the pit when Wull Baxter gets up. Are you gaun up?

JOCK: What am I gaun to do there?

BOB: Feart you get the jile?

JOCK: No, I'm no feart I get the jile.

BOB: What wey are you no' gaun then?

(*Spreads margarine on bread*)

JOCK: Hey! that's butter, and there's a strike on.

BOB: That's no butter, that's margarine.

JOCK: Weel ca' cannie wi' it. If you want tea you'll need to put water in the teapot.

BOB: (*going to fire to fill teapot*) Fancy oor Jenny engaged to a worm like Wull Baxter. I'm ashamed to go doon the street.

(*Sits down and puts sugar in his cup*)

JOCK: (*at third spoonful*) Here! ca' cannie wi' that sugar.

BOB: Don't get excited. Where did you say my mither was?

JOCK: Your auntie has to go to the hospital.

BOB: Oh, what's wrang wi' her?

JOCK: If you kent that you'd be as wise as me, wouldn't ye?
(JOCK *lights his pipe*)

BOB: My uncle, Tam, was up at the Pairish tryin' to get some
money, but he dinna get it.

JOCK: No.

BOB: No, the clerk tellt him he heard his yarn before. But he'll
get it noo if the doctor says it.

JOCK: Ay, he'll get it noo when it's mebbe ower late. (*There is
a short pause*) I ha'e twa horses up the day, Bob.

BOB: By gee! your jam's fairly in the noo.

JOCK: Thirty-five bob. And, if the ither yin comes in, I'll hae
aboot three quid.

BOB: That's the stuff to gi'e them. If you had that every day
you'd be a' richt, eh?

JOCK: Ay, IF. If the Lakes o' Killarney were in Hell you'd get
a shillin' a gallon withoot any trouble.

BOB: Would ye?

JOCK: Ay, if !

BOB: If what?

JOCK: Thick heid! Did you no hear me say that if the Lakes o'
Killarney were in Hell you'd get a shillin' a gallon!

BOB: What for?

JOCK: For the water, of coorse!

BOB: Oh, ay. IF (*Spreading margarine on bread*) IF you hadna
went into the pub wi' the last bookie's money . . .

JOCK: (*interrupting*) Ca' cannie wi' that margarine, I said!

BOB: I'm doin' that, sir, it's no guid onywey.

JOCK: Be damned thankfu' you're gettin' it.

BOB: I'm no' grumblin' (*Pause*) Did you hear aboot Sam
Lindsay?

JOCK: What Sam Lindsay?

BOB: Sam Lindsay, the bookie.

JOCK: No, what aboot him?

BOB: He was pinched on the street the noo.

JOCK: (*jumping*) Eh!

BOB: The polis pinched him takin' bets on the street.

JOCK: (*almost in tears*) I had my bet on wi' him.

BOB: Weel, you can say ta! ta! to your money, the polis took a'
the slips off him.

JOCK: Cripes! that's a blow. Here! ca' canny wi' that breid, are you aware that's a' we ha'e in the hoose?

BOB: Listen! That's them singin' 'The Red Flag'. By gee! there's gaun to be some fun here the day! it'll be anither Waterloo! Can YOU sing 'The Red Flag' yet?

JOCK: Oh, shut up! It's bad enough backin' losers, but it's a damned sicht worse backin' winners, and no' gettin' payed ower.

BOB: I ay tellt ye it was a mug's game.

JOCK: Shut up! I tell ye! And get thae things off the table. I thought Sam Lindsay had mair savvy than get pinched on the street. If I'd only put my bet on wi' Peter.

BOB: Ay, IF!

JOCK: I want less gab frae you, see! But if there's nae pairish money the morn that gramophone o' yours'll need to go to the pawn.

BOB: My mither'll ha'e a say in that.

JOCK: Wha's boss in here, me, or your mither?

BOB: My mither, of course.

(JEAN *enters; she is crying.* LIZZIE *follows, much concerned*)

JOCK: What's the maitter, Jean?

(JEAN *is too much upset to answer*)

JOCK: What has happened?

JEAN: Oh, Jock, she's deid!

JOCK: Deid! Good Lord!

JEAN: Oh, Jock, that's an awfu' sicht doon there; a' the weans greetin' like to break their wee he'rts, and Kate tearin' her hair and cryin' on her mither to speak.

JOCK: Where's the faither?

JEAN: He's awa to the Pairish wi' the doctor's line. But it's ower late noo. Oh, Jock, she's worn awa' tae mothing, lyin' yonder wi' her thin, white face.

JOCK: Is there onything I can dae, Jean?

JEAN: Naething ava', Jock.

JOCK: Christ knows what it's comin' tae.

JEAN: Puir wee things, they'll miss their mither. Gi'ed the bite oot o' her ain mooth, puir sowl. What can God be thinkin' aboot when he lets the like o' this happen.

JOCK: If it's God's will that has ta'en awa' puir Agnes He's a gey queer God, and doesna ha'e much o' a he'rt for the weans it seems.

(JEAN *rises*)

JEAN: Fill the kettle, Jock, I'll need to go doon beside them the nicht. I'll leave Jenny wi' them the morn's nicht.

JOCK: Right o!

JEAN: (*going out*) Puir wee things . . .

(JEAN *goes out*, LIZZIE *following. Jock fills the kettle with water, spilling some on the floor. He puts kettle on fire then goes to scullery; returning with a cloth. He wipes floor awkwardly, and carries cloth away, as if it were a dead rat, by the tail, letting it drop on the way, and has to clean up another mess. He chucks cloth through scullery door. He then lifts floor brush and sweeps the floor, making the best of a bad job. He puts table nearer the window to hide the mess. Then he sits at fireside. Through the silence the booing of a crowd can be heard at intervals, he goes to window and looks out.* BOB *enters excitedly*)

BOB: That's Wull Baxter up the pit, and he's comin' hame between twa regiments o' polis!

JOCK: Are there mony women there?

BOB: Hunners, did you no hear them booin'?

JOCK: Could they not stay in their hooses and leave it to the men?

BOB: Leave it to the men! There's mair fecht in twa women than there is in a hunner men. (*The booing is heard again*) Listen! Are you comin' to see the fun?

JOCK: I ha'e mair to think aboot.

BOB: You're feart you get the jile, I'm no'.

(*He runs out.* JOCK *peers through window. The sound of disorder gets louder. There is one loud 'Boo!' then* JENNY *bursts in*)

JENNY: Oh, faither, there's a riot started doon the street!

JOCK: I kent it would happen. Could thae blasted women no' kept to their hooses onywey. (*Draws aside curtains of window*) God Almighty! there's the crowd has got Wull Baxter awa' frae the polis! They'll lynch him . . . Jenny! shut that door, he's making for here.

(JENNY *stands undecided.* JOCK *makes to lock door.* JENNY *holds him back*)

JOCK: Oot o' my road woman!

(JENNY *struggles.* JOCK *loses his temper, and thrusts her aside as the door bursts open, and* WULL BAXTER *almost falls in, locking the door behind him. The mob is at his heels, shouting madly. A stone crashes through the window*)

JOCK: Oot o' this house!

WULL: They'll kill me, Jock!

JOCK: Oot o' here, you traitor!

(JOCK *makes to eject him when the sound of a police whistle is heard and the screaming of women. Then a stampede, and then silence*)

JOCK: (*at window*) Bloodshed! Bloodshed ower the heid o' you! Oot o' here before I crush the life oot o' ye!

    (WULL *looks piteously at* JENNY. *She hesitates a second, then she goes to door, unlocks it, and opens it. He goes out, and she shuts the door again*)

JOCK: Bloodshed ower the heid o' a worm like that! a traitor! a bloody skunk. And you would . . .

JENNY: (*burying her head in her hands against the door*) Oh! faither! . . .

    (*He looks at her sympathetically as the curtain falls*)

ACT THREE

The same as Acts One and Two. A week later. At rise of curtain, BOB sits at table-side with a soup bowl on his knees, playing on it with two spoons as he would a kettle drum; he whistles a bagpipe tune. JOCK enters from room: jacket off.

JOCK: Is it no' time you were awa' to the soup kitchen?

BOB: I'm waitin' till the last day, it's aboot time noo I was gettin' some o' the thick stuff.

JOCK: Ay, wait till the last, and when you get doon, there'll be nane left.

BOB: That'll be MY funeral.

JOCK: Ay, but you'll be guzzlin' the dinner in here.

BOB: Some hope when YOU'RE there.

JOCK: I don't want ony lip, see!

    (BOB *rattles on the bowl and whistles*)

JOCK: Oh, for God's sake stop that, it gets on my nerves.

BOB: I think I'll join the pipe band.

    (*Has another rattle*)

JOCK: You'll break that flamin' bowl.

BOB: No fear, sir. (*Rattles still*)

JOCK: (*rising*) Are you gaun to stop it?

    (BOB *stops*)

BOB: It's high time we had the dictatorship o' the proletariat here.

JOCK: Did you hear ony word o' Tam Anderson when you were doon the street?

BOB: There's word comin' ower the telephone whenever the trial's finished.

JOCK: (*half to himself*) I wonder hoo he'll get on?

BOB: Ten bob, or thirty days.

JOCK: They're no' tryin' him in the High Court before a jury o' auld farmers and grocers and butchers to let him aff wi' a fine. I wouldna be surprised if he gets six months.

BOB: Away and don't haver! Six months! You're a reactionary. What would he get six months for?

JOCK: If you had seen the summons you wouldna say that; they're just aboot chairgin' him wi' startin' a rebellion.

BOB: But it was Wull Baxter that was the cause o' it, no' Tam Anderson.

JOCK: Ay, but Wull Baxter was helpin' the maisters, he was dain' richt as far as they were concerned.

BOB: But the maisters are no' tryin' him.

JOCK: Are they no? You ha'e a lot to learn aboot your revolutionary movement.

BOB: I ken mair than you ken; it's a revolution that's needed, and you dinna ken that.

JOCK: I ken that when the revolution comes you'll be fillin' your belly some place.

BOB: When the revolution comes, sir, I'll be in the thick o' the dictatorship o' the . . .

JOCK: Oh! shut it!

(JEAN *enters carrying a basin containing potatoes which she puts on the table and begins to pare*)

JEAN: Is it no' time you were awa' to the soup kitchen, Bob?

BOB: I'm waiting on the thick stuff the day.

JEAN: Ay, and you'll likely wait till it's finished.

JOCK: I've just been tellin' him that, but you may as weel speak to the Bass Rock noo as speak to him.

BOB: I dinna ken what you're a' worryin' yoursel's aboot. If I dinna get ony soup it'll be me that'll be hungry, no' you.

JOCK: I dinna want ony backchat, see!

BOB: (*rising*) If there's nae soup left for me there'll be a revolution doon there.

JOCK: Revolution! and if onybody was burstin' a paper bag at your back you'd dee wi' the fricht.

BOB: Oh, you're just a reactionary, when the revolution comes you'll be usin' propaganda for the bourgeois. (*Going out door*) Three cheers for the dictatorship o' the . . .

(JOCK *rises in a hurry, and* BOB *scoots*)

JOCK: They damned Bolshies' are settin' the young yins off their heids.

JEAN: He's only a laddie, man. You're worse than him that pays ony attention.

JOCK: Dictatorship o' the proletariat! and, if you asked him what it meant, he couldna tell ye.

JEAN: Do you ken what it means?

JOCK: Ay.

JEAN: What?

JOCK: It means . . . it means . . . weel, it means if . . . it means a revolution that's what it means.

JEAN: Ay, you ha'e a lot tae learn yet tae, I doot . . . Hoo d'ye think Tam Anderson'll get on the day?

JOCK: Six months!

JEAN: Six months! He'll no get off as easy as that.

JOCK: Then, if you ken, what are you askin' for?

JEAN: Just for fun. They're sayin' doon the street that they'll no' be ower hard on him seein' that the strike's aboot finished. But there's no' much sympathy wi' lawyers and judges, it's hard facts wi' them a' the time, hard, cauld facts; staring you through and through wi' their cauld, grey e'en seein' a' the bad points, but very few o' the guid yins.

JOCK: It's true Jean. Mebbe eichteen months for him, and the strike likely to be finished the day; it's hard lines . . . Ay, it's bad when you think aboot it, oot for seven lang months, hungered and starved just aboot off the face o' the earth, and to go back defeated.

JEAN: Ach! you men dinna ken hoo to strike onywey; you throw doon your tools, come oot the pit, and stand at the street corner till you starve yoursel's back to the pit again. And, when you DAE go back, instead o' strikin' oot for mair on your rate, you fill mair hutches, and would cut each ither's throat to get them.

JOCK: I ken there's a good wheen o' thae kind.

JEAN: You're yin o' thae kind yoursel'. And you're grousin' aboot the langer 'oors you'll need to work, but you'll be awa' to the pit an 'oor before the time, and be an 'oor later in comin' hame frae it. Ach! you dinna ken the first thing aboot strikin', for as often as you've been on strike.

JOCK: D'ye want us to blaw the pits in the air, or what?

JEAN: If you'd slip oot the road and play cricket, and leave it to the women you'd dae mair guid.

JOCK: You ha'e plenty o' gab, if that would win a strike. I was at yin women's meetin', and I couldna hear a word for a week efter it, gab-gab-gab!

JEAN: We ha'e mair than gab, we ha'e courage, and that's what you men dinna ha'e.

JOCK: I'll bet you the next strike'll no' be sae quiet.

JEAN: (*sarcastically*) The next strike! and you'll be breakin' your neck rinnin' up to the pit to get your jobs before the strike's finished.

JOCK: What else can we dae?

JEAN: Huh! I tellt ye. Some men to win a strike.

JOCK: The men were richt enough, it was the leaders that let us doon.

JEAN: And wha put the leaders there? Hoo often dae ye attend the Union meetin's? You tak' nae interest in yer affairs till there's a strike on, then you find oot that you want new leaders. You just get the leaders you deserve.

JOCK: There's a lot no' interested, richt enough: of coorse it's a' for the want o' sense.

JEAN: It's the want o' sense that makes a man buy that paper you're readin', tae, after a' it has said aboot ye since the strike started.

JOCK: Eh!

JEAN: That's a coalmaisters' paper you're readin'.

JOCK: I ken that fine, you dinna need to tell me that.

JEAN: Then what dae you buy it for?

JOCK: Oh, just for the sake o' the pictures.

JEAN: You'd be as weel to stop it, then, and buy 'Comic Cuts'.[10]

JOCK: Where's Jenny?

JEAN: She's doon at the soup kitchen, gi'en them a hand.

JOCK: They tell me they're on their last bag o' tatties.

JEAN: Ay, and as mony tattie pits aboot the place. It doesna say much for you men.

JOCK: I think you want to see us in the jile.

JEAN: The jile! You'd rather lie doon on a tattie pit and dee wi' an empty belly than risk the jile. I canna understand you men.

JOCK: Where did you get THAE tatties?

JEAN: When you were studyin' the form o' the horses.

JOCK: Wull Baxter was doon the street yesterday, I hear.

JEAN: Ay, he was in the toon, at the shippin' office.

JOCK: Gaun off to Canada likely?

JEAN: Ay.

JOCK: Does Jenny ken?

JEAN: He sent a letter to her yesterday.

JOCK: Oh? did he! And what was in it?

JEAN: Wantin' her to go to Canada wi' him.

JOCK: Well, I'll be damned! Did you ever hear sic' neck? What did he say?

JEAN: He's vexed for everything that's happened. Says it was for

Jenny's sake he blacklegged — wanted to get as much as take them awa' frae here.

JOCK: If you dinna watch her she'll slip off wi' him, that's what you'll see.

JEAN: I'm kind o' vexed for him tae, Jock.

JOCK: I tell't ye. See here, Jean, there's to be nae damned nonsense aboot this. Wull Baxter's gaun to Cananda HIMSEL'! What would the neebours say aboot a thing like this?

JEAN: To hell wi' the neebours! they dinna concern me, Jock.

JOCK: It's no' happenin', see!

JEAN: Wha said it was happenin'? I just said I was vexed for him.

JOCK: Ay, but you're fishin' to get roon' the saft side o' me. I see the game a' richt.

JEAN: You'd think you were boss in here the wey you're talkin'. The saft side o' YOU. You havena had ony drink this mornin', ha'e ye?

JOCK: There's something in the wind when you're beginnin' to pity him noo. Vexed for him! and Tam Anderson likely to get the jile ower the heid o' him.

JEAN: He made a mistake, that was a'. And that tinker o' a mither o' his made him go.

JOCK: Where's his letter?

JEAN: She says she burnt it.

JOCK: Then she has mair sense than you.

JEAN: Ay, she tak's it off her faither.

(JENNY *enters, almost in tears*)

JENNY: Ha'e you heard aboot Tam Anderson?

JOCK: No, hoo did he get on?

JENNY: Oh, faither, he's got three years.

JOCK: Three years!

JEAN: Three years! That canna be true, Jenny.

JENNY: Ay, it's true, mither, he's awa' to the jile for three years.

JOCK: Good God! That's cruel. Three years! as quiet a laddie as ever stepped in twa shoon.

JEAN: This'll send Kate mad. Puir sowl, she's hain' her fill o' sorrow the noo. Does she ken, Jenny?

JENNY: No. Will you go doon and tell her, faither?

JOCK: Will I go doon, Jean?

JEAN: (*at window*) Here she's comin'. You'd better go to the room, Jenny.

(JENNY *goes to room*)

JOCK: This is a bad job, Jean.

JEAN: Oh, this strike's gaun to break a' oor he'rts before it's finished.

(KATE *enters. She is very pale and worn-looking*)

KATE: (*holding out her hand*) Here, Jean.

JEAN: What is it, Kate?

KATE: Some money.

JEAN: What is that for?

KATE: Just a wee bit help, Jean.

JEAN: I dinna want it, Kate, you ha'e mair need o' it than me.

KATE: I got the insurance money the day, Jean. Tak' it, noo, or I'll be angry.

JEAN: I'll tak' it, Kate, but I'll pay it back when the strike's finished.

(*She takes the money*)

KATE: Ha'e you seen my faither this mornin', Jock?

JOCK: No, me, Kate.

KATE: He went oot after breakfast time, and he's no' hame yet. He cam' hame gey fu' yesterday.

JOCK: So I suppose.

KATE: D'ye ken, Jean, I'm weary.

JEAN: I'm sorry for you, Kate, but you'll no need to lose he'rt.

KATE: Hoo d'ye think Tam'll get on the day, Jock?

JOCK: I dinna ken, Kate, I don't think they'll be too hard on him.

KATE: Will he get off, d'ye think?

JOCK: I doot he'll no' get off, Kate.

(*He looks at* JEAN, KATE *sees him*)

KATE: Is the word in?

JOCK: I dinna ken, Kate, I havena heard onything.

(*He hangs his head*)

KATE: You HA'E got word. Tell me, Jock. Tell me, Jean. Oh! for God's sake tell me!

JOCK: (*putting his hand on her shoulder*) Kate . . . I ha'ena very guid news for ye . . . you'll need to bear up. They ha'e him awa' for . . . three years.

KATE: (*in whisper*) Three years! . . . three years! . . . Oh! Jock.

(*She buries her head on his shoulder*)

JEAN: (*going to her*) Kate, dearie.

(KATE *cries bitterly*)

JEAN: Puir lass, I'm sorry for ye.

KATE: Three years! Oh, Jean . . . Jean!

JEAN: Come awa' doon wi' me, Kate. Puir Tam!

(*They go out, and* JENNY *enters*)

JOCK: Three years, and we live in a civilised country. If this is

civilisation put me in among the savages. You better go doon
and keep her company a wee while, Jenny.

JENNY: *(in a hysterical kind of way)* Three years? and the miners
are feart for revolution. Ha! ha! ha!

> *(She goes out.* JOCK *takes his pipe from his pocket, it is emp-
> ty. He looks towards door, then hurries to the tea caddie on
> mantleshelf. He fills pipe with tea, and is seated, puffing merrily
> when* JEAN *enters)*

JEAN: Puir lass, she's in an awfu' state.

JOCK: *(puffing)* She's gettin' HER share o' the strike, Jean.

JEAN: God kens she is. And that faither o' her's awa' boozin',
I suppose. You'll need to ha'e a word wi' him; that kind o'
conduct'll no' dae at a time like this; he'll break that lass's he'rt.

JOCK: He has aye been the same, a washoot: the least excuse
and off on the beer. He had the best wife in the country, tae,
but dinna seem to ken it.

JEAN: He'll ken noo, when she's awa'.

JOCK: I'll ha'e a talk wi' him and see if I canna put some sense
into his fat heid. *(Puffs)* What ha'e you for the dinner the day?

JEAN: Tatties and onions.

JOCK: Stovies?

JEAN: Ay *(Coughs)* What kind o' baccy is that you're smokin'?

JOCK: Eh! It's . . . it's some fag ends I got frae Bob.

JEAN: It's surely that, that's an awfu' smell.

> (BOB *enters carryin' his bowl, which he puts on table)*

JEAN: Hullo! did you no' get your soup?

BOB: I was ower late.

JOCK: I tell't ye, didn't I?

BOB: *(to* JEAN) Ha'e you ony dinner, mither?

JEAN: Stovies and onions.

BOB: Some feed!

JEAN: It's better than nane.

BOB: No' much . . . Is it true that the strike's aboot finished?

JEAN: Ay, ham and eggs every Sunday mornin' noo.

BOB: If we had eggs, we could ha'e ham and eggs the noo, if
we had ham.

JOCK: Eh?

BOB: I'm sayin', if we had eggs, we could ha'e ham and eggs.

JOCK: What the flames are you talkin' aboot?

BOB: *(snuffling)* What kind o' baccy is that you're smokin'?

JOCK: What was wrang, there was nae soup?

BOB: Nae money left in the funds.

JEAN: Did you hear aboot Tam Anderson, Bob?

BOB: No, hoo did he get on?

JEAN: Three years.

BOB: Three years! I ken what's needed, it's a revolution that's needed.

JOCK: Oh, for God's sake gi'e that revolution a rest.

BOB: What kind o' baccy is that you're smokin'?

JEAN: (*coughing*) It's fag ends.

BOB: (*jumping*) Where did you get them?

JOCK: Never you mind.

BOB: I havena had a smoke the day. By Gee! When the strike's finished I'll smoke till I'm sick.

JEAN: (*putting on shawl*) I'm gaun doon for something to eat. (*Lifting basket*) Lift off that pot, Jock, you're bound to be tired o' stovies. We'll ha'e ham and eggs the day, supposin' we should never ha'e them again.

    (*She goes out*)

BOB: (*shouting after her*) Bring me a packet o' Woodbines, mither. Ay, if we had eggs, we would ha'e ham and eggs the noo . . .

JOCK: (*interrupting*) Oh! shut up.

BOB: Where did you get the fag ends?

JOCK: I forgot to tell your mither I was needin' baccy.

BOB: She'll mebbe forget the ham and eggs, but she'll no forget your baccy.

JOCK: You better rin efter her and tell her.

BOB: She'll mind richt enough.

JOCK: It's high time the wheels WERE gaun roond; wheen o' ye'll soon no' be able to walk wi' laziness.

BOB: I'm tired.

JOCK: What dain'?

BOB: Rinnin' back and forrit to that soup kitchen on an empty belly. (*Suddenly*) I wonder if she'll mind my Woodbines? (*He jumps and rushes off. JOCK watches him go, and shakes his head. He sits repeating*: If we had eggs, we could ha'e ham and eggs the noo, if we had ham, *in a baffled way. He gives up. Then he lifts pot from fire and takes it to room. LIZZIE enters from school. She takes off her schoolbag, then looks into the cupboard of dresser. JOCK enters*)

JOCK: What are you lookin' in there for?

    (LIZZIE *is startled*)

LIZZIE: I want a piece, daddy.

JOCK: You'll need to wait till your mither comes hame.

LIZZIE: Where is she?

JOCK: Awa' for ham and eggs.

LIZZIE: Ham and eggs!

JOCK: Ay, if we had eggs we could ha'e ham and eggs the noo . . . no, I'm damned if I can get that.

LIZZIE: Eh?

JOCK: Naething.

LIZZIE: I couldna tak' my dinner at the schule the day, daddy.

JOCK: What was wrang wi' ye?

LIZZIE: I got the strap frae the maister, and I was sick.

JOCK: What did you get the strap for?

LIZZIE: Because I dinna ha'e my hame sums richt . . . See, daddy.

(*She holds out her little hand*)

JOCK: Puir wee sowl, you had mair need o' a guid diet the day than the strap. Ower fu' fed, and get their money ower easy, that's what's wrang wi' them. But I'll see him the morn, Lizzie, and he can tak' what he gets frae me, the dirty swine.

LIZZIE: I ken what's needed, daddy, it's a revolution that's needed.

(BOB *enters*)

JOCK: Did you tell her aboot my tobacco?

BOB: No me, she kens to get your baccy richt enough.

JOCK: No, but you would tell her aboot your Woodbines?

BOB: That's what I ran efter her for. That's a fine state o' affairs doon there noo!

JOCK: What's wrang?

BOB: Oh, they're flockin' up to the pit in their hunners to get their jobs back.

JOCK: What are they dain' that for?

BOB: There's a notice up at the pit that every man has to be before the manager before he gets his job back.

JOCK: What's the big idea?

BOB: Every man has to promise to chuck up the Union.

JOCK: Oh! and if we DINNA promise?

BOB: Well, you'll no' get your job back.

JOCK: So that's the wey o' it, they've got their foot on oor necks, and they're gaun to put on the screw. Chuck up the Union! The men'll never agree to that.

BOB: What else can they dae?

JOCK: They can go on the 'dole'. We micht be better on the 'dole' onyway.

BOB: By gee! that's a good idea, I never thoucht o' that. Dinna go near the pit, faither, we ha'e nae buits or claes to start oor work wi' onyway. (*At mirror*) My face is no' half broon, faither.

JOCK: They'll soon take the broon off your face: they'll soon make a mushroom o' ye. It's a hell o' a job, hunger and rags,

water and bad air, and up at fower o' clock on the cauld, snawy
mornin's, and under the heel o' a set o' tyrants for starvation
wages. And what can we dae, just suffer it oot and say naething.

BOB: I ken what's needed . . .

LIZZIE: It's a revolution that's needed, Bob.

JOCK: (*to* BOB) Did you see any signs o' Tam Pettigrew when
you were doon the street?

BOB: Ay, he was comin' oot the pub. As drunk as a sodger.

JOCK: I'm gaun to gi'e that yin a thick ear, that's what's gaun
to happen.

BOB: (*at window*) Here he's comin', faither. He's comin' here.
Will I lock the door?

JOCK: No, let him come in, I'll mebbe sober him up a bit.

BOB: That booze is just a curse, the pubs should be a' shut.

(TAM PETTIGREW *passes the window singing*)

TAM: (*off*) Are ye in!

JOCK: Come in!

(TAM *enters, and stands at door*)

TAM: I'm up to gi'e ye a dram, Jock. I'm Tam Pettigrew, I gi'e a
dram to wha I like and I take a dram . . . when I like . . . that's
me!

JOCK: Are you no' ashamed o' yoursel', Tam?

TAM: Ashamed o' mysel'! What the hell ha'e I to be ashamed
o'? I take a dram when I like . . . and gi'e a dram to wha I
like . . . that's me . . . and always has been me . . . see!

(JOCK *goes to help him to chair.* TAM *pushes him from him*)

TAM: You surely think I'm drunk. I can manage to the chair
myself. (*Walks unsteadily to chair*) I'm Tam Pettigrew . . . I take
a dram when I like . . . and gi'e a dram to wha I like . . . that's
me!

(*He sits down*)

TAM: Gimme a glass, Jock, and I'll gi'e ye a dram.

JOCK: (*to* BOB) Rin doon and tell Kate he's here, she'll likely
be anxious aboot him.

TAM: What's that? anxious aboot me? I know what I'm dain',
there's naebody need to be . . . anxious aboot me . . . Bob!
here's something for fags.

BOB: (*at door*) You shairly think I'd take money frae you. If I
was Kate . . .

JOCK: Rin awa' doon.

(BOB *goes out,* LIZZIE *following, looking at* TAM, *half afraid*)

TAM: Anxious aboot me! aboot ME! Here, Jock, are you tryin'
to be funny? . . . if you are, it's no' gaun to work, see? I'm Tam
Pettigrew, and there's nae man tryin' to tak' his nap aff me, see!

JOCK: D'ye think you're playin' the game, Tam?

TAM: D'ye want a dram, or dae ye no'?

    (JOCK *loses his temper and snatches the bottle from* TAM's *hand*)

TAM: (*rising*) Here! . . . What's the game?

    (JOCK *forces him to his seat*)

JOCK: Sit doon, see? I ha'e something to say to you.

    (TAM *struggles, and* JOCK *has to raise the bottle to strike him*)

JOCK: SIT DOON!

    (TAM *sits, afraid, and much sobered*)

JOCK: A fine sicht you to cheer the he'rts o' your bairns, a lot o' he'rtnin' a drunk faither'll gi'e them. See here, Tam, this conduct'll no' dae: you've got to pull yoursel' thigither; be a man, it's only cowards that droon their sorrows in the pub. Ha'e some respect for the wife you laid to rest.

    (*There is a pause*)

TAM: Jock, my he'rt's broken.

    (*He buries his head in his hands*)

JOCK: Yours is no' the only he'rt that's broken, there's a hoosefu' doon by. And Kate's needin' a' the help you can gi'e her, or there's gaun to be anither death in the hoose.

TAM: I'll never get the better o' this Jock . . . Died o' starvation . . . Them and their strike . . . they've killed her.

JOCK: Noo, noo, Tam, it'll no' dae to lose he'rt that way, it canna be helped noo, and you'll need to put a stout he'rt to a stey brae.

TAM: It COULD ha'e been helped! Them and their bloody strike! The best woman that ever lived. Hoo can I get ower it?

JOCK: You'll never get ower it if you're gaun to boose. You ha'e you're bairns to care for noo. YOU'VE got to take the mither's place, and you'll need to get ower it for their sakes. D'ye think the wife would rest in her grave if she kent o' this cairry on the day?

TAM: Them and their strike . . . Oh! Jock . . .

    (*Enter* KATE, *followed by* JENNY *and* BOB)

KATE: Come awa' doon, faither.

TAM: (*after a pause*) Are you angry wi' me, Kate?

KATE: No me. Come awa' doon and we'll ha'e a cup o' tea.

TAM: Kate, lass, I'm no' playin' the game. Tell me you're no' angry wi' me.

KATE: No, I'm no' angry wi' ye. Come awa doon, the weans are wearyin' on ye.

TAM: Kate, I'm no' playin' the game.

    (JOCK *helps* KATE *to get* TAM *on his feet*)

TAM: Jock, she likes her mither.

JOCK: Ay, ay, Tam. Awa' doon wi' her and get a cup o' tea and you'll sune be as richt as the mail.

TAM: YOU'RE no' angry wi' me, Jock?

JOCK: No' me, Tam.

TAM: (*going out with* KATE) Them and their strike . . . them and their bloody strike! . . .

   (JENNY *follows*)

JOCK: God guide ye, Kate, for you ha'e a big battle in front o' ye.

BOB: The boose is just a flamin' curse.

JOCK: It's a pity for him tae, Bob.

BOB: It's NAE pity for him, he's a washoot. May I choke mysel' stane deid the first time I put that stuff in my mooth.

JOCK: It's easy speakin', but we're no' a' made o' steel. You're young yet, Bob and you ha'e a lot to come through before you can say what you can dae.

   (JOCK *sits at fire*)

BOB: Kate's far too saft wi' him, it's a slap on the kisser he needs.

JOCK: Awa' and meet your mither, she'll be on her road hame noo.

BOB: I ken whit should be done wi' it a'.

   (*He lifts bottle from table, and, unseen by* JOCK, *goes out and smashes it against wall.* JOCK *jumps on hearing the crash.* BOB *enters, rather proud*)

JOCK: What the flames was that?

BOB: That's the stuff to gi'e them, poor it doon the street.

JOCK: (*looking at table*) Here! is that you broken that bottle o' whisky?

BOB: Too true, it's a pity there's only yin.

JOCK: Well, I'll be damned. (*Loudly*) Are you aware a bottle o' whisky costs thirteen shillin's, and here you've sent it sailin' doon the street. Ye flamin' imp!

BOB: (*retreating*) But I thoucht you said.

JOCK: What did I say! WHAT DID I SAY! Thirteen shillin's worth rinnin' doon the street.

BOB: Was you wantin' to pour it doon your ain neck?

JOCK: Shut up, ye flamin' agitator, before I lose my temper wi' ye. Thirteen white shillin's worth runnin'. Oot o' my sicht, see! before I mulligrize ye!

BOB: By gee! it's great, richt enough: tellin' a man aff because he was drunk, and shootin' oot your neck noo because you canna get the same chance.

(JOCK *makes a mad rush after* BOB, *who scoots*)

JOCK: Never heard tell o' such a dirty trick a' my flamin' days. Thirteen white shillin's worth . . . ach! it's enough to break a body's he'rt.

(JENNY *enters*)

JENNY: Faither, you'll need to go doon beside that man, he's still ravin' aboot the strike.

JOCK: (*putting on coat*) A damned guid thumpin' is what HE'S needin' (*Going out*) Thirteen white shillin's worth rinnin' doon the street.

(JENNY *sits at fire side, and, after looking into the fire for a while, takes a letter from her bosom. The canary sings merrily in the quietness.* LIZZIE *enters and* JENNY *hides the letter again in her bosom*)

LIZZIE: Jenny, Wull Baxter wants to see ye.

JENNY: Where is he?

LIZZIE: He's standin' roon' the corner o' the hoose.

JENNY: Tell him to come in.

(LIZZIE *goes out.* JENNY *walks nervously round room. She is facing the fire when* WULL *enters. He halts at door*)

WULL: (*softly*) Jenny.

(JENNY *turns and straightens herself*)

JENNY: What d'ye want here, Wull?

WULL: I'm gaun awa' the morn, Jenny.

JENNY: Weel!

WULL: I canna go withoot sayin' Guid-bye!

JENNY: There was nae need, Wull.

WULL: You're gey hard, Jenny.

JENNY: No, Wull, I'm no' hard, you played a gey hard game wi' ME.

WULL: I thocht I was daein' richt, Jenny. I thocht the men would make a start if somebody took the lead.

JENNY: And you stabbed them in the back; the neebours you ha'e lived wi' a' your days, the men you ha'e kept company wi', the men you ha'e sported wi' . . . ye traitor!

(WULL *is stung by the thrust, and* JENNY *relents*)

JENNY: Oh, Wull, what made you dae it? We were happy . . . ower happy . . . and noo . . .

WULL: We can be happy yet, Jenny. Let us gang awa' thigither . . . awa' frae here . . . awa' where nobody kens me . . . where we'll get peace.

JENNY: It's ower late, Wull, I canna forgi'e ye.

WULL: It was to let us get to Canada, Jenny. It was for your sake.

(JENNY *looks into the fire, but makes no answer*)

WULL: I made a mistake, Jenny, I see that noo, but it's no' ower late to forgi'e me, and let us start a new life . . . The auld days were happy days, Jenny. I could go about wi' my heid in the air, and everybody had a smile for me. But noo . . . everybody has a scowl and a curse . . . God, but I ha'e come through hell.

(*There is a pause*)

WULL: It was the strike to blame, Jenny.

JENNY: (*still looking into fire*) Ay, the strike . . . the strike . . . shattered hopes and broken he'rts.

WULL: We can be happy yet, Jenny.

JENNY: It's ower late, Wull.

WULL: The strike'll soon be forgotten.

JENNY: Ay, but you failed me, failed us a', THAT can never be forgotten.

WULL: If I was to send for you after a while, Jenny . . .

JENNY: It's ower late, Wull . . . (*Holding out her hand*) Guid bye!

WULL: Think it ower for a while . . .

JENNY: Guid bye!

(*He shakes hands with her, and then goes slowly away. JENNY looks into fire. WULL halts at door, watches her for a second or two, then goes out. The bird sings blythly. After a pause, BOB enters*)

BOB: Here! was that Wull Baxter in here?

(JENNY *makes no answer*)

BOB: What was he dain' in here, I'm askin'?

(*Then he sees that she is upset*)

BOB: What's wrang wi' ye, Jenny? Are ye vexed because he's gaun awa'? I wouldna be vexed; he's just a dirty, rotten blackleg.

JENNY: For God's sake, Bob . . .

BOB: I wouldna vex mysel' like that.

JENNY: Ay, you would vex yoursel' tae, Bob; hunger and rags we can get ower but no' the likes o' this . . . Every dream and every hope shattered into a thousand bits. Oh! is there to be nae peace . . . ha'e we ay to be crushed, and crushed, and never get a chance to live! Ha'e we ay to be gropin' in the darkness? nae sunshine ava! Oh, God, dae something to tak' the load off oor shouthers or we'll gang mad!

(*She goes to room. BOB watches her go in wonderment. Then JEAN and JOCK and LIZZIE enter, JEAN carrying a laden basket*)

JEAN: If we had eggs, we could ha'e ham and eggs the noo, if we had ham, eh, Bob?

BOB: Did you mind my Woodbines?

   (JOCK *cuffs his ear off easy chair.* JEAN *hands* BOB *his Woodbines*)

LIZZIE: Is the strike finished, Daddy?

JOCK: (*taking her on his knee*) Finished, dearies, and we ha'e got knocked oot again.

JEAN: (*putting groceries out on table*) Ay, but we're no' gaun to lose he'rt, Jock; we'll live to fight anither day; there's life in the auld dog yet.

   (*Then the sound of voices can be heard singing in the distance, the tune is 'The Red Flag'. A look of pride comes into* JEAN's *eyes, and she listens. Then she speaks, as if inspired by some great hope*)

JEAN: That's the spirit, my he'rties! sing! sing! tho' they ha'e ye chained to the wheels and the darkness. Sing! tho' they ha'e ye crushed in the mine. Keep up your he'rts, my laddies, you'll win through yet, for there's nae power on earth can crush the men that can sing on a day like this.

Notes

1. The General Strike of 1926 was the culmination of a period of intense industrial conflict in Britain following the failure of the first Labour government, headed by Ramsay MacDonald, in 1924. Britain's economic position has been seriously affected by the aftermath of the First World War, and a series of strikes by miners against efforts by owners of the mines to lower their wages had left them worse off than they had been in 1914. When the miners struck for better wages in 1926, the Trades Union Congress called a 'sympathetic' or General Strike of workers in the major unions to support them. After nine days the General Strike collapsed. The miners struggled on alone for several months but in the end were defeated. The Government made 'general' strikes illegal and no left-wing party would hold office in Britain again until 1945.

2. *blackleg*, a strike breaker.

3. *strap*, leather belt or tawse used by teachers on the hands of children, often for academic failure as well as disciplinary reasons.

4. *Pairish*, the Parish Council provided poor relief.

5. *double*, an accumulating bet on the outcome of two horse-races.

6. The Bolshevik Revolution of October 1917 had established a Union of Soviet Socialist Republics in Russia and its former imperial territories. Fear of Russian influence in Britain had been inflamed by the 'Zinoviev letter', which, it was claimed, showed that the Labour Party was acting in the interests of International Socialism. This played a significant part in the failure of the Labour Party to be re-elected after its first term as a minority government in 1924.

7. *Bolshie*, from Bolshevik, the Russian Revolutionaries.

8. *The Red Flag*, anthem of the international socialist movement; sung at Labour Party conferences until the 1990s.

9. *Carnegie*, Andrew Carnegie, Scots multi-millionaire owner of steel factories in the USA.

10. *Comic Cuts*, magazine of comic strips.

Robert McLellan

Jamie the Saxt
A Historical Comedy in Four Acts

(1937)

CHARACTERS

Rab, *apprentice to Nicoll Edward.*
Mistress Edward
Bailie Morison, *an Edinburgh shipping merchant.*
Her Grace Queen Anne of Scotland, *formerly Princess Anne of Denmark.*
Margaret Vinstar, *a lady-in waiting.*
The Laird Logie, *a gentleman of the King's chamber.*
The Lord Atholl
The Lady Atholl
His Grace King James *the Sixth of Scotland.*
Bailie Nicoll Edward, *an Edinburgh cloth merchant.*
The Lord Spynie, *a gentleman of the King's chamber.*
John Maitland *of Thirlstane, the Lord Chancellor.*
The Lord Ochiltree
Lodovick Stewart, *Duke of Lennox.*
Sir Robert Bowes, *resident ambassador from her Majesty Queen Elizabeth of England.*
Sir James Melville
Francis Stewart, *Earl of Bothwell.*
John Colville, *an accomplice of Bothwell's.*
Robert Bruce, *a preacher.*
The Earl of Morton
The Earl of Morton's fair daughter.
Sir Robert Bowes' English servant.

Introduction

Robert McLellan (1907–85) was born in Lanarkshire and spent his childhood on a farm on the Clyde valley. His writing was to be marked by the strong sense of dialect speech that he acquired there. He refused, however, to follow the 'synthetic Scots', i.e. a Scots from any dialect and any historical period, largely derived from dicitionaries, that had been the basis of Hugh MacDiarmid's poetic experiments during the Scottish Renaissance of the 1920s. McLellan's Scots is grounded in a living vernacular, though it was often at its most effective, as in *Jamie the Saxt*, when it was transposed to a historical period where Scots would have been the natural speech of the whole community.

Jamie the Saxt was first produced in 1937 by the Curtain Theatre, an amateur drawing-room theatre established by Grace Ballantyne in Glasgow. Duncan Macrae, then a school-teacher but about to become one of the outstanding actors of the twentieth century, played Jamie, a role which he was to make his own in successive productions.

The play takes place in the period between 1591 and 1593 when the young James VI of Scotland (1566–1625, and later to become James I of England, after the death of Elizabeth I in 1603) was struggling to establish himself against the power of the competing factions and religious groups which had caused much turmoil in Scotland since the Reformation of 1560, and had sought control in Scotland during the period, up to 1585, when James, who was crowned when only one year old, was a minor. McLellan follows closely the accounts of David Moysie's *Memoirs of the Affairs of Scotland* (quotations from which provide the scene locations in each Act) and P. F. Tytler's *History of Scotland* (1882).

Michael Lynch, in *Scotland: A New History* (1992) describes the events surrounding the play's action as follows:

The first crisis of the personal reign came only in 1592, after seven years of almost universal harmony between King, nobles and ministers. It took the form of the celebrated murder in February 1592 of the 'bonnie Earl of Moray'. The only relationship which the well-known ballad bears to reality is that the Earl was indeed bonnie. The feud between him and the

Earl of Huntly was, like most feuds, largely a matter of local
dispute which had been allowed to get seriously out of hand.
When Moray's kinsman, the quixotic figure of Francis Stewart,
5th Earl of Bothwell, became involved the feud spilled over
into court politics. Bothwell's sensational arrest on a charge
of witchcraft along with a coven of North Berwick 'witches'
gives the affair an air of supernatural intrigue which it hardly
deserves; his escape, the repeated failures of James's government to catch him and his increasingly ostentatious raids on
royal palaces, including one on the Palace of Holyroodhouse in
July 1593 when the King was trapped in . . . the privy of his own
presence chamber, lend it a strong whiff of farce. The persistent
demands of Moray's mother for justice, she commissioned a
portrait of the corpse, which lay unburied for six years, add an
element of the macabre.

Despite its eccentricities, this was a prolonged and major
crisis for James's authority, for the Kirk by 1592 had sprung
to the defence of the unlikely figures of both Moray and
Bothwell, victims, as they saw it, of a papist conspiracy. The
fragile understanding between James and the Kirk had broken
down . . . The affair was resolved only through the stupidity of
Huntly and Bothwell, who had decided, ironically, to join forces
in 1594. A major feud which had threatened to pull apart the
carefully constructed coalition of loyalties painstakingly erected
by Maitland [James's chancellor] since 1585 became a rebellion,
which was (as always) much easier for the crown to deal with.
By early 1595 a chastened Huntly was contained and Bothwell
was exiled, never to return. It was the last concerted protest by
magnates in James's reign.

McLellan said that he he was more interested in character
than in theme and *Jamie the Saxt* derives its power from its
presentation of James, once described as 'the wisest fool in
Christendom'.

ACT ONE

*'The Kingis ludging in Nicoll Eduardis hous in Nithreis Wynd',
Edinburgh, VII February, 1591. Evening.*

A room in the house of BAILIE NICOLL EDWARD. In the middle
of the left wall a huge open fire-place. In the middle of the back
wall a door leading to the dining-room and kitchen apartments.
In the back right-hand corner a door leading in from a turnpike
staircase. In the middle of the right wall a window.

Armchairs beside the fire. Against the back wall, to the left
of the middle door, an awmrie, and to the right of the door a
compter. By the window a low bench. In the centre of the floor
a table with paper, pens, ink and candlesticks. A chair behind
the table.

It is late afternoon, and the room derives most of its light from
the fire. The lower half of the window is shuttered, but in the
shutters is a large hole which enables people in the room to put
their heads out and view the wynd below.

MISTRESS EDWARD enters from the dining-room. She carries
a lit candle which she places on the table. She sorts the fire then
moves to the window and looks out through the shutter-hole.
She moves to the table and starts to peer furtively at the papers
on it.

RAB, apprentice to NICOLL EDWARD, comes up the turnpike
stair from the booth below. MISTRESS EDWARD retreats hastily
from the table.

RAB: (*outside*) Mistress Edward!

MRS E: What is't?

RAB: (*entering*) Bailie Morison's doun in the booth. He wants
to ken if the King's back frae the hunt.

MRS E: And did ye tell him no?

RAB: Ay, but he hasna gaen awa. I think he ettles to be askit up.

MRS E: Nae dout. He canna bide awa frae the door whan we
hae the King here. He hates to see his Grace in ony hoose bune
his ain. What is he wantin? His supper, nae dout, and a nicht's
drinking wi royalty.

RAB: Wheesht! He's comin up!

MRS E: Mercy me! Doun wi ye, then.
(RAB *leaves*).

BAILIE M: (*outside*) Mistress Edward!

MRS E: Ay, Bailie, come in. (*He does so*) Dae ye want to see
Nicoll? He's oot wi the King.

BAILIE M: I ken. I want ye to let me bide here till they come
hame. There's a ploy afute i' the Toun. The King maun hear
aboot it.

MRS E: Can ye no ride oot to meet him?

BAILIE M: I maun dae naething to cause suspeecion. Gin I were
seen gaun through the ports it micht haste maitters on.

MRS E: Is it something bye the ordinar?

BAILIE M: Weill Mistress Edward, ye'll ken fine, yer guid man
bein a Bailie himsell, that I maun gaird aye my tongue weill in
maitters that affect the Toun.

MRS E: Oh, is it some Toun maitter. I warn ye Bailie, that the
King daesna like to be deived wi the clash o the Toun whan he
comes in hungert frae the hunt. Can ye no gang to the Toun
Gaird? Hae ye seen the Provost?

BAILIE M: The Provost's at Leith for the horse-racin, and it's
a maitter that the Toun Gaird couldna settle. It micht, I may
tell ye, mean a cry at the Cross for the haill Toun to rise.

MRS E: Bailie! Dinna tell me it's anither o Bothwell's ploys! He
canna ettle to attack the King here?

BAILIE M: My guid wumman, ye need fear naething like that.
Bothwell's mebbe at haund, but he daurna come near the Toun.
It's ower well gairdit against him.

MRS E: And there's nae hairm ettled to the hoose here?

BAILIE M: It's naething like that.

MRS E: I'm gled to hear it. But the Toun micht hae to rise, ye
say?

BAILIE M: It micht, and again it micht no. It'll depend on the
King.

MRS E: Weill, it's a blessin he's a peacable man, and fonder
o his books nor o fechtin. Ye maun sit down, Bailie, and
I'll licht a wheen maur caunles, for the gloamin's weirin
on.

BAILIE M: (*sitting*) Thank ye.

MRS E: (*lighting the candles on the table*) We're leivin in steerin
times.

BAILIE M: Ay.

MRS E: I hardly sleep at nichts, wi the King here. It's a great
responsibeelity.

BAILIE M: Ay, it's aa that.

MRS E: Yon was an awfou nicht doun at the Palace. I hear ye
were in the thick o't.

BAILIE M: Ay, I was gey thrang for a while.

MRS E: Ye suld hae seen the marks on Nicoll's shouthers wi the
clowts he gat. And frae some o his ain toun's-folk, he said. It's

his opeenion that some wha sud hae been fechtin for the King were on the side o Bothwell.

BAILIE M: Weill, Mistress Edward, I wadna woner but he's richt.

MRS E: I'm shair he is. It gars ye woner what the country's comin to, that the like o Bothwell, that's been put to the horn for brekin oot o the Castle jeyl, can fin freinds in this Toun to help him herry the King in his ain Palace! Did ye see the wrack they made o't? I was doun wi the Queen and some of the leddies the ither day, to see hou faur they had gotten wi the sortin o't, and it fair gart my hairt stoun to see the bonnie wuid-wark sae sair hasht. It'll cost a hantle o guid siller afore it's aa as it was, and the King can ill afford it, puir laddie. I may tell ye, Bailie, in confidence, that it'll be a gey lang while afore Habbie Tamson the jeyner's peyed for the wark he's daein doun there the nou.

BAILIE M: Oh that's nae news to me, Mistress Edward. Habbit Tamson the jeyner isna the only man i' the Toun that has an accoont wi the King, though some o us are faur mair loyal nor mention the maitter.

MRS E: Ye're richt, Bailie, ye're richt. Mony a braw bale o fine claith his Grace has haen frae Nicoll that we dinna mention, and nae dout ye hae pairtit yersell wi mair nor ae bonnie nick-nack frae Flanders.

BAILIE M: Weill, mebbe, mebbe. But I'm sayin naething.

MRS E: I ken, I ken. And it daes ye credit. And efter aa what's a wheen bales o claith, or a bit fancy kist, atween loyal subjects and their Sovereign. It's mair shame on the corbies at Coort that rob him o ilka bawbee o the Croun rents. But shame on me, Bailie! Ye'll hae a dram?

BAILIE M: Sin ye speir, Mistress, I'll tak it gledly. The reik o that witch they were burnin at the Cross the day gat fair doun my thrapple.

MRS E: (*pouring a drink*) Ay, it was gey thick for a while, and it maks an unco stink. I woner ye canna gar them dae aa the burnin on the Castle Hill.

BAILIE M: For shame, Mistress Edward, and ye a Bailie's wife! Ye ken fine the folk maun be weill warnt no to meddle wi the Deil, and the burnins on the Castle Hill are ower faur oot o the wey to bring the warnin hame. There hae been ower mony o thae auld beldams at their dirty wark this year.

MRS E: Weill, Bailie, ye're mebbe richt. But drink that up.

BAILIE M: (*accepting drink*) Thank ye. Yer guid health.

MRS E: Aa the same, it isna the puir auld craiturs o witches I blame, sae muckle as the like o Bothwell that sets them on.

Gin ye had heard o aa the spells he's gart them wark against
the King, Bailie, ye'd be fair dumfounert.

BAILIE M: Mistress Edward, naething ye ken aboot their spells
wad dumfouner me. I was at their trials i' the Tolbooth.

MRS E: Ay, ay, Bailie, but there's a lot that didna come oot at
their trials. There's a lot cam oot whan they were brocht afore
the King himsell that maist folk dinna ken. The King can sort
them. He just speirs and speirs at them, and be they eir sae
thrawn, afore lang he has them roun his pinkie.

BAILIE M: Ye'll paurdon me, but he shairly hasna speirt at ony
o them here?

MRS E: Oh ye woner hou I ken. Dae ye see thae papers?

BAILIE M: Ay

MRS E: Dae ye see the writin?

BAILIE M: Ay.

MRS E: It's aa in the King's ain haund. And what dae ye think
it's aboot?

BAILIE M: What?

MRS E: Witches!

BAILIE M: Shairly no!

MRS E: I tell ye it's aboot witches. It's a book he's writin,[1] and
ilka ill notion he worms oot o them efter they're put to the torture, he writes doun there in ink. Bailie, there are queer things
in that book.

BAILIE M: I daursay. Hae ye read it?

MRS E: Me! Read! Na na, Bailie, ye ken fine I'm nae scholar.
But I ken what's in the book for aa that, for there's mony a nicht
efter supper whan we'll sit ben there and talk, and aye the talk's
aboot the book, and the next chapter, and what he's gauin to
write. And it's queer talk, some o it. The things thae beldams
dae, wi taids and cats and cauves' heids, to say naething o deid
men's innards, wad fair gar ye grue.

BAILIE M: It's a woner he isna feart to meeddle wi the craiturs.
Ye wad think he micht bring himsell to hairm.

MRS E: Na na, Bailie, that's whaur ye're wrang. He says they can
dae nae hairm to him wi their spells, because he's the Lord's
anointit. And it's a guid thing, or Bothwell wad hae haen him
lang eir this. (*There is a sound of chatter from the Wynd below*) But
what's that? I hear a steer. (*She has a look through the shutter-
hole*) It's the Queen's Grace hersell, and one o her leddies,
wi the Duke o Lennox and the young Laird Logie. My Lord
Lennox is takin his leave, it seems, and I'm no surprised. The
mair he bides awa frae the King the nou the better.

BAILIE M: Deed ay. It's a peety he canna bide awa frae the

Queen tae. He's aye at her tail. And she daesna seem to dis-
courage him ony. I sair dout, though I'm sweirt to think it, that
she's no aa she sould be.

MRS E: Hoots toots, Bailie, if my Lord Lennox is saft eneugh
to gang trailin ahint her aa day ye canna say it's her faut.

BAILIE M: I wadna gin it were the first affair. Hae ye forgotten
her ongauns wi the Earl o Moray?

MRS E: Ah weill nou, Bailie, there was mebbe something in that.
There's nane but has a saft side for the Bonnie Earl.

BAILIE M: I ken ane wha hasna.

MRS E: And wha's that?

BAILIE M: My Lord Huntly

MRS E: And wha cares for the like o him! But wheesht!
> (*Her Grace* QUEEN ANNE, LADY MARGARET VINSTAR
> *and the* LAIRD LOGIE *appear on the turnpike stair. The*
> QUEEN *stands within the doorway, with the others behind her.*
> MRS EDWARD *curtsies and the* BAILIE *bows low*)

THE QUEEN: (*speaking with a Danish accent*) Ah, Mistress
Edward, ye hae a veesitor! Guid ein, Bailie. Ye are weill, eh?

BAILIE M: Yer Grace, I canna grummle.

THE QUEEN: Grummle, eh?

BAILIE M: I'm haill and hairty.

THE QUEEN: (*doubtfully*) Ah, I see. That is guid. And Mistress
Morison? She is weill, eh?

BAILIE M: Ay, yer Grace, she's weill tae.

THE QUEEN: And the bairns?

BAILIE M: They're weill tae.

THE QUEEN: Ye are aa weill tae, eh?

BAILIE M: Ay, yer Grace, juist that.

THE QUEEN: See, the last time I see ye I couldna speak. I speak
nou. Logie he say I hae a guid Scots tongue in my heid afore
lang.

LOGIE: Yer Grace, ye talk like a native already.

THE QUEEN: Ah Logie, ye flaitter me. But Bailie. My Leddy
Vinstar. Ye haena met her. She is my friend frae Denmark.
Margaret, this is the Bailie Morison. He is a magistrate o the
Toun. He is gey, what ye say, kenspeckle. And he is gey weill-aff.
He has mony ships that sail to Flanders. Eh, Bailie?

BAILIE M: Weill, ane or twa.

THE QUEEN: Ane or twa. He disnae ken. But he kens fine. He
daesna like to, what ye say, blaw his ain horn, eh?

MRS E: He has fower, yer Grace.

THE QUEEN: He has fower. Ye see, he maun hae muckle
gowd. But Mistress Edward, we maun gang and mak ready

for supper. My Lord and Leddy Atholl. They come the nicht, eh?

MRS E: Ay, yer Grace, they suld be here ony meenit.

THE QUEEN: Ony meenit. Guid. And his Grace?

MRS E: He isna back frae the hunt yet, yer Grace.

THE QUEEN: Na. Weill, I gang. The Bailie. Daes he bide for supper, eh?

BAILIE M: Yer Grace, ye'll paurdon me, but I canna.

THE QUEEN: No bide. That is a peety. But I maun gang. Guid ein, Bailie, and tell Mistress Morison I send her my guid thochts.

BAILIE M: (*bowing*) Guid ein, yer Grace, I will that.

THE QUEEN: We leave Logie. He trail ahint Margaret ower muckle.

LOGIE: (*bowing as* MARGARET *curtsies*) I couldna dae that, yer Grace

(*The* QUEEN *and* LADY MARGARET *go up the turnpike stair.* MRS EDWARD *makes a belated curtsy as they go*)

MRS E: Weill, Laird, I maun gang and see that the lassies hae the supper ready to serve. Ye'll keep the Bailie company till the King comes?

LOGIE: Shairly, Mistress, for I see he has a stoup o wine aside him.

MRS E: That's richt. Help yersell.

LOGIE: Thank ye.

(LOGIE *and the* BAILIE *bow as* MRS EDWARD, *with a slight bob, withdraws into the dining-room*)

LOGIE: (*helping himself*) Sae ye're waitin for the King, Bailie? Dinna tell me ye hae turnt a coortier.

BAILIE M: Dinna fash, Laird. I hae mair to dae nor hing aboot the coat-tails o lassies frae morn till nicht.

LOGIE: The coat-tails o the King pey better, mebbe?

BAILIE M: I'm no the King's teyler, Laird, but I dout if they dae.

LOGIE: (*laughing*) Weill said, Bailie. But I didna suggest it was the want o siller that's brocht ye til his Grace. There's sic a thing as warkin yer neb in for the sake o pouer.

BAILIE M: There's sic a thing as wantin to dae his Grace a service, Laird.

LOGIE: And what service hae ye come to dae the nicht?

BAILIE M: He'll learn whan he comes.

LOGIE: (*with a change of manner*) Bailie, whause side are ye on.

BAILIE M: What!

LOGIE: Are ye for the King or Bothwell?

BAILIE M: Hou daur ye ask me that, ye brazen scoondrel!

LOGIE: Come come nou, Bailie, ye needna tak it ill. Ye'll ken that ein aboot the Coort there's mony a man whause colours arena kent, and weill, Bailie, I ken ye're a guid douce member o the Kirk, and maun hae a haillsome hatred o the Papists.

BAILIE M: And what if I hae?

LOGIE: Isna Bothwell Protestant?

BAILIE M: He may caa himsell that, but in my opeenion a man wha meddles wi witches has nae richt to the name. And whan it comes to that, isna the King Protestant himsell?

LOGIE: He's gey chief wi the Papist Huntly, Bailie, and in the opeenion o maist o yer Kirk freinds, a man wha meddles wi idolators has nae richt to the name aither. Shairly, Bailie, as a pillar o the Kirk, ye maun be sair grieved that the King can hae freinds amang the Papists?

BAILIE M: I thocht ye were Protestant yersell, Laird.

LOGIE: Weill?

BAILIE M: Is it no clear? Gin ye can serve the King and be Protestant, as weill can I. But here are my Lord and Leddy Atholl.

(LORD *and* LADY ATHOLL *enter from the turnpike stair*)

LOGIE: (*bowing*) Guid ein, my Lord and Leddy.

ATHOLL: Guid ein, Laird. Ah Bailie, ye're there.

(*The* BAILIE *bows,* LADY ATHOLL *bobs, smiling*)

LADY A: The King isna back yet? I suppose her Grace is up the stair?

LOGIE: She gaed up no a meenit syne.

LADY A: Weill, I'll leave ye. But whaur's my Lord Lennox, Logie? Wasna he alang wi ye this efternune?

LOGIE: My Lord Lennox took his leave at the door. He thinks the Queen'll hae mair peace to her meat gin he bides awa.

LADY A: Oh, sae the King's growin jealous?

LOGIE: Ay, he preached her a lang sermon in the bed last nicht.

LADY A: Dear me, I maun hear aboot that.

(*She bobs hastily and hurries upstairs*)

LOGIE: Weill, Bailie, are ye scandalised?

BAILIE M: I'm beginnin to think his Grace hasna mony freinds aboot his ain Coort, Laird.

LOGIE: (*to* ATHOLL) Ye see, my Lord. Watch what ye say in front o the Bailie. He's a loyal man for the King.

ATHOLL: Dear me, Bailie, ye shairly resent his traffic wi the Papists. I thocht ye were haill-hairtit for the Kirk.

BAILIE M: (*huffed*) Gin ye'll paurdon me, my Lord, I'll tak mysell ben the hoose.

(*He withdraws into the dining-room*)

LOGIE: And that's that.

ATHOLL: Sae the Toun's loyal?

LOGIE: Ay, but there's little in it. They wad be aa for Bothwell gin it werena for his witchcraft. It's a peety he didna stey in jeyl and staun his trial for it, insteid o brekin oot and rinnin wild.

ATHOLL: I daursay, Laird, but Bothwell's like the rest o's. He wud suner hae a haill skin nor risk his life to a trial. What were ye sayin aboot the Queen and Lennox?

LOGIE: The King has the notion that they're mair nor friends. Someane's been clypin.

ATHOLL: The Chancellor again?

LOGIE: Nane else. He had an audience in here last nicht.

ATHOLL: I kent it. God, he's an auld tod! He gat redd o the Bonnie Earl in juist the same wey. I tell ye, Logie, it's time his wings were clipped. When ony bune himsell begin to win favour he sterts his trickery and oot they gang. And aa the time he feathers his nest. Whan eir there's a lump o grun gaun beggin wha gets it? My Lord the Chancellor. It wad seiken ye. It haurdly peys to attend the Coort at aa.

LOGIE: Weill, my Lord, he could be redd oot the morn.

ATHOLL: Hou that? He has the King roun his fingers and the Papists at his back.

LOGIE: We could bring in Bothwell.

ATHOLL: And Bothwell wi the Toun against him for his witchcraft! Na na, Laird. There's nae gaun that gait.

LOGIE: The Toun hates Papery tae, my Lord. Gin the traffic wi the Papists gangs ower faur the Toun'll cheynge its front.

ATHOLL: I daursay, but hou faur will the traffic wi the Papists gang? The King looks aye to the English Queen for siller. He'll get nane as lang as the Papists are at Coort.

LOGIE: There's as muckle gowd in Papist Spain as there is in Protestant England.

ATHOLL: But he daurna touch the Spanish gowd!

LOGIE: Juist that! The Toun wad flee to Bothwell's side at ance, witchcraft or no. I tell ye, my Lord, the tide'll sune turn. And whan it daes we suld be ready, at Bothwell's back!

ATHOLL: Ye seem to be a freind o his.

LOGIE: I hate the Chancellor.

ATHOLL: Ay, weill, we'll see. (*There are sounds of yelling and cheering from the Wynd below*) But there's the rabble in the Wynd. His Grace maun be back frae the hunt.

(MISTRESS EDWARD *enters with a jug of steaming spirits and some stoups*)

MRS E: (*bobbing*) Guid ein, my Lord Atholl. (ATHOLL *bows*) Ye're juist in time. His Grace is in the Wynd.

(*She places the jug and stoups on the compter and goes to the window*)

MRS E: Dear me, it's turnt gey quick daurk. I hope the Toun Gaird's here in time the day, for the rabble herrit the booth twa days syne, and we lost twa bales o claith. (*She pokes her head out of the shutter-hole, looks for a moment and continues*) I canna richt mak oot, wi the wind blawin at the links, but Nicoll maun hae tummlet in a moss-hole. He's thick wi glaur. (*She pokes her head out again*).

LOGIE: He'll be a braw sicht at the table. Her Grace'll be scunnert the nicht again.

ATHOLL: It's Nicoll that peys for the meat, Laird, sae what can she dae?

MRS E: (*withdrawing her head from the shutter-hole*) They're in nou. They'll be gey cauld and tired. But what were ye sayin to the Bailie, the pair o ye? He's sittin ben there like a clockin hen.

LOGIE: He couldna thole oor licht conversation.

MRS E: He says there's some ploy afute i' the Toun. But here they come.

(*The three group themselves and wait, listening. His Grace KING JAMES enters with LORD SPYNIE and BAILIE NICOLL EDWARD. LOGIE and ATHOLL bow low. MRS EDWARD curtsies elaborately. The KING walks in, loosening his jerkin at the neck, and falls plump into a chair. NICOLL EDWARD and SPYNIE also loosen their jerkins. BAILIE MORISON appears at the door of the dining-room, unheeded*)

THE KING: (*entering, almost exhausted*) Ay weill, here we are. (*Falling into his chair*) God, I'm wabbit!

MRS E: (*running to the compter for the jug and stoup*) Here, yer Grace, hae a guid lang dram.

THE KING: Thank ye. And gie ane to Nicoll, for I'm shair he needs it. Yer guid health.

MRS E: Thank ye. (*Passing NICOLL*) Oh Nicoll, ye're a sicht! (*Starting to fill another stoup*) Ye'll hae a dram, Lord Spynie?

SPYNIE: I will that. (*Taking the stoup*) Thank ye.

MRS E: (*facing NICOLL with the jug in one hand and a stoup in the other*) What in aa the warld were ye daein to get intil a mess like that?

NICOLL: (*impatiently*) Gie me a dram. I had a bit tummle.

THE KING: (*taking his nose out of his stoup*) By God he had that! My guid wumman, ye gey near lost yer man the day.

MRS E: Lost my man?

THE KING: Ay lost yer man! It's a woner his neck wasna broken.
He gaed clean ower his horse's heid on Corstorphine Craigs.

MRS E: Oh Nicoll, what hae I aye telt ye! Ye will hunt, and ye
can nae mair sit on a horse nor flee in the air. Drink that up,
see, and then cheynge yer claes.

NICOLL: (*taking his stoup and raising it to his lips*) Ach I'm ower
hungry.

MRS E: Oh but ye'll hae to cheynge. Ye canna sit doun aside
the leddies like that. Yer Grace, I'm shair he maun cheynge his
claes?

THE KING: (*with his nose in his stoup*) Eh?

MRS E: I'm shair he canna sit doun like that?

THE KING: (*coming up for a breath*) Like what? Whaur?

MRS E: He canna gang in for his supper aa glaur.

THE KING: Hoot, wumman, dinna be hard on him. He's stervin
o hunger. (*He buries his nose again*)

MRS E: But he'll fair shame us.

NICOLL: (*having emptied his stoup in one long draught*) Eh?

MRS E: I say ye'll shame us.

NICOLL: Dinna blether, wumman. Fill up my stoup again. (*Suddenly noticing* BAILIE MORISON) But dear me, I didna ken we
had the Bailie in the hoose.

(*All turn and look at* BAILIE MORISON)

MRS E: Oh ay, Bailie Morison cam to see ye, yer Grace, aboot
some Toun maitter.

THE KING: Weill, Bailie, it'll hae to wait. Man, I woner at ye.
Ye hae a Provost, Bailies, Deacons and a Gaird and ye come
rinnin aye to me whan onything gangs wrang. What is it this
time? Has there been anither coo stolen frae the Burgh Muir?

BAILIE M: Na, yer Grace, it's naething like that.

THE KING: Oot wi't, then. God, ye hae a gey lang face. It's
naething bye the ordinar, shairly? (*Eagerly*) Ye haena foun
anither witch?

BAILIE M: Na.

THE KING: Then what's the maitter?

BAILIE M: (*indicating by his manner that the presence of the others
makes him reluctant to speak*) Weill, yer Grace, there's mebbe
naething in it.

MRS E: I'll leave ye, yer Grace, and hae the supper served in
case *I'm* in the wey.

(*She curtsies and leaves, giving the* BAILIE *a resentful look*)

THE KING: Come on Bailie, oot wi't. They're aa in my Cooncil
here bune Nicoll, and he's a Bailie like yersell.

BAILIE M: There are horsemen getherin in Hackerton's Wynd.
They're gaun to ride for Dunibrissel at the chap o seiven.[2]

THE KING: What! Hou did ye fin that oot?

BAILIE M: I was brocht word frae the yill-hoose in Curror's
Close. Some o the men were heard talkin.

THE KING: Whause men were they?

BAILIE M: My Lord Ochiltree's.

THE KING: Sae that's the wey o't? Whaur's Ochiltree the nou?

BAILIE M: At his ludgin in the Schule Wynd.

THE KING: Richt. Gae to the Captain o the Toun Gaird and tell
him to shut aa the ports. Let naebody leave the Toun. Hurry.
I'm gled ye cam. (*The* BAILIE *bows and hurries out*) Logie, ye'll
fin Ochiltree and gar him come to me. (LOGIE *bows and hurries
out*) Atholl, did ye ken o this?

ATHOLL: Na, yer Grace.

THE KING: Did ye see naething?

ATHOLL: No a thing.

THE KING: Ochiltree rade oot o the Toun this mornin. Whan
did he come back?

ATHOLL: I dinna ken.

THE KING: Hae ye been i' the Toun aa day?

ATHOLL: I cam up frae the Abbey aboot an hour syne.

THE KING: Ye wad come in by the Nether Bow?

ATHOLL: Ay.

THE KING: And ye saw nae horsemen?

ATHOLL: Ane or twa, but nane bandit thegither.

THE KING: Were they Ochiltree's?

ATHOLL: Some o them.

THE KING: I kent it! Atholl, ye'll fetch the Chancellor! At ance!
(ATHOLL *bows and hurries out*) God, Nicoll, did ye see his face
the nou? He hates the Chancellor like pousin. Spynie, ye'll haud
the door, and see that nane pass in bune the anes I hae sent for.
(SPYNIE *bows and leaves*) The doors in the Wynd'll be gairdit,
Nicoll?

NICOLL: Ay, but ye shairly dinna lippen to be hairmed here?

THE KING: Na, na, but I'm taking nae risks.

NICOLL: What is it that's wrang?

THE KING: Dinna heed the nou. Ye'll tell yer guid wife to let
the supper stert withoot me.

NICOLL: Ye'll hae to tak a bite, though.

THE KING: Later on, I tell ye.

NICOLL: The mistress'll be gey vexed.

THE KING: I canna help it, Nicoll. Tell her I maun be left alane.
Awa wi ye.

(NICOLL *retires to the dining-room. The* KING *is obviously agitated.* SPYNIE *enters*)

SPYNIE: Yer Grace?

THE KING: Ay?

SPYNIE: Her Grace wad like to ken if ye're gaun ben for supper.

THE KING: Tell her to stert withoot me.

    (*The* QUEEN *enters as he speaks*)

THE QUEEN: What, eh? Ye no come ben for supper?

THE KING: Na, I'm no gaun ben for supper! Stert withoot me!

THE QUEEN: What is it that is wrang?

THE KING: Naething!

THE QUEEN: (*meaningly*) It is Ochiltree, eh?

THE KING: (*angrily*) Hou in aa the warld did ye fin that oot?

THE QUEEN: Spynie. He tell me.

THE KING: Then he suld hae his lang tongue cut oot by the rute! Spynie!

    (SPYNIE *enters*)

SPYNIE: Ay, yer Grace?

THE KING: Try to learn to keep yer mooth shut!

SPYNIE: Eh?

THE KING: Dinna gang tellin the haill hoose what's gaun on!

SPYNIE: I hae telt naebody bune her Grace.

THE KING: Ye had nae richt to tell her Grace! Gin I want her to ken what's gaun on I'll tell her mysell! Oot wi ye!

    (SPYNIE *bows and leaves*)

THE QUEEN: That was nae wey to talk! Ye insult me! What wey suld I no ken what the ithers, they ken? Gin ye dinna tell me I will gang awa! I will stey at Lithgie and no come near!

THE KING: (*pushing her persuasively*) See here, Annie, awa ben and tak yer supper.

THE QUEEN: Haunds aff! Oh I am angert! I ken what it is! Ye are feart I fin oot! Ochiltree he ride to Dunibrissel!

THE KING: No if I can help it!

THE QUEEN: What wey for no? What is wrang at Dunibrissel that Ochiltree he want to gang? The Earl o Moray. He maun be in danger! Ochiltree is his freind!

THE KING: Dinna shout, then!

THE QUEEN: I shout if I like! I yowl!

    (SPYNIE *enters*)

SPYNIE: Yer Grace?

THE KING: What is it nou?

SPYNIE: My Lord the Chancellor.

    (MAITLAND *of Thirlstane enters.* SPYNIE *retires*)

MAITLAND: Ye sent for me.

THE KING: Ay, Jock, the cat's oot o the bag nou!

MAITLAND: What!

THE KING: Ochiltree's back in the Toun! He's raisin men! He means to ride for Dunibrissel!

MAITLAND: He maun be stoppit! Hae ye sent for him?

THE KING: Ay.

MAITLAND: Then threaten him wi the gallows if he leaves the Toun! Hae ye ordert the Toun Gaird to shut the ports?

THE KING: Ay.

MAITLAND: Then we'll manage yet. Hou mony ken what he's efter?

THE QUEEN: I ken what he is efter!

MAITLAND: Eh!

THE QUEEN: He ride to help the Earl o Moray!

MAITLAND: Come come nou, yer Grace, what maks ye think that?

THE QUEEN: He is the Earl his freind!

MAITLAND: But what maks ye think the Earl's at Dunibrissel?

THE QUEEN: It is the Earl, his mither's hoose! He gang there aff and on!

MAITLAND: And what hairm can come to him there?

THE QUEEN: I dinna ken. But I ken ye baith hate him. I ken yer freind Huntly hate him. I ken Huntly is awa north! And ye dinna want Ochiltree to gang! Ye hae some plot!

MAITLAND: Hoots, ye're haverin!

THE QUEEN: Hoo daur ye say like that! I am the Queen!

THE KING: Ay, Jock, watch hou ye talk to her.

THE QUEEN: Ye are a bad ane! Jamie he hate the Bonnie Earl for he is jealous. What wey is he jealous? Because ye tell him lees! Ye dae the same last nicht. Ye say the Lord Lennox he luve me and I trail my skirt!

MAITLAND: Sae he daes and sae ye dae!

THE QUEEN: It is aa wrang! It is bare-faced! But I ken what ye are efter. Ye mak Jamie hate me for ye want to bide at Coort! Ye ken I want Jamie to send ye awa! And ye will gang yet!

THE KING: He'll gang whan I say.

THE QUEEN: He will gang if ye say or no! He is aye ahint the bother, frae the very stert. When ye wantit to mairry me he say no! He say mairry the Princess o Navarre! What wey? Because the English Queen she think I wasna guid Protestant and pey him siller!

MAITLAND: That's a lee!

THE KING: Na, na, Jock, she has ye there.

MAITLAND: It's a lee about the siller.

THE QUEEN: It is nae lee!

MAITLAND: It is a lee!

THE QUEEN: Jamie, ye let him say like that!

THE KING: Hoots awa, there's nae need for me to interfere. Ye can haud yer ain fine.

THE QUEEN: Haud my ain. Oh, ye are hairtless! But I say he will gang!

THE KING: Na na, he's needit.

(SPYNIE *enters*)

SPYNIE: Yer Grace. My Lord Ochiltree.

(OCHILTREE *enters*. SPYNIE *retires*)

THE QUEEN: My Lord, at Dunibrissel? What is wrang?

OCHILTREE: Yer Grace, Huntly left the Toun this mornin wi mair nor a hunder o his men, to mak for the Leith races. He didna gang near them! He crossed the Firth at the Queen's Ferry and rade for Dunibrissel! And the Bonnie Earl's there wi haurdly a man!

THE QUEEN: I kent!

OCHILTREE: There's mair to tell! I gaed to cross mysell, to see what was wrang, and was held up at the Ferry! I was telt that the King and Chancellor had ordert that nae boats were to cross!

THE QUEEN: See! I was richt! It is a plot!

MAITLAND: Sae ye cam back here and stertit to raise yer men, eh?

OCHILTREE: I did, and I'm gaun to ride for Dunibrissel if I hae to fecht my wey oot o the Toun!

MAITLAND: That's juist what ye'll hae to dae, my Lord! The ports are shut against ye!

THE QUEEN: (*to* MAITLAND) Ye will let him gang!

THE KING: Haud ye yer tongue, see!

THE QUEEN: I winna haud my tongue! I will tell Lennox! I will tell Atholl!

THE KING: Stey whaur ye are!

THE QUEEN: I winna!

(*She rushes out*)

THE KING: Spynie! Haud the door!

SPYNIE: (*entering after a short lapse of time and bowing*) Did ye speak, yer Grace?

THE KING: Ye thowless gowk! Did I no tell ye to haud the door?

SPYNIE: I'm hauding the door. Ye shairly didna want me to stop her Grace.

THE KING: Gae oot o my sicht! (SPYNIE *retires with dignity*) Jock what'll we dae?

MAITLAND: Naething. Let them come.

OCHILTREE: Ye'll hae a lot to answer for, yer Grace. Huntly wasna held up at the Ferry!

THE KING: Huntly had a warrant to bring the Earl to me!

OCHILTREE: Oh, sae ye hae tricked me! Yer Grace, I'll nair forgie ye if the Earl comes to hairm. I gart him come to Dunibrissel sae that I could tak Huntly ower and end the feud atween them. Huntly was to cross wi me the morn withoot his men. Nane were to ken bune the three o's and yersell. Ye hae taen a gey mean advantage o yer knowledge!

THE KING: Man, Ochiltree, we didna issue a warrant against the Earl for naething!

OCHILTREE: What has he dune?

THE KING: He was haund in gluve wi Bothwell in the last attack on the Palace!

OCHILTREE: That isna true!

THE KING: It is! He was seen at the fute o the Canongait whan the steer was at its warst!

OCHILTREE: Wha telt ye that? Some o the Chancellor's bribed freinds!

THE KING: Ye'll see them whan they come forrit at the Earl's trial!

OCHILTREE: What wey hae they no come forrit afore this?

THE KING: Because they had to be brocht!

OCHILTREE: Ye hae tortured them! They wad say onything!

THE KING: Hoots awa, man, there's nae need to wark yersel intil a rage!

MAITLAND: Yer freind'll hae a fair trial! What mair can ye ask?

OCHILTREE: If I thocht he wad leive to see his trial!

THE KING: Guid God, man, hae ye no my word for it! (*Suddenly alarmed*) What's that!

(*The door of the dining-room opens and the* QUEEN *enters with* LENNOX *and* ATHOLL)

LENNOX: What's wrang at Dunibrissel?

OCHILTREE: Huntly has a warrant to bring in the Bonnie Earl!

LENNOX: What for?

THE KING: For bein a fause-hairtit traitor haund in gluve wi Bothwell!

LENNOX: Yer Grace, that isna true!

THE KING: It is!

LENNOX: Ye canna prove it!

MAITLAND: Gin we dinna prove it, Lennox, he'll come to nae hairm! He'll hae his trial afore the Lords o the Session!

LENNOX: His trial! Ye sleekit hypocrite! Ye ken as weill as the

rest o's that he winna see the licht o anither day! Didna his
wife's faither the Guid Regent send auld Huntly to the scaffold!
Huntly's been cryin for revenge for years!

MAITLAND: Ach havers!

LENNOX: I tell ye it's murder, though hou ye'll be the better
for't I dinna ken!

ATHOLL: He'll hae bargaint for a gey guid lump o the Earl's
grun!

MAITLAND: Hou daur ye say it! Ye young blaggard, I hae a
damnt guid mind to rin ye through!

OCHILTREE: Ye're in the praisence of the Queen!

THE KING: Ay, Jock, haud doun a wee.

MAITLAND: Hae I to staun here and listen to snash like that!
By god, the government o this country's a gey thankless job!
(*To the Lords*) Certies, but ye're a bonnie lot! We fin oot that
a man's a fause-hairtit traitor, thick as a thief wi ane that has
time and again tried to tak the life o the King, but daur we
bring him to his trial? Na na, his friends at Coort wad stop us!
My Lords, ye're guilty o rank black disloyalty!

THE KING: Weill said, Jock! Ye're traitors, ilka ane o ye! Ye
wad hae yer King gang ilka day in terror o his life! What kind
o country's this, that Bothwell's alloued to leive? Has he no
made sic a wrack o the Palace that I canna bide in it? Has he
no haen aa the witches in Lothian raisin storms on the watter
whan I was crossin ower wi Annie there frae Denmark? Has
he no haen dizzens o them stickin preens in my cley corp, and
brewin pousins for me oot o puddock's bluid? And ye mak a
steer, certies, because we hae sent oot a warrant against ane o
his closest freinds!

LENNOX: By God, yer Grace, if it's Bothwell ye're feart o ye'll
hae to gang in terror nou! Ilka man in Toun or Kirk'll rin to
his side at ance, if Huntly kills the Bonnie Earl the nicht! I tell
ye ye winna move a fute frae yer door withoot bein spat on by
the rabble! The wrath o the Almichty God'll be cried doun on
yer heid by ilka preacher i' the country! They'll thump their
Bibles to some tune nou!

THE KING: Let them thump! They canna rant mair against me
nor they dae at praisent! I daurna put my fute inside a kirk but
they're at my throat for bein friendly wi the Papist Lords! But
dae they eir cry curses doun on Bothwell? Na na! He's oot for
the life o the King! He's a favourite! But I'll waste nae mair
braith. Gin Toun or Kirk winna help me against Bothwell the
Papist Lords will! Jock, hou mony are there i' the Toun the
nou?

MAITLAND: Errol's here, wi Hume and Angus.

THE KING: Hae they ony men?

MAITLAND: Scores.

THE KING: Then tell them to staun bye the Toun Gaird gin ony try to force the ports! Lennox, Ochiltree and Atholl, ye'll gang til yer ludgings and bide there till ye hae leave to move!

OCHILTREE: Yer Grace, ye'll regret this!

THE KING: Is that a threat?

OCHILTREE: It's nae threat to yersell, but if Huntly kills the Bonnie Earl I winna rest till I hae split his croun!

THE KING: The Deil tak ye, man, is there nae Coort o Session? Gin there are ony wrangs they can be richtit there! Awa wi ye, and steer a fute frae yer ludgin gin ye daur! Jock, ye'll see that my orders are cairrit oot!

MAITLAND: I will that!

THE KING: Awa then.

(MAITLAND *goes to the door, then turns, waiting*)

THE KING: Weill, my Lords?

(*The Lords stand for a moment, glaring in anger, then* OCHILTREE *turns and bows to the* QUEEN. LENNOX *and* ATHOLL *follow his example.* MAITLAND *seeing that the Lords are leaving without trouble, hurries downstairs. The Lords go to the door.* OCHILTREE *and* ATHOLL *follow* MAITLAND. LENNOX *turns to the* KING)

LENNOX: Yer Grace, ye tak evil coonsel whan ye listen to the Chancellor!

THE KING: I wad tak waur gin I listened to yersell!

LENNOX: Ye'll see yet!

(*He leaves*)

THE QUEEN: It is dune. Frae this nicht dinna speak. Dinna touch. Dinna come near. I hae supper in my ain room.

THE KING: Awa for God's sake and tak it, then!

(*She stands staring at him. Tears gather in her eyes. She turns suddenly and hurries out*)

THE KING: Spynie!

(SPYNIE *enters*)

THE KING: Is Logie there?

SPYNIE: Ay.

THE KING: Has he haen onything to eat?

SPYNIE: He's juist dune, I think.

THE KING: Let him haud the door, then. We'll gang ben and hae a bite with Nicoll and the Mistress, then I'll hae a quait nicht at my book. The Queen's awa up the stair wi a sair heid.

(RAB *pokes his head in at the door*)

RAB: Yer Grace?

THE KING: Ay, Rab, what is it?

RAB: There were nane o yer gentlemen aboot the door. It's Sir Robert Bowes the English ambassador.

THE KING: What! Guid God, hae I to get naething to eat the nicht at aa! Send him in, Spynie. (SPYNIE *leaves*. RAB *is about to follow*) Rab? (RAB *turns*) Is the Wynd quait?

RAB: Ay, yer Grace.

THE KING: Are there gairds at aa the doors?

RAB: Ay.

THE KING: Awa, then.

(RAB *leaves*. SPYNIE *enters with* SIR ROBERT BOWES)

SPYNIE: (*bowing elaborately*) Sir Robert Bowes.

(*He leaves*)

THE KING: Weill, Sir Robert, this is a queer time o the day for a veesit, but ye're weill come for aa that.

(*He holds out his hand.* SIR ROBERT *kisses it*)

SIR ROBERT: Most Gracious Sovereign, if I call early you are gone to the chase, and if late you have retired to your literary labours.[3]

THE KING: Sir Robert, that soonds like a rebuke. I hope ye dinna mean to imply that naither the sport o the chase nor the airt o letters is a proper employment for a sovereign?

SIR ROBERT: I would suggest, your Majesty, that they must be held subordinate to the arts of war and government, compared with which they are but recreations.

THE KING: Na na, Sir Robert, I dinna haud wi ye there! Hae ye neir thocht, Sir Robert, that it's the weill governt country that kens the maist peace, and the ill the maist bluidshed?

SIR ROBERT: That, your Majesty, can hardly be denied.

THE KING: Then daes it no follow, Sir Robert, that the airt o government precedes the airt o war, for gin the tane is weill practised the tither isna needit?

SIR ROBERT: Undoubtedly.

THE KING: But the practice o guid government, Sir Robert, entails great wisdom?

SIR ROBERT: Most certainly.

THE KING: And whaur can we fin wisdom, Sir Robert, if no in books, that cairry aa the wisdom o the ages? And arena books, Sir Robert, the ootcome o the airt o letters?

SIR ROBERT: They are, your Majesty, indisputably.

THE KING: Then I hae ye nou, Sir Robert, for the airt o letters maun precede the twa ithers, and is therefore a proper employment for a sovereign. But the airt o letters daesna exercise the body, and for that there can be nae better practice, Sir Robert, nor the sport o the chase. The chase demands strength and courage, like the airt o war, and it keeps ane in grant fettle in case war suld arise, but it kills naebody and costs less. Nou there ye are, Sir Robert. I hope ye're convinced.

SIR ROBERT: I am, your Majesty, completely.

THE KING: I'm gled to hear it, and if ye want to improve in debate, Sir Robert, ye suld hae a warstle wi the Logic. Tak a guid look at the Socratic method.[4] Socrates spent his haill life haein arguments, and he wasna bate ance.

SIR ROBERT: I have no doubt, your Majesty, that you will follow most worthily in his distinguished footsteps. But I hope you will meet a less untimely end.

THE KING: Deed ay, Sir Robert, I hope sae, for there's nae king but has his faes. I suppose ye hae some maitter to discuss?

SIR ROBERT: Indeed your Majesty, I have. It hath come to the knowledge of the Queen my mistress that certain of your Lords do harbour Jesuit priests, whose practice is to woo your subjects from the true religion with gifts of Spanish gold.

THE KING: Dear me, Sir Robert. Hou did this come oot?

SIR ROBERT: A certain fellow, your Majesty, a Papist, suspected of traffic with the Cardinal of Spain, was taken prisoner at the Port of London. In his possession were certain papers, your Majesty, which he did attempt to swallow on his way to jail.

THE KING: Guid God, Sir Robert, he's been a gey glutton. And hou did he fare?

SIR ROBERT: His meal, your Majesty, was interrupted, and when the rescued papers were assembled they were traced to the hand of one James Gordon, a Jesuit, who resides in secret at the castle of the Lord Huntly.

THE KING: Weill, Sir Robert, it's a serious maitter. Hae ye brocht the bits o paper wi ye?

SIR ROBERT: Alas, your Majesty, no. They have been retained in London.

THE KING: What! Ye shairly dinne ettle us, Sir Robert, to believe ony chairge against the Lord Huntly till we hae seen the prufe!

SIR ROBERT: Such proof as there was, your Majesty, was sufficient to convince the Queen my mistress. Surely you do not doubt her shrewdness in these matters?

THE KING: Sir Robert, we dinna dout her shrewdness in ony maitter, but she'll shairly see hersell that we can tak nae action against the Lord Huntly on the strength o a second-haund story!

SIR ROBERT: Your Majesty, I think she doth expect you to

accept her royal word. It is her wish that you banish the Lord
Huntly from your presence, and adopt a more rigorous attitude
towards the whole of your Papist subjects.

THE KING: I see. Sir Robert, I'll be plain wi ye. We welcome
aye oor dear sister's royal advice for the better government o
oor puir afflictit country, but she'll paurdon us, shairly, if we
whiles think we ken hou the wind blaws here a wee thing better nor hersell. She's at us aye to herry and harass the Papists,
but she daesna ken, mebbe, that we hae great need o them at
times, and at nane mair nor the praisent. The great affliction
o Scotland the nou isna idolatory! It's the Earl o Bothwell!
And we maun bide as close wi the Papist Lords as if they were
oor very Brithers, till the traitor's heid's on the spike o the
Palace yett! Nou listen, Sir Robert. Gin oor dear sister were
to mak us anither praisent o some siller, sae that we could
fit oot a weill furnisht body o men to bring the blaggard to
the gallows, something micht be done aboot the ither maitter
then!

SIR ROBERT: Your Majesty, the question of money was raised
in my dispatch.

THE KING: (*eagerly*) Eh?

SIR ROBERT: The queen my mistress hath instructed me to say,
your Majesty, that until her wishes concerning the Papists are
regarded, she can make no further grant to your exchequer.

THE KING: The Deil tak her for an auld miser!

SIR ROBERT: Your Majesty!

THE KING: Hoots man, dinna bridle up at me! By God she isna
blate! She wad gar me leave mysell helpless against a man that's
been oot for my bluid for the last year or mair, juist because twa
or three Papists here hae written letters to their freinds abroad!
And aa this, certies, withoot the promise o a bawbee! By God,
Sir Robert, I woner at yer effrontery in comin up the nicht!

SIR ROBERT: Your Majesty, if you have ought to answer when
you have considered the matter further, you will be pleased to
send for me! Till then, I pray, you will allow me bid farewell!
    (*He bows*)

THE KING: Sir Robert, the suner ye're doun the stair the better.
Ye hae held me frae my meat for naething! Spynie!
    (LOGIE *enters*)

LOGIE: (*bowing*) My Lord Spynie's haein his supper, yer Grace.

THE KING: Ay weill, Logie, show Sir Robert doun the stair. I'm
gaun for mine.
    (*He goes into the dining-room. The two who remain sudden-
    ly assume the manner of conspirators. SIR ROBERT beckons*

LOGIE *aside from the door. He takes a letter from his tunic*)

SIR ROBERT: This letter is for the Lord Bothwell. Will you see it safely delivered?

LOGIE: (*looking furtively at each door in turn*) Shairly, Sir Robert.

SIR ROBERT: (*handing over the letter*) The Queen my mistress will reward you well.

(*He leaves quietly.* LOGIE *hurriedly places the letter in an inner pocket and follows him*)

ACT TWO

'*The Kingis chalmer in the palace of Halyroudhous*', Edinburgh, XXIV *July*, 1593. *Morning.*

The KING's bed-chamber in Holyrood House. In the left wall, downstage, a small door leading to a dressing-closet. Upstage from this a large window in a deep recess. In the middle of the back wall a wide fire-place. Right of this a large door leading to the KING's audience-chamber. In the right wall, downstage, a small door leading to the QUEEN's bed-chamber.

Against the back wall, left of the fire-place, a large four-poster bed with elaborate hangings. Left of the bed a carved kist, and right an armchair. By the right wall, upstage from the door of the QUEEN's chamber, a table with a chair behind it.

A narrow shaft of sunlight slants across from a slight opening in the drawn curtains of the window. There is no fire in the grate. The hangings of the bed are drawn close.

The QUEEN enters stealthily from her chamber, tiptoes to the bed, listens, and peeps through the hangings. She tiptoes to the door of the audience-chamber. She opens it quietly. She admits LADY ATHOLL with the EARL OF BOTHWELL and JOHN COLVILLE. The men carry drawn swords. The QUEEN and LADY ATHOLL retire silently to the QUEEN's chamber. BOTHWELL and COLVILLE stand expectantly beyond the fire-place from the bed.

The clock in the steeple of the Canongait Tolbooth strikes nine.

The KING parts the curtains at the far side of the bed and emerges in his nightshirt. He sits on the edge of the bed and rubs his eyes. He rises, parts the window-curtains, and looks out.

THE KING: (*yelling*) Spynie!

(*Starting to loosen his nightshirt he goes into his closet.*
COLVILLE *makes to move.* BOTHWELL *restrains him*)

BOTHWELL: He canna win oot that wey. It's his dressin-closet.
(*A shot is fired somewhere within the Palace. A brawl is started.
More shots follow, accompanied by shouts and the noise of
clashing weapons. The* KING *rushes in from his dressing-closet,
naked, but carrying his shirt. As he comes round the foot of the
bed he sees* BOTHWELL. *He halts, hastily wrapping his shirt
round his loins*)

THE KING: Bothwell!
(*He runs to the* QUEEN'*s door. It is locked*)

THE KING: (*pulling at the handle*) Annie! Annie! Open the door!
Let me in! Annie!
(*He receives no reply. He turns at bay.* BOTHWELL *steps to the
foot of the bed, facing him with his sword held threateningly*)

THE KING: (*yelling at the pitch of his voice*) Treason! Treason!

BOTHWELL: Ay ay, my bonnie bairn. (*Moving round and forcing
the* KING *back into the chair beside the bed*) Ye hae gien oot that
I ettle to tak yer life. It's in this haund nou!

THE KING: (*crouching back in the chair fearfully, almost in tears*)
Ye traitor, ye hae shamed me. Strike and be dune wi't! I dinna
want to leive another day.
(LENNOX, OCHILTREE *and* ATHOLL *appear at the door of
the audience-chamber.* BOTHWELL *and* COLVILLE *suddenly
drop their threatening manner and start to act a pre-arranged
part. The* KING'*s bearing changes. A note of hopeful excitement
creeps into his voice*)

THE KING: Come on Francie, feenish what ye hae stertit! Tak
yer King's life. He's ready to dee!

BOTHWELL: (*dropping elaborately on his knees*) Maist Gracious
sovereign.

COLVILLE: (*likewise*) Maist Clement Prince.

THE KING: (*almost jubilant*) Na na, ye hypocrites, ye needna
kneel! Ye were for rinnin me through!

BOTHWELL: We submit oorsells maist humbly to yer royal
mercy.

THE KING: Ye leers, ye're cheyngin yer tune because the Lords
are here! What are ye daein in my chalmer at aa? Hou did ye win
past the gairds? Arena yer swords drawn nakit in yer haunds?

BOTHWELL: (*holding his sword by the blade and kissing the hilt*)
Yer Grace, my sword is at yer service. (*Presenting it*) Tak it, and
strike my heid frae my shouthers gin eir I hae wished ye ill.

THE KING: (*shrinking back from the sword*) Did eir ye hear sic
rank hypocrasy! My Lords, ye hae him reid-haundit for high

treason! Hack him doun! (*None makes any move to obey*) Come on Lodovick! He cam in here wi bluidy murder in his hairt! Hae I to ask ye twice to redd me o him?

LENNOX: He hasna ettled ony ill, yer Grace.

THE KING: What! Nae ill! Atholl! Ochiltree! (*Neither responds to his appeal. A note of fear creeps into his voice*) Sae ye're aa against me.

OCHILTREE: Yer Grace, ye need fear nae ill to yer person.

THE KING: Dae ye think I dinna ken what that means? Hae I no heard it afore! Ye're for locking me up, are ye, like the auld Lords at Ruthven!5 Ye think to haud me in yer pouer and rin the country for yer ain ends! I tell ye thae days are bye! I'm a bairn nae langer! I'm twenty-seiven year auld, and I hae mair sense nou nor submit to ye! Gin I dinna sign yer enactments what can ye dae? Threaten to kill me? Ye ken ye daurna! The haill country wad turn against ye!

BOTHWELL: Yer Grace, ye hae sair mistaen us.

THE KING: Rise up aff yer knees, man, and end this mockery! Ye hae come to gar me gie ye back yer grun! But ye may threaten till ye're blue i' the face! I winna heed ye!

BOTHWELL: (*having risen at the King's order*) Ye'll hae to! Ye haena a freind!

THE KING: Dae ye think the Toun'll let ye tak me? (*Bells in the Town and Canongait can be heard ringing in alarm*) Hearken to the bells! In ten meenits ye'll be pouerless!

BOTHWELL: The bells can ding till they crack for aa the help the Toun'll gie ye! The Kirk and the Guilds are for me! And ye haena a freind i' the Palace that isna weill tied wi towe.

THE KING: I hae freinds elsewhaur wha winna fail me!

BOTHWELL: If it's Huntly ye mean his haunds are fou! Atholl's seen to that!

THE KING: Atholl, I micht hae kent it! Yer wife's turnt yer heid! She's been up to naething but mischief sin the day I sent her faither to the gallows!

ATHOLL: She has nae haund in this maitter!

THE KING: Then what are ye efter? Ye're for the kirk, nae dout. Ye want Huntly and the ither Papists put to the horn!

ATHOLL: What wey no! They're traitors! They hae plottit wi Spain!

THE KING: They hae grun that lies gey near yer ain!

ATHOLL: They hae grun that suldna belang to them!

THE KING: Juist that! It suld belang to yersell!

ATHOLL: It micht, gin it hadna been for Maitland! What richt has he to dae the sharin?

THE KING: He's Chancellor and daes the will o the Cooncil!

ATHOLL: Then Chancellor and Cooncil maun be cheynged!

THE KING: Hou daur ye say it!

LENNOX: Yer Grace, we want to save ye frae yer supposed freinds!

THE KING: Supposed freinds! Ay, Lodovick, I hae some supposed freinds, some that I cherish like brithers and lavish wi ilka favour at a King's command. And what dae they dae? Hing aboot the tail o Annie's skirt, and try their best to turn her heid!

LENNOX: It's a lee!

THE KING: A lee! Can I no believe my ain een? I catch ye wi yer heids thegither ilka time I turn a corner!

LENNOX: (*gripping his hilt*) Gin ye werena King I wad rin ye through!

OCHILTREE: My Lord, we arena here to threaten his Grace's life!

THE KING: What are ye here at aa for?

OCHILTREE: It's weill ye ken! We had a freind slauchtert in cauld bluid! Justice hasna been dune against his murderers!

THE KING: Justice has been dune! Twa o Huntly's men were beheidit!

OCHILTREE: And Huntly himsell? It was he wha dang the Bonnie Earl doun!

THE KING: He was put in jeyl for it!

OCHILTREE: For seiven days! Then he was alloued oot!

THE KING: He was let oot on a caution!

ATHOLL: And he didna pey it!

THE KING: Ye canna blame me for that!

OCHILTREE: He suld hae been keepit in! He suld hae been sent to the gallows at ance!

THE KING: That was a maitter for the Lords o the Session!

OCHILTREE: Juist that! It was a maitter for Maitland and the rest o his freinds, and they made shair he cam to nae hairm! I tell ye Maitland suld feel the towe on his thrapple tae! It was he wha sent oot Huntly to bring the Earl in!

THE KING: He did it wi my authority!

OCHILTREE: Efter fillin yer heid wi lees! And he did it kennin weill what the upshot wad be!

LENNOX: He wasna the only ane wha kent what the upshot wad be!

THE KING: Eh!

LENNOX: Ye had yer ain reasons for winkin at the murder!

THE KING: By God, Lodovick, gin I werena pouerless ye wad

swallow that! The Bonnie Earl was my best freind till he jeynt wi Bothwell there!

LENNOX: Ye turnt against him afore that! And it was Maitland's faut again! He telt the same lees aboot the Bonnie Earl as he daes aboot me!

THE KING: They werena lees!

OCHILTREE: I tell ye they were, and he'll pey for them dearly!

THE KING: He's peyed eneugh! He was banisht frae the Coort!

OCHILTREE: He's on his wey back nou! Ye sent for him twa days syne!

THE KING: Whaur was I to turn? There wasna ane o ye I could depend on! Even Logie was plottin ahint my back, and he hadna been in jeyl for't for twa days whan ye alloued him to brek oot!

LENNOX: It was ane of her Grace's leddies that let him oot!

THE KING: Wha put her up to't? Ye were aa in the plot!

LENNOX: We were aa against Maitland!

THE KING: My only freind!

LENNOX: Yer warst fae!

THE KING: He hasna betrayed me to traitors! Ye're a queer lot to miscaa Jock! But I winna gie in to ye! I'll set my haund to naething! And gin Bothwell wants his grun back he'll hae to staun his trial for witchcraft!

BOTHWELL: That's juist what I'm here to dae!

THE KING: What!

BOTHWELL: I'm willin to staun my trial as sune as ye like.

THE KING: Then by God I hae ye nou! I hae eneugh evidence to hae ye brunt twice ower!

BOTHWELL: The evidence o tortured auld weemen!

THE KING: The evidence o vicious auld beldams wi the mark o the Deil's cloven fute on their skins!

BOTHWELL: Brunt on wi a reid-hot airn!

THE KING: Stampit on by the Deil himsell! And there's Ritchie Graham the wizard![6] I hae clear prufe that ye warkit a spell wi him to pousin me! He confessed the haill ploy!

BOTHWELL: Efter haein his legs torn gey near aff him!

THE KING: What wey no? The Deil gies strength to his ain! It's aye the warst that hae to be maist rackit to confess!

BOTHWELL: We'll see what the new Lords o the session think o that!

THE KING: The what!

BOTHWELL: We're gaun to cheynge Coort, Cooncil, Session and aa!

THE KING: I tell ye ye shanna! I'll let ye dae yer warst!

BOTHWELL: (*threatening with his sword*) Then by God we'll dae it!

THE KING: (*shrinking back*) Ye blaggard! Tak yer sword awa! Ye daurna kill an anointit King!

BOTHWELL: It's been dune afore this! Think o yer faither![7]

THE KING: A gey wheen gaed to the gallows for that!

BOTHWELL: Then think o yer mither![8] Nane hae suffert for that yet!

THE KING: Hae ye forgotten the steer it rase?

BOTHWELL: Weill I micht, whan her ain son let it pass!

THE KING: What dae ye mean by that, ye leear?

BOTHWELL: Ye could hae saved her gin ye'd tried! The English wadna hae daured beheid her gin they'd thocht ye'd tak a firmer staun!

THE KING: I did aa I could!

BOTHWELL: Ye did naething but bluster wi yer tongue in yer cheek! Ye were feart to offend them in case ye lost yer claim to the succession! Ye're that greedy for the English Croun ye wad sell yer sowl to the Deil for it! (*A murmur outside indicates that the people of the Town and Canongait are gathering below the window*) Colville, see what's gaun on ootbye.

THE KING: The folk o the Toun are here to save me! Let me on wi my sark. (*Concealed from the others, and the audience, by the bed, he hurriedly pulls on his shirt*) I'm gaun to the winnock.

BOTHWELL: Ye're no gaun to the winnock till we hae everything settled.

THE KING: They're here to save me! (*Moving from the bedside*) I'm gaun to the winnock!

BOTHWELL: (*sword in hand*) Mak ae move and I'll cut ye into collops!

COLVILLE: I see Hume the Provost and auld Sir Jamie Melville!

BOTHWELL: Keep back, then!

LENNOX: Wha else are there?

COLVILLE: Juist the rabble o the Toun.

THE KING: The Toun Gaird'll sune be doun!

BOTHWELL: The Toun Gaird's thrang elsewhaur! We hae seen to that! Ye'll hae to come to tairms to save yer face!

THE KING: Whaur are the Bailies?

BOTHWELL: The Bailies are roun at the yett wi the Preachers! They're waitin to be askit in to tak pairt in the agreement!

THE KING: Oh ye deil, to bring the Preachers in! They'll tell the haill story in aa their kirks! Ye'll shame me afore the haill country! Kill me! Kill me! I tell ye! I winna face them!

OCHILTREE: Yer Grace, they needna ken ye were threatent!

THE KING: They ken Bothwell's here! They kent he was comin!

LENNOX: They think he cam to seek his paurdon!

THE KING: I winna hae them in, I tell ye!

BOTHWELL: Ye'll hae to!

> (*The noise below the window increases. There is a little shouting and scuffling within the Palace*)

THE KING: There's help comin!

BOTHWELL: I tell ye ye hae nae chance!

THE KING: Whaur's Spynie?

BOTHWELL: Spynie's on gaird at the yett, for us!

THE KING: Anither traitor!

BOTHWELL: I tell ye ye haena a freind!

> (*The noise below the window increases further*)

COLVILLE: Ye'd better hurry! The croud's growin bigger!

OCHILTREE: I dout he'd better gang to the winnock.

BOTHWELL: (*closing on the King threateningly*) Listen, then. Ye'll hae to grant Colville and mysell remission and gie us back oor grun!

LENNOX: (*Likewise having drawn*) And Maitland maun be keepit frae the Coort!

ATHOLL: (*likewise*) And Huntly maun be put to the horn!

THE KING: (*shouting through his terror*) It's for me to say what's gaun to happen!

BOTHWELL: Ye'll say what's gaun to happen! But ye'll say what we tell ye!

OCHILTREE: Come on, yer Grace, put a face on it.

LENNOX: Ay, come on!

ATHOLL: Time's rinnin short!

COLVILLE: We'll hae to dae something sune! They're aa cryin up!

BOTHWELL: (*sheathing his sword and gripping the* KING *by the shoulders*) Gin ye dinna gie in I'll cairry ye ower to the winnock juist as ye are!

THE KING: (*almost in tears*) Aa richt. I'll gie in the nou. But by God wait!

BOTHWELL: (*to* ATHOLL) Whaur are his breeks?

THE KING: They're in the closet.

BOTHWELL: Fetch his breeks, Lennox.

LENNOX: (*indignantly*) My Lord, ye forget yersell!

OCHILTREE: I'll fetch them.

> (*He goes into the dressing-closet*)

COLVILLE: They're cryin for the Queen tae!

OCHILTREE: (*coming in from the closet*) This is the only pair I can fin.

BOTHWELL: They'll dae. Help him into them.

COLVILLE: (*to* BOTHWELL) They want the Queen, my Lord!

LENNOX: I'll fetch her.

THE KING: See that! He wadna fetch my breeks, but he'll gang for Annie!

LENNOX: I wasna ordert to gang for Annie!

(*As he leaves there is a sudden knock at the door of the audience-chamber*)

BOTHWELL: See wha that is, Atholl.

(ATHOLL *opens the door of the audience-chamber.* SPYNIE *enters*)

THE KING: (*to* SPYNIE) Ye fause-hairtit traitor!

BOTHWELL: Haud yer tongue and put yer claes on!

THE KING: He'll hing for this yet! I want my doublet.

BOTHWELL: Colville, fin the rest o his claes. (COLVILLE *goes into the closet. To* SPYNIE) My Lord, hae ye everything in order?

SPYNIE: Ay, Mar and Glamis pat up a big fecht, but they're awa oot the Lang Gair nou wi their tails atween their legs.

BOTHWELL: Wha else is against us?

SPYNIE: Melville and the Provost are ablow the winnock wi the Toun rabble, but they haena mony o their ain men.

BOTHWELL: Will the rabble gie ye ony bother?

SPYNIE: Na, they juist want to ken if the Queen's safe.

THE KING: They want to ken if *I'm* safe!

BOTHWELL: (*as* COLVILLE *comes in from the closet with a doublet and belt*) Gin ye dinna bide quait ye'll be strippit again! Keep him thrang, Colville. (*To* SPYNIE) Are the Bailies and the Preachers ready?

SPYNIE: They're eatin their heids aff at the yett.

BOTHWELL: Richt, we'll hae them brocht in. Atholl, put them in the ither chalmer and haud them there till we're ready. (ATHOLL *leaves*) Ochiltree, gae oot and treat wi Melville and the Provost. Try to keep them quait. The less steer we hae the better. (OCHILTREE *bows to the* KING *and follows* ATHOLL) Back to the yett, then, Spynie. Wha's haudin the coortyaird?

SPYNIE: Morton. He has it weill in haund.

BOTHWELL: Richt, then.

(SPYNIE *leaves.* LENNOX *enters with the* QUEEN.)

THE KING: (*to the* QUEEN) Oh here ye are! What wey was yer door lockit?

THE QUEEN: It is my ain door. I lock it if I like.

THE KING: Ye maun hae kent they were comin!

THE QUEEN: What if I dae! I telt ye I dinna want Maitland, and ye for bring him back!

THE KING: Ye sleekit jaud! Ye fause-faced jezebel!

    (*There is a sudden crash of broken glass from the window*)

LENNOX: They're throwin stanes at the winnock!

BOTHWELL: We'll hae to hurry! Yer Grace, gae ower and cry doun that ye're safe, but say ae word o bein threatent and I'll hack ye doun!

    (*There is another crash, and a stone lands on the floor*)

THE KING: Guid God, lookat that! Dae ye want to hae me staned?

BOTHWELL: They'll stop whan they see ye.

THE KING: Lennox, gae ye first!

BOTHWELL: It's ye they want, no Lennox!

THE KING: I tell ye I'll be staned.

BOTHWELL: (*drawing*) Ower to the winnock!

    (*The* KING *jumps hastily into the window recess. The murmur below gives way to a profound silence*)

PROVOST: (*from below the window*) Are ye aa richt, yer Grace?

THE KING: (*shouting loudly*) I dinna ken yet, Provost.

PROVOST: Dae ye need help? Say the word and I'll ding the doors doun and redd ye o ilka traitor near ye!

THE KING: Hou many men hae ye?

PROVOST: Abooth three score.

BOTHWELL: Tell him I hae fower hunder!

THE KING: (*to the* PROVOST) Dinna stert ony steer the nou, then. We're in nae danger.

MELVILLE: Whaur's the Queen?

THE KING: She's safe ahint me, Sir Jamie.

MELVILLE: Gar her come forrit. We want to see her.

    (*The murmur rises again*)

THE KING: (*to* BOTHWELL) They want to see Annie.

BOTHWELL: (*to the* QUEEN) Yer Grace, staun forrit aside him. Gie them a wave and a smile.

    (*The* QUEEN *goes to the window. There is a great outburst of cheering*)

LENNOX: That shows whause side they're on.

    (*As the cheering dies a little* MELVILLE'*s voice is heard again*)

MELVILLE: Can we come in?

BOTHWELL: What daes he say?

THE KING: He wants to come in.

BOTHWELL: Tell him to meet Ochiltree at the yett. He can bring the Provost in tae.

THE KING: Gae roun to the yett wi the Provost and meet my Lord Ochiltree. He'll bring ye in.

BOTHWELL: And tell the rabble to gang awa hame.

THE KING: I winna!

BOTHWELL: They can dae ye nae guid! Send them awa hame oot o the wey! If they fecht they'll juist be slauchtert!

THE KING: (*shouting to the rabble*) The rest o ye maun gang awa peacably and quaitly ilka ane til his ain hame. Ye can dae naething but mischief bandit thegither wi weapons in yer haunds. Yer King and queen are in nae danger. Bothwell's here, but he cam in aa humility to seek his paurdon. He's gaun to staun his trial for witchcraft.

> (*A murmur of dissent arises. There are shouts of 'Hang the Papists!'*)

MELVILLE: They dinna want to gang yet. They want to bide and hear what's what.

THE KING: (*to* BOTHWELL) They want to bide.

BOTHWELL: Tell them to gang roun to the Abbey Kirkyard and bide there till we hae come to tairms.

THE KING: Ye can dae nae guid making a steer ablow the winnock. We hae grave maitters o state to discuss. Gin ye're ower anxious for oor safety to leave us yet gae awa roun to the abbey Kirkyaird and bide there for hauf an hour. By that time we'll mebbe hae a proclamation to mak, for we're haein in the Bailies and the Preachers. (*There is a great burst of cheering at the mention of the Bailies and the Preachers. The* KING *shouts through it*) See that they dae as they're telt, Provost, and then mak haste to come in.

> (*The* KING *and* QUEEN *come from the window. The noise of the rabble gradually dies away*)

THE KING: (*to* BOTHWELL) The haill Toun seems to ken what ye're here for! It's weill seen ye hae the Preachers in yer plot!

BOTHWELL: I tell ye I hae aa ahint me bune the Papists!

THE KING: Ye micht hae keepit the Toun frae kennin! They'll be haudin me up to ridicule in their silly sangs! Ye'll destroy the authority o the Croun!

> (ATHOLL *enters from the audience-chamber*)

ATHOLL: (*to* BOTHWELL) I hae the Bailies and the preachers here.

BOTHWELL: Richt. (*To the* KING) Sit doun ower there and stop haverin. (*He indicates the chair beside the table*) Look as dignified as ye can. Hou mony are there, Atholl?

ATHOLL: A dizzen athegither, but they hae chosen three spokesmen.

BOTHWELL: Hou mony Preachers?

ATHOLL: Ane, juist. Maister Bruce, I think.

THE KING: Guid God, we'll suffer for oor sins nou!

BOTHWELL: Haid yer tongue, will ye! Bring them in, Atholl. (ATHOLL *leaves. To* LENNOX) My Lord, dinna staun sae near her Grace or Maister Bruce'll be scandalised. Will ye sit doun, yer Grace? Attend her, Colville.

> (*As* COLVILLE *escorts the* QUEEN *to the chair beside the bed* ATHOLL *admits the* BAILIES EDWARD *and* MORISON *and the Preacher* ROBERT BRUCE. *All bow to the* QUEEN *as they enter.* BOTHWELL, LENNOX *and* COLVILLE *step into the background*)

THE KING: (*before they have finished bowing*) Here ye come. Hech, sirs, but ye're a bonnie lot. Ye mak a conspeeracy against the Croun, and get an ootlawed traitor to dae yer dirty wark.

BRUCE: (*straightening up*) Oor cause is the Lord's!

THE KING: I tell ye it's the Deil's! Whan did the Lord stert to mak use o meddlers wi witchcraft?

BRUCE: It isna even for a King to speir at weys abune his comprehension!

THE KING: Damn ye, man, what isna abune yer ain comprehension is weill within mine!

BRUCE: Curb yer profane tongue and dinna provoke the wrath o the Almichty God! It wad fit ye better to gang doun on yer knees and gie Him thanks for yer delivery, for it maun hae been charity faur abune man's that shieldit ye frae hairm this day!

THE KING: It was my royal bluid that shieldit me frae hairm!

BRUCE: And wha gied ye that?

THE KING: Wha eir it was, he guid nane to yersell!

BRUCE: He ordaint me a Preacher in His haly Kirk!

THE KING: Havers! Ye were ordaint by the Moderator o yer Assembly!

BRUCE: He had the Lord's authority!

THE KING: He had the authority o the ranters wha electit him to office, a wheen delegates frae yer district presbyteries! And wha electit them? In the lang rin it was the congregations o yer kirks, folk frae the wynds and closses o the touns and the cot-hooses o the landward pairishes! I tell ye yer Moderator daes the will o the rabble! He has nae mair claim to the Lord's authority nor the souter wha puts tackets in his shune!

BRUCE: He acts accordin to the Book!

THE KING: The Book maun be interpretit! What richt has he to claim infallabeelity?

BRUCE: He seeks the guidance o the Lord in prayer.

THE KING: Ony donnart fule can dae that! Afore a man can claim authority in speeritual maitters he maun hae ae thing that yer Moderator hasna! He maun hae the pouer by Divine Richt to enforce his decrees! Nou whause poseetion cairries that wi't? No yer Moderator's, I tell ye, but yer King's!

BRUCE: A king's pouer is temporal!

THE KING: It's temporal and speeritual baith! A king's the faither o his subjects, responsible for the weilfare o their minds and bodies in the same wey as ony ordinary faither's responsible for the weilfare o his bairns! He is, I tell ye, for his bluid rins awa back through a lang line o kings and patriarchs to its fountain-heid in the first faither o mankind! And the first faither o mankind was Adam, wha gat his authority straucht frae the Lord, wha made him in His ain image, efter His ain likeness!

BRUCE: Ye forget that Adam sinned and fell frae grace! There was nae salvation till the Saviour cam! And He investit his Authority in His twelve Disciples, whause speeritual descendants are the Preachers o the Kirk!

THE KING: What richt hae ye to say that? Ye're heids are aa that swalt wi conceit that I woner ye acknowledge ony God at aa!

BRUCE: We acknowledge God afore the King, and in his Kingdom we hae authority and ye haena!

THE KING: Ye can hae nae authority withoot the pouer to enforce it! God didna grant ye that!

BRUCE: He grantit it this very day, whan he lent the Kirk the help o His servant Bothwell!

THE KING: Guid God, sae it's God's wark to rise against the Croun! Shairly gin I'm King by God's grace, as ye acknowledged yersells at my coronation, it maun be His will that I suld hae allegiance!

BRUCE: Ye hae oor allegiance in temporal maitters, but whan ye use yer authority to hinder the wark o the Kirk we own nae allegiance bune to God Himsell!

THE KING: And hou hae I hindert the wark o the Kirk? Damn it, it isna fower days sin the three Estates gied ye aa ye could ask for! Ye had an inquisition ordert against seminary priests, and a statute passed against the Mass! And yer stipends were aa exemptit frae taxation! What mair dae ye want?

BRUCE: We want ye to acknowledge oor independence o the Temporal Pouer! We canna haud an Assembly withoot yer consent! And we want an act o attainder passed against the Papist Lords![9]

THE KING: Oho! An act o attainder! What can be mair temporal nor that?

BRUCE: In this case it concerns the welfare o the Kirk!

THE KING: Juist that! I hae ye confoundit oot o yer ain mooth!

Ye're in the horns o a dilemma! Gin the Kirk suld be independent o the Temporal Pouer it daesna need acts o attainder! Gin it daes it canna be independent o the Temporal Pouer! Ye're flummoxed, I tell ye!

BRUCE: Whan the Temporal Pouer interferes wi the weilfare o the Kirk it's for the Kirk to interfere wi it! Ye hae favoured the warst enemies o the Kirk and o Scotland baith, and gin ye winna cheynge yer coorse it maun be cheynged for ye! The Papist Lords hae plottit to betray us to the Spaniard and force us back into the daurkness o idolatry! They wad hae us bend oor knees to the graven image and gie oorsells to mummery and ritual! It canna and it shanna be! They maun be cleaned oot o the country rute and branch, wi fire, sword and the gallows!

BOTHWELL: Amen. We can caa that maitter settled, then, I think.

THE KING: It isna settled! It canna be settled here! It's a maitter for my Cooncil.

BOTHWELL: We had come to tairms, I think, afore oor reverent freind was brocht in. Gin I were ye I wadna stert the haill thing ower again.

THE KING: Yer reverent freind! (*Turning to the others*) Ye wad think butter wadna melt in his mooth, and afore ye cam in he was dictatin to me at the peynt o the sword!

NICOLL: Weill, yer Grace, I wad haud my tongue aboot it. It canna be helpit nou.

THE KING: Na! It canna be helpit nou! But it could hae been gin it hadna been for ye and ithers like ye! Ye suld think shame o yoursell, man, turnin against me wi a lot of grun-greedy Lairds and bumptious fanatics o Preachers! What hairm hae I ere dune the like o ye?

NICOLL: Ye hae dune nae hairm yersell, but ye hae been sair misguidit by yer coonsellors! For yer ain sake they maun be cheynged!

THE KING: Ye turn gey presumptious nou ye hae me pouerless! Misguidit by my coonsellors, forsooth. It'll be a bitter day this if I hae to sit helpless and listen to advice on the government o my country frae a wheen Toun Bailies that keep twa–three hauf-sterved kye on the Burgh Mair and dae a bit tred ahint a coonter!

MORISON: Ye're gey weill indebtit to some of the same Toun Bailies!

THE KING: Sae it's the siller that's botherin ye! Hae I no promised that ye'll baith be peyed back aa I owe ye?

NICOLL: I haena gien the siller a thocht!

THE KING: (*indicating* MORISON) Na, but he has, and he's been peyed back mair nor ony o ye! Glamis the Treasurer sent him some o the Croun plate no a fortnicht syne!

MORISON: Twa cups and an ashet! They werena worth fower thoosand punds Scots! Ye owe me aboot eleeven thoosand!

THE KING: Ye'll be peyed, I tell ye, gin ye'll juist hae patience!

MORISON: I'll hae gey need o patience if Maitland and Glamis are to bide in office! They squander aa yer rents amang themsells and their freinds!

THE KING: It isna for the pat to caa the kettle black! Ye're aa oot for what ye can get!

NICOLL: Yer Grace, ye wrang *me* if ye think that! But ye ance acceptit my hospitality, and I'm grieved to think it suld hae been in my hoose that the murder o the Bonnie Earl was planned!

THE KING: There was nae murder planned!

NICOLL: There was by the Chancellor!

THE KING: Havers!

ATHOLL: It's the truith! He did it for a lump o grun in the Carse o Stirlin that he bargaint for wi Huntly!

THE KING: Wha telt ye that? Ye're sic a glutton for grun yersell that ye canna see past it! The Chancellor gied oot a warrant on my instructions! He had nae thocht o the earl's daith or the Carse o Stirlin aither!

ATHOLL: He's efter aa the grun he can lay his haunds on!

LENNOX: He tried to steal the very grun that was settled on her Grace whan she mairrit ye!

THE KING: Her Grace! What hae ye to dae wi her Grace's affairs? (*To* BRUCE) There's a target for ye, Maister Bruce, gin ye want to rant against ineequity at the Coort! Gie *him* a taste o yer fire and brimstane! Tell him to fin a wife o his ain!

LENNOX: Her Grace is praisent!

THE KING: It'll dae her guid!

THE QUEEN: (*rising*) I am affrontit! (*To* LENNOX) Tak me awa!
(*There is a sudden knock at the door of the audience-chamber and* OCHILTREE *enters.* SIR JAMES MELVILLE *can be seen in the doorway behind him*)

OCHILTREE: (*to the* KING) I hae Sir Jamie Melville here, yer Grace.

BOTHWELL: Whaur's Hume the Provost?

OCHILTREE: He was feart to come in whan he kent oor strength. He's for fleein the Toun.

BOTHWELL: That's him settled, then. We'll hae in Sir Jamie.
(OCHILTREE *motions in* SIR JAMES *who immediately approaches the* QUEEN *as she stands hesitant before her chair*)

MELVILLE: (*bowing over the* QUEEN's *hand and kissing it*) Yer Grace, I'm glad to see ye safe. Is his Grace aa richt? (*He turns and looks round. When he sees the* KING *he approaches him with elaborate courtliness*) Yer Grace, I thank God wi aa my hairt for yer delivery. (*He kisses the* KING's *hand*) I had thocht ye were in peril o yer life.

(*The* QUEEN *quietly resumes her seat*)

THE KING: Ye werena faur wrang, Sir Jamie. That blaggard wad hae killed me gin it hadna been for the steer ye made ablow the winnock.

OCHILTREE: That isna true! (*To* MELVILLE) He's been cairrit awa by the excitement. My Lord Bothwell cam in juist to seek his paurdon and offer to staun his trial.

THE KING: He cam in here to gar me cheynge my Officers o State!

BOTHWELL: And wi aa respect to Sir Jamie we're gaun to dae it!

THE KING: There ye are! Ye hear him! They hae aa been at it!

OCHILTREE: We thocht it time to save ye frae evil coonsel!

BRUCE: And to turn ye frae the Papists to the service o the Kirk!

THE KING: Listen to that! That's hou he thinks he suld address his King. He treats me like some trollop on his stule o repentance that's haen a bairn on the wrang side o the blanket!

BRUCE: Ye're guilty o a blacker sin nor that, for ye're on yer wey to beget Prelacy and Papery!

THE KING: (*shouting wildly*) For God's sake dinna stert again! Save yer braith for the Saubbath!

MELVILLE: (*shocked*) Yer Grace! I'm grieved to hear ye sae faur forget yersell as to tak the name of the Lord in vain!

THE KING: Guid God, sae ye hae come to preach at me tae!

MELVILLE: Gin ye mean I'm in the plot against ye, yer Grace, ye're faur wrang. Ye ken I hae been aye a loyal subject, firm against feids and factions, and thrang for the establishment o order, but I'm an aulder man nor ye are, and hae served yer puir mither afore ye, and I wad be wantin in my duty as a coonsellor gin I didna reprove ye whan ye uttered a word that wasna seemly, or behaved in a wey that didna befit yer exaltit state. And this muckle I will say, though I hae nae haund in this mornin's wark, that the Lords here praisent hae mair in their favour nor the faction o the Papists.

THE KING: The auld sang, Sir Jamie. The auld sang. But cairry on. We hae the haill mornin.

(*As the speech proceeds the Lords gradually sit, obviously wilting*)

MELVILLE: Gin we were to listen for a haill week, yer Grace,

we couldna hear ower muckle guid advice! And I think I may
weill claim to be able to advise ye, for I hae served in mony
a coort abroad as weill as at hame here, and gien a lang life's
study to the warks o the warld's great scholars. The formaist o
a prince's aims, yer Grace, suld be the advancement o the true
releegion, for gin we neglect God we canna prosper. Therefore
ye suld show a guid example, first in yer ain person, for it's
on ye as his sovereign that ilka man's ee is fixed, and second
by yer choice o coonsellors and freinds, for gin the men ye
maist favour are godly and richteous, there can be nae fear in
the minds o yer subjects that their Prince is corrupt. And nou
I maun tak a liberty that I hope ye winna resent, for ye're a
scholar yersell, and ye'll ken what Theopompis answert whan
he was askit hou a king micht best rule his realm. He said, 'By
grantin liberty to ony man that luves to tell him the truith'. Yer
Grace, I'm gaun to tell ye the truith nou. Ye hae brocht aa yer
troubles on yersell by yer ill choice o freinds. Ye hae spent yer
days wi idolators, and offendit the maist o yer subjects. Nae
king can afford to dae that, for as Plutarch said to the Emperor
Trajan, 'Gin yer government daesna answer the expectation o
yer people, ye maun be subject to mony dangers'.

THE KING: Mebbe ye dinna mind, Sir Jamie, what the Senate
o Rome said to Trajan?

MELVILLE: I can think o naething that's contrar to my drift.

THE KING: Weill, Sir Jamie, it's a peety, for it telt him to be
'sparin o speeches'. Haha, eh! Man ye can be gey dreich. (*There
is another knock at the door of the audience-chamber. The Lords rise
again*) Guid God, wha's there nou? The chalmer's that fou we'll
sune no hae room to draw a braith. (*The* EARL OF MORTON
enters) What's wrang, Morton?

(MORTON *bows to the* KING *but addresses* BOTHWELL)

MORTON: My Lord, I couldna bide ootbye anither meenit. The
Danish Ambassadors are growin oot of haund. They hae heard
the steer and think her Grace is in peril.

BOTHWELL: Whaur are they?

MORTON: Lockit in their chalmers. They hae been jabberin awa
in Danish for the last hauf hour. They're tryin to ding the doors
doun nou.

THE QUEEN: (*rising*) I will gang.

BOTHWELL: Ye micht, yer Grace. Sir Jamie, wad ye like to
escort her? My Lord Lennox canna leave us yet.

MELVILLE: (*as* LENNOX *bridles up in anger*) I'm aye at her
Grace's service.

(*He bows stiffly to the* KING, *offers his arm to the* QUEEN *and escorts her from the room. All bow as she leaves except the* KING)

BOTHWELL: My Lord Morton, ye'd better bide. Nou that his Grace has heard Sir Jamie he'll be in a proper mind to settle his affairs.

THE KING: Ye're aa gaun to settle them for me, it seems, sae juist gae straucht aheid. I'm gaun for my breakfast.

BOTHWELL: (*intercepting him*) Ye can hae yer breakfast whan we hae come to tairms! There are folk waitin ootbye to ken what's what!

THE KING: Aa richt, then. Oot wi yer proposals. But mind that onything ye settle here'll need the ratification o my Cooncil or the three Estates.

BOTHWELL: Colville, hae ye that document?

COLVILLE: Ay, my Lord.

BOTHWELL: Read it oot, then.

LENNOX: What document's this?

BOTHWELL: It's a list o the tairms o the agreement we're gaun to mak wi his Grace.

LENNOX: It wasna shown to us!

BOTHWELL: Ye'll hae yer chance nou to discuss it. Richt, John.

COLVILLE: (*reading from a parchment*) We that are here assembled propose that his Grace suld set his haund to the articles herein subscribed:

  Ane: That remission be grantit to Bothwell, his freinds and pairt-takers, for all attempts against his Grace's person in ony bygaen time, and promise made never to pursue him or his foresaids for ony bypast fact, as likewise to repossess them in their lands and hooses.

THE KING: What aboot the blaggard's trial for witchcraft? Has he to be gien back his grun if he's foun guilty?

BOTHWELL: That's a different maitter! This concerns oor attempts against yer person. It'll mak shair that whan I'm cleared o witchcraft there'll be nae trials for treason.

THE KING: Whan ye're cleared! Ye winna be cleared, I tell ye! Ye'll be brunt at the stake!

BOTHWELL: We'll see whan the time comes!

THE KING: It'll hae to come sune! Ye'll hae to staun yer trial afore I sign this!

BOTHWELL: I'm gaun to staun my trial at ance! Gin I'm foun guilty ye can teir this up.

THE KING: Dae ye hear him, the rest o ye! He's gien his promise!

OCHILTREE: He gied his promise afore we brocht him in, yer Grace.

THE KING: (*obviously pleased*) Oho, sae that's the wey o't. Weill weill. Gae on wi yer rigmarole, Colville. Wha wrote it for ye, for it's nae lawyer's job?

COLVILLE: I wrote it mysell!

THE KING: I thocht as muckle.

BOTHWELL: Come on, then.

COLVILLE: Twa: That the Three Estates suld be summoned to meet in November, and an act passed in his and their favours for their greater security.

THE KING: 'His and their favours.' Wha dae ye mean?

COLVILLE: Bothwell's and his foresaids.

THE KING: And wha are his foresaids?

COLVILLE: It means me.

THE KING: Juist that. (*To the others, drily*) It means himsell. G'on, then.

COLVILLE: Three: That during that time,

THE KING: What time?

COLVILLE: (*furiously*) The time atween nou and the paurliament in November!

THE KING: Ye suld hae said sae. Weill?

COLVILLE: That during that time his Grace suld banish from his praisence the Chancellor, the Maister of Glamis, the Lord Hume and Sir George Hume, and likewise ony that belang to their faction.

THE KING: Oho, ye deil, I see nou what ye're efter! Ye're gaun to staun yer trial at ance because ye'll hae the Coort o Session fou o yer ain men!

BOTHWELL: Better that nor fou of the chancellor's men!

THE KING: Ye sleekit scoondrel! Gin they dinna fin ye guilty they'll mak a mockery o justice!

OCHILTREE: We'll see that the trial's a straucht ane, yer Grace!

THE KING: Ye'll be useless, I tell ye! Ye'er in the blaggard's haunds!

BOTHWELL: We haena the haill day to waste! Gae on wi the readin, Colville!

THE KING: Ay ay, let's hear the rest.

COLVILLE: Fower: that frae henceforth the Earl of Bothwell, his freinds and pairt-takers, suld be esteemed as guid and lawfou subjects, and shown sic favour as if they had never offendit.

THE KING: Lawfou subjects! God, it's lauchable. And what else?

COLVILLE: That's aa there is.

LENNOX: What!

ATHOLL: Guid God!

OCHILTREE: What aboot the murder o the Bonnie Earl?

BRUCE: What aboot the Kirk and the Spanish plots?

THE KING: I telt ye he didnae care a rap for the rest o ye!

BOTHWELL: Gin ye'll juist listen, my lords and gentlemen.

THE KING: Ay ay, leave me oot! I dinna coont!

BOTHWELL: Oh haud yer tongue! Gin ye'll juist listen, ye'll see that aa the ither maitters follow frae the anes set doun in Colville's document. I haud the Palace. Ilka gaird in it now's a proved servant o my ain. I haud the Toun tae. I hae it bristlin wi fower hunder men frae the Borders. But for the sake o savin his Grace's face and preservin the dignity o the Croun I maun hae my paurdon cried at the Cross. Agree to that, my Lords, and I'll help ye to keep the Chancellor's faction frae the Coort. Ye'll be able to dae what ye like then.

LENNOX: Ay ay, my Lord, but there's naething o that in yer document! Hou can we be shair that ye'll support us? Oor wants suld be doun in writin tae!

BOTHWELL: Shairly that's a maitter for yersells. There's naething to hinder ye frae drawin oot yer ain tairms whan ye like. But my paurdon comes first. The folk o the Toun ken I'm here. Gin they dinna hear that I'm paurdont they'll be restless and ye'll hae nae hope o a quait settlement.

LENNOX: I wish I could trust ye.

BOTHWELL: Ye'll hae to. What has my reverent freind o the Kirk to say?

BRUCE: I dout I maun consult my colleagues ootbye.

BOTHWELL: The suner ye dae it the better, then.

THE KING: Guid God, hae I to be keepit here aa mornin! I'm stervin, I tell ye!

BOTHWELL: Sterve for a while langer! What dae the Bailies say?

NICOLL: I dout we maun consult oor colleagues tae.

MORTON: I dout sae.

THE KING: Awa and dae it, then, and gar them agree sune, for Francie's richt, deil and aa as he is. The suner the folk are pacified the better. They maun believe I'm reconciled to the blaggard, or they'll think he's forced my haund. Lennox, ye'll see that they're sent hame frae the Abbey Kirkyaird. Let them ken there'll be a proclamation at the Cross the morn. Nou awa oot o here, the haill damt lot o ye! I maun fin my shune and gang for something to eat. I'm sae sair hungert I wad sell my sowl for a bowl o parritch!

BOTHWELL: Yer grace, ye hae juist been saved withoot skaith frae serious jeopardy! I wadna be sae flippant!

THE KING: Gae oot o my sicht, see!

(LENNOX *leaves the chamber.* BRUCE *bows stiffly and follows him. All but* BOTHWELL *proceed to do likewise.* MORTON *is last. As he makes his bow the* KING *addresses him*)

THE KING: Morton, the gentlemen o my chalmer are aa thrang daein Bothwell's wark, sae ye'll mebbe bide and help me to settle my domestic maitters. Francie, *ye* needna bide. I hae seen eneugh o ye this mornin.

BOTHWELL: I had hoped for a bit crack wi ye, yer Grace. I haena seen ye for a lang time.

THE KING: Ye can see me efter I hae haen my meat!

BOTHWELL: Very weill, yer Grace.

(*He bows elaborately*)

THE KING: Awa, ye hypocrite.

(BOTHWELL *leaves*)

THE KING: Morton, ye were on gaird in the coortyaird. Did ye see ocht o Sir Robert Bowes?

MORTON: Na, yer Grace.

THE KING: He hasna been doun frae the Toun, then!

MORTON: No that I ken o.

THE KING: The auld tod's lyin low. Gin he hadna a haund in this mornin's wark I'm nae judge o villains. We'll see hou sune he shows his face. Nou what aboot yersell? I thocht I could coont aye on loyalty frae ye. What turnt the like o ye against me?

MORTON: The murder o the Bonnie Earl.

THE KING: Tach, the Bonnie Earl, he's been deid thir twa years.

MORTON: I was a freind o his faither's.

THE KING: Aa richt, then, dinna stert. Awa and see aboot my breakfast.

(MORTON *bows and leaves. The* KING *who is still in his stocking soles, goes into his dressing-closet. As he does so a pretty fair girl of about sixteen enters by the* QUEEN's *door. She pauses, listening and looking around, as though searching for someone. The* KING *enters with his shoes in his hand*)

THE GIRL: I thocht I heard my faither.

THE KING: Yer faither?

THE GIRL: The Lord Morton.

THE KING: And what are ye daein here?

THE GIRL: I'm a new leddy-in-waitin to the Queen. I cam to tak the place o the Danish leddy that ran awa to mairry the Laird Logie whan he brak oot o jeyl.

THE KING: I see. And whan did ye come?

THE GIRL: Last nicht. And I didna sleep a wink wi aa the comin and gaun in the Queen's chalmer, and this mornin there was a maist awesome steer, and sic a dingin and bangin on doors

wi mells and hammers, and sic a clashin o swords and firin o
pistols as I neir heard in aa my life afore, and I could fin nae
ane to look efter me, and was sae sair frichtent I could hae grat.
I dae sae wish that I could fin my faither.

THE KING: Did he ken ye were comin last nicht?

THE GIRL: Na, for when we cam til the Toun yestrein my mither
gaed to speir for him at his ludgin, and he hadna been near it
for twa days.

THE KING: He wad be awa on some errand for the King, likely.

THE GIRL: Ay, mebbe.

THE KING: Or for the Earl o Bothwell?

THE GIRL: Weill, I dinna ken. Mebbe he was.

THE KING: He wasna a loyal man for the King, then, aye?

THE GIRL: Na, he said the King was whiles ill coonselt.

THE KING: Ye haena seen the King?

THE GIRL: Na.

THE KING: Ye'll hae heard aboot him, though?

THE GIRL: Oh ay.

THE KING: And what hae ye heard?

THE GIRL: That he's faur frae braw, and weirs the maist horrid
auld claes. And he's a gey glutton, and sweirs and drinks ower
muckle. But he's a great scholar and writes poetry.

THE KING: Ye'll no hae heard ony o his poetry?

THE GIRL: Oh ay. My mither said that gin I were to gang til the
Coort I suld ken the King's poetry. I hae some o his sonnets
aff by hairt.[10]

THE KING: And what dae ye think o them?

THE GIRL: Ah weill, they're ower clever for me. They're fou o
pagan gods I neir heard tell o.

THE KING: He'll mebbe tell ye aa aboot them ae day himsell.
But yer faither gaed through that door no twa meenits syne.
He's awa to see aboot the King's breakfast.

THE GIRL: The King's breakfast?

THE KING: Ay. Tell him I'll be in for it as sune as I hae on my
shune.

THE GIRL: (*incredulously*) Are *ye* the King?

THE KING: Are ye disappeyntit?

THE GIRL: (*in an awed whisper*) Yer Grace.
(*She curtsies elaborately and steps backwards a few paces towards
the door of the audience-chamber*)
I didna ken.
(*She curtsies again and steps backwards to the door. With a fur-
ther final curtsy she backs out into the audience-chamber. The
KING stares after her and scratches his head*)

ACT THREE

*'The Kingis chalmer in the palace of Halyroudhous', Edinburgh,
XI August, 1593. Early morning.*

The KING's bed-chamber in Holyrood House. The window-
curtains are drawn close, but the curtains of the bed are open
and the bed-clothes undisturbed. A fire is burning, and there are
lit candles on the table.

The KING, cloaked and booted for travelling, is sitting writing.
He glances up now and again furtively, as though listening for
every sound.

Suddenly he appears to hear something from the direction of
the QUEEN's chamber. He rises silently from his chair and backs
away towards the door of the audience-chamber, concealing the
letter he has been writing. The QUEEN's door opens and the
Earl of Morton's daughter, wearing a cloak over her nightgown,
enters on tiptoe. She carries a shaded lantern. She closes the door
quietly. The KING comes forward to her. They speak softly.

THE KING: Did Lesley manage oot?
THE GIRL: I dinna ken yet. I took him doun to the covert causey,
    but he'll hae to bide there till the mune's daurkent afore he can
    cross the coortyaird. The gairds are aa on the alert.
THE KING: Guid God, I hope he'll manage through. He suldna
    hae left his horse in the stables. If he's catchit wi that letter
    they'll stop me tae. Is there nae word frae the ithers at aa yet?
THE GIRL: They're gaun to bring their horses to St Mary's
    Wynd. Ye hae to leave whan there's a rattle at the winnock.
    Ye maun gang through the Abbey Kirk nave and oot by the
    abbot's door, syne through the kirkyaird to the back yett. Twa
    o them'll meet ye there.
THE KING: Could they no hae met me nearer haund?
THE GIRL: Na. Ogilvy has to rattle at the winnock wi a haundfou
    o stanes, then mak for the wynd by the North Gairdens. He
    daesna want to tak the same gait as yersell in case he's seen.
THE KING: And what aboot the Erskines?
THE GIRL: Ane o them'll hae to haud the horses, and the ither
    twa hae the porter at the yett to deal wi.
THE KING: They micht hae foun some ither way. It'll be gey
    frichtsome crossin that kirkyaird in the daurk.
THE GIRL: It's faur frae daurk, yer Grace. It's that bricht
    wi the mune ye'll hae to hide gey low ahint the heid-
    stanes.

THE KING: (*shivering*) I wish it was aa ower. Is her Grace sleepin soun?

THE GIRL: Ay. Aa wad be as quait as the grave gin it werena for the gairds.

THE KING: Dinna mention graves! I'll see eneugh o them the nicht! Has there been nae steer frae Bothwell or the Lords?

THE GIRL: Na. They had sic a nicht wi the drams that they'll sleep till denner-time the morn.

THE KING: Aa richt, then. I hae a letter I maun feenish. Gae ower to the winnock and listen for the rattle. Will it come sune?

THE GIRL: As sune as Ogilvy kens they hae the horses there.

THE KING: Listen weill, then and be as quait as ye can.

(*The GIRL placing her lantern on the floor, goes to the window. The KING sits down again and goes on with his letter. As he concludes it and is drying the ink the clock on the Canongait steeple strikes three. Both start at the first note*)

THE KING: That's three. They're late.

(*Immediately he has spoken there is a faint commotion from somewhere beyond the interior of the Palace*)

THE KING: What's that?

THE GIRL: (*rushing over to him on tiptoe*) It's frae the ither end o the coortyaird!

THE KING: It maun be Lesley!

THE GIRL: Oh what a shame!

THE KING: The thowless gommeril! Wheesht!

(*The commotion continues. There are a few distant shouts and sounds of people running backwards and forwards. Suddenly there is a rattle of stones on the window*)

THE GIRL: (*excitedly and rather loudly*) That's Ogilvy!

THE KING: (*picking up his letter quickly*) I'll hae them dished yet! Come on!

(*The GIRL picks up the lantern and moves with the KING quickly to the QUEEN's door. Voices are heard suddenly from the QUEEN's chamber*)

THE GIRL: She's wauken!

THE KING: Guid God almichty! (*Pulling her back from the QUEEN's door*) Sh! Oh, what'll I dae?

THE GIRL: Try the ither door! Ye micht win through!

THE KING: It's ower weill gairdit, I tell ye!

THE GIRL: (*hurrying over to the door of the audience-chamber*) It's yer ae chance! Hurry! She micht come in!

(*Voices are heard again from the QUEEN's chamber. The KING hurries over beside her*) Tak ye the lantern! I'll bide here!

(*She gives him the lantern and opens the door. More stones*) *rattle on the window*) There's the rattle again. Oh, man, hurry!

(*The* KING *hurries out nervously. The* GIRL *closes the door quietly, looks anxiously at the* QUEEN'*s door, hesitates, blows out the candles and goes behind the window-curtains. The* QUEEN *enters with* LADY ATHOLL. *Both have cloaks over their nightgowns and the* QUEEN *carries a candle*)

THE QUEEN: The bed! It is toom! He is gaen!

LADY A: I'm share I heard him.

THE QUEEN: And wha else? He daesna speak wi himsell! Look for the Earl Morton his dochter! See if she sleep!

(LADY ATHOLL *hurries out again. The* QUEEN *goes to the door of the dressing-closet, holds up the candle and looks in. There is a knock at the door of the audience-chamber*)

THE QUEEN: (*turning*) Come in.

(SIR JAMES MELVILLE *enters wearing a long nightgown and cowl. He carries a candle*)

MELVILLE: Paurdon me, yer Grace, but I wonert if his Grace was safe. There's been a steer in the coortyaird.

THE QUEEN: The bed! See! He is awa!

MELVILLE: Awa! But whaur can he be?

THE QUEEN: I want to fin oot!

(LADY ATHOLL *enters*)

LADY A: Morton's dochter's gaen tae! She isna in her bed!

THE QUEEN: I kent it! He luve her!

LADY A: But whaur are they?

THE QUEEN: They hide! Ablow the bed! Look!

LADY A: But there was a steer in the coortyaird! They maun hae gaen oot!

THE QUEEN: Sir Jamie! Look ablow the bed!

(SIR JAMES *goes down on his knees to look below the bed. Two pistol shots are heard from beyond the window*)

THE QUEEN: (*looking towards the window*) They bang pistols!

(SIR JAMES *rises quickly from his knees.* LADY ATHOLL *rushes over and draws the curtains from the window. Bright moonlight reveals the* GIRL)

LADY A: (*startled*) Oh!

THE QUEEN: Aha! She is foun! Come oot!

(*The* GIRL *steps forward*)

THE QUEEN: Whaur is his Grace?

THE GIRL: I dinna ken.

THE QUEEN: Sir Jamie? Hae ye lookit?

MELVILLE: He isna there, yer Grace.

THE QUEEN: (*to the* GIRL) Whaur has he gaen?

THE GIRL: I dinna ken.

THE QUEEN: Ye dae ken! Ye lee! Whaur has he gaen? The Queen speirs! Answer!

THE GIRL: I winna!

THE QUEEN: Oho! Ye winna! I will hae ye in the jougs! I will hae ye tied to the Tron! I will hae yer lugs cut aff.

MELVILLE: Yer Grace,

THE QUEEN: Be quait! I speir! I maun be answert! Whaur has he gaen?

MELVILLE: There's mair noise ootbye!

> (*There is some shouting from beyond the audience-chamber. All turn to listen. As they do so the* KING *enters, facing outwards, and closes the door quickly. He turns round to mop his brow and draw a breath of relief, and becomes aware of the others*)

THE QUEEN: Aha! Ye are here! Ye are catchit!

MELVILLE: What's wrang, yer Grace?

THE QUEEN: It is for me to speir!

THE KING: (*in an intense whisper*) Awa to yer bed and leave me alane!

THE QUEEN: I bide till I hear aa! I will hae it oot! (*Pointing to the* GIRL) She hide ahint yer curtains! I hear her speak! I hear ye baith speak whan I wauken! What daes she dae in here?

THE KING: (*still whispering, almost pleadingly*) Dinna shout and wauken the haill Palace!

THE QUEEN: Na! Let nane ken that the King his Grace is catchit wi ane o the Queen's leddies! The Preachers micht ding bang on their big books! They micht peynt fingers!

MELVILLE: (*soothingly*) Ye'd better explain yersell, yer Grace.

THE KING: (*still keeping his voice low*) Haud ye yer tongue! Ye're doitit! The lassie's young eneugh to be my dochter! She was helpin me in maitters o state!

THE QUEEN: Maitters o state! Yer dochter! Huh!

THE KING: (*losing his temper and raising his voice*) Awa to yer beds when ye're telt! I'm no gaun to be talked to like a bairn! What dae ye think I'm daein wi my ootdoor claes on? Daes it look as if I'm up to ony o yer Lennox ploys? I'm gaun to Falkland, I tell ye! I'm gaun to win my freedom!

THE QUEEN: Ye were for takin her!

THE KING: Dinna be stippit! She's in her nichtgoun!

THE QUEEN: She is here and no in bed!

THE KING: She was helpin me to win my wey oot!

THE QUEEN: Ye canna fin yer ain wey oot! Ye need help frae a new lassie! It is lees! She is wi ye aye! She is here afore! I hear souns in the nicht ower and ower again! I thocht! I ken

nou! (*Almost weeping*) O Sir Jamie, I am wranged! He shame
me! The folk! They will talk! They will sing sangs! (*Turning
suddenly on the* GIRL) Awa! Awa or I will claw yer een oot! I
will teir aff yer hair! I will scratch!

(*She rushes towards the* GIRL, *who retreats behind the* KING)

THE KING: Leave her alane! Rin, lass!

(*The* GIRL *hurries out by the* QUEEN's *door. The* KING
intercepts the QUEEN *by holding her with his free hand*)

THE QUEEN: Let me past!

THE KING: (*swinging his lantern threateningly*) Haud aff, see!

THE QUEEN: (*retreating*) Oh ye blaggard, ye wad ding me wi
yer licht!

THE KING: Staun at peace, then!

THE QUEEN: Oh ye are hairtless! Ye dinna care if I am hurt! Ye
say to me like dirt! Ye gar me staun at peace as if I am a cuddy!
(*Turning sobbingly to* SIR JAMES *for comfort*) Oh Sir Jamie, it is
the hin end! He luve her mair nor me!

MELVILLE: (*taking her in his arms. To the* KING) Yer Grace, ye
hae gaun ower faur!

THE KING: Tak her awa oot o here.

MELVILLE: Man, ye wadna talk like that gin ye kent o her
condeetion! It's time yer een were opened! (*To* LADY ATHOLL)
My Leddy, tak her Grace til her bed. Gae awa nou, yer Grace,
and hae a guid greit. Ye're sair ower wrocht.

THE QUEEN: Oh I am dune!

MELVILLE: Ay ay, yer Grace, that's richt, my Leddy. Tak her
awa.

LADY A: (*leading the* QUEEN *out*) Come nou, yer Grace.

(*The* QUEEN, *still sobbing, leaves with* LADY ATHOLL)

THE KING: (*puzzled by* MELVILLE's *manner*) What's come ower
ye?

MELVILLE: (*going to the table*) We'll licht the caunles, I think. I
maun hae a talk wi ye.

THE KING: Leave the caunles alane! The curtains are open!
(*Putting his lantern on the table and rushing over to draw the
curtains*) Damn it, ye'll sune hae the haill Palace doun on us!
What's come ower ye, I'm askin?

MELVILLE: (*lighting the candles*) We'll win faurer, yer Grace,
gin ye'll juist calm yersell and sit doun. I hae something to tell
ye that'll hae a maist momentous effect on yer poseetion as a
monarch. Something, I micht venture to say, that'll cheynge
the poleetical situation in ilka realm o Christendom.

THE KING: Eh?

MELVILLE: Sit doun (*The* KING, *as though hypnotised, sits on the chair beside the bed*) Yer Grace, ye'll ken I play my pairt in the affairs o the Coort wi dignity and reserve, and haud mysell aloof frae the clavers o the kitchen and the tittle-tattle o the Queen's leddies, but in my poseetion as heid gentleman o her Grace's chalmer there's mony a private maitter comes to my notice that I canna athegither ignore, though I hope I keep aye in mind the fact that my poseetion's preeviliged, and gaird ilka secret mair nor it were my ain. Nou if her Grace and yersell enjoyed the intimacy and mutual affection that belang o richt to the holy state o matrimony I wad be spared my praisent predeecament, for nae dout she wad be gey prood to tell ye o the maitter hersell, but to the sorrow o yer subjects ye hae baith gaen the gait that leads to dout and suspeecion, and there's a brek atween ye that can only be mendit by an auld servant like mysell. Yer Grace, I'm gaun to tell ye something that suld gar ye sweir anew the solemn vows ye took at yer nuptials, something that suld gar ye turn again to the bonnie lass ye brocht wi ye frae Denmark, whan yer hairt was lichter nor it is nou, and yer ee was bricht wi luve.

THE KING: (*intensely excited*) Sir Jamie! Is it a bairn?

MELVILLE: Yer Grace, ye may lippen for an heir in the coorse o the comin year.

THE KING: (*soberly*) It's what I hae hoped for wi aa my hairt. (*Pause*) But I'm sair bothert wi douts, Sir Jamie. (*Bitterly*) If I could juist be shair I'll be the faither!

MELVILLE: Yer Grace!

THE KING: Dinna be an auld wife! Ye ken as weill as mysell that the bairn micht belang to Lennox!

MELVILLE: That's juist whaur ye're wrang, yer Grace! I ken it's yer ain!

THE KING: Hou i' the Deil's name can ye ken that?

MELVILLE: Juist listen weill and I'll explain. It taks a lang experience o life, yer Grace, to gie a man a knowledge o human nature, and in that respect I hae the better o ye.

THE KING: Ay ay, ye're auld eneugh to be my faither! I ken that!

MELVILLE: Juist that, yer Grace, but I was young ance, and in my early days I had mony an opportunity for insicht that daesna come the wey o maist men, parteecularly in regaird to the weys o weemen, for was I no ambassador frae yer mither to her Majesty in England?

THE KING: Ye're tellin me naethin I dinna ken! Come to the peynt! Hou dae ye ken the bairn'll be mine?

MELVILLE: I'll tell ye gin ye'll juist hae patience.

THE KING: Hou can I hae patience? I hae tried to leave and couldna win past the gairds, and my friends ootbye hae been catchit! Bothwell'll be in ony meenit! Hou dae ye ken the bairn'll be mine, I'm askin?

MELVILLE: Weill, yer Grace, I'll come to the peynt, but it's a gey kittle maitter to explain in juist ae word.

THE KING: For God's sake try yer best! Oot wi't?

MELVILLE: Ye see, whan her Grace fand Morton's dochter in yer chalmer here she was gey upset.

THE KING: And what aboot it?

MELVILLE: Weill, yer Grace, hae ye eir afore kent her flee intil sic a rage as she did at that lassie, or rack her bonnie breist wi sic mains and sabs? There was mair nor her pride hurt. (*With great point*) She was jealous! Nou think, yer Grace. Wad she hae felt like that gin she hadna kent ye were the faither o her bairn?

THE KING: (*after a long pause, reflectively*) Ye're richt, Sir Jamie. Ye're richt. I see it nou. (*Contritely*) Puir sowl, I haena been guid to her. Nae woner she turnt against me. She gaed daffin wi some o the Lords, mebbe, but then she was neglecktit. I didna pey her eneugh attention.

MELVILLE: And a bonnie lass, yer Grace, lippens aye for attention.

THE KING: Sir Jamie, I sweir I'll mak amends. I'll stert aa ower again. I'll coort her like a laddie. (*Pause*) But I'm ower sair beset the nou. I'm hemmed in wi faes. I can hae nae peace till I win my freedom.

MELVILLE: Ye'll win yer freedom, yer Grace, whan ye show that ye hae nae mair thocht o haein traffic wi the Papists.

THE KING: Wha eir thocht o haein traffic wi the Papists? I'm soond in doctrine. I wadna thole the Papists for a meenit gin they werena my ae hope against Bothwell!

MELVILLE: Naen o the Lords wad hae jeynt wi Bothwell gin ye had keepit the Papists at airm's length frae the stert!

THE KING: Havers! Hauf o them jeynt because o their spite at the Chancellor!

MELVILLE: And had they no just cause? Did the Chancellor no wrang the Bonnie Earl? (*More meaningly*) And has he no wranged my Lord Lennox and her Grace?

THE KING: I dinna ken, Sir Jamie. I woner.

MELVILLE: He filled yer heid wi lees aboot them.

THE KING: Sir Jamie, I had soond gruns for my suspeecion, I hae seen them thegither in mony a compromisin poseetion.

MELVILLE: Ye were neglectin her, yer Grace. She maun hae led him on juist to anger ye.

THE KING: That was nae excuse for him! He was gey eager to be led!

MELVILLE: Let me ask ye this, yer Grace. Hae ye eir foun my Lord Lennox in her Grace's chalmer in the middle o the nicht?

THE KING: Eh!

MELVILLE: I dout there are soond gruns for suspeecion on mair sides nor ane, yer Grace.

THE KING: Sir Jamie, I sweir there's naething in it. The lass was helpin me to win my wey past the gairds. I haena gien her a thocht.

MELVILLE: Yer Grace, gin ye ettle folk to gie a generous interpretation to yer ain ploys, ye maun be ready to be generous yersell.

THE KING: (*diplomatically*) Ye're richt, Sir Jamie. Ye're richt. I maun be generous. I'll mak amends. Listen. The Palace seems quait again, but the steer canna hae blawn ower. Bothwell winna be lang. Dae ye think ye could win at Lodovick withoot bein seen? Try to win him roun. Tell him that I ken I hae wranged him. Say I'll dae aa in my pouer to win back his freindship. Ask him to come in.

MELVILLE: I'll try, yer Grace.

THE KING: Haud on, though, I hae thocht o something else. Yer news has gien me hairt. Dae ye no see? It'll strengthen my poseetion in regaird to the English Croun. What the English want, Sir Jamie, efter aa thae years o wonerin whaur to turn in the event o their Queen's daith, is a settled succession. They'll hae that nou gin they hae me.

MELVILLE: They'll hae to be shair that baith King and heir are soond in releegion, yer Grace.

THE KING: Hae nae fear o that, Sir Jamie. Ance I can redd mysell o Bothwell I'll win my wey clear o the Papists. Man, I wad dearly luve to see her English Majesty's face whan she hears what ye hae telt me the nicht. It'll be a bitter dose for her to swallow, that's a barren stock hersell. Whan ye hae waukent Lodovick, Sir Jamie, try to win through to Sir Robert Bowes. I wad sweir he's been in tow wi Bothwell, but I neir thocht till this meenit to challenge him till his face. He winna daur acknowledge it. He'll hae to tak my side. And I'll mebbe gie him a hint o hou the wind blaws. Man, that wad tickle him up.

MELVILLE: It wad be a queer time i' the mornin, yer Grace, to inform a foreign ambassador that there's an heir on the wey.

THE KING: I want Sir Robert here! I want to play him against

Bothwell! Awa and fetch him whan ye're telt! (*Suddenly*) What's that!

(*A guard beyond the door of the audience-chamber has been heard making a challenge*)

MELVILLE: It soondit like a challenge frae ane o the gairds!

THE KING: It's Bothwell nou! Hurry oot! Gae through the Queen's chalmer!

MELVILLE: But I'll hae to gang the ither wey to win at my claes!

THE KING: Dae withoot yer claes! It canna be helpit! Lodovick'll lend ye something! (*He opens the door of the* QUEEN'*s chamber*) Hurry!

(SIR JAMES *goes into the* QUEEN'*s chamber. There is a scream, then a sound of voices, then silence as the* KING *closes the door. He hurriedly removes his cloak and seats himself in the chair beside the bed. The door of the audience-chamber opens and* BOTHWELL *appears, incompletely dressed, and carrying two letters*)

BOTHWELL: (*as he opens the door*) He's here. Haud ye the door, Atholl, and keep Colville quait. (*Turning into the chamber*) Ay ay, yer Grace, sae ye're haein a quait sit-doun by the fire. Wad ye no feel mair at ease wi yer buits aff?

THE KING: I didna hear ye chappin.

BOTHWELL: I had thocht frae thir twa letters that ye micht be weill on yer wey to Falkland.

THE KING: (*restraining a motion of his hand towards the inside of his doublet*) What twa letters?

BOTHWELL: Ane directit to my Lord Hume, that was taen frae Lesley in the coortyaird. The ither directit to my Lord Huntly, that was foun at the end o the ither chalmer. Ye let it drap, nae dout, whan ye were frichtent by the gairds.

THE KING: Sae ye hae read them?

BOTHWELL: I canna deny it, and what I hae read reflects on yer Grace's honour. Ye're for slippin awa, are ye, withoot setting yer haund to oor agreement?

THE KING: What's to hinder me frae gaun nou? Ye hae gotten what ye wantit! Ye hae frichtent the Coort of Session into lettin ye gang skaithless for aa yer North Berwick ploys!

BOTHWELL: I stude my trial and was cleared!

THE KING: Trial! It was nae trial! It was naething but perjury frae stert to feenish! There wasna a lawyer or a witness that wisna feart to speak against ye! Ye had men airmed to the teeth in ilka close in the Hie Gait! The Tolbooth was like an airmed camp!

BOTHWELL: The case was focht on its merits! Craig my coonsel tore the chairge to shreds!

THE KING: The Prosecution wasna free to speak oot, or Craig wad hae been flummoxed on ilka peynt he raised! The gowk havert the maist illogical nonsense I eir heard in aa my life! Him and his Uvierus! Wha was Uvierus to be coontit an authority? A doctor wha maintained the auld error o the Sadducees in denying the existence o speerits! Uvierus, forsooth! I could hae quotit some authorities! What aboot the Daemonomanie o Bodinus, that's fou o witches' confessions? What aboot the fowerth book of Cornelius Agrippa, that's fou o descriptions o their rites and curiosities? What aboot Hemmingius and Hyperius, that gie ye accoonts o ilka black airt there is, dividit into the fower heids o Magic. Necromoncy, Sorcery and Witchcraft? And yer coonsel had the impiddence to deny speerits athegither, and say that witchcraft was a delusion in the minds o crazed auld weemen! But by God wait! I'm writin a book mysell, and I'll tak gey guid care to controvert him on ilka peynt he pat forrit!

BOTHWELL: I dout yer book'll be ower late to mak ony difference to yesterday's verdict.

THE KING: Verdict! It gars my bluid beyl! Ritchie Graham suld neir hae been brunt! He suld hae been keepit in the Castle jeyl till yer ain trial was ower! He wad hae damned ye!

BOTHWELL: His evidence was brocht forrit!

THE KING: It hadna been taen doun richt! It was aa muddlet! He suld hae been there to clear up aa the obscurities!

BOTHWELL: Weill, yer Grace, it was yer ain coort that brunt him.

THE KING: It suld hae brunt ye tae! Ye're a plague! Ye hae been a constant terror to the country sin ye first brak oot o jeyl! Certies, but yer witchcraft has led ye a bonnie dance! Ye wad neir hae been in bother at aa gin ye had left it weill alane!

BOTHWELL: I hae been cleared, damn ye!

THE KING: Ye tried to hae me drount, I tell ye! Ye tried to pousin me! And for what, Francie? For what? Did the pouer ye had on the Cooncil whan I was in Denmark wi the chancellor gang til yer heid? Did ye think that gin I hadna come back ye wad hae it aa yer ain wey? Ye're a cauld-bluidit, schemin ambeetious scoondrel!

BOTHWELL: (*angrily, with his hands on his hilt*) Dinna let yer tongue cairry ye awa wi it!

THE KING: Tak yer haund frae yer hilt, man! Yer threats cairry nae terrors nou! I ken juist hou faur ye can gang! What hae ye dune wi Lesley and the Erskines? What's happened to Ogilvy? Gin they hae come to hairm I'll gar ye suffer!

BOTHWELL: They're lockit up!

THE KING: Then ye'll let them gang! It's nae crime to be loyal to yer King!

BOTHWELL: They haena been loyal to me!

THE KING: And wha are ye to demand loyalty? Ye mebbe haena been foun guilty, but ye arena an anointit King! I'm gaun to Falkland, I tell ye, and ye hae nae richt to stop me!

BOTHWELL: I hae a richt to stop ye till ye hae signed oor agreement! I was to be paurdont for treason gin I was acquitit o witchcraft!

THE KING: Ye promised if ye were acquitit to bide awa frae the Coort!

BOTHWELL: If I was gien my grun back! And if the Bonnie Earl's murder was avenged!

THE KING: Ye deil, ye mean to stey for ever!

BOTHWELL: I'll stey till then!

THE KING: We'll see what the ithers hae to say aboot that!

BOTHWELL: We'll see what they say aboot thir twa letters!

THE KING: God, ye're the Deil himsell!

(ATHOLL *enters hurriedly*)

ATHOLL: (*to* BOTHWELL) Lennox is here!

BOTHWELL: Eh!

THE KING: Fetch him in! Fetch him in, I tell ye!

(LENNOX *appears as he speaks.* COLVILLE, *very drunk, staggers in behind him*).

BOTHWELL: (*to* ATHOLL, *who looks to him for guidance*) Let him be. Bide ye ootbye, Colville!

COLVILLE: I want to hear watsh gaun on.

BOTHWELL: Pitch him oot, Atholl.

COLVILLE: (*to the* KING *as* ATHOLL *grips him*) Hang the Papists!

(ATHOLL *heaves him out. He then closes the door, remaining on guard, but inside*)

LENNOX: (*ignoring* BOTHWELL *and turning to the* KING) Yer Grace, I heard a steer in the coortyaird and made haste to dress mysell. I thocht ye micht need me.

BOTHWELL: My Lord Duke,

LENNOX: I spak to his Grace!

THE KING: That's richt, Lodovick! Gar him keep his place! He's been staunin there talkin like God Almichty!

LENNOX: What is he daein here?

BOTHWELL: I'll tell ye, my Lord.

THE KING: Ye'll haud yer tongue! Lodovick, I had planned to gang to Falkland to win oot o his wey. Ane or twa o the loyal men in the Palace Gaird were gaun to meet me in St Mary's Wynd wi horses. I thocht it wad be better to slip awa withoot ony steer. I didna want ony bluidshed. But that blaggard fand oot! He winna let me leave!

LENNOX: (*to* BOTHWELL) Ye promised to leave his Grace alane gin ye were acquitit at yer trial!

BOTHWELL: He hasna signed the articles o remission! I was promised back my grun!

THE KING: He says he's gaun to stey till we avenge the Bonnie Earl!

LENNOX: Juist that! He has nae intention o leaving the Coort at aa! My Lord, ye needna think we're blin. Colville's ower fond o his dram to mak a guid conspeerator. He's been braggin o his appeyntment to the new Privy Cooncil!

THE KING: Eh!

LENNOX: He's to be yer Grace's new Lord Secretary!

THE KING: Guid God, the deil can haurdly put pen to pairchment!

BOTHWELL: He's as guid a clerk as ony at the Coort!

THE KING: He's an illeeterate ignoramous! And what's to be yer ain office, whan we're on the subject? Hae I to staun doun and offer ye *my* job?

LENNOX: He's to be Lord Lieutenant, wi Atholl as his depute!

THE KING: A bonnie mess they'd mak atween them! They'd be for herryin and reivin aa ower the country!

ATHOLL: We'd be for keepin yer promise to the Kirk and houndin doun the Papists!

THE KING: Ye'd be for grabbin aa the grun ye could lay yer haunds on! Wha dae ye think ye are, the pair o ye? Dae ye think that ilka Lord and Laird's gaun to staun bye and see the like o ye twa divide the haill country atween ye? There wad be wars, slauchters, spulzies and commotions whaur eir ye gied a tuck o the drum or a blaw o the trumpet! And wha wad pey for yer men? The Croun, think ye? What wad the Burghs hae to say to that? Dae ye think they're gaun to pey taxes to let ye twa rin aboot reivin?

ATHOLL: We'll hae the Kirk ahint us!

THE KING: What'll the kirk avail against the Lords and the Burghs? I tell ye, Francie, ye hae shot ower the mark! Ye suld hae been content wi remission! Ye micht hae gotten that!

BOTHWELL: Ye arena at Falkland yet, yer Grace!

THE KING: And wha'll gar me bide nou? The Toun, think ye, or the ither Lords? Lodovick, fin Ochiltree and Morton!

BOTHWELL: Haud on, my Lord! Ye dinna ken the haill story! Tak a look at thir twa letters.

(*He hands them towards* LENNOX)

THE KING: (*leaning forward and seizing them*) Gie them to me, ye blaggard!

BOTHWELL: Ye see, my Lord, he daesna want ye to ken their contents. They were for my Lords Huntly and Hume, nae less.

THE KING: And what wey no? Ye made a jeyl o my Palace! Had I nae richt to try and win oot? I wrote to the only freinds I thocht I had!

LENNOX: Yer Grace, I dinna blame ye.

BOTHWELL: By God, Lennox, ye hae turnt yer tabard!

LENNOX: I staun whaur I stude aye! I didna bring ye in to usurp royal authority!

BOTHWELL: Ye thocht ye micht usurp it yersell, nae dout!

LENNOX: I had nae thocht bune to save his Grace frae Maitland!

BOTHWELL: What aboot Maitland's freinds, the very men he's for jeynin wi at Falkland!

LENNOX: He needna jeyn them gin he can fin freinds nearer haund! Yer Grace, I'll fetch the ither Lords.

BOTHWELL: (*drawing*) Ye'll bide whaur ye are!

(LENNOX *is about to draw when he hears* ATHOLL *drawing also. He pauses with his hand on his hilt*)

THE KING: Ye murderin blaggards! Ye cut-throat scoondrels

(*There is a knock at the door of the audience-chamber. All turn. The door opens and* MELVILLE *enters, clad in night-gown, cloak and boots. He looks in alarm at* BOTHWELL *and* ATHOLL, *who hasten to sheathe their weapons*)

THE KING: Ye see, Sir Jamie, Ye're juist in time! They were for hackin Lodovick doun! Hae ye brocht Sir Robert Bowes?

MELVILLE: He'll be doun as sune as he can dress, yer Grace.

BOTHWELL: Eh! What gart ye gang for Sir Robert?

MELVILLE: I gaed at his Grace's order!

BOTHWELL: Ye auld meddler! Hou did ye pass the gairds?

MELVILLE: Yer gairds didna see me! They had been ower thrang in St Mary's Wynd! (MORTON *suddenly appears at the door of the audience-chamber and shouts to someone beyond*, 'They're here! Hurry!' *All turn and look towards him.* SIR JAMES *hastens to explain*) Yer Grace, I took the liberty, whan I cam in, to wauken the ither Lords.

(MORTON, *dressed in shirt and breeches, and carrying a naked sword, turns into the room*)

MORTON: What's gaun on?

THE KING: Come in, my Lord. I want ye.

MORTON: (*startled*) What's that!

> (*A sudden thump has been heard. All look towards the door. There are mutterings and exclamations and* OCHILTREE *enters, in shirt and breeches, holding his brow with one hand and his sword in the other*)

LENNOX: What's wrang wi ye?

OCHILTREE: Wha's been fechtin? There's a deid man oot there! I tummlet ower him!

THE KING: It's that deil Colville lyin drunk! Are ye hurt, my Lord?

OCHILTREE: (*rubbing his brow*) I gat a gey sair dunt.

THE KING: Ye'll hae to keep yer freinds in better order, Bothwell!

BOTHWELL: I'm no my brither's keeper!

THE KING: It was ye that brocht the blaggard here! (*To* OCHILTREE *and* MORTON) My Lords, he winna leave the Coort! He threatens to bide and tak office!

OCHILTREE: What! That was nae pairt o the bargain, my Lord.

BOTHWELL: It was! Ye brocht me in to avenge the Bonnie Earl!

OCHILTREE: Ye were brocht in to force his Grace's promise! Ye werena brocht in to cairry it oot!

BOTHWELL: And wha'll dae it gin I dinna bide? He'll rin back to the Papists at ance!

OCHILTREE: We hae his Grace's promise that he'll keep them frae the Coort!

BOTHWELL: He was for sneakin aff this very nicht to Falkland! He had written to Huntly and Hume!

OCHILTREE: I dinna believe it!

LENNOX: (*to* OCHILTREE) Ye canna blame him! He had to fin freinds somewhaur!

BOTHWELL: He promised to hae nae mair to dae wi the Papists!

LENNOX: He didna ken he was to hae nae freedom. He had yer ain promise to leave the Coort!

BOTHWELL: When I was paurdont and gien back my grun!

MORTON: Yer paurdon was cried at the Cross!

BOTHWELL: What guid will that dae if he ance slips through my fingers?

MORTON: Ye canna haud him in yer pouer aye! There maun be some respect for the Croun! Yer paurdon was promised afore witnesses! They'll mak shair ye're gien yer grun back!

BOTHWELL: They'll mak shair! By God it's likely! They'll be ower thrang featherin their ain nests!

OCHILTREE: My Lord, ye dae us wrang!

BOTHWELL: Ye ken I'm richt! (*To the others*) Ye wantit Maitland oot o the wey because his freinds had ower muckle pouer, but ye hadna the guts to force his Grace's haund yersells! Ye had to bring me in! And nou I hae dune it ye're for houndin me oot! Ye're feart that gin I bide I'll hae to share in the favours!

MORTON: Ye hae come oot o't gey weill, my Lord! Ye hae won yer acquittal!

BOTHWELL: Hae I to thank ye for that? I had to staun my trial for't!

MORTON: Ye were shair o the verdict! The Tolbooth was packed wi yer men.

BOTHWELL: By God it was juist as weill! There isna ane o ye wad hae liftit a finger to help me gin I had been foun guilty! Ye're a lot o sleekit, avareecious rats!

MORTON: (*gripping his sword fiercely*) Ye're gaun ower faur!

BOTHWELL: Ay ay, Morton, and ye're the warst o them! I ken what's gart ye cheynge yer tune! Ye lippen for his Grace's favour as the price o yer dochter!

MORTON: (*drawing*) Ye messan! Tak that back!

BOTHWELL: (*likewise*) Ye ken it's the truth!
    (*They start to fence*)

THE KING: (*keeping well out of danger*) Rin him through, Morton! Hack him to bits!

MELVILLE: Stop them!

ATHOLL: (*drawing*) Leave them alane!

LENNOX: (*turning on* ATHOLL) Staun ye back!

OCHILTREE: (*stepping over between* BOTHWELL *and* MORTON *and striking up their swords*) My Lords! Haud doun!
    (SPYNIE *enters hurriedly*)

SPYNIE: For God's sake quaiten doun! Here's Sir Robert Bowes!
    (*All attempt to look respectable*)

THE KING: Whaur is he?

SPYNIE: At the faur door o the ither chalmer. I could hear the steer.

THE KING: Will he hae heard it, think ye?

SPYNIE: I dout sae.

THE KING: Dear me. (*Pause*) Ay weill, bring him in. (SPYNIE *makes to leave*) And Spynie! (SPYNIE *turns in the doorway*) Watch he daesna trip ower Colville. He's lyin drunk at the door.

SPYNIE: Very weill, yer Grace.
    (*He leaves*)

MELVILLE: It's the wark o Providence. We micht aa hae been slauchtert.

THE KING: The credit's yer ain, Sir Jamie. It was ye wha gaed for him.

(SPYNIE *enters with* SIR ROBERT BOWES)

SPYNIE: (*bowing*) Sir Robert Bowes.

(*He leaves and closes the door*)

THE KING: I'm sorry to hae sent for ye at this time o the mornin, Sir Robert, but yer praisence is needit.

SIR ROBERT: (*bowing*) Your Majesty, it is indeed early, and the morning is cold. Your business must be urgent.

THE KING: It's treason, Sir Robert! Naething less! There are some here that wad usurp my authority! Bothwell here threatens to haud me in his pouer! He winna let me leave for Falkland!

SIR ROBERT: Indeed! My Lord Bothwell, I am astounded!

THE KING: Dinna let on to be astoundit at onything he daes! Weill ye ken he's been a terror to me for the last twa year! He raidit Falkland ance! He's raidit the Palace here twice! He cam intil my very chalmer a fortnicht syne wi his sword in his haund to gar me gie him back his grun! And nou he threatens to bide on and tak office!

SIR ROBERT: My Lord, you are ambitious! But surely, your Majesty, you can use your royal authority? Have you not power to send him to the gallows? Or do your Lords, too, turn traitor?

THE KING: To tell ye the truith, Sir Robert, it was the ither Lords that brocht him in.

SIR ROBERT: Your Majesty, I feared it. I have been aware, indeed, of the recent events at your Court, for I follow your fortunes closely, and I make bold to say that the pardon of an outlawed traitor, who hath violated the royal chamber and threatened the royal person, is an act that would be unheard of in an ordered Christian realm. It is an act, your Majesty, which the Queen my mistress, secure in her English Court, and accustomed to the obedience and devotion of her subjects, will hear of with profound amazement.

THE KING: Oh ay, Sir Robert, stert to craw. I could keep order tae gin I had the siller. She can afford to keep a guid gaird.

SIR ROBERT: Her ability to do so, your Majesty, may be due to her shrewdness in the administration of her revenues.

THE KING: It weill micht, Sir Robert! We ken she cuts gey close to the bane!

SIR ROBERT: I fear some insult!

THE KING: Ye needna tak offence, Sir Robert! Ye hae juist as muckle as said that I canna look efter my rents! And ye may fein astonishment at this blaggard's impiddence, and talk aboot yer royal mistress's amazement, but I'll hae ye understaun that

I hae my douts aboot baith her and yer ain guidwill in the maitter. Bothwell here gaed ower the Border when he was first put to the horn! He was alloued by yer royal mistress to gang skaithless! Is it richt, Sir Robert, for ae country to harbour anither's ootlaws?

SIR ROBERT: (*uneasily*) Your Majesty.

THE KING: Ye needna stert to hum and haw! Weill ye ken the deil was gien encouragement! I whiles woner if he wasna gien siller tae, for he keeps a bonnie band o airmed reivers weill filled wi meat and drink! I tell ye, Sir Robert, I winna staun it muckle langer! Yer royal mistress lets on to be freindly, but if aa the help she can gie me against traitors is to hae ye comin in crawin aboot the devotion o her English subjects I'll look for an alliance to some ither country!

SIR ROBERT: Your Majesty!

THE KING: I will, I tell ye! I'm a Protestant! I staun for Episcopacy![11] But suner nor hae my country dividit into factions and wastit wi feids I'll look for help to Spain and my Papist Lords!

MELVILLE: Yer Grace!

THE KING: Haud ye yer tongue! Sir Robert, what hae ye to say to that?

SIR ROBERT: I would ask, your Majesty, if such an alliance would be acceptable to your subjects. (*Cunningly*) Must I remind you of your present situation?

THE KING: (*as if deflated*) Deed, Sir Robert, ye're richt. I had forgotten. I was cairrit awa.

SIR ROBERT: Your Majesty, your outburst is forgiven. It was due, no doubt to your eagerness to excel in argument.

THE KING: Ye're richt again. I aye let my tongue rin awa wi me. Sir Robert, ye winna mention my lapse to her Majesty?

SIR ROBERT: You may rely on my discretion.

THE KING: Thank ye, Sir Robert. (*With a change of manner*) Weill, we haena gotten muckle faurer forrit.

SIR ROBERT: Your Majesty, if you will advise me of the matter in which you seek my guidance, I shall do what I can.

THE KING: Weill, Sir Robert, ye ken what happened a fornicht syne. I was set on by Bothwell and ane o his ootlawed freinds and the ither Lords stude bye them. Efter they had threatent me wi daith they brocht in the Bailies and the Preachers. I had to promise this blaggard his paurdon for treason gin he was acquitit for witchcraft.

BOTHWELL: Ye promised to avenge the murder o the Bonnie Earl and hound doun the Papists for the Spanish plots!

SIR ROBERT: (*soothingly*) My Lord, may I speak with his Majesty?

(BOTHWELL *and* SIR ROBERT *eye each other keenly*)

BOTHWELL: Very weill, Sir Robert.

SIR ROBERT: Your Majesty, I fail as yet to see the point at issue. You do intend, of course, to keep your promise?

THE KING: What wey should I? It was extortit!

SIR ROBERT: I sympathise. Your position was unfortunate. But your promise was given, and before representatives of your governing assembly. It will be to your credit to fulfil it.

THE KING: Nae dout, Sir Robert. Nae dout. But Bothwell promised to leave the Coort!

LENNOX: And he threatens to bide!

SIR ROBERT: My Lord!

BOTHWELL: The agreement hasna been signed yet! His Grace was for fleein to Falkland the nicht withoot haein dune it!

SIR ROBERT: But surely, my Lord, you can rely on your King's honour?

BOTHWELL: He had written to Huntly and Hume!

THE KING: I had to dae something to win my freedom! I wasna gaun to let the blaggard haud me aye in his pouer! Sir Robert, it was my last resort. I wadna hae dune it gin he had left me alane.

SIR ROBERT: (*soothingly*) Your Majesty, I understand. My Lord Bothwell, your promise to leave the Court was no doubt witnessed by others?

THE KING: It was witnessed by the Lords here praisent!

SIR ROBERT: (*airily*) Then, your Majesty, my Lords, there is no difficulty. Let all the promises be kept.

BOTHWELL: Gin I leave the Coort, I tell ye, they'll aa turn against me! I'll be put to the horn again!

SIR ROBERT: My Lord Bothwell, you must be content with his Majesty's assurance, given before witnesses, that your pardon will not be overlooked. No other course can be entertained. Your continued presence at his Majesty's Court will be distasteful to the Queen my mistress, who will lend his Majesty whatever support may be necessary for the enforcement of your obedience.

(*He eyes* BOTHWELL *meaningly*)

BOTHWELL: (*bowing*) Very weill, Sir Robert. We dinna daur offend her Majesty o England.

(*The* KING *stares in turn at* BOTHWELL *and* SIR ROBERT, *puzzled, then exchanges a knowing look with* SIR JAMES MELVILLE)

SIR ROBERT: The matter, your Majesty would appear to be set-tled, but if I may take the liberty to make a suggestion it is that at a more convenient hour you should summon to your Court the magistrates and clergymen who were present on the occasion of your surprise, put the agreement then projected into writing, and append the necessary signatures. That, no doubt, would allay my Lord Bothwell's fears for his freedom and property.

THE KING: Sir Robert, it sall be dune. And I thank ye wi aa my hairt for yer intervention.

SIR ROBERT: (*bowing*) Your Majesty, whilst you are the ally of the Queen my mistress to serve you is my duty.

MELVILLE: If I may be permittit to speak, yer Grace, I suld like to say to Sir Robert that neir in aa my lang experience o coorts and diplomats hae I seen sic a taiglet situation strauchtent oot wi sic economy o effort. Sir Robert, it was maisterly.

SIR ROBERT: Such praise from one so renowned in the art of diplomacy, Sir James, affords me profound gratification. But the hour is yet early, and I would fain to my slumber. Most Gracious Sovereign, I take my leave.

(*He kisses the* KING's *hand*)

THE KING: I hope ye sleep weill, Sir Robert, I could dae wi my bed mysell.

SIR ROBERT: (*bowing towards* LENNOX) My Lords. (*Bowing to* SIR JAMES) Sir James. (*Turning to bow to the company in general when he reaches the door*) Farewell.

THE KING: Atholl, tak the lantern and show Sir Robert oot.

(ATHOLL *lifts the lantern from the table and opens the door*)

SIR ROBERT: (*bowing*) My Lord, I thank you.

(ATHOLL *bows in reply and follows* SIR ROBERT *out. The Lords stand silent, regarding* BOTHWELL *curiously*)

THE KING: Francie, ye may tak yer leave.

BOTHWELL: (*who has been staring sullenly at the door since the moment of* SIR ROBERT's *departure*) By God, the lot o ye, ye'll hear mair o this!

(*He marches out*)

THE KING: (*almost gleefully*) Oho, did ye hear him? Did ye see his face? Did ye watch him wi Sir Robert? There was some-thing atween thae twa! There was, I tell ye! The blaggard's in English pey! Whan eir Sir Robert gied him a glower he was as meek as a mouss! I see it aa! I see it aa nou! My Lords, ye hae been gulled! Yer haill plot against me was an English trap! They hae gotten juist what they wantit, the Papists banisht frae the Coort and the Kirk brocht in at the back door!

LENNOX: The English had naething to dae wi't!

THE KING: Man, Lodovick, can ye see nae faurer nor the peynt o yer neb! What gart Bothwell lie sae low when Sir Robert put him in his place! Was it like him? Dae ye think for a meenit that gin he hadna dependit on Sir Robert's pooch he wad hae stude there helpless? Did ye no hear what he said? 'We dinna daur offend her Majesty o England.' What wey that? Ye ken the blaggard wad daur gey near onything! Has he no daured baith God and the Deil wi his treason and witchcraft? There's but ae thing he wadna daur, I tell ye, and that's to be in want o siller!

MELVILLE: Yer Grace, there's mebbe something in what ye say, but ye suldna hae threatent Sir Robert wi a Spanish alliance!

THE KING: What wey no? That's what gart him come doun aff his midden tap and stert to the business in haund! Sir Jamie, ye may think he was clever, but he was dancin to my tune aa the time! I telt ye he wadna daur tak the blaggard's side! That was the wey I sent ye for him!

MELVILLE: I thocht it was for something else, yer Grace.

THE KING: (*momentarily crestfallen*) God, I forgot. (*Rallying quickly*) But that can keep. I won the peynt at issue. I did, I tell ye. (*Turning quickly to the Lords*) My Lords, are ye pleased wi yersells? It maun gie ye great satisfaction to ken that whan ye thocht ye were savin yer King frae the consequences o his ain folly ye were daein the English will!

OCHILTREE: English or no, yer Grace, it was oor ain will tae!

THE KING: Sae ye think ye hae won what ye want? Ye think that ance I'm redd o Bothwell I'll juist dae what Sir Robert orders? We'll see, My Lords. We'll see. Yer agreement'll hae to be ratified by a Convention o the Three Estates. Dae ye think it michtna be cancelled?

MELVILLE: (*about to start a homily*) Yer Grace,

THE KING: (*continuing rapidly*) What wey no? It'll be cancelled as faur as Bothwell's concerned, or I'm dune wi the lot o ye! I hae ye sortit tae, I tell ye! There isna ane o ye that wants Bothwell to bide, and whan he gangs I hae ye back whaur ye startit!

OCHILTREE: Yer Grace, if I hae to sign the agreement the morn I'll tak my leave. I hae my conscience to think o.

(*He bows stiffly and walks to the door*)

THE KING: Come back! (OCHILTREE *turns*) Sae ye're gaun to Bothwell?

OCHILTREE: That will depend, yer Grace, on hou ye keep yer word.

(*He bows again. The* KING *speaks as he leaves*)

THE KING: Awa ye upstert! (*Whimsically*) But there's something
likeable aboot Ochiltree tae, mind ye.

MELVILLE: Yer Grace, he's neir been kent to brek a promise,
yet he's but a Lord, and ye're a King. And was it no the renowned Isocrates himsell wha said, 'Princes suld observe their
promises, mair nor ither men their solemn aiths'?

THE KING: Ye auld humbug, that was in a letter I ance gat frae
the English Queen!

MELVILLE: It was apt, yer Grace, sae I thocht I wad quote it.

THE KING: Apt, say ye! It was impiddent! I tell ye, Sir Jamie,
ye're ower fond o moralisin at my expense! Ten meenits o ye's
juist aboot as bad as hauf an hour wi ane o the Preachers.

MELVILLE: Yer Grace, I regret my offence, but there's anither
remark o Isocrates' to the effect,

THE KING: Ay ay, Sir Jamie. 'Dinna repute them freinds who
praise what eir we dar, but raither thae wha modestly rebuke
oor fauts.' Ye're aye at that ane. Awa to yer bed wi ye! Ye're
ower auld to be staunin aboot wi haurdly ony claes on. And
whan I think o't, I'll mak ready mysell.

(*He starts to take off his boots*)

MELVILLE: (*bowing*) Guid nicht, yer Grace.

THE KING: Ye mean guid mornin. It'll sune be fower o'clock.

MELVILLE: Yer Grace, ye aye hae the last word. (*Bowing again*)
Guid mornin.

(*He leaves. The* KING *starts to take off his clothes and makes
towards his dressing-closet.* MORTON *steps forward*)

MORTON: Weill, yer Grace, I'll tak my leave tae.

THE KING: (*turning*) Na, Morton, haud on. I want a word wi ye.
(*Retreating as he speaks into the closet*) Lodovick, there's something else I had forgotten. Ye micht fin Spynie and tell him to
see that his gaird daesna ill-use Lesley or Ogilvy or the three
Erskines. Tell him they maun hae their freedom.

LENNOX: Very weill, yer Grace. (*He stands quickly aside, to be
out of the* KING'*s view, and motions to* MORTON. MORTON
joins him) Morton, he'll be speirin at ye. Watch what ye
say.

(MORTON *nods.* LENNOX *leaves*)

THE KING: (*from the closet*) Ye micht pou doun the claes,
Morton, and draw the curtains.

(MORTON *arranges the* KING'*s bed, drawing the hangings
around it except on the side near the fire. The* KING *enters in
his nightshirt*)

THE KING: (*secretively*) Did Lodovick steik the door?

MORTON: (*looking*) Na.

THE KING: Dae it nou then. (MORTON *closes the door and returns to the* KING, *who has seated himsell in the chair by the bed*) My Lord, I'm sair bothert aboot yer dochter. Ye see, the lass took my fancy. She was sae fresh and winsome and sae keen to learn, and weill, ye ken hou I like to haver awa aboot the ancient mythologies and the auld pagan gods and siclike, and ye ken hou little interest yersell and the ithers hae in maitters like that, save for Sir Jamie, and he aye likes to dae the talkin himsell.

MORTON: I ken, yer Grace.

THE KING: Weill, her Grace has been steerin up bother. She has a gey jealous disposeetion, ye see, and she's inclined to let her imagination rin awa wi her. I dout, my Lord, it'll be better for yer dochter's sake if ye tak yer awa, though, mind ye, my Lord, I'll aye tak an interest in her. (*Eagerly*) I'll see her weill endowed. There'll be some grun gaun whan this steer's bye, for that deil Atholl needs his wings clippit, and weill, a nod's as guid as a wink to a blin horse. My Lord, ye'll hae it dune? I'll sairly miss her, but she wad hae nae pleisure here.

MORTON: (*bowing*) Very weill, yer Grace, it sall be dune. Sall I shut ye in and blaw oot the caunles?

THE KING: (*slipping into bed*) Ye micht, my Lord.

(MORTON *closes the hangings and blows out the candles*)

MORTON: Are ye aa richt, then?

THE KING: Cauld a wee, but I'll sune warm up. Guid mornin, my Lord.

MORTON: Guid mornin, yer Grace.

(*He goes out and shuts the door. The chamber is still lit dimly by a faint glow from the fire. Pause. The* KING *suddenly draws aside the hangings, emerges from the bed-clothes and sits on the edge of the bed. He rises and walks to the door of the* QUEEN's *chamber. He opens it. He listens for a moment. He pokes in his head*)

THE KING: (*calling urgently*) Annie!

(*He passes through and closes the door*)

ACT FOUR

'*Nicoll Eduardis hous in Nithreis Wynd*', Edinburgh, *XV September,* 1594. *Late afternoon.*

The room which was the scene of Act 1. The shutters are wide open, giving a view of the opposite side of the Wynd in the light of a sunny afternoon in autumn.

MISTRESS EDWARD is sitting on a bench at the window, working on a piece of tapestry attached to a frame. RAB appears at the door behind her, carrying a large earthenware jar, a basket and a couple of hares. His clothes are soiled with dust and straw. He puts down his jar and basket and holds up the hares.

RAB: See what I hae gotten!

MRS E: (*turning, slightly startled*) Losh, laddie, ye suldna come creeping up ahint folk's backs like that! Ye gart me jag my finger! Whaur did ye fin thae?

RAB: Doun on the Muir. They loupit oot whan the men were scythin the corn. I gat the tane wi a stane and the tither wi a stick. Feel their hin legs. They're burstin wi flaish.

MRS E: Ay, they're braw anes. Ye maun hae been gey quick.

RAB: Quick! Dae ye see that ane? That's whaur the stane gat it, at sax yairds and it loupin for its very life!

MRS E: Yer stane's made an unco mark.

RAB: It gart it rowe alang the grun like a cairt wheel! And see this ane. There's whaur I gat it wi the stick. I gied ae breinge and clapt it on the mooth!

MRS E: Ye haena left mony o its teeth in.

RAB: Wha'll want its teeth? It's the flaish on its banes that maitters.

MRS E: Ay ay. Haud them awa though. I dinna want my claes aa bluid. Had the men their fill o yill and bannock?

RAB: There was plenty o bannock, but the yill sune gaed. It's gey drouthy wark, it seems, wi the stour in their thrapples. Auld Tam frae the stable says his tongue's like leather.

MRS E: It's been like that sin eir I mind. Awa to the kitchen wi yer things and syne back till the booth.

RAB: Ay. (*Picking up his jar and basket*) Mistress Edward, dae ye think I'll be alloued oot airly the nicht?

MRS E: What dae ye want oot airly for?

RAB: Twa o Bothwell's men hae been brocht to the Nether Tolbooth for makin coonterfeit siller. Their hoose was fou o thirty shillin pieces that they'd struck oot o souther.

MRS E: Dear me, they'll catch it for that. Wha are they?

RAB: Johnstones, o a Border clan. They were brocht in by some o the Maxwells. They're to be hurlt through the Toun tied to the wheels o a cairt, and syne hangit on the Castle Hill. Dae ye think I'll be alloued oot in time to see it?

MRS E: Nou Rab, ye needna ask me that. Ye'll hae to hear what yer maister says.

(NICOLL *enters as she speaks*)

NICOLL: What's this?

MRS E: He wants oot in time to see a hangin.

RAB: The twa men o Bothwell's that struck siller oot o souther. They're to be hurlt through the Toun.

NICOLL: We'll see. We'll see. Were ye oot at the hairst?

RAB: Ay.

NICOLL: And hou's it gaun?

RAB: They were scythin the last rig whan I cam awa.

NICOLL: Is aa that's cut stookit?

RAB: Ay.

NICOLL: Grand. The wather can dae what it likes nou. Weill, lad, ye can tak yer supper in yer pooch and gang to the hangin whan the booth's lockit. And let it be a lesson to ye neir to wrang yer maister be he King, Lord, or Toun Merchant. Whar did ye fin thae hares?

RAB: At the hairst.

MRS E: He gat the tane wi a stane and the tither wi a stick.

NICOLL: Grand. Tell the lassies to gie ye a dram.

MRS E: Nou, Nicoll.

NICOLL: Hoots, the lad desairves it. Awa wi ye.

(RAB *leaves*)

MRS E: Sae Bothwell's up to his tricks again?

NICOLL: Ay, but he's gaen ower faur this time. He'll hae nae sympathy nou. Gin ilka body wi a toom pooch were to stert makin his ain siller there wad be nae profit in tred at aa.

MRS E: I suld think no. And that's the man the Preachers are sae fond o. I dinna understaun them at aa.

NICOLL: Wait. I'll let them ken what I think o them. Maister Bruce is comin up in a wee while to hae a talk aboot raisin siller for the raid against the Papists. Aa the Preachers want his Grace to stert it afore the winter comes on, and his Grace aye puts them aff by saying he canna afford to pey for the sodgers. I dout they want me to mak him anither advance.

MRS E: Weill, Nicoll, I wadna dae it.

NICOLL: Dinna fear, I'll watch mysell.

MRS E: Weill, watch yersell. Ye're aye ower saft.

(RAB *enters suddenly*)

RAB: Guess wha's here!

MRS E: Wha?

RAB: Her Grace, wi the Laird Logie and the Danish leddy!

MRS E: O dear me, and I'm sic a sicht! O Nicoll! Oh what'll I dae?

NICOLL: Tach, wumman, ye're aa richt. Fetch them up, Rab.

(RAB *leaves hurriedly, and* NICOLL *goes to the door.* MIS-TRESS EDWARD *pushes the tapestry aside, straightens her dress, pats her hair and prepares to curtsy*)

NICOLL: (*at the door*) Weill, weill, weill. (*The* QUEEN *appears with* LOGIE *and* MARGARET VINSTAR *behind her*) Come awa in Yer Grace. Sae ye're back frae Stirlin?

(*The three enter. Appropriate bows, bobs and curtsies, some of them during the ensuing dialogue*)

MRS E: Yer Grace, this *is* a surprise!

THE QUEEN: We thocht we wad caa in for a meenit in the passin. We canna bide lang. We shanna sit. But ye are pleased to see us, eh?

MRS E: Yer Grace, ye hae dune us an honour.

NICOLL: Ye hae that.

MRS E: And my Leddy Vinstar.

THE QUEEN: Na na, Vinstar nae mair!

MRS E: Oh I forgot!

NICOLL: Ay, Laird, sae ye brak oot ae jeyl and landit yersell in anither.

MRS E: What things men say! Dinna heed him, Leddy Margaret. But I thocht, weill, ye se—

THE QUEEN: Ye woner to see them back at Coort, eh?

MRS E: Ay weill, I thocht the Laird wad still be in his Grace's black books.

THE QUEEN: Na na. I missed my Margaret and wantit her back, sae I twistit him roun my finger. Logie is paurdont.

MRS E: I'm gled to hear it. Laird, did we no lauch the nicht ye won doun ower the jeyl winnock. We wonert what wad happen to my Leddy Margaret, though, for smugglin in the towe raip, and whan we heard that she had rin awa to jeyn ye we gey near rived oor ribs. Was his Grace no gey angert?

THE QUEEN: He was, gey. But whan he gat redd o Bothwell and wantit the Chancellor back at the Coort I said no. I said that gin he didna allou Margaret back wi her Logie he wad hae nae Chancellor. And what could he say?

MRS E: And the Chancellor's back? Times hae cheynged, eh?

THE QUEEN: Mistress Edward, it is different aathegither. There is haurdly an auld face left. Atholl is put to the horn, Ochiltree is oot wi Bothwell, and Spynie is in jeyl, puir man. Logie has been gey luckie.

NICOLL: He has that.

THE QUEEN: Weill, ye see, he mairrit my Margaret, and the rest didna. But the Chancellor, Mistress Edward, ye suld see. He is a cheynged man. He licks my shune like a dug. And he taks pains.

MRS E: Pains?

THE QUEEN: Ay, and they are gey sair. He will talk and talk and then, aa at ance, he will twist his face and girn and haud his back. Puir man, I feel sorry, but it gars me lauch.

NICOLL: I suld think sae.

THE QUEEN: Ay. Jamie his Grace says it is the judgement o the Lord on him for his wickedness.

MRS E: I daursay, for he was a bad ane. But ye haena said onything yet aboot the big event in yer ain life.

THE QUEEN: (*coyly*) Ah, Mistress Edward, haud yer tongue.

MRS E: Is the young Prince keepin weill. What is he like?

THE QUEEN: Ah weill (*shrugging humorously*) he is like his faither.

MRS E: (*forgetting herself*) Aw. (*Recovering*) But ye had a grand christenin. We had a wild day o't in the Toun here. Aa the prentice laddies were dressed up like heathens, wi their faces blackent and feathers in their bannets, and we had ballad-singers and jougglers and tummlers and aa sorts, and ye suld hae seen the bane-fires at nicht. They were bleizin frae aa the hill-taps like staurs in the lift. It was a sair day for the Preachers. They werena pleased.

THE QUEEN: Huh! The Preachers! They made a sang at Stirlin tae. They were flytin at the Lords for dressin up in weemen's claes.

MRS E: They hate to see folk enjoyin themsells.

THE QUEEN: Ye are richt. They wad hae us aye wi lang faces. They say we are ower licht-hairtit at the Coort, and that we maun hae lang prayers mornin and nicht, and lang graces afore and efter meat. They say it in their kirks to the rabble. It is gaun ower the mark.

NICOLL: Weill, yer Grace, I wadna heed them.

THE QUEEN: Naither I dae. I gang my ain wey.

MRS E: Ye're quite richt, yer Grace. I hear the young Prince got some gey grand praisents.

THE QUEEN: (*brightening*) Oh Mistress Edward, it wad hae taen awa yer braith. Frae the States o Holland there was a gowden box and inside, written in gowden letters, a promise to pey the young Prince a yearly pension o a thoosand guilders.

MRS E: A thoosand guilders! Dear me.

THE QUEEN: It is a lot. And gowden cups! Oh Mistress Edward the wecht! Sir James Melville stude aside me to tak the heavy things, and he could hardly haud them. And there were precious stanes frae my ain country, and mair gowden cups, and a fancy kist, staunin on legs, frae her Majesty o England.

MRS E: Mercy me, he's a luckie bairn. And he has a gey hantle o titles for ane no oot o his creddle.

THE QUEEN: Titles! What a rigmarole! I hae it aff by hairt. 'The richt excellent, high and magnanimous Frederick Henry, Henry Frederick' — he is caa'd efter my faither ye see, and the faither o her Majesty doon bye, and we hae it baith weys to please everybody — but I am wanert aff — 'Frederick Henry, Henry Frederick, by the grace o God Baron o Renfrew, Lord o the Isles, Earl o Carrick, Duke o Rothesay, Prince and Great Steward o Scotland.'

MRS E: It's a gey lang screed that.

THE QUEEN: Is is ower muckle. I caa him 'Wee Henry'.

MRS E: (*laughing*) Aye it'll be a lot mair convenient. But I thocht ye wad hae caa'd him by yer ain faither's name.

THE QUEEN: Na na, we caa him by the English name, for some day he will be English King. But Mistress Edward, we canna bide. We hae to see the Provost. Ye maun come to the Palace, some day sune, and see Wee Henry for yersell.

MRS E: Yer Grace, I'll tak ye at yer word.

THE QUEEN: Dae. We sall be pleased to see ye. (*Bobbing*) Bailie, I bid ye guid efternune.

NICOLL: (*bowing*) Guid efternune, yer Grace. I'm sorry ye canna bide. And I'm sorry his Grace isna wi ye.

THE QUEEN: Huh! *He* is doun the Coogait, at the printers'.

NICOLL: Aye at books yet.

THE QUEEN: Aye at books. (*Bobbing*) Mistress Edward, fare ye weill.

MRS E: (*with a curtsy*) Fare ye weill, yer Grace. (*Bobbing*) And ye, my Leddy. (*Bobbing*) and ye tae, Laird. See and bide oot o jeyl this time.

NICOLL: My Leddy Margaret'll see to that.

LENNOX: (*bowing*) My wild days are by nou, Mistress Edward. Guid efternune, Bailie.

NICOLL: I'll come doun.

> (*He follows the visitors out.* MISTRESS EDWARD *watches them go, then takes a seat at the window. She sits staring reflectively at her lap, and wipes her eyes as a few tears gather. She rises and looks out of the window. She waves as the* QUEEN *turns into the Wynd. She sits again, giving her eyes another wipe.* NICOLL *enters*)

NICOLL: What's wrang wi ye?

MRS E: I was haein a wee bit greit.

NICOLL: What aboot?

MRS E: I was juist thinkin.

NICOLL: What?

MRS E: Weill her Grace is sae cantie the nou. I was thinkin what a peety it is that the Lord God haesna seen fit to gie us the blessin o a bairn tae.

NICOLL: Hoot, wumman, think o yer age.

MRS E: Ay, but still.

NICOLL: Tach!

    (RAB *enters*)

RAB: Here's Bailie Morison!

NICOLL: Eh! What daes he want?

RAB: He wants to see ye.

NICOLL: Nae dout. Fetch him up. (RAB *leaves*) He can keep his neb oot o naething. He'll hae heard that I hae Maister Bruce comin up.

MRS E: Watch him, then. I hope he saw her Grace leavin. It'll gie him something to tell his wife.

BAILIE M: (*outside*) Are ye there, Nicoll?

NICOLL: Ay, Bailie, come in.

    (BAILIE MORISON *enters, with* RAB *behind him*)

MRS E: Guid efternune, Bailie.

BAILIE M: Guid efternune, Mistress Edward.

RAB: Can I gang nou?

NICOLL: Hae ye lockit the booth?

RAB: Ay.

NICOLL: Awa then. (RAB *shoots off*. MISTRESS EDWARD *goes to the awmrie for a bottle and glasses*) Sit doun, Bailie.

MRS E: Ye'll hae a dram?

BAILIE M: Weill ay, I will, thank ye. It's gey drouthy wather. I saw her Grace leavin the nou.

MRS E: (*pouring drinks*) Oh ay, she aye taks a rin up if she's onywhaur near.

BAILIE M: Ay, ye seem to be gey weill ben. (*Accepting drink*) Thank ye. Yer guid health.

NICOLL: Guid health.

MRS E: Thank ye.

    (*She bobs and leaves by the dining-room door*)

BAILIE M: I hear ye hae Maister Bruce comin up?

NICOLL: Ay.

BAILIE M: It'll be aboot siller for the raid against the Papists?

NICOLL: Ay weill, I canna say ye're wrang.

BAILIE M: And hou dae ye staun?

NICOLL: Weill Bailie, I dout I can dae nae mair. His Grace is ower deep in my debt as it is.

BAILIE M: That's my poseetion tae, in a wey.

NICOLL: In a wey, eh?

BAILIE M: Weill, ye see, I could afford to lend him mair gin he could offer guid security.

NICOLL: Sae could I. But whaur will he fin that?

BAILIE M: Think. Hae ye no heard aboot the christenin praisents that were brocht to the young Prince?

NICOLL: Damn it, Bailie, we canna tak the bairn's christenin praisents!

BAILIE M: I see nae hairm in it.

NICOLL: It isna richt.

BAILIE M: Man, it's oor ae chance o gettin a bawbee o oor siller back. There's eneugh gowd, frae what I hear, to cover baith what he owes us the nou and a new advance as weill. In fact, Nicoll, it wad be a grand stroke o business.

NICOLL: He wadna hear o't.

BAILIE M: Weill,

NICOLL: Na na. Ye ken he's faur frae eager to stert the raid. He jumps at ony excuse that comes to haund. Poverty's as guid a ane as ony.

BAILIE M: Mebbe. And mebbe no. I think the maitter's worth some thocht.

(MISTRESS EDWARD *comes to the door*)

MRS E: Paurdon me, Bailie. Nicoll, here's Maister Bruce.

NICOLL: Haud on, then. He's aye rantin against self-indulgence. Gie me yer gless, Bailie. (*He lifts the bottle and two glasses*) Fetch him nou.

(*He hurriedly hides the bottle and glasses as* MISTRESS EDWARD *goes for* BRUCE)

NICOLL: (*as* BRUCE *appears*) Come in, Maister Bruce. Come in. (MISTRESS EDWARD *retires and closes the door*) I hae Bailie Morison here.

BAILIE M: (*half-rising*) Nicoll, if ye hae business to discuss I had mebbe better leave ye.

BRUCE: My business micht concern ye tae, Bailie, sae dinna leave on my accoont.

NICOLL: Bide still man. Maister Bruce, will ye sit doun?

BRUCE: (*sitting*) Thank ye.

NICOLL: It's been grand wather for the hairst.

BAILIE M: Deed ay. I haena seen the Muir wi sic bonnie raws o stooks on't for mony a lang year.

BRUCE: The Lord has filled yer girnels, Bailie, as a sign and a portent. He wad hae ye return his liberality in the service o His cause.

BAILIE M: Ay?

NICOLL: Hou that, Maister Bruce?

BRUCE: Oor temporal ruler, as ye weill ken, is pledged to haud a raid against the Papist lords, but he says he hasna the siller to pey for the men. That may be the truith, my freinds, and it may no, but gin the siller were brocht forrit he wad hae to stert.

NICOLL: Ay, Maister Bruce, and what dae ye propose?

BRUCE: Ye'll ken, Bailie, that the Croun has a richt to command men frae ilka Lord, Laird and Burgh in the country, but ye'll ken tae that maist men dinna rise, and that thae wha dae mak a gey scattered force. What I propose is this: that whan it's resolved to haud the raid forrit, and proclamation's made to that effect, ony that want to bide at hame suld be grantit exemption gin they pey for the sodgers to tak their place.

NICOLL: Na, Maister Bruce, it winna dae. The kind that dinna rise when there's a proclamation are juist the very kind that tak a lang time to pey their debts. The winter wad be on lang afore the siller was collectit.

BRUCE: I had thocht, Bailie, that wi this ither siller as security, an advance micht be made to the Croun at ance.

NICOLL: Na.

BAILIE M: Na.

BRUCE: Think weill, my freinds, afore ye harden yer hairts. The cause I ask ye to serve is the cause o the Kirk, and gin ye dinna serve it weill ye canna prosper. For hasna the Lord said, 'If ye walk contrar unto me I sall walk contrar unto ye also. I will lay bare yer fields, and mak yer cities waste, and bring the haill land unto desolation'?[12]

NICOLL: Ay ay, Maister Bruce, but we arena in the Kirk the nou. This is a maitter o business. Ye ask us to mak an advance to the Croun, but the Croun's gey deep in oor debt as it is, and the security ye offer is worth naething. Hauf o the siller ye talk aboot wadna be peyed unless a body o airmed men was sent oot to fetch it.

BAILIE M: And I dout if the ither half wad pey the Croun's praisent debts.

NICOLL: It canna be dune, Maister Bruce.

BAILIE M: Weill, Nicoll, I wadna say that. There micht be some ither wey.

NICOLL: There's nae ither wey, I tell ye. The poseetion's hopeless frae the stert. If his Grace had his hairt in the raid it wad be a different maitter, but ye ken hou he led the last ane. When eir he gat near the Papists he pitched his camp till they had time to retreat, and the Hielands are braid enough to let that

sort o ploy gang on for years. The haill truith o the maitter is,
Maister Bruce, that he winna lead the raid wi ony hairt till he
has houndit doun Bothwell, and that ye winna let him dae.

BRUCE: He can dae that whan he has first served God and the
Kirk! Bothwell's soond in his releegion!

(*There is a faint commotion from far beyond the window*)

NICOLL: He has nae scruples whaur siller's concerned. Listen
to that! Twa o his men are being hurlt through the Toun for
makin coonterfeit thirty shillin pieces!

BRUCE: It's anither o the Chancellor's fause chairges! Bothwell
has naething to dae wi the men!

BAILIE M: What's that!

(RAB *can be heard on the staircase shouting* 'Bailie Edward!
Maister!')

NICOLL: It's Rab!

(RAB *enters breathlessly*)

RAB: There's a fecht on at the Nether Bow Port! Johnstones
and Maxwells! The Johnstones raidit the Nether Tolbooth to
let their twa freinds oot, and the Maxwells that brocht them in
cam doun the Hie Gait to stop it! The Toun Gaird's tryin to
clear the causey!

NICOLL: Guid God! Help me on wi my gear, Rab!

(NICOLL *and* RAB *hurry out through the dining-room door.*
BAILIE MORISON *goes to the window. The commotion grows*)

BAILIE M: Here's his Grace, fleein for his life, wi the Chancellor
pechin ahint him! (BRUCE *goes over beside him*) I believe he's
comin here!

(MISTRESS EDWARD *enters from the dining-room*)

MRS E: What's aa the steer? I'm shair Nicoll daesna hae to gang
fechtin! He'll be slauchtert! It isna richt!

(*The* KING *is heard on the staircase shouting* 'Nicoll Edward!
Nicoll, ye deil!')

BAILIE M: It's his Grace.

(*The* KING *enters in disarray*)

THE KING: Mistress Edward, gie me a dram! I hae been gey
near shot doun, hackit to bits, and staned to daith!

(MISTRESS EDWARD *hastens to pour him a drink.* NICOLL
appears at dining-room door, strapping on his gear)

NICOLL: What's wrang, yer Grace?

THE KING: What's wrang! Yer Toun isna safe! That's what's
wrang! It's fou o Border reivers fleein at ilk ither's throats!

RAB: (*coming in behind* NICOLL *with his pistols*) It's the
Johnstones, yer Grace! They were tryin to brek doun the doors
o the Nether Tolbooth and let oot Bothwell's twa men!

THE KING: Bothwell! I micht hae kent it! There'll be nae peace in the country till the blaggard's ablow the grun! (*Accepting a glass from* MISTRESS EDWARD) Thank ye, Mistress Edward. (*The* CHANCELLOR *appears at the door, breathing heavily*) Ay, Jock, come in and sit doun. Gie him a dram tae, guid wumman, for he's worn oot.

> (MAITLAND *slumps into a chair, and* MISTRESS EDWARD *goes to fetch him a drink. The Town bell begins to ring*)

NICOLL: (*completing his preparations*) There's the Town Bell, thank God. It'll bring the men up frae the hairst. Hurry oot, Rab. Bailie Morison, dinna staun there gawpin. Come on hame for yer gear.

MRS E: Oh Nicoll, watch yersell.

NICOLL: (*leaving quickly*) Ay ay.

> (RAB *and* BAILIE MORISON *follow him out*)

MRS E: (*dabbing her eyes*) Oh I hope he'll be aa richt.

THE KING: Ay ay Mistress, he'll be aa richt. He's as strang as a bull. Are ye comin roun, Jock?

MAITLAND: (*busy with his glass*) Gie me time.

MRS E: (*suddenly remembering*) Her Grace was here no lang syne. I woner if she'll be aa richt.

THE KING: Her Grace, eh? Whaur did she gang?

MRS E: She left to gang to the Provost's.

THE KING: There's nae need to worry then. The fechtin's aa ablow the Tron.

MRS E: I think I'll gang up to the mooth o the Wynd and hae a look, though. It micht be better.

THE KING: Watch yersell, then.

MRS E: Ay, ay.

> (*She goes out in a state of agitation*)

THE KING: Weill, Maister Bruce, what are ye staunin glowerin at? Can the like o ye dae naething? Or are ye sae thick wi Bothwell that ye want his freinds to win?

BRUCE: Ye hae nae richt to blame Bothwell! Ye hae nae prufe that the men are his!

THE KING: Havers! The Johnstones were aye ahint him. They were in his gaird whan he held the Palace last year, and they were alang wi him in the spring whan he cam wi Ochiltree to Edmonstone Edge. Gin it hadna been for my Lord Hume he micht hae marched them on the palace again. And that's the man ye try to shield.

BRUCE: I try to defend him frae the persecution o his enemies! He was first put to the horn on a fause chairge, and whan he was adjudged guiltless, he gat nae remission! And that in spite o yer promise, written by yer ain haund, that he wad be shown sic favour as if he had neir offendit!

THE KING: My promise was cancelled by the Three Estates! And he has little to complain o, the Lord kens. For a man wha's committit sae mony treasons he's been gey weill used. He was paurdont. He was to be alloued to draw his rents. Aa that was askit was that he suld leave the country!

BRUCE: He left the country! He gaed to England!

THE KING: To lie low and plot anither raid! Ye talk aboot brekin promises, Maister Bruce, but if Bothwell has his match in the haill o Christendom he'll be gey ill to fin!

BRUCE: His match is praisent in this very room!

THE KING: Jock! did ye hear that?

MAITLAND: Gin I werena auld and dune I wad split his croun!

BRUCE: I spak the truith, Maitland, as weill ye ken! Didna the King promise that ye and Hume suld be keepit frae the Coort?

THE KING: Guid God, ye canna object to Jock here! He's a dune auld man.

BRUCE: And Hume? Is he dune?

THE KING: Ye ken he's convertit! I argued him roun mysell. He's as guid a Protestant as there is in the country.

BRUCE: He's like aa the ithers ye hae aboot ye, a hypocrite that wad raither ye spent the revenues o the Croun on his ain profligate pleisures nor in the service o God's Kirk! But I tell ye, Jamie Stewart, King though ye be, that gin ye dinna rouse yersell to dae the wark that the Lord has committit to yer haund, the Kirk shall rise in its strength and act withoot ye!

THE KING: The Kirk'll dae what it's alloued to dae, and nae mair. I'm aye its heid yet!

BRUCE: The Lord is its heid, and ye are but a member, and gin ye hinder its wark ye sall be weedit oot!

THE KING: Ye canna weed me oot aither! There can be nae ex-communications withoot my consent! And as for the Papist raid ye canna grummle. I hae promised to stert it whan eir I can fin the siller.

BRUCE: The want o siller's an excuse! Ye ken that gin the folk o the Burghs wad rise to support ye ye wad be for fleein at Bothwell's throat at ance! Ye wad sune fin the siller for that!

THE KING: By God I wish I could! I wad sune fin the men, ay though ye thumpit the brods o yer pulpits till they brak into bits! Rant against me hou ye like, uphaud Bothwell as muckle as ye will, gin I ance fin the siller I'll hound the blaggard doun!

BRUCE: Ye little ken the pouer o the Kirk! There isna a man i' the haill country that wad daur follow ye against the will o the Preachers!

THE KING: The will o the Preachers! Siller's a mair potent motive nor the fear o hell!

BRUCE: Nae dout, amang the unbelievers at the Coort, but I tell ye that to the congregations o the Kirk the will o the Preachers is the will o God! Tak warnin afore it be ower late! Gin ye delay ower lang wi the raid against the Papists the Kirk itsell sall summon the godly to the fecht! Frae ilka pulpit in the country the cry sall gang forth, that the hour appeyntit has come at last, and the sword of the Lord is to be girdit on!

THE KING: Huh! They'd look a bonnie lot! Eh, Jock can ye see them? (MAITLAND *snorts*) Weill I ken what they'd be like, Maister Bruce: a rabble o puir gowks airmed wi heuks. And nae dout yersell and Andrew Melville wad lead them?

BRUCE: They wad be led by my Lord Bothwell!

THE KING: Oho, ye deil!

MAITLAND: (*pushing back his chair and gripping his hilt*) Watch what ye say, sir! Yer words micht cost ye dear!

BRUCE: Ye daurna touch me, and ye ken it! The folk o the Toun wad stane ye!

MAITLAND: (*stepping forward and drawing*) I wad tak the risk!

BRUCE: Tak it, and may the Lord accurse ye! May aa the maledictions that fell upon Judas, Pilate, Herod and the Jews, aa the troubles that fell upon the city o Jerusalem, aa the plagues and pestilences that ever,

(*He breaks off, as* MAITLAND *seems suddenly to be seized with pain. The Town bell stops ringing*)

MAITLAND: (*writhing back into his chair and dropping his sword*) Oh. Oh. Oh.

(*The* KING *and* BRUCE *stare at him in amazement.* MISTRESS EDWARD *enters hurriedly from the staircase*)

MRS E: Yer Grace! (*Noticing* MAITLAND) Guidness gracious, what's wrang!

THE KING: That deil's been cursin Jock. It's brocht on his pains.

MRS E: (*reproachfully*) Oh, Maister Bruce.

THE KING: I'll hae him tried for witchcraft! Leave him. He'll sune come roun. Sit up, Jock and tak anither moothfou. That's richt. Are ye feelin better?

MAITLAND: Gie me time.

MRS E: Yer Grace, My Lord Lennox and Nicoll are bringin a man doun the Wynd.

THE KING: A man, eh?

MRS E: Ay, by the scruff o the neck. Here they are nou.

(*They look to the door.* LENNOX *enters*)

LENNOX: (*to* NICOLL *outside*) Bring him in, Nicoll.

    (NICOLL *enters leading a stranger by the shoulder.* LENNOX
    steps forward and hands the KING *a letter*) Yer Grace, hae a
    look at that.

THE KING: (*indicating the stranger*) Wha's this?

LENNOX: It's Sir Robert Bowes' new English servant.

THE KING: And what's this? Whaur did ye fin it?

LENNOX: I was in the Hie Gait when the steer stertit. Juist when
    it was at its heicht a man made to ride up the Toun frae the
    Black Friar's Wynd and was dung aff his horse by a stray shot.
    This man ran forrit and rypit his pooches. It was that he was
    efter, for whan eir he fand it he made to rin awa.

THE KING: (*unrolling it*) Is it a letter?

LENNOX: It's blank!

THE KING: Oho! No a word on it! Conspeeracy! Weill weill,
    we hae dealt wi blanks afore.[13] Mistress Edward, rin ben to the
    kitchen and fetch a bit o flannel and a hot airn. Hurry! We'll
    sune see what's at the bottom o this. (MISTRESS EDWARD
    hurries out by the dining-room door. To the stranger) Ay ay, my
    man, sae ye hae been foun wi a secret document in yer pos-
    session? Pou him forrit, Nicoll, and put yer sword to his hin end.
    (NICOLL *obeys*) Was this letter for Sir Robert Bowes? (*Silence*)
    Was it, I'm askin? Nicoll, gar him speak.

NICOLL: (*jabbing the stranger*) Answer whan ye're telt!

STRANGER: (*turning on him indignantly, and speaking with a
    Cockney accent as remote from the speech of* SIR ROBERT BOWES
    as RAB's *Edinburgh sing-song is from the speech of* SIR JAMES
    MELVILLE) Avaunt, thou pock-faced villain, sheathe thy sword!
    I know not what thy master asketh!

THE KING: What is he sayin? Tak him by the collar!

    (NICOLL *obeys*)

STRANGER: Unhand me or I'll kick thy paunch, thou bottled-
    nosed bully!

THE KING: Jab him again, Nicoll!

    (NICOLL *obeys*)

STRANGER: Oh!

NICOLL: Staun at peace, see!

STRANGER: Peace! God's light if this be peace! Call for my
    master!

THE KING: He said something about his maister! I'll try him
    in English. Listen, my man. Art thou the servant of Sir Robert
    Bowes?

STRANGER: He is my master! Call him here!

THE KING: Ay ay, but listen. Did Sir Robert Bowes send thee to obtain this letter?

STRANGER: This scurvy dog of a servant choketh me!

THE KING: Eh? What is he sayin, Jock?

MAITLAND: It bates me.

THE KING: Listen again. Did Sir Robert Bowes send thee to obtain this letter?

STRANGER: He is my master!

MAITLAND: Maister! It's aa he can think o!

THE KING: He's donnart! Letter, my man! Letter! Dae ye no ken what letter means? Dost thou see this letter?

STRANGER: How can I see? He has me by the throat! Order thy varlet off!

THE KING: It's hopeless. I wish Sir Jamie Melville was here. He kens aa their tongues.

LENNOX: He's at Halhill the nou.

THE KING: He's aye awa whan he'a maist needit. But we'll persevere. We'll take him word by word. Dae ye hear? Dost thou hear? We shall speak each word separately. Dost thou understand letter?

STRANGER: Call for my master! He will tell thee all!

MAITLAND: Maister again!

THE KING: We're at letter the nou, no maister! I'm haudin it up! Look at it!

STRANGER: I know not what thou sayest!

THE KING: What was that?

MAITLAND: I didna catch it.

THE KING: Can ye no speak ae word at a time?

MAITLAND: Say it in English.

THE KING: Ay ay, I forgot. Canst thou not speak each word separately?

STRANGER: God grant me patience! Dost thou not follow Master? Master, thou addle-pate! Master!

THE KING: Guid God!

MAITLAND: He's at it yet!

THE KING: I dinna like his mainner, aither.

MAITLAND: Naither dae I. Put him in the jougs.

THE KING: Dae ye ken what the jougs are? Dae ye ken what the rack is? Dost thou understand gallows?

STRANGER: Call for my master!

THE KING: Guid God Almichty! Tak him oot and droun him!

MAITLAND: Put him in the jougs!

THE KING: And fetch his maister! We'll see what he has to say! Dinna say what we're efter, though. We'll tak him by surprise.

NICOLL: Aa richt, yer Grace. (*Dragging the* STRANGER *out*)
Come on, see.

STRANGER: Call for my master! Call for my master! (*Turning
his attention from the* KING *to* NICOLL) Oh thou lousy, damned,
abominable rogue!

NICOLL: Haud yer tongue or I'll clowt ye!

> (*He bundles the* STRANGER *out by the staircase door.* MIS-
> TRESS EDWARD *enters from the dining-room with a piece of
> flannel and a hot iron*)

MRS E: Here ye are, yer Grace. I was as quick as I could manage.

THE KING: Ye haena been lang. Gie me the flannel. We'll
spread it here. Then the letter, flat oot. Haud it doun, Jock, till
I fold the flannel ower it. Nou put doun the airn. (MISTRESS
EDWARD *lays the iron on the table. The* KING *picks it up*) Hou
hot is it? (*He tests it*) Ph! Grand. It's juist richt. Nou watch
this.

> (*He starts to iron carefully over the letter*)

MRS E: Whaur's Nicoll, yer Grace?

THE KING: He's awa to the Tolbooth wi the Englishman.
Wheesht the nou. We'll sune see what Sir Robert's up to. (*He
puts down the iron and lifts the flannel*) Look, Jock, it's up!

MAITLAND: It is that!

THE KING: It's in Sir Robert's haund! Juist what I thocht! Sir
Robert's servant maun hae gien it to the horseman in the first
place! Nou let me see. (*He reads excitedly*) It's fou o ciphers!
Jock, ye ken the English code![14] Wha's Argomartes? Bothwell,
eh!

MAITLAND: Nane else! Is it for him?

THE KING: It is! By God, I hae Sir Robert nou! (*He reads*)
America! That's the English Queen hersell!

MAITLAND: America, ay!

THE KING: Oho, then, listen to this! 'Thou (that's Bothwell)
didst by thine own unreasonable demeanour render thyself
too weak to serve America further, and cannot complain that
America now leaves thee to furnish thine own purse.' Oho, eh!
It's what I aye said! He's been in her pey aa alang! (*He reads*)
But there's a bit here I canna richt mak oot. 'As for thy latest
threat, America hath strong hopes that through vee ane emm
thirty-sax pund sterlin . . .'

MAITLAND: The Preachers!

THE KING: Eh! By God, Maister Bruce, sae ye're in towe wi
Sir Robert tae!

BRUCE: It's a lee! There's a mistake!

THE KING: Haud yer tongue and we'll see! It says here 'America hath strong hopes that through the Preachers she may force Petrea . . .' That's me! What rank black ineequity!

MAITLAND: Force ye to what!

THE KING: 'to rise against Chanus'

MAITLAND: Huntly!

THE KING: Juist that! Listen! 'to rise against Chanus in such strength that thy support will avail him nothing.' Guid God! Thy support! Bothwell's!

MAITLAND: Support for Huntly!

THE KING: It canna be!

(*They peer excitedly into the letter. There is a commotion below the window*)

MRS E: There's a steer on the stairs!

(RAB *comes to the door*)

RAB: Here's my Lord Morton!

(*He stands back.* MORTON *enters*)

MORTON: Yer Grace, I hae Colville here! He's gien himsell up!

THE KING: What! Whaur is he?

MORTON: I hae him here! He says he wants to speak to ye at ance!

THE KING: Dinna let him near me! It's a plot!

MORTON: He says he has news for ye alane!

THE KING: It's a trick, I tell ye! Is he airmed?

MORTON: Na.

THE KING: Lodovick! Staun by and draw! Jock! Whaur's yer sword? Pick it up! See that he daesna win near me!

MORTON: Sall I fetch him?

THE KING: Ye're shair he has nae weapon?

MORTON: Ay.

THE KING: Then let him come.

(*They stand expectant.* MORTON *leaves. In a moment he returns and stands within the door.* COLVILLE *enters stained with travel, and throws himself at the* KING's *feet. The* KING *shrinks back*)

THE KING: Keep back!

COLVILLE: Maist Clement Prince.

THE KING: Ye hae said that afore! What dae ye want?

COLVILLE: (*grovelling*) Yer Grace, I hae focht against ye in bygaen times, but I actit as my conscience dictatit, and in the service o the true releegion.

THE KING: Ye leear, ye did it for Bothwell and his English siller!

COLVILLE: The Lord kens, yer Grace, that I thocht he was soond in doctrine. I renounce him nou!

THE KING: Eh?

COLVILLE: He's jeynt the Papist Lords for Spanish gowd!

THE KING: (*quietly*) Say that again.

COLVILLE: He's at Kirk o Memure wi Huntly and the ithers! They hae pledged themsells to kidnap the young Prince and murder Hume and Maitland.

THE KING: (*as* MAITLAND *gasps*) The fiends o hell! Wha telt ye that?

COLVILLE: I hae kent it aa alang! I wantit to mak shair! Yer Grace, ye'll paurdon me? I'll serve ye weill!

THE KING: I wad paurdon the Deil himsell for that news! It's like a dream come true! I can haurdly tak it in! To think o't! To think o't! My warst enemy destroyed by his ain folly! Aa my troubles washt awa by ae turn o the tide! Man, Jock, it's lauchable. It's rideeculous. It's a slap in the face to the Kirk and England baith. Ay, Maister Bruce, ye may weill look dumfounert! That's yer Bothwell for ye! That's the man that was to lead the godly in the service o the Lord! But dinna tak it ill, man! The Lord sall be served! I'll hound doun the Papists for ye nou! (*With a quick change of manner*) Man, Jock, look at him. He daesna seem pleased.

MAITLAND: It's ower big a dose for ae gulp.

THE KING: It is that! He canna believe that the Lord can hae His ain wey o daein His ain wark. That'll teach ye, my man, that it's in the Croun and no in the assemblies o yer Kirk that the Lord invests His authority, for has He no by this very move entrustit leadership to me, and gart ye lick yer vomit!

BRUCE: His will's beyond yer comprehension!

THE KING: His will's as clear as the licht o day! He has peyntit me oot as His airthly Lieutenant! Awa to yer colleagues, man, and tell them the news! Tell them their idol has turnt idolator! Let them cry frae ilka pulpit that the hour has come at last, whan the King sall lead the godly in the service o the Lord, and Bothwell and the Papists sall perish thegither!

BRUCE: May ye hae the Lord's help in the task, for ye'll fail withoot it!

(*He marches out*)

THE KING: Hoho, he didna like it! He lost his tongue athegither! God, it's miraculous! Colville, I'll spare yer heid, man, for ye hae served me weill. Ye can ward yersell wi Morton. My Lord, I mak ye responsible for his safe keepin. Tak him doun to the Palace. I'll speir at him the nicht afore my Cooncil.

MORTON: Very weill, yer Grace.

COLVILLE: (*kissing the* KING's *hand*) Maist Clement Prince. Maist Noble King.

THE KING: I haena paurdont ye yet, mind. Ye'll hae to tell me aa ye ken.

COLVILLE: I hae copies o aa their documents, yer Grace.

THE KING: They're yer ain wark nae dout. Awa wi ye. (COLVILLE *kisses his foot*) Man, ye're a scunner. Watch him weill, my Lord (MORTON *bows*) Rise up aff the flair, man, and tak yersell oot o my sicht! (COLVILLE *bows himself elaborately out of the room*. MORTON *bows and follows him*) He turns my stamack, but he'll be worth his wecht in gowd. Lodovick! Caa my Cooncil for eicht o'clock.

LENNOX: Very weill, yer Grace.

(*He bows and leaves*)

THE KING: (*reaching for the bottle*) Weill, Jock, it's been a grand efternune, Eh, Mistress?

MRS E: It has that, yer Grace. Sall I tak the airn?

THE KING: Leave it. I want it. I'm expectin Sir Robert.

MRS E: Very well, yer Grace. I'll leave ye, I think, and hae the table laid. (*Knowingly*) Will ye bide for supper?

THE KING: (*joyfully*) Mistress Edward, ye're the best friend I hae! I'll clap my sword to yer guid man's back and say 'Arise, Sir Nicoll'!

MRS E: Na na, yer Grace, dinna dae that. The Kirk wad turn against him. Aa the tred in black claith wad gang to Tam MacDowell. Wait till he's retired.

THE KING: Aa richt, whateir ye please. (*Eagerly*) What's in the pat?

MRS E: Cock-a-leekie.

THE KING: Ye maun hae kent I was comin!

MRS E: (*bobbing*) I ken ye like it.

THE KING: I dae that. (MISTRESS EDWARD *leaves*) Jock, I'm bothert aboot siller. It'll tak a lot to cairry on a raid in the Hielands.

MAITLAND: (*who has been helping himself from the bottle*) Damn it, man, ye hae eneugh gowd at Stirlin to pey for a dizzen raids, if ye juist had the gumption to use it.

THE KING: Na na, Jock! Annie wadna hear o't! She wad flee oot at me! I wadna hae the life o a dug! Dinna stert that again!

MAITLAND: It's the ae wey oot.

THE KING: It canna be! We maun fin some ither! And it maun be sune. My haill hairt's set on stertin at ance. Man, think,

MAITLAND: Wheesht!

THE KING: Here they are! Sir Robert! By God, I'll gar him wriggle! Ye'll hae the time o yer life nou!

(NICOLL *enters*)

NICOLL: Here's Sir Robert.

> (SIR ROBERT *enters*. NICOLL *withdraws. The* KING *affects a heavy scowl*)

SIR ROBERT: (*puzzled*) Your Majesty?

THE KING: Weill

SIR ROBERT: You seem hostile.

THE KING: Daes it surprise ye?

SIR ROBERT: It doth, your Majesty, immensely.

THE KING: What dae ye think o that, Jock? He's fair astoundit!

> (MAITLAND *gives a little bark of laughter*)

SIR ROBERT: (*indignantly*) My Lord! Your Majesty!

THE KING: Ay ay, Sir Robert, wark up yer indignation! But ye dinna ken what's comin! Dae ye see that airn? Dae ye see that bit o flannel? Dae ye see this letter? Ay, Sir Robert, ye may weill turn pale. Ye may weill gowp like a frichtent fish. Ye're a proved plotter, a briber o traitors, a hirer o murderers! Whan I think hou ye hae leived amang us, respectit by gentle and simple in the Toun, treatit like a lord at Coort, honoured wi my ain freindship and invitit often to my very table, I tak a haill-hairtit scunner at human nature! There's nae kent form o torture, nae way o inflictin daith, that isna ower guid for ye! Ye're waur nor the warst auld beldam witch that was eir brunt to cinders!

SIR ROBERT: Your Majesty, I am but an instrument of my country's policy.

THE KING: Policy! Jock, he said policy! (MAITLAND *snorts*) Sir Robert, yer mistress daesna ken what policy is. She wantit to stop the plottin o the Papists, and aa she could think o was to mak Bothwell sic a terror to the country that I had to look to the Papists for help. Aa the siller she wared on Bothwell, gin it had been peyed to me at the stert, wad hae redd her o the Papists at ance!

SIR ROBERT: I think she attributed your friendship with the Papists, your Majesty, to your hatred of the Protestant Church.

THE KING: The Protestant Kirk! It's a Presbyterian Kirk! They winna acknowledge their Sovereign as their speeritual heid! They elect men o their ain to tak the place o my bishops in the Three Estates! I woner what the Queen yer mistress wad dae, Sir Robert, if the preachers o her ain Kirk in England denied her authority! Wad she show nae ill will? I ken she wad, for by God, there's nae sovereign in Christendom hauf sae shair o Divine Richt as her Majesty o England! My fecht with the Kirk, Sir Robert, is a fecht against government frae the pulpit, and yer mistress suld be the last to encourage that!

SIR ROBERT: Your Majesty, there was no question of such encouragement. My mistress feared Spanish invasion and the loss of her throne.

THE KING: Spanish invasion! Did she think for a meenit that I wad jeyn wi Spain to put Phillip on the throne o England and destroy my ain claim to succeed her! Ye wad think, Sir Robert, that I had nae intelligence at aa!

SIR ROBERT: Yer Majesty, I assure you.

THE KING: Oh ay, Sir Robert, try to win me roun, but I tell ye that gin I had nae mair sense nor to waste guid siller on a treacherous blaggard like Bothwell I wad droun mysell in the nearest dub. Dae ye ken what he's dune? He's jeynt the Papists!

SIR ROBERT: (*slightly startled*) I thought it possible.

THE KING: Ye thocht it possible!

SIR ROBERT: I did your Majesty, as you will realise from my letter.

THE KING: I realise frae yer letter that ye were gaun to try to force my haund through the Kirk. Dinna try to mak oot, Sir Robert, that ye thocht I wad need any forcin if Bothwell turnt his coat! Ye hae won what yer mistress wantit nou, but dinna try to tak the credit for it!

SIR ROBERT: Am I to understand, your Majesty, that the Papist Lords will be attacked?

THE KING: They will, by God, as sune as I can fin the siller!

SIR ROBERT: (*airily*) Then, your Majesty, all is well. I am certain that the Queen my mistress, when she hath heard of your resolve, will endow you with undreamt of wealth.

THE KING: (*eagerly*) Dae ye think sae, Sir Robert?

SIR ROBERT: I am certain, not only because you intend to serve a cause she hath at heart, but because she must regard you now as sound in your religion, and therefore the most proper person, by your faith as by your birth and endowments, to succeed her on the Throne.

THE KING: Ye think sae, Sir Robert?

MAITLAND: Sir Robert hauds the best caird in the pack, yer Grace. He aye wins ye roun.

SIR ROBERT: (*in protest*) My Lord!

THE KING: Na na, Sir Robert, he's richt! Ye ken hou to play on my hopes o the succession!

SIR ROBERT: Your hopes are brighter now, your Majesty, than the stars of heaven.

THE KING: Awa wi ye. Flaittery wins nae favour frae me. Ye'll hae to show yer guid will in mair solid form. Hou sune dae ye think I can hae some siller?

SIR ROBERT: As soon as the Queen my mistress hears of your resolve.

THE KING: Then let her hear at ance. And I'll write to her mysell. Ye may tak yer letter.

SIR ROBERT: Your Majesty, you are indeed merciful. Have you seen ought of my servant?

THE KING: Ye deil, ye're wrigglin oot aathegither! Yer servant's in the Tolbooth, and he'll bide there the nou! I maun dae something to assert mysell! Gin it werena for the turn things hae taen, Sir Robert, I wad be faur mair severe! Ye wad pack yer kist and mak for the Border! Ye bide on, ye understaun, for the sake o the guid will that maun exist atween mysell and yer royal mistress, but gin I fin ye up to ony mair o yer intrigues I'll ask her to remove ye at ance!

SIR ROBERT: Your Majesty, I understand.

THE KING: Awa and think shame o yersell!

(SIR ROBERT *bows to the* KING, *then, to* MAITLAND, *then leaves. They watch him go*)

THE KING: I couldna be hard on him, for he's fired my hopes. Jock, I *will* pledge the bairn's praisents! They'll be safe nou. I can hae them back whan his mistress pays up. Oho, but fortune's favoured me the day! There's naething in my wey! Aa that I hae wished for is promised at last! Bothwell on the scaffold, the Papists houndit doun, the Kirk in my pouer, England ahint me, and then, in the end, the dream o my life come true! It gars my pulse quicken! It gars my hairt loup! It gars my een fill wi tears! To think hou the twa pair countries hae focht and struggled. To think o the bluid they hae shed atween them, the touns they hae blackent wi fire, the bonnie green howes they hae laid waste. And then to think, as ae day it sall come to pass, that I, Jamie Stewart, will ride to London, and the twa countries sall become ane.

(MISTRESS EDWARD *can be heard off calling* 'Nicoll! Nicoll! Come for yer supper!')

MAITLAND: (*coming out of his trance and reaching for the bottle*) Ay, yer Grace, it's a solemn thocht. But the auld bitch isna deid yet.

(*He places the bottle before the* KING. *The* KING *fills his glass*)

THE KING: (*raising his glass high*) Jock, here's to the day. May the mowdies sune tickle her taes.

(MISTRESS EDWARD *appears at the door of the dining-room*)

MRS E: (*with a deep curtsy*) Yer Grace, the supper's ready.

(*The* KING *and* MAITLAND *eye each other and drink the toast*)

Notes

1. James's *Daemonologie in Forme of ane Dialogue* was published in Edinburgh in 1597.
2. Moysie writes: 'Upone the vii day of Februar or therby, the erle of Huntlie, with sex or sevin scoir of his friendis, past out of the kingis house, and maid thame to giang to ane horse rease at Leithe: bot quhen they wer theare, hafing the execution of a bluddie conspiracie in thair hairte, they past to the Queinies ferrie, quhiar they had causit stay the passing over of all boittis, and past toward the plaice of Donnybirsell besyd Aberdour, perteining to unquhill James Erle of Murray . . . quhaire he was slayne'.
3. James was a critic and poet of some talent, and his court was distinguished by the group known as the Castalian Band. This included William Fowler, Alexander Montgomerie and John Stewart of Baldynneis, and James himself laid down the style of their work in his *Reulis and Cautelis,* sometimes considered to be the first major Scottish work of literary criticism.
4. The young James had as his tutor George Buchanan, one of the outstanding classicists and the major Latin poet of the age. James would have known well the techniques of argument based on Plato's presentation of Socrates and his method of philosophical debate.
5. In August 1582, when he was 16, James had been captured by some of the Scottish Lords and held prisoner at Ruthven Castle until June 1583.
6. Graham was one of the North Berwick witches, supposedly consulted by Bothwell. In November 1590 they admitted meeting the devil in the form of 'a man with a redde cappe, and a rumpe at his taill'.
7. James's father was Darnley, the husband of Mary Queen of Scots, who, having himself been involved in the murder of her servant Riccio, was murdered at Kirk o Field near Edinburgh in 1566. Mary was suspected of having a role in his death and was forced from the throne in 1567.
8. Mary was held captive by Elizabeth I for fifteen years after she was forced to seek protection in England and was executed,

in 1587, for her alleged involvement in a papist plot against Elizabeth.

9. '*Act o attainder*' was an act decreeing a judgment of death or outlawry for treason without a trial.

10. James used some of his sonnets as introduction to his *Essayes of a Prentise* published in Edinburgh in 1585.

11. '*Episcopacy*', as the Scots defined what was to become the English version of protestantism, was not regarded by Scottish protestants as being truly a protestant system because it retained the place within the church of bishops, who were anathema to the reformed Church of Scotland with its democratic basis in the ordinary members of the Church.

12. '*If ye walk contrar unto me . . .*': *Leviticus*, XXVI, 27–32.

13. James had previously had to deal, in 1589, with 'blank' communications from various Scottish lords to other European monarchs. These contained signatures over which appropriate text was to be entered when they reached their destination.

14. The use of 'cypher letters' is presented by Tytler as part of Elizabeth's dealings with Bothwell, and McLellan follows the attributions of names given in Tytler.

Glossary

ablow, below
airn, iron
awmrie, cupboard
booth, shop, stall
breinge, violent movement
brods, boards
bune, except
causey, cobbled roadway
chalmer, room
chappin, knocking
chief, friendly
clash, gossip
cley corp, clay effigy
clowts, blows
clypin, telling tales
compter, sideboard
corbies, crows
cot-hooses, cottages
donnart, stupid
dumfounert, dumbfounded, amazed
dung, knocked
ettled, intended
ettles, is eager
feids, feuds
flummoxed, defeated
flytin at, abusing
gaun that gait, going that way
girnels, granaries
glaur, mud
gommeril, scoundrel
grue, shudder
herry, harry
heuks, reaping hooks
hin end, the end
hurlt, carted
jougs, pillory
kenspeckle, conspicuous
kist, chest

kittle, difficult
lift, sky
lippen, expect
messan, cur
mowdies, moles
pairt-takars, collaborators
ports, town gates
pousins, poisons
preens, pins
put to the horn, proclaimed a rebel
rowe, roll
rypit, rifled
scunnert, disgusted
seminary priests, i.e. Roman Catholic priests
siller, money, coin
snash, abuse
souther, solder
spulzies, raids
steik, shut
stoups, flagons
tabard, coat
taiglet, entangled
ted, trade
teyler, tailor
thir, those
thowless, useless
thrang, busy
thrapple, throat
thrawn, determined, resistant
tod, fox
towe raip, hemp rope
wabbit, exhausted
warstle, struggle, wrestle
winnock, window
yett, gate
yill, ale

James Bridie

Mr Bolfry
A Play in Four Scenes

(1943)

CHARACTERS

Cully
Cohen
Jean
Morag
Mr McCrimmon
Mrs McCrimmon
Mr Bolfry

Introduction

James Bridie was the name used by Osborne Henry Mavor (1888–1951), a practising doctor in Glasgow who began writing plays in the late 1920s and rapidly became a major force in British theatre. *The Anatomist* and *Tobias and the Angel* were both produced in London in 1930, and by the time of his death Bridie had had forty-two plays produced, many of them on London West End stages. He became a full-time writer in 1938.

Throughout his life, Bridie played a key role in the development of Scottish theatre. He was a board member of the Scottish National Players until their refusal to turn professional led to his resignation and then, during the Second World War, was instrumental in the establishment of the Citizens' Theatre in Glasgow, of which he was Chairman until his death. He was also involved in the establishment of the Glasgow College of Drama as an extension of the Royal Scottish Academy of Music and was an adviser to the early Edinburgh Festivals.

Bridie's works have often been compared with those of George Bernard Shaw for their argumentative wit, but Bridie, unlike Shaw, had no strong ideology to assert. He regarded himself as primarily a clever entertainer, diverting an audience for an hour or two, but in fact his plays, like Barrie's, constantly challenge the underlying assumptions and apparent certainties of the modern world.

Mr Bolfry was written during the Second World War: its comic engagement with the conjuring of the devil reflects directly on the rediscovery of the power of evil unleashed by Fascism. The Calvinism that was so much derided by twentieth-century liberal thinkers becomes the medium for confronting — and containing — the threatening reality of an evil which modern rationalism has failed to banish from the world. In this it prefigures the early novels of Muriel Spark and connects to the tradition of Hogg (*Confessions of a Justified Sinner*) and Stevenson (*Jekyll and Hyde*).

Bridie was both the most internationally successful of Scottish-based dramatists and the most important shaper of Scottish theatre in the first half of the twentieth century.

SCENE ONE

A parlour in the Free Kirk Manse[1] at Larach, in the West Highlands of Scotland. It is Sunday afternoon. The furnishing is
austere. Two walls are occupied by bookcases full of forbidding-
looking books. On the other wall are signed engravings of elderly
clergymen. There is a presentation black-marble clock on the
mantelpiece. There are no further concessions to decorative art.
A lanky man in battle-dress is lounging in the only comfortable
chair, with his slippered feet on the mantelpiece. His name is
CULLY. When he speaks, it is with an 'educated' accent. He
wears large horn-rimmed spectacles. Through the window is seen
an autumnal Highland landscape, illuminated, for the moment,
by a watery beam of sunshine. A second soldier enters. He is
small, sturdy, Hebraic and disconsolate. His name is COHEN.

COHEN: (*singing, dirge fashion*) 'Roll out the barrel; we'll have
    a barrel of fun . . . ' Not half, we won't.
    (*He finds a dishcloth in his hands and throws it back through
    the open door*)
CULLY: (*in what he imagines to be Scots*) Hoots mon! Don't ye
    no ken, you cannot sing on the Sabbath Day?
COHEN: Don't I know it!
CULLY: Where have you been, my dear Mr Gordon Montefiore
    Cohen?
COHEN: Cleaning up the crimson dinner dishes. That's where
    I've been.
CULLY: Don't you get enough polishing to do at the Camp?
COHEN: You've said it.
CULLY: Then what's the matter with you? Gone balmy?
COHEN: Not yet.
    (*He sits down and absently takes out a cigarette*)
CULLY: You can't smoke in here, cocky.
COHEN: Hell, no. (*He puts his fag away*) Cor, stone the crows,
    what a dump! What a billet! Cor darn my socks!
CULLY: You've only got your lousy ambition to thank for it.
COHEN: What do you mean ambition? Did I have any ambition
    to get drafted up North to this perishing cold doorstep of a
    country? Did I have any ambition to be billeted on an old holy,
    sour-puss, praying bloody preacher? Tell me, I'm asking you.
CULLY: You were ambitious to be the cleanest, best-behaved
    man in the battery, and that's why they picked you.
COHEN: Oh, indeed. And why did they pick you?
CULLY: God knows. They thought I needed a bit of religion, I

expect.

COHEN: What's the good? Lord love me, what's the good?

CULLY: They'll make you a bombardier all right. This is only a small spot of purgatory, before they receive you into everlasting glory.

COHEN: Bombardier? Not me, they won't. Not with a nose my shape and that old Nazi of a B.S.M.[2] anti-semiting all over the ship. Tin-eyed old beer-tank. What you reading?

CULLY: *Meditations among the Tombs.*[3]

COHEN: So help me, there isn't a decent cemetery to go to, let alone a cinema.

CULLY: Why did you wash the dishes?

COHEN: Something to do. Just to pass the time.

CULLY: Damned liar.

COHEN: Well . . . I thought there might be a bit of fun in it.

CULLY: Was there?

COHEN: No fear! They made her go to the matinee — the after-noon service, whatever you call it — the minute I offered. The nasty minds these holy blokes has.

CULLY: Bad luck.

COHEN: I'll be more careful next time. A bit unsophistkitated but quite a pretty little bit of stuff. And a skirt's always a skirt. And I ain't seen many round hereabouts.

CULLY: I thought you were a respectable married man.

COHEN: Hell, chum, I wouldn't be a married man if I didn't like a bit of skirt. Be reasonable. There ain't no harm in it. Read us a bit. I'm right browned off, and that's a fact.

CULLY: 'Indulge, my soul, a serious pause. Recollect all the gay things that were wont to dazzle thy eyes and inveigle thy affec-tions. Here, examine those baits of sense. Here form an estimate of their real value. Suppose thyself first among the favourites of fortune, who revel in the lap of pleasure; who shine in the robes of honour; and swim in tides of unexhausted riches; yet, how soon would the passing bell proclaim thy exit; and, when once the iron call has summoned thee to thy future reckoning, where would all these gratifications be? At that period, how will all the pageantry of the most affluent, splendid and luxurious circumstances vanish into empty air? . . . '

COHEN: I ain't got that. Who's supposed to have murdered who?

CULLY: Nobody's murdered anybody.

COHEN: Who's this bloke supposed to be talking to?

CULLY: To anybody. To you.

COHEN: He is, is he? Then he don't know me! Swim in tides of unexhausted riches! He don't say anything about skirts, does he?

CULLY: Oh, yes. There's a lot about blokes dying and skirts howling over them. Would you like me to read you a bit?

COHEN: No, I thank you. I thank you kindly, I am much obliged, but I should not think of troubling you. I don't like howling skirts, I like joyful skirts. I'd give a week's pay to see one this moment.

CULLY: You damp down your libido, cocky. There aren't any skirts around here.

COHEN: No. And if there were, there ain't much to make them joyful.

(*He goes to the window*)

What a country!

CULLY: Well, the sun was shining last time I looked out.

COHEN: Yes. You can see across the loch. They say hereabouts when you can see across the loch it's going to rain, and when you can't see across the loch it blooming well is raining.

(JEAN, *a tall, cheerful-looking young lady in a dressing-gown appears in the doorway*)

JEAN: Hello!

CULLY: Oh, hello!

JEAN: (*to* COHEN). Hello! you too.

COHEN: Hello! Miss.

CULLY: Who are you?

JEAN: A joyful skirt.

COHEN: You heard us talking?

JEAN: Yes. I heard you. I hesitated for years. I was too shy to come in, till you said what you liked. So then I came.

COHEN: I'm sorry, Miss. I'm not that sort of a chap at all. I'm not really. But you know how it is, when two blokes gets chinning together.

JEAN: Oh yes. That's all right. May I have a book?

CULLY: Oh, yes. Please.

JEAN: I didn't mean to interrupt you.

COHEN: Not at all. It's a pleasure.

JEAN: I'm the Meenister's niece.

CULLY: No. Really? Are you?

JEAN: Yes. My name's Jean Ogilvie. What are your names?

CULLY: Cully's mine.

COHEN: Gunner Cohen, Miss.

JEAN: What are your first names?

CULLY: Tom.

COHEN: Gordon.

JEAN: Do sit down, Tom and Gordon. I won't be a minute. Are you from the gun position on the hill?

COHEN: Yes.

JEAN: I heard you were billeted here. It must be pretty dull for you.

COHEN: You have said it.

JEAN: Where do you come from? London?

COHEN: Yes. Little shop in the Borough Road.

JEAN: You too?

CULLY: More or less, yes.

JEAN: So do I. I'm a typist and teapot carrier at the Ministry of Interference. I was blitzed about a bit, and they sent me for a week's holiday. That's why I'm still in bed.

CULLY: I see.

JEAN: I only came yesterday. The hills are nice, don't you think?

CULLY: Very nice.

JEAN: How do you like my uncle?

COHEN: He seems a very nice gentleman.

JEAN: And there's no doubt about my aunt being nice, so it's all very nice together — only dull. I must try to see about getting you cheered up a bit. But my uncle's so damned strict.

COHEN: He is a bit, isn't he?

JEAN: Yes. It's funny. He's very intelligent too. I'm no match for him. Are you intelligent?

CULLY: I used to think I was. Cohen certainly is.

JEAN: Then we must tackle him tonight after evening service.

CULLY: It will be a pleasure.

JEAN: Will it be a pleasure to you too? . . . I say, look here, I can't call you Gordon. Haven't you another name?

COHEN: The boys sometimes call me Conk.

JEAN: May I?

COHEN: Yes, if you like.

JEAN: Conk, will you help me with my uncle?

COHEN: Well, if it's not too much of a liberty in the gentleman's own house.

JEAN: But it's for his good. There's lots of things we could teach him.

COHEN: I shouldn't be surprised.

JEAN: Then that's settled. I must run now . . . What's this book? . . . Oh, Greek, damn. Never mind. I feel much better. I think I'll get up.

COHEN: Won't you stay and talk to us?

JEAN: No, Conk. My uncle doesn't think naked women are good for soldiers. He'll be back any minute now. Cheers. I'll see you later.

> (*She goes out before the* SOLDIERS *have time to get to the door-handle. They make polite rushes and get to the door opposite one another*)

COHEN: After you, Claude.

CULLY: Not funny. How do you like her?

COHEN: What do *you* think of her?

CULLY: I don't know. I haven't really seen her yet.

COHEN: It seemed to me like you had a good look.

CULLY: She was putting on an act. She needn't have troubled. I didn't come all the way up to the Heilans to be sparkled at. I'm like old Wordsworth, Mr Conk. I am one of them as likes a solitary Highland Lass to be a solitary Highland Lass.[4] I can get plenty 'Come on, you chaps' stuff where I come from.

COHEN: A bit hard to please.

CULLY: (*resuming his chair and his book*) Yes.

COHEN: Looked a very high-toned bit of stuff to me. You could see she was a lady.

CULLY: There are no ladies nowadays.

COHEN: In that case, I'll mizzle up to the canteen. Coming?

CULLY: No. Remember you've got to be back for supper at eight.

COHEN: Hell, yes . . . (*at the window*) . . . and there's the soft refreshing rain coming. And there's the church coming out. And there's his holiness coming up the path. I can't make it. No dodging the column this time, chum!

> (*He sits down beside the table with a gesture of hopelessness*)

A fatalist. That's me.

> (McCRIMMON *enters. He is a handsome, serious man of about fifty. He wears a turnover collar and a white bow tie. He carries a silk hat carefully in his hand. Behind him come* MRS McCRIMMON, *a pretty little woman of forty, and* MORAG, *the serving-maid, a girl of seventeen*)

McCRIMMON: Morag! Put my hat in the box, girl. And take you great care of the nap this time.

> (MORAG *takes the hat and goes out*)

MRS McCRIMMON: Oh, Mr Cully! The Minister's chair!

CULLY: Sorry, Mrs McCrimmon.

McCRIMMON: Oh, it is all right. It is all right, dear me. A man who defends my country is at liberty to sit in my chair, I'm sure. Sit ye down.

CULLY: No thank you, Sir. Cohen and I were thinking of going out for a walk.

McCRIMMON: It is a nice thing, a walk. You would be too tired maybe to attend the afternoon diet of worship? But I forgot. I am the stupid man. You do not belong to our communion.

MRS McCRIMMON: It's raining now, Mr Cully. Maybe you'd be better to stay in beside the fire. I'll put some peats on it, and the Minister will be in his study at his evening sermon, and I'll be in the kitchen with Morag, so you needn't be bothering yourself.

McCRIMMON: Oh, there is no harm in the young men going for a walk. No harm at all. You were reading?

CULLY: (*showing him the book*) Yes.

McCRIMMON: Well, well. Hervey's *Meditations among the Tombs*. An improving kind of a work in its way, but to my mind he was a greeting bit body, that. And not very sound in his doctrine. But he's dead longsyne, and no doubt he has done you little harm with his greeting.

> (MRS McCRIMMON *is busy with the peats.* COHEN *is helping her*)

CULLY: He makes very soothing Sunday-afternoon reading.

McCRIMMON: The Lord did not give his Day that you should be soothed, young man.

CULLY: Oh? I was always told he did.

McCRIMMON: Those who told you so did you no service. The Day was given for rest of the body, improvement of the mind, and the ordinances of public and private worship.

CULLY: Oh, but, Mr McCrimmon, surely . . .

McCRIMMON: Marget, will you bid Morag put my cup of gruel in the study? You will excuse me, Sir? I have to make some meditations of my own before my sermon.

CULLY: At least I was trying to improve my mind.

McCRIMMON: Indeed, I hope so. And now will you excuse me?

> (MRS McCRIMMON *and* COHEN *leave the fireside.*
> *Exit* McCRIMMON)

MRS McCRIMMON: Now, there's a clean fireside, and I think there's nothing nicer in the whole wide world. Don't you think so, Mr Cohen, and you a family man?

COHEN: You're right. Not that I won't say them turf fires take a bit of getting used to.

MRS McCRIMMON: If you handle them kindly you get a fine steady glow. And the smell of the burning peat is grand.

CULLY: Like a burnt offering on the family altar.

MRS McCRIMMON: You're making fun of me, and that's fine; but I wouldn't make jokes of things like that, Mr Cully. Not of sacred subjects.

CULLY: I didn't think a good Presbyterian would think altars particularly sacred.

MRS McCRIMMON: Maybe not, but they are no subject for levity.

CULLY: I wasn't trying to be funny.

MRS McCRIMMON: That's all right, then.

CULLY: I'll go up and get my boots on. What about you, Conk?

COHEN: I've got my boots on.

MRS McCRIMMON: If you're going for a walk, I wouldn't go anywhere you might be seen during the evening service. There might be talk, and you living with the Minister.

CULLY: Right ho.

MRS McCRIMMON: And you'll be back for supper at half-past eight, will you not? It's only pease brose, but there will be a wee bit of cold ham for the pair of you.

CULLY: Fine. I'll remember.

   (CULLY *goes out*)

MRS McCRIMMON: He seems kind of vexed. I hope I was not too sharp with him.

COHEN: Keep your mind easy. He's been on the mat before sharper-tongued people than you.

MRS McCRIMMON: Maybe he's not very used to the ways of a Minister's house, only being here three days; and none of them the Sabbath.

COHEN: That's it. He's not used to it.

MRS McCRIMMON: He's a fine young fellow. It's a pity he's an episcopalian.

COHEN: He's not that, Mum, whatever else he is. He's C. of E.5

MRS McCRIMMON: Ah, dear me, now, he cannot help his upbringing . . . Look, the fire's glowing fine. It's a homey looking thing, a fire.

COHEN: It is and all.

MRS McCRIMMON: And it growing so dark and gloomy out bye. I think we will have a storm. It is not a nice walk you will be having at all.

COHEN: It helps to pass the time.

MRS McCRIMMON: Och, dear me, with me the time passes without any help. You would think there was scarcely enough of it.

COHEN: It hangs a bit heavy when you're used to city life.

MRS McCRIMMON: And what would you do, now, if you were in the City at this very moment?

COHEN: Well, now you ast me, I shouldn't be surprised if I sat down by the fireside and went to sleep. I'd have read all the

Sunday papers by this time.

MRS McCRIMMON: Tuts, tuts! Sunday papers!

COHEN: But it'd be a comfort knowing there was places I *could* go, if I wanted to.

> (COHEN *heaves a deep sigh and suddenly takes a pocket-book out and pushes a snap-shot at* MRS McCRIMMON *as if it were a pistol*)

MRS McCRIMMON: Oh! What's that?

COHEN: Me and the trouble and strife.[6] Down at Southend. That's the kid she's holding up to get took.

MRS McCRIMMON: What a lovely boy!

COHEN: He's a bit of all right; but he isn't a boy. He's a girl.

MRS McCRIMMON: Amn't I the stupid one! I should have known.

COHEN: Don't see how you could, with all them clothes on.

MRS McCRIMMON: She's a bonny wee lass. How old is she?

COHEN: Eleven months there. Had her third birthday last week. There she is. Sitting in the park with her blooming dawg.

MRS McCRIMMON: My, my, how they grow! She'll be the great chatterbox now.

COHEN: She's like her ma. Got a lot to say and says it.

MRS McCRIMMON: She's got a look of you too.

COHEN: Cor blimey! I hope not.

MRS McCRIMMON: It's about the eyes.

COHEN: She's a way of laughing with her eyes before the rest of her face gets going.

MRS McCRIMMON: What's her name?

COHEN: Gladys. Same as the old lady.

MRS McCRIMMON: You must miss them sorely.

COHEN: Not half, I do. Roll on the time.

MRS McCRIMMON: Roll on the time.

> (*A pause*)

COHEN: No news yet from North Africa?

MRS McCRIMMON: Not yet. He'll be twenty next month. Ninth of November.

COHEN: You don't look like you'd a grown-up son.

MRS McCRIMMON: There's whiles I'm surprised myself.

> (*They turn and look at a photograph of a Seaforth Highlander on the mantelpiece*)

MRS McCRIMMON: That was taken the day he got his commission.

COHEN: You'd be proper and proud of him that day.

MRS McCRIMMON: What's it you say? Not half I wasn't!

> (*She laughs*)

You'll have us all speaking the fine, high English before you've finished with us.

COHEN: You speak first-class English. There's a bit of an accent, if you don't mind my saying so, but I can understand every word you say.

MRS McCRIMMON: Ah, well, now, am I not glad of that? You will be finding us a wild uncivilised lot in the Highlands?

COHEN: I wouldn't go as far as that. You don't get the same chanst as what we get up in London, but I wouldn't call you uncivilised — except on Sundays.

MRS McCRIMMON: Well, well, we've all got our ways of doing things, I suppose. Is it a nice place, London? It'll not be all wickedness with eight million folk in it.

COHEN: I wish you could see our little place in the Borough Road. Above the shop, it is. Nice and handy. And Gladys, she keeps it a treat. Pots and pans shining and a couple of budg-erigars in a gilt cage. And always something tasty after we puts up the shutters.

MRS McCRIMMON: She still keeps the shop open?

COHEN: You bet she does. Twicet she's had the window blown in, but what does she care? Out with the old broom and bucket and on with the job. Cor stone the crows, I shouldn't have the nerve. And I'm supposed to be a soldier.

MRS McCRIMMON: Och, now, you're a very brave soldier too, I'm sure.

COHEN: Not me. I get the willies, sometimes, imagining what's going to happen to me if the Gerries get busy on my gun.

MRS McCRIMMON: You'll be like us up here. You've a strong imagination. There's whiles I can frighten myself more than Hitler and Goering and that lad Rommel[7] could do if they were all in this room waving their pistols and making faces at me. I'll be lying awake at night with my head under the blankets thinking there's devils and bogles and kelpies coming down the chimney, though fine I know there's no such thing. But when they dropped a big bomb on Aberdeen and me at a shop door and knocked over with the blast with all my messages flung mixty maxty, I wasn't afraid at all, at all. I was just angered.

COHEN: That's right. It's the same with Gladys.

MRS McCRIMMON: Not but what I put up a wee prayer, the minute I could think about it.

COHEN: The way you'd hear Gladys howling about the War, you'd think old Hitler got it all up for her benefit. But there's no more howling when it comes to the bit.

MRS McCRIMMON: It's our imaginations. They're an awful

nuisance our imaginations.

(*Enter* JEAN — *now fully dressed*)

My sorrow and my shame! What are you doing up and about, you bad girl?

JEAN: I'm cured, Aunt Maggie. It's the Highland air.

MRS McCRIMMON: You should think shame of yourself. I told you to stay in bed till I said you could get up.

JEAN: You know quite well that I never did what you told me.

MRS McCRIMMON: And that's a true word. You've always been little better than a wayward wee rascal.

JEAN: But I'm interrupting you.

MRS McCRIMMON: (*in some confusion*) Oh, I was just having a wee talk with Mr Cohen. You'll not have met Mr Cohen. He's one of the two gentlemen who are billeted with us.

JEAN: I've met Mr Cohen and Mr Cully too.

MRS McCRIMMON: Dear me, when would that be, now?

JEAN: Never mind. And go on with your wee talk. I'll go and speak to Morag and try to work up a bad cough for next time I come back.

MRS McCRIMMON: You are just terrible, and that's the only one word for you. She has no respect for her elders, Mr Cohen. I'm real sorry for her poor mother. And you'll just stay here and cheer Mr Cohen up, and I'll away ben to the kitchen.

(*Enter* CULLY *in his boots*)

Now, Mr Cully, you're surely not going out on an evening the like of this.

CULLY: It does look pretty black.

MRS McCRIMMON: And there's the mists coming down from the ben. I have seen me lost a hundred yards from the Manse door.

COHEN: I'm not going out, you can bet your life on that.

CULLY: I'll go myself, then.

JEAN: I'll go with you if you aren't going far. Mr Cohen can lend me his waterproof cape.

MRS McCRIMMON: Jean!

JEAN: Well, Aunt Maggie?

MRS McCRIMMON: You're just out of your bed.

JEAN: I told you I was all right now.

MRS McCRIMMON: And apart from all else, do you remember what day it is?

JEAN: Yes. Quite well.

MRS McCRIMMON: What will people think? What will your Uncle say?

JEAN: I haven't the least idea what people will think, and Uncle

Mac can say what he likes, and I'll be delighted. He has a
beautiful, thrilling voice.

MRS McCRIMMON: Oh, but, Jean . . .

JEAN: If you like, I'll promise you one thing. If Gunner Cully
attacks my virtue, I shall defend it heartily. I am feeling very
virtuous tonight.

MRS McCRIMMON: Oh, Jean, that's awful talk! And it's not like
you at all. I don't know what's come over you.

JEAN: Get your mackintosh cape, Conk, will you?

    (COHEN *goes out*)

MRS McCRIMMON: I've half a mind to fetch your uncle.

JEAN: Yes. Do. I haven't seen him today.

MRS McCRIMMON: Oh, Jean! . . . It's all right in England,
dearie, and there's no harm in it, I suppose; but surely you
know what sort of place this is?

JEAN: Yes. It's got the best record for church attendance and
the highest illegitimacy rate in the Kingdom. I don't respect it
for either of these records, much. I'm not very keen on going to
church, and I rather like behaving myself decently. So I propose
to do exactly what I like. I hope you don't mind.

MRS McCRIMMON: Well . . . Don't go too far away, and see
and be back in time for supper. I think I'll let Morag get the
supper ready and go and lie down for a wee bit. I've a kind of
a headache coming on, and it's still an hour and a half to the
evening service.

JEAN: Oh, poor soul! Would you like an aspirin? I've got dozens.

MRS McCRIMMON: No, no. It's only a wee headache. Don't
be late.

JEAN: No. I won't be late. We won't go far.

MRS McCRIMMON: (*going*) I hope you have a nice walk.

JEAN: Please forgive me, Aunt Maggie. I'm an ill-tempered
beast. I must be a bit nervy.

MRS McCRIMMON: Yes. You would be after all those experiences.

JEAN: I wish I weren't going for that walk, but you see I've got
to now, don't you?

CULLY: I say, really, I'm not frightfully keen . . .

JEAN: Shut up . . . You see, Aunt Maggie, don't you?

MRS McCRIMMON: Now don't be asking me if I see or if I don't
see. Away for your walk and don't bother me.

JEAN: But we're friends, aren't we?

MRS McCRIMMON: Och, I've no patience with you. Away with
you and your havering.

    (*She gives* JEAN *a tearful smile and goes out*)

JEAN: The fool I am, fighting about nothing.

CULLY: I don't know. I couldn't see what all the fuss was about.

JEAN: This is a Wee Free Parish. They think it's a mortal sin to be seen on the road with a strange young man — especially on the Sawbath.

CULLY: I gathered that.

JEAN: That's why they stick to hedges and ditches for their — social occasions. Disgusting, superstitious pigs. And they're not only immoral and hypocritical. They're Devil-Worshippers.

CULLY: I'd hardly put it that way.

JEAN: They are. I don't want particularly to go for a walk in the rain with you, but I'm not going to knuckle under to Devil-Worship.

CULLY: What do you mean by Devil-Worship?

JEAN: Have you read any of these books?
   (*Indicating the bookcase*)

CULLY: Two or three. They're very interesting. I've just been cooling off a bit with Hervey on the Tombs.

JEAN: Have you heard any of my Uncle's sermons?

CULLY: No. I've denied myself that pleasure.

JEAN: They don't worship God. They worship the Devil. They call him God, but he's really the Devil. All this holiness and censoriousness is to save their skins from boils and leprosy and their souls from damnation. They think if they flatter this fiend and go through a few — rites of propitiation, he'll let them alone. They're like savages tying red rags outside their caves to keep away demons. I know them. I've lived among them. I'm one of them.

CULLY: You may be right about the particular deity these people believe in, but I think you're wrong about the Devil.

JEAN: How wrong?

CULLY: Anybody who has thought a lot about the Devil has a great respect for him.

JEAN: You mean they cringe to him. That's what I'm saying.

CULLY: No. They don't cringe. None of the fellows I'm thinking about knew how to cringe.

JEAN: Who are they?

CULLY: Milton, Goethe, William Blake, your own Bobbie Burns.

JEAN: Robert Burns to you, please. Well?

CULLY: Even in the Old Testament all they could find against him was that he was rebellious and had a proper pride in himself and tried to educate people.
   (*Enter* COHEN *with soldier's waterproof cape*)

JEAN: Oh, thank you, Conk.

CULLY: Conk's ancestors made exactly the same charges against Christ himself.

COHEN: Never mind about my ancestors. What was your ancestors like in those far-off times? Painted blue, they was.

CULLY: They still are. Come along, Jean, let's get some cold, damp, fresh air.

COHEN: You don't want me to come with you, I don't suppose?
(*He helps* JEAN *on with the cape*)

CULLY: You can come if you like.

JEAN: Yes, do. I've got my own mackintosh upstairs.

COHEN: No, thank you. I'll settle down to a good book.

JEAN: Oh, yes. Good. Do read the Institutes of Calvinism. We want your opinion on them.

COHEN: I've already got my opinion of most of these here books, lady. I hope you have an enjoyable swim.

JEAN: Gosh, yes. It's raining cats and dogs. Still, we must get out sometime. Come on, Cully. We'd better face it. See you later, Conk.

COHEN: Cheery bye.
(*Exeunt* JEAN *and* CULLY. *When they are well away*, COHEN *opens the door carefully, leans against the jamb and whistles low and melodiously with his eyes on the passage ceiling. After a few bars*, MORAG *comes in the door in some trepidation*)

MORAG: What is it you want?

COHEN: Me? I was just whistling.

MORAG: You cannae whistle on the Sabbath. The Minister'll be hearing you.

COHEN: Come in the office.

MORAG: Oh, I couldna.

COHEN: The Missus has gone to lie down. The other two are out. Come in a minute.

MORAG: Well, just for a wee minute.

COHEN: I got something for you.

MORAG: Dear me, what can it be?

COHEN: Packet of chocolate.
(*He gives her packet of chocolate*)

MORAG: Now, are you not the kind man, man, no indeed yes.

COHEN: Like chocolate?

MORAG: Och, I'm most terrible keen on the chocolates. I could be sitting there eating the like for all eternity, whatever.

COHEN: You're pretty easy on the eye.

MORAG: Och, I don't know what you're saying, easy on the eye.

COHEN: Got a boy friend?

MORAG: What would I be doing with boy friends, away up here in Larach? I've no patience with them at all, with their ignorance.

COHEN: What's the matter with me, then?

MORAG: Nothing doing.

(*She pronounces this 'Nuthun DOOOOun,' with a dignified coyness unusual in most uses of the phrase. After a brief attack and a token defence,* COHEN *succeeds in kissing her expertly. They disengage*)

Dear me, aren't you the awful man, and a great danger to the neighbourhood.

COHEN: Not me, and thank you very much. Do you know what that was worth to me?

MORAG: It would not be much to a gallus rascal like of you.

COHEN: It was as good as a hundred Players, four pints of mild and bitter, and a gallon of Rosie Lee. And now you better hop it. I don't want you to be getting into no trouble.

MORAG: Deed yes. This is not the thing at all.

(*Exit* MORAG. COHEN *registers mild satisfaction and then goes to the bookshelf. His spirits drop. He wearily chooses a book, without very much hope; takes it to the table and begins to turn over the leaves with a rather disgusted air. Noise of* CULLY *and* JEAN *in the passage*)

JEAN: No. Wait. I'll take them into the kitchen. You'd better take your boots off before you go into the parlour.

(COHEN *listens, is about to get up, but returns to his book. Presently* JEAN *comes in, a little bedraggled about the head and carrying her muddy shoes in her hand*)

JEAN: Hello, Conk.

(*She puts her shoes at the fireside*)

Thank God there's somebody in the British Army with a little sense. What possessed that man to go out on a day like this, I do not know.

COHEN: You didn't go far.

JEAN: Quite far enough. What a day! It's getting dark, too. Another ten minutes and we'd have been hopelessly lost. We couldn't see a yard in front of us.

(*She takes off her stockings and hangs them on the fire-irons, while she is speaking*)

I asked Morag to bring in a nice cup of tea. She was very doubtful. She rather thought she'd go to Hell if she did. I told her there was nothing in the Bible about having tea between one o'clock and half-past eight. I don't suppose there is, is there?

COHEN: What of it if there is? All that stuff's a lot of hooey, if you ask me.

JEAN: Are you an atheist?

COHEN: I'm an agnostic.

JEAN: Good. We'll make Uncle pull his socks up tonight. Talking of socks, I'd better go up and 'put cla'es on my feet,' or I'll be excommunicated.

  (CULLY *enters, wearing his slippers*)

JEAN: Oh, hello! You've been very quick. I'm just going to tidy up. You'd better dry your shins at the fire.

CULLY: Yes. Thanks.

  (*Exit* JEAN. CULLY *dries his shins at the fire*)

COHEN: Any luck?

CULLY: What do you mean by 'Any luck'?

COHEN: Garn! Errcher!

CULLY: I've told you what I think of the young person. I haven't had time to change my mind. She's not my type.

COHEN: Any skirt's anybody's type in a place like this. You're a Cissy. That's what you are.

CULLY: If you call me a Cissy, I'll fetch you a skelp on the jaw that'll make your teeth rattle.

COHEN: No offence.

CULLY: Take care that there isn't, you cock-eyed gutter-snipe.

COHEN: All right, all right.

CULLY: And if you want to make offensive remarks, you'll kindly keep them strictly impersonal, if you understand what that means.

COHEN: Keep your hair on. Who's making offensive remarks?

CULLY: You were winding yourself up into your most facetious vein. You'd better unwind yourself. I find your facetiáe offensive.

COHEN: Ah, shut up and let me read. It gives me a pain when you talk like a gory dictionary.

CULLY: What are you reading?

COHEN: Never mind.

CULLY: Why can't you keep your temper?

COHEN: I like that. Who lost his temper? You did.

CULLY: I asked you a perfectly civil question and you answered like a sulky kid.

COHEN: A bloke's got to be careful what he says to the great Goramity Mister Cully — him that writes to the Reviews . . . What the Hell's biting you, chum?

CULLY: Nothing. I'm sorry. It's funny how chaps begin yapping like terrier pups when the weather changes. Forget what I said.

COHEN: I accept your perishing apology . . . It's five o'clock.

Five stricken hours till bedtime.

CULLY: Oh, as it's turned out, it may not be so bad.

COHEN: Not so bad as what? A blinding Gerry Concentration camp at the blazing North Pole?

CULLY: I think we'll see some sparks flying.

COHEN: What sparks?

CULLY: Wait and see. Our young lady seems to think she has a mission to assault thrones, dominations, princedoms, virtues, powers, and crack their forced hallelujahs.

COHEN: She seems to think what's it?

CULLY: She's spoiling for a row with his Reverence.

COHEN: I don't see much good in that myself.

CULLY: No more do I.

COHEN: Live and let live, I always say.

CULLY: She says that too. Only she says his Reverence won't let live.

COHEN: Cor blind me, you got to make allowances. If you come to a place where there's niggers what likes bowing down to idols because it does them good, cor blimey, let them get on with it. They didn't ask you to come. They don't want your blooming interference.

CULLY: You're probably right, but she doesn't think so. I think we'll have quite a pretty fight.

COHEN: *He* won't fight. He's too blinking self-satisfied. He's got the Commanding Officer on his side.

CULLY: If he does, she won't have a chance.

COHEN: Yes, she will.

CULLY: You underrate his Reverence. I think you'll find he packs a pretty heavy punch.

COHEN: I never saw a skirt yet get the worst of an argument. All in, of course. No holds barred.

CULLY: We'll see. It might be quite a Pleasant Sunday Evening after all.

(MORAG *comes in with a teapot and three cups and a section of black bun. She is very nervous about it all*)

MORAG: Oh, dear me, I wish to thank goodness Miss Jean would go away back to London. We'll all have our heids in our hands.

CULLY: What's the matter?

MORAG: Oh, where iss she? Drink your tea now quick, like good lads, before the Minister finds out. My sorrow, you cannae say, 'No', to her, she's that birsey.

(*Enter* JEAN. *She has changed her stockings, shoes and skirt and rearranged her hair*)

JEAN: Oh, thank you, Morag. You are a Highland seraph.

MORAG: I may be a seraph or a geraffe or a camomile, but haste ye now, Miss Jean, before the Mistress finds the dirty cups and teapot.

JEAN: Awa wi' ye, you chittering oinseach! There's nobody going to eat you.

MORAG: I wouldna be over sure of that, Miss Jean. Ochonorie! It's a weary day for me.

(*Exit* MORAG, *lamenting. The* OTHERS *sit round the table*)

JEAN: Gather round, chaps. Do you both take sugar?

CULLY and COHEN: Yes, please.

JEAN: What a lot of sugar! I suppose the Army's the generous donor.

COHEN: They get our ration, you see, and neither of them takes it.

JEAN: Thank the Lord for our gallant defenders. Here's mud in your eye.

COHEN: And in yours, Miss.

JEAN: (*picking up the book* COHEN *has left on the table*) 'The Discoverie of Witchcraft,' by Reginald Scot. You been reading this, Conk?

COHEN: Glancing at it. The spelling seems a bit cock-eyed to me.

JEAN: When I was a kid I used to stay here for the holidays. I sneaked in when nobody was about and read this book. I didn't notice much wrong with the spelling then. It frightened me out of my wits. My Uncle found me reading it and gave me the telling off of my life. I still feel beautifully frightened when I only look at the book.

COHEN: Tells you how to raise the Devil and that.

JEAN: Oh, does it? I never got so far as that. You draw cabalistic signs and repeat a spell, don't you?

COHEN: I shouldn't be surprised. Like the old boze in the opera.

JEAN: It would be quite fun to try.

COHEN: A waste of time, if you ask me.

JEAN: I don't know. He might tell us why the Wee Frees behave in that extraordinary fashion.

COHEN: He might if there was any such things as devils.

CULLY: What about the good old Battery Sergeant-Major?

COHEN: Cor stifle me, don't you go calling him up now. He's bad enough in the old monkey kit, but think what he'd be like in red tights! Old Mestify-toffles!

(*He laughs and chokes on his tea.* JEAN *thumps him on the back*)

JEAN: Take it easy, Conk.

COHEN: I'm sorry. I had to laugh. Think of him blowing out flames instead of beer, with his fore and aft hanging to his near side horn. 'Battery, tails up!'

> (*He coughs again. Both* JEAN *and* CULLY *take a hand at thumping him on the back*)

JEAN: Oh dear, oh dear; the man'll choke himself.

CULLY: Pull yourself together, Conk.

COHEN: Easy on. Easy on. It's having a sense of humour. It'll be the death of me.

> (*These lines are spoken simultaneously. As they are being spoken,* McCRIMMON *enters without being noticed and watches the scene with an enigmatic expression on his face.* JEAN *sees him first; knocks the book off the table onto the floor; picks it up and hides it on a chair. Silence falls*)

JEAN: Oh, hello, Uncle Jock.

McCRIMMON: Good evening, Jean. Your aunt did not tell me that you were up and about.

JEAN: I got up this afternoon. I'm ever so much better.

McCRIMMON: That is a blessing.

> (*He sits down at the table*)

JEAN: Will you have a cup of tea?

McCRIMMON: No. I thank you.

JEAN: It has turned into an awful night. Cully and I were out in it for a little.

McCRIMMON: Indeed?

JEAN: Yes. It didn't seem to like us. It drove us in after a very few minutes. I suppose it was a lesson to us to do as the Romans do.

McCRIMMON: What Romans?

JEAN: *You* know. When you are in Rome, you should do as the Romans do. I don't agree with that, do you? I mean, you couldn't do as the Romans do even if you wanted to. And they'd like you much better if you were just yourself. We used to laugh at the Japanese for wearing bowler hats and trying to talk slang. I think we were quite right. They were much nicer in those lovely silk dressing-gowns.

McCRIMMON: No doubt.

CULLY: Of course, there's got to be some sort of compromise, hasn't there? You can be yourself, I hope, without offending the local customs and prejudices.

JEAN: Naturally.

McCRIMMON: We have a very peculiar local prejudice, Mr Cully, in this part of the country. We have a prejudice against desecrating the Lord's Day.

JEAN: Is that remark intended for our benefit?

McCRIMMON: Indeed, I hope that if you conseeder it seriously you may indeed benefit by it.

JEAN: How have we desecrated the Lord's Day, as you call it.

McCRIMMON: Your consciences will tell you that. And it is not I who have called it the Lord's Day.

JEAN: Look here, Uncle, let's get this straight. What are we supposed to have done?

McCRIMMON: You are my guests, and it is unbecoming that I should rebuke you; but, since you ask me, I have found you eating and drinking at unsuitable hours and indulging yourselves in unseemly levity and in that laughter that is like the crackling of thorns under a pot: and this on the day that we are enjoined to keep holy.

JEAN: Uncle Jock, there are nearly seven hundred millions of Christians in this world, and nearly seven hundred millions of them wouldn't see an atom of harm in anything we've done today.

McCRIMMON: To be called a Christian is not to be a Christian. You will find in the Gospel according to St Luke the words, 'Why call ye me, Lord, Lord, and do not the things which I say?'

JEAN: When and where did the Lord tell us not to have tea on Sunday afternoon?

McCRIMMON: In the Fourth Commandment.

JEAN: The Fourth Commandment says nothing about tea.

McCRIMMON: Tea is included.

JEAN: And buns. Like a Sunday School Trip.

McCRIMMON: I have no inclination to listen to blasphemy.

JEAN: It isn't blasphemy.

McCRIMMON: It is blasphemous to mock at the Ten Commandments.

JEAN: The Ten Commandments are a set of rules for a wandering desert tribe. And not very good rules either. An American girl said they didn't tell you what to do. They only put ideas into your head.

McCRIMMON: She would find elsewhere plenty of instructions what to do. And the ideas were there already.

JEAN: Anyhow, they tell us to keep Saturday holy, not Sunday.

McCRIMMON: If you were in a proper frame of mind, I would explain to you why.

JEAN: What do you mean by a proper frame of mind?

McCRIMMON: A state of humility and reverence.

JEAN: You mean I'm to swallow everything I'm told?

McCRIMMON: When you were a child you were not allowed to argue about your medicine.

JEAN: I'm not a child now.

McCRIMMON: Ah, well, now, I'm not so sure of that.

JEAN: I'm nearly thirty.

McCRIMMON: If you were Legion, you'd still be a bairn. You have all the signs and symptoms of infancy.

JEAN: I'm glad to hear it, then. But there's something about out of the mouths of babes and sucklings, isn't there?

McCRIMMON: Hath He perfected praise. I did not observe that you were in the exercise of Praise, when I entered just now. And since then I have not been aware of any high spirit of reverence.

JEAN: I can't revere things I don't believe in.

McCRIMMON: You do not believe in the Word of God as it is revealed in His Holy Scriptures?

JEAN: Oh, I believe lots of it, and I'd like to believe lots more: but when you put on that hangman's face and that awful voice and call it 'The Word of God as it is revealed in His Holy Scriptures', I go all shivery down to my stomach and I don't believe a word of it.

McCRIMMON: (*with a bland seriousness*) Well, now, I have observed the same thing in my conversations with the atheists and infidels from England who come up for the fishing. If I employ the sacred and beautiful words appropriate to the subject, they flinch and flee from my presence. I must even abandon plain English and descend to their baby talk. And yet I find that they have the presumption to set their opinions against the Gospel with not even an educated schoolboy's vocabulary to support them. It is very peculiar. They are so ignorant that their own episcopalian meenisters, poor bodies, in ministering to them have well-nigh lost the power of human speech. I have to wait till I see Father Mackintosh, the priest from Strathdearg, before I can converse in a civilised language forbye the Gaelic.

JEAN: (*helplessly*) Do listen to that, Cully. If anybody dares to speak back to him, he makes a beautiful little speech showing that they're fools and ignoramuses — or ignorami or ignoramae — which is it, Uncle Jock? You know I can only talk baby talk. What am I? An ignorama?

McCRIMMON: The wee bit of Latin I once taught you has gone by the board. Mr Cully will tell you that ignoramus is not a noun.

CULLY: Oh, isn't it?

McCRIMMON: It is not. But I will talk to you in any language you please. What is it you want to know?

JEAN: I don't want to know anything. At least, I don't want to know anything about religion. At least, I don't want to know anything about religion that you can tell me. Because I think you're all wrong. Absolutely and entirely wrong.

McCRIMMON: That is your opinion, is it?

JEAN: It isn't my opinion only. It's the opinion of all decent sensible people. You contradict your own book of words by making your holy day Sunday instead of Saturday; and by denying that it was made for man and not man for it; and by preaching original sin and election and predestination . . .

COHEN: Stop the horses a minute. I like a good argument. It's like the Brains Trust. But I like to know what you're talking about.

JEAN: Original sin means that a baby is damned to Hell Fire even before it's born. Election means that only a little clique will ever get into the kingdom of Heaven and the rest haven't a chance. Predestination means that it doesn't matter two hoots what you do, because it was all fixed long ago. It's all a pack of nonsense.

COHEN: It sounds funny, all right.

McCRIMMON: You do not believe in these doctrines?

JEAN: I do not. I think your premises are wrong and your evidence is phoney. There's nothing in the whole thing that appeals to my reason. And if you don't appeal to my reason, you need no more expect me to believe you than to believe a man who tells me he's a poached egg. There might even be some sense in *that*. Some men look like poached eggs.

COHEN: That's the stuff to give him. Reason all the time.

McCRIMMON: How far away is the sun?

JEAN: I don't know.

CULLY: About ninety million miles.

JEAN: Yes. That's it. I'd forgotten.

McCRIMMON: Who told you?

JEAN: I don't remember. I read it in some book.

McCRIMMON: And you believe it?

JEAN: Yes. Because it can be checked. If it's a lie any expert could disprove it.

McCRIMMON: And when an expert had disproved it you would believe that it was a lie. Very well, then. I will tell you a wee story.

COHEN: But if you don't believe experts, who are you to believe?

McCRIMMON: I will tell you, with your permission, a wee story: Once upon a time there was a wee wee fellow with the finest set

of whiskers that ever you saw and his name was wee Stumpie
Stowsie.

COHEN: Cor blimey!

JEAN: Shut up, Conk.

McCRIMMON: If there was one thing he was fond of it was a
good swim. He would be down in the pond every day and all
day swimming with his whiskers.

One day he was swimming and thinking about nothing at all
and up comes a snail as big as a whale. 'I'll swallow you as
if you was Jonah,' said the snail. 'Come on. Do it,' says the
bold Stumpie Stowsie. So the snail swallowed him, and it was
peaceful and warm in the insides of the snail, and Stumpie was
quite joco, like a tourist passenger on a steamboat sailing round
the Western Isles. But a time came when he thought and better thought, 'Now am not I the silly one, dozing away in the
insides of a great big snail when I might be settling down in a
house of my own with a growing family to keep me cheery?'
So he made a great todo in the insides of the snail till the snail
was for no more of it, and he ups with Stumpie Stowsie and
his whiskers into a forest that ran down to the seashore. So
Stumpie he looks and he looks, and the verdure was that thick
he could see nothing. So he climbs up a big palm tree to spy
out the land.

COHEN: So along comes his Fairy Godmother on a magic
carpet. Good night, children, everywhere.

McCRIMMON: No. It was a kangaroo ass big ass a post office.
But I am wearying you, with my havers.

JEAN: No. Honestly. We're enjoying it. It's like old times. Do
you remember telling stories to Colin and me, on Saturday
nights when we were wee tottums?

McCRIMMON: I do, I do.

JEAN: You tell them so well! I believed every word.

McCRIMMON: You don't believe this one?

JEAN: Of course I do, in a way.

McCRIMMON: In what kind of a way? Would you put your
experts on to prove it or to disprove it?

JEAN: No, of course not.

McCRIMMON: But they would be very pleased, whatever, your
experts. Indeed, now, a whole clacking of experts have been at
that very story, proving it and disproving it till they were nearly
black in the face.

CULLY: I see what you mean.

JEAN: I'm afraid I don't.

CULLY: He's been telling us the story of the Liver Fluke. It swims about in pools until it's swallowed by a water-snail. And then it's puked up onto a blade of grass. And a kangaroo eats the grass and the Fluke lays its eggs in the kangaroo's liver. Unless he does all these things the Fluke can't live. He seems to be very well named.

McCRIMMON: So we are told.

JEAN: What a cad's trick!

McCRIMMON: Are you referring to the Distoma Hepaticum or to your humble relative by marriage?

JEAN: To you. I call it cheating.

McCRIMMON: But you believe my story now, I think.

JEAN: Yes, I suppose so.

McCRIMMON: In both ways?

JEAN: How in both ways?

McCRIMMON: When I took you into a world outside this world you readily suspended what you call your reason and believed in Stumpie Stowsie. When Mr Cully brought you back to earth and told you the story in another way, you believed it in another way without stopping to think. Your marvellous power of reasoning hadna much say in it either way, I'm thinking.

(*He gets up, but stays at the table*)

It comes to this, that you wish to have the eternal world outside our wee temporal world explained to you in the language of the tuppeny-ha'penny general knowledge text-books. Such language is neither adequate nor exact. But I'll do my best. Use your eyes and look round you. Mr Cully and Mr Cohen, you'd be bonny-like soldiers if you had no discipline. For three hundred years Scotland disciplined itself in body, brain and soul on one day of the week at least. The result was a breed of men that has not died out even in this shauchly generation. You don't believe in Original Sin, Jean, you are telling me? Well, now, you could easily have had ten babies by this time if you had not preferred talking and sentimentalising about them. Then you would have found the truth that a baby has every sensual vice of which it is anatomically capable with no spirituality to temper it. You do not believe that mankind is divided into the sheep and the goats — the Elect and the Damned? Use your eyes and look around you. You may pity the Damned — and indeed it is your duty so to do. But you cannot deny that they exist.

You do not believe in Predestination? That is because you do not like it. If you only believe what is nice and comfortable, our doctrine is of no service to you. If I give you a crack on the head with a stick, you need not believe it; you need not believe in your dentist's drill or in the tax-gatherer's demand. Go on. Believe what is agreeable to you. I do assure you that you will be in such a continuous state of surprise that your eyebrows will jump off the top of your head. Even your heathen philosophers *knew* that Predestination was a fact, like Ben Nevis. You can go round it. You can go over it. But you are foolish to ignore it.

Do you believe that the body rises from the grave on the Great Day?

JEAN: I believe that the spirit does.

McCRIMMON: In all my days I have never seen the interment of a spirit. You do not believe that the body can rise again, though every spring and every day in a myriad forms you see that actual thing happening. But it is folly to talk to you. The Lord gave you a spiritual mind with which you might see the truth of these things. But you are afraid of your spiritual sight. And 'deed I can hardly blame you. Yet it is with that sight alone that you can apprehend spiritual truths. Reason is a poor instrument for such a purpose.

CULLY: The Fathers of the Church cultivated the spiritual mind?

McCRIMMON: I believe some of them did.

CULLY: They found in the world outside reason a lot of unreasonable phenomena. They believed in transubstantiation and miraculous liquefaction and the remission of sins by priests and the efficacy of prayers for the dead. They found warrant for all these things on the spiritual level. Yet they are outside reason. Do you believe in them?

McCRIMMON: No.

CULLY: Why? Because your reason rejects them?

McCRIMMON: When I said that reason was a feeble instrument, I did not refer to my own reason. But I must ask you to excuse me. My evening diet of worship is in ten minutes. It is in the Gaelic; and I must think for a little in the Gaelic before I am ready to speak it. In the meantime I would feel very much obliged if you would respect my serious and conseedered opinion that today is a sacred day and should be observed, within these walls at least, with all due decorum.

CULLY: Oh, yes, of course, but . . .

McCRIMMON: I thank you. That is all I wished of you. I shall see you at the evening meal.

(*Exit* McCRIMMON)

COHEN: (*with the gestures of one drowned or dizzy*) Help! Throw me a lifebelt, somebody.

JEAN: I think you scored a hit, Cully. His eyes flashed for a minute, but he broke off the engagement very quickly.

CULLY: And very neatly. He won handsomely on points.

JEAN: Why didn't you chip in earlier?

CULLY: What's the good? He's a professional and we're only drivelling amateurs. We're apt to forget that parsons are professionals. Our English parsons are a bit like our professional soldiers. They want us to forget that they know their job.

COHEN: Why don't you shout him down, like you used to do in the barrack room?

CULLY: He'd beat me at that too. He's a chest on him like a bull.

JEAN: He'd talk the hind leg off the Devil himself.

CULLY: Would he?

JEAN: I suppose so. And he's so utterly wrong. It kills everything that's gay and decent in life. The other churches let you alone. They sometimes go haywire and burn a few heretics, but most of the heretics are Calvinists, so it doesn't matter.

CULLY: He made it look so damned logical for a bit. It's his infernal totalitarianism I can't stand, though.

JEAN: They seem to have a sadistic love for persecution for its own sake.

COHEN: A lot of Nazis.

CULLY: I don't know.

COHEN: What do you mean, you don't know?

CULLY: Do you know who invented modern democracy?

COHEN: The thing we're fighting for? No. Lloyd George?

CULLY: No. Calvin.

JEAN: I don't believe it.

CULLY: You can look it up. His system was a theocracy; but all its officials were elected by vote and responsible to God and to the electors. And everybody in the community voted, so long as he behaved himself.

JEAN: You're on his side?

CULLY: I'm on nobody's side. I'm a sort of Devil's Advocate.

JEAN: I wish we could raise the Devil and get him to speak for himself.

COHEN: You seemed to me to be doing your best.

JEAN: Conk! Your book!

(*She finds* REGINALD SCOT *on the floor*)

We'll follow the printed instructions and have a shot.

CULLY: That's an idea. It will help to pass the time for Conk.

JEAN: They are all in bed before ten. We could sneak down quietly and try at, say, about midnight.

CULLY: I'm on.

COHEN: What's this? a séance?

JEAN: Yes. A sort of a séance.

COHEN: I went to a séance. Spoke to my grandfather. Cor blimey, the poor old perisher had gone off his head. Said he was happy.

JEAN: But what about your beauty sleep?

CULLY: That's all right. Four hours' sleep's enough for the likes of Conk and me.

JEAN: That's a date, then. We'll have to be very quiet.

    (*At door*)

CULLY: Where are you going to?

JEAN: I'm going to church.

COHEN: Cor blimey.

    (*Exit* JEAN)

SCENE TWO

The Same, six hours later. Darkness, except for the dull glow of the fire. Enter CULLY, commando fashion, in gymn shoes. He lights the oil-lamp and turns it low. To him, JEAN.

JEAN: (*in a whisper*) Hello.

CULLY: Hello.

    (*He suddenly embraces her with some violence*)

JEAN: Damn you, what do you think you're doing?

    (*She disengages forcibly and gets in a rousing slap to* CULLY'S *cheek*)

CULLY: Sorry.

JEAN: I should damn well think so.

CULLY: I thought you wanted me to. I didn't know. I'm sorry. You see, I'm not much of an expert at amatory exercises. I never know whether they want to make love or not.

JEAN: What do you mean by 'they'?

CULLY: Oh, anybody.

JEAN: Well, I'm not just anybody. I'm a friendly sort of creature; and when I pass a fellow-creature a cheery-oh I don't intend it as a mating call. Do you appreciate that?

CULLY: Yes. I think so.

JEAN: And do you think you can manage to be friendly with me in a civilised fashion without getting into a continual state of excitement — or pretending to get into one?

CULLY: Yes, of course.

JEAN: That's all right, then. Sit down.

CULLY: Thanks.

JEAN: I'm not a puritan. I suppose I've got the ordinary appetites. But I think it's absolutely disgusting to go cuddling or
guzzling one's way through life. Do you agree, or are you just
the ordinary pig-man?

CULLY: Yes. You're perfectly right. I made a mistake, I've said
I'm sorry. I suppose it was a sort of compliment to your general
attractiveness.

JEAN: It's not a compliment at all. It's a squalid insult. It always
has been, until the last few years. Never mind. You know now
that 'I'm not that sort of girl.' Forget about it. Where's your
friend?

CULLY: I don't know. I suppose he's making his own arrange-
ments.

JEAN: How beastly! Go and fetch him.

CULLY: I shouldn't think he'd like that.

JEAN: Whether he likes it or not, do as I tell you. If you mean
what I think you mean, the sooner you two learn to behave
yourselves the better. You're my uncle's guests, and you must
behave as if you were. Where is he?

CULLY: I think he said something about the wash-house.

JEAN: Wait. I had better go. I know my way in the dark; we
musn't wake everybody up. You wait here and keep cave.

CULLY: You'll get wet.

JEAN: There's a cape in the lobby and it's only a few yards.
(*She goes out.* CULLY *fetches the* DISCOVERIE OF WITCH-
CRAFT *and opens it on the table. The clock strikes twelve.
Re-enter* JEAN *with* COHEN *and* MORAG. *They are both fully
dressed.* MORAG *is in some confusion of spirit, but is inclined
to brave it out*)

JEAN: Come in and sit down here.

MORAG: I'll away to my bed, Miss Jean.

JEAN: You will not. Do as I tell you.
(*All sit down at the table*)
I'm surprised at you, Morag.

COHEN: Aren't you surprised at me?

JEAN: Not a bit.

MORAG: There was no harm in it. No harm in it at all. He was
telling me about the wee talking birds he has got in a cage down
in London.

JEAN: Well, he can go on telling you here. Cully and I don't
mind.

MORAG: This is not the thing. This is not the thing at all. Sitting in the parlour and the Minister upstairs in his bed. It is you that is the surprising one, Miss Jean, I am telling you. Now like a good lady, be letting me away to my bed. I have my washing to do, tomorrow's morning.

JEAN: Sit still. Maybe you'll hear something for the good of your soul.

MORAG: Oh, dear me, let you my soul alone. It is two minutes past twelve, and not the Sabbath day now at all, whatever.

JEAN: That clock is ten minutes fast. It's still the Sabbath day. Sit still and be quiet.

MORAG: Oh, dear me. My sorrow and my pain!

(*She mumbles a little in Gaelic and relapses into silence*)

JEAN: You were going to tell us about the birds, Conk.

COHEN: (*grunts*)

JEAN: Oh, very well, then. We'll get on with the business of the meeting. Have you the book, Cully?

CULLY: Yes.

JEAN: Have you found the place?

CULLY: Yes.

JEAN: Let me see. I've got a bit of chalk . . . Oh, but this is terribly complicated! We have to go out and bathe in a spring; and we've got to have a lion-skin or a hart-skin girdle; and we've got to have chest protectors with words on them; and we've got to have a knife . . .

CULLY: That's all right. We've all bathed quite recently, and a tap's as good as a spring. I've made myself a chest protector, and Conk and I have both got magic belts with brass devices on them. You can have them if you like. Conk, give the lady your belt.

COHEN: I can't. It's keeping up my respectability.

JEAN: You're sure they will do?

CULLY: Yes. I know the drill pretty well. I've written Agla and the mystic signs on my jack-knife. There it is.

(*He opens his jack-knife and throws it on the table*)

JEAN: Hush! Don't make a noise. You're wonderful, Cully.

CULLY: You go ahead and make Solomon's Circle. That's it — on page 244. I'll read a sort of condensed version of the exorcism. It should do well enough. Get cracking, now. Give me a bit of chalk. I'll do the central diagram on the table.

(JEAN *draws a circle round the table and adds certain cabalistic signs.* CULLY *makes marks on the table itself*)

JEAN: Whom shall we call up, Cully?

CULLY: It'll have to be a Duke of the Infernal Regions. They are free from midnight till four a.m. I should think Bealphares would be the best. He's the Golden Devil and a great talker.

COHEN: I thought you sat in a circle with your hands on the table and played 'Lead Kindly Light' on the gramophone.

CULLY: We'll do that too, except the gramophone. Are you ready, Jean?

JEAN: Nearly. What's this word? AGLA . . . EL . . . YA . . . PANTHON.

> (*Standing up*)
> Righty-ho.

CULLY: Give me the book and sit down. Turn down the light, Conk. Not too far, you fool.

> (COHEN *lowers the light*)

COHEN: Do we sit with our hands touching?

CULLY: Yes. Are you ready? Now keep very quiet.

> (*He takes up the knife and points it at all in turn*)

Fugiat omne malignum

Salvetur quodque benignum . . . Say Amen.

OMNES: Amen.

CULLY: *Homo . . . sacarus . . . musceolameas . . . cherubozca*: I exorcise and conjure Bealphares, also called Berith, Beall and Bolfry, thou great and terrible divell, by the sacraments and by the unspeakable name TETRAGRAMMATON. I conjure and exorcise thee, Bealphares, by the virtue of all angels, arch-angels, thrones, dominations, principats, potestats, cherubim and seraphim that thou do come unto us, in fair form of man or womankind, here visible, before this circle and not terrible by any manner of ways; and that thou do answer truly without craft or deceit unto all my demands and questions. Lemaac, solmaac, elmay, gezagra. Josamin, sabach, ha, aem, re, sepha, sephar, semoit, gergoin, letes. Amen. Fiat, fiat, fiat. Amen.

OMNES: Amen.

> (*The light turns blue.* MORAG *begins to whimper softly. There is a crash of thunder and the door swings suddenly open, revealing an elfish little gentleman in a glistening black mackintosh and a tall silk hat. His umbrella is open and dripping with water. He closes it.* MORAG *stands up to her full height and gives a piercing scream, which she checks by biting on the back of her hand*)

MORAG: It's unchancy to bring an umbrella into a hoose and it open. It's unlucky.

COHEN: For God's sake put up the light.

> (*He turns up the lamp with a shaking hand. The* GENTLEMAN *takes off his mackintosh and hat and gives them to* MORAG, *with the umbrella.* MORAG *gingerly puts the umbrella upside*

down at the edge of the fireplace. He is dressed, to the astonish-
ment of everybody, in exactly the same way as the REV. MR
McCRIMMON. His face is amiable and his hair is a silky black.
He comes into the room with a light, springy step and takes his
stance in front of the fireplace, beaming on the conjurors)

THE GENTLEMAN: Well, ladies and gentleman, a most dis-
agreeable evening.

(He lights a big cigar by some sleight of hand and then looks at
the clock)

Your clock is slow, I think. It is just after twelve o'clock, as I
happen to know.

(He smiles benignantly, tucking his hands under his coat-tails.
Enter McCRIMMON, in nightshirt and dressing-gown. MRS
McCRIMMON behind)

Ah, Mr McCrimmon, I believe? I am Dr Bolfry. How do you
do?

McCRIMMON: *(shaking hands uncertainly)* How do you do?

BOLFRY: I am very well, thank you.

(He stands smiling on McCRIMMON)

SCENE THREE

The Same, an hour later. The fire has been stoked up to a
cheery glow, and illuminates BOLFRY with just a suspicion of
red light. He is reclining in the Minister's chair, with his feet on
another chair. A bottle of 'medicinal' whisky is on the mantelpiece, and he is obviously enjoying himself. McCRIMMON, still
in his dressing-gown, sits bolt upright at the far end of the table
with a dazed expression on his face. MRS McCRIMMON, with
her back to the Audience, sits beside him. JEAN is on his other
side. They both appear anxious about McCRIMMON, who is certainly looking very strange. CULLY is next MRS McCRIMMON,
COHEN next JEAN. MORAG, completely pixilated, is just within
reach of BOLFRY, and he is able to lean over and pat her hand
or her knee affectionately from time to time.

CULLY: I see. Yes. That's very interesting. But, you see, Mr
Bolfry, we have got a little away from the conceptions of Good
and Evil that were prevalent in . . . well, in your time. We have
rather a different orientation, if you see what I mean.

BOLFRY: I see exactly what you mean. Your generation is not
what you call orientated at all. Your scientific gentlemen have
robbed you of Time and Space, and you are all little blind,

semi-conscious creatures tossing about in a tempest of skim milk. If I may be allowed to say so, it all comes of thinking yourselves a little too good for your priests. You went prancing away from your churches and schoolrooms. And the first thing you did with your emancipated state was to hand yourselves over body and soul to a number of plain-clothes priests whose only qualification was that they were good at sums. That was very foolish of you. (*To* MORAG) Wasn't it, my dear?

MORAG: Yes, Sir.

BOLFRY: You can't organise and expound the sentient Universe simply by being good at sums, can you?

MORAG: No, Sir.

BOLFRY: Just as I thought. And then you found that even sums were a bit too difficult. If you can't do a quadratic equation, all these pages of incomprehensible figures are too much of a strain on simple Faith. You went to a new sort of old gentleman who said to you, 'Life, my dear brethren, is one long smutty story.'

'Aha!' you said, 'This is a bit of all right. Why wasn't I told this before?' But no amount of licentious conversation with serious-looking professors could cure the ache and restlessness in your souls. Could it, my darling?

MORAG: Whatever you say yourself, Sir.

(*He helps himself to another drink*)

BOLFRY: That's an admirable whisky you keep, Mrs McCrimmon.

MRS McCRIMMON: We only keep it as a medicine. Mr McCrimmon is a teetotaller.

BOLFRY: Everything is a medicine, Mrs McCrimmon. Everybody in this world is sick. Why is everybody in this world sick? A most profitable line of enquiry. Why are we all sick, Morag?

MORAG: I think it is because we're all a bit feared of you, Mr Bolfry.

BOLFRY: Feared of me? Feared of me? Dear, dear. Come, come. You're not afraid of me, are you, McCrimmon?

McCRIMMON: Get thee behind me, Satan!

BOLFRY: What did you say?

McCRIMMON: Avoid thee. Get thee behind me, Satan!

BOLFRY: Perhaps I should not have allowed you to get within that comfortable ring of chalk. You must not speak to me like that.

McCRIMMON: (*throwing over his chair as he stands up*) This is nonsensical. It is an evil dream. Presently I will be waking up. What do they call you, you masquerading fiend?

BOLFRY: I have told you, Sir. My name is Bolfry. In the days of sanity and belief, it was a name not unknown to men of your cloth.

McCRIMMON: You are dressed like a minister. Where is your Kirk?

BOLFRY: In Hell.

McCRIMMON: Are there Kirks in Hell?

BOLFRY: Why not? Would you deny us the consolations of religion?

McCRIMMON: What I would deny you or grant you is nothing to the point. You are a liar and the Father of lies. There cannot be a Kirk in Hell.

BOLFRY: (*twisting suddenly round to look at the portrait of a clergyman hanging on the wall*) Who is that?

McCRIMMON: That is the worthy Doctor Scanderlands of Fetterclash.

BOLFRY: How do you know?

McCRIMMON: It is an engraving of a portrait taken from the life.

BOLFRY: The portrait was bitten into a plate with acid and printed in ink on paper. The black ink and the white paper were arranged according as the light and shadow fell on the Doctor's face and bands and gown; so that the Doctor's friends cried in delight: 'It is the very lineaments of the Doctor himself that we behold!' Would you recognise it as the Doctor if it were all black ink or white paper?

McCRIMMON: If you came here, Sir, at the back-end of midnight to give us a lecture on the Art of Engraving, I can only observe . . .

BOLFRY: Keep your herrings for the Loch, and do not drag them across my path. Without this black and that white, there would be no form of Doctor Scanderlands that we could see?

McCRIMMON: Maybe you are right.

BOLFRY: The Artist could tell us nothing about the Doctor without them?

McCRIMMON: He could not.

BOLFRY: And neither you nor I nor anyone else can tell anything about Heaven or Hell, or this very imperfect makeshift of an Earth on which we stand, without our blacks and our whites and our greys, which are whites mixed with black. To put it in simple words, we cannot conceive the Universe except as a pattern of reciprocating opposites — (*to* MORAG) — Can we, my love? No, of course we can't. Therefore when I tell you that there are Kirks in Hell, I am telling you something that is at least credible. And I give you my word of honour as a gentleman that it is true.

McCRIMMON: What do you preach in your Kirks?

BOLFRY: Lend me your pulpit and I will show you a specimen.

JEAN: Oh, Uncle Jock, do! You may never get such a chance again.

McCRIMMON: Sleeping or waking, dream or no dream, I'll have no blasphemy in this parish.

BOLFRY: Blasphemy? I should never think of committing blasphemy. I think I may say that I know my position better. I am a Duke and a General of Legions. Only gutter devils are impertinent to the Deity . . . But won't you sit down?

McCRIMMON: (*sitting*) I can make nothing of this.

BOLFRY: You disappoint me. You are a Master of Arts. You are a Bachelor of Divinity. You are a theologian and a metaphysician and a scholar of Greek and Hebrew. What is your difficulty? Don't you believe in the Devil?

McCRIMMON: He goeth about like a roaring lion.

BOLFRY: Not when I am sober. Answer my question.

McCRIMMON: I believe in a personal Devil.

BOLFRY: And in Good and Evil?

McCRIMMON: Yes.

BOLFRY: And in Heaven and Hell?

McCRIMMON: Yes.

BOLFRY: And Body and Soul?

McCRIMMON: Yes.

BOLFRY: And Creation and Destruction?

McCRIMMON: Yes.

BOLFRY: And Life and Death?

McCRIMMON: Yes.

BOLFRY: Do you believe in the truth and inspiration of the Bible?

McCRIMMON: Yes.

BOLFRY: Have you read the Book of Job?

McCRIMMON: Yes.

BOLFRY: 'Now there was a day when the sons of God came to present themselves before the Lord, and Satan came among them.'

McCRIMMON: The Devil can quote Scripture for his own purpose.

BOLFRY: An entirely suitable purpose in this case . . . Mr McCrimmon, I believe also in the things of which I have spoken.

McCRIMMON: And tremble.

BOLFRY: Not infrequently. But the point is this: Why, if we

hold all these beliefs in common, do you find anything odd in
my conversation or my appearance here?

McCRIMMON: I don't know.

BOLFRY: Tuts, tuts, man. Pull yourself together. If the Creator
Himself could sit down peacefully and amicably and discuss
experimental psychology with the Adversary, surely you can
follow His example?

McCRIMMON: Mr Bolfry, or whatever you call yourself, it is
plain to me that you could talk the handle off a pump. If you
have a message for me, I hope I have enough Highland courtesy
to listen to it patiently, but I must ask you to be brief.

BOLFRY: Mr McCrimmon, I am not charged with any message
for you. Indeed, I think it will turn out that you and I are
in agreement on most essential points. But these young people have summoned me on a cold and dismal night from my
extremely warm and comfortable quarters. If you had instructed
them properly, all this wouldn't have been necessary. But we'll
let that pass. Do you mind if we go on from the point at which
you rather rudely ordered me to get behind you?

McCRIMMON: Go you on from any point you like. You are
whirling about like a Tee-to-tum.

BOLFRY: Highland courtesy, Mr Cully.

McCRIMMON: And keep your tongue off the Highlands.

BOLFRY: Mr McCrimmon, I may be only a Devil, but I am not
accustomed to be addressed in that fashion.

JEAN: Mr Bolfry . . .

BOLFRY: One moment, please. (*To* McCRIMMON) Unless, Sir,
you are prepared to exercise a little civility, I must decline to
continue this discussion.

McCRIMMON: The discussion, Sir, is none of my seeking — no
more than is your intrusion into my house and family circle. So
far as I am concerned, you are completely at liberty to continue
or to sneck up.

MRS McCRIMMON: Oh, John! That's an awful like way to speak
to a guest.

McCRIMMON: He is no guest of mine.

BOLFRY: That is true. I am Mr Cully's guest. Why did you send
for me, Mr Cully?

CULLY: I'm blessed if I know, now you come to ask.

BOLFRY: The likeliest reason was that you were unhappy and
afraid. These are common complaints in these days. Were you
crying for me from the dark?

JEAN: No. We weren't. My Uncle thinks he has got divine
authority. And he was using his confidence in that and his

learning and his eloquence and his personality to bully us. We
wanted a little authority on our side.

BOLFRY: I see. Thank you very much.

JEAN: He's got the advantage of believing everything he says.

BOLFRY: A great advantage.

JEAN: You can't meet a man like that on his own ground if you
think he's talking nonsense.

BOLFRY: You can't discuss what brand of green cheese the
moon is made of unless you accept the possibility that the moon
is made of green cheese. I see. In what *do* you believe, Miss
Jean?

JEAN: I believe that the Kingdom of Heaven is within me.

BOLFRY: Is that all?

JEAN: That's practically all.

BOLFRY: So far as it goes, you are quite right. But you are also
the receptacle of the Kingdom of Hell and of a number of other
irrelevances left over in the process of Evolution. Until you can
reconcile those remarkable elements with one another, you will
remain unhappy and have the impulse, from time to time, to
raise the Devil.

JEAN: Then we ought to study these what-do-you-call-'ems —
these elements, and try to reconcile them?

BOLFRY: I didn't say you *ought* to. I said you won't be happy
till you do.

JEAN: Then we ought to, oughtn't we?

BOLFRY: If you want equilibrium. If you want happiness.

CULLY: But surely the pursuit of happiness . . .

BOLFRY: Yes, yes. The pursuit. A very different thing from
catching your electric hare. The happiest man is a general para-
lytic in Bedlam. Yet you do not envy him. He is in a state
of death in life. You naturally prefer life in death — probably
because you are used to it . . . You are not favouring me with
much of your attention, Mr Cohen.

COHEN: Sorry, Sir.

BOLFRY: Why not?

COHEN: Well, Sir, if you want to know the honest truth, I'm
bored bloody stiff.

BOLFRY: You say that with an air of some superiority. You must
not be proud of being bored stiff. Boredom is a sign of satisfied
ignorance, blunted apprehension, crass sympathies, dull understanding, feeble powers of attention and irreclaimable weakness
of character. You belie your lively Semitic countenance, Mr
Cohen. If you are alive, Mr Cohen, you should be interested
in everything — even in the phenomenon of a Devil incarnate

explaining to you the grand Purpose in virtue of which you live, move and have your breakfast.

COHEN: It's all hooey, that. There's no such thing as a Purpose. It's a tele—teleo—teleological fallacy. That's what it is.

BOLFRY: Dear me! *Dear* me! Mr McCrimmon, you are an amateur of blasphemy. What do you say to that?

McCRIMMON: The man is wrong.

BOLFRY: Another point on which we are agreed.

COHEN: I can't help it. I'm entitled to my opinion.

McCRIMMON: In what sort of a world have you been living, man?

COHEN: In the Borough Road. Do you know it?

McCRIMMON: Even in the Borough Road, do you find no evidence of Eternal Purpose?

COHEN: Not a bit.

BOLFRY: My dear goodness gracious me, I know the place very well, and it's simply bursting with Eternal Purpose.

McCRIMMON: There's not one brick laid on another, there's not one foot moving past another on the dirty pavement that doesn't tap out 'Purpose, purpose, purpose,' to anybody with the ears to hear.

BOLFRY: Every one of your higher faculties is bent to some purpose or other. You can't make anything happen without a purpose. There are things happening all round you on the Borough Road. How in the world do you think they happen without a purpose behind them?

McCRIMMON: Do you deny to your Maker the only respectable faculty you've got?

COHEN: All I can say is, if I've got a Maker and He's got a purpose, I can't congratulate Him on the way it works out.

BOLFRY and McCRIMMON: (*talking together*) But my dear good chap, you can't possibly sit there and . . . How can you have the presumption to sit there and . . .

BOLFRY: I beg your pardon.

McCRIMMON: No, no. Excuse me. Please go on.

BOLFRY: Not at all. After you.

McCRIMMON: It is not for you to congratulate or not to con- gratulate. Who is able to judge the Creator of Heaven and Earth?

CULLY: Well, who is?

COHEN: Yes, who is? Mind, I don't admit there's any such per- son. But if there is and he give us a critical faculty, we got to use it, see?

JEAN: Conk's absolutely right. You tell us to praise Him. What's the good of praise when you've no chance of blaming? It doesn't mean a thing.

CULLY: What happens to your reciprocating opposites, Mr Bolfry, if we can't be anything but a lot of sanctified Yes Men?

COHEN: Hallelujah all the time. Not much encouragement to the Creator to stick to His job.

JEAN: That's the stuff to give them, Conk! And I thought you were too much the gentleman to open your head.

COHEN: No offence meant, of course.

McCRIMMON: Young man, do you realise that your foolish words are jeopardising your immortal souls?

COHEN: That's all tinky-tonk with me. We ain't got any immortal souls.

BOLFRY: I begin to believe it. Mr McCrimmon, it seems to me we cannot begin our battle for the souls of these persons until they realise that they have souls to battle for.

McCRIMMON: It is terrible indeed. Our duty is plain. We must wrestle with them. We must admonish and exhort them.

BOLFRY: It is my duty no less than yours.

McCRIMMON: But stop you a minute. I know that this is only a dream, but there must be logic, even in dreams. I understand you to say that you are a Devil.

BOLFRY: But I am also, like yourself, a servant of One whom I need not name.

McCRIMMON: I am a very distressed man. You must not quibble with me nor use words with double meanings.

BOLFRY: I am bound by my contract with our young exorcist here to tell nothing but the plain truth. My distinguished relative is in the same position as I. I am the same Instrument of Providence as he who smote Job's body with boils for the good of his soul.

McCRIMMON: That is a way of looking at it. Certainly it is a way of looking at it, whatever.

BOLFRY: More than that, if it is of any interest to you, I am an ordained Minister of the Gospel.

McCRIMMON: Do you tell me that? Where were you ordained.

BOLFRY: In Geneva in 1570.

McCRIMMON: What did you say?

BOLFRY: In Geneva, I said.

McCRIMMON: But in what year?

BOLFRY: The year is immaterial. I can't swear to it within two or three years. But ordained I am. And I have preached, among other places, in the High Kirk at North Berwick, to the no small edification of the lieges.

McCRIMMON: Will you swear to that?

BOLFRY: Mr McCrimmon, my Yea is Yea and my Nay is Nay.

McCRIMMON: It is a most remarkable thing, but from what I have heard from your lips so far, your doctrine appears to be sound.

BOLFRY: None sounder. And now that you are satisfied, I have a proposal to make.

McCRIMMON: What is your proposal?

BOLFRY: I propose that we adjourn to the adjoining sacred edifice and there admonish and exhort our brothers and sister in a place suitable for these exercises.

McCRIMMON: You mean in my Kirk?

BOLFRY: Where else? Is it not the place most suitable for a conversion?

McCRIMMON: It is suitable. But all this is very strange.

BOLFRY: All life is very strange. Shall we go?

McCRIMMON: I cannot enter the Kirk in my nightshirt; though it is true that I have dreamed that same more times than once.

BOLFRY: Go upstairs then and change. I shall wait for you.

McCRIMMON: Well, well. Come with me, Marget . . . And in case I wake up before I come down again, Mr Bolfry, let me assure you that it has been, upon the whole, a pleasure to meet you. I hope I have not passed the stage of learning . . . even from a — a Being of your — your Nature.

BOLFRY: Sir, you are most polite. I hope to be able to reciprocate the compliment.

(*Exeunt* MR *and* MRS McCRIMMON, BOLFRY *holding the door open for them*)

JEAN: I never heard the like of that!

BOLFRY: (*mildly*) Of what, my dear?

JEAN: You're on his *side*!

BOLFRY: What did you expect?

JEAN: I don't know. I certainly didn't expect such a pious Devil!

BOLFRY: My dear young lady, you don't know everything, as you are very shortly to find out.

JEAN: If you want to know my opinion, I think you're drunk.

BOLFRY: Drunk? Dear me! Tut tut, tut tut!

(*He helps himself*)

CULLY: Well, I don't know what you chaps feel, but I'd feel the better of a drink myself.

MORAG: No!

CULLY: What do you mean by No?

MORAG: Don't leave the circle. He'll get you if you leave the circle.

BOLFRY: She's quite right. Quite right. Quite right. You are a percipient little slut, my darling.

JEAN: But . . . I mean, it's all nonsense . . . but what happens on the way to church?

BOLFRY: Nothing. Nothing. The Holy Man will protect you. They have their uses, Holy Men. Not that I am really dangerous. But we are mischievous a little, and fond of experiments. Eve and the apple was the first great step in experimental science. But sit down, Mister Gunner Cully. There is plenty of time. Let us continue our delightful conversation. Let me see. Where were we?

JEAN: Does it matter very much? You're the most inconsequent character I ever met.

BOLFRY: Oh, no, no. I follow the pattern. If there is one. Perhaps that's what's wrong with you young people. You don't seem to have any pattern. The woof, as it were, is flying loosely about in space. There is no drama about your associations. Now, I am very fond of the Drama. I have done a little bit in that way myself. To my mind the really interesting life is that which moves from situation to situation, with character developing naturally in step with that orderly progress. Now what is the matter with the four of you is that you haven't a situation among you. You are a quartette that has forgotten its music. We must do something about it. Let me see. Mr Cully.

CULLY: Well?

BOLFRY: Here we have a common soldier who . . .

CULLY: I'm not a common soldier. I'm in the Royal Artillery.

BOLFRY: Here we have a young intellectual . . .

CULLY: There's no need to use foul language. Call me what you like, but not that.

BOLFRY: Very well, then. Here we have a product of our Universities and Public Schools. I know I am correct there.

CULLY: How do you know?

BOLFRY: Because you can't listen patiently and because you have no manners. Here we have this delicately nurtured youth cheerfully bearing the rigours of the barrack and the bivouac. Why? Has he a secret sorrow?

CULLY: No, I haven't. And I'm bearing the rigours because I've blooming well got to. I was stuck for a commission on my eyesight, but I'll be in the Pay Corps within a month with any luck. And then good-bye rigours of the barrack and the bivouac.

BOLFRY: None the less, an interesting character. A philosopher. An observer of Life. Obviously the juvenile lead for want of a better.

CULLY: Thank you.

BOLFRY: Don't mention it. There is about him a certain air of mystery which we shall presently resolve. The leading woman, on the other hand, is cast along more stereotyped lines. She is what happens in the third generation after one of the many thousand Movements for the emancipation of Women. So is Mr Cully, by the way.

JEAN: What in the world do you mean by that?

BOLFRY: You are only faintly feminine and he is only slightly masculine. All these Women's Movements tend to have a neutralising effect on the Human Race. Never mind. It will make our little drama interesting to the psychologist, and we are all psychologists nowadays. We come now to what used to be called Comic Relief.

COHEN: That wouldn't be me, I don't suppose?

BOLFRY: Yes. There is nothing dramatic about the Poor unless they are very funny or very tragic.

COHEN: Wotjer mean by the Poor? I ain't never had a bob I haven't worked for.

BOLFRY: That is what I mean by the Poor. As for the extremely charming little person on my right, I haven't decided whether she is funny or not. As she is an unsophisticated savage, she is probably significant of something which will no doubt emerge.

CULLY: What about the Minister?

BOLFRY: He will provide Personality. The drama will revolve about him and . . . ah, yes . . . his lady wife. As I had nearly forgotten all about her, she is probably the key to the whole business. There, my dear friends, are the Dramatis Personae. We have now . . .

COHEN: Where do you come in?

BOLFRY: I am the Devil from the Machine. Here we have our Persons in the Play. We know very little about them, because, so far, there is nothing much to know. We cannot imitate the old dramatists and describe them as Cully in love with Jean, Conk, in love with Morag, Jean, in love with Cully, Morag . . .

MORAG: Now, I am not, Mr Bolfry, no indeed at all. And you needn't be saying it.

JEAN: Nobody's in love with anybody else. Not here, anyhow. Why should they be?

BOLFRY: The animals went in two by two for a very particular reason. And when a drama has no other especial interest, it would be unkind to deny it a Love Interest. I think the least you can do is to fall in love as quickly as possible. You are wasting time.

JEAN: Except Conk and Morag.

MORAG: Now, Miss Jean! . . .

COHEN: We told you before we was only talking about budgerigars.

BOLFRY: Budgerigars! Love Birds! Brilliant images of tenderness and desire with every delicate feather-frond alive with passion! We taught them speech that they might teach us their mystery. And what did they say: 'Cocky's clever. Cocky's clever. Chirrup, chirrup. Good morning, good evening.' That's all. And yet how much better do you express the primeval urgencies within you? 'Cully's clever. Jean's clever. Chirrup. Good evening.' I must teach you how to express yourselves better, young enemies of Death. Come, then. Why don't you tell Miss Jean what you think of her, Cully? She would be extremely flattered.

JEAN: No, I wouldn't. He's told me already what he thinks of me, and I've slapped his face. You're a silly old ass. If you've come here to talk about repressions and inhibited personalities, I wish you'd stayed in Hell. You know perfectly well that if it weren't for inhibitions every living thing on this earth would run down in a few minutes.

BOLFRY: Of course it would. And how shockingly you misunderstand me. I love repression. You repress your passion to intensify it; to have it more abundantly; to joy in its abundance. The prisoner cannot leap to lose his chains unless he has been chained.

JEAN: Then what *are* you talking about?

BOLFRY: About you. Come. I'll marry you.

JEAN: But I don't want to marry you.

BOLFRY: No, no. I mean, I'll marry Cully and you. I'll bind you by the strongest and most solemn contract ever forged in heaven. Think of the agonising fun and excitement you'll have in breaking it.

JEAN: No. Thank you very much.

BOLFRY: But why don't you do something? Why is the blood galloping through your not unsightly limbs? Why are the nerve cells snapping and flashing in your head if you are to wrap this gift of life in a napkin and bury it in a back garden.

JEAN: We are doing something.

BOLFRY: Indeed?

JEAN: We're fighting Hitler.

BOLFRY: And who is Hitler?

COHEN: Blind me, I'd 've thought if anybody knew the old basket, it'd be you.

CULLY: Do you mean to tell me that we've all gone to the

trouble of fetching a damned medieval hypothesis out of Hell to tell us what life is all about, and now we have to tell *him*?

JEAN: Mr Bolfry, dearest, Hitler is the man who started the War.

BOLFRY: Is he? I thought I had done that. How is the War getting on? . . . No. Don't tell me. I'll try to guess.

(BOLFRY *helps himself to another drink*)

I should think some lunatic has been able to persuade his country that it is possible to regiment mankind. I should think the people he has persuaded are my old friends the Germans. They are sufficiently orderly and sufficiently stupid so to be persuaded. I should conjecture that mankind has risen in an intense state of indignation at the bare possibility of being regimented. I should think that the regimenters will succeed in hammering their enemies into some sort of cohesion. Mankind will then roll them in the mud for a bit and then pull them out and forget all about them. They will have much more interesting things to attend to — such as making money and making love . . . Ah, there you are, McCrimmon.

(*Re-enter* MR *and* MRS McCRIMMON. MRS McCRIMMON
is carrying a Minister's gown and white Geneva bands)

Well, my dear Sir, time is getting on. Shall we adjourn to the Kirk?

McCRIMMON: No.

BOLFRY: No? But, my dear fellow, I thought it was all arranged.

McCRIMMON: No. This is a dream, of course; but there must be decency even in dreams. Waking or sleeping, I will have no phantasmagorical equivocator preaching in my Kirk.

BOLFRY: A dream, eh? You think this is all a dream?

McCRIMMON: What else can it be?

BOLFRY: What is the difference between a dream and a supernatural happening?

McCRIMMON: The question does not arise. This is nothing but a highly circumstantial dream. I shall laugh at it in the morning.

BOLFRY: The sign of a supernatural event is that it obeys all the laws of Nature except one. You will find that true of every supernatural event from the Burning Bush to the Resurrection.

McCRIMMON: There is truth in that.

BOLFRY: Has your room changed? Have the people around you changed? Does the clock go on ticking? This is not a dream, Mr McCrimmon.

McCRIMMON: I am troubled in my mind, but I can yet hold fast to what there is to grasp. I will have no spectre or Devil preaching in my church.

BOLFRY: (*in a low and sinister voice*) By the Throne of Thunder and the Canopy of Eternal Night . . .

MRS McCRIMMON: Now, now, then, Mr Bolfry, there's no
need to excite yourself. You can preach here quite well. See,
here's the wee reading-desk, and I've brought the Minister's
second-best gown and bands. Put the desk on the table, Mr
Cohen.

(COHEN *puts a small reading-desk on the table*)

There now, that's fine. For Sabbath after Sabbath we had the
diet of worship in this wee room when the Kirk was being done
for the dry rot. We'll pull the chairs round, and Mr Bolfry will
give us the grand sermon, I'm sure.

JEAN: Yes, Mr Bolfry. It would be better. Give me the gown,
Auntie.

BOLFRY: What is there in Creation or beyond it that cannot be
wheedled by women?

(JEAN *and* MRS McCRIMMON *close in on him and invest him
in the gown and bands. He is a little tipsy. The others arrange
the furniture for the Sermon*)

MRS McCRIMMON: Well, well, that's no' very polite talk. Put
your arm through here and content yourself.

JEAN: (*with the bands*) How does this go, Auntie?

MORAG: There's a wee thingummy that catches behind the
collar. Look you, I'll do it.

(MORAG *fastens the bands, while* JEAN *walks round for a front
view.* MRS McCRIMMON *smooths the robe*)

JEAN: You look absolutely beautiful.

(BOLFRY *goes to the fireplace and surveys himself in the picture-
glass. The others sit down round the table in silence.* BOLFRY
turns and goes to the makeshift Pulpit)

BOLFRY: You will find my text in the Gospel according to
William Blake, that Poet and Prophet who walked to the edge
of Hampstead Heath and put his finger through the sky. 'Now
is the dominion of Edom and the return of Adam to Paradise.'

CULLY: Ha! Ha!

BOLFRY: What are you laughing at?

CULLY: Paradise! I can't help it.

BOLFRY: You must not laugh at Paradise.

CULLY: Have a look at your Paradise . . . Hunger and filth and
disease and murder.

BOLFRY: Have a look at your Bible and don't interrupt my Sermon. You sit there in your squalid, drab, killer's clothes, with
your squalid, drab mind and see nothing but your little bodily
rough-and-tumble in your little thieves' kitchen of a world. Look
up! The real War is beyond and about it. The War between

Good and Evil. The Holy War. It is a War not to destroy, but to create. It is like the war between man and woman. If there were no war, God would go to sleep. The Kingdom of Heaven would wilt and wither. Death would conquer both Good and Evil and there would be Nothing. It is unbearable that there should be nothing. The War must go on.

For what, you ask me, do these forces fight? Their War Aims are plain. My Führer fights for the New Disorder; for disorder is perpetual movement and movement is Life. The Enemy has stated clearly his Ten Points, from Mount Sinai in a thunder storm. We must not allow our reverence to stray from one single object. We must not create works of Art, nor devote ourselves to them. We must not conceive or propagate any idea about God that is not strictly true. We must do no work on the seventh day of the week. We must respect the Family. We must not destroy life. We must be faithful to our first love and desire no other woman. We must not live on another man's efforts. We must not lie about our neighbours. We must want nothing that another man has.

To these are added two more powerful commands, spoken quietly on a hot and dusty day. We must love the Holy Spirit with all our strength and we must love Tom, Dick and Harry as ourselves.

To effect these things is impossible. It is admitted by the teachers that to do them is impossible to man; and man is the cleverest thing we know. But to the Holy Spirit, they say, everything is possible. By its Grace, they say, and by forcing the soul through Fire and Water up to Crucifixion itself man will at last achieve the impossible, which will be Victory.

I, the Devil, am Fire and Water. I hoist the gallows and drive the pike between the ribs. Without an enemy, there can be no Victory. Honour me, then, for my part in your triumph. Honour me for the day when you spurn the clouds written with curses, when you stamp the stony laws to dust, 'Loosing the eternal horses from the dens of night'.

McCRIMMON: Rhetoric! Rhetoric! Rhetoric! The Fathers have confuted you hundreds of years back.

BOLFRY: So much the worse for them.

McCRIMMON: You are talking a parcel of old-fashioned Dualistic sophistications. You are a Manichæan.

BOLFRY: You are a liar.

COHEN: Order, order!

McCRIMMON: I do not take issue with you for that word, because you are my own heart speaking in a dream. But it is sorrowful I am that it should be so.

BOLFRY: You are better than your neighbours, Mr McCrimmon. They would say that because a truth was sorrowful or distasteful, or inconvenient, it was therefore not a truth. That is why they will not believe what I have come to tell you; that Victory may go the other way.

McCRIMMON: What do you mean?

BOLFRY: That the Gates of Hell may prevail against the armies of the Cherubim. That Disorder may win the day. If that were not possible, why do you wrestle and pray?

McCRIMMON: God forbid that it should be so.

BOLFRY: God forbade Adam to eat an apple.

JEAN: What will happen if you win this War?

BOLFRY: Man's genius will burst its bonds and leap to meet the sun. The living, glorious animal in you will riot in the fields, and the soul will laugh for joy, naked but not ashamed. Your Self will be triumphant.

When I win, Man will be an individual. You may love your neighbour if you like, but all that is highest in you tells him to keep his distance. You don't know him. You will never know him. You are no longer a thing in a herd, crouching against your neighbour's wool to keep you from the cold. You are a man. You are a woman.

Onward, Christian Soldiers, shuffling along shouldered with your heavy packs, and your blistered feet, and the fear of Hell in your eyes. It's a rocky road to Zion, and what will you find when you get there? Your officers lash you on with curses and punishment and flatter you with Hope. There is no Hope in my country. No man hopes for what he has.

What are the virtues that keep you going? Courage? Honesty? Charity? I have them too. Courage is the reaction to Fear. You are more afraid than I am. Honesty is the reaction to lies. Charity is the reaction to hate and suspicion. My honesty spurns your superstitions. My charity embraces both the sheep and the goats.

My flags are the pride of the Eye and the Lust of the Flesh. Their other names are Art and Poetry, and where they wave the abomination of desolation can never be.

How long, O Lucifer, Son of the Morning, how long? How long will these fools listen to the quaverings of impotent old priests, haters of the Life they never know?

How long will they swaddle their strong limbs in dusty parchments? How long will they shut out the sky from their eyes with prisons of cold stone?

I tell you that all you have and all you know is your Self. Honour your Self and set him free; for the Soul and the Body are one, and their only home is the World, and their only life is the Flesh and their only friend is the Devil.

Let the wild horses loose!

McCRIMMON: (*rising*) In nomine Patris Aeternis, Filii et Spiritus Sancti, conjuro te, Sathanas . . .

BOLFRY: Latin, eh? You've gone Papist, have you? You don't know your own regiment, my man.

McCRIMMON: Away with you! Away with you out of my house!

BOLFRY: Take care, McCrimmon.

McCRIMMON: (*more quietly*) If you are, as I think you are, a bad dream and the voice of my own heart speaking evil, I will tear you from my breast if I die for it.

BOLFRY: Stay where you are. You said there was truth in what I told you —'The sign of a supernatural event is that it obeys all the laws of Nature except one.' Think of that before you act too rashly.

McCRIMMON: You said you were here to free the Self from its shackles. I am my Self, and myself is a Minister of the Gospel. I will follow my inclination, look you. And what is my inclination? It is to have the thrapple of you out by the roots.

(McCRIMMON *suddenly takes up* CULLY's *knife. The* WOMEN *scream.* BOLFRY *backs out of his pulpit and towards the door*)

BOLFRY: You are not very wise, McCrimmon. You are not very wise.

MORAG: Stay in the circle. He will have you. He will have you.

JEAN: Uncle, don't be a fool.

MRS McCRIMMON: Oh, no! Oh, no!

CULLY: Let him be. It's all right. Conk and I will look after him.

BOLFRY: You will have it will you? Come along, then. Let's see you hunt the Devil over the moor.

(McCRIMMON *breaks from* CULLY *and* COHEN *and makes for* BOLFRY. BOLFRY *throws the gown over* McCRIMMON's *head and makes for the door. In a moment* McCRIMMON *recovers himself and, flinging the gown over his shoulder like a cloak, follows* BOLFRY *through the doorway*)

COHEN: Come on, Cully. There'll be murder done.

(*He runs through the doorway*)

CULLY: Murder? Of what?

(*He follows* COHEN)

MRS McCRIMMON: Oh, such a like night to be out! And in his

slippers, too. Well, well. We'll away to our beds.

JEAN: But, Auntie . . . But . . .

MRS McCRIMMON: Och, we're dreaming all this. And I've a hard day's work before me tomorrow when I wake up. And moreover, when I do wake up, I'd like it to be decent-like in my bed. Away to your bed, Morag, girl.

MORAG: You're sure, now, we're only dreaming?

MRS McCRIMMON: What else would we be doing, you silly creature? Away with you to your bed.

MORAG: Well, dear me, good night, then, Mem.

MRS McCRIMMON: Good night, Morag.

JEAN: Good night, Morag.

MORAG: Good night, Miss Jean.

(*Exit* MORAG)

JEAN: Do you think . . . ? I mean to say . . .

MRS McCRIMMON: Och, that girl's head is such a mixty-maxty of nonsensicalities, it'll be all the same to her in the morning, dream or no dream.

JEAN: What will be all the same in the morning? Do you think we *are* dreaming? Are you dreaming the same dream as I am, or are you just part of the dream? Is she dreaming too?

MRS McCRIMMON: I thought you knew enough about the High-lands to know that it is all one whether we are dreaming or not.

(*She begins to tidy up the room, moving the reading-desk to its proper place and shifting the chairs*)

JEAN: I don't think I'm dreaming. I'm sure somebody has been here. It was so absolutely real. It's real now.

MRS McCRIMMON: Maybe Aye, maybe No.

(*She dusts off the chalk marks*)

JEAN: But there was a wee minister — you saw him too.

MRS McCRIMMON: Oh, aye, may be.

JEAN: What are they doing out on the moor? Uncle Jock went after him with a knife.

MRS McCRIMMON: As likely as not your uncle is up in his bed snoring.

JEAN: Why don't you go upstairs and look?

MRS McCRIMMON: What difference would that make? Here or there, it's all one in a dream, if a dream it is. And it's gey like one, I must say. Forbye, I'm going up the stair this minute. I'm blind with sleep. We'll can tidy up in the morning, if there's anything to tidy.

JEAN: I'll wait and see if they come back.

MRS McCRIMMON: Please yourself.

JEAN: But, Aunt Marget . . . if it's a real man . . . if he's chasing a real man, with a real knife . . .

MRS McCRIMMON: Your uncle never did the like of that in his life. That's why I know fine it's a dream. Don't you fash yourself . . . and put out the lamp when you come up.

JEAN: But if it's not a real lamp, what does it matter whether I put it out or not?

MRS McCRIMMON: It's unlucky to set the house on fire, even in a dream. Good night.

JEAN: Good night, Aunt Marget.

> (*Exit* MRS McCRIMMON. JEAN *rubs her eyes, pinches herself, picks up the* DISCOVERIE OF WITCHCRAFT, *looks at it for a moment, slams it shut, and puts it back on the shelf.* JEAN *starts and turns round as* McCRIMMON *enters followed by* CULLY *and* COHEN. *All three look dazed* McCRIMMON *throws the knife on the table and the gown on the chair and stares into the dead fire.* COHEN *picks up the knife, rubs his thumb along the edge and shows it to* CULLY)

COHEN: No blood. He can't have used it.

CULLY: Yes, but . . . the Name I wrote on it. Agla. It isn't there.

COHEN: Rubbed off, I expect.

CULLY: It's damned funny,.

COHEN: It's all damned funny. Do you think we're crackers or what?

CULLY: I don't know what to think.

JEAN: Where's Bolfry?

COHEN: He grabbed his hat and his coat and away he went across the moor like an electric hare with his old Battle of the Nile on his head. His Reverence caught up with him on the edge of the cliff. Then he hit him. With Cully's jack-knife, I thought. Anyways he . . . the . . . Bolfry, I mean . . . he took a leap like a circus acrobat straight out and down into the sea. A 'undred blinking feet down. Into deep water. We couldn't do nothing about it.

CULLY: And where he dived, the water boiled like a pot. You saw it. Why not say so?

COHEN: I won't swear as how I didn't see it. But it might have been anything. Atmospherics or a squall or something.

CULLY: The sea was as calm as a millpond. And the steam rose to the cliff's edge. Damnation, we've all gone mad.

> (*He takes up the knife, rubs it vigorously on his sleeve, closes it, and puts it in his pocket.* JEAN *has been staring at them and automatically straightening the furniture*)

JEAN: Cully, what's happened? What do you think has happened? What do you think, Cully?

CULLY: I'm doing no thinking tonight. Come along, Conk. Let's get down to it. If I stay in this room any longer . . .

COHEN: Look at him.

> (*He indicates* McCRIMMON. *All three watch him as he slowly picks up the bottle and pours the heel of it into* BOLFRY'S *glass. He swallows the whisky neat at one gulp*)

COHEN: That's right, Guv'nor. You need it. Do you a world of good, that, eh?

McCRIMMON: What did you say?

COHEN: I said it'd do you good.

McCRIMMON: (*picking up the empty bottle and looking at it in a mournful, puzzled sort of way*) Do me good, do you think? . . . Well, well.

> (*He turns to* CULLY *and* COHEN)

Gentlemen, I must ask your forgiveness. It seems that I . . . that I have forgotten myself. When I was a Divinity student there was a time when I was over-addicted to alcohol. It is many years ago. I thought that I had conquered the vice. Indeed, I thought it. But it seems I was over-confident. I have been too confident about too much.

JEAN: Perhaps you should go to bed now, Uncle.

McCRIMMON: No doubt but you are right. I cannot conceive how it happened. My head is not yet clear, but my legs seem to be doing their duty. I will go to bed. It is the black disgrace of a fellow I am, and me a Minister . . . Stop you, though, am I right or am I wrong? Was there another person here?

JEAN: How could there be? There's only Cully and Conk and me, Uncle Mac.

McCRIMMON: Dear me, that is so. It is a terrible thing this weakness of mine. I thought for a moment . . . I will go to bed. You will put away this . . . evidence?

JEAN: All right, Uncle Mac, I'll get rid of the dead man.

McCRIMMON: The dead man? . . . Ah, the bottle. Do, like a good girl. I would not like to think . . .

COHEN: That's all okey-doke. We know how to keep our traps shut. We've forgotten all about it already. That's right, Cully?

CULLY: That's right.

McCRIMMON: Tell me, was I violent at all? I seem to recall a lot of noise and rushing to and fro.

COHEN: Nothing out of the ordinary. You were a bit excited, but always the gentleman. My old grandfather used to get a bit that way, but Lord bless you, he meant no harm by it, and he was all right in the morning.

McCRIMMON: There was something I wanted to say.

JEAN: It will do in the morning, Uncle Mac.

McCRIMMON: I will go to bed.

COHEN: Need any help, Guv'nor?

McCRIMMON: No, I thank you. You have been very kind and very forbearing. Good night. Indeed, I am ashamed.

(*Exit* McCRIMMON.)

JEAN: Oh, dear? I wonder. Should we have explained?

CULLY: Explained what?

JEAN: I see. There's that in it.

CULLY: If you can explain, I wish you would.

COHEN: If you ask me, I think we'd best forget about all this. Unless it's a blooming murder and we're all in it.

CULLY: If it's not a murder, I'm damned if I know what it is. But it's not a murder.

JEAN: Are you sure?

CULLY: I'm not sure of anything in the whole Universe.

JEAN: I'm a bit frightened.

CULLY: By God, so am I.

(*He puts an arm round* JEAN)

COHEN: Oh, I don't know. A cousin of the wife's went to one of them spiritualist meetings and seen a trumpet flying through the air. But I says to her, 'If you started worrying about things the like of that, you'd fetch up in the Silly House,' I says.

CULLY: You think there are . . . ? Gosh, I nearly said it.

COHEN: Said what?

JEAN: That there are more things in Heaven and Earth than are dreamt of in our philosophy, Conk.

COHEN: Oh, I don't know. Depends on what your philosophy is. Seems to me if there *was* SOMEONE up topsides — and I'm not saying there is and I'm not saying there ain't — he wouldn't tell the likes of you and me what he was up to. Nor we wouldn't have much idea of what he was gabbing about if he did . . . Do you see the time?

CULLY: Yes, by jove!

COHEN: Only three hours to good old Wakey-Wakey. Good night, Miss. You waiting up a bit, Cully?

CULLY: No.

COHEN: Okey-doke. Good night, Miss.

(COHEN *goes.* JEAN *and* CULLY *have separated and stand looking at each other*)

CULLY: Cully's clever, Jean's clever, chirrup-chirrup, good evening. Only not so damned clever.

JEAN: I'm still frightened.

CULLY: May I kiss you now? Would that help?

JEAN: Oh, no, no, no, no! It would make it worse. But thank you all the same.

CULLY: Good night, then.

JEAN: Good night, my dear.

(*They shake hands and* CULLY *goes.* JEAN *puts out the lamp*)

SCENE FOUR

The Same. The following morning. Bright sunshine. JEAN, in a spectacular dressing-gown, and MRS McCRIMMON have just sat down to breakfast. MORAG has just brought in a cover and coffee.

JEAN: Good morning, Morag.

MORAG: Good morning, Miss Jean. It's fresh herrings and bread-crumbs, Miss Jean.

JEAN: Isn't that splendid! There's nothing I'd like better. Did you sleep well last night, Morag?

MORAG: Yes, Miss Jean. I slept like a top all night, thank you very much. Coffee, Mrs McCrimmon.

MRS McCRIMMON: Thank you, Morag.

(MORAG *goes*)

For what we are about to receive, the Lord make us truly thankful.

JEAN: Uncle Mac isn't down yet?

MRS McCRIMMON: No. He had a disturbed night, your uncle. I wanted him to have his breakfast in bed, but he's coming down. It's a beautiful day.

JEAN: How do you mean a disturbed night?

MRS McCRIMMON: Oh, well. He has the indigestion whiles. And it's an awful thing for not letting you sleep very well. That's a beautiful dressing-gown you're wearing. Have I seen it before?

JEAN: No, Auntie. Didn't Uncle Mac sleep, then?

MRS McCRIMMON: It is very nice. But, mind you, it is hardly what we are used to up in these outlandish parts. I don't say your Uncle will make a remark. He may and he may not. But he may not think it just quite the thing for breakfast. Mind, I'm not saying. But even on my honeymoon I always dressed for breakfast. It was just the way we had. Not that it's important.

JEAN: I'm sorry. I didn't sleep too well either.

MRS McCRIMMON: Did you not, now? You shouldn't have got up. We'd have brought you your breakfast. Are you sure you're feeling all right?

JEAN: Oh, yes. Fine now. But it was a most peculiar night.

MRS McCRIMMON: Was it so? You would be dreaming, maybe. I never pay any attention to such things. Will you be well enough to come down to the village with me today?

JEAN: No. Yes. I think so. Have the two soldiers gone?

MRS McCRIMMON: Ah, yes. They have to be out for their runnings and their jumpings. They have breakfast up at the guns, poor souls. Nice lads, too. We are very lucky, whatever. Mrs McLean up by Offerance, she got some gey funny ones. But these are nice quiet lads.

JEAN: Aunt Marget . . . how did you sleep last night?

MRS McCRIMMON: Oh, very well, I thank you. But nothing puts me up or down, from the moment I put my head on the pillow.

JEAN: I was wondering. I . . . You . . . I had an eerie dream last night, Aunt Marget.

MRS McCRIMMON: Had you, dear? It was a wild night. It is a strange place up here in Larach, but, och, you get used to it. It might be something you ate.

JEAN: That's what I said to Morag. I mean . . .

MRS McCRIMMON: I hope you won't be putting daft ideas into that lassie's head. It's full enough of daftness already.

JEAN: All right, Aunt Marget, I won't. Oh, good morning, Uncle Mac.

(McCRIMMON *enters. He is very solemn*)

McCRIMMON: Good morning, Jean.

(*He sits down*)

Heavenly Father, we thank thee for all these mercies. Sanctify them to our use. Amen. Well, that's a fine day.

MRS McCRIMMON: Yes. Isn't it a beautiful day?

McCRIMMON: It's not often you'll see Larach all over smiles the like of this, Jean. It's a great compliment to our visitor. It can be a wild place, Larach.

MRS McCRIMMON: Indeed, that is so. I hope you don't object to the herring. There wasn't a single egg this morning. I don't know what came over the hens. It would be the storm, maybe.

McCRIMMON: Aye, yes. The storm.

MRS McCRIMMON: And now you two will have to excuse me. We're a wee thing late, and I have to check over the linen for the washing before I go down for the messages.

McCRIMMON: Certainly, my dear. Certainly.

(MRS McCRIMMON *goes out. She turns at the door and makes mysterious signs to* JEAN *from behind her husband's back. He is not on any account to be worried.* JEAN *nods*)

McCRIMMON: A man is a very curious thing.

JEAN: Yes, isn't he?

McCRIMMON: Dear me, I did not think that I would behave like that at this time of day. It is a lesson to me.

JEAN: Oh, it was nothing, Uncle Mac. Nothing, really, at all.

McCRIMMON: Nothing? That one who should be an example to the flock should give way to strong drink like a beast?

JEAN: Beasts don't give way to strong drink. Besides, it wasn't your fault.

McCRIMMON: A bottle of whisky! Mind you, it is not everybody who could drink a bottle of whisky and go up to bed as straight as a die. Pre-war whisky too.

JEAN: But you didn't . . .

McCRIMMON: I must have. It was full on the Lord's morning, because I happened to notice. Forbye it is not the first time, the Lord forgive me. But, Lord helping me, it will be the last. It comes on me about every five years. But never like this time.

JEAN: How? What happened?

McCRIMMON: That's the queer thing. I don't know. I had a whirling vision that I was disputing with Beelzebub himself in this very room and racing over the moor with a knife in my hand. And then I found myself leaning against the mantelpiece finishing off the bottle with the two lads tidying up the room. I aye throw the furniture about a wee. Or I did when I was that way.

JEAN: It was a strange dream.

McCRIMMON: Never have I had a dream so real. I could see Beelzebub as plain as could be — in that chair and then uttering blasphemies in my ears as if he were in the pulpit — in my gown and bands. I mind every word I thought he said.

JEAN: (*breathlessly*) What did he say?

McCRIMMON: I thought you and Marget and the lads were here too. He was telling you all to stamp the ancient Law into dust and revolt against the Armies of the Lord.

(*He laughs*)

Very plausible and persuasive he was, too. I had an answer for him, but he never heard it. I was that angered I struck him with my dirk and threw him into the Firth. It wasn't a bad answer, but I had a better.

JEAN: What was your answer? I mean, what would it have been?

McCRIMMON: (*ignoring her question*) It was my own mind

speaking. We've got the queer, dark corners in our mind and strange beasts in them that come out ranging in the night. A sophisticated black beast yon. I never knew of him. I wonder, now, did I kill him? If I did it was worth it all. Mind you, there were points where he nearly had me.

(*He has been thinking aloud, but he becomes again aware of* JEAN *and turns to her*)

Of course, this was all a dream or a delirium, I canna right say which. But you learn things in these states. It's a kind of a twisted inspiration. I learned one thing.

JEAN: What was that?

McCRIMMON: That mankind turns to Almighty God as a nettle turns to the sun. And if the nettle had a fine, argufying brain in it and a spacious command of words, it could do little better and maybe a good deal worse. We've a thing called Faith in us, Jean, and we've no more command over it than we have over our lungs. Mind you, we can develop our lungs and we can develop our Faith. Maybe, I've neglected that a bit. I was over proud of my head. But in the middle of all the talk it rose up within me and told me to strike the Devil dead . . . in my delirium, mind you. But it was awful like the real thing. A lesson to me.

(MRS McCRIMMON *re-enters, ushering in* CULLY *and* COHEN. CULLY *wears a brand-new Lance-Bombardier's stripe.* COHEN *carries a postbag. He lays it down near the door*)

MRS McCRIMMON: Isn't this a nice surprise? Come in, boys, and have a cup of tea.

COHEN: Look at him. Lance-Bombadier Cully, Non-Commissioned Officer in charge of his Majesty's Mails and the same old Gunner Cohen, Lance Bombardier's stooge to same.

JEAN: Oh, congratulations, Cully.

CULLY: Thanks very much.

COHEN: We thought we'd pop in. No good getting a dog's leg if you don't give the skirts a treat.

CULLY: How are you, Mr McCrimmon?

McCRIMMON: I am well, I thank you. Indeed, remarkably well. And you?

CULLY: I couldn't sleep. Look here, Mr McCrimmon, it's no use pretending and telling lies. It's not fair to you. It's not fair to any of us. You weren't drunk last night.

MRS McCRIMMON: Oh dear me, what a thing to say! As if the Minister would be!

McCRIMMON: (*rising*) What do you mean?

CULLY: Something happened last night that I don't understand, and we've got to thrash it out somehow.

McCRIMMON: Do you mean that the — the — the — experience I had last night was shared by the whole of you?

(McCRIMMON *sits down again in great perturbation of mind.* Mrs McCRIMMON *goes to him to soothe him.* JEAN *sits rigid*)

MRS McCRIMMON: Now, now, now, now. The best thing is to forget all about it.

COHEN: I told you that, Cully. You can't do any good.

CULLY: No, we've got to get it straight. There must be an explanation. We can't leave things that way. Look, Mr McCrimmon, do you know anything about Mass Hypnotism? I know they don't think there's much in it, but you know about the Indian Rope Trick, don't you? And the old necromancers who thought they were raising the Devil, they *did* induce a sort of suggestible state. I mean they sat down and deliberately hypnotised themselves with their spells and magic circles. I mean, what do you think? . . . Of course, you and Mrs McCrimmon weren't here at the beginning of the seance, but it's the only explanation that seems to me natural.

JEAN: You mean there was really nobody here?

CULLY: Yes. There must be a natural explanation. I know the other one's wrong.

JEAN: What other one?

McCRIMMON: That I killed a man. I did not kill a man. How I know, I do not know, but I know it. I did not kill a man.

MRS McCRIMMON: Of course you didn't, now.

CULLY: I'm sure you didn't. It's mass suggestion. Nothing happened. Look at the room. There are no signs of anything happening in this room.

McCRIMMON: It is a peaceful room. Everything is natural. Everything obeys the Laws of Nature. It is the sign of a . . . let me see . . . it is the sign of a supernatural event that everything obeys the laws of Nature except one thing. No doubt you are right.

JEAN: (*suddenly screaming*) The umbrella!! It's Bolfry's.

(*All look towards the umbrella on the hearth. There is a tense pause. Then the umbrella gets up and walks by itself out of the room*)

MRS McCRIMMON: Well, now, isn't that the queer like thing? And with all this havering, I was forgetting about your cups of tea. It isn't long infused, or have you time to wait for some fresh?

(*The* OTHERS *are too astonished to react to this.* MRS

McCRIMMON *pours hot water into the teapot and pours out cups. She talks all the time.* COHEN *and* CULLY, *in a trance-like state, take their cups*)

Well, well, it seems you had a kind of a tuilzie with the De'il, after all. You're not the first good and godly man who did the like of that. Maybe you didn't kill him, but I'm sure you'd give him a sore dunt. And you're none the worse yourself.

It's a funny thing we should be surprised at seeing the Devil and him raging through the skies and blotting out the sun at this very hour. We're all such a nice kind of lot that we've forgotten there's any such person. Poor soul, him roaring away like a raging lion and nobody paying any attention to him with their fine plans to make us all the happy ones.

Will you be having another cup of tea, dear, now? You're looking quite white and peely-wally, and no wonder, dear me.

McCRIMMON: I have nowhere seen such great Faith, no, not in Israel.

MRS McCRIMMON: Drink you your tea.

Och, well, dear me, a walking umbrella's nothing to the queer things that happen in the Bible. Whirling fiery wheels and all these big beasts with the three heads and horns. It's very lucky we are that it was no worse. Drink up your tea.

(McCRIMMON *smiles and takes her hand*)

Notes

1. *Free Kirk Manse*, house of a minister of the Free Church. The Free Church seceded from the Church of Scotland in 1843 and although the main bodies of the two churches reunitied in the 1920s, a segment of the Free Church continued its independent existence — sometimes called the 'Wee Free Church'. The Free Church is committed to the more rigorous elements of the Calvinist theology on which the Church of Scotland was founded.
2. *B.S.M.*, Battery Sergeant Major.
3. *Meditations among the Tombs*, by the Rev. James Hervey, A.M., at one time Rector of Weston Favell, Northamptonshire, written in 1746. The book asserts the fundamentally Calvinistic basis of the 39 articles of the Church of England, and its harmony with the fundamental truths of all protestant religions.
4. *I'm like old Wordsworth . . . Highland Lass*, in Wordsworth's poem 'The solitary reaper', the speaker encounters an isolated young woman singing a Gaelic song, whose beauty he can respond to despite not uderstanding her language.
5. *Episcopalian . . . C. of E.*, in Scotland, Anglicans are referred to by the term that means rule by bishops, the element most opposed by early presbyterianism.
6. *trouble and strife*, wife (Cockney rhyming slang).
7. *Goering and that lad Rommel*, Hermann Goering was the close associate of German Nazi leader Adolf Hitler, and head of the Luftwaffe (the German Air Force). Rommel was Hitler's battle-winning general in North Africa until defeated by the Allies in 1943.

Glossary

angered, grieved, annoyed
awa' wi' ye, go away
ben, within, through, inside
birsey, (birsie) hot-tempered, passionate
body, a person (sometimes used contemptuously)
bogles, ghosts, spectres
bonny, pretty, beautiful
cannae, cannot
dunt, blow, knock
feared, (feart) afraid, frightened
forbye, as well as, besides, in addition to
gallus, (gallows) wild, bold, daring, rascally
gey, rather, very
greeting, weeping, lamenting
havering, talking nonsense
heids, heads
heilans, highlands of Scotland
joco, merry, lively, pleased with oneself

kelpies, water demons haunting rivers in forms of horses
ken, know
kirk, church
longsyne, (lang syne) long ago
messages, shopping
mixty-maxty, jumbled together; a jumble
peely-wally, sickly, ill-looking
skelp, smack, slap
sneck up, shut up, hold one's tongue
thingummy, something one cannot give a name to
thrapple, windpipe, throat
tuilzie, (tulyie) quarrel, fight, wrangle or dispute
unchancy, unlucky
vexed, distressed, grieved

Ena Lamont Stewart

Men Should Weep

(1947)

CHARACTERS

Maggie
Granny
Edie
Marina
Lily
Alex
Jenny
John
Ernest
Isa
Mrs Wilson
Mrs Harris

Introduction

In the 1930s, Scottish writers, like writers in many parts of Europe, were driven by the appalling conditions of the Depression to document the lives of the working classes, and to impress on audiences (mostly middle-class) the depth of the deprivations they suffered. In the West of Scotland, high unemployment, dense housing and encouragement of immigrant workers prepared to work for lower wages produced a downward spiral of social deprivation. The struggle against these terrible conditions was documented in novels such as James Barke's *Major Operation*, published in 1936 and dramatised by the Unity Theatre in 1941.

Ena Lamont Stewart (born in 1912) was the wife of an actor and began writing plays for amateur groups in the 1940s because of her disillusionment with the falsity of plays being put on by professional theatre companies. Her first play, *Starched Aprons* (1942), was about a large hospital but was not produced till after the War when her husband was working with Unity Theatre. *Men Should Weep* (1947) was also produced by Unity and was so successful that it transferred to Edinburgh and London before returning to Glasgow in 1948. Thereafter, however, her work was forgotten until the 1970s.

Most of the works of that period — even with a female protagonist — adopted a fundamentally male perspective on social issues. Ena Lamont Stewart's work is significant in that it presents working-class experience from the point of view of women whose lives have been defined by the success or failure of the men to whom they are — or are not — married, and who are struggling to find an alternative way of valuing their own experience. In *Men Should Weep*, the relationships between men and women, under conditions of extreme pressure, are explored as part of the struggle to achieve a common humanity in defiance of the brutalisation imposed on them by capitalism. In presenting a working-class, female perspective on the modern city, Stewart was, in 1947, well before her time — which may account for the fact that she substantially revised her play when it was revived by the 7:84 Theatre Company in the 1970s, taking out the many melodramatic deaths with which it had concluded and introducing some of the feminist perspectives of the 1960s and 1970s.

ACT ONE

Scene: the kitchen of the Morrisons' home in the East End of
Glasgow. Time: the nineteen-thirties.

Right centre: a window with sink beneath; below this a door to
bedroom. Back centre: kitchen range; left centre: bed recess, curtained; below this door to outside landing. Another door to left
of range leads to another room referred to as 'the back parlour'.

Nappies hang on a string across the fireplace and the table,
dresser, etc., are in a clutter.

CHRISTOPHER, the owner of the nappies, is asleep behind the
closed curtains with MARINA. These children are heard but not
seen.

GRANNY, a shawl over her shoulders, is down left in her rocking chair, sucking a sweetie. All that can be seen of MAGGIE is
her posterior as she hangs out of the window.

MAGGIE: Edie! Ernie! Wull yous two come in oot o that when
ye're tellt! If I've got tae cry on ye again, it'll be the worse for
ye, I'm tellin ye.
    (*She sinks into a chair and sighs, then yawns widely*)
GRANNY: (*giving a companionable yawn*) Eh deary, deary me!
(*Singing, none too tunefully*) 'When the weary seekin rest to thy
goodness flee, when the heavy-laden . . . '
MAGGIE: Aw, cut oot the music, Granny, ma heid's splittin.
Time you wis in yer bed.
GRANNY: No yet, Maggie. No yet. The nicht's ower lang when
ye're aul.
MAGGIE: I canna be as aul as I feel then, for the nicht's a Hell
o a sight tae short for me; seems I'm no sooner in ma bed than
I've tae rise. It's a right for you wi naethin tae dae but sit there
an gant.
GRANNY: Aye . . . that's a I'm fit for noo! Sittin an gantin.
MAGGIE: I wish ye could pit yersel tae bed. Ye're as much bother
as anither wean.
GRANNY: That's right, cest up whit ye're daein for yer man's
aul mither! (*Whining and rocking*) Oh, it's a terrible thing tae
be aul wi naebody wantin ye. Oh, it's time I wisna here!
MAGGIE: Time I wisna here tae; I should be reddin up the place
a bit afore Lily comes. Right enough, if a woman did everythin
that ought tae be done aboot the hoose, she'd go on a day an
a night till she drapped doon deid.
GRANNY: Eh? Whit's that, Maggie? Wha's drapped doon deid?

MAGGIE: There's naebody drapped doon deid, Granny; least-ways, *no here*! You'll no drap! You'll just sit it oot like it was a second roon o the pictures.

GRANNY: I'll be away soon. (*Nodding her head*) Aye. It'll no be lang afore I'm awa. Aye. Ma life's ebbin. Ebbin awa.

MAGGIE: Och, it's been ebbin ever since I met ye; but the tide aye seems tae come in again.

GRANNY: (*setting up a terrible wail*) Oh, that's no nice! that's no a nice thing tae say! But I ken the way it is, Maggie; I'm jist an aul nuisance, takin up room. I'll awa back tae Lizzie's the morn. (*Sets the chair rocking fiercely and cries*)

MAGGIE: Ye're no due at Lizzie's till the end o the month and she'll no take ye a day sooner.

GRANNY: Oh, I'll no bother ony o ye. I'll awa tae the Poorhoose an John can hae me boxed and buried frae there. It's him the disgrace'll fa on, no me.

MAGGIE: Och Granny, stop yer nonsense! Ye ken fine there's nae such a thing . . . leastways it's got a fancy name noo. Onyway, John and me wad never send ye onywhere.

GRANNY: Ye send me tae Lizzie's.

MAGGIE: Aye . . . well . . . Lizzie's tae tak her turn.

GRANNY: She disna want me. She's aye crabbit, is Lizzie. She's got a tongue wad clip cloots. A she's interested in's ma pension book

MAGGIE: Aye, she's a right skinflint, is Lizzie.

GRANNY: She's aye been able tae keep her belly well lined, Lizzie. *She*'s had nae hard times! No like me, a widdy wi weans tae bring up.

MAGGIE: Uch I ken a that. It's ancient history. I live in the present. One day at a time. And, ma Goad! That's enough.

GRANNY: (*sudden shout after a pause*) Goad bless Lloyd George! Him that gie's us wur pension books. (*Singing*) 'Glorious things of thee are spoken . . . '

MAGGIE: Wheesht! Lay aff the hymns. Ye'll waken the weans.
(*Sure enough, she has:* CHRISTOPHER *starts to cry*)
There noo, see whit ye've done ye aul pest! and him teethin, tae.
(*She crosses to the bed and her head and shoulders disappear behind the curtain: she makes soothing noises*)
Shoosh, shoosh, pet; go bye-byes.
(CHRISTOPHER *continues to wail.* EDIE *comes in. She is about eleven, skinny and somewhat adenoidal. She wears a miscellaneous collection of cast-off clothing, her stockings are down about her ankles*)

EDIE: Ma. Ma. Ernest won't come in. I tellt him, but he'll no. Ma. He said a bad word. He said: 'Awa tae Hell'.

(GRANNY *makes an exclamation of horror*)

GRANNY: Oo! Hell is whaur yon lad'll gang. He's needin a guid leatherin, Maggie.

MAGGIE: I hevna the energy. (*To* EDIE) See's ower yon sugar basin, Edie.

(EDIE *hunts out the sugar bowl,* MAGGIE *dips the baby's dummy into it and retires again behind the curtain: the wails cease abruptly. She emerges*)

EDIE : Ma. Ma. I'm hungry, Ma.

MAGGIE: Oh, stummicks! Stummicks! Am I no seeck o folks an their stummicks. Get yersel a piece.

GRANNY: It seems a lang while since I had onythin. There wouldna be a wee drap left in the pot, Maggie?

MAGGIE: If you'll gae aff quiet tae yer bed, I'll mak a wee cup and bring it ben tae ye.

GRANNY: Wull ye? A nice hot cup. Wi sugar and condensed mulk? And a wee bit bread tae dip?

MAGGIE: Aye. Come on. (GRANNY *struggles out of her chair*) That's the girl. Ups-a-daisy! Edie, pit the kettle on and then come and help me get yer Granny oot o her stays.

EDIE: (*wailing*) Aw Ma! Must I?

MAGGIE: Dae whit ye're tellt or I'll tell yer Daddy on ye.

MARINA: (*voice from behind bed curtain*) Mammy, can I hev a piece?

MAGGIE: Are you wakened noo? The lugs you weans has on you! Edie, get Marina a piece. And if ye drap the jeely on the bed, Marina, I'll gie ye the daein ye should have got for spillin yer co-co-a last night.

(MAGGIE *takes* GRANNY *off left.* EDIE *puts on kettle, cuts and spreads bread for* MARINA *and pushes it through curtain*)

EDIE: Mind oot, Marina; the jeely's runny.

(EDIE *is busy with her own piece when there is a brisk knock on the outside door.* EDIE *opens it to* LILLY GIBB, *Maggie's sister: a spare, hard-mouthed woman in her thirties*)

Hello, Auntie Lily. Mammy's busy pittin ma Granny tae her bed.

LILY: Hullo. (*calling*) Hullo Maggie!

MAGGIE: (*off*) Hullo Lily! Edie! I want ye!

EDIE: (*putting down her 'piece'*) Aw Jings!

(*She trails reluctantly off, making a face*)

MARINA: Hullo, Auntie Lily.

LILY: (*going to bed*) Hullo! Are you no asleep yet? Whit's this ye're eatin? Bread and jam at this time o night! Are ye no ashamed o yersel? An y're a jammy; wait till I wipe yer fingers.

(*She has a hunt for a towel which she dips in water and disappears again behind the curtain*)

There noo, off ye go tae sleep.

(*She stands in the middle of the kitchen and surveys* MAGGIE's *muddle: sighs, takes off her coat and ties a towel round her waist, rolls up her sleeves, wonders where to start.*

From the back parlour comes the sound of BERTIE *coughing. It is a TB cough and it continues intermittently throughout the scene. She takes from her shopping bag a tin of baked beans and a bottle of cough mixture, lays them down on the crowded table, then hunts for a teaspoon, wipes it, goes to door, back left*)

Bertie! Bertie dear! I'm comin ben tae see ye. I'm comin wi something nice tae stop yer nasty cough.

(*She goes off with bottle and spoon.* MARINA *starts to sing:*)

MARINA: Jesus loves me this I know
  For the Bi-bul tells me so (*Pause*)
  Did ye ever see a dream walk-in?
  Well I did.
  Did ye ever hear a dream talk-in?
  Well I did.

Auntie Lily! Auntie Lily! I'm singing. D'ye no want tae hear me singing? Auntie *Lil*-y!

(MAGGIE *comes in at a run, swoops down on* MARINA *and extinguishes the song with a smart slap. A howl from* MARINA)

GRANNY: (*off*) Maggie! Maggie! She's pullin the hair oot o ma heid!

MAGGIE: (*hurrying back*) Edie! Whit're you daein tae yer Granny?

(LILY, *coming back with bottle and spoon meets her*)

MAGGIE: I'll be ben in a minute, Lily; Goad, if it's nae yin, it's anither.

MARINA: Auntie Lily, I'm wantin a drink.

LILY: Ye're no gettin one. Go tae sleep.

MARINA: Auntie Lily, I'm needin a drink of *wat*-ter!

(LILY *gives her a drink.* EDIE *comes in, goes across to the window and shouts out:*)

EDIE: Ernest! Ernest! You've tae come in at once. Ma's gonna wallop the daylights oot o ye . . . Auntie Lily, Ernest'll no come in. I came in when Mammy shouted on me; but Ernest'll no come in, so he'll no.

LILY: (*dry*) Fancy that! aren't you a wee clever? (*Surveying her with distaste*) Pull up yer stockings. Have ye nae suspenders?

EDIE: *Suspenders*? No.

LILY: Well, have ye nae garters?

EDIE: No, Auntie Lily.

LILY: Well, have ye nae elastic in yer breeks?

EDIE: I've nae breeks.

(MAGGIE *comes in*)

LILY: Maggie, has she no got a pair o knickers tae her name?

MAGGIE: They're wore oot. I'll see whit I can get doon at the Mission — if I've onything left efter settlin the grocer.

LILY: (*despairing*) Maggie, ye're aye in the same pickle.

MAGGIE: Lily, money disnae stretch. Ye pit oot yer haun for yer change and whit d'ye get? A coupla coppers. A ten shillingy note's no a ten shillingy note ony langer. I dinna ken whit they dirty rotten buggers in Parliament are daein wi ma money, but they're daein *somethin*. John says . . .

LILY: Ach, I'm no wantin tae hear whit John says aboot they bliddy capitalists. I've heard it a. It wisnae they bliddy capitalists gie'd you a the weans, wis it?

MAGGIE: (*with her hearty laugh*) No that I mind o!

LILY: John should think shame o himsel.

MAGGIE: Whit way? He's a man and I'm a wumman. We're flesh an blood.

(EDIE, *all ears, looks from one to the other*)

EDIE: Are you no flesh an blood, Auntie Lily?

MAGGIE: No, she's jist skin an bone.

(CHRISTOPHER *wakens up and starts to cry*)

He's teethin.

LILY: He canna *aye* be teethin!

(MAGGIE *dips the dummy in the sugar bowl and the crying stops as she disappears behind the curtain*)

Ye shouldna gie him sugar, Maggie; it's bad for worms.

MAGGIE: Ach! Worms!

LILY: Y're wastin him. As if it wisnae bad enough lettin him walk too soon and gie'in him rickets . . .

MAGGIE: He has nutt got rickets!

LILY: Whit else is bowly legs but rickets?

MAGGIE: Bringin up weans is no as easy as it looks, Lily. Old maids are awfu good at the criticisin.

LILY: I hope ye don't think I'm envyin you because you managed tae get the haud o a man. Look at ye! Dae ye never rin a comb through yer hair?

MAGGIE: (*turning to the grinning, listening* EDIE) Edie, rin you aff tae yer bed.

EDIE: Aw, Mammy! No yet!

(*She scratches her head vigorously*)

LILY: Here! Has she got somethin?

MAGGIE: Edie, wis you scratchin? Come here! (*Seizes her and examines her head without mercy, heaves a sigh of relief and thrusts her away*) Thank Goad! that's one thing I wull not have in this hoose . . . a loose.

EDIE: Mary Harris has got them, so she has. Teacher says so.

MAGGIE: Mary Harris! And her up this very close! Jist wait till I get the haud o that lazy mother o hers, I'll gie her a piece o my mind. Listen you tae me, Edie, there's tae be nae mair playin wi Mary Harris till she's got her heid cleaned. We've no very much this side o respectability, but there's aye soap and water.

LILY: Tae look at her, ye wouldna think it.

EDIE: I wis playing in the back coort.

MAGGIE: Nae back-chat. Get oot the soap and flannel and dae yer neck in case the teacher taks it intae her impident heid tae look the morn.

(EDIE *drifts around*)

EDIE: Ma, I canna find the flannel.

MAGGIE: Noo, whaur did I lay it doon? I did Christopher before he went oot ta-tas . . .

LILY: How you ever find onythin in this midden beats me.

MAGGIE: Oh, here it is. It beats me tae sometimes. Edie, bend ower the sink till I scart some o this dirt aff ye.

LILY: D'ye no tak aff her dress tae wash her neck?

MAGGIE: Awa for Goad's sake! It's no Setterday nicht.

LILY: She's old enough tae dae it hersel. The way you rin efter they weans is the bloomin limit. Nae wunner y're hauf-deid.

MAGGIE: I'm no hauf-deid!

LILY: Well, ye look it.

MAGGIE: I canna help ma looks ony mair than you can help yours.

LILY: The difference is, I try. Hev ye looked in the mirror since ye rose the morn?

MAGGIE: I havena time tae look in nae mirrors; and neither would you if ye'd a hoose an a man an five weans.

LILY: Yin o they days your lovin Johnnie's gonna tak a look at whit he married and it'll be ta-ta Maggie.

MAGGIE: My lovin Johnnie's still ma loving Johnnie, whitever I look like. (*Finishing off* EDIE) Comb yer hair noo, Edie . . . I wonder whaur it's got tae? (*They both look for the comb*)

EDIE: I canna find it Ma. Auntie Lily, could you lend us yours?

LILY: (*starting to look in her bag, then thinking better of it*) I didna
bring it the night.

EDIE: I've nae beasts, Auntie Lily.

LILY: Jist the same, I didna bring it. Scram aff tae yer bed.

MAGGIE: Aye, Edie, get aff afore yer feyther comes in frae the
library.

LILY: Oh, is that whaur he is?

(EDIE *takes down from wall key to the outside W.C. and goes
off*)

MAGGIE: Whaur else wad he be? He disna go tae the pubs noo.

LILY: Oh aye! I'd forgot he'd went 'TT'.

MAGGIE: Ye ken he's 'TT'; but ye jist canna resist a dig at him.
He hasna been inside a pub since Marina was born.

LILY: That's whit he tells you, onywey.

MAGGIE: My, the tongue you hev on you, Lily; it's a pity ye
had yon disappointment; ye might hev been real happy wi the
right man and a coupla weans.

(LILY *holds out her sleeve and laughs up it*)

LILY: Dae you think *you're* happy?

MAGGIE: Aye! I'm happy!

LILY: In this midden?

MAGGIE: Ye canna help havin a midden o a hoose when there's
kids under yer feet a day. I dae the best I can.

LILY: I ken ye do. I'd gie it up as hopeless. Nae hot water. Nae
place tae dry the weans' clothes . . . nae money. If John wad
gie hissel a shake . . .

MAGGIE: You leave John alane! He does his best for us.

LILY: No much o a best. O.K. O.K. Keep yer wig on! Ye're
that touchy ye'd think ye wis jist new merriet. I believe ye still
love him!

MAGGIE: Aye. I still love John. And whit's more, he loves me.

LILY: Ye ought tae get yer photies took and send them tae the
Sunday papers! 'Twenty-five years merriet and I still love ma
husband. Is this a record?'

MAGGIE: I'm sorry for you, Lily. I'm right sorry for you.

LILY: We're quits then.

MAGGIE: Servin dirty hulkin brutes o men in a Coocaddens
pub.

LILY: Livin in a slum and slavin efter a useless man an his greetin
weans.

MAGGIE: They're *my* weans! I'm workin for ma ain.

LILY: I'm *paid* for ma work.

MAGGIE: So'm I! No in wages . . . I'm paid wi love. (*Pause*)
And when did you last have a man's airms roon ye?

LILY: *Men*! I'm wantin nae man's airms roon me. They're a dirty beasts.

MAGGIE: Lily, yer mind's twisted. You canna see a man as a man. Ye've got them a lumped thegether. Ye're daft!

LILY: You're *saft*! You think yer man's wonderful and yer weans is a angels. Look at Jenny . . .

MAGGIE: (*instantly on the defensive*) There's naethin wrang wi Jenny!

LILY: No yet.

MAGGIE: Ye wis like Jenny yersel once and don't you forget it. There wis naebody fonder o dressin up and rinnin aroon wi the lads.

LILY: I went oot respectable! No wi a the riff-raff o the toon, an a dressed up like a bloomin tart wi peroxided hair.

MAGGIE: You mind yer tongue, Lily!

LILY: I'm only tryin tae tel ye tae keep yer eye on her, I'm in the way o hearin things.

MAGGIE: Whit d'ye mean? Come on! Whit're ye gettin at?

LILY: I'm saying nae mair. But jist you watch her. Yon Nessie Tait's a right bad lot, and her and Jenny's as thick as thieves.

MAGGIE: (*troubled, she sighs*) I canna blame Jenny for being fed up. Wi Granny aside her, and Edie snorin wi her tonsils. Jist the same, it hurts terrible tae hear her goin on an on aboot leavin hame. I'm sure it's no ma fault! I've din ma best! I've din ma best for every yin o them!

(*She starts to cry. LILY stands and looks at her helplessly. She too sighs*)

LILY: I ken ye've done yer best. Ye've done great. But . . . ye havenae had a life fit for a dog! I jist wish there wis something I could dae for ye.

MAGGIE: (*wiping her tears away with her hands, she shakes her head at LILY*) O Lily, ye dae plenty; ye've aye been good tae the lot o us.

LILY: I dae whit I can . . . but it's nae much.

MAGGIE: Oh aye, it is. There wis yon black puddin ye brung intae us on Wednesday and the gingerbreid on Sunday, forbye a the cest-affs and the odd bobs . . .

LILY: Och, that's naethin. I brought ye a tin o baked beans the night. They'll mebbe dae yer dinner the morn.

MAGGIE: If they're no ett afore.

LILY: There ye are, see! Jist like you! I bring ye somethin for the morn's morn and it's ett afore ma back's turned. Och well, they're your beans . . . Hev ye been back tae the hospital wi Bertie yet?

MAGGIE: (*perturbed*) Naw . . . no yet. I wis that tired, I jist
couldna think tae get masel dressed an trail awa up yonder.

LILY: I thought the doctor said ye wis tae go back for an X-Ray?

> (*When very agitated,* MAGGIE *'combs' her hair with her fingers:
> she does this now*)

MAGGIE: I'll tak him up next week.

LILY: Aye Maggie, ye've no tae pit it aff. He's nae weel, the wee
chap. If you cannae go, whit's wrang wi John takin him? Whit's
he got tae dae wi himself when there's naethin daein for him
at the Burroo?

MAGGIE: Oh . . . he'll no go . . . no wi'oot me. He disnae like
it . . . amang a they gossiping wifies, he says, an weans yellin
in his lugs an fa'in ower his feet.

> (LILY *gives a snort of disgust*)

LILY: Jist like him! Leave a the dirty work tae the women!

MAGGIE: It's no that . . . John's . . . *sensitive.*

> (LILY *looks as if she is about to explode: she manages to control
> herself*)

LILY: Well . . . onywey . . . somebody's got to see tae Bertie. I
hope the bottle I brought him'll help.

MAGGIE: Did ye get it frae the chemist, Lily?

LILY: Aye. Of course! Whaur did ye think I'd get it?

MAGGIE: It cost ye money.

LILY: Forget it.

> (EDIE *comes in. She hangs up the W.C. key.* ERNEST *is right
> behind her; he gives her hair a good hard tug and she yells*)

EDIE: Ow! Let go ma hair, ye cheeky beggar.

> (*She hacks his shins. He retaliates*)

MAGGIE: (*seizing him roughly and clouting his ear*) Did I no tell
you you wis tae come in hauf an oor ago? Did I? (*Clout*) Did
I? (*Clout*) Well, you dae whit ye're tellt. (ERNEST *wriggles just
out of reach*) Come you here when I want tae hit ye! (*With a
final clout she pushes him away and brushes back her dishevelled
hair*) Noo, get you tae that sink and wash yer face an hands.

> (ERNEST *feebly soaps the flannel and washes a small area round
> his mouth and nose, then he draws it gently across the backs of
> his filthy hands and dries himself*)

LILY: Some wash!

ERNEST: Hullo, Auntie Lily. Did ye bring us onythin the night?

LILY: Aye, but ye're no gettin ony the now.

ERNEST: Aw! I'm hungry. Whit is it? A pie?

LILY: Never you mind.

ERNEST: A black pudden? . . . a white pudden? Aw, go'n; tell
us.

MAGGIE: It's a tin o baked beans; it's for yer dinner the morn.

ER: Aw, can we no get eatin them the night?

MAGGIE: (*looking out of the corner of her eye at* LILY) Certainly *nutt*!

ERNEST: Aw! Can I hev a jeely piece, then?

MAGGIE: (*sighing*) Yon loaf wis new at tea time.

> (*She cuts and spreads bread which* ERNEST *takes and climbs on to the sink, eating wolfishly*)

ERNEST: Ma! I can hear the Bones's wireless. Ma! It's playin jazz! O great! . . . O Ma, I wisht we had wan. Ma, when'll we get a wireless?

LILY: When yer Daddy's heid bummer o Fairfield's!

ERNEST: Ma Daddy disnae work in Fairfield's.

LILY: Your Daddy disnae *work*.

MAGGIE: Some day we'll hae a wireless, sonny.

LILY: Aye. And get a grand pianny when ye're aboot it.

ERNEST: When we get a wireless, I'm gonnae listen tae a the bands.

> (*He seizes a spoon and starts to beat out a jazz rhythm on a tin tray.* MAGGIE *tears both of them from his hands and brings him off the sink with a smart jerk which lands him on the floor*)

MAGGIE: (*pointing to the bed*) There's weans asleep in there!

> (ERNEST *climbs back on to the sink. Noises from above indicate a brawl: this gets louder*)

ERNEST: (*nodding towards ceiling*) That's him bashin her.

> (LILY *and* MAGGIE *raise their eyes to the ceiling*)

MAGGIE: Puir soul! . . . (*To* LILY) Is that no fair awfu? At it again! Canna keep aff the bottle, him.

LILY: I jist canna understand a woman let's her man bash her aboot. Catch *me* bidin wi him!

MAGGIE: If ye've got weans, ye've got tae pit up wi the fella that gied ye them . . . My! That wis a dunt! The plaster'll be doon!

LILY: I'll chap up tae them.

MAGGIE: Aye, tak the brush — no that it'll dae ony good; they'll never heed, she'll be that busy dodgin . . . My! . . . I bet she'll hae a black eye the morn, but she'll never let dab how she got it. (*She clouts* ERNEST *off the sink*) Get you aff tae yer bed and don't sit there listenin tae yer elders.

> (ERNEST *goes off*)

LILY: I see y're skelpin Ernest aboot plenty. I hope it does some good. Mebbe that's whit's wrang wi Alec; ye didnae skelp him enough when he was wee.

(MAGGIE *runs her fingers through her hair: looks at* LILY: *shakes her head*)

MAGGIE: (*agitated*) Don't start, Lily; don't start. I'm no needin your opinion!

LILY: Eh? Whit's up wi you?

MAGGIE: I'm no needin ony advice frae you, Lily. No aboot Alec. (*Long pause*) I took it once. (*She nods grimly at* LILY).

LILY: Ach! Yon rubbish again! ye're daft!

MAGGIE: Ye cannae deny Alec's aye been delicate . . .

LILY: There's naethin delicate aboot him noo — except the way he takes money aff ye . . . When did ye see him last?

MAGGIE: Oh . . . nae that lang since.

LILY: Well, when ye dae see him . . . ach . . . never heed.

MAGGIE: He's no owin you onythin is he?

LILY: If he is, it's naethin tae dae wi you. Did he no come roon at the week-end? (MAGGIE *shakes her head*) The dirty wee whippet! He can aye come runnin when he's wantin something; the rest o the time you can go tae the hot place for a he cares! . . . An him wi his pockets fu efter the dugs on Saturday. He couldnae even bring a poke o sweeties for the weans.

MAGGIE: Wha tellt ye he'd won at the dugs?

LILY: Isa was boastin aboot it. He's bought her a swagger coat aff his winnins.

MAGGIE: He'd gie that bizzom the eyes oot o his heid. Whit he sees in her . . . she's a right bad lot, yon.

LILY: Aye, but you try an tell *him* that! It seems tae me, Maggie, that the mair ye cairry on wi ither men, the mair yer ain man thinks o ye. If ye sit at hame washin oot the nappies an blackleadin yer grate, all the attention ye'll get's a bashin on a Saturday.

MAGGIE: Alec'd never lift a finger tae Isa.

LILY: I wouldnae bet on that . . . if she riles him enough. Goad help her if he starts, for he'll no ken when tae stop. Ye mind yon tempers? Mind the time he jist missed me wi the breid knife?

MAGGIE: (*covering her face with her hands and cringing*) Lily, I've enough tae keep me aff my sleep at nights wi'oot you rakin up the past.

LILY: I'm sorry, Maggie . . . I didna mean tae upset ye.

MAGGIE: It wis the day efter he threw the knife at you he got intae yon ither trouble . . .

LILY: Maggie, forget it . . .

MAGGIE: I'm no likely tae forget it . . . the polis . . . and the Court . . . and yon Probation Officer.

LILY: There's naebody but you remembers.

MAGGIE: The neighbours does . . . Mrs Harris and Mrs Bone . . . and yon Wilson wumman . . . every time her an Alec comes face tae face, I can see her rememberin.

LILY: He was only a lad.

MAGGIE: There's times I think he's no much mair than that yet.

> (JOHN *comes in carrying books under his arm. He is a big, handsome man. He puts down his books, gives* MAGGIE *a pat: they exchange warm smiles. He goes to sink and has a glass of water*)

Ye dry, John? I'll pit the kettle on. I've jist minded I promised yer auld lady a cup in her bed.

JOHN: She a right?

MAGGIE: Oh aye. Jist as usual . . . greetin an eatin.

JOHN: (*turning to* LILY *with as much of a smile as he can muster*) An how's Lil?

LILY: I wish you'd leave aff cryin me Lil. Ma name's Lily.

JOHN: An it couldna suit ye better.

LILY: Whit d'ye mean by that, eh?

MAGGIE: Don't you two stert up! I've had enough the day. (*To* LILY) He didna mean onythin.

LILY: Well if he didna mean onythin he shouldna say onythin!

JOHN: Goad help us!

LILY: (*to* MAGGIE) Whit aboot yon ironin?

MAGGIE: Och, never heed. I'm that tired it wad kill me tae watch ye.

LILY: It'll be steamie day again afore ye've got that lot done.

MAGGIE: Well, I canna help it.

JOHN: Yous women! Ye've nae system.

LILY: Oh, I suppose if *you* was a wumman you'd hae everythin jist perfect! The weans a washed and pit tae bed at six, an everythin a spick an span. Naethin tae dae till bedtime but twiddle yer thumbs. Huh!

JOHN: I'd hae a system . . .

LILY & MAGGIE: He'd hae a system!

JOHN: Aye, I'd hae a *system*! ony man wull tell ye, ye can dae naethin properly wi'oot ye hae a *system*.

LILY: And ony wumman'll tell ye that there's nae system ever inventit that disna go a tae Hell when ye've a hoose-fu o weans an a done aul Granny tae look efter.

MAGGIE: Never heed him, Lily. Ye should see him tryin tae mak the breakfast on a Sunday; ye'd get yer kill! If he's fryin bacon, he's fryin bacon, see? He's no keepin an eye on the toast an on the kettle, an breakin the eggs intae the pan a at the same time.

JOHN: Well, it's no ma job. If it *wis* ma job . . .

MAGGIE: We ken: ye'd hae a system.

LILY: Well, if you're sure there's naethin I can dae, Maggie, I'll awa.

MAGGIE: Och no, wait and hae a wee cup wi us.

LILY: Naw . . . I'll mak yin at hame and hae somethin tasty tae it. A rarebit, mebbe.

JOHN: (*winking at* MAGGIE) Aye, you dae that Lily; nae use hintin for ony rarebites here.

LILY: (*not having seen the wink*) I like that! Hint! the cheek! It was me brung yon tin o baked beans that's sittin up on your dresser this minute, John Morrison!

MAGGIE: Och, he's only pullin yer leg, Lily.

LILY: If that's a sense of humour I'm glad I hevna got one. Yous men! I wouldna see one o you in ma road.

JOHN: Oh ho! If a man jist crep ontae your horizon, ye'd be efter him like a cock at a grosset.

LILY: (*hauling on her coat*) I'm no stayin here tae be insultit. Ye can keep the beans, Maggie, but that's the last ye're gettin frae me till ye learn some folks their manners. Aye. And ye can tell yon precious Alec o yours that the next time he maks enough at the dugs, tae get fleein drunk in the middle o Argyle Street, he can pay me back ma ten shillingy note.

(*She stamps out of the room, slamming the door*)

MAGGIE: Ye shouldna tease Lily, John. Yin o they days she'll tak the huff and no come back, and whaur'll I be then?

JOHN: Puir Lily! Goad help her . . . (*Sotto voce*) the interferin bitch. Nae wunner she couldna get a man.

(*A burst of coughing from* BERTIE)

Whit aboot Bertie's X-Rays? Did ye tak him up tae the Hospital?

MAGGIE: I'll go tomorrow. (*Suddenly*) could you no . . . come wi me?

JOHN: Maggie, I'm on casual labour; ye never ken whit's comin up. There might be work and there might no . . .

MAGGIE: Aye . . . that's right . . . it's jist . . . I get sick tae ma stummick up there . . . and the wee chap . . . the nurse ca's oot the name an . . .

JOHN: Get Mrs Harris tae go wi ye . . . or Mrs Wilson.

MAGGIE: Aye, I could dae that . . . Is there onythin for ye the morn?

JOHN: Three days . . . or mebbe four . . . Hundreds o us, Maggie, beggin for the chance tae earn enough for food and a roof ower our heids.

(*There is a knock at the door*)

MAGGIE: You go, John. It'll likely be yin o the neighbours.

(JOHN *admits* MRS. HARRIS *and* MRS. WILSON: *both are highly excited and 'puffed oot'*)

JOHN: Come in, Ladies, come in. It's aye open hoose here.

MAGGIE: I hope it's no marge; I've nane.

MRS HARRIS: I like that! Ye'd think we never come near ye except tae borry a wee tate this or that. We come in tae tell ye there's been an accident at your Alec's.

(MAGGIE *jumps to her feet, eyes staring*)

MAGGIE: Whit's happened?

JOHN: (*bitter*) Has the Polis got him again?

MRS HARRIS: The Polis is there; but they're no efter Alec.

MRS WILSON: It's the street. Your Alec's street. The hooses has collapsed. The close next Alec's is the worst; they've pit a the fowk oot o it, and they've yon wee red lamps . . . me and Mrs Harris wis jist new oot o the pictures and we seen the crowd, an I thought it wis a fire, but here, that's whit it wis . . .

MRS HARRIS: Jist like an earthquake it wis . . . like yon fillum wi Jeanette McDonald and Clark Gable. There's a sink sittin oot in the open air . . .

MRS WILSON: And ye can see right intae a bedroom and there's a chest o drawers . . .

MRS HARRIS: And a pair o troosers hangin by the braces and nae man inside them.

MAGGIE: Did ye see oor Alec?

MRS WILSON: Naw, we didnae see *him*.

MRS HARRIS: Nor Isa neither.

MRS WILSON: But they said there wis nae deiths. Yin chap got his heid split, but that wis a the casualities as faur as we ken.

MRS HARRIS: Your Alec must hae been oot somewhere.

MAGGIE: You'll gae roon, John, and see?

MRS HARRIS: Och, I wouldna bother ma bunnet, Mr Morrison. The Polis would hae come roon for ye . . . Alec kens a the Polis hereaboots.

JOHN: Ye mean the Polis a kens Alec.

MRS HARRIS: Whichever wey ye like tae pit it. It's a guid job it wis only a sub-let; he'll hae nae furniture tae flit.

MAGGIE: John, are you goin roon? If you're no, I am.

JOHN: Aye, I'll go, but I'll be lucky if I find him this side of midnight. They'll be oot at the dancin, and when they dae come

hame they'll be that pie-eyed they'll no care whether they've a
hame or no.

MRS WILSON: Still, ye should go, jist tae see it. Whit a mess! I
wunner when they hooses wis built?

JOHN: The industrial revolution.

MRS WILSON: Eh? I never kent we'd had a revolution! I thought
it wis still tae come. Ma man says . . .

JOHN: It's a damned nuisance, that's whit it is! Well, we're no
havin them here, Maggie; they can find another room.

MAGGIE: They'll no can find anither room the night, John.

JOHN: Naw . . . well . . . they can look for one the morn; gie
themselves somethin tae dae instead o lyin in their beds.

    (*He goes off*)

MRS WILSON: My, thae men! Nae a word o sympathy! They're
right hard nuts.

MAGGIE: That's jist talk. If onythin wis tae happen tae ony o
the weans, John would tak it bad. They canna staun up tae
things like a wumman. They loss the heid and shout.

MRS WILSON: (*nudging* MRS HARRIS) Did yon picture the night
no gie you an awfy thirst? Yon time they wis swillin doon the
champagne, ma tongue wis fair hingin oot.

MAGGIE: I've jist made some — tea, I mean. No champagne.
Sit doon. I promised a cup tae Granny a while back . . . it's a
wunner she hasnae yelled.

MRS WILSON: How's she keepin, puir aul soul?

MAGGIE: Jist the same. She'll see *me* oot, I think.

MRS HARRIS: Aye, it's a trial for ye right enough. Wait till she's
bedridden though, it'll be a Hell o a sight worse.

MAGGIE: That's right, look on the bright side.

MRS HARRIS: When's she due at Lizzie's?

MAGGIE: No till the end o the month.

    (MAGGIE *pours and hands tea*)

MRS WILSON: Ta. Whit'll ye dae if ye have tae pit up Alec and
Isa?

MAGGIE: Granny'll jist have to go tae Lizzie.

MRS HARRIS: Puir soul! Yon Lizzie, she'd screw the teeth oot
o yer heid if she could get onythin for them in the pop-shop.
Did Granny ever get yon brooch she lost last time she wis wi
Lizzie?

MAGGIE: No.

MRS HARRIS: I tell't ye. She'll never see it this side o Hell.

MRS WILSON: It's pathetic, so it is, the way Granny comes wi
yon aul bed o hers, and taks it wi her when she goes. Old folks
is an awfu problem.

MRS HARRIS: They're no the only problem. Eh, Mrs Morrison?

(MAGGIE *rises*)

MAGGIE: I'll jist tak a keek in at Granny.

MRS WILSON: Problems! She hasnae hauf got them. Puir Maggie. And she's no the only yin on this stair. The Bones wis at it again last night. He got overtime paid him.

(MRS WILSON *draws down one eye with a forefinger and nods*)

MRS HARRIS: Overtime? Is that whit she ca's it? Ach well, onyway, it's dough. And we can a day wi a bit extra. But there's some men ye jist canna talk oot o bein honest.

MRS WILSON: Roon aboot here, the yins that's honest's feart they get nicked.

MRS HARRIS: Oh, I wouldnae say that; I wouldnae say that . . . *He*'s honest — her John.

(*She nods through the door through which* MAGGIE *now appears*)

MAGGIE: Dead . . .

MRS HARRIS: (*screeching*) *Dead?*

MAGGIE: Dead tae the world. Sorry I've nae biscuits.

MRS WILSON: Never heed; I've a sweetie left ower frae the pictures.

(*She produces a poke and hands them round*)

MRS HARRIS: Jenny no in the night?

MAGGIE: No.

MRS WILSON: I see she's got a new yin. Wee dark chap. I seen them the ither night.

MAGGIE: Did ye? Fancy that. Hope ye took a guid look.

MRS WILSON: I see she's become yin o they platinum blondes.

MAGGIE: Aye . . . John disnae like it.

MRS HARRIS: Somebody must hae tellt her that gentlemen prefers them. Wait till your Edie an ma Mary gets sterted! It'll no be lang the way they're gaun on these days.

MAGGIE: Here! That reminds me! Ma Edie says the teacher says your Mary's got beasts in her heid.

MRS HARRIS: (*A long screech of indignation*) Oh, the cheek! Beasts! Whit a thing tae say!

MAGGIE: Can you deny it?

MRS HARRIS: Oh, wait till I get ma haunds on yon bitch o a teacher!

MAGGIE: Can you deny it?

MRS HARRIS: I never heard the like!

MAGGIE: You look me in the eye, Mrs Harris, and tell me your Mary's got nae beasts!

MRS HARRIS: It's no fair, so it's no . . .

MAGGIE: See! She canna deny it!

MRS HARRIS: Ach well . . . whit's an odd louse?

MAGGIE: I'll tell ye whit an odd louse is: it's the mither o a hale battalion that's no content tae bide on hame grun. So jist you get something frae the chemist's, or I'll get the Sanitary tae ye.

MRS HARRIS: (*rising, with swelling bosom*) Oh, the Sanitary, is it? If you're for bringin in the Sanitary, there's a thing or two aboot the dunny stairs no being washed when it's a certain party's turn. Am I no right, Mrs Wilson?

MRS WILSON: (*apprehensively*) Never heed the dunny stairs. Come on!

(*She plucks at* MRS HARRIS*'s sleeve*)

MAGGIE: Are you insinyatin that I don't take ma turn o the close?

MRS HARRIS: No, I'm no insinyatin. I'm *telling* ye.

MRS WILSON: Come *on*!

MRS HARRIS: I'm comin.

(*She stalks with dignity at the heels of the scurrying* MRS WILSON)

MRS WILSON: (*to* MRS HARRIS) Fine you ken there's naebody does the dunny till it comes up their humph.

MAGGIE: (*shouting after them*) Mind! she's na playin wi ma Edie till she's cleaned.

MRS HARRIS: Ye needna fash yersel. I wouldna let her!

(*They go.* MAGGIE *slumps in her chair*)

MAGGIE: Aw Goad! (*Sighs*) I'll need tae buy her aff now wi some tattie scones or snowballs . . . or something. (*She looks at* LILY*'s tin of beans*) . . . No, she's no gettin they beans.

(*The lights dim out. Some hours later. Space has been cleared, centre, for a mattress on the floor with pillows, blankets, old coats,* MAGGIE *is making up this 'bed' as well as she can. She has on a nightdress covered by her coat*

JOHN, ALEC *and* ISA *come in. They all carry a share of* ALEC *and* ISA*'s belongings.* ISA *has on a tawdry dance dress: she and* ALEC *have had too much to drink, but only* ALEC *is maudlin*)

JOHN: Don't make such a bloomin row; ye'll waken the hale hoose.

ALEC: (*flinging down a battered suitcase*) I'm no makin ony row. (*Aggressive*) An I'm nae wantin ony favours! Can I help it if the bloody roof fa's in?

JOHN: Mind yer langwidge; ye're in ma hoose, no in a pub.

MAGGIE: (*hovering anxiously, placating*) Are ye a right, Alec?

ALEC: Aye . . . I'm a' right . . . Tae hear him, ye'd think I'd knocked doon the tennyment!

JOHN: You couldna knock doon an empty midden-bin.

ALEC: There ye are! That's whit ma feyther thinks o me. (*To* JOHN) Ye've aye been the same tae me. Despisin . . . Despisin. (*He turns slowly and unsteadily to* ISA) An her, her there . . . she's jist the same. I've got a wife an I love her. I love ye, Isa. I love ye. (*He paws her, she gives him a push*)

ISA: Aw shut up ye wee nyaff.

ALEC: I love her, but she disna love me. When I want tae kiss her she shoves me aff . . . like that. (*His drunken gesture catches* ISA *in the stomach*)

ISA: Ow! Ye drunken . . .

MAGGIE: John, pit him tae his bed.

ISA: Aye, that's right, Daddy; pit yer wee boy tae his bed.

JOHN: (*to* MAGGIE) Whaur's he tae lie?

MAGGIE: Whaur *can* he lie? . . . Aside Bertie an Ernie. Isa, you'll need tae share wi Jenny an Edie an Granny; I've pit through blankets for the sofa.

ISA: Some sleep I'm gonna get. (*She sits down and kicks off her high-heeled slippers*) Goad! Ma taes are tramped tae pulp. Whit a rammy it wis the night.

JOHN: Paying oot good money tae get battered aboot in yon crowd . . .

ISA: *You* never went tae the dancin, eh? Hee-haw!
 (*She looks him over appreciatively and gives him a 'certain smile'*)

ALEC: She shoves me aff . . . but she disna shove *him* aff.

ISA: Stow it.

ALEC: I seen ye. I seen ye the night. Jist wait. Jist you wait!
 (*His eyes have difficulty focusing, but they have a very nasty look.* MAGGIE *gives a little moan of distress*)

ISA: That's whit he's like when we hev a night oot. He mixes them and I've got tae get somebody tae cairt him hame. Gie's a haun wi him, for Goad's sake!
 (ALEC *is swaying about in his chair, and muttering*)

JOHN: (*To* MAGGIE) Is he gonna lie aside Bertie stinkin o stale beer?

MAGGIE: Whit else can we dae, John!

JOHN: Bertie's nae weel. (*He looks at his sprawling son*) Whit I'd like tae dae is kick him oot o the hoose.

ISA: Aye, pit him oot on the stairheid.
 (MAGGIE *starts to cry*)

MAGGIE: It's terrible! Whit's tae be done!

ISA: He's useless. I'm seeck fed up wi him.

MAGGIE: *You* hevna helped him ony.

ISA: Ach, he wis a rotten tattie lang afore I was daft enough tae get landed wi him. If ye ask me, I've improved him. He'll dae whit I tell him, that's mair than you can say. I can twist him roon ma little finger. Come on, pimple! (*Takes him with a practised hand by the back of his collar and jerks him off his chair*) Well? Are ye gonna let me cairry him masel? Gie's a haun . . . I'm wantin ma bed. (*As she and* JOHN *take* ALEC *off, right:*) Nighty-night. Sleep tight.

MAGGIE: Haud yer row! The bairns is sleepin.

> (*She stands looking at the bedroom door, hands working nervously.* JOHN *comes out. They look long at each other without speech: then* JOHN *comes to* MAGGIE: *he takes her in his arms and 'pets' her*)

JOHN: You get intae bed, Maggie and rest yersel. (*Pause*) If ye can.

> (MAGGIE *doesn't move: she watches him sit down and light a Woodbine*)

Ma son! (*Pause*) I used tae think, when he was wee, it'd be rare when he grew up. He'd go tae the night-school an learn a trade . . . we'd be rare pals, him an me. (*Pause*) An look whit I've got!

MAGGIE: (*bursting into tears*) I've din ma best wi him! I have! I have!

JOHN: I'm no blamin *you* Maggie. If I'm blamin onybody, I'm blamin masel. A man's got nae right tae bring weans intae the world if he canna provide for them. (*Turning to her*) It's a wunner ye don't hate me.

MAGGIE: (*wiping her cheeks with her hands*) Don't talk daft. It's because things have aye been right atween you an me that I can struggle on.

JOHN: Struggle! Aye, ye've hit on the right word — struggle . . . *Weans*! They roast the heart an liver oot o ye!

MAGGIE: Aye . . . but it's as if they wis tied on tae ye . . . they'll tug awa till the day ye dee.

JOHN: Ye're right. I can get that mad at Jenny I could . . . then she looks up at me wi that wee smile o hers an I can feel . . . I can *actually feel* ma heart turnin intae butter.

MAGGIE: Jenny's your pet.

JOHN: (*smiling*) Aye. Canna deny it. Didna see her the night. I suppose she was in bed time I got back wi that pair in there. (*He nods towards door.* MAGGIE *doesn't answer: she puts a hand up to her mouth, afraid he'll pursue the question: then she gets into the bed*) Well, I don't know whit's done it, the excitement or the vexation, but I'm damned hungry. Is there onythin tae eat? Hey! Whit aboot Lily's beans?

MAGGIE: Whit aboot tomorrow?

(*Hunts in drawer*)

JOHN: Ach, tomorrow! Whaur's the tin-opener? Goad! It's never twice in the same place, Maggie.

MAGGIE: I've nae system (*She giggles*).

(*He finds the tin-opener, opens the tin, finds a pan and heats the beans, stirring and tasting*)

MAGGIE: Pit some o them aside for the weans the morn.

JOHN: Aye . . . right. A wee bit Ayrshire bacon would go great wi these.

(*They exchange a look of greedy longing and lick their lips*)

MAGGIE: It says on the tin: Beans wi pork.

JOHN: Pork? (*He lifts out a cube of something*) Could be onythin. Blubber. (*He eats it*) Aw, I've ett it a, Maggie! the hale square-inch o it!

MAGGIE: Aw, ye greedy thing! Fancy no haufin it wi me. (*Giggles*)

(*He hands her a plate of the beans*)

That's ower much, John! I said keep some for the weans.

JOHN: You eat that lot; I've kept some.

(*They eat. In the silence, there is a prolonged fit of* BERTIE*'s coughing: they look at each other*)

Maggie, ye'll need tae . . .

MAGGIE: I ken, I ken. I wull go; but I'll hae tae bother Mrs Harris tae mind Granny and the weans . . . an I had words wi her the night.

JOHN: Yous women! Whit wis it this time?

MAGGIE: She said I didnae tak ma turn o the dunny stairs, and I said her Mary had somethin in her heid.

JOHN: I've tellt ye an tellt ye! Can ye no keep yersel *tae* yersel?

MAGGIE: No, I canna. It's only rich folks can keep theirselves tae theirselves. Folks like us hev tae depend on their neighbours when they're needin help.

(*He finishes his beans and takes away the plates.* MAGGIE *lies back with a sigh*)

JOHN: (*looking at her*) Ye're dead beat, Maggie. It's been too much for ye . . . Isa an Alec . . .

MAGGIE: Aye . . . I'm gey tired right enough.

JOHN: Some day we'll hae a real bed, Maggie.

MAGGIE: On legs? I hevnae been on a bed since I wis in the Maternity wi Marina.

JOHN: Here, that'll dae! I'm no wantin nightmares . . . I'd better
lock up.

MAGGIE: Och, never heed . . . y're no needin tae lock the door.

JOHN: (*turning quickly towards her*) So . . . she's no in?

(MAGGIE *shakes her head*)

Whaur is she? Who's she wi?

MAGGIE: She didnae say; she disna tell me onythin noo.

JOHN: By Goad, she'll tell me somethin! I'm for nane o this
traipsin roon the toon till a oors.

(*He opens the window. A crowd of drunks are rolling homewards
singing 'I'm alone because I love yew, love yew with all my
heart' with mouth-organ accompaniment*)

Listen tae that! Goad knows whit sort of scum's on the streets
at this time o night. She's no getting aff wi this.

MAGGIE: Whit's the use? She pays nae attention when ye speak.

JOHN: She'll pay attention tae me!

(*He looks out of the window, left and right, then closes it*)

Nae sign o her.

MAGGIE: It's they lassies she's got pals wi since she went tae
the Sauchiehall Street branch. She'll no bring me naethin frae
the shop noo . . . that feart the girls'll think onythin o her gettin
hame a few bashed tomaties an some ower-ripe bananas. I miss
them; it wis a rare wee help . . . Marina loves a chipped apple.

JOHN: Oh, so she'll no bring hame ony bashed fruit noo? I'll see
aboot that! Ma word! Wait till ma lady shows up the night!

MAGGIE: (*alarmed*) Ye've no tae be rough wi her, John.

JOHN: It strikes me it's *past* time tae be rough wi her. She's
changed a lot, Maggie! Jenny was never impident . . . (*Remembering the old* JENNY) Jenny was aye a kind wee lassie, aye
ready for a laugh — for a she'd be a bit cheeky at times . . . but
nae . . . yon hard look she's got aboot her this last while
back.

MAGGIE: I didnae tell ye, but . . . she's wantin tae leave hame.

(JOHN *turns slowly, absolutely shocked*)

JOHN: *Leave hame*? (*Pause*) Leave . . . *us*? Naw, she wouldna dae
that. No Jenny. It's jist talk . . . (*Pause*) She *couldna* leave us!
Whaur would she gae?

(MAGGIE *shakes her head*)

MAGGIE: Aye, it'll jist be talk. She'll be in soon, John. Come
tae bed.

JOHN: D'ye think mebbe I should gae oot lookin for her?

MAGGIE: No! Ye'll only vex her. Come tae bed.

JOHN: *Goad*! Time was she was feart o angerin *me*! (*Strongly*)
She's ma lass, and it's up tae me — aye and you — tae see

that she behaves hersel! Vex her? I'll vex her a right! (*Pause*)
Sh! Whit was that?

MAGGIE: Bertie. I'd better awa through wi anither dose . . .

JOHN: I thought I heard someone at the close-mouth.

> (BERTIE *starts to cough: intermingled with it is* JENNY's *laugh,
> distant*)

MAGGIE: (*struggling up*) Oh, I'm that tired! Every bloomin night
I've got tae rise . . .

JOHN: Stay whaur ye are; I'll see tae Bertie.

MAGGIE: The bottle's on the dresser, tak ben a spoon wi it.

> (*As soon as* JOHN *has gone out, there is the sound of* JENNY
> *and a man talking softly, laughing together.*
>
>   MAGGIE *goes quickly to the window and listens. When she
> hears* JOHN *returning, she scuttles back to bed.* JOHN *sets down
> bottle and spoon, opens door and stands, listening*)

MAGGIE: Come tae bed, John.

JOHN: Jenny's doon there wi a fella.

MAGGIE: If she's safe hame, ye needna worry . . .

JOHN: I'm gaun doon.

> (*He puts on his jacket*)

MAGGIE: Don't go doon, John . . . ye'll only vex her, I tell ye!
Speak tae her in the morning.

JOHN: Whit's the matter wi ye, Maggie? Are ye no carin whit
sort o a life Jenny's leadin?

MAGGIE: I'm no wantin her tae leave hame! I'm no wantin ony
trouble atween the three o us.

JOHN: She's got tae be spoke tae.

> (*He goes out.* MAGGIE *sits up straight, her eyes straining at
> the door through which presently come angry voices: then* JOHN
> *comes in holding* JENNY *by the arm. She is about eighteen, made
> up boldly for the nineteen-thirties: her lipstick is spread over her
> mouth, her coat and blouse undone, her hair tousled*)

JENNY: (*furious*) Leave me go!

> (*She shakes herself free and she and* JOHN *stand glaring at each
> other.* MAGGIE *is watching fearfully*)

JENNY: Makin a bloomin fool o me in front o ma friend!

JOHN: Where hae you been till this time o night?

JENNY: That's nane o your business. I'm grown up noo.

JOHN: Don't you speak tae me like that. I asked ye where ye'd
been.

JENNY: An I tellt ye! Nane o your damned interferin business!

MAGGIE: Jenny! John!

> (JOHN *takes* JENNY *by the shoulders and shakes her*)

JOHN: Where wis ye? Answer me!

JENNY: At the pickchers.

JOHN: The pickchers comes oot at hauf ten. Where wis ye efter?

JENNT: (*sullen*) Wi Nessie Tait an a coupla friends.

> (*He lets her go and she flops into a chair, glaring sullenly at him and rubbing her shoulder*)

JOHN: I don't approve o yon Nessie Tate.

JENNY: That's a peety. I dae.

JOHN: Ye impident little bitch! What I ought tae dae is tak ma belt tae ye.

JENNY: Jist you try it!

JOHN: The next time you come in here at this time o night wi yer paint smeared a ower yer face, I wull! Look at yersel!

> (*He drags her over to a mirror, then propels her, resisting, to the sink, where, holding her head under his arm, he scrubs off her make-up*)

There! And in the future, you'll let yer hair grow tae the colour God meant it tae be an leave it that wey.

JENNY: Mebbe I wull . . . an mebbe I'll no. It jist depends.

JOHN: I'm wantin nae mair sauce frae you, Jenny. I'm speakin tae ye for yer ain good. Whit'll the neighbours think, you comin hame at this time o night an staundin in the close wi a man.

JENNY: Whit dae I care whit the neighbours thinks? An I suppose *you* never stood in a close yersel?

> (ERNEST *appears at the door of the back parlour and stands there in his bare feet and wearing an old coat over tattered pyjamas, taking everything in*)

JOHN: I ken ma ain sex, Jenny, an it's you I'm thinking aboot.

JENNY: Ye can save yer breath, well. I ken how to look efter masel. I'm no as green as I'm cabbage lookin . . . an talking aboot cabbages . . . I'm chuckin the shop.

JOHN: Ye're daein whit?

JENNY: You heard. I'm done wi the fruit an veg. Look whit they done tae ma hauns! Scoopin up clarty tatties an carrots the rats has been at, forbye yon aul skinflint that's the boss aye gaun on at ye, an aye checkin the takins. Naw, I've had enough o that.

JOHN: And whit, may I ask, dae ye propose tae dae, my lady?

JENNY: I've got a job.

MAGGIE: (*eagerly*) Oh whit kind, Jenny? Whit kind?

JENNY: In a joolers. Yon wis ma new boss I wis wi the night.

> (JOHN *and* MAGGIE *look at each other, disturbed*)

JOHN: Is that so? Whaur's his shop? I'm yer fayther an it's ma right tae have a word wi this . . . new boss.

JENNY: (*rather scared, but determined*) You've a fat chance o that, for I'm no tellin ye. (*As he takes her by the shoulders*) I'm no tellin ye naethin! I'm no tellin ye whaur I'm workin. I had enough o Ma waitin at the shop door every Friday closin time, wi Christopher yellin and Marina rinnin aboot, an Ma askin for chipped apples an bashed tomaties an disgracin me afore the hale shop.

MAGGIE: I didna mean tae aggravate ye, Jenny. It wis jist that I wis aye needin yer money sae sair . . .

JOHN: The impidence o ye! It's your duty tae hand ower every penny ye earn tae her that's looked efter ye a yer days.

JENNY: Oh, is that so? Well, ma duty's finished. From noo on, what I earn is mines. It's no ma job tae keep your weans. It's *yours*.

MAGGIE: Jenny!

JENNY: I didnae ask tae be born. No intae this midden. The kitchen's aye like a pig-stye . . . there's never ony decent food, an if there wis, ye'd hae nae appetite for it . . . an sleepin in a bed-closet in aside a snorin aul wife. Naw. I've had enough. I'm gonna live ma ain life.

JOHN: (*placating*) Things'll no aye be like this, Jenny. I ken it's no the hame for you yer Mammy an me would like, but it's no oor fault . . . It's . . . it's the way things are.

JENNY: Ach! It's aye bad luck wi you. Every time ye loss yer job, it's bad luck.

JOHN: Well, so it is bad luck! There's a depression on! D'ye no understaun?

JENNY: I understaun fine. (*She looks at him contemptuously, thrusts her face towards him*) Some men gets on an makes money, depression or no. Ithers hasna the brains.

(JOHN *has caught her drink-laden breath*)

JOHN: You've been drinkin!

JENNY: (*a slight suggestion of fear underlies her aggression*) Whit aboot it?

JOHN: Whit have you been drinkin?

JENNY: Water!

JOHN: By Goad! If ever a girl asked for it! (*He shakes her roughly*) Whit have you been drinkin?

JENNY: Jist . . . a coupla gins.

JOHN: (*letting her go suddenly*) Right ye are, ma lady! Right ye are! No content wi paintin her face an dyin yer hair an stayin oot hauf the night, ye're drinkin gin! Cairry on! Ye'll land in the gutter, and when ye dae, ye needna come tae me tae pick ye up.

(EDIE *appears at the other door*)

JENNY: Ye needna worry! When I leave this rotten pig-stye I'm no comin back. There's ither things in life . . . so you'd better hang on tae yer job this time. If ye can!

(JOHN *hits her across the face.* EDIE *screams and runs across to her mother and gets in beneath the blankets.* JOHN *and* JENNY *face each other in a frozen silence, broken by* EDIE's *frightened sobbing: her mother's soothing noises.* MARINA *wakens up*)

MARINA: Mammy, is ma Daddy drunk?

MAGGIE: No, no pet. It's a right. Go tae sleep.

MARINA: I canna get tae sleep, Mammy . . . Is ma Daddy angry?

JOHN: (*to* JENNY) Clear aff you, tae yer bed.

(JENNY *marches off with her nose in the air, watched by* MAGGIE. JOHN *goes to the bed and opening the curtains, quietens* MARINA. *We can't hear what he says*)

MARINA: A right, Daddy. I'll go tae sleep. (*Pause*) Wull *you* go tae sleep if I go tae sleep, Daddy?

JOHN: Aye, I'll go tae sleep. (*Puts his head in his hands and whispers:* Christ! *He turns and sees Ernie still standing in the doorway*). Whit are *you* daein oot o bed? Clear aff!

(*He assists* ERNEST *off with a kick, then walks slowly to the window and looks out into the night*)

MAGGIE: (*timid*) Come tae bed, John.

(JOHN *does not answer. He lights a fag-end and continues to stare out of the window*)

ACT TWO — SCENE ONE

Scene: The same. A week later.

The kitchen is fairly tidy. GRANNY's bed-ends and mattress are propped against the wall: she is sitting, dressed in her outdoor clothes and surrounded by her worldly belongings. MRS HARRIS and MRS BONE are keeping her company.

GRANNY: It's awfu tae be aul an kicked aboot frae yin hoose tae the ither.

MRS HARRIS: Aw, cheer up, Granny. Have anither strippit ba. Whaur did ye pit them? (*Rummages through one of the bags and locates sweets*) There ye are! (*She pops one into* GRANNY's *mouth.* GRANNY *takes it out again, looks at it, and, satisfied, sucks contentedly*) That'll keep her quiet for a wee while. Hoo's yer keeker the day? (*Peers at* MRS BONE's *mahogany-coloured eye*) Och, it's no near as bad as the last yin ye had. Whit did ye bump intae this time?

MRS BONE: The mangle . . . Mrs Morrison's shairly bein kep a lang while at the hospital. I hope it's naethin serious wi wee Bertie; yon's an awfu-like cough he's got. Nicht efter nicht I hear him hechin awa.

MRS HARRIS: Aye. Chests is chancy things. I mind when oor Wullie had the pewmony, I wis up a day an a nicht. No a wunk o sleep did I get till he'd past the crisis . . . and there wis his feyther, lyin snorin his heid aff.

MRS BONE: They men!

MRS HARRIS: Aye, they men! But if their nebs is rinnin, they think they're deein.

MRS BONE: I hope it's no pewmony wi Bertie, but I wouldnae be surprised, I wouldnae be surprised . . . I'm never surprised at onythin! I mean, aboot the human body I'm no surprised.

GRANNY: Eh dear! I'm deserted! Lizzie's forgot me!

MRS BONE: Nutt at a! Of course ye're no deserted. She'll be here in a wee minute. (*To* MRS HARRIS) Puir aul thing!

GRANNY: I ken the way it is; I'm nae that dottled that I dinna ken i'm no wantit. I'm naethin but an auld nuisance tae Maggie an Lizzie.

MRS HARRIS: Whit an idea! Ye're no an aul nuisance at a! I'm shair they'll miss ye something *terrible* when ye go.

GRANNY: They'll no miss me. But they'll miss ma pension tae buy a bit bacon on a Friday nicht. Maggie aye bought a bit bacon wi ma pension. No that I got ony; I jist got the smell o it an a bit dipped breid. (*Pause*) She said I'd nae teeth tae chow wi. Wait till she's aul hersel wi nae teeth.

MRS HARRIS: Aye, it's a terrible bad arrangement that. When ye loss yer teeth, ye should loss yer appetite wi them.

GRANNY: Eh, deary dear! I'm wearied waitin.

MRS BONE: (*giving* MRS HARRIS *a dig in the ribs*) Sing us a wee song, Granny, tae pass the time.

(GRANNY *turns her head slowly and looks long at* MRS BONE)

GRANNY: (*reproving*) Singing's for rejoicin.

MRS BONE: (*with a giggle*) Oo, that's me pit in ma place!

GRANNY: An I'm no gettin up an dancin the Hielan Fling for ye either. (*Darkly*) I'm jist sittin here . . . thinkin . . . there's on-gauns in this hoose . . . yon lassie that Alec's mairret on . . .

MRS HARRIS: Isa.

GRANNY: Aye, Isa. She's a tink. A tink. Maggie should rin her oot o the hoose. Mark ma words.

MRS BONE: Oh aye, Granny; we'll mark them.

(*There is a peremptory knock on the door*)

That'll be Lizzie. Jist the cheeky kind o knock she'd hae.

(MRS HARRIS *opens the door to* LIZZIE, *a hard-faced harridan about fifty*)

LIZZIE: (*ignoring the others*) Well? Ye ready?

MRS BONE: Ready? She's been sittin here waitin on ye for the last hauf-oor.

LIZZIE: Got a yer claes packed? And yer pension book?

GRANNY: Aye, Lizzie; it's here.

LIZZIE: See's a look at it.

(GRANNY *starts to fumble with her bag.* MRS BONE *goes to help her*)

Hev they men no been for the bed yet?

MRS HARRIS: If they'd hae been for the bed it wouldna be staunin up against yon wa, would it?

LIZZIE: (*taking pension book from* MRS BONE) Here! Ye've drawn this week's. Ye got the money?

GRANNY: Naw, Lizzie . . . I gied it tae Maggie.

LIZZIE: Oh? So Bertie gets new socks at ma expense, does he? And whit does she think you're gonna live on for the next week? Air?

MRS HARRIS: Ach, leave the puir aul wife alane. Shairly ye can scrape up a bit tae eat for her; it's no as if ye wis takin in a big hulkin brute o a man tae feed.

LIZZIE: I'm no takin in naebody tae feed. Folks that canna pay for their meat'll find nae room in ma hoose.

MRS BONE: Oo! An her yer puir dead husband's mither. Oo! I'm surprised at ye, Lizzie Morrison.

MRS HARRIS: I thought you said you wis never surprised — at anythin human.

MRS BONE: That's jist whit I said: *anythin human.*

(*They both stare hard at* LIZZIE, *then shake their heads at each other*)

LIZZIE: I've tae earn every penny that comes intae ma hoose.

MRS HARRIS: Aye, we ken that. An ye don't dae sae bad either, ye aul miser. Buyin up aul claes for a copper or twa an sellin them at sixpence a week . . .

MRS BONE: Or she'll loan ye the dough tae buy them outright — at fifty percent.

MRS HARRIS: Aye, she's got a right kind heart, she wouldnae see ye stuck; no if she could mak a guid thing oot o it.

LIZZIE: Ye're jealous! Ye hevna the brains tae mak a bit yersels. But ye're no above tradin wi me when it suits ye. Aye, an gettin a bargain.

MRS HARRIS & MRS BONE: A bargain? Frae *you*?

(*They look at each other and shake their heads*)

MRS HARRIS: I canna mind ony bargain.

LIZZIE: Whit aboot yon veloory hat ye bought aff me?

MRS HARRIS: Veloory hat? Veloory hat? . . . Oh, ye mean yon scabby aul felt bunnet wi the moultin bird on tap? Oh aye, I mind! If yon wis veloory, I'm a wally dug.

LIZZIE: It wis veloory. It belanged tae a lady in Kelvinside whaur I did a bit on a Saturday.

MRS BONE: A bit whit? Pinchin?

LIZZIE: Here! I could pit ye tae the Polis for that.

MRS HARRIS: No roon aboot here ye couldnae. They a ken ye.

GRANNY: Oh, I'm nae wantin tae leave here! I wisht I could bide wi Maggie till I dee!

LIZZIE: Bide then!

GRANNY: Ye ken I canna bide. Alec an Isa's needin the room.

MRS HARRIS: Some folks is right selfish. You've naebody but yersel tae think aboot, an ye'll no tak the aul wife aff Maggie's hauns wi'oot kickin up a fuss.

(LIZZIE *sits down and loosens her coat*)

MRS HARRIS: I thought you wis in a hurry tae get aff?

LIZZIE: I'm sittin right here till Maggie comes hame wi whit's left o Granny's pension.

MRS BONE: Huh! Whit a hope you've got! Whit d'ye think'll be left?

LIZZIE: Aye . . . mebbe y're right . . . In that case, I'll jist hae tae tak whit she bought.

(*She gets up and goes to open food cupboard.* MRS HARRIS *grabs her*)

MRS HARRIS: Here! Mrs Bone and me's in chairge o this hoose till Lily comes; you keep yer dirty aul neb oot of the cupboards or we'll shout for the polis.

MRS BONE: An y're no wantin *them* . . . No efter whit happened last Christmas. Wis it ten days she got, d'you mind, Mrs Harris for yon wee fraud wi the Club Fund?

MRS HARRIS: Aye. Ten days. It wis right bad luck her bein fun out, wasn't it?

(*A sharp knock on the door.* MRS HARRIS *lets in* LILY. *She looks around, surprised*)

LILY: Maggie no hame yet?

MRS BONE: No yet, Lily. They're keepin her a lang while at the hospital.

LILY: And the men hasnae come for the bed?

MRS HARRIS: Aw well, ye ken whit they Hoggs' men is; aye like the coo's tail and as much cheek when they dae show up.

(LILY *turns to* LIZZIE)

LILY: Well, Lizzie . . . nae sense in the baith o us hangin on . . . I'm here noo.

LIZZIE: Aye. So I see . . . Didnae expect tae see you. Hev they sacked ye at last?

LILY: I'm servin the night. I can shairly get a bit of the day tae masel. No that it's ony o your business.

LIZZIE: Funny tae me the way you can aye be bobbin in an oot o Maggie's. Ye must hev an awfu nice boss . . . Or mebbe you're awfu nice tae him, eh?

LILY: Jist whit dae ye mean by that?

MRS BONE: Tak no notice o her, Lily. Her tongue's that rotten it'll drap aff yin o they days.

> (*There are sounds of girlish laughter on the stairs and a cheeky rat-tat-tat on the door.* LILY *opens it to* ISA, JENNY *and* ALEC. *The girls are arm-in-arm and are convulsed with laughter at some joke not shared by* ALEC *who looks glum*)

ISA: Aw Goad! the aul yin's no awa yet.

JENNY: I tellt ye we'd rin intae them. It taks a stick o dennymite tae shunt Granny.

ISA: Whaur's ma dear mither-in-law? Oot at the jiggin?

LILY: Cut oot the impidence. Ye ken fine she's at the hospital wi Bertie.

ISA: Keep yer wig on. I jist thought she'd hae been here tae welcome me wi oot-stretched airms.

LILY: You'll get *ma* ootstretched airm in a minute.

> (JENNY *and* ISA *look at each other, lift their shoulders, heave mock sighs*)

JENNY: (*to* ISA) See whit I mean, Isa?

> (*They both slowly survey the other women, looking them over, up and down and shaking their heads*)

ISA: Aye Jenny. I see whit ye mean . . . Ach well . . . they canna help it. (*To* ALEC *who has found himself a chair of some sort*) Get aff that an let me sit doon!

ALEC: No, I'll no! I had it first. (*For a brief moment he faces her boldly, then he wilts and removes himself to lean morosely against the wall*)

MRS BONE: (*enviously*) My, Isa! I could dae wi a leaf oot o your book!

> (ISA *gives her a long hard stare*)

ISA: Oh aye . . . You're the yin that lives up the stair? . . . Ye lost the battle years ago, hen.

JENNY: (*to* GRANNY) Well, ye've got plenty o company noo, Granny.

GRANNY: Aye. Plenty o company.

JENNY: (*to the room*) She's got plenty o company, she says.

MRS BONE: (*rising*) Well, I'm shair I'm no one tae stay whaur I'm no wantit. Come on, Mrs Harris.

MRS HARRIS: Aye. Comin. (*To* JENNY) You're a right cheeky wee bizzim, Jenny Morrison. Serve you right if the next time your Mammy's needin me or Mrs Bone, we'll no come; an *you'll* hae tae bide in.

JENNY: Oh, but I'll no be here! I've seen the last o you auld tea-sookin tabbies. This little birdie's flyin awa frae the nest . . . Pit *that* in yer pipe and puff it oot tae the neighbours.

MRS BONE: An whaur is the little birdie flyin tae, may I ask?

JENNY: Ye can ask, but that disnae mean ye'll be tellt.

ISA: High time ye wis flyin, Jenny. Whit a nest!

LILY: You wis glad enough tae fly in here when yon midden ye wis in fell doon aboot yer ears.

ISA: Oh aye, but we're jist bidin meantime tae help the aul folk oot wi the rent. Ten shillins a week we're payin. Aren't we, Alec?

ALEC: (*surprised*) Eh? Oh aye. Aye. That's right.

LIZZIE: Gettin ten shillings aff yous and takin Granny's pension tae? Who says I'm no takin yon groceries?

LILY: (*grabbing her arm*) I says.

(*There is a loud thump on the door.* JENNY *lets in the removal men.* MRS HARRIS, MRS BONE *who had been ready to go, sit down again*)

1ST MAN: Hya, Granny! For the road again, eh? My, the rare time you hae tae yersel.

(GRANNY *bows her head and starts to cry*)

Aw, cheer up.

GRANNY: I'm nae wantin tae gae wi Lizzie. I'd raither bide wi Maggie.

1ST MAN: (*straightening up and looking at the grim-mouthed* LIZZIE) Aye. Imphm.

LILY: Come on, Granny. Ye ken Maggie's had ye near a year and there's nae the room! And aside frae the room, Maggie's tired oot wi Bertie . . . (*Looking balefully at* ISA *and* ALEC) . . . an a her ither troubles. So come on, be a good girl. Eh? For Maggie.

(*She helps* GRANNY *to her feet and collects her belongings. Meanwhile the second man has been whistling under his breath and giving* ISA *and* JENNY *the eye*)

2ND MAN: D'ye fancy blondes or brunettes, Joe?

1ST MAN: Jist so lang's they're (*He illustrates 'curved'*) I tak them as they come. (*He goes 'click-click' to* JENNY *who tosses her head*)

2ND MAN: (*grabbing bed-end*) Old iron, old iron, any any any

old iron. It's a wunner tae me this buggerin bed disnae walk
doon the stairs an oan tae the lorry itsel.

GRANNY: I'll no be callin oan ye again, lads; I'll no gang doon
they stairs again, oxtered by Maggie an Lizzie. Next time it'll
be ma box.

LILY: Och Granny, dinna talk daft.

GRANNY: Na na, Lily. I ken . . . the Lord has beckoned me.
(JENNY *and* ISA *snigger*)

ISA: Well, next time he beckons, jist you go.
(GRANNY *sets up a terrible wail. The* 1ST MAN *approaches*
ISA *grimly: she looks up, surprised*)

1ST MAN: Ye didna mean that, did ye? *Did ye?* (ISA *is taken
aback*) Tell yer Granny ye didna mean it.

ISA: She's no ma Granny.

1ST MAN: Tell her ye didna mean it.

ISA: I didna mean it.

1ST MAN: She didna mean it, Granny.

ALEC: (*unsticking himself from the wall and cackling*) He soarted
you, Isa! He soarted you!

(ISA *turns a vicious look on him and he wilts*)

ISA: Jist you wait!

2ND MAN: Come oan, come oan, get a move oan. Here, we'll
tak the bed doon first an come back for the mattress.
(*They go out with the spring*)

MRS HARRIS: My, whit a rare-looking chap yon big fella is. And
nice, tae. Bet he has his fun, eh?

JENNY: It's no likely tae be wi you, hen.

MRS HARRIS: I've ma ain man!

JENNY: Aye. So ye hev. We've met on the stairs. Heavy breather.

MRS HARRIS: Well, he's gettin oan!

JENNY: Oh, is that it? I've whiles thought he wis trying tae get
aff.

(JENNY *and* ISA *clutch each other and giggle.* MRS HARRIS
glares at them)

LIZZIE: (*to* GRANNY) Well, if ye've had yer greet, we'll get on.
(*To* LILY) An I'll get yon pension money oot o Maggie. I'm no
as saft as I look.

ISA: Saft? *Saft?* They dug you oot o a quarry.

LIZZIE: If I wis you, Alec, I'd wallop that impident wife o yours
till she wis black and blue.

ISA: Wallop me? He wouldna dae that tae me, would ye,
sweetheart?

(ALEC *grins foolishly, and shuffles his feet. The men come
back*)

1ST MAN: Ups-a-daisy! (*To* ALEC) Here, Mac, like tae gie's a
haun wi the bed-ends? That'll let him tak doon the matt*r*ess.
  (ALEC *makes a move to comply*)

ISA: Here you! Whit d'yous think ma husband is? A bloomin
cairter?

2ND MAN: Ye don't mean tae tell us you're merriet tae *him*?
  (*He gives a long low whistle and shakes his head*)

1ST MAN: Come oan, cut it oot! We'll pit the mattress oot on
the stairheid.

2ND MAN: Aye, a right. Cheerio girls. Sorry we canna gie ye
a lift on the lorry, Granny, but we're no allowed tae cairry
livestock.

LIZZIE: We'll tak a penny on the tram, and if yous two's no at
the hoose in hauf an oor, I'll ken whaur tae look for ye.

1ST MAN: That's a right sweetheart; come right in and we'll let
ye staun us a pint.
  (*They clatter off, whistling*)

JENNY: Bloomin cairters! Cheek!
  (LIZZIE, *none too gently, takes* GRANNY'*s arm*)

LIZZIE: Come on then.

GRANNY: Leave go! I canna rin awa!
  (*In the doorway, left wide open by the removal men, stands*
  MAGGIE. *She carries* BERTIE'*s clothes over her arm and his
  boots, laces tied together, dangle from her fingers. She is sobbing.
  They all look up at her*)

LILY: (*running forward*) Maggie?
  (MAGGIE *leans against the door-jamb and sobs helplessly*)

MAGGIE: They've kep him in.

NEIGHBOURS: Aw! Naw!

GRANNY: Maggie, Maggie, she says ye're tae gie back ma last
week's pension.

MAGGIE: Fancy them keepin him in . . . I never thocht . . .

MRS HARRIS: Is it the bronchitis, Mrs Morrison?

MAGGIE: No, its no bronchitis . . . it's TB.
  (LILY *comforts her*)

MRS BONE: I kent it! I kent it! I says tae *him*, I says, yon's a
TB cough!

LILY: Shut up, you! Don't cry, Maggie. (*She puts her arms round*
  MAGGIE *and leads her towards the chair occupied by* ISA *to whom
  she hisses:*) Shunt, you! (ISA *gets up*) It's better for Bertie tae
  be in the hospital; they'll pit him right there. Doctors are that
  clever noo.

MRS HARRIS: TB! My! That's bad. Puir wee fella!

MRS BONE: (*giving her a poke in the ribs*) Och awa! They can

dae a soarts o things wi lungs. Ma sister Mary's hubby went
up regular tae hae a lung taken oot and blew up an pit back.

JENNY: Whit a lot o rot!

MRS BONE: I'm tellin you, Miss Cleversticks! There's a big word
for yon operation. Numey-somethin.

JENNY: Lungs is no penny balloons. (*To the still sobbing
MAGGIE*) Och, Mammy, don't cry (*Pause*) Mammy! (*To* ISA)
Ma Goad! Did I no tell ye? It's like this a the time! Yin trouble
efter anither! I've never kent it ony different! D'ye *blame* me?

(ISA *gives* JENNY *a sympathetic head-shake and they sigh in
unison*)

ISA: Like we said . . . it's no livin, is it?

GRANNY: Maggie, I'm awa tae Lizzie's.

LIZZIE: Aye, we're awa. (*With an effort*) Sorry about the wean,
Maggie. Ye should hae went up wi him afore. Come on then,
Granny, or they men'll be at the hoose afore us.

GRANNY: I can manage masel.

(*At the door,* GRANNY *looks back at the crowd, then at
MAGGIE, but MAGGIE is too upset to notice*)

MRS HARRIS: (*as the door closes behind them*) Och, the puir aul
soul.

LILY: (*appealing to both neighbours*) See! (*She indicates the sag-
ging heap that is* MAGGIE) Thanks very much for helping oot,
but . . .

MRS HARRIS: That's a right, Lily. Ye're welcome, any time.

MRS BONE: (*a pat on* MAGGIE's *back as she goes out*) We'll tak
a wee look in later tae see if there's onythin new.

(MRS HARRIS *and* MRS BONE *go off together.* ALEC, *who
has slipped immediately into a vacated chair, chews his nails,
his eyes on* MAGGIE)

MAGGIE: He looked that wee in yon hospital cot, and the doctor
said . . . he said . . . why was he no attendin the chest clinic?
He was angry. He said something tae the nurse . . . (*She breaks
into helpless sobs again*).

LILY: (*taking the little shoes from* MAGGIE's *finger and folding
BERTIE's clothes*) Never heed, Maggie; never heed they doctors;
they're aye crabbit at they clinics . . . Whaur's John?

MAGGIE: He jist saw me ontae the tramcaur at the hospital
gates; he said he'd . . . (*She raises her eyes and looks pointedly at
JENNY*) . . . be hame later.

LILY: Oh! Aye. I get ye. (*She turns to look at* JENNY *who stares
back at her resentfully*).

(*In the following silence,* ALEC *gets up and crosses to his mother, sits on the arm of her chair and pats her back. She puts*

up a hand which he takes: she gives him a watery loving smile)

MAGGIE: Ye a right, Alec? An Isa?

ISA: Oh aye! I'm a right. Sorry aboot Bertie, but he's faur better aff in the hospital.

JENNY: Aye, he couldna get well in this midden o a place, Mammy.

MAGGIE: Tae think I ever grudged gettin up tae him in the night!

JENNY: Och, *Mammy*!

MAGGIE: Jenny . . . ye'll no leave us . . . will ye?

JENNY: *(sighing)* Mammy, there's nae *difference*. Aye, I'm gaun. I'm jist waitin till Nessie gets back frae the factory so's I'll no go intae a cauld hoose. *(As MAGGIE looks at her with eyes full of reproach)* Uch! *(She turns her face away)*

MAGGIE: Ye're breakin yer daddy's heart, that's whit ye're daein! (JENNY *doesn't answer)* Ye'll . . . ye'll come back an see us . . . often, Jenny?

JENNY: Aye . . . well . . . I'm no makin ony proamises. *(She gets up and goes towards bedroom)* Ma, ye've got Daddy an Lily an Alec an the weans. Ye'll no miss me oot o the hoose. I'm hardly ever in it.

(JENNY goes into the bedroom)

MAGGIE: I dinna ken whit way we bring weans intae the world at a. Slavin an worryin for them a yer days, an naethin but heartbreak at the end o it.

ALEC: Aw, come on Ma, cheer up. *(He smooths her hair: she looks up at him gratefully, lovingly, and lays his hand to her cheek. ISA looks at them and laughs)*

ISA: Mammy's big tumphy! G'on, ye big lump o dough!

(ALEC disengages himself from his mother and grins feebly)

LILY: My, You're a right bitch, Isa. Yin o they days you'll get whit's comin tae ye. Alec's no as saft as he looks.

ISA: Is he no, Auntie? I'm right gled tae hear it.

(JENNY comes in with a suitcase)

JENNY: Well, I'm awa. Cheeribye, everybody.

LILY: Goodbye. And good riddance tae bad rubbish.

(JENNY sticks out her tongue)

MAGGIE: Jenny, whit am I goin tae tell folks?

JENNY: Folks? Ye mean the neighbours? If they've got the impidence tae ask, tell them it's nane o their bloomin business.

MAGGIE: Oh Jenny, Jenny! Whit's happened tae ye, Jenny?

JENNY: Whit's happened? I've wakened up, that's whit's happened. There's better places than this. Jist because I wis born here disnae mean I've got tae bide here.

LILY: Gie yer Mammy a kiss.

JENNY: (*she wavers for a moment, then tosses her head*) I'm no in the mood for kissin. Cheerio, Isa. Mind whit I tellt ye.

ALEC: Aboot whit? (*He creeps forward, suspiciously to* ISA) Whit did she tell ye, eh?

ISA: (*pushing his face away*) A bed-time story; but no for wee boys.

(MAGGIE *looks helplessly on, combing her hair with her fingers*)

LILY: Clear aff then, if ye're gaun!

ISA: Ta ta, Jenny. See ye roon the toon.

JENNY: Aye. Ta ta.

(*The door opens.* JOHN *comes in. He and* JENNY *look at each other*)

JOHN: (*wretched*) I thought ye'd hev gone.

JENNY: Naw. Jist gaun.

(*He lowers his eyes from her face and stands aside to let her pass. He turns and watches her from the doorway until her footsteps die away and the outside door bangs. Then he turns to* MAGGIE. LILY *goes over to* ISA, *gives her a shove, indicating the bedroom door: does the same to* ALEC *who follows* ISA, *but with a backward look to* MAGGIE *and* JOHN. LILY *goes off by the other door*)

MAGGIE: (*pointing to the pile of clothes with the little scuffed shoes on top*) John, they've kep him in.

(*She starts to cry again: he comforts her*)

JOHN: I wis afraid o that; but it's better, Maggie, it's better.

MAGGIE: I didna want him kep in; I didna want him left in a strange place! He'll be feart! He'll be cryin for his Mammy!

JOHN: I ken, Maggie. I ken. He'll be cryin for his Mammy the way I'm cryin for Jenny. (*Pause*) Ma first bonnie wee girl. Aye laughin. Ridin high on ma shoulders . . . Tell me a story, Daddy . . . Tie ma *soo*-lace, Daddy . . . (*Despairing*) An I couldna mak enough tae gie her a decent hame. So! She's left us! She's as guid as deid tae us.

MAGGIE: Naw! Ye've no tae say that! She'll come back.

JOHN: (*shaking his head*) Nae. Naw. She's deid tae me.

(*He sinks down into a chair and is silent*)

If I could hae jist . . . jist done better by ye a. If I could hae . . . (*Head in hands, eyes on floor*) . . . If! If! . . . Every time I've had tae say 'no' tae you an the weans it's doubled me up like a kick in the stomach.

(*He lifts his head and cries out:*)

Christ Almighty! A we've din wrong is tae be born intae poverty!

Whit dae they think this kind o life does tae a man?

Whiles it turns ye intae a wild animal. Whiles ye're a human question mark, aye askin why? Why? *Why?*

There's nae answer. Ye end up a bent back and a heid hangin in shame for whit ye canna help.

(*Fade out lights*)

SCENE TWO

Scene: The same. A month later. Afternoon.

ALEC and ISA are quarrelling in the bedroom: their raised voices are heard off. ISA comes out in a soiled, tawdry negligee with her hair about her shoulders, a cigarette hanging from her lip.

ISA: Aw shut up! I'm sick o yer jawin.

ALEC: (*appearing behind her, half dressed*) I am tellin ye, Isa, I'll no staun much mair! I'm jist warnin ye. That's a.

ISA: An I'm warnin you! If you think I'm gaun on like this a ma life, ye've anither think comin. You're no the only pebble on ma beach, no by a lang chalk. If you want tae keep me, it's time ye wid be makin a bit o dough again. I canna live on air.

ALEC: (*placating*) Come an we'll go tae the dugs the night, Isa; mebbe we'll hae a bit o luck.

ISA: Aye. *Mebbe.*

ALEC: Mind last time I won . . .

ISA: Aye, an I mind the last hauf dizzen times ye lost . . . Whit did you dae wi yon bag?

ALEC: I flung it ower a wa.

ISA: Ye stupid fool! I'm needin a bag.

ALEC: It's no safe, Isa . . . ye've got tae get rid o the evidence . . . the Polis . . .

ISA: Three quid an a handfu o coppers! A fat lot o use that is tae me. Why the Hell did ye no pick on a toff? We wis in the right district.

ALEC: She looked like a toff; honest, Isa! She'd on a fur coat . . .

ISA: Whit kind o fur? Rabbit? You're that dumb ye wouldnae ken. Next time, I'm no jookin up a lane, I'm staying wi ye.

ALEC: No ye're no! It's no safe. Ye've got tae be able tae rin fast.

ISA: Rin! That's a you're guid for. Rinnin. It's aboot time I wis daein the rinnin. I'm sick fed up wi you. If I'd went wi Peter Robb I'd hae a fur coat an it wouldna be rabbit. An he's got a caur . . .

ALEC: You say Peter Robb tae me again an I'll kill ye! I wull!
  I'll kill ye!
    (*He gets hold of her by the throat: she makes 'strangling' noises.
    He panics and drops her*)
ISA: (*frightened first, then angry*) You . . . ! Ma Goad! (*She rubs
  her throat*) You'll pay for that!
ALEC: Isa! Did I hurt ye? I didnae mean tae hurt ye . . . I lost
  ma heid.
ISA: Get oot! Clear aff oot o ma sight!
ALEC: Isa, I'm sorry. I jist see red when ye talk aboot Peter
  Robb. I canna see naethin but him an you taegether . . . an the
  way ye wis last night, cairryin oan wi him.
ISA: Aye! Ye can use yer hauns a right on a wumman; but if ye
  wis hauf a man, ye'd have kicked his teeth in last night.
ALEC: He's bigger nor me . . . he'd have hauf-killed me!
ISA: Fancy me mairryin a rat like you. The joke wis on me a
  right.
ALEC: Isa, I'll hae plenty again . . . you'll see . . . I've a coupla
  pals that's got ideas . . . wait on, Isa! I'll get ye onythin ye
  want . . . a fur coat an crockydile shoes . . . ye said ye wanted
  crockydile shoes . . . I proamise, Isa! I proamise! . . . if ye'll stay
  wi me . . . I love ye, Isa; honest, I dae. I love ye.
ISA: *Love*! Hee-haw! There's nae sich a thing. There's wantin
  tae get intae bed wi someone ye fancy . . . or wantin someone'll
  let ye lie in yer bed an no have tae gae oot tae work; but there's
  nae love. No roon aboot here, onyway. Don't kid yersel.
ALEC: (*trying to take her in his arms*) That's no true! I love ye.
  I'm no fit for onythin when you're oot o ma sight. I'm lost . . .
  waitin on ye comin back . . . I get tae thinkin . . . an wonderin
  whaur ye are . . . and if . . .
ISA: If I'm behavin masel? Well, hauf the time, I'm no.
ALEC: Isa!
ISA: Aw shut up! (*She pushes him away*) Ye're ae wantin tae slob-
  ber ower me. If ye wis onythin decent tae look at it wouldna
  be sae bad, but ye're like somethin that's been left oot a night
  in the rain. G'on, blow! I canna staun yer fumblin aboot —
  unless I'm canned. Get oot ma way. I'm gonnae get dressed.
    (*She slams the bedroom door in his face. He stands looking at it.
    MAGGIE comes in. Clearly she is dead beat. She has a shabby
    bag in one hand and a little jar of jelly in the other. She gets the
    jar on the table and sinks into a chair. ALEC has not moved*)
MAGGIE: Alec? Whit's the matter?
ALEC: (*as if coming out of a trance*) Eh? (*He turns slowly to her*)
MAGGIE: Is there somethin wrang?

ALEC: Naw. 's a right.

MAGGIE: You an Isa's been at it again.

ALEC: She's threatenin tae leave me, Mammy!

MAGGIE: Ye'd be better aff wioot her.

ALEC: Don't you stert! I don't care whit you think! She's mines, an I'll no let ye speak against her, d'ye hear?

MAGGIE: All right, all right . . . Aw, look at they dishes still sittin frae the mornin! Does nane o ye think o me comin hame tae this?

ALEC: Aw shut up, shut up!

> (*He suddenly sweeps everything off the table, then stands staring at the mess on the floor*)

Aw, I'm sorry. I didnae mean tae . . . I'll help ye clear it up. (*He looks up, pleading*) Mammy? Mammy?

MAGGIE: (*on her knees*) Ye've broken the dish o jelly Mrs Ferguson gie'd me tae tak up tae Bertie . . . the nurse said he could get a wee tate on his breid. Well . . . there's nae use greetin. Are the weans a right?

> (ALEC *takes the debris from her and disposes of it at the sink*)

Did Isa gie them their dinners? I asked her . . .

ALEC: She's jist new up.

MAGGIE: Jist new up? It's no fair! Naebody lifts a haun tae help me! I've tae go oot charrin a day and then come hame tae this! . . . Whaur's yer feyther?

ALEC: Hevna seen him.

MAGGIE: I suppose you wis in yer bed tae, a mornin?

ALEC: I wis tired!

MAGGIE: Too tired tae go doon tae the burroo? At least yer feyther does *that*.

ALEC: Whit's the use? There's nae jobs.

MAGGIE: Nae work for the men. Aye plenty for the women. Oh, I'm that sick I could see the hale lot o ye in Hell! (*Taking out her purse*) Would ye gae doon tae the chip shop and get a coupla pies and some chips for wur tea?

ALEC: (*squinting into her purse*) Aye. A right Ma.

MAGGIE: Get ninepenny worth o the chips an a tin o condensed. An then rin across tae the baker an see if there's ony stale tea-breid left. An if ye can find Edie an Ernest, send them up . . .

ALEC: Ma, whit aboot a packet o fags?

MAGGIE: There's nae money for fags.

ALEC: Jist five Woodbine'll dae. I'm needin them.

MAGGIE: Ye're no needin them, Alec. Ye're jist *wantin* them; an ye'll hae tae dae a lot o wantin afore ye're deid.

ALEC: (*shouting*) Aw shut up preachin at me! Ma nerves is a tae Hell! . . . I feel like cuttin ma throat.

MAGGIE: Whit wey is that tae talk?

ALEC: There's nae use livin . . . naebody cares whit happens tae me.

MAGGIE: Alec, ye ken that's no true.

ALEC: If I chucked masel intae the Clyde naebody'd care. I wisht I could! . . . But she's right . . . I hevnae the guts!

MAGGIE: Alec, whit is it, son?

ALEC: She says she's gaun wi Peter Robb. She says I'm nae use. Ma, I canna staun it if she goes wi him! I canna staun it!

MAGGIE: My Goad! I'll gie that girl a piece o ma mind for gettin you intae this state. It's woke me up a bit tae find oot the way you twos been livin . . . ye're shakin, Alec. Hev ye had onythin tae eat the day?

ALEC: A cup o tea.

MAGGIE: We should hae some spirits in the hoose. Whaur's Isa? Is she oot? (ALEC *points to the bedroom*) Isa! Isa! Alec, lie doon a wee minute, ye're that white.

> (*She helps him over to the bed:* ALEC *is play-acting for all he's worth, leaning on her and half-whimpering*)

ALEC: Oh ma, ye're that guid tae me.

> (ISA *comes out of the bedroom. She has a tawdry lacy, low-cut slip on, and over it a dirty 'film-starish' negligée*)

ISA: Whit's a the row?

MAGGIE: (*emptying contents of purse on table*) Alec's shiverin; he can hardly staun on his feet. Rin doon quick an get's a gill o whisky.

ISA: A *gill*? There's no much in a gill.

MAGGIE: An get a packet o Woodbine tae. An here! You've tae leave aff tormentin him!

ISA: Me? Tormentin him? I'm no tormentin him!

MAGGIE: Aye are ye! Threatenin tae leave him when ye ken he's that daft aboot ye. Goad kens why, for ye're a worthless slut if ever there wis yin.

ISA: You keep yer insultin names tae yersel, ye dirty aul bitch!

MAGGIE: I'll learn you tae ca me a bitch!

> (*She slaps* ISA's *face. At this moment* JOHN *comes in*)

JOHN: Here! Whit's a this?

ISA: She hit me! She's that rotten tae me!

JOHN: Maggie! Whit dae ye think ye're daein?

MAGGIE: Naethin she didnae deserve. She ca'd me a bitch.

JOHN: Well, ye're certainly actin like yin.

MAGGIE: John!

JOHN: Ma Goad! Whit a Hell o a hoose tae come hame tae!

MAGGIE: It's no ma fault! I've din a hale copper-fu o washin an scrubbed three floors an the hale lot o yous had naethin tae dae but lie in yer beds! Ye couldna even wash up a dish for me. It's me that aye has tae dae twa jobs when you get the sack!

JOHN: Aw, shut up harpin on that string. It's no ma fault. I've been oot lookin for work.

MAGGIE: Aye, I've seen yous men lookin for work. Haudin up the street corners, ca'in doon the Government . . . tellin the world whit *you'd* dae if you wis rinnin the country . . .

JOHN: Shut yer mouth or I'll shut it for ye!

MAGGIE: (*shocked*) John! (*Pause*) Whit I meant wis . . . ye could hae tidied the place up afore ye went oot.

JOHN: Tae Hell wi this Jessie business every time I'm oot o a job! I'm no turnin masel intae a bloomin skivvy! I'm a man!

ISA: (*softly*) Quite right. A woman disnae respect a man that's *nae* a man. (*To* MAGGIE) Well, whit aboot this whisky?

JOHN: Whit's this? *Whisky?* There's nae drink comin intae this hoose!

ISA: It's for Alec. He's nae weel, *she* says.

MAGGIE: He's lyin doon.

JOHN: If he's nae weel it's mair likely because his system's poisoned wi the stuff a'ready. Alec! Get oot o that bed an show yer face!

MAGGIE: I tell't ye he's nae weel, John.

(JOHN *goes across to the bed and drags* ALEC *out*)

JOHN: Get ootside and breathe some fresh air, at least whit passes for fresh air roon here. Ye're gettin nae whisky. D'ye understan?

MAGGIE: (*turning on him fiercely*) Who earned that money? You or me?

(JOHN, *as if he had been shot, drops* ALEC *and turns away, slumps down in a chair and puts his head in his hands.* ALEC *craftily sneaks some of* MAGGIE'*s cash and slinks out.* MAGGIE, *resentful, eyes first* ISA *and then the demoralised* JOHN)

ISA: That's the stuff! He's needin somebody tae tak him in haun. He's beyond me. (*She cries, not very convincingly*) I cannae dae naethin wi him.

MAGGIE: Oh, wull ye listen tae her! See they crocodile tears? It's a wunner ye can squeeze oot a drap frae they wee marble eyes!

JOHN: Don't cry, Isa; he's nae worth it.

MAGGIE: It's her that's the worthless yin! If she'd leave him alane . . .

JOHN: Maggie! That's no fair! she's upset.

MAGGIE: (*bitterly hurt at* JOHN's *perfidy*) Oh, yous men! Big saft idiots the lot o ye.

JOHN: It's *your* fault. You spoiled him frae the day he wis born. He's still your wee pet lamb no matter whit he gets up tae.

ISA: Aye, he's jist a great big baby. If he disnae get whit he wants, he greets; tears rinnin doon his cheeks. It fair scunners me. I like a man tae *be* a man. Staun up for hissel.

MAGGIE: (*to* JOHN) And I like a man . . . (*Her voice breaking*) . . . tae stand up for his wife.

> (*She seizes her coat and hauls it on, jams on her terrible old hat — this should be black or dark brown — and goes to the table to pick up her money: when she sees how little* ALEC *has left her, she can't help making a small sound.* JOHN *looks up*)

JOHN: Here! Whaur d'ye think you're gaun?

> (*She looks at him coldly and doesn't answer. She goes out. There is a pause, then* ISA *laughs*)

ISA: Oh ho! Ye've done it on yersel noo, Daddy. She's in the huff. She'll no be speaking tae ye.

JOHN: (*uneasy*) Och no . . . no. Maggie disnae take the huff . . . hardly ever.

> (ISA *comes up close*)

ISA: Ye'll get the cold shoulder in bed the night, eh? Nae fun and games!

JOHN: (*genuinely shocked*) Isa! Mind who ye're speakin tae!

ISA: I'm speakin tae you and why should I no? Ye're a man as well's ma faither-in-law.

> (JOHN *moves away, goes to window, pulls aside the curtains: throws up the sash and looks right, then left*)

Goad! I'm freezin tae death! (*She hugs her arms and shivers*) Pit doon the sash.

> (*He does so: returns, troubled*)

JOHN: I should hae gone tae the shops for her and let her hae a rest.

ISA: The shops? She's awa lookin for her wee boy in case he gets intae mischief.

JOHN: We shouldnae hae criticised him, Isa.

> (*He smiles at her. They both burst out laughing*)

ISA: My! Your eyes when ye laugh . . . (*Pause*) Listen, don't you bother yer bunnet; it's no you she's mad at; it's me. She cannae staun the sight o me. Never could.

JOHN: Och, I wouldnae sae that, Isa.

ISA: Right frae the stert. I took her wee boy away frae her.

They're a the same, mothers. The first yin's aye his mither's big tumphy.

JOHN: Aye . . . weel . . . mebbe they cannae help it.

ISA: Mebbe no; but Goad help the wife that gets stuck wi the tumphy.

JOHN: She's been a guid mother tae the lot o them, Isa, and Goad knows we've had a tough time.

ISA: Aye . . . well . . . but she's been lucky. Lucky wi her man.

JOHN: Come aff it, Isa!

ISA: I mean it! I think you're great. Ye've . . . ye've an *air* aboot ye.

JOHN: An air?

ISA: Aye. As if ye wis somebody.

JOHN: Hee-haw! In these claes?

ISA: There's some can see whit's *under* the claes — if ye ken whit I mean. If you wis single, you could get a job in Canada, or Australia. Or even England . . . but ye're stuck; pinned doon here wi Maggie and the weans.

JOHN: (*feebly*) Y're no tae say onythin against Maggie, Isa.

ISA: Oh, I'm no. She's a good sort. Kind o ready wi her hands . . . (*She feels her cheek*) . . . but nae wunner wi a they weans tae skelp aboot. Of course, that's her life . . . she disnae care . . . I mean aboot whit she looks like.

JOHN: The kids has tae come first. And once ye've a faimly ye begin tae forget whit ye used tae look like when ye's a few bob tae spare tae posh yersel up. Ye get intae the way o thinkin that it's nae worth botherin.

ISA: (*bending towards him*) It's a night oot on the toon you're needin; make ye forget yer troubles.

JOHN: When ye're on the dole, Isa, ye're lucky if ye can skin a packet o Woodbine.

ISA: Aw, it's a right shame! D'ye no hae the odd . . . (*She 'fingers' a couple of notes*) . . . win at the dugs? D'ye never get a tip?

(*For a moment the light of remembrance dear comes into his eyes, then fades: he looks at his boots*)

JOHN: Naw. It's nae worth it, Isa . . . the way ye feel efter.

ISA: Och, a coupla aspirins and a guid dose . . .

JOHN: Aspirins is for sair heids; no for bad coansciences.

ISA: (*shakes her head sorrowfully*) And you in the prime o life. It's a right shame, so it is.

JOHN: Shut up Isa, will ye? Juist shut up. I've had *nae* prime. I got married. Nae trainin. Nae skill; juist a labourer when there wis labourin needed; and when there's nane . . . the Buroo. And

there's nae escape that I can see. (*With an effort*) But thanks a
the same, Isa.

    (*His head is bent. Impudently she tickles the back of his neck*)

ISA: Whit for, Daddy?

JOHN: (*jerking up*) Here! Behave yersel. You're asking for
trouble!

ISA: Whit sort o trouble had ye in mind, Daddy?

JOHN: Don't ca me Daddy!

    (*She giggles. He smiles at her. Then, into the kitchen burst* EDIE
    and ERNEST)

ERNEST: Whaur's Mammy?

JOHN: Gettin in the messages, whit you should be daein for
her. When I wis your age I'd hev got a good leatherin . . . you
should be in here when your Mammy gets hame tae see whit
she wants.

ERNEST: Aw cripes! Ye cannae pit yer heid in the door but
someone's jawin ye.

JOHN: Cut it oot. Get on and redd this place up a bit.

ERNEST: I dinnae ken whaur tae stert!

JOHN: Neither dae I.

    (EDIE *starts to clear the table by the simple expedient of sweeping*
    things on to the dresser)

EDIE: I'll set the table. Is the kettle on, Isa?

ISA: Look and see. I'm nae wantin tea here; I'm gaun oot tae
mines.

EDIE: Gaun oot tae yer tea! My! . . . In a rest-u-rant? Ye lucky
dog!

    (ISA *goes off to bedroom*)

ERNEST: She'll be gaun wi yon big fat bookie she wis wi last
night; he's got an Armstrong-Siddley. I seen it!

JOHN: (*giving him a clout on the ear*) You keep yer trap shut.

    (ERNEST *makes a great row, holding his ear and trying hard*
    to cry. MAGGIE *comes in. She doesn't look at* JOHN *but goes*
    to the table and puts down a loaf, a tin of milk and a parcel of
    chips. Then she takes off her hat and coat)

JOHN: (*sheepish*) Ye werena lang.

    (*She looks at him, stoney eyed.* EDIE *looks anxiously from one*
    to the other and ERNEST's *crying dies to a whimper.* MAGGIE
    lifts the kettle to put it on)

EDIE: (*eagerly, taking it from her*) I'll dae it, Mammy.

    (*She fills the kettle and sets it on the cooker.* JOHN *picks up his*
    library book and turns his back on the lot of them. ERNEST *sits*
    too, but his eyes follow his mother about: he is not used to this
    silent, grim-mouthed woman. The smell of the chips is too much

*for him, and, while his mother busies herself cutting the loaf, he
creeps to the table, opens the parcel up and sneaks out a chip:
EDIE steals up on him as he is stretching out for another and
hits him. He lifts his foot to give her a kick on the behind and
MAGGIE, turning at that moment, sees the scuffed toe-caps of
his boots and what remains of her self-control gives way. She
screams at him:)*

MAGGIE: Look at yer new boots! (*She seizes him, shakes him and
hits him*) Ye've kicked the taes oot o them again! I'll learn ye
tae play fitba' in yer best boots. (*Crying hysterically, she belabours
ERNEST who tries to get away, yelling, but she holds on*) Whaur
d'ye think I'll find the money for anither pair? Oh, I cannae
staun ony mair o this . . . I cannae staun it!

   (*She collapses in a storm of weeping. EDIE joins in out of fear
   and sympathy, and JOHN jumps up in alarm. He goes to calm
   her but she shouts at him:*)

Leave me alane! Leave me alane! I hate ye! I hate the hale lot
o ye!

   (*In a storm of tears she blunders out of the room. JOHN gathers
   the two frightened children to him and sits down an arm around
   each*)

JOHN: Wheesht, wheesht, the baith o ye; wheesht. Listen. Listen tae me. Edie, Ernie, listen. I'll try tae explain. (*He sighs*)
Yer Mammy's no really angry at ye . . . (*the children's tears stop
in a series of sobs and hiccoughs*) Your mammy's just tired. She's
been oot a day cleanin ither folks' hooses, and mebbe we ought
tae hae helped mak things a bit easier for her. (*EDIE nods her
head vigorously*) . . . When women gets that tired they kind o
loss their heids; ye unnderstaun?

EDIE: I wis feart, Daddy. I've never been feart o' ma Mammy
before.

JOHN: She'll be sorry ye were feart, Edie.

ERNEST: Daddy, am I no tae get playin fitba again? I hevnae got
nae ither boots; the auld yins crushed ma taes. I'm the centre-
forward! Ma chinas'll kill me if I'm no in the team. Some o
them's got real fitba boots. Daddy, could you no get us a pair
o real yins?

JOHN: I'll try, son. I'll try.

ERNEST: Bobbie Gray got his at the barras.

JOHN: (*a gleam of hope*) Oh aye . . . there's the barras. We'll need
tae see whit Mammy says.

ERNEST: (*a despairing cry*) Aw naw! She's a wumman; she
cannae unnerstaun men!

EDIE: I'm awfu hungry, Daddy and the chips is gettin cold.

ERNEST: (*desperate*) Wull ye try, Daddy, wull ye?

   (JOHN *bows his head, holds it between his hands and groans*)

JOHN: (*to himself*) Try. Try. As if I didnae try.

   (EDIE *plucks his sleeve*)

EDIE: So could we no juist hae wur tea, Daddy? Mebbe ma Mammy's gone tae her bed.

JOHN: Aye. We'll hae wur tea.

   (*The children sit at the table and dive into the chips.* JOHN *slowly and painfully locates the tea pot and makes tea. He sets out cups: lifts the teapot and looks at the door through which* MAGGIE *had disappeared plainly wondering if he dare take her a cup. The door opens and she appears, her face begrutten, but calm*)

MAGGIE: Well, come on then, come on! Which o yous has found the strength tae mak the tea! (*In a whisper to* JOHN) I'm sorry. Couldnae help masel. Think I'm needin something tae eat.

JOHN: (*patting her*) That's a right, lass.

   (EDIE *offers her mother the chips*)

MAGGIE: Naw, hen! I'm no for a chip. They gie me the heart-burn. (*She sits down and stretches for bread and butter: with a piece halfway to her mouth she stops and gives a kind of laugh*)

   Heartburn! I wonder whit kind o a male idiot called indigestion heartburn? Ma Goad! I could tell him whit heartburn is! Ma Goad! Couldn't I no!

ACT THREE

Aftenoon of Christmas Day.

   The kitchen is clean, tidy and festive: decorations, vase of pa-per flowers, etc. A wireless set to which ERNEST's ear is glued. He has on new football boots and between them — which from time to time he caresses — and the jazz to which he listens in ecstasy, he is in a world of his own.

   MAGGIE in a new dress, is bustling in and out: GRANNY is back in her rocker in the corner: she sighs, shakes her head: smiles now and again: even gives an occasional cackle to herself.

MAGGIE: Och Ernie! that's enough o that hootin an tootin. Why do they no keep tae the tune the man made?

ERNEST: Ma! It's *swing*!

MAGGIE: I ken it's swing; and they deserve tae swing for it. (*She listens*) Yon's no music.

ERNEST: Ma, it's the latest! Listen! (*In awe and admiration*) that's Louis Armstrong on the trumpet! Dazzlin!

MAGGIE: He's clean lost control.

ERNEST: He's improvisin. That means daein a sort o turn.

MAGGIE: Well, you dae a turn for me, son — wi yon knob.

ERNEST: *Ma*!

MAGGIE: Turn the knob. I'm no sufferin ony longer. See, oot ma way! (*She gives him a clout and fiddles until she gets choir boys afloat on carols*) There noo! *That's* music. Holy music. (*She sings with the choristers*)

ERNEST: (*sotto voce*) Who's wantin holy music?

    (*He starts dodging about the kitchen, trying imaginary tackles, dribbling, etc. MAGGIE polishing her few bits of brass-ware, still helping the choir boys, pays no attention to him. GRANNY's old head turns slowly from the footballing ERNEST to the carolling MAGGIE*)

GRANNY: I cannae understaun this hoose. There's aye a din, even when ye're supposed tae be happy. (*To ERNEST who has got dangerously close to her*) Keep awa frae ma bunion wi they tacketty boots!

ERNEST: Tacketty boots. Cripes! They's fitba boots, Granny.

GRANNY: I ken they're fitba boots, and the kitchen's nae a footba pitch.

ERNEST: (*doing imaginary headers*) Cripes! Wummen!

GRANNY: Whit wey d'ye no gang ootside wi yer fancy boots an play wi a real ba?

ERNEST: Because I'm waitin on ma Daddy.

MAGGIE: (*singing to 'Oh, come all ye faithful'*) He's waitin on his Daddy, he's waitin on his Daddy wha's oot at the shops.

GRANNY: Mair spendin. Ye'll rue the day. I'm tellin ye.

    (JOHN *comes in looking happy and confident. He unwinds the muffler he wears and flings it aside disclosing a smart collar and tie: he keeps his other hand behind his back, holding a brown paper hat bag tied at the neck with string*)

ERNEST: Hurry! Daddy! Did ye get it for me?

JOHN: No yet, Ernie. Haud yer horses. You're no the maist important pebble on ma beach. (*He grins across at MAGGIE*)

ERNEST: Aw Daddy, ye promised ye'd bring me back a ba.

GRANNY: Gie him a bat on the ear instead, John.

JOHN: You buzz aff ben the back parlour; you and me's gaun oot later. It's yer Mammy's turn noo. Maggie! Here.

    (ERNEST *goes reluctantly.* MAGGIE *turns down the choristers and comes over*)

MAGGIE: Whit is it?

JOHN: (*beckoning her closer*) Nievy-nievy-nick-knack, which haun will ye tak?

MAGGIE: Is it ma Christmas?

JOHN: Whit d'ye think? Come on. Nievy-nievy . . .

(*She deliberates: chooses one hand, he shifts, teasing her before he hands over the hat bag*)

MAGGIE: It's a hat!

GRANNY: (*screwing round to see*) Mair money than sense. Ye'll rue the day, the baith o the two o ye. Waste not, want not. Ye'd think ye'd won on they fitba thingammies.

JOHN: (*while* MAGGIE *is busy undoing her present*) Listen, aul yin. This is the first Christmas I've had a decent job for ten year; it's gonnae be the best. The *best*! It's gonnae be somethin for Maggie and me tae remember when we're a coupla toothless aul has-beens.

(GRANNY *snorts.* MAGGIE *has torn off the paper and brought out a red hat: it is a bright hat but not fussy: it might be felt with a bow. It is not a comic piece with a feather sticking up or even lying down. She is quite overcome*)

MAGGIE: Oh John!

JOHN: (*his pleasure matching hers*) Well, come on then; let's see ye in it.

(MAGGIE *is sorting out the front from the back:* JOHN *sees the price ticket still dangling and rushes to tear off the tag which he pockets*)

MAGGIE: Watch! Ye'll rive oot the linin! (*Fondly*) Ye great muckle ham-fist . . . Did it . . . cost an awfu lot, John?

JOHN: Ye don't ask the price o presents, Maggie. Ye forgot that, didn't ye? (*He smiles ruefully*) Nae wunner. Let's see ye in it.

(MAGGIE, *at a small mirror, settles the hat on her head with care, turning to* JOHN *for approbation. He nods. She gives him a kiss, almost in tears. He puts his arms round her, patting her back.* GRANNY *gazes at them and tut-tuts*)

GRANNY: Fancy you wi a red hat. Yon's nae a colour for an aul wife, Maggie.

JOHN: We didnae invite your opinion, Granny.

GRANNY: Weel, I'm giein it ye for naethin. Black would hae been better . . . When's she gonnae wear yon? There's nae weddin comin aff that I ken aboot. A red hat!

JOHN: She can wear it whenever she wants.

GRANNY: Maggie never gets further than the Copey; when they're a done gawpin at it in there, she'll hae a face tae match it.

MAGGIE: Never heed her, John. I think it's lovely. (*She strokes it*) Wait till Lily sees it!

GRANNY: A red hat! It's no as if she ever sets fit in the kirk door. A croshay bunnet would hae done her as weel.

MAGGIE: Aw shut up, Granny! You're spoilin it on me! (*To* JOHN) Did ye get a wee thing for her Christmas?

JOHN: Naw. I wis too busy trying hats on a wee lassie in C & A's. I'll get her something when I gae oot wi Ernie. No that she deserves it, the aul soor-dook.

MAGGIE: That'll dae ye; she cannae help being a done aul wife.

GRANNY: I heard ye! I heard ye! Wait on, Maggie, wait on. Yer ain day'll come by yer son's fireside. Nae wantit.

JOHN: Goad! Whit can ye say?

MAGGIE: Granny, it's Christmas and John's got a job. We're a gaun tae have a merry Christmas.

JOHN: Aye, and you too. When ye waken the morn, ye'll find a stockin hangin on yer bed-rail.

GRANNY: A stockin? (*She sniggers*) A stockin! Stockins is for weans.

JOHN: Aye, that's right.

MAGGIE: I think I'll chap Mrs Bone for a wee cup wi us. Her man'll be oot on the batter.

(*She knocks on ceiling. There is an answering thump*)

JOHN: Well, I'll tak Ernie oot for his fitba.

MAGGIE: Aye, and get wee Marina's pianny. And if it's ower dear, see if ye can get a dolly's tea-set.

JOHN: Aye. Right. (*Shouting*) Ernie! Ernie! Come oan! You and me's for aff. The wummen's gatherin.

(MAGGIE, *still with her hat on, puts on the kettle and sets out cups, etc.* ERNIE *comes in whistling and bouncing an imaginary ball.* JOHN *tackles and they career around,* GRANNY *guarding her feet*)

MAGGIE: Mind ma polished lino!

(*A knock on the door.* JOHN *lets in* MRS BONE *who is closely followed by* MRS HARRIS)

JOHN: Come awa ben. Maggie's got the kettle on.

MRS BONE: Ta. I chappit Mrs Harris in the passin.

JOHN: Quite right.

MRS HARRIS: Thanks, Mr Morrison. I like yer tie. Daein' fine noo, aren't ye?

JOHN: Fine.

MRS HARRIS: Drivin a van, isn't it? They'd hae tae learn ye?

JOHN: (*winking to* MRS BONE) Naw I kent it by instinct.

MRS HARRIS: Fancy!

JOHN: Are ye ready, Ernie?

MRS BONE: Ernie, ye got yer fitba boots! My! Rangers'll be signin ye.

ERNEST: Rangers be damned. I'm Celtic.

MAGGIE: Ernie, mind yer langwidge.

ERNEST: Och, I ken mair nor that. I ken (*He counts on his fingers and mouths words until:*) An f . . . (*The women screech and* JOHN *and* MAGGIE *reach over to clout him: he dodges and runs off.* JOHN *follows him as far as the door*)

MRS BONE: Gaun oot, Mr Morrison? Gettin intae trainin for Hogmanay, eh?

JOHN: No me. It's nae worth it. Ta ta a. Enjoy yersels.
　　(*He goes off*)

MRS HARRIS: I like yer decorations. Quite festive. We didna bother this year. (*As she accepts tea and is offered a piece of Christmas cake:*) Ta. Oh my! Did ye get a parcel frae the Mission?

MAGGIE: Naw. John brung that in frae Lipton's. Eat up. Come on!

MRS BONE: The kids at the Treat?

MAGGIE: Aye. Yon ladies at the Mission's awful nice. Real toffs. *Kelvinside.* A present, and their tea, an 'Away in a manger' an a wee prayer. Marina's been prayin Tae Jesus for the fairy aff the tap o the tree. Whit'll I say tae the wean if Jesus disna come up tae scratch?

MRS BONE: That's whit ye get for sendin her tae the Sunday School. They teachers! They tell the kids: 'Ask an it shall be given ye', an there's the hale jing bang o them praying like Hell for the yin fairy!

MRS HARRIS: Aye. And the yin that gets it wull no hae it lang. The rest'll hae its wings aff an its croon bashed afore ye can say winkie . . . Alec an Isa oot?

MAGGIE: Aye.

MRS HARRIS: Daein their Christmas shoppin, eh?

MAGGIE: (*her happy face clouding*) I wouldna ken whit they're daein.

MRS BONE: (*leaning across and patting* MAGGIE) I wouldna worry aboot him, Maggie.

MAGGIE: (*startled at first, then rattled*) I'm no worryin. I've nae need tae worry.
　　(*A knock on the door*)
　　It's open. Come awa in.
　　(MRS WILSON *comes in: at the sight of the trio round the table, she throws up her hands in great surprise*)

MRS WILSON: Oh, a pairty? Hope I'm no intrudin?

MAGGIE: Nut at a. Draw up a chair. Mind! The back legs is shoogly.

MRS WILSON: I'll no swing on them. (*Accepting tea*) Ta . . . Aw, the lovely! Who done them?

MAGGIE: John an the kids . . . Whit else d'ye see aside the decorations?

MRS BONE: I see ye've got Granny back.

> (*They all turn and look at* GRANNY *who is asleep with her mouth open*)

MRS HARRIS: I seen the bed come.

MAGGIE: She wis greetin tae come for her Christmas. Lizzie doesna hold wi Christmas. (*Pause: she looks round at them*) Well? I'm waitin . . . I'm *waitin*! Ma *hat*!

MRS BONE: Well, we couldna pretend we didna notice it . . .

MAGGIE: But . . . ye don't like it?

MRS BONE & MRS HARRIS: It's lovely, Maggie! Lovely! But . . . whit the hell made ye take *red*? It's an awfu fierce colour. (*Their voices are a confused jumble*)

MAGGIE: I didnae pick it. It wis John. (*Shy, reminiscent*) When him and me wis coortin, I'd a red hat and he fair fancied me in it. Used tae meet me at the corner o Renfield an Sauchie . . .

MRS BONE: Simpson's Corner!

MAGGIE: Aye, Simpson's Corner. Said he could see ma red hat bobbin through the Setterday nicht crowds. So it's a kind o a . . .

MRS HARRIS: I ken. It's tae mind ye o the days when ye first kissed and cuddled doon the dunny. Quite the romantic, your John. Mines wouldna hae noticed if I'd met him at Simpson's Corner wi a floral po on ma heid.

MRS WILSON: Aye! Them wis the days! I mind the first time Wilson took me tae the La Scala . . .

MRS HARRIS: The *La Scala*!

MRS WILSON: Aye. The La Scala. Back stalls. I wis that excited I didna notice there wis silver paper on ma toffees till I wis hauf-way through the poke! Ma Goad, the pain I had in ma stummick! . . . Thought I wis sent for! Ach well . . . nice tae look back on. Coortin days. They're the best. (*She sighs*)

MRS BONE: Aye. Guid job we've nae crystal balls, eh? . . . How's your Lily? Is she workin?

MAGGIE: Aye, but she's aff the efternoon; she'll be comin by.

MRS WILSON: A nice girl, Lily. Pity she missed the boat.

MRS BONE: Considerin the number o boats that sinks, she's as weel swimmin alang by hersel. Ma Goad, Maggie Morrison, but you're right lucky. There's no mony men that's been used tae a dram can stay TT. Mines is aye proamisin; but he canna resist the smell o a cork.

MAGGIE: Well, there's nae use kiddin on I didna hae ma troubles; but John's learned his lesson. He kens I'd close the door on him if he sterted up again on the bottle.

MRS BONE: Wull ye tell me how ye can close the door on yer man? Mines would jist batter it doon.

MAGGIE: Ye can close the doors o yer heart on him, and once ye've done that tae yer man, batterin wull no get him back in.

MRS HARRIS: My! Ye're that poetic, Maggie. The doors o yer heart!

(GRANNY *wakens up with a start, presumably out of a disturbing dream*)

GRANNY: Aw! Aw! Whaur am I? (*Comin to*) Aw! Aw! Ma Goad! I thought they wis efter me!

MAGGIE: Who, Granny?

GRANNY: The men . . .

(*The women laugh*)

MRS HARRIS: Ye're past it, Granny.

GRANNY: The bad men . . . They wis efter ma money.

MAGGIE: Ye've been dreamin, Granny. Here's a wee cup o tea an a biscuit.

(GRANNY *takes the tea: she turns the biscuit over and grumbles to it quietly*)

GRANNY: It's only chocolate on the wan side. Himph! Cheats!

(*A knock at the door.* MAGGIE *opens to* LILY)

LILY: Hullo. Oh? Open hoose?

MAGGIE: Hullo Lily. Ye're jist in time for a cup and a wee tate cake.

LILY: Cake? Hev ye cut it already, Maggie? Tomorrow's Christmas. (*She looks round the company and gives them a nod and a half-smile*) Ye a well? Lookin forward tae yer Christmas stockin? (*She doesn't expect or get an answer. The women become subdued and a little uneasy*) Maggie! (*Staring at the hat*) D'ye mean tae say ye bought that? It's new!

MAGGIE: No, Lily. I didna buy it: it's John's Christmas tae me.

LILY: (*very dry*) Oh. Quite nice.

(MAGGIE's *face falls: she takes off the hat and holds it uncertainly, stroking it. At this point* GRANNY *provides a diversion by dropping half her biscuit in her tea*)

GRANNY: Maggie, Maggie! I've loss ma biscuit!

MAGGIE: (*putting the hat down on top of the wireless set, she goes*

to GRANNY) OCH, GRANNY, YE CANNA DUNK A CHOCO-
LATE BISCUIT! (*She fishes out the soggy biscuit with a teaspoon
and feeds it to* GRANNY) There noo! Finish up yer tea an stop
yer nonsense.

    (*She turns to see* LILY *taking the hat off the wireless and going
off with it*)

Here!

LILY: I'm jist gonna put it past for ye, ben the room.

MAGGIE: (*with unusual command*) Leave it whaur it is! (*More
quietly*) John'll like tae see it when he comes in.

    (LILY *shrugs. She takes a parcel from her bag and hands it to*
MAGGIE)

LILY: Here's yer Christmas.

    (*The women stretch their necks*)

MAGGIE: Aw thanks, Lily, but ye shouldna hev. I've a wee
somethin for you, tae.

LILY: (*smiling at her*) Ye shouldna hev.

MRS HARRIS: Are ye no openin yer present, Maggie?

    (MAGGIE *looks enquiringly at* LILY *who shrugs*)

LILY: If ye like; but tomorrow's Christmas.

    (MAGGIE *tears at the paper: the others watching to see what
will emerge: a pair of yellow gloves, cotton*)

MAGGIE: Aw thanks, Lily; they're jist whit I wis needin.

    (LILY *nods and goes across to* GRANNY. *The women hand
round and examine the gloves*)

LILY: Hullo Granny. Enjoyed yer tea?

    (*She takes cup.* GRANNY *gives a small belch*)

GRANNY: Was yon tea? Tasted mair like co-co-a.

MRS WILSON: (*about the gloves, in a whisper*) A bob the pair in
Woollies.

LILY: Whit's the matter wi Woolworth's if Woolworth's is a ye
can afford?

MRS WILSON: Lily, ye've picked me up a wrang! I said she'd
hae been better wi woolly yins, seein it's winter.

MAGGIE: Woollen gloves is no dressy.

    (*She smoothes them, smiling. Alex comes in*)

ALEC: Ma, Isa been in?

MAGGIE: No, son.

ALEC: Are ye sure?

MAGGIE: Well, I hevnae seen her an I've been in a day. Is there
onythin wrang, Alec?

    (*Without answering,* ALEC *goes into the bedroom*)

MRS HARRIS: We must be the invisible wummen.

LILY: Ye'll need tae excuse him; he never had nae mainners.

MRS WILSON: He's aufy kind o white and starey-eyed.

MAGGIE: (*on the defensive*) Whit d'ye mean, eh?

MRS BONE: She didnae mean onythin.

MRS WILSON: I juist meant . . . he's no lookin very weel.

MAGGIE: Alec's delicate.

    (ALEC *comes out*)

  Alec, there's tea in the pot, would ye like a cup?

ALEC: Naw. Aw well . . . aye, I'll hev a cup.

    (MAGGIE *rises*)

LILY: Sit doon, Maggie; I'm nearer the pot.

    (*She gives* ALEC *his tea*)

MAGGIE: Whaur hev ye been a day, Alec?

ALEC: Juist . . . roon aboot.

MRS HARRIS: He's no giein onythin away, are ye, Alec?

    (*She gives him a dig in the ribs, he jumps nervously, spilling his tea*)

ALEC: Watch whit y're daein, ye aul fool!

MAGGIE: Alec!

    (ALEC *rises in a silence*)

MRS WILSON: Awful pretty, the decorations, aren't they no?

LILY: Aye. They fairly took wee Christopher's fancy, they streamers and yon chain. I wish we could hae bought a wee tree, though. Mebbe next year . . .

MRS BONE: Yon's a lovely tree they hev in Bertie's ward in the Hospital.

    (ALEC *is standing, staring at nothing: the women look at each other, uneasy*)

MRS WILSON: Ony word o gettin him hame, Mrs Morrison?

MAGGIE: No yet. But he's back frae the Sanitorium; so it shouldnae be lang.

MRS BONE: Oh? I thocht he wis gaun back tae the Sanny.

MAGGIE: Gaun back tae the Sanny? Of course he's no gaun back! The Sanny's for . . . whit-ye-may-ca-it . . . ye ken . . . like yon place at Saltcoats.

MRS BONE: Ye mean the Convalescent?

MAGGIE: Aye. (*Pause*) Alec, ye've hardly touched yer tea. Are ye nae wantin it efter yer Auntie Lily pourin it?

ALEC: (*suddenly spinning round and glaring at the women*) Aw right! Aw right, I'll drink it if that'll shut ye up. Yous wummen! Yap, yap, yap a' day. (*He slurps his tea: takes a hunk of cake* MAGGIE *is timidly proferring and turns his shoulder to the company. They exchange looks and shrugs. After a silence:*)

MRS BONE: Well, I'm right gled tae hear the wee chap's tae get hame.

LILY: Aye, the hoose is nae the same wi yin o them away.

(MRS HARRIS, *silently*, to MRS BONE, *mouths 'two' and holds up two fingers, nodding*)

LILY: (*who has seen this*) Aye.

(ALEC, *still chewing, dumps down his cup and starts for the door*)

MAGGIE: Alec! Are ye gaun oot again?

ALEC: Aye. (*He glowers at her: she subsides nervously*)

MAGGIE: If Isa comes lookin for ye, whit'll we say?

ALEC: (*stopping still on way to door*) I'll . . . I'll . . . (*Agitated*) Never you heed! I'll see her masel . . .

(*He looks at them all in a half-demented way*)

You'd like tae ken, wouldn't ye? You'd like tae ken!

(*He hurries off.* MAGGIE *rises and runs after him, right out of the room*)

MAGGIE: (*off*) Alec! Alec! Wait!

MRS WILSON: Ken whit? Whit did he mean?

LILY: *Uch*!

MRS BONE: Puir Mrs Morrison. If it's nae yin o them, it's anither. Here, Lily, we didnae tell ye we seen Jenny.

LILY: Ye seen her? When?

MRS BONE: Mrs Harris and me. Oh . . . no that lang since.

MRS HARRIS: Aye, no that lang efter she'd went.

LILY: Where?

MRS BONE: Roon aboot the Poly. It was gettin dark, but it was her a right.

MRS HARRIS: Aye. Oh aye. Nae mistake.

MRS WILSON: (*eagerly*) Wi a man?

MRS BONE: Naw!

LILY: It's a wunner.

MRS HARRIS: Huh! If ye'd seen her ye wouldnae wunner. Whit a sight! (*To* MRS BONE) Wasn't she no? A right mess.

MRS WILSON: Fancy! Her that wis aye so smart.

LILY: She was too smart for her ain guid, was oor Jenny.

(MAGGIE *comes back*)

MAGGIE: Whit aboot Jenny?

LILY: Naethin special. Juist that it's Christmas and we were sayin . . . sayin how smart she aye was.

MAGGIE: (*fondly*) Aye. She paid for the dressin, did Jenny . . . Mebbe if she could see us the night, wi the decorations, and the wireless; she's never set fit in the door since she left. Whiles I dream aboot her, and aye in the morning I'm sayin mebbe she'll . . . pop in on me.

LILY: Dreams go by contrare-y, Maggie. She said she wouldnae come back and it's obvious she's no comin back. Forget her.

MAGGIE: Forget her! It's weel seen you never had a faimly, Lily.
Once they've been laid in yer airms, they're in yer heart tae the
end o yer days, no maitter whit way they turn oot.
(*There is a thumping from upstairs.* MRS BONE *jumps up as
if she had been shot*)

MRS BONE: O Goad! That's him wakened. See ye later. Ta for
the tea.
(*She runs out*)

MRS HARRIS: (*rising in leisurely fashion*) Fancy that! I'd like tae
see ma man thump doon for me; I'd thump him!

MRS WILSON: Think I'd better move juist in case Wilson is
waiting on his tea. I'll tak a wee look doon the morn tae wish
ye a Merry Christmas.
(*There is a thud on the door*)

VOICE: Is ma wumman there? Well, tell her tae get the Hell oot
o it. I'm wantin some atten-shun.

MRS HARRIS: Ask for it politely and ye'll mebbe get it!

MRS WILSON: Come on, then, before he gets angry at ye.

MRS HARRIS: (*following* MRS WILSON *out*) It's him that's wantin
me; I'm no needin *him*. (*Over her shoulder as she goes, with a
coarse laugh*) 'Cept for his wages. Ta ta then. Ta ta Granny.
(*She goes off*)

LILY: Whit a relief!

MAGGIE: Oh, They're no bad . . . they're coorse but kind.

LILY: Aye. So lang's ye keep on the right side o them. I thought
they were never goin tae shift. Mind you and me wis goin
tae hae a wee run up toon and see the shops? Are ye fit for
it?

MAGGIE: (*brightening immediately*) Oh aye! I'll pit on ma new
hat. (*She considers the sleeping* GRANNY) Whit aboot her?

LILY: Gie her an aspirin and stick her in her bed. (*They both
advance on Granny*) Talk aboot a ball and chain!

MAGGIE: Come on, Granny, waken up so's we can pit ye tae
bed. You got an aspirin, Lily?

LILY: Aye, I've aye got one in ma bag.

MAGGIE: Bash it up and mix it wi jam while I get her oot o her
chair.

GRANNY: I'm quite happy sleepin in ma chair.

MAGGIE: Ye'll be mair comfortable in yer bed, Chookie.

GRANNY: Whit are you up tae, eh? I aye ken when you ca me
Chookie ye're up tae somethin. Ye're gaun oot! Y're gaun oot
tae leave me.

LILY: (*advancing with the aspirin*) Whitever gied ye that idea,
Granny? Open up! Come on, that's a good girl.

GRANNY: (*backing*) I'm nae needin nae medicine, Lily. Ye ken fine ma bowels is aye rinnin awa frae me.

LILY: Awa an chase yersel, then.

> (MAGGIE *and* LILY *cackle loudly,* GRANNY *is outraged, glaring and spluttering at them*)

MAGGIE: Och, it's no fair laughin at her. Swallow it doon, Granny an ye'll get a sweetie.

GRANNY: I'm no gaun tae ma bed.

LILY: Ye've nae choice the night. See, here's a bit vanilla taiblet.

> (GRANNY *takes the tablet and looks at it suspiciously, turning it over before she puts it in her mouth. While she is chewing,* MAGGIE *and* LILY *grab her and take her off at a smart trot. Her protestations are heard off.* LILY *comes back, tidies up a bit, eats a piece of tablet, puts on her coat and hat.* MAGGIE *returns*)

LILY: Has she cooried doon?

MAGGIE: Aye, nae bother. I jist whipped aff her tap things an rolled her under the blankets. She'll doze aff fine. Come on, quick, Lily; I'm dyin tae see they posh shops up Sauchie. (*She sets her new hat on her head and admires herself in the mirror*)

LILY: When you've finished admirin yersel . . .

MAGGIE: (*turning to* LILY, *happy*) Oh, Lily, this is a rare Christmas! I'm that happy! (*Pause*) Leastways, I would be if only . . .

LILY: Aye, I ken.

MAGGIE: If I'd Bertie hame. And Jenny. Jenny was aye a great girl for Christmas; she'd hang up her stocking, (*Sighs*) an orange an a penny — if she wis lucky.

LILY: We aye managed something, between us, for the kids.

MAGGIE: It wis you, Lily. It wis you did the stockins; I hevna forgot.

LILY: I'm yer sister, for Goad's sake! Nae weans o ma ain tae keep me aye skint. *Come oan!*

> (*They go off*)

Time lapse. Stage blacked. In the distance a salvation army band is playing Christmas carols: the music gets louder throughout the following scene.

Up lights slowly. Pause. ISA walks in: she listens: looks cautiously about her. Slips across to bedroom, listens again at the door then goes inside. Sound of drawers being opened and shut. While she is in, the band, distant, plays 'Oh, come all ye faithful'. At the end of the chorus, ISA emerges hurriedly with a shabby suitcase and a coat over her arm (*imitation fur*). She has a smart new outfit on. She has a look in the mirror and powders her nose, settles her hat: then, picking up her case and coat, makes for the door. Opens it to find ALEC, wild-eyed, on the threshold. For a moment she sags: then recovers.

ALEC: (*near hysteria*) So ye're back are ye? Whaur wis ye last night?

ISA: (*scared but bold*) Oh, did ye miss me?

(ALEC *shuts the door with his foot, then advances: she retreats*)

ALEC: Whaur wis ye? Isa! Whaur wis ye?

ISA: Whit does it maitter whaur I wis?

ALEC: Wis ye . . . wi . . . *him?*

ISA: Aye! I wis! An I'm gaun wi him an you canna haud me back.

ALEC: (*deadly quiet voice*) Isa, I tellt ye, I tellt ye if you ever left me, I'd find ye, an I'd kill ye. (*Advancing*) You said I hadnae the guts. You laughed at me. D'ye mind? d'ye mind laughin at me? . . . You said I wisna a man. (*Sudden shout*) I'll show you! I'll show you!

(*He whips out a knife and flicks the blade.* ISA *lets out a scream of fear*)

ISA: (*backing*) Naw! Naw, Alec! *Naw!* Ye wouldna dae it tae me! Ye wouldna mark me!

ALEC: Mark ye. (*Whisper*) Whit makes ye think I'd stop at spoilin yer face for ye?

(ISA *starts to scream for help at the top of her voice. Her screams panic him: he drops his knife and chases her as she makes for the window: they struggle, he gets his hand over her mouth: she nearly gets away, and inflamed, he gets his hands round her throat. When she is making choking noises and he feels her body going limp, he has another panic and releases her: she sinks to the ground. He bends over her, shaking. Silence except for his rasping breath. She gives a moan*)

ALEC: Isa! Isa! Isa!

(*He is on his knees beside her, rocking himself like a baby and weeping; when she is able, she struggles to a sitting position and massages her throat. She looks at his shaking shoulders with disgust*)

ISA: I'm still alive . . . but ye near aboot strangled me.

ALEC: Tell me it's no true! (*Sobbing*) Tell me it's no true that ye're leavin me for Peter Robb.

ISA: (*her look of scorn and disgust changes to a crafty one*) Of course it's no true. I wis kiddin ye on. Wanted tae see whit ye'd dae. Ye're that saft, Alec! Ye believe everythin ye're tellt.

(*Stands up*) Goad! Yon wis rough, Alec! That's mair like a man!

> (*He looks up at her with grateful, begging eyes: his sobs die*)

I never meant yon aboot Peter. I wis tryin tae frighten ye; tryin tae get ye tae . . . tae get a move on oot o this!

ALEC: (*on his feet, cringing*) I wull! I wull, Isa! Jist gie me a chance!

> (*She moves away from him: he follows her, dog-like. He suddenly sees the suitcase and turns on her*)

Ye're lyin! Ye're lyin! Ye *are* gaun wi him!

ISA: I'm no. Honest, I'm no.

ALEC: Whit's in the suitcase then? Whaur are ye gaun a dressed up?

ISA: Whaur am I gaun wi the suitcase? (*Pause*) Whaur d'ye think, stupid? I've got us a room an kitchen. I canna stick it here wi Granny an the weans an yer Mammy; she disna like me, yer Mammy. So I says tae masel, it's up tae me tae find a place for me an Alec.

ALEC: Is that right? Dae ye mean it?

ISA: Why would it no be right? You an me'll get on better awa frae here. (*She comes up very close to him*) Mind when we had wur ain wee place? (*Arms go round his neck*) Mind? Mind the way ye used tae rake doon the ashes and pile on the coals in yon aul kitchen range so's we could (*Her body pressing against his*) lie an watch the shadows on the wa? You used tae say . . . firelight . . . wis the thing . . . tae see me . . . lyin in the glow . . .

ALEC: (*his arms coming slowly round her*) Aye, I mind, Isa. I mind. I'll never loss the picture o you . . . you were that beautiful . . . an you were mines. O Isa, Isa! I'd dae onythin for ye, onything in the world if ye'd . . . if ye'd love me like ye used tae.

> (*He is babbling against her shoulder. She starts to kiss him: she kisses him until his knees buckle*)

(*Whisper*) Isa . . . come on . . . there's naebody in . . . (*She draws away a little, measures with her eyes the distance between suitcase and door*) Oh, Isa, the way ye've been gaun on, ye've been drivin me aff ma heid. (*Over his shoulder she gives a sneering grin, at the same time stroking the back of his head and murmuring: Aw!*) Isa, come wi me . . . (*He starts to pull her towards the bedroom*) I canna dae wi'oot ye.

ISA: Aye, Alec, sure . . . but a minute. I'm needin a drink efter a that . . . (*She massages her neck*).

ALEC: Aw, there's no a drink here. Ye ken Mammy.

ISA: Well, for Goad's sake, ye've shairly got a fag on ye?

ALEC: (*her sharp tone makes him pathetically anxious to please her*) Oh aye, aye, I've got a fag.

> (*He produces a crumpled packet of Woodbine. She takes one: waits. He feels in his pockets feverishly while she stands, cigarette between her lips, waiting. He brings out a single match, and while he is striking this on the sole of his shoe, she puts out a foot smartly and trips him up, grabs her coat, bag and case, overturning a chair as she races to the door. ALEC collapses in a sobbing heap. Then, rage possesses him and he drags himself up*)

I'll get them . . . I'll get the baith o them.

> (*Lights down. The salvation army band is now outside the house. The stage remains empty: then MAGGIE and LILY come in. They look around the room, then at each other*)

MAGGIE: Whit's been gaun oan here?

> (*She looks towards open door of bedroom, crosses, goes in: we hear her opening and shutting drawers. LILY takes off her coat and hat and rights the fallen chair. In doing so, she sees the knife on the floor and exclaims, runs to pick it up: examines it fearfully*)

LILY: Aw, thank God! (*Looks at it with an expression of disgust and flicks the blade back. Just as MAGGIE comes out of the bedroom, LILY has quickly put the knife into her handbag*)

MAGGIE: She's rin oot on him. Her clothes is awa.

LILY: Whit aboot his?

MAGGIE: (*shaking her head*) She's left him.

> (*She feels for a chair and sits down*)

LILY: She didna get aff wi'oot a fight — by the look o things.

> (*MAGGIE gives a moan of fear and squeezes her hands together*)

MAGGIE: Lily! Oh, ma Goad, Lily!

LILY: Naw, naw, it'll be a right. He'll turn up the morn.

MAGGIE: Lily, I'm feart . . . I wish John'd come hame.

LILY: Listen! Alec hasnae the guts tae dae onythin tae her. Even if he could find her, and that's no likely. She'll be aff wi anither man.

MAGGIE: An him that saft aboot her. The dirty wee bitch!

LILY: So he's better aff wi'oot her. Don't you worry, Maggie. Alec kens fine the only hole he can coorie intae is here, wi his Mammy. (*Some rowdy revellers pass beneath the window*) Hear that lot? Drunken sots!

> (*MAGGIE sits slumped in misery*)
> (*Watching her, in sudden fury*) Aw the hell wi him! The rotten wee bastard! He's spoilt yer Christmas!

(MAGGIE *shakes her head*)

MAGGIE: I spoilt *him*. I've aye cairried a load here (*hand on her heart*) aboot Alec. I've been punished for whit I did, Lily. Punished.

LILY: Naw, naw . . . *naw!* The way Alec is had naethin tae dae wi . . . (*She stops, helpless*) We've had this oot afore . . . ye didna harm the wean, Maggie . . . 'cept that ye've *kept* him a wean, tryin tae make up . . .

MAGGIE: I ken. I ken. I've aye felt guilty. (*Pause*) It looks tae me, Lily, there's nae end tae trouble. Nae end tae havin the heart tore oot o ye.

LILY: I don't suppose there is. It's jist life, Maggie! (*Pause*) Life! Ye don't ken the hauf o it . . . and neither dae I. Come oan, gie me yer coat. (*She pulls MAGGIE to her feet, takes off her coat and gently removes the red hat which she puts back on the wireless set. MAGGIE is still in a state of shock*) Wee cup o tea, hen? (MAGGIE *shakes her head*) Aw, come on, come on . . . (*Then she gets out with an effort, because it is so foreign to her:*) darling.

(*She holds out her arms and MAGGIE topples into them: they rock together soundlessly, LILY patting MAGGIE's back. After a moment, LILY sets MAGGIE gently back in her chair and smoothes her hair and kisses her. MAGGIE is now composed*)

MAGGIE: Lily, I've said it often tae ye . . . whaur would I be wi'oot ye?

LILY: I'm yer sister. Faimly type, me.

(*There is a knock on the door. MAGGIE jumps to her feet and stares, scared, at the door, then at LILY*)

LILY: It's a right; that's no a polis knock, a wee tap like yon. I'll see.

(LILY *opens the door and reveals JENNY. They look at each other, JENNY uncertainly, LILY with a hard appraisal of JENNY's nice, but not tarty clothes, her hatless, blonded hair*)

Well! I didnae recognise yer Ladyship efter a this time.

(*She drops JENNY a curtsey and stands aside. JENNY has a swift look round the room before rushing into MAGGIE's arms*)

MAGGIE: O Jenny, Jenny! The times I've dreamt o this!

(*She holds her off and looks into JENNY's face, then holds her tight again*)

Why did ye no write tae me, Jenny? No even as much as a postcard.

JENNY: I couldna write. And I couldna come, Mammy. (*Pause*) I've had ma troubles since I walked oot o here.

LILY: Ye've got ower them noo, by the look o ye. Ye werena dressed up like a fillum star last I heard o ye.

JENNY: Mebbe no, Auntie Lily. (*To* MAGGIE) Can I . . . tak
aff ma coat? (MAGGIE *eagerly rushes to receive it: she smooths
it, smiling, lays it tenderly over the back of a chair*) Whaur's the
others? the weans? An Alec an Isa? . . . An . . . ma Daddy?

MAGGIE: The kids went tae the Mission treat; Alec an
Isa's . . . (*She drives her fingers through her hair*) They're oot tae.

LILY: But no taegether. We think she's fun a sugar-daddy. (*Pause
while she looks hard at* JENNY) There seems tae be quite a few
aboot. Funny that! I heard there wis a depression on . . .

    (JENNY *turns her back on* LILY)

JENNY: Mammy, Bertie . . .

MAGGIE: Oh, Bertie's gettin on fine. Still in the hospital, but
gettin on fine.

JENNY: (*gently*) Mammy, I've been up. I've seen the Sister and
the doctor. Mammy, you and ma Daddy's got tae *dae* somethin!
The sister said she spoke tae ye, and the Lady Almoner, I seen
her tae. Mammy, why d'you no listen tae them at the hospital?

MAGGIE: (*guilty and bewildered*) I dae . . . I try . . . but I get that
excited. They hospitals make me feart and ma heid gets intae
a kind o a buzz. When I'm oot the gate I canna rightly think
back on whit they said tae dae . . .

LILY: Jenny, whit're ye gettin at?

JENNY: Mammy seems tae think they're lettin Bertie hame; but
they're no. *No here.* No tae this. Mammy, ye've tae see the
Corporation for a Cooncil hoose.

MAGGIE: A Cooncil hoose! A Cooncil hoose! Yer Daddy's been
up tae that lot till he's seeck scunnert. Ye've tae wait yer turn
in the queue.

JENNY: But if they kent aboot Bertie . . .

LILY: Is this whit brought ye back, Jenny?

JENNY: It's whit gied me the courage tae come. Least . . . it was
ma Daddy's face . . . in the water . . . (*More to herself than the
others*) . . . there wis lights shimmerin on the blackness . . . it
kind o slinks alang slow, a river, in the night. I was meanin tae
let it tak me alang wi it.

    (MAGGIE *gives a gasp*)

MAGGIE: Whit kind o talk is this, Jenny? Did ye no think o us?
Yer Daddy an me?

JENNY: Think o ye? O aye, Mammy, I thought o ye. But thinkin
jist made me greet. I was that ashamed o masel . . . Isa and me,
we were that rotten tae ye, the things we said.

MAGGIE: That's a bye, Jenny.

JENNY: Naethin's ever *bye*, Mammy; it's a there, like a photy-
album in yer heid . . . I kept seein ma daddy, the way he used

tae sing tae me when I wis wee; I seen him holdin ma bare feet
in his hands tae warm them, an feedin me bread an hot milk oot
of a blue cup. (*Pause*) I don't know where you were, Mammy.

LILY: Ben the back room wi the midwife, likely. (*Pause*) It's as
weel ye came tae yer senses; yon's no the way tae tak oot o yer
troubles; a river. But ye're daein fine noo? Ye merriet?

JENNY: No.

LILY: Oh. Livin in sin, as they ca it these days, eh?

JENNY: (*suddenly flaring up*) Aye, if ye want tae ca it sin! I don't.
The man I'm livin wi is kind, an generous.

LILY: Oh aye, we can see that. We've had an eye-fu o yer wages
o sin.

MAGGIE: (*mournful*) Aw Jenny, I wisht ye'd earned it.

LILY: (*coarse laugh*) Oh, she'll hae earned it, Maggie. On her
back.

MAGGIE: *Lily!*

LILY: So the Bible's a wrang, is it? The wages o sin's nae deith;
it's fancy hair-dos an a swanky coat an pure silk stockins.

JENNY: You seem tae ken yer Bible, Auntie Lily. I never pretended tae. But I'm happy, an I'm makin *him* happy. We've a
nice wee flat in a clean district, wi trees an wee gardens.

LILY: A wee love-nest oot west! Great! Juist great — till yer tired
business man gets tired o you an ye're oot on yer ear.

JENNY: Well, you hevnae changed, Auntie Lily. I've got tae
laugh at you.

LILY: Laugh awa. I'm no mindin. I've kept ma self-respect.

JENNY: Aye. An that's aboot a ye've got.

MAGGIE: Oh, stop it! Stop it! (*Her hands to her head*) I wis that
happy . . .

JENNY: Mammy, I'm sorry. We'll sit doon properly an talk. (*She
draws a couple of chairs together, deliberately excluding* LILY *who
moves off a little, but keeps within ear-shot and stands, back resting
against the table — or the sideboard — watching*) I've got plans
for you.

MAGGIE: Plans?

JENNY: Aye. For gettin yous a oot o this.

MAGGIE: Och Jenny, pet; you wis aye fu o dreams.

LILY: Aye. Dreams. Fairy-tales. She went awa an impident wee
bissom an she's come back on Christmas Eve, kiddin on she's
a fairy wi a magic wand.

JENNY: (*she doesn't even look at* LILY) Listen, Mammy. We canna
wait for a hoose frae the Cooncil, it'll tak too lang; but mind!
Ye've tae get ma Daddy tae speak tae them. (MAGGIE *nods*)
So, while ye're waitin, ye're goin tae flit tae a rented hoose.

MAGGIE: Jenny, ye need a lot o money tae flit!

JENNY: I've got it. (*She opens her handbag and produces a roll of notes that makes* MAGGIE's *eyes bulge. She gasps*) There's plenty for the flitting and the key money forbye.

(JOHN *comes in. He stops at the sight of* JENNY *and at first his face lights up: then his lips tighten*)

JOHN: Well! Well! *Well!* (*Pause*) Whit's brought you back tae the nest? The Christmas spirit?

MAGGIE: *John!*

JOHN: Oh aye, I can see you two's fallen on each ither's necks. (*Pause*) But I've no forgotten the way you walked oot o this hoose.

JENNY: (*head bent*) I mind. I'm sorry.

JOHN: So am I. (*Pause*) And there's somethin else I mind. (JENNY *looks up at him. Pause*) I mind nights when your mother sobbed hersel tae sleep worryin an frettin aboot you.

(JENNY *bends her head again*)

MAGGIE: That's a past, John.

JOHN: She sobbed hersel tae sleep, night efter night; and I had tae lie aside her an listen. (*Pause*) I didna care very much for you, Jenny, lyin there listenin.

(*There is a silence.* MAGGIE *starts to 'comb her hair'*)

LILY: Well, she's hame noo, an Maggie's happiness wis shinin oot o her face till you come in wi yer Holy Joe stuff.

JOHN: You keep oot o this; it's faimly business.

LILY: Oh, I'm no in it; I'm jist an interested spectator.

JOHN: (*to* JENNY, *after a good look at her clothes*) I don't suppose ye're thinkin o bidin?

JENNY: No.

JOHN: Naw. I didna think ye'd be for bidin.

(*He picks up her coat, has a good look at it, flings it aside*)

JENNY: And neither is ma Mammy bidin! Or the kids! You can dae whit ye like. I'm takin a hoose for them in a decent pairt o the toon.

JOHN: You're . . . daein . . . *whit?*

MAGGIE: It's true, John. Jenny says . . .

JOHN: I'd an idea I wis the heid o this hoose.

MAGGIE: John, Listen! Jenny's got the key money, an she kens . . .

JENNY: I've a friend factors property; I can get ye a four room an kitchen, rare an open, near a park. An . . . I'll can help ye wi the rent.

JOHN: Oh, you'll can help wi the rent? Oh, very fine! Very fine! I'll fair enjoy havin ma rent paid by one o your fancy men.

JENNY: Mammy, tell him why.

MAGGIE: It's . . . it's Bertie. The hospital's no lettin him back here.

JENNY: It's rotten, this hoose. Rotten. Damp. Ye ken yersel. It's a midden lookin oot on ither middens. It's got rats, bugs . . .

MAGGIE: No bugs, Jenny! We've never had bugs!

JENNY: There's ithers roon aboot that has. Daddy, if Bertie comes back here, he'll . . . he'll never get better.

JOHN: But . . . but he's gettin on well. They tell't us that at the hospital. (*To* MAGGIE) Didn't they no?

MAGGIE: (*agitated*) Aye, but they did say something aboot it . . . asked me questions, the Lady Almoner did . . .

JOHN: Whit questions? Why did you no tell me aboot this?

MAGGIE: I didna want ye worryin. I didna think there wis onythin tae be done.

JOHN: If there is onythin tae be done, it'll be done by me.

LILY: Well, why did ye no *dae* somethin? When wis you up at the Cooncil last aboot yer hoose? Yer hoose that's aye supposed tae be comin, *some* day. Trouble wi you, ye've nae fight in ye.

JOHN: I tell't you tae keep oot o this!

LILY: Why should I? Maggie's ma sister! An I've had tae fight hauf your battles for ye, John Morrison or the hale lot o ye would hae been oot on the street mair than once!

(JOHN *cannot answer: his hatred of* LILY *and her truth turns his mouth to a grim line: his hands open and close, open and close. The others wait for him to speak*)

MAGGIE: (*with placating smile and a note of pleading*) John, it's juist a wee help till we get a Cooncil hoose wi a wee bit garden at the front and a real green tae hang oot the washin.

JENNY: (*still holding her fat roll of notes now exhibits it*) I've got the cash. Ca it a loan if ye like.

MAGGIE: There's plenty for the flittin and the key money.

JENNY: Fifty pounds.

(*She comes forward and offers it to* JOHN)

JOHN: Ye can tak that back tae yer fancy man. We're wantin nane o yer whore's winnins here.

MAGGIE: *John!*

LILY: (*shouting*) It's no for *you!* It's for Bertie an the ither weans, ye pig-heided fool!

JOHN: (*to* JENNY) If ye'd earned it, I'd be doon on ma knees tae ye. But ye're no better than a tart. We tried wur best tae bring you up respectable so's ye could marry a decent fella . . .

JENNY: Marry a decent fella! I never had a chance! Every time

I got whit you would ca a decent fella an he saw me hame frae
the dancin, he'd tak one look at the close an that's the last I'd
see o him. Did you ever provide me wi a hoose I could bring
a decent fella hame to? Did ye?

JOHN: I done ma best! There's naebody can ca me a lay-about!
I worked when there wis work tae get!

LILY: Oh, ye must mind, Jenny, he's no tae blame. Nae man's
ever tae blame. It's they dirty rotten buggers in Parliament, or
they stinkin rich bosses . . .

JOHN: Haud yer rotten tongue, ye frozen bitch!

JENNY: (*sudden sour laugh*) I've often thought the way it would
be when I come hame. I was gonna make up for the way I left
ye. An here we are, Christmas eve, fightin ower ma . . . whit
wis it? . . . ma whore's winnins. I've been savin an savin so's I
could help ye, an mak friends again, an be happy.

> (*She cries, head bent, standing forlornly before* JOHN *who looks
> down on her grimly.* MAGGIE *watches, waits: then suddenly
> she stops combing her hair and rises. She takes the money out
> of* JENNY'*s hand and interposes herself between them*)

MAGGIE: (*with uncharacteristic force*) An so we wull be happy!
Whore's winnins, did ye ca this? . . . An did I hear ye use the
word 'tart'? Whit wis I, when we was coortin, but *your* tart?
(JOHN *is startled and shocked. In an urgent whisper,* MAGGIE
imitates the JOHN *of her 'coortin' days*) Let me, Maggie, g'on,
let me! I'll mairry ye if onythin happens . . .

JOHN: (*a hurried, shamed glance towards* LILY) Stop it, Maggie!
Stop it!

> (*He moves away from* MAGGIE, *but she follows, still whispering.*
> LILY, *arms a-kimbo, eyes a-gleam, laughs coarsely, and hugs
> herself*)

MAGGIE: Aye, I wis your whore. An I'd nae winnins that I
can mind o. But mebbe it's a right being a whore if ye've nae
winnins. Is that the way it goes, John? (*Pause. She draws breath
and her voice is now bitter*) And don't you kid yersel that I didna
see the way ye looked at yer ain son's wife trailin aboot the
hoose wi her breasts fa'in oot o her fancy claes. (*Coming right
up to him and completing his humiliation before* LILY *and* JENNY)
I'm no sae saft I didna ken why it wis (*urgent whisper*) Maggie!
Come on, quick, ben the back room . . . lock the door . . . it'll
no tak minutes . . .

JENNY: Mammy, Mammy! *Stop!*

> (JOHN *has sunk into a chair. He covers his face with his hands.
> There is a silence:* MAGGIE'*s breathing loses its harshness: she
> looks down upon him: she sags*)

MAGGIE: Aw . . . aw . . . (*She wipes her face with her hands and sighs*) Aw, I shouldna have said they things.

LILY: Why no? Ye wouldna hae said them if they wisna true.

MAGGIE: (*shaking her head*) Naw. There's things atween husbands and wives shouldna be spoke aboot. I'm sorry. I lost ma heid.

JENNY: (*kneeling at her father's feet*) Daddy . . . Daddy . . . forget it. It disna matter. Daddy? (*She tries to draw his hands from his face*) When I wis wee, you loved me, an I loved you. Why can we no get back? (*He does not answer, but he lets her take one of his hands from his face and hold it in both of hers*)

MAGGIE: Dinna fret yersel, Jenny. I can manage him . . . I can aye manage him.

> (*She is still holding the roll of notes. She looks away into her long-ago dream and a smile breaks over her face*)

(*Very softly*) Four rooms, did ye say, Jenny? (*Pause*) Four rooms. Four rooms . . . an a park forbye! There'll be flowers come the spring!

Glossary

Armstrong-Siddley, motor
  manufacturer
bizzim, disruptive child
Burroo, Unemployment
  Bureau
C & A's, chain store
charrin, domestic cleaning
chinas, mates, friends
clip cloots, cut cloths
close, entrance to a tenement
cooried, settled, cuddled
Copey, Co-operative
  Association store
coppers, coins, small change
croshay, crochet
done, exhausted, expired
dunny, outhouse in tenement
  back court
gant, yawn
gey, somewhat, very
grate, metal section of
  fireplace
grun, ground
hale, whole
hechin awa, panting
humph, comes up their,
  when it suits them to
  do something, when
  something occurs to
  them
jawin, talking
jeely, jelly
jookin, dodging

Kelvinside, affluent district
  of Glasgow
kill, get yer, to die laughing
loss the heid, go mad, daft
  or angry
merriet, married
midden-bin, dustbin
Mission, charity institution
nebs, noses
nyaff, orig. a small dog, a
  twisted or stunted person
pickchers, the pictures,
  cinema
piece, sandwich
pie-eyed, drunk
Poly, dance hall
rammy, crush, crowd
rive, rent, tear
soor-dook, sour mouth, bitter
steamie, public laundry
TB, tuberculosis
tate, piece
tattie, potato
tink, tinker
Treat, party for children
tumphy, stupid person, idiot
veloory, velour, form of
  velvet
wally dug, china dog,
  ornament
wean, child
winnins, profits
wireless set, radio

Roddy McMillan

The Bevellers

(1973)

CHARACTERS

Joe Crosby
Peter Laidlaw
Bob Darnley
Dan Matchett, the Rouger
Charlie Weir
Norrie Beaton
Leslie Skinner
Alex Freer
Nancy Blair

The play is set in the basement bevelling shop of a glass firm in Glasgow.

Introduction

Roddy McMillan, who began his career with the Glasgow Unity Theatre, was one of the most distinguished of Scottish character actors, famous for his leading role in the television series *Para Handy*. His first play, *All in Good Faith*, was written in the 1950s, but thereafter he concentrated on acting until, in 1972, his part in Bill Bryden's play, *Willie Rough*, about the Glasgow shipyards in the period after the First World War, inspired him to complete a play based on his early experiences of a bevelling factory. *The Bevellers* was first performed in 1973 at the Royal Lyceum in Edinburgh, in a period when it was vigorously engaged in the promotion of new Scottish works.

McMillan's play is significant as a fine example of 'workplace drama', focusing on the induction of an 'innocent' youth into the harsh industrial environment which dominated the lives of the majority of Scottish working-class men. Like most in its genre, it balances the destructive effects of a mechanised life of labour against the pride in skill and the sometimes brutal camaraderie which sustain the characters' sense of their own humanity. Some of its most effective theatrical effects, however, derive from the author's knowledge of the trade involved. For the original production the actors studied bevelling, and it has to be recalled in reading the play that the characters are almost all onstage throughout, hard at work while the talk proceeds.

John Byrne's *The Slab Boys* (1978) was to develop this genre in comic fashion; Tony Roper's *The Steamie* (1987) was to translate it to the working environment of housewives. 'Workplace drama' allowed the lives and the voices of Scottish working-class people to be directly represented in ways which no other literary genre could achieve.

The Bevellers was to be Roddy McMillan's only major piece of dramatic writing but one into which he put his experience both of industrial society and of the craft of theatre.

BOB, PETER, CHARLIE, and JOE are all getting ready for work in the morning, taking off their jackets, and putting on their working aprons.

The ROUGER carries his bike down the stairs; LESLIE SKINNER, the Manager, then brings NORRIE downstairs.

LESLIE: Here's the new boy, Bob. Smart boy he looks. Name's Beaton — that right, lad? Norman Beaton.

NORRIE: That's right, Mr Skinner.

LESLIE: This is Mr Darnley, the foreman.

BOB: Boys call ye Norrie?

NORRIE: Aye.

LESLIE: Well, I suppose that's what they'll call you in here. Show him the job, Bob. I'll ring down for you in a wee while. Couple of items I want to show you. Stick in, boy, you'll do fine. Good effort the day, the rest o' you lads.

    (LESLIE *climbs the stairs and goes off*)

BOB: Well seen it's Monday mornin. 'I'll ring doon fur ye, Bob.' Ah'll be up an' doon that bliddy stair like a yo-yo. I can feel it in ma watter. Dae ye know whit bevellin is, young Norrie?

NORRIE: Naw.

BOB: It's a' ower the bliddy place, though no wan in a million wid recognise it. No so much o it nooadays, right enough. Time wis there wisnae a boozer or a half-decent shitehouse in the country withoot a sample o the bevellers' craft screwed tae the wa'. Can ye no guess?

NORRIE: Tae dae wi gless, int it?

BOB: Now there's a boy wi his eyes open. Comes intae a bevellin shop where the stuff's stacked on its edges an' says it's tae dae wi gless. A'right, son, let me show ye this.

ROUGER: Watch him, young-yin. He might show ye the gless version o the golden rivet.

BOB: Haud yur tongue, Rouger. See this mirror here, Norrie. That's what we call a mirror, but it's no done yet. No silvered. Well, that kinna border-bit round the gless is a bevel. If that wis woodwork, they might call it a chamfer. Not tae be confused wi yur champer, of coorse. An' there's a few other kinna jobs that's a' in the trade, like the arrisin, the polishin an' that. But ye'll soon see it a'.

NORRIE: An' is that whit I'll be learnin, the bevellin?

BOB: No right away, naw. Ye start at the feedin-up. Joe'll tell ye aboot that. It's his job ye're gettin. C'm'ere, Joe. This is Norrie

Beaton, he's gaun tae the feedin-up. Get him an apron.

JOE: Hullo. Crosbie's the second name.

NORRIE: How ye?

JOE: Better noo ah'm aff the feedin-up.

BOB: Don't gie the boy a bad impression. Feedin-up's no a bad job. It's an easy job, an' wan that ye must learn before ye start bevellin.

JOE: Aye, whitever ye say yursel'.

BOB: Aye, well, show him how tae mix the pomas. No too thick, no too thin. Then show him how tae make the brush.

JOE: OK. Ower tae the bench here.

ROUGER: Whit d'ye say this boy's name wis?

BOB: Beaton. Norman Beaton. Kinna film star's name that, int it?

ROUGER: Naw Teuchter name, I wid say. That right, eh? Teuchter name yours, int it?

NORRIE: Whit?

ROUGER: Teuchter, teuchter. Ye no know whit 'teuchter' is?

NORRIE: Naw.

ROUGER: This is a very dim youth. You'll learn something here, I'll tell ye. Hear that, Charlie, he never heard o a teuchter.

CHARLIE: Innocent, eh!

ROUGER: Doe-eyed.

CHARLIE: He'll soon loss it. Clear and press, a hundred an' eighty, hah!

> (CHARLIE *snatches at an imaginary weight and holds it aloft.*
> *The* ROUGER *pretends to tickle his armpit*)

ROUGER: Tickle, tickle.

CHARLIE: (*immediately furious, dropping his arms*) Whit have I said aboot that before, Rouger? One o these times I'll hoist you by the ballocks an' chip ye ower the mill.

ROUGER: Aw, easy, easy, fur Jesus' sake. Bit o fun.

CHARLIE: Or maybe ye'd like a small tournament, jist you an' me. There's the bar in the corner, hundred and twenty pounds. Ten snatches right up, eh?

ROUGER: Wait a minute. That's your game, the liftin, int it? You're on a cert. Whit dis that prove? Superiority in wan field of exertion. I mean, you come oot the road wi me on the bike sometime, I'll show you a fast wheel an' a flash o ma arse as ah leave you gaspin on the highway.

CHARLIE: Never mind the cycle talk. There's the bar. Ten snatches, whit ye say?

BOB: Aw, snatch yur fuckin drawers! Ye're like a coupla weans. Get yur aprons on an' start graftin. A good effort the day now, as Leslie says. Too much shaggin the dog in here lately.

(*They all break up and start moving towards their wheels*)

PETER: Don't worry aboot the Rouger, son. He might try somethin' on wi ye. Don't be feart. He's full o crap. Jist tell him tae come an' see me at the mill. I'll put a hauf-inch level on his tail. Mind, noo.

NORRIE: Is it always like this?

JOE: Worse sometimes. Bevellers are a' mad, ye know. Peter therr couldnae blow a feather aff his nose withoot havin a rigor.

NORRIE : A whit?

JOE: A fit. Takes fits, ye know.

NORRIE: Straight up?

JOE: Aye, jist noo an' again.

NORRIE: Works wi gless an' takes fits? That must be dangerous.

JOE: Oh whit! Ye see him startin tae jerk a wee bit. Next thing Bob's shoutin, 'Never mind the man, save the bliddy job!'

NORRIE: Whit happens?

JOE: Ach, jist lie him doon for five minutes, he gets up bran' new.

NORRIE: Naw, but I mean, ye wunner they let him carry on.

JOE: Nae choice. Cannae get men like him nooadays.

NORRIE: Is he good?

JOE: The best. Noo, look, ye jist take a haunful o pomas an' stick it in the basin. Then ye take the watter an' mix it slowly tae it's jist right. Too thick it clogs the grooves, too thin it skooshes all over the shop and disnae polish.

NORRIE: How d'ye know when it's right?

JOE: Ye jist learn. That's aboot right noo, feel that. Right, noo fur the brush. This pile o straw here an' some string, it's easy. (*Proceeds to make the brush*)

NORRIE: That's a funny name that, Rouger, int it?

JOE: That's no his name, his right name's Dan Matchett. We call him Rouger because he works wi the rouge. See a' that red stuff ower at his wheel. That's the rouge.

NORRIE: That's a hell of a mess. Whit's it dae?

JOE: Peter pits the bevel on at the mill. Grinds it on wi the hard wheel, the carborundum. Then he pits it on the sander. That's a slightly softer wheel. Efter that it goes tae the polishin — that's Bob's job. Then it goes tae the rougin — that pits the gloss on it.

NORRIE: Whit are the other wheels?

JOE: Wan's Charlie's an' wan's mine. They're vertical fur daein' edges an' . . .

(*Suddenly the noise of glass applied to the various wheels blots out all other sound*)

NORRIE: (*putting his hands over his ears*) That's a hell of a noise.

JOE: Ye get used tae it.

(*The noise recedes after a short time*)

BOB: No ready yet, Joe?

JOE: Coupla shakes.

NORRIE: That a real weight-liftin thing ower therr?

JOE: Aye, it's Charlie's. Brought it in hissel'. Practises wi it at dinner-time sometimes.

NORRIE: I'd like tae see him liftin that.

JOE: He'd lift that an' you alang wi it. Don't needle him — he might dae it.

NORRIE: He pit the breeze up the big-fella anyway, didn't he? Does he lose the head easy, that Charlie fella?

JOE: Not always. Fact, sometimes he's very good-tempered. Disnae like anybody takin him down. Winches this bird that works up next door in the printin-works. Noo ye see how tae make the brush? Ye jist take enough straw and fold it, tie it in two places away fae the middle, and cut the ends wi the chisel.

NORRIE: I fancy I could dae that.

JOE: The secret's ye tie it tight — it's got tae be tight. That's it, Bob! (*He carries the basin and brush over to the polishing wheel*)

BOB: Right noo you sit there, son, jist beside the wheel. Take the brush, dip it in the pomas. Feed it up on tap o the wheel when I'm usin the surface, and feed it intae the groove when I'm daein the edges. Try it noo, but easy.

(NORRIE *soaks the brush and plunks it on the wheel, as* BOB *touches it with the glass. The pomas squirts up into* BOB's *face*)

BOB: (*wiping the pomas away with his apron*) Aw, Jesus Christ, naw, naw! No so hard, an' no so much pomas. I've got tae be able tae see tae dae this job, Norrie. Try it again — a wee bit easier.

(NORRIE *tries again. This time the brush flies out of his hand and lands over by the bench*)

NORRIE: Sorry, Mr Darnley.

BOB: Away and pick the bliddy thing up. Gie it a run through in the trough. That's it, jist enough tae take the grit oot o it. It's no needin a haircut an' a shampoo. Noo, wance mair, nice an' easy.

NORRIE: That better, Mr Darnley?

BOB: Aye, that's better. Jist pit some on when ye think it needs it. An' stop callin us Mr Darnley. Bob'll dae. But no Bobbie — I'll no stand for Bobbie.

NORRIE: Aye, right.

BOB: Ye see the idea? Noo that bit o the bevel's still rough, but this bit here that I'm polishin is a bit smoother, see that? *(He wipes the glass and holds it up to the light)*

NORRIE: That's great.

BOB: Well, it's no exactly great, but it'll be a'right. Merr pomas.

NORRIE: Is that ma job, then? Jist sittin here dabbin the brush?

BOB: Refer tae it as feedin-up fae noo on. Like everything else, ye start at the beginnin. It's amazin how much ye pick up when ye think ye're idlin'. I wis feedin-up when I wis fourteen. Sometimes I think I havenae learnt it a' yet. This is a craft, ye know, not jist a common trade. Wan o the few, an' wan o the auldest. Put your mind tae this, ye'll get a job anywhere. Merr pomas. Ah, ye see, that wis you gaun a wee bit heavy again — but don't worry, the time'll come when ye'll be able tae judge it, an' that'll be somethin' learnt, that right?

NORRIE: Aye.

BOB: Is this yur first job?

NORRIE: Aye.

BOB: Ye'll be able tae bung yur mother a couple o poun' at the end o the week noo, eh?

NORRIE: Naw.

BOB: Ye gaun tae keep it a' tae yersel?

NORRIE: Naw, I didnae mean that. Ma mother's deid. Died when ah wis thirteen. Two years ago.

BOB: That a fact, son? Yur faither's still livin, though?

NORRIE: Oh aye. There's ma da, ma sister, an' me.

BOB: An' yur sister looks efter ye, like?

NORRIE: Aye. She's got a job tae, though.

BOB: Yez'll be quite a well-doing wee family, then?

NORRIE: Aye, no' bad.

BOB: Whit dis yur faither dae?

NORRIE: Docker.

BOB: Good job, good job. Merr pomas. She'll wid have been quite young, your mother? When she died?

NORRIE: Forty-four, I think.

BOB: That's young. Must've been sudden, eh?

NORRIE: Aye, it wis during the school holidays it wis. I wakened up wan mornin, an' there wis this noise in the kitchen. A lot o voices. I went through an' they widnae let me in. I jist saw her lyin in a chair. That wis it.

BOB: Ah didnae mean tae make ye greet noo.

NORRIE: Ah'm no greetin. It's a long time. Two year.

BOB: Aye, a long time fur a boy tae be withoot his old-lady.

Hear that, youz fullas. This boy here's been tellin me aboot his oul'-wife dying, and he's no greetin. No much wrang wi a boy that can dae that, eh?

ROUGER: Eh, whit's that, who's dyin? Who's deid?

BOB: Norrie's oul'-lady. He wis jist at school at the time.

ROUGER: Whit wis wrang wi her? (NORRIE *doesn't answer*) . . . It's a'right, young-yin, we're no tryin tae extract ye. Jist askin whit happened tae her.

NORRIE: Heart-attack.

ROUGER: By Jees, eh. That's tough luck. Hey, Bob, wee bit fire on this side here.

> (*The* ROUGER *holds out the glass.* BOB *gives it a wipe and holds it up to the light*)

BOB: Aye, ye're right. Ah'll gie it a touch. Noo, Norrie, jist gie the brush the least wee sensation on the wheel therr . . . ach, I better dae it masel'.

ROUGER: That the only time yur mother wis ever sick?

NORRIE: Naw. Eh, she wis sick wance before — a couple o year before she died.

ROUGER: Hospital, wis she?

NORRIE: Naw, naw.

ROUGER: Couldnae have been too bad, then, wis she?

NORRIE: Oh, she wis bad. It wis in the middle o the night. She suddenly had these terrible pains. She wis moaning — nearly screaming. I had tae go tae the polis station, fur them tae call a doctor.

BOB: Whit time o night wis that?

NORRIE: Hauf past two — three o'clock.

ROUGER: An' wis she a'right efter that?

NORRIE: Aye, a while efter the doctor came.

ROUGER: Did ye see her?

NORRIE: Naw, ma oul'-man told me tae go back tae bed. She wis a bit better in the mornin.

ROUGER: Nae merr pain, eh?

NORRIE: You're hell of a nosy. Whit ye want tae know fur?

ROUGER: Nothin'. Jist askin.

BOB: Ye must've been only eleven year auld then. No much wrang wi a boy that'll go fur a doctor for his mother at three o'clock in the mornin an him only eleven year auld. Did yur big sister no go wi ye?

NORRIE: She wis bubblin. She couldnae go.

ROUGER: Got a sister, eh? Tell her ah'll take her out some night.

NORRIE: Aye, likely. That your bike over therr?

ROUGER: Yes! Nice machine, int it?

NORRIE: 'S all right.

ROUGER: Like tae get yur leg ower it?

NORRIE: Widnae mind.

ROUGER: Leg ower yur sister?

NORRIE: She widnae pish on you if ye were on fire.

ROUGER: Now . . . I'll remember that.

BOB: Therr ye are, then. That should be a'right. Jist blend it in
easy. That should dae . . . (*The bell rings and the* ROUGER *goes
back to his wheel*) That's him started. Ye ever see wan o' thae
monkeys on a string, Norrie? That's whit he thinks ah am. Got
tae take the apron aff every time ye go up the sterr in case
there's some conshiterified bloody eediot in the office. Whit's
the time? Clock's stopped, bi-Christ! Hey, Joe, see the time —
show Norrie here how tae keek, then gie that clock a dunt an'
see if it'll go.

> (BOB *goes off upstairs.* JOE *goes to the back of the shop, mounts
> a box, and puts his eye to the roof*)

NORRIE: Whit ye daein? Whit can ye see?

JOE: The pavement up there's wan o' thae glazed gratings.
There' a hole in the gless, an' if ye judge it right ye can see the
Greek clock.

NORRIE: Gaun tae let us swatch it?

JOE: Sure. Jist pit your eye up there.

> (NORRIE *goes up*)

NORRIE: Aw, Christ, I think I've blint masel'.

JOE: Don't pit your eye hard against the hole, it's full o muck.
Try it again and jist squint a wee bit tae the left.

NORRIE: Cannae sae anythin'.

JOE: Nae wunner, ye've got your eye shut.

NORRIE: Eh, oh aye. I think I can see somethin' noo.

JOE: Can ye see the coffin-end corner?

NORRIE: I think so — aye!

JOE: Jist move a wee touch tae yur left and look up, ye'll see the
Greek steeple wi the clock.

NORRIE: Got it, bang in the sights. That's great, int it?

JOE: Oh, aye, great, but whit the hell's the time?

NORRIE: Twenty past nine. Naebody in here wear watches?

JOE: Naw. Too much stour and damp. Even that oul' clock's
got a touch o the cramp. (*He goes up to the clock, which is on the
wall just above* BOB's *wheel*)

PETER: Hey, Norrie — is that your name? Well, c'm'ere, ah want
ye. See this brush? Take it up in your airm, yur right airm, and
ower yur shouther. That's right . . . noo, jist you stan therr fur
a wee while, an' if ye feel like it, jist take a wee about-turn noo

an' again. Anybody comes, shout, 'Beware the amber bead!'
(NORRIE *is holding the brush like a sentry, though he doesn't realise it.* PETER *darts into the lavvy under the stairs.* NORRIE *stands quite still for a bit, until* BOB *appears carrying an old mirror down the stairs*)

BOB: The hell ye daein staunin therr, ya bliddy eediot! Pit that thing doon an' come ower here tae ah show ye somethin'. Somethin' that came oot the Ark. An' as for you, Peter Laidlaw, you should have merr sense. I hope a bliddy crocodile gets ye.

NORRIE: Sorry, Bob.

BOB: Don't be sorry, be sensible. Joe, leave *that* rush job the noo an' start on *this* rush job. I want ye tae show the young fella here how tae dismantle this oul' mirror. Go easy wi it. If anything happens tae it, Leslie'll bastricate ye.

JOE: Is it worth somethin'?

BOB: Tae you an' me it widnae be worth a pump, but tae the oul' cow that brought it in it's the light o the world. I wunner where Leslie digs them up. They come in here wi their broken-doon, oul'-fashioned fol-de-rols an' expect us tae gie them back tae them bran' new. Ye'd think we hidnae enough work o wur ain. I think Leslie must be gettin his mutton oot o it. Dirty oul' midden. Anyway, she wants it touched up an' re-silvered. Noo, watch the surface. If ye lay it on the face, lay it on straw or plenty paper.

JOE: No much tae it, Bob. Jist a hauf dozen wee tacks.

BOB: Go ahead, then. I'll feed-up tae the boy's ready.

JOE: Right, we'll lay it on the slant so's the glass disnae touch the bench. You haud wan side, an' ah'll ease the tacks oot.

NORRIE: Ye think it's very ould?

JOE: Oulder than you an' me pit thegither, I'll tell ye that. Might even be an antique. Nae bother, see. Jist two merr . . . therr we are. We take the back aff, Bob?

BOB: Aye, go ahead, go ahead.

JOE: (*easing the back off, and separating the glass from the frame*) That's it.

BOB: Jist haud on tae it, ah'll finish this side.

NORRIE: Hey, Joe! Look at this oul' paper that came oot the back. *Evening Times*, October the fourteenth, 1921! 1921! Ye were right, it is oulder than you an' me pit thegither. Look at that, whisky three an' fourpence a bottle.

JOE: Bit chipped on the side here, Bob.

BOB: Aye, aye. Hey, Peter, c'm'ere a minute. Rouger, you, tae. Charlie have a look at the edges.

NORRIE: 'Fordyce's Annual Sale — women's stockings, wan an'

six a dozen.' Hey, Rouger, look at this oul' paper I foun' oot the mirror. It's ancient history.

ROUGER: Nae five-poun' notes in the back o it? Nae confessions tae rape and murder concealed in a secret groove? See the paper. Yah, that's a lot o pap. 'Ladies' combinations, every size.' That's disgustin, that. Look at ye, you're slaverin like a dog wi the dicky itch. Get away! (*He throws the paper away*)

NORRIE: Hey, easy, easy. I want tae read that paper. (*He bends down for the paper. The* ROUGER *catches him a soft kick on the arse, and he falls against the bicycle*)

ROUGER: Watch that bike, teuchter!

NORRIE: Bugger you and yur bike. Ah'm nae teuchter.

ROUGER: Ha-ha, so ye've learnt whit it is suddenly.

NORRIE: Naw, ah havenae.

ROUGER: I'll tell ye sometime. No as bad as ye think.

BOB: That's quite a chip oot the side right enough. D'ye think it wid staun the slightest touch o the grinder, Peter?

PETER: Never. It wid shatter instantly.

BOB: Aye, I wis thinkin that masel'. Mebbe a wee rub wi the blockin-stone, then?

PETER: Aye, that might dae it. Need tae go dead easy, a' the same.

BOB: We'll a' need tae go very careful wi it. Hear that, Rouger? You hear that, Charlie?

(CHARLIE *is revealed with the weight-bar over his head. He brings it down and with a great* 'Yah!' *drops it. The whole place trembles*)

BOB: In the name o the lantern Jesus, have ye nae fuckin sense? I'm tellin everybody tae keep the heid wi this auld merchandise here, and you're flingin ton weights a' ower the place. It's blohoorable, so it is. Diabastric and blohoorable!

CHARLIE: Nae herm done.

BOB: I've tellt ye a hunner times, this is a glesswork. Ye've only been here nine year, ye should know by noo that this is the last place for a contraption like that. But ye'll get it oot o here. Ye'll get it oot that back door by the end of the week.

CHARLIE: Will you cairry it oot?

BOB: Aw, shite! You want tae grow up. Classic beveller, you! Strong back — weak heid!

CHARLIE: Must keep the strength up, Bob.

BOB: How much strength dis it take tae lift three feet o quarter-inch plate?

ROUGER: Aw, this strength o' yours — whit ye gaun tae dae wi it?

CHARLIE: Use it when the time comes.

ROUGER: Like hauf-past ten at night when you're lumberin Nancy up the high-road? Don't blush, Charlie, we a' know you're a wee bit short o strength in the right place.

CHARLIE: Not at all, I've got it when the time comes.

ROUGER: Oh, ye've got it a'right, but where are ye hidin it?

BOB: Be quiet an' pey attention. You're a bliddy mixer, Rouger. I think you were born wi a needle up yur arse. I must decide the best wey tae tackle this thing.

PETER: I could settle that fur ye.

BOB: How?

PETER: I'll just drap it.

BOB: Ye wull, like hell! Don't you start, Peter, we've had enough kiddin this mornin'.

ROUGER: He might drap it anyway.

(*The bell rings from upstairs*)

BOB: (*tearing off his apron as he goes upstairs*) Whit dis he want noo?

(BOB *goes off*)

PETER: Whit did you mean therr, Rouger?

ROUGER: Mean aboot whit?

PETER: When you said I might drap it anywey.

ROUGER: So ye might, so could anybody.

PETER: That wisnae it, you meant me special.

ROUGER: Oh, ye know me better than I dae masel', like?

PETER: Ah know ye fur a big-mouthed, dyin gett.

ROUGER: It's you that might have the big mouth shortly.

PETER: Any time ye like. Dinner-time, any time, oot the back door therr. I'm no much, but I'll have a go wi the likes o you any time ye fancy it. Arse-holer!

ROUGER: Better watch it, ye'll be foamin at the mooth soon.

PETER: That's it, int it — that's whit ye meant? I might take a wee turn an' drap it. That's whit ye meant. Couldnae haud yur tongue in front o the boy therr. Ye must let *him* know.

ROUGER: It's you that's lettin him know.

PETER: Whatever he says, son, it's no epilepsy — no epilepsy! Take a wee tightness in the throat sometimes — constriction — looks bad, but it's no malignant. So, if this big, lousy, squeezed-up pox-eye tells ye anything different, ye'll know him fur a five-star bastart liar.

ROUGER: You might get yur go sooner than ye think.

PETER: Go! You? I've seen merr go in a haun-reared, Abernethy fuckin biscuit. Ya common, schoolboard-faced, sodomistic pig, ye!

(*The* ROUGER *moves towards* PETER. *As he goes,* CHARLIE
grips his arm tightly. It's obviously a grip of steel)

CHARLIE: Away ye go, Peter.

(PETER *goes*)

ROUGER: Let go the grip, Charlie.

CHARLIE: Try and get away.

ROUGER: This is atween him an' me.

CHARLIE: Whit's on ma mind's between me an' you.

ROUGER: The strength kick again, 's 'at it?

CHARLIE: That's it.

ROUGER: Aye, well, while you're at it ye might try shaftin some o
it through tae that hot-arsed wee barra up in . . . oh . . . Christ,
Charlie . . . you'll break ma fuckin airm!

CHARLIE: A'right . . . Noo, ah'm tellin ye, you lift her name
again in here, an' ah'll split ye — take ye apart!

(CHARLIE *lets go. The* ROUGER *and* CHARLIE *move away
to their wheels.* NORRIE *goes to his seat with the paper*)

NORRIE: Hey, Joe, Joe, listen tae this — in this paper. 'Parents in
the Anderston district of Glasgow are invited and encouraged to
view the new school to be opened soon, to accommodate children of school age in the district. Classrooms and other facilities
will be open to inspection for two weeks from the fourteenth of
November 1921, which is the fortnight preceding the school's
opening date, November twenty-eighth. The school, which will
cater for infants, juniors, and advanced division scholars, will
be known as Finnieston Public School.'

Joe — that's the school ah went tae — honest — Finnieston
School. I cannae believe it. Imagine that, eh, oor school, an'
here's this oul' paper tellin ye when it opened. That's great, int
it? D'ye think ah can keep this paper? Ah'll show it tae the boys.
Might even take it in tae show it tae ma oul' school-teacher.
Therr ye are, Joe — want tae see it?

JOE: Away ye go, an' don't bother me. Ah've this set tae finish
aff the day.

NORRIE: But — d'ye no want tae look at it?

JOE: Beat it ah'm tellin ye, blow!

NORRIE: A'right, a'right.

(BOB *comes down the stair and puts on his apron*)

BOB: A'right then, Norrie, come on, we'll get wired in. An' youz
get wired in, tae. Cannae go up the sterr but ye're a' squealin
murder. I'm tellin yez — if there wis bevellers tae be got ah'd
bag the hale bliddy lot o ye. Me tae! I'd bag me tae fur no baggin
yez a' years ago. Now then, as Leslie says, a good effort! Think
a strong fart wid dae him some good. Feed up, son. Whit's that

in yur haun?

NORRIE: It's this oul' paper that came oot the mirror.

BOB: Whit year?

NORRIE: 1921.

BOB: Nae photies in it, ah'll bet ye.

NORRIE: Naw, jist readin. It's got a paragraph aboot the open-ing o oor school in it, askin the mothers and faithers tae go an' inspect it before it opens.

BOB: Whit school was that?

NORRIE: Finnie — Finnieston.

BOB: Doon Anderston wey, eh?

NORRIE: Aye, d'ye know it?

BOB: Naw. Cowcaddens wis wherr ah wis brought up. Used tae be a bevellin shop doon your wey. Ye know Elliot Street? Aye, well, doon therr. Quite unusual that. The trade wis maistly centred up roon aboot Cowcaddens. Lot o Irishmen in it, tae. Hard men — hard drinkers, a lot o them. Piece-workers, and no often steady work. Used tae wait in the pub tae a few jobs came in and go intae the shop when the gaffer sent fur them. Merr pomas, son. Of course, sometimes they'd been in the pub that long they wernae able tae go tae their work when they wer sent fur. Strong men they were. Had tae be. Some o these jobs they had in the oul' days wid have ruptured ye. Every man saw the job right through — start tae finish — and they had tae be fast at the game. There wis plenty o men tae step intae their shoes if they wernae. Merr pomas. Ye see, Norrie — noo listen — try and get used tae knowin when the wheel needs a bit merr pomas — no hiv me tellin ye a' the time. When the wheel's dry, ye can smell the burnin, see? Try some again . . .

(NORRIE *uses too much pomas, and it squirts up into* BOB *'s face*)

Holy Jesus! Ye had it right, therr — noo ye're away back again. Enough, but no' too much, see. Doot ye widnae have lasted long in the oul' days Norrie. But ye never know, ye might jist see a job like wan o the ould yins quite soon. This very day, in fact. There's a big job lying through therr, an' ah've a feelin Leslie's gaun tae tell us tae drap everything an' get oan wi it this efternoon. That reminds me, ah've got somethin' tae dae. In the meantime, you can cairry these two jobs up tae the silverin.

NORRIE: Up the sterr is that?

BOB: Past the cuttin-table an' through the door.

NORRIE: OK. (*He grabs the glass awkwardly*)

BOB: Easy, son, easy for the . . . noo, listen. Always haunle gless gently. If there's two jobs thegither, make sure there's always a bit o paper in between when ye're carryin' them. Like that,

see, at the tap. Lift them up easy — wan haun at the bottom
an' wan haun on the edge. Haud them a bit tae the side so
that they're no movin' in front o ye. Try that. That's no bad.
Careful up the sterr, noo, and if they gie ye somethin' tae bring
doon, jist take it slow. That's the stuff.

(NORRIE *goes off*)

Now, I'll away and phone my granny. (*He goes to the lavatory
his head round the door, shouting to Peter*) How's that comin wi
the hand-block, Peter?

PETER: It's fragile — very fragile — but it'll be a'right, ah think.

BOB: Well, don't spend too much time oan it. We'll jist fake it
the best wey we can an' sen it up.

PETER: Don't know who first bevelled this thing, Bob. Think
it must have been ould Alex Freer when he wis on the wine.
See that?

BOB: Well, ah, cannae see roon corners. Jist a minute. A wee
bit aff the true, eh?

PETER: The rocky road tae Port Dundas.

BOB: Ach well, that'll nearly dae it. Christ, ye're right. I think
whoever did this job wis either blind or workin in the dark. Ye
seen any sign o ould Alex Freer these days?

PETER: Naw, it's a while noo. Last time I saw him he couldnae
see me.

BOB: He'll never get aff the juice. Well, as long as he disnae
come roon here tappin us we'll be a'right. Last time he came
in he looked like a bliddy ghost. He wis the colour o pomas.

PETER: That's the wine, Bob, the dadlum.

BOB: Aye, good tradesman he wis. He might be deid fur a' we
know.

PETER: Aye, he wis fadin away. Ye feel he wid just slide doon
a gratin an' disappear.

BOB: Bring that ower tae the polisher when you're ready. Take
your time noo, Norrie, an' jist haud it right!

(NORRIE *carries a couple of pieces of glass down the stairs*)

Good. Noo drap it first on tae yur shoe — that's it — an' lean
it against the wa' — a wee bit oot at the bottom. That's it. See,
that's a wee bit merr ye've learnt.

NORRIE: That gless is sherp. Think ah've cut ma haun.

BOB: See it. Naw, that's nothin'. Jist the skin. See these. A few
cuts therr, eh? But that's nothin' either. You ask John the cut-
ter tae show ye his haun's sometime. He's got millions o wee
cuts.

NORRIE: I don't think ah'd fancy that. Gettin ma hauns a' cuts,
ah mean.

BOB: That's funny. When we were boys we couldnae wait tae get wur hauns lookin like bevellers'. Used tae compare them, and sometimes ye'd gie them a wee roughin-up wi a sherp bit o gless tae hurry them on.

NORRIE: That sounds a bit daft tae me.

BOB: Well, son, maybe you're no cut oot tae be a beveller. Never mind. It's no often ye get a real cut, unless there's a flaw in the job an' it comes away in yur haun. Mind wan time when ah wis feedin-up — the beveller wis workin in the groove and the job cracked. Well, see the wey your brush skited aff the wheel therr, same thing happened tae the job. It planed right across the shop and caught this other fulla on the thigh. It went through aprons, troosers, the lot. Severed his hamstring, an' though they got him tae the hospital in time, he never walked right again. That frighten ye, eh?

NORRIE: It's no hell of a cheery.

BOB: Come on, we'll get intae it again. Ye might no believe this, but ah've seen me wi near a mornin's work done by this time. Feed up. Noo watch it — jist got ma heid away in time therr, didn't ah?

NORRIE: The feeder-up no find this a monotonous job?

BOB: Maybe a wee bit, but no too bad. How, you find it monotonous?

NORRIE: Ah thought when ah wis workin time wid fly. Seems as if ye jist sit here lookin at the clock.

BOB: Well, ye should be lookin at the job instead.

NORRIE: Is it a'right if ah keep this oul' paper?

BOB: Tae hell wi the paper. Pey attention.

NORRIE: Naebody seems tae care aboot it except me. I mean, it's kinna historical. I wis gaun tae try an' show it tae ma oul' school-teacher.

BOB: Listen, son, schooldays are over. Noo forget the fuckin paper, an' jist keep yur mind on the job. That wey, we'll get along fine.

NORRIE: Aye, right, sorry.

BOB: Stop apologisin. Jist dae the job. (*The pomas squirts up again*)

NORRIE: I'm sorry, Bob, so I am. I'll . . . I'll . . .

BOB: It's no a hard job this, Norrie, an' ah think you're quite a sensible lauddie, but you're no concentratin. Noo, ah'll tell ye again . . . (*The bell rings*) . . . aw, Jesus Johnnie, therr that bastart bell again. Oan wi the apron — aff wi the apron. Ye'd think, bi-Christ, I wis a hure on a hard day. Rouger, c'm'ere! Finish that other side or this bliddy thing'll never get done.

(*The* ROUGER *takes over.* NORRIE *feeds pomas. It's too much.
It squirts into the* ROUGER's *face*)

ROUGER: Ya bastart, ye tried that.

NORRIE: Naw, honest, ah didnae, ah didnae mean it.

ROUGER: Ye did, ya swine. Don't try anythin' funny wi me.

NORRIE: No kiddin, ah couldnae help it.

ROUGER: See that ye dae help it. Feed up right. Bliddy teuchter,
a'right, that's you.

NORRIE: Ah don't even know whit you're talkin about.

ROUGER: Hielan, Hielan, Stupit Hielan. Nae wunner they used
tae eat folk like you.

NORRIE: Whit?

ROUGER: Hielanmen, they used tae eat them. But their meat
wis tough — tyuch — teuch! That's how they called them
teuchters.

NORRIE: Ah'm no' Hielan.

ROUGER: Yur oul'-man, then?

NORRIE: Naw.

ROUGER: Your oul'-lady? Don't like talkin aboot her, dae ye?

NORRIE: Whit should ah talk aboot her fur?

ROUGER: Cat's fur! Ye ever seen it oan a fuckin dug?

NORRIE: Whit ye gettin' at?

ROUGER: Big innocent game noo, eh. Oot at three o'clock in
the mornin gettin a doctor. That wisnae cat's fur, wis it?

NORRIE: She was ill. Anywey, it's nane o your business.

ROUGER: Oh, you're right. It wid have held tight if it had been
ma business.

NORRIE: Whit the hell ye talkin aboot?

ROUGER: A miss, wis it, eh?

NORRIE: A whit?

ROUGER: Don't come it. You know. A miss. Couple o snorts
o penny-royal, an' bang goes the baby. Mis-carriage, wis it?

NORRIE: She was sick in the middle o the night . . .
she . . . she . . .

ROUGER: Abortion, wis that it?

NORRIE: You're a stinkin big bastart! Don't you talk aboot ma
old-lady like that.

ROUGER: She drapped it, didn't she? (NORRIE *dives at the*
ROUGER, *who holds the job in one hand and the boy at arm's
length with the other.* CHARLIE *and* JOE *look on, but do nothing*)
Got ye gaun noo, haven't ah? Look at him, feet an' a'. She wis
like the man wi the barra — it wis in front o her.

PETER: Whit ye daein tae that boy, ya dirty big sod, ye? Can ye
no let nothin' alane? Lea' him go or I'll come ower there an'

pit ma boot in yur cobblers.

ROUGER: You couldnae pit yur boot in shite. No time ye had a wee convulsion?

PETER: Ya midden! Ya misbegotten, Parish-bred midden! Liberty-taker! Ould men an' wee boys, it's a' you're good fur.

(The ROUGER *gives* NORRIE *a shove. He lands on his back and begins to cry.* BOB *comes down the stair)*

BOB: I don't know whit you're daein therr, but get on yur feet. Whit ye greetin fur?

PETER: He's greetin because that . . . big, long-distance sod therr wis tormentin him.

BOB: Ah'm no askin you, Peter. You seem tae be gettin intae a hell of a lot o trouble, son, fur yur first day.

NORRIE: Ah didnae start any trouble.

BOB: Whit happened?

NORRIE: It wis . . . it wis . . . cannae fuckin tell ye.

BOB: Ye don't hiv tae tell me who wis aback o it. Whit wer ye sayin tae the boy, Rouger?

ROUGER: Nothin' much. He no tell ye hissel'?

BOB: Ye've got him greetin anyway. If you'll no say whit's goin on, an' he'll no say whit's goin on, we'll never know, wull we? Honest tae God and Jesus, Rouger, you're a needle o the first bliddy mettle. Ah wis readin aboot folk like you. Psychopaths they call them. Ye hear that? Psychopaths!

ROUGER: Aw aye, that's thon wee special roads fur ridin the bike on, int it?

BOB: Wan o these days you'll run intae it, an' ah hope ah'm therr tae see it.

ROUGER: That's been said before.

BOB: Dry up noo, Norrie, it cannae be as bad as a' that.

NORRIE: You don't know whit it wis. He said somethin' aboot ma mother.

BOB: You Charlie, could ye no have done somethin' fur the boy?

CHARLIE: No ma business.

BOB: Nothin's your business, except your sodie-heided weight-liftin. A'right, Norrie, ah don't know whit he said tae ye, but it's no the worst ye'll hear. In this game or any other. Feed up, noo. Come on, come on, move. Feed up.

NORRIE: Ah'm chuckin it.

BOB: Ah tellt ye. You're no in the school noo. You're wi the big men ootside. Yur faither cannae come divin up tae see the heid-maister an' tell him somebody's been unkind tae his wee boy. That's in the past. Make up yur mind tae it, you'll get a lot o knocks afore you're done, specially fae the likes o the

Rouger therr, and if you want tae chuck it on the first day,
that's up tae you, but ye havenae made much o a stab at it, hiv
ye? So either feed up, or take aff yur apron an' pit yur jaicket
on. (NORRIE *lifts the brush and starts feeding-up*) We'll likely be
makin a start on that big job sometime in the efternoon. Then
ye'll see somethin'. Ye'll see a bit o the trade as it used tae be.
Four-handed we'll be tae this job, inchbevel all round. We'll hiv
tae use the trestle-board. There's no much o that kinna stuff
goin aboot these days.

NORRIE: Whit's it fur?

BOB: Some daft dancin-school wants a matchin mirror fur wan
that got broke. Hey, whit's the time? Joe, pit the watter on fur
the tea. Ye forgot aboot it. It's hardly worth while noo before
dinner-time.

JOE: That's *his* job noo.

BOB: He'll dae it the-morra. An' a' the rest o yur jobs, tae.

JOE: Hope that means runnin doon tae the bettin-shop fur ye.

BOB: Less o yur lip, Joe . . . Christ, that reminds me. Ah backed
three winners on Friday an' didnae collect the money. Ought
tae hiv a few quid comin back. Noo, where'd ah pit the ticket?
Aye, in ma jaicket. Norrie, take a run doon tae the bettin-shop
an' pick up the money fur us. They should jist be open noo. Oot
the back door, up the sterr and a hunner yards doon the street
on this side. Ye cannae miss it. Run like hell, an' if anybody
sees ye, kid on you're no therr. Think ye can dae that?

NORRIE: Sure, nae bother.

BOB: On ye go, then. It's a lovely day ootside. Ye'll enjoy the
run.

(NORRIE *goes out the back door. The* BEVELLERS *concentrate,
swaying gently at their wheels. A moment of peace settles on the
shop, and they start to sing. In contrast to what has gone before,
the song is sweet and sentimental*)

ALL: Meet me tonight when the clock strikes nine
Down in the glen where the stars brightly shine
And we will walk, love, over the hill.
Meet me tonight by the old water-mill.

Evening will come at the close of the day
And to the glen we will both make our way
Your hand in mine, love, over the hill
Meet me tonight by the old water-mill.

(*They hum the end of the song again to a close, and break off
slowly.* JOE *goes for the tea and hands it round.* NORRIE *comes
back*)

NORRIE: That's it, Bob. Jist a few pence short o eight quid.

BOB: Champion, champion. Jist aboot whit ah thought masel'. No bad fur dollar roll-up, eh?

ROUGER: You're hunted — enchanted.

BOB: Jist makin up fur a' the cripples ah've backed since the season started.

PETER: By Jees, Bob, you're a dab at the accumulators. Ye always back wan stotter. Makes up for a' the stevers.

BOB: You're right, Peter. Jist aboot this time last year ah had two bob — ten pence — gaun fur me on a four-horse roll-up. Jist over fourteen poun' it got me.

JOE: An' ye didnae forget the boy that ran wi the line.

BOB: Ah'm no forgettin him this time either. Therr haf a quid. But there wer two o' yez this time. You went wi the bet, and the boy here picked it up. So, a dollar each.

JOE: Whit! Ah've been daein it for donkeys! He comes in here new, an' the first day he goes, he's on a dollar?

BOB: That's right. Ye wur greetin therr a wee while ago for Norrie tae go tae the bettin shop. That wis before ye knew ah had a treble up. So a dollar tae you, an' a dollar tae the boy.

JOE: (*giving* NORRIE *the money*) Therr ye are — Pontius.

NORRIE: Ah didnae ask fur it.

BOB: Never mind him. Get yur tea.

JOE: Don't think there's enough left fur him.

BOB: Well, whit d'ye no pit plenty on fur?

JOE: Ah jist pit the usual on. Ah forgot aboot him.

NORRIE: That's a'right, ah've got ma flask.

ROUGER: Oh, a flask, eh? Whit aboot that, Joe? Ye hear that, Charlie? Lord Fauntleroy's sister's sent him tae his work wi a flask an' sandwiches.

CHARLIE: Ye don't need a flask in here. Plenty gas in the ring.

NORRIE: It's jist tae go wi ma dinner piece.

CHARLIE: Ye eatin yur dinner in here?

NORRIE: Aye. D'yez no a' dae it?

CHARLIE: Ah think merr o ma gut than eatin ma chuck in here.

NORRIE: Dis naebody dae it, then?

JOE: You'll be on yur tod in here the minute the whistle goes.

ROUGER: Only wan other man in here at dinner-time.

NORRIE: Who's that?

ROUGER: The beveller's ghost!

JOE: Aye, him an' the rats.

NORRIE: Jesus Christ!

ROUGER: Ye'll be sittin therr an' ye'll feel this cauld thing creepin up the back o yur neck. Ye look roon, an' therr it is, glowin in the dark, the beveller's ghost.

PETER: Ach, the beveller's arse! Don't believe them, Norrie. Many's the good kip ah've had in here at dinner-time, stretched oot on the bench.

NORRIE: Ah didnae believe them anyway.

ROUGER: No much — it wis hingin fae ye.

NORRIE: 'S a lot a junk, that ghost stuff.

PETER: Ah'll no be havin a kip the day a' the same. Ah'll be joinin Bob on a wee toddle doon tae the boozer fur a gless o that class lager. Ye settin them up the day, Bob?

BOB: Don't mind. No every day ye get a wee turn at the bookies. Ye're a' invitit.

CHARLIE: No me, Bob. Thanks a' the same. Ye know me.

BOB: Good enough, wan less.

JOE: Ah'm on fur a half pint.

BOB: You've had yur dollar. You, Rouger?

ROUGER: Don't know. Ah want tae go fur a spare inside tube fur the bike. If ah get back.

BOB: Ye might be too late then.

ROUGER: That'll no bother me.

BOB: Suit yersel'.

(CHARLIE *lifts the weight-bar above his head and lets it fall with a great gasp. Everyone freezes. Nobody says anything*)

ROUGER: That's how tae spend yur dinner-time, young-yin. Try liftin Charlie's weight.

NORRIE: No me. Many times can you dae that, Charlie?

CHARLIE: Often as ye like, within reason. I'll show ye. Wance merr fur luck, eh?

PETER: Aw, Charlie, we're a' fuckin galvanised wi you drappin that thing.

CHARLIE: I'll put it doon nice an' easy this time, like a feather.

(CHARLIE *lifts the bar again, holds it there, brings it down with one break, then sets it gently on the floor*)

CHARLIE: That satisfy ye, eh, young fulla?

NORRIE: You must have some strength.

ROUGER: Aw aye, an' some knack, tae — ye learn the knack through practice.

CHARLIE: Ye fancy tryin tae learn it, then?

ROUGER: Ah've got some knack o ma ain. Shovin that thing ower yur heid a couple times might look snazzy, but you try shovin a bike up tae Dalmally an' back in wan day. See who'd hiv the knack then. Knackered merr like you'd be.

CHARLIE: Widnae waste ma time.

ROUGER: We wernae wastin time yesterday, ah'll tell ye. We

caught six riders fae the Troy Wheelers just below the Falls o Falloch. Four o us, an' six o them. They knew we were on their tail and tried tae shake us on the climb. Suddenly the road ahead wis clear, an' wan o oor boys shouts 'Jump!' We wer out the saddles like jockeys. As one man we sprinted up the hill an' left them fuckless. We danced away fae them! Burnt off they were — burnt right off! An' that wisnae knack, that wis pedallin, Mac, shovin an' pedallin.

CHARLIE: Bravo. So, how d'ye fancy makin yur name, Norrie? On the bike, or on the bar here?

NORRIE: Don't think ah fancy either o them.

CHARLIE: Ye can sit straight on a bike though, can't ye?

NORRIE: Who cannae?

CHARLIE: So try gettin that thing two inches aff the flerr.

NORRIE: Don't want tae.

CHARLIE: Jist hiv a wee crack at it.

NORRIE: Nae point, ah'd never dae it.

CHARLIE: Jist tae get the feel o it — get a sense o the resistance.

NORRIE: Ah think you're kiddin me.

CHARLIE: Naw, naw, c'm'ere. Pit baith hauns on the bar — a wee bit further apart — noo bend at the knees and jist get the feel o it. (NORRIE *does so and strains at the bar*)

NORRIE: If I try any harder I'll go through the flerr.

(ALL *the men laugh. There is a move towards resuming work. The* ROUGER *spots the red cloth peering out of* NORRIE's *pocket. He whips it out*)

ROUGER: Here, wipe the sweat aff yursel' . . . whit the hell's this?

NORRIE: Give us that, you.

ROUGER: Oh aye, gie's back ma drawers. Whit ye daein' wi these? (*He holds up a pair of red ladies' briefs*)

NORRIE: Give us them, ah said.

ROUGER: Cairry these aboot in yur pocket a' the time, dae ye?

NORRIE: Naw ah don't.

ROUGER: Doin yur knee-creeper an' blaggin them aff the washin lines, then. Is that it?

NORRIE: They're no mine.

ROUGER: Well ah hope tae Christ they're no. We've had a few queeries in here, but never wan o that kind before.

NORRIE: Ach, work them up your nose. Ah don't care.

JOE: Wherr d'ye get them?

NORRIE: Ye'll no believe us anyway, so whit the hell's the use o tellin' yez?

BOB: Aye well, Norrie, ye must admit it's a kinna unusual article fur a boy tae hiv aboot him.

NORRIE: Ah don't care, they're no mine.

ROUGER: Yur sister's, 's 'at it? Takes his sister's knickers oot wi him. Some boy, eh?

NORRIE: You keep the sister oot o' it! Some bird up at a windae shouted at me as ah wis comin doon the back sterr and threw these things ower.

ROUGER: Oot the work next door?

NORRIE: Aye.

ROUGER: An' you picked them up an' kept them?

NORRIE: They fell right on ma heid. Ah wis in a hurry. Bob said ah wis tae hurry an' no let anybody see me. Ah jist stuck them in ma pocket. Meant tae throw them away later.

ROUGER: Oh, we'll believe that, oh aye. Nae wunner ye're takin yur dinner in here, eh?

NORRIE: Ach, away you an' peddle yur duff.

ROUGER: Whit ye tellin us? Some young fox up therr hauls aff her drawers an' chucks them oot the windae fur ye?

NORRIE: They wernae fur me.

ROUGER: Oh, fur somebody else, then?

NORRIE: Ah don't know.

ROUGER: Naebody in here knows any o the birds in therr, except Charlie.

NORRIE: Ah don't know, ah'm tellin' yez.

ROUGER: Hidin it, eh? Feart somebody might lift ye ower his heid an' drap ye like a fifty-sixer?

NORRIE: Aw, shut it!

CHARLIE: All right, boy, speak up.

NORRIE: Charlie, ah didnae want tae say anythin' . . .

CHARLIE: Never mind that. Jist tell whit wis shouted.

NORRIE: Ah cannae mind.

BOB: The boy cannae mind. Come on, back tae work, if that's whit ye call it, sittin on yur jacksies hauf the mornin.

CHARLIE: Listen, Bob, it's no often ah go against ye, but ah'm gaun tae hear the version o' this, wance an' fur a'.

NORRIE: Aw, right then, it's no ma fault. There wis two or three o these lassies up therr. The windae wis slung open. Wan o them seemed tae be tryin tae stop the others throwin these things, but they came flyin ower the windae, an' wan o them shouted, 'These are fur Charlie. Tell him Nancy says they're on fire and he's the man wi the hose.' (*The men laugh*)

CHARLIE: (*deeply humiliated*) Ya little bastart!

BOB: Naw, naw, Charlie. The boy wis keepin it quiet, but you made him speak. That no right, noo? Peter?

PETER: Aye, fair enough. Boy wantit tae keep his mouth shut. Whit the hell's it matter anyway? Only a bunch o lassies skylarkin'.

CHARLIE: Suppose you're right. OK, son, forget it. Joke's on me. But it's over. Jist keep that in mind, everybody.

BOB: Whit's the time therr? God stiff me, ah believe that clock's stopped again. Nae wunner the tea-break went on so long. Dae ye know how tae squint the time up therr, Norrie?

NORRIE: Aye, think so . . . (*He toes to the hole in the glass grating*) It's jist leavin hauf-past.

BOB: Whit! Oh buggeration! We've less than hauf-an-oor o the mornin left an' we've hardly turned a wheel. Ah well, wan o these days. Set that clock, Norrie.

(NORRIE *goes up to the clock*)

NORRIE: The hauns are stiff, they'll hardly turn.

BOB: Well, spit on it — right on the spindle. That usually dis it.

(NORRIE *spits on it*)

NORRIE: Ah think that's it noo.

BOB: Come on then, get some pomas on, an' mind my eye.

(BOB *and* NORRIE *start to work*)

NORRIE: Did you think the mornin went past quick, Bob?

BOB: Past quick? It vanished, disappeared. How d'you no?

NORRIE: It seemed quite long tae me. In school you've got different periods. Time goes quick.

BOB: Back at school again, are ye? Take ma advice, son. Put it behind ye, unless you're thinkin o gaun back there, are ye?

NORRIE: Naw, nae chance.

BOB: Got tae make the break sometime. So stick in. You might think this is a rough trade and rough folk in it. But that's jist because we havenae broke away fae the oul' days — no a'thegither anyway. Ye cannae wipe oot years o' hard men an' hard graft jist because the machinery changes a wee bit. No that it's a' that different, mind you. The wheels are a wee bit different here an' there, like the carborundum stone. That used tae be the ould mill wi the hopper feeder and a sand-drip. That's when boys younger than you really grafted. Cairryin pailfuls o saun an' sievin it in the trough beside the mill. They still use them in wan or two places yet, an' if somethin' had tae go wrang at Peter's end we might have tae use it yet, but it's no likely. As ah said, there wis a lot o Irishmen in this game at wan time. Haill families o them. It wis wan o the few trades open tae them. The Rouger's oul' man wis a beveller. You think he's twistit. Ye want tae have seen his oul' man. They worked on

piece work, each man seein his job through fae start tae finish, an' they had tae shift. The Rouger's faither wis a beaster.
He'd collect his ain wages at the end o the week an' take the
Rouger's tae. That wis the last they'd see o him tae the pubs
shut on Setturday night. They wer lucky if he had enough left
tae get them pigs' feet fur the rest o the week. So maybe it's
no surprisin that he's a wee bit rough. Course they wurnae a'
like that, the oul' yins. Some o them could cut a design wi a
wheel that wis merr like somethin' ye'd see in the Art Galleries.
Ah wis never a' that good at figure-work masel'. But some o
them raised families an' even put them tae the University. Ah
see some lawyers' names aboot the toon an' ah can mind their
faithers. Bevellers. Hard men, but good bliddy men, some o
them. Aye, aye. Ye find the time long, then?

NORRIE: Jist keep glancin up at the clock a lot. Disnae seem tae
move much.

BOB: Ah well, it's no much o' a clock. Whit kinna stuff did they
learn ye at school?

NORRIE: Usual. Bit o maths, science, techy-drawin, composition an' that.

BOB: Whit wer ye good at?

NORRIE: English.

BOB: English?

NORRIE: Aye. Might no talk it very good, but ah wis a'right
when it came tae writin it doon.

BOB: Wisnae exactly ma best subject. Mebbie you're wan o these
fullas wi the itch.

NORRIE: Eh?

BOB: Ah've noticed. There's roughly three kinds o blokes get
loose efter school. Wan's like me. Plods along, learns a trade
and disnae see much further than a week's work an' his wages
at the end o it. A wee bit o security tae keep the wife happy.
Other kind's the wan wi a bit o education. They run businesses,
buy a hoose, an' never seem tae be short o a few nicker. They
might be dumplins, but that bit o education makes the difference. They're usually solid. Third kind's the wans wi the itch.
Ah don't mean scratchin theirsel's or anythin' like that. A kind
o internal itch. They'd come in an' look at a job like this an' say,
'Bugger that — ah'm off!' They might cast aboot fur a while
before anythin' turns up, but it usually happens. They might
be the kind that tries tae knock aff a couple o wage-vans an'
get seven year fur their bother, but they're no exactly the really
itchy wans. Naw, the fullas ah'm talking aboot don't seem tae
need whit the rest o us need. They've a kinna instinct, an' it

gets them through. Some o them turn intae bookies, some do well at the buying an' sellin, but occasionally ye get wan an' he really makes a name. Nae real start in life, but he's got the itch. We had a fulla like that in oor class in school. He wis good at composition, tae.

NORRIE: Ah don't feel very itchy now.

BOB: Ah well, we'll see. You're feedin up better. (*The bell goes*) Stiff me, that's Leslie again. He's got the itch, but ah widnae like tae tell him where it is.

> (BOB *goes off upstairs. The* ROUGER *and* JOE *start to talk together, hatching something*)

ROUGER: Hey, Norrie! Ye really fancy that bike, eh?

NORRIE: How, ye giein it away?

ROUGER: Naw, but ye could always have a gander at it.

NORRIE: Much'll it cost us?

ROUGER: Jist thought ye might be interested tae have a look. See these gears here, many permutations ye think's in the cogs therr?

NORRIE: You tell us.

ROUGER: Twelve. A dozen choices when you're nickin along. Hills, flats, corners, take yur pick.

> (NORRIE *moves towards the bike and becomes absorbed.* JOE *snatches the old newspaper*)

NORRIE: Whit kinna frame is it?

ROUGER: Continental. Top stylin. The lightest frame on the road.

NORRIE: Much it cost ye?

ROUGER: Best part o fifty quid for the frame itsel'. Wheels, gears, brakes, extra. Worth a hundred nicker as it stands.

NORRIE: That's no a bike, that's a space-ship.

ROUGER: Feel the position.

NORRIE: Position?

ROUGER: The relationship between the saddle, the rider, and the haunle-bars.

NORRIE: Whit's that got tae dae wi it? Ye no jist get on an' shove?

ROUGER: That's gringo talk. You see a rider wi his position right, ye know he's a pedaller. Ye see a bloke wi his arse in the air, ye know he's a plunk, a Joseph. Ye can always spot the pedallers weighin thursel's up in shop windaes as they pass.

NORRIE: Ah widnae mind whit ah looked like if ah had that thing under me.

ROUGER: Ye'd get the knock before ye reached Old Kilpatrick.

NORRIE: Ah've shoved a bike before this.

ROUGER: Ye'd get fire in yur gut. Jist like that fire behind ye.

    (NORRIE *turns round and sees a small blaze on the floor*)

NORRIE: Whit's that fur?

ROUGER: Ye no feel it cauld?

NORRIE: No me.

JOE: Ould papers make very good burnin.

NORRIE: Ye no feart ye set fire tae that straw?

JOE: No chance.

ROUGER: Don't think ye heard him right. Ould papers make good fires. Nice and dry.

NORRIE: (*looking towards his bench*) 'S 'at that paper that came oot the mirror?

ROUGER: You're gettin warm. But no so warm as that crap aboot yur oul' school.

    (NORRIE *tries to kick out the fire and rescue the paper but it's too late*)

NORRIE: Whit ye want tae dae that fur?

ROUGER: Jist a wee game. New boy — first day. Ye've got tae gee him up a wee bit.

NORRIE: Ah don't mind ye takin the rise, but the paper wis somethin' else. D'ye burn the lot o it?

ROUGER: Mebbe no.

    (JOE *holds up the rest of the paper.* NORRIE *dives for it. The* ROUGER *collars him, while* JOE *puts the rest on the fire*)

NORRIE: You're a coupla animals. Liberty-takers. Yez knew ah wanted that paper.

ROUGER: Teacher's pet. Gallopin back tae get a pat on the heid fur bein a good boy.

NORRIE: Ah thought you wur gaun tae be ma mate in here, Joe.

JOE: No chance, Mac.

NORRIE : Lousy bastards.

    (BOB *comes down the stair*)

BOB: Whit's that burnin?

ROUGER: Gaun, tell him. Tell the teacher. The big bad boys set fire tae his paper.

BOB: You get some watter on that at wance, Joe, or I'll land ye a severe kick in the arse. Rouger, ye're a lousebag plain and simple. It wis daein ye nae herm tae let the boy hiv the paper, but ye couldnae leave it, could ye? Ah knew yur oul' man. Ah widnae hiv crossed him, but he wis straight in his ain wey. You! When they bury you, they'll use a twisted coffin.

ROUGER: Ma oul' man wis a pig, an' when he got tae the age when he wis past it, ah let him know it, too.

BOB: Aye, don't tell us. Ah mind o his last days at the job. Ye used tae thump him on the chest an' say, 'Gaun, ya dirty oul' pig, ye.'

ROUGER: Mebbe he'll no be the last oul' man tae feel that.

BOB: If that's me you're talkin aboot, ah'll tell ye somethin'. Ye wernae bred fur it. Ah'd cut ye fae yur heid tae yur arse, or ah'd find them that wid dae it fur me. Joe, don't let me catch you at that caper again.

JOE: Only a bit o kiddin, Bob.

BOB: Ye might've burnt the shop doon. Aw right, Norrie, don't staun therr like a stumor. Mix some merr pomas or somethin', but stir yur ideas — the lot o ye. Peter, Charlie. C'm'ere, ah want yez. We're gettin that big mirror-plate through right now. Leslie says we've tae try an' get it started by two o'clock this efternoon, so gie's your efforts, an' we'll get it through against the sterr therr.

JOE: You want me, Bob?

BOB: When ah want you, ah'll ask ye. Any oul' gloves aboot the place?

CHARLIE: They're baith fur the right haun.

BOB: Like the rest o the stuff in here. Two o everythin' — bugger all o nothin'.

ROUGER: Ah hivnae got wan.

BOB: Good. Mebbie ye'll do wan o yur arteries in.

(BOB, PETER, *and* CHARLIE *move through to the side of the shop*)

JOE: You've got me in bad wi the gaffer.

NORRIE: Ah got ye in bad? Ah didnae dae anythin'.

JOE: You and yur manky oul' paper.

NORRIE: Well, ye knew ah wanted tae keep it 'cause it wis ould.

JOE: Ould papers oot o ould mirrors are ten a penny in this job.

NORRIE: Ah didnae know that. Yez didnae need tae burn it anyway.

JOE: Ach, get bottled.

(BOB, PETER, *and* CHARLIE *begin to appear carrying the glass plate.* LESLIE *comes down the stair*)

LESLIE: Is that you bringing it through now, Bob?

BOB: We're no exactly takin it oot the back door.

LESLIE: See you don't mark the face.

BOB: We're jist lookin for rough corners tae gie it a dunt against.

LESLIE: Careful with the step down, then.

BOB: Aye. The wan-legged man'll go first.

LESLIE: It's all right kidding, Bob, but that's a valuable job. Watch the step, Peter.

PETER: Thanks for remindin me. Ah'd never noticed it before.

LESLIE: You're all in good humour today, I can see that.

BOB: We're a' jist tryin tae get this thing fae wan side o the shop tae the other.

LESLIE: Where are you putting it down?

BOB: We'll lie it alangside the sterr therr. If you'll get oot the road, that is.

LESLIE: Sorry, sorry. You think that's the safest place for it?

BOB: It's the only place fur it. Unless you know somewhere in this shop that ah havenae seen before.

LESLIE: No need for the sarcasm, Bob. Just seeing things right.

BOB: Jist a minute, Leslie. Ah'll talk tae ye in a minute. Now then, fullas, put it doon easy against the lavvy boards and the haun-rail.

LESLIE: You'll have to be careful when you're going into the doings.

BOB: Ma end doon first. Easy, noo, Charlie, easy, Peter. Your end, Rouger, aboot a foot oot at the bottom. That's it. Well noo, that wisnae so bad, wis it, Leslie?

LESLIE: No, quite good, quite good. You laddies be careful going up the stairs. No jumping. You hear that, sonny?

NORRIE: Yes, Mr Skinner.

LESLIE: I suppose you're right, Bob. That's just about the best place for it.

BOB: It's nice an' near the grinder anywey.

LESLIE: When do you think you'll make a start on it?

BOB: Well, we've a few odds and ends o rush jobs tae clear up first. Mebbe two o'clock or hauf-past.

LESLIE: How's that mirror coming along?

BOB: That's wan o the odds an' ends. Right efter dinner-time ah'll gie it a polishin.

LESLIE: Well, as long as you get the big one started this afternoon.

BOB: Honest, ah don't know whit the panic is. We'd be better giein this a full day.

LESLIE: No. Must get it started sometime today.

BOB: You're the boss.

LESLIE: I'll look down later and see how you're managing. How will you tackle it?

BOB: Same wey we always tackle that size o job. A man tae each corner, an' the trestle-board underneath for support. Peter'll do the bevel.

LESLIE: Your best effort, Peter. Keep the bevel true. Use the measuring-stick. Inch bevel all round.

PETER: Aye, right, Leslie.

LESLIE: I'll be off, then. Remember what I told you, boys. Watch the stairs.

(LESLIE *goes off — and stumbles on the stair*)

ROUGER: Inch bevel all round now, Peter. Use the measuring-stick.

PETER: I havenae used a measuring-stick in twenty year. When ah dae a job, it's bang on. Nae merr, nae less.

BOB: That man wid drive ye tae drink, so he wid.

PETER: He disnae hiv tae drive me. You're still settin them up, ah hope, Bob.

BOB: Mebbie you shouldnae go the day, Peter.

PETER: The day wan lager sets me aff ma stroke ah'll chuck it.

BOB: Ah, well, it'll no be long noo. Some bliddy mornin this has been.

ROUGER: Whit aboot this yin here, eh? 'Yes, Mr Skinner.'

BOB: Whit d'ye want him tae say — ye want him tae call the manager by his first name, an' him a new boy?

ROUGER: He calls you Bob.

BOB: Aye, 'cause ah told him tae. Right, back tae the graft for the wee while that remains o the mornin. Try an' clear up some o the small stuff.

(ALL *return to their wheels and settle again. The singing takes over, and they begin humming the same tune as before.*

The whistle goes shortly. ALL *rush for their jackets and go off upstairs, the* ROUGER *taking his bike.* NORRIE *remains downstairs. At the foot of the stair* PETER *turns*)

PETER: Ye can leave a couple o the lights on, but don't touch anythin' ye shouldnae.

(PETER *goes off*)

NORRIE: Aye, right.

(NORRIE *is left alone. He takes a flask and sandwiches from his piece-bag and settles on the bench beside his wheel. After a moment he goes to his jacket and returns with a comic, in which he soon becomes absorbed — so absorbed that he doesn't notice old* ALEX FREER *coming slowly, like a shadow, down the stair.*

Old ALEX *gets very near to* NORRIE *and stands looking round vacantly. He puts out a thin hand and touches* NORRIE)

NORRIE: (*leaping up on to the bench and backing away*) Jesus Christ! Ya whey-faced oul' bastart, ye come near me, ah'll break every bit o gless in the shop ower ye!

ALEX: Eh . . . Eh . . . Wait, noo . . . don't be feart, son.

NORRIE: Ye might be a fuckin ghost, but you touch me an' ye'll be sorry ye ever snuffed it!

ALEX: Aw, ah'm no' a ghost, son. Sometimes ah wish ah wis,

an' sometimes ah feel like wan, but ah'll just hiv tae wait ma time. Sorry if ah gied ye a fright.

NORRIE: Wit ye daein in here?

ALEX: Ah'm nae stranger here. I wis doon here before ye wur born. Best years o ma life wer spent doon here, among the pomas an' the wheels an' the slurry.

NORRIE: The whit?

ALEX: The slurry — the grindings o the gless that gethers at the bottom o the wheels. You must be new here. When did ye start?

NORRIE: This morning.

ALEX: Ye'll no have learnt a' the names fur the different wee bits an' pieces roon aboot the trade yet. The burning, the slurry, the culet. Ye know whit culet is?

NORRIE: Naw.

ALEX: Well, it's no much, but it sounds like something. The scrap gless in the box below the bench therr. The shards, the spikes, the remains o ould jobs bunged away an' forgot aboot — that's culet.

NORRIE: Naebody told me.

ALEX: Sometimes ah feel like a bit o ould culet masel'. Sometimes in the mornings I feel as if the culet's inside me. Apexes, corners, an' wee sherp slithers o gless trying tae bust their wey oot ma inside. It's no gless, of course, it's jist the wey ah am sometimes in the mornings.

NORRIE: Wur ye lookin fur somebody?

ALEX: Ye could say that, aye. Ah try tae stey away, no bother anybody, but then the time comes when ah miss the smell. Ye've noticed the smell? Aye, ye wid. The burning at the polisher, an' that peculiar smell fae the edgers. It's no like anythin' else ah can think o. A kinna funny, limy smell. Nearly sweet. I noticed it the first time ah ever went intae a bevellin shop, an' ah can smell it noo.

NORRIE: Is it Bob you're looking fur?

ALEX: Aye, Bob. Maybe Peter, or any o the ould-yins. The young-yins, they're different. Widnae gie ye a smell o their drawers if their arse wis studded wi diamonds. Sit doon, son, hiv yur piece. Ah'll hiv a wee sate, tae. Ye're no sure o me yet, are ye? It's a'right, ah'll sit a wee bit away fae ye. Gaun, don't bother wi me. Ah'm Alex Freer . . . . (NORRIE *sits down cagily, and* ALEX *takes a place down the bench from him*) Whit's making ye hiv yur piece inside?

NORRIE: Jist thought that's how they wid a' dae it.

ALEX: They used tae, right enough. Nothin' else fur it at wan time. Different noo. No very often they stey in at dinner-time noo. Peter sometimes if he's needin a wee sleep. If he's been feelin a wee bit dizzy or that. An' a very odd time, Bob.

NORRIE: They're no here the day. Bob backed a few winners, an' Peter an' him are in the pub.

ALEX: Are they? By Christ if ah'd known that, ah widnae be here, ah'll tell ye.

NORRIE: Could ye no run doon? Ye might catch them.

ALEX: Run? Ha-ha, Jesus, that's a good yin. Run, eh? Whit's yur name?

NORRIE: Norrie.

ALEX: Well, Norrie, the thing ah want maist right noo is a big gill o wine, but ah couldnae run if they wer at the bottom o Pitt Street giein it away in barrels.

NORRIE: Ye no feelin well?

ALEX: Aye, ye could pit it that wey. Mebbie ah could manage a wee drap o yur tea, if ye've any tae spare.

NORRIE: Aye, sure. Ye want a bit piece?

ALEX: Naw, nae piece, nae piece.

(NORRIE *pours out some tea and hands it over.* ALEX *stretches out his hand, which shakes violently*)

NORRIE: Ye cauld or somethin'?

ALEX: Ah'm cauld, ah'm hot — ah'm sweatin, ah'm shiverin. (*He gets the cup to his mouth. It rattles against his teeth*) God take care o us! Cannae even . . . cannae even . . . aw, never mind, son, it's a wee bit too hot anywey.

NORRIE: Sure ye widnae like a bit o piece?

ALEX: Naw, naw. Oh, Jeez, ah'm exhausted. Whit's on yur piece?

NORRIE: Sausage.

ALEX:: Cannae mind the last time I had a sausage. Listen, son . . .

NORRIE: Whit?

ALEX: Aw, never mind . . . cannae ask ye that. Ye jist started this mornin, eh?

NORRIE: Aye.

ALEX: Ye gaun tae stick it?

NORRIE: No sure. Hiv tae wait an' see.

ALEX: Don't, Norrie boy, don't. Get away fae it. Ye spend yur days grindin gless, an' at the finish yur life's like slurry at the bottom o the wheel. Yur back's like the bent bit o an oul' tree an' yur hauns are like jaurries aboot the knuckles. Ye never get away fae the sound o watter drippin in yur ears. The damp gets in at the soles o yur feet an' creeps right up tae yur neck.

Yur face turns tae the colour o pomas an' ye cannae stop it. That Rouger, he tries tae keep the shine on his face by gallopin like a bliddy eediot oot on that bike o his, an' Charlie thinks he can pit aff the evil day liftin that stupit weight o his ower his heid, but they cannae stop it. Somethin' breks doon in the chest, an' the sound o yur voice gets thin, an' wan day you're an oul' man like me, bent an' brittle. Don't stey at it, Norrie. Get somethin' else — anythin'. Get intae the sun an' the fresh air. Get a job on a motor, a van, anythin', but don't stey at this trade. Fur if ye dae, it'll bend ye.

NORRIE: Aye . . . well . . . hivnae made up ma mind aboot it.

ALEX: Take ma word, make it up soon.

NORRIE: Thought ye said ye couldnae stey away fae the smell?

ALEX: That's right, oh, that's right. Efter a while it gets intae ye, an' wance it gets under ye, it's very hard tae make the brek. Ah'm no sayin there urnae some lovely things aboot this trade, but it's a' in the end-product, like. A bit o figure-work or a good — a beautiful mirror — well bevelled an' set — will staun against anythin' in any craft. Ah've seen work by some o the oul' fullas that wid bring wee needles intae the corners o yur eyes it wis that lovely, but take ma word — it's no worth it. The price fur a' that work has got tae be peyed.

NORRIE: How long have ye been stopped workin?

ALEX: A few year. Must be five or six anyway. Come in here sometimes an' see the boys. Sometimes they bung us a few bob tae get's a gless o wine. Ah'm a wine-mopper, ye know.

NORRIE: 'S 'at how you're shakin?

ALEX: That's how, son, that's how. Ye can imagine me haudin a three-foot plate wi a shake like that on, eh?

NORRIE: Dangerous fur ye.

ALEX: Dangerous fur everybody else. Ah'm no sayin the trade did that tae me. That might have happened anyway. But sometimes, stuck doon here wi the mill gaun, the shaddas an' the watter drippin, on bad days ah used tae think, 'This is how it must be efter the big trumpet blaws', an' ah'd grab ma jaicket an' dive oot the back door fur a glass o the ruby red. Time came when ah couldnae come in at a'. No tae work anyway. How long before the rest o them come back?

NORRIE: Good forty minutes yet anyway.

ALEX: Well, ah cannae stey here. The wee funny things are beginnin tae jig aboot at the side o ma eyes. Must try an' see the boys on the road up.

NORRIE: Whit if ye don't see them?

ALEX: Don't know. When it's like this ye never know. Jist hiv tae suffer, ah suppose, jist hiv tae suffer.

NORRIE: Wid a dollar be any good tae ye?

ALEX: Ye mean ye wid give us a dollar?

NORRIE: Aye.

ALEX: Oh, give us it, Norrie, give us it. Ah wis gaun tae tap ye a wee while ago therr, but you're jist a young boy.

NORRIE: (*gives him the money*) . . . Thanks. A dollar's quite a lot the wey ah'll drink it. At least the tap o ma heid'll no come aff. Thanks. Ah'll away noo. Ye'll never know whit this means . . . it might no make a' that much difference in the long run . . . but the day, anyway . . . I'll be safe fur the day, anyway. Cheerio, Norrie. You're a kind boy.

> (ALEX *goes.* NORRIE *sits for a long moment before picking up his comic and starting to read and eat again*)

ACT TWO

NORRIE has finished eating and is now roaming around the shop. He has a crack at CHARLIE's weight, but can't budge it. He swings on a thick rafter that juts out from the wall, then, spotting an old loft high up on the side wall, he climbs up into it to see what's there.

Just then, the ROUGER comes down the stair carrying his bike, and puts it down.

ROUGER: Anybody here? Wherr are ye, teuchter? Come oot, come oot, we're sellin fruit!

> (NORRIE *peeps out from the loft, but doesn't answer. The* ROUGER *looks around the shop and decides he's alone. He, too, goes to* CHARLIE's *weight and has a go, but can't lift it more than shoulder-high.* NORRIE *watches*)

ROUGER: Bastart! Five an' a half feet o fuck-all, an' he pits this thing up like a bag o straw. By Christ, ah ever see him oot the road, ah'll burn him, ah'll burn him down tae the rim o his jacksie.

> (*The* ROUGER *tries the weight again, but with no more success. He lets it drop on to the floor, and the noise is followed quickly by a rattle at the back door. The* ROUGER *goes through to answer it.* NORRIE *stays aloft.* NANCY's *voice is heard, off*)

NANCY: Charlie here?

ROUGER: No the noo. Come on in.

NANCY: No if he's no here.

ROUGER: 'S a'right, he'll be in a minute.

NANCY: Jist tell him ah wis here, eh?

ROUGER: Tellin ye straight, he'll be back in a shake. Come on in. Nothin' tae be feart o.

NANCY: A'right, ah'm comin, but you keep yur distance, ye hear?

ROUGER: Sure, sure. Jist fixin the bike.

(NANCY *appears. She is wary of the* ROUGER, *who is slamming the back door and throwing the bolt*)

NANCY: Whit's a' the security fur? Leave that back door open.

ROUGER: Ah'm no botherin ye. Ye want tae open the door, naebody stoppin ye.

NANCY: You'll no be stoppin me anywey an' chance it.

ROUGER: That's whit ah'm sayin', int it?

NANCY: Jist mind it.

ROUGER: You got somethin' against me? (*He goes to his bike and fiddles about*).

NANCY: Whit d'ye mean?

ROUGER: Ye're comin on as if ah wis gaun tae dive ye or somethin'. Ye hardly know me.

NANCY: Ah know ye a'right. Ah widnae trust you wi a deid cat.

ROUGER: How dae you know aboot me — Charlie been wisin ye up on the shop gossip?

NANCY: Ah jist know, that's a'.

ROUGER: Oh, ah've heard o them, but ah didnae think we had wan o them in here.

NANCY: Wan o whit?

ROUGER: The kind that run tae their mammies or their birds or their wives. 'See whit a bad boy Rouger is — see whit a good boy, me.'

NANCY: Say that in front o Charlie.

ROUGER: You that implied it, no me.

NANCY: Ah'll tell him — see who's smilin then.

ROUGER: Ah don't know whit you're losin the brow fur. You pit the needle intae me, ah stick it back. Nothin' wrang wi that.

NANCY: Ah'm balin out o here.

ROUGER: Suit yursel'. Go or stey, ah'm no botherin ye.

NANCY: Ye mind opening that door then?

ROUGER: Ah don't mind. Jist gie's a minute, an' ah'll open it.

(*There is a moment of truce.* NANCY *looks around the place. She is keenly aware of the* ROUGER, *and not entirely disenchanted*)

NANCY: How can ye work in a place like this?

ROUGER: It's no that bad.

NANCY: It's a dump. Places like this should be demolished.

ROUGER: Maist o them are, but we're still here.

NANCY: Ah widnae work here if ye gave me a mink Rolls-Royce.

ROUGER: Ye'll be gettin that any day noo. Ah mean, when you an' Charlie walk down the aisle.

NANCY: Oh aye, that'll be the day.

ROUGER: Ye no set the date yet?

NANCY: I think the calendar's stopped.

ROUGER: Whit, ye mean tae say Charlie's no sweatin tae get ye signed up?

NANCY: You ask too many questions.

ROUGER: Nae offence. Jist thought ye wanted tae air yur feelins.

NANCY: Aye, but ah don't want tae broadcast them.

ROUGER: Right. Ah heard nothin. Well, that's that. Wull ah open the door fur ye then?

NANCY: Ye in a hurry tae see me aff noo?

ROUGER: Naw, naw. Ah like talkin tae ye. In fact ah like you.

NANCY: Save it, Santy. How can you like me, ye don't even know me?

ROUGER: Well, the cat can look up the queen's drawers, can't it?

NANCY: That's enough! Excuse me!

ROUGER: It's jist a wey o speakin. Ah've seen ye stacks o times, an' in ma ain wey ah've liked ye. Havenae said much tae ye, but then ah don't know wherr ah stand, dae ah?

NANCY: Ye stand wherr ye've always stood, big-yin, right oot in the rain.

ROUGER: That's no exactly fair, is it? Ah mean, fur a' you know, ah could be wan o the nicest fullas in the city.

NANCY: Ah'll never know anythin' aboot that.

ROUGER: Up tae you. Wer ye supposed tae see Charlie?

NANCY: Aye. Said he'd see me at the front o the work at a quarter past.

ROUGER: He must have left late. He sometimes dis a bit o trainin wi the weight therr. Maybe he forgot.

NANCY: Trainin fur whit? The Possilpark Olympics?

ROUGER: Gettin his strength up. Ah mean, a lovely girl like you.

NANCY: Flattery'll get ye nowhere.

ROUGER: Naw, genuine. Ah think you're a lovely girl.

NANCY: The compliments are bowlin me over.

ROUGER: Ah mean it. Terrific body, smashin face, the lot.

NANCY: Don't let *him* hear ye sayin that.

ROUGER: He'll never hear it unless you tell him.

NANCY: You're dead crafty, aren't ye?

ROUGER: Strike me dead, ah mean it, genuine. If ah wis Charlie you'd be right up on the old pedastal fur ma money.

NANCY: Ah used to think you wer a dead-head. Gettin quite romantic in yur ould age.

ROUGER: I'll say it again, you don't know me, Nancy. Sit doon a minute, an' if ye'll no fly off the handle, I'll tell ye whit ah think.

(NANCY *sits, takes out a cigarette, and lights it*)

NANCY: Fag?

ROUGER: Don't use them. Savin ma strength fur the big event.

NANCY: D'ye think it'll be worth it when the time comes?

ROUGER: No swankin now. If you were ma bird, ah wid look efter ye in a wey Charlie disnae, I don't think.

NANCY: Didnae know ye told fortunes.

ROUGER: See a fulla day in, day out. Jerkin that bar therr ower his nut a hunner times a session disnae mean tae say he's got confidence in the right places.

NANCY: You're daein the talkin.

ROUGER: Ye can tell me if ah'm wrang, but ah believe the strong-man stuff is strictly fur the onlookers. Whit's he like in the heat o the moment, when the defences are down, or when anythin' else is down, fur that matter? Noo don't get the spur. Has he ever set the brush on fire? In the clinch, ah mean?

NANCY: You'd like tae know, widn't ye?

ROUGER: Naw, but you should know. You should know the difference. Four year ye've been waitin, haven't ye? Waitin fur the man behind the muscle tae give ye a charge. Jist wance.

NANCY: Whit ye gettin at?

ROUGER: It's simple. He blouters hissel' intae a trance, breakin tissue, buildin the frame, an' for what? Another night when he leaves ye like a cauld pie on the doorstep.

NANCY: Mebbie ah'm not that kinda girl.

ROUGER: Ye are, Nancy, ye are. You're just waitin for the moment. It might come in a wey that wid surprise ye.

NANCY: Like when?

ROUGER: Let me pit it tae ye this wey. Charlie's a champ fae the finger-nails up. Ah'm like steel fae the waist doon. Ah've got power therr, Nancy. That machine ower therr, that bike, has built me somethin' you couldnae imagine in yur wildest fantasy.

NANCY: Ah think it's time ah wis leavin.

ROUGER: Jist hang on for a minute, Nancy. Jist a couple o shakes an' let me state ma case, and if you fancy it, prove it.

NANCY: The men'll soon be here.

ROUGER: We've jist got time. You said you've nothin' against me. Jist you let me take care o you for a minute, an' ah'll have somethin' lovely against you.

(NANCY *is almost mesmerised. The* ROUGER *slips his arms around her and half-presses her on to the bench. She is hooked. His hands engulf her, and she almost succumbs then*)

NANCY: No here! For God's sake, no here!

ROUGER: Ower here, then. The straw — a lovely bed for a lovely deed, hen. Come on, don't draw back now. I'll take care o ye, Nancy, that's it, that's it. Ye'll be a'right wi me.

(NANCY *allows herself to be led to the straw. The* ROUGER *is a snake-pit of fumbles. Partially out of sight, they seem to be at the moment of her undoing, when suddenly she looks up, catches sight of* NORRIE, *who has been watching fascinated, and screams, 'Who's that up there?' The pair scramble to their feet,* NANCY *pulling up her drawers, the* ROUGER *buttoning up in a fury of frustration.* NANCY *flies to the back door and disappears. The* ROUGER *spots* NORRIE)

ROUGER: Ya knee-crept, Jesus-crept, swatchin little fucker, ah'll cut the bliddy scrotum aff ye! Ah'll knacker an' gut ye, ah'll eviscerate ye! Ya hure-spun, bastrified, conscrapulated young prick, ah'll do twenty year fur mincin you. Ye hear me? Ah'll rip ye fae the gullet tae the groin, ah'll incinerate ye! Ah had her — right therr — ah had her, spreadeagled, waitin fur the knife — an' you blew it. You blew the chance o pittin wan in her, an' wan on Charlie. He's never had her, but ah wid have had her. Another minute, ah wid have scored where he's never scored, an' you shankered it, ya parish-eyed, perishin bastart. Well, whit she didnae get, you'll get. Come doon here, come doon ah'm tellin ye, ah'll pit a shot in your arse that'll feel like thunder. Come doon, ah tell ye, or are ye gaun tae stey up?

NORRIE: Ah'm feart tae stey up, but ah'm feart tae come doon.

ROUGER: You better, young-yin. Ye see this culet? Ah'll make a bayonet o this an' come up therr an' get ye. Ah'll stow ye in the rubbish, an' the rats'll guzzle whit's left o ye. Ah'm comin up!

NORRIE: Naw, don't, don't, Rouger, ah'm comin doon. Don't touch us, eh, don't touch us. Ah never meant tae watch ye, honest, ah'll no say anythin'. (*He drops to the floor*)

ROUGER: (*grabbing him*) By Christ, ye'll no say anythin', or ah'll tell them a' ah blocked ye 'cause ye wanted it. Ah'll dae that anywey.

(*He begins hauling* NORRIE *towards the straw*)

NORRIE: Lea's alane, ya dirty pig. Ah'll tell Charlie when he comes doon that sterr.

ROUGER: Ye'll whit? Ye'll no live that long! Ah'll hiv you stuffed an' parcelled in a coupla shakes.

LESLIE: (*Off*) Whit the hell's the row down there?

(*The* ROUGER *lets go of* NORRIE *and moves to the bottom of the stair, blocking the way out*)

ROUGER: Nothing, Leslie, nothing. Jist a bit o kiddin.

LESLIE: That's a terrible noise. Sounds like a bad day at Hampden. No more of it, now.

ROUGER: Yes, Leslie. Right ye are.

LESLIE: (*off*) See to it, then.

ROUGER: (*moving towards* NORRIE) Whit wis that you said aboot Charlie?

NORRIE: Said ah widnae tell him.

ROUGER: Or any o the others?

NORRIE: Them either.

ROUGER: Right. Ah'll gie ye another chance. You say nothin' tae anybody, specially Charlie, an' ah'll let ye aff this time.

NORRIE: Too true you'll fuckin let me aff, 'cause Charlie widnae let you aff.

ROUGER: Noo, don't needle me. Say nothin', we'll forget the haill thing. But you tell him, an' ah'm no kiddin, ah'll take a cuttin oot the culet box, an' they'll be stitchin you for ever.

NORRIE: Ye don't think ah'll be staunin here waitin fur it, dae ye?

ROUGER: Ye mean ye'll be takin a powder?

NORRIE: Ah'll no be loiterin.

ROUGER: An' whit wid ye say before ye go?

NORRIE: Ah widnae be wastin time.

ROUGER: Ha-ha, by Jeez, ah pit the wind up ye therr, didn't ah? Ye don't think ah mean a' that, dae ye?

NORRIE: Bliddy sure ye did.

ROUGER: Not at all. Whit ye take me fur? Ye heard me tellin Leslie it wis jist a bit o kiddin. That's a' it wis.

NORRIE: Widnae be kiddin if Charlie got tae hear aboot it.

ROUGER: Ah now, Norrie, ye cannae blame me therr, eh? Every man fur hissel', when it comes tae that. Ah mean, Nancy's quite a doll, isn't she?

NORRIE: Well, you leave me alane, an' ah'll be sayin nothin'. Nane o ma business anywey.

ROUGER: That's you screwin the nut now. We'll jist keep Charlie oot o this, 'cause if you open your mouth . . . ah'll get tae ye quick, believe it.

NORRIE: Jist keep yur hauns aff me.

ROUGER: Sure, sure. Peace an' love, eh?

NORRIE: Piece an' fuckin jam.

ROUGER: Ha-ha . . . that's good, that. (*The men's voices are heard returning.* BOB *and* PETER *come down first, followed soon afterwards by* JOE) Remember, no grass. Ye dae, I'll dig you up. New kipper, you.

PETER: Bob, you can take the drawers aff the bookies every day in the week, an' it'll give me pleasure tae stand alongside ye and drink the proceeds.

BOB: If ah make it wance a year ah'm no complainin. Buy ye another pint next year.

PETER: Where'll we a' be then?

BOB: Wi any luck we'll a' be somewhere. No so sure aboot the shop here. It's on its last legs.

PETER: Aye, like the trade.

BOB: Widnae say that, Peter. Maybe no the same class o work as there used tae be, but ther'll always be room fur a good man.

PETER: Well, right now ah havenae got room fur a' that lager. Ah'll away an' pour the totties. 'Oh dropping, dropping, dropping, dropping, hear the pennies fall . . . '

(PETER *goes to the lavatory.* JOE *arrives. The* ROUGER *keeps squinting at* NORRIE)

BOB: Ye enjoy yur piece, Norrie?

NORRIE: No bad.

BOB: Ye no go oot at a'?

NORRIE: Didnae bother.

JOE: The ghost no get ye?

NORRIE: Aye, he wis here.

BOB: Who wis that, then?

NORRIE: Said his name wis Alex. Alex Freer.

ROUGER: Ye didnae tell me that.

NORRIE: Ye never asked us.

BOB: Wis he right in the shop here?

NORRIE: Aye.

ROUGER: Wis he away before ah came in then?

NORRIE: Aye.

ROUGER: Ye sure aboot that?

NORRIE: Well, ye didnae see him here, did ye?

BOB: Christ, dae ye no know if he wis here?

ROUGER: He might have went oot the back . . . door.

BOB: Ye'd have seen him then, widn't ye? Whit ye gettin intae an uproar fur?

ROUGER: Jist askin.

BOB: Ye sure you're here the noo?

ROUGER: Naw, ah'm up on the rafters, higher an' higher.

(PETER *reappears from the lavatory*)

BOB: Hear that, Peter? Ould Alex Freer wis in here, an' the Rouger's no sure whether he saw him or no.

PETER: How, wis he invisible?

ROUGER: A'right, forget it. Jist thought he might have slipped away as ah came in.

BOB: Whit's up wi you?

ROUGER: Nothin'. Nothin's up wi' me.

NORRIE: He left a while before the Rouger got here.

PETER: Whit wis he wantin'?

NORRIE: He wis lookin fur you an' Bob.

PETER: Whit d'ye tell him?

NORRIE: Said yez wer doon in the pub.

PETER: That should have been enough tae sen' him gallopin.

NORRIE: He wis kinna shaky.

BOB: Ye mean he wisnae chasin us up tae the boozer when he left here?

NORRIE: Ah'm no sure.

PETER: Did he no put the tap on ye fur the price o a gill?

NORRIE: Naw, but ah gave him a dollar anywey.

JOE: Ye mean the dollar Bob gave ye, ye bunged that oul' stumor?

NORRIE: Ah suppose it wis.

JOE: That's a good yin, eh. First day here he carries the gaffer's stash, then throws away the dollar he gets bunged fur it.

NORRIE: Didnae mean it that wey. Jist felt sorry fur the man.

JOE: Whit ye make o that Rouger?

ROUGER: Very ungrateful boy, that. Devious-like.

NORRIE: Aye, like some other people no a mile away fae here.

BOB: Ach, whit's the odds? His dollar, wisn't it? Alex Freer look bad?

NORRIE: He wis sick.

BOB: He'll no get better. Hey, that whistle hasnae went. Time we were started.

(CHARLIE *runs down the stair in a fury*)

PETER: See any sign o ould Alex in yur travels, Charlie?

CHARLIE: Saw naebody — naebody — nutt anybody!

(CHARLIE *slings his jacket and goes to the weight. He lifts it straight up six times and then lets it fall with a smash. The men cringe and go to their wheels, starting up one by one*)

BOB: Whit's eatin ye, Charlie?

CHARLIE: Forty-five minutes ah stood on that corner. Not a sign, not a whiff. By Jeez, she'll wait fur me, ah'm tellin ye.

ROUGER: (*on hot cinders, watching* NORRIE) Nancy no show up, or somethin'?

CHARLIE: That's right — or somethin'. I'm staunin therr like a motionless pump . . . forty-five . . . fuckin minutes . . .

ROUGER: Ye must be angry, Charlie, no often we hear you swearin.

CHARLIE: Yeh. By Christ ah'm angry, ah'll . . . ah'll . . .

(*He goes to the weight again and snatches it overhead*)

BOB: Aw naw, Charlie, naw. Ye'll hav us a' in the nut-hoose if ye drap that thing again. (CHARLIE *smashes it down*) That's the grand bastart finale, Charlie Weir! Noo ah don't give a shite if Nancy's running ye shammy-leggit, you're in here tae work, so leave the bleedin heart ootside an' start graftin, an' get that bliddy earthshaker oot o here fur wance an' fur a'. Nine shell-shocked, pile-drivin bliddy year we've had o it, so finish now, finish! Ye get it oot o' here . . . ah don't care how ye dae it — ye can stuff it in yur back pocket or ram it up yur nose, but oot it goes . . . Friday at the latest.

ROUGER: That's short notice you're giving him, Bob.

(CHARLIE *is not sure where he is. He blinks and gets to work*)

BOB: You get tae yur work, plaster arse. Noo listen, everybody, we get a' the odds and ends an' rush jobs cleared up before we start on the big job this efternoon. Get stuck intae it, now. Norrie, ye got plenty o pomas therr?

NORRIE: Aye.

BOB: Right, where's that oul' mirror nou?

(ALL *work for a short spell during which the grinder screeches its loudest, and then goes quiet as* PETER *approaches* BOB)

PETER: Eh Bob, ah'm sorry tae bother ye. Ah should have noticed it before, but the grinder's pretty faur worn doon. Ah don't know if there's enough left in it tae see the big job through.

BOB: That's a' we need. Ah wish tae hell ye had seen that before, Peter. Nae time tae set a new wheel in noo.

PETER: Naw.

BOB: That's a problem right enough. Any suggestions?

PETER: No unless we use the ould mill tae we get a new wheel on. It wid be the day efter the morra before the new yin wid be right fur a job like that.

BOB: Nothin' left in that wheel therr at a'?

PETER: Oh aye, but it might no be enough. Might be doon tae the metal before we knew it.

BOB: We'll have a look at it. Norrie, you run up the sterr an' tell Leslie ah wid like tae see him. Let him come doon here fur a change. (NORRIE *goes off upstairs.* BOB *and* PETER *go to the grinder*) . . . Ah don't think that's too bad, Peter. I think it'll jist last. Whit d'ye say yoursel'?

PETER: It could last, mebbie. On the other hand, ye know how it goes. Wan minute ye've got a grinder, the next minute you're through tae the wheel.

BOB: Ah wid chance it anywey. But jist in case, we'll get the boys tae sieve some saun fur the oul' mill. Hey, Joe, when Norrie comes doon start gettin' a wee load o saun ower here an' sieve it. Peter, have a look at the belts and see they're a'right. Well, come on, Joe, get crackin.

JOE: Whit, sievin saun?

BOB: Aye, sievin saun, whit d'ye think?

JOE: It's two year since ah sieved saun — ah don't know if ah can dae it noo.

BOB: Oh aye, ye'll have forgot the intricacies. Ye cairry saun tae the mill and run it wet through the sieve. That's a hell of a lot tae forget, right enough.

JOE: That's no ma job any mair, Bob. Ah'm bevellin noo.

BOB: We're a' bevellin! You've done the job before, so show the boy, an' if it ever needs done again, he'll dae it. Get the pails ready, he'll cairry some fur ye.

JOE: Ah hate sievin saun.

BOB: Ye'll hate gettin a kick in the arse if ah land ye wan. Whit d'ye make o it? Open bliddy rebellion fae the junior staff. If there wis a war on they wid take ye oot in a Mexican hat an' shoot ye. (NORRIE *returns down the stair*) Whit kept ye?

NORRIE: He wis on the phone. He says you've tae go up.

BOB: Whit — ye mean tae say he couldnae even . . . right! Ah'll go up an' ah'll tell him a few things. Jist wance, ye want a wee conference wi the heid o the hoose an' whit happens? He'll no even come hauf wey tae meet ye. (*He starts to mount the stair*)

NORRIE: Yur apron, Bob.

BOB: Ach, bugger the apron. You get wi Joe an' learn how tae sieve saun.

NORRIE: Whit's a sieve?

BOB: Oh by Jeez, ah've heard everythin' noo. Whit's a sieve? Ah'll away up before ma arteries start tae chuck it.

    (BOB *goes off upstairs*)

JOE: Right you! See if ye can cairry a pailful o saun.

NORRIE: Ah'll go pail fur pail wi you anytime an' chance it.

JOE: Ye should be daein' it by yursel'. No ma' job noo.

NORRIE: Ah'll hiv tae learn it first, win't ah?

JOE: Imagine, never heard o a sieve before.

NORRIE: Ah'm waitin fur you tae tell me.

JOE: Rouger, this yin disnae know whit a sieve is.

ROUGER: Oh, riddle me ree, wan two three, up Mick's arse in the breweree.

NORRIE: Thanks fur wisin us up.

ROUGER: Ah said it, didn't ah? Riddle me ree, riddle, riddle, riddle. Never heard o' a riddle? An' ah don't mean a conundorum. The other kind.

NORRIE: Wan o these roun' things?

ROUGER: That's right — wi the meat safe in the end o it.

JOE: Now ye know — so full up two pails an' carry them ower. (NORRIE *fills the pails. They are heavy, and he doesn't find it easy.* JOE *has taken his load out of sight beyond the grinder*)

PETER: That's the stuff, young fulla. Pit muscles on ye, that.

NORRIE: Aye, a' we need's the ankle-chains.

(JOE *returns for more sand*)

JOE: Moanin already. Instant greetin-face. Wan load o saun, an' he's knackered.

NORRIE: You lay affa me. I might be out ma class wi everybody else in here, but ah'll give you a run fur it any time ye fancy it.

JOE: Mebbe ah fancy it right now. (NORRIE *drops the sand,* JOE *is a fraction unsure. Just then,* BOB *comes down* . . .) Ah'll see you later.

PETER: Don't let him rummle ye, son. Him an' that Rouger, they're a coupla poe-naggers.

BOB: Some game this, eh? Ye go up the stair tae ask for a bit o' advice, an' whit dae ye get? 'You're the foreman, Bob, you know the job and what's required, it's your responsibility.' That's the manager fur ye.

PETER: Well, he didnae know hissel', did he?

BOB: You're right. Nearly shat hissel' when ah brought it up. Never mind — hauf-past two or earlier we get on wi the big yin. Ma decision. Much saun ye got through therr?

JOE: Eight pails.

BOB: That'll dae. Start sievin it. Back tae the polisher, Norrie . . . (*He works for a short spell at the old mirror, then holds it up to the light, and decides it's all right*) Right, Rouger, ye can take this thing an' gie it a finish. Don't waste too much time on it.

(*The* ROUGER *takes the mirror, and* BOB *lifts another job. Suddenly there's a splintering of glass.* CHARLIE *turns away from his wheel. He has a bad cut on his left hand*)

CHARLIE: Christ, ah'm wounded! Ah'm goutin like a punctured bliddy pig.

ROUGER: (*first to move*) Let us see that. Oh, that's bad, Charlie, very bad. Better get Leslie tae phone the ambulance.

CHARLIE: Naw, nae ambulance, nae hospitals! It's jist across the palm. Ah'll get it bandaged up in the office.

BOB: Right enough, Charlie, it looks gey bad.

CHARLIE: It's no too deep, it'll be a'right wi a bandage.

ROUGER: Never. That's serious, that. Need's stitchin, ah'm tellin' ye. Good anaesthetic, ye'll no feel a thing.

CHARLIE: Nae hospitals, ah said!

BOB: Ah think ye better see a doctor anywey.

CHARLIE: Nae doctors! Ah'm seein nae doctors!

ROUGER: Ye'll feel nothin', Charlie, honest. They'll clean it oot wi a bit o spirit — well, that's sore, right enough — an' shove the old needle in, draw it thegither, an' you're bran' new.

CHARLIE: Shurrup, Rouger! Ah'm no gaun anywhere. Ah'm gaun up that sterr an' get a dressin on it.

BOB: Ah'll come wi ye.

CHARLIE: Ah'll go masel'. Stey away fae me, everybody.

(CHARLIE *goes off upstairs*)

ROUGER: Therr goes the hero fur ye. Mister Universe. He wis shitin hissel' sidie-weys in case he had tae go tae the hospital.

BOB: That wis a bad cut.

ROUGER: Aye, palm o his hand. Nae merr hair growin therr fur a while, eh?

PETER: You're a monster, Matchett. A diabonical, lousy big twat. Your mate cuts hissel', an' you're crawin. You're an imbecile.

ROUGER: Ach, away you an' fa' aff the spar.

BOB: Peter's right. Everybody's bad luck's your excuse fur laughin.

ROUGER: He'll no be slingin that weight o his aboot so handy noo, ah'll wager ye.

BOB: That's wherr he's always had ye, isn't it?

ROUGER: Had me nothin'. Every man tae his ain exertion. Ah'll be nickin up the Lochside this weekend at the goin rate fur all good pedallers — somethin' he knows nothin' about — while he's greetin ower his sore mitt an' soilin his drawers in case he has tae go tae the doctor. He's knackerless. If he ever gets a hard on, he'll think it's a fart that's went the wrang wey.

BOB: Go an' finish that job.

ROUGER: Wan dab, half a jiffy, it's yours.

BOB: Whit we gaun tae dae aboot that job if Charlie's oot the game? Widnae like tae trust Joe as the fourth man.

PETER: Charlie might jist manage it.

BOB: Very doubtful. Did ye get a look at that cut?

PETER: Naw, ah wisnae too keen on a close inspection.

BOB: Couldnae tell if it wis really bad or no. Ye know, Peter, it's a while since ah've seen a really bad injury at the job. Ah wis tellin the boy earlier aboot the day a hauf plate came off the polisher an' caught a man in the back o the leg. He never walked right again.

PETER: That Eddie McCance?

BOB: Aye, did ye know him?

PETER: Heard aboot him up in the Northern Glass.

BOB: Ah believe he finished up therr.

PETER: Nice an' near Lambhill Cemetery.

ROUGER: That's you, no much tae it, as you said. Whit's next?

BOB: Jist use yur eyes. Plenty lying aboot.

ROUGER: You're the gaffer.

BOB: Come on ower, Norrie. We'll set this back in its frame. Go tae ma inside pocket, an' ye'll find a paper therr — seein these intelligent fullas had the good sense tae set fire tae the ould yin. A'right, noo, hauf a dozen tacks or so, an' it'll be restored tae its former glory. Wee tap wi the hammer and jist bend them over gently. That'll haud it lovely. Jist a wee couple merr an' we'll be home. Therr we go. Mind you, when ye see it in that frame, it's right. Aye, dead right. Ah didnae gie it much o a glance when it came in, but noo ah see it, it's all of a piece. Gless and frame in wan union, quite delicate and nicely balanced. Ah don't know who the oul' fulla wis that set his haun tae the bevellin — an' mebbie he wisnae seein too straight when he did it — but ah can read him — ah can see he wis wan o ma ain kind. As ah said before, he wid take it through a' the stages fae the mill tae the rouger, an' if he earned seven an' tanner fur his day's work, he thought he wis king of the land. When ah look in a gless, Norrie, ah don't jist see masel', ah see the age o the job, the quality, the craftsmanship, and the style. Ah can very near see the face o the man that wis therr before me. Here's Leslie comin wi Charlie.

(LESLIE *and* CHARLIE *come down the stairs.* CHARLIE*'s hand is bandaged, and* LESLIE *is carrying a crystal bowl*)

LESLIE: He's not too bad, Bob. Bad enough, you know, but not so bad that he'd have to go to hospital.

BOB: Are ye sayin' that fur Charlie's sake or the sake o the big job therr?

LESLIE: No . . . eh . . . the job comes into it, of course, but Charlie says he can manage.

CHARLIE: That's right, ah'll manage.

BOB: Aye, but will ye manage yur corner at the job?

CHARLIE: Ah said ah'll manage. I've still got wan good haun.

BOB: It's no the good haun ah'm worried aboot, it's the other yin.

CHARLIE: This good haun' o mine is better than two o anybody else's in here. An' if anybody didnae hear that, they better flush their ears oot.

BOB: Naebody's questionin yur strength, Charlie, but ye need a coupla hauns for this job.

CHARLIE: Look, wan good haun tae support the board an' the other tae keep ma end steady. Ah'll be fine. Ah'll rest the left yin on tap o the job, an' it'll be dandy.

BOB: A'right, if you say so. It's your haun.

LESLIE: You'll get a start made this afternoon, Bob?

BOB: That's whit ah said, an' that's whit we'll dae. Listen, Leslie, dae us a favour. Tell me whit a' the rush is aboot. I mean, why start the day?

LESLIE: I promised the job for delivery on Thursday. If we don't get on with it today, it'll still be down here on Wednesday. It's got to be up the stair tomorrow afternoon at the latest.

BOB: I wish ye widnae pit us a' on the rack like that, Leslie. Whit's that ye've got wi ye?

LESLIE: Well, actually, Bob, it's a small emergency that just came in.

BOB: Ye don't mean ye want us tae tackle that the noo?

LESLIE: Let me explain, Bob . . .

BOB: Aw, Jesus Johnnie, Leslie, give us a break.

LESLIE: It's a small crisis, Bob. An old friend brought this in just before Charlie came up the stair.

BOB: Oh aye, upset, wis she?

LESLIE: It wasn't a she, it was a he. And he was upset. Look, see the rim there. There's the tiniest piece out of it. It's a presentation — an office presentation — and by some accident somebody has knocked a small chip out of it.

BOB: They should take it back tae the shop an' say it's a bad yin.

LESLIE: Don't think they haven't tried it. They were chased. Anyway, the presentation's at five o'clock this evening. You know, small office party and a few drinks.

BOB: Oh, that's fine, we'll a' go alang.

LESLIE: Come on, Bob, can you fake this so as the chap will never notice it?

BOB: Let us see it. Where is it? Oh, therr? No much in that. If they cannae get that past him he must have microscopic eyes.

LESLIE: They don't want to take a chance he'd spot it. What do you say, Bob?

BOB: A'right, leave it wi us. Wee touch o the handstone an' the polisher, it'll be bang in front.

LESLIE: Good, good. Then you'll start the big one, eh?

BOB: Ah'd like the boys tae get a drap o tea first.

LESLIE: Sure, sure. But right after that?

BOB: As you say, Leslie, right after that.

LESLIE: Thanks, Bob, I'll leave you to it, then.

    (LESLIE *goes off upstairs*)

BOB: Ah've said it before, an' ah'll say it again. Skinner by name an' Skinner by nature. Nae wunner ould Alex went on the sauce. Joe, make the tea.

JOE: It's made.

BOB: Thank you, son. Anythin' bad ah've said aboot you the day, Joe, cancel it. You're a good, clever, conscientious boy. Get yur tea lads, quick as ye can. Peter, a wee touch o the handstone on that crystal. Ah'll smooth it aff on the polisher when you're done.

    (ALL *get their tea. Distantly a pipe band is heard. It gets nearer, accompanied by the sound of marching feet overhead*)

NORRIE: Whit's that?

PETER: Must be that time o the year again.

ROUGER: Aye, the bastarts.

NORRIE: Is it the army?

ROUGER: No quite, but it could be.

PETER: Happens every year at this time. The Academy boys. The Officers Corps, or whatever they call them. Aff tae the summer camp.

ROUGER: Bunch o ponced-up parasitical twats. Mummies and daddies walking alongside the darling boys to see them off at the station.

NORRIE: Wish ah wis gaun wi them.

ROUGER: You'll never see it. Not if ye had six lifetimes.

    (*The band and procession draw nearer and pass by overhead.* ALL *listen quietly until they pass. Then* PETER *hands the bowl over to* BOB, *who touches it very gently on the polisher*)

ROUGER: Naw, naw. You'll never be amongst it, young-yin. They're up there, an' you're doon here, an' even if ye wer grindin yur guts tae get up therr amongst it, next year when they go by you'll still be doon here, like the rest o us.

NORRIE: No me. Ah'll no be here.

ROUGER: No good enough fur ye, 's 'at it?

NORRIE: Didnae say that.

ROUGER: Ye fancy yoursel' up therr wi that mob?

NORRIE: Jist fancy gettin away tae hell oot the road. See a bit o the country.

ROUGER: But ye think ye'd make the grade wi the grandees up therr?

NORRIE: No ma style.

ROUGER: But a' this is no yur style either?

NORRIE: Whit ye talkin aboot? Fae whit ah've heard, you're never done gaun on aboot divin oot the country yursel'.

ROUGER: Aye, but on ma terms. Shovin that bike up the road's a different thing a'thegither fae kiss-my-arse and daddy's bankbook. Whit are *your* terms?

NORRIE: No money anyway. Mebbie a job on a van or somethin'. That oul' man, Alex, wis tellin us tae blow this job and get oot in the fresh air.

ROUGER: Ye listen tae him ye'll end up in Carrick Street Model. Did ye believe him?

NORRIE: Don't know. Made sense the wey he said it.

BOB: Don't think ye fancy this game much, young fulla.
    (*He gives the bowl a wipe and lays it down*)

NORRIE: Don't like some o the folk in it.

BOB: It's a hard trade wi crude beginnins. Some o that's bound tae have rubbed aff. We're a wee bit on the rough side. Mebbie as time goes on you'll no notice it so much.

NORRIE: Aye.

BOB: Well come on then, fullas, it's now or never. Yur eye in, Peter?

PETER: Bang on.

BOB: Ye fit, Charlie?

CHARLIE: Yes!

BOB: Right! We'll get stevered intae the big yin therr. Youz young fullas might see another job like that in yur lifetimes again, but it's no' likely. We'll start on the grinder therr, but any sign o the wheel packin in, we transfer tae the ould mill. Right, Peter?

PETER: Right.

BOB: Rouger, you an' Joe bring the big trestle-board through fae the back. We'll lie it up against the job an' jist ease it gently ower tae the horizontal. (JOE *and the* ROUGER *go for the board. It is a large wooden frame of four crossed spars. The men complete the operation of placing the board against the plate and tilting it over to the horizontal.* PETER *goes to the corner which will be nearest the grinder.* BOB *calls instructions to the men*) Easy, noo, lads. Wan step at a time tae we get used tae it. Jist keep it steady when Peter gets his corner on tae the wheel. The board'll take up the vibration.

(*Just then*, LESLIE *hurries down the stair*)

LESLIE: Hold it, Bob. Hold it, boys.

BOB: Hold it? We've jist got tae hold it. We cannae drap it on the fuckin flerr.

LESLIE: No need to use that language in front of young boys, Bob.

BOB: These young boys have got words we've never even heard o. Whit's the panic?

LESLIE: You didn't forget that bowl, did you?

BOB: Christ, is that a' ye want tae ask? We're staunin here wi this thing in wur hauns, an' you're worryin aboot some stupid article that some half-arsed cowboy'll use for a chanty in the middle o the night.

LESLIE: You don't have to be so crude.

BOB: It's lyin ower therr. Gie it a wipe, an' it'll be champion.

LESLIE: You managed to get the mark out?

BOB: Aye, aye. Noo, will ye kindly take a walk up these sterrs an' leave us in peace?

LESLIE: You might be the foreman here, Bob, but you are talking to the manager.

BOB: The manager that didnae gie me much co-operation when I was askin fur yur ideas a wee while ago. It wis up tae me, ye said. A'right, then, it's up tae me an' ah'll see the job done. Away you an' staun up at the front door an' scratch yur arse.

(LESLIE *leaves*)

A'right noo, mind whit ah said, jist take it easy, an' we'll put a bevel on this thing that ye could hing in a palace. (*The job begins.* NORRIE, *standing by, holds his ears. All seems to be going well when* PETER'*s face begins to tighten, unnoticed by the others. Then he begins to jerk, and the plate flaps wildly*) Mind the job, fur Christ's sake, mind the job! Joe, grab Peter's end. Norrie, get the haud o Peter an' lie him doon. Ye hear me, Norrie, stir yur arse fur fuck's sake, an' get Peter on tae that low bench. (NORRIE *is rooted and can't move*) Rouger, leave your end tae Charlie and grab Peter. Don't be rough wi him, noo. That's it, lie him doon. Jist leave him, an' gie's a haun wi this thing. Norrie, ya useless young bugger ye, get oot the road. Right, lads, quick as ye can, get this thing against the wa'. Up she goes, easy, noo. How's Peter? Jist leave him, he'll come oot o it soon. Charlie, ye look as though you're in some bother wi that haun.

CHARLIE: It wis fine tae ah had tae take the full weight o the end.

(LESLIE *appears*)

LESLIE: What's going on?

BOB: Ach . . . Peter took wan o his turns. He's lyin oot on the bench therr.

LESLIE: Is it just the usual or is it worse, do you think?

BOB: How the hell dae ah know, ah'm no a doctor. He looks like he always looks when this comes on him. Have a glance at him yursel'.

LESLIE: No, I'll leave that to you and the men. You've dealt with it before.

BOB: Aye, an' ah suppose we'll deal wi it again the next time it happens.

LESLIE: Is the job all right?

BOB: Oh, that's whit's on yur mind? I knew it couldnae be Peter.

LESLIE: That's unfair, Bob. You know Peter's been kept on here despite his disability.

BOB: An' because ye couldnae get his like anywhere else.

LESLIE: I won't argue with you. I'll be in the office if you need me.

　　　(LESLIE *goes*)

BOB: Whit's up wi ye, Norrie? You're staunin therr like a stumor.

NORRIE: He's dead, isn't he?

BOB: Who, Peter? Not at all.

NORRIE: Ah've only seen wan . . . I mean . . . he looks like it.

BOB: Ye'll see him worse than that, mebbie, if you're here long enough.

NORRIE: Ah'll no see him. Ah'm chuckin it.

ROUGER: He's movin a wee bit noo.

CHARLIE: Bob, ye mind if ah go up tae the end o the shop?

BOB: Naw, on ye go, Charlie. Ye'll have tae go tae the hospital wi that thing.

CHARLIE: Aye, we'll see.

ROUGER: Ah don't want tae be around when the likes o that happens again. Ah thought we were a' gaun tae be minced.

BOB: Don't make it any worse than it wis. If it had been an ordinary job it widnae have looked so bad.

ROUGER: Couldnae have been much worse. Leslie's right, he's lucky he's got a job.

BOB: An' this shop's lucky it's got Peter. He's got the best eye o any beveller ah ever met, tae any fraction you like tae quote. An' he can horse it wi anybody . . . he's no feart tae bend his back.

ROUGER: You'll no hear a bad word aboot him, will ye?

BOB: No fae you anywey. You're always tryin tae make oot he's epileptic when he's no. He's had a' the tests, an' they've told him he's no epileptic, not that it wid worry me in the least if he wis.

ROUGER: Whit dae you think's up wi him, then?

BOB: Ah don't know. Some kind o tension when he's excited or upset.

ROUGER: Jist as well he's got you fur a china.

BOB: That's right, an' don't you forget it. (PETER *sits up slowly*) A'right, then, Peter, how ye feelin?

PETER: Ah? Aye. Whit time is it?

BOB: How ye doin, oul' son? You're gey faur away.

PETER: Ah wis supposed tae meet . . . this big fulla at the corner . . . he had a parcel fur me.

BOB: Sure, sure. Wid ye like a wee drap tea tae clear yur heid? Joe, any merr tea left?

PETER: Took me a' ma time . . . ye know . . . ma fingers were thon funny wey . . . an' then . . .

BOB: Jist slipped away, did it?

PETER: Fell aff the spar. Aw, God love us . . . that you, Bob?

BOB: Aye.

PETER: Are we late?

BOB: Naw, we're no late, plenty o time.

PETER: We're in the shop?

BOB: That's right.

PETER: That's funny, ah thought . . .

BOB: Easy, Peter.

PETER: Ah pass out?

BOB: Yes.

PETER: Ah break anythin'?

BOB: Naw, naw. Come on, ah'll take ye tae the back door fur a wee bit air.

PETER: Aye, sure. That big bastart tell me tae fa' aff the spar?

BOB: Ah believe he mentioned it.

PETER: He wis right then, wisn't he? Stuck in ma mind.

(BOB *and* PETER *go to the back door*)

JOE: You challenged me a while ago.

NORRIE: Naw, ah didnae.

JOE: Ye said ye fancied yur chances anywey.

NORRIE: Ah wis browned off.

JOE: Ah wisnae needlin ye a' that much.

NORRIE: Naw, but he wis.

ROUGER: Now, mind your mouth, you.

NORRIE: Don't worry, I'm saying nothin'. A' ah'm waitin fur's the five o'clock whistle an' ah'm jackin it in.

JOE: When, the day?

NORRIE: Aye.

JOE: Less than wan day at the job, an' you're turnin it up already?

NORRIE: Ah'd never be any use at it anywey.

ROUGER: How dae ye know?

NORRIE: Ah jist know.

ROUGER: Like it's a' right fur the common grafters, but no fur the likes o you.

NORRIE: It's nothin' tae dae wi that.

JOE: Ah don't get it. It's a job, int it — it's a trade. Whit'll yur oul'-man say when ye tell him?

NORRIE: He'll say try somethin' else.

ROUGER: Whit wis it finally got ye? Seein Peter, wis it?

NORRIE: Didnae help.

ROUGER: Ah thought that sickened ye. Remind ye o somethin'?

NORRIE: You keep our mouth shut, an' ah'll keep mine.

ROUGER: Ah'm easy.

(BOB *comes back with* PETER)

BOB: He's no hissel'. Try a wee drap o that tea, Joe. Take Peter wi ye.

JOE: He said he's leavin the day, Bob.

BOB: Who?

JOE: Him, Norrie.

BOB: 'S 'at a fact? Well, ah don't suppose wan boy here or therr'll make any difference tae this trade. (*He goes to the foot of the stair*) Hey, Leslie, Leslie, ye hear me? Wid ye mind comin tae the heid of the sterr fur a minute, ah want a word wi ye? Take that tea slow, Peter, it'll dae ye good. Ah think ye can pit yur jaicket on, tae. Listen, Leslie, ah think we better a' pack it in fur the day. Charlie's no fit, an Peter should go hame. Ah'll have tae see him up the road. Nae sense in the rest hingin on. Whit dae ye say?

LESLIE: Hold on, Bob, I was on the phone. I'll have to finish the call and think about it.

BOB: There's nothin' tae think aboot. If me an' Peter are no here, there's nothin' the rest can dae.

LESLIE: I'll finish this call an' blow the whistle. It might take a few minutes.

BOB: Got tae be manager, hisn't he? He'll blaw the whistle, but in his ain time. Can ye manage yur jaicket, Charlie?

CHARLIE: Ah'll be a'right.

(BOB *and* CHARLIE *begin preparing to leave*)

NORRIE: Ah'm sorry, Bob. Wisnae you ah meant when ah said ah didnae like some o the folk in here.

BOB: Jist as well ye told me that. Ah widnae have slept the night.

NORRIE: An' ah'm sorry aboot the job. Ah mean leavin.

BOB: Don't apologise tae me. You're no comin tae the trade, so forget it. This time the morra ah'll have forgotten you. It's nae insult tae me if you don't want tae work at this job. Ah didnae think ye wid stick it long anyway. That's the wey it goes. New folk don't want tae come intae the game, an' some o them that are at it don't give a toss fur it. So save yur apologies. Makes nae odds tae me. How ye shapin up, Peter?

(JOE *and* ROUGER *have been whispering together and now approach* NORRIE)

ROUGER: Jist wan thing you missed in this job, Mac.

NORRIE: Whit wis that?

ROUGER: Ye didnae get baptised.

(*The* ROUGER *and* JOE *grab* NORRIE *and rush him to the trough, where they shove his head under the water.* JOE *lets go quite soon; but the* ROUGER, *who has* NORRIE *by the hair, holds him under till he almost passes out.* BOB *intervenes*)

BOB: Whit ye daein, Rouger, fur Christ's sake, ye want tae kill the boy?

ROUGER: Jist wettin his heid.

BOB: Ye couldnae let him go, could ye? You had tae get the needle in. Ye might've droont him, ya bliddy eediot.

ROUGER: Fuck him. He's no wan o us.

BOB: He didnae deserve that, anyway.

(*The* ROUGER *collects his bike and brings it to the foot of the stairs to join the others.* NORRIE *recovers slowly. The whistle goes.* ALL *begin to leave*)

NORRIE: Hey, Charlie, Nancy wis in here at dinner-time. The Rouger tried tae shag her.

(ALL *stop. There is a long silence*)

BOB: Come on, Peter, ah'll take ye up the road.

(BOB *and* PETER *leave.* JOE *is merely a bystander.* CHARLIE *considers his hand, but advances slightly on the* ROUGER)

CHARLIE: Ah'm wan-handed, Rouger, but if whit that boy says is true, ah'll take you, ah'll take you, an' ah'll mash ye intae the slurry.

ROUGER: He's a liar, Charlie. Honest tae God on the old-lady's grave, ah'll give ye ma genuine Bible oath, he's a liar.

CHARLIE: Whit made him say it?

ROUGER: Ah don't know, ah really don't know. He jist couldnae take the kiddin, ah suppose, an' made it up fur badness.

CHARLIE: Ah believe ye. Now, you listen, boy, that's the second time you've raised Nancy's name the day, an' each time ye soiled it.

(CHARLIE *punches* NORRIE *in the stomach, and* NORRIE *folds up.* JOE, *the* ROUGER, *and* CHARLIE *go up the stairs.* NORRIE *lies on the floor gasping in pain. After some time, he gets to his feet and begins weeping deep, hard sobs which come from the pain in his body. He supports himself on the trough, but seems unable to make any kind of decision. At last* LESLIE *comes down the stair*)

LESLIE: What's the matter with you, sonny, have they been giving you a rough time? It sometimes happens with new boys. They haven't really hurt you, have they? That's all right, then. I think you better get up the stair. Where's your jacket? I'll get it for you. This bag belong to you, too? All right, come on then, up you go. Your stomach sore, eh? Ah, you'll be all right. Away home to your mother, and you'll be all right.

Glossary

bag, sack, dismiss
blooters hissel, exhausts himself, gets drunk
boozer, pub
bunged, paid, usually illicitly
Carrick Street Model, hostel for the homeless
champer, potato masher
chanty, chamber pot
china, friend, mate
chuck, food
chuckin it, giving up, resigning
crawin, rejoicing, crowing
diabastric and blohoorable, (invented expletives)
dollar roll-up, a form of bet
fifty-sixer, a, fifty-six pound barbell
get wired in, get to work, get going
grafter, hard worker
grass, informing, telling tales
gringo talk, outsider's talk
jacksies, backsides
peddle your duff, sell your goods
piece workers, workers paid by the number of pieces of work they complete rather than by the hour or week
pit the breeze up, scare
poe-naggers, people who worry a child on its pot
pour the tatties, go to the toilet, urinate
shaggin the dog, wasting time
shammy-leggit, crooked legged
sodie heidit, stupid
stour, dust, dirt
Teuchter, Highlander, Gaelic speaker
rummle, rumble, rummage
shitehouse, toilet
stumor, idiot
takin a powder, running away
wine-mopper, alcoholic

Donald Campbell

The Jesuit

(1976)

CHARACTERS

Father John Ogilvie
Archbishop Spottiswoode
Lady Rachel Spottiswoode

Soldiers in Spottiswoode's service:
Andrew
Will
Wat
Sandy

Doctor
Hangman

[*The language of the characters*:
Ogilvie speaks English with an officer-class accent. Spottiswoode
speaks Scots, although conventional English spelling is used for
many of the words. This is to allow the actor freedom to modulate
the degree of Scots in Spottiswoode's speech at different points in
the play. For the sake of uniformity, a similar orthography is used
with Lady Spottiswoode. The soldiers all speak an Edinburgh
dialect of Scots.]

Introduction

Donald Campbell was born in Wick, Caithness, in 1940 and established his reputation as a poet in the 1970s with volumes such as *Rhymes 'n Reason* (1972). He has lived mostly in Edinburgh and his poetry follows the model of Edinburgh poets such as Robert Garioch, whose contemporary use of Edinburgh urban dialect is mixed with an awareness of the traditions of Scots from the eighteenth century. Both Garioch and Campbell are particularly aware of the work of the eighteenth-century poet Robert Fergusson, whose poems use vernacular speech to display the richness and variety of the lower-class social world of urban Scotland.

Campbell's dramatic work focuses on historical periods or geographical locations in which Scots is the normal speech of the community and where the author does not need to justify the use of Scots in purely artistic — rather than naturalistic — terms. *The Widows of Clyth* (1979), for instance, explores the impact on a small community of a fishing tragedy, and gets its dramatic effects from the authenticity of the characters' speech. *The Jesuit* exploits effectively a modernised version of the Scots of the last age before English became the language of the ruling classes.

The historical conflict which *The Jesuit* explores is still a live issue in Scotland, since religion remains a matter of significant division, manifested in the country's divided educational system, which allows children to attend non-denominational or Catholic schools. Sectarianism continues to haunt Scottish life, the often unacknowledged basis of community identity from the accepted confrontations of football supporters to the underlying religious biases of political parties.

John Ogilvie was the first Scottish cleric to be sanctified. By focusing on this character, seen in the light of his contemporary elevation to sainthood, Campbell dramatises key issues of Scottish tradition and the ways in which a past Scotland — the Scotland of pre-Reformation Catholicism — relates to a Scotland where Catholicism has played a crucial role in defining modern Scottish identity — if only by challenging the traditional conceptions of Scotland as a resolutely Calvinist country.

'It has plesit God to cast in my hands a Jesuit, that calls himself Ogilvie . . . In his bulget we haif found his vestementis and other furniture for the masse with some bookis and reliques of S. Ignatius, S. Margaret, S. Katherin and other thair saints; also some writtis amongst qhiche the principal is a Catalogue of things left be Father Anderson, a Jesuit in Scotland qho semis to be furth of the countrey. Thairby your Majestie wil persaif the furniture of bookis and vestementis that haif in store against the day they looke for, and sum of thair freindschip with qhom the samin is reservit.' *Archbishop John Spottiswoode to James VI, October* 1614.

'If nothing could be found but that he was a Jesuit and had said Mass they should banish him the country and inhibit him to return without licence under pain of death. But if it should appear that he had been a practiser for the stirring up of subjects to rebellion or did maintain the Pope's transcendent power over kings and refused to take the Oath of Allegiance they should leave him to the course of law and justice.' *King James's reply.*

'If the King will be to me as his predecessors were to mine I will obey and acknowledge him for my King but, if he do otherwise and play the runagate from God, as he and you all do, I will not acknowledge him more than this old hat.' *Father John Ogilvie S.J., Speech at his trial, March* 1615.

ACT ONE — SCENE ONE

Glasgow 1614. An ante-room in the provost's house at four o'clock on a bitterly cold October afternoon. The room is small, furnished only by a table, a chair and a short bench. On the table (which is on the left side of the room) is a decanter, two goblets and a jug of water. Opposite the table is a small fireplace in which a freshly-lit fire is blazing. The bench is between the fire and the table, lying along the wall beneath the window. The window is open and the howling of an angry mob can be heard outside.

WILL: (*off*) Come on, man! Get aff yer knees! Get a move on!

ANDREW: (*off*) Dinna talk tae him, Wullie! For Christ's sake, dinnae jist talk tae him! If he winna move, gie him yer fuckin buits!

> (ANDREW, OGILVIE *and* WILL *enter from the right. The soldiers are contrasting types —* ANDREW *is a grizzled veteran,* WILL *a raw recruit. Both are plainly frightened but disguise their fear in different ways —* WILL *takes it out on* OGILVIE *and* ANDREW *takes it out on* WILL. OGILVIE *is a fair-complexioned man in his middle thirties. He has had a bad mauling from the mob — his face is a mass of scratches, his shirt is torn and open at the waist and a swordless scabbard is twisted round his back. He grips his cloak rather desperately in his right hand. He takes two steps into the room and falls, exhausted, flat on his face.*
>
> ANDREW *goes to the window and pulls it shut, blocking off the noise of the mob which is, in any case, beginning to die away)*

WILL: Aw Jesus Christ! (*kicks* OGILVIE *in the kidneys and spits on him*) Ye papish bastard! Damn ye . . .

> (OGILVIE *groans and tries to rise, but cannot manage it.* WILL *kicks him again and* ANDREW, *hurrying across the room, shoulders* WILL *out of the way)*

ANDREW: Jesus Christ, laddie, ye've nae fuckin idea have ye?

> (*Stepping across* OGILVIE's *body, he turns him over and tries to lift him but cannot manage it. He grunts, straightens, and turns on* WILL *in a fury*)

ANDREW: That's right, Wullie, that's right! That's whit ye draw yer fuckin wages for — staunin there like a spare prick at a hooer's weddin! For Christ's sake, laddie, catch a grup at the ither end afore I catch a grup o you!

> (WILL *comes forward and together they lift* OGILVIE *on to the bench. He half-sits, half-lies there, shivering in a semi-conscious*

condition. They stand back and look at him for a moment, wiping their brows and spitting and generally assuming the attitude of men admiring a finished job. ANDREW *turns and picks up* OGILVIE's *cloak — which he dropped when he fell — and throws it over* OGILVIE's *body.* ANDREW *then turns to the table and pours himself a stiff drink*)

WILL: Hi, hi, ye cannae dae that!

ANDREW: Cannae dae whut?

WILL: That's the Airchbishop's drink . . .

ANDREW: (*smouldering*) The Airchbishop — can get *stuffed!* (*Takes off the drink*) Bluidy man, he can take a runnin fuck at hissel! And I'll tell him that when I see him anaa, you see if I dinna! Jesus Bluidy Christ, he's aff his fuckin heid! (*Pours another drink and takes it immediately*) Twa men — twa men. A hauf-airsed wee laddie and a buggered auld man, no even twa real men tae tak a prisoner through thon rammy! Wullie, the man's a heid-case!

WILL: Aye, it was a haurd ane, richt enough! The mood thae folk were in — tae tell ye the truth, Andro, I didnae think we were gaun tae make it! Naw! Christ, I dinnae mind tellin ye, Andrew, I was a wee bit feart gettin . . .

ANDREW: Aw, ye were, were ye? Well, thanks for tellin me pal! Thanks a lot! Because wance or twice oot there, I was getting the distinct impression that you were aa set tae shoot the craw and leave me on my jaxy!

WILL: Aw, come off it, Andro! I wadnae dae that!

ANDREW: Too right ye wadnae! Too fuckin right ye wadnae! (*Turns his attention to* OGILVIE) Look at him! (*Laughs*) That's him! That's the lad! That's the lad that sterted aa the trouble! (*Laughs again*) Christ, if this wasna sae serious, ye could piss yersel laughin at it! Whit that mob werenae gaun tae dae tae that puir bugger lyin there! And whit for? Whit for, eh?

WILL: (*with some embarrassment*) Hi, Andro, screw the nut eh?

ANDREW: Eh?

WILL: Ye ken fine!

ANDREW: Aw I dae, dae I? Well, I'm sorry, son, but I'm no shair that I dae. I'm no shair that I ken whit this boy's done — whit *ony* man could hae possibly done — tae turn the fowk o this toun intae a gang o fuckin animals. Because that's whit . . .

WILL: Aw come aff it, Andro, come aff it! Ye ken fine whit that oot there was aa aboot! That bugger there's a Pope's man!

ANDREW: A Pope's man? A Pope's man! The Pope, is it? Bugger the Pope! I didnae bring the Pope through thon rammy. I didnae risk my life for the Pope. And gin I did, son, and gin I did, they'd hae as little reason for it as they had wi this ane!

WILL: Aw, for Christ's sake, Andro! Whit's the matter we ye? Here, ye're no gonnae stert feelin sorry for him, are ye? He's a dangerous Jesuit priest! He's been saying the Mass aa owre the place!

ANDREW: The Mass? Dae ye tell me that? (*Whistles through his teeth*) Ha, that maun be a gey wanchancy thing tae dae, eh? Dangerous man, that. Aye, oh aye! Masses, eh? Jesus Christ. Dearie me. They'll shairly hing him for that.

WILL: (*ignoring* ANDREW's *sarcasm*) Serve him right anaa! B'Christ, hingin's owre guid for the like o that! See if it was me, I'd burn him. I'd pit the bastard on that fire here and nou! Papes, they're bastards! Bastards! I'd pit every fuckin pape in Scotland on that fire gin I had my wey; every fuckin pape in Scotland . . .

(WILL *advances towards* ANDREW *as he speaks, aimlessly wandering about the room.* ANDREW *seizes him by the lapels of the tunic and pulls him to his face*)

ANDREW: Ye little . . . (*He is so full of anger that he can say no more. He pushes* WILL *away from him with a gesture of contempt*) I'm sorry tae disappoint ye, son. He'll no hing. No for sayin Masses.

WILL: (*bewildered by* ANDREW's *assault, has all but lost interest*) Naw? Will he no? (*Suddenly realises the import of what* ANDREW *has said*) Whit for no?

ANDREW: Because it's the law! This is his first offence — he'll maybe no even get the jile. Likely he'll get off wi a fine.

WILL: A fine! Christ, dae you mean tae tell me . . .

ANDREW: Aye. We brocht that man (*Points to* OGILVIE *who has now recovered sufficiently to be able to sit up and take an interest in the conversation*) through aa that — and aa he'll get is a fine.

WILL: A fine! It's no right, Andro, it's no right! (*Pauses and thinks before he says any more*) Listen, Andro, if his kind got back, if the papes got the pooer . . .

ANDREW: Wullie, Wullie, Wullie! (*Gentler*) Wullie! Hou often dae I hae tae tell ye, son? Gin ye're gonnae be a sodger, gin ye're gonnae be ony kind o sodger — for Christ's sake, son, dinnae tak onythin tae dae wi politics!

WILL: *Politics?* Whae's talkin aboot politics? This is religion!

ANDREW: Politics, religion, whit's the fuckin difference in this day and age? (*Suddenly weary, he passes his hand across his eyes and looks about him*) Whaur the hell has Spottiswoode got tae? Gode, I swear that man'll be the daith o me yet? He'll drive me tae the grave, b'Christ he will. See you that's talkin aboot

Pope's men and religion? Well jist you keep an eye on the guid
Airchbishop, that's aa! God, I whiles think he's hauf-roads tae
bein a Pope's man himsel — and if we ever get anither Catholic King, I'll gie ye three guesses whae'll be the Airchbishop o
Glesca! See if you want tae keep yer job . . .

WILL: Shote!

> (*Slow heavy footsteps are heard outside on the stair.* ANDREW
> *throws the dregs of his goblet on the floor and tries to dry the
> goblet on the tail of his tunic while* WILL *tries to straighten*
> OGILVIE *on the bench and bring him round by slapping his
> cheeks.* OGILVIE, *who is fully conscious by this time, pushes*
> WILL *away.* SPOTTISWOODE *enters. He is a biggish, heavy-
> set man in his middle age. He wears a long black cloak and
> a tight-fitting skull cap. Apart from the merest hint of a smile
> his face is quite expressionless. Both soldiers go to him and kiss
> his hand.* SPOTTISWOODE *never takes his eyes off* OGILVIE
> *from the moment he sees him.* OGILVIE *rises to his feet as soon
> as* SPOTTISWOODE *enters*)

SPOTTISWOODE: (*a statement rather than a question*) This is the
man.

ANDREW: Aye, m'lord. (*Clears his throat*) We had a bit of a
job bringing him owre, m'lord. The mob were — eh — unco
coorse. We very near didnae manage . . .

> (SPOTTISWOODE *has been gazing thoughtfully at* OGILVIE
> *and listening to* ANDREW *with the slightest of attention. He
> now turns to* ANDREW *with a nod*)

SPOTTISWOODE: No doubt it went sair with ye. (*Looks at*
ANDREW *expectantly*)

ANDREW: (*sighs and takes a small pouch and papers from the inside
of his tunic*) We fund this at his ludgins, m'lord.

SPOTTISWOODE: (*taking the pouch and papers with a cursory
glance*) Guid. (*Thoughtfully, with a dismissive shake of his head*)
Attend me.

> (ANDREW *and* WILL *begin to leave. As they reach the
> door,* SPOTTISWOODE *suddenly, without turning, calls after*
> ANDREW)

SPOTTISWOODE: Andro!

ANDREW: M'lord?

SPOTTISWOODE: Gif ye think it is necessary to bawl at the top
of your voice anent sic matters as the richts and wrangs of the
orders I see fit to give ye — will ye please make an effort to mod-
erate your language? It is — nocht seemly for the Airchbishop's
man to be heard effing and blinding aa owre the Toun House
of the Provost of Glasgow. (*He turns his head to look sternly over*

his shoulder at ANDREW)

ANDREW: (*without expression*) M'lord.

(SPOTTISWOODE *waves the soldiers away. When they have gone, he suddenly smiles warmly and shakes his head. He returns his attention to* OGILVIE *going to the table, taking off his cloak and draping it over the chair. As he is taking off his cap, he speaks to* OGILVIE)

SPOTTISWOODE: Captain Roderick Watson, is it no?

OGILVIE: (*somewhat shakily*) I think — perhaps it would be better to dispense with that name. It is a completely false one and to continue the pretence further would serve little purpose. My name is . . .

SPOTTISWOODE: Ogilvie. John Ogilvie. (*Drops his cap on the table*)

OGILVIE: (*biting his lip*) That is perfectly correct. You have the advantage of me, sir.

SPOTTISWOODE: (*amused*) Just so, Master Ogilvie. Just so. (*Rubbing his hands together*) Nou. Would ye take a dram? Ye look in sair need of it?

OGILVIE: That is very kind of you. I would be most grateful.

(SPOTTISWOODE *picks up the goblet that Andrew has used, examines it for a moment, purses his lips and looks sceptically towards the door. He tosses the goblet in his hand, lays it aside and pours* OGILVIE's *drink into a fresh goblet*)

SPOTTISWOODE: Water?

OGILVIE: Please.

(SPOTTISWOODE *pours some water into the drink and hands it to* OGILVIE)

OGILVIE: Thank you.

SPOTTISWOODE: And you are of noble bluid, I understand?

OGILVIE: I am — and all my people before me.

SPOTTISWOODE: (*conversationally*) Sir Walter Ogilvie of Drum?

OGILVIE: My father.

(SPOTTISWOODE *smiles and, sitting down, turns his attention to the papers. He begins to read, then looks up solicitously*)

SPOTTISWOODE: Sit ye doun, Master Ogilvie, sit ye doun. There is no need for you to stand.

OGILVIE: Thank you — but I prefer it.

SPOTTISWOODE: (*with a slight shrug*) As ye please.

(SPOTTISWOODE *reads one paper, lays it aside with a sharp sniff of breath and frowns up at* OGILVIE. *He picks up the second paper and asks his next question casually as he spreads it out*)

SPOTTISWOODE: And you have been saying Masses in the City

of Glasgow?

OGILVIE: (*mildly*) If to do so is a crime, then it will be necessary to prove it — with witnesses.

> (SPOTTISWOODE *leans back in his chair and regards* OGILVIE *with a kind of stern speculation before he speaks*)

SPOTTISWOODE: To say the Mass in His Majesty's Dominions — ye maun be maist siccarly assured — is a crime. (*Leans forward and re-commences his study of the paper*) And I have any amount of witnesses.

> (SPOTTISWOODE *spends little time with the second paper, laying it carefully on top of the first. He picks up the pouch and empties the contents on to the table. There are a number of bones and a small hank of grey hair*)

SPOTTISWOODE: Oh aye. Relics. (*Picks up the hank of hair rather gingerly between his thumb and forefinger and glances enquiringly at* OGILVIE)

OGILVIE: (*crosses himself*) A lock from the head of the blessed St Ignatius.

SPOTTISWOODE: (*nods without comment, lays the hair down and leans back in his chair with interlocking fingers*) I am given to understand that ye have been furth of Scotland this long while — twenty-two year, to be exact, the maist of your days?

OGILVIE: You appear to be remarkably well informed.

SPOTTISWOODE: Master Ogilvie, what garred ye return?

OGILVIE: My vocation.

SPOTTISWOODE: Which is?

OGILVIE: To save souls. (*Proudly*) To unteach heresy.

SPOTTISWOODE: Indeed? Sic a michty vocation would be of necessity — require a michty authority. But where is yours, Master Ogilvie? Since ye did not get it from the King or from any of his bishops . . .

OGILVIE: The King is a layman — as are all his so-called bishops. None of them are competent to place authority, spiritual authority that is, on any man.

SPOTTISWOODE: (*slightly mocking*) The *King* is a layman?

OGILVIE: He has not had his first tonsure — and he is certainly not a priest!

SPOTTISWOODE: And you are?

> (OGILVIE *gives a little start, hesitates, then laughs*)

OGILVIE: Since you are so certain that I have been saying Masses, you must be positive that I am a priest!

SPOTTISWOODE: (*acknowledging the point with a faint smile and nod*) Aye. But let us return to my original question. From where do you derive your authority?

(OGILVIE *pauses, looks seriously at* SPOTTISWOODE, *finishes his drink, and lays the goblet carefully on the table. Taking a deep breath, he delivers his next speech as if he were giving a lecture*)

OGILVIE: Christ's sheep were committed to the charge of Peter. Any man who would feed them must first seek his authority from the Apostolic See. Preserved there — through an unbroken line of succession — is the authority and power given in the first instance to the Prince of the Apostles. 'Thou art Peter and upon this rock I will build my church; and the gates of hell shall not prevail against it!' (*Pauses and lets the passion of the quotation subside*)

Thus was Simon, son of John, made the strong rock of the Church that he might be Cephas and be called Peter. By the simple method of working back through all the Pontiffs, I can trace my authority to him — and through him to the Lord Jesus Christ.

(*There is a short silence between them*)

SPOTTISWOODE: (*with a sigh*) Aye. The Petrine Claim.

OGILVIE: The Truth.

SPOTTISWOODE: (*sternly*) That, Master Ogilvie, is treason!

OGILVIE: (*equally sternly*) that *Master Spottiswoode*, is faith!

SPOTTISWOODE: (*snapping*) And ye would sign a declaration to the sic effect?

OGILVIE: (*hotly*) In my own blood if need be!

SPOTTISWOODE: I hardly think so. *Father* Ogilvie. I hardly think so. I hardly think that that will be necessary. Plain ink, no doubt will do just as well! (*Pushes his chair back savagely and walks a few steps away from* OGILVIE *before swinging round to address him again*)

It is the law of the land — the law of this realm — that the King — His Sovereign and Maist Gracious Majesty King James the Saxt — demands and is entitled to the allegiance and lealty of his subjects — of aa his subjects — in aa matters touching their lives. Aa matters — temporal *and* spiritual. That is the law. Did ye ken that?

OGILVIE: The law of the land is the law of man. The laws of God are not to be changed so readily.

SPOTTISWOODE: Maybe no. The fact remains that ye deny allegiance to the King in this matter and in aa religious matters?

OGILVIE: I do.

SPOTTISWOODE: And would render up sic allegiance to the Pope?

OGILVIE: I would.

SPOTTISWOODE: And if the Pope took it into his head to depose a king on the grounds of heresy, ye would uphold and
support the Pope's richts in the matter?

OGILVIE: (*guardedly*) I do not know whether the Holy Father
has, or would claim such a right. It is true that many learned
doctors of the Church have asserted that this is the case . . .

SPOTTISWOODE: Never mind the doctors of the Kirk, Faither.
I'm speiring at you!

OGILVIE: It is not an article of faith. If and when it becomes so,
I will die for it — and gladly. Until then, I do not need to pass
an opinion to anyone — and certainly not to you. You have no
right . . .

SPOTTISWOODE: Aye, Aye, I ken. I'm a layman. No had my
first tonsure. I've no bloody rights ava! (*Pauses, looks seriously
at* OGILVIE) I must warn ye, Faither Ogilvie, that sooner or
later, ye will be forced to answer that question. Your very life
micht weill depend on the answer ye give. So. Aince mair. Gif
the Pope took it into his head to depose a king on the grounds
of heresy, would ye uphold and support the Pope's richts in
the matter?

OGILVIE: (*with some hesitation*) I assume you are asking me
whether or not I would condone regicide. I fail to see why
you cannot ask me the question straight out. I am opposed to
regicide, Master Spottiswoode, I am opposed to murder — the
murder of a king or the murder of a beggar. As a Christian and
as a Catholic, that is the only answer I give you.

SPOTTISWOODE: And gin I asked ye as a Jesuit, what answer
would ye gie me then?

OGILVIE: What do you mean by that, sir?

SPOTTISWOODE: Let us get doun to specifics, Faither Ogilvie.
There are others in your order who have less scruple when it
comes to murder.

OGILVIE: I haven't the faintest idea what you are talking about.

SPOTTISWOODE: Oh, have you not? Perhaps I am being less
than plain. Does not the name of Henry Garnett mean anything
to you? Faither Henry Garnett and the Gunpowder Plot?

OGILVIE: That is a monstrous slander! Father Garnett was a
good and holy man!

SPOTTISWOODE: (*snorting*) Holy man! Garnett was a traitor, a
willing accomplice to the attempted murder of his king!

OGILVIE: That is a lie! Father Garnett was executed by the English for refusing to betray a penitent — and he was not obliged
to do that for anything in the world.

SPOTTISWOODE: Ha! Was he no? Let me tell ye, Faither

Ogilvie, that if any man was to confess sic a crime to me, I'd no lose much time in turning him in.

OGILVIE: Nobody should confess to you.

SPOTTISWOODE: Maybe no! But the fact remains that there was a Jesuit priest involved in the Gunpowder Plot. I ken that and so do you . . .

OGILVIE: I know no such thing!

SPOTTISWOODE: (*scornfully*) Ach, he was up to his oxters in it! What's more, barely a year of his Majesty's reign has gone by without some plot or intrigue or some scheme or other of a traitorous and seditious nature being uncovered. And on every single occasion there's been a Jesuit at the foot of it! And nou here you come owre from France with your English manners and your assumed name and (*snatches up the papers in his fist*) this neiveful of sedition in your kist. At this very minute . . .

OGILVIE: This is preposterous! What are you charging me with? If you're looking for traitors, why don't you try Robert Bruce? I'm told he lives near here and you have plenty of evidence . . .

SPOTTISWOODE: (*ignoring the question*) At this very minute there are twenty-seven . . .

OGILVIE: Are you afraid to answer me then? Why don't you arrest a presbyterian traitor? Why don't you . . .

SPOTTISWOODE: (*shouting him down*) Jesuit priests working against the well-being . . .

OGILVIE: What about the Seventeenth of September riots? Why don't you drag Robert Bruce in here?

SPOTTISWOODE: . . . and security of this nation.

OGILVIE: (*shouting almost into* SPOTTISWOODE'*s face*) What about Robert Bruce? Answer me, you imposter, answer me you *God-damned king-worshiping Heretic!*

(SPOTTISWOODE *knocks* OGILVIE *down with a full-blooded punch to the jaw. He stands over him, panting with rage*)

SPOTTISWOODE: At this very minute, there are twenty-seven Jesuit priests working against the guid-keeping and security of this nation of Scotland — and I am Airchbishop of Glasgow and hae no need to answer to any one of them! (*Turns to the door*) Andro! Andro!

(ANDREW *and* WILL *enter at the double*)

SPOTTISWOODE: Take this man out of my sight!

ANDREW: Aye, aye, m'lord! Whaur tae?

SPOTTISWOODE: (*angrily*) The Castle, ye fool! Where ither? Get me lowse of him!

(OGILVIE *rises slowly to his feet as the soldiers advance. He stares at* SPOTTISWOODE *who has turned his back on him*)

OGILVIE: Who made you my executioner? (*Spits on the floor at*
    SPOTTISWOODE*'s feet*) And who made you Archbishop? Better
    butcher than bishop!
SPOTTISWOODE: (*without turning*) Get him away!
        (*The soldiers lead* OGILVIE *out*)
        SPOTTISWOODE *goes to the table and pours himself a drink.*
        He gathers the papers together carefully, re-dons his cap and
        picks up his cloak. Finishing his drink, he sighs and stares into
        space for a few moments)
SPOTTISWOODE: Robert Bruce — oh damn Robert Bruce!
        (*Hurls the empty goblet into a corner of the room*)
    God damn him!
        (SPOTTISWOODE *stamps out*)

SCENE TWO

The following January. A corridor in the Palace of the Archbishop
of Glasgow. ANDREW is on his own, happed up for a journey
and carrying a shield and spear. He looks distinctly cheesed off
as WILL similarly attired, enters briskly.

WILL: Nae sign o them yet?
ANDREW: No chance!
WILL: Sandy's got aathing organised at the gate and Wattie and
    the ither lads are staunin by with the horses.
ANDREW: (*nodding*) Guid.
WILL: Here, though. Gin we dinnae get a move on, we'll hae a
    job winnin awa. There's a fair crowd buildin up ootby.
ANDREW: Ach, the Airchbishop's no bothert! No him! No wi *us*
    ridin aside him tae tak aa the stanes and glaur they'll be chuckin
    at *him*. Och! I'm fair wrocht tae daith wi aa this ditterin aboot!
WILL: Whit are they jawin aboot, onywey? They've been in there
    for mair nor an 'oor!
ANDREW: Christ knows! Ogilvie'll be argyin the toss again, I
    shouldnae wonder.
WILL: (*laughing*) Weill, I hope the Airchbishop disnae lose the
    heid and thump him this time! Oh he's a funny ane that Ogilvie!
ANDREW: Funny's no the ward. Bluidy bampot if ye ask me.
WILL: Christ, no hauf! Tellt me aince — when I brocht him in
    his meat like — tellt me aince that he didnae mind the jile! Nae
    kiddin, Aye! Said he was servin his destiny, fulfillin his desti-
    ny — I cannae mind right what he said but it was somethin aboot
    his destiny. And he's aye crackin bawrs and laughin, ken? Aye

that cheery. Damn shair I wadnae find muckle tae be cheery
aboot gin I was in he's place! Christ, ye ken whit it's like in
there, Andro?

ANDREW: Aye, Oh aye.

WILL: He's no been oot of that place for geynear three month.
It's cauld and it's damp and it's pitch-black and fair crawlin
wi rats. And there's this muckle iron beam at the fit o the bed.
Ogilvie's chyned til it by the ankles and it's a gey short chyn!
He gets naethin but parritch tae eat and water tae drink. If he's
aff his heid bi now, it's nae wonder!

ANDREW: He was aff his fuckin heid afore he gaed in there if
ye want my opinion.

WILL: Aye. Maybe he was anaa! (*A thought strikes him*)

Here but! I didnae tell ye aboot this mornin. (*Laughs at the
recollection*)

I gaed in there aboot — och, echt o'clock it wad be — brocht
him in his parritch and some clean claes and that. (*Laughs
again*)

He's lyin there, aa clairty and bleary-eyed among the rats and
the shite (*Laughs*) and his feet're stuck hauf-roads up tae the
ceilin wi this bluidy chyn! I gets in there and I says tae him I
says 'Hello there, Faither! Hou're ye daein the day?' And ye
ken whit? He's lyin there (*Laughs and shakes his head*) and he
says tae me, he says 'Oh, Will' he sayd — aa englified ken? —
'Oh Will!' he says 'It's past joking when the heid's aff!'

(*They both laugh*)

ANDREW: Christ, that'll dae!

WILL: Past joking when the heid's aff! Oh Jesus — Andro, I
geynear creased mysel! It was the way he said it, ken? Aa English
and that (*mimics*) 'Past joking when the heid's aff,' Aw Christ!

ANDREW: (*serious again*) I wonder — maybe his heid'll really
be aff efter they've done wi him in Embro.

WILL: Here, when we get hame — tae Embro like — what's the
chances of a couple o days aff? I'd like tae get up the road —
see my Maw.

(ANDREW *grins broadly and chuckles to himself*)

WILL: What's the joke? Whit are ye laughin at?

ANDREW: Naethin. Naethin. It's jist — eh, want tae see yer
Maw, eh?

WILL: Aye! I've no seen her for a while and — weill, I mean tae
say, she's no gettin ony younger. Whit's the maitter wi that?

ANDREW: Naethin. Naethin at aa! (*Wipes the smile from his face*)
Aw, never mind, Wullie. Never mind, son. It's jist my sense
o humour. I daursay we'll get some time away when we're in

Embro — tae stert wi onywey. Later on, I'm no saw shair.

WILL: Later on? Are we gonnae be in Reekie for a while then?

ANDREW: A few weeks, I reckon. Depends.

WILL: Depends on whit?

ANDREW: Depends on hou muckle trouble they get frae Ogilvie.
Ach Ogilvie! Buggers like him gie me the boke, so they dae!

WILL: The Papes?

ANDREW: Naw! The nobility — nobility like thon! Rich men
wi bees in their bonnets! Ach, they scunner me! I tell ye this,
Wull — I've seen Ogilvie's like afore nou! He can caa hissel a
Jesuit, a pape or whitever ye like — at the hinner end, he aye
minds that he's Sir Wattie Ogilvie's son. And nae matter whit
he's suffered here in Glesca, he kens up here (*Taps his temple*)
that the men that'll be sittin in judgment on him in Embro are
his ain kind — gentlemen like himsel! sae he argies the toss,
stands up tae the Airchbishop — aw he's the brave, brave boy
richt enought! Crackin jokes and aa the rest o it! But aa the
time, Wullie, he kens that he can say the ward and walk oot o
here free as air! And he thinks that efter he's been in Embro
and aa the talkin's done, that's jist exactly whit he's gonnae
dae! But that's jist where he's mistaken, son. When we get tae
Embro . . .

SPOTTISWOODE: (*off*) Andro! Andro!

ANDREW: At last! Christ, dinnae tell me . . . Come on, Wullie!

WILL: (*taking* ANDREW's *arm*) Andro, whit were ye gonnae say?
Whit'll happen when we get tae Embro?

(ANDREW *looks at* WILL *and grins*)

ANDREW: Och, ye'll mebbe get tae see yer Maw! Come on, son.
We're aff!

(*Both exit*)

SCENE THREE

Edinburgh a few days later. Ogilvie's room in Spottiswoode's
house in the Canongate. A barely furnished room containing no more than a bed, a table and two chairs. OGILVIE is
seated at the table, writing. An empty chair is opposite the table. SPOTTISWOODE enters. OGILVIE glances up briefly but
continues to write.

SPOTTISWOODE: Guid afternoon Faither. And hou are ye the
day?

OGILVIE: (*continues writing, finishing with a flourish of his pen*)

As well, my Lord Archbishop, as can be expected. Really Spottiswoode, these questions that you ask me are ridiculous!

SPOTTISWOODE: (*raising one eyebrow*) It is your answers which interest me, Ogilvie — no your opinion of the questions. (*Indicates the paper on which* OGILVIE *had been writing*) Ye have finished?

> (OGILVIE *rather sourly pushes the paper across the desk and walks away.* SPOTTISWOODE *seats himself on the empty chair and begins to read the paper*)

SPOTTISWOODE: (*reading*) 'Whether the Pope be judge and have power *in Spiritualibus* over His Majesty, and whether that power will reach over His Majesty even *in temporalibus* if it be *in ordine ad spiritualia* as Bellarmine affirmeth.' Aye. Well, we aa ken the answer to that ane. Nane of us has the power to speir sic a thing of ye.

OGILVIE: (*turning*) Nor I to answer such a question! Let us be quite plain about this — just what is it that you are asking me to pronounce on? This matter has been hotly contested by two of the most brilliant minds in Europe — namely King James and Cardinal Bellarmine. Father Francisco Suarez has also written on the subject and I, as a Jesuit and a good Catholic, naturally incline to the Jesuit and Catholic point of view — but, my good Spottiswoode, I am a very junior and unimportant Jesuit and it would be hardly fitting for me to enter publicly into such a controversy. Besides, what possible purpose could be served by any answer I might give? It would affect the issue neither way.

SPOTTISWOODE: (*sighs and shakes his head incredulously*) Faither Ogilvie, whiles ye bumbaze me! Never mind. (*Reads on*) 'Whether the Pope has the power to excommunicate kings (especially such as are not of his Church) as His Majesty?' Hmm. Faither Ogilvie, I fear that I am unable to understand your answer. The Pope, ye say, can excommunicate His Majesty? I do not understand that.

OGILVIE: What is there to understand? Of course the Holy Father has the power!

SPOTTISWOODE: But — by your own argument — His Majesty is a heretic. And if His Majesty is a heretic, he cannot be a Catholic.

OGILVIE: (*with a long-suffering sigh*) A simple analogy. An outlaw is outside the law as far as the protection of the law is concerned — but he can be apprehended and tried and convicted by and according to the law. In just the same way a heretic is outwith Mother Church as far as her blessings are concerned but is still subject to her justice — and to her punishment.

SPOTTISWOODE: I see. We are aa spiritual outlaws then?

OGILVIE: Yes.

SPOTTISWOODE: Even the youngest bairn baptised the day by a Calvinist minister?

OGILVIE: Yes. Yes. The Pope acquires his authority over man by baptism. Man enters Christ's flock through baptism and the Pope is the shepherd of that flock.

SPOTTISWOODE: (*sighs*) Man, d'ye ken what ye're saying? There's scarce a man in Scotland'd have his bairn baptised under sic conditions!

OGILVIE: That is a matter of opinion. It may be true of those who despise Christ and serve the Devil — it is certainly not true of the faithful. And there are many more of these in Scotland than you, perhaps, imagine.

SPOTTISWOODE: (*sighs again, reads on*) 'Whether the Pope has power to depose kings by him excommunicated? And in particular whether he have the power to depose the King, His Majesty.' Aye. Aye. the auld sang. Nane of us has the authority.

OGILVIE: No.

SPOTTISWOODE: 'Whether it be no murder to slay His Majesty, being so excommunicated and deposed by the Pope?' And here we are again! No spiritual jurisdiction! Can ye no, in aa conscience, give your opinion?

OGILVIE: No.

SPOTTISWOODE: Ye gave it to me! Ye told me that ye despised murder! Why could ye no have said the same to the Commission?

OGILVIE: You have my answer there. You'll have to be satisfied with that.

SPOTTISWOODE: (*reading on with a withering look in* OGILVIE's *direction*) 'Whether the Pope has power to assoyle subjects from the oath of their borne and natural allegiance to His Majesty?' (*Sighs deeply*) With your customary arrogance, ye condem the Oath of Allegiance. (*Lays the paper aside*)

OGILVIE: I most certainly do.

> (SPOTTISWOODE *bows his head wearily, rubbing the bridge of his nose between his thumb and forefinger. After a moment, he looks across at* OGILVIE)

SPOTTISWOODE: Faither, d'ye ken wha framed these questions?

OGILVIE: No.

SPOTTISWOODE: Ye have no idea?

OGILVIE: No. I assumed that it was a joint decision — yourself and some, perhaps all, of your colleagues on the Commission.

Is it not so?

> (SPOTTISWOODE *shakes his head, taps the table, rises. He walks about a little, folds his hands purposefully behind his back*)

SPOTTISWOODE: Faither Ogilvie, I'll leave ye without any doubts. The answers ye have given to these questions will send you to the gallows. You are going to hang.

OGILVIE: I am not afraid to die.

SPOTTISWOODE: Aye, I thocht ye'd be pleased! (*Loses his temper momentarily, leans over the table towards* OGILVIE) But I am nocht concerned with the smaa-boukit ambitions of your vanity! (*Turns away and faces about until his temper is under control*)

These questions are speired at you by no lesser person than His Gracious Majesty King James the Saxt of Scotland and First of England! (*Pauses to glower at* OGILVIE) When ye were arrested in Glasgow — on that same night — I scrieved a letter to the King, I thocht — and still think — that ye were involved in a plot to murder His Majesty. Oh Faither Ogilvie, ye have been used in a maist merciful manner! *I* would hae given ye the boots — and micht yet! But His Majesty thocht otherwise. These questions were put to ye in order that ye micht have the chance to prove your lealty and allegiance to your King! Well, they have disproved it! They demonstrate quite clearly how small a value ye place upon your King and your country — the insolence and provocative nature of these answers will put a rope about your thrapple! Mind on that when ye mount the gallows!

OGILVIE: I do not know what you want of me. I have given the only answers I possibly could. I have replied with all the honesty and sincerity that I could muster.

SPOTTISWOODE: Certes, Man! It's not a question of honesty or sincerity but of tact! There's little wrong with the substance of your answer — it's the manner of the replies! Have ye read what ye hae scrieved? In every single instance — forby the ane anent the Pope's power of excommunication — ye deny the authority and jurisdiction of the King's Commission!

OGILVIE: Do you expect me to affirm it?

SPOTTISWOODE: Ye are no required to affirm or to deny! Aa ye had to say — aa ye *hae* to say is that ye do not ken! Ye'll get away with your answer anent excommunication — the King and the other Commissioners'll be as bumbazed as I was by it, but they'll no pay it muckle heed. As for the others, ye can just say what ye've just this minute said to me — ye are only a humble priest, no very important, and ye have no opinion in the matter.

OGILVIE: And such a reply would release me?

SPOTTISWOODE: No from the King's Justice. There's aye the matter of the Masses ye have said — ye maun be tried and punished for that. But ye'll no hang for saying Masses.

OGILVIE: I see. (*Thinks about it for a moment*) You are, of course, aware that I have yet to stand trial?

SPOTTISWOODE: (*irritably*) Ye'll stand trial when the nature of your crime can be determined. It is the purpose of the King's Commission to gather evidence for the trial. This (*indicates the deposition*) would make any trial for treason a formality!

OGILVIE: And if I answer as you advise?

SPOTTISWOODE: In any trial for treason, the process of law would be open to ye. In practice, I doubt very much whether sic a charge would be brocht.

OGILVIE: But I would be charged with saying Masses?

SPOTTISWOODE: Of course. Charged, convicted and banished from His Majesty's dominions.

OGILVIE: You seem remarkably sure of the outcome!

SPOTTISWOODE: These are troubled times we live in, Faither Ogilvie.

OGILVIE: Indeed they are, Archbishop, indeed they are! (*Pauses thoughtfully*) Why are you doing this, Spottiswoode?

SPOTTISWOODE: I beg your pardon?

OGILVIE: Why are you doing this? Why are you trying to persuade me to change my deposition? After all, you said just now that you believed me to be involved in a plot to murder the King. You are quite mistaken but I shan't argue about it — you are obviously persuaded otherwise. In your eyes, I am a potential assassin. Why should you seek to allow me to escape with my life?

SPOTTISWOODE: There are larger issues at stake.

OGILVIE: Larger than the King's safety?

SPOTTISWOODE: Larger than the life of one extremely ineffectual conspirator! Look, Ogilvie. If you are banished, I will be quit of ye — alive or dead, it's aa the same to me!

OGILVIE: (*with a deep breath*) Then I am afraid that it will have to be dead. For I cannot and will not change my deposition.

SPOTTISWOODE: Certes man, are ye wyce?

OGILVIE: Wise or foolish, I will not change my deposition.

SPOTTISWOODE: Damn you, John Ogilvie, for a bloody fanatic! What on God's earth d'ye hope to gain from this?

OGILVIE: Gain? I have no thought of gain. I am as in love with life as any man — but I will not change my deposition!

SPOTTISWOODE: But why, man, why? After aa I hae tellt ye?

OGILVIE: There are too many considerations. Far too many.

SPOTTISWOODE: Considerations? Certes man — there maun be plenty of considerations to gar a man die for his faith — there's nothing byordnar about that! But this is phraseology, a trick of speech, no mair nor that! With just a wheen changing of words, ye micht be as free as air! My God, man — ye cannae die for an attitude, a pose! Hou in the warld can sic a thing be justified?

OGILVIE: It can be justified because I justify it! That is enough.

SPOTTISWOODE: Pride!

OGILVIE: Not pride but dignity! The dignity of Mother Church. (*Sighs*) You can neither understand nor sympathise. How can you when you do not know what dignity means? We speak in different tongues, Spottiswoode. You and I, we speak in different languages. When you accuse me of attitudes and poses, you do no more than judge me by your own standards. You call yourself Archbishop of Glasgow — what is that but a pose? What is that but a cynical attitude towards a noble and ancient office? You are no more Archbishop of Glasgow than I am — but it's little you care about that! You are quite happy to be an imposter as long as it serves your purpose. So I can expect nothing from you. (*Suddenly angry*)

But I know very well what you expect from me! You would have me go before this illegal commission and — what's the expression — play the daft laddie! That's it, isn't it? That's what you want. Then you would spank the daft laddie's bottom and kick him out of the country — kick *me* out of my own country — hoping, no doubt, that Catholicism would go with me! Oh My Lord Archbishop, how mistaken you are! I may not be more than a priest — and not a very significant one at that — but when I take my place before that court, I will be the representative of the Church of the Risen Christ! And if my faith is to be defiled and humiliated in this land, this will not be the hand that does it! I will not change my deposition.

SPOTTISWOODE: (*stonily*) Then ye maun take the consequences.

OGILVIE: Do you think I'm not ready for that?

SPOTTISWOODE: It will mean daith — and worse than daith!

OGILVIE: (*scornfully*) Oh Spottiswoode, what a wonderful hangman you'd make! Do you think that I care in the least for your threats? I haven't asked you for any favours and I never will. I despise you, Spottiswoode. I despise you and your threats and your damned heretic malice! Do what you can and see if it makes any difference to me! I'll willingly suffer more in this cause than you and your henchmen can ever inflict!

SPOTTISWOODE: Will ye suffer the boots?

OGILVIE: Oh stop making those threats! Whatever you are going to do to me, do it! You won't frighten me with threats! I'm not a hysterical woman, you know. You don't frighten me! All you do is to give me fresh heart — your threats are like the cackling of so many geese! Do what you have to do, Spottiswoode! Do not talk about it! I am not afraid. When are you going to understand that? *I am not afraid.* All I ask is that, whatever you do, you do quickly.

SPOTTISWOODE: The boots'll no be quick.

OGILVIE: Damn your boots! I am not afraid of your boots!

SPOTTISWOODE: Are ye no? (*Looks at* OGILVIE *thoughtfully for a moment, then turns to the door. He looks once at* OGILVIE'*s back before calling out*) Wattie! Are ye there? Come in a minute. I want ye!

> (WAT *is a middle-aged man of medium height, rather squat in appearance and wearing a perpetually dour and surly expression*)

WAT: M'lord?

SPOTTISWOODE: (*to* OGILVIE) Wat is a great authority on the boots, Faither Ogilvie. (OGILVIE *glances over his shoulder at* WAT, *then looks away*) I'll let him take a look at ye and then he'll maybe be guid enough to explain to ye just exactly what is entailed. Wat?

> (*Hands on hips,* WAT *walks slowly round* OGILVIE, *keeping a distance of approximately six feet between himself and the priest. He is carefully examining* OGILVIE'*s legs, behaving rather like a tradesman who has been asked to measure for a job of work and is making a preliminary inspection. Eventually he stops and addresses himself to* SPOTTISWOODE)

WAT: I'll dae the richt ane first, m'lord. That's the usual. (*Squats beside* OGILVIE'*s right leg.* OGILVIE *eyes him apprehensively all the time*) Generally get mair purchase on that leg. Mair muscle, ye see.

SPOTTISWOODE: (*nodding*) Aye.

WAT: Fower splints, m'lord. Ane here, (*indicating the inside of the leg*) ane here, (*indicating the outside of the leg*) ane here (*indicating the back of the leg*) and ane here (*indicating the front of the leg*). Fower tichteners. Ane at the ankle, ane on the shin — jist ablow the knee — ane on the thigh — jist abune the knee — and ane on the thigh again, jist ablow the hip. (*Stands up and stretches*)

There's been a wheen airgument aboot the best place tae drive in the wedge — Oh! (*Takes a wooden wedge from the inside of* his tunic and holds it up for them both to see) This is the wedge. As I say, there's been a bit o airgument aboot the best place to drive it in. Some say that ye're better wi the ootside o the leg (*Laughs*) — I think that's daft. I mysel prefer to drive the wedge in on the inside. Ye get mair purchase, m'lord. D'ye understand? (*Demonstrates on his own leg*) The wedge has got mair tae drive intae. (*Sniffs speculatively*) Purchase is the secret in this game m'lord. Gin the wedge was big enough and I could get the purchase, I could drive it frae the tap o the hip-bane aa the way through tae the sowls o the feet!

OGILVIE: (*hoarsely*) And how far will you drive it in my case?

WAT: (*addressing* OGILVIE *directly for the first time*) Depends. Depends mainly on the Airchbishop but it depends on yersel anaa. I'll be hammerin awa wi the mallet richt up til the minute I'm tellt tae stop.

SPOTTISWOODE: (*all but crying out to* OGILVIE) Three blows of the mallet will gar the marrow spurt from your banes!

WAT: (*with some relish*) Jist sae, m'lord. Jist sae.

SPOTTISWOODE: That will be enough for nou, Wat. Away ye go.

WAT: (*taking his leave*) Thank ye, m'lord. (*Grinning wolfishly at both of them*) I'll be at yer service whenever ye need me.
    (*Exit* WAT)

SPOTTISWOODE: Well. Nou ye ken what's in store for ye.

OGILVIE: I certainly do.

SPOTTISWOODE: And ye will not change your deposition?

OGILVIE: No.

SPOTTISWOODE: (*exasperated*) Ogilvie, ye are beyond me! I swear your perversity leaves me speechless! Ye would thole sic a torment as thon rather than make a reasonable deposition . . .

OGILVIE: (*incredulously*) Reason? What are you talking about? The boots are hardly instruments of reason!

SPOTTISWOODE: There would be no need for the boots — nor, indeed any other method — if ye would but purge the arrogance and pride from this deposition! Ogilvie, I beseech ye — in the name of the Lord Jesus Christ I beseech ye — do not make me do this thing to you. Change your deposition! For the love of God, man, have some sense!

OGILVIE: Sense? Who are you to talk of sense to me? We are beyond that now. Good Lord, Spottiswoode, even if I had been willing before to do as you ask, I cannot do so now. Can't you see that? If I did, I would seem to have been moved and led by feeling, like a beast — and not by reason, like a man. You cannot move me by reason and you will not move me by feeling. But try your boots, Spottiswoode! Try them and see how far you get! Try your boots and I'll show you that, in this cause, I care as much for your boots as you for your leggings! For I know myself born for greater things than to be overcome by *sense!* I put my trust in the Grace of God and you can do whatever you like! I will ask you for nothing — and I will neither alter nor add to anything I have said!

SPOTTISWOODE: (*turning to leave*) Ye won't? Very well. Only mind on this — the pain ye suffer wilna be the pain of the martyr. Ye maun think what ye like — you are no martyr, John Ogilvie, and aa the suffering in the warld winna make ye ane!

(*Exit* SPOTTISWOODE. *Somewhat shakily,* OGILVIE *goes to the table and takes his seat. He draws a piece of paper towards him and begins to write. Before he has written two words, he breaks down and weeps uncontrollably. He beats his fist on the table repeatedly*)

OGILVIE: I am not afraid! I am not afraid! I am not afraid!

SCENE FOUR

That same evening in the soldiers' quarters. The dining room or, more accurately, the room in which the soldiers eat. There is a longish table with benches on either side. On the wall, there is a rack where the soldiers hang their coats, swords, etc. WILL is at the table taking a meal. His sword and helmet are on the rack. ANDREW enters, whistling, a plate of food in one hand, a mug of beer in the other.

ANDREW: Ye got back then?
WILL: Aye.

(ANDREW *lays his food and drink on the table and talks to* WILL *as he unbuckles his sword and hangs it up, placing his helmet on top of it*)

ANDREW: Hou'd ye get on, well? (*Grins*) See yer Maw?
WILL: Aye.
ANDREW: (*coming forward and sitting down*) Faimly aaricht?
WILL: No sae bad. Whit's the joke?
ANDREW: Joke?
WILL: Aye, ye're laughin aa owre yer ugly face. Whit's the big joke?
ANDREW: Nae joke, Wullie. Nae joke. Honest.

(WILL *looks unsure, but does not pursue the matter.* ANDREW *grins and begins to eat. He eats quickly with plently of noise but no talk. When he is finished, he pushes back his plate, picks up his mug and grins at* WILL)

ANDREW: Come on well, let's hear it! Gie's aa yer news!

WILL: (*surlily*) Naethin tae tell, Andro.

ANDREW: (*with look of disappointment*) Aw here! Dinnae tell me! Dinnae tell me ye didnae get yer hole?

WILL: (*choking with outrage*) Whit's that tae dae wi you?

ANDREW: But here I thocht we were gonnae be pals, you and me! (*Tongue in cheek*) Comrades-in-arms, like?

WILL: There's some things ye keep tae yersel.

ANDREW: Aw haw! So ye did get yer hole?

WILL: Naw! I mean if I did — whether I did or didnae — I wadnae tell you!

ANDREW: (*shrugs*) Suit yerself! (*Takes a slug of beer, grins wickedly*) I did.

WILL: Eh?

ANDREW: I did.

WILL: You did what?

ANDREW: Got my hole.

WILL: Aw — ye did, did ye?

ANDREW: Oooh Aye! (*stretches himself in reminiscence*) Had tae pey for it like! Cannae expect onythin ither at my age. But, oh Jesus . . .

WILL: (*sighs, pulls a long face*) Ye clairty auld tyke! And did ye no dae onythin else?

ANDREW: Och, jist the usual! Gaed oot and got fou, got intae a fecht, got a hooer and got my hole. Whit else is there for an auld sodger? And forby — the toun's no the same.

WILL: (*without much interest*) Naw?

ANDREW: Naw! Ye'll haurdly credit this, Wull, but there was a time I could walk through the Gressmerket and get stopped by every second bugger I met. They were aa my friens, I kent them aa. And nou? Nou they're aa deid — deid or no able tae get oot. I haurdly ken a saul in Embro nou, son. See whit ye're comin tae? (*takes another drink*) Wha'd be a sodger, eh? Wha'd be a sodger?

WILL: (*smiles*) Come aff it, Andro. Ye wadnae cheynge it!

ANDREW: Huh? Dae I hae ony option? Still. Ye're richt, I suppose. It's been my life. And it's no sae bad in a job like this — nae action tae speak o, forby the bit dunt wi the flet o the sword ye whiles dole oot jist tae keep yer haun in. Protectin His Lordship's presence frae the blandishments o a worshippin Glesca population! Huh! Staunin gaird on heid cases like Ogilvie!

WILL: Here aye! The Faither! Hou's he gettin on?

ANDREW: Ogilvie? Ach, the sooner we're shot o him the better! I dinnae ken whit wey they dinnae jist hing the bugger and be done wi it!

WILL: (*troubled*) Been actin up again, has he?

ANDREW: Ach, ye've nae idea! Still, he'll soon be sortit!

WILL: Hou's that?

ANDREW: I reckin he's for the buits. The buits'll brak him.

WILL: The buits? I've heard o them? Are they awfy . . .

ANDREW: Aye they're a sair thing, laddie. An awfy sair thing!

WILL: Ach, it's a shame! The Faither's no sic a bad sort o cheil, ye ken! It's an awfy pity! Ach, whit wey dae they hae tae torture him, onywey? They ken he's a priest, a Jesuit! That should be mair nor enough tae hing him! Whit wey dae they hae tae gi him the buits?

ANDREW: Politics, Wullie. I've tellt ye afore. Naethin tae dae wi us. Mair nor likely, Ogilvie kens somethin and Spottiswoode wants tae find oot. Politics.

WILL: Well, I think it's a fuckin shame! Gin his Lordship was gonnae gie the Faither the buits he should hae done it months ago, b'Christ! This is bluidy awful! (*Pauses obviously upset by the news*) Will they get somebody in?

ANDREW: What for?

WILL: For the buits! Will they get somebody in tae gie them tae him?

ANDREW: Ye're jokin!

WILL: Well, wha gies him the buits then?

ANDREW: I'll gie ye three guesses!

WILL: (*jumping to his feet*) Here, here, jist a minute! Screw the nut, eh? Screw the fuckin nut! I didnae sign on for that.

ANDREW: Ye're in the airmy nou, boy. And in the airmy — even this yucky wee airmy — ye dae whit ye're tellt! Which reminds me — ye better get awa up and relieve Wattie. The puir bugger'll be starvin bi nou!

(*Rather reluctantly*, WILL *goes to the rack and takes down his sword and helmet*)

WILL: That's aaright, Andro, but I signed on for a sodger — no a bluidy torturer!

ANDREW: (*wearily*) Forget it son! Forget it for nou! It wadnae be you that'd be rammin the wedge intil his leg in ony case . . .

WILL: Maybe no, but it's oot the bluidy box for aa that!

(WILL *goes to the door, pauses, hitches up his sword*)

WILL: Ye'll be on the nicht watch?

ANDREW: (*absently*) Aye.

WILL: See ye the morn then!

(*Exit* WILL. ANDREW *sits staring into his drink. Eventually, he drains the mug and stands up.* SPOTTISWOODE *enters*)

ANDREW: (*turning*) M'lord.

SPOTTISWOODE: (*raising his hand*) It's aa richt, Andro, it's aa richt! Ye can stand easy! I'm sorry about this — hae ye finished your dinner?

ANDREW: Aye, m'lord.

SPOTTISWOODE: Guid. Well, get armed then and come on up the stairs. I want a word with ye. (*As* ANDREW *gets ready*) Ogilvie, Andrew. It's about Ogilvie. What d'ye think?

ANDREW: (*belting on his sword*) He'll brak gif ye gie him the buits, m'lord. Shair as daith!

SPOTTISWOODE: Mm. Ye dinnae care for the boots, do ye Andro?

ANDREW: I'm a sodger, sir. It's aa in the day's wark.

SPOTTISWOODE: Aye, aye, aye. But ye dinnae care for them, do ye. Yersel, I mean! It's no a job ye like?

ANDREW: Wattie's yer man for the buits, m'lord. No me. (*Hesitates*) As I say, I'm a sodger — I'm trained tae fecht, no torture. Naw sir, I dinnae care for the buits.

SPOTTISWOODE: I'll be frank with ye, Andro. Neither do I. And in this case — in this case I question their effectiveness. I'm thinking that it micht be better to consider something else.

ANDREW: (*all ready*) Whatever ye say, m'lord.

SPOTTISWOODE: Come away up the stair. We'll hae a blether aboot it.

(*Exit* SPOTTISWOODE, *followed by* ANDREW)

SCENE FIVE

(OGILVIE's *room, nine days later. The bed has been removed and* OGILVIE *is seated at the table. He is a terrible sight. His shirt is torn to shreds, his hair is in disarray, there are enormous black rings about his eyes and scratch-marks and streaks of blood all over his hands and arms. He has been denied sleep for the past eight days.*

It is four o'clock in the morning. ANDREW, *on the night watch, is seated on the edge of the table. He has shed his sword, helmet and tunic and has no other weapon except for a dagger which he keeps in a leather sheath strapped to his bare arm.* OGILVIE's *head falls on his chest and his eyes close.* ANDREW *slaps him hard across the face several times*)

ANDREW: Come on, Faither, come on! Ye ken ye cannae get

tae sleep! (ANDREW's *slapping has had no effect so he draws the dagger and jabs at* OGILVIE's *shoulder several times*) Wake up, man, wake up, wake up!

 (OGILVIE *staggers back out of his chair like a startled beast. He stumbles once or twice but eventually manages to stand up fairly steadily, albeit in a stooped position*)

OGILVIE: (*peers in* ANDREW's *direction, shading his eyes with his hand*) Who — who is it this time? Andrew? Is it you, Andrew? You'd never believe . . . Is it you, Andrew? Yes. Yes, it *is*! It *is* you, Andrew. I know it is. You're the one. You're the one who never says anything. You never say anything. Well, very little anyway. So it must be you, Andrew. It must be . . .

ANDREW: Aye, Faither, it's mysel.

OGILVIE: Oh. Oh. I knew it. I knew all the time that it was you. I knew it but I hoped — oh, never mind! I hoped — I hoped it might be one of the others. Because you're the worst, Andrew, did you know that? The worst, the very worst of the lot. The very worst (*Laughs*) of a bad, bad lot! (*Laughs louder*) The Praetorian Guard of His Heretical Holiness! (*Bitterly*) Bunch of workshy know-nothings and broken-down has-beens! Sandy — God, Sandy's bad enough! He talks and talks and talks and talks. He hardly stops for breath. His tongue chisels away all the way into the farthest extremities of my brain! Oh, I know all about you. Andrew — what a great warrior you were, all the battles that you fought! Sandy makes it sound like some great legend (*Laughs*) — a great legend that goes on and on and on and on! (*Shakes his head*) Sandy — poor Sandy — Sandy is a bore. But he's not the worst — no, no, not by a long chalk he's not the worst. Neither is Will — oh my God, Will, Will, what am I saying? Will's the best! The only one of the whole damned lot of you with a morsel of charity in him. He's a good boy, Wullie — a very good boy. Now don't mistake me! Don't misunderstand! He does his job, he keeps me awake — nothing else you hear? (*Softer*) But he's kind. He's considerate. He talks to me — he talks to me without shouting, without argument, without — without — without . . . oh dammit, what's the word, what's the word! What I mean to say is that, when he talks to me he listens to what I say, there are no barriers between us, no implacable stone walls! I have not talked to another living being, the way that I sometimes talk with Will, for many a long, long day. And perhaps I never will again. And if he could just — if I could get him to — Oh, no, no, no, no, it's useless, useless! He will not listen. He's a heretic, another damned heretic just as you . . . just as you (*Gives* ANDREW *a shifty suspicious look*) all are! (*Whispers*)

Andrew? Andrew? Is that right? Are you a heretic?

ANDREW: Eh?

OGILVIE: A heretic. I asked you if you were a heretic. Are you a heretic?

ANDREW: If ye say so, Faither.

OGILVIE: No! *Not* if *I* say so! *I* am not *you*! It's not for me to tell you whether or not you are a heretic. It's not for me to say! It's for you. You. It's your own decision! The facts are before you, you can make up your own mind. You don't *have* to be a heretic, you know. You don't have to be! (*Suddenly weary, he passes his hand across his eyes*) I was a heretic once, did you know that?

ANDREW: (*more to himself than to* OGILVIE) Wadnae surprise me, Faither.

OGILVIE: Eh? What was that? What did you say? It wouldn't surprise you, It wouldn't surprise you, eh? Why not? Why not, pray? Do I look like a heretic! Do I sound like a heretic! Do I behave like a heretic? What am I doing here if it would not surprise you?

ANDREW: (*uneasily, not really wanting to talk*) Jist passin a remark, Faither. Didnae mean ocht by it.

OGILVIE: No? No? It occurs to me Andrew, that you do not care for heretics. Is that right? (ANDREW *says nothing*) Now Andrew. I asked you a question. I want an answer. I get the distinct impression that you do not greatly care for heretics. Andrew, am I right? (*Again* ANDREW *says nothing*) Andrew, I am talking to you! I am asking you a question and I want an answer right now. Do you or do you not care overmuch for heretics? (*Still* ANDREW *says nothing.* OGILVIE *bunches up his fist and shakes it at him*) You! You! You! Oh you! I might as well try to communicate with a rock as bother with you! You are always this way. You hardly say a word. Sandy speaks too much and you speak too little and Wat (*recoils as if in pain*). Wat! Oooh that twisted pig, Wat! (*Holds out his hands to* ANDREW) Have you seen this, Andrew? Have you seen Wat's latest? Clever wee Wattie's latest trick to torment Father Ogilvie? He took ten nails, Andrew, ten nails and drove them — one at a time, with his mallet — right under my fingernails! Oh, the cunning little bastard, why did he have to do that! His ingenuity, his bestial ingenuity knows no bounds! (*Pauses to recover his somewhat fragile composure*) And yet and yet, I'll tell you something — I prefer, I *much* prefer Wat to you. Yes. Yes. His torture, his physical torture, is far more bearable than the torment that your silence inflicts on me! (*Pauses to gather his thoughts and puts them into words*) Wat enjoys himself you know — he *enjoys* himself. You'd never guess it from his expression — that dour, heretical, swinish little face — but he *does* enjoy himself. Everything he does — every new source of pain that he invents comes from up here. (*Taps his head*) Nobody tells him. Nobody gives him orders — how he must think and rack his brain for originality! He brings his tortures to me with all the enthusiasm and delight of a devoted father with gifts for his new baby! Mind you, there's nothing personal in it! It has nothing to do with *me*! But I am a Catholic, you see — and Wat is strong, strong against the papes! Oh aye! So he doesn't worry about me at all — and he enjoys himself. But Andrew — it works both ways. D'you understand what I mean? D'you understand? D'you understand what I'm trying to say? Wattie doesn't think of me as a human being at all — that's why he can approach his work with so much equanimity. But, you see, it works both ways. I don't think of him as human either! No! And when he was hammering those nails into my hands, there was a part of me — not all of me, I admit, just a part, a small part — that was enjoying it every bit as much as he was! Can you understand that? Eh? (ANDREW *looks sceptical but says nothing.* OGILVIE *laughs*) You don't believe me, do you? You don't believe that anyone could enjoy it! (*Thrusts his hands in front of* ANDREW's *eyes so viciously that* ANDREW *recoils, reaching for his dagger*) But I did, I tell you — I did. You see, Andrew, when Wat was tapping in the nails — the nails into my fingers — there were no complications, no extraneous considerations. There was a confrontation going on, a divine confrontation, that had nothing to do with Wat or myself, with the logic or wisdom of my beliefs or the logic or wisdom of his, with his cruelty or my pain. No, no, it was more than that, much more. We were only the instruments, the weapons of a conflict that was ultimately between the Almighty on my side and the Devil on his. Now do you understand why I hate you more than the others? Now do you understand why I asked you that question? Now do you understand why I *must* know what you feel about heretics? (*He has wound himself up almost to breaking point and now begins to weep*) Why don't you answer me? Why don't you say something? Why do you just stand there and smirk?

ANDREW: Naethin to say, Faither!

OGILVIE: That's what you always say! (*Mimics*) 'naethin to say, Faither'. Don't try to fool me, Andrew. Don't try to pretend to me that you are a man of few words — because I know different! (*Turns wearily away, worn out by his fury but turns back almost immediately in a more composed, if intense, vein*) Andrew. I am not a fool. I'm not a child. Eh? I know, you know. I know why you won't talk to me. I know. You will not talk to me, you refuse to talk to me, you are afraid to talk to me because you (*Points*) are a Catholic!

 (ANDREW *gives a scornful, embarrassed laugh but says nothing*)

OGILVIE: How long have I been without sleep. Andrew. How long? Must be — a week? Must be. Eh? Is it a week? It must be that at least! Even so. Even so, Andrew, after all this time, after all this time without my natural rest — even so, there are periods, there are short spells when I have complete, absolutely complete lucidity. There are periods when I am as awake and as aware as ever I was. And believe me, Andrew, I am fully awake now! (*Goes quickly to* ANDREW *and takes him by the shoulders*) Andrew, I am going to ask you a question. I am going to put a question to you. And if you refuse to answer — or if you should answer falsely — Andrew, Oh Andrew, Andrew you will surely be damned! (*Takes a deep breath*)

Now. Tell me. Are you or are you not a Catholic?

ANDREW: (*hesitates, looks* OGILVIE *in the eye, turns away*) That was a while syne. A lang while syne.

OGILVIE: (*exulting*) You are! You are! I knew it! I knew it! You are a Catholic. Heaven be praised!

ANDREW: (*angry and embarrassed and evasive all at the same time*) My faither was! My mither was!

OGILVIE: (*without noticing the evasion*) Your mother — your mother was a Catholic? Is that right? Is that right now, Andrew? (*Turns away as if in a dream*) So was mine, Andrew. So was mine. Oh Andrew, it is the Catholic women who are the backbone of our faith — the Catholic women. There are many — I myself have known many, a great many men who were holy, truly holy. But I never met any man who was as holy as my mother. (*Closes his eyes as if in prayer*) Oh you are a woman of great faith. What you have desired will be accomplished for you. (*Turns again to* ANDREW) Tell me, Andrew. Where do you worship?

ANDREW: (*amused*) Worship, Faither?

OGILVIE: Worship. Yes. Where do you worship? Where do you receive the Mass.

ANDREW: (*shaking his head*) I never worship, Faither.

OGILVIE: (*shocked*) Never.

ANDREW: Naw!

OGILVIE: Then how . . . how do you serve your faith?

ANDREW: Faither (*With some hesitation*) I hae nae faith.

OGILVIE: No faith? No faith? This — what d'you mean, you've lost your faith? Is that it? Have you become a heretic? (ANDREW *turns away, says nothing*) Answer me, Andrew. Answer me. You're not going to turn dumb again, are you? Just when you've started to talk? Don't you understand Andrew? Don't you understand that I cannot bear those silences? I cannot bear your terrible silences!

ANDREW: (*savagely*) Faither, I hae nae faith. Leave it at that!

OGILVIE: But Andrew — a man cannot live without faith!

ANDREW: (*turns savagely once more, suddenly smiles gently*) Faither, I am forty-twa year auld.

OGILVIE: Oh Andrew. Oh Andrew, Andrew, Andrew. Oh — Oh Scotland. What kind of country have you become? What depths of barbarism have you reached? When a man can stand before his priest without shame and tell him that he has lost his faith! (*Turns to* ANDREW *again*) So. You are beyond even the evil sin of heresy. You are a pagan. You have lost your faith. (*Suddenly savage*) Well, I have not lost mine! That is why I am here. That is why I am enduring this — this torment! That is why I will endure all this and more! Spottiswoode — did you know that Spottiswoode threatened me with the boots. Yes. The boots. (*Smiles and shakes his head*) I think he broke poor Wattie's heart when he decided not to use them. And he told me — Spottiswoode did — he told me, he said to me that I was lucky. Lucky! (*Mimics*) 'Ye hae been used in a maist merciful manner, Faither Ogilvie'. (*Laughs bitterly*) You're all fools, do you know that? (*Slaps his leg*) What's this. Eh? It's a leg. That's all. A leg. What good is a leg to a priest? To carry him into chapel, that's all. To carry him into chapel. *I can be carried into chapel!* Don't you understand? Take my leg, take both my legs! Take my arms! I do not need them, they are of no use to me! But you, you . . .

(*Suddenly he screams and staggers about with his head in his hands.* ANDREW *stands by, aghast and helpless, looking towards the door every now and again as if unsure about going for help.* OGILVIE *turns on* ANDREW *forcing him up against the wall and ranting at him in a voice that seems stretched to breaking point:*)

OGILVIE: You, you, you, what are you doing? What are you doing to me? What are you doing? You are driving a wedge into my mind! You are crushing my brains and my reason is running from my skull in rivers of grey! (*Pushes himself away from*

ANDREW *who now seems considerably alarmed*) You are driving me mad! You take my mind, you take my body, you take my reason, you take my comfort. Very well, then! Take it — take it all! I have no use for it, for any of it! I tell you only this (*Gathers himself together in one last defiant bellow*) You shall not have my faith!

    (OGILVIE *collapses.* ANDREW *rushes to him and tries to bring him round, without success. He goes to the door and bangs on it repeatedly*)

ANDREW: Sandy! Sandy! Whaur are ye, ye donnert bugger! Wake up, for Christ's sake! I want ye!

SANDY: (*off*) Is that yersel, Andro?

ANDREW: Whae the bluidy hell d'ye think? Come in here, for Christ's sake! I'm needin ye!

    (*The door opens and* SANDY *enters. He is a wiry little man, extremely talkative and of roughly the same age as* ANDREW)

SANDY: Is it the Faither? I heard aa the rammy. Away again, is he?

ANDREW: Aye. Come on, gie's a haun wi him.

    (ANDREW *bends over* OGILVIE's *body, taking him by the armpits.* SANDY *follows, dithering and talking all the time*)

SANDY: My my my my, Andro, I'll tell ye straucht. I cannae be daein with this wey o warkin. I tellt the Bishop, I says tae him, I says . . .

ANDREW: Shut yer bluidy face and get on wi it!

SANDY: (*unperturbed*) . . . this offends my sense o professional decorum . . .

ANDREW: (*struggling with* OGILVIE) Jesus Christ, Sandy! Get him up! (*Together they manage to get* OGILVIE *to his feet*) Right. Twice roun syne let him faa. Come on.

    (*They half-walk, half-drag* OGILVIE *twice round the room.* SANDY *keeps on talking*)

SANDY: They'd hae been far, far better wi the buits — far far better. I've said frae the start that this was a daft-like wey o warkin — wastin aa this time and no even a cheep of whatever it is the Airchbishop wants. Ye can say whit ye like, Andro. Ye can say whit ye like. It's jist no right that professional sodgers like you and me should be asked tae tak on duty like this. This is Wattie's game, this. The torture tredd. It micht be aaricht for Wattie — aye, it micht be aa very weill for Wattie! No for me. I ken wappins, I tellt the Bishop, I ken wappins, been a sodger aa my days, that's *my* tredd. I says tae Spottiswoode I says . . .

ANDREW: (*with long-suffering patience*) Are you fuckin finished?

(They have once more reached the centre of the room)

SANDY: *(slightly cowed)* Weill, ye ken whit I mean.

ANDREW: Dae I? Jesus Christ, I sometimes wonder if ye ken yersel! Have ye got him?

SANDY: *(taking a firmer grip on* OGILVIE's *arm)* Aye.

ANDREW: Are ye ready?

SANDY: Aye.

ANDREW: Right, Wan. Twa. Three.

(They stand back and allow OGILVIE *to keel forward on his face.* OGILVIE *rises to his hands and knees and shakes his head)*

OGILVIE: *(rising)* My God. Oh My God. *(Shouting)* My God! I have kept my promise! I have made you known to the men you gave me! I have given them your word and they have received it! My God, My God, I pray for them, these men. I pray for them and them alone because these are the men you gave me. Let them be with me, Oh Lord! Let them be with me in my hour of glory. Let them be with me in the glory you will give me! Let them be with me that they might see, that they might know that the glory that is mine is the glory of Almighty God! Father, the world does not know you as I know you . . . the world does not know . . . Father . . . the world . . .

(He is reeling and tottering and obviously about to fall over again)

ANDREW: Watch him!

*(ANDREW *and* SANDY *manage to catch* OGILVIE *safely but his falling weight makes both of them stagger back. They stand, holding* OGILVIE, *and panting for breath)*

SANDY: Jesus Christ! Andro, he's weill awa nou. Did ye hear whit he was sayin? He's haverin nou — we'll no get onything oot o him gin we keep this up! He'll no last the nicht. Aw Andro, when I think o aa that you and me hae seen through thegither — I never thocht I'd see the day that . . .

ANDREW: Shut up, Sandy! Shut up! Gie yer fuckin erse a chance, will ye? Christ, ye never stop!

SANDY: *(hurt by* ANDREW's *rebuke)* I'm sorry, Andro. I didnae mean tae . . . Will we tak anither turn?

ANDREW: Naw, naw, it'll dae nae guid. We'd jist tire ane anither oot. We'd better gie the drap anither try tho. Are ye ready?

SANDY: Aye.

ANDREW: Richt. Wan. Twa. Three.

*(OGILVIE *keels forward again.* ANDREW *and* SANDY *go to him.* ANDREW *kneels down and listens to his heart)*

OGILVIE: You're damned, Andrew! You are going down to the burning fires of hell! You have thrown away your faith and you cannot be saved or released from your damnation! God is not mocked. Andrew, God will not be mocked. I know where you are, I know where you live. I know the spirit that burns within you, the flame, the dying flame, the dying flame which yet might live! Wake up, Andrew, before it's too late and the fire consumes you. Wake up, wake up, wake up! Feed that flame that it might not die! There are few here in Scotland who have kept their clothes clean — but wake up, only wake up and I tell you that you will walk with me dressed in the purest of white raiment. You will walk with me dressed in the raiment of the blessed of Christ. Oh, I know you do not love me as you must have done once — I know you do not love me now as you did then. Only turn from your sins and do as you did then — turn from your sins, I beseech you, turn from your sins! For if you do not turn from your sins I will come and I will find you and I will leap upon you like a thief in the night! Listen to me, Andrew! Listen to me if you have ears! Listen to me if you have ears! Listen to me if you have ears!

> (OGILVIE *collapses again and, this time,* SANDY *and* ANDREW *are so horror-struck by him that they do not even try to catch him. He lies on the floor gabbling for a moment before passing out again*)

SANDY: (*breathlessly*) He's gane badgy!

ANDREW: (*glancing dazedly at* SANDY) Guid God! Guid God!

> (SPOTTISWOODE *enters briskly, followed by a* DOCTOR, *a severe-looking young man*)

SPOTTISWOODE: What's happening here? What's the trouble? Andrew?

> (THE DOCTOR *goes to* OGILVIE *and starts examining him.* ANDREW *takes a step back and looks at* SPOTTISWOODE, *shaking his head*)

SANDY: Gin ye want my opinion, M'lord, I'd say that he's gey near it. I mean to say, sir, echt days and nine nichts, I mean tae say . . .

SPOTTISWOODE: (*completely ignoring him*) Andro. What d'ye think?

ANDREW: (*hesitates before he answers*) I dinnae ken, m'lord. Shair as daith, I dinnae ken. I thocht that . . . weill, I didnae think he had it in him, I didnae think he had the smeddum tae see it through this far. And nou — nou I hae the idea, I'm jist as shair that he'll see it through till daith. Daith and worse nor daith. I think he's past tholin ony mair o it.

DOCTOR: M'lord, gin this man is no let to sleep within the hour, he'll no survive.

SPOTTISWOODE: Ye're siccar o that?

DOCTOR: Aye, m'lord.

   (SPOTTISWOODE *paces the floor, hands behind back, deep in thought*)

SPOTTISWOODE: Very well. Andro. Sandy. Bring him a bed.

   (*Exit* ANDREW *and* SANDY *hurriedly, followed by the* DOCTOR)

SPOTTISWOODE: Damn ye, John Ogilvie. Damn ye!

   (*Exit* SPOTTISWOODE)

ACT TWO — SCENE ONE

About a month later. Ogilvie's quarters in Spottiswoode's Castle in Glasgow. As the scene opens, OGILVIE is discovered sitting on the bed reading a book. He looks up from his reading, closing his eyes, committing a passage to memory. The high-spirited laughter of a woman is heard off. OGILVIE lays the book aside, frowning, rises to his feet. Enter ANDREW, and, sweeping in behind him, LADY RACHEL SPOTTISWOODE. A tall, handsome woman she is dressed in a floor-length cloak and is slightly tipsy, she keeps her arms under the cloak folded across her chest, and glances about the room with a rather exaggerated inquisitiveness.

ANDREW: (*grumpily*) Faither, ye hae a visitor. The Leddy Rachel Spottiswoode.

   (*Looking rather uncertain*, OGILVIE *steps forward, inclining his head in the merest suggestion of a bow*)

OGILVIE: (*guardedly*) Madam, this is an unlooked-for pleasure.

   (RACHEL *gives a slight nod and moves past* OGILVIE, *downstage and across, speaking as she does so*)

RACHEL: Weill, Faither, this is hardly what I'd been led to expect. (*She stops one step away from the end of the bed and turns to address* OGILVIE *direct*)

Ye seem to be byordnar comfortable here. They maun be treating ye better nou nor they did when ye were in Embro!

OGILVIE: (*pleasantly*) Madam, it is still . . .

RACHEL: Is that richt, Andro? Ye'll hae been tellt to treat the Faither a wee thing kinder here in Glesca nor ye did in Embro?

ANDREW: That's no for me to say, m'leddy.

RACHEL: (*giggles*) Andro's no very pleased wi me, Faither. Are ye, Andro?

ANDREW: No my place to be pleased or displeased, m'leddy.

RACHEL: Och, wad ye listen to him, Faither? It's my husband, ye see. He's feart the Airchbishop'll get to ken that I've come to see ye!

ANDREW: He's shair tae, m'leddy. And *he'll* no be pleased.

(OGILVIE *is looking distinctly unhappy by this time*)

OGILVIE: In that case, madam, perhaps it would be better . . .

RACHEL: Och, Faither Ogilvie, dinna you start! There's nae need to fash about John. I ken weill enough hou to handle *him*. I'll tell him myself — in my ain guid time. Andro, as I was just this minute passing the servants' quarters, I've a notion I heard the sound of merriment and conviviality. (*Flatly*) I suggest that ye go and get yourself a drink.

ANDREW: (*hardly able to contain his outrage*) I am on duty, m'leddy.

RACHEL: (*irritably*) Aw, Andro, dinna you be sic an auld fash! (*Smiles with mischief*) Faither Ogilvie's a braw-looking cheil richt enough — but he's a man o the cloth and a perfect gentleman, I'm shair. I don't suppose that there's the slightest chance that my honour will be in danger whatsoever!

ANDREW: (*growling*) Madam . . .

RACHEL: Andro, that's enough! Dinna argue. Dae what I tell ye. Away ye go! Shoo!

(*Reluctantly, glowering at them both,* ANDREW *takes his leave.* OGILVIE *watches him leave somewhat helplessly*)

OGILVIE: Well, madam — would you care to take a seat?

(OGILVIE *goes to take the chair from the desk.* RACHEL *steps over to the bed and sits herself down on it*)

RACHEL: That's very kind of ye, Faither.

(*Perplexed,* OGILVIE *sits down on the chair himself*)

OGILVIE: Well! (*Pauses*) I'm afraid that I'm unable to offer you any kind of refreshment.

(RACHEL *laughs and rises. She throws back her cloak to reveal that she has been holding a bottle and two goblets, hiding them presumably from Andrew*)

RACHEL: No need for apologies, Faither! I brocht my ain!

(*She places the bottle and the goblets on the table, and, slipping off her cloak, throws it on to the bed.* OGILVIE *rises to his feet.* RACHEL *uncorks the bottle and begins to pour*)

RACHEL: Say when, Faither.

OGILVIE: That will be sufficient madam.

(RACHEL *hands him the goblet and pours out a drink for herself*)

RACHEL: (*Grins*) Here, I wonder what Mistress Calder and the ither douce leddies o Glesca toun'd say, gin they could see me nou? On my lane wi a man — a Catholic priest! — sipping wine at this time o the nicht! Tut, tut, tut! (*Confidentially, coming*

closer to him). But then Faither Ogilvie, Mistress Calder and the
ither douce leddies o Glesca toun consider me a harlot and a
tippler in any case — so we'll no worry about them, eh?

(*She moves away from him and takes up her seat on the bed*)

OGILVIE: Well, Lady Spottiswoode — your very good health!

RACHEL: (*raising her glass*) And yours, Faither. (*Takes a sip*) Tell
me — are ye keeping better nou?

OGILVIE: Oh yes! Yes, I've quite recovered from my (*Pauses*)
my experience in Edinburgh.

RACHEL: That's fine, then.

(OGILVIE *nods and pauses for an instant*)

OGILVIE: Tell me, my lady, what can I do for you? (*Smiles
guardedly*) I take it you've not come to interrogate me?

(RACHEL *laughs*)

RACHEL: Hits, na, Faither. I ken nocht o sic maitters! I wadnae
ken where to start! Just a wee social visit, that's aa! There's been
sic a lot o clash about the toun anent the ongoings o Faither
John Ogilvie that I thocht — ach, I had a notion to come and
see ye, that's aa! (*Pauses*) Efter the morn's morn, I michtna get
the chance.

OGILVIE: (*warily*) No. No. That's true.

RACHEL: Aye! (*Changing the subject*)
They tell me, Faither, that ye left Scotland when ye were nae
mair nor a laddie?

OGILVIE: That's correct. I've spent most of my life on the
Continent. I only returned last year.

RACHEL: Shairly . . . it maun hae been a thocht to come back?

(OGILVIE *pauses a minute before answering, moving away from
her downstage*)

OGILVIE: I have a vocation to serve, madam. It is not for me
to be afraid of the conditions in which I must serve it.

RACHEL: (*smiling*) Dinna mistake me, Faither. That's no what
I meant. I was just thinking that Scotland — the place and the
folk — maun seem unco strange til ye after aa this time.

OGILVIE: (*faintly surprised*) Strange? No. No, not really. I was
happy enough in Europe, but Scotland, after all, is my native
land — I am no foreigner here!

RACHEL: Mmm. (*Change of subject*) And did ye manage to see
your family?

OGILVIE: My family? (*Suspicious of the question, pauses before re-
plying*) Yes. Yes. I paid a short visit to Banff shortly after I
arrived.

RACHEL: (*pleasantly*) Oh, they'd be pleased to see ye!

OGILVIE: (*laughs bitterly*) Pleased? No, madam, they were hardly pleased!

RACHEL: (*rising in concern*) Were they no? But shairly your faither . . .

OGILVIE: My father! (*Laughs again*) My father — and my step-mother and all the rest of them — are heretics! Surely you don't imagine that they'd kill any fatted calves for me?

(RACHEL *sits down on the edge of the desk*)

RACHEL: Och, I'm no sae shair! Bluid's thicker nor water when aa's said and done!

OGILVIE: Water perhaps, madam! Other elements are made of sterner stuff. (*Sighs and walks towards her*) Look, my lady. My father was asked to make a choice — years ago — between his title and his land on the one hand and his faith on the other. Well you know the choice he made. And if he were asked to make a similar choice — between his property and his blood — which do you think he'd choose?

(RACHEL *drains her goblet*)

RACHEL: Puir Johnnie! Puir, puir Johnnie Ogilvie! No had much o a homecoming, have ye, son?

(OGILVIE *resumes his seat*)

OGILVIE: (*with irony*) It certainly has left a lot to be desired!

RACHEL: Still, your faither maunnae hae been sae bad! I mean, ye'd shairly hae been a heretic yourself gin he hadnae sent ye . . .

(OGILVIE *rises angrily from his seat*)

OGILVIE: Oh that! That, madam, is the greatest irony of all! It was the dying wish of my mother — my real mother, that is — that I should be given a Catholic education. That desire was never honoured until my father married my step-mother — the Lady Douglas — and she saw the opportunity to rob me of my heritage — to seize the title and the property that should be rightfully mine and give them to her own bastard brats! Well, very soon now, I shall be given a greater title — and believe me, madam, there's none of them will have any part in that!

(RACHEL *lays her goblet aside thoughtfully*)

RACHEL: Faither, d'ye ken wha ye put me in mind o? Wullie Scott.

(OGILVIE *looks puzzled*)

RACHEL: Och, it's an auld tale. There was this laddie in the Borders — Wullie Scott was his name. A cattle thief. Naethin byordnar in that, of course — they're aa cattle-thieves in the Borders, ye ken. Anyway. Wullie was reivin the kye o a man cried Murray — and Murray keppit him at it. In the normal wey o things, Murray wad hae hinged Wullie Scott and that wad hae

been that. But it seems that Murray had a problem. He had a
dochter — an ill-faured bitch bi the name of Meg — muckle-
moued Meg they cried her — and he couldna get onybody to
mairry her and take her aff his hands. So he tellt Wullie, he
said 'See here, Scott. I'll gie ye the choice. Ye can hing — or
ye can mairry my dochter. What's it to be?' Wullie took ae look
at muckle-moued Meg — and he says 'I'll hing!'

OGILVIE: (*huffily*) I fail to see the analogy, madam. I am no
criminal.

RACHEL: I didnae say ye were, Faither.

> (*Enter* ANDREW. *He sees the bottle on the desk and eyes*
> RACHEL *with suspicion*)

RACHEL: Ah, it's yourself, Andrew. Aye, I suppose I'd better
awa. (*She picks up her cloak and takes it over to* ANDREW) We
hae sic a feck o visitors the nou — I'd better go and do my
hostess. (*She hands the cloak to* ANDREW, *who holds it for her*)
Thank ye kindly for the refreshment. (*She indicates the bottle and
winks at* OGILVIE) It's been grand talking to ye.

OGILVIE: Likewise, madam.

RACHEL: I trust it'll aa go weill for ye at the trial the morn.

> (OGILVIE *shrugs.* RACHEL *turns to go, then stops*)

RACHEL: Oh, by the way, Faither. I never tellt ye the end o the
tale. Wullie Scott didnae hing, Naw. He thocht about it and
decided that discretion was the better pairt o valour. I heard
tell that Meg was a guid enough wife till him and that, in time,
he even learned to love her.

OGILVIE: Madam, I could never learn to love heresy.

RACHEL: (*smiles*) Faither, I fear ye dinna take my meaning yet!
Guid nicht wi ye!

> (*Exit* RACHEL *and a relieved* ANDREW. OGILVIE *watches
> them go, puzzled*)

SCENE TWO

The courtyard of the Castle later that night. WILL, on guard duty,
walks back and forward thoughtfully, holding his spear over his
shoulder. He hears a step and comes to the alert.

WILL: Whoa! Stop richt there, whaever ye are!

> (THE DOCTOR *steps out of the shadows*)

DOCTOR: It's aaricht, Wullie. It's just mysel!

> (WILL *relaxes*)

WILL: Doctor! Ye gied me a wee gluff there! Ye're shairly out of yer bed late the nicht, are ye no?

(*They approach each other in a friendly manner*)

DOCTOR:. Aye! Just canna get to sleep, Wull! I keep thinkin about the trial the morn.

WILL: (*nodding sadly*) Aye!

DOCTOR: Tell me, Wullie . . . what d'ye think the outcome'll be?

WILL: O the trial?

DOCTOR: Aye.

WILL: That's no for me to say, Doctor. Tae tell ye the truth, I'll no even be there. I'll no be on duty.

DOCTOR: Aye, but ye've shairly some idea! Will they hing him, d'ye think?

(WILL *pauses, looks at the Doctor a trifle guardedly, turns away*)

WILL: It looks like it, doctor. Aye. It shairly looks like it!

DOCTOR: Mmm. It strikes me ya wadna be aathegither happy about that, Wullie.

(WILL *turns to him suspiciously*)

WILL: What d'ye mean bi that?

DOCTOR: (*innocently*) Naethin! Just that Faither Ogilvie and yourself seem to get on sae weill thegither that I'd hae thocht . . .

WILL: Ogilvie's a prisoner. I'm a gaird. Naethin chynges that!

DOCTOR: Na? That's no what I heard.

WILL: Aye, and whit did ye hear?

(THE DOCTOR *smiles*)

DOCTOR: I'm no shair if I can say, Wullie. It concerns a patient o mine, ye see. It michtna be ethical for me to tell *onybody* what I ken. Still, a doctor's no the same as a priest, is he? Whiles, a doctor micht feel it's his duty to betray a professional confidence . . .

WILL: (*shaking his head*) I'm no wi ye, doctor. I've no got a clue o what ye're talkin about!

DOCTOR: I'm talkin about a patient o mine — a man cried Mayne. John Mayne. Ken wha I mean?

WILL: (*shocked rigid*) Oh!

DOCTOR: Aye. Oh Wullie, ye've been an awfy silly laddie!

WILL: I didna mean ony hairm! It was just a wheen letters for his freins — his faither and his brithers and that — just tae let them ken hou he was! There was nae hairm . . .

(DOCTOR *goes to him and lays his hand on his shoulder*)

DOCTOR: Of course no! Of course there wasna! Still, gin the bishop was to find out . . . (WILL *looks alarmed*) Aw dinna fash, Wullie! Dinna fash! I'll no say a word. Like I said, it wadna be ethical . . .

WILL: (*relieved*) Thanks a lot, doctor! I'll no . . .

> (THE DOCTOR *looks about him before drawing a yellow parchment from the inside of his coat*)

DOCTOR: Only there's a wee complication. Ane of Faither Ogilvie's brithers has sent him a reply!

> (WILL *backs away from* THE DOCTOR)

WILL: Naw! No chance!

DOCTOR: What for no, Wullie? I mean, in for a penny . . .

> (*Enter* WAT, *none too sober*)

WAT: What the hell's gaun on here?

> (*Both* WILL *and* THE DOCTOR *are terrified*)

DOCTOR: Oh! It's yersel, Wattie! (*Pauses uncertainly for a moment*) I've just brocht this message round for the bishop. Wullie here seems to think it's owre late in the day to bother him wi it (*Goes to put the paper back in his pocket*) but it doesna maiter. It'll keep til the morn.

> (WAT *steps up to* THE DOCTOR *suspiciously and puts his hand out*)

WAT: See's it here!

DOCTOR: It's aaricht, Wat. I tellt ye . . .

> (WAT *snatches the parchment from his hand*)

WAT: I'll just tak a wee look at it just the same!

> (THE DOCTOR *turns away, very frightened.* WAT *unfolds the parchment and gazes at it for a few moments without expression. He looks up at* WILL)

WAT: What's the maitter wi this? Eh? Naethin the maitter wi this! See, you take it, gie it tae the bishop the morn. (*Turns to* THE DOCTOR) Save ye a trip back, eh doctor? (*Turns back to* WILL) See? Simple! Nae bother! (*Burps and claps* WILL *on the shoulder*) I'm awa tae my bed!

> (WAT *moves off, then stops suddenly, turns slowly and looks at both of them suspiciously, shrugs as if he couldn't care less, then exits.* THE DOCTOR *heaves a huge sigh of relief*)

DOCTOR: Right! I think I'd better get awa nou, Wullie . . .

> (WILL *strides over to him*)

WILL: Just a second, doctor. (*Holds up the document*) I'll deliver this. I've nae option nou — sae I'll gie it tae the Faither. But I'm thinkin that you want tae be grateful, doctor, that nane o us can read.

> (*Without another word,* THE DOCTOR *makes a hurried exit.* WILL *puts the parchment inside his tunic*)

SCENE THREE

About a month later. Spottiswoode's study in the Castle of the
Archbishop of Glasgow. It is a well-furnished, comfortable room,
the most dominating features of which are: on the right a writing
desk and chair, in the centre a large fireplace with comfortable
chairs on either side, on the left a small table with a decanter,
water and goblets. It is well past midnight and the fire has died.
SPOTTISWOODE sits on the left of the fireplace, a book in one
hand and a goblet of wine in the other. He sighs and, laying the
book aside on his lap, takes a sip of the wine. His wife, LADY
RACHEL SPOTTISWOODE, dressed in a nightgown and carrying
a candle, enters from the right.

RACHEL: (*reprovingly*) John! Are ye wyce, man? For heaven's
sake, what ails ye? Ye should be in your bed!
(SPOTTISWOODE *looks up at her, shakes his head and sighs*)
SPOTTISWOODE: (*absently, almost defensively*) I hae been read-
ing the epistles of the apostle Paul.
RACHEL: (*sarcastically*) Oh. I see. Are ye to be examined in them
then? — the morn's morn — that ye maun bide up aa nicht in
preparation?
SPOTTISWOODE: (*with a faint smile*) Woman, your wit is sour.
(RACHEL *comes forward and places her candle on the mantle-*
piece)
RACHEL: I ken. It's the time of nicht — and the sair trial of
haeing sic a husband as I hae.
(*She sits down opposite him*)
SPOTTISWOODE: (*still smiling, rises and takes his goblet over to*
the drinks table) Hae I been sic a bad husband to ye, lass?
RACHEL: (*turning in the chair to smile at him*) No, John. No. Ye
ken better than to speir that. But there was a time when ye'd
tell me aathing — a time when ye'd bring aa your sair bits to
me.
SPOTTISWOODE: And do ye think that time has gane?
RACHEL: It looks like it, John. It shairly looks like it. St Paul,
it would seem, has mair to offer in the way of comfort than I.
(SPOTTISWOODE *laughs loudly*)
SPOTTISWOODE: Rachel, there can be smaa comfort for me in
these times we live in. The office I hold in our Kirk is hardly
a comfortable ane! Will ye tak a cup of wine with me m'lady?
RACHEL: Dearie me. (*Sighs*) Just a small one please, John!
SPOTTISWOODE: (*grinning*) For the stomach's sake?
RACHEL: Aye.

(*As* SPOTTISWOODE *pours the drinks, the smile leaves* RACHEL*'s face and she becomes apprehensive. She turns away from him*)

RACHEL: John — I went to see John Ogilvie the nicht.

SPOTTISWOODE: (*turning, astounded*) You — what?

RACHEL: I went to see John Ogilvie the nicht.

SPOTTISWOODE: Certes, woman! Whiles ye go past it! What would Mistress Calder and the leddies o the congregation . . .

RACHEL: (*With a wave of her hand*) P-y-e-e-h!

SPOTTISWOODE: P-y-e-e-h yourself! Rachel! What in creation garred ye do a thing like thon! Ogilvie has set this toun on fire! If it is kent — and certes, it will be kent! — that Spottiswoode's wife . . . (*Hands her the goblet*) I do not ken where ye got the gumption!

RACHEL: (*taking the goblet*) Weill — I maun admit to being a wee thing leerie about it myself — so I took a rather large glass of this before I went. So they'll maist likely let on that I was fou at the time!

(SPOTTISWOODE *is about to take his seat. He turns on her, fuming and speechless. Looking at her, his temper fades and he smiles and shakes his head hopelessly*)

SPOTTISWOODE: Rachel, oh Rachel! What am I to do with ye?

RACHEL: (*seriously*) What am I to do with you, John? I'm sorry if I've offended or upset ye by going to see Ogilvie — but I'd hae thocht myself a sorrier wife gin I had stayed away! John, d'ye no understand? I had to try to discover what it was about this man that was bothering you.

SPOTTISWOODE: (*irritably*) Bothering me! Huh! It's no Ogilvie that bothers me!

RACHEL: Is it no? I'm no so sure! John, ye've no been yourself this while past — ill-tempered, growling and snarling aa owre the place, biding up gey near aa nicht, tossing and turning when ye do come to your bed . . . Na, na, my mannie, ye'll na tell me that it's no John Ogilvie that's bothering ye! This aa started on the very day he was arrested! Your bad humour started then. I had a notion to speak with the man that had put ye in sic a humour! So I went to see him.

SPOTTISWOODE: And are ye any the wiser?

RACHEL: I am not! I fail to see what there is to worry ye about this man! I canna help but feel sorry for him, but he's a wrong-headed fool! He micht be a cliver fool, but he's a fool just the same.

SPOTTISWOODE: D'ye tell me that, woman? A clever fool?

RACHEL: Ye needna laugh! Ye ken fine what I mean! The man

has faith enough, I daresay! Faith of a kind — but is it the Christian faith? I beg leave to doubt it. I jalouse that even a papist micht beg leave to doubt it! That man cares for nobody but himself — his ain hurts and grievances! And how can he hae any sympathy with the concerns and conditions of ordinary folk? He kens nocht about them. He has charm enough to spare and a braw sharp tongue — he'd make a bonnie courtier no doubt. What does he ken o the sufferings o Scotland? He maybe kens principle and argument. He kens nocht o flesh and blood!

SPOTTISWOODE: Principle is necessary, m'dear, in any undertaking — and so is argument. Flesh and blood survive and flourish on the guid maintenance of baith. (*Gets to his feet thoughtfully and walks about*) What troubles me in this matter is no Ogilvie's faith — I have never doubted nor grudged him that for an instant. He is a man of great faith, of great courage — and of not inconsiderable intellect. Really Rachel, John Ogilvie is a maist byordnar man. I wish we had a few like him in our Kirk. Paul tells us — as ye weill ken — that every man should bide the way he was when God called him. I cannot blame Ogilvie for his faith — in his own way, he is as true to his principles as, in his place, I would hope and pray to be to mine.

RACHEL: Aye. Maybe. But ye ken as weill as I do that there is mair to this than John Ogilvie's faith! Since Paul appears to be in favour the nicht, I would commend to you the advice given by Paul to the Romans anent their responsibilities to the authorities of the State!

SPOTTISWOODE: (*shaking his head irritably*) Oh it's no that, Rachel! It's no that, it's no that!

RACHEL: Weill what is it then?

SPOTTISWOODE: Ye ken what men say about me — and what they said about your faither?

RACHEL: (*hotly*) And you ken me weill enough to ken that I do not care a docken for what men say. My faither stood fast against the papes — and against the presbyterians! You have done the same and I'm proud of ye baith! What time of day is this to be bothering about what men say?

SPOTTISWOODE: Rachel, I am a man of the cloth! It is my business to take tent of what men say. And they say that we were bocht — that we served the King no out of conviction but for the stipend.

RACHEL: Och, John. Ye ken that's no true.

SPOTTISWOODE: Aye! Aye! But d'ye no understand? We were

taking a gamble — your father and myself and the others —
we were taking a gamble with our own guid names, with our
reputations. We kent that it would take time but what we were
ettling to effect was a reconciliation — we thocht and gif the
Catholics could bend a wee bit and the presbyterians could
bend a wee bit, we could bring them aa intil ae strang kirk. Ae
kirk in Scotland and peace in the land!

RACHEL: Aye. That's what ye've aye wanted.

SPOTTISWOODE: It was the King's plan but it was us who had
to carry it out — it was men like your faither and me who had to
take the gamble. We kent that it would be a gey hard trauchle.
A hard ane and a lang ane — your faither died still trauchling.
But we kent anaa that it was the only way. And nou (*sighs*) nou
we are going to spoil it aa. The morn's morn John Ogilvie will
be tried and condemned and the haill thing — years of work —
will aa be up in the air!

RACHEL: But John — it's no siccar yet that Ogilvie's to hing!

SPOTTISWOODE: Is it no! Losh woman, ye ken yourself — ye
have seen Ogilvie, ye have spoken to him. Is it no obvious what
he's after? He pants after the martyr's croun like a dog at a
bitch! And they'll gie it to him, thae men that you tell me no
to take tent of!

RACHEL: Och, John!

SPOTTISWOODE: Oh aye, they will. Since we came back from
Edinburgh, John Ogilvie's name has been on every lip. Gif —
no. — *When* he mounts the gallows, the Scottish Catholic community'll take him to their hearts and there will be blood. It'll
be war aa owre again! As for Ogilvie, he'll hae got what he
socht, what he returned to Scotland for. Glory, Rachel, Glory
and a place in the bloody history of our country! What does he
care if the rivers of Scotland run black with the blood of her
people, as long as he gets his glory!

RACHEL: But John, that's no your wyte . . .

SPOTTISWOODE: Did I say it was? Woman, d'ye no understand
yet? I hae given everything — my capabilities, my intellect, my
honour and my — *oor* guid name — everything to ae single
course of action. And the morn's morn, I maun sit doun in that
court yonder and watch aa the work that I hae done — and,
what's worse — the work I micht hae done being brocht doun
and connached by ane fushionless fanatic!

RACHEL: (*Going to him*) John, John, my love, ye're making owre
muckle of this! (*Sighs*) Ye said one true thing anent Ogilvie —
he's a byordnar man. There's no mony'd have stood what he's
stood — I ken what ye did to him in Embro, John — and if

he wants his martyrdom, he's surely earned it. But it'll be an empty thing, folk'll forget aa about it in no time! Hing him, John, hing him and ye'll never see his like again!

SPOTTISWOODE: Will I no? (*Breaks away from her*) I'm no sure. Oh gin I just had the power, gin I could just get him to listen! Gin I could persuade him! Persuade him to change his mind . . .

RACHEL: (*With an empty laugh*) Recant? Fegs John, he'll never do that!

SPOTTISWOODE: Gin he doesna, I'm feared. Gin he doesna I'm feared that I'll be hinging him again and again and again. Owre and owre and owre and owre! Martyrs are a queer-like breed, Rachel — they hae a way of turning into saints. Saints! Saint John Ogilvie — can ye no imagine it? Oh Rachel, I look intae that young man's een and I see a dream — a dream that is alowe with a bitter hatred. And it is a hatred that he has never learned — it is a hatred that he has only dreamed. Oh God! Rachel, how does a man learn sic hatred — how can a man learn to dream sic dreams?

RACHEL: (*quietly*) John, I'm sure I dinna ken.

SPOTTISWOODE: No more do I, love, no more do I. (*Savagely*) but, shair as daith, I'd better learn! I'd better learn gin my work in Scotland is to mean ocht ava! For I hae a dream of my own Rachel, I hae a dream of my own! Christ's sheep maun aa be brocht thegither in ae fauld! (*Stops and smiles a little at his own emotion*) Paul again, Rachel. Gin we dinna aa eat thegither at the same table, there will be some wha maun gang hungry — while ithers get fou! I want a Kirk in Scotland that will serve aa men. I want a Kirk in Scotland that will bring Catholic and Protestant thegither in the ae faith, in the ae life; I want peace in the land and britherhood and guidwill amang aa men — as the Guid Lord aye intended it should be! That is *my* dream, Rachel, a dream that is biggit nocht on hatred but — I pray to God! — on love!

RACHEL: Ogilvie can never change that, John.

SPOTTISWOODE: No, but he can stop the dream from coming true! He can set the clock back twenty years! Ogilvie can change reality — and it is reality that is important, no dreams! That is a lesson we maun learn here in Scotland! (*Gives a bitter laugh*) D'ye ken what is the maist absurd thing in this haill business? My auld teacher, my auld lecturer here in Glasgow — Andro Melville — preached the doctrine of the Twa Kingdoms. The temporal and the spiritual. D'ye mind? D'ye mind when King Jamie was seventeen year auld and auld Maister Andro took a grip of him by the arm and tellt him he was 'nocht but God's silly vassal'? Aye, aye. Maister Andro was aye strang for the Lord and against the King! Nou Andro Melville's in the Tower of London for exactly the same reason that John Ogilvie's doun the stair! Would it no gar ye laugh? Gin it wasna so deathly serious would ye not see the humour? Melville, wha railed against the 'Harlot of Rome' and Ogilvie wha cries 'damn aa heretics' with geynear every second breath, are both facing death for geynear the exact same reason. Catholic and Protestant could aye unite better in death than they could in life! But where's Scotland aa this time — where's the sheep that we were aa tellt to feed? They're aa starving to death!

RACHEL: (*thoughtfully*) John, d'ye mind if I tell ye something?

SPOTTISWOODE: Woman, I'd like fine to see the day when I could stop you!

RACHEL: You're a clever foo anaa! Ye are. Oh I'm no complaining! Ye hae great faith, great learning, great generosity and great compassion. But ye've barely enough imagination to fill this cup!

SPOTTISWOODE: Woman, what time o day is this . . .

RACHEL: Na, na, na, na, na! Just you haud on and leave me have my say! Ye're sitting there, raxing yourself to daith, biding up aa nicht, pouring owre puir auld Paul looking for some divine answer to your predicament — and aa the time, there's a simple solution to the hail affair staring ye in the face gin ye only had the gumption to take a look at it!

SPOTTISWOODE: There is, is there? And what is that, woman?

(RACHEL *goes to the mantlepiece and retrieves her candle*)

RACHEL: (*turning to him with the candle in her hand*) Ye're siccar that he'll be condemned the morn?

SPOTTISWOODE: As siccar as I'm standing here.

RACHEL: And ye'll keep him in thon cell there, with a lock on the door and an armed guard ootbye?

SPOTTISWOODE: Aye.

RACHEL: So. Send the guard awa. Unlock the door. What would ye think of that gin you were Ogilvie?

SPOTTISWOODE: Ye think he'd run.

RACHEL: (*Going slowly to the door*) Ogilvie's young — he's time yet to be a martyr. (*Grins*) And I ken what Andro Melville would do in he's place! (*Sweeping out*)
Come awa to your bed!

(SPOTTISWOODE, *bewildered, gazes at her departing presence*)

SCENE FOUR

The following day in the late afternoon. The armoury at Spottiswoode's Castle in Glasgow. It is a roughly furnished but rather cosy room which the soldiers use as a sort of common room in their off-duty periods. There is a rack of spears along the length of the back wall and, in front of this, a long low table with a number of stools all about it. WILL is seated at one end of the table, polishing his helmet and ANDREW is at the other, sharpening his sword with a whetstone. WILL's sword and ANDREW's helmet lie on the table. They talk as they work.

WILL: Andro?

ANDREW: Aye?

WILL: Were you ever mairrit?

ANDREW: (*laughing*) Naw, no me!

WILL: Whit for no?

ANDREW: Oh, a lot o reasons! Never kent a lassie I fancied enough — at least, I never fancied a lassie that fancied me! (*Looks at* WILL *thoughtfully*) Thinkin aboot it yersel like?

WILL: Aye. I'd hae tae get oot o here . . .

ANDREW: Oh aye! Sodgerin's nae life for a mairrit man!

WILL: . . . But I'm no worried aboot that. I was thinking o packin it in onywey. Nae offence and aa that, Andro, but I dinnae want tae end up like you and Sandy — or, worse yet, like Wattie.

ANDREW: Well, it's up tae yersel, son.

WILL: Aye. Andro, the Faither says I cannae get mairrit — no really mairrit — gin I dinnae get mairrit in a Catholic kirk.

ANDREW: Haw, ye dinnae want tae listen tae the Faither, Christ! He's said a lot, has he no, and see whaur it's got him.

WILL: Aye, but if I did! That would mean that I'd hae to be a pape afore I could get mairrit! If the papes won like?

ANDREW: (*laying down the sword and looking at him*) Wullie, ye're a chynged laddie, dae ye ken that? Ye're an awfy chynged laddie. Jist a few short months syne ye were aa for burnin every pape in sicht! D'ye mind when we brocht Ogilvie in? D'ye mind whit ye were wantin tae dae tae him then?

WILL: I didnae ken the Faither then; I didnae ken — I had nae idea o hou mony folk in Scotland were still papes at hert. Aw, I'm no one o them, dinnae fash yersel aboot that! But I hae tae look oot for mysel and for —

ANDREW: For yer maw?

WILL: For the lassie that I want tae mairry! There are places in

Scotland whaur the ministers hae tae tak swords intil the pulpits wi them! Aye! Gin the papes were tae get back . . .

ANDREW: Wullie, I'll set yer mind at rest! The papes arenae comin back, son. The papes are never comin back!

WILL: (*sceptically*) I dinnae ken hou ye can be sae shair.

ANDREW: Dae ye no? Weill, I'll tell ye. The papes arenae comin back because the gentry — Faither Ogilvie's ain kind — 'll never let them. Christ, the reason — I winnae say the only reason — why the papes got kicked oot of the country in the first place was so's thae buggers could get their hauns on the ferms and the big hooses and aa the property and treisour that belanged tae the Roman kirk. Ye'll no tell me that they're gonnae hand aa that back for a daft-like thing like religion? (*Laughs*) Ye'll no tell me that Tam o the Cougait's gonnae gie back Melrose Abbey so that the papes can stop a laddie like you frae gettin mairrit!

WILL: (*nodding, still troubled*) Mebbe ye're richt, Andro, mebbe ye're richt. Still, gin the Faither hings . . .

(WILL *is interrupted by the excited entrance of* WAT *and* SANDY)

WAT: That's it, then. The pape's tae hing!

WILL: When?

SANDY: On the tenth. Jesus Andro, ye should have seen this! (WILL *picks up his sword and helmet and leaves the room*) Here, whit's the maitter wi the boy?

ANDREW: Never mind him. He's got a lot tae learn, that's aa.

SANDY: Aye, Him and the Faither's been gettin gey chief this last wee while. He'll be upset by the news.

WAT: (*taking the seat that* WILL *has vacated*) Aye and he's no the only ane either! Ye want tae have seen the greetin in the coort the day, Andro — eh, Sandy? No aa weemen either!

SANDY: (*coming round and taking his seat beside* ANDREW) Aye, Ogilvie's taen the trick wi them richt enough. Wadnae mind bettin there'll be a puckle trouble nou!

WAT: B'Christ there will! You jist watch! See, that's the thing wi papes — they worm awa intae people, turn them against their ain kind. They should hae hung that bugger months syne! See whit he's done tae young Wullie. He was a guid laddie that, at one time. But see nou? I'll tell ye this — if there is trouble, I'll be awfy careful aboot turnin my back on him. In my opinion . . .

ANDREW: (*angrily*) That's the trouble wi aa you buggers — ye're aa fu o yersels, ye've aa got opinions! Weill, I've an opinion anaa! (*Picks up his sword and hits the table with it*) That's it there! And if there is trouble, Wattie, and I see you turnin yer back on *onybody*, I'll soon enough gie ye my opinion, son! You bet I will!

(WAT *glares back hatefully at* ANDREW *but says nothing*)

SANDY: Aye, he will anaa! He will! (*Pause*) Andro . . .

ANDREW: Aaricht, Sandy. Aaricht. I can see that I'm gonnae get it aa sooner or later — I can see ye're fair burstin tae let it aa oot — sae it micht as weill be nou. Whit happened at the trial?

SANDY: (*enthusiastically*) . . . Weill, Andro, seein ye asked, I'll tell ye. It was somethin. It was somethin tae see aaricht! Nou, I'd hae thocht that — efter whit happened in Embro — that the Faither'd have calmed doun a wee, behaved himself like? Not a bit of it! My, my, but did he no gie them laldy! I'll say this for him — he's fit for them aa in a slangin match. Is that no richt, Wat?

WAT: Oh aye.

SANDY: He said he didnae gie a rotten fig for the jury, that the judges were aa like flies swarmin roun a lump o shite — weill, he didnae say shite, bein aa pan-loaf and a priest and that, but we aa kent whit he meant — he said he wadnae set doun holy things afore dugs and — tae cap it aa — he tellt the haill coort that the King was nae mair tae him nor an auld hat! Christ, ye want tae have seen Spottiswoode's face! If looks could kill, there'd be nae need for a hingin!

ANDREW: In ither wards, he pit the raip aroun his ain thrapple! I thocht he wad. (*Stands up and, taking his sword, holds it up to the light and looks along the edge*) And it's a bluidy waste, d'ye ken that? A man wi he's smeddum and brains could dae a haill lot o guid!

WAT: (*Sneering*) Ye're shairly gettin auld, Andro. Auld and saft! What guid is there in a papish priest? There's owre mony o the fuckers in Scotland as it is!

ANDREW: (*coldly*) He has echt days and nine nichts of pure bluidy hell in Embro. You ken that, torturer, you gave him the maist o it — and he never even looked like breakin! In spite of yer nails and yer mallet and yer clairty wee mind, he never came near tae beggin for mercy! And as far as the law's concerned, bein a papish priest isnae a hingin maitter.

WAT: (*smugly*) But he's no hingin for bein a papish priest! He's hingin for bein a traitor — he wadnae tak the Aith o Allegiance!

ANDREW: Then he should hae got the jile until he did! Och, it's no for me tae say that he shouldnae be punished — I'm no even sayin that he shouldnae hing! It jist seems tae me that it's a gey donnert thing for a man like Ogilvie, wi aa his smeddum and brains, tae fling his ain life awa like that! Ach whit gars me grue the maist is the fact that aa this argy-bargy is aboot sweet fuck-all! (*Holds the naked sword up before him*) The haun that hauds this sword has killed mair men nor I hae years o my life — and whit for? Whit some bluidy jyner said or didnae say in Palestine hundreds o years syne! Christ, it gies me the boke tae think o it! (*Looks at* WAT) You'll mebbe no mind on this, but Sandy will. Back in the year o' 96. . .

SANDY: Oh aye. I mind aaricht. The seventeenth o September riot. I mind thon aaricht!

ANDREW: The seventeenth o September. In Embro. There was a mob o thousans that day — aa bearin wappins and wantin tae kill the King. And at the heid o them aa was the meenisters. Bruce. Welsh. Black. 'For God and the Kirk' they cried 'For God and the Kirk!' And on the ither side — on the ither side, there was anither mob. And they were shoutin 'For God and the King!' God and the King! The bluid and the snot ran through the streets o Embro like a torrent that day!

WAT: Oh, aye, I mind on that that anaa. It was a sair business richt enough — but it was aa King Jamie's wyte . . .

ANDREW: Oh was it? Aaricht weill, whaur's King Jamie nou? He's still got his croun on his heid — at least, it's no the same croun but a bigger ane — and whaurs Robert Bruce? Whaur's John Welsh? Huh! The King's on his throne and meenisters are in their pulpits yet! It's aye the same — the meenisters and the priests and the high-heid anes'll dae the argyin and the stirrin up — but when it comes tae the killin and the dein, weill there's nane o them can lift up the deid they left on the streets o Embro that day. And they're never satisfied. When Ogilvie hings we'll hae anither riot, this time on the streets o Glesca. And it'll no be the meenisters that'll dae the fechtin or the killin or dein — it'll be you and me and Sandy and young laddies like Wullie!

WAT: (*laughing, quite insensitive to what* ANDREW *is saying*) Be fair, Andro! Be fair! It'll be Ogilvie anaa!

ANDREW: Aw fine Ogilvie. Ogilvie'll gae til the gallows and hae his craig stretched — fine for him! That's what he wants, that's whit he's efter! They'll mak a martyr oot o'm nae doubt — pent his pictur and hing it up on the Vatican waa! Great for Ogilvie! But whae'll fecht the battles that he'll leave ahint him? No John Ogilvie. He's away! (*Sighs and sheaths his sword*) And so am I. Better get back tae work, back tae the bluidy job!

(ANDREW *picks up his helmet and walks towards the door somewhat wearily*)

WAT: (*Addressing* SANDY *but really taunting* ANDREW) It's like

I was sayin, Sandy. Ye cannae trust thae papes. They get in aawhere — even here.

(ANDREW *stops and considers* WAT *amusedly*)

ANDREW: What's the maitter, Wattie? Ye're shairly no gonnae tell me that ye're worried aboot turnin yer back on me?

WAT: (*rises, walks towards the centre of the room*) Turnin my back? I made up my mind on that score as far as you were concerned a while syne.

(SANDY *rises and moves away from the table, behind* WAT *who is facing* ANDREW *from the middle of the room*)

ANDREW: (*very quietly*) And what dae ye mean bi that, son?

WAT: I mean that you're a pape — I mean that you're a Pope's man. I mean that I wadnae trust ye as far as I can throw ye!

ANDREW: (*stiffens, goes very quiet*) I hope you're feelin lucky, son!

WAT: Ha! Listen tae the hard man! I dinnae need luck for you, ye tired auld priest's (SANDY *very quickly draws his sword and prods* WAT *in the back with it*) bastard!

SANDY: (*laughing*) Ha, ha! Wattie, ye werenae mindin yer p's and q's. I micht be a pape anaa for aa ye ken! Will I disarm him, Andro?

ANDREW: Naw! (*Strides forward and gives* WAT *the back of his hand across the face*) Ye daft cunt! I micht hae killed you! Comin the haurd-case! You stick tae yer buits and yer mallet and yer nails! Because the next time you try onythin like thon, the best you can hope for is tae be flung in a cell withoot a door in it. D'ye understand?

WILL: (*wiping his cheek where* ANDREW *struck him*) I micht hae kent that the pair o ye wad hing thegither.

ANDREW: We aa hing thegither! We aa hing thegither — or we aa end up deid! That's the rule, Wattie. For Christ's sake, get it intae yer thick heid and forget aboot papes and protestants and bein feart aboot turnin yer back! We'll forget aboot this — you jist mak shair it disnae happen again, richt? (WAT *makes no answer*) Richt?

WAT: (*reluctantly*) Aye.

(ANDREW *nods and exits.* SANDY *sheaths his sword.* WAT *returns to where he was sitting*)

SANDY: Christ, Wattie, that was a daft-like thing tae try. What got intae ye?

WAT: Ach, I got pissed off wi him! Him and aa that talk aboot the seventeenth o September! Christ, ye'd think the papes'd never done onything!

SANDY: I'll no argy wi ye, Wattie. But ye're a lucky bugger

tae be sittin there the nou. Andro's a haurd man, Wat. He's
no lived as lang as he has for naethin. His sword'd have been
through your guts afore ye'd got yer ain clear o the scabbard!
Jist dinnae try that again, son. I'm warnin ye!

WAT: Aye? Weill maybe . . . (*Looks towards the door*) . . . but I
still say ye cannae trust thae papish bastards!

SCENE FIVE

Ogilvie's room in the Castle on the night of the 9th March 1615.
It is slightly more comfortable than his quarters in Edinburgh
(inasmuch as there is a small fire) but it is just as barely furnished.
OGILVIE, dressed completely in white is seated at a table writing.
He finishes, sands the paper, folds it and goes to the door and
knocks.

OGILVIE: Will! (WILL *enters.*)

OGILVIE: (*handing* WILL *the paper*) This is the last. You know
where to take it.

WILL: Aye.

(WILL *takes the paper from* OGILVIE, *puts it inside his tunic*)

WILL: (*with a sigh and a shake of the head*) Oh Faither, this is
the last for me anaa!

(OGILVIE *gives a speechless, unsteady smile but says nothing. Quickly, somewhat impulsively,* WILL *doffs his helmet and
kneels before* OGILVIE. OGILVIE *is taken aback for a second,
then smiles and places his hand on* WILL's *head*)

OGILVIE: Nomine Patris et Filis . . . The Lord bless you and
keep you. (WILL *gives a small, choked sob*) Oh Willie. Willie!
Arise, my son, arise! (OGILVIE *takes him by the shoulders and
brings him to his feet, talking to him gently and kindly*) You must
not grieve for me, Will! Do you not remember when I told
you — a long time ago — that this is my destiny? Tomorrow
my destiny will be fulfilled. Tomorrow — they are going to put
a crown of precious stones upon my head! (*He looks at* WILL
inquiringly. WILL *nods*) So no tears, boy. Go now. Go and give
my messages and my story to my brethren that the world shall
know what happened here.

(WILL *nods again and turns.* SPOTTISWOODE *enters and
stands at the door. Coming face to face with him,* WILL *freezes*)

SPOTTISWOODE: Ye hae secured your prisoner, Wull?

WILL: (*shakily*) Aye aye, m'lord. M'lord . . .

SPOTTISWOODE: Guid. Ye'd best get awa to your men nou.

Ye'll no be wantit again the nicht. (*When* WILL *hesitates*) Go, boy! It's aaricht!

(WILL *goes but stops briefly at the door*)

WILL: Guidby, Faither.

OGILVIE: (*quietly, with a kind smile*) Goodbye, Will. Take care!
(WILL *leaves*)

OGILVIE: (*rather too eagerly when* WILL *has gone*) Will has been very good to me. I am most indebted to you for putting him at my disposal. I have given him some letters for my family, he has promised to see that they are delivered safely . . .

(OGILVIE *lets his rather guilty words trickle away into silence*)

SPOTTISWOODE: Family? The Heretics? Ye make a damned poor liar, John Ogilvie. Did ye ken that?

OGILVIE: (*with some heat*) Spottiswoode, I had hoped never to see you again and do not in the least know what you hope to gain by coming here tonight! But since you are here — and will no doubt state your business in due course — I would thank you to spare me your insults for I am completely beyond them now!

(*Ignoring him,* SPOTTISWOODE *paces the floor a little in thought*)

SPOTTISWOODE: Tell me, Faither. Did ye hae any success with the boy?

OGILVIE: Boy? What boy?

SPOTTISWOODE: The laddie! Wullie! Did ye manage to convince him of the true faith?

OGILVIE: That's for you to find out!

SPOTTISWOODE: Aw, Faither, come on! I'm no going to set up a new trial at this time of day! I was only voicing a professional interest, that's aa! And gin ye dinnae wish to tell me, I'll no press ye! (*Pauses*) Houever, I would be interested to ken if ye tried. Did ye? Did ye try?

OGILVIE: (*taken aback*) As a matter of fact — since you ask — I didn't. (*Laughs*) I didn't. I never even thought of it. I gave him some instruction — Look, Will is no catholic, believe me when I tell you that! Please do not persecute him on my account!

SPOTTISWOODE: No, no, no, no, Faither Ogilvie, ye misunderstand me! I'm no interested in the laddie! I ken him for an honest young man and a loyal and faithful servant! It's you that interests me, Faither Ogilvie, you! Ye didna try, ye tell me? Forgive me, Faither — I'll no doubt ye, never fear! — but I find that a wee thing strange.

OGILVIE: Not all that strange. Right from the start — from the very day I was taken into captivity — I realised that I had to

be strong, that I had to raise my voice and shout. I knew that
if I did otherwise, I was lost! That is to say, my cause was
lost — there was never any hope for me personally and I knew
it. I knew that I had to be strong, I expected nothing from my
jailers but blows and abuse. I certainly never expected charity.

SPOTTISWOODE: And yet ye got it from Wullie?

OGILVIE: Yes. Yes. I never asked for it, I certainly never begged
for it — and yet, without I myself doing anything at all, Will
changed — he changed from a rough-tongued, bigoted youth
into a warm-hearted and decent fellow man. I do not know
how I would have kept my sanity and my courage without him.
And I? I gave him nothing! Oh he would occasionally ask me
a question about faith or behaviour and I would give him my
opinion — but I did not minister to him. I gave him nothing!

SPOTTISWOODE: Faither Ogilvie. Will is damned. Will is going
straight to the fires of hell!

OGILVIE: (*outraged*) That's a terrible thing to say!

SPOTTISWOODE: Aye, maybe! But I dinna say it — you do!

OGILVIE: I have never said any such thing!

SPOTTISWOODE: Have ye no? And what have ye been saying
this last half-year? You tellt me — in Embro last January —
that even the youngest bairn baptised by a presbyterian minister
was damned!

OGILVIE: I never said that — I said that he was within the Pope's
authority as far as . . .

SPOTTISWOODE: . . . punishment is concerned. I ken. And
what if he bides outwith the Pope's authority? What if he never becomes a Catholic? He's damned! You said that, Faither
Ogilvie, you believe that! You had the chance to save Wullie's
soul — according to your own beliefs — and you threw it away.
Ye didna try!

OGILVIE: Do not seek to burden me on the gallows with a lost
soul! There are other priests!

SPOTTISWOODE: Aye. There *are* other priests — or will be.
There are episcopalian and presbyterian ministers as well —
wha kens? Willie micht weill win to heaven yet! Houever, let
us no get into *that* argument! I didna come here the nicht to
burden your heart with a lost soul — I came for quite another
purpose. (*Very carefully, he pauses to frame his words*) Faither
Ogilvie, when first we met and I speired at ye what had garred
ye return to Scotland, ye tellt me — as I mind — that it was
to save souls. To 'unteach heresy' was the phrase, as I mind?

OGILVIE: That is correct. That is why I came.

SPOTTISWOODE: Ye haena had muckle success, hae ye?

SPOTTISWOODE: (*sighs exasperatedly*) Since you seem to be unable to understand what I mean, let me put it another way. Are you a Christian — or are you a Jesuit?

OGILVIE: (*looks at* SPOTTISWOODE *speculatively for a moment, then suddenly laughs*) You do! You want me to recant! You want me to save my life by denying my faith!

SPOTTISWOODE: (*snorts*) It's no possible for a traitor to recant. Damn the Pope to hell if ye like, it'll do you no good. But is your lealty to the Society of Jesus mair important than your lealty to Our Lord Himself? Would you live for Christ — or die for Ignatius? That's the question that I'm speiring at you!

OGILVIE: Spottiswoode, I have been condemned to die — but in condemning me, you and your like condemn all our ancestors, all the ancient bishops and kings, all the priests — all that was once the glory of Scotland! Do you not understand that to be condemned with all these old lights is a matter of gladness and joy for me. God lives, Spottiswoode, posterity lives and the judgment of posterity will not be so corrupt as yours. You call my religion treason . . .

SPOTTISWOODE: (*snapping*) But what *is* your religion?

OGILVIE: I am a Catholic man and a priest. In that faith I have lived and in that faith I am content to die . . .

SPOTTISWOODE: Rhetoric. Sheer, empty-headed, bloody-minded rhetoric. To put Catholicism before Christianity is bad enough — but no man will ever be condemned to death in Scotland for that! But you put your Jesuitism before your Christianity and your Catholicism! That is why you are going to hang! Certes, Ogilvie, you are an ignorant man! Your ignorance appals me. What do you ken of folk — plain ordinary common Scottish folk! What do you ken and what do you care that men will kill and die, women will be widowed and bairns will be orphaned because of you and your illbred pride? What do you ken of Scotland — guidsakes man, what garred you return after all these years? Ye canna even speak the language! What do you ken of religion? Oh aye, ye've been well trained and can quote Holy Scripture by the mile — but what is your religion to you? 'Feed my sheep' said the Lord — but you hae a gey funny notion of how to feed sheep! You'd feed sheep by killing kings! And that's what it all comes doun to — your religion, I mean. Christianity is a religion of life — the god you serve is a god of daith!

OGILVIE: (*stiffly*) In your judgment perhaps. Posterity, as I have said, will take a different view.

SPOTTISWOODE: Posterity! Ha! And what will posterity hold

OGILVIE: Time alone will tell about that.

SPOTTISWOODE: Time? (*Nods*) Faither, ye are due to hing the morn's afternoon. Ye'll be aware, no doubt, that the courageous — if perverse — manner in which ye hae conducted yourself in the course of the various hearings has attracted a certain popular element, a mob following. And ye will be aware anaa that there is a certain anti-Catholic element in this city. By the morn's nicht, there could be riots. We are expecting riots. We are expecting blood to flow on the streets of Glasgow.

OGILVIE: (*unhappily*) That is not a consideration that I am in a position to entertain.

SPOTTISWOODE: No. But ye will appreciate that as a man of God and as spiritual leader of this community, I am anxious to avoid needless bloodshed?

OGILVIE: I, too, am a man of God, Archbishop — but if there are riots because of me tomorrow night, it will not be the first time that men have spilled blood over religion — nor, I fear, will it be the last. I repeat — I am in no position to think about it.

SPOTTISWOODE: Faither Ogilvie, do you esteem your life a success? Do you feel that there is nothing left for you to achieve?

OGILVIE: If I could serve my faith in the clean air of freedom, there would be a great deal. But if I cannot live without compromising my faith? (*Smiles sadly*) It is another consideration I am in no position to entertain.

SPOTTISWOODE: Your faith? Oh, aye. Nou, there's a question . . . (*Pauses carefully, regards* OGILVIE *thoughtfully*) Tell me, Faither Ogilvie, what *is* your faith?

OGILVIE: (*angrily*) Surely I have made that plain enough by this time!

SPOTTISWOODE: Ye havena — that's just what I'm saying! Oh, ye've speechified and argued and swaggered and bragged your way throughout this whole affair — but you have just this minute admitted to me that you had the chance to save the soul of one young man from eternal damnation — and that you did not even try! So I want tae ken, John Ogilvie. What *is* your faith.

OGILVIE: I thought you said that you would not burden my heart with a lost soul!

SPOTTISWOODE: Nor will I! For Wullie is my responsibility and his soul is *not* lost — nor will it be while I hae ocht to do with it! So forget about Wullie — what about yourself?

OGILVIE: You want me to recant!

for you?

OGILVIE: It is not important what it will hold for me, but some day we may have a Catholic Scotland again and if my action . . .

SPOTTISWOODE: A Catholic Scotland! There will never be a Catholic Scotland any more than there will be a Presbyterian or Episcopalian Scotland! But that's no important — perhaps some day there'll be a Christian Scotland. And how will posterity judge you then?

OGILVIE: (*hotly*) As a man who stood by his principles against the threats and tortures of pagans and unbelievers!

SPOTTISWOODE: D'ye think so? D'ye really think so? What you call your 'principles' will be long-forgotten political issues in less than twenty years' time! And then history will see ye as ye really are — the false shepherd who betrayed his flock in the vain hope of winning a martyr's croun!

OGILVIE: And who are you to accuse me of betrayal, you — you Judas! You who betrayed your own cause to the sinful vanity of a decadent and Godless King!

SPOTTISWOODE: I micht hae kent that sooner or later ye wad hae brocht that ane up — but ye needna hae bothered! That charge has been made afore this with greater eloquence than even you can summon — *and* my conscience is clear. I had guid reasons for what I did!

OGILVIE: (*laughing*) Oh, no doubt! Hundreds of reasons for leaving your presbyterian ministry and thousands of reasons for taking on your episcopalian diocese!

SPOTTISWOODE: Certes but you're the sharp ane! You're the sharp ane richt enough. With half a dozen wits as sharp as yours I could chynge Scotland, I could chynge the warld!

OGILVIE: Then it's as well that I'm going to the gallows because you're going straight to hell!

(SPOTTISWOODE, *struck dumb with horror, stiffens and balls his fists.* OGILVIE *immediately regrets his words*)

OGILVIE: Pardon me, m'lord. That was not well said. Whatever our intentions, it seems that we always end up shouting at each other. I know that you did not change your church for material gain — and I believe that you know, that you must know in your heart that I am no death worshipper! God knows I do not want to die! I am as in love with life as any man! But there is no way out of my situation — no way at all.

SPOTTISWOODE: There is one way — that's why I'm here the nicht.

OGILVIE: (*hopelessly*) I cannot go back on anything that I've said.

SPOTTISWOODE: There's no need to. The locks hae been removed from aa the doors and my men hae their orders. Gin ye should decide to leave the Castle the nicht, there's nane will detain ye.

> (OGILVIE *seems about to make some outraged reply, but something in* SPOTTISWOODE'*s expression makes him hold his tongue. Instead, he moves to his chair and sits down wearily*)

OGILVIE: And where do you think I could go? What kind of reception do you think I would receive from my brethren were I to run away at this hour?

SPOTTISWOODE: That would be up to yourself. But ye are yet a young man — young for a priest at any rate. In time . . .

OGILVIE: Yes, I suppose I might be able to live it down. I would be able to preach again — might even be able to . . . some day . . . to come back to Scotland. (*He glances enquiringly at Spottiswoode*)

SPOTTISWOODE: (*doubtfully*) Weill . . .

OGILVIE: No. No. I would never be able to come back to Scotland.

> (OGILVIE *sits brooding in his chair, his head turned away from* SPOTTISWOODE. *There is a set of rosary beads lying on the table. Absently,* OGILVIE *reaches over and picks them up, laying them on his lap.* SPOTTISWOODE *senses that he is tempted by the offer of freedom*)

SPOTTISWOODE: (*with passion*) Ogilvie! Save yourself, Ogilvie! Save yourself! In the name of the Lord Jesus Christ, I beseech you . . .

> (OGILVIE *turns, looks at* SPOTTISWOODE *wordlessly, then looks away*)

SPOTTISWOODE: (*throwing his hands in the air*) Fare ye weel, Faither Ogilvie. One way or the other, fare ye weel!

> (SPOTTISWOODE *starts to leave*)

OGILVIE: (*rising stiffly to his feet*) My Lord Archbishop! (SPOTTISWOODE *turns expectantly towards him*) There is just one thing before you leave.

SPOTTISWOODE: Aye?

OGILVIE: (*extending his hand*) I would require your hand.

> (SPOTTISWOODE *almost responds. He looks at the outstretched hand and then at* OGILVIE)

SPOTTISWOODE: No. No. This is no game, Faither, This is no game.

> (SPOTTISWOODE *turns and goes, leaving* OGILVIE *standing with his hand outstretched. Slowly,* OGILVIE *lets his arm fall to his side*)

SCENE SIX

The hangman's quarters, within sight of the gallows. OGILVIE
kneels in prayer, with his rosary wound round his fingers and
his eyes tightly shut. THE SOLDIERS stand by watching him
patiently. Their swords are drawn and they carry shields. In the
distance, the sound of drums can be heard.

SPOTTISWOODE enters impatiently, followed by THE HANG-
MAN. Both check as they see OGILVIE at prayer. OGILVIE
finishes praying, opens his eyes, and rises unsteadily to his feet.
He sees SPOTTISWOODE as he turns.

OGILVIE: My Lord.
SPOTTISWOODE: (*quietly*) Ye are ready now? (OGILVIE *nods.*
  SPOTTISWOODE *looks about himself in exasperation and says to
  no-one in particular*) Better get on wi't then!
    (*Exit* SPOTTISWOODE. THE HANGMAN *approaches*
    OGILVIE *with bowed head.* OGILVIE *goes to meet him, taking
    him lightly by each sleeve*)
OGILVIE: Be of good heart, my friend. I have forgiven you
  already. Will . . .
    (WILL *turns as he calls.* OGILVIE *goes to him and embraces
    him*)
OGILVIE: Take care, my son! My time has come. Take care.
    (WILL *chokes with emotion, turns away*)
OGILVIE: Sandy! Goodbye to you!
    (SANDY *pumps* OGILVIE*'s hand*)
SANDY: Here's tae ye, Faither. Here's tae ye!
OGILVIE: Wat!
    (WAT *turns away and spits*)
OGILVIE: Andrew! Can I just say that . . .
ANDREW: (*roughly*) Say naethin, Faither! The time for words
  is past! (*Prods* THE HANGMAN *with his sword*) Come on, you!
  Get on wi't (*Turns to the other soldiers*) Right. Sandy and me'll
  tak it frae here! (*They prepare to move off*)
WILL: Andro . . .
ANDREW: Aye?
WILL: Can I no come instead o Sandy?
    (ANDREW *and* SANDY *exchange wise smiles*)
ANDREW: Been on the gallows afore, have ye?
WILL: Naw, but . . .
ANDREW: Then I'm no wantin ye! (*Softer*) Listen, son. Ye ken
  there's gonnae be trouble — bound tae be. There's no an awfy
  lot o room up by the scaffold thonder. Mair nor twa o us and

we'd just be gettin in ane another's road. Best leave it tae Sandy
and me, son — we're auld hands at this gemme.

SANDY: Aye, Andro's richt, son. You listen tae Andro. Him and
me, we've . . .

ANDREW: (*to* SANDY) You shut up! (*To* THE HANGMAN)
Come on! Let's dae the job.

> (*They are about to move off again, when* OGILVIE *suddenly
> stops dead and turns to them all*)

OGILVIE: Wait! (*Looks pointedly at* ANDREW *who makes a pained
expression*) I have one last word for you all. If there are any
hidden Catholics among you, I would welcome your prayers —
but the prayers of heretics I will not have!

> (ANDREW *explodes with anger*)

ANDREW: Get him oot o here!

> (THE HANGMAN *takes* OGILVIE *by the arm, but* OGILVIE
> *stands his ground.* ANDREW *comes forward and pushes*
> OGILVIE *in the chest with his sword hand. Between* THE
> HANGMAN *and* ANDREW, OGILVIE *is pushed and hauled
> off the stage, followed by* SANDY.
>
> WILL *watches them leave anxiously. Unconcerned,* WAT
> *sheathes his sword*)

WAT: He doesnae trust ye, son.

> (*A huge roar is heard from outside*)

WILL: (*sheathing his sword*) What's that?

WAT: The auld fella. Andro. I'm sayin he doesnae trust ye.

WILL: (*absently*) Aye? Weel, he's richt enough, I suppose.

WAT: Aye, ye see, it doesnae dae tae get owre chief wi a prisoner,
Wullie. It doesnae dae, son.

WILL: Does it no? Weel, Andro kens I'll aye dae the job. He
kens he can rely on me.

WAT: He does, does he? Huh! That's mair nor I wad dae!

WILL: What for no, eh?

WAT: Aw, come on, son! Ye're jokin! See ye there the nou — ye
were near greetin! I'm gaun up tae the gallows tae hing a man —
wi a big mob like that ane ootby — and the boy that's meant
tae be helpin me's greetin like a wean acause the prisoner's tae
be hung? Foo! Forget it, son! No danger!

WILL: Aye, weel, it wisnae you that was gaun tae the gallows in
any case!

WAT: So what? What the hell's the odds whae goes up? The
thing is, Wullie — ye're no reliable. Ye took up wi that pape
and there's nane o us can depend on ye!

WILL: Aye, so ye say — but Andro doesna think that! Neither
does Sandy. Ach, you, ye dinnae understand onything, you

dinnae! I'll no deny I thocht a lot on Faither Ogilvie — but I'm no ashamed o that! He's a guid man . . .

WAT: Is he . . .

WILL: You shut yer mooth! He's worth ten o you ony day o the week!

WAT: Aw, is that right? Weel, listen son, I'll tell ye somethin aboot your precious Faither Ogilvie. He's a crappin bastard! He's got a big yellae streak rinnin aa the wey doun his back!

(*A huge roar is heard from outside. They pause as they hear it*)

WAT: I ken. I ken Ogilvie's kind weel enough. And I'm tellin you, Wullie . . .

WILL: Aw, you get stuffed!

WAT: Listen, d'ye want me tae prove it tae ye? I'm a torturer, son — and part o my tredd's kennin when a man's feart and when he's no. I kent he's kind the minute I clapped eyes on him.

WILL: Aye, when ye went tae meisure him for the buits!

WAT: Aye, he didnae get the buits, though, did he? He got somethin worse, I reckon. And I'm no shair but that *that* didnae brak him. I'm no shair but he didnae cough his load tae the Archbishop.

WILL: Balls! Whit the hell are they hingin him for then?

(*Another huge roar is heard from outside. Again they pause*)

WAT: I dinnae ken. But I ken this; mind when he was in Glesca first, just efter the arrest? What was he like? Eh? Ye ken yersel. Doun in the dungeon amang the rats and aa the shit and filth o the day! A twa-hunner pund wecht chyned til his leg! Aye. And hou's he been this past while? A different story. A wee room o his ain, a table, a chair, a bed, visitors tae see him, buiks tae read, wine tae drink, Lady Spottiswoode . . . Even you have tae admit there's somethin twisted about that!

WILL: There's just the wan thing that's twisted aboot here . . .

WAT: Listen, hou d'ye fancy a wee bet? Eh? Hou d'ye fancy a wee wager that they'll hae tae turn him aff.

WILL: Turn him aff? What's that?

WAT: Shove him aff, ye fule! He'll get tae the tap o the scaffold syne put up a fecht! They'll hae tae gie him the heave!

WILL: Naw! Naw! No chance! No him! Never him!

WAT: Aye, we'll see then, eh? Just you wait! We'll see.

(*Enter* SANDY *running*)

SANDY: (*out of breath*) Jesus Christ, I never saw anythin like thon in aa my born days!

WAT: What happened, Sandy! Tell us what happened!

(SANDY *leans against* WILL *for support. He is out of breath for the duration of his speech*)

SANDY: Aw, wait'll I catch my braith! Lads, I'll tell ye . . . Oh
my God!

WILL: What happened, Sandy? What happened?

SANDY: The Faither — he goes up there quite checko, ye ken?
Kisses the scaffold — aye, kisses the bluidy scaffold. Then this
laddie manages tae get up on the gallows.

WAT: What then?

SANDY: Aw, Andro sorted him aaricht. Nae messin. Boom,
boom. Puir laddie. I hope he wasnae thinkin o gettin mairrit.

WILL: Never mind him! What about the Faither?

SANDY: Ogilvie takes his rosary and he slings it intae the
crowd . . .

WILL: Aye, that'd be him right enough.

SANDY: Aye, weel, we get him aa tied up and the hangman
takes him up the scaffold. He had a bit o a job o it, what wi
Ogilvie's hands bein ahint his back and that — but onyway,
he gets him up. Ogilvie's chantin awa at this Latin prayer aa
the time. The hangman gets him up — and he says tae him
'Say it, John. Lord have mercy on me. Lord, receive my soul'
and Ogilvie says it 'Lord, have mercy on me. Lord, receive my
soul', and then . . .

WAT: Aye! Aye! What happened then!

SANDY: Aw, Christ I dinnae ken! There was a struggle . . . the
hangman couldnae manage . . . Andro had tae sclim the ladder
and shove the Faither aff!

WAT: I tellt ye! I tellt ye! The bastard crapped it at the last! I
tellt ye he was yella, Wullie! I tellt ye! (*Slaps one palm against
the other*) Put it there, son! Put it there!

    (WILL *loses his temper completely and goes for* WAT)

WILL: Shut up, you! Shut up, shut up, shut up! I'm seik and
tired o listenin tae your sneerie tongue . . .

SANDY: Hi, Wullie, what's this? Keep the heid, son, eh? Keep
the heid!

WAT: (*sneering*) Cannae take it, eh?

    (WILL *pushes* SANDY *aside*)

WILL: I tellt you tae shut up! Shut up — or you'll take it! Ye'll
take it frae me! Aa richt!

WAT: Naw! No aaricht! I've taen about as muckle as I can
thole . . .

    (SANDY *tries to restrain* WAT)

SANDY: For the love o Christ, Wattie! Wad ye no . . .

    (WAT *throws* SANDY *to one side*)

WAT: Oot the road! Nae hauf-airsed wee pape's gonnae tell

me . . .

> (WAT *draws his sword.* WILL *lets out a yell of anger and draws his sword too. He aims a great two-handed sweep in* WAT's *direction. At that precise moment,* ANDREW *bursts in, hauling* WAT *out of the way of the blow and throwing him to one side.* WILL *is thrown off balance and the impetus of the blow spins him round.* ANDREW *grabs him by the belt and the scruff of the neck and throws him to the other side of the stage)*

ANDREW: What the fuckin hell dae you pair of stupit bastards think ye're airsin about at? I tellt ye, did I no? I tellt ye baith — but you, ye stupit fuckers, ye wadnae listen! (*Pauses breathless, exasperated with them*) It's done! It's finished! And that's an end tae it!

Glossary

aince mair, once more
alow, alight
anent, about
badgy, in a heap, unconscious
bampot, madman
bawrs, jokes
boke, gies me the, makes me
   sick
bumbaze, bamboozle
chief, friendly
clairty, dirty
claes, clothes
connached, wasted, destroyed
ditterin, dithering
dunt, hit, strike
effing and blinding, swearing
flet, flat
fushionless, feeble
geynear, nearly
glaur, mud, dirt, ooze
gluff, a whiff, a twinge, a
   scare
hinner end, the back, the last of
hits, hoots (exclamation of
   doubt, surprise)
jaxy, own, by oneself
kist, chest
laldy, gie them, punishment,
   beating

lowse, set free
ludgings, lodgings
neiveful, handful
parritch, porridge
rammy, crush, struggle
Reekie, Edinburgh (Auld
   Reekie)
screw the nut, get sensible,
   take care
scunner, to sicken
shoot the craw, desert
siccarly, securely, surely
smeddum, mettle, spirit,
   courage
*spare prick at a hoer's
   wedding,* unnecessary
   man at a prostitute's
   wedding
speiring, asking
tent, to take, to take
   care of
tholin, bearing, suffering,
   tolerating
wappins, weapons
ward, word
wrocht tae daith, fed up
   (wrought to death)
wyce, sensible, wise
wyte, blame

Liz Lochhead

Mary Queen of Scots
Got Her Head Chopped Off

(1987)

CHARACTERS

Fiddler
La Corbie
Mary
Elizabeth
Hepburn O'Bothwell
Knox
Dancer/Riccio
Darnley/Leicester

All other characters are taken by the company.

Introduction

Liz Lochhead was born in Motherwell in 1947 and began writing poetry while a student at Glasgow School of Art. Her first collection was published in 1972, and many others have followed, with a *Collected Poems* appearing in 1984. Lochhead is probably still better known as a poet than a dramatist, yet her poetry always contained a strong sense of individual voice, and a potential for performance. Some of her best work took the form of dramatic monologues, which she regularly performed at readings: with the Lost Poets, in the early 1980s, or later with her Festival Fringe group The Nippy Sweeties — *Quelques Fleurs* (1991) offers good examples of these.

Her development towards full-scale drama was therefore a natural one, though her plays still retain a strongly poetic element — in the songs or lyric sections which appear in *Mary Queen of Scots Got Her Head Chopped Off*, for example. A poetic aspect appears in another way in the subtlety of the play's construction, its last scene suddenly throwing a different light on earlier ones, and demanding that audiences work out for themselves, through the historical action they have just witnessed, answers to some of the questions about the nature of Scotland asked at the beginning of the play.

Lochhead's challenging tactics were complemented by the staging of the first production, by Communicado Theatre Company, alert to some of the more innovative movements in contemporary European theatre, in Poland especially. Mixing music and physicality into a fluid, inventive, performance style, the company's actors successfully managed the radical transitions between roles which the play demands — between Queen and maid, for example, highlighting Lochhead's question 'when's a queen a queen / And when's a queen juist a wummin', and the constructed, performed nature of both political power and gender role which this question raises.

Questions of gender role and of shifting relations of power between men and women also concern Lochhead in much of her poetry, and in plays from *Dracula* (1985) to her Festival success of 1998, *Perfect Days*. She has written several other stage-plays, including *Blood and Ice, Same Difference*, and *The*

Big Picture, as well as revues, plays for television and scripts for radio: she worked for a time as writer in residence for the Royal Shakespeare Company, and with Communicado on *Jock Tamson's Bairns*, a large-scale, multi-media investigation of Scottish character and identity which was one of the centrepieces of Glasgow's year as European City of Culture in 1990. Her 1986 adaptation of Molière's *Tartuffe* for Edinburgh's Royal Lyceum confirmed what a flexible, resourceful vehicle Scots has become for stage translation. The language of *Mary Queen of Scots Got Her Head Chopped Off* might be equally well described, in Lochhead's own terms, as 'a totally invented . . . theatrical Scots, full of anachronisms, demotic speech from various eras and areas . . . proverbial, slangy, couthy, clichéd, catch-phrasey and vulgar . . . deliberately varied in register'.

ACT ONE

SCENE ONE — SCOTLAND, WHIT LIKE?

> *(Alone,* FIDDLER *charges up the space with eldritch tune, wild and sad, then goes. Enter into the ring, whip in hand, our 'chorus', LA CORBIE. An interesting, ragged ambiguous creature in her cold spotlight)*

LA CORBIE: Country: Scotland. Whit like is it?

It's a peatbog, it's a daurk forest.

It's a cauldron o' lye, a saltpan or a coal mine.

If you're gey lucky it's a bricht bere meadow or a park o' kye.

Or mibbe . . . it's a field o' stanes.

It's a tenement or a merchant's ha'.

It's a hure hoose or a humble cot. Princes Street or Paddy's Merkit.

It's a fistfu' o' fish or a pickle o' oatmeal.

It's a queen's banquet o' roast meats and junkets.

It depends. It depends . . . Ah dinna ken whit like your Scotland is. Here's mines.

National flower: the thistle.

National pastime: nostalgia.

National weather: smirr, haar, drizzle, snow.

National bird: the crow, the corbie, le corbeau, moi!

How me? Eh? Eh? Eh? Voice like a choked laugh. Ragbag o' a burd in ma black duds, a' angles and elbows and broken oxter feathers, black beady een in ma executioner's hood. No braw, but Ah think Ah ha'e a sort of black glamour.

Do I no put ye in mind of a skating minister, or, on the other fit, the parish priest, the dirty beast?

My nest's a rickle o' sticks.

I live on lamb's eyes and road accidents.

Oh, see, after the battle, after the battle, man, it's a pure feast — ma eyes are ower big even for *my* belly, in lean years o' peace, my belly thinks my throat's been cut.

> *(Laughing,* LA CORBIE *cracks whip for* THE ENTRANCE OF THE ANIMALS. *In a strange circus our characters, gorgeous or pathetic, parade:* MARY, ELIZABETH, HEPBURN, DANCER/RICCIO, KNOX, DARNLEY *all dirty and down on his luck. They circle, snarling, smiling, posing. And halt. Drumbeat ceases. With both Queens by the hand, parading them)*

Once upon a time there were *twa queens* on the wan green island, and the wan green island was split inty twa kingdoms. But no equal kingdoms, naebody in their richt mind would insist on that. For the northern kingdom was cauld and sma'. And the people were low-statured and ignorant and feart o' their lords and poor! They were starvin'. And their queen was beautiful and tall and fair and . . . Frenchified. The other kingdom in the island was large, and prosperous, with wheat and barley and fat kye in the fields o' her yeoman fermers, and wool in her looms, and beer in her barrels and, at the mouth of her greatest river, a great port, a glistening city that sucked all wealth to its centre which was a palace and a court of a queen. She was a cousin, a clever cousin a wee bit aulder, and mibbe no saw braw as the other queen, but a queen nevertheless. Queen o' a country wi' an army, an' a navy and dominion over many lands.

(*Burst of dance from* DANCER, *a sad or ironic jig*)

Twa queens. Wan green island. And ambassadors and court-iers came from many lands to seek their hauns . . .

SCENE 2 — THE SUITORS

(MARY *and* ELIZABETH *raised up at either corner. Others alter-nate between ambassadors, courtiers or commoners to each in turn. A dance, a mad tango, to music.* LA CORBIE *watching*)

AMBASSADOR I: (*To* ELIZABETH) To the most esteemed royal court of Her Majesty Queen Elizabeth of England from His Majesty *King Philip of Spain* whose hand in marriage —

LA CORBIE: King Philip of Spain?

ELIZABETH: Our bloody dead sister's widower? We think *not*, Cecil . . .

ENGLISH COMMONER 1: I 'ates the bastern Spanish Spanish bastards!

ENGLISH COMMONER 2: At least 'es no bloody *French*!

ELIZABETH: A *king*! We do not think we could marry a *king*!

AMBASSADOR 2: (*to* MARY) Pray accept this jewelled miniature with a portrait by our esteemed limner Sanchez Coello of Don Carlos of Spain, whose bride perhaps . . . ?

LA CORBIE: The King o' Spain's son, Don Carlos?

MARY: (*delighted*) A Catholic!

SCOTS COMMONER 1: (*disgusted*) A *Catholic* — well we canny hae that.

SCOTS COMMONER 2: At least he's no *French*!

ELIZABETH: On the other hand, Cecil, do contrive to keep the ambassador dangling. Do dandle the odd demi-promise, lest Philip o' Spain should try to get a nibble . . . elsewhere!

MARY: (*delighted*) A Catholic! At least he is a good Catholic, even if he's not a king in his own right.

(*We have by now noticed* Mary's *strange accent — a French-woman speaking Scots, not English, with, at the beginning of the play, getting subtly less as it proceeds, quite a French accent*)

ELIZABETH: I cannot allow her to marry a powerful *Catho-lic* . . .

AMBASSADOR 4: (*to* MARY) Félicitations, Madame la plus belle Reine Marie d'Ecosse from Catharine de' Medici, la reine de France, mère du roi Charles, who wishes you should consider her son *Henri de Valois.*

LA CORBIE: Henri de Valois?

SCOTS COMMONER 2: Ah'd raither *Spain* nor bliddy France —

MARY: My own Francis's wee brither! But he's no thirteen year aul' . . . How could ma belle-mère think o't?

ENGLISH COMMONER 1: I'm taking bets on it. Pickering! Ten to one its Pickering for King of England.

ENGLISH COMMONER 2: Pickering, never!

ELIZABETH: (*overhearing*) We do not think we could marry a subject!

ENGLISH COMMONER 2: We know what subject she'd have —

ENGLISH COMMONER 1: If he hadna a wife already!

AMBASSADOR 5: (*to* MARY) What think you of the King of Denmark?

AMBASSADOR 3: (*to* ELIZABETH) From the King of Sweden on behalf of his son, Eric —

SCOTS NOBLE 1: (*to* MARY) The queen should mairry a Hamilton!

SCOTS NOBLE 2: No she shouldnae! She should mairry a Douglas.

SCOTS NOBLE 3: A Gordon!

SCOTS NOBLE 2: By God and she better no'!

SCOTS NOBLE 3: Wha says she'll no'?

SCOTS NOBLE 2: I dae!

LA CORBIE: A Lennox-Stewart, that's wha she should mairry!
    (SCOTS NOBLES 1, 2 *and* 3 *all draw their swords*)

SCOTS NOBLES 1, 2 *and* 3: (*Together*) Ower ma deid body!

ELIZABETH: If we, the Queen, were to follow our own nature's inclinations it would be this: we would rather be a beggar woman and single than a queen and married.

AMBASSADOR 9: (*to* ELIZABETH) Archduke Ferdinand of Austria.

AMBASSADOR 6: (*to* MARY) Archduke Charles of Austria?

AMBASSADOR 9: (*to* MARY) Archduke Ferdinand of Austria?

AMBASSADOR 6: (*to* ELIZABETH) Archduke Charles of Austria?

ELIZABETH: Methinks they do try to play me and my Scotch cousin off against each other. We must keep the Emperor of Austria sure that Charlie or Ferdie will land him the fat salmon England until it is too late for him to net the skinny brown trout of Scotland.

AMBASSADOR 2: (*to* MARY) Don Carlos of Spain.

(*He gives* MARY *a miniature. She holds it*)

MARY: Don Carlos, certainly, to judge from his likeness is very comely . . .

LA CORBIE: I hope they dinna tell her the truth!

(*Note of discord, a beat's freeze as* DANCER *parodies twisted grotesque cripple*)

MARY: Aye, Don Carlos looks braw . . . He'd be the most *politik* marriage . . .

ELIZABETH: Back to Scotland with you, and let it be clearly known to your mistress, that should she marry Don Carlos of Spain, or make any other powerful Catholic match in Europe, then we shall be forced to regard her as our enemy. We shall never recognise her or her progeny as heirs to the throne of England.

SCOTS AMBASSADOR: Your majesty, Queen Mary has been despairing of pleasing you by her choice of husband, or of you ever granting her right of succession.

ELIZABETH: Despair! Such a mean, unqueenly emotion. Methinks she doth give up hope too easily. Although it might be thought that to ask a monarch to name her own successor were to ask her to embroider her own winding sheet.

SCOTS COMMONER 1: They say Don Carlos isnae a' there.

SCOTS COMMONER 2: Neither was her first wan, the Frenchy.

LA CORBIE: Naw, with wi' him it wis his baws never drapped! This yin is a pair stutterin' slaiverin' waggin' baw-faced dafty that takes black-oots, and that they hae to chain up when the mune's oot, or e'en the scullery boys are no safe.

MARY: I shall marry Don Carlos of Spain!

ALL: Olé.

(*Tango ends and we are left with only the two queens and* LA CORBIE, *in the lull, on stage*)

ELIZABETH: Do not really wish to marry? I? I will marry. I have said so. I hope to have children, otherwise I shall never marry.

(MARY *and* ELIZABETH *come together*)

MARY: Indeed I wish that Elizabeth was a man and I would willingly marry her! And wouldn't that make an end of all debates!

LA CORBIE: But she isny. Naw, she isny. There are two queens in one island, both o' the wan language — mair or less. Baith young . . . mair or less. Baith mair or less beautiful. Each the ither's nearest kinswoman on earth. And baith queens. Caw. Caw. Caw.

SCENE THREE — QUEENS AND MAIDS

LA CORBIE: (*rhyming*) Ony queen has an army o' ladies
    and maids
That she juist snaps her fingers tae summon.
And yet . . . I ask you, when's a queen a queen
And when's a queen juist a wummin?
    (*She cracks her whip, and the hectic and garish but proud*
    ELIZABETH *bobs a curtsy, immediately becoming* BESSIE)
MARY: Bessie, do you think she'll meet me?
BESSIE: Aye, your majesty, she'll meet wi' ye face to face at York, an' you're richt, gin ye talk thegither it'll a' be soarted oot. If ye hunt a' they courtiers and politicians an' men awa!
LA CORBIE: She shall never meet you face to face.
MARY: They say she wears my portrait I sent her in that wee jewelled case hangin' fae her girdle. And she sent me an emerald.
LA CORBIE: Oh aye . . . !
MARY: I'm shivering . . . (*Laughing it off unsuccessfully*) Maytime, and it's cauld enough to gie me *chair de poule* . . . Ah dinna think Ah'll ever understand this country o' mine.
BESSIE: The doctor says we have to mak' shair you dinna get a' melancholick, your majesty.
MARY: Three years! I mind me and the Maries oot on deck chitterin' in oor fine French frocks peerin' through the glaur o' the air for ae glimpse o' my kingdom! Three years and I havena seen it yet!
BESSIE: Naw, naw, ye've never seen your country! You've never made your progresses through the length and breadth o' the land.
MARY: The stour o' the air clears, then, sherp, kafuffle atween a Lennox an' Hamilton, a Hamilton and a Douglas . . . Haar fae the sea . . . Cauld . . . rebecks and chanters a pretty masque and a goldhaired bairn presents me wi' a filigree hert that's fu' o' golden coins, new minted. Clouds. A flytin' fae Knox. Daurkness. A mad poet tries to mak' a hoor o' me. Wisps . . . A revel! Smoke . . . A Banquet for the ambassador new fae Spain. Fog. A bricht affray in the Canongate, a bloody clash at the

Butter Tron, a murdered bairn in the Grassmarket, sunshine, and a ragged, starvin' crowd o' cheerin' cheerin' weans jostle to touch ma velvet goon as I go by. My kingdom. Alternately brutal and boring. And I canny mak sense o' it at a'.

BESSIE: It's the weather, it's yir sair side. Doctor says we'll hae to gie ye duck eggs whiskit up in wine tae keep the mist o' yir melancholia awa'.

MARY: It's daein' nothin', Bess! The Queen. And nae power tae mak' my country flourish.

I want to marry, Bessie, I want to marry and begin my reign at last.

BESSIE: In good time. A guid man in guid time, madam.

LA CORBIE: Aye, gie her a guid man, she'll gie him a guid time!
(And with a drumbeat, or a flash of lightning — change, ELIZABETH, proud queen, is on a pedestal, preening, as MARY becomes, in that instant, modest MARIAN, ELIZABETH's gentlewoman)

ELIZABETH: Marian, what do they say she is like?

MARIAN: I don't know, madam.

ELIZABETH: Is she fairer than me? What do they say?

MARIAN: They say she is the fairest queen in Scotland, and you are the fairest queen in England, madam.
(ELIZABETH pinches MARIAN's cheek and laughs. They get playful, parodic . . .)

ELIZABETH: And how do you know this?

MARIAN: *(laughing)* Because I heard you ask her envoy Melville.

ELIZABETH: And what did he say — when I pressed him?
(She pinches her face again)

MARIAN: That *you* were the whiter, their queen 'very lusome'.

ELIZABETH: And who is the higher?

MARIAN: She is!

ELIZABETH: Then she is too high.

MARIAN: *(laughing)* You told him!

ELIZABETH: What are her other amusements?

MARIAN: She writes poems apparently . . .

ELIZABETH: Poems? In English?

MARIAN: In French. And in 'Scots'. *(Scornful laugh)*

ELIZABETH: What else?

MARIAN: She plays on the lute and the virginals.

ELIZABETH: And does she play well?

MARIAN: 'Tolerably well. For a queen.'
(Them laughing together)

ELIZABETH: And does she dance?

MARIAN: She dances. She dances, though not so high or so

disposedly as you, your majesty.

> (*They laugh. A beat's pause*)

> (*Hesitating*) Madam, you know I love you well.

ELIZABETH: Yes, Marian, like all good subjects, I hope.

MARIAN: Then, madam, I beg you marry the Earl of Leicester, for there is such scandal, a babble getting louder and louder all the time.

> (ELIZABETH *light and playful all through this*)

ELIZABETH: They say what, Marian?

MARIAN: Madam, I think you know right well.

ELIZABETH: I cannot imagine what they would say about Us.

MARIAN: Just that . . . you behave together as if you were married already.

ELIZABETH: We do love him right well, indeed.

MARIAN: And he you — madam, I do not think much heed is paid to the bad things some people say, and if you married . . .

ELIZABETH: I have always said I shall marry — if I marry — as queen and not as Elizabeth. You think because my subjects love me as their queen they'll have me marry where I will?

MARIAN: Madam, I know so. Marry my Lord Leicester, and live in happiness, that England shall be a peaceable kingdom.

> (ELIZABETH*'s smile says 'perhaps'. Is she tempted? We think so . . .*)

LA CORBIE: (*indicating* ELIZABETH)

> Och, when a Queen wad wed,
> Or tak' a man tae bed,
> She only does whit ony maid funns chancy.
> So dinna argue the toss,
> Just show them wha's boss —
> You're the Queen so mairry wha ye fancy.

ELIZABETH: (*to herself, thinking of him*) Robert Dudley, my darling, my Lord Leicester . . . . my love.

LA CORBIE: Oh, in England there's a wild floo'erin love

> That the saicret daurkness nourishes
> But in Scotlan' — in the braid daylicht! —
> The daurk bloom o' hatred flourishes.

SCENE FOUR — KNOX AND MARY

(*Sudden lighting change, completely different mood as we go from intimacy in England to a parodic public parade in Scotland, as* KNOX, *in bowler hat and with umbrella, stands on back pedestal, marching. Two men, stamping, sway a big sheet like a blank banner behind him, swagger on the spot with exaggerated Orangemen's gait. Music and hoochs and ugly skirls.* KNOX *is ranting*)

KNOX: I, John Knox, do preach the evangel of Jesus Christ crucified, by repentance and faith. And justification by faith alone.
Moved by my god and in humble obedience to him wha is
abune us a', I hae been commandit to blaw the first blast o' the
trumpet against the monstrous regiment o' women, an abomination against nature and before God; and to disclose unto
this my realm the vanity and iniquity of the papistical religion
in all its pestilent manifestations in Sodom priesthooses and
poxetten nunneries.

(*Parade stops abruptly, lights change, white sheet is spread over
pedestal, making it a table. Roll of bread is placed upon it.* MARY
and KNOX *sit. Others, behind, listen and pray*)

MARY: John Knox, mair nor three years, I hae borne wi' you in
a' your rigorous manners o' speakin' oot, baith against masel'
and ma French uncles. And yit I hae socht your favour by a'
possible means.

KNOX: When it shall please God to deliver you frae that bondage
of darkness and error into the one true religion your majesty
shall find the liberty o' my tongue as a soothing balm unto ye.
For inside the preaching place, madam, I am not master of
myself but the mere instrument of him who commands me to
speak plain and flatter no flesh upon the face of the earth, nor
wait on the courts o' princes or the chaummers o' ladies.

MARY: But what have ye to do with my marriage? What are ye
in this commonwealth?

KNOX: A subject born within the same. Albeit I be neither earl,
lord nor baron within it, but however low and abject I am in
your eyes, it is ma duty no less to forewarn of what I foresee
hurtin' it than I were o' the nobility. And gin the nobility should
consent ye marry ony husband wha isna o' the one true faith
then they do as muckle as lies within their power to renounce
Christ, to betray the freedom of the realm and in the end to
do small comfort to yourself.

LA CORBIE: Corbie says by the bones of your beloved mother
you must destroy this man.
    Knox, nox as black as nicht, nox lik' a' the bitter pousons,
nox lik' three fearfu' chaps at the door, did ding her doon.
Knox did lead the rebels. Knox did break yer mither's heart
and Knox did laugh when she did dee. Hark at him — 'The
Guid Lord says, and I agree wi' him!' Hark. Cark Cark.

MARY: Maister Knox, I see in you yin wha is convincit he be
moved by love of God, but is in truth fired raither by hatred
o' mankind.

LA CORBIE: Cark! Aye tell him!

KNOX: There is yin abune us a' madam, wha is the best judge, the only.

MARY: You raised up a part of this nation — ma subjects — against ma mither, and against me, their prince, anointed by God. You hae written a treasonous treatise o' a book against ma just authority. You have been the cause of great sedition and greater slaughter in England —

KNOX: By the richt worshipping of God men learn from their hearts to obey their just princes.

MARY: But ye think that I hae nae just authority?

KNOX: Your majesty, if this realm finds no inconveniency in the regiment o' a woman, then that which they approve shall I not further disallow.

MARY: Except within your own heart and breast . . . ?

KNOX: My heart is God's. But I shall be as weill content to live under ye as Paul was tae live under Nero.

MARY: Sae ye will gie to Caesarina whit is Caesarina's?

KNOX: I see madam kens her scriptures.

MARY: I ken ma scriptures. I hae baith heard and read. (*Pause*) Maister Knox, because I am by nature douce, and queyet, dinna think I hae nae convictions or beliefs locked in ma silent heart — though I dae not *trumpet* them abroad.

KNOX: Well, if I did blaw the first blast of the trumpet, madam, against the monstrous regiment o' women — this blast was neither against your person or your regiment, but against that bloody Jezebel o' England!

MARY: I am shair my guid cousin Elizabeth would be maist disconcertit to ken Maister Knox, wha doth profess the same faith as she, cried her a Jezebel!

KNOX: The Jezebel is Bloody Mary before her as weel you ken! Wha did practise murderous and several slaughter amang the hedgerows, till the vera weans o' the serfs o' the loyal lords wha did profess the true faith, did lie wi' their guts a' skailt oot amang the stubble o' the field, while the air was stinkan' and corruptit wi' the thick smoke fae the fires o' burning martyrs and ministers o' the truth.

MARY: And you will bid my subjects obey me?

KNOX: Madam, I will.

MARY: Then they shall obey you and not me. Their lawful prince. Like I say, Maister Knox, I hae heard and read.

KNOX: So, madam, did the Jews wha crucified Christ Jesus read both the law and the prophets — and interpretit them as suitit themsel's.

MARY: And do ye no interpret as suits you?

KNOX: I believe only what God plainly speaks in his word.

MARY: And yet the same words sound different to my ears!

KNOX: For instance: the Mass.

A god of bread! A god of breid, it is idolatory. Nay, I say that it is *mair* idolatory tae mak' a god of breid than when the heathens in their daurkness made fause idols. Consider a god o' wood or a god o' stane — well a god o' bread is mair miserable. This god will putrify in a single season. The rain or snow can mak' saps o' sicc a god. Ony durty maid in a scullery can mak' a god tae rise in a warm an' yeasty corner! Rats and mice will require nae better dinner than roon white gods enough! Show me in the Bible whaur Christ Jesus at his Last Supper did command the Mass? — I tell you nae mention is made o sicc in a' the scripture.

MARY: Ye are ower sair for me!

> (*She breaks down sobbing.* KNOX *is uncomfortable, genuinely. Stirring of certain pity, perhaps lust*)

KNOX: Madam, in God's presence I swear that I never delightit in the weeping of ony o' God's creatures. As I can scarcely staun' the tears o' my ain wife or ma ain young sons when ma ain haund is forcit to correct them, faur less can I rejoice in the greetin' and howlin' and bawlin' o' yir majesty.

> (*Gently he goes to touch her. She recoils*)

But I hae tae thole your saut tears, rather than I betray my God or nation by my silence.

MARY: Yet will I in my realm and in ma heart silently defend the Kirk o' Rome. And I will marry wha I please. Ye will grant to me guid tolerance — as I hae *aye* granted to you and your Reformit Kirk.

KNOX: Madam, I shall never be seduced by the Siren song o' toleration. I fear you dinnae understaun this country ye are queen o'.

> (KNOX *is bowing out*)

MARY: Nevertheless I will marry wha I please.

KNOX: I pray God grant you the wisdom of Deborah among the Israelites.

> (*Exit* KNOX, *taking his hat and umbrella again.* MARY, *shaking, is left alone on her knees praying with* LA CORBIE *looking with some sympathy on her*)

LA CORBIE: Gin ye want to gag Maister Knox you will hae tae abolish the Mass and embrace his cauld kirk.

MARY: And is there nae comfort in his kerque?

LA CORBIE: Aye. Cauld comfort. But there are those wha say

it a' the better suits the climate.

MARY: And you think gin I sat on St Giles's hard pews on a Sunday I'd sit surer oan ma ain throne a' week lang?

LA CORBIE: Nae doot aboot that!

 He has cowped the Queen o' Heaven so how could he worry 'bout cowpin' a mere earthly queen?

MARY: Then the Protestants dinnae love oor Blessed Virgin?

LA CORBIE: Knox has torn the Mother of God from oot the sky o' Scotland and has trampit her celestial blue goon amang the muck and mire and has blotted oot every name by which ye praise her — Stella Maris, Star of the Sea, Holy Mother, Notre Dame, Oor Lady o' Perpetual Succour.

MARY: But if he hae torn her frae the blue sky what has he left in her place?

LA CORBIE: A black hole, a jaggit gash, naethin'.

MARY: But how should I live without Our Lady?

LA CORBIE: Easy. You hae livit withoot yir earthly mother, sae ye can live without your heavenly yin.

MARY: I will marry wha I can love!

 (*Exit* MARY)

SCENE FIVE — REPRESSED LOVES

LA CORBIE: Sae oor Queen wha'd rule by gentleness
 Is but a pair fendless craiture —
 An' in Englan' the Lass-Wha-Was-Born-To-Be-King
 Maun dowse her womanische nature.

 (ELIZABETH *is lying down, asleep. She rolls over moaning and murmuring*)

ELIZABETH: Leicester? Dad . . . Dad . . . Mother? Robert?

 (*In dream lighting and strange music, very stylised,* FIDDLER *comes on with a doll whose head is off and she holds it separate by the hair. She is like a child and she is crying her eyes out. But slowly, silently. In real time and like a child,* ELIZABETH, *still asleep, is crying for her dead mama — and her dead dreams of marrying* LEICESTER *too, probably — and tossing and turning*)

No! No! Don't . . . don't kill her. Dad? Want my Mam. Want Robert!

 (*Shadowy figure — Dad — puts something — not a crown but an improvised and very clear representation of one — on* FID-DLER's *head. Everyone cheers weirdly. Dad-figure chucks doll away*)

Don't want — I want — Don't want to be Daddy's little princess. Yes!

(*All the men throw* FIDDLER *from one to the other, kissing her. Her crown keeps nearly falling off but she holds it on. They blindfold her, spin her round, a game of blindman's-bluff. She goes to one man very slowly, deliberately, head held high. They are 'married' by the others. She turns round to kiss him, eyes shut, trusting. He steals her crown. All the 'dream-people' laugh in a surreal, nightmarish, horrible way.* ELIZABETH *wakes up with a cry. Dream snaps out. She is sobbing and crying*)

Robert!

(*Enter* MARIAN)

MARIAN: Madam . . . What on earth's the matter? Bad dreams again, only a dream. Ssh.

(*Comforts her like a child,* ELIZABETH *is sobbing all through next*)

ELIZABETH: I couldn't have married him, Marian . . .

MARIAN: Well . . . no madam. Perhaps not.

ELIZABETH: I told him! I said, Leicester, if I married you and we lay down together as King and Queen, then we should wake as plain Mister and Mistress Dudley. The Nation would not have it.

MARIAN: Surely the scandal would have died down? Can't you marry him secretly and —

ELIZABETH: She trumped us. His bloody wife. Why couldn't she let him decently divorce her? Oh no, she has to commit suicide. Now everyone is sure he murdered her. If he'd bloody murdered her, he'd have done it a lot better than that. Made quite sure it looked as though she took her own life.

MARIAN: Marry him secretly! In six months . . . a year . . . everyone will have forgotten she ever lived.

ELIZABETH: Too late! I've told him I want him to marry Madam o' Scots.

MARIAN: Who?

ELIZABETH: Queen Mary and take him off to Edinburgh.

MARIAN: Madam!

ELIZABETH: Why not? I hear she is very attractive, though I've yet to set eyes on her.

MARIAN: But, madam —

ELIZABETH: Oh yes! Bit on the tall side, of course, and hair that reddish colour that makes the complexion sickly looking — oh, and a virgin too, although she has been married. Altogether doing it exactly the wrong way round for my taste, but still, she is a Queen after all, so —

MARIAN: He loves you!

ELIZABETH: I'm sure she'll make him happy, that'll shut all

their mouths and we'll have a loyal Englishman — I think we may depend on him to remain a loyal Englishman — in her bed. Well, we really cannot have her married in France again, else the French King can straddle England with one foot in Calais, the other in Edinburgh, and piss down on us all fire, brimstone and poison. Besides, I have already broached it with the Scotch Ambassador.

> (MARIAN *looks on her with amazement.* ELIZABETH *holds her defiance, then suddenly it crumbles, breaks, and she is sobbing in real abandonment and agony.* MARIAN *holds her, hushes her. Soon she calms again*)

No more. What shall it profit a woman if she can rule a whole kingdom but cannot quell her own rebellious heart. Robert, you are more dangerous to me than a thousand, thousand Northern Catholics poised and armed. I am not proud I love him — but I am proud that loving him, still I will not let him master me.

LA CORBIE: But when a queen wud wed, or tak' a man tae bed,
She only does whit ony maid funns chancy!
Dinnae argue the toss, juist show them wha's boss
You're the Queen — so mairry wha ye fancy.

> (*Enter* HEPBURN, EARL OF BOTHWELL, *as a huntsman, and* DANCER *as a stag — no costume, just the highland stag dance, a bit of this passionate, awesome, folk dance — as others, with horn noises, make a hunting motif to intrtoduce this brute but magnetic character. Then* MARY *is with him, alone.* BOTHWELL *defiant,* MARY *in attitude of reprimanding schoolteacher*)

MARY: Alison Craik, Earl Bothwell!

BOTHWELL: Wha?

LA CORBIE: He kens her!

MARY: You ken her!

BOTHWELL: Dae I?

MARY: I ken you dae.

BOTHWELL: Well, your majesty, you ken, I kinna ken a' the lassies I ken. So mibbe you ken mair than I dae . . .

MARY: (*like a formal accusation at first*) Alison Craik is the dochter of thon respectable Edinburgh merchant, whase hoose near the Saut Tron ye did rudely invade and enter, wi' ma pair auld uncle d'Elboeuf a' fired up wi' drink and his brains addled.

BOTHWELL: Oh, that Alison . . .

MARY: Ma pair gyte auld uncle, Bothwell!

BOTHWELL: Aye, his auld hurdies werena fit to gan whaur his new youthfu' and fair French-style fancies would have led him tae lie . . .

LA CORBIE: Caw! Caw!

MARY: Ye led him to wickedness, Bothwell! Drunkenness and rapine, Ah'll no hae it!

BOTHWELL: Ah dinna expect ye'll get offert it vera often. No in your station in life.

LA CORBIE: Caw! Caw canny.

MARY: *Naebody* speaks to the Queen lik' that.

BOTHWELL: And that's jist wha Ah am. Naebody. Ah widnae let naebody bother you, your majesty.

MARY: Apparently you are naebody. Naebody to be chidit by the Kirk Assembly. The excellent Protestants were vera quick tae complain and denounced fae the pulpit ma pair auld uncle wha couldna go whaur you dinna lead him.

And did they chide you?

BOTHWELL: Noo, wha are you worrit aboot — your auld uncle or . . . the fair Alison.

MARY: I want, in my realm, Maister Hepburn o' Bothwell, that women should sleep sound in their beds.

LA CORBIE: You tell him!

BOTHWELL: Because dinna, you ken. Worry aboot Alison. She's jist a tail.

(MARY *gasps. They hold a moment.* MARY *cannot look away. Cannot reply*)

A brass nail, a hure, a daw, a penny-jo. (*Pause*) O, a pricey penny-jo, her faither is a city merchant. (*Pause*) Sleepin' sound isny lik' Alison, if a' Ah've heard be true . . . though, mind, she sleeps the sleep o' the just. The just-keistit that is . . . (*Pause*) No' that Ah've a bad word for ony lass that is an honest hure . . . But Alison Craik is the Earl o' Arran's hure. And the Earl o' Arran is a bloody Hamilton . . . So I had her. (*Pause*) She wisna unwilling. (*Pause*) She wisna unwilling, but yir auld uncle d'Elboeuf wisna able . . . (*Pause*) Sae the Kirk Assembly are makkin' a mountain oot o' a mowdie-hill . . . At least in uncle d'Elboeuf's case . . .

MARY: (*impotently*) Because he is a Hamilton! Ah'll no' have you nobles o' this yin nation aye at each ither's throats lik' terriers.

BOTHWELL: Well, madam, I fear you are queen o' the wrang kintra. Terriers we are, it is our nature. Be a while afore ye mak' kittocks o' us, or wee saft-moothed spaniels to stick oor heids in yer lap . . . and fawn ower each ither while we wait for yir favours.

MARY: I'm your queen. And in three years in this country I canna depend on any o' ye to show me royal respect as I am due, although in every way I try — (*Into tears*)

LA CORBIE: Don't greet!

BOTHWELL: Madam, I hae the greatest respect for my anointed queen, whase grace and beauty gladdens my heart and whase gentleness and clemency does tame my savagery.

LA CORBIE: Aye well, there's mibbe somethin' tae be said for weepin' . . .

BOTHWELL: And whase courage and swiftness in the chase does quicken my spirit and speed my ain steed in pursuivance of the quarry.

MARY: I didna ken ye took such pleasure in hunting.

BOTHWELL: In the chase? Aye. When there's a fine white hind dancin' afore me through the trees, and I glisk it, then lose it again, glisk it, lose it . . . but my hound, my pointing hound, doth throw back his liver-coloured chops and bay! Because my hound and I can smell it. Glintin' through the trees in the gloamin' daurk. Hunting? Aye! When I am honoured to be in the Queen's party. Hae we no shared minny's an exhaustin' day's sport, your majesty? And yet ye turned me doon. I humbled masel' but you widna mairry me . . .

(MARY, *her back to him now, finds it difficult not to respond*)

MARY: Nae mair Alison Craiks!

(*She is in control again*)

BOTHWELL: (*bowing*) Your majesty.

MARY: Nae mair tiltin' at Hamiltons!

BOTHWELL: But, your majesty, there is a history to this dispute.

MARY: I dinna want to hear your history!

(*A drumbeat*)

Bothwell, as well as queen I am widow. And maiden. And I would hae all unprotectit women in my realm honoured in their privacy!

BOTHWELL: I ken. You are heart-sorry for Alison Craik.

MARY: And I tell you if there is any mair of this I will be forcit to outlaw you, to put you to the horn!

LA CORBIE: Caw!

BOTHWELL: (*aside*) Put me to the horn would you, my leddy? I tell you Ah'll pit you to the horn and you'd be glad to rin outlawed wi' me.

MARY: Bothwell —

BOTHWELL: Nae mair tiltin' at Alison Craik. Nor at Arran the Hamilton gin he 'gree no tae tilt at me.

MARY: Go then. And keep the peace, James Hepburn, I charge you, keep peace.

(*He bows out.* BESSIE *comes on*)

Bessie, do you think it's true he is a warlock?

BESSIE: A warlock, your majesty, why?

> (*She is behind the Queen, rubbing her shoulders*)

MARY: He frichtens me.

BESSIE: Aye, madam, but Ah dinna think there is anything'
eldritch or extraordinar' in that . . .

MARY: But how then would he hae the power tae disturb me
so?

> (*But* BOTHWELL, *braces loose over his shoulders, in his grubby
> undervest and old corduroys, has entered like a ghost and, behind
> BESSIE, kisses BESSIE's neck lewdly. A swaying shudder runs
> with a gasp through BESSIE straight through MARY herself.
> Sexual current as electric shock. Lights change. MARY exits.
> BESSIE becomes proud ELIZABETH again*)

LA CORBIE: Twa Queens, yae nicht push their plates awa'
When they sit doon tae sup.

Yin doesnae ken whit's steerin' her

— Yin doesnae ken whit tae steer up!

> (ELIZABETH *now is speaking to maid MARIAN, a whisper*)

ELIZABETH: He is here, Marian?

MARIAN: Yes, madam.

ELIZABETH: And none saw him who could carry tales to my
Lord Leicester?

MARIAN: I think not, madam . . .

ELIZABETH: Go then, send him in . . .

> (DARNLEY *looking young and nervous, enters and kneels*)

ELIZABETH: Cousin!

DARNLEY: Your Majesty.

ELIZABETH: Do get up, let me look at you. Well, I haven't seen
you since you were but a beardless boy — and now you are
grown such a fine long lad. How old are you?

DARNLEY: Nineteen, madam, almost —

ELIZABETH: Old enough, eh? Cousin, the Scotch Ambassador
and I have been discussing you lately, wondering whether we
are to allow you to take yourself off to Bonnie Scotland. What
think you?

DARNLEY: Madam I don't know what to say, you surprise me
so!

ELIZABETH: Oh nonsense! You know how your Mama Lennox
has been two–three years at wheedling at me. 'Will I help her
to restore your father and your site to his rightful lands and
estate in Scotland?'

> (*Foxy*) What do you suppose your mother really wants?

DARNLEY: Madam, I know she desires nothing more than justice for my father, an end to his banishment from his own homeland. He's an old man, your Majesty!

ELIZABETH: Oh we're all old to you Henry!

DARNLEY: Twenty years! Since before I was even born. Exiled, unfairly stripped of his lands by the Scottish Crown.

ELIZABETH: Yes, yes, and of course your Mam wants him to die happy and be buried on his own soil. Commendable, such uxoriousness. (*He doesn't understand*) That means nice-little-wifeyness, Henry. Do sit down, Henry! Henry, your Mama and I are both grandchildren of Henry the Seventh of England! You are aware of that?

DARNLEY: Yes, of course, ma'am.

ELIZABETH: There are even some who say she has a close claim to succeed me!

DARNLEY: Madam, I think you know my mother is your most loyal and most humble subject.

ELIZABETH: (*too quickly*) Even though she is a Catholic like the Scotch bitch! (*Recovers*) Perhaps, Oh, Henry, some of my advisors and statesmen are a very suspicious sort of people, you know I really cannot keep up with them! They try to convince me your mother has big ambitions for her little son and before Queen Mary's poor wee French runt had begun to rot in his coffin, Mum had sent you and your brother off on French holidays, a-commiserating with the young widow.

DARNLEY: I was but a child then!

ELIZABETH: So was she, Henry, but you're both all growed up now. But I know you would never think to marry a lady so much older than you.

DARNLEY: Only three years!

ELIZABETH: Ah yes, but, Henry, when the difference is the wrong way round and the maid is older than the man it puts the balance out of kilter. Don't think of it! You are a right loyal subject of England, Henry Darnley?

DARNLEY: Madam you know I am.

ELIZABETH: Exactly. I will tell my ministers so! I'll explain it all to them — The old Dad etcetera, I think you may depend on it. We will allow you to go!

DARNLEY: My father will be —

ELIZABETH: Except —

DARNLEY: Ma'am?

ELIZABETH: Well . . . can I trust you to keep a confidence? Maybe I shouldn't tell you this but . . . you see negotiations are well advanced with the Scotch Ambassador that Queen Mary will marry my Lord Leicester.

DARNLEY: Leicester, but he is your . . .

ELIZABETH: My favourite! Yes. But wise monarchs should keep no favourites. I am determined there shall be no other English rival to Leicester for the hand of the Queen of Scots. And it's been troubling me a little, just in case — no fault of your own — but what if the Scotch Queen should take it into her head to prefer *you*, being there, to *him*, being here? You do see my little difficulty? Remember, when you are in Scotland you'll be beyond my power. Why, you could pretend to be a Catholic yourself and woo her and me not able to stop you! Honestly, were I not so confident of your loyalty, I could not let you go.

(*It sinks in she has said yes*)

DARNLEY: May I?

ELIZABETH: I've signed the paper already. You may go. And . . . you may go!

DARNLEY: Your Majesty. (*Begins to leave*)

ELIZABETH: Young Henry, be careful, I hear it's a cold, dire, rough place. Worse than Yorkshire.

(ELIZABETH *and* DARNLEY *exeunt*)

LA CORBIE: (*exclaims:*)

Though the wind blaws snell doon the Canongate the day
There's ne'er an honest bairn nor a rogue less
As through the toun, in fine processioun
Comes the Queen, and her cooncil, in progress.

Gaberlunzies in duds and pair drabs in their rags
Can feast their een on hoo the Queen and the court dress
Though their teeth micht chitter they dinna fell bitter —
Naw, they cheer at *Queen Mary's progress*!

SCENE SIX — MARY QUEEN OF SCOTS'S PROGRESS AND JOHN KNOX'S SHAME

(*Bright professional music from shoulder-high fiddler. In a procession the Queen is passing but instead of seeing her we see the crowd who are watching, cheering hurrah! and waving bits of rag.* MARY *is now* MAIRN, *a wee poor Scottish beggar lass;* ELIZABETH *is* LEEZIE, *her tarty wee companion. They are just wee girls of thirteen or so, in love with royalty and splendour. The whole set of Brueghel grotesques is cheering*)

MAIRN: The Queen! The Queen! She's comin'.

LEEZIE: Aw, she's beautiful, eh, Mairn?

MAIRN: Lovely.

LEEZIE: Mind you, we'd be braw in brae claes . . .

MAIRN: Ah don't think Ah could lukk lik' the Queen, Leezie . . .

LEEZIE: Aye ye could, if yer froack wis French velvet, wi' a siller-lace collar.

    (*Suddenly a shower of small coins and squabbling and fighting over it.* JOHN KNOX *looks on in disgust*)

KNOX: And thus oor pair, fair bairns o' Scotland reduced to fechtin' ower trashy scraps o' glisterin' tin coins that French hoor scatters fae her progress. By smilin' an' dauncin' does she steal the people's hearts away from the true priests and the true religion. Starvin'. The people are starvin'. But inasmuch as they hunger for earthly sustenance, a hundredfold were they famisht for the spiritual food of true redemption. Till the Lord God did deliver them.

    (*Everybody except* KNOX, LEEZIE *and* MAIRN *exit.* LEEZIE *and* MAIRN *are rolling on the ground among the dirt, laughing, whispering and staring at* KNOX)

LEEZIE: He wis. He wis starin'. Gaun'. Ask him, Mairn!

MAIRN: Dinna, Leezie, dinna. Ah canny.

LEEZIE: Starin' ett ye! He'll ken ye the next time, honestly! Lukks lik' he's juist back fae a funeral! He'll be definitely wantin' a wee bit rumplefyke then . . . (*Shouts*) Haw, maister, ma pal wants tae ken if ye want tae go wi' her?

MAIRN: Come awa', Leezie . . .

KNOX: Awa' tae hell wi' ye, ya jauds!

MAIRN: Leezie! Leezie, yon's . . . John Knox! Oh — ah!

LEEZIE: Maister, buy us wir denner . . .

KNOX: Awa' and pray the Lord tae forgive ye. You're nobbut weans!

LEEZIE: Well, yon's no whit ye said last week!

    (*She runs off, wild coarse laughter, a rude sign, a flashed bum, or a bent arm.* KNOX *right at* MAIRN *and everything freezes.* LEEZIE *in her cheeky running away;* MAIRN *suddenly straight and tall, totally* MARY *in our eyes, and in* KNOX*'s, as he chides a cheeky wee harlot on the cauld Canongate.* KNOX*'s hand raised in anger but stayed in awe*)

KNOX: By Christ. Ah'll tan yir arse fur ye ya wee hoor o' Baby-lon. Lukk at ye! Wi' yir lang hair lik' a flag in the wind an advertisement o' lust tae honest men an' they big roon een lik' a dumb animal, slinkan alang the road wi' yir hurdies hingin' oot yir sark an' yon smell aff ye, ya durty wee fork-arsed bitch ye. Nae wunder it is written in the Guid Book that your kind are the very gate and port o' the devil — Ah'll leave the rid mark o' ma haun on your white flesh afore Ah —

    (*Moment of ambiguity passes, it's a wee tart again,* KNOX *is back in control of himself)*

Awa' and behave! Pray God forgive you and sin nae mair.

(*By now the hysterical girls have fled*)

(*Song sung by* LA CORBIE; *repeated by the company*)

LA CORBIE: In papische days wi' evil ways

The sinner sins and then he pays.

The blind bishop he canna preach

For playin' wi' the lasses.

The friar flatters a' in reach

For alms that they possesses.

The curate his creed, he canna read —

But noo we are reformit.

Hoo shall the meeinster creesh his palms

Or his cauld bed be warmit?

(BOTHWELL *comes, speaks to* KNOX)

BOTHWELL: A wee burd tells me the Queen isna pleased wi' you! Well, you arena feart, ma freen, speakin' oot lik' yon!

KNOX: The marriage o' our Queen is in all men's mouths, Bothwell, sae it is ma duty to denounce France and decry Spain and to preach against allowin' her a papish marriage. For by the same act o' takkin' a man tae her bed, she makks a king tae a people.

We, the people, should choose a husband fur a lassie raither than a silly wee furrin lassie should choose a king for a hale people.

BOTHWELL: Well, you tell her! You arena feart . . .

KNOX: Why should the pleasin' face o' a gentlewoman affray me? I hae lookit in the faces o' many angry men and no' been afraid, no' above measure.

BOTHWELL: Well, Ah'm mair feart o' a pleasin' female face nor an angry male yin onyday. No that Ah'd ever let a quine ken it. They're lik' dugs — show them fear and they are forcit tae bite ye.

KNOX: She's only a silly spilte wee French lassie, Bothwell.

BOTHWELL: Only a silly spilte wee French lassie wha could cowp the kirk and cut your heid aff, John Knox.

KNOX: She's only a queen.

BOTHWELL: (*as they begin to exit*) And what's a queen?

KNOX: Juist a silly, spilte, wee lassie.

(*And they are gone*)

LA CORBIE: Yestreen the Queen was wyce enough

To forswear all desire

From love, and the keist-and-rummle o' love

She flinched, as at fire.

But noo . . . the Queen and Lord Darnley
Close-closeted thegither
Young Lord Darnley's on his sickbed
But baith o' them hae a fever.

SCENE SEVEN — DARNLEY AND A FEVER

(*Suddenly we're there with* DARNLEY *in bed,* MARY *by his bedside*)

DARNLEY: Your majesty, is it you?

MARY: Yes, it's me. It's Mary.

DARNLEY: This is humiliating.

MARY: Wheesht!

DARNLEY: Measles! A childhood complaint, it's —

MARY: I had it in France when I was a wee wee girl!

DARNLEY: You poor little thing, so far away from your mother too.

MARY: Aye. I grat full sore for her!

DARNLEY: I don't know how she could have sent you away. You must have been such a pretty child.

MARY: I dinna ken 'boot that. But I missed her. (*Pause*) She had to dae it though to keep me safe an' soond. There were plenty plots to steal the infant Queen and rule in her stead. (*Pause*) If I had a child though . . . I dinna think I could send ma ain bairn awa'.

DARNLEY: Poor Mary!

MARY: Oot on the deck, ready tae embark, an' Ah wis sae excitit — I'm a great sailor, ye ken, I wis the only wan no seeck a' the wey tae France — but, ma mither, she wis greetin' an' roarin' and stitchin' wee medals o' the Blessed Virgin intae ma claes tae keep me safe, I didna ken whit was the maitter, I didna realise hoo lang it'd be e'er I'd see her again.

DARNLEY: My mother's a Catholic too!

MARY: Is she?

DARNLEY: Oh yes. I can't imagine my mother ever sending me away!

MARY: No' even for your ain guid?

DARNLEY: I don't think so! (*Laughing*) I'm glad she's not here now, she'd be rushing around with junkets and milk jellies and broth to get my strength back up!

MARY: I brocht you some broth! I forgot! That wis why I came! It'll be cauld noo, I'll go get some mair.

DARNLEY: Mary, don't — I'm not hungry!

MARY: Do ye no want onything?

DARNLEY: No. Just . . . stay with me, Mary.

(*Music.* DANCER *holds up parasol over* ELIZABETH *as she enters, puffing on a clay pipe*)

ELIZABETH: And really it has proved remarkably simple. All we had to do was keep it nice and complicated. Well, once Philip withdrew Don Carlos — although clearly the boy was an idiot, even Mary couldn't have married him — well, we pushed for Leicester, hinted we might be about to ratify on the succession question, if we got her married to an Englishman and a Protestant but, alack, our heart was not in it . . . A weakness of course, must be a bit of the old *Dad* in me, must cut it out . . . but secretly we were somewhat relieved when the old religion bit was a little too much for Mary to swallow. Well, we might have got somewhere if Master Knox could have been persuaded to be a little less confrontational — really there is no *moderation* in the man — but I was glad really when she would have none of my Robert. Then the measles! What a stroke of luck, poor Darnley all flushed and fevered, and Queen Mary playing nursemaid, brought out her tender feelings, most affecting . . . And now they are to be married. All it took was for me to *expressly* forbid it and he was irresistible. Which should keep her busy at home sorting out the snarls and quarrels that lad'll cause among her nobility! Too busy to indulge in any mischief among my disenchanted Catholics . . . And it does let my lord Leicester off the hook. Pity really, there were no more *piquant* nights than those ones he were never sure if he were off to the *Tower* or to *Scotland* in the morning.

SCENE EIGHT — A WEDDING

(*Music and the shivery sound of* LA CORBIE'S *voice as slowly* MARY, *with a white stole over her head, and* DARNLEY *enter. Solemn. Erotic.* LA CORBIE's *Wedding Song*)

LA CORBIE: Oor Queen has mairrit her a knight
His curls are fair as ony child
Sma' is his mooth and his manner douce
His eyes are meek and mild.

Oor Queen has mairrit her a knight
She fondles him an' he were her pet
He moves sae spry and his voice sae high —
Yon long lad he is a-growin' yet . . .

Oor Queen has mairrit her a knight
His cheek as saft as ony baby boy
Soon may she declare a son and heir
To be oor nation's joy.

   (*Others carry on a sheet by four corners and place it flat out on the floor*)

ALL: And we hae made to them a bed
  We made it large and wide
  That Mary oor Queen and the Lord Darnley
  Micht lay doon side by side.

MARY: And each o' ye draw oot a pin
  A pin frae oot ma mournin' gear
  Alas, alack, in weeds o' black
  To show I hae a widow been
  And ever sin' I hae been wrapped in
  Ma mournin' gear, ma mournin' gear,
  For many a long and weary year.

   (*A pin is drawn out by each person in turn and all together sing* LA CORBIE*'s song again as the couple face each other and* MARY *unlooses her long hair and shakes it free*)

And I shall loose ma long rid hair,
Ungimp ma girdles o' the plaited silk
Slip frae ma sark and in the dark
Ma bodie will gleam as white as milk
And I shall be dressed in nakedness,
My briests twa aiples o' desire
And you shall hae the brichtest jewel
That nestles in my brooch o' red-gowd wire.

   (MARY *and* DARNLEY *have each taken an end of the sheet and circled slowly, intent on each other, and twisted it into a rope, tighter and tighter. The drum stops. They move a step or two towards each other and the corded sheet twists in the centre to a love knot.* DANCER, *swift, snatches it immediately away*)

ACT TWO

SCENE ONE — SEIGNEUR RICCIO, A FORTUNE, A BABY, AND A BIG BABY

   (DANCER *completes bravura jig, then becomes* RICCIO, *with his old typewriter, typing away efficiently.* MARY *is there and* LA CORBIE. *We create a picture of fast, secretive, well-established and intimate hard work.* RICCIO *has a slight hunchback and*

an elaborate embroidered brocade waistcoat — fine clothes his
wee vanity . . . LA CORBIE snaps fingers)

MARY: Twa copies, seigneur Davy, yin tae the Papal Nuncio,
yin tae the Cardinal o' Lorraine — ssh! Carefu', carefu', no' a
word tae naebody, no' tae the King, no' even tae Bothwell.

(RICCIO, *fingers to his lips, a wee gesture of a smile. He turns*
letters into paper aeroplanes, sends one flying to each of the wings,
goes back to typing. MARY sits down and looks at her belly. She
isn't very obviously pregnant yet)

Please mak' it be true, mak' it a' richt enough. And mak' it a
boy — for your ain sake.

(RICCIO *looks at her, shakes his head and wags his finger, then*
goes on typing)

LA CORBIE: And is that what we'd expect to see, no' three
month efter yir weddin'. Whaur's yir bonny young groom? Eh?
Eh?

(RICCIO *rips out the sheets of paper, takes them over to* MARY.
She plucks a feather out of LA CORBIE's *coat sleeve and signs*
flamboyantly)

MARY: And you ha'e the stamp we ha'e made up o' the King's
signature?

(RICCIO *produces it flamboyantly and rubber-stamps each paper*
with a thump, blows on them and puts them in his pocket)

Aye . . . oan the richt-hand side, o' coorse. *Mine* must aye hae
the pride o' place, because it is the name you read first! On the
left. (*Pause*) O, Riccio, Riccio, you dinnae think it was . . . petty
o' me to withdraw the silver ryal?

(RICCIO's *familiar hushing gesture; he comes and starts mas-*
saging her temples. We realise RICCIO *is to* MARY: *guru,*
confidant, secretary and PA, 'alternative' healer, fortune-teller,
adviser, and silent as a psychiatrist to boot. As well as musi-
cian and occasional mimer and jester — these are demonstrated
during this scene, variously)

I don't think so, there was nae choice. I couldna allow it as a
coin o' the realm.

(LA CORBIE *does a coin trick, conjures up on*e)

LA CORBIE: The silver ryal, a commemorative coin worth thirty
shillings, Scots, to celebrate the love of King Henry for Queen
Mary —

(LA CORBIE *bites the coin*) Is it genuine?

MARY: The damnable cheek of it — Henricus et Maria, Deo
Gratia *Rex* et Regina Scotorum! Wrang order.

LA CORBIE: Whom God hath jined together let nae man cast
assunder.

(*The silver ryal turns magically into two*)

MARY: Sometimes I think he doesn't realise we proclaim him King without even ratifyin' it wi' the council . . . I wish Henry widna harp and carp aboot the crown matrimonial a' the time, for it widna be politick to grant him it.

LA CORBIE: Even if you wanted tae . . .

MARY: So, Henry Darnley, you ha'e nae richt to ma throne eftir ma death — even if it werena for you, ma son. (*Pause*) If you are a son. Och I widna wish for ye to be a lassie.
  Whit think ye, Davy Riccio, boy or girl?

  (RICCIO *shuts* MARY's *eyes, leans her back, takes a ring on a ribbon from his pocket and swings it like a pendulum above her belly*)

LA CORBIE: Whit is't then? Widdershins an' it's a boy! —

  (RICCIO *pauses, then makes a cheeky wee wiggling baby's penis of his crooked little finger at his crotch*)

RICCIO: Ragazzo!

MARY: Thank God, a son.

LA CORBIE: Funny! Yesterday it went the other wey and still ye said, oh aye it wis a laddie! Dowsers an' diviners an' fortune-tellers, ever noticed how they aye tell ye whit they think ye want to hear?

MARY: Make him strang! (*Pause*) Davy Riccio — tell ma fortune!

LA CORBIE: (*producing them as if by magic*) Ta-rocco!

  (*They are Tarot, of course, outsize.* RICCIO *takes them, spreads them in a circle, spins*)

MARY: Only you, Davy, only you said I wis richt to marry Henry Darnley. You cast ma cairts for me — an' you chartit ma birth staurs — time an' again we turnt up the same cairt.

RICCIO: (*turning it up again*) Gli Amanti!

MARY: The lovers. 'Numero six.' 'A choice.' Except there wis nae choice at a', you kennt that! (*Fierce and smiling to remember it*) Though even ye couldna hae fortellt the anger o' ma nobles! Damn them a'! Damn England for harbouring the bloody rebels, Ah'll depend on France and Spain afore England, Ah'll show them a' I was richt tae follow ma destiny an' marry the man I loved.

LA CORBIE: Love-*ed*. Note the past tense.

MARY: Noo, we hae tae cast three, is that no' richt?
  (*First card*)

MARY and RICCIO: (*together*) Il diavolo!
  (*Second card*)

RICCIO: Numero tredici —

MARY: (*shivering*) The unnamed card . . .

RICCIO: La morte.

> (MARY *tries to laugh*)

MARY: Ah ken that's supposed to be a lucky caird, dinna cairds aye mean the opposite! But it frichts me a' the same!

LA CORBIE: A skeleton wi' a grin as wide his ain scythe. Airms and legs in the broken earth. A crowned head, cut aff, in the boattom corner. Only a picture! Colourt in ower crudely by some Admon Kadmon trickster at a tally fair! La morte!

MARY and RICCIO: (*as the third card goes down*) Justizia!

MARY: (*Relieved*) Justice, well yon's a lucky caird, eh Davy?

LA CORBIE: Oh aye, an' — lik' chance — it'd be a fine thing.

> (RICCIO *smiles, massages her feet and ankles, a reflexologist incarnate.* LA CORBIE *has picked up the rest of the pack when* MARY *has put it down. She fans them*)

An' whit else is in here? There's . . . the world, il mondo, la ruota, the wheel o' fortune; the ruined tower; the wummin pope; the hangin' man; il pazzo, the fool, zero.

> (*On the word 'fool'* DARNLEY, *bottle in hand, appears*)

The King — nay, the knave, the knave o' cups!

> (*And she shows that card.* HENRY DARNLEY *is there, supported by* BOTHWELL *and* BESSIE. DARNLEY *sees* RICCIO *with a bare royal foot in his hands, on his lap*)

DARNLEY: What in hell's name is going on? Leave my wife alone — I'll bloody well —

> (DARNLEY *makes a drunken lunge*)

LA CORBIE: He will!

BOTHWELL: C'moan, man, wheest . . . !

> (BOTHWELL *bows low at* MARY *and* RICCIO *after struggling with his drunken burden, settling him on stool*)

Madam, at your service. Seigneur Davy . . .

MARY: Bothwell, hoo daur you let him get intae sicc a state?

BOTHWELL: Madam . . . Ah nivir encouraged him. Ah . . . did advise him that mibbe he should caw canny. But he is the King. (*Shrugs*)

MARY: He's only a laddie.

> (BOTHWELL *shrugs again, ruffles* DARNLEY'*s drunken head*)

BOTHWELL: Ah ken, Ah ken . . . he hasna yet the heid for it yet.

DARNLEY: I'll tell you where I have been. I have been making friends among your nobles. On *your behalf.* You make no attempt to understand them or make them your allies. I'll tell you where I have been. On Tuesday, after the hunt, a great day's sport, we came upon a deserted little cove . . . near Aberdour. Very rocky . . . Bothwell and I swam a race across it. All the other nobles cheered. And I won. Didn't I, Hepburn . . . ? I won!

MARY: (*sharply*) Bothwell, I thocht I had askit ye for your help?

BOTHWELL: Madam, I hae missed ma ain dinner and ridden fifteen miles tae bring him safely hame, he isna ma responsibeelity . . .

MARY: Maister Hepburn, I am sorry. Bessie, tak' the Earl o' Bothwell doon tae the kitchens directly and wake someone, middle o' the nicht or no'! Somethin' hot for the Earl o' Bothwell.

(BESSIE *curtsies,* BOTHWELL *bows and both go.* DARNLEY *lurches up to* MARY, *breathes in her face*)

DARNLEY: Ah Mary, Mary. I'm sorry . . . Give me a kiss.
(*She recoils*)

Leave us alone, Seigneur Riccio!

MARY: Davy, stay exactly where you are!

(RICCIO *stays. Begins typing fast as if to say I'm not here or listening.* DARNLEY *crumples in humiliation. Pause. Begins causing what impotent bother he can. Slurring a lot*)

DARNLEY: Clack, clack, clack, like the tongues of foreigners . . . Italians. French . . . Only thing I can stand about the bloody French is the wine. (*Sings drunkenly*) 'Oh — oh — Give me twelve and twelve o' the good claret wine/ An' twelve — and twel' o' the muskadine . . . '

Mind you the Scotch are as bloody bad, God made the Highlander out of a lump of dung . . . Then for the bloody Lowlander, He decided to economise on even that basic raw material . . . What are you writing? (*Pulls sheet out of typewriter, crumples it up*) Because it's too late at night. Go away, Seigneur Davy, I want to kiss my wife.

(RICCIO *frozen*)

My lovely wife. My beautiful wife. D'you know she is the Queen? Therefore she must be beautiful. (*Pause. Touches* MARY'*s hair*) She is though.

MARY: Davy, leave us.

(RICCIO *bows, goes quickly with relief.* DARNLEY *is sobbing, like a child*)

DARNLEY: Oh, Mary, Mary, I am sorry.

MARY: (*not bitterly*) Aye, Henry, aye. You aye-weys are.

DARNLEY: Mary, Mary, I love you, hold me!

(*She is rocking him and cradling him like a child. Lips to his hair*)

MARY: Wheesht, wheesht, Henry! Ssh. (*Rocks him*)

LA CORBIE: Yin big bairn, and yin on the wey!

SCENE TWO — RUMPLEFYKE

LA CORBIE: Haw — somethin' hoat for the Earl o' Bothwell!
   (BOTHWELL *in undervest and braces loose,* BESSIE *dishev-
   elled. He grabs her and kisses her.* BESSIE *giggling, all sexy
   terror*)
BESSIE: Dinna!
   (*She bites his mouth in a passionate kiss. He jumps apart*)
BOTHWELL: Ya jaud ye, ye are as sherp as ye are soople.
BESSIE: Wheesht! The Queen'll hear us, or somebody'll —
BOTHWELL: The Queen! She's likely busy da'en the same —
   (BOTHWELL *kisses* BESSIE *passionately*)
BESSIE: I dinna think sae!
BOTHWELL: Richt enough, he's ower fou tae even pish straight.
   (*Pause*) Ah wunner if he cin still pit a smile on her face?
BESSIE: Whiles. (*Pauses*) But no' vera oaften.
BOTHWELL: Hoo dae ye ken?
BESSIE: Ah ken fine! (*Pause*) What do you want to talk aboot
   the Queen for?
BOTHWELL: Ah dinna!
   (*They kiss again*)
BESSIE: Bothwell, ma mistress kens naethin' o' the happiness
   you hae taught me.
BOTHWELL: Ah should hope no'! The difference in oor ranks!
   Besides I am a married man.
BESSIE: You ken fine whit Ah mean. I'm sure she has never
   kennt it for hersel'.
BOTHWELL: Whit?
BESSIE: Love.
BOTHWELL: And her mairrit tae sicc a handsome long lad?
BESSIE: Ah'm sayin' naethin'!
BOTHWELL: And she doesna love him?
BESSIE: Mibbe aye — mibbe hooch aye.
BOTHWELL: Pair, pair Queen! Nae wunner her an' Davy Riccio
   are sae thick thegither.
BESSIE: Noo dinna you start ony daft —
BOTHWELL: You're no' tellin' me it's true that the Queen and
   Davy Riccio —
BESSIE: Davy Riccio is as ugly as sin . . . He is a humphit back't
   wee puggy monkey o' a man!
   (BOTHWELL *kisses* BESSIE *lewdly*)
BOTHWELL: Does he kiss her lik' this? And does he stick his
   haun' —
BESSIE: Dinna! You're makkin' me shudder.

BOTHWELL: Makks a lot of women shudder so Ah've heard. Makks them shiver when they see their smooth milk skin up agin' greasy, creashy, warted skin, when they run their haun ower the bone-hard knarl o' the hump —

BESSIE: Dinna!

BOTHWELL: Oh aye! There is a big attraction — beauty wad fain keist wi' ugliness, its opposite!

BESSIE: Naw —

BOTHWELL: Oh aye, oh aye, ma lassie, when you ken the weys o' the warld as weel as this auld tod-fox o' a man, here, does —

BESSIE: Does it no' occur tae ye maybe she loo'es Davy Riccio because he is the only man wha has ever touched her withoot he wants tae tummle her?

BOTHWELL: Och! Mibbe I should stap tummlin' ye and ye'd loo'e me a' the better . . . ?

BESSIE: Dinna!

> (*She reaches for him, easily teased.* BOTHWELL *kisses her, she kisses back*)

BOTHWELL: A'richt, mibbe Ah'll no' . . . *Touchin'* her, though! Ah hae heard it said a cat cin lukk at a queen, but never that a durty wee lowborn furriner can run his hauns a' ower her. Nae wunner the King droons his pair hornit heid in his cups, an' the rumours —

BESSIE: He is a healer.

BOTHWELL: Och, Ah bet!

> (*Pause*)

What was a' yon wi the bare feet then? By God, the king was *bleezin'* . . .

BESSIE: It's a healin' airt! (*She holds out her bare foot*) Ilka bit o' yer feet is . . . lik' a map o' the rest o' yir body — oh I dinnae ken, but yir ankle-banes are your briests . . .

> (BOTHWELL *is sucking at her ankles,* BESSIE *running her hands down her body*)

. . . and the gimp-bit is your waist — an' when you touch that bit on the fit it soothes that bit o' the body. It works!

> (BOTHWELL *runs his hand over instep, tickles between her toes*)

BOTHWELL: Ah'm tickery-Riccio . . . Ah'm Seigneur Davy . . . an' you're the Queen . . . brawer than the Queen by faur . . .

BESSIE: I'm no'!

BOTHWELL: Oh aye. An' Ah'm Riccio! Touch ma hump. Gaun'. It's hard and gnarlit, but it's got a bone in it. Go an' . . . It's lucky . . . a hunchback . . . Touch it! Touch. (*Whispers*) Touch.

SCENE THREE — WHISPERS, RUMOURS, SOUCHS AND CHATTERS

> (*The whole company devise a moving motif of laughter, whispers, passing letters, espionage. Eventually we reveal* MARY *and* RICCIO *in a tableau of work.* MARY *speaking French fast,* RICCIO *typing fast. A paper aeroplane swoops and loops across in front of them and lands. Silence.* MARY *looks at it.* RICCIO *looks at it.* MARY *goes and picks it up.* RICCIO *to her side, takes her arm and shakes his head trying to stop her opening it. She unfolds it though, and reads*)

MARY: 'Seigneur Davy — beware o' the bastard.' (*Pause*) Whit does this mean?

LA CORBIE: The bastard? That could be a'most hauf the court!

> (RICCIO *takes it, screws it up into a ball and kicks it, as if into a wastepaper basket*)

RICCIO: Parole! Parole!

> (*And shakes his head, unimpressed, unafraid*)

LA CORBIE: Rumours, souchs and chatters i' the court, an' in the streets gowsters mairch vaunty an' crawlin' chauntin' oot hatred tae the Catholics.

SCENE FOUR — KNOX AND BOTHWELL

> (*And our ragged troop swagger on like an Orange Walk singing out hatred in 'The Good and Godly Ballad'. Bringing on* KNOX *and* BOTHWELL *for their confrontation. Good and Godly Ballad*)

ALL: (*quietly, as if distant*) Up wi' the hunt. Up wi' the hunt
Tis noo the perfect day
Jesus oor King is gane hunting
Wha likes to speid they may.

(*Louder*) Yin cursit fox lay hid in rocks
This lang and mony yin day
Devouring sheep whaur he micht creep
Nane micht him fricht away.

(*Louder still*) It did him guid to lap the bluid
Of young and tender lambs
Nane could he mis for all was his
The young yins wi' their dams.

(*Crescendo*) That cruel beast, he never ceased

By his usurpit power
Under dispense to get oor pence
Oor souls to devour.
   (*Stamping, getting louder than ever*)

The hunter is Christ that hunts in haste
The hounds are Peter and Paul
The Pape is the fox, Rome is the rocks
That rubs us on the gall.
   (KNOX *and* BOTHWELL *peel off from the rabble band of singers, become themselves, and continue a conversation they've been having*)

KNOX: I sympathise (as I am shair the Guid Lord does) wi' the zeal which inspires destruction and indiscipline, although of course I condemn the act itsel'. (*Pause*) And ye were saying . . . ? 'Boot the Queen . . . ?

BOTHWELL: Och, I wis gey suspeecious o' her tae, when she arrivit, and I hae much watcht for ony dissemblin' I'd see there. And there is nane.

KNOX: You see nane?

BOTHWELL: Nane.

KNOX: Then beware o' yir ain een, Bothwell. Beware of women, the charms o' their hair — beware for adultery begins wi' the eyes. Are ye mair virtuous than David? Are ye wiser than Solomon? Are ye stronger than Samson?

BOTHWELL: Ah am an ordinary man, but kinsman, I see . . . a wummin wha in six years in this country —

KNOX: Has in her ain private chapel ilka Sunday heard the filthy popish Mass.

BOTHWELL: Aye, in private. She has never heard Mass said in public. Ye ken how strang Ah am agin the Mass —

KNOX: Bothwell, it were mair fearfu' tae me that yin Mass be heard in this realm than ten thousand men, armed and bristlin', were landed in a hundred foreign men o' war upon oor shores.

BOTHWELL: And has she restored yin Scotch Catholic or yin abbey? Ye hae *dingit* doon the nests. The rooks *are* flown awa. Never tae return! Oh, the Queen does maintain her diplomatic contacts wi' the Pope and a' Catholic Europe. Whit does it avail her? Jist words. 'Parole, Parole.' There are three things they can send. Promises. Hard cash. Soldiers.

   Hae they armed her? Hae they fattened oor skinny Scotch coffers? I say we maun maintain her safely on this throne — otherwise foreigners will be *forcit* to intervene to uphold the vera *idea* o' sovereignty and legality.

On oor throne we hae a Catholic who has aye in word and deed affordit oor New Truth toleration.

And she is oor Queen. Anointed by God.

KNOX: She says. And God says we are his, we belong to him, justified by faith alone, and his election.

BOTHWELL: But I tell ye, Knox, there is a plan — you *ken* there is a plan — to bring doon the Queen and bring chaos to the realm.

KNOX: (*sharp*) What wind have ye, o' this?

God — in his infinite mercy — aft-times does yase wicked men to punish other wicked men . . .

BOTHWELL: Maister Knox, stop hiding ahint your holiness just for once. I care naethin' for Davy Riccio —

KNOX: Seigneur Davy is a poltroon an' a vile knave.

BOTHWELL: Exactly. But I care *less* for him-that-ye-cry oor bold, young King.

KNOX: He is a Protestant.

BOTHWELL: Is he? Oh aye, is that whit he is these days. Chynged his mind again, has he? If a' his hums and haws were hams and haggises, the country wad we weel fed!

KNOX: And he is the King.

BOTHWELL: The Queen's man . . .

KNOX: The King. And he kens he disna want to hae to rock Seigneur Davy's son in the royal cradle.

BOTHWELL: It is Henry's bairn she is big wi'. But wicked men — aye, Knox, ye dae ken wha they are and only ye can stap them — are yasin' Henry Darnley's weakness as their strength.

KNOX: Hoo dae ye mak' that oot?

BOTHWELL: I ask ye, the vera men wha rebelled agin the Queen when she mairrit Darnley, and wha were pit tae the horn and banisht tae Englan' — they loo'e Darnley sae weel six months later that it is a' for advancement o' him abune the Queen that they are plottin' a' this mischief? Acht! —

KNOX: I ken naethin' o' ony mischief.

BOTHWELL: Ye could forbit it, skail the hale thing fae the pulpit and stap it.

KNOX: I am a man o' God. I care naethin' for politics.

BOTHWELL: Because in this instance ye think the hail cowp will benefit ye and yir kirk.

KNOX: God's kirk, Bothwell. (*Pause*) Plots and mischief? And whit benefit is there to you in stappin' it? Keeping' a'thing sweet for you and for her whase favour an' influence yu hae ingratiated yoursel' intae by crawling flattery?

BOTHWELL: I dinna think either Queen nor maid ever accusit

me o' flattery.

KNOX: Oh aye there is honey-flattery and there is sourrock-flattery. Such is the perverseness o' women I hear they like the sherp taste better.

BOTHWELL: As I love my kirk, and my country, so I love my Queen. Nae mair. (*Pause*) Besides, the Crown cowps and the bliddy English will be up ower-rinnin' us again.

KNOX: Elizabeth is a Good Protestant . . .

BOTHWELL: I love the Scottish crown.

KNOX: Oh aye. And what it will provide ye wi'?

BOTHWELL: And ye wad suffer treason . . .

KNOX: James Hepburn, Earl o' Bothwell, kinsman — I tell you I am a man o' God. My God has charged me, loud and plain, in the words o' his ain Guid Book, no' tae meddle wi' the temporal filth o' politiks. And it is my duty to obey my God. As God's kirk teaches its truth by the preachin' o' the word, the spreadin' o' the word *demands* that all people be educated to read so that they may freely read and feed at his word, but there be nothin' temporal or political in educating equally all God's subjects. If the kirk fight to feed them and claithe them it is only sae that they can maintain on earth God's *heavenly* kingdom.

If the word of God teaches men that all earthly palaces and power systems are robbers' caves then the punishment o' wicked princes is the *duty* of their subjects.

I will leave it unto God to deal with the prince o' this realm. I am shair the good Lord will protect her, if she deserve to be protectit. Neither I, nor the yane true kirk have ony richt tae interfere. And I'd advise you no' tae either, Maister Hepburn O'Bothwell.

(*Noise of bones, then* LA CORBIE *announces flamboyantly, tumbling a long string she has been setting up all during the last, a standing chain of dominoes, with a clatter*)

LA CORBIE: Dominoes!

(*Which has got us straight into scene 5 with a pile of dominoes already laid out on the table, spread*)

SCENE FIVE — MUMMERS AND MURDERERS

(LA CORBIE *moves off to the side, observing, as a very pregnant* MARY, BESSIE *and* RICCIO *are playing dominoes. It's very domestic and easy*)

BESSIE: Ah'm chappin'.

(*She does.* MARY *plays a domino, wins*)

MARY: Och, kickin!

BESSIE: They do say a boay kicks mair . . .

LA CORBIE: An' that's juist on the inside, wait till he gets oot.

> (DARNLEY *bursts in looking weird, pale and strange. He is drunk*)

MARY: King Henry — so you jine us?

DARNLEY: And you aren't pleased to see me? It's me. Your husband. To while away the night with my sovereign, my wife, and my unborn son . . .

MARY: Of coorse we are pleased to see ye, Henry, maist gratified you have deserted mair congenial companions for our sake.

DARNLEY: . . . yes, with my sovereign, my wife, my unborn son and . . . assorted servants and menials, of course. Do excuse me, I did not *prostrate* myself before you all in greeting.

MARY: King Henry, you are drunk.

DARNLEY: Right you are, Queen Mary!

> (*He drinks*)

Not drunk. No. Just merry. And wishing to share my merriment with my poor lumpen wife.

I wonder if there can be a God, He arranges things so unfairly, eh? 'Deed it's true enough you women get all the pain and burden, us men get all the pleasure. Isn't that so, Seigneur Riccio?

MARY: Sit doon, Henry, if ye are going to drink a loving-cup with us.

DARNLEY: A loving-cup. I will indeed.

> (*He drinks. Sound of music approaching, and masked and strange* — to BESSIE's *alarm* —)

BESSIE: Whit's that? Queen Mary, dinna let —

> (— *the* MUMMERS *burst in,* 1 *and* 2 *and* 3, *with a fiddle*)

DARNLEY: Only a troop of travelling players. Here to entertain us.

LA CORBIE: Mmhm!

> (*The* MUMMERS *stand like stookies*)

DARNLEY: What are you going to perform for us tonight then?

LA CORBIE: Ah wonder . . .

> (*They stand like stookies*)

DARNLEY: Ha! Dumbshow . . . haha . . .

> (*Suddenly the* MUMMERS *move, a little sign shoots out on a stick with the legend* THE MASK OF SALOME)

MUMMERS: Tara!

MUMMER 1: 'The Mummers' Masque of Salome.'

MUMMER 2: A mellow-drama that entails

Sex and lust at the court of King Herod

— Plus the Dance of the Seven Veils!

(*A rude fart-noise on a horn thing and a quick burst of juggle, very staccato, not at all merry but horribly sinister*)

LA CORBIE: Oh good, the Bible! Ah love a story with a bit of blood and guts in it.

(MUMMER 3 *pulls out an inflated cushion with a very cardboard crown on it.* MUMMERS 1 *and* 2 *exaggerated hands in the air and 'Ooh'*)

MARY: Wha the hell *are* you?

DARNLEY: Just mumbling mummers, poor travelling players . . .

(*The* MUMMERS *offer* DARNLEY *the crown*)

(*Very bitter*) Not at all! *The crown does not fit me!*

(DARNLEY *places it on* MARY'*s head*)

Tara! Hail the King!

MUMMER 1: The King, he was called *Herod* —

He was King of all the Jews —

And he fell in love with his brother's wife

— Which was: Exceeding Bad News.

MUMMER 2: Because a man called *John the Baptist* —

MUMMER 1: Said 'Herod! Upon my life

It is written in the Law of the Prophets

Thou shalt not BLEEP-BLEEP Thy Brother's Wife.'

(*The silly Marx Brothers horn comes in handy quite often during all this*)

MUMMER 1: Herod looked at John the Baptist

And his face turned deathly pale —

MUMMER 2: Said: 'I'm the one that gives the bleeding orders'

And he clapped the poor prophet in gaol.

MUMMER 1: Herod said:

MUMMER 2: 'A king can mairry wha he likes

Holy Joes like you can wheesht their din!'

And he promptly turned back to his feastin'

And got boozin' and beastin' in.

MUMMER 1: To assuage his Foul Lust, nothing fur it but he must

BLEEP the brother's wife in an adulterous lee-aison

Then he done-in the brother so they could marry one another —

MUMMER 2: Acht! For murder, och! It's aye the silly sea-aison!

MUMMER 1: Noo the honeymoon's *been* for the *King* and new Queen

And they are back to auld claes and parridge.

And the palace is the home y them and *Salome* —

MUMMER 2: That's the new Queen's dochter by her first

marriage.

(DARNLEY *has been thrown Salome-kit*)

DARNLEY: Salome! That's *moi*!

(*And he dons crude yashmak/falsies costume, and begins lumbering grossly and drunkenly.* MUMMER 1 *skelps him, he quietens down, disconcerted to find himself their puppet*)

MUMMER 1: Now, Herod was throwin' a wee stag night
For some visiting pot-entates.
Says the Queen:

MUMMER 2: 'Haw, ony chance Salome cin dae a wee dance
For the entertainment, like, o' you and yir mates?

(*And they lead out* DARNLEY *as gross Salome*)

MUMMER 1: Now Salome had always been . . . big for her age
Sortae . . . lamb dressed up as mutton.
Buxom and pretty wi' a tassel on each titty
And a jewel in her belly button.

(*Salome begins to dance sand-dance and mock striptease*)

MUMMER 1: So Salome done the seven veils
— At furst it wis jist fur a laugh —
She hooched, shimmied and skirled
Shook, shoogled and birled
Till they shouted, 'Get them aff!'

MUMMER 2: Salome's mammy's look said, 'Go for it!'
So she didnae mess aboot —

MUMMER 1: An' soon — sweet sixteen wi' slanty een —
She stood in her birthday suit.
— Herod said!

(*And they force a bit of paper on* MARY, *forcing her to read Herod's part*)

Herod said! —

(*He repeats more forcefully and, flustered,* MARY *reads out:*)

MARY: 'Och, Good Lord! Lassie, name your reward
Ask for anything — yon wis great!'

DARNLEY: (*as Salome*) 'Give me the head of John the Baptist —
With some parsley, on a plate!'

(*And* DARNLEY *points right at* RICCIO. *All three* MUMMERS *rush at him, pull him to the ground, knives out and as he screams and clutches at* MARY's *skirt they stab him viciously and drag him off*)

RICCIO: Justizia! Justizia! Sauvez ma vie! Justizia!

(*And* MARY, DARNLEY, BESSIE, LA CORBIE *left.* MARY *cradling belly, stunned, staring at* DARNLEY, *who is crumbling at the real and actual violence. He begins to sob.* MARY *runs at him then*)

MARY: Kill me! Go on. Kill me tae. Kill me an' your ain bairn. Go an, ye micht as well. Plunge the knife in. Tear yir ain son oot o' ma tripes an' strangle him wi' yir ain hauns. Because if you dinna he will grow up tae be revenged on ye. Kill me. Kill me. Kill me!

(*He is in such a frenzy he might. But* MUMMER 1 *grabs his wrist very hard, holds it there.* MUMMER 2 *draws his sword against* DARNLEY's *throat*)

MUMMER 1: I wouldna dae that, young Henry . . .

MUMMER 2: (*tuts*) Regicide, that is.

MUMMER 1: Killing a king! Very nasty . . .

MUMMER 2: That's no' hoo we dae things here in Scotland

MUMMER 1: Never been heard of!

MUMMER 2: Not all through history . . .

MUMMER 1: *I've* never heard of it, have you, Jimmy?

MUMMER 2: Naw, Jock!

(*Pause*)

Not nice to kill a member of the fair sex either.

MUMMER 1: Not nice at the best of times but to kill wan that's thon wey wi' a bairn . . .

MUMMER 2: We couldnae hae it, Tam!

MUMMER 1: Neither we could, Wullie.

(*Pause*)

Even though we are at your service, King Henry. (*Bows*)

MUMMER 2: Behind you all the way, King Henry, we're your men, yes sir.

MUMMER 1: Aren't we, Rab?

MUMMER 2: A' the wey, Geordie.

DARNLEY: Is he dead?

(MUMMERS *chuckle very softly*)

MARY: Wha are ye? Wha are ye an' wha did this?

(LA CORBIE's *next speech is a rhythm to herself as* MUMMERS/MARY/DARNLEY *drama stays unbroken, continues above it. She's circling and drumming herself up with this, a quiet frenzy*)

LA CORBIE: There's Ruthven and Morton and Lindsay
and Lethington
Ormiston, Brunstane, Haughton and Lochlinnie
There's Kerr o' Fa'donside, Scott, and Yair and Elphinstone
There's Ballantin' and Douglas
There's Ruthven and Morton . . .

(*Continues over the next and fades out*)

MUMMER 1: King Henry, we need ye a wee minute, don't we, Jake?

MUMMER 2: We dae that, Eck. (*To* DARNLEY) Ye see . . . some
o' the townspeople are clamourin' at the windaes —

MUMMER 1: There's been a wee bit o' a disturbance an' they're
wonderin' if the Queen's a'richt.

(*They begin to go,* DARNLEY *flanked by* MUMMERS. MUM-
MER 1 *suddenly wheels back*)

(*At* MARY) There's nae windaes in here, Ah warn ye, there's
twa big strang men staunin' by that door wi' the twa-handit
sword and if ye try and get oot they will cut ye intae collops!

(*He wheels back and exits.* MARY *is left with* BESSIE *in the
silence now.* LA CORBIE*'s litany has stopped too. Exits.* MARY,
LA CORBIE, BESSIE *alone*)

LA CORBIE: Blood!

MARY: He has killed oor maist special servant wha I loo'ed richt
well, I hate him.

LA CORBIE: Aye hatred can be got in an instant lik' a bairn
is, fattens faster in the wame an' is, whiles, a lot langer in the
nursin' o' it.

MARY: (*to her child*) O' so much are ye yir faither's bairn I fear
for ye in the future.

LA CORBIE: A bairn's bairns are ill tae prosper. Blood. Whit
does that cry oot for?

MARY: Nae mair tears. I will think o' a revenge. Bessie . . .
Bessie, when they sen' ye for claes for me — Ah'm gonny
pretend ma labour has sterted, they'll hae to get me a midwife, we maun somehow get hand o' ma black box wi' Davy's
foreign correspondence and somehow smuggle a message tae
somebody, Bothwell, onybody wha will help us!

(*Snap lighting change, music moves us instantly on in time*)

SCENE SIX — SWEET BABY JAMES, AUNTIE
ELIZABETH AND A SORER SICKBED FOR
DARNLEY THIS TIME

(LA CORBIE *wheels on baby, first loop of her circle . . . she sings
a sinister wee song which is also a familiar Scottish west-coast
lullaby*)

LA CORBIE: Wee chookie burdie
Tol-a-lol-a-lol
Laid an egg on the windae sole
The windae sole it began to crack
And wee chookie burdie roared and grat.

(LA CORBIE *wheels him.* ELIZABETH *revealed soliloquising à
la Act One. She has a letter and a Polaroid snapshot of a baby*

as if from proud new parents, and a hand mirror)

ELIZABETH: And so she has a son and heir. They do say he is perfect. (*Looks at photo*) Well, 'James of Scotland', are you going to end up my heir for want of a better or a nearer? Surely not . . .

(LA CORBIE *wheels pram into focus*)

LA CORBIE: Wee Jamie eh? Born tae be King James the Saxt o' Scotland. Some day. If ye live sae lang . . . An awfy big name for sicc a wee rid-faced scrawny shilpit wee scrap o' humanity, eh? Dinna greet. Aye wha's the lucky laddie tae have made it this faur, eh? Eh?

ELIZABETH: A son and heir . . . and I am of but barren stock. 'The Virgin Queen'. Too old to whelp now at any rate.

LA CORBIE: Wheest, wheest, does your mammy love yir daddy, eh? Eh? Does she no? Ach well, son, you'll no' be the first bairn i' the world conceivit in love and born intae hate.

(*Lights reveal* DARNLEY *in his surgical mask lying on sickbed,* MARY *with a bowl of something, spoonfeeding him*)

DARNLEY: Love me, Mary.

MARY: Sup this up, Henry . . .

DARNLEY: But you will love me again, Mary . . . ? When I'm better?

MARY: Aye, Henry . . . when you're better.

DARNLEY: Doctor said he didn't think it'd mark my face. You don't think I'll be marked for ever? Surely smallpox doesn't always —

MARY: Likely no, Henry.

DARNLEY: It's disgusting to you, isn't it? What if I'm all pocked . . . Mary, could you ever let me back into your bed again, with my face all —

MARY: It'll leave nae mark, Henry.

DARNLEY: Want to come back to your bed, be a proper husband again, Mary.

MARY: Eat. You're weak.

DARNLEY: Don't say that word. It's been a taunt at me ever since I was a boy.

MARY: You're still but a boy, Henry.

DARNLEY: And God help me but it's true! I'm weak. Wicked men used me, you were right, they would have killed me too. They used my weakness, my — is loving you a weakness? They made me jealous, I was a mad person, not myself, it wasn't — Jealousy! It was a poison, it filled me up, they manipulated me, it wasn't my fault.

MARY: Wheesht. Eat.

DARNLEY: It was my fault.

MARY: Aye but it wisna a' your fault, Henry. You're . . . only young yet. I tellt you.

DARNLEY: It's a long time ago now, Mary. I've changed. Honestly I'm not the same person! And our fine son is growing, eh?

MARY: Fat and bonny.

DARNLEY: I tell you, this last year . . . ever since that night — (MARY *shrugs*)

MARY: We hae ither secretaries.

(ELIZABETH *crumples letter and photo*)

ELIZABETH: I do think it's hard to think of her so happy and me not! Dark deeds, bloody murders, plots against her life and throne, and she wins out again and again. All those involved just scatter when Darnley deserts them, most of the original rebels are pardoned and back in favour in Edinburgh, such is the wheel of fortune, and she is — if my spies tell me true — quite reconciled to the child-husband. All her people love her, she has a husband and a fine healthy son.

(*Pause*)

Such is the wheel of fortune! . . . 'Oh, madam, you never wanted to marry!' How the hell do any of them know what I wanted! Shut up! Shut up!

(*Pause*)

I don't know what I wanted (*Looks at her coiffure in the mirror*) Lord! Grey hairs. Pluck them out.

LA CORBIE: Aye, King James the Saxt. Some day. And mair, mair than that, shall be. Some day. Wheesht. But watch ma lambie, watch! Listen, once upon a time, aye, aye, oot on the open moor, caw, caw, an' there was a moose thocht it was lord o' a' the heather, and there was a foumart's den an' it lay toom and empty. Sae the wee moose moved in and thocht it wis in heaven. Till the foumart cam' back an' ett it fur its supper.

(LA CORBIE *wheels off out of focus*)

DARNLEY: We'll be happy again, you'll see.

MARY: Aye, Henry.

DARNLEY: And I can come to your bed again?

MARY: Once . . . you're better o' the smallpox, aye.

DARNLEY: I wish I could come back to the palace.

MARY: Soon.

DARNLEY: But you will stay here?

MARY: Aye, Downstairs. Richt ablow ye. I'm your wife.

DARNLEY: Will you come and sit with me tonight? We could have music.

MARY: No the nicht, Henry. I hae tae gang tae a weddin' — ma best page is tae be merrit at the palace and I canny no' go to the feast o' ma favourite, it widnae be lucky.

DARNLEY: Don't go.

(MARY *is arching and trying to fasten beads*)

MARY: I must. (*Pause*) Fasten ma necklace, Henry.

(*She bares the nape of her neck, hair forward, all vulnerable as in beheading pose, almost. An echo, a premonition of it. He fastens clasp and kisses her neck, burying his face in her hair*)

DARNLEY: You smell beautiful. Amber, isn't it? I wish it could drown out all the camphor of this sickroom, I wish, I wish —

(*He probably'd like it to drown out guilt, everything.* MARY *bursts suddenly*)

MARY: Henry, come with me to the wedding! Get up, Henry Darnley! Come and dance wi' me!

DARNLEY: Mary, you know I'm sick, I can't go out of doors.

MARY: Of course you canna. Guid nicht, Henry.

DARNLEY: Kiss me?

(*She does. Goes calmly from him. Straight to where* BOTHWELL *is waiting for her. She goes into his arms. They dance*)

BESSIE: (*when she sees*) Oh, naw Bothwell. Bothwell! I'm your Bess! (*She starts to scream. But gets whirled away in a mad dance, a hideous anachronistic waltz, they la-la out and spin, staccato, like mannikins, each with imaginary partner*)

MARY: To hell in a white petticoat wi' you, Bothwell. Aye I will go. I maun go.

BOTHWELL: Ah only hud tae bide ma time . . .

MARY: An' thegither we shall hae justice!

(MARY *and* BOTHWELL *kiss and sink down to the floor in love-making, rolling over and over. Drums are building up to a crescendo.* DARNLEY *where she left him on his sickbed stirs, murmurs her name*)

Justice!

(*And this time the very word makes an enormous explosion happen as* DARNLEY *at Kirk o' Field goes up. As smoke clears everyone else but* MARY *and* BOTHWELL, *who are still writhing in love-making on the floor, begins the accusatory chant*)

ALL: Burn the hoor! Burn the hoor! Burn the hoor!

(*And* BOTHWELL *to his feet and runs one way.* MARY *another. The stage is empty but for clearing smoke.* LA CORBIE *alone, singing her not particularly full of pity 'Lament for Lord Darnley'*)

We Twa Corbies.

LA CORBIE: Twa weet black corbies in the snaw
  Wi' naethin' in oor wames ata'
  Tae the other yin Ah did say
  'Whaur sall we gang and dine the day

  In ahint yon auld fail dyke
  I ken there lies a new slain knight
  And naebody kens
  Naw, naebody kens
  That he lies there
  But his hawk and his hound and his lady fair.

  His hound is to the hunting gane,
  His hawk to fetch the wildfowl hame,
  His lady has ta'en another mate,
  And we may freely mak' our dinner sweet.

  Ye'll sit on his white hause-bane
  And I will pike oot his braw blue een
  And wi' wan lock of his gowden hair
  We shall theek oor nest when it grows bare.

  Aye, his lady's ta'en another mate
  So he shall be oor dinner sweet
  And ower his white banes when they are bare
  The wind shall blaw for ower mair.'

> (*The wind starts up, blowing out the back curtain and what snow and rose petals are still strewn on the stage.*
>
> *Then with some homely clanks of his metal pail, suddenly, on his hands and knees,* KNOX, *with his sleeves rolled up, is scrubbing, scrubbing, the souch of his scrubbing brush on bleached board as if to rub out an indelible stain.* ELIZABETH *comes to another part of the stage.* KNOX *scrubs on in slow motion as she speaks, and* LA CORBIE, *with the pram again, is pushing it back and forward 'shoogling' it as she sits watching the end of it all*)

ELIZABETH: Why me? Why? Why help her? Why does she come here, throwing herself on my mercy? Merciful God, I cannot *afford* to be merciful.

ADVISER 1: Kill her now.

ADVISER 2: It were a kindness.

ELIZABETH: I cannot welcome her here at court. I cannot help restore her to her throne in Scotland. I cannot be seen to condone rebellion against a rightful prince.

ADVISER 2: Exactly.

ADVISER 1: And you cannot keep her in prison indefinitely.

ELIZABETH: She is my honoured guest.

ADVISER 1: Yes and some day she'll escape.

ADVISER 2: The focus of every Catholic hope, of every anti-Elizabeth faction in England.

ELIZABETH: Is she a witch?

ADVISER 1 *and* ADVISER 2: Ask the Scotch.

ELIZABETH: They split her from her Bothwell, drive him from their shores, they seize her infant son, strip her of her crown, lock her in a castle in the middle of an island and throw away the key. And still she can charm some man into helping her escape. God help me, why does she come to England when she could have sailed to bloody France!

(*And* MARY, *all alone, is lit up on the other side of the stage. She holds out her empty arms around an imaginary* BOTHWELL *and spins in a bitter parody of that dance together ta-ra-ing the same made waltz tune, then stops still*)

MARY: I said: 'To hell in a white petticoat wi' you Bothwell, oh aye I will go, I maun go.' Wis it love? No, no' whit you thocht, Jamie Hepburn, oh aye, ye were richt I did . . . aye did . . . lust for ye. Wis that whit it wis? At the time I wis ower innocent to ken whit wis steering me. But I ken noo, Bothwell, I ken noo. Dinna think it wis lichtsomely or in love that I lay me doon wi' ye, in the daurk. Naw, it wis in despair. Oh and wi' a kinna black joy I reachit oot for you to cover me and smother me and for yin moment, snuff oot the hale birlin' world in stillness. And ilka dawn I woke up wi' ye, I saw disaster a' mapped oot for me, clear as my Davy's magic cairds. The ruined tower, the hangin' man, the Empress on her Throne, Judgement . . . and a' thing smashed and skailt for ever tummelin' a' aroon.

(*She sinks down on her knees caught in her tight spot and at the other side of the stage, balancing her, is* ELIZABETH *in — quite literally — her tight spot. All alone too . . . but for those men and their paper and their pen*)

ELIZABETH: My subjects love me! I am the Virgin Queen! I love my good cousin Queen Mary and will keep her my honoured guest in all luxury in the lavish hospitality of my proudest castle. For her own safety.

And my so-called 'wise advisers' would have to trick me before I would consent to sign a warrant for her death.

Would have to trick me. Trick me. Trick me!

(*Her manic repetitions begin to sound like instructions to invisible advisers. KNOX's scrubbing speeds up again. Is it bloodstains on an executioner's block that are proving indelible?*)

SCENE SEVEN — JOCK THAMSON'S BAIRNS

Through the back curtains, one by one, come all our characters, stripped of all dignity and historicity, transformed to twentieth-century children by the rolling up of trouser legs, addition of a cardigan or pair of socks: FIDDLER, WEE BETTY (Elizabeth), WEE HENRY(Darnley), JAMES HEPBURN (Bothwell), RICHIE (Dancer/Riccio), and one by one KNOX baptises them by pouring a cup of dirty water from his pail over their heads, soaking them. They move off slowly and begin miming childhood games. KNOX takes off his pail, comes back, with his trouser legs rolled up and with a muffler, as WEE KNOXXY, a loner, who goes off to his own corner. Downstage, though, BETTY and FIDDLER have got WEE HENRY cawing their rope for them. One skips and both sing.

WEE BETTY *and* FIDDLER: Queen Mary, Queen Mary,
 My age is *sixteen*
 My faither's a wino on *Glesca* green.
 He's drank up the Broo that should dress me up braw.
 Och, will nae bonny laddy come tak' me awa?
 A! B! C! D! E!

   (*MARIE appears, by herself, very prominent, an outsider. She stands silent*)

 On a mountain
 Stands a lady.
 Who she is I do not know.
 All she wants is
 Power and glory.
 All she wants is a fine young man.

   (*The two wee girls see MARIE, sign at each other. BETTY wolf-whistles*)

WEE BETTY: Get her!

FIDDLER: Get swanky!

WEE BETTY *and* FIDDLER: Big banana feet and legs long and lanky!

   (*JAMES HEPBURN wolf-whistles*)

JAMES HEPBURN: Hello, stranger!

WEE BETTY *and* FIDDLER: Hiya, stranger!
 I hope yir maw
 Thinks you're braw!
 Naw, naw

Nae chance! Nae danger!

RICHIE: That's a sin. She's a wee orphan.

WEE BETTY: Little Orphan Annie!

Show us your fanny.

FIDDLER: (*shocked*) Oh-a!

(WEE BETTY *and* JAMES HEPBURN *guffaw, lewd children*)

WEE BETTY: What's your name anyway!

MARIE: Marie.

WEE BETTY: Marie? Whit school do you go to?

JAMES HEPBURN: She means urr ye a left-fitter?

Haw, stranger, d'you eat fish oan a Friday?

WEE BETTY: You a Tim?

JAMES HEPBURN: You a Fenian?

WEE BETTY: Are you a Pape?

MARIE: I'm a Catholic. Ih-hih.

WEE BETTY: Ih-hih? How you mean, mmhmm?

MARIE: Just.

(*Pause*)

WEE BETTY: (*very savage*) Well, away and get converted!

Go an' get born again.

Away an' jine the Bandy Hope, the Tabernacle and go on a
crusade up the Tent Hall tin hut and get saved or somethin' —
Away and get saved for a sweetie.

(*The mention of 'getting saved' reminds them all of* WEE
KNOXXY)

WEE BETTY, JAMES HEPBURN, WEE HENRY *and* RICHIE:

Wee Johnny Knox

Peed in the jawbox

When he thought his mammy wisnae lookin'.

She hit it with a ladle

That was lying on the table,

Walloped him, and gie'd his heid a dooking!

(*They torment him with this but* WEE KNOXXY *tries to ignore
them, singing to himself*)

WEE KNOXXY: I'm H.A.P.P.Y.

I'm H.A.P.P.Y.

I know I am, I'm sure I am,

I'm H.A.P.P.Y.

I'm S.A.V.E.D.

I'm S.A.V.E.D.

I know I am, I'm sure I am,

I'm S.A.V.E.D.

JAMES HEPBURN: Haw! Get Knoxxy!

(*Some grab* WEE KNOXXY, *some* MARIE)

WEE BETTY: Stick his heid up her skurt!

(*They shove* WEE KNOXXY*'s head up* MARIE*'s skirt, holding both.* WEE KNOXXY *is struggling furiously and crying in real terror.* MARIE *too*)

THE REST: A queen cried Mary hud a canary
Up the leg o' her drawers!

WEE KNOXXY: Yuck it, Youse! Yuck it. Dinnae! Ah doan't like lassies. Ma faither says I'm no' tae play wi' lassies.

(*They drop him, afraid of his terror, it's too real.* MARIE *is a sobbing shamed victim, ignored*)

WEE BETTY: Goan' then! Get tae! Away an' play wi' yoursel' then!

JAMES HEPBURN: Aye, git!

WEE BETTY: Skoosh!

RICHIE: Skedaddle.

WEE BETTY: See you later, alligator!

(*And in sudden spite she pulls* MARIE*'s cardigan over her head.* JAMES HEPBURN, *who's been no slouch at being part of the torturers, suddenly grabs* MARIE, *runs with her*)

JAMES HEPBURN: Leave the lassie alane!

(*All turn on them, including* WEE KNOXXY, *who sees how to taunt back*)

WEE KNOXXY: Haw, Hepburn! Ah think you love her.

WEE BETTY: So do I, I think you love her! You gonny marry her?

JAMES HEPBURN: Nut.

WEE BETTY: Aye, you urr! James Hepburn loves Marie Stewart!

THE REST: James Hepburn loves Marie Stewart!

James Hepburn loves Marie Stewart!

JAMES HEPBURN: Ah jist says, lea' the lassie alane!

(*He pulls what's tied and bundled over her head and* MARIE *is free, looks right into his eyes. He into hers. She spits right in his face*)

Right!

THE REST: Fight! Fight! Fight! Fight! Fight!

JAMES HEPBURN: I am the axeman.

THE REST: Kiss the axe.

WEE KNOXXY: Pardon the executioner.

THE REST: And kiss the axe!

ALL: Mary Queen of Scots got her head chopped off.

Mary Queen of Scots got her head chopped off!

WEE BETTY: And eftir you're deid, we'll share oot yir froacks and pu' a' the stones oot yir brooches, and gie yir golden slip-

pers a' away to the Salvation Army, and we'll gie' the Saint
Vincent de Paul —

JAMES HEPBURN: Sweet fuck all!

WEE BETTY: And eftir you're deid
　　We'll pick up your heid
　　Up aff the flair
　　By the long rid hair —

JAMES HEPBURN: Wallop!

WEE HENRY: Haw-haw! It was just a wig!
　　Yir heid goes —

JAMES HEPBURN: Wallop!
　　And it stoats alang the flair like a great big —
　　Tumshie!

ALL: Wallop! Bum . . . bum . . . bum . . . bum.

WEE HENRY: Skoosh!

ALL: *Splat!*
　　(*Pause*)

WEE BETTY: And her wee dug . . .
　　(*Mock tearful*) Her lovely wee dug . . .
　　Her lovely wee dug
　　Wi' the big brown eyes that loved her *so* much . . .
　　Comes scooshing oot fae under her crimson skirts where it
　　has been hiding —
　　— And skites aboot among the blood barking and shiting
　　itself!
　　　(*Shriek of harpy laughter from* WEE BETTY, *totally wild,
　　　hysterical. Silence.* LA CORBIE *is wheeling the pram on the spot
　　　back and forth as she sits. She plays with a marigold head the
　　　old childhood dandelion game, flicks the golden head off*)

LA CORBIE: (*very quietly*) Mary Queen of Scots got her head
　　chopped off.
　　Mary Queen of Scots got her . . . head . . . chopped . . . off.
　　　(*And all around* MARIE/MARY *suddenly grab up at her throat
　　　in a tableau, just her head over their hands. Very still in the red
　　　light for a moment then black*)

Glossary

abune, above
baw, ball
baws, testicles
chair de poule, goose flesh
chancy, lucky, auspicious
chauntin, chanting
craiture, creature, being,
  person
creesh, grease
douce, gentle, kind, pleasant
fendless, defenceless, shiftless
flytin, scolding
foumart, polecat
funns, finds
gaberlunzies, beggars, tinkers
gimp-bit, slimmest part
gin, if
glisk, catch sight of
gowsters, chancers, riff-raff
haar, mist
horn, put to the, to outlaw,
  denounce as a rebel

hurdies, hips, buttocks
just-keistit, recently bedded
keist, lechery
kittocks, women (derogatory),
  loose women
lye, pasture land
maun, must
rumplefyke, sex
saicret, secret
shilpit, feeble, pathetic
shoogling, shaking, trembling
skailt, scattered, spilt
smirr, fine rain
souchs, scrapes
sourrock, sour
theek, thatch
tod-fox, crafty
toom, vacant, empty
tumshie, turnip
vaunty, boastful
wyce, wise, sensible

John Byrne

Your Cheatin' Heart
A six-part television drama
(1990)

MAJOR CHARACTERS

Cissie Crouch
Frank McClusky
Fraser Boyle
Dorwood Crouch
David Cole
Billie McPhail
Jolene Jowett
Shirley
Tracey
Diner in the Bar-L
Young Woman in the Bar-L Ladies' Room
Spencer The Barman
Timberwolf Tierney (aka *The Tall Cowpoke*)
Cherokee George
Eric The Barber
Prison Chaplain
Aberdeen Matron
Elderly Neighbour
Radio DJ
Cissie's Child
Drew
Tamara Macaskill
Engineer (in radio car)
Tonto
Barman at the OK Korral
Policewoman
Limping Man
Ralph Henderson
Roxanne
Nurse
Newsvendor
MC at Ponderosa
Libo Ragazzo
Secretary
Milkman
The Toad
Jim Bob O'May
'Jonathan Ross'

Introduction

John Byrne is as well known as an artist and illustrator as he is a dramatist. He was born in 1940 in Paisley and his experiences in a local carpet factory were to become the basis of his first successful play, *The Slab Boys* (1978). A 'workplace drama' in which the limitations of working-class experience are pitched against the possibilties of a life as an artist, *The Slab Boys* explores ground which has been fundamental in the representation of Scottish working-class culture since Archie Hind's *The Dear Green Place* was published in 1965, and which is represented in this anthology by Roddy McMillan's *The Bevellers*. In Byrne's work, however, Scotland becomes a place where a world of international popular art rubs shoulders with the confined and claustrophobic world of Scottish provincialism. Through the juxtaposition of American mass culture with local vernacular culture, Byrne explores the limits of both, and the fact that Scotland is the site of a ludicrous conjunction of cultures which are apparently alien to one another and are yet places in which individual characters can be equally at home.

In *Your Cheatin' Heart*, Country & Western — itself, of course, from Scottish and Irish origins in folksong — combines with Glaswegian vernacular culture in the same ways that *The Slab Boys* trilogy combined mid-twentieth century Scottish life with the the world of Hollywood films, or his earlier and very successful television series, *Tutti Frutti*, combined it with rock music. Byrne's texts are often accompanied by his own drawings of characters (as in the cover illustration of this volume), and emphasise the extent to which they must be understood as the products of a multi-media culture.

Byrne's importance lies in the fact that no other modern Scottish dramatist is so conscious of the media through which Scottish people engage with the modern world, and the ways in which this shapes their experience as a condition of being 'between' cultures rather than inhabitants of a single culture. In this respect, Byrne's television drama is both a profound representation of the complexities of modern Scotland and a challenge to the ways in which traditional theatre has tried to encompass Scottish experience.

Friday

Glasgow at dusk. A ghostly sickle moon scythes its way between the dark rain clouds that hang over HM prison Barlinnie,
(known affecionately to Glaswegians by its 'Cowboy' nickname,
the 'Bar-L'). In the visiting room of the prison Cissie Crouch,
beanpole-skinny and wearing a dark grey and white horizontally-
striped suit buttoned to the throat and with a number tag stitched
to the breast pocket, sits across the visiting room table from her
husband Dorwood. His features are pale, impassive. He is dressed
in jeans and an unshowy cowboy shirt, his hair neatly groomed.
The atmosphere in the room is tense, as one might expect. A
female prison officer, hands folded behind her back, stands at
a not-quite-discreet-enough distance from the couple. Neither
Cissie nor Dorwood speaks to the other. Cissie reaches a tentative
hand across the table. Dorwood draws his hands away. A distant
bell sounds. Dorwood scrapes back his chair and stands up. The
female prison officer crosses and unlocks a door. Dorwood pulls
on his denim jacket and moves to the door.

CISSIE: Dorwood?
> (*Cissie half-rises in her seat. Dorwood reaches the door, stops,
> and turns*)
DORWOOD: The suit isnae funny, Cissie.
> (*Cissie's face falls. A male prison officer appears in the doorway,
> takes Dorwood by the arm and leads him out. The female of-
> ficer hands Cissie her bag. We hear the men's footsteps fade off
> down the corridor. Cissie crosses to the door, and emerges from
> the visiting room into the corridor as Dorwood is being escorted
> back to his cell, her face distorted into an angry mask*)
CISSIE: (*loudly*) If you weren't in here I wouldnae have to wear
this funny suit!

* * *

> (*The 'Bar-L' is Glasgow's newest piano bar and grill. It is even-
> ing, and the ziggurat neon sign flashes in the dark. Inside Cissie
> is taking down a banquette's order in her pad*)
CISSIE: Yeh, the specials are really nice . . . would you care for
some cornbread with that?
> (*The Bar-L is not a 'fun pub' but a straight eatery set out along
> New York lines: baby-grand surrounded by barstools at one end
> of the room, semi-circular banquettes around the walls, and a bar*)

for cocktails, dining, and serious posing. The one concession to frivolity — aside from the establishment's name — is the waiting staff's livery: the two other waitresses, Tracey and Shirley, are, like Cissie, togged out in modishly-cut 'convict' trouser suits. David Cole, the black American manager, immaculate in white tux, sits at the piano, his fingers caressing a medley of 40s hits from the keyboard. Spencer, the barman, spends his afternoons at the movies and is a big Tom Cruise fan. Cissie crosses to the bar)

CISSIE: Give us a Margherita, will you?

(Spencer displays the enviable dexterity of a juggler as he handles the order. Cissie turns round, rests her elbows on the bartop, and lets out an exhausted sigh)

DAVID COLE: Hey, you.

(Cissie looks around, wondering who it is he's talking to)

DAVID COLE: Yeah, you . . . Jessie.

CISSIE: Cissie.

DAVID COLE: C'mere.

(Cissie crosses to the piano)

CISSIE: What?

(David Cole carries on playing)

DAVID COLE: How long you been workin' here?

(Cissie's lip curls)

CISSIE: What's this, a variation on 'how many fingers am I holdin' up?' I told you when I started, I never touch the stuff . . . that cocktail's for a customer.

(Cole's mood darkens)

DAVID COLE: Hey, don't get sassy with me, Red . . . five days awready, an' nobody's seen you crack a smile.

(He segues into Billy Joel's 'Just the Way You Are')

CISSIE: So, what you tellin' me?

DAVID COLE: Lighten up or take a hike, that's what I'm tellin' you.

(Cissie touches a forelock and tries to turn the contemptuous twist of her mouth to a smile)

* * *

(It's night-time, and on a gap-site in a rundown part of the city there is an eruption of crackling on a two-way radio, the single intelligible word of which is an 'over' at the end)

FRANK: I'm positive it's about here someplace.

(Billie McPhail is standing by her taxi. She is wearing a New York Police Department leather jacket, baggy trousers, and short cowboy boots. She reaches into the cab and unhooks the mike)

BILLIE: (*on radio*) Car Fourteen, say again, over?

(*Frank McClusky, your quintessential 'new' Glaswegian, is standing a few yards distant, with the toecaps of his stout brogues submerged in a scummy cesspool, and his eyes peering into the gloom of the 'bombsite'. Frank is dressed in an enormous Burberry, belted but unbuttoned so that it flaps decorously around the turnups of his Harris Tweed pegbottoms. His shirt is a Japanese/French co-production retailing at around £150 and looking like it's been slept in more than once*)

FRANK: It's a low-rise buildin' with a pokey hat on the roof.

(*He paces across the rubble-strewn wasteland*)

BILLIE: With a what on the roof?

(*Frank scrapes the sole of his shoe along the ground and wishes a pox on all dog-owners*)

FRANK: A pokey hat. Used to be Ragazzo's ice-cream works.

(*There is a short eruption of static over the radio*)

BILLIE: (*on radio*) Naw, I cannae Jolene. I'm stuck out here in the middle of the Okeyfenokey Swamp[1] with a boy scout in a belltent lookin' for a low-rise buildin' with a pokey hat on the roof. Give Car Twenty-Six a shout, over.

(*There is another short burst on the radio*)

BILLIE: (*on radio*) Naw, a pokey hat, over. (*To Frank*) Don't tell me you've spent . . .

(*She glances at the meter. The fare is £8*)

BILLIE: . . . Just to come out here an' buy yourself a wafer? We musta passed umpteen ice-cream vans on the road in.

FRANK: Used to be, I said . . . it's now a very snazzy piano bar and grill specialisin' in Soul Food. Wish to Christ I could remember the name of it . . .

(*He stares up at the stars*)

BILLIE: You're not the only one. (*On radio*) Car Fourteen, you there, Jolene, over?

FRANK: Flang its portals open to the cognoscenti last Monday night . . .

(*There is a short burst on the radio*)

BILLIE: (*on radio*) Yeh, piano bar an' grill specialisin' in Soul Food, Duke Street area, over?

FRANK: I was away coverin' a clambake in Seamill which is how come I missed the launch . . .

(*There's another short burst on the radio*)

BILLIE: (*on radio*) Naw . . . Soul . . . guy says you have to get a boat out to it, over.

(*Frank wanders off across the 'bombsite'*)

FRANK: You mebbe read my piece in the *Echo*?

BILLIE: *Echo?*

FRANK: *Echo.*

(*Another eruption of static on the radio*)

FRANK: My piece about the clambake, naw?

BILLIE: (*on radio*) Hold on, I'll ask. (*To Frank*) Jolene wants to know is it The Clappy Doo in Clyde Street? She's got that in her yella pages under 'Sole, Haddock & Whiting'.

(*Frank fixes Billie with a bilious stare*)

* * *

(*Back in the Bar-L Shirley and Tracey are in a huddle behind the kitchen door marked 'out'. As Cissie enters the 'in' door, Tracey hides a copy of the* Glasgow Evening Echo *behind her back*)

CISSIE: (*loudly*) Four Claws, two Grits, one Gumbo.

(*Cissie turns to go, gives Shirley and Tracey a look, then leaves. Shirley makes a grab for Tracey's tabloid*)

SHIRLEY: Quick, give us a look.

TRACEY: Stop crowdin' us . . .

(*She opens the paper and finds a big publicity picture of the Deadwood Playboys, Dorwood Crouch, Fraser Boyle, and Dwane Devlin, onstage in colour, together with a grainy black and white photograph of Dorwood and Dwane being led handcuffed from the court under a banner headline: 'DEADWOOD DUO'S SHAME AS SHERIFF CRACKS DOWN ON COWBOY COKEHEADS'*)

SHIRLEY: (*reading*) 'Dwane & Dorwood Hit Trail to Pokey! . . . In Clydebank Hold-Up Trial' . . .

(*Her brows knit. She looks at Tracey*) . . . Pokey? Like in hat, naw?

TRACEY: Pokey, like in prison, ya dope . . . they got put away for nine years.

SHIRLEY: Aaah, that's how come the face is trippin' her? S'that him there?

(*She points at the paper*)

TRACEY: Naw, that's Dwane . . . Listen to this . . . (*Reads*) 'Thirty-four-year-old Crouch, speaking for the first time during the two-day trial, said that he and fellow "Playboy", Dwane Devlin, forty-two, were "poleaxed" when police stopped Devlin's Fiesta in Faifley and found . . . '

SHIRLEY: (*interrupting*) You ever dined out in Faifley? I wouldn't recommend it. Carry on.

TRACEY: (*reads*) ' . . . and found a quantity of cocaine and a hammer, later identified as the one used in the Post Office raids, concealed inside a pair of brand-new size 10^1/$_2$ cowboy boots on the back seat. Giving evidence, D.C. Douglas Weir of Strathclyde Serious Crime Squad, said that when challenged, the Clydebank-based Country singer said . . . '

SHIRLEY: (*interjecting*) Aw, look, he's quite nice.

(*She leans close to paper*)

TRACEY: 'Yes, they are mine but I have never seen those dot dot drugs or that dot dot hammer in my . . . ' Where? Get your noddle out the road.

(*Another article on the same page has the headline 'PISMO CLAMS "HIT THE SPOT" IN SEAMILL'. It carries the byline 'Rab Haw' — a corruption of the name 'Robert Hall', the legendary nineteenth-century 'Glasgow Glutton', who is said to have consumed four cows, two sheep, and forty-four black puddings at one sitting — together with a head-shot of Frank McClusky*)

SHIRLEY: Not him . . . him there.

(*Shirley points to the Deadwood Playboys' picture where Fraser Boyle is flanked by Dwane and Dorwood, overstamped in red with '2 yrs' and '7 yrs' respectively*)

TRACEY: What . . . him in the middle? He didnae even get indicted Shirley.

SHIRLEY: You don't have to get indicted to qualify as a hunk.

TRACEY: It says here he sells fish . . . what's got into you?

(*She looks askance at Shirley*)

SHIRLEY: Shut your mug . . . what does it say about *her*?

TRACEY: *Her* who?

SHIRLEY: Look out.

(*Cissie re-enters the kitchen*)

CISSIE: (*loudly*) Five Chitlin', one Baby Ribs, one Chilliburger!

(*Tracey stuffs the newspaper inside her jacket*)

SHIRLEY: (*to Cissie*) If you need a hand out there just . . .

(*Cissie sweeps out again*)

SHIRLEY: . . . give us a shout. (*To Tracey*) Her . . . I want to hear what it says about . . .

(*Cissie's head reappears round the door*)

CISSIE: Sorry to disappoint you, girls, but it doesn't say anythin' about *her* 'cos *her* refused to talk to that rag, right?

(*Her head disappears again. Shirley looks at Tracey, and Tracey looks away*)

★ ★ ★

(*In another part of the city on an abandoned factory site Billie perches on the taxi wing, mike in hand, while Frank prowls*) *around the 'ghost town')*

BILLIE: (*on radio*) See when you're comin', Jolene, gonnae bring all my stuff over, over?

(*There is a garbled response over the radio*)

BILLIE: (*on radio*) 'Cos I'm never gonnae get back in time to get changed, this galoot's got us drivin' all over, over.

(*Another longer incoherent eruption over the radio*)

BILLIE: (*on radio*) Naw, they're in gettin' soled an' heeled, the ones I wore to the Cowdenbeath Rodeo with the frogs on them, over.

(*By now Frank has fallen into conversation with a filthy-looking individual in ragged topcoat and matted hair. Money changes hands between them*)

BILLIE: Aw, brilliant . . . If you want to know where the nearest snazzy Soul Food bar is, ask your friendly neighbourhood wino.

(*She hooks the mike back up inside the cab*)

BILLIE: (*loudly*) This meter's still runnin'!

(*While Billie resticks her collection of Patsy Cline cut-outs on to the glass partition Frank parts company with the derelict and makes his way back to the taxi*)

FRANK: Bumped into an old school chum.

(*He replaces his now empty wallet in his hip pocket*)

BILLIE: Yeh . . . 'gaudeamus igitur'² . . . gonnae just gimme the fare an' I'll blow? Me an' Jolene's got a gig at the Cactus Club at half ten.

FRANK: Dropped outta dental college, he was tellin' me.

(*Billie glances at the meter as Frank delves into his Burberry pocket and brings out a crumpled newspaper 'poke' full of blackened shellfish*)

BILLIE: Call it fifteen quid, okay?

FRANK: (*shocked*) Fifteen quid?

BILLIE: Cash . . . we stopped takin' cowrie shells back in '49.

FRANK: You get any funnier an' we'll get you a balloon on a stick . . . this's my doggy-bag from the Clambake . . .

(*He takes a pin from his lapel and prises a particularly unappetising-looking wulk from its shell*)

BILLIE: An' I'm supposed to stand here an' watch you eatin' it? Fifteen quid . . . hurry up.

FRANK: I don't want to purchase the heap, sweetheart . . .

(*He pops the wulk into his mouth*)

FRANK: Besides, I've already got myself a motor . . .

(*He cracks open a disgusting mussel*)

FRANK: You ever had a hurl in the front seat of a white T-bird?

BILLIE: Naw, an' unless you cough up pronto you're for a doin' in the back seat of a Black Maria. Fifteen quid, cash . . . c'mon!

* * *

(*A battered delivery van with a faded fishmonger's name on the side draws up outside the Bar-L and the driver climbs out. Fraser Boyle is a muscular man in his middle thirties with a bruiser's 'handsome' features. He is dressed in an interesting mix of old-style 'trail-wear' and 'new-wave' Western gear, a pair of well-worn, highly ornamented cowboy boots on his feet. Boyle looks up at the Bar-L sign, dons a pair of leather gloves, and slams the van door*)

* * *

(*Inside the bar Cissie is serving drinks to a banquette, and she glances up as Boyle enters from the street*)

DINER: Aaargh . . . what you givin' us!

(*Cissie has just served a plate of Crawdaddy Claws in the diner's lap*)

CISSIE: What you ordered. Here.

(*She chucks a napkin at the disgruntled diner and beats a retreat in the direction of the rest rooms*)

SHIRLEY: (*to Tracey*) Lemme see that newspaper a minute.

(*David Cole breaks off after sharing a joke with customers*)

DAVID COLE: Enjoy yourselves, huh?

(*He slides off the banquette and crosses to the door where Boyle is chewing gum and rubber-necking*)

* * *

(*Cissie enters the ladies' powder room and leans her back against the door, her fists clenched. A young woman, repairing lipstick in the mirror pouts in Cissie's direction*)

YOUNG WOMAN: Long're you in for?

CISSIE: (*Preoccupied*) What?

YOUNG WOMAN: The outfit . . . it's cute.

* * *

(*Back in the bar David Cole speaks to Fraser Boyle*)

DAVID COLE: I think you maybe lost your way, man . . .

(*He takes Boyle's elbow*)

BOYLE: I've came about the fish.

(*He disengages Cole's hand from his elbow*)

DAVID COLE: Fish? What you talkin' 'bout, fish?

BOYLE: Red snapper, blue snapper, conger eel, turbot . . .

(*Boyle heads towards a corner banquette*)

BOYLE: . . . Angel fish, queenies, lobster, wulks . . .

DAVID COLE: Sure, sure . . . lemme redirect you to the street, huh?

> (*He catches up with Boyle and takes a firm grip of his arm*)

BOYLE: You werenae listenin', big boy . . .

> (*Again he prises Cole's fingers from his sleeve*)

BOYLE: . . . like, I've been sent to take your 'order', yeh?

> (*He plonks himself down in the corner banquette. Shirley approaches*)

SHIRLEY: Hi, there . . .

> (*She gives Boyle a big smile and sets a glass of iced water down in front of him*)

SHIRLEY: What can I get you, Mr Cole?

DAVID COLE: Later, honey . . .

BOYLE: I'll've pinta lager, gorgeous.

DAVID COLE: Give 'im a beer. (*To Boyle*) Listen, punk, I don't know who the hell you are but . . .

SHIRLEY: (*interrupting*) Will that be lite, ultra-lite, root, or regular?

> (*She bares her teeth at Boyle in what she imagines to be a sexy grin*)

DAVID COLE: Jus' give 'im a goddam beer, Shelley!

SHIRLEY: Shirley. Sure.

> (*She smiles over her shoulder at Boyle and sashays off to the bar, tray held high. Boyle's eyes follow her*)

DAVID COLE: Awright, so what's with the fish, huh?

BOYLE: Relax, man . . . I'm to be your go-between . . .

> (*He turns to face Cole*)

BOYLE: . . . meetin's set up for the morra.

> (*He takes a pencil stub from his ear and a grubby order pad from his jacket pocket*)

BOYLE: (*loudly*) So, that's four box of flounder, five box of haddie, an' six dozen lobster . . . D'you want the lobster humanely put down?

SHIRLEY: (*to the barman*) Pour us a Longlife, Spencer.

> (*She glances over her shoulder at the corner banquette*)

SHIRLEY: (*to Tracey*) Told you he was a doll, didn't I?

TRACEY: Yeh, the kind you'd like to stick pins into.

* * *

> (*Back at the abandoned factory site Frank is leaning against the passenger door of the taxi wolfing down the remainder of his Clambake leftovers. The taxi's bonnet is up, and Billie is underneath it*)

FRANK: You sure you don't want to try some? Friend of mine in Aberfoyle flies a planeload of this scoff across to Maxim's[3] twice a week.

BILLIE: (*under bonnet*) Thanks, I'll bear that in mind next time I phone up for a res . . . ha! It's just fell into place!

FRANK: Good, you can drive us back to the *Echo*, I've got a feelin' I might've . . .

BILLIE: (*emerging*) 'Crabmeat Crepes A Feast of Fun for Fifties Freaks at Faifley's "Pancake Roadhouse"', right?

FRANK: Eh?

BILLIE: I thought I recognised the kisser, I just couldnae put a quote to it.

FRANK: God, fancy you rememberin' that.

BILLIE: How could I ever forget?

FRANK: You and my Features Editor.

BILLIE: That's where Dorwood took us for my birthday . . . talk about bum steers?

> (*She reaches in to the taxi and unhooks the mike*)

FRANK: Who's Dorwood?

> (*He stuffs more seafood into his mouth*)

BILLIE: Typical . . . doesnae even read his own newspaper. (*On radio*) Car Fourteen to base, over? (*To Frank*) Dorwood Crouch and the Deadwood Playboys, they're a Country an Western outfit.

FRANK: Away.

BILLIE: Correction . . . used to be a Country an Western outfit. (*On radio*) You there, Jolene?

FRANK: Ah . . . crossed over to Motown, have they? A suitably lumpen compromise.

> (*There is a burst of static over the radio*)

BILLIE: (*on radio*) Yeh, Jolene, you'll find a coupla thumb picks in my coat, gonnae chuck them in your saddle bags for us, over?

> (*After a 'Ten Four' on the radio she hooks the mike up*)

BILLIE: You ever listen to any their albums?

FRANK: Thought you were a gonnae ask her to phone up a garage . . . Jolene, naw?

> (*Billie goes back under the bonnet*)

BILLIE: They brung their last one out as a tribute to Johnny Cash . . . played it all through their trial on Radio Clyde . . .

> (*Frank piles more shellfish into his mouth*)

BILLIE: Dorwood and the Deadwoods . . .

> (*She pops her head out*)

BILLIE: Live at the Bar-L.

(*Frank gags on his seafood cocktail*)

BILLIE: S'up with you?

FRANK: Bugger me, that's it!

BILLIE: Ironic? Yeh, that's what I said to Jolene.

(*She bangs the bonnet shut*)

* * *

(*Cissie is cautiously checking the banquettes at the Bar-L for any sign of Fraser Boyle. Frank enters from the street*)

FRANK: (*over shoulder*) Chuck moanin', you'll get your dough!

(*Billie trails in his wake*)

FRANK: (*surprised*) Hey, it is quite snazzy

(*He casts his eyes around the interior*)

BILLIE: Nineteen fifty, right!

FRANK: Bevis Hillier[4] you ain't, shorty. That plasterwork is almost certainly art deco . . .

(*He looks at Billie*)

FRANK: . . . Awright, awright, ersatz deco but it's still a lot earlier than . . .

BILLIE: (*interrupting*) Your taxi fare, it's nineteen pounds fifty.

(*Shirley approaches them, a big smile at the ready*)

SHIRLEY: (*to Frank*) Hi, can I find you a stool?

FRANK: Naw, I'll just kill her with my bare hands . . .

SHIRLEY: I'm sorry?

FRANK: It's her that should be apologisin' . . . twenty quid for a world tour of the City Centre?

(*Billie leans forward*)

BILLIE: You couldnae cash this balloon a cheque, could you?

SHIRLEY: Pardon me?

FRANK: Not to mention the Hank Williams[5] tapes an' a short-wave bandit called Jolene . . .

(*He shrugs off his Burberry*)

FRANK: I'll perch up at the Steinway,[6] if you don't mind, sweetheart.

(*He piles his coat into Shirley's arms*)

SHIRLEY: It's a Blüthner.[7] (*Loudly*) Tracey?

BILLIE: Look, if I don't get my dough I'm phonin' the polis.

(*Frank catches sight of Cissie making her way back to the kitchen*)

FRANK: (*smitten*) Yeah, you do that.

(*Tracey strolls up*)

SHIRLEY: (*in passing*) Stick this jerk at the pianna, will you?

BILLIE: Ho, I'm talkin' to you.

TRACEY: (*to Frank*) Hi, are you together?

FRANK: What you talkin' about, I'm always together . . .

(*He spills his cigarettes on to the floor as he tags along behind Tracey who leads the way to the piano*)

FRANK: (*over his shoulder to Billie*) Sixties' patter's obviously back in.

(*But Billie is no longer there. Cissie exits from the kitchen, and Frank tries catching her eye*)

FRANK: Right on, yeah?

(*He walks straight into the piano*)

FRANK: (*softly*) Ohyah.

TRACEY: Can I get you a drink?

(*Frank glances in Cissie's direction*)

FRANK: Yeah . . . bring us somethin' long an' cool, will you?

TRACEY: Tonight's Specials are Lobster Creole in a Blue Cheese Dip and Crawdaddy Claws with a side order of Clam Chowder . . .

(*Frank pales at the very mention*)

TRACEY: Sorry, what was your bar order again?

(*Billie's head appears above the piano lid*)

BILLIE: Big glass of ginger, plenty ice.

FRANK: I thought you were away phonin' the . . . bwoop!

(*His hand flies to his mouth*)

BILLIE: You shut your face or I'll tell them who you are.

TRACEY: How . . . who is he?

FRANK: 'Scuse me . . . bwoop.

(*He slides off the piano stool, and hotfoots it for the men's room*)

BILLIE: Did I ask for ice? I cannae quite . . .

TRACEY: (*loudly*) One Seven-up, out the freezer!

(*She moves off. Cissie appears at Billie's other shoulder, order pad at the ready*)

CISSIE: Hi, would you care to order?

(*She gives Billie a dazzling smile as David Cole passes on his way back from the men's room. Billie glances at her Hopalong Cassidy[8] watch*)

BILLIE: Yeah, I suppose I might have somethin' before Jolene . . .

(*Cissie slips away as soon as David Cole has gone past*)

BILLIE: . . . gets here.

(*She looks around for Cissie*)

TRACEY: (*to Shirley*) Night Of A Thousand Stars, did you say? There's another one just hightailed it into the lavvy.

* * *

(The men's room is deserted. The painful sound of retching reverberates around the marble-tiled walls. Just visible in the gap under a cubicle door is a pair of well-worn highly ornate cowboy boots)

FRANK: *(Echoey)* Aw, God . . .

(The boots are joined by a pair of stout brogues in the next cubicle but one. The brogues are attached to a pair of Harris Tweed pegbottoms on their knees. There is a long moment of silence. Then . . .)

FRANK: *(Echoey, sings)* 'Well, since ma baby left me, I found a new place to dwell . . . '

* * *

(Frank has his head down the faux-marble toilet bowl, his hand groping for loo paper)

FRANK: *(Sings)* 'It's down at the end of Lonely Street, call' Heartbreak Hotel . . . doo-doo doo-doo . . . heartbreak is so lonely . . . doo-doo doo-doo . . . doo-doo doo-doo . . . Heartbreak so lonely, I could . . . '9

(There is a splintering crash as the cubicle door is booted in. Frank lifts his head out of the toilet bowl as Fraser Boyle's gloved fist smashes into his face)

* * *

(Out in the bar Jolene, splendid in fringed jacket and Stetson hat, has joined Billie by the piano . . .)

JOLENE: What d'you mean, what kept me? I'd to put away all my maps an' hose out the drivers' toilets. That's your rodeo boots . . .

(She plonks a pair of boots on the piano lid)

JOLENE: Car Twenty-Six says you can get Western-style Odor Eaters from the wee cobbler's next door to the bookie's shop in Maryhill Road.

(Billie looks suitably embarrassed)

BILLIE: Thanks, Jolene.

(Jolene tugs at the bandana knotted round her throat)

JOLENE: God, it's really bilin' in here, d'you think we could ask somebody to open a windae?

(David Cole resumes his seat at the piano and launches into a selection from the recent Broadway musicals catalogue)

BILLIE: Gonnae shuttup, Jolene?

JOLENE: *(to Cole)* Give us the nod if you're gonnae play any Jim Reeves numbers . . . 10

(She gets a dig from Billie)

JOLENE: . . . so we can skedaddle. (*To Billie*) What you pokin'
us for? I should've got Car Twenty-Six to get you these in-
soles . . . did the guy not tell you them frog boots were rubber
when you tried them on?

BILLIE: Aw, God . . .

    (*Billie covers her face with her hands*)

JOLENE: (*to Cole*) You don't happen to know anybody that wants
to buy a moped, do you?

    (*Cissie approaches them on her way to the kitchen*)

JOLENE: (*loudly*) 'Scuse me? (*To Billie*) D'you want a plate of
chips?

    (*Billie's head sinks slowly on to the piano lid*)

BILLIE: I'm not with you, Jolene . . .

JOLENE: God, look who it is, Billie!

    (*Cissie sails past into the kitchen*)

CISSIE: (*From kitchen*) Five Tamali, one Devildog!

BILLIE: I'm not with you, I said.

JOLENE: It's her that used to sing with the Driftin' Tumbleweeds
before they split up.

    (*Billie looks up*)

BILLIE: Where?

JOLENE: The big skelf in the car smash hairdo, she just went
through that door.

BILLIE: Och, your bum.

JOLENE: Cross ma heart an' hope to die, she just shoved that
door open an' went straight through it. D'you not remember the pair of us done a duet with her at the OK Korral in
Kilwinning?[11] Dorwood was on the jumbo . . .

BILLIE: Comin' back from Kentucky?

JOLENE: The twelve-string jumbo, quit actin' it . . . you were
wearin' this stupit poncho an' she had on these brilliant
buckskin chaps . . . d'you remember now?

BILLIE: Naw, I don't, it's about ten years since we last played
the OK, an' it was you that was wearin' the stupit poncho, not
me, right!

             * * *

    (*Meanwhile, in the men's room at the Bar-L Fraser Boyle has
removed his gloves, and is running his knuckles under the tap*)

FRANK: You'll never guess who else I bumped into the night.

    (*The loo flushes, and Frank emerges from the cubicle, jacket in
hand. His nose is swollen and bloody*)

FRANK: Gordon Smart.

    (*He crosses to the basins, and chucks his jacket on top of Boyle's fish order book)*

BOYLE: Wee guy with a humph?

FRANK: Naw, that was Wee Humphrey . . .

> *(He turns the taps on)*

BOYLE: I don't recall any Gordon Smart, sure you got the name right?

FRANK: You must . . . he was the only guy in the entire history of St Saviour's that could say the whole of the *De Profundis*[12] without wettin' his trousers . . .

> *(Frank examines his damaged nose in the mirror)*

FRANK: . . . big yella teeth . . . used to wear a Cecil Gee shurt with a monogram on the pocket.

> *(He gives his face a tentative splash)*

BOYLE: Cecil Gee? Nup, doesnae get the recollective juices goin'.

> *(He gives his knuckles a suck)*

FRANK: Lugged his homework books about in a toilet bag with succulents all over it . . .

BOYLE: With what all over it?

FRANK: . . . succulents. Big fan of Wishbone Ash an' the Beverley Sisters.[13] His Maw was an invalid . . . never away from the chapel.

BOYLE: Hold on, hold on . . .

FRANK: Snappy dresser.

BOYLE: Snappy dresser . . . wore these weird shurts wi' somebody's initials on the pocket.

FRANK: You want to see him now.

BOYLE: Doin' well, is he?

> *(Boyle moves to the hand-drier)*

BOYLE: Couldnae draw cowboys, as I remember.

FRANK: Cannae draw teeth either. Not long dropped outta dental college, he was tellin' me.

BOYLE: S'that what he done? Somebody told me he'd snuffed it. What about yourself, what you been up to?

> *(He stabs on the hand-drier, rendering Frank's résumé of his career totally inaudible, but he carries on anyway)*

FRANK: *(Under hand-drier racket)* Aw, this 'n' that . . . managed to get a job sellin' holy pitchers an' second-hand pullovers off a stall at the Barras when I left St Saviour's, that lasted about a fortnight . . . then I went into surgical hosiery, stuck for seven months, it was murder . . . what'd I do then? Aw, yeh . . . saw this advert for a Mobile Librarian in the *Dundee Courier* . . . spent the next year an' a half drivin' about Angus in a converted ambulance dolin' out

True Detective an' cowboy books to the natives . . . thought I was gonnae go off ma head . . . eventually got the heave for chuckin' fourteen hundredweight of Annie S. Swans[14] into a skip in Forfar . . . took to ma bed for a year, read a lotta Descartes . . . which is where I got the notion to go to university . . . plan was to read French literature but that would've meant learnin' French so I settled for philosophy an' economics . . . bought myself a Hofner Senator[15] to replace the one ma old man made into a coffee table . . . started goin' wi' this knockout doll wi' buck teeth an' a Ferrari, managed to clinch a pretty poor 'second',[16] got myself a job on the *Evening Echo*, spearheadin' their telephone advertisin' department . . . shifted us from there on to the Rab Haw column when the incumbent went down wi' dysentery after dinin' out in Faifley . . . been there ever since . . .

(*As the blower whines to a stop, Boyle recrosses to the mirror to comb his greased-back pompadour*)

FRANK: How's about you?

(*He crosses to the roller-towel*)

FRANK: Last I heard you were studyin' for the priesthood.

★ ★ ★

(*Billie is driving the taxi, and Jolene is crammed in the back with the moped, accordion case, guitar, 5-watt amp and togs*)

BILLIE: (*over shoulder*) I promise you, Jolene, I remember distinctly your Mum gettin' the knittin' pattern out of her *Woman's Realm*[17] . . . it had these big reindeers gallopin' round the hole you put your head through.

JOLENE: They werenae reindeer, they were caribou . . . an' it was the *Red Star Weekly*. The *Woman's Realm* never done ponchos . . . tea cosies, yes . . . ponchos, naw.

BILLIE: You wanted to look like Emmylou Harris, remember.

JOLENE: Aye, well you ought to know, it was you that wore it . . . an' you looked like bloody *Rolf* Harris,[18] so there!

BILLIE: What was it we sang again . . . you, me, and the beanpole?

JOLENE: I thought you couldnae remember?

BILLIE: I cannae, what d'you suppose I'm askin' for? It wasnae 'Pistol Packin' Mama', was it?

JOLENE: Don't be ridiculous.

BILLIE: 'Tennessee Wig Walk'?

JOLENE: Naw!

BILLIE: What was it, well?

JOLENE: See if you ever tell anybody I wore a poncho I'm gonnae batter your melt in, Billie McPhail!

(*Billie muses momentarily*)

BILLIE: Naw, I'm pretty sure it wasnae a Kristofferson[19] number, Jolene.

* * *

(*By now Cissie has started clearing empty glasses from the Bar-L piano top. Fraser Boyle emerges from the men's room, pulling his gloves on. He spots Cissie, does a double take, then approaches stealthily and places his face close to her ear*)

BOYLE: Boo.

CISSIE: Waaaaah!

(*She drops the tray with a crash. David Cole's head appears above the banquette*)

TRACEY: There she's tryin' to get off with your lumber, Shirley.

CISSIE: I might well ask you the same . . . what does it look like I'm doin'? Out my road.

(*She bends down to clear up the broken glass*)

BOYLE: Yeh, smart thinkin' . . . best not goin' near all thon dough till the dust settles.

CISSIE: All what dough? Lift your feet.

BOYLE: You been in to see the boy yet? I dig the hairdo.

CISSIE: What boy is this?

BOYLE: Naw, you suit it, honest . . . lotsa guys would get put off, not me. Dorwood . . . up the Bar-L . . . listen, do us a favour, will you? Next time you're in to visit him, tell him Fraser Boyle managed to get him back his Dobro.

(*Cissie's face comes up level with Boyle's*)

CISSIE: Dobro?

BOYLE: Aye, s'a geetar with resonator pan in the middle . . . the guy he lent it to just lost all his fingers in an unlucky . . .

CISSIE: (*interrupting*) I know what a Dobro is, I'm just wonderin' how come you couldn't've told him about it yourself . . . were you not in court this mornin'? Shift.

(*She tries to push past, but Boyle blocks her way*)

BOYLE: Have a heart, sugar. I'm hardly goin' to stand up in the public benches an' go 'Scuse me, Dorwood, sorry to hear you're gettin' locked down for seven years but I've got your Dobro sittin' outside in a brown paper poke' . . . that cruel I'm arenae.

CISSIE: Hold on, hold on . . . is this the same Fraser Boyle that stood at the curb an' sang two verses of 'Ole Shep'[20] 'cos next door's alsatian just went under a Dodge City delivery truck, while his eld . . .

Your Cheatin' Heart

BOYLE: *(interrupting)* Naw, you've got it all wrong, darlin' . . .

CISSIE: . . . while his elderly mother was lyin' in a hosptal bed gettin' penicillin jags for lockjaw?

BOYLE: Naw, you've definitely got it . . .

CISSIE: *(interrupting again)* I think we can drop the Mr Sensitive act. If you've got anythin' to give to Dorwood, you give it to him, I'm not your dogsbody!

(She shoves him aside and heads for the kitchen)

BOYLE: Ho, come back here, you've got it all wrong . . .

(Cissie disappears into the kitchen, and Shirley crosses to the piano)

SHIRLEY: Hi, can I get you somethin'?

BOYLE: Stupit bitch, it was an airedale.

(Shirley's smile evaporates)

SHIRLEY: Okay, cool it cowboy, I'm not a mind-reader. *(Loudly)* One Airedale! *(To Boyle)* D'you want a slice of lemon in it?

* * *

(In the men's room Frank is investigating the damage done to his nose in the mirror)

FRANK: Awright, so we all of us revere His Pelvic Majesty's memory but God Almighty . . .

(A diner enters and crosses to one of the cubicles)

FRANK: He was exactly the same at St Saviour's . . . set fire to six of the Janitor's rabbits when he sluiced all his Elvis pin-ups down the urinals . . . welded the woodwork teacher's goggles to the front bumper of his Lambretta[21] after gettin' three outta fifty for his plywood cutout of 'The King',[22] when we were supposed to be makin' coat pegs outta gash timber for the *Gang Show*.[23]

(He picks up his jacket)

FRANK: If you're thinkin' about stickin' your napper down the pan an' givin it laldy, don't whatever you do, pick anythin' from the Sun Records[24] catalogue, pre-'57 . . .

(He slips his arms into the jacket sleeves)

FRANK: *(continues)* . . . he's liable to burst in here an' splatter your brains all over the sanitary-ware.

(He picks up Boyle's order book)

FRANK: Stupit grizzly's left his Filofax[25] . . .

* * *

(In the smoky back-room of a pub, that doubles as the Cactus Club on alternative evenings, Billie and Jolene are onstage singing)

TOGETHER: ' . . . and went back to the wild side of life'.
> (*Billie executes a nifty side-step in her Cowdenbeath rodeo boots and allows Jolene to squeeze a spirited solo from her accordion*)

JOLENE: (*over music*) Nineteen pounds fifty! I wish you'd told me, I'd've went in there after the bugger.

BILLIE: Aw, shuttup, you gave me a big enough showin' up in that joint without bargin' into the Gents'.

JOLENE: *I gave you* a showin' up?

BILLIE: Yeh . . . an' these are not rubber, they're Composition Nugahide, its melted into the soles . . . She holds up a boot for inspection and then leans into the mike.

BILLIE: (*Sings*) 'If I had the wings of an angel . . . '

★ ★ ★

> (*Back at the Bar-L Cissie is leaning up against the back of an unoccupied banquette reading Tracey's* Echo. *Frank sneaks up behind her and peeks over her shoulder*)

FRANK: Aw, well done.

CISSIE: (*surprised*) I wish people wouldn't keep doin' that! What d'you want?

FRANK: I thought one of the other dolls was goin' to beat you to it.
> (*Frank plucks a pen from Cissie's pocket and starts scribbling on a small card from his coat pocket*)

FRANK: Who's the lucky guy?

CISSIE: You're not talkin' to me, are you?

FRANK: If you take my advice, you'll give the Pancake Road-house in Faifley the go-by.
> (*He hands the card to Cissie*)

CISSIE: What's this? (*Reading*) 'Bon appetit. That fabulous "Dinner for Two" is yours. Signed Rab Haw'.
> (*Frank's signature and phone number are scrawled along the bottom of the card*)

FRANK: Any problems just ring that number . . . there's one or two of the eateries listed overleaf that aren't fully conversant with the scheme as yet but we're hopin' to . . .

CISSIE: (*interrupting*) I don't know what it is you're sellin' but it's no sale. Sorry.
> (*She stuffs the card back into Frank's top pocket*)

FRANK: Naw, naw. I know when I've been rumbled. Here . . .
> (*He takes the card from his pocket and hands it to Cissie*)

CISSIE: Too right you have.
> (*She rams the card back into Frank's top pocket*)

FRANK: Okay, so you didn't go through the ritual of rappin' me

on the raincoat with your rolled-up copy of the *Echo*, an recitin'
the rubric 'You are Rab Haw and I claim my intimate candlelit
dinner for two' but rules are there to be bent. Please . . .

(*Cissie takes the thrice-proffered card*)

FRANK: That entitles you and your partner to the free sparkling
red of your choice . . .

(*Cissie rips the card in two . . .*)

FRANK: . . . plus a second cup of coffee . . .

(. . . *and rips the two pieces into four . . .*)

FRANK: . . . and the Black Forest gateau.

(*Cissie tears the four pieces into eight . . .*)

FRANK: If they've got any.

(*Cissie lets the torn pieces of card flutter to the floor*)

FRANK: You didn't happen to notice where the hardnut in the
high heels went, did you?

(*He tries nonchalantly glancing round the room and fails*)

CISSIE: You'll be a friend of his yeah?

FRANK: Depends what you mean by a friend . . . we don't
exchange Christmas cards or nothin'.

(*He holds out Boyle's order book*)

FRANK: He left his . . .

CISSIE: (*interrupting*) Quick, order somethin'.

(*She shoves Frank into the banquette and whips out her pad*)

FRANK: Eh?

CISSIE: . . . and would that be with the Clam Chowder or
without the Clam Chowder?

(*She gives Frank a big smile as David Cole 'circulates' in their
direction*)

FRANK: Er . . . without, I think. This's a wind-up right?

DAVID COLE: Hey . . . the footwear, man.

(*He regards Frank's brogues with wry amusement*)

FRANK: Aw, naw, don't tell me . . .

(*Frank bends down to inspect the soles of his shoes to discover
what he's stood in*)

DAVID COLE: Outtasight, baby . . . outtasight.

(*He moves off, chuckling*)

FRANK: What is this, Sixties Patter Fortnight?

CISSIE: S'that what they call you in these parts, yeah?

FRANK: What?

CISSIE: The Footwear Man?

(*Frank snatches pen from Cissie*)

FRANK: (*Writing*) . . . cheeky waitresses.

(*He folds his 'Reporter's Shorthand Notepad' shut and hands
the pen back to Cissie*)

CISSIE: Come off it, you can buy they notebooks in Woolie's.[26]

FRANK: Yeh, you tell that to the big guy in the white tux when he opens the morra night's edition an' there it is starin' him in the kisser . . . 'Bolshie Broads and Bum Service Bug Our Man at Bar-L' . . . give us that pen back, I forgot to take down your number.

CISSIE: Don't act it, you're not a reporter.

FRANK: I'm an investigative journalist, you're just after droolin' over my picture in the *Echo*.

CISSIE: Your tonsils. Where?

(*She unfurls the newspaper and starts riffling through it*)

FRANK: Don't *you* act it . . .

(*He snatches the paper*)

FRANK: . . . there I am there in the mid . . . hey, there's Dorwood . . .

CISSIE: Gimme that.

(*She attempts to snatch the paper back*)

FRANK: It's one of those days, innit? You ever read Koestler's *The Roots of* . . . [27]

(*Cissie manages to grab the paper*)

CISSIE: What the bloody hell has Koestler got to do with Dorwood gettin' sent to jail for seven years!

FRANK: Seven years? What'd he do, a cover version of 'Tiny Bubbles'?[28]

(*Tracey has noticed Cissie laying into Frank with the shredded* Evening Echo *and goes over to the manager*)

TRACEY: I don't like to bother you, Mr Cole, but I've got a feeling one of the diners might like a word.

(*She jerks a thumb over her shoulder*)

★ ★ ★

(*As the sickle moon melts into a slithering serpent on the rippling waters of the river Clyde, Frank, leaning on a parapet, flicks idly through Fraser Boyle's forgotten order book*)

FRANK: I remember once when I was about ten I had to wait seven weeks for a letter to arrive from my pen-pal in the States . . .

(*He fingers a brown envelope he has found between the pages of the order book*)

FRANK: . . . thought I was goin' to die before it got here.

(*He holds the envelope up to the light*)

FRANK: Seven years . . . ?

(*Cissie sits hunched up on a bench, Frank's outsize Burberry belted tightly around her. She leans an arm on the benchback, one hand held to her forehead*)

FRANK: . . . I'm not sure I could wait that long for anythin'.

CISSIE: If that's an invitation, the answer's 'Get lost, buster.'

FRANK: Naw, I didn't mean it like that, I meant . . .

(*Cissie looks at him*)

FRANK: . . . I didnae, honest. I'm not that kinda guy.

CISSIE: You're all that kinda guy.

(*She stands up*)

FRANK: You don't believe in makin' it easy, do you? I'm tryin' my best to be sympathetic here.

CISSIE: Well, don't bother, it's nauseatin'.

(*Cissie takes off across the bridge nearby*)

FRANK: (*Getting up*) Look, I realise you must be upset at losin' your ball'n'chain but it wasn't entirely my . . .

(*He takes off after her*)

CISSIE: If that's meant to be an apology it's only just this side of adequate . . . try rephrasin' it.

FRANK: An apology! Listen, ya lanky big get . . .

(*He catches up with Cissie and grabs her sleeve*)

CISSIE: Uh uh . . . Start again.

FRANK: Who was it was batterin' lumps outta who back there, hmmmm?

CISSIE: Think yourself lucky, if you'd been a man I'd've socked you in the teeth . . . an' just in case you got the wrong end of the stick from that rotten rag you work for, Dorwood didn't do any of that stuff they said he did . . . he might be a header but he's hardly into snortin' coke an' holdin' anybody up with a hammer.

FRANK: How can you be so . . .

CISSIE: (*interrupting*) Because I know Dorwood, don't I?

(*She sets off again*)

FRANK: (*to himself*) Yeh, an' so does at least one Patsy Cline-clone[29] of my acquaintance . . .

(*He starts walking after Cissie*)

CISSIE: God almighty, it's all I can do to get him to hold up a shelf while I put the nails in, he's that feeble! As for drugs . . .

FRANK: How's about Dwane, mebbe it was him that put Dorwood up to . . .

CISSIE: (*interrupting again*) Dwane's just a dumplin'. If you want to know who the real culprit is . . . och, what's the point, you're like all the rest . . . why don't you just beat it?

(*She stops and looks at Frank*)

FRANK: Eh?

CISSIE: You heard . . . blow . . . vamoose.

(*She pulls Frank's Burberry round her and strides angrily off*)

FRANK: How can I vamoose? This's my night for gettin' the grease stains out of my Burberry, dammit!

★ ★ ★

(*Outside the Cactus Club Billie and Jolene are loading their gear into the taxi*)

BILLIE: Wonder how Dorwood's gettin' on, eh?

JOLENE: At least he'll be gettin' somethin' to eat where he is . . .

BILLIE: You know perfectly well we've got to make up the short-fall in wur taxi float, which is still seven bucks short, by the way . . . I'm gonna have to stop off at my mother's an' ask for a bung . . . 'time is it?

JOLENE: Ten past twelve, God, I could happily bite the reindeers off a poncho, she'll not still be up, will she?

BILLIE: Who willnae?

JOLENE: Your Maw.

(*They climb into the taxi, Billie in the front and Jolene in the back*)

BILLIE: Jolene, my 'Maw' died on the fourteenth of March, you wore thon shurt with the tommyhawks on it to her funeral . . .

JOLENE: Aw, yeh, so I did . . .

BILLIE: . . . a bung off our Raymond I'm talkin' . . . (*She starts the engine*) He's strippin' the wallpaper in the lobby.

JOLENE: What's he doin' that for?

BILLIE: My Mammy always hated it.

JOLENE: That's what I mean, what's he doin' it now for?

BILLIE: 'Cos he's got his work to go to durin' the day . . . honest to God, see you, you can be right obtuse at times, Jolene.

(*She revs the taxi engine*)

★ ★ ★

(*On a street corner near the river Frank and Cissie are still arguing*)

FRANK: You take that off again and you're getting smacked, right!

(*He pulls the Burberry tight around Cissie*)

CISSIE: Right!

FRANK: Right!

(*He lets go*)

CISSIE: I'll post it on to you, right!

FRANK: Right!

(*They walk on*)

CISSIE: You don't know what it's like goin' back to an empty

flat an' his Wranglers are all shrivelled up over the radiators an'
the phone never goes an' the clingfilm's come off his Randy
Travis[30] records an' lies about the carpet like ectoplasm an'
the neighbours stuff things through your letterbox an' write
these foul letters an' you cannae get anythin' from the grocer's
without payin' cash an' . . .

   (Frank stops)

FRANK: You'll post what on to me?

CISSIE: This coat.

FRANK: Talk sense, by the time you get it into a Jiffy Bag you'll
not have enough spittle left to lick the . . . don't you dare take
that off again, I'm warnin' you!

   (He grabs Cissie by the lapels)

CISSIE: Aaaaarg, ma chest!

★ ★ ★

   *(Back at his flat, Frank is standing in the middle of a chaotic
kitchenette, a piece of charred toast on the worktop in front of
him)*

FRANK: *(shouts)* D'you want me to spread some butter on it?
Or mebbe you'd prefer some . . .

   (He takes a grimy container down from the shelf)

FRANK: . . . treacle?

   (He unscrews the top of the container and sniffs the contents)

★ ★ ★

   *(In the adjoining room, Cissie, in a pair of Frank's pyjamas,
is perusing a pinboard. It is covered in newspaper clippings and
snapshots — including one of a youthful Frank with big guitar and Elvis leer — restaurant invites, yellowing book reviews,
Doris Day[31] cutouts, unpaid bills, publishers' rejection slips, et
al. Cissie's attention is caught by a clipping from the* Glasgow
Herald *dated 1976. It shows a line of mug shots with a headline above that reads 'Kelvinside Four jailed for incitement'.
The 'K4' — two male and two female — are: Henderson (M),
Brolly (F), Melon (F), and McClusky — a younger Frank.
The sub-heading under the photographs reads: '90 days apiece
for pot-smoking "Maoists"'.[32] Frank wobbles through from
the kitchen with a tray)*

FRANK: Wire in.

   *(He places the tray with non-matching crockery on a low table.
The studio apartment, a converted loft in a one-time cheese factory, is a large airy room with bare floorboards, a mattress, a
battered typewriter, a broken — but still working — telephone,*

a 50s' wireless set, a 30s' armchair, and 'enormous potential'.
It is also unbelievably untidy)

CISSIE: You not havin' any?

FRANK: I ate awready.

(Cissie bites into the toast and freezes)

FRANK: Marmite. 'Many sugars?

CISSIE: I don't . . . thanks.

(She picks up a mug and crosses to the window)

CISSIE: 'Long've you lived in this dump?

FRANK: Aw, about six . . . what d'you mean, this dump? I'll have you know this property's listed in at least one agent's books as a 'des con enviably adj to "Merchant City"'33 . . .

(Cissie looks out of the window at a clutch of winos huddled around burning garbage on the wasteground opposite)

CISSIE: Yeh, an' these'll be some of the 'merchants' havin' themselves an informal Round Table tête-à-tête over a glass of Buckfast34 'Nouveau', I presume?

FRANK: Where?

(He joins Cissie at the window)

CISSIE: I've just twigged . . .

(She turns away from the window and wanders back across the room)

FRANK: Twigged what?

CISSIE: . . . how come, after claimin' to be an investigative journalist, you were at some pains to point out the difference between your 'part-time food an' wine correspondent with shoogly shorthand and an overdraft that would choke a Clydesdale' and your 'hard-nosed crime reporter with one foot in the underworld an' . . . '

FRANK: *(interrupting)* Aw, God, we're not harpin' back to that again.

CISSIE: Naw, naw, I don't blame you . . . I mean, ex-junkie jailbirds with extreme political views cannae be too careful when it comes to . . .

FRANK: *(indignantly)* 'Ex-junkie jailbirds' nothin'! It was the two dames that rolled this big joint an' got me an' that other mug at the end there to pap eggs at the Home Secretary . . .

(He peers at the pinboard)

FRANK: . . . it was the Home Secretary, wasn't it? Anyway, some balloon that arrived on campus to deliver a two-hour diarretic on 'inner city unrest' an' to raffle a set of water-skis on behalf of the Toryglen Young Conservatives.

CISSIE: It says here you were 'Maoists'.

FRANK: That's only 'cos we ran outta ammunition an' my

compadre, Henderson, high on moral outrage an' a hefty dose
of marijuana, flang what was left of his carry-out Chinky
at the Rector . . . look, we know that Fraser Boyle wasn't in
the motor the night Dorwood got arrested for the simple
reason that he stayed behind at the what-d'-you-me-cry-
it . . .

CISSIE: OK Korral.

FRANK: . . . to pack up their banjos 'n' stuff, it said it in the
paper.

CISSIE: An' you believe everythin' you read in the paper, right?

FRANK: Not all of it, naw . . . the trouble with you is you just
cannae face up to the fact that you married a nutter.

CISSIE: An' the trouble with you is you just don't listen . . . I'm
the first to admit he's a nutter. I mean, who in their right
senses jacks in a deep-sea divin' career to become a Deadwood
Playboy?

FRANK: Deep-sea divin'?

CISSIE: That's what he got into after The Driftin' Tumbleweeds broke up . . . things were fine till he bumped into
Fraser Boyle in a submersible just south of Piper Omega[35] an'
started swappin' Country albums with a trouble-shooter called
Dwane . . . we all know what happened then. What sticks in my
craw is that Fraser Boyle's still at liberty to drive about in his
fish motor dispensin' threats an' menaces along with the lemon sole an' God-only-knows-what-else, while dopey Dorwood
keeps his gub shut an' carries the can for the next seven years!

FRANK: Lemme get this right . . . are you sayin' it was Boyle
that tipped off . . .

CISSIE: Who else would it be! He was eaten up with envy right
from the off . . . whatever Dorwood had, Boyle wasnae happy
till he'd wasted it . . . the big Everly Brothers[36] picture he had
in the bathroom, Boyle blacked their teeth out . . . the Hank
Williams souvenir toaster he got from the States, Boyle put
Kraft cheese slices in it . . . the Slim Whitman[37] autographed
doyley his Auntie Kathleen got at the Empire[38] in 1955, Boyle
made it into a parachute . . . he's a jealous bastard, the guy.

FRANK: An' not just jealous . . . I've seen him puttin' squibs
in a school chum's blazer an' tyin' his wrists to the fire
extinguisher . . . d'you want to see the scorch marks?

CISSIE: So you'll help me nail him, yeh?

(*Frank stuffs his shirt back into his trousers*)

FRANK: I wish I could but I can't . . . I just cannae . . . you want
to see the workload I've got . . . two screenplays, four hard-
back reviews, one of them for the *TLS*[39] . . . not to mention an

overdue anthology of Georgian poetry⁴⁰ and a probing piece
on Potato Puffs for the Christmas issue of the *Grocer*.

(*There is a knocking at the front door*)

FRANK: . . . Who the hell can that be at this time of night?

(*He crosses to the hallway*)

FRANK: (*to Cissie*) Help yourself to more coffee.

CISSIE: Yeh . . . thanks.

(*Frank exits to the hallway. There is more knocking*)

FRANK: That's right, chap the door down!

(*Cissie crosses to the kitchen and surveys the mess of burnt pots, manky dishes, the remains of a thousand frozen dinners, overflowing buckets, filthy cooker . . . and is appalled*)

CISSIE: God what a cowp.

(*She hears voices from the hall*)

FRANK: Aw, naw, I thought I'd got shot of you . . .

JOLENE: Okay pal, taxi money, stump up.

FRANK: Ohyah!

* * *

(*On a parapet by the riverside the pages of Boyle's order book flutter in the breeze. A filthy mit with horny nails closes over the book and picks it up. A derelict with a toilet bag covered all over in succulents, leafs through the book, removes the carbon paper and blows his nose on it. As he is about to drop the order book into a litter bin a brown envelope falls out on to the pavement. The derelict drops the book into the bin and bends to retrieve the envelope. He peels back a corner flap, lifts it to his nose and sniffs*)

* * *

(*In the Bar-L a selection of jazz-tinged Smokey Robinson⁴¹ hits underpins the hum of conversation from the late-night diners. There is a faint screech of brakes from outside, followed by the slamming of a van door. Fraser Boyle shoulders his way in from the street, knocking Tracey aside in his headlong dash for the men's room*)

TRACEY: That's your cowpokes for you, Shirley . . . cannae hold their Airedales.

* * *

(*Cissie has finally located the coffee pot under some debris in Frank's kitchen and is pouring some into a mug when Frank appears in the doorway*)

FRANK: Er . . . I hate to ask, but I don't suppose you could see your way to lendin' me nineteen pounds fifty, could you?

BILLIE: (*shouting from the hall*) Naw, Jolene . . . don't!

   (*There is splintering crash from the hall*)

* * *

   (*There is another splintering crash as Fraser Boyle boots in the cubicle doors on the Bar-L men's room*)

2 THE EAGLE OF THE APOCALYPSE AND THE SIDEWINDERS OF SATAN

Saturday/Sunday

There is a Turneresque[42] sunrise over the river Clyde. Through the mist a River Police launch can be seen. A tattered topcoat is being dragged from the water. As the ragged coat is hoisted aboard, a toilet bag covered all over in succulents bobs to the surface. A brown envelope floats in the middle of the powdery scum that forms on the undulating waters.

* * *

(*Frank McLusky is scrubbing his teeth in front of the bathroom mirror. There is the sound of a hoover from the other room, and he hears a muffled voice shouting at him*)

FRANK: (*loudly*) What'd you say?

(*He turns his head. His face contorts in agony*)

FRANK: Aaaaahyah . . .

(*Frank, in boxer shorts, woolly vest, and thick socks, clutches at his lower back with one hand while gripping the basin with the other . . . his toothbrush jammed in his mouth. Cissie Crouch appears at the bathroom door clutching the hoover. She is wearing Frank's Burberry over Frank's pyjamas*)

CISSIE: (*over noise*) I meant to ask you last night but you looked that cosy tucked up in your armchair I didn't like to waken you.

FRANK: (*unintelligibly*) How very thoughtful!

CISSIE: Hang on . . .

(*She disappears*)

FRANK: (*unintelligibly*) Jesus God . . .

(*The hoover noise dies down, and Cissie reappears in the doorway*)

CISSIE: Naw, I thought mebbe with you workin' at the *Echo* you might have one or two contacts on the Country scene, that was all.

FRANK: (*unintelligibly*) Yeh, I'm quite pally with the guy that . . .

(*He reaches up and extracts the toothbrush from his mouth with some difficulty*)

FRANK: I'm quite pally with the guy that does the 'Farming Outlook' column on a Wednesday . . .

(*He bends stiffly and splashes water on to his face*)

FRANK: . . . cycles up from Maybole[43] with his copy in a

sheepskin briefcase . . . chuck us that towel, will you?

(*Cissie's face clouds over*)

CISSIE: The Country *music* scene.

(*She chucks a towel at his head*)

FRANK: Ah, it's a 'scene', is it? I've always regarded it as a 'disaster area', myself . . .

(*He squeezes past Cissie, drying his face on the towel. The apartment has been tidied up beyond recognition*)

FRANK: What you askin' for?

CISSIE: Because it's a good ten years since I set foot in . . .

(*Frank takes the towel from his face and looks around the room*)

FRANK: (*interrupting*) Hey, you've hung up my togs.

(*Frank's 'wardrobe' has been salvaged from the decks and hung neatly on a row of hangers*)

CISSIE: Yeh, that's gonnae be a slight problem . . .

FRANK: I thought I'd lost that . . .

(*He points to one of the shirts*)

CISSIE: . . . you're gonnae look a right haddie goin' round the clubs in any them get-ups . . .

FRANK: . . . an' there's my corduroys! I was positive they'd walked.

CISSIE: . . . people are just goin' to clam up.

(*Frank pales*)

FRANK: Please . . . don't say stuff like that.

(*He slips his arms into the sleeves of his newly found shirt*)

CISSIE: Well, they are . . . we'll have to think about gettin' you some different . . .

FRANK: (*interrupting*) Naw, I meant, please don't mention clams.

CISSIE: Are you goin' to listen to me?

FRANK: I'm listenin' . . . I'm listenin'.

(*He wanders across the room*)

CISSIE: You an' Dorwood're about the same build, right?

(*Frank pops his head into the kitchen*)

FRANK: *And* you've done the kitchen . . .

(*Frank goes into the now-sparkling kitchen*)

FRANK: . . . Good God, you managed to get the grease off the dishes. I've just been chuckin' them in the bin.

(*Cissie appears at the doorway behind him*)

CISSIE: Did you mean what you said last night?

FRANK: What . . . 'This armchair's givin' us gyp. I wish that doll in the bed would invite me over to share my own mattress'?

(*He starts filling the kettle*)

FRANK: 'Course I meant it . . . ooooow . . .

(He puts his hand to his lower back)

CISSIE: About doin' somethin' to help Dorwood . . . gimme that.

(She takes the kettle and plugs it in)

FRANK: Aw, yeh . . . Dorwood . . . I'd forgotten all about him . . .

(Frank inches his way out of the kitchen, clutching on to the doorframe)

FRANK: . . . I was rather hopin' that you had as well . . . ohyah . . .

CISSIE: *(from the kitchen)* Yeh, I'll bet you were.

FRANK: I mean, it's hardly as if I know the guy . . . you either, come to that. An' I didn't say I'd help him, I said, I'd try an' think of somebody that might.

(He crosses the room laboriously to where his corduroy pegbottoms are)

FRANK: . . . or you could have a word with the Polis . . . tell them it's all been a ghastly mistake. I'm quite sure you'll get a sympathetic . . .

CISSIE: *(interrupting)* Will you stop soundin' off for a second an' listen!

(Frank freezes, his back to Cissie, bent double with his trousers halfway up his legs)

FRANK: Watch it, Ginger . . . just because I let you red up my kitchen, rearrange my wardrobe, an' lend me nineteen pounds fifty for a taxi, that does not give you licence to . . .

CISSIE: *(firmly)* Shut up. And you needn't bother haulin' up those trousers, they're only comin' straight back off again.

FRANK: I'm sorry, I didn't quite catch . . .

CISSIE: You heard . . . get them off.

(Frank makes to turn round)

CISSIE: Stay where you are, I'm just about to step out of these pyjamas of yours.

FRANK: Good God, she's serious . . . *(Aloud)* What made you . . .

(His voice cracks. He clears his throat)

FRANK: what made you change your mind? You must be nuts about this Dorwood to plump for such a ploy . . . or was it catchin' sight of a manly calf that . . .

CISSIE: *(interrupting)* Don't look, I said!

FRANK: You'll understand, of course, that I'm possibly not at my best first thing in the mornin' . . . what guy is? 'Specially not after spendin' the night curled up like a kirby grip in my unfavourite armchair . . .

(He hobbles across to the mattress, clutching on to his trousers, still bent over)

FRANK: . . . but I think I can promise you a forenoon of unparalleled ec . . . *(He bends further to slip his trousers off)*

FRANK: *(softly)* . . . ahyah.

(Cissie tucks a borrowed shirt into the waistband of some borrowed trousers)

CISSIE: What size are you?

FRANK: *(still bent over wrestling with his trousers)* I beg your pardon?

CISSIE: Size . . . how big?

FRANK: Big? What d'you mean, 'big'?

CISSIE: Dorwood's a ten and a half.

FRANK: *(to himself)* Ten and a half? Good grief . . .

CISSIE: You'll be about the same, I fancy . . .

(She rolls up her trouser legs and slips her feet into her shoes)

FRANK: *(quietly)* Centimetres, we talkin' about, yeh?

(Still bent double, Frank measures out $10^1/_2$ cm with his hands)

FRANK: I think that most medical men . . .

(He starts to shuffle painfully across to the mattress again)

FRANK: . . . or indeed, most medical women, come to that'll tell you that size is totally irrevelant . . . in fact, I have it on good authority . . .

CISSIE: *(interrupting)* Not when it comes to cowboy boots, it isnae.

(She looks around for her bag)

CISSIE: You don't want to be scliffin' your feet in them.

FRANK: Scliffin' my what?

CISSIE: Or mebbe you do, you're such an oddball.

(She regards the seat of Frank's boxer shorts with a raised eyebrow)

FRANK: You ready yet?

CISSIE: I'll not be long.

FRANK: *(quickly)* Naw, take your time . . . no rush. Hey, we never did settle on what I should call you . . . '4-8-4', perhaps? Mrs Crouch sounds a bit stiff in the circum . . .

(He hears the front door slam)

FRANK: . . . stances . . . hullo?

(He manages to twist round and look with considerable effort. The room is now empty)

FRANK: Well, that's her missed a treat.

(He straightens his back, and slowly hauls up his corduroys)

FRANK: . . . aaaaaaaaaaaaaaaargh.

★ ★ ★

(*Tracey is standing at the counter in the Bar-L, a white 40s style plug-in telephone to her ear*)

TRACEY: (*on phone*) Yeh, hang on . . .

(*She holds the receiver against her chest*)

TRACEY: Give him a shout, Shirley.

SHIRLEY: (*shouts*) Telephone, Mr Cole.

TRACEY: (*on phone*) If it's a banquette you're after we're fully . . . aw . . .

SHIRLEY: What we supposed to do with this?

(*She holds up Cissie's 'convict' suit*)

DAVID COLE: (*to Tracey*) Who is it?

TRACEY: The toilet wrecker . . .

DAVID COLE: Huh?

(*He takes the receiver from Tracey who returns to her sweeping up*)

DAVID COLE: (*on phone*) Yeh, David Cole, who is this?

(*Tracey bends down and retrieves the torn fragments of a 'dinner for two' invitation card from the floor*)

SHIRLEY: It's never gonnae fit anybody . . .

DAVID COLE: (*still on phone, voice rising*) . . . That's your responsibility, man, I ain't got no more.

SHIRLEY: . . . not even if he puts an advert in the *Echo* for a stiltwalker. Check the gams . . .

(*She holds the trouser legs against her own*)

DAVID COLE: (*on phone*) . . . Awright, awright, relax . . . relax lemme find out, huh?

(*He looks around for Tracey, who is busy piecing together the invitation card with Frank's signature and phone number on it*)

DAVID COLE: (*to Tracey*) The weirdo in the wing-up footwear, honey?

TRACEY: (*to Shirley*) You don't fancy a pancake tea in Faifley, do you?

★ ★ ★

(*Cissie has now returned to Frank's apartment and is standing in the doorway draped in several cowboy shirts with a pair of jeans over her arm. She has changed into her own clothes. Frank is standing in the middle of the room looking down at the very new cowboy boots on his feet*)

CISSIE: Try strollin' up an' down for a bit.

FRANK: Backwards an' forwards, d'you mean?

(*Frank takes a few tentative steps in his unfamiliar footwear*)

FRANK: Ohyah . . .

CISSIE: Don't point your toes out, it makes you look a right jessie.

FRANK: Nup, they're killin' us . . .

(*He cockles over and starts limping*)

CISSIE: Keep goin' they just need breakin' in . . . Dorwood never even got to wear them.

FRANK: Lucky Dorwood. What they made out of . . . teak?

CISSIE: What shirt d'you want?

FRANK: I don't want a shirt, I've got a shirt.

CISSIE: Here . . . try on these Wranglers.

(*She loops the jeans over his shoulder*)

FRANK: S'that where you wear them, yeh?

CISSIE: Stop actin' the goat.

(*Frank reaches out and leans against the wall*)

FRANK: Would it look stupit if I wore my slippers to the OK Korral? I'm pretty sure the Kilwinning Chapter of the 'Kid-on Cowpokes' wouldnae object to a tenderfoot turnin' up in his baffies . . . you could stitch some fringes round the toecaps, give them a sort of devil-me-care Western look, naw?

CISSIE: Are you gonnae take this seriously or . . .

FRANK: (*interrupting*) Aw, c'mon, Cissie, you're jokin'. What the hell'm I gonnae discover that the whole of the Strathclyde CID . . . okay, okay, I'm walkin' . . . look, I'm walkin'.

(*He strides to and fro, his arms swinging*)

FRANK: How's that?

CISSIE: You're not meant to *walk*, you're meant to . . .

(*She buries her face in the cowboy shirts she's holding*)

CISSIE: (*Muffled*) . . . aaaaaaargh!

FRANK: Meant to what . . . mosey, you mean? Lemme try some moseyin' for you . . . watch.

(*He starts moseyin' around the room*)

FRANK: You're not watchin', Cissie.

CISSIE: (*looking up*) Forget it, awright! It was a stupit idea in the first place . . . gimme those off.

FRANK: Naw, naw . . . I just need a bit of practice . . . right, who's this?

(*He does his John Wayne walk for her*)

FRANK: He was in Fort Apache and Space Dudes Eat My Ka-ka . . . d'you give in?

(*The telephone at his feet rings. Frank bends his knees and picks up the receiver*)

FRANK: (*on phone*) Big Bill Campbell . . . Naw, don't hang up, it's me, Tamara . . . hi. (*To Cissie*) One of my colleagues on the *Echo* . . . (*On phone*) What can I do for you, sweetheart?

CISSIE: (*interrupting*) You can post that stuff on to us, okay?
  (*She stuffs the shirts into her bag*)
FRANK: (*to Cissie*) Naw, wait, this might be the very person
  we're lookin' for . . .
  (*Cissie crosses to the door*)
FRANK: (*to phone*) Can I call you right back, Tama . . . what?
  yeh, yeh, right . . . hang on till I get a pencil . . .
  (*He lays the receiver aside*)
FRANK: (*to Cissie*) Silly bugger's on a carphone . . . you're not
  away, are you? This dame works on the Crime Desk . . .
  (*He hunts around for something to write with*)
FRANK: It was her that wrote up that stuff on Dorwood's trial.
  God, see when you tidy up, it's chaos . . .
  (*He hears the sound of the front door slamming again*)
FRANK: . . . Cissie?
  (*He starts limping across to the door, only to be brought up short
  by Tamara's small but insistent voice from the phone. He doubles
  back and picks up the receiver*)
FRANK: (*on phone*) Listen, Tamara, I want you to do me a
  big favour, d'you remember the coupla cowboys that just
  got . . . what?

* * *

(*Fraser Boyle is in a telephone box in Candleriggs. He's holding a 'Dinner for Two' card, sellotaped together, with Frank
McClusky's phone number on it. He listens to the engaged signal, and slams the receiver down. He picks it up again and dials
Directory Enquiries*)
BOYLE: C'mon, ya imbecile! (*To phone*) Yeh, City Centre
  area . . . Name of McClusky . . . naw, k-y, like in Jelly . . . F for
  Francis . . . naw, I've got the number, I just need an address to
  go with it . . . gonnae hurry up, it's a matter of life an' death!

* * *

(*Frank is still on the phone to Tamara*)
FRANK: (*on phone*) Holy God . . . poor old Gordon, that's tragic . . . I'm really choked . . . naw, I am . . . I happened to bump
  into him last night quite by . . . wait a minute, the guy was a
  hobo, what you phonin' me for? I hadnae clapped eyes on him
  since . . . what!
  (*Frank stands up alarmed*)
FRANK: Fingerprints . . . what d'you mean, fing . . . what envelope! All I gave the durty dropout was a 'Dinner for
  Two' card an' a coupla qu . . . aw, God, it's just occurred to

me . . . where'd you say they found his . . . naw, skip it, how the hell should I know how the sod got his manky mitts on a . . .

(*He's interrupted by a loud banging at the front door*)

FRANK: . . . listen, I'll have to go, Tamara, there's somebody at the . . . Christ, the Polis . . .

(*There is more loud banging*)

FRANK: (*on phone*) . . . I hope their computer gets a virus, tell them. Aw, an' listen . . . tell the Features Editor not to worry, I'll keep in t . . . hullo? Buggeration.

(*He slams the phone down, grabs his Burberry, and hobbles across to the window in his cowboy boots. The banging at the front door continues as Frank throws the window up. At the front door Fraser Boyle bends down and flips open the letterbox with his gloved finger*)

BOYLE: (*loudly*) Kissogram44 for McClusky . . . open up!

(*A long moment of silence is shattered by a sickening crash as Boyle barges in through the door. Once inside he stops and looks around, his eyes light on a blind flapping in the breeze*)

BOYLE: Aw, classic . . . empty room, open windae, flappin' drapes . . . bugger's legged it down the fire escape.

(*He clumps across the bare floorboards in his highly-tooled Western footwear. Frank cowers in his bathtub behind the half-open bathroom door, and listens*)

BOYLE: Exceptin', there isnae one.

(*Boyle's clumping footfalls come to a heart-stopping halt outside the bathroom door. A rivulet of perspiration trickles the length of Frank's still-swollen nose and falls with a soft plop on to his bunched up Burberry. A floorboard creaks. The half-open bathroom door is pushed full open by an unseen hand. Frank sinks lower in the tub and draws his knees up towards his chin. A pin might be heard to drop in Dennistoun.45 Then . . .)*

BOYLE: (*echoey, sings*) 'Well, since ma baby left me, I've found a new place to to dwell . . . '

(*Boyle, eyes shut, hands braced against the doorframe, has his head thrust inside the echo chamber of the bathroom*)

BOYLE: (*sings*) 'It's down at the end of Lonely Street, call' Heartbreak Hot . . . '

(*He breaks off*)

BOYLE: For God's sake, get a grip, Fraser . . .

(*He pushes himself backwards off the doorframe and sets about searching the living-room. Frank, still in the bathtub, twitches spasmodically at each crash and bang as Boyle systematically demolishes the apartment. The 'studio' is now reduced to an even worse shambles than it was prior to Cissie's tidy-up exercise. As a final PS, Boyle picks up Frank's treasured Hofner Senator guitar, places an ear to one of the F-holes, and gives it a shake before raising it above his head and bringing it crashing down on to a low table. Frank stuffs the Burberry into his mouth in an effort to stifle the involuntary squeal of anguish upon hearing the awful splintering 'twang' resonate round and around the bathroom. A deadly silence ensues. Then . . .)*

BOYLE: *(quietly sings)* . . . 'Heartbreak is so lonely, baby . . . heartbreak is so lonely . . . doo doo-doo . . . heartbreak is so lonely, I could . . . '

(The front door slams. Slowly, very slowly, Frank straightens his legs and lowers the Burberry from his face. He stares at the ceiling for several seconds)

FRANK: I know you don't exist, but thanks a million . . . ya bastard!

★ ★ ★

(The OK Korral in Kilwinning is a 'bona fide' Western saloon with cowboys and cowgirls of all ages, sizes, and shapes, crowding the tables and bar. Billie and Jolene, collectively advertised as 'The McPhail Sisters', are onstage at the far end of the room giving it big licks on a somewhat old-fashioned PA system. At the other end of the room, perched on a bar stool, and aloof from the crowd, sits Cissie, a glass of once-sparkling water in front of her)

BILLIE AND JOLENE: *(together, sing)* 'Why does the world keep on turning? Why do the stars shine above? Don't they know it's the end of the world, it ended when I lost your love . . . I wake up in the morning and I wonder.'

(Jolene takes an accordion solo)

JOLENE: *(over music)* Don't look, Billie, but look who's proppin' up the far end of the bar.

BILLIE: Where? I cannae see . . . aw, yeh, I've spotted him.

JOLENE: It's not a him, it's a her . . . Spotted who?

BILLIE: The guy with the speech impediment that wanted you an' I to go with him to Lourdes.

JOLENE: Lourdes?

BILLIE: Aye . . . d'you not remember he came up to us in the Wells Fargo an' he was walkin' all funny?

JOLENE: Aw, wee Desmond, you mean? Don't talk daft, it wasnae Lourdes he wanted took, it was the loo, he'd got his galluses all twisted.

BILLIE AND JOLENE: *(onstage, sing)* ' . . . don't they know it's the end of the world, it ended when I lost your love.'

(*Billie and Jolene finish their song and their set, and leave the stage. There is a smattering of applause followed immediately by the clamour of conversation as the assembled 'cowpokery' return to their refreshments*)

BILLIE: You don't want to push your luck an' do an encore, naw?

JOLENE: Naw, I think we'll just hoof it for the hills . . . you didnae tell anybody who we were, did you?

(*At the other end of the room a tall cowpoke, with hands and forearms smothered in tattoos, edges up to the bar beside Cissie*)

TALL COWPOKE: Howdy Slim . . . *High Noon*,[46] is it?

(*Cissie reacts with a blank stare*)

TALL COWPOKE: All on your ownsome . . . (*To barman*) Give us a big Glen Campbell, chief, an' whatever the little lady's huvvin'. (*To Cissie*) Whit you fur hen?

CISSIE: I'm fine, thanks . . . an' we'll have less of the little lady.

TALL COWPOKE: Somebody give you a dizzy, yeh?

CISSIE: Nobody gave us a dizzy, gonnae just vanish?

TALL COWPOKE: Now, that isnae what I'd cry 'neighbourly', honeybunch.

CISSIE: What you gonnae do, shoot me? I said I was fine . . . I'm fine, okay?

TALL COWPOKE: (*sotto voce, to barman*) Little lady's hud a dizzy . . . give it a coupla minutes an' bring us another big wanna these an' a Malibu, awright? Here . . .

(*He hands the barman a fiver*)

TALL COWPOKE: . . . bung whatever's left over into the boattle fur the weans's wigwam party.

(*He picks up his glass and turns to Cissie*)

TALL COWPOKE: 'Time was he supposed to be here at?

(*Cissie ignores him*)

TALL COWPOKE: Eh?

(*Cissie continues to ignore him*)

TALL COWPOKE: I guess you don't rightly know who I'm are, right?

(*Billie and Jolene have now started to pack up their gear by the side of the stage*)

JOLENE: Look, Billie, there she's talkin' to Timberwolf Tierney, what d'you suppose she's bitin' *his* ear about?

BILLIE: Away over an' ask her.

JOLENE: Naw, I couldnae, I'd be too . . . stop that, you.

BILLIE: She'll be orderin' up a set of louver doors, he's got them on special offer.

JOLENE: How, what's up with them?

BILLIE: Same as what's up with all his stuff, they're all . . .
(*Sniffs*) You been eatin' garlic?

> (*Frank, Burberry buttoned up to the neck, makes his way backwards into the OK Korral bar from the street. He turns, this way and that, spots Cissie and presses his way through the crowd towards her*)

TALL COWPOKE: . . . an' that wan there wi' the daurk herr's
'Geronimo' . . .

> (*He is giving Cissie a guided tour of his tattoos*)

CISSIE: What about that one with the pigtails an' the face like
a burst tamatta . . . that wouldnae be Sittin' Bull,[47] would it?
Or have I got it wrong?

TALL COWPOKE: That's ma girlfriend.

CISSIE: Whoops . . .

TALL COWPOKE: See, it's got it roon there at the tap . . .
'Roxanne' . . . boy took it affa Polaroid of her . . .

CISSIE: (*quickly*) Naw, I'm sure it's a good likeness.

TALL COWPOKE: (*slowly*) Aye, it is.

> (*He drains what's left in his glass*)

TALL COWPOKE: Right, that's me . . . don't furget yur brochure . . . you'll fun yur dinette doors wi' yur prairie oyster
motif on page two . . . ready-to-hang, fourteen quid. S'yur man
handy wi' a hammer?

> (*Frank slides up to the bar behind Cissie*)

FRANK: Don't turn around but guess who this is?

TALL COWPOKE: Better late than never, eh?

> (*He gives Cissie a wink and takes off*)

CISSIE: I don't have to turn around, I got a whiff of the raincoat
from two blocks away . . . what you doin' here? I thought you
told me . . .

FRANK: Yeh, but that was before Big Gordon OD'd . . . pretend
you're not with me.

CISSIE: I don't have to pretend . . .

> (*She turns to face Frank*)

CISSIE: . . . who's Big Gordon?

FRANK: 'The Boy Most Likely', Class of '68, St Saviour's High.

> (*Frank turns away to try and catch the barman's eye*)

FRANK: . . . thought you said you didnae know anbody?

CISSIE: Who, that geek that just left? Don't be . . .

FRANK: (*interrupting*) God, these boots arenae half tight . . .

> (*Cissie reaches down and lifts the tails of Frank's Burberry. He is wearing cowboy boots and Dorwood's Wranglers*)

FRANK: . . . yeh, okay, okay, I've decided to take on Dorwood's case.

(*He removes Cissie's hand and smooths down his raincoat*)

CISSIE: You've what?

(*Frank turns to face her*)

FRANK: Well, not take it on, exactly . . .

(*He takes a pair of Ray-bans[48] from his raincoat pocket and puts them on*)

FRANK: . . . look closer into it, as you might say.

CISSIE: What made you change your mind? Not that I'm not grateful, you understand . . . wasnae anythin' to do with Big Gordon, was it?

FRANK: D'you ever catch the Hitchcock movie, *The Wrong Man*? Hank Fonda was in it . . . [49]

(*The barman comes up and places a large malt whisky and a Malibu on the counter in front of them*)

BARMAN: It's paid for, Stevie . . . Malibu's to your left.

FRANK: Just saved me burstin' a ten-spot, Jim . . . (*To Cissie*) Played the bass fiddle in a night club orchestra.

(*He hands the Malibu to Cissie*)

CISSIE: Who . . . Big Gordon?

(*Frank picks up the whisky and sniffs at it*)

FRANK: Hank Fonda. This isnae funny, sweetheart.

CISSIE: Penny's dropped, has it? Cheers.

(*She upends the glass and pours its contents on to the floor*)

★ ★ ★

(*Over at the Bar-L David Cole in Ray Charles-type wraparound shades is seated at the Blüthner purveying Ray Charles-type wraparound R 'n' B.[50] Fraser Boyle, in identical shades, is perched on a bar-stool by the piano, a tall glass clutched in his gloved fist*)

DAVID COLE: (*not looking at Boyle*) So what happened?

BOYLE: (*not looking at Cole*) Nothin' happened . . . he wasnae in, was he?

DAVID COLE: You didn't hang around

BOYLE: Just as well I never . . . another five minutes an' the joint was gonnae be hoachin' with SAS.[51] Accordin' to my sources the guy's some kinda left-wing dev . . .

(*He breaks off as Shirley passes*)

BOYLE: Gonnae freshen that up for us Gorgeous?

(*Shirley takes his glass*)

SHIRLEY: Mr Cole?

(*Cole shakes his head. Boyle waits till Shirley is out of earshot*)

BOYLE: 'Course, that's me all over, innit? Mr Trustin . . . the

Gestapo's got his life story an' a full set of dabbities on file an' there's me swappin' pleasantries with the guy in the toilets.

DAVID COLE: Yeah, what you gonna do 'bout my doors, man?

BOYLE: (*interrupting, shouting at Shirley*) Ho, ask the fruitcake to go easy on the lemon scliffs, will you?

DAVID COLE: Hey, I'm talkin' to you, meathead . . . you wrecked my goddam men's room, huh?

BOYLE: Aye, awright, awright, I'll get my joiner to come over an' have a look-see, stop buggin' us about it, I've got enough on my plate with this missin' merchandise an' havin' to go round all my customers replicatin' their fish in a jotter!

DAVID COLE: So what do I tell the Man from Motown when he calls?

BOYLE: Just tell him everythin's cool, yeh?

DAVID COLE: Everythin' better be cool 'cos this dude from Motor City don't mess with no amateurs, you know what I'm sayin'?

BOYLE: You tell this dude not to fret himself, these people are pros . . . when the boys an' me met up with them in thon back room in Derry[52] it wasnae just our side that were blindfolded . . . don't laugh, that was a gag. Believe me, there's nothin' amateur about these guys.

DAVID COLE: I wasn't talkin' about those guys, stupid.

BOYLE: Eh? Who were you talkin' ab . . .

SHIRLEY: (*interrupting, loudly*) One Ball Breaker, plenty lemon scliffs!

(*She bangs the drink down in front of Boyle*)

* * *

(*In the Lone Star Chinese restaurant in downtown Kilwinning Billie and Jolene are seated in a booth scanning menus*)

JOLENE: . . . Yeh, fine, but if we get the Lone Star Dinner-for-Three, an' the Cantonese Banquet over the page, we just need another two dishes an' you can wrap whatever beancurd you don't want in your neckerchief . . .

(*In the far-end booth Frank and Cissie are eating*)

FRANK: Cherokee what?

CISSIE: Cherokee George . . . I've got his address in my bag . . .

(*Frank manipulates his chopsticks and manages to convey a single Singapore noodle to his mouth*)

CISSIE: . . . the only problem is you're gonnae have to get whatever lowdown he's got while you're in gettin' one done . . . d'you want that other pancake?

FRANK: Help yourself . . .

(*He makes a note in his shorthand notebook open on the table*)

FRANK: . . . while I'm in gettin' one what done?

CISSIE: A tattoo . . . pass me the Hoi Sin.

FRANK: (*looking up sharply*) What?

CISSIE: The Hoi Sin sauce, you just put your elbow in it . . . Thanks.

FRANK: I know this's goin' to strike you as wantonly perverse, given that I said I'd look into Dorwood's case, but I don't think I fancy gettin' a tattoo done . . . naw, cancel that . . . if I was asked what was the most obscene thing a human being could . . .

CISSIE: (*interrupting*) It doesn't have to be anythin' elaborate.

(*She spoons some Hoi Sin sauce on to her pancake*)

FRANK: Aw, sure . . . coupla rattlesnakes an' 'Howdy, Stranger' across here in 'American Gothic' . . .

(*He draws his chopsticks across his forehead*)

FRANK: . . . in exchange for what, the name an' address of the nearest skin graft clinic?

CISSIE: You're just bein' stupit now.

(*She arranges some cucumber and spring onion on a saucy pancake*)

FRANK: And you're bein' perfectly sensible, are you? S'up with me just takin' along a shorthand notebook an' askin' this Cherokee what's-his-name to . . .

CISSIE: (*interrupting*) The guy isn't goin' to talk into a shorthand notebook, ya mutt . . . we're tryin' to infiltrate a closed community here . . . what d'you think I put you into camouflage for? Look, you don't imagine I'd ask you to go visit this party if I didn't reckon we were on to somethin'? Everybody that's anybody on the Country scene's been to Cherokee George, includin' Fraser Boyle, right?

(*Frank pours himself a glass of wine*)

FRANK: So?

(*He offers some wine to Cissie who refuses*)

CISSIE: So, it's like goin' to confessions to these dingbats, they all unburden themselves to their tattooist, don't they?

FRANK: You tell me . . . I get the distinct impression I've just landed on Mars an' I've left my Baedeker[53] in my other boilersuit.

(*Frank downs his glass and pours himself another*)

CISSIE: You remember that illustrated geek I was talkin' to in the OK?

FRANK: The one you didnae know, yeh?

CISSIE: I don't know him, he just came up an' started givin' me a guided tour of his torso . . . I gathered from him that . . . s'up. You're not tellin' me you're chicken, are you?

(*She places some shredded duck on the pancake and rolls it up*)

FRANK: I'm not sayin' another dicky burd . . . how's your duck?

CISSIE: My duck's awright.

(*She takes a bite out of the pancake*)

FRANK: 'Awright' is not an officially recognised Rag Haw rating . . . on a scale of one-to-ten, I'm talkin'?

(*Cissie ignores him*)

FRANK: A four, mebbe?

(*Cissie carries on munching*)

FRANK: Higher . . . lower?

(*He waits, pencil poised over his notebook*)

FRANK: C'mon, Crouch, I want to get this written up an' posted off to my editor . . . I might be on the run but I still have to earn a crust . . . a five, a two . . . what?

CISSIE: You show me your bluebird, I'll let you know how I score the duck . . . right?

FRANK: What blueburd?

JOLENE: (*muffled in the distance*) They want to get some Hoyt Axton[54] on their hi-fi, that's hellish . . .

* * *

(*The same evening finds Frank leafing through a tattoo design catalogue. He is sitting in a dentist's chair, shirt sleeves rolled up, his Burberry hanging by the pay phone. The tiny, insalubrious back street tattoo parlour has peeling walls festooned with bleeding hearts, writhing snakes, and voluptuous mermaids. A thin layer of brownish grease has embalmed all surfaces. Oriental tintinnabulation carries on in the background*)

FRANK: Naw, naw, they're very handsome, I was just wonderin' if you had somethin' a bit less . . . y'know?

CHEROKEE GEORGE: (*leaning close*) Did you say 'meadow pipit'?

FRANK: Okay, forget the meadow pipit . . . 'much is that one?

(*He points to a particularly gruesome troup of vultures in the catalogue*)

CHEROKEE GEORGE: Aw depends where you want it done, pal.

FRANK: Up the Royal under a general anaesthetic, I would've thought.

(*Frank gives a little laugh, Cherokee George remains stony-faced at this witticism*)

FRANK: You not got anythin' from the Disney archive I could

look at?

CHEROKEE GEORGE: Disney?

FRANK: 'Disney' matter . . . I'll come back another time when you're better dressed . . .

   (*He makes to get up from the chair*)

CHEROKEE GEORGE: I know your face from someplace, ya cheeky bastart.

   (*He places a hand on Frank's chest*)

FRANK: D'you mind not doin' that, I'm an asthmatic . . . (*Coughs*)

CHEROKEE GEORGE: It wasnae the cages at Peterheid, was it?

FRANK: Naw, it was livin' up a close in Possilpark, my whole family's got it . . . (*Wheezes loudly*)

CHEROKEE GEORGE: Who was it you said put you on to me?

   (*He fixes Frank with his wall eye*)

FRANK: Aw . . . er . . . I don't think you'd know her . . . him, I mean . . . Big Ted . . . Tex . . . Big Tex . . .

CHEROKEE GEORGE: Big Tex what?

   (*Cherokee George puts his face next to Frank's and breathes on him*)

FRANK: . . . mebbe it was Wee Tex . . . yeh, come to think of it, he wasnae all that tall . . . in fact, 'm not all that sure his name was Tex, now that you mention it. Rex, naw? Lex? Yeh, that was it . . . Lex Somethin'. Or was it Rudy? Randy? Don't know any Randys, naw?

CHEROKEE GEORGE: I've definitely saw your face someplace . . . just cannae put ma finger on it.

FRANK: (*interrupting*) Jody? Jesse? Wayne? Dwane? Clint?

   (*George's eyes narrow*)

CHEROKEE GEORGE: Did you say 'Dwane'?

FRANK: Did I?

CHEROKEE GEORGE: Wasnae Dwane Devlin, was it?

FRANK: Dwane Devlin . . . ?

   (*Frank snaps his fingers*)

FRANK: That's who it was . . . the Deadwood Playboys, right?

CHEROKEE GEORGE: Only your most decorated pedal-steel player in the business . . . aye, I done some of my best work on Dwane . . . s'a matter of fact, I was workin' up a special for him when he got flung into the slammer. Somethin' along they lines you were after, was it?

FRANK: Was it?

   (*There is a whooshing sound as Cherokee George depresses the dentist's chair pedal and Frank finds himself being lowered rapidly backwards. Frank's eyes alight on a grubby notice affixed to the ceiling warning potential customers about the possible dangers of contracting the Aids virus)*

FRANK: (*to himself*) Aw, my God, that's all we need . . . (*To George*) You are goin' to be wearin' some kinda gloves, I take it?

CHEROKEE GEORGE: 'Course I'm are . . .

FRANK: That's somethin' . . . lemme find you a very small blueburd on page . . .

(Frank flicks through the catalogue that he is still clutching)

CHEROKEE GEORGE: . . . freeze the gonads offa gopher in here.

(He pulls on a filthy pair of fingerless Fair Isle gloves and uncorks a bottle of methylated spirits)

FRANK: Naw, I'm sorry, that isn't quite . . .

CHEROKEE GEORGE: (*interrupting*) Page twenty-three.

(He drenches a cotton wool swab with meths)

FRANK: Page what?

(He flicks through the catalogue)

FRANK: Good grief.

(Frank finds the page, he swallows in horror as he sees a picture of 'The Eagle of the Apocalypse in a Titanic Death struggle with the Sidewinders of Satan')

FRANK: Er . . . 'scuse me I don't really think . . .

(He is cut off in mid-sentence by the high-pitched whine of a tattooing 'gun')

CHEROKEE GEORGE: Here, hold that a second . . .

(He hands the tattooing 'gun' to Frank and sets about securing him to the chair with a stout leather strap)

FRANK: (*alarmed*) What you doin'?

CHEROKEE GEORGE: That's not too slack for you, naw?

FRANK: Oooow!

(Cherokee George takes the 'gun' from Frank)

CHEROKEE GEORGE: Better have a slug of this 'fore we get tore in, eh?

(He tilts his head back and takes a swig from the meths bottle)

FRANK: Aw, my God . . .

* * *

(The Irish ferry is berthing at the Sealink terminal at Stranraer. Fraser Boyle, a pay phone to his ear, watches)

BOYLE: (*on phone*) . . . not that Bar-L, ya mug, this's a Yankee-style establishment I'm talkin' about . . . some vandal's put all their toilet doors in, I'm doin' the boy a favour . . . how quick can you . . . never heed what Roxanne wants to do, this's an emergency!

* * *

(Cissie's apartment is a veritable shrine to 40s' and 50s' cowboy 'collectables', most of which are in the process of being wrapped up and packed into tea-chests. Cissie hands a steaming mug to Frank who sits ashen-faced, his Burberry draped around his shoulders, his left arm in an improvised sling)

CISSIE: Well?

FRANK: *(shakily)* Give us a chance, I havenae tasted it yet . . .

CISSIE: You'll get that other arm in a sling if you're not careful . . . what'd you find out, I'm askin'?

FRANK: That I don't go a bundle on guys with Red Indian nick-names tyin' me up an' stickin' needles into me, then chargin' sixty-five quid plus VAT for the privilege, but I could've told you that before I went . . .

(He takes an exploratory sip from his mug)

FRANK: . . . mmmm, Melrose's Darjeeling,55 my very fav . . .

CISSIE: *(interrupting)* It's Bovril,56 an' if you don't hurry up an' tell me what you discovered it's goin' straight down the front of your Wranglers, right!

FRANK: *(indignantly)* Dorwood's Wranglers . . . I wouldn't be caught dead in a pair of . . .

CISSIE: Hurry up, I said!

FRANK: Aaaaaarg, my arm! Quit shoutin' will you! D'you ever hear . . . *(Lowers voice)* D'you ever hear Dorwood talkin' about a buncha guys callin' themselves . . . God, what was it again?

CISSIE: Callin' themselves what?

FRANK: This is really aggravatin' . . . I kept repeatin' it to myself all the way here on the bus . . .

CISSIE: Repeatin' what? C'mon.

FRANK: . . . tch . . . it was on the tip of my tongue, dammit . . . Somebody Somebody and Somethin' Somethin' . . . I told Cherokee what's-his-face I was doin' a profile on the Playboys for *Country Life* . . . an' I'd give his tattoo parlour a plug if he filled in some background detail on the Deadwoods person-nel for us . . . which is when he brought up this other buncha brainless bandits . . . beg your pardon, this other band . . .

* * *

(Meanwhile, back at the Sealink terminal in Stranraer, Fraser Boyle flicks a cigarette butt away as a convoy of trucks disem-barks from the ferry. Boyle crosses the yard to the parked fish van. As he does so a Winnebago57 with 'Jim Bob O'May and the Wild Bunch' lettered on the side rolls down the ramp and joins the convoy heading for the exit gate. Boyle turns the key

in the van's ignition and nudges his way into line behind the Winnebago)

* * *

(In Cissie's apartment Frank is still wrestling with his memory)

CISSIE: Forget about this other band, what'd he say about Fraser Boyle, ya dooley?

FRANK: I'm comin' to that, I'm comin' to that . . . he seems to've been particularly palsy-walsy with Dwane . . . you havenae got a drink, have you?

CISSIE: Dwane Devlin?

FRANK: You know a lotta Dwanes, do you? An' you can cut the dooley, I've just been through the most horrendous experience of my . . .

CISSIE: *(interrupting)* Yeh, fine, just get on with it, hurry up.

FRANK: Quit badgerin' us, I'm tryin' to collect my thoughts! This's bloody goupin'! Right, where was I?

CISSIE: Rabbitin' on to no good purpose about some other band . . . will you get to the point, McClusky!

FRANK: I'm gettin' to the point . . . if you'd chuck harassin' me for a second an' pin your ears back you might just latch on to the nub of this narrative!

CISSIE: Don't shout!

FRANK: *(loudly)* It's you that's shoutin'! Calm down . . . calm down . . . *(Calms down himself)* So, in bet . . . *(Clears throat)* So, in between beltin' down a half-litre of meths, workin' round my vaccination mark an' my polio injection, Cherokee what-d'-you-call-him lets slip about how Boyle wasnae all that heartbroken when the other two band members got busted 'cos he, Boyle, had already got his marchin' orders from the Deadwoods an' was about to . . .

CISSIE: *(interrupting)* Dorwood never mentioned that to me . . . carry on.

FRANK: . . . an' was about to buddy-up . . . naw, sorry, I tell a lie . . . his exact words were 'do a deal with' . . . and here I quote . . . 'a buncha bog-hoppin' badhats from the back-of-beyond called . . .

CISSIE: Called what?

FRANK: . . . hold on, hold on!

(He screws his eyes shut in a desperate bid to recollect their name. Cissie waits with bated breath. Frank opens his eyes. There is a deathly pause . . .)

FRANK: *(matter of fact)* Nup, it's away . . . gonnae chuck us a cushion? This arm isnae half . . .

(Cissie rams a cushion at his back)

FRANK: . . . ahyah!

CISSIE: See you, you're hopeless . . . that's the last time you're gettin' sent for a tattoo!

★ ★ ★

(In the Bar-L Timberwolf Tierney — aka Tall Cowpoke — adjusts his holster with its new hammer slung around his waist like a gunbelt and sniffs. His 'entourage' — apprentice, Drew, and girlfriend, Roxanne — lounge against the fittings awaiting instructions from their leader)

TRACEY: *(to Tall Cowpoke)* I'm just after tellin' you, the boss isnae here, he's went for a haircut . . . *(Loudly)* Shirley? You talk C 'n' W, come an translate for us . . . *(To Tall Cowpoke)* . . . he's away gettin' scalped, yeh?

★ ★ ★

(Cissie is trying to attend to Frank's wounds, but he shrinks away as she reaches out towards the dressing on his upper arm)

CISSIE: Don't be a sap, I'm not goin' to hurt you . . . I just want to . . . look, we're not gonnae get very far if we don't trust each other . . .

(Frank raises a skeptical eyebrow)

CISSIE: Trust me, Frank . . .

(Frank deliberates)

CISSIE: *(softly)* . . . trust me.

(Frank hesitates. He looks into Cissie's eyes, and relaxes somewhat)

FRANK: Awright, I trust you, but don't go an' . . . ooooooooooow!

(Cissie peers at the spot on Frank's upper arm from which the dressing had been so untimely ripped)

CISSIE: What is it?

FRANK: That was bloody excruciatin', ya . . . ! What d'you mean, what is it?

(Cissie looks at a hideously discoloured and totally unidentifiable wound on Frank's upper arm)

FRANK: It's the 'Eagle of the Apocalypse in a Titanic Death Struggle with the Sidewinders of Satan', innit!

CISSIE: Aw, yeh . . . so it is.

FRANK: Aw, God, I think I'm goin' to . . . bwoop.

CISSIE: Here . . . hold this under your chin.

(Frank grabs the proffered newspaper and runs to the bathroom)

CISSIE: *(shouts)* An' don't use the wash-hand basin, d'you hear!

* * *

(In a side-street in Candleriggs[58] Boyle's fish van and Jim Bob's Winnebago are parked. A motorcycle cop dismounts and starts slapping parking tickets on everything in sight. In the Winnebago Boyle is talking to the Outlaw who is guarding Jim Bob's inner sanctum)

BOYLE: Naw, hey, listen . . . tell Jim Bob I'll get him a 'taste' for later on the night an' he can let us know how much you guys want to order up for the European market . . .

(The Outlaw carries on watching TV)

BOYLE: . . . I had to return the sample I had to my suppliers . . . wasnae just your top-notch quality, know what I mean?

(The Outlaw turns a bloodshot eye on Boyle, Boyle sidles towards the door. The Outlaw goes back to watching Kind Hearts and Coronets *on his Sony[59] as Boyle makes his exit. Boyle leaves the trailer and finds the motorcycle cop putting a ticket under the fish van's wiper)*

BOYLE: *(to cop)* Ho, that fish motor's mine, I'm on a mercy dash to the Sick Children's Hospital with a loada cod liver oil capsules!

* * *

(In a fashion shop nearby Jolene, all in black, turns this way and that in front of a full-length mirror)

JOLENE: Well, what d'you reckon?

BILLIE: I reckon it's about time we made some more phone calls, we're onstage at the Ponderosa the morra night an' we still havenae . . .

JOLENE: *(interrupting)* Och, stop annoyin' us, there's a thousand guys'll jump at the chance.

BILLIE: We don't want a thousand, we just want a couple, Jolene.

JOLENE: We'll get wurselves a couple, will you quit worryin' about it, Billie?

BILLIE: I cannae help worryin' about it, we're advertised on all the Wild Bunch posters as The McPhail Sisters and Friends, a right pair of numpties we're gonnae look turnin' up on wur tod.

JOLENE: Speak for yourself . . . there's no way I'm lookin' a numpty.

BILLIE: Naw?

JOLENE: What d'you mean, naw?

BILLIE: You seen the price that is?

JOLENE: Where?

> (*She examines the price ticket dangling from the hem of the blouson she is modelling*)

JOLENE: Good God, they're jokin'!

BILLIE: What about the wee guy that used to play with Big Norrie's Texas Handful? We could try givin' him a call.

> (*Jolene shrugs off the overpriced blouson*)

JOLENE: Yeh, I suppose we could, but you'll need an awful lotta change . . .

> (*She selects a green leather jacket from the rack*)

JOLENE: . . . he's in Tristan da Cunha with the Territorials[60] . . . gonnae hold that for us?

> (*Billie holds the leather jacket while Jolene slips her arms into its sleeves*)

BILLIE: Okay, what about the guy with the stigmata that used to turn out all them tepee lampshades for Timberwolf Tierney's DIY shop, was he not quite an accomplished . . . awright, awright, scrub him. That leaves an amputee with an autoharp an' the big guy from Bearsden with the steel plate in his heid . . . let's face it, Jolene, the McPhail Sisters cannae come up with any Friends.

JOLENE: Don't talk garbage, Billie, 'course we can.

BILLIE: Awright, name two . . . name one, you cannae.

JOLENE: There's wee Desmond.

> (*She strolls up and down in front of the mirror*)

BILLIE: Jolene, wee Desmond cannae even say his own name right, we're talkin' about wur big chance here.

JOLENE: Okay, how's about the boy MacIndoo?

BILLIE: MacIndoo?

JOLENE: You forgot all about him, didn't you?

BILLIE: I sure did . . . who the hell's the boy MacIndoo?

JOLENE: Don't tell me you don't remember the big fulla in the bi-focals that ran up all the bridesmaids' frocks for our Jinty's weddin'?

> (*She executes a twirl*)

JOLENE: Him an' his pal used to front The Desparadoes . . .

> (*Billie buries her face in the garment rack*)

JOLENE: . . . I'll get him to bring along your poncho.

* * *

> (*Cissie is now clearing up her apartment and is wrapping cowboy memorabilia in sheets of newspaper and packing them into tea-chests. The loo flushes*)

CISSIE: (*loudly*) There's a half-bottle of Listerine in the medicine cabinet . . . use it.

> (*She picks up her Gene Autry radio and runs her fingers over its smooth bakelite contours*)

FRANK: (*from bathroom*) Naw, it's okay. I washed my hair last Monday.

> (*Cissie flicks the radio on and off, and then on again. Jim Bob O'May's version of* 'Your Cheatin' Heart' *comes surging faintly forth before spluttering out. Cissie turns the radio over and prises the back off with her fingernail. In the bathroom Frank, looking pale, is already investigating the contents of the medicine cabinet and has come across a cracked snapshot of a smiling Cissie, Dorwood and a small child of about four in a cowboy suit*)

CISSIE: (*from living-room*) D'you find it?

> (*Frank looks at the photo for some moments*)

FRANK: (*loudly*) This'll be Dorwood junior, yeh?

> (*Cissie's eyes widen in disbelief*)

FRANK: (*from bathroom*) I said this'll be Dorwood junior, yeh?

CISSIE: (*to herself*) Aw naw . . .

> (*She withdraws a tightly-rolled bundle of twenty pound notes and then an avalanche of them tumbles out of the radio on to the carpet*)

* * *

> (*Back at George's tattoo parlour the sound of wheezy snoring can be heard while Jim Bob's* 'Your Cheating Heart' *plays over the radio. Cherokee George's manky socks are resting on the dentist's chair, there is a pair of discarded boots and an empty meths bottle on the floor. The shop door rattles, and the unmistakable features of Fraser Boyle's face are pressed up against the glass panel*)

BOYLE: Right ya dozy half-breed . . .

> (*He takes a step away from the door and raises a boot*)

* * *

> (*The Tall Cowpoke is shaking his head while surveying the extensive damage to the cubicle doors of the Bar-L men's room*)

TALL COWPOKE: Tch, tch, tch, tch . . . Drew, away oot tae the covered wagon an' get Roxanne tae start makin' oot some invoices . . .

> (*He takes a hammer from his gunbelt and smashes at a door hinge*)

TALL COWPOKE: . . . c'mon move yursel'.

> (*His apprentice finishes blowing his nose on the roller towel and ambles across to the door*)

TALL COWPOKE: (*shouts*) An' bring us a coupla lengths a timber . . .

>   (*The Tall Cowpoke takes a swing at the bottom hinge of a cubicle door, and it falls drunkenly on to the WC pedestal*)

TALL COWPOKE: . . . thuv had some bloody cowboy daein' thur carpentry fur them.

★ ★ ★

>   (*Frank is outside Cissie's apartment rattling the door handle*)

FRANK: Cissie? It's me . . . Frank . . . What you locked the door for? C'mon, I kept my side of the bargain . . . I want to know how you scored the duck. Cissie?

Sunday

The rising moon over Barlinnie prison catches the bony contours
of Dorwood Crouch's head, making him appear like an over-
inked etching by Rembrandt. Dorwood shuffles his way along the
prison rooftop towards the shelter of a chimney stack, a cheap
transistor radio clutched to his ear. A loose slate skitters down
the frosty pitch of the roof while Jim Bob O'May and the Wild
Bunch's version of the Hank Williams classic 'Settin' the Woods
on Fire', an upbeat anthem to incendiarism, fights a losing battle
with the fading batteries.

* * *

(*Cissie chucks Frank's Burberry around his shoulders*)

FRANK: What's this?

CISSIE: What does it look like?

FRANK: It looks like a particularly roomy marquee but I can tell
from the absence of guy ropes that it might just be my . . . where
am I goin'?

CISSIE: Home, where'd you think?

(*She escorts him to the front door of her apartment*)

FRANK: Thanks to you I no longer have a home. It's been
ransacked . . .

(*Cissie opens the door*)

FRANK: . . . not to mention bein' put under surveillance ever
since Big Gordon got fished out the Clyde . . . I'll have to find
a bed an' breakfast joint an' lie low till all this blows over . . .

CISSIE: Fine, I hope you'll be comfy.

FRANK: That's it? I get myself indelibly lumbered with the
'Eagle of the Apocalypse', supply you with vital information
concernin' Fraser Boyle an' a band whose name escapes me
for the moment, the significance of which we've barely touched
upon, an' all that's on offer is a not-so-hot Bovril and a decidedly
cool 'I hope you'll be comfy' . . . what is this?

CISSIE: Yeh, that was a bit remiss . . .

FRANK: I'll say it's remiss! Do you have any notion just how
painful . . .

CISSIE: (*interrupting*) . . . I hope you'll be very comfy, now beat
it before I . . .

FRANK: (*interrupting*) What the hell's got into you? Twenty-four
hours ago you were on your bended knees beggin' me to look

into Dorwood's case, to which end I've lost my apartment, shelved my better judgement, an' acquired a tattoo, now you cannae wait to get shot of me . . . no explanation, nothin'.

CISSIE: What's to explain? You goofed . . . bye.

(*She gives Frank a shove and tries closing the door on him*)

FRANK: Ow! This could turn septic on us, ya big ungrateful midden!

CISSIE: (*sotto voce*) Quit yelpin', will you! If it gets back to Dorwood that I've had a guy up the house he'll kill me!

FRANK: (*interrupting*) Aw, I goofed awright . . . when I let you talk me into forkin' out sixty-five quid for this monstrosity when I could've got my motor outta . . . what d'you mean, I goofed?

CISSIE: Screwed up . . . goofed . . . couldn't remember.

FRANK: I'm still in a state of post-tattoo shock, for Christ's sake!

(*The elderly neighbour from upstairs shouts down*)

NEIGHBOUR: Is that you, Mrs Crouch?

CISSIE: (*sotto voce, to Frank*) See that. I told you to keep your voice down!

(*She hauls Frank back inside and closes the front door swiftly and silently*)

FRANK: What've I done now?

CISSIE: (*interrupting*) Shhhhhhhhh!

NEIGHBOUR: (*from upstairs*) Cooeeee?

(*Cissie presses a finger against her lips and herself against the wall. Some moments pass*)

FRANK: (*sotto voce*) She the one that shopped you to Dorwood that time?

CISSIE: (*sotto voce*) In green biro, you want to've read the lies! He was nearly goin' off his head . . .

FRANK: The old bastart!

CISSIE: Told him I was goin' out with other guys while he was on remand.

FRANK: An' were you?

(*Cissie gives him a kick on the shin*)

FRANK: Ooooooow!

CISSIE: Shhhhhhhhhhh!

(*Cissie places an ear against the door*)

CISSIE: She's still out there . . . listen.

(*Frank listens at the door*)

FRANK: I cannae hear anythin'.

CISSIE: Listen!

(*They listen. There is complete and total silence*)

FRANK: Aw, yeh . . . a sort of low-decibel hum, right?

(*He moves his face closer to the back of Cissie's neck*)

FRANK: (*confidentially*) My old boy got one of them put in last Easter ... four an' a half hours on the operatin' table ... surgeon told my mother he was good for another ten years at least ... gave up the ghost on the M90 two months back ... passin' motorist tried to revive him with a set of jump leads an' a hockey stick but he was a gonner.

CISSIE: Chuck that!

FRANK: Naw, it's true ... cross ma heart an' hope to ...

CISSIE: (*interrupting*) Not that ... that!

FRANK: What?

CISSIE: Breathin' on me!

FRANK: Anybody ever tell you what a beautiful ... shhh!

CISSIE: What?

FRANK: Listen ...

CISSIE: Listen what! I cannae hear any ...

FRANK: Her pacemaker either conked out or ...

(*He hauls the door open*)

CISSIE: What're you doin'?

FRANK: It's awright, she's away.

CISSIE: Good, so are you ... bye.

(*She shoves Frank out of the door on to the landing*)

FRANK: Ho, ya rotten big ... !

(*And slams the door shut behind him. Frank tugs at his Burberry which is trapped in the door. He bends down and flips the letter box open*)

FRANK: Sixty-five quid plus VAT you owe me!

(*He turns to the neighbour who has appeared from upstairs*)

FRANK: Just delivered them a pizza ... never even gave us a tip.

* * *

(*Dorwood sits, cold and dejected, hunched up against the chimney stack as the sporadic and feeble reception finally gives up the ghost and the transistor radio dies. He gives the radio a disgusted dunt, bangs it against the side of the chimney and then launches it high into the blackness*)

* * *

(*A big red Chevrolet Drophead hoves into view, and draws up outside Bruno's Late Nite Barber Shop. David Cole, ultra-cool in his belted topcoat and shades, steps out. Inside, Bruno's remains unaltered since the 1950s, right down to the row of latest hairstyles, 'Olympic', 'Tony Curtis', 'Blow-wave', 'Jeff Chandler', the Bush portable atop the Brylcreem dispenser, and Eric, whose name is spelled out on his overall pocket in red, and in stick-on plastic letters across the fly-blown mirror. Eric's own favoured coiffure is a slightly-elevated 'Tony Curtis' that might easily be mistaken for a rug. Jim Bob's 'Settin' the Woods on Fire' carries on over the radio. Eric swoops low for a final snip at the back of a customer's head. David Cole enters, unbelts his topcoat, and hangs it up as the final chords of 'Settin' the Woods on Fire' fade on the Bush portable. Eric holds up a two-handed mirror and his customer in the chair nods his approval)*

RADIO DJ: . . . Jim Bob O'May and the Wild Bunch there with a sizzling cut from their *Lean 'n' Tasty* album . . . seventeen minutes past the hour . . .

(Eric plucks the towel from his customer's shoulders and gives it a shake. The customer gets up from his chair, still wearing a barber's sheet. As the customer and David Cole pass, Cole slips a package to him in exchange for some folded banknotes. Cole takes his place in Eric's chair. The customer removes the sheet and passes it to Eric who throws it over Cole and tucks the corners into the back of his collar)

RADIO DJ: . . . no need to remind Jim Bob fans that the boys are back in town on the first leg of a European Tour that kicks off in Wishaw tomorrow night, with local support act The McPhail Sisters and Friends, before heading up country to Aberdeen . . .

* * *

(Across town, in the Bar-L men's room a grubby ghetto-blaster is tuned to the same radio station)

RADIO DJ: . . . You're tuned to *The Old Chisholm Trail* on 289 metres . . . six pairs of those Wild Bunch tickets to be won in our great phone-in competition directly after the news headlines from Ward Ferguson . . .

(The Tall Cowpoke emerges from the end cubicle)

RADIO NEWS READER: . . . Cheers, Dunky . . . and we go straight over to the radio car and *Evening Echo* reporter, Tamara MacAskill, for an update on the rooftop protest at HM Pris . . .

(The Tall Cowpoke stabs at the 'off' button)

TALL COWPOKE: How we daein', young Drew?

DREW: . . . Jist drivin' hame this last . . .

(There is a loud hammering)

DREW: . . . screwnail.

(Drew emerges from another cubicle and pulls its door shut behind him. The replacement door with its high-gloss finish and Western-style pokerwork decoration doesn't quite manage to close

properly. The other cubicle doors, with the exception of the not-too-badly-damaged original end door, have been patched or nailed over with hardboard sheeting, and are slightly at odds with the badly-hung replacement door and the art deco surroundings. The apprentice joins the master as they assess their handiwork. The Tall Cowpoke takes the hammer from Drew and slips it into his 'gunbelt')

TALL COWPOKE: Coupla coats a dark stain an' I defy embody tae spot the difference . . .

(Drew stabs a black-nailed finger at the ghetto-blaster 'on' button)

TAMARA: . . . between the shower block and the prison laundry.

* * *

(As the radio news reporter speaks into her in-car microphone, under the prison wall, Dorwood totters unsteadily along the apex of the roof high above)

TAMARA: No attempt has been made so far this evening to bring the man down owing to the treacherous conditions on the roof . . .

(Dorwood's foot slips on the frosty slates and he teeters for a moment before regaining his equilibrium)

TAMARA: . . . but prison authorities are expected to move in at first light to help de-escalate what could very well be a repetition of the violent rooftop demonstrations we saw earlier in the year at a number of Scottish institutions . . . a spokesman for the governor assured journalists just before we came on air that every effort is being made to contact the prisoner's wife who is thought to be still living at the couple's luxury maisonette in Clydebank . . . Tamara MacAskill for Radio Kelvin News, Riddrie.

(Tamara leans down to the radio car window)

TAMARA: Brian . . . d'you fancy a quick coffee or d'you think we should hang around in case he plunges to his death? I'm easy . . .

* * *

(Frank is still standing outside Cissie's front door. He can hear the telephone ringing inside)

FRANK: The very least you could do is phone us a taxi . . .

(He tugs at the trapped Burberry)

CISSIE: *(from inside)* There's a box at the corner.

(The telephone keeps on ringing)

FRANK: Yes, positively rib-tickling . . . how d'you expect me to dial for a taxi with this!

(*He waves his sling at the door*)

CISSIE: (*from inside*) Get a bus!

FRANK: Aw, first class . . . you know fine well I cannae risk usin' public transport with my face plastered all over the papers every Tuesday and Friday!

(*He tugs fiercely at his Burberry, and there is a ripping noise*)

CISSIE: (*at letterbox*) Stop exaggeratin', your own mother wouldn't recognise you from that photograph . . .

(*Her fingers appear through the letterbox*)

CISSIE: . . . it's this big.

FRANK: That big!

(*The telephone stops ringing*)

FRANK: 'Much d'you want to bet that was my Features Editor? I'm supposed to be at a sushi restaurant in East Kilbride right now!

* * *

(*Fraser Boyle stands in Cherokee George's tattoo parlour stamping up and down and blowing into his hands, his breath steaming in the icy atmosphere. There is the sound of running water*)

CHEROKEE GEORGE: What'd you say?

(*Cherokee George lifts his head out of the sink, his teeth chattering, groping for a towel*)

BOYLE: I said, I've tried everyplace . . . soon as you mention Cole they don't want to know . . . God, it's bloody chitterin'.

CHEROKEE GEORGE: You're no' kiddin' . . . freeze the gonads . . .

TOGETHER: . . . offa gopher in here.

BOYLE: Aye, very apt . . . so what time does your guy normally deliver at?

CHEROKEE GEORGE: What guy?

(*George stops drying his hair and looks up from under the towel*)

BOYLE: What guy . . . your supplier! What d'you suppose I kicked the door in for, I've ran out, haven't I!

CHEROKEE GEORGE: Awright, awright, hing loose . . . you should've kicked it in a bit earlier, I'm no' that long off the phone to his missus . . . God, ma heid . . .

(*Boyle snatches the pay-phone from the wall*)

BOYLE: Here . . . tell her you want another six bags . . .

(*George takes the phone*)

BOYLE: . . . c'mon, I've got people waitin' for us!

(*George sticks his finger in the dial*)

CHEROKEE GEORGE: Better have some readies on you, this

boy doesnae take cards or nothin' . . .

BOYLE: Get a move on, it's freezin'!

CHEROKEE GEORGE: Six, did you say? (*To phone*) Aye, hullo, George Tierney here . . . could you ask your man to stick another six bags on to that order, love?

BOYLE: An' it better no' be cut with nothin' or you're for it.

CHEROKEE GEORGE: (*on phone*) Hold on . . . (*To Boyle*) D'you want any logs, she's askin'?

    (*Boyle's expression changes*)

BOYLE: Logs? What you talkin' about, logs?

CHEROKEE GEORGE: (*to phone*) Naw, jist the Grade One Smokeless, darlin' . . . ta.

    (*He hangs up*)

CHEROKEE GEORGE: Be here at the back a nine, he's got four ton a nuggets to drop off at the Blind Basket showrooms . . .

    (*He drops the towel over his face and starts drying his hair*)

CHEROKEE GEORGE: What?

    (*George lifts the towel from his head just as Boyle's fist comes crashing into it*)

* * *

    (*Frank hunches morosely in the back of a taxi, his Burberry draped over his shoulders, nursing his tattooed arm*)

BILLIE: (*on radio*) Car Fourteen to base . . . come in base, over? (*Over shoulder to Frank*) Jolene said it was a lassie's voice that phoned . . . good job for you it was dark.

    (*There is a short eruption over the radio*)

BILLIE: (*on radio*) Yeh, Jolene . . . let your fingers do the walkin' . . . B an' Bs, South Side, over? (*To Frank*) This you gettin' evicted, yeh?

FRANK: Naw, this is not me gettin' evicted . . . shuttup.

BILLIE: What's the long face for . . . well?

FRANK: I wasnae aware I had a long face.

BILLIE: Any longer an' you could tuck it into your underpants . . . somebody die, yeh?

FRANK: Not yet but there's still time . . . give it a rest, will you?

BILLIE: There's definitely somethin' up, I can tell . . .

    (*There is another unintelligible interruption over the radio*)

BILLIE: (*on radio*) Naw, B an' Bs, Jolene . . . YMs, one-star hotels, flop-houses, over. (*To Frank*) Is it your kidneys, mebbe?

FRANK: Is what my kidneys?

BILLIE: Made you go that funny colour?

FRANK: What funny colour?

BILLIE: Like a peely-wally satsuma.

FRANK: Aw, yeh, thanks, that's cheered me up no end, that has. If you must know, I've just had myself tattooed . . . awright?

BILLIE: Tattooed?

FRANK: Yeh . . . tattooed!

BILLIE: What with, your name an' address in case you turn up lost again?

(*There is an incomprehensible message over the radio*)

BILLIE: (*on radio*) S'that includin' all the ones over the page, over.

(*There is a short response*)

BILLIE: (*on radio*) Naw, put your phone down . . . d'you want to try . . . lemme think . . . d'you want to try . . . ?

FRANK: They canna all be full up, surely to God?

BILLIE: (*on radio*) I'm puttin' you on hold, Jolene . . . (*To Frank*) Did you say somethin'?

FRANK: I said, there has to be one that has a vacancy, naw?

BILLIE: One what? (*On radio*) You still on hold, Jolene, over?

FRANK: One of the boardin' houses . . . s'that not what you were talkin' to her about?

BILLIE: Her?

(*Another short eruption over the radio*)

FRANK: Her on the walky-talky.

BILLIE: If it's any of your business, which I venture it isnae, 'her' on the walky-talky an' I happen to be discussin' the chances of comin' up with a coupla sidemen, at short notice, to help beef out the McPhail Sisters' lineup when me and Jolene . . .

FRANK: The McWho Sisters?

BILLIE: . . . when me an' Jolene go out on this mini-tour with Jim Bob O'May an . . .

FRANK: . . . The Wild Bunch! Yahoooooooo, that's it!

BILLIE: (*coldly*) Yahoo, that's what?

* * *

(*On the prison roof Dorwood is attempting to roll a cigarette in the cold and windy conditions. Tamara is shouting to him from the street below*)

DORWOOD: (*loudly*) C . . . I . . . double S . . . (*To himself*) damn an' bugger it. (*Loudly*) . . . I . . . E!

TAMARA: (*shouting*) D'you want me to give her a message?

DORWOOD: (*shouting*) What?

TAMARA: (*shouting*) Any message?

DORWOOD: (*loudly*) Naw, just tell her I want to see her . . . I don't trust these animals.

(*Tamara leans down to the car window*)

TAMARA: (*to engineer*) Did you manage to get that address, Brian?

DORWOOD: (*loudly from the roof*) Ask her to bring us two hunner Bensons an' somethin' to eat, the grub in here's diabolical!

TAMARA: What's he wittering on about now.

ENGINEER: They want to get a marksman out here an' pick the bugger off . . .

ENGINEER: I said, they want to get a police marksman out here . . .

DORWOOD: (*loudly*) There's my redundancy money off the rigs inside the Gene Autry wireless, tell her.

(*Tamara leans down to the car again*)

TAMARA: (*to engineer*) Something about Jean, is that what you got?

ENGINEER: He's just after tellin' us the wife's name was Cissie, what one we supposed to bring back, the wife or the fancy wumman?

DORWOOD: (*loudly*) I was savin' up to take her an' . . . I was savin' up to take us to Nashville, if she asks you.

* * *

(*Billie's taxi is parked outside Cissie's apartment block, the radio continues to give out incomprehensible messages. Billie is leaning against the cab, mike in hand*)

BILLIE: (*on radio*) Say again, over?

(*There is a burst of static in reply*)

BILLIE: (*on radio*) Naw, Jolene, forget about the B an' Bs, I'm back at the pick-up point with Rab Haw gettin' to grips with this other business, over.

(*Cissie and Frank are both slumped on the back seat in the darkened interior of the taxi. Cissie has a coat pulled over her nightclothes*)

CISSIE: Are you actually tellin' me this's what you chapped me up for?

BILLIE: (*on radio*) Naw . . . 'Haw' . . . as in 'Haw, you', over.

CISSIE: I've never heard anythin' more ridiculous in my life . . .

(*The static continues*)

FRANK: (*interrupting*) I told her you wanted to be billed under your maiden name.

BILLIE: (*on radio*) Hold on I'll ask . . .

CISSIE: You don't even know my maiden name . . . bloody cheek!

(*Billie's head appears through the window*)

BILLIE: (*interrupting, to Frank*) Jolene wants to know what outfits you've played bottleneck for an' how come her an' I's never
heard of any them?

CISSIE: Och, I'm away back to my bed . . .

   (*She climbs out of the taxi*)

FRANK: (*to Billie*) Just tell Jolene that Ry Cooder's got my home
number an' I've got his, okay?

   (*He clambers out of the taxi after Cissie*)

FRANK: (*to Cissie*) Hoi, come back here . . .

   (*Cissie stops to retrieve her slipper*)

BILLIE: (*on radio*) You there, Jolene, over?

   (*Frank catches up with Cissie*)

FRANK: It's not any more ludicrous than you askin' me to go
visit Cherokee Georgie Boy . . .

CISSIE: Yeh, it is.

FRANK: . . . you've done it before.

CISSIE: Scab off.

   (*Frank catches her by the arm*)

FRANK: Listen, I didn't go through hell gettin' this on my
arm just so I could wake up handcuffed to the bedpost
in some crummy roomin' house with Gordon Smart on my
conscience . . . stop actin' the . . .

CISSIE: Scab off, I said!

   (*She pulls away from him*)

FRANK: . . . stop actin' the prima donna! If you were serious
about helpin' you-know-who you wouldn't hesitate . . .

CISSIE: (*interrupting*) If your referrin' to Dorwood why don't
you . . .

   (*Frank clamps his free hand over Cissie's mouth*)

FRANK: (*sotto voce*) Shhhhhhhh, d'you want to blow it! If the
McWhat-d'-you-call-them Sisters get wind that joinin' their
band's just an excuse for a covert operation we'll get the bum's
rush . . . as far as they're aware, I'm a Chet Atkins[61] playalike
with an NUJ[62] card an' you're just some dumb outta-work
waitress that used to yodel a bit with the Tumblin' Driftwoods,
let's keep it like . . . ooooooow!

   (*He withdraws his hand from Cissie's mouth with a set of her
   teethmarks on it*)

CISSIE: Driftin' Tumbleweeds an' that was ten years back . . .
what makes you think I'm all that desperate to get back onstage
an' start apein' Tammy Wynette!

FRANK: You don't have to ape Tammy Wynette,[63] just doll
yourself up an' I'll cover for you . . . you want to get the dope
on Fraser Boyle an' clear Dorwood's name, don't you?

(*Cissie turns away*)

FRANK: Well, don't you?

CISSIE: Look there's somethin' I really ought to tell you . . .

FRANK: What? Naw, lemme guess . . . you're chicken, right?

(*Cissie turns to face Frank*)

CISSIE: What'd you say?

(*There is a short eruption over the radio*)

BILLIE: (*on radio*) . . . naw, I reckon she would be hunky-dory, it's wur slide-guitar picker I'm still a bit dubious about . . . he's only got the one . . .

FRANK: (*loudly*) Aaaahyah!

BILLIE: (*on radio*) . . . as you were, Jolene . . . lemme check if he doubles on mouth harp, over.

* * *

(*Tracey is peering curiously through the Bar-L men's room door*)

TRACEY: (*to occupants*) . . . it's awright, I'm just lookin' . . .

(*She withdraws her head and closes the door*)

TRACEY: . . . aw, my God . . .

(*Shirley passes on her way to the kitchen*)

SHIRLEY: Don't tell me, they've left the joint a shambles?

TRACEY: Have a gander.

(*She holds the door open again. Shirley hesitantly steps forward to have a peek*)

SHIRLEY: (*to occupants*) It's awright, I'm just look . . . aw, my God . . . The big guy's gonna do his nut!

* * *

(*A grimy Mercedes, with a bashed-in front fender, pulls up outside Bruno's barber shop and stops behind David Cole's car. Three men get out. The driver leans against the bonnet while his two companions, one limping and one, a short man called Tonto in a baggy check suit, go into the shop. Eric glances up from razor-stropping as the bell above the front door jangles. Jim Bob O'May and the Wild Bunch's version of 'It Keeps Right On A-Hurtin' plays over the radio. The limping man and the short man pull their balaclava masks down over their faces and the limping man eases himself down on to a bentwood chair, his gammy leg stuck out in front of him. David Cole, with hot towels covering his face, is unaware that anything untoward is going on. Eric carries on stropping. The short man rolls up his companion's right trouser leg. Strapped to the limping man's leg with broad strips of adhesive tape is a sawn-off shotgun. The short man starts to remove the tape, but the limping man*) *indicates that he will remove the rest of the tape himself. The short man crosses to the mirror and picks up a shaving mug and brush. Eric carries on stropping. The short man works up lather in the mug. The limping man, sawn-off shotgun in one hand, is trying to rid his other hand of the tiresome tape. The short man crosses the room and relieves the limping man of the unwanted tape, and is now lumbered with both shaving mug and tape. The limping man waves the shotgun at Eric. The short man crosses to Eric who relieves him of the tape. Eric slices at the tape with the razor. The tape promptly sticks to the razor and won't come off. The limping man now crosses to the Bush portable and turns the volume up)*

DAVID COLE: *(from under towels)* Hey, c'mon, what's with the loud music, man?

(The music carries on)

DAVID COLE:*(loudly)* Whatsamatter, you deaf or . . .

(There are sounds of a scuffle under the closing bars of the record. David Cole feels hands on his towels)

DAVID COLE: . . . git that thing outta ma face, what the hell you doin'?

RADIO DJ: . . . the Wild Bunch and 'It Keeps Right On A-Hurtin', and that comes with special birthday greetings for seven-year-old Trento Capaldi of Bishopbriggs who'll be nine this coming Friday . . .

(There is a deafening shotgun blast, and pink shaving foam splatters the radio)

RADIO DJ: . . . four pairs of fabulous Jim Bob tickets still up for grabs as we go back to the phone-lines . . .

* * *

(Billie's taxi is still parked outside Cissie's apartment block. The radio is now tuned to the Country music station)

RADIO DJ: *(over radio)* . . . who's on line one?

(Frank walks towards the taxi and opens the passenger door and climbs into the back seat)

RADIO DJ: Line 2? Anybody on line two? Okeydokey, we'll go to line three . . . are you there, line . . .

(Billie flicks the radio off)

BILLIE: Well, what's the verdict?

FRANK: Jury's still out.

BILLIE: Meter's still runnin'.

* * *

(Meanwhile the radio car is prowling the streets nearby with

Tamara and the radio engineer inside)

TAMARA: (*into carphone*) D'you want to read that back, Trish?

(*Tamara peers out of the car window at the passing houses*)

TAMARA: (*to engineer*) D'you remember what number he said?
(*into carphone*) That should be 'robbery' not 'rubbery', Trish.

ENGINEER: I don't know what you're botherin' for, bugger'll be
tucked up in his cell wi' the latest Hank Jansen[64] right now . . .

TAMARA: (*into carphone*) No . . . colon, dash, new para.

ENGINEER: . . . five years in the forces, that's what they want
to give these wastrels . . .

TAMARA: (*into carphone*) Right, thanks, Trish . . . get them to
send out a photographer . . . bye.

(*She replaces the phone*)

ENGINEER: . . . army sniper wi' an M16 would've saved us all
this trouble.

TAMARA: There it is . . . 'Campsie Quadrant'.

(*The carphone bleeps*)

ENGINEER: (*into carphone*) Meals On Wheels,[65] yes?

TAMARA: If you turn left just here, Brian . . .

ENGINEER: (*into carphone*) What d'you want?

TAMARA: . . . no, left . . . left. You've driven right past it.

ENGINEER: Forget it, you've got an appointment at the hairdresser's.

(*He hands the carphone to Tamara*)

TAMARA: Hairdresser's?

★ ★ ★

(*Billie and Frank are still sitting in her taxi outside Cissie's
apartment block*)

BILLIE: Right, you ready? This's your starter for ten . . .

(*She consults some notes on her lap. Frank sticks his head out of
the window as the radio car speeds past. He watches it disappear
down the street*)

BILLIE: . . . You're on your own, no conferring . . . who wrote
the 1955 Tennessee Ernie hit, 'Sixteen Tons'?

FRANK: I could be wrong, but was that not Tamara MacAskill?

BILLIE: Naw, Merle Travis . . . that's ten points to me. Who
wrote . . .

FRANK: It's me to go . . . Who wrote *Mein Kampf*?[66] Picture
clue . . . it's a book.

BILLIE: Er . . .

FRANK: Must hurry you . . .

BILLIE: Vangelis?[67]

FRANK: No, Hitler. Who wrote 'Oh Lonesome Me'?

BILLIE: Don Gibson![68]

FRANK: Naw, not that 'Oh Lonesome Me', the other one . . .
d'you give in?

BILLIE: (*indignantly*) There wasnae another one.

FRANK: 'Fraid there was, Shorty . . . George Stafford . . . came
ninth in the egg an' spoon at St Saviour's Sports . . . scratched
it on the back of Libo Ragazzo's neck, two verses an' a chorus. Big tall guy with no eyebrows . . . his old lady was a
beachcomber . . .

(*There is a rap at the steamed-up passenger window*)

FRANK: . . . wasnae a hit, mind you.

(*He slides the window down. Cissie stands there hugging herself
in the cold*)

FRANK: (*to Cissie*) Yes?

CISSIE: We need to talk.

FRANK: I'm right in the middle of a quiz.

CISSIE: We need to talk now.

(*Frank looks at Billie*)

BILLIE: You heard.

(*Frank climbs out of the taxi*)

FRANK: So talk.

CISSIE: Not here . . .

(*She takes his arm and leads him off along the street*)

CISSIE: . . . you know when you were in the bathroom?

FRANK: Throwin' up, yeh?

CISSIE: Please . . .

FRANK: I forgot to screw the top back on the Listerine[69] bottle.

CISSIE: This's serious!

FRANK: Ow!

CISSIE: D'you remember that Gene Autry wireless . . . ?

FRANK: Do I remember that Gene Autry wireless what . . .
profile . . . documentary . . . request show . . . what?

CISSIE: (*interrupting*) We've got a Gene Autrey[70] wireless . . .
radio . . . bakelite . . . about this size . . . 1949 . . . Dorwood
bought it off one of the roustabouts up in Aberdeen for
eighty-seven quid.

FRANK: S'that a bargain, yeh? I mean, I don't know about these
things.

CISSIE: I'm not talkin' about whether it was a bargain or not,
I'm talkin' about what was inside the bloody thing!

FRANK: You mean, like valves an' stuff. (*Shakes head*) You don't
mean like valves . . .

CISSIE: Eighteen thousand quid, I've just counted it.

FRANK: An' it cost how much, eighty-seven? Sounds like a

bargain to me, Crouch.

CISSIE: You know what this means, don't you?

FRANK: Er . . . (*Ponders*) Christ, this's worse than *University Challenge*[71] . . . lemme think, lemme think . . .

CISSIE: Somebody hid it there, ya dummy!

FRANK: Ah, right, I'm with you now . . . the roustabout was usin' it as a piggy bank an' you've mislaid his address so you cannae . . . ow! Chuck punchin' us!

BILLIE: (*shouting out of taxi window*) Okay, what's the score . . . I've got Jolene screamin' over the radio at us . . . you doin' it or you not doin' it?

* * *

(*Fraser Boyle is still pacing around the tattoo parlour, waiting while Cherokee George listens into the telephone*)

CHEROKEE GEORGE: Better have some ready cash on you, this boy doesnae take cards or nothin' either . . .

(*Boyle puffs on a cigarette*)

BOYLE: (*irritably*) I've got ma fish money . . . get on with it!

CHEROKEE GEORGE: . . . six, did you say?

(*He turns his head to address Boyle, his blackened eye shining*)

CHEROKEE GEORGE: (*on phone*) Aye, hullo, Indian Love Call here . . . I've got a client that's severely in need of a six-pack urgent . . .

BOYLE: An' it better no' be cut with nothin' or you're for it.

CHEROKEE GEORGE: (*on phone*) Where d'you want him to make the drop? No' here, I've got the coalman comin' . . .

BOYLE: Ask him to meet up with us at . . .

CHEROKEE GEORGE: What about the Cactus Club? He knows where that is . . .

BOYLE: Aye, an' so does every narc in the city . . . tell him to make it the Bar-L.

CHEROKEE GEORGE: That no' a bit tactless? Boy just got paroled last Wednesday there . . .

BOYLE: No' the Bar-L, ya clown . . . the noo pianna bar in the old ice-cream works . . . I'll be there in twenty minutes, tell him.

(*He moves towards the door*)

CHEROKEE GEORGE: (*on phone*) Hullo, you still there, Tonto?

* * *

(*Fraser Boyle appears in the doorway of the tattoo shop. A large sheet of crumpled cardboard covers the broken glass panel which Boyle kicked in. Boyle shivers, turns up his jacket collar, sticks*

*his hands into his jacket pockets and hurries off to where the fish
van is parked. A few moments later, Cherokee George appears.
He looks up and down the street*)

CHEROKEE GEORGE: (*to himself*) Aw, brilliant . . . how they
supposed to recognise wan another?

(*He has another look up and down the street before going back
inside the parlour and slamming the door. A few moments later,
he reappears. He checks busted door panel*)

CHEROKEE GEORGE: An' I'm doin' this guy a favour?

(*He shakes his head in incomprehension*)

★ ★ ★

(*Cissie is slumped on the floor of her apartment in front of the
empty fireplace, her eyes glued to the TV with the sound turned
down. On the screen Dorwood, Dwane, and Fraser Boyle play
and mouth the words to 'Your Cheatin' Heart'. At the end of
the song Dorwood slips off his Dobro, hands it to Boyle, and
crosses to talk to Jonathan Ross[72] on The Last Resort set. The
doorbell rings. Cissie continues watching TV. The doorbell rings
again*)

NEIGHBOUR: (*from landing*) Are you there, Mrs Crouch?

(*Cissie struggles to her feet, crosses to the living-room door, and
closes it. The doorbell rings again*)

NEIGHBOUR: (*from landing*) Mrs Crouch?

(*Cissie hits the rewind button on her video commando, spools
back, and turns up the volume on the Deadwood Playboys' 'Your
Cheatin' Heart'*)

★ ★ ★

(*On the Barlinnie Prison rooftop Dorwood stares intently at a
snapshot of a child. He runs his thumb across the photo. He sits
crouched against a chimney stack with the distant 'whoop-whoop'
of police cars in the air around him*)

★ ★ ★

(*In a street nearby the Tall Cowpoke, Drew and Roxanne are
driving in their 'covered wagon' as police cars and an ambulance,
blue lights flashing, rush past them in the opposite direction*)

TALL COWPOKE: 'Much d'you want tae wager that's some
stupit wean goat its heid stuck in the palin's?

★ ★ ★

(*Fraser Boyle's fish van pulls up short outside the Bar-L Piano
Bar, Boyle jumps out and clamps a pair of wraparound shades*

to his face despite the darkness. Inside, Spencer the barman is preparing a cocktail. Shirley and Tracey rush to and fro with orders)

TRACEY: *(to Shirley, en passant)* Some long haircut the big guy's gettin', is it not?

(Fraser Boyle enters from the street and crosses to the bar)

BOYLE: *(en route, to Tracey)* Ho, do us a favour, Gorgeous, there's somebody gonnae be lookin' for us . . .

TRACEY: You're not kiddin' . . . do yourself a favour an' beat it before he gets here . . .

(She moves on to serve at a banquette)

TRACEY: *(to diners)* Who'd the Gumbo?

(Boyle carries on to the bar)

BOYLE: *(to Shirley)* Ho, do us a favour, Gorgeous, there's somebody gonnae be lookin' for us only I'm no' too sure they know . . .

SHIRLEY: *(interrupting)* You said it, bub . . . I'd make myself scarce, if I was you . . . he'll be here any minute. *(To Spencer)* Two club sodas, one tequila.

BOYLE: *(to himself)* What is this? *(To Spencer)* 'Scuse me, pal, there's somebody gonnae be lookin' for us only I'm no' too sure they know who I'm are . . .

SPENCER: Aw, I'm pretty positive they do . . . don't worry, I'll bring you some grapes.

BOYLE: *(to himself)* Call it paranoia but there's somethin' funny goin' on here . . .

(Shirley moves off with some drinks and Tracey passes the bar on her way to the kitchen)

TRACEY: *(to Boyle)* You still here . . . God, you're no' feart.

BOYLE: *(to Spencer)* Have you had a call from a dozy half-breed, by any chance?

SPENCER: *(loudly)* Shirley . . . have we had a call from a dozy half-breed?

BOYLE: Soon as I've been to the toilet somebody's for a doin' . . .

(He heads off towards the men's room)

* * *

(The street outside Bruno's Late Nite Barber Shop is cordoned off with uniformed police officers stationed outside the scene of the crime. Plain-clothes men are dusting a big American car for prints, while others are ferrying plastic bags from the shop to a police van. Tamara MacAskill is filing her radio report)

TAMARA: ... The man leading the murder inquiry, Chief Inspector Docherty of Strathclyde Regional Crime Squad, did make a brief statement to reporters a few minutes ago but declined to name the victim of this brutal and apparently motiveless crime ...

(*Tamara stands, mike in hand, a few yards from the radio car. Behind her, two ambulance men carry a bodybag to the waiting ambulance*)

TAMARA: ... I have with me, however, an eye-witness, Mr ...

ERIC: ... Eric.

TAMARA: ... Eric Tierney ... Tell me, Eric ...

(*Eric leans into the mike*)

ERIC: I never seen nothin'.

TAMARA: ... I believe you were actually on the premises when the two men ...

ERIC: (*interrupting*) I never seen nothin' but I'd like to say hullo to my elderly mother in ward ten at Stobhill Hospital ...

POLICE SERGEANT: (*approaches, gesticulating*) Haw, you ... bawheid ... get you back in this vehicle!

TAMARA: (*to Eric*) ... you did say, did you not, that one of the killers had what you describe as a 'Fats Domino-type' accent, is that correct?

ERIC: Naw, hen, that was the big fulla that got his face blew off his heid ...

(*He leans close to the mike again*)

ERIC: ... if you're listenin' to this on your headphones, Ma, I want you to know that I'm awright an' that George and Tommy'll be up on Thursday wi' your gift tokens ...

(*The police sergeant appears at Tamara's side*)

POLICE SERGEANT: Right, miss, you an' the crew back into the motor an' bugger off ... c'mon, shift yourself!

(*He starts hustling her towards the radio car*)

TAMARA: (*into mike*) I am now being forced backwards towards the radio car but not before I've had a chance to ask Mr Tierney if ...

ERIC: (*loudly*) I never seen nothin'.

POLICE SERGEANT: (*to Eric*) Get you into that van an' keep your mouth shut or you're for a sore face, m'boy.

TAMARA: (*loudly*) ... Tamara MacAskill, for Radio Kelvin's *Crime Beat* ... Tobago Street. (*Off-mike*) Stop pushing, ya big shite!

* * *

(*The radio is on inside Billie's taxi*)

RADIO DJ: And we'll be rejoining *Evening Echo* reporter, Tammy MacAskill, later in the show for more news on that sensational barber shop slaying . . .

    (*Frank reclines in the back seat of the taxi, his eyes closed*)

RADIO DJ: . . . five minutes to the top of the hour on the Dunky Chisholm show . . . two pairs of buckshee Wild Bunch tickets still on offer after this one from The Deadwood Playboys . . .

    (*The opening chords of* 'Lovesick Blues' *come crashing in over the airwaves*)

FRANK: (*opening eyes*) That is all I need . . . (*To Billie*) . . . gonnae turn that off?

    (*Billie turns the volume up*)

FRANK: Not up . . . off!

BILLIE: (*over shoulder*) Whereabouts are we headed? You never said.

FRANK: (*above song*) I thought Jolene was lookin' up her Yella Pages?

BILLIE: I cannae hear you.

FRANK: (*loudly*) Yella Pages!

BILLIE: Naw, that was Creedence Clearwater, d'you want to give us a shout when we get there?

FRANK: Get where?

* * *

    (*Tonto, a short, thickset individual in a baggy suit, enters the Bar-L from the street. His eyes sweep the banquettes. Tracey is leaning against the bar waiting for Spencer to prepare a drinks order. Tonto crosses and perches on the stool next to her*)

TONTO: (*to Spencer*) Gless a wine, Butch.

    (*He takes a loose cigarette from his top pocket, sticks it in his mouth, and strikes a match against the bar counter*)

TRACEY: D'you mind?

    (*Tonto pats his jacket pockets*)

TONTO: Sorry, darlin', that's ma last wan . . . I'll keep you ma dowt.

    (*Tracey turns away in disgust*)

TONTO: Ho, dae us a favour. I'm supposed tae be meetin' somebody only I'm no' too sure if I know whit they luk like . . .

    (*He casts his eyes around*)

TRACEY: I wouldnae worry about it, if they've caught sight of you first, chances are they've legged it awready.

    (*She takes her tray of drinks and moves off*)

TONTO: Eh?

SPENCER: Red or white?

TONTO: Rid ur white whit?

SPENCER: I can let you have a nice Chardonnay at two seventy-five.

TONTO: Naw, jist the wine, Jim . . . in a tumbler . . . fur drinkin', yeh?

(*Shirley crosses over to the bar*)

SHIRLEY: Would you care for a glance at tonight's Specials?

(*She hands Tonto a menu*)

SHIRLEY: There's a Vegetarian Ragout set in a Guacamole Cassis on the back at seven fifty or you might prefer the Crab and Kiwi Junket with continental leaves at six twenty-five?

TONTO: No' got any squerr crisps, naw?

SHIRLEY: Excuse me . . .

(*Two uniformed police officers enter the bar from the street. Fraser Boyle emerges from the men's room, wraparound shades in one hand, his other covering his eyes. He glances up and spots Shirley crossing to speak to the police officers*)

BOYLE: Oh oh.

(*He clamps his shades back on and disappears back into the men's room. As the two police officers cross to the bar, Tonto slides off his stool, slips on his Ray-bans and casually sidles towards the street exit. As soon as he reaches the street he hurries off towards a dark alleyway by the side of the building. Tonto enters the alleyway and hastens down it, glancing backwards towards the street. Just ahead of him a pair of highly-ornamented cowboy boots appear at a small ground floor window. Suddenly Fraser Boyle drops from the window in front of Tonto who crashes into him*)

BOYLE: Ho, ya . . . !

TONTO: Sorry, pal, never seen you there . . . you awright?

(*He checks to see that Boyle is physically intact*)

BOYLE: Aye, I'm fine, I'm fine . . . chuck pawin' at us.

(*Boyle draws away and fingers his jacket lapels, turning the collar up*)

TONTO: S'long as yur awright . . . nice jaikit . . .

(*He turns and hurries off. Boyle dusts himself off and starts walking in the opposite direction, towards the street. After a few paces he stops*)

BOYLE: (*to himself*) Aw, naw . . .

(*He pats his hands up and down his jacket, then he slips his hand inside*)

BOYLE: (*loudly*) Ho, come back here, ya durty vermin!

(*He turns round and sets off at a gallop along the now deserted alleyway*)

* * *

(*Cissie is kneeling in front of her fireplace, her face illuminated by flickering flames. She has rigged up the Gene Autry wireless to run off the mains and the McPhail Sisters' version of 'These Two Empty Arms' is playing through it. As she listens Cissie is feeding the small blaze in the fireplace with twenty pound notes, of which there is a dwindling pile on the hearthrug. 'The Last Resort' video is running on the TV set at fast forward, again with the sound turned down. The telephone dangles at end of its cord. The front doorbell rings, while Billie and Jolene's voices blend in bitter-sweet harmony. Cissie continues to feed bank notes on to the flames. The front doorbell rings again*)

RADIO DJ: (*as record fades*) . . . The McPhail Sisters, Billie and Jolene, disappearing down *The Old Chisholm Trail* with that track from the Radio Kelvin compilation CD, *Country Comes to Calton* . . . Dunky Chisholm with you for the next three and a half hours . . . exactly 10.30 by my trusty Tom Mix[73] timepiece, the latest news headlines from Ward Ferguson . . .

(*There is a news jingle on the radio*)

RADIO NEWS READER: Radio Kelvin News at 10.37 . . .

(*There is a prolonged knocking at Cissie's front door*)

RADIO NEWS READER: . . . Strathclyde Police issued a description tonight of the two men wanted in connection with the brutal murder of . . .

(*The banging gets heavier*)

RADIO NEWS READER: . . . in a City Centre barber shop.

CISSIE: (*loudly*) If that's who I think it is, I'm not in!

RADIO NEWS READER: The men . . . one in his early-to-mid thirties, the other with a limp . . . are said to be armed and extremely dangerous . . .

POLICEMAN (*from landing*) Police, open up!

CISSIE: Bloody hell . . .

(*She scoops up the remainder of the bank notes and piles them on to the fire*)

RADIO NEWS READER: . . . on a somewhat lighter note, the roof top protest at a Glasgow jail has now . . .

(*Cissie reaches across and pulls the plug from the wall socket. On the landing outside a policeman and a policewoman are standing with Cissie's elderly neighbour from upstairs*)

POLICEWOMAN: (*into personal radio*) Naw, still no joy, Chief.

NEIGHBOUR: D'you want a hatchet to break the door down?

(*The policewoman leans down to the letter box*)

POLICEWOMAN: (*loudly*) If you're in there, love, will you . . .

(*The door swings open suddenly*)

CISSIE: (*coldly*) Yes!

POLICEWOMAN: Mrs Crouch?

NEIGHBOUR: Aye, that's her awright.

CISSIE: (*to neighbour*) Drop dead, ya old nuisance.

POLICEWOMAN: It was just to let you know your husband's fine.

NEIGHBOUR: She's had one of her fancy men in there . . . tarted up to the nines . . .

CISSIE: (*interrupting. To policewoman*) Fine? What you talkin' about, he's 'fine'?

* * *

(*Tamara MacAskill is standing by the open door of the radio car, talking into the mike*)

TAMARA: (*into mike*) . . . the prison officer, 48-year-old Mr Donald Ritchie, sustained only minor facial injuries and a fractured pelvis when the 34-year-old rooftop demonstrator landed on top of him in the exercise yard below.

(*Looking up the prison wall above the radio car it is possible to see a trail of broken slates that marks the trail of Dorwood's downward progress*)

TAMARA: (*into mike*) Both men are reported to be reasonably comfortable in separate wards of the prison hospital this evening . . . Tamara MacAskill, Radio Kelvin News, Riddrie . . . (*To engineer*) . . . I wonder if the paper managed to get a shot of him coming off the roof . . . d'you want to give them a ring, Brian?

ENGINEER: (*on carphone*) Aye, here she is . . . hold on . . .

(*He hands the carphone out of the car window*)

ENGINEER: (*to Tamara*) . . . sounds like the boyfriend.

TAMARA: I don't have a boyfriend, I've got a husband. (*On carphone*) Hi . . . who's this?

FRANK: (*on phone*) . . . I don't need a hot water bottle or nothin', I'm quite prepared to rough it . . . hullo, Tamara?

* * *

(*Billie is sitting in her parked taxi, radio mike in hand*)

BILLIE: (*on radio*) . . . when, there the now, over?

(*There is a short bark over the radio*)

BILLIE: (*on radio*) You might've given us a shout an' I could've switched it on . . . what'd it sound like, over?

(*There is a long incomprehensible message over the radio*)

* * *

(*Frank is still in the phone box, he dials a number and gets the unobtainable tone. He replaces the receiver, but remains inside the phone box*)

* * *

(*Meanwhile Cissie stands at the window of her apartment and watches as a drizzling rain starts to fall*)

* * *

(*On the roof of Barlinnie prison a well-thumbed snapshot of a child flutters in the night breeze on the dark slates near a chimney stack*)

Monday

In the slowly lightening morning Billie's taxi is parked outside a scruffy two-storey building, on the ground floor of which is Ronnie's Radio Taxis. As the wintry sun struggles manfully to clear the rooftops, an elderly hobo shuffles along the icy pavement, dipping every so often to examine some item of interest in the gutter. There is the faint sound of music on the thin air.

The hobo pauses to rifle a litter bin. A stray cur wanders across the street to sniff at the trail of rubbish in the hobo's wake. As he shuffles abreast of the parked taxi, the hobo sees a discarded Lanliq bottle dully glinting in the feeble rays of the watery sun. He bends to investigate.

The passenger door of the taxi inches open and Frank McClusky's bleary features appear opposite the hobo's at the ground level. It is apparent that Frank has spent the night sleeping on the taxi floor. Frank looks at the bottle in the hobo's mitt.

FRANK: Naw, I'll stick with my usual, pops . . . pint of Head and Shoulders[74] an' a half-dozen rolls . . .

* * *

(*The rehearsal room above the taxi office is still and bare now, except for a mike stand in the middle of the floor and a 5-watt guitar amp in a battered black case*)

* * *

(*Across town, in stark comparison to the quietness of Ronnie's Radio Taxis, an ambulance with a police and prison van escort pulls up at the gates of the huge Victorian Glasgow City Hospital. The vehicles pull off through the gates following signs for the Neurology Unit*)

* * *

(*The rehearsal room is now in use again. Jolene idles across to the window as her fingers wander across the accordion keys*)

JOLENE: (*over music*) You didnae happen to catch the news on the radio last night, did you?

(*Billie is concentrating hard on perfecting her fingerwork on a somewhat convoluted guitar riff*)

JOLENE: Billie?

BILLIE: (*Preoccupied*) What?

JOLENE: You didnae happen to catch . . .

    (*Billie abandons her riff*)

BILLIE: Naw . . . an' nor did I happen to catch wur album track's first outing 'cos somebody never thought to get in touch . . .

    (*She carries on strumming while Jolene takes over the melody*)

BILLIE: . . . what you askin' for?

JOLENE: Naw, nothin', I was just curious.

    (*Jolene leans forward and peers through the icy window*)

JOLENE: Yeh, the roofs do look quite slippy . . .

BILLIE: The what?

JOLENE: . . . there's a wee auld guy just fell all his length on to a stray pooch out here.

BILLIE: On to a which?

    (*Jolene watches the dog struggle out from underneath the hobo, yelping. Frank emerges from the taxi in all the confusion, a pair of cowboy boots in his hand*)

FRANK: (*to stray cur*) Don't let him sit on you, son . . . take a bite out his bum . . .

    (*The dog looks at Frank, snarling viciously*)

FRANK: . . . ahyah, bugger!

    (*He hotfoots it across the pavement in stocking soles and heads for the taxi office as the stray cur rounds on him.*

    Upstairs, Jolene and Billie are still talking)

JOLENE: Okay, so we've got wurselves a geetar-picker, what about wur chantoose?

    (*They hear the sound of barking and door-slamming from downstairs*)

                   ★ ★ ★

    (*In the waiting room of the City Hospital there is a mixture of visitors and outpatients, all of them silent and sullen. A young man, with a shaven head, his face covered in defiant tattoos, chomps on gum, blowing intermittent bubbles and cracking them loudly. Next to him is an older woman with her husband and two young women. They're all watching Cissie, who paces to and fro in front of them, pulling on a cigarette*)

FIRST YOUNG WOMAN: (*loudly*) She's smokin'.

OLDER WOMAN: (*to Cissie*) This's supposed to be a hospital.

SECOND YOUNG WOMAN: What aboot hur? She's smokin'.

    (*She accepts a cigarette from her companion, as the older woman's husband takes a packet from his pocket*)

OLDER WOMAN: (*to husband*) Get you those away.

YOUNG MAN: Err she's smokin' . . .

> (*The young man takes a wad of gum from his mouth and hands it to the older woman*)

YOUNG MAN: . . . huv that.

> (*He takes a cigarette from the older woman's husband, breaks the tip off and sticks it in his mouth. There is a great plume of smoke as everyone lights up*)

OLDER WOMAN: (*sotto voce, to husband*) Just you wait till I get you home!

HUSBAND: (*between coughs*) Good Christ, wumman, it's the only pleasure I've goat . . .

> (*Tamara MacAskill's head appears round the waiting room door, as the husband has a coughing fit*)

TAMARA: Is there a Mrs Crouch here?

OLDER WOMAN: Hell bloody mend you!

> (*Cissie whips round*)

CISSIE: How is he?

TAMARA: I was just about to ask you the same thing . . .

> (*She enters the room and closes the door quietly behind her*)

TAMARA: *Evening Echo*, d'you mind having a word? I'm doing a follow-up story on Dorville.

CISSIE: Dor-wood.

TAMARA: Sorry?

> (*Tamara delves into her bag for a shorthand notebook*)

CISSIE: Dor-wood!

> (*Cissie starts pacing again, lighting a fresh cigarette from a dogend*)

TAMARA: I just need a couple of details from you . . .

> (*She flips the shorthand pad open*)

CISSIE: Yeh, like gettin' his name right . . . slope off.

TAMARA: I believe you were quite active on the Western music scene yourself at one time, is that true?

> (*All eyes swivel from Tamara to Cissie*)

CISSIE: Last night he's fine, this mornin' he's in for a brain scan . . .

> (*All eyes swivel from Cissie to Tamara*)

TAMARA: How long've you been married?

CISSIE: What the hell kind of a jail is it that lets them exercise on the bloody roof in this weather . . .

TAMARA: D'you have any kiddies?

CISSIE: . . . he's a deep-sea-diver, for God's sake!

TAMARA: Did it come as a bit of a shock to you when he got into the lower reaches of the charts earlier this year with . . .

CISSIE: (*interrupting*) I wish to God he still was instead of harin'

about the country with a bandana round his nut singin' Gene
Autry numbers with a bunch of deadbeats an' drug addicts . . .

TAMARA: Gene Autry . . . of course . . .

(*She writes in her notebook*)

CISSIE: . . . at least I knew where he was when he was trauchlin'
about the sea-bed in his . . .

TAMARA: (*interrupting*) . . . something about his 'redundancy
money'?

CISSIE: . . . what'd you say?

(*She stops dead and looks at Tamara. All eyes swivel to Tamara*)

TAMARA: Shouted down to the radio car, wanted you to fetch
him food and cigarettes . . . of course, Brian and I thought . . .

CISSIE: Aw, my God . . .

TAMARA: . . . are you all right? You're as white as a sheet.

CISSIE: Naw, I'm fine, I'm fine . . .

(*A nurse appears at the waiting room door*)

NURSE: Is there a Mrs Crouch here?

★ ★ ★

(*Frank is seated on the floor of the rehearsal room while Jolene
is trying to force a cowboy boot on to one of his feet*)

JOLENE: It's pretty obvious they've swole up durin' the
night . . .

FRANK: Don't be ridiculous, if they'd swole up durin' the night
I'd be able to get my feet into them this mornin' . . . ohyah . . .

BILLIE: So who we gonnae phone?

JOLENE: What about the wee cobbler's in Maryhill Road?

FRANK: Yeh, get him to send over a coupla gallons of thon
stretchy paint, this's murder . . .

(*Billie fixes them with a baleful look*)

BILLIE: To replace the beanpole.

FRANK AND JOLENE: (*together*) Aw . . .

★ ★ ★

(*Fraser Boyle presses his finger to the doorbell of Cissie's apartment, and keeps it there. He has a guitar case in his other hand.
The elderly neighbour passes the landing on her way upstairs.
She is wearing a slightly scabby fur coat over an overall and
slippers and is carrying a half-pint carton of milk*)

NEIGHBOUR: Tch, tch, tch, tch, tch, tch . . .

(*Boyle keeps his finger on the doorbell and watches the woman
disappear upstairs. The apartment door is suddenly thrown open
and Cissie appears. She is now dressed in a riding suit with a
long divided skirt*)

CISSIE: I told you awready, I don't want to talk to any report . . .

(*She breaks off on seeing who it is*)

CISSIE: (*to herself*) . . . aw, God.

BOYLE: Thought you werenae in . . .

(*He places a boot over the doorstep and leans against the doorframe*)

CISSIE: I've just this minute got back, what d'you want? I'm in a hurry.

(*She closes the door against Boyle's foot and peers through the remaining gap*)

BOYLE: I've brung the boy's Dobro.

CISSIE: You've what?

BOYLE: Brung his Dobro. S'a geetar wi' a resonator pan in the middle, d'you no' remember me tellin' you about it in the . . .

(*Cissie reaches out and takes hold of the guitar case*)

CISSIE: (*interrupting*) Yeh, fine, I'll see that he . . . (*Breaks off*) are you tryin' to be comical?

BOYLE: Naw, too quick, Gorgeous . . . that's what you say after I've asked you.

CISSIE: Asked me what?

BOYLE: If you can lend me some dough?

CISSIE: Are you tryin' to be comical?

BOYLE: See? That's what all your best double acts've got . . .

CISSIE: You know he fell off the roof, don't you?

BOYLE: (*interrupting*) . . . timin'. What?

CISSIE: Dorwood . . . he fell off the roof last night . . . it was on the news.

BOYLE: You're kiddin' . . .

(*He looks up the stairwell*)

CISSIE: Not this roof . . . D-Wing, he's in intensive care, I've just come back to get his rosary beads!

BOYLE: That bad? Jesus . . . look, I'll let you have it back, Friday . . .

CISSIE: Let me have what back Friday?

(*The elderly neighbour reappears from upstairs and passes across the landing*)

NEIGHBOUR: Tch, tch, tch, tch, tch, tch . . .

CISSIE: (*loudly*) He's only bringin' Dorwood's Dobro back!

BOYLE: (*loudly*) I'm only bringin' the boy's Dobro back . . . (*To Cissie*) . . . d'you want me to run after the auld bag an' give her a kickin'?

CISSIE: Beat it, ya louse.

(*She tries closing the door but the guitar case gets in the way*)

BOYLE: Heh, c'mon, sweetheart, I'm tryin' to be nice to you

while ma best buddy's in the jile, yeh?

(*He leans a hand against the door panel*)

CISSIE: The only time you ever try to be 'nice' is when you're after somethin', an' right now your best buddy' isn't in the jail, he's in a locked ward at the City Hospital with a suspected cerebral haemorrhage!

BOYLE: What's that — nose bleeds, yeh?

CISSIE: If he dies you've had it . . .

BOYLE: Dies?

CISSIE: You've had it, anyhow . . . now, get!

(*She tries forcing the door shut*)

BOYLE: I wouldnae do that, Gorgeous . . . if there's one thing that drives me nuts it's . . .

CISSIE: Bugger off!

BOYLE: . . . awright, awright, you're upset, I can see that . . . tell you what I'll do . . . save you gettin' this door rehung . . . I'll come inside an' you an I'll discuss how much you want to give us over a cuppa coffee, how's that?

(*He forces the door open and shoves his way past Cissie into the flat*)

CISSIE: Hoi, come back here, where the hell d'you think you're goin'?

* * *

(*Frank, one boot half-on, hirples towards the door of the rehearsal room*)

FRANK: (*to Billie*) I'm only goin' to wash my gizzard . . .

BILLIE: Don't you do a runner, d'you hear?

(*Frank pauses at the door, gives a quick glance down, looks across at Billie, then exits*)

JOLENE: (*shouts from downstairs*) You there, Billie?

(*Billie consults her song-list on the floor in front and carries on working out chords on the guitar*)

FRANK: (*shouts from outside door*) What one's the toilet?

JOLENE: (*shouts from downstairs*) Billie?

BILLIE: (*loudly*) How's wee Desmond fixed, can he do it?

JOLENE: (*still shouting*) I wasnae phonin' wee Desmond, I was phonin' the boy MacIndoo . . .

BILLIE: (*loudly*) Can the boy MacIndoo do it?

JOLENE: (*shouting, but tailing off*) I'm just about to phone wee Desmond.

(*Frank finds the drivers' toilet. It is a very basic affair with peeling walls and graffiti-covered doors. He opens one of the cubicle*) *doors and looks inside. He frowns)*

FRANK: Well, one thing's for sure . . . I'm certainly not doin' an Elvis down that one . . .

* * *

(Cissie's Gene Autry radio is on, 'Don't be Cruel' blaring from it)

BOYLE: *(sings along)* ' . . . if you don't come round, at least, please telephone . . . '

(In the kitchen Cissie removes a coffee mug from the oven, with the aid of a dish towel, and places it on a tray)

BOYLE: *(still singing)* ' . . . don't be cruel, to a heart that's true . . . '

(Boyle is perched on the arm of a chair, with the radio on his lap)

BOYLE: *(singing)* ' . . . don't want no other love . . . baby, it's still you . . . '

(He breaks off as Cissie enters with the red-hot mug on a tray)

BOYLE: . . . I remember the night me an' Dorwood bought this off the boy up in Oilsville . . .

CISSIE: Here . . . grab that.

(Boyle lays the radio aside and takes hold of the mug handle in his gloved hand)

BOYLE: . . . cheeky sod wanted two hunner bucks for it . . .

(He raises the scalding mug to within a half-inch of his lips)

BOYLE: . . . I goes like thon.

(He lowers the mug and gives his 'radio seller' look)

BOYLE: He goes like that, I goes . . .

(He raises the scalding mug to his lips again)

BOYLE: So, tell me, how's the boy?

(He lowers the mug without its having touched his lips)

CISSIE: On the critical list.

BOYLE: Not that 'boy', the boy, yeh?

(Boyle raises the scalding mug to his lips and is just about to drink . . .)

BOYLE: I don't see his pitcher up . . .

(He lowers the mug and looks around the bare walls)

BOYLE: . . . in fact, I don't see any pitchers up . . . this you doin' a moonlight?

(He gets up and crosses to some packing cases, mug in hand)

CISSIE: Come outta there.

BOYLE: I remember you used to have a big coloured-in snapshot of him in thon cowboy gear I bought for his Christmas.

(Boyle pokes around the tea-chests)

CISSIE: What cowboy gear? You bought him a baseball cap an' a pair of Johnny Sheffield swimmin' trunks that nearly drowned him . . .

(*Cissie gets up and goes over to Boyle and stuffs some crumpled notes into his top pocket*)

CISSIE: . . . there's twenty-seven quid there, drink up an' disappear.

(*Boyle lays aside the scalding mug without having set a lip to it and reaches for the crumpled notes in his top pocket*)

BOYLE: They werenae Johnny Sheffield swimmin' trunks, they were Johnny Mack Brown junior competition chaps, he would've grew into them . . .

(*He smooths the crumpled notes out*)

BOYLE: . . . you no' heard nothin', naw? Must be comin' up for startin' school . . . what's that, about a year?

CISSIE: Seven months. When're you leavin' so I can fumigate the place.

BOYLE: Seven months? No' long in goin' in, eh? Any luck an' he'll've forgot all about you . . . 'much did you say was here?

CISSIE: What d'you need it for? Thought you were makin' plenty off that fish . . . don't sit there countin' it!

BOYLE: (*interrupting*) . . . twenty-two, twenty-three, twenty-four . . . I make it twenty-five. Twenty-five quid isnae gonnae purchase what I'm after . . . naw, hold on, there's two stuck tegither . . . lemme start again . . . one . . . two . . . three . . . four . . .

CISSIE: Are you goin' to leave right now or do I have to get on that phone?

BOYLE: Who are you gonna phone, your Probation Officer?

(*He laughs*)

BOYLE: Seven, eight, nine . . .

CISSIE: I mean it!

BOYLE: . . . eleven, twelve, thirteen . . . what'd you get him for his burthday? November, innit? Or did you forget? Naw, naw, that's perfectly understandable . . . takes a good coupla years for the old brain cells to knit back into place after takin' that kind of a doin' . . . fourteen, fifteen . . . you still go to the meetin's yeh? Sixteen, seventeen . . .

CISSIE: I'm warnin' you . . .

(*Lena Martell's*[75] 'One Day at a Time' *is playing low on the radio*)

BOYLE: . . . ho, there's your theme tune.

(*He reaches out and turns the volume up*)

BOYLE: (*sings along*)' . . . show me the way, one day at a

time . . . '

CISSIE: Get that off.

BILLIE: S'up . . . no' makin' you thirsty, is it?

CISSIE: Get it off, I said!

(*She makes a breenge for the radio, but Boyle grabs a hold of her, laughing. Cissie attacks him with her fists*)

BOYLE: Ho, chuck that!

(*He grabs Cissie by the wrists*)

CISSIE: (*enraged*) Aaaaargh . . .

BOYLE: S'no' ma fault he got took into care . . .

CISSIE: . . . I'm gonnae kill you!

BOYLE: Aye, like hell you are . . . it's a blue do when a peace-lovin' guy cannae check up on his kid's welfare without some crazy doll . . .

CISSIE: (*interrupting*) Who said he was yours!

BOYLE: C'mon, Gorgeous, you werenae that drunk you cannae recall all they times when Dorwood was splashin' about in the deeps an' you an' me were . . .

(*He pulls Cissie close*)

CISSIE: You an' me were what! Quit maulin' us . . .

(*She struggles to get free*)

BOYLE: . . . used to be right friendly us guys . . . d'you no' remember?

(*He starts kissing Cissie's neck*)

CISSIE: You're forgettin', I'm an amnesiac . . . gerroffa me . . .

BOYLE: Lemme remind you . . .

(*He kisses her throat*)

CISSIE: . . . chuck that. (*Softening*) Chuck it, I said . . . naw, please, Fraser, don't . . . pl . . .

(*Boyle's mouth is on hers. Cissie continues to struggle during the long embrace but her struggles grow less until she melts*)

BOYLE: (*coming up for air*) . . . d'you remember now?

(*Cissie reaches down and unbuckles Boyle's belt. She unzips his jeans. Boyle's eyes roll, and shut*)

BOYLE: (*hoarsely*) She remembers . . . aw, God . . .

CISSIE: (*huskily*) d'you mind if I . . . ?

BOYLE: (*quickly*) . . . naw, naw . . . do it, do it . . .

CISSIE: You sure you want me to?

BOYLE: (*eyes shut*) . . . sure I'm sure, just hurry up an' . . .

(*Boyle's eyes burst open in horror*)

BOYLE: . . . waaaaaaaaaaaaaaaaaaaaagh!

(*Boyle clutches at his scalded crotch with both hands*)

CISSIE: One for the souvenir album, right!

BOYLE: Ya bitch!

(*Cissie chucks the now empty coffee mug at him, grabs the Dobro case and makes a beeline for the front door*)

* * *

(*Outside the Bar-L Tracey is fixing a hand-printed notice to the front door. It reads: 'WE ARE CLOSED NEAREST SOUL FOOD BAR "THE DIXIE CUP", 418 W12 ST. NYC.' Tracey goes back inside and crosses to the banquette where Shirley sits, in her street clothes, with the early edition of the* Evening Echo. *There is a head and shoulders picture of David Cole on the front page of the paper under a big headline which reads, 'Barber Shop Slaughter', with a smaller picture of barber Eric next to a sub-heading of 'Close Shave for Eric'*)

TRACEY: What'd Detroit say when you phoned? D'you tell them he got murdered?

SHIRLEY: They never said nothin' . . . just to pay off the kitchen staff, lock everythin' up, an' somebody from some lawyer's office, I didnae quite catch, would be along to pick up the keys . . . that could be any time. What'm I supposed to do, sit about here an' wait to get my head blown off?

TRACEY: That's what you get the extra one seventy-five a week for, Shirley. I'll get you a coffee.

(*Tracey crosses to the bar*)

SHIRLEY: What d'you reckon it is, some kinda vendetta? There's that Italian guy with the hair round the corner . . .

TRACEY: The fishburger franchise?

SHIRLEY: . . . he also does filled rolls. You don't know what gets into some people . . . I'm just readin' in here about a lassie that got both her ears bitten off at a dance in the City Chambers an' she's not even heard from the Polis . . . don't gimme any sugar, I want to get into they cream culottes I got for Wee Sandra's twenty-first on Thursday.

(*She flicks over another page in the newspaper*)

SHIRLEY: Aw, my God . . . hey, Tracey, look at this, who's that?
(*She holds the newspaper up to show a picture of Dorwood, his head bandaged so that only the eyes show, under a headline which reads: 'SLIPPERY CUSTOMER FOR HIGH JUMP SAY DOCS'*)

TRACEY: The Invisible Man?

SHIRLEY: Naw, it's him . . . big thingmy's husband . . . accordin' to this he's at death's door.

* * *

(*Dorwood lies on a bed in his hospital room. Only his eyes show*

*in his bandaged head, and they are shut. There is a knock at
the closed door. The prison officer at Dorwood's bedside folds his
newspaper, gets up, and crosses to unlock the door. The prison
chaplain enters and walks across to the bed. He lays out his last
rites paraphernalia)*

★ ★ ★

*(In another part of town Cissie is trudging through the freez-
ing streets with Dorwood's Dobro. She eventually finds a phone
box, dumps the Dobro on the ground, and searches through her
pockets for some money)*

★ ★ ★

*(In Ronnie's Radio Taxis' office Jolene sits straddled on a chair
with her chin resting on her hands. She's chomping on some
gum. Billie stands in the entrance holding the door open)*

BILLIE: *(loudly)* Are you gonnae get a move on up there! *(To
Jolene)* Have you phoned to cancel yet?

JOLENE: I'm waitin' to hear back from wee Desmond . . .

BILLIE: I thought you spoke to him awreday an' he couldnae
do it?

JOLENE: I'm just after buyin' myself a new rigout.

BILLIE: What kinda answer's that? Are you gonnae hurry up!
(The telephone on the table rings)

JOLENE: I told him to get his mother to call . . . *(On phone)*
Ronnie's Radio Cabs, s'that you, Mrs Devaney?
*(Frank comes clomping down the stairs, one boot on, the other
still only half-on)*

FRANK: You don't happen to have a very long shoehorn, by any
chance?

BILLIE: Out.
(She jerks a thumb towards the street)

JOLENE: *(on phone)* Hold on . . . *(To Billie)* Will we accept a
transfer-charge call from a Glasgow telephone box?

FRANK: Or a half pound of margarine might do the trick . . .

BILLIE: *(to Jolene)* Is it for a taxi?

FRANK: Naw, it's for this stupit boot . . .

JOLENE: *(on phone)* Is it a taxi they're after?

BILLIE: *(to Frank)* Right you . . . adios.

JOLENE: *(to Billie)* Who d'we know cried . . . *(On phone)* what
was their name again?

★ ★ ★

(The prison chaplain anoints Dorwood's bandaged forehead.

Dorwood lies still in his bed)

CHAPLAIN: Through this holy anointing may the Lord in his love and mercy help you with the grace of the Holy Spirit.

PRISON OFFICER: Amen.

CHAPLAIN: Lord Jesus Christ, our Redeemer, cure the weakness of your servant, Dorwood . . . heal his sickness and forgive his sins. Expel all afflictions of mind and body, mercifully restore him to . . .

(There is a deep sigh from Dorwood and the prison chaplain leans his head down towards the bed)

CHAPLAIN: *(with renewed urgency)* . . . may you live in peace this day, may your home be with God in Zion, with Mary, the virgin Mother of God, with Joseph and all the angels and saints.

(He makes the sign of the cross over Dorwood)

PRISON OFFICER: Amen.

* * *

(Fraser Boyle comes hobbling painfully into the living-room of Cissie's apartment, sticking a wet flannel down the front of his jeans. He hobbles across to the phone and picks up the receiver. He rattles the rest up and down and listens. He takes the receiver away from his ear and glares at it)

BOYLE: Ya bitch . . .

(He picks up the handset, rips its cord from the wall, and smashes the lot into the fireplace. He takes a swing at the TV and boots the screen in)

BOYLE: . . . bitch!

* * *

(Billie's guitar is propped up against the wall of the taxi office, Jolene's accordion sits on the table. The phone is off the hook. Jolene, with a large pair of shears in her hand, is concentrating on cutting up two sets of old street maps, selecting the least tatty sections from each, and sellotaping the pieces together into one large, if slightly misleading, entity)

JOLENE: You never mentioned what outfits you played with . . .

(Frank sits on the stairs, still struggling in vain to get the remaining boot on)

FRANK: Naw?

JOLENE: We asked you several times but you kept goin' to the toilet.

FRANK: It was that brown lentil lasagne Shorty made for supper last night . . . if there's one thing . . .

JOLENE: *(interrupting)* That was Boston Bean Broulé an' it was me that made it . . .

FRANK: (*quickly*) Naw, naw, it was very . . . I might even write
a piece about it . . . in fact, I saved some on my shurt so I could
send it away an' have it analysed . . . look.

(*He displays a stain on his shirt front*)

JOLENE: You're askin' for a fat lip.

FRANK: Am I?

JOLENE: Chuck tryin' to be smart, I've had better patter off a
bumper sticker. Were they mostly all Country, yeh?

(*Frank has returned to his ongoing struggle with the recalcitrant
boot*)

FRANK: Were what mostly all . . . ?

JOLENE: Your outfits?

FRANK: Naw, this's just camouflage . . . I tend towards a Harris
tweed two-piece an' a brogue pump, myself . . . aw, sorry . . . bands we talkin' about? Country-ish, yeh . . . you ever
come across The Texas Chainsaw Trio? They had a bazooka
in their lineup . . .

JOLENE: A bazooki, you mean?

FRANK: Naw, a bazooka . . . they were heavily into martial
rock at the start . . . blew a big hole in the boy Henderson's
good cardigan at one of the university hops, his Maw had
a leary . . . that's when we swapped over to 'swamp music' . . . lead singer was the spittin' double of Jerry Reid . . .

(*He tugs at his boot*)

FRANK: . . . or was it Al Reid? I'm not too sure . . . you
wouldnae like to give us a hand with this, would you?

JOLENE: Here . . . why don't you just cut the legs off an' have
them as slip-ons?

(*Jolene holds out her shears*)

FRANK: That's an idea.

(*He goes to take the shears, but Jolene snatches them away*)

JOLENE: God, you would, as well . . . there must be four hunner
bucks' worth of boot there . . .

FRANK: You reckon?

JOLENE: . . . more like seven or eight hunner . . . I used to go
out with a guy an' he had a pair that were identical, only newer.

FRANK: They don't come any newer . . . any newer an' they're
still chewin' the cud.

JOLENE: He only ever wore them the once.

FRANK: I'm not surprised.

JOLENE: Took us to this pancake roadhouse in Faifley when I
passed my drivin' test . . . you ever been there?

FRANK: Only the once.

JOLENE: I'm not surprised . . . you couldnae tell what was the pancake an' what was the plate, they were identical.

FRANK: Mebbe you're meant to gnaw them, naw?

JOLENE: We tried that, you still couldnae tell.

FRANK: Naw, the boots . . . mebbe you're meant to gnaw them?

JOLENE: Gnaw them?

FRANK: Yeh, gnaw. Here . . . d'you fancy gnawin' that for us?
(*He holds the boot out to Jolene*)

FRANK: S'what your Eskimo does with his footwear of a mornin' . . . gets his old lady to gnaw it for him . . .

JOLENE: (*ignoring boot*) So what's with you an' the beanpole?

FRANK: . . . softens them up a treat . . .

JOLENE: Last time me an Billie bumped into her was ten years back . . .

FRANK: . . . feart yur fillin's'll fall out, yeh?

JOLENE: . . . where's she been hidin' all this time?

FRANK: S'far as I know she hasnae been hidin' . . .

JOLENE: Good friend of mine said she seen her up in Aberdeen last Christmas with a toddler in a go-chair . . . you an' her winchin', yeh?

FRANK: Naw . . . an' chuck referrin' to her as 'the beanpole', her right name's Cissie.

JOLENE: What's that short for . . . Cystitis?

FRANK: Now you're askin' for a fat lip.

JOLENE: Aw, yeh? Like who's gonnae gimme one . . . you?

FRANK: Could be.

JOLENE: Away you go, you couldnae hang a fat lip on a Hallowe'en cake if I gave you a pipin' bag fulla marzipan.

* * *

(*Boyle is in a phone box in the street near Cissie's apartment*)

BOYLE: (*on phone*) . . . naw . . . 'Winnie' like in 'pooh', an' 'bay-go', as in 'bay-go' . . . 'Winnie . . . bay-go' . . . what? Naw, that's the make of trailer they're in, the party's name is Jim Bob O'May . . . naw . . . Bob, capital O, apostrophe, M-a-y, as in 'Darling Buds of . . . ', they've got one of these portaphones, you must've number . . . he's no' got an address, that's what I'm sayin' . . . I've just looked, they're no' there . . . what d'you suppose I'm phonin' Directory Enquiries for? They've moved . . . what? 'Cos they got fed up gettin' parkin' tickets, how the hell should I . . . hullo?

(*He takes the receiver away from his ear and stares at it*)

BOYLE: Ya cheeky . . . !

* * *

*(Cissie has now arrived at the rehearsal room and sits with Frank
in one corner while Billie and Jolene sit in the other. Billie is tuning her guitar while Jolene straps her accordion on. Cissie bends
down to the guitar case on the floor, and springs the catches)*

FRANK: Boy, am I glad to see you, they were all for givin'
us the heave an' getting wee MacIndoo an' boy Desmond
in . . . what'd you say this was . . . a Dumbo?

CISSIE: Dobro . . . Dopyera Brothers, 1932 . . . it's got a resonator pan in the middle . . .

FRANK: Ah, yeh, right . . . *(To Billie and Jolene)* S'got a
resonator pan in the middle . . .

CISSIE: Dorwood only ever played it the once so watch it . . .
(She lifts the Dobro out of its case)

FRANK: C'mon, you're talkin' to the guy that inherited a
Skiffle-jo . . .

CISSIE: How's the arm?
(Frank takes the guitar from her)

FRANK: Naw, that's the neck . . . looks awright to me, s'not
warped or nothin' . . .
(He runs a thumb across the strings)

CISSIE: That arm.
(She gives Frank's tattoo a prod)

FRANK: Ohyah . . . sore . . . kept me up all night . . .
(He slips the Dobro around his neck)

FRANK: . . . that an' the brown lentil lasagne . . . so, what made
you change your mind? Not that I'm not grateful. I thought
I was never gonnae see you again . . . wasnae anythin' to do
with . . .
(He footers with the tuning pegs)

FRANK: . . . your discoverin' somethin'?

CISSIE: Yeh, I discovered where that eighteen grand came
from . . .

FRANK: Naw, I meant somethin' to do with you an' me.

CISSIE: *(interrupting)* . . . an' how much I loathe that crummy
slug.

FRANK: . . . okay, so it's a banal scenario . . . boy meets
girl . . . boy falls head over heels . . . boy gets head punched
in . . . boy gets tattoo . . .

CISSIE: Give us a coupla quid, will you?

FRANK: . . . boy parts with all his dosh . . .
(Frank produces a single one pound note)

CISSIE: That's just eighteen fifty you owe me.
(She pockets the pound note)

FRANK: . . . tell me about this toddler.

CISSIE: (*sharply*) What toddler?

BILLIE: You ready, you pair?

(*She and Jolene make their way to the mike*)

FRANK: I'm ready . . . what d'you want to kick off with . . . 'Billy Goat Gruff'?

(*Billie and Jolene freeze in their tracks*)

FRANK: It's about the only cowboy number I know all the verses to . . .

★ ★ ★

(*Fraser Boyle's fish van lurches to a halt outside Timberwolf Tierney's — aka The Tall Cowpoke's — DIY store in Cowcaddens.*[76] *Boyle climbs gingerly out, a lumpy newspaper-wrapped parcel under his arm. He hobbles painfully across the pavement. Inside the store Roxanne is serving a customer*)

ROXANNE: Is it furra boudoir? (*Loudly*) We goat any they 'easy-assemble' wardrops in stock? Thur's a customer oot here luckin' fur a tallboy. (*To customer*) Jist the wan, aye?

(*Boyle shoves the door open and hobbles in*)

ROXANNE: (*loudly*) Jist the wan. (*Greeting Boyle*) Well, how-dy, stranger . . . huvnae saw you since the hot-dog stall at the Cowdenbeath Rodeo . . . this you hud yur vasectomy? (*Loudly*) Ye there, Timber?

(*In the backshop Drew and the Tall Cowpoke are sitting with their feet up enjoying a late lunch. Drew is poring over a crossword on the 'Fun Page' of the early edition of the* Evening Echo)

DREW: (*reads*) 'Seven across . . . "Asbestos underpants no an-swer to Jerry Lee's outsize spherical blazers?" . . . five, five, two, an' four . . . '

(*Boyle hobbles through into the backshop clutching his parcel*)

DREW: (*musing*) . . . 'Asbestos underpants no answer to . . . '

TALL COWPOKE: (*to Boyle*) Ye want some coffee? Still hoat . . .

(*He pours himself a cup. Boyle dumps the parcel on the table and unwraps it*)

DREW: (*musing*) ' . . . Outsize spherical blazers?'

BOYLE: 'Much?

(*The Tall Cowpoke eyes Cissie's Gene Autry radio*)

TALL COWPOKE: Whit is it, a cigarette boax?

(*Boyle plugs the radio into a socket*)

DREW: (*musing*) ' . . . Asbestos underpants?'

(*The radio stutters into life playing the Wild Bunch Fiddlers' version of Jerry Lee's 'Great Balls of Fire'*)

TALL COWPOKE: Aah . . . s'a musical cigarette boax . . .

BOYLE: S'a Gene Autry wireless, ya mug.

(*Boyle switches the radio off as Roxanne enters the backshop*)

ROXANNE: D'ye no' hear me shoutin'?

(*The Tall Cowpoke examines the radio*)

TALL COWPOKE: Where d'ye pit the fags, in the back?

ROXANNE: (*to Drew*) Away oot an' ask that customer is it aw wan if it's a 'vanitry' unit? I cannae see any wardrops . . .

TALL COWPOKE: (*to Boyle*) Tenner suit ye?

(*He pulls a wad of bills, receipts, banknotes, and invoices from his dungaree pockets*)

BOYLE: That's worth at least a hunner, ya doughball . . . if she hadnae took the Dobro I wouldnae've came here.

ROXANNE: (*to Drew*) They come in rid, off-white, an' olive, tell him.

(*Drew chucks his newspaper aside and slouches out to the front shop, stuffing a fried egg roll into his face*)

BOYLE: Make it fifteen.

TALL COWPOKE: I huvnae goat fifteen . . .

ROXANNE: (*loudly, to Drew*) Thur's wan olive left . . .

(*The Tall Cowpoke sifts through the litter from his pockets*)

TALL COWPOKE: . . . two fives . . . three wans . . . four two bob bits . . .

ROXANNE: (*loudly to Drew*) . . . naw I tell a lie, it's avo-cadda . . .

TALL COWPOKE: . . . an' them's yur invoices.

BOYLE: What invoices?

TALL COWPOKE: I'm gonnae huv a joab gettin' squerred up offa cadaiver, umn't I?

(*Boyle runs an eye down the invoices*)

BOYLE: (*reads*) 'Seventeen hinges . . . five pund of screw-nails . . . '?

TALL COWPOKE: D'ye want tae dae a cheque?

(*He slides Drew's ballpoint pen across the table to Boyle*)

BOYLE: I've awready done a check . . . last night . . . couldnae believe ma . . . 'cadaiver', what 'cadaiver'?

TALL COWPOKE: Yankee boy . . . goat hissel offed at the herrdresser's . . .

(*He picks up the* Echo *and folds it to the front page*)

BOYLE: Got hissel' what?

ROXANNE: (*loudly, to Drew*) . . . unless he wants tae go fur the beej, which I personally think luks clatty.

(*Boyle snatches the paper from the Tall Cowpoke's hand*)

BOYLE: . . . Holy Christ.

* * *

(Shirley is seated at one of the Bar-L banquettes, a plug-in phone to her ear, and a pen poised over the 'Sits Vac' page of the Evening Echo. A long list of vacancies has been scored through in felt-tip)

SHIRLEY: *(on phone)* . . . yeh, I've eaten there myself, I must say it was very nice . . . would you like me to bring along my diploma from Hamburger University?

(There is a rattle at the Bar-L front door)

SHIRLEY: *(on phone)* No, this was the three-day residential course in microwave technology and personal hygiene . . .

(The front door rattles again)

SHIRLEY: *(on phone)* . . . no, hygiene . . .

(The rattle gets more insistent)

SHIRLEY: *(on phone)* . . . sure, no problem . . . see you then, then . . . thanks, bye.

(She replaces the receiver and circles the Pancake Roadhouse vacancy. The front door rattles violently)

SHIRLEY: *(loudly)* Yeh, awright, I'm comin'.

(She gathers up a bunch of keys. She sees a shadowy figure fuzzily visible on the other side of frosted-glass deco door. She sticks the key in the lock, makes a half-turn, and hesitates)

SHIRLEY: *(to herself)* Yeh, that's right, get your stupit head blown off. *(Aloud)* We're shut. Who is it?

* * *

(Inside the taxi office Billie stands by the front door, straining her eyes in the gathering dusk. Frank and Jolene sprawl in their chairs)

FRANK: . . . Doris Day, your bahookey.

JOLENE: It was so Doris Day . . . *(To Billie)* Who sang 'Windy City' on the *Perry Como Hogmanay Special* in 1958.

BILLIE: *(looking out of the door)* If she's not off this next bus that's it . . .

FRANK: *(to Jolene)* D'you give in?

JOLENE: If this's another one of your trick questions you're gettin' that boot rammed down your gullet . . .

BILLIE: *(turning)* I don't know if you realise, Jolene, but we're in serious trouble here . . .

JOLENE: Naw, we're not, we'll catch up . . . *(To Frank)* Right, this's for twenty points . . . what famous Country singer . . .

FRANK: *(interrupting)* You havenae answered the previous question . . .

BILLIE: *(interrupting)* I'm not talkin' about your stupit game! I'm talkin' about the beanpole!

FRANK: Chuck callin' her that, I've awready chastised her for . . .

BILLIE: Shuttup!

(*Billie paces the length of the room and stands with her hands against the wall, looking at the floor*)

JOLENE: (*sotto voce, to Frank*) What famous Country singer appeared in the John Ford movie, *My Darling Clem* . . .

FRANK: (*interrupting*) Roy Acuff!

BILLIE: Shuttup, I said!

* * *

(*Ralph Henderson, of Melon, Brolly and Henderson, solicitors, stands inside the Bar-L Piano Bar and Grill and casts his eyes upwards to the art deco detail around him*)

SHIRLEY: . . . Tracey an I's wiped the surfaces an' turfed all the perishables out the back for the bin motor, Mr . . . ?

(*Shirley, dressed for going home, pulls on her gloves*)

SHIRLEY: . . . sorry, I didn't catch your name through the glass.

HENDERSON: Henderson . . . Ralph (*Pronouncing it 'Raif'*), Melon, Brolly and Henderson . . . Jamaica Street.

(*He passes a business-card to Shirley*)

HENDERSON: Tell me something.

SHIRLEY: . . . Shirley.

HENDERSON: . . . is that a pokey hat?

(*Shirley's hand instinctively goes to her head*)

SHIRLEY: Naw, it's a beret.

HENDERSON: No . . . up there.

SHIRLEY: Where?

(*She follows Henderson's gaze upwards*)

SHIRLEY: Aw, yeh . . . so it is.

(*She and Henderson ponder the frieze for some moments*)

HENDERSON: Don't let me keep you.

SHIRLEY: Naw, right. If you ever find yourself footloose in Faifley an' feel like a pancake, give us a phone . . .

(*She moves towards the door*)

SHIRLEY: . . . I've left wur uniforms folded inside the Blüthner . . . bye.

(*She goes out into the street. Moments later Tonto enters the bar*)

TONTO: Thought that gabby doll wis never gonnae go . . . where d'you want us to start?

* * *

(*In a corridor of the Glasgow City Hospital Cissie is standing in front of a grim-faced nurse)*

CISSIE: What d'you mean I'm too late? I'd to come on the bus, I've brought his bedsocks an' his rosary beads . . .

NURSE: I am awful sorry, Mrs Crouch.

(Cissie pushes a hospital room door open and stares at an empty bed, its sheets thrown back)

CISSIE: Sorry? What you tellin' me sorry!

* * *

(Jim Bob's Winnebago is parked in the darkness outside the Ponderosa club in Wishaw. Jim Bob and his band The Wild Bunch are onstage inside the club for a soundcheck. Jim himself is in a crumpled linen suit. He leans into his mike and delivers the words of Hank Williams' lament 'Your Cheatin' Heart' with an off-handed conviction)

* * *

(Billie is driving the taxi on the road to Wishaw. Frank and Jolene are crammed into the back seat with all sorts of clothing and equipment)

BILLIE: . . . Naw, *you*'re gonnae have to explain.

FRANK: Me? Why me?

BILLIE: *(over shoulder)* 'Cos it was you that got us into this mess!

FRANK: S'not my fault she vanished off the face of the earth.

BILLIE: It was you that gave her the quid!

JOLENE: I told you we shoulda hung on till Mrs Devaney phoned.

BILLIE: What time we supposed to be on at?

JOLENE: Lemme find out . . . pull over here.

(The taxi pulls up at the corner where a newsvender has his pitch)

NEWSVENDOR: *(hoarsely)* Err's yur *Times*, *Echo*, feeeeenell!

(Jolene leans her head out of the cab window and whistles. The newsvendor flips an Echo *out of the bundle under his arm and crosses to the taxi)*

NEWSVENDOR: Err's yur thirty-five pee, sweetheart.

(He holds out the folded copy of the Echo*)*

JOLENE: I thought it was only twenty?

NEWSVENDOR: Err's yur fifteen pence delivery charge, darlin'.

JOLENE: Err's yur fifty, get yourself some elocution lessons.

(The taxi pulls away from the kerb. Jolene flicks through the pages of the Echo*)*

FRANK: Hey, is that not . . . ?

(He gestures at a picture on the front page)

BILLIE: (*over shoulder*) You found it?

JOLENE: Gimme a tick, I'm still . . .

　(*She carries on flicking the pages*)

JOLENE: (*to herself*) . . . aargh!

　(*Frank bends his head to get another view of the front page. He sees David Cole's picture*)

FRANK: Mebbe it's just me but this guy on the front page . . .

　(*Jolene suddenly rips out the page with Dorwood's 'Invisible Man' picture and scrunches it into a ball. Underneath are the entertainment listings*)

JOLENE: . . . quarter past.

　(*She chucks the scrunched-up paper ball into the space between the front seats*)

BILLIE: (*over shoulder*) Quarter past what? It's nearly ten to the now . . .

　(*Frank eases the scrunched-up paper ball towards his hand, and picks it up. He surreptitiously un-scrunches it*)

JOLENE: Aw, naw . . .

BILLIE: What?

JOLENE: . . . naw, it's awright, I thought I'd left my new rigout back at the ranch . . .

　(*Frank steals a sideways squint at the torn-out page with Dorwood's picture on it*)

JOLENE: . . . I got the fright of my life there.

　(*Frank mouths the report on Dorwood's 'Fight for Life' in astonishment . . . until it is snatched from his grasp by Jolene.*

　He looks at her as she scrunches the page up into a ball again and stuffs it in the ashtray)

★ ★ ★

(*A straggle of cowboys and cowgirls make their way towards the dimly-lit entrance to the Ponderosa Club. The Tall Cowpoke's 'covered wagon' pulls up alongside the Winnebago, and the Tall Cowpoke, Drew, and Roxanne disembark*)

★ ★ ★

(*Cissie stands thumbing a lift along the darkened Wishaw road. A snatch of Jim Bob O'May's version of 'Your Cheatin' Heart' hits her ears as a van drives past. She breaks into a run as the van's brakelights flash on some twenty yards up the road. Cissie reaches the van, slides the door open and clambers gratefully aboard. 'Your Cheatin' Heart' is still on the radio*)

CISSIE: You're not goin' anywhere near . . .

　(*Fraser Boyle leans across Cissie and locks the van door*)

BILLIE: 'course I'm are . . .

CISSIE: Aaaargh . . .

> (*Meanwhile, in the back of the van, two eyes glint through the slits in bandages behind the fish crates in the darkened interior as they lurch towards Wishaw*)

Monday/Tuesday

Ralph Henderson, divested of his camel coat and suit jacket, is standing up to his armpits in a sinkful of polythene-wrapped frozen, partly-frozen, defrosting and defrosted lobsters in the kitchen of the Bar-L. The kitchen itself is in chaos, as if someone has been searching unsuccessfully for something. Henderson chucks yet another red herring into the sink. There is a series of crashes and splinterings from elsewhere in the building. Henderson wipes his hands on his trouser seat and crosses to the kitchen door. He walks into the dim and deserted bar. Tonto limps in from the men's room.

TONTO: Nothin' in the toilets either . . .
    (*Tonto chucks a length of splintered doorframe on to the floor*)
HENDERSON: Have you searched his office?
TONTO: Ripped it apart . . . came across a perra slingbacks an' a Billy Daniels LP . . . apart fae that . . . zilch.
HENDERSON: It's got to be here somewhere . . .
HENDERSON: . . . you can't lose ten kilos that easily in a joint this size!
    (*Up on top of the building above their heads, nestling inside the giant glowing Ragazzo's half-round 'pokey hat' cornet shell, is a brown paper-wrapped polythene bag of pure Bolivian cocaine, tipping the scales at something just under 18 lbs*)

* * *

(*Up the road at Wishaw, Jim Bob's Winnebago gleams bulbously in the moonlight outside the Ponderosa Club. Just inside the door of the club Frank is clutching the receiver of a pay-phone to his ear*)
FRANK: (*on phone*) . . . Sorry Trish, I'm having to shout . . .
    (*Onstage Jim Bob O' May is belting out a lively version of 'Jambalaya'*)
FRANK: (*on phone*) . . . there's a buncha Hibernian ho-downers hollerin' into my left earlobe, I'm just phonin' to check is you got my Peking Duck copy?
    (*Frank is clutching a copy of the* Evening Echo *in his other hand*)
FRANK: (*on phone*) . . . naw . . . 'Duck', Trish . . . 'king' as in 'Cole', 'Duck' as in 'David' . . .

(*He casts an eye down Tamara MacAskill's front page account of David Cole's murder*)

FRANK: (*on phone*) . . . correction . . . 'Donald' . . . sorry, say again?

(*He hears a continuous beep-beep as the pay-phone runs out of money. Frank wedges the phone against his ear, Echo between his teeth, and delves both hands into his Burberry pockets. He stuffs a ten pence piece into the slot and plucks the newspaper from his mouth, leaving a large chunk of the front page adhering to his bottom lip*)

FRANK: (*on phone*) . . . naw, as in 'hoi polloi' . . . it's an oriental . . . (*spits*) . . . oriental ketchup, you spread it on your . . . (*spits*) . . . naw, your pancakes . . . (*spits*).

(*Backstage, in the dressing room, Jolene is standing in her striking new rigout singing along with Jim Bob who's playing over a tinny tannoy, and applying yet another coat of Carmine Lip Gloss to her already dazzling mouth. Billie opens the dressing room door and eyes Frank on the phone down the corridor*)

FRANK: (*on phone*) . . . lemme talk to Tamara, I've just went an' swallowed that murder story of hers . . . (*spits*).

JOLENE: So?

(*Billie closes the door and looks at Jolene*)

BILLIE: So I spoke with the management.

JOLENE: And?

BILLIE: We're on at the drinks interval.

(*Billie's eyes sparkle*)

JOLENE: Aw, well done, McPhail. I thought this was meant to be wur big chance?

(*Jolene turns away in disgust*)

BILLIE: It still is wur big chance, there's a wee guy sittin' right in the front row wi' a leather coat an' a pony-tail . . .

(*She weighs her words carefully*)

BILLIE: . . . he's smokin' a Gooloise.[77]

* * *

(*Boyle's fish van is trundling along the wet Wishaw road, the wipers are slapping in time to 'You are my Sunshine' which is playing over the radio. Boyle eyes Cissie*)

BOYLE: Stop lookin' at us like that . . . I'm doin' the pair of you a big favour gettin' the boy out the country. (*Over shoulder*) Y'awright back there, Dorwood?

CISSIE: 'Fraid he was goin' to spew up the truth on his sick bed, is that it?

(*She turns to the grill opening behind the front seats*)

CISSIE: (*loudly*) What possessed you to go along with this far-
cical notion! Not only have you scuppered any chance of me
gettin' my son back, you're goin' to wind up gettin' another
five years, ya numbskull!

BOYLE: (*over shoulder*) Don't listen to her, ole buddy . . . this
time next week you're gonnae find yourself on the Costa Blanca
doin' 'China Doll' for one of the best bands to break outta
Belfast in a blue moon.

CISSIE: (*over shoulder*) I'd take the five years . . .

(*There is a moan from Dorwood in the back of the van*)

CISSIE: (*to Boyle*) He's just had a brain scan, ya scumbag!

BOYLE: An' I've just had a fried egg roll on top of a nervous
stomach, quit screamin' at us!

CISSIE: Aw, naw . . .

BOYLE: What?

(*Up ahead in the road is a line of disembodied luminescent stripes
and waving lights. They loom out of the murky dark on the
motorway approach road*)

BOYLE: That's aw we need . . . (*Over shoulder*) . . . don't want
to alarm you, good buddy, but we're comin' up to a line of
berrs at a road block . . . (*To Cissie*) . . . any funny business an'
you're dead meat, darlin'.

(*Boyle slows the van down and stops at the road block. He winds
the window down and sticks his head out as a policeman moves
towards them waving his torch*)

BOYLE: S'up, you lost somethin', you guys?

(*Boyle shields his face as the policeman's torch sweeps the cab*)

POLICEMAN: D'you want to turn that racket down a bit?

BOYLE: D'you want to get that searchlight out ma face?

POLICEMAN: Turn it down!

(*Cissie reaches over and turns the radio volume down low*)

POLICEMAN: You didnae happen to pick up any hitchhikers on
your travels, did you?

(*His torch beam plays over Cissie in the passenger seat*)

BOYLE: Just the wife here, we're goin' to the Stations of the
Cross in Carluke . . . what's all this in aid of?

POLICEMAN: S'your back doors unlocked?

BOYLE: Sure, help yourself . . .

CISSIE: (*involuntarily*) Aw, Jesus . . .

(*She puts a hand to her face as Boyle punches her hard on the
thigh*)

CISSIE: . . . ow!

(*The policeman returns to shine his torch into the cab*)

POLICEMAN: D'you say somethin', love?

BOYLE: Not me, pal.

(*Boyle turns to Cissie*)

BOYLE: Y'awright, sweetheart?

(*He rubs his hand along Cissie's thigh*)

CISSIE: (*tartly*) I'm fine.

(*Cissie knocks Boyle's hand from her leg. He turns and leans his head out of the window*)

BOYLE: (*confidentially to policeman*) Fine she says . . . just had a bone marra transplant to her hip-joint . . . quack reckons that's her showbiz career curtailed . . . used to dance wi' the Muppets.

POLICEMAN: Switch your engine off.

(*The policeman moves around to the rear of the van. There are now several other vehicles that have been stopped and the occupants are being questioned by other police officers*)

BOYLE: (*loudly, to anyone*) Some how-d'you-do this, eh?

(*At the back of the fish van the policeman grabs the rear door handle and hauls one half of the double doors open*)

POLICEMAN: Bloody hell . . .

(*The policeman takes a step backwards, his hand to his face, as the acrid stench of dead fish hits his nostrils*)

BOYLE: (*loudly, to anyone*) Any you drivers know if there's a ten o'clock Mass in Larkhall the night?

(*Unwilling to get any closer, the policeman gives the van interior a cursory sweep with his torch, and satisfies himself that it's empty of passengers, before kicking the door shut with the toe of his boot. Dorwood, crouched behind the unopened half of the van doors, puts a hand to his injured head as the other door bangs shut*)

POLICEMAN: Right, get this stinkin' heap outta here . . .

(*Boyle smiles to himself as he turns the ignition key and the engine coughs into life. The policeman comes up alongside the cab*)

POLICEMAN: . . . C'mon, move.

(*Boyle lets the clutch out, and the fish van lurches off, only to stall some five yards up the road. Dorwood and the crates in the back are thrown forward in the dark*)

DORWOOD: (*on hands and knees*) C'mon, move!

(*The engine revs, splutters, and dies . . . Beads of sweat break out on Boyle's brow as he turns the ignition key again. The engine wow-wows ominously*)

CISSIE: C'mon, move . . .

(*Horns begin to beep behind them*)

BOYLE: (*loudly*) Awright, shurrup wi' the horns!

(*He tries the ignition key again, as the policeman comes up*) *alongside the cab*)

POLICEMAN: (*to Boyle*) You are bein' a right bloody nuisance, you are . . . (*To drivers behind*) Shurrup! (*To Boyle*) You got a handle, yeh?

BOYLE: Handle? Aye . . . Fraser. How?

(*He turns the ignition key once more*)

CISSIE: A startin' handle, ya mug.

BOYLE: Aw. (*To policeman*) Yeh, there should be one in the b . . .

(*The starter motor suddenly catches, and the engine roars impressively*)

BOYLE: . . . I don't believe it.

POLICEMAN: Right, Fraser . . . beat it.

(*The fish van weaves its way between the police vehicles at the road block and sets off along the motorway*)

BOYLE: Eeeeeeeeeeeeeha!

(*Cissie peers anxiously through the grill opening in the back wall of the cab*)

CISSIE: Yeh, dead jammy but what if that cop'd had to hunt in the back for the startin' hand . . .

(*She turns her head as Boyle reaches under the dashboard and produces an enormous lethal-looking navy Colt revolver*)

CISSIE: . . . aw, my God.

BOYLE: Good for him I got it goin', innit?

(*He brandishes the revolver in front of the grill*)

BOYLE: (*over shoulder*) . . . wrapped inside a lassie's scarf on top of a wardrobe in your apartment . . . 'much did we give thon mad guy for it . . . four quid? (*To Cissie*) Four quid.

(*The van inches over into the adjoining lane*)

CISSIE: Watch out!

(*She grabs the steering wheel and brings the van back into line as a car, horn blaring, overtakes them on the outside*)

BOYLE: Flang in three live rounds along with it, as I recall . . .

(*He holds the revolver up and squints into the chamber*)

CISSIE: (*loudly, to grill*) What in God's name were you doin' with a gun, ya lunatic!

(*Boyle spins the chamber against his leg and brings the gun up to Cissie's temple*)

BOYLE: . . . one for him, one for you . . .

CISSIE: (*defiantly*) Yeh, go on, I dare you.

(*Boyle cocks the hammer*)

BOYLE: . . . an' one for Junior.

(*Cissie's face remains impassive*)

CISSIE: You utter shit.

BOYLE: (*over shoulder, to Dorwood*) Ho . . . d'you hear what she's cryin' us, ole buddy? (*To Cissie*) That isnae very ladylike, sweetheart . . .

(*His voice takes on a harder edge*)

BOYLE: . . . wouldnae take me that long to get up to Aberdeen an' back in this jalopy so don't get surly, d'you hear?

(*He presses the gun barrel against the side of Cissie's head*)

BOYLE: (*over shoulder*) Remind me to let you have the wee fulla's address . . . you can drop him a postcard from wherever you happen to be on this European tour with Jim Bob . . . (*To Cissie*) Don't worry, he's wi' a nice family . . . foster-da's a telephone engineer . . . foster-ma's a total abstainer . . . there's two older kids an' a spaniel . . . 'Trixie'. Couldnae be happier. C'mon, smile . . .

(*He de-cocks the revolver and removes it from Cissie's temple*)

BOYLE: . . . I got your man out the jile, didn't I?

(*There is a moan from Dorwood in the back*)

BOYLE: Beg your pardon . . . hospital.

(*He sticks the gun into the waistband of his Wranglers . . . and winces slightly as he does so*)

BOYLE: (*over shoulder*) 'Much did we say, old pal . . . two grand, was it? (*To Cissie*) Two grand . . . cash.

(*Dorwood's face appears at the grill opening*)

DORWOOD: D'you think we could stop for a minute? I don't think I'm feelin' too hot . . .

BOYLE: Relax, we've no' got far to go.

DORWOOD: (*to Cissie*) Did that doll get in touch with you about ma redundancy money?

(*Cissie stares straight ahead*)

CISSIE: What redundancy money?

DORWOOD: The doll off the *Echo* . . .

(*Dorwood goes into a coughing fit*)

DORWOOD: . . . aw, God . . .

BOYLE: (*to Cissie*) Whereabouts were you headed anyhow? (*Over shoulder*) You want to keep an eye on this little lady of yours, ole buddy . . .

DORWOOD: (*between coughs*) . . . I planked it inside thon radio.

BOYLE: . . . out cruisin' the highways in her best duds while you're laid up in a hospital bed gettin' the last sacraments?

DORWOOD: (*feebly*) . . . know the one I mean?

BOYLE: (*to Cissie*) That just isnae tactful, darlin' . . .

DORWOOD: (*weakening*) I know I shoulda told you about it . . .

(*His face disappears from the grill*)

DORWOOD: . . . but I wouldnae've got legal aid.

(*Dorwood goes into an enfeebling coughing bout*)

BOYLE: That is one sick boy back there . . . yessiree, one very sick boy.

* * *

(*Frank is still at the pay-phone in the Ponderosa Club*)

FRANK: (*on phone*) . . . naw . . . 'wood', Tamara . . . as in 'or would you rather be a fish?' . . . the guy that fell off the roof, I was readin' your piece in the taxi but you didnae mention what hospital he was . . .

(*He hears continuous beep-beeps as the pay-phone runs out of money again*)

FRANK: . . . dammit . . .

(*There is applause behind him as Jim Bob and the Wild Bunch finish a number. Frank searches frantically through his coat pockets*)

FRANK: (*on phone, through beeps*) . . . I'm tryin' to find out if Cis . . . if his wife . . . naw, I cannae tell you where I am . . . it doesnae accept incomin' calls any . . .

(*The line breaks . . .*)

FRANK: . . . how . . . bugger.

(*Frank gives up his fruitless search for dough, hangs up the receiver, and leans his forehead against the wall. Behind him Jim Bob launches into 'Tenessee Waltz'. Down the corridor in the dressing room Billie is sitting with the Dobro on her lap singing along with Jim Bob on the tannoy. There is no sign of Jolene*)

BILLIE: (*singing*) ' . . . when an old friend I happened to see . . . introduced him to ma darlin' and as they were waltzin', ma friend stole ma sweetheart from me . . . '

(*Jolene enters the dressing room*)

BILLIE: (*singing*) . . . 'I remember the night . . . '

JOLENE: I thought you said the wee guy in the front row was from one of the music papers?

BILLIE: Well, that's what I . . .

JOLENE: (*angrily*) He's a wumman's hair stylist, I've just checked. See you, Billie McPhail!

(*She tears off her new blouson and chucks it across the room*)

BILLIE: What you doin'? We're on after this number . . .

(*Jolene stalks off towards the walk-in closet, goes in and slams the door*)

BILLIE: Jolene?

JOLENE: (*from closet, muffled*) Lea' me alone!

(*The Wild Bunch go into a fiddle-led instrumental break on the*

*tinny tannoy. Frank is still standing in the corridor with his fore-
head pressed against the wall next to the pay-phone. The Tall
Cowpoke ambles along the corridor, opening doors and peering
inside)*

TALL COWPOKE: *(loudly)* Y'err, Roxanne? *(To Frank)* You
huvnae saw a burd wi' a T-shirt an' a biro waunnerin' aboot
backstage, huv ye, pal? *(Loudly)* Y'err, honeybunch?

(He opens the door nearest Frank and sticks his head inside)

TALL COWPOKE: Woops.

(He closes the door)

TALL COWPOKE: *(to Frank)* T-shurt's goat Dave Dee, Dozey,
Wozey, Mick'n'Dick[78] oan the front . . . biro belangs tae the
shoap . . .

*(He wanders off along the corridor. Frank heaves a sigh, straight-
ens up, and heads towards the emergency exit doors leading to
the car park. Hands thrust forlornly in his raincoat pockets, he
has a dirty great smudge on his forehead)*

TALL COWPOKE: *(muffled)* Y'err Roxanne?

* * *

*(Ralph Henderson is at the wheel of his white BMW driving
along to Wishaw. Tonto sits in the passenger seat next to him)*

HENDERSON: *(on carphone)* . . . no, stay put, I'm on my way
there n . . . don't shout at me, I've just spent a fruitless ninety
minutes up to my armpits in dead crayfish!

*(Tonto leans forward in the passenger seat and peers through the
windscreen)*

HENDERSON: *(on carphone)* Never mind what for . . .

*(Tonto takes a pair of shades from his top pocket and slips them
on. He leans forward and peers through the windscreen)*

HENDERSON: *(on carphone)* . . . did you book us a table at that
Italian joint?

*(Tonto gives Henderson a nudge and points through the
windscreen)*

HENDERSON: *(on carphone)* Okay, okay, I'll do it . . . talk to you
later.

*(A policeman waves down the approaching BMW at the road
block. Henderson lowers the window)*

HENDERSON: 'Evening, officer . . . Ralph Henderson . . . Melon, Brolly and Henderson . . . what seems to be the problem?

*(The policeman bends down and flashes his torch into the
car)*

* * *

(*Tamara MacAskill replaces the carphone, draws a scarlet finger-nail carefully underneath a moist eye. She glances at her reflection in the rear-view mirror, sniffs, checks her watch, and picks up a portable tape recorder from the front passenger seat of her car. There is a light tap on the windscreen. Tamara glances up and sees Frank McClusky's face pressed against the window. She draws back startled*)

TAMARA: Wah!

(*Frank leans down to the driver's window of the parked radio car*)

FRANK & TAMARA: (*together*) What're you doing here? I've just been talking to you . . .

FRANK: . . . at the office, naw?

TRACEY: . . . God, what a fright.

(*She sniffs and pushes the car door open*)

FRANK: There's me huntin' through ma pockets for loose coins when I could just . . .

(*Tamara clambers out of the car clutching her tape recorder*)

TAMARA: (*interrupting*) I'm waiting to interview this Irish chap for the ten o'clock news . . . my God, you look awful . . .

(*She looks Frank up and down*)

FRANK: I'm on the run, Tamara . . .

TAMARA: . . . I mean, you don't look too terrific at the best of times but . . . ha!

FRANK: 'Ha'?

TAMARA: What on earth have you got on your feet!

(*Frank's eyes follow Tamara's*)

FRANK: Aw, these? These're Dorwood's.

TAMARA: Oh, I thought for a second they were cowboy boots, I was going to ask what got into you.

(*She fumbles with her car keys*)

FRANK: Allow me.

(*Frank takes the keys and locks the radio car door*)

FRANK & TAMARA: (*together*) You don't happen to know . . .

FRANK: . . . know what?

TAMARA: . . . no no, carry on, what were you going to ask?

(*She discovers that the tape recorder mike lead has got inexplicably and inextricably fankled in Frank's Burberry belt*)

FRANK: You don't happen to know when Big Gordon's gettin' buried, do you?

(*They set off across the car park together, Tamara puzzling over the problem with her mike lead*)

TAMARA: When who's getting what?

FRANK: Gordon Smart . . . guy they fished out the Clyde . . .

(*Tamara squints across the car park at Jim Bob's trailer*)

TAMARA: (*interrupting*) Does that look like a 'Wendy-bagel' to you? Sorry, what were you saying?

(*She stops and grapples with the mike lead and the raincoat belt*)

FRANK: . . . his Maw was a cripple . . . turned up at the school prize giving one year in the back of the boy Ragazzo's ice-cream motor . . .

TAMARA: You don't happen to know any Italian restaurants around here?

FRANK: . . . Big Gordon won himself a Palgrave's *Golden Treasury* . . . [79]

TAMARA: There used to be one in the High Street with venetian blinds but it's all boarded up.

FRANK: . . . Libo Ragazzo half-inched it out his toilet bag . . . Fraser Boyle fashioned a one to ten thou pop-up model of Graceland[80] outta *The Cotter's Saturday Night*[81] . . . I'd quite like to be at his funeral.

TAMARA: Lago di Something? . . . He's got this thing about Ossobucco.

FRANK: Lago di Lucca . . . I devoted a half-column to it last month, guy sent me a death threat through the post. Who's got this 'thing' about . . .

TAMARA: Ralph.

FRANK: Ralph?

TAMARA: Spent our entire honeymoon stuffing himself.

FRANK: Aw, that Ralph? Thought you an' him went to Michigan, naw?

TAMARA: Is this belt stitched to the back?

FRANK: I'm only goin' by what Trish in Copy told everybody . . .

TAMARA: Damn!

(*She sucks a broken fingernail*)

FRANK: . . . I used to know a Ralph only this guy called himself Raif, like in Vaughan Williams[82] . . . nice big chap . . . tone deaf . . . we got arrested together at university . . . last I heard he went into the army, got posted to Northern Ireland . . . havenae seen him since . . . I think that belt's stitched to the back . . . is it?

★ ★ ★

(*A young man and his girlfriend come round the corner and peer through the front door of the Bar-L into the darkened interior. A voice comes out of the shadows*)

VOICE: Thurshut.

(A man's unattractive features glow in the shadows as he drags hard on a cigarette butt. He flicks the butt away and limps out under the street lamp)

GIRLFRIEND: Their pokey hat's on.

LIMPING MAN: Where?

(The limping man and the young man step into the street and look up at the Bar-L roof. Ragazzo's pokey hat glows fitfully against the black velvet of the night sky)

YOUNG MAN: Aw, aye, so it is.

LIMPING MAN: Soon fix that, hen.

(The limping man draws back an arm with a half-brick on the end of it. The young man and his girlfriend look up, their eyes following the flight path of the missile. There is a crash, followed by the sound of a burglar alarm going off)

* * *

(In the car park of the Ponderosa, Tamara, with Frank in tow on the end of her microphone lead, walks over to the Winnebago and rattles the door. A bouncer appears at the door of the club, opens the door and pins it back)

MC: *(from club)* Thank you, ladies an' gen'lemen, that's your refreshments interlude right now . . .

FRANK: *(to Tamara)* What time you goin' back to Glasgow at?
(A sweating Jim Bob and his band tear out of the club towards the Winnebago. Tamara whirls round and points her microphone at them)

TAMARA: Hi . . . Tamara MacAskill, Radio Kelvin, did someone give you a ring about a possible interview regarding Jim Bob's alleged involvement with the INLA?[83]

(Frank pretends to be a passer-by. The Tall Cowpoke wanders by, still looking for Roxanne. Inside the dressing room Billie listens to the MC over the tannoy. Jolene is still hidden in the closet)

MC: . . . your pub next door here does some very tasty Kentucky ham vol-a-vongs . . .

BILLIE: *(to closet)* We're on, Jolene!

* * *

(On a slip road, off the motorway, Fraser Boyle's fish van sits, bonnet up, with its engine smoking. Boyle has removed his jacket, rolled up his sleeves, and is leaning over the mudguard to investigate the problem. Boyle straightens up and removes the navy Colt from his waistband. He sets it down nearby before leaning over the engine again. Cissie is sitting in the van behind the steering wheel)

DORWOOD: Yeh, so you keep sayin' but I was goin' bananas in that joint . . .

CISSIE: (*over shoulder*) Are you callin' me a liar?

   (*Dorwood's knuckles whiten as he pushes his face up against the grill*)

DORWOOD: What about all these letters I've been gettin'?

CISSIE: What letters?

DORWOOD: In green biro! You have so been seein' guys, I can tell!

CISSIE: Och, away an' don't be stupit.

BOYLE: (*loudly, from under the bonnet*) Okay, turn over!

   (*Cissie reaches for the ignition key*)

DORWOOD: See if I find out . . .

   (*The rest of his words are drowned out by the chung-chung of the engine before it coughs and dies*)

DORWOOD: (*continues*) . . . an' that isnae just an empty threat, right!

* * *

(*Billie appears at the entrance of the Ponderosa, she casts around the car park in panic. She spots Frank over by the Winnebago with his ear to the door. She rushes across to him*)

BILLIE: C'mon, you're wanted . . .

   (*She grabs hold of Frank and tries hauling him away from the trailer*)

FRANK: (*sotto voce*) Beat it, Shorty, can you not see I'm tied up!

BILLIE: C'mon, I said!

   (*She grabs Frank by the scruff of his shirt collar and pulls him out of his belted Burberry like a caterpillar from a cocoon*)

FRANK: Ooooooooooooow

   (*Billie drags Frank bodily across the tarmac leaving his raincoat dangling by the microphone lead from the Winnebago door*)

* * *

(*The white BMW peels off the motorway, and takes the road to Wishaw. A short way along they see a fish van parked by the verge. A man steps into the road, and waves his arms. Tonto leans forward in his seat and peers out through the windscreen*)

TONTO: We don't want any fish, dae we?

   (*Fraser Boyle's face contorts into a silently cursing mask as the BMW sweeps past. Tonto swivels round to look back down the road*)

HENDERSON: Lago di Lucca . . .

   (*Henderson passes a slim address book to Tonto*)

HENDERSON: . . . quiet table for two . . . 10 o'clock.

> (*Tonto takes the address book, picks up the carphone, and punches in a number*)

TONTO: What aboot the wife, she no' comin', naw?

* * *

> (*Billie has just arrived on the Ponderosa stage. There are five patrons, presumably teetotallers, dotted around the room, all looking badly in need of cheering up*)

BILLIE: (*into mike*) Howdy . . .

> (*The hair stylist with a ponytail and a leather coat sits in the front row munching a hotdog from a doyley*)

BILLIE: (*turning head*) . . . is this mike on? (*Into mike*) Howdy, Wishaw . . .

> (*She runs her plectrum across the guitar strings*)

BILLIE: . . . I'd like to introduce you to a coupla McPhail Sisters' Friends this evening . . . would you welcome, on the slide guitar . . . Mister Frank McCusker.

> (*Frank is busy hunting for a socket in the amplifier to plug the Dobro jack into*)

FRANK: McClusky.

> (*He disappears behind the amp*)

BILLIE: And replacing Jolene Jowett on vocals . . . (*To Roxanne*) . . . What's your second name again?

> (*Roxanne leans forward from the stage so that the hair stylist in the front row can finger her tresses*)

FRANK: (*behind amp*) McClusky!

BILLIE: (*into mike*) . . . Rexene McClusky.

> (*Billie hits the opening chords of* 'Silver Threads and Golden Needles')

FRANK: (*to anyone*) Any you guys seen a bottleneck?

ROXANNE: (*to hair stylist*) Naw, no' like hurs . . . somethin' stylish, yeh?

> (*She crosses to the mike*)

BILLIE: Thanks a bunch. (*To Frank*) In G.

> (*Roxanne launches into the opening verse. Roxanne's voice comes belting over the tannoy into the dressing room backstage. The closet door creaks open, and Jolene appears, eating her way through a packet of biscuits. She stares at the tannoy*)

JOLENE: Ya cheeky bitch . . .

> (*A fountain of digestive biscuit crumbs arcs across the room*)

JOLENE: . . . that's ma number!

* * *

(*Boyle is still fiddling about under the bonnet of the immobilised fish van. There is no response from the cab, and Boyle emerges, his hands blackened with grease*)

BOYLE: (*loudly*) Try that, I said!

(*There is still no response. Boyle takes a couple of paces away from the engine and looks into the cab. There is no sign of Cissie. He gallops round to the back of the van. The rear doors are gaping wide. But there is no sign of Dorwood apart from a trail of bandages snaking across the verge. Boyle spins round and runs out into the road. His head swivels this way and that. He reaches for the revolver at his waist . . . and panics. Then he remembers and races back to the van. There is no sign of the navy Colt where he left it*)

BOYLE: Aw, naw . . .

(*He strikes his palm on his forehead leaving a big black oily mark*)

* * *

(*Cissie is standing alone at the side of the Wishaw road keeping a lookout for oncoming cars*)

CISSIE: (*to Dorwood, in bushes*) Keep down, they're hardly goin' to pull up for a guy in his PJs . . . you could be an escaped lunatic.

(*She steps out into the road to thumb down the approaching headlights*)

CISSIE: (*to herself*) What'm I sayin'? You are an escaped lunatic.

(*There is a roar as several vehicles race past her. A shivering Dorwood emerges from the roadside undergrowth and draws a flimsy hospital blanket round his shoulders*)

DORWOOD: (*to disappearing tail lights*) Aye, cheers, pal . . . wait to you're on the run an' aw you've got on your feet's a perra bedsocks! (*To Cissie*) You might've thought to bring us ma new boots instead of these useless items . . .

(*Dorwood looks down at his sodden feet and sneezes*)

CISSIE: I wasn't to know you were goin' walkabout, was I?

DORWOOD: Me neither . . . one minute I'm at death's doorstep, next minute Fraser Boyle's got his leg over the winda-sill an' him an' I's makin' a break for . . . (*Looks around*) . . . where in God's name . . . (*Sneezes*) . . . are we?

(*Cissie peels her jacket off*)

CISSIE: Here. . . .

(*She places the jacket around Dorwood's shoulders*)

DORWOOD: What you doin'? Get that offa me.

(*He shrugs Cissie's jacket off his shoulders on to the ground. Cissie*)

*looks down at the jacket, and then up at Dorwood. Cissie bends
down, picks up the jacket and replaces it around her husband's
shoulders)*

DORWOOD: Somethin' up wi' your hearin'?

(He shrugs Cissie's jacket on to the ground again)

CISSIE: Pick that up.

DORWOOD: You pick it up, it's your . . . *(Sneezes)*

CISSIE: D'you want to catch pneumonia? Pick that up when
you're told.

DORWOOD: Away to . . . *(Sneezes)* aaaah, ma head.

CISSIE: Quit moanin' about your stupit head an' get that
jacket . . .

DORWOOD: *(interrupting)* Moanin'? Who's moanin'? All I've
done is bite the bullet ever since I dove Christ-knows-how-many
feet offa that roof! *(Sneezes)* ahyah . . .

CISSIE: Bite the bullet? Don't make me laugh, you've done
nothin' but feel sorry for yourself ever since you got arrested . . . an' you shouldn't've been on the bloody roof, you
should've been in your room!

DORWOOD: Cell, Cissie . . . they don't put you in a room, they
lock you up in a . . . *(Sneezes)* . . . cell!

CISSIE: Yeh, whatever . . . just pick up the jacket an' . . .

DORWOOD: *(interrupting)* There were three other galoots in
there along wi' us . . .

(He starts pacing to and fro in a vain effort to get warm)

CISSIE: The jacket, Dorwood.

DORWOOD: . . . One for stickin' a bottle-opener through his
girlfriend's neck, one for sawin' the thumbs off a security guard,
an' the other one was . . . *(Sneezes)* . . . bloody Dwane. One
toilet, four guys . . . it was worse than bein' on the road, for
Christ's . . .

(He turns to find himself staring down a gun barrel)

DORWOOD: *(tailing off)* . . . sake. What the hell're you doin'
with . . .

CISSIE: *(interrupting)* Pick up the jacket, Dorwood.

(She waves the gun at him)

CISSIE: Pick up the jacket unless you want to die!

(Dorwood reaches down and picks up the jacket)

DORWOOD: Yeh, go on, I . . . *(Sneezes)* I dare you.

CISSIE: From exposure, ya nitwit! Right, get it on . . . c'mon,
hurry up!

DORWOOD: You're just out to humiliate me, that's what you're
out to do . . .

(He puts his arms through the sleeves)

CISSIE: What're you talkin' about, humiliate you? I'm tryin' to prevent you from gettin' pleurisy, ya . . .

DORWOOD: This's a lassie's jacket!

CISSIE: It's a what?

DORWOOD: This! It's been made for a lassie . . . look at it!

CISSIE: What the hell does it matter who it was made for as long as . . .

DORWOOD: (*interrupting*) A helluva bloody lot, it matters! If this ever gets near the papers the fans're gonnae go . . . (*Sneezes*) . . . the fans're gonnae go mental!

(*He pulls the jacket on and stands there*)

DORWOOD: They'll crucify us . . . look at the state of me . . . aw I need's a shoulder bag an' wur album's out the charts for evermore!

CISSIE: Mental, did you say?

DORWOOD: Yeh, awright, Miss Intellect, so they don't aw read wee print an' tune into Channel Four movies, but the one thing they do do is go out an' buy Country music secure in the knowledge that Hank Snow[84] isnae gonnae stroll onstage at the Grand Ole Opry[85] in a wumman's evenin' gown!

CISSIE: I thought Hank Snow was dead?

DORWOOD: Willie bloody Nelson, well! Don't get smart . . .

CISSIE: Och, I give up . . . do you seriously mean to tell me that you would rather catch pleurisy than . . .

DORWOOD: Too bloody right, I would!

(*Dorwood gets the jacket half-off when he is overtaken by a violent sneezing fit*)

CISSIE: That's right . . . die, ya dope!

DORWOOD: (*recovering*) Yeh, that would suit you just fine, wouldn't it?

CISSIE: Too bloody right, it would!

(*Dorwood struggles manfully to escape from the jacket, but he is hampered by the hospital blanket underneath and by the tightness of its lassie's sleeves*)

DORWOOD: Well, I hate to disappoint you, sweetheart, but you ain't gonnae be left a single parent for some considerable . . . (*Loud sneeze*) . . . ah, Jesus, ma napper . . .

(*Still trapped in the jacket, Dorwood lurches forward and leans himself against Cissie, exhausted. Cissie looks down at him and for the first time she sees a lurid gash in the middle of a shaven spot on Dorwood's skull*)

CISSIE: Aw, my God . . .

(*She sticks the revolver inside her shirt and reaches out to touch the ugly wound*)

DORWOOD: (*bent over*) Don't touch it!

CISSIE: I wasn't goin' to touch it . . . 'many stiches did you get? One, two, three . . .

DORWOOD: Forty-seven . . . naw forty-nine.

CISSIE: (*peering close*) It's not very neat, is it?

DORWOOD: They didnae get a seamstress in to do it, naw!

CISSIE: It looks awful sore . . .

DORWOOD: It is awful sore! I havenae slept a wink since it happened, kept wakin' up wi' the skitters.

CISSIE: Kept wakin' up with the what?

DORWOOD: The skitters! In case they started clubbin' us again . . .

CISSIE: In case who started . . .

DORWOOD: (*interrupting*) . . . didnae have a mark on us . . . fell on top of the screw that was tryin' to talk me down, shattered his pelvis, broke all his top teeth . . . his pals just couldnae see the funny side, started knockin' lumps outta ma . . . ach, what d'you care?

CISSIE: Talk sense, ya dummy, of course, I care! We'll sue!

DORWOOD: Sue?

CISSIE: Sue!

DORWOOD: Sue who?

CISSIE: The Governor, the prison authorities, the Home Office!

DORWOOD: Don't talk romantic, it's ma word against theirs, innit? 'Prisoner was resisting recapture, m'lord . . . the officers were obliged to exercise restraint . . . '

CISSIE: Restraint? They've smashed your skull in!

DORWOOD: (*loudly*) I know they've smashed ma sk . . . ooooow!
    (*He holds on to his head*)

CISSIE: There must've been witnesses that saw what happened.

DORWOOD: Yeh . . . Dwane . . . I clocked his wee beady eyes keekin' out into the playground just before I went under.

CISSIE: We'll get him to testify. If he can identify the lousy pigs that . . .

DORWOOD: (*interrupting*) Dwane Devlin? Dwane couldnae identify himself in the mirror if you gave him his passport pitcher. (*Softly*) Ohyah . . .

CISSIE: I thought you an' Dwane were quite close?

DORWOOD: Never trust a guy with a tattoo of Farley Granger on his bum . . .
    (*His body starts to heave*)

DORWOOD: . . . I used to lend that swine shurts an' everythin' . . .

CISSIE: (*tenderly*) C'mere . . .

(*She holds him close*)

DORWOOD: (*between sobs*) . . . got them back, cuffs were all frayed, collars were absolutely manky.

DORWOOD: Did you really get the last sacraments, yeh?

(*Dorwood wipes his eyes on Cissie's shirt collar*)

DORWOOD: Did I what?

CISSIE: The last sacraments? Fraser Boyle said you'd got . . .

DORWOOD: (*interrupting*) 'Course I got the last sacraments, they thought I was gonnae snuff it, didn't they! (*Sneezes*) Ahyah, bastart!

CISSIE: First thing we have to do is to get you out of that wet stuff an' into some proper clothes . . .

DORWOOD: Aye, very good . . . what d'you suggest, poppin' into the nearest Co-operative outfitters an' pickin' something off the rail? We're in the middle of Nowhere Gulch, for Christ's sake!

CISSIE: Don't raise your voice, you'll only aggravate that gash . . . s'not itchy, is it?

DORWOOD: Naw, just very painful! Aaaaah . . .

CISSIE: Don't worry, it'll get itchy . . . d'you remember when Thomas's buggy turned over an' . . . (*She stops herself*)

DORWOOD: Naw, I don't . . . was that when you were hittin' the sauce, yeh?

CISSIE: (*looking away*) He only ever had a wee tiny scar . . . just here . . .

(*She puts a finger to her hair, just behind her ear*)

CISSIE: . . . shaped like a tortoise . . . (*Quickly*) . . . d'you want to start walkin'?

DORWOOD: Walkin'?

CISSIE: Not much point in hangin' about here, Fraser Boyle could be along in that clapped-out fish truck any minute . . .

(*She pulls the jacket up over Dorwood's shoulders*)

DORWOOD: Yeh, what is it with you an' Fraser? I always thought you an' him got on like a house on fire.

CISSIE: S'that what he told you?

(*She fastens Dorwood's jacket buttons*)

DORWOOD: Listen, if it hadnae've been for Fraser Boyle I wouldnae be standin' here right now.

CISSIE: Exactly, C'mon . . .

(*She starts walking Dorwood along the road*)

DORWOOD: Didnae relish handin' him a measly two grand for gettin' us out the country, s'that what it is? Eh? S'that what it is, Cissie?

CISSIE: How in God's name was Fraser Boyle goin' to get you

out the country . . .

DORWOOD: Simple . . .

CISSIE: . . . he cannae even get his motor started!

DORWOOD: . . . one of the Wild Bunch lends us an Irish passport, I get ma snap taken, we hand the lot over to a guy called
Cherokee George, George does the business, 'Jim Bob's your
uncle' . . . Naw, listen, listen . . . their Hawaiian guitar player's
wife's expectin', he'll be quite happy to hop it back to Derry
while I fly outta Hamburg for the States . . . it's all arranged.
All you have to do is hand over the two Gs to Boyle, change
the rest of ma redundancy dough into travellers' cheques, stick
them in an envelope an' . . .

CISSIE: (*interrupting*) Promise me somethin', Dorwood . . .

DORWOOD: Don't worry . . . soon as I hit Nashville I'm gonnae
mail you out two 'plane tickets . . . one for you. One for . . .

CISSIE: (*interrupting*) . . . naw, somethin' else, Dorwood.

DORWOOD: Yeh, what?

CISSIE: Promise me you'll resist the urge to pen the definitive
work on British constitutional history.

DORWOOD: British constitutional what?

CISSIE: They don't have Irish passports in Derry, they have
United Kingdom passports, same as you an' I have got!

DORWOOD: Aw, yeh? So how come I'm to give Fraser Boyle
two thousand quid for gettin' us . . .

    (*Dorwood stops walking*)

CISSIE: (*interrupting*) An' somethin' else you ought to know . . .
you don't have any 'redundancy dough' so that's the entire
enterprise knocked on the head.

    (*She starts walking Dorwood along the road again*)

DORWOOD: What d'you mean, I don't have any redundancy
d . . . (*Sneezes*).

CISSIE: 'Cos I burnt it . . . pick your feet up . . .

DORWOOD: . . . it's tucked inside thon Gene Autry . . . (*Stops
dead*) What'd you say?

CISSIE: . . . your feet . . . pick them up.

DORWOOD: You burnt it!

CISSIE: Just the money, your Gene Autry radio's quite safe, I
put it in the tea-chest along with . . .

DORWOOD: (*interrupting*) Eighteen thousand quid . . . you actually burnt eighteen . . .

CISSIE: (*interrupting*) It's your own fault, you should've told me
about it . . . I presumed it was the proceeds from . . .

    (*Cissie turns round as Dorwood drops to his knees and starts
    beating his head on the tarmac*)

CISSIE: . . . stop that, ya headbanger!

(*She grabs Dorwood by the scruff of his lassie's jacket and pulls him into an upright kneeling position. She can see his blood-flecked face in the lights of the approaching cars*)

DORWOOD: (*ferociously*) Waaaaaaaaaaaa . . . choo!

★ ★ ★

(*On the Ponderosa Club stage Billie and Roxanne are harmonising sweetly on 'These Two Empty Arms'. Jolene stands at one side of the stage, a little apart from the others, with her accordion strapped to her chest, and a face like fizz*)

JOLENE: (*to Billie*) Away, ya two-faced get!

(*Frank, bent over his amplifier, glances across at Jolene*)

JOLENE: (*to Frank*) Not you . . . her, there. (*To Billie*) Yeh, you, ya insect!

ROXANNE: (*between verses*) S'up wi' yir associate?

BILLIE: I forgot to bring her poncho.

(*Frank shuffles over to Jolene and starts fingering her blouson*)

JOLENE: (*to Frank*) . . . go on, have a guess . . . seventy-nine fifty, reduced from three hundred an' eighty-four, an' she's got the gall to invite a two-pound T-shirt in a Sixties hairdo onstage to do all ma numbers? . . . She can sing nane, McPhail!

(*Billie and Jolene's voices drift through the air and out into the dark car park outside. Tonto, who has been examining the Burberry's sleeves sticking out of the Winnebago door, steps smartly back into the shadows as the door is opened and Tamara is 'shown out'*)

TAMARA: (*to outlaw*) All right, all right, I'm going, there's no need to shove . . . ow!

(*The outlaw rips the tape reel out of the recorder and hurls the machine across the car park. Tamara stumbles across the tarmac to retrieve it. Tonto slips out of the shadows and into Jim Bob's trailer as Tamara gathers up the tape recorder and hurries across the car park towards the white BMW, with Frank's discarded raincoat dragging along behind. Onstage, Frank has accidentally solved the Dobro amplification problem, and takes off on a shaky bottleneck solo that gains in confidence — if not immediately in polish — as it intertwines with Jolene's accordion on the instrumental break in* 'These Two Empty Arms')

BILLIE: (*to Jolene*) Okay, so Ry Cooder,[86] he isnae, but he's got wee Desmond tanked.

(*The Tall Cowpoke and Drew materialise beside the hair stylist in the front row*)

JOLENE: Yeh, if we play wur cards right we might get a free

perm . . . chuck tryin' to sook in, McPhail.

ROXANNE: (*to Tall Cowpoke*) S'up wi' your face?

TALL COWPOKE: (*to hair stylist*) Did you gi'e hur an estimate furra herrdo?

> (*Frank's raincoat is now to be seen hanging from the mike lead outside the rear passenger door of the white BMW. Inside the car Tamara is gesticulating at Ralph Henderson*)

TAMARA: For heaven's sake, you're a solicitor, Ralph, there must be something you can do . . . those tapes are Radio Kelvin property.

> (*The carphone rings, and Henderson snatches at the receiver*)

HENDERSON: (*into carphone*) Yes?

> (*In a phone booth near the Bar-L a limping man, covered all over in a fine layer of white powder, is trying to talk into the upside-down pay-phone receiver*)

LIMPING MAN (*into phone*) Hey . . . (*Sniffs*) . . . whooo!

* * *

> (*Cissie and Dorwood have finally reached the Ponderosa Club car park. A shivering Dorwood crouches behind Tamara's radio car as Cissie surveys the scene from its shadow. Roxanne, The Tall Cowpoke and Drew all wander across the tarmac arguing*)

ROXANNE: Whit'd ye go an' drag us away fur?

> (*Cissie ducks out of sight beside Dorwood*)

ROXANNE: I wisnae especially wantin' a vol-a-vong . . .

DORWOOD: (*to Cissie*) Bring us somethin' to eat, will you?

CISSIE: (*sotto voce*) Shhhhhh!

> (*The Tall Cowpoke, Drew and Roxanne make their way past the radio car towards a nearby pub*)

TALL COWPOKE: (*to Drew*) Did you get that biro affa hur?

> (*Cissie eases herself cautiously upright after they have passed by*)

CISSIE: (*sotto voce, to Dorwood*) Wait here, okay?

* * *

> (*From her seat in the BMW Tamara catches a glimpse of Cissie, crouched low, zig-zagging her way across the car park towards the club*)

TAMARA: (*watching Cissie*) Just as well I got it down in shorthand . . .

> (*A preoccupied Henderson replaces the carphone*)

HENDERSON: Hmm?

> (*Boyle's fish truck limps into the car park and conks out alongside the 'covered wagon'. Cissie slips into the club as Boyle climbs down from his cab and makes his way towards Jim Bob's trailer,*)

pulling his jacket on as he goes. Tonto emerges from the Win-
nebago and crosses towards the BMW. Boyle and Tonto pass
each other. Boyle hirples on a few paces, then freezes, one arm
in the air, his jacket half-on. He turns)

BOYLE: Ho!

* * *

(Billie and Jolene, their faces up against the microphone onstage,
harmonise the last line of their song)

BILLIE AND JOLENE: *(singing)* ' . . . just out of reach of these
two empty arms . . . '

BILLIE: Ooooow!

JOLENE: Sorry, was that your toe?

FRANK: Ha, look who's here . . .

(Cissie makes her way towards the stage)

CISSIE: *(to hair stylist)* 'Scuse me.

(The McPhail Sisters and Friend wind down, Billie and Jolene
exchanging 'bodychecks'. There is a pitiful smattering of applause
from the assembled few)

FRANK: *(to Cissie)* . . . you just missed my big solo.

* * *

(Out in the car park a frustrated Fraser Boyle is left clutching
on to Frank's Burberry as the white BMW roars away, tyres
screaming. A straggle of cowboys and cowgirls returning from the
nearby pub give Boyle a wide berth as he wallops the raincoat
on the tarmac in fury)

* * *

(Cissie is standing in front of the stage engaged in a secretive
conversation with Frank who is crouching in front of her)

CISSIE: *(sotto voce, to Frank)* C'mon, hurry up, he's goin' to
catch his death out there!

FRANK: What about me? I'm supposed to stroll about in ma
underpants an' a pair of cowboy boots?

CISSIE: Don't be daft, he needs the boots as well . . .

(She makes a grab for Frank's foot)

FRANK: Ho, chuck that!

(Just offstage in the corridor Billie and Jolene continue their
argument)

BILLIE: What was I supposed to do, go out there an' tell the
world that you were in the huff?

JOLENE: I was not in the huff, I was incommunicado!

BILLIE: You were in a bloody closet, Jolene!

(Jim Bob and the Wild Bunch file past them on their way onstage)

JOLENE: That's right, tell the entire . . .

BILLIE: Shh.

JOLENE: Don't shh me, ya wee . . .

BILLIE: Shhhh!

JOLENE: What?

(Billie nods in the direction of the stage where Cissie is standing by the microphone)

CISSIE: *(sings)* ' . . . the world looks small and green and the snow-capped mountains white . . . From a distance the ocean meets the stream . . . '

(Frank stands with his back to the audience filling in on bottle-neck, while Jim Bob and the band pick up on the number. Cissie stands at the mike, Jim Bob's guitar slung around her neck)

FRANK: *(to Jim Bob)* If I suddenly gallop offstage it's nothin' personal.

(A hapless Fraser Boyle stands at the back of the club, silently cursing, as the cowboys and cowgirls resume their seats after the drinks interval. Billie and Jolene wander back onstage to fill out the sound on guitar, accordion, and voices. Dorwood hunkers down beside Tamara's car listening to the distant music. He glances up at the rumbling DC10 in the night sky above him. He shivers)

* * *

(Libo Ragazzo chucks his leather bag into the stretch limo parked outside the 'Arrivals' lounge at Glasgow airport. He climbs in after it. The car pulls away smoothly. A young woman in glasses is sitting next to Ragazzo. She glances up from some documents she's going through)

YOUNG WOMAN IN GLASSES: *(in Italian)* Been a lotta changes since you left . . .

(Libo Ragazzo stares out through the window at the passing city)

RAGAZZO: Mm . . .

YOUNG WOMAN IN GLASSES *(In Italian)* . . . don't forget you've to phone Detroit before . . . *(She glances at watch)* . . . Signor Ragazzo?

RAGAZZO: Huh?

(He turns his head)

YOUNG WOMAN IN GLASSES: *(in Italian)* Detroit . . . you've to telephone before . . .

RAGAZZO: *(interrupting)* Si, grazie.

YOUNG WOMAN IN GLASSES: Prego.

RAGAZZO: (*after some moments, in Glaswegian*) Bung annurra big Bell's[87] in there, honeybunch.

(*He holds out his tumbler in a gold-ringed mitt. A little while later the limo pulls up at the front of the Holiday Inn*)

* * *

(*The McPhail Sisters and Friends are belting out 'From a Distance' from the stage of the Ponderosa. Outside in the car park Dorwood turns up his jacket collar and wraps his arms around his shivering body. By now Tonto has got into the back seat of the BMW and has his head between his knees. He is going through his hair with his hand. Tamara leans forward to Henderson*)

TAMARA: Ralph, there's something you're not telling me.

(*Inside the club Cissie and the McPhail Sisters and the Wild Bunch and Friends build towards the climax of 'From a Distance', with Jolene and Cissie harmonising on vocals. There is a momentary pause at the end of the song. Then the cowboys and cowgirls in the audience are on their feet, whooping and hollering. Suddenly, a loud bang is heard from outside the club. The applause dies quickly, and heads in the audience turn away to look. In the confusion Cissie slings Jim Bob's guitar around her back and feels about in her shirt for the revolver*)

CISSIE: Aaaaaaaaaaaagh . . .

* * *

(*Outside in the moonlight the navy Colt snags in Dorwood's fingers as it falls to the ground*)

Friday

'Ragazzo's' pokey hat, perched atop the roof of the Bar-L, has a jagged hole in the front, from which a single naked bulb sinks weakly. There is stoned laughter and whoops of delight from the dark as the burglar alarm dies away and the light bulb goes out. In the street below the white BMW turns the corner and moves along towards the bar. Tamara MacAskill sits in the back seat as far away from Tonto as she can get, her face buried in her hands. The Deadwood Playboys' version of 'Hello, Mary Lou' plays on the car radio. Tonto leans forward, taps Henderson on the shoulder, and points through the windscreen. Henderson looks, and sees a man swaying on the street corner ahead, a brown paper-wrapped parcel in his hand dribbling its contents on to the pavement.

TAMARA: Ralph, will you please tell me what's going on ... who are these people?

* * *

(*In the car park of the Ponderosa a circle of concerned and curious cowboys and cowgirls huddle around the radio car.*
In the middle of the circle are the Tall Cowpoke, Roxanne and Drew. The Tall Cowpoke holds his hand to his ear and blood trickles between his fingers)
ROXANNE: Chuck pullin' faces, it's only a crease.
TALL COWPOKE: Crease? A hauf-inch closer an' that wis me ... brains blootered aw err the tarmac.
ROXANNE: It's a car park, no' an erradrome. (*To Drew*) Away an' ask the bouncer fur some ointment.
DREW: You no' be better knottin' a tourniquet roon his froat, naw?
ROXANNE: Jist get us the ointment, Drew.
TALL COWPOKE: It's a bullet wound, no' a midgie bite. (*To Drew*) Ask him furra big gless a firewatter, it's goupin' somethin' chronic, tell him.
  (*Drew slopes off. A voice rises behind the onlookers*)
BOYLE: 'Scuse me, pal ... out ma road ... 'scuse me ...
  (*Fraser Boyle forces his way through the crowd*)
BOYLE: ... boy made his escape in a motor ... y'awright?
ROXANNE: Efter they vol-a-vongs? Yur jokin'.

BOYLE: I'm talkin' to Timberwolf.

ROXANNE: *He* didnae huv any vol-a-vongs. Scram.

(*She pushes Boyle aside and applies a 'kerchief to the Tall Cowpoke's injured ear*)

TALL COWPOKE: Watch ma herr.

BOYLE: (*to Roxanne*) I wouldnae go buyin' him too many stereo albums for his Christmas, sweetheart.

* * *

(*Frank is at the wheel of the radio car speeding away from the Ponderosa. Cissie is sitting next to him peeling the shirt off him as he drives*)

CISSIE: (*over shoulder*) I'm goin' to murder you . . . what'd you go an' take a pot-shot at that guy for?

DORWOOD: It wasnae meant to be a pot-shot . . .

(*Dorwood is lying on the back seat pulling up his Wranglers*)

DORWOOD: . . . it was meant to even up the score for aw they hammer hold-ups.

CISSIE: I thought you'd killed yourself!

FRANK: No such joy.

DORWOOD: (*to Cissie*) You've got a lotta explainin' to do . . .

CISSIE: Like what?

(*She thrusts the top half of Dorwood's prison pyjamas at Frank. The carphone starts ringing*)

DORWOOD: . . . like, who is this idiot, an' how come he's wearin' aw ma stuff!

FRANK: Somebody better answer that.

* * *

(*Also speeding away from the Ponderosa, Jim Bob's Winnebago has taken the Aberdeen road. A taxi appears a little way behind them, with Billie and Jolene inside*)

JOLENE: Did you get a load of the beanpole? Bang! She was out that door like her tail was on fire . . . nosey big get.

(*Jolene is changing in the back seat*)

JOLENE: I havenae seen anybody shift that quick since our Jinty got a call-back for the Coatbridge[88] panto.

BILLIE: She wasnae too bad a singer, mind you.

JOLENE: Yeh, I know, but she was a good head an' shoulders bigger than all the other six dwarfs . . . the boy MacIndoo's sister was playin' Snow White . . . you ever seen a Snow White wi' a stookie leg an' a poncho?

BILLIE: I'm not talkin' about your Jinty, I'm talkin' about Cissie what's-her-name.

JOLENE: Crouch.

BILLIE: Eh?

JOLENE: Crouch . . . her name's Crouch. Don't tell me you didnae tumble?

BILLIE: Tumble? You don't mean . . . ?

JOLENE: They've got a four-year-old kid, for God's sake . . .

BILLIE: . . . the bastard.

JOLENE: . . . what'd I do wi' that coat hanger?

(*Suddenly the taxi comes to a juddering halt*)

JOLENE: Woh!

* * *

(*In the hotel suite at the Holiday Inn Libo Ragazzo is pacing to and fro with a telephone in his hand and the receiver clamped to his ear. He is wearing a bathrobe, and his hair is still wet. The bedside radio is playing Billie and Jolene's version of 'Quicksilver'*)

RAGAZZO: (*into phone*) Naw, person to person . . . an' make it snappy, it's nearly six o'clock.

(*He crosses to the window and peeks out. He glances at his wristwatch*)

RAGAZZO: (*into phone, angrily*) Detroit time, I'm talkin' . . . hurry up.

(*He gives his wrist a shake, and holds his watch to his free ear*)

RAGAZZO: (*into phone*) Hullo?

(*Billie and Jolene's singing fades over the radio*)

RADIO DJ: The McFabulous McPhail Sisters there with yet another track from our Radio Kelvin *Country Comes to Calton* compilation CD . . . six and a half minutes to eke out before the Midnight News on Kelvinly casual 289.

(*With the phone still clamped to his ear Ragazzo crosses to the TV set, he prods the 'on' button with his big toe, and flicks through the channels. He pauses to stare fixedly at the mute re-run of a Deadwood Playboys 'Your Cheatin' Heart' video extract which is followed by a newsreader mouthing to the camera. He checks his watch again*)

RADIO DJ: . . . let me just confirm that time check for you . . . it's coming up to seven . . . no, eight . . . eight and a half minutes past twelve . . .

RAGAZZO: (*agitated*) C'mon, for God's sake . . . (*Into phone*) . . . hullo!

RADIO DJ: . . . a gentle reminder that you're tuned to the top rated . . .

(*There is an abortive news jingle on the radio*)

RADIO DJ: . . . in the West . . . Dunky Chisholm standing in for Ward Ferguson in the Midnight Newsroom, and we kick off with a bit of excitement down at the old Rancho Ponderosa tonight, and I don't just mean Jim Bob O'May's one and only Central Scotland appearance before . . . and I'm told that we have made contact with the radio car . . .

RAGAZZO: (*into phone*) Hullo?

RADIO DJ: (*to radio car*) . . . Hullo, Tamara?

RAGAZZO: (*into phone*) Is that you, Phil?

FRANK: (*into carphone, over radio*) Aw naw, it's that clown off the wireless . . .

RAGAZZO: (*into phone*) Naw, it's me . . . Libo.

RADIO DJ: (*to radio car*) Is that you, Brian?

FRANK: (*into carphone, over radio*) Hullo? You're through to . . .
    (*There is a burst of static over the radio*)

RAGAZZO: (*into phone*) Libo Ragazzo, d'you want me to talk up . . . hullo?

RADIO DJ: (*to radio car, over static*) I'm sorry, I can't hear you . . .

FRANK: (*into carphone, over radio*)` . . . but if you'd like to leave a message please speak after the tone.

RAGAZZO: (*into phone*) I wish I could, but I'm in Glesca . . .

FRANK: (*into carphone, over radio*) Thank you.
    (*Frank whistles a tone into the carphone*)

RADIO DJ: (*to radio car, overlapping whistle*) Could you ask Tamara to fill us in about this latest shooting incident down there in Wishaw?

RAGAZZO: (*into phone*) . . . naw, Glesca . . . G-l-a-s-g-o-w.

RADIO DJ: (*to radio car*) I believe that one of the Wild Bunch may've lost an eye, how accurate is that report . . . hullo?

RAGAZZO: (*into phone*) . . . I'm here to pick up that stuff you were inquirin' about.

FRANK: (*into carphone, over radio, distant*) Ohyah!
    (*There is a clunk over the radio as the carphone is hung up*)

RADIO DJ: Hullo?

RAGAZZO: (*into phone*) Naw, naw, absolutely no problems on that score, Phil, just to let you know I'll be back in Flowerdale Sunday night . . .
    (*There is a knock at Ragazzo's hotel room door*)

RADIO DJ: (*off-mike*) We've lost them, Kathy.
    (*There's another knock at the door*)

RAGAZZO: (*into phone*) Can you hold on a second, there's some-body . . . (*Loudly*) . . . who is it? I'm on the phone! (*Into phone*) You still there, Phil?

RADIO DJ: Hullo?

RAGAZZO: (*into phone*) Yeh, I know I promised, but . . .

    (*Ragazzo hears a muffled voice from outside the door*)

MUFFLED VOICE: Room service, that's yur sangwidge order.

RAGAZZO: (*into phone*) . . . naw, c'mon, hey, listen, I've still
  got most of that dough in Detroit, all you have to do is call ma
  wife an' she'll . . .

    (*There is a sudden crash and a splintering noise as the hotel
    room door comes crashing down into the room. Ragazzo whips
    round in a fury*)

RAGAZZO: . . . I told you I was on the fff . . . (*breaks off*) . . .
  wait a minute, you urnae Room Serv . . . what you doin'?

RADIO DJ: Okay, if there's anybody still awake down there in
  Wishaw and you happen to've been at tonight's historic Jim
  Bob gig . . .

RAGAZZO: (*shouting*) What you doin'! Naw, don't . . . woyah.

RADIO DJ: . . . why not give us a call on Freephone, 0800.

    (*Ragazzo's body slumps on to the floor, the telephone with it*)

TELEPHONE RECEIVER (*distant*) Ciao, Ragazzo.

    (*As Tonto stands over Ragazzo's crumpled body a hypodermic
    syringe falls from his hand and oozes its vile contents on to the
    carpet. Ragazzo gurgles weakly*)

RADIO DJ: . . . 775.

* * *

    (*The radio car sits outside the New Pancake Roadhouse diner
    in an otherwise deserted parking lot. The radio is playing*)

RADIO DJ: . . . 772. *A Country Comes to Calton* CD to the first
  phone-in eyewitness to get through to the *Crime Beat* studio
  before we go off the air at 2 o'clock. Seven, sorry, nine minutes
  after midnight . . . Ward Ferguson, if we can find him, with
  the *Weather Outlook* for ranch-hands in the Glasgow area after
  this one from . . .

    (*Frank reaches forward to snap the radio off before sinking out
    of sight in the driver's seat*)

* * *

    (*Inside the Pancake House Cissie squeezes ten pence into the juke-
    box, while Dorwood perches on a stool at the counter, scanning
    the large overhead pancake menu. Dorwood is dressed in clothes
    previously worn by Frank — including boots. On his head he
    wears an improvised hat fashioned from a Radio Kelvin Coun-
    try Comes to Calton plastic bag. He has borrowed Frank's
    Ray-bans. Cissie presses the 'select' button on the jukebox and a*

Scottish country danceband version of 'Your Cheatin' Heart'
comes up. Cissie crosses to the window overlooking the car park)

DORWOOD: *(still scanning menu)* If that's supposed to get ma
goat, it doesnae. *(Loudly)* How's about some service out
here . . . ho!

(He bangs on the counter with a sugar dispenser. Cissie stands
at the window, her eyes closed. Shirley, a pac-a-mac over her
waitressing outfit, struggles up the road towards the diner, lugging
a large pail of pancake mix. She stops under a streetlight, puts
the pail down and looks at the front page of the late edition of
the Evening Echo. *She scans the report about Dorwood's escape*
from custody. Accompanying the report are two photographs: one
straightforward mug shot, the other a snap showing Dorwood's
head wound. Shirley screws up her face in disgust as she crosses
the parking lot. Cissie disappears from the window. Dorwood
swings round from the counter to face the door as Shirley enters)

DORWOOD: No' before time.

(Shirley gives the jukebox a kick in passing. Its volume drops)

DORWOOD: How does yur Three Egg Pancake Special come?

SHIRLEY: Wi' three eggs an' a pancake.

(She crosses the room, slings the Echo *on the counter-top, dumps*
the pail, and removes her pac-a-mac)

SHIRLEY: What's your companion after?

(She nods towards a figure sitting in the corner, the Radio Kelvin
'hat' pulled low over her eyes)

DORWOOD: Lemme ask.

(He swivels round to face Cissie)

DORWOOD: D'you want a coffee?

SHIRLEY: Aw, my God, what happened to your . . .

(She breaks off. Her eyes dart to the Evening Echo *on the*
counter)

DORWOOD: Make that one Special an' two coffees.

(He swivels round to face Shirley)

SHIRLEY: Sure . . . lemme . . . er . . . lemme check out back an'
see if the hens've laid any . . . er . . .

(She edges away from the counter and gropes for the back door
handle)

SHIRLEY: . . . any pancakes.

(Shirley edges out of the back door of the diner and rushes around
the side of the building. She gallops past the radio car in the car
park and heads for a telephone box some hundred yards further
up the road. Frank hears her footsteps and sits bolt upright in
the driver's seat. He casts around, eyes unfocused. He sees Cissie
come bursting through the front door of the diner, Dorwood behind

her. She hauls the passenger door open and stuffs Dorwood inside)

FRANK: (*groggily*) Okay, where's ma pancake?

CISSIE: Move!

(*She chucks the car keys at Frank and jumps in beside him*)

DORWOOD: (*to Frank*) You heard . . . move.

(*The radio car roars into life, reverses out on to the road, and bucks off in the same direction taken by the galloping Shirley*)

FRANK: That is a very fetching chapeau . . . all you need is a pair of polythene pantaloons an' . . . hey, is that not what's-her-features from the Bar-L?

(*The car slows down as it comes level with a flagging Shirley*)

FRANK: D'you want me to stop an' give her a . . .

(*There is a smacking noise*)

FRANK: . . . ohyah!

(*The car accelerates away, leaving an exhausted Shirley to catch her breath by the roadside*)

★ ★ ★

(*Billie's taxi is parked at the side of the road in darkness. Billie leans against the taxi wing and scuffs her toe along the ground. Jolene leans out of the passenger door, lights two cigarettes and offers one to Billie*)

JOLENE: I still am your best pal, I wouldn't've told you if I didnae think you knew awready . . . I thought you knew awready . . . you sure you didnae know awready?

(*Jolene puffs on both cigarettes*)

JOLENE: Everybody else we know knew awready.

BILLIE: Yeh, thanks.

HENDERSON: Aw, c'mon, it could be an awful lot worse, at least you're not . . .

(*Billie stops scuffing and looks up*)

JOLENE: . . . aw, naw, don't tell me.

BILLIE: Don't you start, it was an accident!

JOLENE: Aw, my God in Heaven, when did this happen?

BILLIE: (*interrupting*) Mind your own business.

(*She stomps off up the road*)

JOLENE: It is ma business, I'm your best . . . where you off to?

(*Billie carries on walking*)

JOLENE: Come back here.

(*Billie gets swallowed up in the darkness*)

JOLENE: Billie?

(*Jolene steps on to the road and chucks the cigarettes away. An owl hoots*)

JOLENE: Billie!

BILLIE: (*in distance*) What?

JOLENE: You forgot the can for the diesel.

(*She holds up a jerry can*)

* * *

(*From a deserted approach road there is a distant view of Aberdeen, icily silvered by the dawn creeping up over the sea. The silence is gradually eroded by a low hornet-like hum that grows into a throaty rumble. A line of motorbikes appears over the horizon like so many Indians in a 'B' western. Riding at the head of the extended 'V formation flanking Jim Bob's Winnebago, is a squat man astride a massive Harley Davidson, in aviators and a peaked cap, the studs embedded in the back of his sawn-off scrotum-hide jacket identifying him as 'The Toad'. The Toad's obvious role model is the young Brando of* The Wild One *fame.*[89] *Behind 'The Toad' come the rest of the Loons O'Lucifer (Buchan Chapter) as they ride into the granite city limits. Fraser Boyle's fish van, coming at the oil capital from a different direction, brakes violently at the crossroads, despite the green light, as the line of bikers cross in front of it. Boyle sits behind the wheel and stares balefully as a seemingly endless procession of bikers passes in front of the van windscreen*)

CHEROKEE GEORGE: Whit you stoppin' fur? Yur lights're at green.

(*Boyle stops chewing and turns his head. Cherokee George sits hunched up in the passenger seat. He is wearing Frank's Burberry and still sports the black eye doled out to him in Glasgow*)

CHEROKEE GEORGE: Jist plough through the bastarts . . . Too late, yur lights've went tae . . .

(*The fish van takes off across the junction, narrowly avoiding a collision with a newspaper truck travelling in the opposite direction to the convoy and assiduously following traffic-light instructions to proceed. Horns blare*)

CHEROKEE GEORGE: . . . that's right, get the pairy us kilt!

* * *

(*A bundle of newspapers thump down on to the doorstep of an Aberdeen seafront café. There, on the front page of the* Aberdeen Press & Journal, *is the headline: 'MAFIA BAGMAN FOUND SLAIN IN SCOTTISH HOTEL'. A large photograph of the dead Libo Ragazzo in his bathrobe accompanies the news item. There is a smaller picture of a hypodermic needle 'similar to the one found at the scene of the crime'. In the listings box to the right of the page is the info: 'Former North Sea Diver sought in Grampian Region — see page 4'. Frank, in prison-issue pyjamas, Dorwood's cowboy boots on his feet, and wearing a hospital blanket poncho, plucks a newspaper from the bundle as the delivery boy reboards his truck heading off along the promenade. Frank flicks through the* Press & Journal *pages. He looks at a smiling picture of Dorwood in a cowboy hat. The headline above the picture reads: 'PANCAKE WAITRESS SHIRLEY: "I WAS PETRIFIED".' Frank's lips move silently as he reads the article. There is a hum as a milk float approaches. Frank's lips stop moving. He leafs quickly back to the front page)*

FRANK: *(to himself)* Jeesus . . .

(On the front page the dead Ragazzo wears a curiously peaceful expression on his bloated face. The milkman crosses the pavement with a crate of yoghurts and deposits it on the café doorstep. He picks up the empty crate and re-crosses to his float. He dumps the empty crate in the back of the float, picks up a crate of milkshakes, and repeats the journey, pausing on the way back to peer over Frank's shoulder at the front page of the newspaper)

MILKMAN: Quine next door till us has the perfect double o' that dressin' gown, onnly in reid.

(He goes back to the float, chucks the second empty crate in to the back, and climbs aboard. Frank shivers, folds the newspaper, and crosses to the crates of yoghurt and milk shakes)

* * *

(In a narrow backstreet lane in Aberdeen dockland a young police constable is standing by the now abandoned radio car. He is reeling off the car number plate into his personal radio)

POLICE CONSTABLE: *(into radio)* Echo, six, one, niner, Tango . . . Foxtrot . . . Jitterbug . . .

(Boyle's fish van appears at the far end of the narrow lane and drives down it towards the radio car and the policeman. The young constable steps out on to the cobbles to examine the radio car driver's door. Boyle brakes sharply some twenty yards away and reverses speedily all the way back up the street)

POLICE CONSTABLE: *(into radio)* . . . no sign of forced entry, over.

(There is a blurred response from HQ over the radio. Boyle's van reaches the top of the narrow street, backs round the corner out of sight, and reappears a few seconds later crossing the gap. The carphone inside the radio car starts to ring. The young police constable peers in through the window. Ralph Henderson sits at the wheel of his white BMW, driving through the outskirts of Aberdeen, carphone to his ear)

HENDERSON: Tammy?

(*He holds the phone out to a white-faced Tamara sitting beside him. Tamara stares straight ahead*)

HENDERSON: (*replacing carphone*) Tell you what, why don't I take you to that little French place this evening? Chappie hails from Provence . . . serves up a passable *bourride* by all . . .

(*Tamara makes a grab for the carphone*)

HENDERSON: . . . uh, uh.

TAMARA: Ooow.

HENDERSON: (*sweetly*) You don't imagine I'm going to let you talk to anyone, do you?

★ ★ ★

(*Frank makes his way along the deserted seafront promenade towards a distant beach shelter. His arms are loaded with milk shake and yoghurt cartons. A growing rumble causes him to turn his head and look behind him. Cissie sits shivering with her back against the beach shelter, the Dobro case on the bench on one side of her and Dorwood stretched out on the other, his head in her lap. The Winnebago and its biker escort pass behind the shelter. First one, then several, empty milk shake cartons come sailing over top of the shelter roof. Dorwood stirs slightly, his stockinged feet rubbing together. The convoy passes along the promenade towards the fairground site. Frank appears round the side of the shelter, two yoghurt cartons in his hand*)

FRANK: Hi, how's the boy?

CISSIE: Still asleep, what kept you!

(*Dorwood lets out a moan*)

FRANK: Loons O'Lucifer had the milk shakes, I'm afraid.

(*He sits down on the bench at Dorwood's feet and passes a yoghurt carton to Cissie*)

FRANK: I'll've the turnip one.

CISSIE: Did you manage to get a newspaper?

(*She examines her yoghurt label*)

FRANK: Yeh . . . boy Ragazzo's dead.

(*He peels the top off his carton and dips his tongue into the yoghurt. Dorwood lets out another moan*)

FRANK: There's a bit about hubby on page 4.

(*He produces the* Press & Journal *from under his poncho. Cissie grabs the paper and leafs through it*)

FRANK: It's not really turnip, it's turnip an' raisin.

(*He upends the yoghurt down his throat*)

CISSIE: (*reading*) The rotten pig, I always knew she was a clipe.

FRANK: You know I love you, don't you? Who's a clipe?

CISSIE: Shirley . . . she phoned the cops right enough . . . they know we're here.

FRANK: Naw, they don't . . . it says 'Sought in Grampian Region', that could be anywhere within a radius of . . . ho, wake up . . . (*He gives Dorwood a dunt*) . . . how big is 'Grampian Region'?

(*Dorwood comes to with a start*)

DORWOOD: (*groggily*) Wha . . . ?

CISSIE: (*sotto voce, to Frank*) What're you doin'!

DORWOOD: (*non compos mentis*) Where am I?

FRANK: Grampian Region, cops're after you.

(*He takes the yoghurt carton from Cissie and spoons a dollop into his mouth with his fingers*)

CISSIE: (*clapping Dorwood on the back*) It's okay, you were asleep.

(*She shoots Frank a filthy look*)

FRANK: Bleagh!

(*He spits a mouthful of yoghurt on to the ground*)

DORWOOD: (*to Cissie*) What you done wi' ma boots?

FRANK: (*to Cissie*) You might've warned me it was banana!

CISSIE: (*to Dorwood*) He's got them.

(*She hides the newspaper behind her back*)

FRANK: (*to Cissie*) An' you've got the cheek to talk about Shirley bein' a clipe? (*To Dorwood*) I was only wearin' them to go for . . . (*Pointedly at Cissie*) . . . the newspaper.

(*He hands the banana yoghurt to Dorwood*)

DORWOOD: What's this?

(*Dorwood peers at the carton*)

FRANK: (*to Cissie*) Gonnae get that for us?

(*He holds a leg out*)

DORWOOD: Ho, what's he doin' wi' ma boots? (*To Cissie*) Eh? What's he doin' wi' ma boots on!

CISSIE: God spare me from all this.

(*She buries her face in her hands*)

FRANK: (*to Cissie*) I'm not surprised you want a divorce, does he have to say everythin' twice over?

DORWOOD: Divorce? What's he talkin' about, divorce! (*To Frank*) What're you talkin' about divorce!

FRANK: Correction . . . thrice over.

DORWOOD: (*to Cissie*) I thought you told me this guy was brought in by the Samaritans to keep you off the booze?

(*Frank looks up from tugging at Dorwood's boots*)

CISSIE: (*through fingers, to Frank*) I had to tell him somethin'.

DORWOOD: What've you been sayin' to him?

(*He chucks the yoghurt carton away and grabs Cissie*)

CISSIE: Aaargh!

DORWOOD: What've you been tellin' this geek about our private business!

CISSIE: Chuck that!

FRANK: Ho!

(*He prods Dorwood in the back*)

DORWOOD: What!

FRANK: There's no call to add to this mess.

(*He points to the litter on the floor*)

DORWOOD: Listen, ya . . .

(*He lets go of Cissie and rounds on Frank. Cissie gives him a shove, forcing him to wade through the yoghurt puddle in his bedsocks*)

DORWOOD: . . . aw, naw!

(*He stares down at his claggy feet*)

FRANK: Here, lemme give you these boots.

* * *

(*Jim Bob's Winnebago and the attendant Loons O' Lucifer have come to rest by the Aberdeen beach pavilion. A Loons O'Lucifer motorcycle 'Guard of Honour' has been lined up, leading to Jim Bob's trailer door. The Toad slowly dismounts from his machine and removes his sawn-off scrotum-hide jacket. Standing there in his sleeveless black T-shirt, one cannot help but be struck by the bold tattoo on the Toad's beefy bicep. Though not exactly alike in every detail, the tattoo is strikingly similar to the one that Frank will carry on his upper arm to the grave. A Lieutenant moves forward with sheets of tissue paper and a bottle of 'Ferguzade'.*[90] *The Toad folds his colours and places them reverentially between the sheets of tissue paper. The Toad has a slug of 'Ferguzade' and he and his Lieutenant move forward between the two rows of bikes. The Loon nearest the Trailer door gives it a respectful tap with the toe of his jackboot. There is a low murmur of expectant Loons. Fraser Boyle's fish van pulls up unnoticed and parks nearby. The Toad adjusts his aviators and gives his peaked Brando cap a little twitch. Inside the van Boyle lights a half-cigarette and passes it to Cherokee George*)

CHEROKEE GEORGE: D'you see wit I see?

(*He presses his nose against the windscreen*)

BOYLE: I don't want to see what you see, I havenae been at the meths, ole buddy.

CHEROKEE GEORGE: Naw, oan the boy's airm . . . it's the dead spit of the wan I done fur that pal a Dwane's the other day there.

BOYLE: What pal a Dwane's?

CHEROKEE GEORGE: Big glaikit-luckin' sod, turnt up out the blue in a raincoat no' aw that dissimilar tae . . .

(*He breaks off and examines the Burberry he's wearing*)

CHEROKEE GEORGE: . . . haud oan, where'd you say you bought this?

(*The Toad reappears at Jim Bob's trailer door and raises a triumphant forearm*)

CHEROKEE GEORGE: . . . awyah!

(*The fish van takes off suddenly and weaves its way past the beach pavilion, just clipping the Toad's mighty Harley in passing. The big machine teeters on its stand. The Toad stops dead in his tracks. All heads turn and an unearthly hush descends as the Toad's beloved sickle crashes in slow motion to the concrete. There is a collective gasp of incredulous Loons as the fish van drives unconcernedly off along the promenade*)

★ ★ ★

(*Jolene sits on one of the fold-down seats of the taxi, her back to Billie. She's strumming Billie's guitar*)

JOLENE: (*sings*) 'I cry myself to sleep each night an' wish that I could hold you tight . . . ma life's so empty since you went away . . . ' (*Breaks off, to Billie*) You thought up any names yet? (*Sings*) 'The pillow that I dream upon . . . ' (*Breaks off*) Or there's Randy? (*Sings*) 'An' it keeps right on a . . . ' (*Breaks off*) Naw, scrub Randy, you don't want any crass individuals passin' remarks . . . (*Sings*) . . . hurtin' since you've . . . '

(*The taxi comes to a juddering stop*)

JOLENE: (*breaks off*) What you stoppin' for?

★ ★ ★

(*Later that afternoon Frank and Cissie are seated in a stationary Waltzer bucket on the carnival site. The afternoon light is fading and, except for the occasional Loon passing in the middle distance, the site is deserted*)

FRANK: So?

CISSIE: So what?

(*Frank removes his prison-issue pyjama top and slips an arm into the sleeve of Cissie's jacket*)

FRANK: So what? I told you I loved you, didn't I?

(*He gropes behind his back without success for the other sleeve*)

CISSIE: Look, I'm only lendin' you a jacket, for God's sake.

FRANK: (*interrupting*) Naw, back in that beach bunker, you pretended not to hear me.

*(The 'Eagle of the Apocalypse' on Frank's upper arm has healed
and lends his otherwise spindly limbs a certain macho credibility)*

CISSIE: I was readin' my yoghurt.

(The Toad makes his way around the Waltzer towards them)

FRANK: Aw, yeh?

THE TOAD: Ho!

CISSIE: I don't think we should be here.

*(She makes to get up. Frank breaks off groping for the other
sleeve and takes hold of her arm)*

FRANK: Sit where you are.

(The Toad draws level with their bucket)

FRANK: So what's with the 'Ho', Jim?

(He turns to face the Toad)

THE TOAD: 'Hojim'?

FRANK: You're just after shoutin' 'Ho!', I trust that wasnae at
us? *(Aside, to Cissie)* You might've told me he was built like a
bus shelter!

(The Toad peers at Frank's tattoo, then at his own)

FRANK: We were just goin', it was her that wanted to sit here.

(He starts getting up)

CISSIE: It was not!

THE TOAD: Nae sweat, min . . .

(He presses Frank back into his seat)

THE TOAD: . . . I didna ken ye wur a Loon, ken?

FRANK: Yeh, right. *(To Cissie)* What's a 'Loonken'?

THE TOAD: *(leering over Cissie)* Fit Chapter ye wi'?

CISSIE: *(to Frank)* You tell him.

FRANK: Chapter? Aw . . . er . . . The Devil-dogs . . . Carfin.

CISSIE: *(to The Toad)* Chuck oglin' us.

THE TOAD: *(to Frank)* Fit'd she say?

FRANK: *(apologetically)* I think it's your after-shave. *(Sotto voce,
to Cissie)* D'you want us to die?

THE TOAD: Ho!

(He leans forward and pokes Frank)

THE TOAD: *(close to Frank's face)* S'nae a bad-lookin' quinie . . .
if I ever loss the errial aff me sickle I'll ken far tae come till.

(He winks and swings off along the Waltzer)

CISSIE: What'd he say?

FRANK: Biker talk . . .

(He locates the missing sleeve and sticks his arm down it)

CISSIE: D'you not feel stupit in that?

FRANK: What . . . this?

CISSIE: Accordin' to Dorwood it buttons up the wrong side.

FRANK: Accordin' to Dorwood the entire planet buttons up the wrong side . . . has he always been that narky?

CISSIE: You'd be that narky if you'd got seven years for somethin' you didn't do.

(*She gets up to go*)

FRANK: You don't still believe that nonsense, do you?

CISSIE: Of course I believe it, I'm married to him, amn't I?

FRANK: You could put a tune to that an' sell it to Tammy Wynette . . . naw, wait, don't go, Cissie!

(*He grabs her arm*)

CISSIE: Leggo ma arm, I've got to go an' hunt for . . .

(*Frank pulls her close*)

CISSIE: . . . what you doin'?

(*Frank leans forward and kisses her tenderly on the lips. He breaks away and looks at her for some response. She regards him balefully*)

FRANK: Well?

CISSIE: (*shaking her head*) Nup . . . sorry.

FRANK: Awright . . . c'mere.

(*He takes her in his arms and presses his lips to hers, and they sink down into the bucket locked in an embrace. Suddenly the lights around them come on as the Waltzer comes to life. A husky steam organ version of 'Your Cheatin' Heart' begins to play as the Waltzer buckets start to move. The volume of the music swells. In the control booth of the Waltzer the Toad, oil-can in hand, is tinkering with the speed and volume controls as Frank and Cissie spin past him. The Waltzer whirls round at breakneck speed and still Frank and Cissie embrace. Cissie's hair corkscrews behind her as the lights shed a rainbow across her cheek. Slowly, the Waltzer begins to slacken its reckless pace, and the steam organ starts to run out of puff. The bucket begins to rotate at a more leisurely speed, and the lights start going out one by one. The Waltzer finally grinds to a halt where it started. Cissie sits there, eyes shut, knuckles white on the handlebar as the steam organ wheezes out a final grace note. Frank looks at Cissie, then looks away. Cissie slowly opens her eyelids*)

CISSIE: (*softly*) Wow.

* * *

(*Dorwood stands on the seashore at the water's edge, the incoming tide lapping over his one cowboy boot and one bedsock. He stares out to sea and steels himself against the icy spume carried on the evening breeze. A supply vessel battles through the waves on her way out to the far-off rigs. Dorwood looks down at the revolver and checks the chamber. Two slugs left*)

★ ★ ★

(Cherokee George and Fraser Boyle are sitting in the fish van on the edge of the carnival site eating fish and chips out of newspaper. Cherokee George has a fresh black eye to keep the other one company)

CHEROKEE GEORGE: You want to know somethin'?

(Boyle stares through the windscreen as one or two fathers and small sons wander forlornly between the boarded-up stall and sideshows. The Loons o' Lucifer, in contrast, cluster around Snowy's mobile fish, chip and coffee stall which sits in a pool of light on a patch of ground vacated by the showman's caravan)

BOYLE: Naw, but I can tell from the way you're munchin' that you're gonnae to ad to ma aready bulgin' catalogue of totally useless information.

(Cherokee George scrunches up his chip paper, smacks his lips, and wipes his hands down the Burberry)

CHEROKEE GEORGE: That hus tae be the worst fish supper I've ever hud in ma life.

BOYLE: Didnae deter you from molocatin' it, I notice.

CHEROKEE GEORGE: It wis me that bought them . . . d'you want a beverage?

(He opens the van door)

BOYLE: Aye, get us a hot choclit . . . an' listen . . . don't you go an' do a bunk, that stuff's up here someplace an' I'm gonnae need a good buddy to give us a hand to get it off the get that's got it an' get it to Jim Bob afore he gets on that boat the morra, get me?

(Cherokee George weighs this up for several seconds)

CHEROKEE GEORGE: What happens if they don't huv any hot choclit?

★ ★ ★

(On another part of the carnival site Frank and Cissie meander between the boarded-up booths, Frank's arm around Cissie's shoulder, hers around his waist)

FRANK: If that gets too heavy gimme a shout an' we'll dump it.

(Cissie is lugging the Dobro case. She looks at Frank)

FRANK: What?

CISSIE: Nothin' . . . I'm just tryin' to picture what you were like as a toddler.

(She leans her head on his shoulder)

FRANK: Much as I am the now . . . totally irresist . . . aw, naw.

(He stops dead)

FRANK: Is this Friday?

CISSIE: I think so . . . why?

FRANK: I forgot to phone in ma copy.

CISSIE: Copy?

FRANK: For the 'Rab Haw' column. What time d'you make it?

CISSIE: What you goin' to phone in? You havenae eaten anythin' all day.

(*She turns her gaze upwards to the sky and Frank joins her in staring upwards. A blanket of twinkling stars covers the heavens*)

FRANK: I had a turnip yoghurt at breakfast time.

CISSIE: Turnip an' raisin.

FRANK: I just need to find myself a telephone . . .

CISSIE: Look!

(*A shooting star traverses the velvet black sky and burns itself out*)

FRANK: (*looking down and around*) Where?

CISSIE: That means you can make a wish.

FRANK: Aw . . . I thought you'd spotted a phonebox.

(*Cissie stands with her head tilted back, and her eyes shut now*)

FRANK: Cissie?

(*She lowers her gaze and looks at Frank*)

FRANK: (*swallows*) God, see when you look at me like that, you put all thoughts of turnips an' raisins right out of ma head.

(*He leans forward and kisses her. Cissie drops the Dobro case on to Frank's foot — the one without the cowboy boot on — and puts her arms around him*)

FRANK: (*softly*) Ohyah.

(*Cissie leans forward and kisses Frank*)

FRANK: 'Know how it slipped ma mind?

(*He picks up the Dobro case and puts his arm around Cissie. They walk on*)

FRANK: I wasnae wearin' ma Rab Haw rain . . .

(*He breaks off as he sees Cherokee George stroll between the booths up ahead wearing Frank's Burberry and looking exactly like Dopey from the Seven Dwarves*)

FRANK: . . . coat.

(*He looks at Cissie. Cissie looks at him. They both look at the now-empty gap between the booths. Frank drops the Dobro case and breaks into a lop-sided trot. Up ahead Cherokee George picks his way between the parked motorbikes by Snowy's stall to get to the counter. He squeezes himself between some lounging Loons and slaps a couple of coins down*)

CHEROKEE GEORGE: Wan coffee, wan choclit, baith hot.

(*Snowy, the lugubrious stallholder, carries on wiping the counter-*)

top with a filthy cloth)

CHEROKEE GEORGE: You want tae get a big sign up there . . . 'The Worst Fish Suppers in Scotland, Bar None'.

(*He looks around at the assembled Loons, failing to notice that they are all happily munching on Snowy's renowned fish suppers*)

CHEROKEE GEORGE: (*to Loons*) I've scoffed a few fish suppers in ma time an' I don't mind tellin' youse people, that wis the worst fish supper I ever hud in ma life.

(*The Loons stop munching*)

CHEROKEE GEORGE: Naw, straight up, it hus tae be the worst fish supper I ever hud in ma life. Seriously.

(*He turns back to Snowy*)

CHEROKEE GEORGE: Bung a coupla broon sugars in the choclit, will you, Chief? S'fur the boy in the fish motor.

(*He turns once more to the Loons*)

CHEROKEE GEORGE: Goat tae keep the bastart sweet, eh?

(*Frank is peering round the corner of Snowy's stall and watching the commotion. Cissie stands behind him*)

FRANK: (*over shoulder*) 'Course I want it back but this may not be the most opportune . . .

CHEROKEE GEORGE: Waaaaaaaaaagh!

CISSIE: (*distressed*) Can you not go an' help him?

(*She leans over the top of Frank and tries peering round the corner*)

FRANK: (*straightening up*) Help him? That's the guy that landed me wi' this!

(*He taps his tattooed arm*)

CISSIE: Cherokee George? What's he doin' in Aberdeen?

(*There is a sudden roar from a mighty Harley Davidson*)

CHEROKEE GEORGE: Aaaaaaaaaaaaa-aaaaaaaaaaaaargh!

(*The Toad roars through the gap between booths with Cherokee George roped by his ankles to the back of his bike, getting dragged along the ground in Frank's Burberry*)

FRANK: (*laughing*) There's your answer. (*Stops laughing*) Hey, ma good coat!

* * *

(*Billie and Jolene are cruising along the Aberdeen promenade in the taxi. Jolene is sitting up in the back seat*)

JOLENE: Aw, look, Billie, the Shows!

(*She presses her nose against the window*)

BILLIE: (*over shoulder*) Yeh, an' they're shut.

JOLENE: So they're shut? Still the Shows, innit? God, you're that crabbit, gettin'.

(*They hear the roar of the Harley as the Toad circles the showground in search of the fish van*)

CHEROKEE GEORGE: Waaaaaaaaaaa-aaaaaaaaaaaaaaooooooh!

JOLENE: See that? Somebody's enjoyin' theirself.

(*She sticks her tongue out at the back of Billie's head*)

★ ★ ★

(*The white BMW is parked discreetly not far away from the beach pavilion and Jim Bob's Winnebago*)

HENDERSON: 'Fraid we'll have to take a raincheck on that *bourride*, sweetie . . . don't think you're quite up to it, hmm?

(*Tamara is slumped in the back seat. She looks like she's dead, but her eyes are open and she is still breathing . . . just. Henderson picks up the carphone*)

HENDERSON: Believe me, the people who were eliminated were scum, Tammy . . .

(*He punches in a number*)

HENDERSON: . . . the sort you write about in that little newspaper of yours. (*Into phone*) Hi, we spoke last night, I'm in a position to deliver.

(*He reaches behind him and adjusts Tamara's collar*)

HENDERSON: (*into phone*) . . . no, not quite that much . . . about six, seven kilos . . . all right . . . six . . . listen, I can just as easily . . . (*Listens*) . . . wise fellow.

(*He replaces the receiver*)

HENDERSON: Back in a jiffy, darling . . . don't go 'way, you hear?

(*He reaches out and touches Tamara's cold cheek. He smiles. Henderson gets out of the car and goes around to the boot. He turns the key and throws the boot-lid open. He reaches in, removes a parcel, and reaches up to close the lid. A revolver barrel glints in the moonlight and Henderson freezes as the gun is placed just behind his ear*)

DORWOOD: Nice an' easy does it.

(*Henderson closes the boot-lid nice and easily*)

DORWOOD: Right, start walkin'.

(*Henderson steps away from the car*)

DORWOOD: Slow! walk slow, I've only got the one boot.

(*He brings the gun down and jabs it into Henderson's back, forcing him forward towards the roadway traversing their path to Jim Bob's trailer*)

DORWOOD: I just hope she's gonnae be okay in that motor, or that's three murders that're gonnae appear on the charge sheet alongside whatever else you've been . . . get that down!

(*He knocks Henderson's upraised right arm down to his side*)

DORWOOD: D'you want everybody to know I've got a gun at your back?

HENDERSON: (*over shoulder*) So you tell me . . . I've only got your word for . . .

DORWOOD: (*interrupting*) Try me.

(*Dorwood cocks the gun. Henderson arrives at the kerb and stops*)

DORWOOD: What you waitin' for, the lollipop man?

(*He prods Henderson in the back with the revolver. But Henderson stays put*)

HENDERSON: I've just wet myself.

DORWOOD: So, you get scurvy legs . . . walk, I said!

* * *

(*Billie's taxi is approaching the beach pavilion, Jolene scrunches up her fish supper paper*)

JOLENE: God, that was scrumptious, how was yours?

(*Billie leans forward and peers through the windscreen. Through it she sees Henderson and Dorwood cross the road in front of them*)

JOLENE: I don't recall our Jinty goin' deaf when she fell pregnant. Hoi, I'm talkin' to you, McPhail.

(*Billie slows down and turns around to Jolene*)

BILLIE: You're never gonnae believe this, Jolene, but guess who I've just seen!

(*She turns back to look through the windscreen again. The road ahead is now completely deserted*)

JOLENE: Wasnae the boy MacIndoo was it?

(*The taxi shrieks to a halt and Billie leaps out. She stands looking around her in the headlight beams*)

JOLENE: Wee Desmond, naw?

(*Jolene makes to get out of the taxi*)

BILLIE: I swear to God, Jolene . . .

JOLENE: Don't be ridiculous, Billie, what would Dorwood be doin' up in Aberdeen?

(*She rushes up to Billie*)

JOLENE: He's just after fallin' off a roof in Glas . . . (*Stops*)

(*Billie turns to face her*)

BILLIE: He's just after what?

* * *

(*Dorwood holds the revolver against Henderson's temple as they press themselves against Jim Bob's trailer in the dark near the beach pavilion*)

★ ★ ★

(*Approaching the cliff-edge Fraser Boyle sees a crumpled coat on the ground. He gathers up the tattered Burberry and inches closer through the moonlight to the cliff edge*)

BOYLE: Hullo! Y'err, George?

(*Below him, on the rocky beach, Boyle can see his van sitting on its nose, rear doors agape*)

BOYLE: (*shouting down*) George? (*Loudly*) Ur you down there, ya dozy half-breed!

(*He can hear the waves crashing on the distant beach below*)

BOYLE: (*to himself*) Ach, I give up . . .

(*He turns away and starts walking*)

CHEROKEE GEORGE: (*distant*) I still think that wis the worst fish supper I ever hud in ma life!

(*Boyle stops, turns, and heads back to the cliff-edge*)

★ ★ ★

(*Back in town a police patrol car cruises along the seafront promenade. An indecipherable message can be heard over the car radio, the single intelligible word of which is an 'over' at the end. As the police car's tail lights disappear along the promenade, Frank and Cissie emerge from their hiding place*)

FRANK: We could always go to the nearest bingo hall an' get the manager to flash a message up on the screen . . . 'Will Dorwood Crouch, last seen wearing one cowboy boot . . . '

(*They pass the discreetly parked white BMW. Frank stops by the driver's door*)

CISSIE: I wish I could remember what pubs we used to . . . (*Breaks off*) . . . come away from there!

FRANK: Be with you in a second . . .

(*He tries the handle and the door opens*)

FRANK: . . . I just want to make a quick phonecall to ma Features Editor.

★ ★ ★

(*Onstage inside the beach pavilion Jim Bob O'May and the Wild Bunch are brewing up a storm*)

JIM BOB: (*sings*) 'Well, I never felt more like singing the blues . . . '

(*There is the sound of an exultant roar from the assembled Loons o' Lucifer*)

JIM BOB: ' . . . 'cos I never thought that I'd ever lose your love, dear . . . '

(*Loon bops with Loon in the aisles*)

JIM BOB: (*sings*) ' . . . why'd you leave me this way . . . '
> (*Jim Bob and the Wild Bunch give the classic early 50s hit big licks from the beach pavilion stage. Few of the bopping Loons pay much heed to the pedal-steel player, who keeps somewhat out of the limelight under his stetson, or to the fact that he is wearing only one cowboy boot under his pedal-steel guitar table*)

* * *

> (*Frank has climbed inside the white BMW and is speaking on the carphone*)

FRANK: . . . aw, an' listen, could you ask one of the paramedics to bring us somethin' to eat . . . anythin' but yoghurt . . . we're starvin' . . . thanks.
> (*He replaces the phone and leans out of the open door*)

FRANK: Be here in two minutes, how is she?
> (*Cissie and Tamara, acting like a bendi-toy are walking to and fro beside the car. They hear a police whoop-whoop nearby*)

CISSIE: You can see how she is . . . if we hadn't found her she'd've snuffed it . . . (*To Tamara*) . . . C'mon, walk, dammit!
> (*Frank climbs out of the car and goes over to them. He examines an ugly bruise on the inside of Tamara's forearm with a tiny red puncture mark at its centre*)

FRANK: D'you suppose this's self-inflicted or . . .
> (*He breaks off as the police car whoop-whoop approaches*)

FRANK: . . . Oh, oh, that's me then.
> (*He raises his arms above his head and walks to meet the oncoming red, white and blue flashing lights*)

CISSIE: Where the hell d'you think you're goin'!

FRANK: (*over shoulder*) It's okay, Hank Fonda got off when they found out it was a case of mistaken . . .
> (*The patrol car speeds straight past him and on towards Jim Bob's trailer*)

FRANK: . . . identity.
> (*A disgruntled Frank lowers his upraised arms, he looks across towards the trailer*)

CISSIE: Hoi, quit sulkin' an' come an' help me with her!

* * *

> (*An Aberdeen matron with a small dog on a lead stands in the beach pavilion parking lot a few yards distant, as two police patrol officers bend over Henderson's body. One of his officers turns Henderson on to his back. Henderson's face is a white powdery mask*)

FIRST PATROL OFFICER: He's nae been out for his Hallowe'en, has he?

(*The matron's dog starts yapping*)

MATRON: Quiet Monty!

SECOND PATROL OFFICER: (*into personal radio*) Y'there, HQ, over?

* * *

(*Inside the pavilion Jim Bob and Jolene are sharing the vocals, leading the Wild Bunch through a rockin' Country version of the Bellamy Brothers' 'Let Your Love Flow'.*

Backstage in the dressing room Billie stands staring into the mirror, her face cupped in her hands. Jim Bob and Jolene's duetting voices are playing over the tannoy)

BILLIE: (*in answer to song*) Yeh, sure, no problem!

(*Her head drops on to the dressing table top. Jim Bob and Jolene combine in joyous harmony over the tannoy. Some flashing blue lights pass the dressing room window as two ambulances speed Tamara and Henderson to hospital*)

* * *

(*Further down the beach, away from the pavilion, Cissie and Frank sit a few feet apart on a beach shelter bench. Frank runs his fingers over the Dobro strings as a wintery sun claws its way up the beach. He eases awkwardly into a slide-guitar version of 'Your Cheatin' Heart'. Out in the distant sea, a Norwegian ferryboat forges its way towards the far horizon. The sun has now risen and Cissie's hair looks burnished by its light. The Dobro lies beside its case on the bench. Frank is gone*)

* * *

(*Frank is at the wheel of a taxi, speeding out of Aberdeen on the way to Glasgow. Billie and Jolene are asleep in the back amid a pile of clothes, amps, guitars and other clutter. Frank notices a man slumped by the roadside ahead of the taxi. As the car approaches a dishevelled looking Fraser Boyle stands up, holding out a tattered raincoat with the word 'Glesca' daubed across the back*)

FRANK: (*to himself*) Yeh, some hope.

(*He gives a laugh as the taxi sails past Boyle*)

FRANK: (*laugh dies*) Ho, wait a minute, that was ma Burberry!

(*He turns to look back, and sees Boyle's diminishing figure behind him*)

* * *

(*Cissie stands in front of the beach shelter looking out to sea.*

Walking behind the shelter, along the promenade, is a woman hand in hand with a small boy about four years old. As the boy and the woman pass along the promenade, Cissie picks up the Dobro case, quits the beach shelter and heads off along the beach in the opposite direction. Beside one of her footprints in the sand there is a brief glimpse of gunmetal as the sun catches on the navy Colt revolver.

Cissie walks on)

Notes

1. *Okeyfenokey*, the Okefenokee swamp is in Florida.
2. *'gaudeamus igitur'*, student song, 'let us rejoice therefore while we are young . . .'
3. *Maxim's*, a famous Parisian restaurant.
4. *Bevis Hillier* was among the first to revive interest in Art Deco styles in architecture and art; see *Art Deco* (1997).
5. *Hank Williams*, American country singer, 1923–53.
6. *Steinway*, a make of piano.
7. *Blüthner*, a make of piano.
8. *Hopalong Cassidy*, hero of 28 Western novels written by Clarence E. Mulford in the 1920s, '30s and '40s. He was played in films by William (Bill) Boyd, who made over 65 movies with Paramount and United Artists, which were later turned into television programmes.
9. Words of Elvis Presley's first hit record, *Heartbreak Hotel*, 1956.
10. *Jim Reeves*, American country singer (1923–64), who died in a plane crash at a time when he was achieving international success for country music in competition with the new wave of rock groups such as the Beatles.
11. *Kilwinning*, small town in Ayrshire.
12. *'De Profundis'*, prayer: 'Out of the depths I have cried to Thee, O Lord'.
13. *Wishbone Ash*, English rock group of the 1970s; *Beverley Sisters*, popular British singing trio in the 1950s.
14. *Annie S. Swan* (1859–1942), popular Scottish novelist (who also wrote under the names of Mrs Burnett Smith and David Lyall), and is sometimes associated with the 'Kailyard' movement in Scottish literature.
15. *Hofner Senator*, style of electric guitar.
16. *'second'*, Second Class Degree.
17. *Woman's Realm*, popular women's journal.
18. *Emmylou Harris*, an American country singer, b. 1947; *Rolf Harris*, Australian artist, singer and performer on British television, b. 1930.
19. *Kris Kristofferson*, American rock and country singer and film star, b. 1936.

20. *'Ole Shep'*, sentimental country song about the death of a dog, written by Red Foley. Elvis Presley sang it at his first audition at the age of ten and it remained one of his favourites.

21. *Lambretta*, a scooter.

22. *'The King'*, Elvis Presley (1935–77).

23. *Gang Show*, variety show staged by Boy Scouts.

24. *Sun Records*, owned by Sam Philips, the company which recorded Elvis Presley's early records in Memphis, Tennessee.

25. *Filofax*, personal organiser, diary.

26. *Woolie's*, Woolworth's department store.

27. *Arthur Koestler* (1905–83), novelist and writer of books on the history of science. His *The Roots of Coicidence* (1972) is a study of apparently chance happenings which he believed not to be accidental.

28. *Tiny Bubbles*, sentimental popular song sung by such Scottish entertainers as Andy Stewart.

29. *Patsy Cline* (1932–63), American country and pop singer who died in a plane crash.

30. *Randy Travis*, American singer, b. 1959.

31. *Doris Day*, American singer and actress, born Doris Mary Ann Von Kappelhoff in 1924; famous for her role in the comedy Western, *Calamity Jane*, 1953.

32. *Maoists*, followers of the Chinese communist leader, Chairman Mao, and, in the 1960s, an alternative to the discredited communism of the Soviet Union.

33. *Merchant City*, gentrified area of Glasgow; *'des con enviably adj'*, desirable accommodation enviably adjacent to.

34. *Buckfast*, very cheap wine.

35. *Piper Omega*, an oil platform in the North Sea.

36. *Everly Brothers*, Phil and Don Everly, American singing duo successful in the 1950s and '60s.

37. *Slim Whitman*, early American country singer, b. 1924.

38. *Empire*, Glasgow theatre.

39. *TLS*, Times Literary Supplement.

40. *Georgian poetry*, the anthologies of Georgian poetry were published before and during the First World War and included the work of poets such as Rupert Brooke.

41. *Smokey Robinson*, American soul singer, b. 1940.

42. *Turneresque*, nineteenth-century English land- and seascape painter J. M. W. Turner was famous for his depiction of sunsets, such as *The Fighting Temeraire*.

43. *Maybole*, small town in Ayrshire.

44. *Kissogram*, a message and a kiss delivered in parody of a telegram delivery.

45. *Dennistoun*, populous area of Glasgow.

46. *High Noon*, western film of 1952 starring Gary Cooper and Grace Kelly, directed by Fred Zinnemann.

47. *Sitting Bull*, Native American chief (1831–98) who defeated General Custer at the Battle of Little Big Horn in 1876 in the struggle to preserve the way of life of the aboriginal peoples of North America. Died after being arrested by State authorities.

48. *Ray-bans*, high-class sunglasses.

49. *Alfred Hitchcock*, British director of thrillers.

50. *Ray Charles*, American pianist and singer, b. 1930, and blind from the age of seven.

51. *SAS*, Special Air Services, British special operations troops.

52. *Derry*, or Londonderry, city which was focus of the 'Troubles' in Northern Ireland from the 1960s and a centre of paramilitary activity on both sides of the religious divide.

53. *Baedeker*, American guide book.

54. *Hoyt Axton*, singer, songwriter and actor, b. 1938; his mother Mae Boren Axton co-wrote Elvis Presley's *Heartbreak Hotel*.

55. *Melrose's Darjeeling*, a make of tea.

56. *Bovril*, a beef extract drink.

57. *Winnebago*, an American mobile home, recreational vehicle.

58. *Candleriggs*, area of Glasgow.

59. *Sony*, television; *Kind Hearts and Coronets*, a popular television series.

60. *Tristan da Cunha*, island in the South Atlantic; *Territorials*, Territorial soldiers of the British army reserve.

61. *Chet Atkins*, American guitarist, b. 1924.

62. *NUJ*, National Union of Journalists.

63. *Tammy Wynette*, American country and western singer (1942–98), famous for her record, 'Stand By Your Man'.

64. *Hank Jansen*, one of over twenty pseudonyms used by Victor George Charles Norwood, writer of popular fiction.

65. *Meals on Wheels*, charity service which delivers meals to the elderly and housebound.

66. *Mein Kampf*, Adolf Hitler's personal statement of his political beliefs.

67. *Vangelis*, Greek composer (b. 1943), best known for his music for the 1981 film, *Chariots of Fire*, about the Scottish Olympic athlete, Eric Liddell.

68. *Don Gibson*, American country singer.

69. *Listerine*, proprietary mouthwash.
70. *Gene Autrey*, 1907–98, American singer and star of film Westerns. He was ranked top Western star 1937–43, and became one of the richest men in America from his investments in radio and broadcasting companies.
71. *University Challenge*, television quizz show involving students from British colleges and universities.
72. *Jonathan Ross*, British talk show host.
73. *Tom Mix*, star of silent films whose career did not survive the arrival of the talkies; he was born in Driftwood, Pennsylvania and died in a car accident in 1940.
74. *Head and Shoulders*, proprietary dundruff shampoo.
75. *Lena Martell*, Scottish child singer whose career failed as she grew up.
76. *Cowcaddens*, district of Glasgow.
77. *Gooloise*, Gauloise, a French cigarette.
78. *Dave Dee, Dozey, Beakey, Mick and Titch* were a British pop group of the 1960s.
79. *Francis Turner Palgrave* (1824–97) was editor of *The Golden Treasury*, a popular anthology of English poetry, first published 1861.
80. *Graceland*, home of Elvis Presley in Memphis.
81. *The Cotter's Saturday Night*, famous poem by Robert Burns (1759–96), first published in the Kilmarnock edition, 1786.
82. *Ralph Vaughan Williams* (1872–1958), English composer.
83. *INLA*, Irish National Liberation Army, breakaway faction of the Irish Republican Army (IRA).
84. *Hank Snow* (1914–99), Canadian country singer.
85. *Grand Ole Opry*, a radio programme that started in 1925 playing Country music; it later became a theatrical venue and a television programme presenting Country and Western music. Elvis Presley made one of his early appearances there in 1954.
86. *Ry Cooder*, b. 1947, famous for slide guitar blues playing.
87. '*Bung anuurra big Bell's*', put another shot of Bell's whisky.
88. *Coatbridge*, small town in Lanarkshire, and an unlikely event for acting fame.
89. Marlon Brando's role in *The Wild One* provided the iconic image for bikers in black leather.
90. *Ferguzade*, Scottish bottled drink similar to Lucozade.

Glossary

baffies, slippers
bahookey, bum, backside
beej, beige
berrs, bears, slang for
 police
bilin, boiling, hot
bin motor, dustbin lorry,
 garbage truck
buckshee, free
bung, sum of money, loan,
 illicit payment
call back, second audition
chuck moanin, stop
 complaining
clatty, dirty
cowrie shell, African unit of
 exchange
craw, gullet
dabbies, fingerprints
dizzy, give you a, fail
 to keep a date, stood
 up
dogend, butt-end of a
 cigarette
dough, money
fit, what (Aberdeenshire
 pronunciation)
firewater, whisky, spirits
flang its portals open, opened
 for business
fruitcase, lunatic, 'nut
 case'
furra, for a
gams, legs
gaudeamus igitur, let us
 rejoice therefore (student
 and school song)
get, offspring, bastard
Glesca, Glasgow
goupin, throbbing

Gs, thousands
handle, name
hardnut, tough guy
headbanger, madman
heave, got the, dismissed,
 fired
hoachin, crowded, teeming
hoi polloi, the lower
 classes
jaikit, jacket
jotter, exercise book,
 notebook
ken, know
kid-on, pretend
loon, boy, adolescent
louver doors, slatted
 doors
manky, dirty, smelly
melt, face (from 'you've
 got a face like a melted
 welly')
molocatin, devouring
morra, tomorrow
noddle, head
numpty, stupid
nutter, nut case, lunatic
OD'd, overdosed
pac-a-mac, plastic raincoat
panto, pantomime, Christmas
 theatrical show
peely-wally, pale, sickly
pegbottoms, style of trouser
perra, pair of
pokey hat, triangular hat,
 ice-cream cone
PJs, pyjamas
quinie, girl, young woman
red up, clean up
rubbernecking, looking around
 in search of

rug, hairpiece
sashays, walks with a
   swing
sickle, cycle
skitters, diarrhoea
slammer, gaol
slingbacks, a style of shoes
stookie leg, leg in plaster
snazzy, sophisticated
tamata, tomato
tanked, defeated

thumb-pick, plectrum for
   thumbing strings of a
   guitar
tod, on wur, alone (on our
   own)
togs, clothes
tux, tuxedo
umpteen, numerous
Wranglers, a style of
   jeans
zilch, nothing

Sue Glover

Bondagers

(1991)

CHARACTERS

Liza, *a very young farm worker (or 'bondager'), facing her first 'hiring' away from home*

Maggie, *a woman with numerous children, married to one of the farm workers.*

Sara, *Maggie's age or a good bit older. Works on the farm with her daftie daughter*

Tottie, *Sarah's daughter, about fifteen. A daftie*

Ellen, *the farmer's wife. Formerly a farm worker like the others, now risen to the status of a lady*

Jenny, *another young farm worker, slightly older than Liza*

Two Warders (non speaking).

Bondagers were the women workers of the great Border farms in the last century. Each farm worker was hired on condition he brought a female worker to work alongside him — if not his wife or daughter, then some other girl that he himself had to hire at the Hiring Fair, and lodge and feed alongside his own family in his tiny cottage.

The play is set on a Border farm of 1860. Act One, with the exception of the opening scene (the 'Hiring'), takes place in the summer; and Act Two in winter.

The bondagers' dress was distinctive, almost a uniform: boots or clogs; full skirts with two or three petticoats; 'headhankies' — i.e. kerchiefs that covered their heads, and could, when work required, be tied over the chin, or even over the whole lower part of the face when the dust and dirt was really flying; and black straw bonnets with red ruching (trimming). Muddy and sometimes shabby, maybe, but beguiling.

Introduction

Sue Glover was born in Edinburgh and lives in North-East Fife, writing for television and radio as well as the theatre. Unlike many successful late twentieth-century plays, often by Glasgow-born writers, Glover's work concentrates not on the city but on country life, sometimes in remote settings: St Kilda in *The Straw Chair* (1988); the Borders in *Bondagers* (1991); Shetland in *Shetland Saga* (2000). Political and economic pressures — such as the exploitation of labour in the nineteenth century examined in *Bondagers*, or merciless, global capitalism at the end of the twentieth in Shetland Saga — are felt just as acutely in these remote contexts, inexorably determining the daily struggles of characters' lives.

These lives, however, are shown as still more significantly shaped by the politics of gender. Glover follows playwrights such as Liz Lochhead and Rona Munro in the extent of her concentration on women's experience — most obiously through the all-female cast of *Bondagers*, but also in the other plays named, and in *The Seal Wife* (1980) and *Sacred Hearts* (1994). These plays show women doubly oppressed — by difficult conditions of life and labour generally, but specifically by the social construction of their roles as wives or lovers, and often by lurking male uneasiness about their sexuality.

Bondagers examines a range of these conventional roles, and suggests some hope of changing or escaping them in Liza's rejection of marriage and child-bearing as women's inevitable destiny. Glover's regular use of folk-song and ballad leaves phrases such as 'woo'd and married and a'' resonating disturbingly throughout the play, but its staging is consistently affirmative, too: dance, song, and even the collective movements of farm labour suggest a choric solidarity among the women, determined to help each other through harsh conditions. Throughout the action, too, there are hints of altogether different possibilities offered by a new life in Canada, along with characters' eerie prescience of inhabiting a rural world itself on the edge of radical change.

(LIZA, SARA, JENNY, TOTTIE *in the market place, for the Hiring Fair.* MAGGIE *at home*)

VOICES: (ALL *the cast, cutting in on each other's phrases, some of the phrases can be repeated. Low whispers at first, growing louder*)
The Hiring, the Hiring, the Hiring . . .
Hiring Fair, Hiring Fair, Hiring Fair . . .
What a folk/What a crowd/What a carts/What a people/What a noise!
Ye get a' the clash at the Hiring.
Ye get a' the fun at the Fair.
I'm blythe to see ye
Tam / Andra / Jenny / Meg / William / Neil / Geordie / Joe / Jane / Jack.
What fettle? Fine fettle. How's the cow? Doing grand. How's a' wi you? How's the bairns . . . and the cow? How's the wife . . . and the cow?
Did you ken about Davie / Jockie / Tam / Sandy / Nathan / Ned / Mary / Betsy / Bob?
What's the crack? / Heard the crack from Langriggs / Redriggs / Smiddyhill / Smiddyford / Horsecleugh / Oxencleugh / Whitehas / Blacksheils / East Mains / Westlea.

(*During this* LIZA *is wandering, jostled by the crowd, looking for a place to stand*)

VOICES (*these phrases more distinct*)
The Hiring, the Hiring Fair.
First Monday in February.
Coldest Monday in February. Eight o'clock. Soon as it's licht.
See the farmers bargain wi the hinds.
See the hinds bargain wi the bondagers.
See the bonny bondagers stand in a row.

(LIZA *has chosen her place, waits to be hired.* SARA *and* TOTTIE *are also standing now together, waiting to be hired*)

FIRST VOICE: (*low whisper*) The coldest Monday. Soon as it's licht. (*Louder, taunting*) No bondager worth a puckle's left after ten o'clock.

LIZA: (*outwardly defiant — not* in *answer to the voice, and never speaking directly to the audience*) I'll be gone long afore ten. Bound over. Hired. See if I'm not. Broad shoothers, short back, strong legs.

SARA: Stand here Tottie, stand still now.

LIZA: — I'll not take the arle from the first that comes.

I'm only going to a well-kept hind.

I can shear come harvest. I'm good with the horses.

I'll fettle the horses — but not your bairns.

I'll redd up the steading — but not your house.

I'll work a' day — but not in your bed.

SARA: Tut, lass, dinna talk that way.

LIZA: — Broad shoothers, short back, strong legs.

The good name of Tam Kerr, deceased, to live up to,

And my brother Steenie, over the seas.

JENNY: No bondager worth a puckle's left after ten o'clock.

LIZA: I'll be hired by ten of the clock . . . I'll take the arle by ten of the clock.

SARA: Stand straight, Tottie, dinna look sweer.

JENNY: No cottar wife's hired till the back o twelve. *Gin* she's hired.

SARA: (*to* TOTTIE:) Look sonsie, can't you?

TOTTIE: I'm hungry.

SARA: Maybe we'll buy a tuppeny loaf after?

TOTTIE: After what?

SARA: After we're hired.

JENNY: *Gin* she's hired!

TOTTIE: There's the Maister o Langriggs — maybe we'll get to Langriggs.

SARA: Maybe. Look sonsie, now.

VOICES: (*each line spoken singly, in turn, by the cast*)

Ten bolls of oatmeal

Fifteen bushels barley

Six bushels pease

Twelve hundred yards potatoes, planted

A peck of lint, sown

Three pounds sheep siller

Grass for the cow

The privilege of keeping hens

Four carts of coals

FIRST VOICE: It is customary to give them their meat during one month of harvest. They may keep a pig. Their wives must shear in harvest. The hinds are also bound to hire and keep a field worker, a female servant called a bondager, commonly paid ten pence a day. (. . .) The hinds complain of this; the wives even more so.

MAGGIE: (*at home. Very busy. Washing clothes, churning butter — or knitting — she knits on the hoof, whilst she's watching a porridge pot, or rocking the cradle. Not directly to audience*) Coldest Monday since Hallowe'en. I should have put straw in his shoon. He's

well respected, my man Andra. Any farmer would be thankful
to hire him. He was up afore dawn to be there for the Hiring.
Kirk claes. Kirk shoon. And a shave like he hasnae had since
the kirn. Three things a hind depends on: a good wife, a good
cow — and a good razor.

FIRST VOICE: A good hind needs a good maister.

MAGGIE: He can take his pick o maisters.

FIRST VOICE: A good hind needs a good bondager.

MAGGIE: He can take his pick o bondagers . . . gin he knows
how. But some o those lassies wear two faces — one for the
hiring, and another for the farm! Just so long as the lass can
shear — I can't work harvest, not with the bairns. Just so long
as she takes to the bairns!

LIZA: I'm not going to any place hoatchin wi bairns!

SARA: (*to* LIZA) Tuts, lassie — there's bound to be bairns!

MAGGIE: See and pick right, Andra. Pick a good maister! Dinna
say yes to the first farmer that slaps your hand and offers a
dram. There's questions to be asked! Two rooms! I'd like a
house with two rooms. The maister at Langriggs bigged a new
row of houses — all with the two rooms . . .

SARA: We don't hope for much, Tottie and me. Day and way.

LIZA: I want a place on a big farm. Plenty lassies for the crack.
Plenty plooman for the dancing!

MAGGIE: A house near the pump. A roof without holes.

SARA: (*coming in on Maggie's line*) A roof without holes.

SARA *and* MAGGIE: Good pasture for the cow.

SARA: Kindness for Tottie — she's slow — she has days.

TOTTIE: Bad days! Bad days!

LIZA: No bairns underfoot.

MAGGIE: And if it's a good place — maybe we'll stay — not just
the year . . . longer. Same house, same farm, same kirk, same
neighbours . . . (*Realising it's an unlikely notion*) Aye! Well! —
so long as it's dry for the flitting.

SARA: (*coming in on her last line*) So long as it's dry for the flitting.

TOTTIE: I doubt it'll rain for the flitting, Mammy!

LIZA: I'll buy a new hat for the flitting.

SCENE TWO

   (LIZA, TOTTIE, ELLEN. LIZA *walking away from the fair*,
   TOTTIE *comes after her*)

TOTTIE: (*to* LIZA) You, you, you. What farm are you going to?

What farm?

> (LIZA *not answering, doesn't think much of* TOTTIE. TOTTIE *insistent*)

What farm?

LIZA: Blacksheils

TOTTIE: So are we. Which hind will ye work with?

LIZA: Andra Innes.

TOTTIE: We're on our own. Mammy and me. (*Trying to keep* LIZA*'s attention*) There's ghosts at Blacksheils. Up on the moor.

LIZA: (*not impressed by ghosts*) Is it still Maister Elliott farms Blacksheils?

TOTTIE: The one that married Ellen. Ellen Rippeth that was. She worked with us at Blacksheils. Not last year. Before. Before she set her cap at the maister.

LIZA: I know.

TOTTIE: *You* weren't there.

LIZA: I was at Billieslaw. Over the hill. I was bondager to my brother.

TOTTIE: Set her cap at him, and married him and a'. That's how we got hired. For the sake o lang syne.

LIZA: Ellen Rippeth never gave any favours.

TOTTIE: Ay, she does. She's the mistress now.

ELLEN: (*practising using a fan, elegantly, expertly*) Learn to use a fan? I can single turnips in the sweat; shaw them in the sleet — I can surely use a fan! Take tea with the gentry? They talk about turnips. Yield, rotation, manure. They know about turnips. Their shoes are shiny, clothes clean, shoothers dry. We were soaked to the skin by half past eight, in the mist, in the morning. Frost, snow, sun, wind, rain; single, shaw, howk, mangle, cart. Aye. We kenned about neeps!

SCENE THREE

> (LIZA *and* MAGGIE. MAGGIE *is busy, very.* (*The baby and the porridge pot both at once.*) LIZA *arrives with her bundle of worldly goods*)

LIZA: I'm Liza. The bondager.

MAGGIE: I'm Maggie, his wife. You'll have seen the bairns, they're playing round the doors.

LIZA: Which are yours?

MAGGIE: All of them, nearly.

LIZA: The wee laddie that kicks?

MAGGIE: (*serene*) Kicks? Oh, no, never — you must have got

in the way. My bairns wouldna kick. Now. Then. (*Proudly*) We've the two box beds. So you can share the other one with the bairns.

LIZA: I'll not. I'll not sleep with bairns. I'll sleep in the roof.

MAGGIE: (*serene*) The older bairns sleep in the roof.

LIZA: A couple of bairns, he said, at the Hiring!

MAGGIE: (*serene*) Andra said that? No, no — you'll have got it wrong. Andra would never deny his ain bairns! You were gabbing to some other hind, nae doubt! Here — see to the pot while I see to the babby. (*She is busy with the baby*) Liza Kerr? Steenie Kerr's sister? There were only the two of you after Tam crossed the Jordan. And a whole house to yourselves? But lassie — naebody round here has a bed to hissel'! I dinna ken anyone that sleeps alone — save the plooman up in the steading — mind you, from what I hear, there's one of the dairymaids — still, it's early days yet to pass judgement. You'll soon love the bairns. You're a lassie, after all — you're bound to love them. (*Sharp appraisal*) Can you shear?

LIZA: Aye

MAGGIE: You'll do!

SCENE FOUR

> (*All of them, except* ELLEN. *They are singling turnips. In their large hats and headhankies tied over their chins, they are not individually recognisable. The five of them are part of a larger squad, the 'field' onstage is part of an enormous field — thirty or forty acres. They work fast, each moving along her own drill, keeping more or less in pace with the others.* (TOTTIE *is slower, maybe much slower.*) *The dialogue, when it comes, is fast, fragmented, overlapping. It comes in spurts with pauses between. And they never stop working. Obviously the gist of the dialogue is important, equally, though, every phrase does not have to be heard. The only lines that have to be spoken by particular characters are* JENNY's *and* LIZA's.*
>
> *Two of them sing.*)

Woo'd and married and a'
Kissed and carried awa
And is no the bride well off
That's woo'd and married and a'

I'd bind more rags round your hands, if I were you lass!
I've nane.

Straw, then, Rope. We'll have to mak mair.

The saddler's come! That's him just passed the gate!

Aw, now, there's a bonny callant!

He'll no be staying more than a week!

That's what makes him bonny!

I'll get a bit crack with him when I redd up the stables!

I'll redd up the stables.

No, you'll no!

Saddler's mine!

    (*Laughter. Pause*)

Is he married, the saddler?

No.

Can he dance?

Can he dance!

Fiddle and dance all at once — as good as yon dancing maister

frae Jeddart!

We'll hae a big dance, then!

I'll hae a bit dearie!

    (*Laughter*)

Ye're an awful lassie, Jenny!

A'body wants the saddler!

A'body want a bit dearie!

(*Singing*) Woo'd and married and a'

Kissed and carried awa

Was she nae very well off

Was woo'd and married an a'

Was Sara married?

Dinna ken. Was Sara married?

Dinna ken.

She was going to marry Wabster, my mother said.

She was never married.

She was never neglected.

    (JENNY *and* LIZA *together*)

JENNY: Can ye spin, Liza — ye get to work up at the Big House
if ye can spin.

LIZA: Don't want to spin.

JENNY: It's good work on a rainy day. Better than being laid
off. And you get your meat, sitting down in the kitchen.

LIZA: I can't spin.

Ye ken yon plooman with the curls?

Kello?

By, he can dance! Tappity with his clogs — and a kind of singing

he makes all the while — right there in the glaur, at the tweak
o a bonnet.

Is he a Gyptian?

Dinna ken. His eyes are black!

Of course he's a Gyptian!

A mugger!

A tinkler!

Maister Elliott hiring Gyptians!

The maister's brown as a peatbog himself!

Maister's a gentleman!

Married one of us, though!

He's still a gentleman!

Maybe the other gentry don't think so!

Nellie makes a braw lady!

Aye — the besom!

Mistress Ellen.

Mistress *Elliot*!

Was she no very well off

Was woo'd and married an a'

(*Shouts coming from the far end of the field*) Ye can stop now,
stop at the end of the drill. We're stopping — Jenny! Liza!

>   (*They rest on their hoes, flex their backs, leave the field.* JENNY
>   *and* LIZA, *slightly apart from the others. Stop to talk*)

JENNY: You're lucky biding with Maggie. She keeps a good
kitchen.

LIZA: I'm aye starving all the same. And I sleep with the bairns.

JENNY: So do I — I'm glad of the bairns!

LIZA: Could you not sleep in the roof?

JENNY: And have him creeping all over me?

LIZA: Who?

JENNY: Who! Who do you think? (*As* LIZA *gapes, astonished*)
Close your gob, Liza, the flies'll get in!

LIZA: But — his wife?

JENNY: It's his bairns keep me safe, and not his wife. I can teach
ye to spin, Liza. If you're wanting work up at the Big House.

LIZA: (*suddenly irritable*) I'm not wanting work at the house.

JENNY: Oh, well —! (*Walking off, then stops to call back at* LIZA)
besom you!

SCENE FIVE

>   (LIZA *and* TOTTIE. LIZA *on her own. She slumps, tired,
>   leaning against or sitting on something, starts unwinding the rags*

that were bound round her hands. TOTTIE *comes on; stands
and stares at her.* LIZA *still uncertain of* TOTTIE)

LIZA: Go away! Shoo!
  (*This has no effect. Tries a frightening face or gesture*)
  Aaaaaargh!

TOTTIE: *for a moment impassive, then, grinning, copies her.*

TOTTIE: Aaaaaaargh! (*Gives* LIZA *a shove*) Maggie says to come
  and mind the babby for its girny and she has to milk the
  coo.

LIZA: If it's girny, it's wet, if it's wet it's likely mingin'. (*Sweetly*) You mind the babby, Tottie. Go on. Go and sing to
  bee-baa-babbity.

TOTTIE: Don't you like babbies? You're a motherless bairn. *And*
  a fatherless bairn. And you've no brother either, for he's gone
  to Canada.
  (LIZA *tries to ignore her. She lies or slumps, wanting to
  rest, pulling her headhankie right up and forward, hiding her
  face*)

TOTTIE: My daddy's gone to Canada. My daddy's been away
  for a hundred year. (*The word is a talisman for her*) Sas-
  katch-e-wan. Sas-katch-e-wan. (*A silence*) There's dancing
  tonight.

LIZA: Where?

TOTTIE: In the turnip shed. The saddler's fetching his fiddle.
  Maybe ye'll hae a bit dearie.

LIZA: What's that supposed to mean?

TOTTIE: That's what Jenny always says. 'A'body needs a bit
  dearie.'

LIZA: Away and see to the babbity!
  (LIZA *walks away*)

TOTTIE: Where are you going?

LIZA: To the pump. To wash off the glaur!
  (TOTTIE *goes over to the cradle*)

TOTTIE: Bee-baa-babbity. Are ye wet? Ugh! Are ye mingin'?
  UUUUgh! (*Hastily, in case she sets it howling*) Don't cry,
  don't cry. (*Very matter-of-fact, as if to someone much older*) I'll tell you a story. I'll tell you about the ghostie. It's
  true. I was up on the moors. The maister sent me. With
  a message for the herd. And the mist came doon — and
  roon — and doon. I was feared. And I shouted for the herd.
  But the mist smoored my words. And then I heard, very
  close: 'Shoough . . . shoough . . . shooough . . .' — a plough
  shoughin through the ground, and whiles whanging a stane
  or twa. And a man, calling to his beasts: 'Coooooooop,

coooooooop'. Like a crow. I could feel the beasts on the ground, I could feel them through my feet. Oxen. I could smell them. I wanted to walk with the plooman till the mist parted. I shouted. But the mist swirled roon and smoored a'thing. After, Jock the herd said: (*She copies his patronising tone*) 'Naebody ploughs there, Tottie — the only rigs there are the lang syne rigs. Ye can see the marks still. Hundreds of year old. But ye'll no see ony plooman, and ye'll no see any plough.' Aye. But I heard him though . . .

VOICES: (*low whispery*)

Lang syne ploughman

Lang syne rigs, rigs, rigs, rigs.

Lang syne barley, barley, barley, barley

Barley means bread, oats means bread, pease means bread

Bread of carefulness

Never enough bread.

CHILDREN'S VOICES: (*or the cast on stage as children; loud, matter-of-fact, unkind*)

Tottie's seen a bogle, Tottie's seen a ghostie.

Tottie's a softie, Tottie's a daftie.

TOTTIE: (*cutting into these lines*) I'm not, stop it. I'm not.

FIRST CHILD: Sixpence in the shilling.

TOTTIE: Stop it! No!

SECOND CHILD: No all there.

TOTTIE: I am! (*Upset, blundering about, wanting to shove, shout down her tormentors*)

CHILDREN: (*jeering, laughing*)

Your mammy lay with Wabster

Gat ye in the cornrigs

Cleckit in the barley rigs

Coupled

Covered

Ploughed

TOTTIE: Married! (*Upset, aggressive — she has blundered into or pushed the cradle, it's rocking wildly*)

FIRST CHILD: In the cornrigs?

TOTTIE: Yes.

SECOND CHILD: In the *cornrigs*?

TOTTIE: Yes. Yes. She had a babby. It was me.

FIRST CHILD: (*soft, sly*) And where's your daddy now?

TOTTIE: (*whisper*) Sas-katch-e-wan . . . Sas-katch-e-wan.

(*She goes to the cradle, blundering, whimpering. She has to steady the cradle, and in doing so quietens herself*)

SCENE SIX

> (SARA, TOTTIE, ELLEN, LIZA. TOTTIE *is maybe still by the
> cradle.* SARA *busy cleaning horse tack, or patching/sewing sacks,
> or winding the home-made straw rope into neat oval balls: any
> wet-weather work.* ELLEN — *adjusting, admiring her clothes,
> hat? umbrella?* — *half pleased at her elevated status, but half
> laughing to herself*)

ELLEN: Sweet wheaten bread, and tea, and cream and sugar
and ham! All this for breakfast! Brought by a servant girl better
dressed than I ever was till now. A table like snow, a floor like
a looking-glass; china, lace. Great wide windows to let in the
sun — to look out on the fields. Every field fifty acres square.
Hedges trim. No weeds. No waste.

> (TOTTIE *stares at her, delighted to see her. Admires and is
> fascinated by* ELLEN. ELLEN *has always tolerated* TOTTIE,
> *with an offhand but genuine acceptance*)

ELLEN: I saw you hoeing the fields this morning. I watched till
you left off because of the rain.

TOTTIE: We don't know what to call you now.

SARA: We must call her Mistress Elliott now.

ELLEN: Aye. That's what you cry me.

> (*Seeing* TOTTIE'S *grinning welcome,* ELLEN *goes to her, hugs
> her.* TOTTIE'S *reciprocating hug is uninhibited, wholehearted*)

SARA: (*fearful of* ELLEN'S *gown*) Mind now, Tottie.

ELLEN: I wear this one to take tea.

SARA: There's no tea here, Nell!

ELLEN: I have just taken tea — at Langriggs.

> (*As awkwardness. She sits down very carefully.* TOTTIE *gapes
> at her happily.* SARA *motions to* TOTTIE *to start work*)

TOTTIE: (*still with her eyes on* ELLEN) Ellen Rippeth-that-was.
Like a lady now. She sits like a lady.

ELLEN: It's the stays. Can't bend forrard. Can't bend back. I'm
tied up every morning — let loose at bedtime.

TOTTIE: Who ties you — the maister?

ELLEN: (*to* SARA) D'you mind Betty Hope? The maister's auld
mither hired her for my maid.

SARA: She's got the sort of face that comes in useful for a wake.

ELLEN: Nae crack from Betsy. It's hot in here.

TOTTIE: It's wet out there!

SARA: Too wet for work. The lassies are throwing their money
at the packman. The lads are in the stables, larking.

TOTTIE: Larking.

ELLEN: By, it rained for the flitting. I watched the carts from

the window, coming down the loan. Bung fu': beds, bairns,
clocks, dressers, grandpas, geraniums — a'thing drookit.

SARA: I've a hundred rheumatisms since the flitting. Maggie's
bairns have the hoast yet.

ELLEN: My shoothers are always dry now. If my stockings are
soaked, or my shoes, someone fetches another pair.

SARA: 'And was she no very well off — / That's woo'd and
married an a'!'

ELLEN: Here, Tottie — let loose my stays! (*shows* TOTTIE *where
to loosen the laces under the bodice*)

SARA: (*shaking her head at* NELL's *old ways*) Mistress Elliott!
  (ELLEN *flops on the straw.* TOTTIE *imitates her.* SARA *never
  stops working*)

TOTTIE: Bad Nell!

ELLEN: Not now! I'm a married lady now!

TOTTIE: Are you having a baby? Is it in there yet?

ELLEN: No . . . Not yet.

SARA: (*after a pause; softly*) There's time enough.

ELLEN: A hind wouldn't think so! Some of them would have
you swelled before they called the banns, even!

SARA: Och, now, Ellen —

ELLEN: Well, it's true!

SARA: Not at Blacksheils. The maister wouldn't stand for it.
He's stricter than the minister.

ELLEN: He's — he's — a fine man. Keeps his passion under
hidlings, though!

SARA: And his mother, the widow?

ELLEN: She calls me 'the new blood'. 'No sense growing prize
turnips, Gordon, without prize sons to mind them!'

SARA: Well, you know what they say: the bull is half the herd.
  (ELLEN *lolls in the hay. More like the bondager she used to be*)

ELLEN: Is that true for folk, as well as beasts?

SARA: Must be. Surely.

ELLEN: He had a son. It died before it got born. It killed its
mother before it was even born.

TOTTIE: How could a baby kill you?

SARA: The Elliotts have farmed here since I don't know when.
His grandfather drained those cold fields of clay. He died before they were ever first cropped. Look at them, now. Tatties,
clover, the finest neeps in Europe. People come from all over —
Germany, England — just to look at Blacksheils, and talk with
the maister.

ELLEN: A son for Blacksheils. Of course he wants a son.

TOTTIE: (*tormenting* ELLEN, *pulling at her*) How could a bull be half the herd? How could a baby kill you?

ELLEN: Babies are mischief. Like you, Tottie! No telling what they'll do.

> (LIZA *appears*)

SARA: It's Liza, Mistress Elliott, Liza Kerr. Andra's bondager.

TOTTIE: (*to* LIZA) You must cry her Mistress Elliott, now.

> (LIZA *gives a bob*)

ELLEN: (*getting up, brushing off the straw — but not put out at being caught lolling there by a servant*) I would hardly have known you. You've grown.

> (ELLEN *is going*)

LIZA: Steenie's in Canada.

ELLEN: Yes, I heard. I hope he's well?

> (LIZA *doesn't answer.* ELLEN *goes*)

LIZA: (*muttering after her*) No thanks to you if he's well. No thanks to you!

TOTTIE: (*softly*) Sas-katch-u-wan.

LIZA: Steik yer gab, you!

> (*Gives* TOTTIE *a shove, as she goes*)

TOTTIE: Sas-katch-e-wan.

SCENE SEVEN

> (ELLEN, MAGGIE, SARA. *They are not 'together', but in their separate areas*)

ELLEN: Steenie Kerr. He was only a bairn. Lovesick loon! Heart on his sleeve. Scratching my name on the steading walls.

SARA: Poor Steenie. I felt heart-sorry for him.

ELLEN: He played on pity. Punished me with other folk's pity. Used me.

MAGGIE: She led him a dance.

SARA: Well, he wouldn't take no.

MAGGIE: She drove them a' wild, the plooman.

SARA: Such a beautiful summer.

MAGGIE: Not for Steenie.

SARA: They were a' mad for dancing — danced every night. Till the first field was cut. And the night of the kirn — the moon was so bonny, a real harvest moon.

ELLEN: I was angry. I'll show you, I thought. Steenie, all of you. I felt angry. Wild. The maister was there in the fields every day, keeping an eye on things. In the fields. At the kirn . . . Ye'll hae a dance. maister? . . . Anither dance, maister? . . . And ye'll hae a bit mair dance, maister . . . He looked that — modest! He made me laugh. He made me want. Stricter than the minister, a'body said. I'll have him in the hay, efter, I thought. Why not? A'body needs a bit dearie. And then I thought — never mind the hay, Nell — ye can mak it tae the bed. Ye can mak the Big Hoose. Ye'll can cry the banns. I could see it in his eyes. Feel it in his bones. (. . .) He cried out when he loved me. Not blubbing like Steenie, not like I wasn't there at the end, but like he was wanting to take me with him . . . Just a bit dearie. And what do I get? A'thing. I got a'thing.

SCENE EIGHT

(MAGGIE, SARA, LIZA, JENNY)

MAGGIE: Did you hear about Marjie Brockie? Buckled up wi Jamie Moodie! Buckled up at Coldstream Brig. Ca' that a wedding?

SARA: It's legal.

MAGGIE: The minister wouldn't say so. Folk should marry in kirk with the full connivance of the Almighty. A lad and lass walk into the inn, and someone says 'Who's the lass, then?' and the lad says 'O, she's my wife'! Ca' that a wedding?

SARA: Well, it's legal!

MAGGIE: It's a scandal!

SARA: It's cheaper that way. Kirk weddings cost. No wonder they run off to Coldstream under hidlings. After the fair. Or after the kirn.

LIZA: Did you run away to Coldstream?

SARA: No, Liza. We were handfasted, Patie and me. We lived together, man and wife, for nearly a year, to see how we would do.

MAGGIE: Handfasting! And who's left holding the bairn?

SARA: But that's what they're waiting for, often as not, to see if there's a bairn. It's the baby leads them to the kirk, eventually.

MAGGIE: Or sends the man fleeing. To Canada, for instance.

SARA: Patie loved the baby. She was a queer bit babby, wheezy and choky. He knew she wasn't quite natural. But he loved her, you mustn't think he didn't, she was ours. He was restless, though. He wanted — something, adventure, Canada. It was me said no, I wouldn't go. This parish was my calf-ground: Langriggs, Blackshiels, Billieslaw; the fields, the river, the moor up yonder with the lang syne rigs. Patie loved the land. 'Her'. But maybe I loved her more. When it came to the bit. When it came to Greenock — and even there the land seemed foreign.

And the sea; and the ships. A sad, sad place. A great crush of folk, all quiet, and a highland lass singing. Then a voice cried out, loud: 'Hands up for Canada! Hands up for Canada!' A rushing, like wings, all the hands held high. And the baby screamed like she'd never grat before. Such a stab in my heart it made the milk spurt from me. I couldn't step forward. I couldn't go on. And Patie couldn't stay. I knew he couldn't stay. He crossed the ocean; I looked for the carter to take us back home. Patie Wabster. I think of him every day, many times every day.

MAGGIE: Fourteen years! He'll have bairns of his own now.

SARA: I hope so surely. He was made for happiness, Patie.

(LIZA *and* JENNY *are all ears, gripped by all this*)

MAGGIE: Well! (*She hasn't heard so much of this story before, is shocked, disapproving, of* SARA.) Well, you've made your bed, you must lie on it.

SARA: (*laughs easily*) I've no leisure for my bed!

MAGGIE: As ye sow, shall ye reap! A cottar wife's bound to be hard-wrought!

SARA: (*serenely*) Day and way!

MAGGIE: (*annoyed, and shows it in the way she is working, with thumps and bangs — feels* SARA *should be regretful and guilty about this*) Well, it takes all sorts! . . . There's naught so queer as folk! . . . (*Exasperation*) A kirk wedding would have bound you both! . . . (*More to* LIZA *now*) You have to bring them to account. Andra wouldn't ask me. He *wouldn't*. He was never going to ask. So when he was standing with a crowd of the lads, I flew to his neck and measured him for the sark. His wedding sark.

(LIZA *and* JENNY *start to giggle at this*)

MAGGIE: Once word got round I was sewing him a sark, well, he had no choice, he had to call the banns. And not before time.

(MAGGIE *either goes offstage, busy on some errand, or busies herself with some work; has left* SARA *and* LIZA *on their own*)

SARA: (*to* LIZA *and* JENNY) She doesn't understand. And neither do you, I daresay. And neither did I, at the time. Patie was lovely, like no one else. Happy, clever. But he needed to wander, he wanted the world. I have to bide still, I have to stay where I am.

JENNY: But you don't bide still — you flit every year!

SARA: (*laughs*) Aye, so I do! But I never flit far. I've never been further than the three, four farms; never been further than — oh — twenty miles, maybe.

LIZA: But you went as far as Greenock once.
   (*An assent from* SARA)
LIZA: I could go to Canada.
SARA: Well, you could. And join your brother.
LIZA: Saskatchewan. I could go there. Is it a big place?
SARA: It's a place I think about every day. But I don't know what
it's like. I wonder: do they have peewees. Patie loved the pee-
wees, he'd never plough a peewee's nest, he'd steer the horses
round it. We understood each other. Tottie's part of that, part
of Patie and me. That makes her special.

SCENE NINE

   (JENNY, LIZA, TOTTIE. *Night. Candlelight. They have a
candle, a looking-glass, an apple. With lots of shushing, they
arrange themselves, so that* TOTTIE *has the candle,* JENNY *the
glass,* LIZA *the apple.* LIZA *places herself in front of, and not
too near, the glass. A clock begins to strike twelve. This is what
they've been waiting for. Immediately, solemnly,* LIZA *bites into
the apple, throws the bitten-out chunk over her left shoulder.*
TOTTIE *wants to retrieve the bite of apple —* JENNY *restrains
her. They take the apple from* LIZA, *hand her a comb. Ceremo-
niously she combs her hair, staring all the while into the mirror,
peering into the space over her shoulder in the mirror. The others are waiting expectantly,* TOTTIE *tries to look in the glass,
obscuring* LIZA'S *own view of it, they signal* TOTTIE *to move
away. Suddenly* LIZA *bursts into excited laughter, doubles up,
dances around, gives a 'hooch' of delight.*

   TOTTIE *and* JENNY *crowding, cutting each other's lines, in
a rush:*)
JENNY: Did you see him, Liza?
TOTTIE: Which one, Liza?
JENNY: Was it the Gyptian?
TOTTIE: Was it Kello?
JENNY: Black-eyed Kello?
LIZA: *still dancing about, laughing, nodding 'yes', clutching at*
JENNY.
TOTTIE: Do me! My turn!
JENNY: (*sternly*) No!
TOTTIE: I want to see my man! Give me an apple! (*She looks
for the apple piece that* LIZA *threw over her shoulder*)
JENNY: Sumph! It's past twelve o the clock! You can't tell
fortunes now!

(*She or* LIZA *blows out the candle*)
You can't see anyone now!

SCENE TEN

(LIZA, MAGGIE, SARA, TOTTIE, JENNY . . . *and later*
ELLEN. *They are stopping for a piece-break, milk or water, and
bannocks of some kind.* MAGGIE *has brought the food along to
the field for them*)

TOTTIE: He was shouting — in the turnip shed. Shouting at
the neeps. Nobody there, just neeps.

MAGGIE: It's a speech. For the meeting! He'll be practising his
speech.

JENNY: For the Soirée!

LIZA: (*the title — an official one — sounds glamerous to her*) The
Plooman's Soirée!

SARA: Go on, then, Tottie, tell us — what did he say?

TOTTIE: He said — we are not penny pies.

LIZA: 'Gentlemen! We are not penny pies.
We must continue to press for the six-pound rise!'

TOTTIE: Yes, that's what he said.

SARA: Six pound!

MAGGIE: Rowat of Currivale gives farm servants a grand wage,
and lost time.

SARA: Lost time?

LIZA: What's that?

MAGGIE: I dinna rightly ken. But he gives them it.

SARA: Dunlop of Smiddyhill's promised to mend up his houses.
Planks on the floor. *And* in the loft.

MAGGIE: Every year the maisters promise to mend up the
houses! But syne it's time for the Speaking, and syne the Hiring,
and syne the Flitting — and where are the promises?

MAGGIE *and* SARA: Snowed off the dyke!

SARA: If we didn't flit every year, they'd have to mend up the
houses.

MAGGIE: If the houses were mended up, we wouldn't want to
flit ae year.

SARA: (*quite cheerful*) Tinkers, that's all we are!

TOTTIE: Penny pies. We are not penny pies.

MAGGIE: A six-pound rise would do me fine, and a new house
even finer — but what we really need is an end to the bondage.
(*Surprise from the others*)

MAGGIE: (*slightly abashed*) Lots of folk are beginning to speak out against the bondage.

(*Others not convinced*)

MAGGIE: I've barely a shilling a week to spare for her.

LIZA: I earn my keep!

JENNY: A shilling! Is that all we're worth?

MAGGIE: Barely a shilling for all that food —

LIZA: I'm aye starving —

JENNY: Even a horse can't work without food!

MAGGIE: She takes the bed from my bairns, and the warmth from my fire —

LIZA: (*furious*) Where d'you expect me to —

SARA: (*restrains her*) She doesn't mean you — (*To* MAGGIE) Maggie! (*To* LIZA) It's the bondage she's angry at!

MAGGIE: Flighty, giddy bits o lassies! Pay no heed to the hind, or his wife!

LIZA: I'm not *your* servant!

MAGGIE: I'm not *your* washerwoman!

SARA: This'll never do now, fraying like — tinklers!

TOTTIE: Penny pies!

MAGGIE: Remember Rob Maxwell two year ago at the Hiring? Pleading with a bondager — a woman he didnae ken from Eve — begging her to take the arle as if his very life depended on it!

SARA: Well, but it did. For his ain wife had bairns, and without a female worker who would have hired him? No maister round here.

MAGGIE: And remember how that young bondager turned out? Remember a' that?

LIZA: What?

MAGGIE: Never you mind. But a poor unsuspecting hind shouldn't have to hire by looks. A sweet face won't shift the sharn.

LIZA: And what about us? It works both ways.

JENNY: Ay, both ways. How can we choose a decent hind by his looks?

MAGGIE: That's just it — the farmer should hire you lassies, not the hind.

LIZA: We'd still get picked by our looks.

MAGGIE: Andra's picked by his looks too, come to that.

LIZA: They'd still pinch our arms and gawp at our legs!

JENNY: We'd still have to sleep with the bairns — or worse!

MAGGIE: The maister should hire all the bondagers himself — ay, and lodge them too.

SARA: Now, where could he lodge them, Maggie?

LIZA: In the Big Hoose!

JENNY: In the big bed! Oooh-ooh!

LIZA: We should have a meeting!

SARA: Who?

LIZA: Us! The lassies! There's as many of us as them! More lassies than men, come harvest!

(MAGGIE *and* SARA *shrug off her anger, won't see the point*)

LIZA: We should make the speeches!

MAGGIE: What do you want? A six-pound rise? And what would you spend it on? Ribbons, ruching? (*To* SARA) Do you know how much this besom owes the draper?

LIZA: We don't get much!

MAGGIE: I wish I had it. I hunger my bairns, whiles, to feed you! And you spend your money at the draper's!

JENNY: We don't get much compared to the men.

MAGGIE: A man's got a family.

LIZA: Sara's got a family.

SARA: Oh, but we're not doing men's work. We canna work like men.

ELLEN: 'Don't be ridiculous, Ellen,' says the maister. 'We can't do away with the bondage. I can't employ a man who hasn't a woman to work with him. One pair of horse to every fifty acre, one hind for every pair of horse, one bondager for every hind. That's the way it's done,' he says. 'I'm all for progress,' he says, 'but I won't do away with the bondage,' he says. 'We need the women. Who else would do the work? . . . Women's work, for women's pay.'

LIZA: (*or all, taking phrase by phrase, in turn. She is kirtling up her skirts, putting on the sacking apron*) Redd up the stables, muck out the byre, plant the tatties, howk the tatties, clamp the tatties. Single the neeps, shaw the neeps, mangle the neeps, cart the neeps. Shear, stook, striddle, stack. Women's work.

ELLEN: Muck. A heap of it — higher than your head. Wider than a house. Every bit of it to be turned over. Aired. Rotted. Women's work.

LIZA: (*forking the dung*)

Shift the sharn, fulzie, muck

Sharn, sharn, fulzie, muck.

Shift the sharn, fulzie, muck . . . *etc.*

ELLEN: (*on top of* LIZA's *words*) Muck is gold, says the maister.

LIZA: (*forking, digging*)

Sharn, sharn, fulzie, muck

Sharn, sharn, fulzie, muck.

ELLEN: Muck's like kindness, says the maister, it can be

overdone.

LIZA: (*to* ELLEN) You mind what it was like, cleaning your claes
after this? My new bonnet — it stinks. My claes, my skin.

SARA: It's Maggie who washes your claes.

LIZA: (*to* Ellen) What was the job you hated most?

ELLEN: Howking tatties. I'm long — here — in the back. At the
end of the day I used to scraffle on all fours. I couldn't get to
my feet till I was halfway down the loan. Can you shear?

LIZA: Aye.

ELLEN: Striddle?

LIZA: Aye!

ELLEN: Are you good?

LIZA: Aye. It's the corn I love best. It's the whisper it gives when
it's ripe for the sickle.

ELLEN: I love the speed of it all, the fury. Faster, faster, keep
up with the bandster; faster, faster, and better your neighbour.
I felt like yon Amazon in the Bible. No one could stop me, if
Mabon himself had stood before me, I'd have cut him in two
with a swipe o my sickle. I gloried in the shearing. I'll miss the
hairst.

(LIZA *and* ELLEN *smile at each other*)

SARA: I remember my mother and her neighbour each had a rig
of corn on the village allotment. My mother was gey thrang, all
her life. Too much to do, no time to do it. One night, when
the corn was ripe, she couldn't sleep. The moon was full. So
she went out to shear her corn. And as she sheared, every now
and then, she'd take just a bitty from her neighbour's rig, just
as much as would make bands to tie her sheaves. Syne she
went home and slept the last hour or two till day, glad the work
was done. But in the morning passing the field, she saw she'd
reaped the wrong rig, her neighbour's rig. The corn she'd stol-
en to bind her sheaves was her own corn — and she still had
her own rig to shear. O, but she grat! It was a punishment, she
said.

SCENE ELEVEN

(MARY, LIZA, SARA. *Evening.* SARA *is working quietly —
in her garden or her house (sewing? hoeing?), near enough to
hear/overhear* LIZA *and* MAGGIE. MAGGIE *is busy (so is her
tongue, she scarcely draws breath during the first part of this
scene). She could be churning butter — it calls for steady rhythmic
movement, she wouldn't be able to leave her work till the milk*

was turned. LIZA is not so busy: adding ribbon to her petticoats, or ruching to her bonnet.)

MAGGIE: You must draw *all* the milk off each milking. Well, I've told you before, it's no use milking if you don't milk her right — she'll draw all the milk that's left back into herself, and come next milking she'll give a bit less —

LIZA: Coo, coo, I'm sick o the coo.

MAGGIE: — you'll only get the same next time, as you took from her the time before. We need all the milk she can give. I can't bake flourocks without good cream —

LIZA: I could eat a coo, I'm starving!

MAGGIE: — Andra's fond of flourocks. *You* eat them fast enough — And what about the teats, Liza? I said wash the teats with alum and water —

LIZA: Horses — aye. Coos — no.

MAGGIE: — I said to wash the warts on her teats. Poor coo. A' you bondagers are the same. You know nothing of coos, or kitchens or bairns —

LIZA: Bairns — never!

MAGGIE: The milking's important, Liza, can't you see. I can't feed the family without it!

LIZA: You've plenty of your own if your coo runs dry.

MAGGIE: *(stops short, at last, for a moment anyway)* Aye, I have. And don't think I'm not proud of it. Oh, you wait. Wait till you're wed. Wait till you've a man to feed —

LIZA: Oh, wait. You wait. You'll ken! You'll see!

MAGGIE: Wait till you've bairns. You'll ken. You'll see! Canna bake, canna milk, canna sew, canna spin. Wait till you're wed!

LIZA: I'm not getting wed. I'll be a cottar wife like Sara.

SARA: *(more to herself than to them)* You want to be like Sara? It's day and way for Sara. Every year gets harder for Sara.

LIZA: *(coming in over SARA's words)* I'm not getting wed. Not yet. Not for years. The sooner you wed, the more bairns you get.

MAGGIE: That's what you wed for — bairns!

LIZA: Why?

MAGGIE: Why? Why! *(Can't think what to say, can't see why she can't think what to say)* Why, they keep the roof over you when they're older, that's why. They keep things going. Wull and Tam will soon be half-yins, getting halfpay, and when they're grown there'll be Jim and Drew, and the girls will make bondagers in time. Meg can work with her daddy. Netta can work with Wull or Tam. It'll be grand. We'll can take our pick at the Hiring. Ay, we'll be easy then. Soon enough.

LIZA: All in the one house — all in the one room? And what about him (*Indicating the cradle*), he'll not be grown, and Rosie's still wee — and how many more? Easy! You'd be easier without.

MAGGIE: Without what?

LIZA: Bairns.

MAGGIE: Fields aye need folk.

LIZA: Bairns for the maister?

MAGGIE: What's a hoose without bairns?

LIZA: If you think they're so bonny, what are you greeting for?

MAGGIE: Me?

LIZA: What do you greet for nights?

MAGGIE: No, not me — it must have been one of the wee ones — Rosie cries —

LIZA: 'Bake, cook, sew, spin, get wed, have bairns.' Natter, natter. Nothing about fighting him off in the night!

MAGGIE: (*a gesture: meaning 'you're havering'*) Now . . . where was I . . . what was I going to do next . . .

LIZA: I hear you! I hear you nights! Do you think I don't hear you?

MAGGIE: Now, what was I doing . . .

LIZA: You sit on by the fire, hoping he'll sleep. You fetch moss from the peat moor to stuff up your legs, I've seen.

SARA: (*calling out from her own house, or garden*) Liza, fetch me some water, would you?

LIZA: It's bad enough listening when folk are — happy. But when they're pleading, crying — giving in —

SARA: Liza! Go to the pump for me, there's my lass!

MAGGIE: (*very upset, loath to admit it to herself*) What's day is day . . . and night is night.

SARA: Liza!

(LIZA *insouciant, unrepentant, fetches some receptacle for water, and goes off to the pump*)

MAGGIE: . . . and the bairns are my days! (*She starts — or resumes — some piece of work, then stops, goes to the cradle*) Aye . . . wee lamb . . . my wee burdie . . . (*Picks him up.*) She doesna ken ought. Just a muckle great tawpie, that's all she is. (*Begins to nurse the baby*) Dinna go to sleep my burdie. Tak your fill.

(*It is she who is being comforted by the nursing, rather than the baby*)

Now . . . Now . . . I ken where I am now. I canna feel dowie when you tug like that. A' the bairns at the breast. A' the folk in the fields. A' the bonny folk. A good harvest is a blessing to all. That's right. Tak yer fill, burdie, I ken who I am when you're there.

SCENE TWELVE

> (LIZA, TOTTIE, *all.* LIZA *is waltzing — humming, or lala-ing the tune ('Logie o Buchan'). Then starts to make up words for the tune, dancing hesitantly, searching hesitantly for words. Sings some or all of this)*

LIZA: O, the plooman's so bonny wi black curly hair
He dances so trig and his smile is just rare
His arms are so strong as he birls me awa
His black eyes are bonny and laughing and bra
His name it is Kello, the best o them a'
His name it is Kello, the best o them a'

> (*Waltzing with an imaginary partner now, more confident, repeating the song more confidently . . .*
>
> A laugh from TOTTIE, *who has been hiding, watching. She appears, kissing her own arm with grotesque kissing noises, sighing, petting noises.* LIZA, *annoyed, gives her a shove or tries to —* TOTTIE *shoves back, hard*)

TOTTIE: Tinkler, tailor, beggar — *Kello! (More kissing noises)* Tinkler, tailor, beggar — *lover!*

LIZA: Tak yer hook, you — go on.

TOTTIE: I looked in the glass. I looked in the glass too. It was twelve o'clock, so I saw. I saw my man. You know who I saw?

LIZA: You haven't a glass. Jenny's the only one with a glass. Away wag yer mou somewhere else. Go on!

TOTTIE: Jenny went with the saddler. I saw them in the rigs. Not our rigs. The lang syne rigs up by the moor. You can hide up there, the furrows are deep. The ghosts'll get them if they don't watch out. Her claes were way up. Woosh! She's getting wed to the saddler. That's what you do! Woosh!(. . .) I've seen you too. You went with the Gyptian. In the turnip house.

LIZA: I never did. I was dancing, that's all. He was showing me the steps. And he's not a Gyptian.

TOTTIE: Woosh!

LIZA: Daftie! Come on, I'll show you the steps. Come on, come here.

TOTTIE: I know the steps!

LIZA: I want to go over the steps. If you don't know them right, no one will ask you. You want to dance at the kirn, don't you?

> (LIZA *holds out her arms, but* TOTTIE *declines to dance with her.* LIZA *starts waltzing again, singing.* TOTTIE *watches for a*

*while, then suddenly breaks into a raucous clog (or boot) dance,
in fast reel or jig time: rough, spirited, noisy. And, like* LIZA,
sings her own accompaniment:)

TOTTIE

Liza loves the plooman

Bonnie black-eyed plooman

Kello is the plooman

O, he's no a tinkler

O, he's no a mugger

O, he's no a Gyptian

He's a black-eyed plooman

Bonnie black-eyed plooman, *etc.*

   (Which kills LIZA's *waltz. She stares amazed —* TOTTIE's
*dancing may lack finesse, but it's wholehearted, makes you want
to dance with her.*

   *The others appear, join in. Someone bangs the ground with
a graip (or hoe) handle, beating time, they are all singing*
TOTTIE's *rhythm now, same tune, same lines, but each singing
different lines to each line of the music. The dance is becoming
the kirn, has led into the kirn. It stops abruptly:)*

VOICES: *(toasts, asides, conversation)*

The kirn, the kirn, the kirn, the kirn

What a folk/a'body's here/mind the bairns

A good harvest/best for years/best in my time.

TOTTIE: *(listing the repertoire of dances)* Reel o Tulloch, ribbon
dance pin reel, polka.

VOICES:

All the corn standing and none to lift

I can't stay late because of the bairns

Will you look at Marjie's petticoats!

The saddler's shed his hair doon the middle!

TOTTIE: Tullogorum, petronella, strathspey, scotch reel.

VOICES:

A good harvest's the envy of none

And a blessing to all

(Toast) Welcome to the maister

(Toast) Thanks to the maister for the harvest home

And the use of the barn

And the beer and the baps

We've a good maister

(Toast) To the maister

And a better mistress

(Toast) To the mistress

Health and Prosperity

A good harvest is a blessing to all
And the envy of none
> (*They shush each other to silence as someone starts to sing —
> maybe Burns — the song entitled 'Somebody':*)

My heart is sair — I darena tell —
My heart is sair for somebody;
I could wake a winter night
For the sake o somebody.
Ohon! for somebody!
O-hey! for somebody!
I could range the world around,
For the sake o somebody!

Ye Powers that smile on virtuous love,
O, sweetly smile on somebody!
Frae ilka danger keep him free,
And send me safe my somebody.
Ohon! for somebody!
O-hey! for somebody!
I was do — what wad I not?
For the sake o somebody!

SCENE THIRTEEN

> (JENNY, LIZA, MAGGIE, TOTTIE, SARA. *Dawn, or just af-
> ter, the morning after the kirn.* JENNY *and* LIZA *arriving home,
> fits of giggles. High from lack of sleep and the night's events.*
> MAGGIE *has heard them coming, she's already up — splashing
> her face with water? fetching water? something — and 'nursing
> her wrath'*)

MAGGIE: I'll thraw your neck when I come to you, lass. I'll
dadd your lugs. I'll skelp you blue.

LIZA: We were only dancing!

MAGGIE: Dancing! He was dragging you down the loan!

JENNY: He'd had a drop! They'd all had a drop.

MAGGIE: Gyptians! Steal the clothes off your back — and a
whole lot more!

LIZA: Kello's not a Gyptian.

JENNY: It was the kirn, Maggie.

LIZA: We were dancing!

MAGGIE: Where to? Coldstream?
> (*Renewed giggles*)

And for the love of the Lord, stop that laughing. You cackled and screeched all through the kirn!

JENNY: She wasn't going to Coldstream *really*! She wasn't getting wed or anything!

LIZA: (*mockingly*) Oooh-ooh! Buckled up at Coldstream!

MAGGIE: You weren't? Were you? By, you'd see —!

LIZA: You'd lose your bondager if I got wed. That's all that bothers you.

MAGGIE: Get ready for work, go on, the pair of you. The steward won't brook lateness after the kirn. Especially not after the kirn. He'll have a thumping head on him this morning. And not the only one. Gin you were mine — I'd shake you, lass!

(SARA *has appeared, been milking her cow or fetching water or firewood*)

SARA: Is Tottie not up yet?

(*They stare at her blankly*)

SARA: Still sleeping with the bairns, is she?

(MAGGIE *shakes her head, is about to say 'no'*)

SARA: I left her last night dancing with the bairns.

MAGGIE: Well, she wasn't with me, Sara.

SARA: (*worried, but not unduly*) I thought she was sleeping at your place. Now where can she be?

MAGGIE: The hayloft, probably.

(JENNY *and* LIZA *exchange looks*)

SARA: She didn't want to leave with me. She wanted to dance.

JENNY: She followed us a way.

SARA: You've seen her then —?

JENNY: last night.

SARA: Well, but now, where is she now?

MAGGIE: (*angry, to* LIZA *and/or* JENNY) You should have kept an eye on her.

JENNY: ⎫ Why? She's a pest.
LIZA: ⎬ She's a pest
JENNY: ⎭ Traipsing after us.

MAGGIE: She's been girny lately. Thrawn.

SARA: She's been having bad days.

LIZA: What's the fuss? She never goes far. She's too daft to get far.

(*They catch sight of* TOTTIE)

SARA: Tottie, burdie, where have you been? Come here. You're a bad girl, going off like that, where have you been?

TOTTIE: (*triumphant, but wary too — keeps her distance*) I've been married.

(*'Ooh-ing' or giggles again from* LIZA *and* JENNY)

SARA: Oh, it's a notion she takes. Like the dancing.

MAGGIE: (*to* JENNY, LIZA) She was with you then?

SARA: Where have you been, Tottie?

TOTTIE: I've been with my man. Getting wed. Liza wouldn't go. He didn't want her anyway.

    (*Each time they approach her she withdraws*)

JENNY: You've never been to Coldstream and back, not without wings.

LIZA: You can't wed, you're not sixteen.

TOTTIE: I'm not the bairnie now! I know things. I'm wed.

MAGGIE: It's their fault, putting ideas in her head.

LIZA: ⎱ Us!
JENNY: ⎰ She wasn't with us!

TOTTIE: I was! I was. They were going to Coldstream brig, they were laughing and dancing, they were having a wedding. I wanted to go too. But they shouted at me, Liza and Jenny and Kello and Dave, and Dave threw a stone. So I hid. Then I heard them running across the field, Liza and Jenny, running and stopping to have a bit laugh, and running and stopping and laughing and running. But the ploomen didn't run cos they'd had too much ale, they couldn't loup the dyke, they stayed in the loan. So I went and asked them could I go to Coldstream instead, and Kello said yes.

LIZA: Kello.

JENNY: You've never been to Coldstream!

LIZA: She's making it up, she talks like that all the time.

TOTTIE: I'm going to have a clock and a dresser and a bed. And a baby.

    (*The silence gratifies her*)

LIZA: Who said?

    (TOTTIE *starts laughing, almost dancing* (*or lolling about in the hay, as* ELLEN *did earlier*)*, hugging herself with satisfaction — at last night's, as well as this morning's, attention*)

MAGGIE: What did he do? Tottie? Which one was it, and what did he do?

SARA: There's blood on her skirt.

MAGGIE: (*slapping at, or shoving at* JENNY *or* LIZA, *whichever is nearest*) Your fault, bitches!

    (*As she speaks the farmyard bell — maybe just two iron bars banged together — is heard in the distance*)

MAGGIE: That's the steward in the yard. You're late. Go on, the pair of you, hurry up, go on. No sense everyone being late.

SARA: Tell the steward we're both sick, Tottie and me. Tell him we're sick.

MAGGIE: And Jenny — both of you — keep your gob shut!

LIZA: (*to* TOTTIE) Was it Kello?

MAGGIE: Tak your hook, Liza!

TOTTIE: (*calling after her in triumph*) You're the bairnie now, Liza!

(LIZA *and* JENNY *go slowly towards the field, collect their hoes, tie on their headhankies, aprons, etc*)

TOTTIE: It was Kello I saw in the glass. Yon night I took a loan of Jenny's glass.

(MAGGIE *and* SARA *say nothing, don't know what to say — to* TOTTIE, *to each other*)

TOTTIE: He said we hadn't got all night, we'd never get to Coldstream, we should go in the rigs. We were wed in the rigs. Lift your claes! Woosh! I wanted a look at his prick, but I couldn't see right, it was still half dark. And he never lay me doon at all, he pushed me agin the stack. 'We'll smoor the fleas together,' he says. 'It canna hurt if we smoor a wheen fleas.' But it hurt. I'm hurt.

(*But just when she seems distressed and ready to be comforted, she starts laughing again, excited, gleeful*)

LIZA: They'll tell the steward and the maister.

JENNY: (*to* LIZA) What'll they do to that Kello, eh? What'll they *not* do!

MAGGIE: There's always trouble after the kirn!

JENNY: (*looking to the fields*) They're ploughing already. I can see the horses. *He's* turning up the stubble, your Kello —

LIZA: Not mine!

MAGGIE: Go to work, Sara. I'll see to her now. Leave her here with me. If you don't work, you don't get paid. And the steward'll be angry if you're not in the field, it'll make him angrier at Tottie.

SARA: (*more angry than sad, for once*) At *Tottie*?

(*But* SARA *can't go*)

JENNY: (*to* LIZA) What'll you say when you see him, Kello?

LIZA: I won't see him — I won't look!

JENNY: If he speaks to —

LIZA: I'll spit!

MAGGIE: (*looking to fields*) They're ploughing already. Ploughing for winter.

SARA: Come home now, bairnie!

TOTTIE: Not the bairnie now!

MAGGIE: Trouble — it comes like the first nip of frost. Sure as frost after harvest.

LIZA: I wish it was last night again. I wish it was the kirn still.

MAGGIE: Sure as winter.

JENNY: I wish the summer would last for ever.
LIZA: I wish we were still dancing!

ACT TWO — SCENE ONE

> (*It is dark, at first we barely see the characters on stage. The different sections of chorus here come fast on top of each other, sections actually overlapping — until* MAGGIE *and* SARA *speak individually, in character*)

A SINGLE VOICE: (*tune: traditional*)
  Up in the morning's no for me
  Up in the morning early
  When a' the hills are covered in snow
  Then it is winter fairly . . . (*Last line more spoken than sung*)

VOICES: (*in a spoken round*)
  When a' the hills are covered in snow
  Then it is winter fairly . . .

> (*As the round finishes, voices still saying* 'Winter . . . winter . . . winter . . .
>
>   *A burst of noise: a rattle of tin cans, or sticks clattering together, or a stick drumming on tin — or something like. It was Hogmanay, not Hallowe'en, when kids went guising in the Borders*)

A CHILD: (*calling out in a mock scary way*) OOooooh!

A CHILD: (*calling out, merry*)
We're only some bits o bairns come oot to play
Get up — and gie's oor Hogmanay!

> (*Some laughter, children's laughter. The rattle/drumming noise. If possible an impression of the laughter fading to distance — as if the children have retreated, and the adults, and adult worries, are coming to the centre of the stage*)

VOICES: (*singly, in turn*)
  Cold wind: snow wind
  Small thaw: mair snaw
  The snow wreaths
  The feeding storm
  The hungry flood

> (SARA's *and* MAGGIE's *speeches here more definite, more individual*)

SARA: The dread of winter. All summer long, the dread of it. Like a nail in the door that keeps catching your hand. Like a nip in the air in the midst of the harvest.

A VOICE: (*whispery, echoey*) Cold wind: snow wind.

MAGGIE: (*brisk, busy*) There's beasts to be fed, snaw or blaw!

VOICE: Cold. Ice. Iron.

MAGGIE: (*with a certain satisfaction*) A green yule makes a fat kirkyard!

(*As* TOTTIE *starts speaking, light comes on her. Her voice gets louder. She is brandishing a graip — maybe there are tin cans or something else tied to it that make a noise when she brandishes. She is swathed for winter — as are the rest of the cast here, but not quite so wildly — straw-rope leggings, her arms covered in extra knitted oversleeves; fingerless mits, shawl, and headhankie pulled protectively well around the face. A right tumshie-bogle*)

TOTTIE: (*voice becomes less childish, harsher, more violent as she recites*)

Get up auld wife and shake your feathers

Ye needna think that we're a' wheen beggars

We're only some bits o bairns come oot to play

Get up — and gie's oor Hogmanay!

(*Aggressive now, hitting out maybe — whanging the straw bales/stack/hedgerow with the graip or just beating about with it, or beating the ground*)

Hogmanay — Hogmanick

Hang the baker ower the stick

When the stick begins to break

Take another and break his back.

(TOTTIE, LIZA, SARA — *and* MAGGIE, *who talks with them, but has work to do in her own 'home area'*)

SARA: Tottie!

TOTTIE: No!

SARA: We'll be late for the field, Tottie.

TOTTIE: I want to play.

MAGGIE: Don't be daft, now.

TOTTIE: (*with menace*) Not!

MAGGIE: The maister'll be after you.

TOTTIE: A' the men are after Tottie!

SARA: Tie up yer claes, we're going to the field.

TOTTIE: I'm playing!

SARA: We've to work, Tottie. No work, no shillings.

MAGGIE: You're too big to play!

TOTTIE: I'm married now!

MAGGIE: Leave her be. What's the use when she's this way?

SARA: If I leave her be she'll go deaving the men.

TOTTIE: I'm going guising. Going to guise the ploomen in the chamber.

SARA: No, you're not. You're not to go there, Tottie. Leave the men alone.

TOTTIE: (*violent. She's still apart from them, by herself*)

'Hogmanay, Hogmanick

Take another and break his back' . . .

A'body wants Tottie. A' the men are after Tottie.

    (LIZA *watching all this, watching* SARA *and*
    TOTTIE, *miserable for herself and them*)

MAGGIE: Best leave her for now. Best get moving. You'll make
the steward angry if you're late — aye, and the maister. No
work, no pay.

SARA *goes towards the field.* TOTTIE *sulking.*

MAGGIE: (*with venum, she's meaning* LIZA) Dirt! . . . Dirt!

    (LIZA, *utterly miserable, follows* SARA *towards the field*)

SCENE TWO

    (TOTTIE *by the stacks/bales.*
     TOTTIE *a slow, sour version of her former jig/song*)

Tottie loves the plooman

Tottie's black-eyed plooman

Kello is the plooman

    (*Throws herself against the stack, beats at it a bit with her body,*
    her arms, her fists)

Not fair. Wasn't there. Not fair. Didn't come . . .

'Away up the moor, Tottie,' he says 'I'll meet you up
   on the moor.'

But he didnae, Kello.

There was a man there, but it wasnae him.

Twixt me and the sun. Just the one man.

He stood in the rigs, the lang syne rigs.

'A week's work done in a day,' he cries.

'We don't need folk. We don't need horses.

Machines without horses.

We've plenty bread now,' he cries

'Too much bread.'

He was pleased. He was laughing.

But I wasnae feared. (*She's laughing a bit, it pleases her*)

For he wasnae the ghost.

I was! I was the ghost!

VOICES: (*whilst speaking these lines, they are moving into posi-*
tion, still muffled on headhankies, mitts, etc., still 'hauden-doon' by
winter. Spoken quite matter-of-factly, either singly, turn by turn, or
in unison)

Barley means bread
Pease means bread
Oats means bread
Wheat means bread
Corn means bread

TOTTIE *(in the middle of the above, on top of their words — the voices do not pause)*

MAGGIE: Best leave her for now. Best get moving. You'll make the steward angry if you're late — aye, and the maister. No work, no pay.

SARA *goes towards the field.* TOTTIE *sulking.*

MAGGIE: *(with venum, she's meaning* LIZA*)* Dirt! . . . Dirt!

    (LIZA, *utterly miserable, follows* SARA *towards the field*)

SCENE THREE

ELLEN: *(polite teatime voice — a teapot or cakestand? — she's talking to the foreigners visiting the show farm of Blacksheils)* Progress? Progress! The key to progress is rotation: Maister Elliott's six-course rotation. Famed throughout the land; throughout Europe. Corn, potatoes, turnips, and swedes, clover, and rye grass, with a good stock of sheep and cattle. Sixty tons of farm manure. Twelve hundredweight of artificials. Wheat yields — up! Potato yields — up! The rent? — up! — naturally. Raised by the Marquis according to our yields. Rotation! Rotation of course applies also to the workforce. On farms of this size we have to be exact. Twenty men and eight women in winter, eighteen extra women and boys in summer. The steward can't do with less, the master can't pay for more.

   (Not talking to the visitors here) If Jimmy Eagan's too frail
      now to work,
Then he and his family must move elsewhere,
For his house is needed for a younger hind,
And his wife and three daughters are surplus to requirements.
If Tam Neil's lad is ready for the fields,
The family will have to seek a new place at the Hiring,
We've too many young boys at Blacksheils already,
We don't need more half-yins,
We need more hinds,
We need more bondagers and unmarried ploughmen.

   (To the visitors again) Of course, they never move far . . . ten, fifteen miles . . . they're used to it. Some welcome it . . . 'So long as it's dry for the flitting!'

(*No longer addressing the visitors*) 'Please God: Keep them dry for the flitting' . . . He's a fair man, the maister. He'd have built a new row of houses by now — if it wasn't for the Marquis raising the rent. 'I overlook small faults in a good workman,' says the maister. 'I've lived here all my life,' he says 'I know this place like I know my own hand. I know the Border peasant: honest, industrious, godfearing . . . '

He never knew me, never knew my name even, till I set my cap at him. The first year of marriage, I still had the face of a bondager: white below, where the kerchief had been tied, the top of my cheeks and my nose dirt brown. The ladies stared, and smiled behind their fans. But I'm all pale now, I'm a proper lady now.

Not once has he asked me what it was like: to live in the row, to work in the fields. Not once . . . They've made a lady of me now.

SCENE FOUR

(MAGGIE, TOTTIE, SARA, LIZA . . . *and* ELLEN *later. All working, or about to.* MAGGIE *working in, or for, her own house.* LIZA *filling baskets or a barrow with neeps to feed the beasts (or crushing the neeps in the crusher).* SARA *helping* TOTTIE *to 'breech her claes', i.e. kittle up her skirts, so that they're almost like trousers, ready for work*)

SARA: Has he spoken to Andra, the maister?

MAGGIE: No. Not yet. Has he spoken to you?

SARA: (*shakes her head*) No. Not yet. Not to anyone yet. Not that I've heard. (*Without conviction*) Well, there's time . . .

LIZA: There's hardly any time. It's past Hogmanay.

(*A pause. Uneasy*)

SARA: Maister Elliott always speaks well before the Hiring. He's good that way.

MAGGIE: Not long till the Hiring now.

LIZA: First Monday in February.

(*Uneasy pause*)

MAGGIE: He's bound to keep some on. The steward; the herd. And he's well pleased with Andra, he'll be speaking to Andra. (*to* SARA) Ellen'll see that you're kept on, don't fret.

SARA: Tottie's had bad days. Too many bad days.

MAGGIE: And who's to blame? Kello. Well, they won't keep him on, that's for sure. It's a wonder he wasn't sent packing before — straight after the kirn! Mind, the same could be said for some other — dirt!

SARA: That's not right, Maggie, that's not fair!

MAGGIE: You don't know the half of it. Don't know the half
of her! Flaunty piece of — dirtery!

> (SARA *wants to smooth this, but can't.*
>
>   MAGGIE, SARA, LIZA, *all speaking and shouting at once
> here:*)

MAGGIE: (*to* LIZA) Her father must be turning in his grave.
Dirt. If the maister only knew, he'd send her packing. Dirt —
that's all she is.

LIZA: (*incoherent, upset*) My father — aye, he must — at you —
at you and your man. What do you expect me to do — what?
If my father knew — if Steenie was here — he'd — if he — it's
not right — it's not.

MAGGIE: Just like her mother. Maisie Kerr — no better than
she should be. Tinkler trash!

SARA: That's not true, Maggie, that's not true at all!

LIZA: Liar! That's a lie!

ELLEN: What's all this? All this noise? Haven't you work enough
to keep busy? The maister's sick of all this clamjamfray. Where's
Tottie — Tottie? — Tottie, come here —

> (TOTTIE *comes, without enthusiasm.* ELLEN *hugs her, but she
> doesn't reciprocate*)

ELLEN: Why haven't you been working? Bad girl. Wild girl! (*says
this nicely, cajolingly, but* TOTTIE, *sulky, is trying to break away*)
You used to be a good worker, Tottie. You've got to be good.
Hey, now, promise me, now — you'll be a good girl now.

> (TOTTIE *retreats to stack, bale, somewhere*)

ELLEN: (*to* SARA) The steward's been grumbling to the maister.
She deaves all the men, she throws herself at Kello.

MAGGIE: Kello shouldn't be here. They should have sent him
away.

ELLEN: Yes. I know.

MAGGIE: Then why did they not?

ELLEN: Because she wouldn't say. Tottie wouldn't say. (*To*
TOTTIE.) You should have told them, Tottie, you should have
told them what happened to you.

MAGGIE: She said it all to us. Don't they believe it? There was
blood on her claes.

ELLEN: I know.

MAGGIE: He should have been punished.

ELLEN: (*knowing how feeble this is*) They did punish him, the
men.

MAGGIE: Oh — they douked him in the trough, and kicked him

round the yard. But they feel sorry for him now. Some of the lads admire him, almost, some of the lassies even. It's Tottie they're angry at now.

(LIZA *very silent, very subdued — and very resentful*)

SARA: He changed Tottie. He stole her.

MAGGIE: They laugh and swear at her now.

ELLEN: 'I keep a steward to manage my workers.' That's all the maister says, that's all he'll say. 'I won't keep a dog and bark for myself.'

MAGGIE: He barks when it's lassies causing the trouble. He sent Minnie packing . . . almost before we'd time to find out why!

ELLEN: And the steward won't budge. 'It takes two,' he says, 'Takes two to smoor the fleas.' You know how they are — maisters, stewards — they leave things be, till the turn of the year. They leave it till the Speaking, and let the bad ones go. Leave it till the Hiring, and let them go.

MAGGIE: (*with some satisfaction*) No one'll hire Kello. That's for sure!

ELLEN: I wouldn't be so certain. He's good with the horses, he's a hero with horses.

MAGGIE: (*with a venomous look at* LIZA) Folk like that are left till last at the Hiring! Lads or lassies!

SARA: It's us who'll get left, Tottie and me.

ELLEN: You won't need to go to the Hiring, Sara. You can stay on here, you know that surely. But see she behaves. If she won't do any work, at least keep her quiet — and away from the men. For the maister won't stand for all this — nonsense.

(SARA *obviously feels this is easier said than done*)

ELLEN: She throws up her skirts, she rushes at Kello, the other men have to pull her away.

SARA: (*very quietly*) He changed Tottie, he stole her.

MAGGIE: If she hated him now — if she feared him, even — well, that would make sense.

SARA: She's angry at him — but not that way.

ELLEN: You know what they say? 'Well, no wonder,' they say. 'No wonder what happened, just look at the way she behaves, poor Kello, poor man, it wasn't his fault, he'd had a few, mind, why not, at the kirn, and what was she doing there out in the field — asking for it.' That's what they say.

SARA: I know.

MAGGIE: (*going off, brisk, busy*) Not the only one asking for it. And not just in the fields, either! Sleekit piece of dirtery!

SARA: (*to* TOTTIE; *as she talks, she fetches* TOTTIE, *and ushers her reluctantly off*) We'll spoil a few moudies in the far field,

Tottie, eh? You like doing that. Fetch your hoe, we'll give the
moudieworps a gliff!

ELLEN: (*she has been aware of* LIZA's *reactions, and the vibes from*
MAGGIE *throughout this scene*) Liza!

LIZA: I've the beasts to feed.

ELLEN: (*signals* LIZA *to come nearer*) There's Mary and Jenny
to see to the beasts. Tell them I needed you up at the House.
It's no more than the truth — there's flax to be spun!

LIZA: (*miserable, awkward, won't meet* ELLEN's *eye*) Can't spin.
I don't want to spin.

ELLEN: (*though never sentimental, touched now by* LIZA's *misery*)
Don't listen to Maggie, what she said about your mother, it isn't
true. She's jealous, that's all. Your father was fierce — but
a'body liked your mother.

LIZA: How would you know?

ELLEN: Steenie tole me. Over and over.

    (LIZA *wants very much to go*)

ELLEN: Liza. It wasn't your fault. About Kello and Tottie.
You're not to blame. Don't let them blame you. Jenny's not
blamed. She holds up her head. Don't let them blame you.

LIZA: (*frustrated, near to tears*) It's not just that . . . It's *her*!

ELLEN: Maggie?

LIZA: *Him*!

ELLEN: Kello?

    (LIZA *shakes her head*)

ELLEN: Andra!

    (LIZA *nods*)

ELLEN: (*incredulous*) Andra!

LIZA: (*blurting this, chopping it up*) It's not my fault. It's not. Just
because I — because — because of Kello — since the kirn —
Maggie — they all think — they all think I'm — word gets
round — it's not my fault — I haven't done anything . . .

ELLEN: (*disbelief — not tragically shocked, because she can't take
Andra all that seriously — maybe a hint of mirth already in her
voice*) Andra.

LIZA: (*upset*) She won't — I can't help hearing them at night —
and then he — I hate it, hearing them — she won't let him,
she won't touch him — and then he — he comes and stands
by the other bed. I keep the curtains drawn, I hug the bairns
close, the two on the outside, and the wee one between me
and the wall — but they sleep like the dead — he stands there,
I can hear him — *she* can hear him, that's the worst, she can
hear him, I hear her listening — but it's not my fault — it's
not my fault — it's not . . .

ELLEN: But he doesn't — does he? — *Andra*? What does he do?

LIZA: Nothing. He stands there. Breathing.

(ELLEN *can no longer hold in her laughter, fairly snorts with mirth*)

LIZA: (*outraged at this response*) It isn't funny. It isn't my fault.

ELLEN: Andra! It would be like going to bed with a tumshie! (*Beginning to laugh again*)

LIZA: (*in self-defence*) He isn't in my bed. (*Almost in defence of him*) I don't think he's a tumshie! He's got awful bonny legs.

ELLEN: Oh?

LIZA: I've spied them through the curtains.

ELLEN: Ah.

LIZA: I like working with Andra. That wall-eyed mare, the one that kicks, she was ramming me tight against the stable wall, I was losing my breath, but Andra came along and roared and whacked her, he showed me how to roar and whack, she's been quiet with me since.

ELLEN: (*laughter threatening again*) Ummm.

LIZA: I don't want him in my bed, whatever Maggie says. I don't want him at all. I'm not a bad girl.

ELLEN: I know that, Liza. I know you're not bad. (*Without remorse, quite fondly*) Ellen Rippeth was bad, Ellen Rippeth-that-was . . . I was douce with Steenie, though, I wasn't bad to Steenie . . . Have you heard from Steenie?

(LIZA *shakes her head*)

ELLEN: Saskatchewan. Are they douce there, I wonder?

LIZA: You sent him away.

ELLEN: (*brisk*) Thistles!

LIZA: Steenie left because of you.

ELLEN: Bonnets! He set off for Canada like you set off for Coldstream brig — he never made up his mind — he'd no mind to make up. You're two of a kind — you and your brother — fresh pats of butter still waiting on the stamp. He was ower young, Steenie. I didn't love him, Liza.

LIZA: (*muttering*) You don't love the maister, either.

ELLEN: What?

LIZA: But you love the maister, do you?

ELLEN: (*very quietly*) Almost. Almost.

(*A pause. Each lost in her own thoughts — of the maister; of Kello*)

LIZA: Kello can ride the maister's black mare — make it dance, and turn in a ring. He stands on its rump, whilst it circles around, he keeps his balance, he takes off his jacket, his waistcoat, his kerchief. (*She is moving, dancing really, as she recalls watching Kello, in the summer, in the paddock*) . . . A red-spotted kerchief. He aye keeps his balance, the mare canters round, and around, and around, and when Kello jumps off, he turns in the air, right round in the air, and lands on his feet . . . A red-spotted kerchief . . . His eyes are aye laughing, he dances so trig. He showed me the steps. He stroked my hair.

ELLEN: Tinkler, sorner, seducer — thief!

LIZA: (*taken aback, then braving it out*) I know.

ELLEN: That's all right then, so long as you know. The maister locks the doors at night to keep him away from the dairymaids. So now he meets with the hedger's wife instead — when he's not walking over to Langriggs at night. The parlourmaid there — they meet in the woods. Bella Menteith. Huh! Who would have thought! Well, she's no chicken — and so perjink!

(*It's a kick in the teeth for* LIZA. ELLEN *didn't mean to say as much*)

LIZA: (*face-saving; lying*) I knew all that! A'body kens that!

(LIZA goes)

SCENE FIVE

(ELLEN, MAGGIE, TOTTIE. TOTTIE *appears — maybe been hiding nearby for a while*)

ELLEN: (*softly, taking account of* TOTTIE's *presence, but not directly to her*) A'body kens that. Don't they, Tottie?

TOTTIE: (*ditto: not directly to* ELLEN *at this point*) 'I'll meet you,' he says. He keeps on saying — 'Away up the moor — down by the mill — along by Craig Water — I'll meet you there, soon — I'll meet you there later.' But he doesnae.

ELLEN: You don't want to see Kello, Tottie. He's a bad man.

TOTTIE: Yes, he is.

ELLEN: Then you must leave him alone.

(TOTTIE *still has her hoe, she's been hoeing down molehills. She attacks the ground, or something, haybale, something, with her hoe*)

TOTTIE: Foxton field's plagued with moudies — moudie hillocks all over the field. Ten, two, a hundred moudies!

Hogmanay, Hogmanick

Find the moudie and break its neck

Find its hillock and ding it doon.

Ding! Dang! — Bang! — Seven hillocks, seven moudies!

(*Well aware of* ELLEN, *half an eye on* ELLEN)

Moudiewort, moudiewort, run to the Tweed

For your hillock's danged doon, and we all want you dead
Ding, dang — damn! (*repeats this with quieter pleasurable
concentration*) Damnation! Damn! Damn!
   (*But* ELLEN *is walking away, maybe not right offstage*)
Hell! Damn! A hundred moudies! Yes, he's bad. I know where
he bides. He bides in the chamber up above the new stables.
He's to fetch me a clock, still. And a bed. (*She's by the cradle
now*) Hasn't he, babby? Eh? Wee babby. Bee-baw-babbity.
   (MAGGIE *bustling in:*)

MAGGIE: Now then, Tottie, keep away from wee Joe. You
shouldn't be here — you've work to do. Mind what Mistress
Ellen told you.

TOTTIE: I'm minding the babby.

MAGGIE: No, no. Not now. Take that hoe out of here. You're
not to mind the babby any more, he's — he's too big for you
to mind now.

TOTTIE: He's not. I'm bigger.

MAGGIE: (*losing patience; has the baby in her arms now, waiting
for* TOTTIE *to go*) Away you go now, Tottie, get that hoe out
of here!
   (TOTTIE *gives the cradle a push, maybe with her hoe, and goes,
leaving the cradle rocking.* MAGGIE, *still holding the baby, follows* TOTTIE *a little way, but not offstage, to make sure she's
really going*)

SCENE SIX

ELLEN: (*not talking directly to* SARA *yet — nor to* MAGGIE) I like
the idea of a winter baby. Swaddled in shawls. I'd feed him in
bed by the light of the fire. I'd keep him safe from the feeding
storms. When spring burst on us, he'd be fat as a lamb, he'd
laugh at the leaves.

MAGGIE: (*muttering*) Lie in bed? All right for some! (*Busy,
busy . . . self-righteousness increasing*) Lying in bed! With a baby
to look after? (*Seems to calm down . . . and then it gets to her
again. With scorn and envy*) Lying in bed! Huh!
   (*She goes. Meanwhile* SARA *appears, with some quiet kind of
work, maybe knitting: she would be knitting as she walked*)

ELLEN (*to* SARA): What do I have to take, Sara? What do I
have to do? Don't say: 'Time enough!' Don't say: 'Be patient!'
I need a child now! Nor for me — well, not for me only — for
the maister! (. . .) Sara?
   (*But* SARA *can't think what to say*)

ELLEN: It was your mother brought me into the world. She knew all the cures. My mother always said she did. You know them, too, don't you?

SARA: Be happy, Nell. You were happy as a lark, once. And so was the maister.

ELLEN: He has things on his mind. Yields per acre, tiles for drainage . . . mortgage for mortgage . . . I don't know what. I'm useless in that great house! Dressing up; pouring tea. His mother minds the house, Betty Hope minds me. I'd shift the sharn if it'd help; mangle the neeps, feed the beasts. I watch him at his desk, writing, counting. He doesn't even know I've come into the room. He breaks my heart. I only want it for him. I'm plump, I'm greedy, I'm healthy! Damn it, why can't I swell? It happens soon enough for those who don't want it, who don't even think about it!

SARA: Then don't think about it, Nell.

   (*Exasperation from* ELLEN)

There's time.

   (*More exasperation*)

Be patient!

ELLEN: Sara!

SARA: And don't let him sit at his desk all night. You can't fall for a baby while he sits at his desk!

   (*They laugh*)

ELLEN: (. . .) There's a herb. It cures a'thing, my mother used to say. It grows round these parts. I don't know its name. But it looked like a docken, I remember she said that.

   (SARA *shakes her head very slightly, as she continues knitting or whatever*)

ELLEN: You know about it, don't you? You know where it grows?

SARA: It cured cuts and wounds. We put the leaves on the wound, and bandaged them round. I never knew it to fail for things like that. For sickness too, and fevers, and wasting.

ELLEN: Barrenness?

SARA: (*gently*) Nell —

ELLEN: Tell me where it grows. I'll fetch some. I'll dig it up. Tell me what to do with it. Eat it? Wear it? I'll wrap myself in it from head to heel.

SARA: It used to grow at Craig's Pool. It never had a name. 'The leaves by Craig Water', that's what we cried it. But — I'm not sure it would have cured barrenness, Nell —

ELLEN: I could try.

SARA: You aren't barren, Nell — you're spun dizzy with nerves.

You just need to —

ELLEN: Craig's Pool — on the crook of the river?

SARA: The leaves don't grow there now.

ELLEN: Where else do they grow?

SARA: That's the only place we ever knew of. But they don't grow there now. The maister had a wall built, some years ago — to keep the river from flooding the fields. He had the bank raised. They moved tons of earth. And build a braw dike, and a paving on the bank so we could wash the linen.(. . .) Nobody thought. We used the leaves all the time — your mother was right, we used them for a'thing . . . well . . . (*Partly her sensible opinion, and partly trying to comfort* ELLEN *in her dismay*) not so much for babies, Nell, some women tried, but I don't —

ELLEN: I could have tried. I could have tried.

SARA: Nobody thought to save any of the roots. Nobody gave it any thought . . .

SCENE SEVEN

(*All except* ELLEN. TOTTIE *brandishing a letter*, LIZA, *desperate, furious, trying to get it back. A silent, quite vicious struggle, shoving, wrestling, pinching, kicking. And* TOTTIE *wins*)

LIZA: Give it me.

TOTTIE: No.

LIZA: It's mine.

TOTTIE: No.

LIZA: It's not yours.

TOTTIE: Sas-katch-e-wan.

LIZA: It's not yours.

TOTTIE: My daddy's been away for a hundred year.

LIZA: You can't read anyway.

TOTTIE: I can so, I can.

Collop Monday,

Pancake Tuesday,

Ash Wednesday,

Bloody Thursday.

Lang Friday.

Hey for Saturday afternoon;

Hey for Sunday at twelve o'clock,

Whan a' the plum puddings jump out o the pot.

(*Throughout this recitation* LIZA *is trying to shut her up, shout her down:*)

LIZA: That's not reading. You can't read. Daftie! You can't read,

Tottie!

(TOTTIE *is upset.* LIZA *beginning — slightly — to take pity on her, but still irritated and fearful for her letter. A moment's pause.* TOTTIE *gets out the letter — keeping it well away from* LIZA'S *snatching hands, begins to 'read' it:*)

TOTTIE: (*'reading' the letter*)
'Here's tae ye a' yer days
Plenty meat and plenty claes
Plenty porridge and a horn spoon.
And another tattie when a's done.' (. . .) I can so, I can read.

LIZA: Here. I'll read it to you. (. . .) It's a story. There's a story in the letter — from Steenie, my brother. I'll read you the story.

(*Very slowly* TOTTIE *gives in, gives* LIZA *the letter. As* LIZA *opens the letter* TOTTIE *suddenly changes mood, all excitement, all smiles. jumps, dances about, laughing, yelling, yelling at the top of her voice*)

TOTTIE: Hey-ey! Oooo-oh! Hey-ey! Liza's got a letter. Liza's reading a letter. A letter. A story. A story. A letter. Sas-katch-e-wan!

(*They all come forward, as for a story: it is, for them*)

LIZA: (*reads*) 'Dear Sister: I am writing letting you know I am in good health. The country is good if a man keeps his health. The land costs eleven shillings and thruppence an acre, but we must take up our axes and cut down the trees. Should he not take land, a man gets four shillings a day and his meat which is no bad wage. Donald McPhail is here, I am staying with him still, he has sixty acres, and Walter Brotherston from Coldstream, one hundred acres.

'The winter here is long. The ice floats in the lake like so many peats, and some the size of a house. The Indians say that Hell is made of snow and ice, and they say that heaven is alive with buffalo. There is buffalo everywhere for eating, they belong to no master. There are no masters here, and no stewards, and no pride. If a man be civil he is respected. I have dined with gentlemen and been asked to say the grace. My — (*She stops dead, astonished*) my wife —'

(*They wait for enlightenment, amused, curious*)

LIZA: (*reads*) 'My wife Emily joins with me in her best respects to you. This letter is brought by her father, Mr Monroe, who is going home to Edinburgh owing to his health.'

(*They wait — surely there's more?*)

LIZA: (*reads*) 'Your loving brother, Steenie.'

(*But surely there's more?*)

LIZA: (*reads*) 'PS. Tell John Mackintosh if he comes he need bring no axes, just the clothes for the voyage.'

    (LIZA *stares at the letter, nonplussed, lonely*)

TOTTIE: (*softly*) Buffalo . . . Buffalo . . .

MAGGIE: Men!

SARA: But it's a grand letter, Liza, and grand news of Steenie. You must write to the wife, you'll get more crack from his wife.

JENNY: (*suddenly, merrily, jigging about*)

Woo'd and married and a'

Kissed and carried awa!

    (*She and* TOTTIE *jigging about, trying to get* LIZA *to jog/dance also — but* LIZA *is still taking in the news of the letter, half-thrilled at the news, at* any *news, half let-down . . . bewildered . . . at the gaps in the news, at the fact that Steenie, now married, belongs to her less.* TOTTIE *and* JENNY *dance around her, jostle, even push her, but she doesn't join in*)

TOTTIE, JENNY:

And is no the bride well off

That's woo'd and married and a'!

    (*They're all thinking over the news.* LIZA *is silent, holding her letter, tracing the seal, the writing, with her finger. She pays only intermittent attention to the ensuing conversation, goes off to some quiet corner to sit with her letter, or goes offstage*)

SARA: Walter Brotherston! A hundred acres! (*She starts to laugh*) Well, he was a young limmer and no mistake! Remember the night of that kirn at Westlea?

MAGGIE: (*frosty*) I certainly do.

SARA: (*enjoying herself*) There were half a dozen bairns — the wee ones, just babies — sleeping in the hay at the farthest end of the barn. Oh, they were good as gold, not a cheep out of them, and of course around dawn everyone started for home, and the mothers were tired out, and the babies sleeping like the dead. So it wasn't till later, till they were all home, that they found out what Walter had done!

MAGGIE: He should have been whipped!

SARA: It wasn't just him, it was Jamie as well. They'd changed the babies round. They'd changed all the clothes, the bonnets and shawls. Six babies! — and all of them home with the wrong mother!

JENNY: But they'd notice, the mothers!

SARA: (*laughing*) Eventually! What a squawking and screeching across the fields — it sounded like a fox had got amongst the hens.

MAGGIE: (*muttering under* SARA's *words*) A swearing scandal, that's what it was!

SARA: The blacksmith's bairn was away up the hill with the shepherd and his wife! And Maggie's wee Tam ended up in the village, who was he with again, Maggie, was it Phoebe?

MAGGIE: (*grim*) I went to feed and change my bairn — and he'd turned into a lassie! Oh, you can laugh. But there's many a baby been changed by the Gyptians — so what was I to think? He was never a Christian that Walter Brotherston — and neither's that scoundrel Jamie Dodds. They aye watch him at the kirk! He'll more likely take money out the plate than put anything in.

JENNY: And when he does put something in, it's only a halfpenny.

SARA: There's plenty he gives that no one knows of. He gives to the needy. Many a time.

MAGGIE: (*grudgingly*) He's a grand worker. I'll grant you that.

SARA: Ay. (. . .)The maister will be keeping *him* on, likely.

(*A pause. These days they are all nagged by the same thought*)

SARA: Has he spoken to Andra yet, the maister?

MAGGIE: No. Not yet. Has he spoken to you?

SARA: No.

JENNY: You don't need to fret, Sara. Ellen said you were biding on.

SARA: Well, he hasn't spoken yet.

MAGGIE: Maybe he's waiting till he's paid his rents. He'll be paying the rents on Friday — down at the inn. They say the Marquis'll be there to collect in person this year. And the usual grand dinner for the tenants.

JENNY: Hare soup. And goose. And plum pudding. And whisky 'as required'.

(*They dwell on this in silence. The conversation is becoming desultory, the scene ends (and light fades) quietly, conversationally*)

JENNY: The chimneypiece at the inn takes up most of one wall. I've seen it from the yard, I've keeked through the window. They don't need candles with a blaze like yon.

(*They dwell on this too*)

TOTTIE: Plum pudding. Buffalo.

JENNY: I wish I was a hedgehog . . . or a frog . . .

TOTTIE: You're a cuckoo!

JENNY: I wish I was. A frog. A cuckoo. I don't know what they do in the winter, those beasts. But you never see them working the fields.

(*Everyone has left by now, except* TOTTIE)

TOTTIE:
Buffalo, buffalo, run up to heaven
For they want you all dead.
And you'll soon be all gone.
(*Suddenly boisterous*) Hey for Sunday at twelve o'clock
When all the buffalo jump out the pot!

I can read, I can. I can write, too. I can write a grand letter.
'Dear Kello, what fettle? I am in good fettle, hope this finds
you in the same. Did you see me in the glass? I saw you in the
glass when the clock struck twelve. I want a clock that strikes
twelve. I want to lie down right, not leaning up agin the stack.
I want a plaidie on the bed, it canna hurt that way. "Come under my plaidie, the night's going to fa'."' (*She is maybe almost
half-singing the next line, very softly, very low*)

Come in frae the cold blast, the drift, and the snaw
Come under my plaidie, and lie down beside me
There's room here, dear lassie, believe me, for twa.

SCENE EIGHT

(VOICES/CHORUS. LIZA, MAGGIE, SARA, JENNY,
TOTTIE. *Couple of days since previous scene. Winter after-
noon/evening. Already dark. Lamps or candles.*
  From the beginning of the scene TOTTIE *hears and is aware of
the commotion, but keeps separate from it . . . as if, by ignoring
it, the commotion might simply disappear.*
  As the lights go up, there is a great howl from LIZA. *Then:*)
LIZA: Sara! Andra! Jenny! Maggie! Davie! Sara! Andra!
  (*All this goes fast:*)
VOICES:
  What now?/ In the name of heaven?/It's only Liza!
  Is that Liza?/What a racket!/Where's the fire?
  What's happened?/These lassies!/What's wrong?
LIZA: Get the maister — Oh — God! — someone — doctor —
  he's hurt. He's lying all — He's lying all crooked. Bleeding.
  Dying.
VOICES: (*coming in halfway through* LIZA'S *last speech.*
  Who's hurt?/Where?/Who's hurt?
  What's happened?/Shush now!/Calm down
  Who's hurt?/Lying?/Dying?/Bleeding?
  Where is he? Where?
  There, lass, shush now

Let her speak

LIZA: It's Kello. It's Kello. He's lying all crooked on the stable
floor. At the foot of the ladder that leads to his chamber. Bella
found him, Bella —

VOICES:

Bella Menteith!

Bella Menteith?

Hush, well —!

Shush, let her speak!

LIZA: She shouted on me. She's there with him now. He's —
It's Kello.

VOICE(S): Why didn't you run to the house?

LIZA: There's no one there.

VOICE(S): Jenny, run to the house.

LIZA: There's no one there.

VOICE(S):

It's the day for the rents

They're down at the inn

They're all at the inn

The steward

The maister

But where's the mistress?

LIZA: There's no one there.

VOICE(S):

Fetch water

Whisky

Lineament

Prayer . . .

　　　(*A pause. Fearful*)

LIZA: (*quietly*) There's blood coming out of him. Out of his head.

SARA: (*to* JENNY, *in fact, but as if to several*) Fetch the trap. For
the doctor. Go on now.

MAGGIE: Yes. Fetch the trap. Go and harness the mare.

　　　(MAGGIE, LIZA, SARA *are now watching 'the others' (i.e.*
　　　JENNY) *go.* LIZA *obviously not keen to go back to the stables.*
　　　TOTTIE *still ignoring it all.* SARA *can't move — neither towards*
　　　the stables to help, nor towards TOTTIE, *whom she is acutely*
　　　aware of)

MAGGIE: (*going now too*) I'll follow them on. If you'll mind the
bairns. Keep the bairn safe from — (*She means from* TOTTIE)

SARA: Yes, Maggie.

MAGGIE: (*on her way*) Lying all crooked! That's rich — for a
Gyptian! (*A dart at* LIZA) Nothing but trouble!

　　　(*All this time* TOTTIE *has been determinedly trying to ignore*

the rumpus, trying not to care (and not to be noticed), birling the
handles of her hoe or graip to and from one hand to the other,
or fiddling, doodling, in some other way)

LIZA: (*in shock, really*) Bella Menteith. I was going to the dairy.
She called from the yard, from the stable door.

SARA: Who else was there?

LIZA: No one.

SARA: *She* found him?

LIZA: He fell. There's blood coming out of him where he fell.

SARA: She saw him fall?

LIZA: She found him. I don't know. Kello. He's dying.

SARA: Oh, now, you don't know that. I've seen several given up
for dead. Why, my own — (*Breaks off, looks at* TOTTIE, *very
softly*) my own . . .

LIZA: Bella Menteith. She's no chicken!

SARA: Are you sure there was no one else there?

LIZA: There was no one about. I went to the Big House. There
was no one about.

SARA: (*she's comforting* LIZA, *calming her*) It's the day for the
rents. They'll still be at the inn. They'll sit long at the dinner.
The Marquis is there . . .

LIZA: But Andra, and Tam, and —

SARA: They'll be playing pitch-and-toss at the back of the inn.
With the stable boys. There'll be whisky going spare from
the tenants' dinner. If the farmers drink, why shouldn't the
men?

LIZA: But not Kello . . . Kello was here . . . Bella Menteith . . . Maggie thinks . . . I wasn't going to the stables, I was
going to the dairy . . .

SARA: (*ushering* LIZA *over to the cradle*) Go and sit with the bairns,
my burdie. Go on now, till Maggie gets back. Look after wee
Joe. (*Takes her arm, pats her, soothes her — but it's* TOTTIE *who's
on her mind*) Tottie?

TOTTIE: No.

SARA: Where have you been?

TOTTIE: No.

SARA: Where have you been?

TOTTIE: Nowhere.

SARA: You went to the stable?

TOTTIE: No.

SARA: Then where have you —

TOTTIE: NO.

(*Big and strong, or small and wiry — she's more than a match
for* SARA *when roused, as now — she pushes, or threatens* SARA,

and moves away. But she's scared . . . and she doesn't move all
that far, stays onstage somewhere. SARA turns away, but stays
onstage somewhere)

SCENE NINE

(MAGGIE *is summoned before the maister. He's trying to piece*
together what really happened. She is answering his questions.
The others are present, also summoned to the maister's 'Inquiry'.
There are whisperings before/just as MAGGIE *speaks* — Bella
Menteith's *name being whispered)*

MAGGIE: Bella Menteith! Well, she's wrong, Maister Elliott. It
wasn't like she said. Tottie wasn't — Tottie wouldn't —
(*Listens to the maister's questions*)
Yes, sir. Well: Liza came screaming, and I ran to the stables, and
Kello was lying at the foot of the ladder, and Bella Menteith —
(*Listens to the maister's questions*)
Yes, sir. It was dusk. It was getting on for dark. But there was a
light in the stables and another in the chamber. But they were
all down at the inn, the men, so why would Kello —?
(*Listens to the maister's questions*)
No, sir. I never saw Tottie. I saw Bella Menteith. Kneeling over
Kello. There was straw in her hair.
(*Listens to the maister's questions*)
Yes, sir, I know that, sir. I know what she says. She said it all
to me too, right there in the stables; she said she happened to
be passing and she heard an argy-bargy and saw Tottie on the
ladder, and that Tottie must have pushed him and that all Tottie
said was 'it serves yourself right!' She said Tottie laughed and
laughed up there on the ladder and yelled 'it serves yourself
right'. I don't believe her, Maister Elliott. It wasn't like she said.
(*Listens to the maister*)
Yes, sir — I know Tottie deaves all the men — Yes, sir, I know
she's always after Kello, but she never wished him harm, sir,
she's only a bairn. That night of the kirn — there was blood on
her claes. He got off scot-free. She thought she was married —
(*But the maister cuts her short*)
Yes, sir (. . .) Thank you, sir.
(*She is dismissed, turns away, and her next words are not for*
the maister, but to herself, or maybe for SARA, *and the others*)
Bella Menteith! It wasn't like she said. There was straw in her
hair.

(*As* MAGGIE *goes,* SARA *is putting on a black shawl, picking up a bible*)

CHILDREN: (*or children's voices*)

Doctor, doctor, quick, quick, quick!

The black-eyed ploughman's sick, sick, sick!

Look at the blood coming out of his head!

Doctor, doctor, surely he's —?

SARA: So he died, and was waked. With pennies on his eyes and salt on his breast . . . Poor Kello. He was daft himself, if the truth be known. But he had that knack — horses, women — they softened at the very sound of his voice. And yet . . . no heart . . . no thought . . . no soul. That's what was wrong. If the truth be known. He wasn't all there. Poor young Kello. He was the one who wasn't all there.

CHILDREN: (*or their voices. They are running around, playing at ghosties, laughing, enjoying scaring each other*)

Ooooooooh! Here's Kello!

Here's a ghostie/Here's a bogle!

Ooooooooh! Here's Kello!

Kello's coming to get you!

Tottie's seen a ghostie, Kello's ghostie!

Tottie's a daftie!

No all there!

Here's Tottie — Oooooh!

(*Shrieks of delighted fear. If they are present, and not just voices, they are flapping cloths — aprons, headhankies? — as they dart for* TOTTIE, *then dart away again in fear.* TOTTIE *trying to catch them, or hit at them*)

Hideaway, hideaway!

Hogmanay, Hogmanick!

Hang the baker!

Hang Tottie!

Tottie's going to jaaaail!

Stone walls, iron bars.

They're going to put you awaaay!

Hang the baker ower the stick.

Hang the rope round Tottie's neck.

(TOTTIE *lunges at them. They shriek — and run away. They are hiding somewhere, giggling, whispering, shushing*)

MAGGIE'S VOICE: (*insouciant, without serious censure*) Now then, my burdies, what are you up to? Eh?

CHILD'S VOICE: Tottie's in a swither!

SCENE TEN

> (TOTTIE, *two* WARDERS, MAGGIE, SARA. MAGGIE *and*
> SARA *are working somewhere, preferably in the field, away from
> the rest of the action.* SARA *knows what is about to happen, but
> can't bear to be there.*
>
> TOTTIE *still upset, relieved the taunting bairns have gone. Ap-
> proaches the cradle, but warily since nowadays she's not allowed
> near. She picks up the baby's cane rattle — the old type with a
> bell inside the cane ball. Plays with it a bit . . . goes on playing
> with it while she's talking — her story seemingly less important
> than her concentration on the toy, as children seem, when they're
> trying to impart something that deeply troubles. She doesn't look
> at the baby, wrapped in her own world)*

TOTTIE *(not so maternal to the baby as she used to be)* I'll tell you
a story if you like — it's true . . . He was up there in the chamber. He heard me coming up the ladder. Creepy, crawlie up the
ladder. 'We don't need you!' he shouted. 'We don't need you
now! Tak your hook, you!' He tried to kick me off the ladder.
He hadn't any boots on, but I fell off, he made me fall. Ding!
And the ladder fell. Clatter! — Bang! And he fell, Kello, from
the top, from the trapdoor . . . dunt!

> *(Two figures in grey cloaks — WARDERS — are creeping up
> on her. One of them is holding a blanket, or sheet — or maybe
> they are holding it between them.*

He wasn't hurt bad — he didn't make a noise. Then she started
to scream up there in the chamber. Her! Huh! She couldn't
get down — and it served herself right — he was giving her
the clock and the dresser and the bed — he was giving her the
baby — Whoosh! — I heard. Creepy, crawlie up the ladder —

> *(She breaks off somewhere in the last line as she senses the two
> behind her, turns round sharply. They have the sheet ready for
> the capture.)*

(Faltering, placating, retreating) What fettle? Do you want a
story? I'll tell you a story. I'll tell you a story of Jackanory.

> *(They have taken hold of her, one on each side. She is para-
> lysed with fear, so doesn't struggle, at first. They wind the sheet
> around her)*

TOTTIE: No!

SARA: *(she stops work, she's in pain,* TOTTIE's *anguish is piercing
her)* Oh, no!

> *(The* WARDERS *make a straitjacket of the sheet; in two or three
> well-practised movements, that take* TOTTIE *by surprise, they
> have made her their prisoner)*

TOTTIE: No! No!

> (*The two* WARDERS *are hustling* TOTTIE *away.*
>
> SARA *and* TOTTIE *both cry out 'NO' two or three times —
> not in unison — but we can hardly tell which cries come from
> whom*)

MAGGIE: (*has been watching* SARA *anxiously*) Sara?

SARA: (*flatly, not speaking to* MAGGIE) No.

MAGGIE: Sara?

SARA: No.

MAGGIE: (*not directly to* SARA. *Even* MAGGIE *realises* SARA *is
beyond conventional comfort at a time like this*) You can't keep
your eyes in the back of your head. She'll be looked after where
she's going. Poor maimed creature. The sheriff was right —
she'll be better off there. Lucky it's not the jail. (*Lower*) Lucky
it's not the noose! And you won't have to pay for her keep. The
well-off pay, but not the poor. There's a ward for the paupers —

SARA: No!

MAGGIE: I didn't mean ought. Be sensible, Sara — look at it
this —

SARA: I'll pay for my daughter, Patie's daughter. I'll pay.

ELLEN *has appeared by now.* LIZA *also — but not with* ELLEN.

SARA: (*turning to* ELLEN, *a plea:*) I'll work.

> (*But* ELLEN *doesn't speak*)

MAGGIE: (*to* ELLEN, *a reminder*) It's only ten days till the Hiring.
The maister hasn't spoken yet.

ELLEN: The maister's out. The Elliotts are out. The lease is
up — out — terminated. The great Lord Marquis has had
enough: the foreign visitors, the mortgages, the politics. Maister
Elliott got above himself, it seems: he supports the six-pound
rise, he's standing for parliament. The Marquis is angry, very
angry. The lease is up and not to be renewed. There'll be no
Speaking at Blacksheils. Not this year. We'll be moving on too.
Like the rest of you.(. . .) Will you come with us, Sara? I won't
keep Betty Hope on. I'd rather have you.

SARA: (*she is still in shock at* TOTTIE'S *incarceration*) But where
will you go?

ELLEN: (*a gesture — where indeed?*) We'll not get a lease round
these parts. The Marquis owns all the farms round here.

SARA: (*refusing the offer*) These fields are my calf-ground.

ELLEN: (*softly*) Mine too.

SARA: I've nothing else now.

> (ELLEN *turns away, goes*)

MAGGIE: (*getting back to work again, picking up a bucket to feed or
milk the cow*) It'll be cold for the Hiring. Bound to be. It's been

a long winter — and more snow to come! (*Wistfully*) I'd like a
house with the two rooms. Maybe we'll get to Langriggs . . .
    (MAGGIE *goes off*)

SARA:

She would tell me these stories, she said they were true.
She 'saw' them, she said, on the moor, in the mist.
In a hundred years — more —
We'll be ghosts in the fields,
But we'll cry out in vain,
For there'll be no one there.
Fields without folk.
Machines without horses.
A whole week's harvest
All done in one night,
By the light of great lamps . . .
Not the light of the moon,
They won't wait for the moon . . . no need for the moon . . .

LIZA: Sara? . . . We'll maybe both get to the same farm, Sara.
If we do — will you teach me to spin?

Glossary

arle, pledge
besom, woman of low repute, disruptive child
bigged, built
clanjamfray, gathering
cottar, inhabitant of a cot-house or cottage
dearie, affection, flirtation
deaving, annoying, deafening noise
drookit, wet through, soaked
fulzie, dung, soil
half-lins, adolescents
hinds, hired labourers
glaur, mud, dirt
gliff, a fright
handfasted, betrothed by joining hands for cohabitation before marriage

hidlings, hidden, secret hiding places
moudies, moles, molehills
moudieworps, moles
sharn, dung
shaw, cut off the foliage (of a vegetable)
sonsie, cheery, thriving
sorner, one who sponges on another, an idle person
steik yer gab, close your mouth, shut up
sweer, reluctant, slow, lazy
trig, smart, active, brisk, neat, tidy
tumshie, turnip
tumshie-bogle, scarecrow (with turnip for face)
thraw, wring

Chris Hannan

Shining Souls

(1996)

CHARACTERS

Margaret Mary
Prophet John
Mandy
Billy 1
Charlie
Nanette
Ann
Stuart / Vince
Billy 2
Max

Introduction

Chris Hannan was born in 1958 in Glasgow, the setting for
many of his plays. Yet Hannan has remarked that 'in theatre
as . . . in company . . . to avoid repeating yourself is just basic
courtesy', and if life in the West of Scotland is a recurrent
theme it is one that Hannan has configured in radically different
ways, and interspersed with a number of other interests. Among
his early Traverse plays, the historical *Klimkov: Life of a Tsarist
Agent* (1984) was followed by *The Orphan's Comedy* (1986), using
contraceptives to educate its audience in the basic principles
of contemporary world economics. Of his two 1990 successes,
The Evil Doers and *The Baby*, the former was a Glaswegian city
comedy and the latter set among riots following the death of the
dictator Sulla in pre-Christian Rome.

Hannan avoids following other playwrights as assiduously as
he avoids repeating himself. Only *Elizabeth Gordon Quinn* (1985)
seems close to an established idiom of Scottish theatre, apparently
following earlier plays such as Bill Bryden's *Willie Rough* (1972)
in its setting among the rent strikes and agitation of the Red
Clydeside period of the First World War. Yet Hannan hardly
celebrates the solidarities of this period in any straightforward
way, concentrating instead on an extraordinary central character
determined to remain aloof from what she considers the more
common people around her. A female figure convinced of her
own superiority and that society does not exist was bound,
in 1985, to suggest affinities with Margaret Thatcher, but it
is on the character herself, rather than her wider significance,
that Hannan's attention is concentrated — consistently with his
preference for theatrical situations where 'emotions outrun or
shortcircuit or otherwise cut across objective political forces at
work'.

Objective political forces might likewise be seen at work
in the typically Glaswegian landscape of Barrowland poverty
and urban stress of *Shining Souls*. Yet the play depicts
impoverishment in financial or imaginative terms partly redressed
in spiritual or metaphysical ones — as if Hannan was
extending the conclusion reached in his friend Simon Donald's
play *The Life of Stuff* (1992), that 'what makes us . . . came
from the inside of a star . . . everybody . . . no matter what

they're like as a person . . . is made from stardust'. Looping between the mundane and the stellar, Hannan's extraordinary dialogue repeatedly presses the play beyond realism and towards expressionism, projecting the inner feelings of characters preoccupied not — only — by the ordinary forces of city life, but by other powers which seem to transcend them, remaining, forlornly, just in view but mostly out of reach. Such tactics show Hannan to be one of the most original and promising of playwrights to emerge in the late 1980s and 1990s, able to exploit some of the idioms — such as gritty Clydeside realism — which have served Scottish theatre well in the past, but also to move on into new dimensions beyond them.

ANN enters as if she's come home from being out all night. She's in her early forties.

ANN: Mandy! Are you up yet? — Mandy! It's six o'clock in the morning! You've had plenty sleep (you've been asleep for nine year).
> (*She starts hunting out some candles. The candles have been used already and are stuck in saucers and a variety of household crockery. She lights the candles and marks out a space. Then she exits into the — presumed — interior of the house. There's a silence. Then a strange yelp of fright, something which sounds almost not human. Then, more subdued, voices. ANN re-enters with Tarot cards and waits inside the ring of candles. MANDY enters, wearing a white dressing-gown over pyjamas. This is ANN's twenty-year-old daughter*)

MANDY: How's the bride?

ANN: Oh, y'know . . .

MANDY: What time is it?

ANN: (*furious*) Oh for chrissake Mandy, what kinna question's that?

MANDY: What?

ANN: Just don't start me, OK? This is my wedding-day supposed to be, I've got enough terrors in my life without you and Time ganging up on me. It's about six.

MANDY: Aw mammy.

ANN: *Yes* aw mammy! Six o'clock already and I still haven't decided the least wee detail. And on top of everything else I'm alive.
> (*Beat*)

MANDY: I thought you were going to sleep here last night.

ANN: So I did! Then I got fed up and went round to Billy's.

MANDY: Which Billy's?
> (*Beat*)

ANN: Two's wrong. I should have learned that from my numerology. Three's harmony, two's confusion. Things get torn in two, two is how things start. Coming home from Billy's I thought, I've got two men in my life, I've got to choose. I've got to make a decision.

MANDY: And did you?

ANN: Yes.

MANDY: What decision did you make?

ANN: I decided to trust my woman's instincts.

MANDY: I see.

ANN: Should I?

MANDY: No.

ANN: No?

MANDY: It was your instincts that got you into this mess.

ANN: O god. — Please, Mandy, read my cards before it's too late: I'm in a situation that's goannae engulf me before I can do a thing about it.

MANDY: I can't

ANN: What do ye mean you can't?

MANDY: I don't believe in the cards any more. I'm a Christian.

ANN: (You're the only one that's dark enough to read me.) You're a what?

MANDY: I'm a Christian.

ANN: You're cute as hell, I'll say that much. Give the cards a good shuffle, I don't want the same bad cards I always get.

MANDY: *You* have to shuffle. You're the seeker.

ANN: I'll jinx them.

MANDY: Shuffle the cards and ask them your question.

> (ANN *kneels beside the candles, shuffles, lays the cards down on the floor. Then* MANDY *joins her, lays out the first card*)

MANDY: The Two of Swords. There's two men in your life.

ANN: I know that! What have I to do?

MANDY: The woman is blindfold and holds a sword in each hand. You've a choice. But you don't trust yourself. Why should you, you're a mess — and if you can't trust yourself who can you trust.

> (MANDY *lays down the second card, across the first*)

The Moon. The Moon is Diana. The Moon is unfaithfulness. There's two men in your life and you're cheating on both of them. That's on one level. On another level it's worse than that. Everything in this world is a resemblance. Everything under the moon could be something else . . .

> (*She lays down four cards one after another, each one as bad as the next*)

ANN: Oh god. — Oh hell. — Oh my god. — Bloody hell.

> (*The cards are so bad,* ANN *can hardly look at them. She's shielding her eyes with her fingers.* MANDY *wants to get her to look at them*)

MANDY: The cards are neither good or bad. The cards are a reflection. To understand the cards what you have to do is look for the pattern. What's the pattern? Look. Are you looking? What do you see? Can you see a pattern?

ANN: Let me look.

MANDY: What's the pattern?

ANN: I'm no sure . . .

MANDY: There's none. You asked me to blind you and I'm blinding you. The cards are a reflection. The cards are saying your past and your future, your future and your past are going round in circles. You're uncreated, like when space was nothing but a dark wind and Time hadn't begun yet. You're a mess, without either —

ANN: Mandy!

MANDY: What?

ANN: Stop it! I'm. I've got Billy. Then I've got Billy. I'm. Mess? I'm Mess? I'm. *Twiced*! I've said to Billy he can move in with me today . . .

MANDY: Which Billy?

ANN: . . . I had to tell him *something*, to explain why I'm getting married to *Billy!*

MANDY: I see.

ANN: (*quietly*) I'm guilty as hell.

MANDY: You keep making it worse.

ANN: I know that.

MANDY: You keep making it worse!

ANN: So do ye see my problem! — I know pills arenae the an- swer, Mandy, and the nurses have far nicer emergencies than me to clean up after (the wee angels) — but I mean it, Mandy (I feel like shite-and-abortion as it is) so tell me something good's going to happen or I'll go up to that wardrobe in the boys' bedroom with my pills and never come out again.

(MANDY *lays out three more cards*)

MANDY: Let's look for the good then. I ignore the Devil: you're in chains to the flesh but you know that already. And in looking for the good what you've to remember is the cards are neither good or bad. They're ambiguous.

ANN: Ambiguous?

MANDY: Two-faced. Like a lie. To make you look more deeply beyond just what you can see. Look at all the twos you've got. On one level you're being told you've got two chances. On a higher level you're being told that the two must become one. You've two men in your life and you only need one. — So. Are you calmer now? You've too much dualism in your life. Will we see what the outcome is?

ANN: Will it be good?

MANDY: The cards only reflect.

ANN: OK. Let's see.

(MANDY *turns over the last card. They stare at it. It's The*

Hanged Man. To ANN *it's an image of despair*)

MANDY: The Hanged Man. — There's two ways to look at this card. This is a card you have to look at twice.

(MANDY *doesn't have the heart to go on.* ANN *gets up*)

MANDY: I'll put out the candles.

(ANN *exits.* MANDY *puts out the candles*)

SCENE TWO

(*A street. The same summer morning.* CHARLIE *and* MAX *enter. About two months ago* MAX *found* CHARLIE *crying in a pub and took him back to his unfurnished flat. They share a flat, an addiction to gambling and continuous cash-flow problems.*

It's early morning and this may affect their voice-levels)

CHARLIE: This is her.

MAX: Where?

CHARLIE: There.

MAX: Which one?

CHARLIE: That one — I had a premonition of this. Walking down the road? Maybe no this. I'd a premonition of something. Walking down the road? I thought, either this is déjà vu or it's already happened, one of the two. — Have I done this before?

MAX: What?

CHARLIE: Have I came here to ask the former person I made my vows to to lend us some dinero?

MAX: Yeah.

CHARLIE: Yeah?

MAX: That's my recollection.

CHARLIE: What did I say to her?

MAX: You said we were skint some reason.

CHARLIE: I know we were skint, ya toxin. What reason did I say?

MAX: All I remember is you cried and she gave you some dosh.

CHARLIE: Because we don't want to repeat the same reason do we.

(CHARLIE *gets a fag-packet out, lights a fag, puts the fag-packet back in his pocket*)

CHARLIE: Right. It's time she was up anyway. On you go, shout her up.

MAX: Give us a fag will ye.

CHARLIE: Naw.

MAX: Give us a fag till I wake up chrissake.

CHARLIE: I don't have any fags! We're skint, remember?

(*Beat*)

MAX: I might be more in tune with myself in the mornings if you'd stop talking in your sleep.

CHARLIE: How, what do I say?

MAX: If you slept in another room.

CHARLIE: It's the floorboards.

MAX: What about them?

CHARLIE: I don't like them do I. They hurt my back.

MAX: That's good for it fuckssake. I sleep on the exact same floorboards you do, you don't hear me yelling for mercy. Get your thoughts in order before you go to sleep like I do and you'll sleep like a mummy. — Give us a fag will ye.

CHARLIE: How many generations do I have to listen to this!

MAX: I cannae wake up a near-stranger at half past seven on a Saturday morning unless I get some sustenance, can I? I'm doing you a favour here!

CHARLIE: Eh?

MAX: You blew my giro.

CHARLIE: I blew your giro?

MAX: Correct.

CHARLIE: You're steeped, Max.

MAX: Am I. You blew my giro on the dogs.

CHARLIE: I blew half your giro on the dogs. Which, you owed me from last week when you blew half my giro on the dogs.

MAX: I don't mind carrying ye, Charlie. I've been carrying ye ever since the night I met you bawling your eyes out in that pub and carried ye back to my flat. I'm no looking for plaudits. What I will say, it's no been easy. Now you want to borrow some dinero from your wife and you want me to shout her up at half past seven on a Saturday morning for the reason that if yir father-in-law saw you he'd chase ye with a hammer and tongs: I call that a favour, what do you call it? — She's your wife.

CHARLIE: Yes she's my wife, exactly she's my wife. Therefore it's my wife and therefore it's me that's to stand here and tell her a lot of lies, all so's we don't have to mug some seven-year-old for his fags that shouldnae be smoking in the first place so he's entitled to a good kicking and you're doing me a favour. Get honest with yourself.

(Slight pause)

MAX: I don't know what I'm saying do I, I haven't had a fag yet. — So I just shout her name, get her to come out?

CHARLIE: Yeah.

MAX: What's her name again — Veronica?

CHARLIE: Margaret Mary.

MAX: I knew it was something papish. So I just shout her name, wake her up?

CHARLIE: And don't wake her da.

(CHARLIE *stands aside.* MAX *stands under the window*)

MAX: Margaret Mary. — Margaret Mary. — Margaret Mary. — Nothing.

CHARLIE: Nothing?

MAX: The dozy pape's went and died in her sleep.

CHARLIE: Try it again.

MAX: You try. (Fuckn Romeo.)

CHARLIE: Try it a bit louder.

MAX: I don't want a whole nest of papes falling on top of my napper do I.

CHARLIE: Try it no too loud and no too quiet.

(CHARLIE *stands aside again*)

MAX: Margaret Mary. — Margaret Mary.

CHARLIE: Nothing?

MAX: Dead.

CHARLIE: It's got to be getting on for — what? —

MAX: – half seven, eight. The day's half gone, put it that way . . .

CHARLIE: Unreal.

MAX: . . . history.

CHARLIE: When is this country going to wake up? — Come on we'll go, I'll cry if I stay here.

(*As they start to go*, MARGARET MARY *enters below in a nightie and dressing-gown*)

MARGARET MARY: Charlie.

CHARLIE: Margaret Mary. It's me.

MARGARET MARY: You'd better go. You've woke my da. What is it?

CHARLIE: I need to talk to you.

MARGARET MARY: I don't have any.

CHARLIE: It's no that.

MARGARET MARY: Last time I gave you money my da belted my ma in the jaw.

CHARLIE: Is that, is money the only thing we've got in common? I need — time.

MARGARET MARY: I've gave you years, Charlie. I don't understand you; one minute you're saying we're finished and you never want to see my ugly face again and the next you're back at my door crying your eyes out. — I can hear my da starting, I'd better go back in.

(MARGARET MARY *starts to go back inside*)

CHARLIE: Margarita darlin! It's my mother. This is all so wrong but you asked me so I'm telling you. She's lying across at the Southern. She got taken very bad again through the night and — I didnae want to say this — apparently this is it.

MARGARET MARY: I don't know what to say to you, Charlie.

CHARLIE: Shock. — I *said*, I *said*: 'all I wanted was some time'. I got rushed into it. Nobody knows for sure when it actually happened but she got rushed to the Southern three or four in the morning.

MARGARET MARY: O god.

CHARLIE: So . . .

MARGARET MARY: Oh god.

CHARLIE: I've been up since five which explains what time it is. Time? Y'know?

MARGARET MARY: So how did you hear?

CHARLIE: My brother Vincent came round earlier on. He was very good, y'know? This is all wrong Margaret, I know that. My life's all wrong. At least I can say that now. At least I can see it. Whether I can retrieve the situation, that's another thing I don't know. Something like this happens you think about your cliché life. Y'know? What have I ever gave. Y'know? What have I ever gave. — So I came, just, thought you'd want to know. The day I married you my mammie was so proud of me. Then when we split up and I walked out on ye she told me I was rotten to the core and if she never saw me again it would be too soon. Which: she relented (thankfully). — She thought the world of you. — So. We're just going to jump a bus across to the Southern. (*Dying, so we can see her any time.*)

MARGARET MARY: Wait here, OK? I'll be back in a minute.

> (MARGARET MARY *goes inside. Long silence. Both* CHAR-
> LIE *and* MAX *are in tears*)

MAX: You OK?

CHARLIE: Eh?

MAX: OK?

CHARLIE: Yeah. I'm OK.

MAX: D'you think she believed you?

CHARLIE: I think so.

> (CHARLIE *gets his fag-packet out, lights a fag*)

CHARLIE: She's gone for her purse.

> (CHARLIE *takes a draw on his fag. Then he holds the fag out
> to* MAX)

Here.

> (MAX *stays where he is*)

MAX: Y're some man, you.

CHARLIE: Here.

    (MAX *crosses to* CHARLIE, *to accept the fag*)

MAX: Y're some man.

CHARLIE: I'm anointed.

    (*Self-congratulation, yes, but he's disgusted with himself too.* MARGARET MARY *comes out with her purse*)

CHARLIE: Listen Margaret Mary pet, don't —

MARGARET MARY: Here. Here's a tenner.

CHARLIE: Right. What for?

MARGARET MARY: Just take it. You'll need something for taxis or something.

CHARLIE: Right. Don't if you haven't got it.

MARGARET MARY: Take it.

CHARLIE: Listen, thanks. Because I'm skint the now. So this is . . . can't think of the word . . . good.

MARGARET MARY: I better go in, Charlie. I'm in my dressing-gown. — The wee man misses ye. He keeps asking where his daddy is.

CHARLIE: How is the wee man?

MARGARET MARY: He misses ye. It's no so bad for me but he's no even three yet, it's hard for him to understand why you've gone. So I told him you were in the jail, I thought that would be the easiest. You should hear him. I say to him, 'Where's your daddy, John Paul?' And he goes, 'He's in the pokey!' Anyway. I better let you get on.

CHARLIE: I'll come round later, let you know how she is etcetera.

MARGARET MARY: Or even just phone me.

CHARLIE: Or phone. I'll phone you, phone you, phone will be better, for the both of us.

MARGARET MARY: I have to go.

    (CHARLIE *watches her go*)

CHARLIE: Margaret Mary.

    (MARGARET MARY *stops*)

CHARLIE: You know the worst of it? The worst thing is (stop me if it gets too painful) the worst is I feel OK. Deep down it's like — quiet. Earlier on, that was different again. Walking down the road etcetera? No idea what I'm going to say to you or (worst comes to worst) what my reactions will be. Jumps, head, routines, somersaults. But now I'm standing here talking to you, I feel good again. It's happened (my mammie I'm talking about) or its goannae happen or it might have even happened. Maybe it's because of my Aunt Netty. She used to *make up* people that had died in Canada or some place nobody was going to check up on her so she could tell people the bad news.

MARGARET MARY: Charlie, you don't have to.

CHARLIE: I don't have to . . . ?

MARGARET MARY: You don't have to . . . explain.

CHARLIE: The point being (I know I don't have to) the point being (I know I don't have to I want to) the point being (I've lost my place). The point is my mammy's dying and so painfulness or sad or whatever it is I'm feeling, anything I say makes sense for once because I've got feelings again. Like, when you're in love. And there's no more Time. Or death. Or Time. — That's how I said Aunt Netty. Death made her feel good too. — You go in, darlin'. You look cold.

> (MARGARET MARY *exits. Silence.* CHARLIE *puts the tenner in his pocket*)

CHARLIE: Whereabouts round here do we get a paper? (I don't even know what's got a card today.)

MAX: (Newmarket.)

CHARLIE: (Newmarket.) Eh?

MAX: Eh?

CHARLIE: Paper?

MAX: Might as well.

CHARLIE: I know that. I'm saying, where?

MAX: Did we pass a shop?

CHARLIE: Did we?

MAX: I think so. Yeah. Yeah I think we did.

CHARLIE: Right. Let's get away from here.

> (VINCENT *enters. He's a lot older than* CHARLIE. *He's wearing a suit. He's done well for himself in life*)

VINCENT: Charlie?

CHARLIE: Vincent? How's my big brother? I just came round earlydoors to see if MM wanted a hand with the wee man. But she chased me, which, I can see her point of view too.

VINCENT: (*disordered but not particularly fast*) No address so no way to contact you. So then yesterday, y'know? She got taken very bad again, rushed to hospital. She's had a bad night, Father Frank Saint Alphonsus got out of his bed to give her the Last Sacraments. She's doing good, the women are all saying she's done it before and come out the other end, but the doctor more or less gave me the nod that this was it.

CHARLIE: Slow down, Vincent. OK? Slow down. Who are we talking about here?

VINCENT: Yir mother.

CHARLIE: Right. Fine. You never said that.

VINCENT: I've got the car.

CHARLIE: Naw, Vincent. Naw. Don't get me wrong.

VINCENT: I'm going back there anyway.

CHARLIE: Vincent. Don't. OK? Don't.

VINCENT: I'm going back there anyway.

CHARLIE: Don't make me say something I'll regret. I hear a day after everyone else?

VINCENT: I explained.

CHARLIE: OK, forget it. It's done now. I need to go home (go to the hospital like this, are ye daft?). Change, get my thoughts (somersaults here) get my thoughts in order. OK?

VINCENT: She's Ward 22.

CHARLIE: Right. What hospital?

VINCENT: Sorry: brain, wrong, car, gears . . . She's across at the Vicky.

CHARLIE: Right. The Vicky did you say, or the Southern?

VINCENT: The Vicky.

CHARLIE: Right, I'll see you later, Vincent. I'll see you later on, eh? Whenever.

VINCENT: She's been asking for ye. You were her favourite, Charlie. You were her wee baby boy.

    (VINCENT *exits*)

CHARLIE: What's happening?

MAX: What's going on?

CHARLIE: That was a disgrace, that was.

MAX: What?

CHARLIE: Did ye see the suit he had.

MAX: That was a disgrace, that was. I'm sorry, Charlie, I know he's your brother but people like him get to me. People like him, it's all on the outside.

CHARLIE: That was an utter disgrace, that was. I hear a day after everyone else?

MAX: I don't even want to think about him, Charlie! — One thing anyway, you knew before he told you.

CHARLIE: Eh?

MAX: Yir mother, OK, you can call it coincidence —

CHARLIE: She's no been well has she.

MAX: So OK, in *that* sense (I'll retreat). But come on, Charlie: *you* get honest, *you* get honest. You didnae need Vincent to tell ye — you knew. Because she's your mother, that's how, because you're closer to her than your own skin. Likes of (when you were saying it to Margaret Mary?) . . . You were in tears, Charlie. You were in tears.

MAX: We were all in fuckn tears.

(*Beat*)

CHARLIE: Right. I'll need to get myself a suit.

MAX: You want a suit?

CHARLIE: I cannae go and see my mammie like this, can I. I want her to see me the way I looked on my wedding-day. Y'know?

MAX: Listen, Charlie, don't say nothing more, OK? (y'll offend me.) The suit's — understood. Understand?

CHARLIE: I want her to be proud of me, y'know.

MAX: Correct. — How much money have we got?

CHARLIE: I've got a tenner. How much you got?

MAX: I'm penniless (as y'know). — Right. So!

CHARLIE: A tenner's a tenner.

MAX: We've got a tenner.

CHARLIE: We could go to The Barras.

MAX: We'll go to The Barras then.

CHARLIE: Pick up something cheap.

MAX: Correct.

CHARLIE: We better get you some fags, eh son? — Right then. Fags suit and we'll be brand new. OK, Max?

MAX: OK, Charlie

CHARLIE: OK, son? Then we can go across to the Southern Vicky wi a bit of dignity and a bunch of flowers and see her proud.

MAX: You're going to be fine, Charlie son, I'll watch out for ye, son. So long as you exercise a wee bit caution, you'll be fine. A day like today: these are the kinna days ye have to watch. These are the days that can tempt ye. I've come across these kinna days before, you have to watch and no get carried away with your emotions.

(CHARLIE *nods and goes*)

It's hard, I know that.

(CHARLIE*'s gone*)

But ye cannae get carried away with a tenner.

(MAX *goes*)

SCENE THREE

(*The same street, later on.* ANN *and* MANDY *enter. They've been shopping and* MANDY*'s holding a bride's wedding-bouquet*)

MANDY: Where are you going? *We* live *here.*

ANN: Oh! so we do.

(ANN, *who's blindly walked past where she lives, stops. She goes back a step or two towards the house, then stops again*)

MANDY: What time's Billy coming?

ANN: Which Billy?

MANDY: Either.

ANN: I forget what times I told them. Anyway, you know what like they are, they'll both be early. I suppose I should count my blessings. Most women would be happy with just the one lovely man . . .

MANDY: Are ye coming in?

ANN: Or could we maybe just . . .

MANDY: Just?

ANN: . . . escape . . .

> (BILLY 1 *enters. He's carrying one of those metal cases hireshops give you suits in and some flowers*)

BILLY 1: Ann.

ANN: Billy.

BILLY 1: I got you some flowers.

ANN: Oh Billy. You shouldn't've.

BILLY 1: Ahch, I wake up on my wedding-day to find it's the most gorgeous day in the history of the universe since the effn rainbow? — I'd no choice. Did you sleep?

ANN: Where?

BILLY 1: Last night?

ANN: Uh huh.

BILLY 1: I lay in my bed sat up lay in my bed sat up lay in my bed sat up. Then I heard the first bus.

ANN: I got a coupla hours.

BILLY 1: Nervous?

ANN: Kind of.

BILLY 1: All last night I stayed awake thinking am I sure, am I absolutely sure? Have I got enough love in me to last thirty forty years? And the truth is, Ann who am I kidding? I'm in chains to you like the seas in chains to the moon. If I'm an ocean you're its heart. Wherever you want to go, I'll race you.

ANN: Billy, I told Billy I'd 'speak' to you, I'm telling you that to let you know. I'm no saying I will 'speak' to ye, I'm just telling you what I told Billy.

BILLY 1: When were you talking to Billy?

ANN: Oh Billy darlin'. I had a sentence about it but it's gone.

MANDY: Here comes BILLY 2.

BILLY 1: Make up another sentence quick then!

ANN: I wish other women had my problems.

BILLY 1: Ann —

> (BILLY 2 *enters, carrying three suitcases and some flowers*)

BILLY 2: Ann.

ANN: Billy!

BILLY 2: I brought you some flowers.

ANN: Oh Billy!

BILLY 1: I like the suitcases, Billy. Don't not come back and visit now and again.

BILLY 2: How, where am I going?

BILLY 1: You tell me.

BILLY 2: Have you *spoken* to him yet?

ANN: I *said*.

BILLY 2: You *said*?

ANN: I have to 'speak' to you too, Billy.

BILLY 2: Don't go back on me now, Ann. After last night?

ANN: Shhh, I know.

BILLY 1: 'Last night'? Who's he talking to, Ann?

BILLY 2: The plans we made. How it would be. Even the en suite shower in the bedroom I promised to build. — We were made for each other, Ann. I know I cannae, like, talk, Ann. And OK Ann, I don't have a vocabulary or even just ordinary words so you'll have to make do or make up your own but I love you so many different ways a day an hour my heart brain can't keep up.

(ANN *crosses to* BILLY 2)

ANN: Oh Billy! See last night? I don't pretend to understand it or even remember what happened. It was the night before I made my wedding vows wasn't it. One minute I was lying in my bed reflecting on the vows I was going to make and the next I was ringing your bell. I suppose my instincts were telling me to panic so I fled the house and ran to you —

BILLY 2: — where you always run.

ANN: — where I always run.

(BILLY 2 *gives her his flowers*)

BILLY 1: I feel sadness more than anything. He's no listening to ye, Ann. He's no listening to what you're *not* saying.

BILLY 2: If you give me your keys Ann I'll let myself in, while you —

ANN: — while I — ?

BILLY 2: — while you Billy.

(ANN *comes back to get the keys out of her handbag*)

BILLY 1: Is he deaf, what's she just told you Billy, what're you just after telling him Ann? Open your eyes, Billy, she said no!

ANN: Mandy, will you hold my flowers while I get into my bag to get my keys?

(MANDY *doesn't take the flowers*)

MANDY: Oh look: everybody's watching us from their windows. Even the black alsatian that baby-sits for the four-year-old across the street is watching. The four-year-old's probably away making the toast.

ANN: Will you hold my flowers, Mandy.

BILLY 1: See last night, Billy: how did you interpret it.

BILLY 2: How did I interpret it? I took it, me and Ann's lying in bed . . .

BILLY 1: (*hurrying* BILLY 2) . . . right, fine, right . . .

BILLY 2: . . . making plans together . . .

BILLY 1: Fine, right, fine . . .

BILLY 2: . . . lying in bed making plans . . . how much detail do ye want, Billy? I took it, she'd came running to me the night before she called off her wedding.

BILLY 1: You took it wrong then, as I suspected. Face it, Billy. She was being polite. She was seeing you one last time wasn't she. She's too effn nice, that's her problem.

BILLY 2: It's all down to interpretation isn't it, you take it one way I take it another. I listen to what Ann says, you listen to what she doesnae say.

BILLY 1: See last night, Ann?

ANN: Don't expect me to feel guilty, Billy, you're the one that's got some explaining to do. If you're that worried about marrying me you stay awake all night then *no wonder* I've got my doubts.

MANDY: Oh, there's the four-year-old now — standing on a chair up at the window — wave!

(MANDY *takes the flowers from* ANN)

MANDY: Aw, I thought she was waving. She's just kinna wiping the window with her toast.

BILLY 1: See last night? You only hurt yourself, beautiful. Like you always do. Ever since the day I held you close on the couch and you told me your life and I understood, you knew it was me and you and no one else for ever. And you being you (and what with the two tragedies you've had in your life) you had to make things hard for yourself. Then Billy comes along and he's the perfect obstacle. I mean, I happen to think you've got enough depressants in your life without Billy but I understand. I even understand last night, that's how I can be so stupid (philosophical about it). Because I know how badly you must be hurting.

(BILLY 1 *gives* ANN *his flowers. She takes them. There's a pause*)

ANN: Don't make it harder for me then.

BILLY 1: I'm trying to make it easier, Ann.

ANN: That's what's making it harder, Billy.

BILLY 1: (*fearing the worst*). What're you saying to me, Ann.

ANN: I wish I could start again Billy but I can't, I wish I could take my ugly face off and start all over again Billy but I can't, and meantime Billy, meantime, I don't like ye *looking* at me the way you look at me.

> (ANN's *crying*)

BILLY 2: She's crying Billy, *chrissake!*

BILLY 1: Yeah Billy, you're perched there like a sad omen. She's waiting on you to take the hint and fly away.

BILLY 2: Will you give me the keys Ann, because the quicker I get inside the quicker I don't have to punch someone.

BILLY 1: That's the difference between me and you: violence.

BILLY 2: So give me the heart keys seizure now Ann!

BILLY 1: Ann, are you going to explain violence to him!

MANDY: Violence? You said that was the difference.

> (ANN, *not wanting to get sandwiched between the two* BILLYS, *moves forward out of the firing line*)

BILLY 1: It's your decision, Ann.

BILLY 2: She's made her decision, Billy.

ANN: Billy — I've said the same words to the both of you, Billy. I've said 'I love you' to him too Billy. I can't trust myself to open my mouth any more. I've decided I can't go on; I've decided I can't make a decision; I've decided I can't nothing, no until I get a new (I'm only being practical) a new (I'm only being realistic) a new big (space to hang in).

> (*Pause*)

BILLY 2: Is it a big wardrobe you mean?

> (ANN *turns away from him*)

Is it a big wardrobe she means?

> (MANDY *turns away from him*.

Is the one in the boys' bedroom no big enough? I mean, if it was big enough for the two boys . . .

ANN: (*fierce, warning*). Billy!

BILLY 1: Billy. Back off.

BILLY 2: I can understand you no wanting to use it right enough, given the, given the, given the (throat's dried). — You can keep it to hang *me* in, Ann. Eh Ann? You can keep it to hang *me* in.

> (*Beat.* ANN *moves towards the house*)

ANN: I better put these flowers in a vase.

BILLY 2: We could pick up a good-size wardrobe at The Barras. Ann, wardrobes coming out the walls there.

ANN: It'll take the both of ye to carry it.

BILLY 1: If that's what you want, Ann.

ANN: OK.

BILLY 2: And then will you make a decision, Ann.

ANN: Yes.

(ANN *exits. The two* BILLYS *collect their stuff*)

MANDY: Listen, seen as how this is the only decision you're going to hear all day, I thought I'd better let you know I've decided that today's the day, OK? She's hardly looked the road I walk on for nine year. Today's the day she's going to look me in the face.

(MANDY *exits after* ANN)

BILLY 2: Sphinx? Is that the word for it?

BILLY 1: Word for what?

BILLY 2: She's gave us a task hasn't she.

BILLY 1: What chance have you got, Billy son. She's no even testing you. She's testing me. You can come to the Barras if you want son, help me cart the wardrobe back. You'll be carrying your own coffin.

(*The* BILLYS *exit in the direction of the house*)

SCENE FOUR

(*The next four scenes are set in The Barras: a market-place which spreads out over several streets, lanes, buildings and yards. In this scene we're in a space behind a street of stalls. We see the back of the stalls, so maybe we see the backs of two or three stall-holders and hear their spiels.* NANETTE *enters carrying a soapbox, followed by* PROPHET JOHN. PROPHET JOHN *has an antagonistic relationship with himself, the world and with his own gift of prophecy. His energy is, in the true sense of the word, daemonic. When the spirit is upon him he is very powerful; but at all other times he is extremely bad-tempered and irritable. There's an anger in him he tries to contain but can't.* NANETTE *puts down the soapbox, gets out a flask from her bag*)

NANETTE: D'you want some soup?

PROPHET JOHN: What kind of soup.

NANETTE: Some soup I made.

PROPHET JOHN: 'Some soup I made.'

NANETTE: D'you want some?

(*Beat*)

PROPHET JOHN: No.

NANETTE: No?

PROPHET JOHN: No!

NANETTE: It's good home-made soup.

PROPHET JOHN: No thank you.

NANETTE: Are you no hungry?

(*No reply*)

Eh? Are you no hungry, John?

(*She holds out a cup of soup*)

Here. — Here.

PROPHET JOHN: Nanette, will you stop please murdering me.

NANETTE: Eh?

PROPHET JOHN: 'Eh?'

NANETTE: Cheesey peeps!

PROPHET JOHN: I've indicated that I don't wish to be a part of your soup. Don't keep on keeping on.

NANETTE: There's no need for language.

PROPHET JOHN: What language did I use?

NANETTE: (*avoiding*) Anyway!

PROPHET JOHN: What bad language did I use?

NANETTE: What about here? You'll get a good crowd here. There's plenty people come to the Barras on a Saturday. I'll stay and help build your crowd but then I'll have to get back and mind my stall. — Eh? What about here?

PROPHET JOHN: I've got nothing to say.

NANETTE: The spirit will speak. — Eh?

PROPHET JOHN: No! — Nobody listens to me.

NANETTE: Och, away ye go! You 'speak' to plenty people. You 'speak' to a right good few of us. When the spirit takes you you're like to Noah's dove. There's plenty that won't listen I'm no saying that, and there's plenty that listen but don't hear I'm no saying that. They can't hear the words of the spirit unless the spirit opens their ears can they. — Eh?

PROPHET JOHN: I've been struck dumb. — The spirit. The spirit's like a lion in the land. He's roaming the land looking for prey. He wants the flesh from my bones. He wants the air from my lungs. He wants the tongue from my head. Then he'll stand up in my bare bones and prophesy. — Who am I? Am I a prophet like Ezekiel? Or Isaiah? Or Jeremiah? Or Amos? Or Zechariah? Or Habbakuk? Or Hosea? Or Daniel? Or Malachi?

(PROPHET JOHN *is now, in spite of himself, in the possession of his daemon — and at this point* ANN *and* MANDY *enter, followed by the two* BILLYS)

I went to Death and said 'Where do I go to find Wisdom?' And Death said, Death said 'I don't know!' 'I don't know,' Death said, 'I only hear rumours of her.' — Yes! Yes! Yes, Israel, yes I'm a prophet! Your prophets, Israel, are like ruin-haunting jackals. Don't come too close — better to stand at the outskirts of the camp and listen to the jackals barking in the distant ruins. Why have you come here? What is it you want?

BILLY 1: Ann, we'll go take a look at —

BILLY 2: — take a look at wardrobes Ann.

BILLY 1: Are you coming. Ann?

PROPHET JOHN: 'Does a girl forget her ornaments, does a bride forget her wedding-wreath? Then why have you forgotten me?'

ANN: You two go on.

(*The* BILLYS *exit*)

PROPHET JOHN: 'Does a woman forget her jewellery or a bride her wedding-sash? Yet you have forgotten me days without number.'

(CHARLIE *and* MAX *enter.* MAX *opens a fresh cigarette-pack, puts two fags in his mouth, lights them, inhales. Then he opens his paper and studies the racing form (and that's him happy for the rest of the scene).* CHARLIE *watches and listens*)

PROPHET JOHN: Once there was a woman. — Yes, Israel! Yes! Revile me! Denigrate me! Heap abuse upon my head! Is it me that says this? — no! — Once there was a woman in the land of Israel. One night she was lying with her husband in their tent and she heard Yahweh God of Israel speak to her saying, 'Does a girl forget her ornaments or a bride her wedding-wreath? Then why have you forgotten me?' And she listened to Yahweh God of Israel and left me sleeping in the tent and stole away. When I arose that morning he could smell her perfume on our sheets, the scent of cinnabar on our pillow; and I waited for her day and night and night and day. I looked for her on the road-sides and sought her out in the cities; as well in the temple as in the jackal-haunted ruins; and everywhere I went I shouted, 'Does a woman forget her jewellery or a bride her wedding-wreath?' Then how come you've forgotten me.

ANN: (*to* NANETTE) Is he speaking to me?

NANETTE: When the spirit descends the spirit descends.

(PROPHET JOHN *takes his coat off and approaches closer to* ANN)

PROPHET JOHN: 'Does a girl forget her ornaments or a bride her wedding-sash? Yet you have forgotten me days without number.'

(*He throws his coat over her head — and holds her strongly by the arms. He does this with authority and power.*

CHARLIE *and* MANDY *look on, concerned, but held back from interfering by the sense that some power is present and no way of knowing whether the power is violent or healing*)

PROPHET JOHN: (*to* ANN) There is a lion in the land. He

wants the breath from your body. He wants the flesh from your haunches. He wants the bones you stand up in. After he's eaten he'll fall asleep.

(PROPHET JOHN *embraces* ANN *strongly. She seems to yield to this. But to* CHARLIE *the embrace is becoming uncomfortably strong — like the embrace of a lion — and* CHARLIE *decides to intervene*)

CHARLIE: Haw! You! Enough! Down! Drop it! Leave! Back! Back!

(PROPHET JOHN *lets go of* ANN *and backs away to a safer distance.   Now* CHARLIE *is beside* ANN *and holds her, to calm her. But* ANN *wants to get the coat off her head and is distressed and doesn't want to be touched*)

CHARLIE: It's OK, it's OK, it's OK, it's OK.

(*He gets the coat off her head*)

ANN: Who are you?

CHARLIE: I'm —

(ANN *feels very naked and needs to hide herself somehow; with her hands, with words; while she sorts herself out*)

ANN: I'm OK, it's OK, I'm OK, I'm fine, I'll be fine.

CHARLIE: Are you sure?

ANN: I'm OK, it's OK, I'm all, I'll be fine, I'm fine, I'm all outside in.

CHARLIE: He was kind of mauling you there.

ANN: I don't know how it happened, he kind of (it's my own fault, I let him!) he kinna undid me.

PROPHET JOHN: The lion stands over his prey.

CHARLIE: Back!

PROPHET JOHN: (*a bit on the back foot, wary*). Is there no god in Israel that you have to go and consult oracles? Is there no god in Israel that you go and consult Beel-Zebub, god of Ekron; or the goddess-whore of Babylon. I fed you full and you became adulterers, well-fed roving stallions, each one neighing for his neighbour's wife. And because you have broken your covenant with me the Lord your God who is a jealous god, I am coming to trample you underfoot in the valley of Jezreel and raise you up as a cloud of dust.

CHARLIE: (See people that shout) I can shout at people too you know! I'm going to hunt you, my friend, you're everything that's all wrong the modern world: where's your structure (ya ugly big ride ye) where's your shape? (You're like a burst binbag) can you no keep anything in? Eh? Can you not keep nothing in? Does the word 'pish' mean nothing to you? Because it's about time you took a few lessons from a three-year-old and

delineated a few lines! You're you, I'm me; this is outside, you
should be inside; put your rubbish inside a binbag and then
outside in the bin — and don't spill it all over the streets (I
don't want to slip on your leftovers do I). I've got enough going on in my jumps, somersaults, suit, head without having to
intermingle my thoughts with yours. So g'on! Away home to
the bedsit; away home and cry in the wilderness; away home
and listen to yourself!

   (CHARLIE *uses this speech to drive* PROPHET JOHN *and*
   NANETTE *from the stage. He also uses* PROPHET JOHN's
   coat. He completes this expulsion by throwing PROPHET
   JOHN's *coat after him. It's a job well done*)

CHARLIE: (*fast, straight, without a pause*), I applaud a man like
   that, who is he? Some people would condemn the man but no
   way no way no way I agree with him: if he's saying everything's
   all wrong the modern world then yes, correct, everything is all
   wrong, (him included). Are you OK?

ANN: Yes. I don't know how I get myself into these things, I
   don't seem to have any self-control.

CHARLIE: What is it you're looking for?

ANN: I wish I knew!

CHARLIE: You must be looking for something.

   (CHARLIE *indicates the Barras*)

ANN: Aw, you mean, what am I looking for? I thought you meant
   what am I looking for?

CHARLIE: I'm looking for a suit. I like to wear a suit, even just no
   for anything special, y'know: I'm too old-fashioned, that's my
   problem. For the reason the old dear's a hunner and something
   (seventy odds). Sad. Y'know? So! Don't make me a stranger
   next time, what's your name again?

ANN: Me? Emm, Ann.

   (CHARLIE *offers his hand and they shake*)

CHARLIE: Charlie. Don't make me a stranger, Ann. — And
   who's this? Are you two related in any way? Because she's lovely
   enough to be your sister.

ANN: Mmmm, she's my gaughter.

CHARLIE: She's your what?

MANDY: I'm her gaughter. Gandhi.

CHARLIE: It's a pleasure to meet you, Mahatma. You see and
   keep your mammie out of trouble. — Well, if it was another
   day. But today (to draw a line) today's a day to get the head
   down and graft away and if it breaks my heart that's all to the
   good. — OK, Max?

   (MAX *is still reading* The Sporting Life *and working out*

accumulators)

Max are you coming? Suit Max suit — c'mawn, c'mawn, cmawwwn — look at the state of him — look at the state of ye, Max — because see life, Max, you can not-live life all you want but you can't not-live death.

> (*And with that bon mot,* CHARLIE *exits, followed by* MAX. ANN *checks off-stage to see where he's gone to*)

ANN: Where has he been all my life!

MANDY: Did you think he was good-looking?

ANN: I wouldnae say he was good-looking. But he was so sad and so complicated and so dignified and so decisive and so (I dunno) so handsome.

MANDY: He seemed quite keen.

ANN: D'you think so?

MANDY: Yeah. He was quite keen on you too for a bit but he kinna lost interest.

ANN: D'you think so?

MANDY: Mmmm.

ANN: What makes you think that?

MANDY: Aw c'mon, I don't want to say it: it's no very nice. OK: let's just say there's a lot less to you than meets the eye. I mean, you don't even have a character. It's like, 'Who are ye?' I mean, a man shows the least interest in you and your wee heart's panicking like a flock of pigeons, or like you're goannae die in the next two minutes.

> (ANN *is dumbstruck for a moment*)

ANN: Are you looking for a fight?

MANDY: Maybe.

ANN: 'Maybe.'

> (ANN *starts to walk towards the same exit* CHARLIE *exited*)

MANDY: Where are you going?

ANN: I'm just going to see if Charlie needs any help choosing a suit.

MANDY: OK. I just think he kinna lost interest in ye.

> (BILLY 2 *enters*)

BILLY 2: We've seen a good-sized wardrobe, Ann, if you'd like to come and see it.

ANN: (*furious*) I'll be right there, Billy, stop nagging me, will ye, you've been biting my ear all bloody day!

BILLY 2: It's a good size, I'll say that. It's just round the corner, Ann, so: whenever.

ANN: (*shouting*) OK, Billy, I'm coming!

> (BILLY 2 *goes*)

MANDY: I'll see you later on, OK?

ANN: Why, where are you going?

MANDY: Nowhere. — Do you think sex and violence are different?

ANN: Eh?

MANDY: I think they can both be an end in themselves.

ANN: You're no too old for a slap on the tits milady.

MANDY: So you agree then. — I'll let you get on, you'd better go and Billy.

ANN: Mandy! Will you get back here!

    (MANDY*'s exited in the same direction as* CHARLIE)

Oh for goodness sake, Mandy, you're more shallow than a bloody — mirror! Right. I see. That's the way it's to be, is it. We're going to tear each other's faces off all day and see who's the ugliest?

    (ANN *goes off in the direction of the* BILLYS)

Good grief. All I want is one happy day.

SCENE FIVE

    (*Interior. Racks of second-hand suits. The perimeter is lined with pairs of second-hand shoes.* CHARLIE *and* MAX *enter*)

CHARLIE: Suits.

MAX: Quiet in here.

CHARLIE: Shoes an' all.

MAX: You want shoes an' all?

CHARLIE: I'm just indicating the shoes.

MAX: You want to try some on?

CHARLIE: Naw.

MAX: Naw.

CHARLIE: Shoes are a man's character. You don't get that second-hand do ye.

    (CHARLIE *approaches the suit-rack. He doesn't touch the suits, just looks at them*)

MAX: The dead . . . The dead have no taste have they. — why do I want to clear my throat in here? What do I want to keep out? What do I want to expel? — I'm a wee bit concerned getting, Charlie. You're too vulnerable, Charlie. You're too wide open.

    (CHARLIE *goes round to the other side of the suit-rack from* MAX. *They can't see each other*)

MAX: D'you see a suit you like?

    (MANDY *enters unseen*)

MAX: Charlie? D'you see a suit you like? — I've seen days like this happen before. Some days it's like the day's out to hunt ye.

So beware, Charlie. Suit, I respect that. But I see a man that lives more invisible than that, more private. Like your voice, Charlie. Your voice, Charlie . . . is like a secret that you're keeping even from yourself.

(CHARLIE *touches the sleeve of one of the suits, lets it go*)

CHARLIE: Let's get out of here.

MAX: You don't want a suit?

CHARLIE: I want to visit my mammie in a suit someone hasnae got old and died in a coupla times.

MAX: You want a new suit?

CHARLIE: Correct.

MAX: Correct. — How much money we got?

CHARLIE: A fiver . . . odds.

MAX: You need to eat, Charlie. This is the unfortunate thing. Certain things, Charlie, whether we like them or no . . . money, Charlie, or . . . hunger. I know I'm hungry. I'm dizzy getting. Can I suggest something? Can I suggest we've reached an impasse? — Charlie? Can I suggest we've reached an impasse?

CHARLIE: Yeah.

MAX: Good. So therefore can I suggest (see if this gets us any further forward) can I suggest we get ourselves something to eat then go to the bookie's? — (see if that gets us any further forward).

CHARLIE: Put on an accumulator?

MAX: Correct.

CHARLIE: (*straight*) I've a bad feeling, Max. I've a bad bad feeling, Max. I'm no sure my mammie's goannae wait till the fourth favourite comes in at Newmarket, Max, y'know. That's my feeling.

MAX: Charlie (fuckssake, Charlie). Are you OK?

CHARLIE: I've a bad sick feeling, Max. Y'know? How bad it is I don't know. It's bad enough.

MANDY: Do you need any help?

MAX: Naw.

MANDY: Jesus says Follow me. Follow me and I'll save you. I'll lead you out of the darkness and into the light. I'm a Christian.

MAX: Charlie?

(CHARLIE *appears from round the other side of the suit-rack*)

MANDY: Hiya, it's me. I've come to save ye.

CHARLIE: Good enough. You got any money?

MANDY: Eh?

(CHARLIE *produces a fiver*)

CHARLIE: Look: fiver: is this on its own or have you got a mate for it.

MANDY: Is this a trick?

CHARLIE: Yes. So back off.

(MANDY *produces a fiver*)

MANDY: There. Now what?

CHARLIE: This is a lighter. See? What you do is wrap the fiver round your wrist then burn a hole through it.

MANDY: Why?

MAX: Because ye cannae do it, that's why.

CHARLIE: Impossible.

MAX: Can't be done.

MANDY: I see. What's the point then?

CHARLIE: Watch. I've got a fiver you've got a fiver. I give you my last lonely fiver which is the only company I've got in the entire world, OK? Now you give me your fiver.

MANDY: OK.

(*They exchange fivers*)

CHARLIE: Thanks, Gandhi: You're a Christian. So now you've got my one and only last fiver even though that leaves me with fuck-all fuck-all and my insides like a half-full can of lager the morning after a party that someone's used for an ashtray. — You burn a wee hole through that fiver onto your wrist you keep it. That's the bet. You fail to burn a hole through it I get my fiver back.

MANDY: I don't like pain. Why don't you try it?

CHARLIE: You're offering the bet to me?

MAX: Yeah.

CHARLIE: OK, give me my fiver then.

MANDY: You can use the fiver of mine you've got.

(*Beat*)

CHARLIE: You're offering the bet to me?

MANDY: Yeah.

CHARLIE: OK. I accept.

MANDY: Is there a trick?

CHARLIE: Are you giving the bet to me?

MANDY: Yeah.

CHARLIE: Sure?

MANDY: Yeah.

CHARLIE: Good. Yes there's a trick.

MAX: Caveat emptor.

CHARLIE: Have you seen boiling chipfat? (So I can teach you.)

MANDY: In the chippie.

CHARLIE: That's the trick: agony. The chippie, the chipfat spits up at him he can accept that. But he doesn't stand there and pour the chipfat over his wrists does he. So that's the question.

How much *pain* can I endure? How much *pain* can I inflict *upon* myself? How much pain can I endure to inflict upon myself? OK, Christian?

MANDY: Yeah, that sounds like it might be quite good.

    (CHARLIE *lights his lighter*)

CHARLIE: OK, Max?

    (MAX *comes across and holds the fiver against* CHARLIE'*s wrist.*
    MANDY *finds a good place to watch the trick from*)

CHARLIE: OK, Christian? You watching?

    (*In the dim interior light* CHARLIE *holds the lit lighter to his face*)

CHARLIE: OK, Max?

MAX: I'm OK, you OK?

CHARLIE: I've got a bad bad feeling, Max. — I want to take this slow. OK? I want to approach the pain.

    (*Slowly* CHARLIE *brings the lighter to his wrist and holds it there. It's painful*)

MANDY: Is it hurting yet?

    (CHARLIE *can't bear the pain*)

CHARLIE: OK, that's it, I'm no doing it. OK, Christian? Give me my fiver back (I'm only being honest with ye) give me my fiver back or I'll cut your eyes open.

MAX: You'd better do as he tells you, gorgeous.

CHARLIE: You'd better do as he tells you, gorgeous, because I am not a well man suddenly and my insides being empty there's no much to stop me from slapping you about the place. Bad? You don't know how bad badness can be, so don't fanny me around because I don't have the time!

MAX: You're in grave danger, darling.

CHARLIE: Because how no well I am (I've no been living good, have I) and how no well I am I'm waiting for a sign from God — that's (only fair) let you know the danger you're in.

    (*In the face of this storm of violence* MANDY *is reasonably serene*)

MANDY: You lost the bet. You owe me a fiver.

CHARLIE: Can someone translate her for me? I'm lost.

MANDY: I bet you're the type that mugs wee seven-year-olds for their fag-money. Are ye?

MAX: Right, you: fuck off while we're still being pleasant.

MANDY: Not until you give me my fiver.

MAX: Is she on drugs?

CHARLIE: Give her the fiver ya diddy.

MAX: Eh?

CHARLIE: You're standing there like a miserable wet shiteyarsed sheep bleating in the rain.

MAX: Am I.

CHARLIE: Give her the fiver, ya grass-muncher.

> (MAX *hands over the fiver*)

MAX: I'm losing the plot here, Charlie.

MANDY: So. Do you see my Christian breastplate of faith? Do you see how unscathed it is?

CHARLIE: I'm stood here admiring ye.

MANDY: Good, I'm glad.

CHARLIE: 'God.' (You're gorgeous, by the way.)

MANDY: Am I?

CHARLIE: 'God.' OK, I can accept that. Because I give up. I'm beat. I'm nothing. I'm a bad bad feeling. And likes of with my mammie across at the Vicky dying . . . Y'know? So shirt shoes and a suit someone hasnae died in a coupla times, I can prepare myself, away across to the Vicky and break my heart. Obviously.

MANDY: And you want help?

CHARLIE: I apologise for raising my voice back there. I'm too complex, that's my problem. I do things (wrong!) — things do things (even that's no quite true).

MANDY: And you want help?

CHARLIE: Listen: I'm sorry. Right? Yeah.

> (CHARLIE *thinks she's going to give him the two fivers now and holds out his hand.* MANDY *just looks at him*)

MANDY: You're in a bad way aren't ye. It's like you're too many, or it's like you're too open, y'know?, like the river or something and you've got infested with the dead bodies and then you open your mouth and they all come pouring out. I hope you don't mind me saying that.

CHARLIE: No. I . . .

MANDY: I'm just shining a light. It might take you a while to get used to it seen as how you've been in the dark so long.

CHARLIE: . . . no, I think I see what you're hinting at.

MANDY: OK, you can come with me then.

> (MANDY *starts to exit*)

CHARLIE: Where to?

MANDY: I'll take you home with me if you want. We've got loads of men's clothes — so bath, shirt, shoes, a couple of suits, and you can go and see your mammie looking brand new. OK?

CHARLIE: That would be — very kind of ye.

MANDY: OK then. Follow me.

> (MANDY *exits.* CHARLIE *and* MAX *make a move in the same direction*)

MAX: Charlie. I'm no goannae ask you what's happening because whatever it is it's not food mouth stomach: but see the art of conmanship, Charlie: the art of conmanship, Charlie, is to con the other person. Otherwise you're Santa Claus ya cunt.

CHARLIE: I got carried away with the truth didn't I. I'd no idea what I was saying.

(CHARLIE *exits in same direction as* MANDY)

MAX: Charlie, if I don't eat shortly I'm goannae have to hurt somebody. I'm goannae have to eat somebody. — Charlie? — Charlie?

(MAX *exits in the same direction as* CHARLIE)

SCENE SIX

(*Exterior, the Barras.* MANDY *enters followed by* CHARLIE. MAX *traipses on after them*)

CHARLIE: It's good of you to do this for me, Christian. Do you do this a lot?

MANDY: No.

CHARLIE: I mean, I acknowledge your goodness taking me into the bosom of your family. Will your ma be there too?

MANDY: Why d'you ask that?

MAX : Can we pause here Charlie to (take stock) break her arm, Charlie? Charlie, can we pause here to take stock? Because we've passed the hot dogs.

MANDY: Eh? Why d'you ask that?

CHARLIE: It's just the way my somersaults, jumps, double-back mind works. I'm no trying to exclude your ma (she's lovely too). I'm concerned what she might say.

MANDY: I'll just tell her I'm trying to save ye.

MAX: I'm running out of excuses for ye, Charlie. Your mother can only last so long (the truth, Charlie), your mother's only an excuse for so long!

MANDY: Do you ever think 'I'm alive!'?

CHARLIE: I am alive.

MANDY: But do you never, like, think 'I'm alive!' and, like, you're so happy you want to tear your scalp off.

CHARLIE: Listen, life's no a good subject for me the now.

MANDY: If I was a tree, like, in the country (we got sent to a home there once), if I was a tree, like, in the country and I was, like, really tall and it was, like, a really nice sunny day, I'd be so happy I'd topple over. I wouldn't be able to stand up.

CHARLIE: You're an angel, you are.

MANDY: Don't worry: I'm not as good as I look.

CHARLIE: You're giving me hope. — To be honest with you
Mandy: I haven't been living good. Time. Y'know? You marry,
have a kid, leave them. Then you think, did I do that? Then,
once upon a time, there was the cherubim, seraphim, thrones,
dominions, powers; virtues, principalities; archangels, angels.
Nice. Y'know?

> (*The two* BILLYS *enter carrying a huge big fucker of a ward-
> robe, followed by* ANN. *We see them as if in long-shot. An image
> accompanied by music.* MANDY *sees this and wants to exit*)

MANDY: Anyway. Let's get going.

MAX: Charlie, have you forsaken leave of your senses? Are you
going to let her wander off with your cash?

> (CHARLIE *turns round to talk to* MAX — *sees the vision*)

CHARLIE: Max, why don't you —. — Look at that. Look at
that, Mandy.

MANDY: Oh uh huh.

CHARLIE: How do you interpret that? The two men walk be-
hind a woman carrying a coffer. The woman's wearing black.
So right away we're talking about Fate, yeah? I look at that and
I want to know the whole sad story. Who's she? Who are they?
What have they done to make her so unhappy? She looks so
sad and so womanly and so longing . . .

MANDY: I sometimes think men should be blinded at birth. I
don't mean that to be horrible, their mothers could do it.

MAX: Blind would be fine by me.

MANDY: So they learned how to not look.

MAX: Blind me so long as she put something in my blind deluded
mouth.

> (ANN *turns, looks at* CHARLIE *and* MANDY)

CHARLIE: She's looking at us.

> (*The* BILLYS *exit, followed by* ANN. CHARLIE *tries to find a
> position onstage where he can continue to watch* ANN *offstage.*
> MANDY *goes up to* CHARLIE, *touches him gently on the arm*)

MANDY: Don't let the devil steal your eyes away.

> (CHARLIE *doesn't look at her, his gaze fixed offstage on* ANN)

CHARLIE: She's stopped.

MANDY: Haven't you got something better to look at?

CHARLIE: She's turned round.

MANDY: You think you're looking but you're not, you're
drowning.

CHARLIE: It's Ann.

MAX: I don't comprehend this. To me this passes —. This is
past —.

CHARLIE: She's coming back.

MAX: I've passed out.

> (CHARLIE *takes up a position to await* ANN's *arrival*. ANN *enters, talking over her shoulder*)

ANN: I seem to be the only one that can see ahead to what's coming. Ambulances? They have to wait till a thing's happened don't they. Till after everything's all over and they might as well not have effn bothered. — Oh look who it is. My daughter Mandy. Has she been showing you her character, Charlie?

CHARLIE: She's been trying to save me, haven't you, Mandy?

ANN: What have you been saving him for, later?

CHARLIE: She's very kindly offered to take me back to your house, Ann.

ANN: Has she? You watch your step, Charlie, she's trickier than a mirror — see when it looks at ye? Oh look. Here come my two workers, Charlie.

> (*The* BILLYS *come on carrying the wardrobe*)

ANN: Are you two going to follow me all the way home!

BILLY: What way are you going, Ann!

ANN: No, Billy!

BILLY 1: 'No'?

ANN: I'm no walking the two miles home behind a stupid big thing like that.

BILLY 1: Could you no have thought of that before?

ANN: Fate, Charlie.

CHARLIE: We meet again, eh?

ANN: You can *explain* it.

CHARLIE: You can *explain* it.

ANN: Still doesn't *explain* it.

CHARLIE: Fate.

BILLY 1: Can we put this down, Billy?

BILLY 2: I'm waiting on Ann to tell me, Billy.

CHARLIE: Would you no be better transporting it by van?

BILLY 1: Yeah. You got one?

CHARLIE: We must know somebody between us that's got a van some kinna transport.

> (*They don't*)

BILLY 2: I've got a brother-in-law in Germany drives a big artic.

BILLY 1: Billy, can we put this down?

BILLY 2: Billy, we put it down: then what?

BILLY 1: Then I demolish ye, ya big wall.

CHARLIE: I mean, if there's any way, Ann, I can help you . . . not *help* . . . if there's any way I can not *help* you *something* you, then I'd be only too glad.

ANN: Uch, Fate, Charlie: you can't escape it. I had these two sons. First Robert hung himself. Then Martin?

(ANN *imagines she's got the sequence in the wrong order and 'corrects' herself*)

ANN: What did I say there? First *Robert* hung himself. Then *Martin*. I don't know what was the bigger shock. It was a shock the first time wasn't it. Then when we found *Martin* in the boys' wardrobe like his twin brother that was another shock. Like seeing things. You can't blame Robert. He wasn't to know the future was he. You can't blame Martin either, he was only copying his twin. You're white as a sheet, Charlie, what did I say, did I say something wrong?

CHARLIE: No. It's just . . . some days you know you're being told something. Y'know? You're being told to get real or something. Y'know? How though?

BILLY 1: Talk to Billy. He's so real it's untrue.

BILLY 2: I might no be clever, Billy, but I can lift heavy things.

ANN: You just follow your instincts, Charlie. Well! I'll go and look for something else I forgot. Mandy, will you go home and open the door for them? — I'll see you two later. — I hope I bump into you again, Charlie. — I'm going to throw myself into the arms of Fate.

(ANN *crosses the stage back in the direction of the Barras*)

BILLY 1: Ann, will you —. Billy, will you —.

CHARLIE: Is she OK? Should someone no go after her?

(ANN *has now exited*)

CHARLIE: Should some bastard not, I think someone should go after her, Mandy.

MANDY: Why?

CHARLIE: I'll go after her then, if no other bastard's going to.

MAX: Charlie son, have you lost your sense of smell? Have you lost your sense of foreboding? Because I swear, Charlie, you go and loss yourself in ghostland you will be beset, beset, Charlie, and torn to pieces by your own hands.

(CHARLIE *exits after* ANN. BILLY 1 *drops his end of the wardrobe.* MAX *loses the place*)

MAX: OK, Christian? I've been as Christian as I can be without actually striking you. OK? You stand there while I look for a weapon, and it'll be a big blind one-eyed lump of wood with a fucking five-inch nail where its cyclops eye should be and we'll see who's blind then!

(MAX *hunts around for a weapon*)

BILLY 1: OK, Billy: lift.

(*The two* BILLYS *lift the big wardrobe and set off in the same direction as* ANN. MAX *locates a suitable weapon and advances on* MANDY)

MAX: OK, Christian? I promised you . . .

MANDY: Not the now, Max . . .

MAX: . . . this is the bastard cyclops is going to explain violence to you . . . !

MANDY: . . . we're going to the bookie's . . .

MAX: . . . violence that I can't seem to explain to you, except by returning to the original Greek!

(MAX *drops his weapon.* MANDY *sets off in the direction of the bookie's*)

MANDY: We can get something to eat on the way.

MAX: You're okay you. You're alright by the way. Charlie, man: the smell of bad luck off the holy jinx creeps like a sweating urinal, I have to sleep the same room as him because he's frightened he gets the fears! You're okay you. You've doubled your money, put it that way.

(MANDY'*s gone*)

MAX: You've got ten notes on yir tail. Charlie, man: I've been carrying that thing all day.

(MAX *exits after* MANDY)

SCENE SEVEN

(*Another corner of The Barras. A couple of handcarts with junk on them which may just be temporarily untended but look as if they've been abandoned for good. Only one of the stalls looks slightly more alive. It's decorated with heart-shaped crimson and silver balloons.* NANETTE *and* PROPHET JOHN *come on carting boxes of singles.* NANETTE'*s a trader.* NANETTE'*s got one box,* JOHN'*s got four*)

NANETTE: The thing is John how literal I take things. Everything to me is as straightforward literal as the manna in the desert or the burning bush. So when you say once there was a woman I take that to mean once there was a woman, John. Am I right?

PROPHET JOHN: Yes.

NANETTE: I'm no jealous: (the Lord has been with me ever since I was a wee girl, he won't desert me now). So there was a woman.

PROPHET JOHN: Yes!

NANETTE: I'm just asking! — Cheesey peeps. — I'm only inquiring, John! — So what was she like?

PROPHET JOHN: She's dead.

NANETTE: Well I can't compete with that can I. I'm only here in the flesh. I'm only clothed like the lilies of the fields, finer than the robes of Solomon. — How did she die? — Eh?

PROPHET JOHN: 'Eh?'

NANETTE: Oh forget it then, effn forget it. If you cannae see what's in front of your eyes . . .

(ANN *enters, looking behind her*)

ANN: Hi there, I'm looking for a single I lost.

NANETTE: Whatever it is we've got it here. This is all the singles here you've ever tried to forget, I cry just looking at the titles. Tell me a rotten single and I've got it.

ANN: Have you got Tom Jones doing The Skye Boat Song?

NANETTE: I could look for you. John, you away and speak to her by the upstairs café.

(PROPHET JOHN *and* ANN *stare at each other*)

ANN: You're . . . He's . . .

NANETTE: Uh huh. On you go John hurry up!

(PROPHET JOHN *exits*)

NANETTE: Did he 'speak' to you, dear? He 'speaks' to a few of us . . . eight or nine just. We call him Prophet John. Uh huh yes uh huh. When the spirit takes him he has wings like to Noah's dove, but when the spirit deserts him again he's like a slave.

(NANETTE *is thumbing through a long box of old singles looking for the Tom Jones. Basically though she doubts its existence*)

NANETTE: The Skye Boat Song?

ANN: It's no for me.

NANETTE: Are you sure?

ANN: Yes!

NANETTE: The one about Bonny Prince Charlie they made us sing at school to teach us how Scottish we were?

ANN: He loaned it to me . . . my boyfriend . . .

NANETTE: Aw.

ANN: I *predicted* I'd ruin it. I left it lying out till it warped didn't I. Then I panicked, put it under the grill on just a low flame, to try and flatten it out again? That only seemed to make it worse.

NANETTE: I see.

(*She goes on looking. She sings the first verse of 'The Skye Boat Song' in a sort of questioning tone as much as to say, 'Are you sure you're thinking of the right song?'*

Speed bonny boat, like a bird on the wing
'Onward!' the sailors cry.
Carry the lad that's born to be king

Over the sea to Skye . . . ?

Eff this. I can think of better things to do with my index finger! I'll see if it's listed. You look through that box there.

(ANN *starts to look through a box of singles*)

ANN: Are they in any order?

NANETTE: It's just a whole load of rubbish dear people have flung out: what's the sense putting them in any order!

(CHARLIE *enters*)

CHARLIE: Ann.

ANN: Charlie.

CHARLIE: I hope you don't mind me following you, Ann. I came just to say —

ANN: What?

CHARLIE: Ach. Nothing.

ANN: It's OK. Say it.

CHARLIE: It's just that I left the wife. So I've no right to even anything, mouth that I am. What I came to say is: sadness. Y'know? You marry, have a kid, leave them.

ANN: It's the order things happen in isn't it.

CHARLIE: What is?

ANN: Sadness. It's a jumble.

NANETTE: I don't see it listed. I don't mind trying to help you dear (we all need help don't we?) . . .

CHARLIE: I get confused as well, Ann (if that's any consolation to you, Ann) (can I call you Ann, Ann). Why when there's so much sadness and confusion in the world can we not reach out and comfort each other.

ANN: It's not just the world is it. Even the galaxies are drifting apart . . .

CHARLIE: . . . I know . . .

ANN: What chance have people got?

CHARLIE: I'm trying to get across to the Vicky. Yeah. My mammy's dying . . .

ANN: Aw.

CHARLIE: Yeah. She's no even my mammy. I thought she was my mammy till I came home from school one day and saw this nice lady sitting on the couch and my mammy said this is your mammy, Charlie, say hello. So I said hello, then I went out and played at . . . (kicking a ball against a wall) . . . till the long slow night came in. — It turned out my mammy was really my granny. Which explains why she's a hunner odds (seventy something).

ANN: Awwwwww, Chicory Tip.

CHARLIE: Aw yeah.

ANN: We used to think these singles were forever.

CHARLIE: What does forever mean anyway, am I right. I used to say that to Margaret Mary (the wife, left her), what does forever mean, Margaret Mary? That was half the problem with me and her, what she meant by forever and what I meant was two entirely different things. Ahch, what's it matter, it's over . . . Infinity . . . y'know? . . . infinity was beyond her. All I'm saying is (you're lovely by the way) all I'm saying is . . . it doesn't have to be forever.

ANN: Don't look now, here come my two deadly rivals.

> (*The* BILLYS *enter with wardrobe, sweat pouring off them and out of breath*)

BILLY 1: OK, Billy? Can we put this thing down now?

BILLY 2: (*fucked*): Is it OK to put this thing down now, Ann?

ANN: If you want, Billy.

> (*The* BILLYS *put the wardrobe down*)

BILLY 1: OK, Ann? OK? All I need is a minute so can everyone no move for thirty seconds. OK, Ann? Because can I explain something, Ann: what the fuck *is* it with you today? I'm thirty three four now, most men have been married twice the time they're my age never mind none, so this is my big day too, right? We said that, didn't we. We said this was my big day too.

ANN: I know we did, Billy.

BILLY 1: Well can you stop treating me as though I'm Billy. You even tell him you love him Ann, you even Ann sleep with him — so he thinks that means something doesn't he.

ANN: It does mean something.

BILLY 1: I *know* that. But how's he supposed to know you don't mean it the same way as you mean it with me when you treat me the exact same way as you treat him I mean, *I'm* perplexed so how d'you think Billy feels?

BILLY 2: I feel fine, Ann.

CHARLIE: Are these two annoying you, Ann?

BILLY 1: I'm *perplexed*, Ann. Y'know? I'm fucking fucked actually.

ANN: Billy, if I could say what I wanted to say, if I could speak the words and hear myself saying them without the dogs of hell tearing my throat out, then I promise, I would. — I'm hoping Fate speaks. I've cast my bread upon the waters and I have to wait and see what the waters bring back up.

> (PROPHET JOHN *enters and gives a single to* ANN)

PROPHET JOHN: Here. I fun it by the upstairs café.

ANN: Oh god.

BILLY 1: What is it, Ann?

(ANN *takes the single and crosses over to* BILLY 2)

ANN: Billy, look what I found. I don't know if it's Fate or what it is, I do believe Fate speaks . . . I could wish she didn't and maybe we don't always understand her . . . which is maybe just as well at times . . . but when Fate speaks . . .

(*She gives him the single*)

ANN: . . . what we say or don't say, when Fate speaks our poor words fall short.

BILLY 2: I don't believe it.

NANETTE: Och . . . it's not unusual.

BILLY 2: Naw. That was the second single the so-called white man with the Motown voice released. This is something else. This is an all-time one-off recording also from 1965 that doesnae even exist.

NANETTE: I thought that.

BILLY 2: Decca denied this single down the phone, so did Tom's manager. I got a wee bit obsessed about it, y'know? Latterly the T. J. Newsletter refused to correspond with me on the subject and my wife deserted me for another fan. I had a single that nobody could explain how it had come to be, or why. Then I got a letter from an Italian called Umberto Eco. It turns out The Skye Boat Song was only ever released by an independent label in Naples that got liquidated shortly after, and I had one of the few copies still extant. That's why I was upset when Ann toasted it. I went back to her after a fortnight. I couldn't even fall out with her in the end. That was a shock to me. I couldn't even fall out with her. I went back and told her, she was the all-time one-off of all time.

BILLY 1: He can't see it Ann.

BILLY 2: She was the all-time one-off of all time.

BILLY 1: It's code, Billy: think. Why's she being so nice to you for christssake.

BILLY 2: We have our own code, Billy . . . nothing's broken it yet . . .

NANETTE: How much would you say that single was worth, Billy?

(MANDY *enters, followed by* MAX)

MANDY: Charlie. I'm still shaking. I won so much money I don't know if it's good.

MAX: The first off at Newmarket, Charlie son.

MANDY: We placed the first and second. I won so much money I don't know if it's good.

NANETTE: Hallelujah.

BILLY 2: Ahch! We're all winners today!

ANN: How much did you win?

MAX: A monkey-load, an effn ape-load.

CHARLIE: How much?

MAX: Bollocks plenty, put it that way.

CHARLIE: I suppose, on the question of how to split it Mandy, I suppose half . . .

MANDY: . . . half . . .

CHARLIE: . . . stake-money was yours and half, the other half . . .

MANDY: . . . was the fiver you lost when you gave me that stupit bet, I suppose. I suppose if I thought the money was a sign to you to believe in me . . . and lead you down the path . . .

ANN: I warned you, Charlie. Tricky? She's trickier than a crowd of sheep (see when they run at ye).

MANDY: Do you want to count it?

> (MANDY *crosses to* CHARLIE *and hands him the wad of cash, which he proceeds to count*)

MANDY: We could go and get you some new togs.

CHARLIE: Yeah.

ANN: How much is it, Charlie?

NANETTE: How much is it, Charlie?

CHARLIE: (Fucking) back off (fuckssake).

MANDY: Back off, he can't breathe.

CHARLIE: This is . . . what's the word, Mandy . . . I'm moved. Y'know? I cannae even count right.

> (MARGARET MARY *enters*)

MARGARET MARY: Can I speak to you a minute?

CHARLIE: Here I am. I'm listening.

> (MARGARET MARY *would like to speak to* CHARLIE *in private.* CHARLIE*'s not interested. He's holding onto the (as yet undivided) cash*)

MARGARET MARY: I'm sorry about your mammy. I'm sorry I didnae believe you this morning. After you came to see me I went inside and phoned your sister and it turned out your mammie was taken bad. So I followed you here.

CHARLIE: What can I say? I tell you my mammy's dying and you don't believe me? I was in tears. You were in tears.

MARGARET MARY: I know.

CHARLIE: What did you think we were crying for?

MARGARET MARY: It was sad.

CHARLIE: Sad?! (All I want to do is break my heart. You'd think that would be easy. Apparently naw, apparently it's a long bastard slog.) Sad?!

MARGARET MARY: I've been crying ever since to make up for

it. I feel so sorry for ye, Charlie. It's times like this you need yir family isn't it and to know they're thinking about you and hoping you'll come through and that if you want anything Charlie or need anything you only have to ask Charlie, because I'm still your wife, no matter.

CHARLIE: Sad?! (I've lost the place here.) Sad?! Because I don't want to humiliate you, Margaret Mary, in front of complete strangers, but you're humiliating yourself, sweetheart. I'm bewildered. I am. When the former person you made your vows to treats you like — then let the shad come up and cover me and take me down — because I'm bereaved of excuses for her. I come to you to let you know my own mammie is dying and you think I'm lying in order to get a tenner off ye.

(MARGARET MARY *turns her back on him, embarrassed, humiliated, wanting this to stop*)

I'm sorry Margaret Mary but it's true. I wish it wasnae true as well Margaret Mary, I really do. You gave me a tenner, Margaret Mary! You know what I'm saying? You gave me a tenner!! What does that make me? I'm no even going to try and imagine what it makes me. Because when the former person you made your vows to turns her back on you then let the sun peck my eyes out as far as I'm concerned because darkness has covered the earth and money? Money? I'll money ye! I'll give you money!

(CHARLIE *tears the wad of money in half*)

MANDY: Charlie!

(CHARLIE *tears the money in four*)

MANDY: Charlie!

(CHARLIE *tears the money in eight, and throws it in the air to fall like confetti*)

ANN: Oh god!

NANETTE: Cheesey peeps!

MAX: Oh Charlie.

BILLY 2: I hope he's going to clear that mess up.

ANN: What happened, Mandy?

MANDY: You saw him.

ANN: Did he tear it up?

NANETTE: I think so.

ANN: It was like violence or something, wasn't it. The way it stands out, bright as confetti after the rain . . .

(CHARLIE *crosses to the wardrobe, upon which* BILLY 1 *is sitting disconsolate*)

CHARLIE: OK Billy, we've got a job to do: let's get this thing shifted — come on come on come on son — shape up and show some effn dignity.

BILLY 1: I'll see you back at the house, Ann. This is to show you that I understand. You've said things to Billy in the past that maybe you shouldn't've said but you've said them therefore: whatever: etcetera that I don't need to say. Don't take too long though because I'm beginning to start no being able to focus or even see things. OK?

(BILLY 1 *walks away home*)

CHARLIE: What's up wi you? Eh, what's up wi him? OK Billy, it's down to us two. Come on, Billy, come on, wake up son or you'll get left behind.

(BILLY 2 *crosses to help* CHARLIE *shift the wardrobe*)

BILLY 2: I'll see you back at the house, Ann.

CHARLIE: Come on, Billy; before the wind blows through me.

(BILLY 2 *and* CHARLIE *exit with the wardrobe.* MAX *starts picking up the torn pieces of money*)

ANN: How much are your knickers, pet?

NANETTE: 50p a pair, fresh from M and S this morning. They don't come cheaper 'less you knock them yourself.

ANN: Give us ten. So how much is that I owe ye . . . ?

NANETTE: . . . Nanette. Ten pair of knickers is a fiver and a fiver for the Tom Jones.

ANN: Right, we better get on . . . What is it your name is, pet?

MARGARET MARY: Margaret Mary. You're the woman lives next close along from me.

ANN: (*shocked*) Oh, so I am! Well, we better get on . . .

MARGARET MARY: I'm sorry about your two boys. The two boys that went and hung themselves?

ANN: Oh uh huh. So are you Charlie's wife?

MARGARET MARY: I believe marriage is for life. Do you?

ANN: Yes. Oh uh huh. That's why I'm no sure if I'm in favour of it.

MARGARET MARY: I believe marriage is for life. Charlie said to me this one time he wanted a divorce. I went Charlie, even if you're no married to me I'd still be married to you!

ANN: Anyway. We better get on, Margaret Mary: I'm maybe getting married this afternoon.

NANETTE: D'you hear that, John — a wedding!

ANN: We'll see we'll see we'll see: I've asked the minister to come round and if it happens it happens. I'm under no illusions. Anyway you're all very welcome, Nanette, the more the merrier, Margaret Mary, 36/3 Arcadia Street, Nanette: no promises but whatever happens something will happen: there'll probably be a . . . (an every-man-for-himself-type-thing) . . .

NANETTE: D'you hear that, John — a buffet!

ANN: Och, it's a chance to wear a hat, isn't it. So will we see you there?

MAX: What about me?

ANN: What about you?

MAX: See Charlie (I feel sad for the deaf blind jinx creep, he's a pal). Look, if ye want me to come along, y'know? Because fair enough, I will then: I've carried him this long . . .

> (ANN, MANDY *and* MARGARET MARY *exit.* MAX *traipses after them.* PROPHET JOHN *and* NANETTE *start to pack up, close their stall*)

NANETTE: I still don't believe that single. I can't imagine it or hear it or picture what it sounds like. I don't know where the hell you got it from. — So d'you fancy a wedding? I think we should go. We've been invited. She must be a bit desperate or she wouldn't have asked us. So, d'you fancy a wedding. Eh?

PROPHET JOHN: 'Eh?'

NANETTE: Eh, miserable?

PROPHET JOHN: I do.

ACT TWO

There are two locations; the backgreen and the boys' bedroom. Mainly the backgreen should create a sense of spaciousness and light. The wardrobe from Act One has been left out here, abandoned to the sun. The boys' bedroom is very small and is wholly dominated by a big wardrobe in which two boys have hung themselves. The boys' bedroom is above and beyond the backgreen. It's later the same day, about three o'clock on a hot afternoon. There is the sound off of a party. Then someone puts on a record and we hear the pulsing intro of a song which turns into Tom Jones' legendary version of The Skye Boat Song. BILLY 1 enters the backgreen from stage left, dressed as a bridegroom. He's carrying BILLY 2's suitcases which he puts on the ground then sits on, to wait. After a bit MARGARET MARY comes out. In the conversation that follows they don't really engage with each other, their minds engaged with what's happening elsewhere.

MARGARET MARY: So.

BILLY 1: Good enough.

MARGARET MARY: D'you think so?

BILLY 1: I'm just sitting here waiting on Billy to come and retrieve his suitcases.

(*Beat*)

MARGARET MARY: What time's the minister coming?

BILLY 1: He's late — So. Good enough. So how's it going up there? Everybody enjoying theirselves?

MARGARET MARY: Uch . . .

BILLY 1: Naw naw, good enough. It's a wedding! It's a happy event! And (good enough) you want people to share your happiness don't ye.

MARGARET MARY: I don't mind people being happy. It's a happy event. I just think you should've the ceremony first then go wild. What's the minister going to say when he gets here and sees all the carry-on.

BILLY 1: Ahch, they're only carrying on.

(*Beat*)

MARGARET MARY: It's Charlie I feel for. You know Ann and Mandy are only having a carry-on with him and I know Ann and Mandy are only having a carry-on with him but by the time Charlie realises Ann and Mandy are only having a carry-on with him he'll be a wee pile of bones that they've left.

BILLY 1: Ahch well. Good enough.

(*Beat*)

MARGARET MARY: It's Charlie I feel for. He's in fairyland as it is without (dope) and (carry-on). It's time he woke up, got a suit and remembered who he is. — He's a different man in his suit. You should've seen him at his wedding. He looked so handsome. I looked nice as well but he looked so handsome. When he made his vows he was that serious he looked like a young priest. — It's Charlie I feel for. He's like the man in the gospels that found treasure in a field. He's delighted, so he leaves the treasure where he found it and goes off and gets drunk. Then next day he goes looking for the field again and can't find it.

(*Beat*)

BILLY 1: I wonder very much Marie-Therese if you would leave me alone here.

MARGARET MARY: I'm Margaret Mary.

BILLY 1: I wonder very much Mary Margaret if you would leave me alone here.

(ANN *enters the boys' bedroom in a bad mood, slamming the door behind her*)

ANN: She's been dogging my steps all bloody day — the wee minx!

(MARGARET MARY *doesn't move*)

MARGARET MARY: Where's the ceremony to be?

BILLY 1: Out here.

MARGARET MARY: Out here?

BILLY 1: Ann always wanted to be married in a garden.

MARGARET MARY: Aw.

BILLY 1: Yeah (y'know) nice.

> (MARGARET MARY *still doesn't want to go*)

MARGARET MARY: I'll wish you all the best then.

> (MARGARET MARY *exits in the direction of the house.* BILLY
> 1 *crosses to the wardrobe. A strong light comes onto the ward-
> robe in the boys' bedroom where* ANN *is now sitting on the bed.*
> BILLY 1 *leans his head against the wardrobe*)

BILLY 1: Ann? Ann? Are you thinking about me? — Remember
the time you phoned me from your house. 'Billy? It's me. I
can't speak: I've got Billy here.' Then you put the phone down.
Dead, nothing — That's the difference between me and Billy:
all the different things I heard in your voice, all the different
things you couldn't say. — I wish you'd get ready, Ann. Put
on some wee thing you've never worn for Billy, one tiny wee
thing Ann you've never worn for Billy and never will. And I
promise: when today's all over you'll look back and see, you
were only ever faithful to me.

> (*In the boys' bedroom,* ANN *starts talking to someone outside
> the door*)

ANN: I don't know what to say to you. Ugly? I didn't know what
ugly was till you. Don't pretend you're no there. I can hear
you. I can hear you not breathing. — Creep, creep, creep. —
Don't pretend you're not there, Mandy, I heard you creeping
up (you've been on the creep all day). — It's Charlie I feel for.
It's Charlie my heart goes out to. What chance has he got with
you sitting on his knee pointing your tits at him. I hope you
don't think I'm competing with ye. I'm just trying to make sure
Charlie has a pleasant time. I stumbled and fell onto his knees
by accident — and don't give me one of your looks! There can
only be one of everything, Mandy. There can only be one of
each thing. Don't let the twins confuse you. The twins were
the same thing. It was the same thing with the twins. Don't
jumble everything up till it's all the same hideous mess.

MANDY: Have you made your decision yet?

ANN: Eh?

MANDY: Have you made your decision yet?

ANN: Eh? Yes, I've made my decision. Are you happy?

MANDY: What decision did you make?

ANN: Wait and see. So you're happy then?

MANDY: I'm happy if you're happy.

ANN: Is that what you say to your men? 'I'm happy if you're happy.'

MANDY: Are you happy?

   (*Beat*)

ANN: Nine years. Nine bloody years. I don't blame Martin. I can't blame Martin. He was only copying his twin. He wanted to be with his twin didn't he. He wanted to be the same thing as his twin. Faithfulness. That's what Martin teaches us. Faithfulness. — We can all learn lessons from the dead, Mandy. — Do you hear me, Mandy?

MANDY: I'm going back to the living-room.

ANN: Mandy! I'm warning you!

   (ANN *gets up off the bed, crosses to the door, opens it.* MANDY's *gone*)

BILLY 1: I'm ready when you're ready, Ann.

   (ANN *exits after* MANDY. PROPHET JOHN *and* NANETTE *enter the back-green from the direction of the shops*)

NANETTE: We're here, we're here, I hope we've no missed any of the excitement. Oh here, I'm quite excited, would ye believe that? I'm in as big a tizz as the bride. D'you like my hat? You don't think it's too orange? I mean, it's no that I want to show my colours but I didnae want to buy a hat I'd only wear the once, where this is a hat I'll get good use out of. — So! Where's the bride and groom?

BILLY 1: I'm the groom. Billy.

NANETTE: Oh look, John, this is the groom!

PROPHET JOHN: Can I shake your hand, Billy? Billy, can I shake your hand? Billy, can I shake your hand? Billy, can I shake your hand? Billy, can I shake your hand?

NANETTE: He wants to shake your hand, Billy.

   (PROPHET JOHN *and* BILLY *shake hands.* JOHN *is looking at* BILLY *like he wants to eat him*)

PROPHET JOHN: You're very welcome, Billy, I have prepared a sacrifice, I have consecrated my guests. Welcome.

NANETTE: Why don't we go inside and have some food, John? Eh?

   (PROPHET JOHN *doesn't want to go inside having found his prey in* BILLY 1 *whom he shadows throughout the rest of this scene.* BILLY 2 *enters the back-green from stage left the direction of the house. He goes to pick up his suitcases*)

BILLY 2: I've come to get my suitcases, Billy.

BILLY 1: Confident, Billy?

BILLY 2: You only have to observe the facts. You?

BILLY 1: Why don't you leave your suitcases till we talk, Billy?

BILLY 2: Will you stop calling me Billy, Billy . . .

BILLY 1: Can we talk?

BILLY 2: . . . let's leave our personalities out of this!

BILLY 1: That suits me.

(BILLY 2 *puts down his suitcases*)

BILLY 1: I can say what I've got to say in seven sentences. OK?
Then it's up to you. OK?

BILLY 2: I'm OK, you OK?

BILLY 1: Can we be pleasant then?

BILLY 2: Talk.

BILLY 1: Fine. — I don't dislike you, Billy . . .

(BILLY 2 *goes mental, comes forward towards the other* BILLY,
*hand in inside pocket of his jacket — i.e. as if he's loaded, got
a chib or whatever*)

BILLY 2: I'll chisel your eyes out!

BILLY 1: . . . what the fuck . . .

BILLY 2: I'll hammer this up your nose, pal.

BILLY 1: . . . fuck did I say!

BILLY 2: 'I don't dislike you, Billy.' I'll jump on your face, son.

BILLY 1: I was trying to be pleasant (ya arse) I apologise. Can
I take it back? OK? I take it back. Can we start again?

BILLY 2: Don't call me Billy.

BILLY 1: I've apologised!

BILLY 2: Keech-features.

BILLY 1: Right. Fine. I'll start again. OK? I don't dislike you.
OK? Why should I. Many many ways we're very similar.

BILLY 2: Haw.

BILLY 1: Many many ways (what did you say?) many many ways
we're (haw?) many many ways we're (tragic). Identical.

BILLY 2: I hope you know what you're talking about, Billy.

BILLY 1: Ann, OK?

BILLY 2: Keep it to the facts, OK?

BILLY 1: OK OK, Ann, OK? So. I'm confident. You say you're
confident.

BILLY 2: I'm confident.

BILLY 1: OK then: Ann doesn't marry me today, I walk from
here to death's door and I don't come back ever, because I
won't know the way any more. You're confident, you back out
till after today when she's all yours. You've got your suitcases:
are you going to walk? — Are you going to walk?

(MAX *enters pursued by a bear. The bear is* CHARLIE. CHAR-
LIE *is followed by* ANN *and* MANDY, *then* MARGARET
MARY, *all from the direction of the house*)

CHARLIE: Max!

ANN: Charlie!

CHARLIE: Max!

MANDY: Charlie!

CHARLIE: Tell me what you said, ya toxin! (He opens his mouth
I try to not inhale.) Tell me what you said, ya pollutant!

> (BILLY 2 *picks up his suitcases and starts to walk but in the
> direction of the house rather than the shops*)

BILLY 1: That's the wrong direction, my friend.

MAX: You heard what I said.

BILLY 1: So therefore you don't love her then.

CHARLIE: You're dead.

MAX: I said when are you going to wake up?

BILLY 2: You're dead.

MAX: Am I.

> (BILLY 1 *backs off the* BILLY *stand-off to look for a weapon*)

MARGARET MARY: Will I jump next door and find you a suit,
Charlie?

CHARLIE: Margaret Mary! It won't fit!

MARGARET MARY: It will!

CHARLIE: It won't!

> (MARGARET MARY *exits stage left.* BILLY 1 *has now found
> a weapon, big lump of metal, with which he faces* BILLY 2)

CHARLIE: What's going on here! Can I call for a period of calm?
First Max, now her?!

ANN: We'll find you a suit easy enough, if that's what you want.
Billy's got two suits.

BILLY 1: OK, Billy?

> (BILLY 2 *stands there for a moment then backs off to look for a
> weapon.* ANN *crosses to* BILLY 2*'s suitcases and starts to look
> through them for a suit.* BILLY 2 *has picked up a bottle which
> he's considering using as a weapon*)

BILLY 1: OK, Billy?

BILLY 2: I won't keep you long Billy.

BILLY 1: Don't keep me long, Billy.

BILLY 2: I won't keep you long, Billy.

BILLY 1: He's thinking.

BILLY 2: Is he?

> (BILLY 2 *breaks the bottle and comes forward to face* BILLY 1.
> *Meanwhile* ANN *has found a suit which might be suitable*)

ANN: Billy!

BILLY 1: (*playing 'cool'*) So what are you saying, Billy?

ANN: Billy!

BILLY 1: (*'cool'*) So you're not going to walk then?

ANN: Billy! Has this suit been to the laundrette lately? I think it has, Charlie.

(*Getting no reply,* ANN *crosses to* CHARLIE *and holds the brown suit against him to see how it is for size*)

BILLY 2: (*playing 'reluctant'*). I'm going to have to cut you a fresh mouth, Billy.

BILLY 1: (*'cool'*) Face it, Billy: you're a nice person. Even Ann says it.

BILLY 2: (*'cool'*) He's upset. What you upset about, Billy?

BILLY 1: (*'cool'*) I'm fine, Billy.

BILLY 2: (*'cool'*) What you upset about, ugly?

BILLY 1: (*'cool'*) I'm a wee bit pushed for time today, Billy, can we commence?

BILLY 2: (*'cool'*) You do everything in a hurry, eh Billy? Even Ann says it.

(CHARLIE *is holding the brown suit against his body while* ANN *has backed off to get a better look — into the path of the two* BILLYS)

ANN: . . . I don't know . . . I can't seem to make up my mind . . .

BILLY 1: Out the way, Ann.

BILLY 2: Ann, out the way.

BILLY 1: Ann!

BILLY 2: Out the way, Ann!

(ANN *notices the* BILLYS *are close to a fight*)

ANN: I'm trying to make up my mind, Billy!

CHARLIE: Calm down, Billy. OK Billy, calm it.

MANDY: Charlie, you come out the way!

CHARLIE: Calm down or I'll sort the two of you out.

BILLY 2: Out the way, I can't see him.

BILLY 1: Out the way you.

BILLY 2: Where's the bull?

BILLY 1: Or I'll mistake you for Billy.

BILLY 2: He'll stampede all over you!

BILLY 1: I'll stamp you into the ground! I'll rip out your teeth and sow them into the earth! I'll obliterate you!

(STUART *the minister enters stage right from the direction of the shops, taking in the scene almost without a pause*)

STUART: OK, we ready? I'm running late (I've got a date to-night) spent the last four hours with a woman wanted to see me said she was depressed (the reason I'm late). I just shouted at her. I said you've got seven kids, you live in a toilet and your man gets out of jail next week, of course you're depressed! The trick at a wedding's to remember their names. How you doing, wee man (I call her wee man). I know the bride: how are you,

Ann?

ANN: Uch . . .

STUART: Are you as nervous as me?

ANN: I suppose every bride's the same (that's getting married).

STUART: Last minute doubts?

ANN: Emm . . .

STUART: OK, Billy?

> (STUART *goes to shake* BILLY 1*'s hand.* BILLY 1 *drops his weapon*)

STUART: Good. You, me and Ann are going inside for a blether. Shift!

> (STUART *indicates with his thumb for* BILLY 1 *and* ANN *to move it, and off they go stage left*)

STUART: The rest of you stay here till we see what the story is. There's ten commandments, far too many, right? Pick one and try and keep it till I get back.

> (STUART *exits.* PROPHET JOHN *and* NANETTE *follow*)

NANETTE: John, will you try and remember you're a guest.

> (CHARLIE*'s focus is off-stage, with* ANN: *concerned about her fate*)

CHARLIE: I'm no too keen on the minister. I've got a good mind to go and stick one on him. Eh? Because he's a minister that entitles him to be ignorant? Ann can do without that (the peril she's in) she can do without being ordered around by an ignorant wee nyaff.

MANDY: Och, he's OK.

CHARLIE: He's not OK, Mandy. He's inexorable. — Has Ann used him before.

MANDY: Yeah. Twice.

> (BILLY 2 *leaves his suitcases and exits in the direction of the house*)

CHARLIE: If there's one thing that upsets me, it's ignorance.

MANDY: I'm hot, are you hot? D'you fancy an ice-lolly?

CHARLIE: You got any money?

MANDY: Yeah.

CHARLIE: It's a bit sticky getting.

MANDY: I'll treat you.

CHARLIE: OK, wee man. I maybe do need to cool down.

MANDY: C'mon then.

MAX: I'll wait here. I'll be here when you get back. OK? — The seasons I can contend with, Charlie. The seasons I can be philosophical about. I'd be happier if something blotted out the sun for good so that was that and we didn't have to live with false hopes but the best I can do meantime is (fuck the seasons) pay no heed to them.

CHARLIE: What's up with you?

MANDY: Does he want an ice-lolly too?

CHARLIE: What's up with you, torn face?

(MAX *gets some of the torn-up money out of his pocket and flings it at* CHARLIE)

MAX: That's what's up with me! When are you going to wake up and come out of the land of strangers, Charlie? When are you going to wake up and acknowledge your debts? I came up big today, I placed a first and second at accumulated odds of 33/2 and won a monkey-load of money which I handed over to you, Charlie, to divide, Charlie, divide according as you saw fit and now I can't put it together again!

(*Beat*)

CHARLIE: I owe ye money, is that it?

MAX: I estimate twenty notes. That's how I see it.

CHARLIE: Yeah?

MAX: That's my interpretation.

CHARLIE: When do you want it?

MAX: When can you get it?

CHARLIE: When do you want it?

MAX: I don't want to be unreasonable.

CHARLIE: Would a few days hence be acceptable?

MAX: You got any securities you can give me meantime?

CHARLIE: Meantime?

MAX: I'm the loser meantime. I've got the worry.

CHARLIE: Correct. — C'mon, wee man.

(MANDY *and* CHARLIE *exit in the direction of the shops*)

MAX: I'm the one that has to calculate for the both of us!

(CHARLIE's *gone*)

MAX: I don't know how you're going to account for yourself today.

(MAX *crosses the stage, shouts up at* MARGARET MARY's *house*)

MAX: Margaret Mary? Margaret Mary?

(MAX *exits in the direction of the house. There's a knock on the door in the boys' bedroom. Then another knock. Then in comes* PROPHET JOHN *followed by* NANETTE)

NANETTE: John. I don't think we should be here. — This is a bedroom, John.

(*She closes the door behind her, maybe goes to sit on the bed*)

NANETTE: I don't see a wedding do you. She's got plenty suitors, I'll say that much (she's got more men than sense). She's got more men than places to put them all. — I think we should

go, John. I don't know what I see but I don't see a wedding.
And I don't much like what I do see. D'you hear me, John?
Eh? We're here as guests today.

   (PROPHET JOHN *goes up to the wardrobe and knocks on it*)
PROPHET JOHN: Speak, prophet!
NANETTE: What is it, John? Is it the spirit? Is he close? Is he
strong?
PROPHET JOHN: Speak, prophet!
   (*The wardrobe rebuffs him*)
PROPHET JOHN: He says 'No!' He says 'Go!' He says 'Eff
off!' They have run into the arms of the goddess. They have
committed abominations. They have worshipped Asherah and
performed rites.

Danced like wine!
Red like wine!
Like skin turned outside in!
Like the little knot, the little knot that won't untie.
They danced like wine!
Red like wine!
They saw visions!
Bees!
— clambered out of the sticky sun.
Bees!
— clambered out of the sticky sun.
(*He stands in front of the wardrobe and opens his arms to it*)
Open your arms, sun!
Open your arms, sun!
Open your arms, sun!

      (*The* PROPHET *falls onto his knees, then lies on the floor and
      tries to curl up.* NANETTE *covers him with something, then goes
      and sits on the bed*)
NANETTE: It's OK, John. It's OK, son. You'll be OK. You'll
be OK in a minute. Do you want me to talk to you? You keep
quiet for a minute. Will I tell you a dream I had? It was a valley
and it was up to its waist in bones. I was lying there on top of
the bones and I was nothing but a skeleton myself. When all
of a sudden there's an avalanche. An avalanche of bones falls
on the valley like a deluge and I get pushed under. And when I
come to the surface again the valley is up to its neck in bones.
It's nice and peaceful. My bones are all broken and I can see
them, scattered here and there, shining in the sun. — You can
rest there for a bit. Then we'll skeedaddle. OK?

      (MANDY *and* CHARLIE *enter stage right from the shops, with*

ice-lollies. They wander on in silence . . . together but not real-
ly . . . CHARLIE's focus is in the direction of the house, where
ANN is)

CHARLIE: I hope Ann's OK. — Silence. — I hope she's (I hope
I'm wrong) I hope this silence isn't ominous. — I'm trying to
think my way into her mind. Y'know? Her past.

MANDY: Y'can only inquire so much.

CHARLIE: The mind . . . ?

MANDY: Mmm.

CHARLIE: The mind only goes so far . . .

MANDY: A healthy mind.

CHARLIE: The mind only (I'm out of my depth here) the mind
only goes so far till it's out of its depth? Yeah. I see that.

MANDY: A healthy mind varies its obsessions.

   (*Beat*)

CHARLIE: I'm a thinker to my cost. First Robert then Martin.
What did I say there? First Robert, then Martin. And nobody
found a reason?

MANDY: Uh huh.

CHARLIE: Uh huh?

MANDY: Mmm.

CHARLIE: Uh huh naw or uh huh aye?

MANDY: It all came out at the fatal inquiry.

CHARLIE: They said a reason?

MANDY: Yeah.

CHARLIE: Yeah?

MANDY: Yeah.

CHARLIE: What?

MANDY: They said Robert was unhappy.

CHARLIE: Right. And was he?

MANDY: Yeah. Then it turned out we knew he was unhappy
and we'd never done nothing about it. Then when Martin went
and done it as well that was easy, he even left a note. He said
he hoped he'd see us both soon.

   (*She's won his attention now. Physically they are quite close*)

CHARLIE: You're some soldier, wee man.

MANDY: I don't normally get personal like this.

CHARLIE: I shouldnae even be here. I'll say that much for me.

MANDY: You should.

CHARLIE: I know. I know that. It's like 'What am I doing here?'
You know? Whether whether I'm deregulated or something —
I don't exclude that Mandy I can't exclude that I don't exclude anything which is maybe why I'm so deregulated . . . So,
whether whether I'm deregulated or not . . .

MANDY: So you feel . . .

CHARLIE: Yeah. I do.

MANDY: You feel . . .

CHARLIE: I'm hypnotised.

MANDY: I'm glad. I thought you might be too weak. Jesus says 'Follow me!'

CHARLIE: She's beautiful. You're lovely too.

> (*Beat*)

MANDY: That's not what you said when we were sitting on my bed.

CHARLIE: What did I say when we were sitting on your bed?

MANDY: I see.

CHARLIE: I remember Max came in and he said something.

MANDY: Forget it.

CHARLIE: I don't take it back, I'm just asking what I said.

MANDY: Aw don't greet! Is my character too strong? Jesus says 'Follow me!' What's her character? — she's got two men, that's her character. She believes in numbers. I mean, she believes in numbers (the more the merrier). Or then she tries to improve her character because it's so weak so she gets three men. — Fine okay fine, 's fine. You're weak, I'm strong; you're lonely, I'll be with you; you're lost and I'll save you.

> (*Beat*)

CHARLIE: I'm trying to think what to say. — See Robert and Martin (which is admirable). See the (Robert and Martin) questions I asked you.

MANDY: You asked me questions so I answered them.

CHARLIE: I admire that. What I'm saying, I went question and you went answer (which, good enough).

MANDY: I was showing you my character.

CHARLIE: I admire that. What I'm saying, it's good you've recovered.

> (*Beat. Then* MANDY *turns and exits*)

CHARLIE: What? Did I say something wrong? What did I say? I said it's good you've recovered. I think that's what I said. Is that no what I said? — I'm lost here. Does she want me to follow her, is that it? Oh god. She's coming back.

> (MANDY *enters*)

MANDY: I tell you my secrets and you say them back to me in different words?

CHARLIE: Naw, Mandy.

MANDY: I tell you my dreams and you interpret them?

CHARLIE: Naw, Mandy.

MANDY: I put my heart out on a dish and you lick it?

CHARLIE: Mandy —

MANDY: Where am I: Babylon? Here's another question: the king of Babylon had a dream so he summons all the wise men and fortune-tellers and says to them 'I had a dream. Tell me what it means.'

CHARLIE: What was the dream?

MANDY: No! 'No!' the king says ('f you're so fucking smart!) 'Tell me what I dreamt first. Then you can interpret it.'

CHARLIE: . . . guess?

MANDY: Guess wrong and you're dead! 'You tell me what I dreamt then I'll know you're the One.' See? We don't worship the sun do we. The sun can no more think than we can. The sun can no more think ahead.

CHARLIE: no more think ahead

MANDY: no more think

CHARLIE: think ahead than any other sunstroked bastard that can't think ahead.

MANDY: the sun

CHARLIE: heatloss! (is all sun is)

MANDY: fat sun no more think ahead than think, all it wants to do is pish its fat shine away till it's over!

CHARLIE: You're crying.

MANDY: I'm not.

CHARLIE: She's crying.

MANDY: I am not crying.

CHARLIE: What are you crying for, snottery?

MANDY: . . . anybody can ask questions. I want someone that can see right through me, someone that can see the back of my face.

(*He's behind her. They are physically very close again. If she were to turn they would be as close as they could be without actually touching*)

MANDY: So. Do you see now who I am?

CHARLIE: Yes. I do.

MANDY: And do you believe in me?

CHARLIE: Yes. I do.

MANDY: Say it then.

CHARLIE: I believe in you.

(*She embraces him.* In the boys' bedroom PROPHET JOHN *bestirs himself, gets up*)

NANETTE: OK? — Will we go? — I'm no jealous, John: I just think we should go and have a nice day somewhere. We'll see if we can sneak away when nobody's looking.

(PROPHET JOHN *exits the boys' bedroom, followed by*

NANETTE. *Out the back-green . . .*)

CHARLIE: Will we sit down?

MANDY: Where?

CHARLIE: Do you not want to?

MANDY: Uh huh. Do you want to?

CHARLIE: Out the way somewhere maybe?

    (ANN *enters the back-green*)

ANN: I see. Uch well.

CHARLIE: Ann.

ANN: Uh huh. Oh well. So long as you're happy.

CHARLIE: She's just been crying, Ann. Haven't you, wee barra.

ANN: So long as she's happy. How about you, Charlie?

CHARLIE: . . . I'm happy if you're both happy . . .

ANN: Did you hear that, Mandy?

MANDY: Uh huh.

ANN: We're all in harmony.

CHARLIE: So, are we going to have a happy ending?

ANN: (*fierce*) Are you fucking stupit?

CHARLIE: I meant, is there going to be a wedding?

ANN: Yes there's going to be a wedding! — Stuart says people
think a wedding's a happy ending but it's not.

    (MARGARET MARY *enters, carrying a suit.* MAX *is with her*)

MARGARET MARY: Charlie. I brought you the suit.

CHARLIE: Margaret Mary: look: I appreciate the bother you're
giving me. But just because a suit fits one man doesn't mean
it's going to fit a completely different man, especially when one
of the men is a twisted wee jobby like your da!

MARGARET MARY: Try it on.

CHARLIE: He's an animal, Mandy. The last thing I want to be
seen dead in is his shitey brown suit.

MARGARET MARY: It's the suit you wore to your wedding isn't
it.

    (*Pause*)

CHARLIE: It just shows how wrong ye can be.

MARGARET MARY: Remember?

CHARLIE: It was the proudest day of my life.

MARGARET MARY: You looked really handsome in it . . . I
looked nice too, I suppose.

MANDY: Can I see it, Margaret Mary?

CHARLIE: It's a good suit.

MAX: It is a good suit. I've had a wee look at it myself.

MARGARET MARY: We wanted the best didn't we.

CHARLIE: It was a symbol of the way we wanted things to be
wasn't it.

MARGARET MARY: Remember our wedding? Remember the downpour when we came out of the chapel? Downpour? It was like a sea dropped on us! Remember? By the time we got into the cars the bridesmaids' dresses were transparent, they were crying, I was crying, my mammie was crying. The rain! Then my uncle Peter stood up at the reception and sang 'Pennies From Heaven'. Remember? So that was it: my Aunt Celine walked out on him there and then. She ended up in Australia eventually, at her sister's. Remember? Then Uncle Peter went and died and Aunt Celine sent us a postcard.

(*Beat*)

CHARLIE: Listen: thanks, MM.

MARGARET MARY: Uch! You can go and visit your mammie now, looking half-decent.

CHARLIE: Listen: thanks, OK? At a time like this ye need reminded.

MARGARET MARY: I better go to the shop, get some confetti. Och (y'know). Nice. Let me see you in your suit before you go, OK?

(MARGARET MARY *exits in the direction of the shops*)

MANDY: Come on then, Charlie.

ANN: Where's he going?

MANDY: You can get changed in my room.

ANN: Let me see if he's got everything, Mandy.

MANDY: See what?

ANN: See men! She's put a freshly ironed shirt in there for him.

MANDY: Some people would give up.

ANN: She tries doesn't she. She's a trier.

(*There's been no visible struggle but* ANN *now sets off with the suit*)

ANN: Come on, Charlie: we can get changed together.

MANDY: He can use my room if he wants.

ANN: He can use the boys' bedroom.

MANDY: He can use either.

ANN: He can use the boys' bedroom, Mandy. The last time I opened the door to her room Charlie she had a fox in there!

MANDY: A fox?

ANN: I couldn't believe it either, Charlie, the smell was inedible.

(BILLY 2 *enters the back-green to retrieve his suitcases*)

BILLY 2: I've come to get my suitcases, Ann.

ANN: OK, Billy.

BILLY 2: You better go and get ready, Ann.

ANN: OK, Billy. Come on, Charlie.

(ANN *exits towards the house*)

MAX: I'll be keeping my eye on ye, Charlie. That suit's your
one possible possession. I don't want to lose ye. OK?

MANDY: Charlie, I don't want to lose ye either.

> (CHARLIE *exits in the direction of the house.* MAX *retreats in
> the direction of the shops, to somewhere he can cover all exits*)

BILLY 2: I've just come to get my suitcases, Mandy. Then I'll go.
Ahch, just disappear is the best thing. — How y'doing anyway,
wee man?

MANDY: Och . . .

BILLY 2: Because you tend to get a wee bit forgotten at times.
How y'feeling?

MANDY: Och . . .

BILLY 2: Ahch, I'm no too bad. Some ways (now it's happened)
I feel more calmer or more tranquiller or more serene, like when
I walked out of my bus-crash into that field of cows. How you
feeling?

MANDY: Och . . .

BILLY 2: Yeah, I know: I'm as bewildered as you are by it. —
She says she still wants to see me though.

MANDY: Listen: if I don't see ye again, all the best.

BILLY 2: Treasure.

> (MANDY *exits in the direction of the house.* BILLY 2 *wanders
> over to the back-green wardrobe, leans against it. A strong light
> comes onto the wardrobe in the boys' bedroom*)

BILLY 2: The way you touched me, Ann. The sex, Ann. Was
the sex too good, is that it? Was it too much? I'm sorry Ann if
it was too much at times . . . your nipples are the highest I've
been. Or is it because I don't know many words? Because I'm
too sensible? If I could only get out of (I'm in a lift. I'm in a
high-rise. I'm in a lift in a high-rise. I get out different floors.
Four doors. Back in the lift. I wish I was a horse on glue I'd
kick more pints of blood out that lift than it knew it had!) If
I could only get out of my mind! Would you love me then?
I try. I want to. The views would be something else. I nearly
can. I can hear but I can't see. A screaming flock of voices?
You calling 'Billy! Billy!' — the horse is true, Ann. These kids
found it in a field. They put some of their glue in a plastic bag,
Ann, used it as a nose-bag. Then they stuck the horse in our
lift. They both got broken, Ann.

> (*He takes off his tie and makes it into a noose*)

Why I'm doing this, Ann . . . because I'm broken, Ann
and . . . just to be the closest to you I can be . . .

> (BILLY 2 *goes inside the back-green wardrobe.* ANN *and*
> CHARLIE *come in the boys' bedroom*)

ANN: This is the boys' bedroom.

CHARLIE: Right.

ANN: Uh huh.

CHARLIE: Right.

ANN: This is where the boys slept.

CHARLIE: Is it OK to sit on the beds?

ANN: Yes!

(*They continue to stand*)

ANN: I better go and get ready.

CHARLIE: I spoke to Mandy. It was good, Ann. She helped me to see 'What am I looking for?' Right? Why all the questions? I know all I need to know. What a good feeling. I know all I need to know.

ANN: I've told Billy and Stuart to go out the back and wait. I won't be long.

CHARLIE: Right.

(ANN *goes.* CHARLIE *starts to get changed into his suit.* BILLY I *and* STUART *enter the back-green from the direction of the house.* BILLY I *crosses the entire stage, making sure the other* BILLY *has gone*)

BILLY I: He's gone. He's gone and left his suitcases. — I think Ann will go through with it now. Eh? D'you think she'll go through with it?

STUART: I hope so, Billy. I hope so.

(*Then they start waiting: whistling, jiggling keys or coins or whatevers in their pockets*)

BILLY I: Listen to that.

STUART: What?

BILLY I: Nothing. The day. What time's it?

STUART: Late.

BILLY I: This time of day (day like today) the day's got no memory. Kids. Wee weans. Remember? We used to spend hours. — What time's your big date?

STUART: It's no a date, Billy.

BILLY I: You said it was a date.

STUART: I was kidding. I'm having someone round to my flat.

BILLY I: Yeah?

STUART: And cooking for them. Which is why the time.

(*They wait some more*)

BILLY I: Who?

STUART: It's no a date, Billy. It's a man.

BILLY I: Good enough.

STUART: He's a very pleasant, very young, naive young Catholic man I met on a train-journey in Morocco. Anyway he phoned me up to say he's going through a crisis of some kind and could we meet up.

BILLY 1: I see. Are you hoping to turn him?

STUART: Eh?

BILLY 1: Are you hoping to convert him? If he's a naive young Catholic . . .

STUART: I don't think I'd want to change that, Billy . . . (We all go our own sweet way to perdition.)

(*Inside the boys' bedroom,* CHARLIE, *suit on, a new man, raises his hand to knock on the wardrobe door when someone knocks on the bedroom door*)

CHARLIE: Who is it?

ANN: It's Ann. Can I come in?

CHARLIE: Come on in, Ann.

(ANN *comes in, wearing her wedding outfit, and closes the door behind her*)

ANN: They're waiting on me.

CHARLIE: You look great.

ANN: You look great too.

CHARLIE: Like a bride and groom.

ANN: Is it OK to sit on the bed?

CHARLIE: Yeah!

ANN: I come here a lot.

CHARLIE: Sit.

ANN: Sit.

CHARLIE: Think.

ANN: Think.

CHARLIE: 'Why?'

ANN: Or think about 'a person'.

CHARLIE: A person?

ANN: Is that what I want to be? (I don't think a person's very applicable nowadays.) She's a person, supposedly. Mandy. Or she tries. She beavers away like a fox. — She hates me coming here. She stands outside and listens. Listen.

(CHARLIE *looks at the bedroom door, listens*)

ANN: I don't say nothing. I keep her hanging on.

CHARLIE: I like Mandy, to be truthful.

ANN: She haunts me. — Martin used to come here a lot too. After his brother hung himself. That big effn wardrobe spoke to him. So Martin said. He heard voices. — Faithfulness. That's what Martin teaches us. He wanted to be with his brother didn't he. I've said that to Mandy. After Martin went and hung himself? She went and took against him, I had to say to her, 'He wanted to be with his brother, Mandy!' — Martin came back from the dead and explained everything. He explained he was dead and Robert was dead too. I said, 'Oh Martin, explain to me!' He said, 'I've explained.' It was good though, we stayed up all night having a laugh. I kept thinking he'd go, I kept thinking 'He's going to go!' Then the ceiling fell in. I thought I was dreaming but no, I was found on the floor bleeding from the ears and a cracked skull to ponder. The ceiling was good as new though.

CHARLIE: Who found you?

(*Silence.* CHARLIE *looks again at the bedroom door*)

ANN: The dead are like kids, Charlie. The dead are like wee kids. They don't know the difference between one thing and another. A pavement? That's something to play with. They pull bricks out the pavement and dump them on the road don't they. A fence is another thing. A fence is a joke round here. They laugh at a fence. They take things apart till you can't tell the difference between one thing and another. — Come here and sit beside me.

(CHARLIE *crosses and sits on the bed*)

CHARLIE: Ann . . . any way I can console you Ann . . . You're no ugly, that's one thing I will say.

ANN: Oh Charlie . . . What am I going to do now . . .

CHARLIE: Whatever, Ann . . .

ANN: What's my instincts telling me?

CHARLIE: Maybe just . . . no to think too much . . .

ANN: I suppose we're all only skin deep. I'm glad you like Mandy.

CHARLIE: I like Mandy.

ANN: She used to be lovely. I'd look at her when she was wee, when she was asleep. You know how: tulips at night, when they close up? Uch, I suppose she's still lovely.

CHARLIE: She's nice. She's nice enough. She's a nice person.

ANN: She wants to save you.

CHARLIE: She wants to save me from . . .

ANN: . . . save you for . . .

CHARLIE: . . . save me from . . .

ANN: . . . sin . . .

CHARLIE: . . . yeah? . . .

ANN: . . . is that what you want? . . .

CHARLIE: . . . sin? . . .

ANN: . . . mmm . . .

CHARLIE: . . . we all want to be good . . .

ANN: . . . I know . . .

CHARLIE: . . . we maybe just don't know how . . .

ANN: . . . what's my instincts telling me? They've all gone away and fled . . .

CHARLIE: . . . yeah? . . .

ANN: . . . yeah . . .

(CHARLIE *touches* ANN. ANN *moves into him*)

CHARLIE: . . . what are we doing? . . .

(ANN *and* CHARLIE *start kissing*)

ANN: . . . what's happening? . . .

CHARLIE: . . . I don't know . . .

ANN: . . . I can't remember what's even happening . . .

(ANN *and* CHARLIE *are now climbing all over each other. They look as if they're heading for wild sex . . . erogenous zones are being handled . . . * MANDY *comes through the bedroom door*)

MANDY: Right you: out!

ANN: Mandy!

MANDY: Out!

ANN: Oh she's ugly, oh she's ugly! Oh look, I've left half my face on Charlie.

MANDY: You can put your face back on, on the way.

ANN: How do I look, Charlie?

CHARLIE: Ugly. I'm kidding. You look fine, Ann.

ANN: Are you sure?

CHARLIE: Yeah.

ANN: Wish me all the best then.

CHARLIE: I wish you all the best, Ann.

(ANN *goes*)

MANDY: Wish us all the best, Charlie.

CHARLIE: I wish you all the (so I'm — what? — I'm something to be torn apart by horses? — yeah?)

(MANDY *goes out the bedroom door. Out the back-green . . .*)

BILLY 1: Has it gone dark?

STUART: Patience, Billy, patience: (we'll all be in glory soon enough).

(CHARLIE *goes out the bedroom door.* PROPHET JOHN *enters the back-green with a mattress and some bed-sheets, followed by* NANETTE)

NANETTE: John, I'm beginning to lose my patience, John, where are you going with Ann's sheets!

(PROPHET JOHN *starts making up a bed*)

NANETTE: John, what on earth are you playing at! John, I think we should go, John. I came here hoping for a wedding as I'm sure Billy did and I'm no staying for a lot of carry-on. We're guests here.

(PROPHET JOHN *goes to shake* Stuart's *hand*)

PROPHET JOHN: Can I shake your hand, pastor? Can I shake your hand, pastor? Can I shake your hand, pastor?

(*They shake.* PROPHET JOHN *holds* STUART *in his grasp*)

PROPHET JOHN: (*to* STUART) My bride has many names. She was taken from her bed in the secret of the night, and driven from the land, herself and her handmaidens and her counsellors. I know her as Asherah. I've prepared a marriage-bed.

NANETTE: Ahch, yir arse in parsley! C'mon, John, c'mon, we're going, we're off, quick before Ann comes out here and obliterates you or I do it for her! — Oh, smelly knickers: too late, here she comes. Here comes the bride.

(MARGARET MARY *and* MAX *enter the back-green from the direction of the shops*)

BILLY 1: Ann?

NANETTE: She's on her way.

BILLY 1: Oh god. So she is.

MARGARET MARY: What's happening?

NANETTE: Surprise! There's going to be a wedding after all.

BILLY 1: Can we get lined up then! Can we get into some kind of order here instead of standing around looking surprised!

(*They get into a line-up of sorts;* NANETTE *starts dah-dah-dahing the bridal march and* PROPHET JOHN *awaits his bride.* ANN *enters at speed, followed by* MANDY)

ANN: I'm here, I'm here.

MARGARET MARY: Awwwww.

BILLY 1: Ann, you look — glorious.

ANN: Do I?

MARGARET MARY: So she does.

ANN: For once.

BILLY 1: Not for once.

ANN: Not for long.

STUART: Will we get lined up then?

MAX: Where's Charlie, has he sneaked off? Eh? Because I know Charlie, and I can tell you he's a hole for snakes.

STUART: OK, Billy?

BILLY 1: I'm —

STUART: OK, Ann?

BILLY 1: — ecstatic.

ANN: Quick, before I'm old.

(*They are now more or less lined up.* PROPHET JOHN *has placed himself beside* ANN *like he's the groom*)

STUART: We'll keep it short. Ann, Billy, want to get married and here we are. The bride's lovely, the groom's a fine-looking man, it's a lovely day. What do I know? The great thing is: we hope.

ANN: Did you invite your fat pal, Mandy?

MAX: No.

ANN: Naw. I'm her only interest in life.

STUART: Hope, like Noah's dove sent out upon the face of the Flood; hope which, without it there is no living. A wedding is all about hope. We hope maybe for a happy ending or maybe we hope to do something that will stand for all time.

ANN: Her fat pal's no even her pal, she's just a big fat stupit lassie. You don't see her for months and then you come home from work and there's ugly lying on the couch under a duvet and six empty cans of diet coke, feeling sorry for herself. How many abortions does she intend to have?

STUART: And yet nothing stands for all time. Everything, thankfully, passes. So spend your days with the one you love, all the lovely futile days God gives you under the sun.

(STUART *now moves to the service proper and a slightly less casual more solemn tone*)

STUART: Unless the Lord builds the house, those who build it labour in vain. Billy, Ann, we have come here in the presence of God and these witnesses so you can be joined in marriage. As God made a covenant with his people in the desert so now you will make a covenant with each other. This is not something to be entered into lightly or unadvisedly but thoughtfully and reverently. Cherish today and the vows you are about to make.

This man and this woman are about to pledge themselves before God and man. I therefore ask you all — if you know any reason why this man and this woman may not lawfully be joined in marriage to speak now since no one speaks, let us ask God's blessing on this union. Almighty Father —

MARGARET MARY: Can we stop this?

ANN: It's like —

BILLY 1: Like what?

ANN: Like. Does anyone else feel it? Like the sun's fell off his chariot in the sky.

NANETTE: I think maybe.

ANN: Is some one missing?

MAX: Is it you do you think?

ANN: Apart from me.

STUART: It's not too late to stop.

ANN: No! I'm just saying.

STUART: Billy, if you'd like to take Ann's hand — and say after me the words of the covenant. I, William Shearer —

PROPHET JOHN: I do.

STUART: I, William Shearer —

(CHARLIE *enters from the direction of the house in a dionysiac rage*)

CHARLIE: I've just come to say I'm off. I'm off, Ann. I'm off, Mandy.

ANN: OK, Charlie

CHARLIE: OK?

ANN: OK. See you again mibby.

CHARLIE: OK. Max, are you coming, son? (I feel sorry for you Billy, I fucking pity you to fuck). C'mon Max: let's get out of here: because the one *good* thing about Max (someone dipped the evil bastard in poison) he's a lying fuck but fuck me (I mean it) Max *lies* . . .

ANN: . . . (don't, Charlie) . . .

CHARLIE: . . . Max is steeped, but he's never deceived me, Ann, he's never deceived me Mandy, he's never led me on to believe, Mandy, or led me into a bedroom Ann and played with me, or tore me in two. I'm no saying I like the jobby fuck and there's a side to Max I don't like but yeah. Yes. Absolutely. Yes! How close I am to Max, Billy, I once hospitalised the cunt . . .

BILLY I: . . . (what's going on) . . .

CHARLIE: . . . once hospitalised the cunt. It was his idea. I agreed, I said fine. We were skint so right so fine so OK we go out to look for a shop to rob . . .

STUART: . . . (look, Charlie, do ye mind) . . .

CHARLIE: . . . you can put this in a sermon, Stuart. So we go under the motorway and past the gasworks across . . .

MARGARET MARY: . . . (glory be) . . .

CHARLIE: . . . across terrain more suited to the camel until we gets to the local shopping-centre. The problem being society, the shops where we live have all been burnt to a crisp or scalped or fucking *robbed* . . .

NANETTE: . . . (glory) . . .

CHARLIE: . . . we gets to the shopping-centre (I get angry about this). The lack of choice is a scandal even from the shopping point of view. They've got a half-shut Paki shop.

Time (This is about three weeks ago.)

We're watching the Paki shop.

Time.

When I'm angry I show it, Billy (one of my good points).

I *know* the Paki. I go there for my bread, fags don't I. His name's Hami, he's an Indian.

What Time is, Time's an explosion . . . naw, *explosion* and then what Time is, Time's meantime.

I goes, 'Max, you want me to go *in* there?' He goes, 'Yes.'

I goes, 'You want me to go *in* there and rob him with nothing but my bare hands?' Max goes, 'Pretend it's not you.'

(CHARLIE *snaps his fingers*)

CHARLIE: Aw man. I . . . *went*. I crossed the Jordan. I . . . whhhho! I . . . went. There was no nothing, no sky, no ground, no Time. Or like . . . Time. It was . . . alleluia . . . it was . . . what's the word, what's the word . . . good. Across the Jordan . . .

(CHARLIE *snaps his fingers*)

. . . then you come back. I look down and there's Max like the skin off some dead animal, like a fucking pelt. I'd very near mauled him to death. I'd very near killed him with my bare hands, Billy. — So d'you get me, Billy? Am I in disguise some kind, some kinna cloak. I've came out here Billy, I've came out here Ann, cloaked in violence, cloaked in violence, to scatter the truth to fuck! The reality is, Billy. And that's the reality.

(BILLY 1 *finds* ANN, *who's wishing she was invisible somewhere*)

BILLY 1: (*shell-shocked*) Ann, after all my best efforts . . . ? — I'm on the verge here . . . — So did something mibby happen you can't explain while I was out here with Stuart waiting to get married . . . ? — Are we food for the gods, is that it . . . ?

ANN: Don't look at me, Billy.

BILLY 1: I don't know where to look . . . Nobody does . . .

ANN: Charlie?

CHARLIE: Yeah?

(ANN *crosses to him*)

ANN: Oh Charlie. How can I say it? It's a hellish mess and I don't want to be here either. You said it better than me. You shone. I want to go, 'cross' . . .

CHARLIE: Cross . . .

ANN: Across . . .

CHARLIE: To.

ANN: You can take my face off. Across where pretend who's not me . . . Across and murder the whole contents of my brain and hang them from the branches of a tree and have a laugh. And yeah. You know? Yes! And no come back.

CHARLIE: You want to . . . cross the shining river . . .

ANN: And no come back.

CHARLIE: And no come back.

ANN: You can pick my bones.

(*Three slow dull knocks come from inside the back-green wardrobe. Everyone has a near heart-attack*)

ANN: Oh god.

MARGARET MARY: Oh god.

ANN: Oh god.

(*Three more slow dull knocks*)

ANN: Oh god. Who is it? Oh god. Who'll hide me?

BILLY 1: I'll go and look, Ann.

(BILLY 1 *goes to open the wardrobe door.* ANN *picks up a stone, to protect herself*)

ANN: You'd better watch it, Martin! D'you think this is an ugly mask I've got on? Try taking it off then! Try taking it bloody off and I'll show you ugly will turn to stone! I'm infested, I'm multiplying, I'm snakes, I'm Legion. It's you that can't look at me, it's you that can't bear to look at me!

(BILLY 1 *opens the wardrobe door.* ANN *sees Martin. Or rather,* ANN *hallucinates Martin. The anger that's released in her is powerful, free-flowing and channelled directly against Martin. At some point during her next speech* BILLY 2 *steps out of the wardrobe, with the tie tied around his neck, and starts walking towards her*)

ANN: Martin! Martin, ya wee snake! Ya wee rat! You can go right back down that tunnel! You can go right back down that tunnel, son! What do you want now? The skin off my back? The bones I stand up in? You've already got them, you've already taken them away and buried them, son! Don't you come near me, don't you come near me — or I swear to God I will let the dogs tear you apart.

CHARLIE: Who'll strike the first blow?

PROPHET JOHN: We all will.

MAX: I'll pelt him!

NANETTE: I'll obliterate him!

MANDY: Stupid old creep!

MARGARET MARY: I'll bloody wedding him!

(MARGARET MARY *throws her confetti at him, violently*)

BILLY 2: Ann, Ann —

ANN: Get away!

BILLY 2: It's me, Ann. It's Billy.

ANN: Who?

BILLY 2: Billy. I tried my best Ann. I wanted to just be the closest I could be to you. I used my tie Ann. It broke Ann. I'm sorry.

(ANN *is well out of it. Apparently she can't even trust her eyes. She feels ugly. She feels hellish ugly*)

CHARLIE: Can I help you, Ann?

ANN: Who are you? Eh? Who are you?

CHARLIE: Charlie, Ann.

(ANN *doesn't seem to know a* CHARLIE)

ANN: Charlie?

CHARLIE: You need help, Ann.

ANN: I don't know a Charlie. Will you do me a favour, Charlie? You know the big hanging thing in the boys' bedroom? Will you take it away for me? You're the only one I can ask, Charlie.

CHARLIE: Now?

ANN: Oh please Charlie, save my life.

(*Pause*)

CHARLIE: Come on, Max: follow me.

(CHARLIE *exits in the direction of the house.* MAX *goes after him.* NANETTE *and* STUART *are around* ANN. ANN'*s putting on some fresh make-up*)

MARGARET MARY: Is she OK? Are you OK, Ann? Is she OK? Is that it? Are you OK, father? Is Ann Ok? It's OK, I'll be fine in a minute. I'll be fine in a minute, Mandy.

(ANN *is still fixing her face. When she says the next line it's not clear which of the* BILLYS *she's addressing*)

ANN: Billy, this is the last I want to see you. I've made my decision. I love Billy. I love Billy to bits. I only went out with you to confuse things and once I started I got all mixed up. I wanted to be fair to the both of you (oh god, what a mess) . . . I knew I was cheating on the two of ye and I wanted to make up for it by showing ye I was a horrible lying cow that wasn't worth bothering about anyway. Then, as time went on, I lost my flavour.

(*She's crying*)

ANN: I'm sorry, Billy. I tried to tell you. I thought you might take the hint when I told you I was getting married to Billy but no. I suppose I led you to believe (which I was, I was!) I was scared. I was scared witless. I was really scared, Billy. I was frightened in case everything worked out the way I wanted them to, and what would I do then?

(CHARLIE *and* MAX *enter the boys' bedroom*)

BILLY 2: I'm sorry, Ann. I wanted to carry your burden, Ann. I'm no very clever, Ann, but I can lift heavy things: and all I ever wanted was to put all your sadness in a box, Ann, and carry it away, even supposing it was heavier than plutonium, Ann: which, it would be, Ann, it would be. — What I would say, Ann: if you really want me to go, if you want me to believe you, say it to my face.

(CHARLIE *and* MAX *carry the wardrobe out of the boys'* *bedroom.* ANN *turns and looks at* BILLY 2)

ANN: I want you to go, Billy.

(BILLY 2 *starts to exit in the direction of the shops. As he does* *so* ANN'*s fear mounts: it looks like everything is going to turn* *out the way she wants them to and what will she do then?*)

ANN: Billy!

(BILLY 2 *stops*)

What if everything turns out the way I want them to?

BILLY 2: I hope they do, Ann.

(BILLY 2 *exits*)

BILLY 1: I knew, Ann, when the day was over you'd look back and see, deep down you were only ever faithful to me.

ANN: Oh Billy.

STUART: Will we leave you two alone to talk?

ANN: No! I want to ask Billy a question.

BILLY 1: You ask me any question you want the answer's the same, Ann: I love you.

ANN: Billy, will you stop trying to scare me away like a ghost!

(*When she asks* BILLY *the question* ANN *seems almost to be* *looking more at* MANDY, *as if she's asking her the question as* *well*)

Suppose I was ever to be happy, Billy. Suppose I was ever happy. Would you despise me?

BILLY 1: No.

ANN: Would you hate me?

BILLY 1: No.

ANN: You wouldn't loathe me?

BILLY 1: No, Ann.

ANN: I'm no saying I will be happy. I'm just saying suppose I was. I mean, it's been nine year now. It's been nine year now hasn't it, Stuart.

STUART: Nine years, Ann.

ANN: They'd have grown up and left me by now. The thing is I made them a promise when they died: I swore I'd never forgive myself and I've been true as my word. So if I was ever to be happy; which, I'm no saying I will be, Mandy; I'm only raising the spectre that I might be —

(MANDY *turns on her heels and walks off in the direction of the* *house*)

Mandy! Will you get back here! Do you think I don't feel guilty enough as it is, I'm guilty as all hell!

(ANN *sees* CHARLIE *and* MAX *off, coming with the ward-* *robe*)

ANN: Oh and look who's coming to cheer me up, my two under-takers. Billy, will you stand next to me. Stuart, will you stand next to me.

(BILLY I *and* STUART *stand next to* ANN. CHARLIE *and* MAX *enter carrying the wardrobe*)

CHARLIE: Is Mandy OK? She seems a wee bit upset.

ANN: She's a wee bit upset, Charlie.

CHARLIE: It's just that she seems a wee bit upset, y'know.

ANN: She'll be fine.

CHARLIE: Are you OK?

ANN: I'll be fine. (If I don't fall to pieces.)

CHARLIE: We'll be fine.

ANN: Thanks for doing your undertaker, Charlie. Will you promise me something?

CHARLIE: Of course Ann.

ANN: I don't want to see that dumped somewhere, vandalised the middle of the road or some back-green.

CHARLIE: I'm disappointed you can say that, Ann.

ANN: And I don't want to see you again either.

(*Beat*)

CHARLIE: Come on, Max. It looks like we're on our own, son.

MAX: Looks like it, Charlie.

CHARLIE: Come on, Max. We better go son.

MAX: On you go then son.

(CHARLIE *doesn't move*)

CHARLIE: I wish you all the best Ann. Today (to draw a line) it's no been all bad. Many many ways I've succeeded. I've prepared myself and underchanged my thoughts. And now that I've done as much as I can here, which, I think I have done Ann, I can go on from here. OK, Max?

MAX: I'll follow you, my friend.

(CHARLIE *and* MAX *carry the wardrobe off in the direction of the shops. As the wardrobe passes,* MARGARET MARY *makes the sign of the cross and bows her head while* STUART *and* BILLY *hold* ANN, *who physically shrinks, as at the interment of a loved one. Nobody speaks till the wardrobe is gone*)

BILLY I: Would you maybe say a few words, Stuart . . . ?

STUART: . . . a few words . . . ?

BILLY I: . . . I thought you might oblige us with a few words of comfort . . .

STUART: Would we no be better getting a drink down us, Billy! I've been on the go since seven this morning, I've hardly been off my feet yet, I've had poverty drugs depression bereavement bronchitis and sheer bloody misery all day and I've still to write tomorrow's sermon preaching the good news.

ANN: I've still got Mandy to face.

STUART: OK, Ann; let's get you inside.

ANN: Ask Margaret Mary in for a drink, will ye Billy.

BILLY 1: Margaret Mary, will you come in for a drink?

MARGARET MARY: OK. — I wanted there to be a wedding so much.

BILLY 1: There might be a wedding yet. — Stuart, will you stay and have a drink, Stuart? I mean, you won't run off and leave us?

STUART: It's OK, Billy: I'll phone my friend and cancel him.

BILLY 1: Thanks, Stuart. Because we're nearly there. We're nearly there, Ann. We're very nearly there, Margaret Mary. — Love. Love will find a way.

(*Like people after an interment,* ANN, STUART, BILLY *and* MARGARET MARY *drift off in the direction of the house.* NANETTE *wants to go with the others but first she has to get rid of* JOHN. *She goes and picks up* ANN's *sheets*)

NANETTE: You're some piece of work, John. I won't blaspheme by saying you were put together so badly nothing will make you right again. I hope in God and I hope you walk in his light one day but I never want to see the outside of your face or the inside of your mind for as long as I have breath.

(NANETTE *exits in the direction of the house carrying the sheets.* PROPHET JOHN *exits the other way.* MANDY *enters the boys' bedroom. The summer afternoon turns into a summer's evening. It's now about ten o'clock, so it's still light outside. Maybe we hear the sounds of a long summer night, wee boys and girls still playing in the streets after a long hard day of it, but mostly quiet.* MANDY's *sitting on the bed in the boys' bedroom. Outside the door is* ANN)

ANN: Mandy! Will you come out of there? Everybody's still waiting. They're all round at Margaret Mary's house waiting on us. — I'm sorry about Charlie. I don't know what that was all about. You know how when you get something stuck in your teeth? — Mandy? Are you on your own in there? — We can't Mandy on like this. We can't Robert Martin for good. That's what Charlie teaches us. We're too stuck together. — Is it because I said I might be happy?

(ANN *enters the boys' bedroom*)

ANN: Is it because I said I might be happy? — I didn't mean it, Mandy. I admit it's crossed my mind that maybe the time has come to maybe foresee a future, which is why I like to get my cards read. I admit I maybe hoped, I do admit that. But as quick as I hoped I just as quick despaired, Mandy, and that's the gospel truth. — You know me, Mandy: I believe a lot of rubbish. I even believe in happy endings. Do you not? Do you not believe in happy endings, Mandy?

MANDY: Are you fucking stupit!

ANN: Mandy!

MANDY: Eh? Are you stupit, ya dippit cow!

ANN: I've never denied I'm stupid.

MANDY: I've carried you for nine years, ya mongol! I've had dreams about it, dreams where I'm carrying this big mongol over my shoulder like a big stupit carpet and the mongol's crying and I can taste his tears in my mouth, these warm tears, and I try to spit them out without him seeing. I've had nine years of it. And now you want to get married and live happy ever after? If you're going to be somebody else, who am I going to be! — There are rules. There have to be rules. Otherwise how will I know you're you, ya Martian. — You're you and I'm me; you're weak and I'm strong; you despair and I hope; I lead and you follow; that's the rules and if we keep the rules, if we keep the rules, if we don't keep the rules then it's pandemonium. I don't like you any more than you do; I don't want to be me either: I don't want to be me any more than you want to be you: but I accept my responsibilities. That's the way things are and we just have to get on with it.

ANN: (*fierce*). Right you: out! This is the end. I don't care if it's happy or no I just want an end so as I can start and if Billy's going to be daft enough to marry me the least I can do is try to be happy. If I try for long enough maybe I'll get the hang of it again.

(*The unfortunate turn of phrase reminds her of the boys' wardrobe and she looks guiltily in the direction where the wardrobe used to be*)

ANN: I mean, I'll maybe get into the swing of it again. — Oh, I give up.

(ANN *crosses over and sits on the bed, suddenly tired and defeated*)

MANDY: So they're all round at Margaret Mary's.

ANN: I can't get married here.

MANDY: So they're all round at Margaret Mary's.

ANN: Margaret Mary said why not have the ceremony in her house.

(*They sit there*)

MANDY: I don't like sudden changes.

(CHARLIE *and* MAX *enter the back-green from the direction of the shops.* CHARLIE *crosses the extent of the back-green. He shouts up at the house)*

CHARLIE: Mandy! Mandy!

   (In the boys' bedroom . . .)

ANN: How are we ever going to get out of here?

MANDY: Do you want to?

ANN: If you want to.

MANDY: OK. On you go then.

ANN: OK.

   (Neither of them move)

ANN: It's just that Stuart's been very patient.

MANDY: On you go then.

   (Uncertainly, ANN *stands up)*

ANN: Come on then.

   (MANDY gets to her feet and actually moves part of the way across the room)

ANN: Are we going?

   (MANDY stops dead)

MANDY: I think so.

   (ANN starts to move across the room towards the door, moving with blind courage)

MANDY: Are we going then?

   (ANN stops dead)

ANN: We seem to be.

MANDY: D'you think I'll ever have a baby?

ANN: Do you want a baby?

MANDY: I'd probably get pregnant then lose it. I can't seem to hang on to anything.

   (Beat)

ANN: I'll miss them, Mandy.

   (ANN goes out the bedroom door. MANDY *follows. Out the back-green . . .*)

CHARLIE: Mandy!

   (A big dog barks in the distance. CHARLIE *turns round, sees* MAX *is still there)*

CHARLIE: You still here?

MAX: You know I am.

   (CHARLIE takes off his suit jacket. He walks over to MAX, *holds it out to him)*

CHARLIE: There. Take it.

MAX: Eh?

CHARLIE: Take it.

MAX: What does this mean?

CHARLIE: Take it.

MAX: You're asking me to take it?

CHARLIE: Correct.

MAX: Are you 'giving' it to me.

CHARLIE: Yes.

MAX: What happens if I take it?

CHARLIE: Take it and see.

MAX: I'm anticipating.

    (CHARLIE *drops it, turns his back and walks away*)

MAX: Charlie, have I upset you in some way? Is it to do with the seasons? Look, I apologise if I spoke my mind, ya huffy cunt. OK? I'm sorry. Naw, I'm no sorry, why should I be sorry, at least I speak what's in my mind. You, I have to pull your insides out and read your entrails, ya omen.

    (MAX *indicates the jacket*)

Here's an example. A jacket? What's that mean? That's no use to me.

CHARLIE: Take it, ya jackal.

MAX: I mean, I pick that up (I'm anticipating) I pick that up (that's immaterial to me) I even so much as pick that up before I even so much as picked that up Time would come to an end rather than watch or look on or even countenance an act so abject as to be beneath a maggot. And if you think I'm capable of that Charlie then maybe the time has come to go our separate ways.

CHARLIE: OK.

MAX: OK?

CHARLIE: OK, leave the jacket and fuck off.

MAX: OK. Fine. — What about tonight? — It's dark getting. It's a bit late to be out hunting somewhere to stay. — You're welcome to come back to the house.

CHARLIE: I'll be OK.

MAX: You can't sleep out, Charlie.

CHARLIE: I'll make a hole.

    (*Beat*)

MAX: OK, well you know where I am, Charlie. — I never anticipated this. I never anticipated I'd be saying adios amigo. — Anyway, you know where I am, Charlie. I'll be back at the house waiting on ye.

    (CHARLIE*'s still not looking at him.* MAX *has no alternative but to just go.* CHARLIE *sees* MANDY *and* ANN *on their way to* MARGARET MARY*'s and calls over to them*)

CHARLIE: Mandy! Come here a minute.

MAX: (*offstage*) We've only got a minute.

CHARLIE: This'll only take a minute.

(MANDY *enters from the direction of the house, fairly closely accompanied by* ANN)

CHARLIE: How's the wee barra?

MANDY: No bad.

CHARLIE: How's the wee barra? Come over here, till I have a wee word with you.

(CHARLIE *wants to detach* MANDY *from* ANN)

MANDY: You'll have to be quick, we're going to get married.

CHARLIE: The both of ye?

MANDY: Yeah.

CHARLIE: You're getting married too?

MANDY: We're both going to get her married — Margaret Mary said we could have the ceremony in her house.

CHARLIE: I've come to get the day. Get the day in some kind of perspective. My mammie died, sadly.

MANDY: Aw.

CHARLIE: Yeah. I never seen her. We'll get the body back on Monday. So . . .

MANDY: What's your favourite part of the body?

CHARLIE: Whose body?

MANDY: Your body.

CHARLIE: I don't have one.

MANDY: Everybody has a body. I like my neck.

ANN: Mandy! What a thing to say!

MANDY: I quite like my eyes now that I've found my tones. I take blues and pinks and sunsets, any colour you see in the sky. She's earth. She's more brown and green.

(*Beat*)

CHARLIE: Today (to get the day) I've had worse days thankfully. I've admired your christian breastplate of faith. There was even a moment today when I was happy. You led me to believe . . . And I believed.

MANDY: Good.

CHARLIE: Do you believe me?

MANDY: Uh huh.

CHARLIE: And . . . I felt (that) I was no longer alone. Y'know?

MANDY: Yeah.

CHARLIE: Y'know?

MANDY: You're too sad and old for me.

(*Slight pause*)

CHARLIE: I'm disappointed you can say that. I am. How can you say that? Fuck. Y'know? I'm describing a moment Christian when I felt like an effing Christian. Don't forsake me that moment when — when — as I remember it, as I remember it — I no longer wanted to strike anyone. My blood stopped clawing me; and I was glad enough for two.

MANDY: Aw, that's nice.

CHARLIE: I was glad enough for two.

MANDY: We have to go.

CHARLIE: I have to go too.

MANDY: OK.

CHARLIE: Tell me to be good.

MANDY: Be good.

CHARLIE: I will, I will. And you take care now, you see and take care.

MANDY: I'll say a wee prayer for you.

(MANDY *turns to* ANN, *smiles*)

MANDY: Are you excited yet?

ANN: No! Don't be daft!

MANDY: Are you not excited? I am.

ANN: I'm too tense.

(*Suddenly* MANDY *throws some confetti over* ANN. ANN *squeals in excitement, fear, concern for her hair, clothes*)

MANDY: (*sings*) Over yonder valley
  Where the green grass grows
  Sits Ann Fairley
  Washing all her clothes
  And she sang and she sang
  And she sang so sweet
  She sang Billy Shearer
  Across the street.

(ANN *joins in the second verse. Then, as* ANN *tries to get the confetti out of her clothes,* MANDY *exits. The tension between them over* CHARLIE *has now completely evaporated*)

MANDY: C'mawn, mammie! We'll be late!

ANN: Wait for me, Mandy! — Oh god. Oh god. Oh god. Oh Billy darlin', I'm coming, I'm coming.

CHARLIE: Will you tell Margaret Mary the bad news?

ANN: Oh uh huh.

CHARLIE: She'll want to know.

ANN: I'll let her know.

CHARLIE: Don't let it spoil your happy event.

ANN: Do I look OK?

CHARLIE: If I was the groom I'd be a happy man.

ANN: Aw, that's nice. Oh Billy darlin', I hope I don't cry too much. All I want is to have one happy day one day.

(ANN *exits in the direction of the house.* CHARLIE *watches till she disappears from his sight. Then he thinks about going away.*

He doesn't know where to go. He crosses the stage, stops, covers his face. Maybe he sits down)

CHARLIE: 'What is it, Charlie son? Are you OK? You're awfy quiet, son. You were out awfy late. Were you playing football? Ah you stick in, Charlie son, you'll be playing for the Celtic one of these days. You're awfy quiet, son. Was it the nice lady? Did the nice lady scare you? It's OK. She's gone. She'll no come back again, son, I've seen to that. I'm your mammy, son, always have been, always will be. — Have you said your prayers? We'll say a prayer then I'll tuck you in. OK? Will we say a prayer? I'll say the words and you say them after me.'

(The words of the prayer are spoken with a pause after each phrase in which we imagine the seven-year-old CHARLIE repeating the words after his mammie/granny)

'Hail, holy queen . . .

mother of mercy . . .

Hail, our life . . .

our sweetness and our hope . . .

To thee do we cry . . .

poor banished children of Eve . . .

To thee do we send up our sighs . . .

mourning and weeping in this vale of tears . . .

Turn then, most gracious advocate . . .

thine eyes of mercy towards us . . .

and after this our exile . . .

show unto us the fruit of thy womb Jesus . . .

O clement . . .

O loving . . .

O sweet Virgin Mary.'

(Silence, CHARLIE wipes his eyes. Then gets to his feet and starts to make a move. Then from offstage there is the sound of applause, pleasure, a happy event. CHARLIE hears it, stops, looks up in the direction of MARGARET MARY's. Then goes. It gets dark)

Copyright Permissions